# THE
# BIBLE
# EXPOSITION
# COMMENTARY

## VOLUME 2

# THE
# BIBLE
# EXPOSITION
# COMMENTARY

## VOLUME 2

### WARREN W.
# WIERSBE

Chariot Victor Publishing
A Division of Cook Communications

Chariot Victor Publishing
A division of Cook Communications, Colorado Springs, Colorado 80918
Cook Communications, Paris, Ontario
Kingsway Communications, Eastbourne, England


14  15  16  Printing/Year  01  00  99

Unless otherwise noted, Scripture quotations are from the *King James Version*. Other quotations are from the *Holy Bible, New International Version* (NIV), © 1973, 1978, 1984, International Bible Society. Used by permission of Zondervan Bible Publishers; the *New American Standard Bible* (NASB), © the Lockman Foundation 1960, 1962, 1963, 1968, 1971, 1972, 1973, 1975, 1977; *The New Scofield Reference Bible* (SCO), © 1967 by Oxford University Press, Inc. Reprinted by permission; *The New Testament in Modern English,* Revised Edition (PH), © J.B. Phillips, 1958, 1960, 1972, permission of Macmillan Publishing Co. and Collins Publishers; the *New King James Version* (NKJV), © 1979, 1980, 1982, Thomas Nelson, Inc., Publishers; *The New Testament: An Expanded Translation* by Kenneth S. Wuest (WUEST), © 1961 by the Wm. B. Eerdmans Publishing Company, Used by permission; *The New Testament in the Language of the People* by Charles B. Williams (WMS), © 1966 by Edith S. Willliams. Used by permission of Moody Press, Moody Bible Institute of Chicago; *The Living Bible* (TLB), © 1971 by Tyndale House Publishers, Wheaton, IL 60189; *The Amplified Bible* (AMP), © 1954, 1958 the Lockman Foundation. Used by permission of Zondervan Publishing House; the *Revised Standard Version of the Bible* (RSV), © 1946, 1952, 1971, 1973, the Division of Christian Education, National Council of Churches of Christ; the *American Standard Version* (ASV). Used by permission.

Recommended Dewey Decimal Classification: 220.7
Suggested Subject Headings: BIBLE, NEW TESTAMENT, COMMENTARY


Library of Congress Catalog Card Number: 89-60158
ISBN 1-56476-031-6

# Contents

# EPHESIANS

## OUTLINE

**Key theme:** The believer's riches in Christ
**Key verse:** Ephesians 1:3

I. **DOCTRINE: OUR RICHES IN CHRIST—chapters 1–3**
   A. Our spiritual possessions in Christ—1:4-14
   1. From the Father—1:4-6
   2. From the Son—1:7-12
   3. From the Spirit—1:13-14
   First Prayer—for enlightenment—1:15-23
   B. Our spiritual position in Christ—2:1-22
   1. Raised and seated on the throne—2:1-10
   2. Reconciled and set into the temple—2:11-22
   Second Prayer—for enablement—3:1-21
   (vv. 2-13 are a parenthesis)

II. **DUTY: OUR RESPONSIBILITIES IN CHRIST—chapters 4–6**
   A. Walk in unity—4:1-16
   B. Walk in purity—4:17–5:17
   1. Walk not as other Gentiles—4:17-32
   2. Walk in love—5:1-6
   3. Walk as children of light—5:7-14
   4. Walk carefully—5:15-17
   C. Walk in harmony—5:18–6:9
   1. Husbands and wives—5:18-33
   2. Parents and children—6:1-4
   3. Masters and servants—6:5-9
   D. Walk in victory—6:10-24

## CONTENTS

# CHAPTER ONE
# SAINTS ALIVE!
*Ephesians 1:1-3*

She had gone down in history as "America's Greatest Miser," yet when she died in 1916, "Hetty" Green left an estate valued at over $100 million. She ate cold oatmeal because it cost to heat it. Her son had to suffer a leg amputation, because she delayed so long in looking for a free clinic that his case became incurable. She was wealthy, yet she chose to live like a pauper.

Eccentric? Certainly! Crazy? Perhaps—but nobody could prove it. She was so foolish that she hastened her own death by bringing on an attack of apoplexy while arguing about the value of drinking skimmed milk! But Hetty Green is an illustration of too many Christian believers today. They have limitless wealth at their disposal, and yet they live like paupers. It was to this kind of Christian that Paul wrote the Epistle to the Ephesians.

### The Author (Eph. 1:1a)
Some names in history we identify immediately, and "Paul" is one of them. His name was originally "Saul" (Acts 7:58); and, since he was from the tribe of Benjamin (Phil. 3:5), it is likely he was named after the first king of Israel (1 Sam. 9). Unlike his namesake, however, Saul of Tarsus was obedient, and faithfully served God. As a devoted rabbi, Saul became the leader of the antichristian movement in Jerusalem (Acts 9:1-2; Gal. 1:13-14). But in the midst of this activity, Saul was "arrested" by Jesus Christ and was converted (Acts 9:3ff; 26).

Saul of Tarsus became Paul, the apostle to the Gentiles (Acts 9:15). While he was ministering in the church of Antioch, he was called by the Spirit to take the Gospel to the Gentiles, and he obeyed (Acts 13:1-3). The Book of Acts records three missionary journeys that took Paul throughout the Roman Empire in one of the greatest evangelistic endeavors in church history. About the year 53, Paul first ministered in Ephesus but did not remain there (Acts 18:19-21). Two years later, while on his third journey, Paul stayed in Ephesus for at least two years and saw that whole vast area evangelized (Acts 19:1-20). During these years, he founded a strong church in the city

that was dedicated to the worship of the goddess Diana. For a description of Paul's ministry in Ephesus, read Acts 20, and for an explanation of the opposition to Paul's ministry there, read Acts 19:21-41.

It was nearly ten years later when Paul wrote to his beloved friends in Ephesus. Paul was a prisoner in Rome (Eph. 3:1; 4:1; 6:20), and he wanted to share with these believers the great truths the Lord had taught him about Christ and the church. Compare Ephesians 6:21-22 with Colossians 4:7-9 and Philemon to get a better understanding of the historical background. Onesimus, a slave, ran away from Philemon, his master, who lived at Colosse. While in Rome, Onesimus met Paul and was converted. Tychicus, one of the pastors of the church at Colossae, which may have met in Philemon's house, was also in Rome to discuss some problems with Paul. So Paul took advantage of the presence of these two men to send three letters to his friends: the Epistle to the Ephesians, the Epistle to the Colossians, and the Epistle to Philemon. At the same time, he sent Onesimus back to his master.

So, the letter was written from Rome about the year A.D. 62. Though Paul was on trial for his life, he was concerned about the spiritual needs of the churches he had founded. As an *apostle,* "one sent with a commission," he had an obligation to teach them the Word of God and to seek to build them up in the faith (Eph. 4:11-12).

### The Assembly (Eph. 1:1b-2)
Are you surprised to find Paul addressing his letter to *saints?* After all, saints are dead people who have achieved such spiritual eminence that they have been given that special title, *saints.* Or are they?

No word in the New Testament has suffered more than this word *saint.* Even the dictionary defines a *saint* as a "person officially recognized for holiness of life." Who makes this official recognition? Usually some religious body, and the process by which a person becomes a saint is technically known as *canonization.* The deceased person's life is examined carefully to see whether he qualifies for sainthood. If the candidate's character and conduct are found to be above reproach, if he has been responsible for working at least two miracles, then he is qualified to be made a saint.

As interesting as this procedure is, we do

not find it authorized in the Bible. Nine times in this brief letter, Paul addresses his readers as saints (Eph. 1:1, 15, 18; 2:19; 3:8, 18; 4:12; 5:3; 6:18). These saints were alive, not dead, though once they had been "dead in trespasses and sins" (Eph. 2:1-3). And it is clear that they had never performed any miracles, though they had *experienced* a miracle by trusting Christ as Saviour (Eph. 2:4-10). The word *saint* is simply one of the many terms used in the New Testament to describe "one who has trusted Jesus Christ as Saviour." The person is "alive," not only physically, but also spiritually (Eph. 2:1). You will find Christians called *disciples* (Acts 9:1, 10, 19, 25-26, 36, 38), *people of the Way* (Acts 9:2) and *saints* (Acts 9:13, 32, 41).

The word *saint* means "one who has been set apart." It is related to the word *sanctified,* which means "set apart." When the sinner trusts Christ as his Saviour, he is taken out of "the world" and placed "in Christ." The believer is *in* the world physically, but not *of* the world spiritually (John 17:14-16). Like a scuba diver, he exists in an alien environment because he possesses special equipment—in this case, the indwelling Holy Spirit of God. Every true believer possesses the Holy Spirit (Rom. 8:9; 1 Cor. 6:19-20), and it is through the Spirit's power that the Christian is able to function in the world.

Now for the important question: How did these people at Ephesus become saints? The answer is found in two words: "faithful" and "grace" (Eph. 1:1-2). When Paul addresses his letter to the "saints . . . and faithful in Christ Jesus" he is not addressing two different groups of people. The word *faithful* carries the meaning of "believers in Christ Jesus." These people were not saved by living faithful lives; rather they put their faith in Christ and were saved. This is clear from Ephesians 1:12-14, 19.

The word *grace* is used twelve times in Ephesians, and refers to "the kindness of God toward undeserving people." Grace and mercy often are found together in the Bible, and they certainly belong together in the experience of salvation. *Grace* and *faith* go together, because the only way to experience grace and salvation is through faith (Eph. 2:8-9).

The phrase "in Christ Jesus" is used twenty-seven times in this letter! It describes the spiritual position of the believer: he is identified with Christ, he is in Christ, and therefore is able to draw on the wealth of Christ for his own daily living.

## The Aim (Eph. 1:3)

Each book in the Bible has its own special theme and message, even though it may deal with many different topics. Genesis is the book of *beginnings;* Matthew is the book of the *kingdom;* Galatians is the book of *liberty.* Ephesians 1:3 states its theme: *the Christian's riches in Christ.*

**The source of our blessings.** "Blessed be the God and Father of our Lord Jesus Christ." God the Father has made us rich in Jesus Christ! When you were born again into God's family, you were born rich. Through Christ, you share in the riches of God's grace (Eph. 1:7; 2:7), God's glory (Eph. 1:18; 3:16), God's mercy (Eph. 2:4), and "the unsearchable riches of Christ" (Eph. 3:8). Our Heavenly Father is not poor; He is rich—and He has made us rich in His Son.

J. Paul Getty, one of the richest men in the world, was worth an estimated $1.3 billion. The weekly income of some of the "oil sheiks" runs into the millions. Yet all of this wealth is but "pennies" when compared with the spiritual wealth we have in Christ. In this letter, Paul explains to us what these riches are and how we may draw on them for effective Christian living.

**The scope of our blessings.** We have "all spiritual blessings." This can be translated "all the blessings of the Spirit," referring to the Holy Spirit of God. In the Old Testament, God promised His earthly people, Israel, material blessings as a reward for their obedience (Deut. 28:1-13). Today, He promises to supply all our needs "according to His riches in glory by Christ Jesus" (Phil. 4:19), but He does not promise to shield us from either poverty or pain. The Father has given us every blessing of the Spirit, everything we need for a successful, satisfying Christian life. *The spiritual is far more important than the material.*

The Holy Spirit is mentioned many times in this letter, because He is the one who channels our riches to us from the Father, through the Son. Not to know and depend on the Holy Spirit's provision is to live a life of spiritual poverty. No wonder Paul began his Ephesian ministry asking some professed Christians if they really knew the Holy Spirit (Acts 19:1-7). We might ask professed Christians today, "Did you receive the Holy Spirit when you believed? If the answer is no, then you are not saved." "Now if any man have not the Spirit of Christ, he is none of His" (Rom. 8:9). Unless you have the *witness* of the Spirit (Rom. 8:15-16), you cannot draw on the *wealth* of the Spirit.

**The sphere of our blessings.** Our blessings are "in heavenly places in Christ." Perhaps a clearer translation would be "in the heavenlies in Christ." The unsaved person is interested primarily in *earthlies,* because this is where he lives. Jesus called them "the children of this world" (Luke 16:8). The Christian's life is centered in *heaven.* His citizenship is in heaven (Phil. 3:20); his name is written in heaven (Luke 10:20); his Father is in heaven; and his attention and affection ought to be centered on the things of heaven (Col. 3:1ff). Evangelist D.L. Moody used to warn about people who were so "heavenly minded they were no earthly good," but that is not what Paul is describing. "The heavenlies" (literal translation) describes that place where Jesus Christ is right now (Eph. 1:2) and where the believer is seated with Him (Eph. 2:6). The battles we fight are not with flesh and blood on earth, but with satanic powers "in the heavenlies" (Eph. 6:12).

The Christian really operates in two spheres: the human and the divine, the visible and the invisible. Physically, he is on the earth in a human body, but spiritually he is seated with Christ in the heavenly sphere—and it is this heavenly sphere that provides the power and direction for the earthly walk. The President of the United States is not always seated at his desk in the White House, but that executive chair represents the sphere of his life and power. No matter where he is, he is the President, because only he has the privilege of sitting at that desk. Likewise with the Christian: no matter where he may be on this earth, he is seated in the heavenlies with Jesus Christ, and this is the basis of his life and power.

When she was young, Victoria was shielded from the fact that she would be the next ruling monarch of England lest this knowledge spoil her. When her teacher finally did let her discover for herself that she would one day be Queen of England, Victoria's response was, "Then I will be good!" Her life would be controlled by her position. No matter where she was, Victoria was governed by the fact that she sat on the throne of England.

The fact that Paul is writing about wealth would be significant to his readers, because

Ephesus was considered the bank of Asia. One of the seven wonders of the world, the great temple of Diana, was in Ephesus, and was not only a center for idolatrous worship, but also a depository for wealth. Some of the greatest art treasures of the ancient world were housed in this magnificent building. In this letter, Paul will compare the church of Jesus Christ to a temple and will explain the great wealth that Christ has in His church. Paul has already used the word riches; but you may want to check other "financial" words such as *inheritance* (Eph. 1:11, 14, 18; 5:5) and *fullness,* or *filled* (Eph. 1:10, 23; 3:19; 4:10, 13; 5:18). Paul is saying to us, "BE RICH!"

**The Analysis**

Paul's letter to the Ephesians is as carefully structured as that great temple of Diana, and it contains greater beauty and wealth! We *inherit* the wealth by faith and invest the wealth by works. Without this balance, our spiritual riches do us no good.

# CHAPTER TWO
# HOW RICH YOU ARE!
*Ephesians 1:4-14*

One of the funniest cartoons I ever saw showed a pompous lawyer reading a client's last will and testament to a group of greedy relatives. The caption read: "I, John Jones, being of sound mind and body, *spent it all!*"

When Jesus Christ wrote His last will and testament for His church, He made it possible for us to share His spiritual riches. Instead of spending it all, Jesus Christ paid it all. His death on the cross and His resurrection make possible our salvation.

He wrote us into His will, then He died so the will would be in force. Then He arose again that He might become the heavenly Advocate (lawyer) to make sure the terms of the will were correctly followed!

In this long sentence, Paul names just a few of the blessings that make up our spiritual wealth.

## Blessings from God the Father
### (Eph. 1:4-6)

*He has chosen us (v. 4).* This is the marvelous doctrine of *election,* a doctrine that has confused some and confounded others. A seminary professor once said to me, "Try to explain election and you may lose your mind. But try to explain it away and you may lose your soul!" That salvation begins with God, and not with man, all Christians will agree. "Ye have not chosen Me, but I have chosen you" (John 15:16). The lost sinner, left to his own ways, does not seek God (Rom. 3:10-11); God in His love seeks the sinner (Luke 19:10).

Note that God chose us even before He created the universe, so that our salvation is wholly of His grace and not on the basis of anything we ourselves have done. He chose us *in Christ,* not in ourselves. And He chose us for a purpose: to be holy and without blame. In the Bible, election is always *unto* something. It is a privilege that carries a great responsibility.

Does the sinner respond to God's grace against his own will? No, he responds because God's grace makes him willing to respond. The mystery of divine sovereignty and human responsibility will never be solved in this life. Both are taught in the Bible (John 6:37). Both are true, and both are essential.

You will note that all three Persons in the Godhead are involved in our salvation (see also 1 Peter 1:3). As far as God the Father is concerned, you were saved when He chose you in Christ in eternity past. But that alone did not save you. As far as God the Son is concerned, you were saved when He died for you on the cross. As far as God the Spirit is concerned, you were saved when you yielded to His conviction and received Christ as your Saviour. What began in eternity past was fulfilled in time present, and will continue for all eternity!

*He has adopted us (v. 5).* Here we meet that misunderstood word *predestination.* This word, as it is used in the Bible, refers *primarily* to what God does for saved people. Nowhere in the Bible are we taught that people are predestined to hell, because this word refers only to God's people. The word simply means "to ordain beforehand, to predetermine." Election seems to refer to *people,* while predestination refers to *purposes.* The events connected with the crucifixion of Christ were predestined (Acts 4:25-28). God has predes-

tined our adoption (Eph. 1:5), and our conformity to Christ (Rom. 8:29-30), as well as our future inheritance (Eph. 1:11).

*Adoption* has a dual meaning, both present and future. You do not get into God's family by adoption. You get into His family by regeneration, the new birth (John 3:1-18; 1 Peter 1:22-25). Adoption is the act of God by which He gives His "born ones" an adult standing in the family. Why does He do this? So that we might *immediately* begin to claim our inheritance and enjoy our spiritual wealth! A baby cannot legally use this inheritance (Gal. 4:1-7), but an adult son can—and should! This means that you do not have to wait until you are an old saint before you can claim your riches in Christ.

The *future* aspect of adoption is found in Romans 8:22-23, the glorified body we will have when Jesus returns. We already have our adult standing before God, but the world cannot see this. When Christ returns, this "private adoption" will be made public for everyone to see!

*He has accepted us (v. 6).* We cannot make ourselves acceptable to God; but He, by His grace, makes us accepted in Christ. This is our eternal position which will never change. Some translations read "which He freely bestowed on us in the Beloved" (NASB). Or, "He has *be-graced* [literal translation] us in the Beloved." The idea is the same. Because of God's grace in Christ, we are accepted before Him. Paul wrote *Philemon* to encourage him to accept his runaway slave, Onesimus, using the same argument. "If he owes you anything, I will pay it. Receive him as you would receive me" (Phile. 17-19, paraphrased). The parallel is easy to see.

## Blessings from God the Son
### (Eph. 1:7-12)

We should not think that each Person of the Godhead works independently, because they all worked together to make possible our salvation. But each Person has a special ministry to perform, a special "spiritual deposit" to make in our lives.

*He has redeemed us (v. 7a).* To *redeem* means "to purchase and set free by paying a price." There were 60 million slaves in the Roman Empire, and often they were bought and sold like pieces of furniture. But a man could purchase a slave and set him free, and this is what Jesus did for us. The price was His own blood (1 Peter 1:18ff). This means that we are free from the Law (Gal. 5:1), free from slavery to sin (Rom. 6), as well as free from the power of Satan and the world (Gal. 1:4; Col. 1:13-14). If we were slaves, we would be poor, but because we are sons, we are rich!

**He has forgiven us (v. 7b).** The word *forgive* means "to carry away." This reminds us of the ritual on the Jewish Day of Atonement when the high priest sent the scapegoat into the wilderness (Lev. 16). First the priest killed one of the two goats and sprinkled its blood before God on the mercy seat. Then he confessed Israel's sins over the live goat, and had the goat taken into the wilderness to be lost. Christ died to carry away our sins so they might never again be seen (Ps. 103:12; John 1:29). No written accusation stands against us because our sins have been taken away! Sin made us poor, but grace makes us rich.

**He has revealed God's will to us (vv. 8-10).** This letter has much to say about God's plan for His people, a plan that was not fully understood even in Paul's day. The word *mystery* has nothing to do with things eerie. It means a "sacred secret, once hidden but now revealed to God's people." We believers are a part of God's "inner circle." We are able to share in the secret that God will one day unite everything in Christ. Ever since sin came into the world, things have been falling apart. First, man was separated from God (Gen. 3). Then man was separated from man, as Cain killed Abel (Gen. 4). People tried to maintain a kind of unity by building the Tower of Babel (Gen. 11), but God judged them and scattered them across the world. God called Abraham and put a difference between the Jew and the Gentile, a difference that was maintained until Christ's death on the cross. Sin is tearing everything apart, but in Christ, God will gather everything together in the culmination of the ages. We are a part of this great eternal program.

**He has made us an inheritance (vv. 11-12).** The *King James Version* reads, "In whom also we have obtained an inheritance," but "in whom also we were made an inheritance" is also a possible translation. Both are true and the one includes the other. In Christ we *have* a wonderful inheritance (1 Peter 1:1-4), and in Christ we *are* an inheritance. We are valuable to Him. Think of the price God paid to purchase us and make us part of His inheritance! God the Son is the Father's love

gift to us; and we are the Father's love gift to His Son. Read John 17 and note how many times Christ calls us "those whom Thou hast given Me." The church is Christ's body (Eph. 1:22-23), building (Eph. 2:19-22), and bride (Eph. 5:22-23); Christ's future inheritance is wrapped up in His church. We are "joint-heirs with Christ" (Rom. 8:17), which means that He cannot claim His inheritance apart from us!

## Blessings from God the Holy Spirit (Eph. 1:13-14)

We move now from eternity past (Eph. 1:4-6), and history past (Eph. 1:7-12), to the immediate experience of the Ephesian Christians. The Holy Spirit had worked in their lives, and they knew it.

**He has sealed us (v. 13).** The entire process of salvation is given in this verse, so we had better examine it carefully. It tells how the sinner becomes a saint. First, he hears the Gospel of salvation. This is the good news that Christ died for our sins, was buried and rose again (1 Cor. 15:1ff). The Ephesians were Gentiles, and the Gospel came "to the Jew first" (Rom. 1:16). But Paul, a Jew, brought the Gospel to the Gentiles as he shared the Word of God with them.

The Ephesians "heard the Gospel" and discovered it was for them—"your salvation" (Eph. 1:13). Even though the Bible teaches election, it also announces, "Go ye into all the world and preach the Gospel to every creature" (Mark 16:15). A soul-winner does not discuss election with unsaved people, because it is a family secret that belongs to the saints. He simply announces the truth of the Gospel and invites men to trust Christ, and the Holy Spirit does the rest. D.L. Moody used to pray, "Lord, save the elect—and then elect some more!" The same God who ordains the end, the salvation of souls, also ordains the means to the end, the preaching of the Gospel in the power of the Spirit.

Having heard the Word, the Ephesians believed; and it is this faith that brought salvation (Eph. 2:8-9). This pattern follows what Paul writes in Romans 10:13-15, so read that passage carefully. It is God's plan for evangelism. When the Ephesians believed, they were "sealed with the Spirit." "After that ye believed" should read "*when* ye believed." You receive the Spirit immediately on trusting Christ. This is not an experience subsequent to conversion. (Read Acts 10:34-48.)

What is the significance of this sealing of the

Holy Spirit? For one thing, it speaks of a *finished transaction*. Even today, when important legal documents are processed, they are stamped with the official seal to signify the completion of the transaction. This sealing also implies *ownership:* God has put his seal on us because He has purchased us to be His own (1 Cor. 6:19-20). It also means *security and protection*. The Roman seal on the tomb of Jesus carried this meaning (Matt. 27:62-66). So, the believer belongs to God, and is safe and protected because he is a part of a finished transaction. According to John 14:16-17, the Holy Spirit abides with the believer forever. It is possible for us to grieve the Spirit and thereby lose the blessings of His ministry (Eph. 4:30). But He doesn't leave us.

Another use for the seal is as a mark of *authenticity*. Just as a signature on a letter attests to the genuineness of the document, so the presence of the Spirit proves the believer is genuine. "If any man have not the Spirit of Christ, he is none of His" (Rom. 8:9). It is not simply our lip profession, our religious activity, or our good works, but the witness of the Spirit that makes our profession authentic.

**He has given us an earnest (v. 14).** *Earnest* is a fascinating word! In Paul's day, it meant "the down payment to guarantee the final purchase of some commodity or piece of property." Even today you will hear a real estate agent talk about earnest money. The Holy Spirit is God's first installment to guarantee to His children that He will finish His work and eventually bring them to glory. The "redemption of the purchased possession" refers to the redemption of the body at the return of Christ (Rom. 8:18-23; 1 John 3:1-3). "Redemption" is experienced in three stages:

• We *have been redeemed* through faith in Jesus Christ (Eph. 1:7).

• We *are being redeemed* as the Spirit works in our lives to make us more like Christ (Rom. 8:1-4).

• We *shall be redeemed* when Christ returns and we become like Him.

But the word translated *earnest* also means "engagement ring." In Greece today you would find this word being used that way. But, after all, isn't an engagement ring an assurance—a guarantee—that the promises made will be kept? Our relationship to God through Christ is not simply a *commercial* one, but also a personal experience of love. He is the Bridegroom and His church is the bride. We know that He will come and claim His bride because He has given us His promise and His Spirit as the "engagement ring." What greater assurance could we want?

We have examined a number of basic Bible doctrines in this chapter, all on the theme of our riches in Christ. It would be profitable for us to review what these verses teach us.

1. *True riches come from God.* It is a source of great encouragement to know that Father, Son, and Holy Spirit are all working on my behalf to make me rich. God not only gives us "richly all things to enjoy" (1 Tim. 6:17), but He gives us *eternal* riches without which all other wealth is valueless.

A distraught wife sought out a Christian marriage counselor and told her sad story of a marriage about to dissolve. "But we have so much!" she kept saying. "Look at this diamond ring on my finger. Why, it's worth thousands! We have an expensive mansion in an exclusive area. We have three cars, and even a cabin in the mountains. Why, we have everything money can buy!"

The counselor replied: "It's good to have the things money can buy provided you don't lose the things money can't buy. What good is an expensive house if there's no home? Or an expensive ring if there's no love?"

In Christ, you and I have "what money can't buy," and these spiritual riches open up to us all the wealth of God's vast creation. We enjoy the gifts because we know and love the Giver.

2. *All of these riches come by God's grace and for God's glory.* Did you notice that after each of the main sections in Ephesians 1:4-14, Paul has added the purpose behind these gifts? Why has God the Father chosen us, adopted us, and accepted us? "To the praise of the glory of His grace" (Eph. 1:6). Why has the Son redeemed us, forgiven us, revealed God's will to us, and made us part of God's inheritance? "That we should be to the praise of His glory" (Eph. 1:12). Why has God the Spirit sealed us and become the guarantee of our future blessing? "Unto the praise of His glory" (Eph. 1:14).

We often have the idea that God saves sinners mainly because He pities them, or wants to rescue them from eternal judgment, but God's main purpose is that He might be glorified. His creation reveals His wisdom and power, but His church reveals His love and grace. You cannot deserve or earn these spiritual riches; you can only receive them by grace, through faith.

3. *These riches are only the beginning!*

There is always more spiritual wealth to claim from the Lord as we walk with Him. The Bible is our guidebook; the Holy Spirit is our Teacher. As we search the Word of God, we discover more and more of the riches we have in Christ. These riches were planned by the Father, purchased by the Son, and presented by the Spirit. There is really no need for us to live in poverty when all of God's wealth is at our disposal!

My friend was discussing money matters with his wife and neither of them realized that their little son was listening. Finally the boy broke in with the suggestion, "Why don't you just write one of those pieces of paper?" Junior did not understand that it was necessary to have money in the bank to back up "those pieces of paper." But we never face that problem when it comes to our spiritual wealth.

A little devotional book by Charles Spurgeon is entitled *A Checkbook on the Bank of Faith*. A promise from the Bible was given for each day of the year, along with a short devotional message. The author described each promise as being as good as money in the bank to anyone who would claim it by faith, as a person would write a check against his bank account. By faith we can claim God's promises and draw on His limitless wealth to meet every need we may face.

# CHAPTER THREE
# READ THE
# BANKBOOK
*Ephesians 1:15-23*

On January 6, 1822, the wife of a poor German pastor had a son, never dreaming that he would one day achieve world renown and great wealth. When Heinrich Schliemann was seven years old, a picture of ancient Troy in flames captured his imagination. Contrary to what many people believed, Heinrich argued that Homer's great poems, the *Iliad* and the *Odyssey*, were based on historic facts and he set out to prove it. In 1873, he uncovered the ancient site of Troy, along with some fabulous treasure which he smuggled out of the country, much to the anger of the Turkish govern-

ment. Schliemann became a famous, wealthy man because he dared to believe an ancient record and act on his faith.

We discovered that we were "born rich" when we trusted Christ. But this is not enough, for we must grow in our understanding of our riches if we are ever going to use them to the glory of God. Too many Christians have never "read the bank book" to find out the vast spiritual wealth that God has put to their account through Jesus Christ. They are like the late newspaper publisher, William Randolph Hearst, who invested a fortune collecting art treasures from around the world. One day Mr. Hearst found a description of some valuable items that he felt he must own, so he sent his agent abroad to find them. After months of searching, the agent reported that he had finally found the treasures. They were in Mr. Hearst's warehouse. Hearst had been searching frantically for treasures he already owned! Had he read the catalog of his treasures, he would have saved himself a great deal of money and trouble.

Paul desired the Ephesian Christians to understand what great wealth they had in Christ. Paul knew of their faith and love, and in this he rejoiced. The Christian life has two dimensions: faith toward God and love toward men, and you cannot separate the two. But Paul knew that faith and love were just the beginning. The Ephesians needed to know much more. This is why he prayed for them, and for us.

In the prison prayers of Paul (Eph. 1:15-23; 3:14-21; Phil. 1:9-11; Col. 1:9-12), we discover the blessings he wanted his converts to enjoy. In none of these prayers does Paul request material things. His emphasis is on spiritual perception and real Christian character. He does not ask God to give them what they do not have, but rather prays that God will reveal to them what they already have.

Before we study Paul's four requests in this "prayer for enlightenment," we must notice two facts. First, enlightenment comes from the Holy Spirit. He is the "Spirit of wisdom and revelation" (Isa. 11:2; John 14:25-26; 16:12-14). With his natural mind, man cannot understand the things of God. He needs the Spirit to enlighten him (1 Cor. 2:9-16). The Holy Spirit reveals truth to us from the Word, and then gives us the wisdom to understand and apply it. He also gives us the power—the enablement—to practice the truth (Eph. 3:14-21).

Second, this enlightenment comes to the heart of the believer (Eph. 1:18). Literally this verse reads, "The eyes of your heart being enlightened." We think of the heart as the emotional part of man, but in the Bible, the heart means the inner man, and includes the emotions, the mind, and the will. The inner man, the heart, has spiritual faculties that parallel the physical senses. The inner man can *see* (Ps. 119:18; John 3:3), *hear* (Matt. 13:9; Heb. 5:11), *taste* (Ps. 34:8; 1 Peter 2:3), *smell* (Phil. 4:18; 2 Cor. 2:14), and *touch* (Acts 17:27). This is what Jesus meant when He said of the people: "They seeing see not, and hearing they hear not" (Matt. 13:13). The inability to see and understand spiritual things is not the fault of the intelligence but of the heart. The eyes of the heart must be opened by the Spirit of God.

## That They Might Know God
### (Eph. 1:17b)

This, of course, is the highest knowledge possible. The *atheist* claims there is no God for us to know, and the *agnostic* states that if there is a God we cannot know Him. But Paul has met God in the person of Jesus Christ, and he knows that a man really cannot understand much of anything else without a knowledge of God.

This willful ignorance of God led mankind into corruption and condemnation. In Romans 1:18ff, Paul describes the stages in man's devolution: from willful ignorance of God to idolatry (substituting a lie for the truth) to immorality and indecency. Where does it begin? It begins with an unwillingness to know God as Creator, Sustainer, Governor, Saviour, and Judge.

The believer must grow in his knowledge of God. To know God personally is salvation (John 17:3). To know Him increasingly is sanctification (Phil. 3:10). To know Him perfectly is glorification (1 Cor. 13:9-12). Since we are made in the image of God (Gen. 1:26-28), the better we know God, the better we know ourselves and each other. It is not enough to know God only as Saviour. We must get to know Him as Father, Friend, Guide, and the better we know Him, the more satisfying our spiritual lives will be.

A believer said to me one day after a Bible lesson, "I'm sure glad I came! You gave me two good verses to use on my wicked neighbor!" Surely there are times when we use God's Word as a sword to defeat the enemy, but that is not the primary purpose behind the writing of the Bible. As the familiar hymn puts it: "Beyond the sacred page / I seek Thee, Lord. / My spirit pants for Thee / O living Word."

## That We Might Know God's Calling
### (Eph. 1:18a)

The word *called* is an important word in the Christian's vocabulary. The word *church* is a combination of two Greek words that mean "called out." Paul never tired of testifying that God called him "by His grace" (Gal. 1:15); and he reminded Timothy that the believer has a "holy calling" (2 Tim. 1:9). We have been "called out of darkness into His marvelous light" (1 Peter 2:9), and have even been "called to glory" (1 Peter 5:10). God calls us by His grace and not because of any merit that we may possess.

Paul wants us to understand the hope that is ours because of this calling (Eph. 4:4). Some callings offer no hope, but the calling we have in Christ assures us of a delightful future. Keep in mind that the word *hope* in the Bible does not mean "hope so," like a child hoping for a doll or a bike at Christmas. The word carries with it "assurance for the future." The believer's hope is, of course, the return of Jesus Christ for His church (1 Thes. 4:13-18; 1 John 3:1-3). When we were lost, we were "without hope" (Eph. 2:12); but in Jesus Christ, we have a "living hope" (1 Peter 1:3) that encourages us day by day.

Dr. Kenneth Chafin, a well-known Baptist author, tells about the pastor and deacon who were visiting prospective members and drove up to a beautiful suburban home surrounded by a velvet lawn and gorgeous landscaping. Two expensive cars stood in the driveway, and through the picture window, the men saw their prospect, lounging in an easy chair and watching color TV. The deacon turned to his pastor and said, "What kind of good news do we have for *him?*"

How prone we are to confuse prices and values. Ephesus was a wealthy city. It boasted the temple of Diana, one of the wonders of the ancient world. Today, Ephesus is an archeologist's paradise, but all of its wealth and splendor are gone. But the Christians who once lived there are today in heaven, enjoying the glory of God!

The hope that belongs to our calling should be a dynamic force in our lives, encouraging us to be pure (1 John 2:28–3:3), obedient

(Heb. 13:17), and faithful (Luke 12:42-48). The fact that we shall one day see Christ and be like Him should motivate us to live like Christ today.

## That We Might Know God's Riches (Eph. 1:18b)

This phrase does not refer to our inheritance in Christ (Eph. 1:11), but His inheritance in us. This is an amazing truth—that God should look on us as a part of His great wealth! Just as a man's wealth brings glory to his name, so God will get glory from the church because of what He has invested in us. When Jesus Christ returns, we shall be "to the praise of the glory of His grace" (Eph. 1:6).

God deals with us on the basis of our future, not our past. He said to cowardly Gideon, "The Lord is with thee, thou mighty man of valor" (Jud. 6:12). Jesus said to Andrew's brother, "Thou art Simon . . . thou shalt be called Cephas [a stone]" (John 1:42).

Gideon did become a mighty man of valor, and Simon did become Peter, a rock. We Christians live in the future tense, our lives controlled by what we shall be when Christ returns. Because we are God's inheritance, we live to please and glorify Him.

This truth suggests to us that Christ will not enter into His promised glory until the church is there to share it with Him. He prayed for this before He died, and this prayer will be answered (John 17:24). Christ will be glorified in us (2 Thes. 1:10), and we will be glorified in Him (Col. 3:4). Knowing this should lead the believer into a life of dedication and devotion to the Lord.

## That We Might Know God's Power (Eph. 1:19-23)

By making us His inheritance, God has shown His love. By promising us a wonderful future, He has encouraged our hope. Paul offered something to challenge our faith: "the exceeding greatness of His power to us-ward who believe" (Eph. 1:19). So tremendous is this truth that Paul enlisted many different words from the Greek vocabulary to get his point across: *dunamis*—"power" as in dynamo and dynamite; *energeia*—"working" as in energy; *kratos*—"mighty"; *ischus*—"power." Ephesians 1:19 can be translated, "What is the surpassing greatness of His power toward us who believe, according to the operation of the might of His strength." He is talking about divine dynamic, eternal energy, available to us!

After all, what good is it to have wealth if you are too weak to use it? Or if you are so afraid of robbers that you cannot really enjoy it? John D. Rockefeller was the world's first billionaire. It is said that for many years, he lived on crackers and milk because of stomach troubles caused by worrying about his wealth. He rarely had a good night's sleep, and guards stood constantly at his door. Wealthy—but miserable! When he began to share his wealth with others in great philanthropic endeavors, his health improved considerably and he lived to be an old man.

We Christians need power for several reasons. To begin with, by nature we are too weak to appreciate and appropriate this wealth, and to use it as it should be used. "The spirit indeed is willing, but the flesh is weak" (Matt. 26:41). To turn this vast spiritual wealth over to a mere human being, living by human wisdom and strength, would be like handing an atomic bomb to a two-year-old. God's power enables us to use God's wealth.

But there is a second reason why we need God's power. There are enemies who want to rob us of our wealth (Eph. 1:21; 6:11-12). We could never defeat these spiritual foes in our own power, but we can through the Spirit's power. Paul wants us to know the greatness of God's power so that we will not fail to use our wealth, and so that the enemy will not deprive us of our wealth.

The power is seen in the resurrection of Jesus Christ. In the Old Testament, people measured God's power by His creation (Isa. 40:12-27) or by His miracle at the Exodus of Israel from Egypt (Jer. 16:14). But today, we measure God's power by the miracle of Christ's resurrection. Much more was involved than merely raising Him from the dead, for Christ also ascended to heaven and sat down in the place of authority at the right hand of God. He is not only Saviour; He is also Sovereign (Acts 2:25-36). No authority or power, human or in the spirit world, is greater than that of Jesus Christ, the exalted Son of God. He is "far above all," and no future enemy can overcome Him, because He has been exalted "far above all" powers.

But how does this apply to you and me today? In Ephesians 1:22-23, Paul explains the practical application. Because we are believers, we are in the church, which is Christ's body—and He is the Head. This means that there is a living connection between you and Christ. Physically speaking, the head controls the body and keeps the body functioning properly. Injure certain parts of the brain and you handicap or paralyze corresponding parts of the body. Christ is our spiritual Head. Through the Spirit, we are united to Him as the members of His body. This means that we share His resurrection, ascension, and exaltation. (Paul will amplify this later.) We too are seated, in the heavenlies (Eph. 2:6), and all things are under our feet.

No wonder Paul wants us to know "the exceeding greatness of His power to us-ward"! Apart from this power, we cannot draw on our great wealth in Christ.

I recall going to the hospital with one of our church members to try to get her husband to sign a paper that would authorize her to draw on his private checking account so she could pay his bills. The man was so weak he could not sign the paper. She finally had to get witnesses to verify his "X" on the document. His weakness nearly deprived her of his wealth.

The power of the Holy Spirit, through the resurrected, ascended Christ, is available to all Christians—by faith. His power is to "us-ward who believe" (Eph. 1:19). It is grace that supplies the wealth, but it is faith that lays hold of the wealth. We are saved "by grace, through faith" (Eph. 2:8-9), and we live "by grace," through faith (1 Cor. 15:10).

In the four Gospels, we see God's power at work in the ministry of Jesus Christ, but in the Book of Acts, we see that same power at work in ordinary men and women, members of the body of Christ. What a transformation took place in Peter's life between the end of the Gospels and the beginning of Acts. What made the difference? The resurrection power of Jesus Christ (Acts 1:8).

The greatest power shortage today is not in our generators or our gas tanks. It is in our personal lives. Will Paul's prayer be answered in your life? Will you, starting today, begin to know by experience God—God's calling—God's riches—and God's power?

# CHAPTER FOUR
# GET OUT OF
# THE GRAVEYARD
*Ephesians 2:1-10*

Having described our spiritual *possessions* in Christ, Paul turns to a complementary truth: our spiritual *position* in Christ. First he explains what God has done for all sinners in general; then he explains what God did for the Gentiles in particular. The sinner who trusts Christ has been raised and seated on the throne (Eph. 2:1-10), and believing Jews and Gentiles have been reconciled and set into the temple (Eph. 2:11-22). What a miracle of God's grace! We are taken out of the great graveyard of sin and placed into the throne room of glory.

Perhaps the easiest way for us to approach this long paragraph is to see in it four specific works.

### Sin's Work against Us (Eph. 2:1-3)
A publisher asked me for a full-length portrait that they could "blow up" and use as a life-size display at their convention booth to promote my tapes. A friend of mine took the picture, and it was a new experience for me. I had been accustomed to sitting for head-and-shoulder photographs, but standing for a full-length photo was something new. I had to watch my posture, the feet had to be placed just right, and the arms and hands—usually forgotten—had to be in just the right position. Fortunately, my photographer friend is an expert, and we managed to get a decent picture in a short time. In these three verses, Paul gives us a full-length picture of the terrible spiritual condition of the unsaved person. Note his characteristics:

*He is dead (v. 1).* Of course, this means spiritually dead; that is, he is unable to understand and appreciate spiritual things. He possesses no spiritual life, and he can do nothing of himself to please God. Just as a person physically dead does not respond to physical stimuli, so a person spiritually dead is unable to respond to spiritual things. A corpse does not hear the conversation going on in the funeral parlor. He has no appetite for food or drink; he feels no pain; he is dead. Just so with the inner man of the unsaved person. His spiritual faculties are not functioning, and they cannot function until God gives him life. The cause of this spiritual death is "trespasses and sins" (Eph. 2:1). "The wages of sin is death" (Rom. 6:23). In the Bible, *death* basically means "separation," not only physically, as the spirit separated from the body (James 2:26), but also spiritually, as the spirit separated from God (Isa. 59:2).

The unbeliever is not sick; he is dead! He does not need resuscitation; he needs resurrection. All lost sinners are dead, and the only difference between one sinner and another is the state of decay. The lost derelict on skid row may be more decayed outwardly than the unsaved society leader, but both are dead in sin—and one corpse cannot be more dead than another! This means that our world is one vast graveyard, filled with people who are dead while they live (1 Tim. 5:6).

**He is disobedient (vv. 2-3a).** This was the beginning of man's spiritual death—his disobedience to the will of God. God said, "In the day that thou eatest thereof thou shalt surely die" (Gen. 2:17). Satan said, "Ye shall not surely die" (Gen. 3:4), and because they believed this lie, the first man and woman sinned and experienced immediate spiritual death and ultimate physical death. Since that time, mankind has lived in disobedience to God. There are three forces that encourage man in his disobedience—the world, the devil, and the flesh.

The world, or world-system, puts pressure on each person to try to get him to conform (Rom. 12:2). Jesus Christ was not "of this world" and neither are His people (John 8:23; 17:14). But the unsaved person, either consciously or unconsciously, is controlled by the values and attitudes of this world.

The devil is "the spirit that now worketh in the children of disobedience." This does not mean that Satan is personally at work in the life of each unbeliever, since Satan as a created being is limited in space. Unlike God, who is omnipresent, Satan cannot be in all places at one time. But because of his demonic associates (Eph. 6:11-12), and his power over the world system (John 12:31), Satan influences the lives of all unbelievers, and also seeks to influence believers. He wants to make people "children of disobedience" (Eph. 2:2; 5:6). He himself was disobedient to God, so he wants others to disobey Him too.

One of Satan's chief tools for getting people to disobey God is lies. He is a liar (John 8:44),

and it was his lie at the beginning of human history, "Ye shall not surely die," that plunged the human race into sin. The unsaved multitudes in today's world system disobey God because they believe the lies of Satan. When a person believes and practices a lie, he becomes a child of disobedience.

The flesh is the third force that encourages the unbeliever to disobey God. By *the flesh* Paul does not mean the body, because of itself, the body is not sinful. *The flesh* refers to that fallen nature that we were born with, that wants to control the body and the mind and make us disobey God. An evangelist friend of mine once announced as his topic, "Why Your Dog Does What It Does," and, of course, many dog lovers came out to hear him. What he had to say was obvious, but too often overlooked: "A dog behaves like a dog because he has a dog's nature." If somehow you could transplant into the dog the nature of the cat, his behavior would change radically. Why does a sinner behave like a sinner? Because he has the nature of a sinner (Pss. 51:5; 58:3). This sinful nature the Bible calls "the flesh."

Is it any wonder that the unsaved person is disobedient to God? He is controlled by the world, the flesh, and the devil, the three great enemies of God! And he cannot change his own nature or, of himself, overcome the world and the devil. He needs outside help, and that help can come only from God.

**He is depraved (v. 3b).** The lost sinner lives to please the "desires of the flesh and the wishes of the mind" (literal translation). His actions are sinful because his appetites are sinful. When you apply the word *depraved* to the unsaved person, you are not saying that he *only* does evil, or that he is incapable of doing good. You are simply saying that he is incapable of doing anything to merit salvation or meet the high standards of God's holiness. Jesus said that lost sinners do good to each other (Luke 6:33), and to their children (Luke 11:13), but they cannot do anything spiritually good to please God. The natives on Malta who kindly assisted Paul and his friends after the shipwreck certainly did good works, but they still needed to be saved (Acts 28:1-2).

**He is doomed (v. 3c).** By nature, children of wrath! By deed, children of disobedience! The unsaved person is condemned already (John 3:18). The sentence has been passed, but God in His mercy is staying the execution of the sentence (2 Peter 3:8-10). Man cannot save himself, but God in His grace steps in to make salvation possible. "But God!"—what a difference those two words make! This leads to the second work.

### God's Work for Us (Eph. 2:4-9)

The focus of attention now is on God, not on sinful man. "Salvation is of the Lord" (Jonah 2:9). We are reminded of four activities that God performed on behalf of sinners to save them from the consequences of their sins.

*He loved us (v. 4).* By nature, "God is love" (1 John 4:8). But God would love even if there were no sinners, because love is a part of His very being. Theologians call love one of God's attributes. But God has two kinds of attributes: those that He possesses of Himself (intrinsic attributes, such as life, love, holiness), and those by which He relates to His creation, especially to man (relative attributes). For example, by nature God is *truth;* but when He relates to man, God's truth becomes *faithfulness.* God is by nature *holy;* and when He relates that holiness to man, it becomes *justice.*

Love is one of God's intrinsic attributes, but when this love is related to sinners, it becomes *grace* and *mercy.* God is "rich in mercy" (Eph. 2:4) and in "grace" (Eph. 2:7), and these riches make it possible for sinners to be saved. It comes as a shock to some people when they discover that we are not saved "by God's love," but by God's mercy and grace. In His mercy, He does not give us what we do deserve; and in His grace He gives us what we do not deserve. And all of this is made possible because of the death of Jesus Christ on the cross. It was at Calvary that God displayed His hatred for sin and His love for sinners (Rom. 5:8; John 3:16).

*He quickened us (v. 5).* This means He made us alive, even when we were dead in sins. He accomplished this spiritual resurrection by the power of the Spirit, using the Word. In the four Gospels, it is recorded that Jesus raised three people from the dead: the widow's son (Luke 7:11-17), Jairus' daughter (Luke 8:49-56), and Lazarus (John 11:41-46). In each case, He spoke the Word and this gave life. "The Word of God is quick [living] and powerful" (Heb. 4:12). These three physical resurrections are pictures of the spiritual resurrection that comes to the sinner when he hears the Word and believes (John 5:24).

But our spiritual resurrection is much greater because it puts us in union with Christ: God "made us alive together with Christ." As members of His body we are united to Him (Eph. 1:22-23), so that we share His resurrection life and power (Eph. 1:19-20).

*He exalted us (v. 6).* We are not raised from the dead and left in the graveyard. Because we are united to Christ, we have been exalted with Him and we are sharing His throne in the heavenlies. Our physical position may be on earth, but our spiritual position is "in heavenly places in Christ Jesus." Like Lazarus, we have been called from the grave to sit with Christ and enjoy His fellowship (John 12:1-2).

*He keeps us (vv. 7-9).* God's purpose in our redemption is not simply to rescue us from hell, as great a work as that is. His ultimate purpose in our salvation is that for all eternity the church might glorify God's grace (Eph. 1:6, 12, 14). So, if God has an eternal purpose for us to fulfill, He will keep us for all eternity. Since we have not been saved by our good works, we cannot be lost by our bad works. Grace means salvation completely apart from any merit or works on our part. Grace means that God does it all for Jesus' sake! Our salvation is the gift of God. (The word *that* in Eph. 2:8, in the Greek, is neuter; while *faith* is feminine. Therefore *that* cannot refer to *faith.* It refers to the whole experience of salvation, including faith.) Salvation is a gift, not a reward.

Salvation cannot be "of works" because the work of salvation has already been completed on the cross. This is the work that God does *for* us, and it is a finished work (John 17:1-4; 19:30). We can add nothing to it (Heb. 10:1-14); we dare take nothing from it. When Jesus died, the veil of the temple was torn in two, from the top to the bottom, signifying that the way to God was now open. There is no more need for earthly sacrifices. One sacrifice—the Lamb of God—has finished the great work of salvation. God did it all, and He did it by His grace.

Sin worked against us and God worked for us, but the great work of conversion is but the beginning.

### God's Work in Us (Eph. 2:10a)

"For we are His workmanship created in Christ Jesus." The Greek word translated "workmanship" is *poiema,* from which we derive our English word "poem." It means "that which is made, a manufactured product." In other words, our conversion is not the end; it is the beginning. We are a part of God's "new creation" (2 Cor. 5:17), and God continues to work in us to make us what He wants us to be. His purpose is to make us more like Christ (Rom. 8:29).

But how does God work in us? Through His Holy Spirit, "both to will and to do of His good pleasure" (Phil. 2:13). Christ finished His work of redemption on the cross, but He arose from the dead and returned to heaven. There He carries on His unfinished work of perfecting His church (Eph. 4:7-16; Heb. 13:20-21). Christ is equipping us for our walk and our work here on earth. To do this, He uses three special tools: the Word of God (1 Thes. 2:13), prayer (Eph. 3:20-21), and suffering (1 Peter 4:11-14). As we read God's Word, understand it, meditate on it, and feed on it, the Word goes to work in our lives to cleanse us and nourish us. As we pray, God's Spirit works in us to release power. And as we suffer, the Spirit of God ministers to us. Suffering drives us back to the Word and prayer, and the cycle is repeated.

Too many Christians think that conversion is the only important experience, and that nothing follows. But this is wrong. We can use the resurrection of Lazarus as an example. After Jesus raised Lazarus from the dead, He said, "Loose him, and let him go" (John 11:44). In other words, "This man is now alive. Get him out of the graveclothes!" Paul has this concept in mind in Ephesians 4:22-24 when he writes, "That ye put off concerning the former conversation [behavior] the old man, which is corrupt . . . and that ye put on the new man, which after God is created in righteousness and true holiness." Colossians 3:1 has the same message: "[Since] ye then be risen with Christ, seek those things which are above."

The same resurrection power that saved you and, took you out of the graveyard of sin can daily help you live for Christ and glorify Him. At great expense to Himself, God worked for us on the cross. And today, on the basis of that price paid at Calvary, He is working in us to conform us to Christ. God cannot work in us unless He has first worked for us, and we have trusted His Son. Also, He cannot work through us unless He works in us. This is why it is important for you to spend time daily in the Word and prayer, and to yield to Christ during times of suffering. For it is through the Word, prayer, and suffering that God works in you.

The Bible shows many examples of this principle. God spent 40 years working in Moses before He could work through him. At the beginning of his ministry, Moses was impetuous and depended on his own strength. He killed an Egyptian and had to flee Egypt, hardly a successful way to start a ministry. But during those 40 years as a humble shepherd in the desert, Moses experienced God's working in his life, a working that prepared him for forty more years of magnificent service.

There are other examples. Joseph suffered for thirteen years before God put him on the throne of Egypt, second to Pharaoh. David was anointed king when he was a youth, but he did not gain the throne until he had suffered many years as an exile. Even the Apostle Paul spent three years in Arabia after his conversion, no doubt experiencing God's deeper work to prepare him for his ministry. God has to work in us before He can work through us; and this leads to the fourth work in our passage.

### God's Work through Us (Eph. 2:10b)

We are "created in Christ Jesus unto good works." We are not saved by good works, but saved unto good works. The famous theologian John Calvin wrote, "It is faith alone that justifies, but faith that justifies can never be alone." We are not saved by faith plus good works, but by a faith that works. The basic Scripture on this theme is James 2, where the writer points out that saving faith always results in a changed life. It is not enough to say that we have faith; we must demonstrate this faith by our works.

The Bible speaks of many different kinds of works. There are "the works of the Law" which cannot save (Gal. 2:16; 3:11). There are also "the works of the flesh" which are listed in Galatians 5:19-21. Paul spoke of "works of darkness" (Rom. 13:12; Eph. 5:11). The "dead works" in Hebrews 6:1 seem to be "works that lead to death," since "the wages of sin is death" (Rom. 6:23). The "works of righteousness" in Titus 3:5 refer to religious works, or other good deeds, that sinners try to practice as a means of salvation. Isaiah declared that "all our righteousnesses are as filthy rags in His sight" (Isa. 64:6). If our righteousnesses are filthy, what must our sins look like!

The "works" Paul writes about, in Ephesians 2:10, have two special characteristics. First, they are "good" works, in contrast to "works of darkness" and "wicked works." If you contrast Ephesians 2:10 with Ephesians 2:2 you will see that the unbeliever has Satan working in him and therefore his works are not good. But the believer has God working in him, and therefore his works are good. His works are not good because he himself is good, but because he has a new nature from God, and because the Holy Spirit works in him and through him to produce these good works.

It is too bad that many believers minimize the place of good works in the Christian life. Because we are not saved by good works, they have the idea that good works are evil; and this is a mistake. "Let your light so shine before men, that they may see your good works, and glorify your Father which is in heaven" (Matt. 5:16). We do not perform good works to glorify ourselves, but to glorify God. Paul desired that Christ would be magnified in his body, even if it meant death (Phil. 1:20-21). We should "abound to every good work" (2 Cor. 9:8), and be "fruitful in every good work" (Col. 1:10). One result of a knowledge of the Bible is that the believer is "thoroughly equipped for every good work" (2 Tim. 3:17, NASB). As believers, we are to be "zealous of good works" (Titus 2:14). Our good works are actually "spiritual sacrifices" that we offer to God (Heb. 13:16).

It is important to note that we do not manufacture these good works. They are the results of the work of God in our hearts. "It is God which worketh in you both to will and to do of His good pleasure" (Phil. 2:13). The secret of Paul's good works was "the grace of God" (1 Cor. 15:10). Our good works are evidence that we have been born again. "Not everyone that saith unto Me, 'Lord, Lord,' shall enter into the kingdom of heaven; but he that doeth the will of My Father which is in heaven" (Matt. 7:21). Our good works are also testimonies to the lost (1 Peter 2:12). They win us the right to be heard.

A pastor friend told about a Christian lady who often visited a retirement home near her house. One day she noticed a lonely man sitting, staring at his dinner tray. In a kindly manner she asked, "Is something wrong?"

"Is something wrong!" replied the man in a heavy accent. "Yes, something is wrong! I am a Jew, and I cannot eat this food!"

"What would you like to have?" she asked.

"I would like a bowl of hot soup!"

She went home and prepared the soup and, after getting permission from the office, took it to the man. In succeeding weeks, she often visited him and brought him the kind of food he enjoyed and eventually she led him to faith in Christ. Yes, preparing soup can be a spiritual sacrifice, a good work to the glory of God.

But these works are not only good; they are also "prepared." "Good works which God hath before ordained [prepared] that we should walk in them" (Eph. 2:10). The only other time this word is used in the New Testament is in Romans 9:23: "vessels of mercy, which He had afore prepared unto glory." The unbeliever walks "according to the course of this world" (Eph. 2:2), but the believer walks in the good works God has prepared for him.

This is an amazing statement. It means that God has a plan for our lives and that we should walk in His will and fulfill His plan. Paul is not talking about "kismet"—an impersonal fate that controls your life no matter what you may do. He is talking about the gracious plan of a loving Heavenly Father, who wills the very best for us. The will of God comes from the heart of God. "The counsel of the Lord standeth forever, the thoughts of His heart to all generations" (Ps. 33:11). We discover God's exciting will for our lives as the Spirit reveals it to us from the Word (1 Cor. 2:9-13).

It would be helpful to close this chapter with a personal inventory. Which of these four works are you experiencing? Is sin working against you because you have not yet trusted Christ? Then trust Him now! Have you experienced His work *for* you—*in* you—*through* you?

Are you wearing the "graveclothes" or the "grace-clothes"? Are you enjoying the liberty you have in Christ, or are you still bound by the habits of the old life in the graveyard of sin? As a Christian, you have been raised and seated on the throne. Practice your position in Christ! He has worked *for* you; now let Him work *in* you and *through* you, that He might give you an exciting, creative life to the glory of God.

# CHAPTER FIVE
# THE GREAT PEACE MISSION
*Ephesians 2:11-22*

"Peace in our time! Peace with honor!" Some of us still remember those words of British Prime Minister, Sir Neville Chamberlain, when he returned from conferences in Germany in September 1938. He was sure that he had stopped Adolf Hitler. Yet one year later, Hitler invaded Poland, and on September 3, 1939, Great Britain declared war on Germany. Chamberlain's great peace mission had failed.

It seems that most peace missions fail. I read somewhere that from 1500 B.C. to A.D. 850 there were 7,500 "eternal covenants" agreed on among various nations with the hope of bringing peace, but that no covenant had lasted longer than two years. The only "eternal covenant" that has lasted—and that will last—is the one made by the eternal God, sealed by the blood of Jesus Christ. It is Christ's peace mission that Paul explains in this section, and three very important words summarize this great work: separation, reconciliation, and unification.

## Separation: What the Gentiles Were (Eph. 2:11-12)
In the first ten verses of Ephesians 2, Paul has discussed the salvation of sinners in general, but now he turns to the work of Christ for Gentiles in particular. Most of the converts in the Ephesian church were Gentiles, and they knew that much of God's program in the Old Testament involved the Jews. For centuries, the "circumcision" (Jews) had looked down on the "uncircumcision" (Gentiles) with an attitude that God had never intended them to display. The fact that a Jew had received the physical mark of the covenant was no proof he was a man of faith (Rom. 2:25-29; Gal. 5:6; 6:15). Those who have trusted Christ have received a spiritual circumcision "made without hands" (Col. 2:11).

But since the hour that God called Abraham, God made a difference between Jews and Gentiles. He made this difference, not that the Jews might boast, but that they might be a blessing and a help to the Gentiles. God set them apart that He might use them to be a channel of His revelation and goodness to the heathen nations. Sad to say, Israel kept this difference nationally and ritually, but not morally. Israel became like the lost nations around her. For this reason, God often had to discipline the Jews because they would not maintain their spiritual separation and minister to the nations in the name of the true God.

The one word that best describes the Gentiles is *without*. They were "outside" in several respects.

**Without Christ.** The Ephesians worshiped the goddess, Diana, and, before the coming of the Gospel, knew nothing about Christ. Those who claim that pagan religions are just as acceptable to God as the Christian faith will have a problem here, for Paul cites the Ephesians' Christless state as a definite tragedy. But then, keep in mind that every unsaved person, Jew or Gentile, is "outside Christ" and that means condemnation.

**Without citizenship.** God called the Jews and built them into a nation. He gave them His laws and His blessings. A Gentile could enter the nation as a proselyte, but he was not born into that very special nation. Israel was God's nation, in a way that was not true of any Gentile nation.

**Without covenants.** While the blessing of the Gentiles is included in God's covenant with Abraham (Gen. 12:1-3), God did not make any covenants with the Gentile nations. The Gentiles were "aliens" and "strangers"—and the Jews never let them forget it. Many of the Pharisees would pray daily, "O God, I give thanks that I am a Jew, not a Gentile."

**Without hope.** Historians tell us that a great cloud of hopelessness covered the ancient world. Philosophies were empty; traditions were disappearing; religions were powerless to help men face either life or death. People longed to pierce the veil and get some message of hope from the other side, but there was none (1 Thes. 4:13-18).

**Without God.** The heathen had gods aplenty, as Paul discovered in Athens (Acts 17:16-23). Someone in that day said that it was easier to find a god than a man in Athens. "There be gods many and lords many," wrote Paul (1 Cor. 8:5). But the pagan, no matter how religious or moral he might have been, did not know the true God. The writer of Psalm 115 contrasted the true God with the idols of the heathen.

It is worth noting that the spiritual plight of the Gentiles was caused not by God but by their own willful sin. Paul said the Gentiles knew the true God but deliberately refused to honor Him (Rom. 1:18-23). Religious history is not a record of man starting with many gods (idolatry) and gradually discovering the one true God.

Rather, it is the sad story of man knowing the truth about God and deliberately turning away from it! It is a story of devolution, not evolution! The first eleven chapters of Genesis give the story of the decline of the Gentiles; and from Genesis 12 on (the call of Abraham), it is the story of the Jews. God separated the Jews from the Gentiles that He might be able to save the Gentiles also. "Salvation is of the Jews" (John 4:22).

God called the Jews, beginning with Abraham, that through them He might reveal Himself as the one true God. With the Jews He deposited His Word, and through the Jews He gave the world the Saviour (Rom. 9:1-5). Israel was to be a light to the Gentiles that they too might be saved. But sad to say, Israel became like the Gentiles, and the light burned but dimly. This fact is a warning to the church today. When the church is least like the world, it does the most for the world.

## Reconciliation: What God Did for the Gentiles (Eph. 2:13-18)

The "but now" in Ephesians 2:13 parallels the "but God" in Ephesians 2:4. Both speak of the gracious intervention of God on behalf of lost sinners. "Enmity" is the key word in this section (Eph. 2:15-16); and you will note that it is a twofold enmity: between Jews and Gentiles (Eph. 2:13-15) and between sinners and God (Eph. 2:16-18). Paul describes here the greatest peace mission in history: Jesus Christ not only reconciled Jews and Gentiles, but He reconciled both to Himself in the one body, the church.

The word *reconcile* means "to bring together again." A distraught husband wants to be reconciled to his wife who has left him; a worried mother longs to be reconciled to a wayward daughter; and the lost sinner needs to be reconciled to God. Sin is the great separator in this world. It has been dividing people since the very beginning of human history. When Adam and Eve sinned, they were separated from God. Before long, their sons were separated from each other and Cain killed Abel. The earth was filled with violence (Gen.

6:5-13) and the only remedy seemed to be judgment. But even after the Flood, men sinned against God and each other, and even tried to build their own unity without God's help. The result was another judgment that scattered the nations and confused the tongues. It was then that God called Abraham, and through the nation of Israel, Jesus Christ came to the world. It was His work on the cross that abolished the enmity between Jew and Gentile and between sinners and God.

***The enmity between Jews and Gentiles (vv. 13-15).*** God had put a difference between Jews and Gentiles so that His purposes in salvation might be accomplished. But once those purposes were accomplished, there was no more difference. In fact, it was His purpose that these differences be erased forever, and they are erased through the work of Christ in reconciliation.

It was this lesson that was so difficult for the early church to understand. For centuries, the Jews had been different from the Gentiles—in religion, dress, diet, and laws. Until Peter was sent to the Gentiles (Acts 10), the church had no problems. But with the salvation of the Gentiles on the same terms as the Jews, problems began to develop. The Jewish Christians reprimanded Peter for going to the Gentiles and eating with them (Acts 11), and representatives of the churches gathered for an important conference on the place of the Gentiles in the church (Acts 15). Must a Gentile become a Jew to become a Christian? Their conclusion was, "No! Jews and Gentiles are saved the same way—by faith in Jesus Christ." The enmity was gone!

The cause of that enmity was the Law, because the Law made a definite distinction between Jews and Gentiles. The dietary laws reminded the Jews that God had put a difference between the clean and unclean (Lev. 11:44-47). But the Gentiles did not obey these laws; therefore they were unclean. Ezekiel the prophet reminded the priests that their task was to teach the Jews "the difference between the holy and the profane" (Ezek. 44:23). The divine ordinances given by God to Israel stood as a wall between the Jews and the other nations. In fact, there was a wall in the Jewish temple, separating the court of the Gentiles from the rest of the temple areas. Archeologists have discovered the inscription from Herod's temple, and it reads like this:

No foreigner may enter within the barricade which surrounds the sanctuary and enclosure. Anyone who is caught doing so will have himself to blame for his ensuing death.

It was this wall that the Jews thought Paul and his Gentile friends crossed when the Jews attacked him in the temple and threatened to kill him (Acts 21:28-31).

In order for Jews and Gentiles to be reconciled, this wall had to be destroyed, and this Jesus did on the cross. The cost of destroying the enmity was the blood of Christ. When He died, the veil in the temple was literally torn in two, and the wall of separation (figuratively) was torn down. By fulfilling the demands of the Law in His righteous life, and by bearing the curse of the Law in His sacrificial death (Gal. 3:10-13), Jesus removed the legal barrier that separated Jew from Gentile. For centuries, there was a difference between them. But today, "there is no difference between the Jew and the Greek. For the same Lord over all is rich unto all that call upon Him. For whosoever shall call upon the name of the Lord shall be saved" (Rom. 10:12-13).

In Jesus Christ, Jew and Gentile become one. "He is our peace" (Eph. 2:14). Through Christ, the far-off Gentile is made nigh (Eph. 2:13, 17), and both Jew and Gentile are made one. The consequences of Christ's work are, then, the destroying of the enmity by the abolishing of the Law, and the creating of a new man—the church, the body of Christ. The word *abolish* simply means "to nullify." The Law no longer holds sway over either Jew or Gentile, since in Christ believers are not under Law but under grace. The righteousness of the Law, revealing God's holiness, is still God's standard. But this is fulfilled in the believer by the Holy Spirit (Rom. 8:1-4). It took the early church a long time to get accustomed to "there is no difference!" In fact, some religious groups have not learned the lesson yet, for they are trying to get Christians back under Law (Gal. 4:8-11; 5:1; Col. 2:13-23).

Christ "is our peace" (Eph. 2:14) and He made "peace" (Eph. 2:15). That verb *to make* in Ephesians 2:15 means "to create." The church, the body of Christ, is God's new creation (2 Cor. 5:15). Everything in the old creation is falling apart because of sin, but in the new creation there is unity because of righteousness. "There is neither Jew nor Greek, there is neither bond nor free, there is neither male nor female: for ye are all one in Christ Jesus" (Gal. 3:28). You may contrast the old position of the Gentiles with their new position and see how wonderfully Christ worked on their behalf on the cross:

| Old Position | New Position |
|---|---|
| "without Christ" | "in Christ" (Eph. 2:13) |
| "aliens" | "a holy nation" (1 Peter 2:9) |
| "strangers" | "no more strangers" (Eph. 2:19) |
| "no hope" | "called in one hope" (Eph. 4:4) |
| "without God" (Eph. 2:12) | "The God and Father of our Lord Jesus Christ" (Eph. 1:3) |

**The enmity between sinners and God (vv. 16-18).** Not only did the Gentiles need to be reconciled to the Jews, but both the Jews and the Gentiles needed to be reconciled to God! This was the conclusion the Apostles came to at the Jerusalem Conference recorded in Acts 15. Peter said that God "put no difference between us [Jews] and them [Gentiles], purifying their hearts by faith. . . . But we believe that through the grace of the Lord Jesus Christ we shall be saved, even as they" (Acts 15:9, 11). It was not a question of the Gentile becoming a Jew to become a Christian, but the Jew admitting he was a sinner like the Gentile. "For there is no difference: for all have sinned and come short of the glory of God" (Rom. 3:22-23). The same Law that separated Gentile and Jew also separated men and God, and Christ bore the curse of the Law.

A man stopped in my office one day and said he wanted to get help. "My wife and I need a re-cancellation!" he blurted out. I knew he meant "reconciliation." But in one sense, "re-cancellation" was the right word. They had sinned against each other (and the Lord), and there could be no harmony until those sins were cancelled. A God of love wants to reconcile the sinner to Himself, but a God of holiness must see to it that sin is judged. God solved the problem by sending His Son to be the sacrifice for our sins, thereby revealing His love and meeting the demands of His righteousness. It was truly a "re-cancellation" (see Col. 2:13-14).

Jesus Christ "is our peace" (Eph. 2:14). He "made peace" (Eph. 2:15), and He "preached peace" (Eph. 2:17). As the Judge, He could have come to declare war. But in His grace, He came with the message of peace (Luke 2:8-14; 4:16-19). Jew and Gentile are at peace with each other in Christ, and both have open access to God (Rom. 5:1-2). This reminds us of the rent veil at the time of Christ's death (Matt. 27:50-51; Heb. 10:14-25). Reconciliation is complete!

## Unification: What Jews and Gentiles Are in Christ (Eph. 2:19-22)

Paul has repeated the word "one" to emphasize the unifying work of Christ: "made both one" (Eph. 2:14); "one new man" (Eph. 2:15); "one body" (Eph. 2:16); "one Spirit" (Eph. 2:18). All spiritual distance and division have been overcome by Christ. In the closing verses of this chapter, Paul gives three pictures that illustrate the unity of believing Jews and Gentiles in the church.

*One nation (v. 19a).* Israel was God's chosen nation, but they rejected their Redeemer and suffered the consequences. The kingdom was taken from them and given to "a nation bringing forth the fruits thereof" (Matt. 21:43). This "new nation" is the church, "a chosen generation . . . a holy nation, a peculiar people" (Ex. 19:6; 1 Peter 2:9). In the Old Testament, the nations were reckoned by their descent from Shem, Ham, or Japheth (Gen. 10). In the Book of Acts, we see these three families united in Christ. In Acts 8, a descendant of Ham is saved, the Ethiopian treasurer; in Acts 9, a descendant of Shem, Saul of Tarsus, who became Paul the apostle; and in Acts 10, the descendants of Japheth, the Gentiles in the household of the Roman soldier, Cornelius. Sin has divided mankind, but Christ unites by His Spirit. All believers, regardless of national background, belong to that "holy nation" with citizenship in heaven (Phil. 3:20-21).

*One family (v. 19b).* Through faith in Christ, we enter into God's family, and God becomes our Father. This wonderful family of God is found in two places, "in heaven and earth" (Eph. 3:15). Living believers are on earth; believers who have died are in heaven. None of God's children are "under the earth" (Phil. 2:10) or in any other place in the universe. We are all brothers and sisters in the one family, no matter what racial, national, or physical distinctions we may possess.

*One temple (vv. 20-22).* In the Book of Genesis, God "walked" with His people (Gen.

5:22, 24; 6:9); but in Exodus, He decided to "dwell" with His people (Ex. 25:8). God dwelt in the tabernacle (Ex. 40:34-38) until Israel's sins caused "the glory to depart" (1 Sam. 4). Then God dwelt in the temple (1 Kings 8:1-11); but, alas, again Israel sinned and the glory departed (Ezek. 10:18-19). God's next dwelling place was the body of Christ (John 1:14), which men took and nailed to a cross. Today, through His Spirit, God dwells in the church, the temple of God. God does not dwell in man-made temples, including church buildings (Acts 7:48-50). He dwells in the hearts of those who have trusted Christ (1 Cor. 6:19-20), and in the church collectively (Eph. 2:20-22).

The foundation for this church was laid by the Apostles and New Testament prophets. Jesus Christ is the Foundation (1 Cor. 3:11) and the Chief Cornerstone (Ps. 118:22; Isa. 8:14). The cornerstone binds the structure together; Jesus Christ has united Jews and Gentiles in the church. This reference to the temple would be meaningful to both the Jews and the Gentiles in the Ephesian church: the Jews would think of Herod's temple in Jerusalem, and the Gentiles would think of the great temple of Diana. Both temples were destined to be destroyed, but the temple Christ is building will last forever. "I will build My church" (Matt. 16:18). The Holy Spirit builds this temple by taking dead stones out of the pit of sin (Ps. 40:2), giving them life, and setting them lovingly into the temple of God (1 Peter 2:5). This temple is "fitly framed together" as the body of Christ (Eph. 2:21; 4:16), so that every part accomplishes the purpose God has in mind.

As you look back over this chapter, you cannot help but praise God for what He, in His grace, has done for sinners. Through Christ, He has raised us from the dead and seated us on the throne. He has reconciled us and set us into His temple. Neither spiritual *death* nor spiritual *distance* can defeat the grace of God! But He has not only saved us individually, He has also made us a part of His church collectively. What a tremendous privilege it is to be a part of God's eternal program!

This leads to two practical applications as we close this study.

First, have you personally experienced the grace of God? Are you spiritually dead? Are you distant from God? Or have you trusted Christ and received that eternal life that only He can give? If you are not sure of your spiritual position, I urge you to turn to Christ by faith and trust Him. Like the nation of Israel, you may have been given many spiritual privileges, only to reject the God who gave them. Or, like the Gentiles, you may have turned away from God and lived deliberately in sin and disobedience. In either case, "there is no difference, for all have sinned and come short of the glory of God" (Rom. 3:22-23). Call on Christ—He will save you.

Second, if you are a true believer in Christ, are you helping others to trust Him? You have been raised from the dead—do you "walk in newness of life"? (Rom. 6:4) Do you share this Good News of eternal life with others? You are no longer at enmity with God, but are you spreading the Good News of "peace with God" with those who are still fighting Him?

Jesus Christ died to make reconciliation possible. You and I must live to make the message of reconciliation personal. God has "given to us the ministry of reconciliation" (2 Cor. 5:18). We are His ambassadors of peace (2 Cor. 5:20). Our feet should be shod "with the preparation of the Gospel of peace" (Eph. 6:15). "Blessed are the peacemakers, for they shall be called the children of God" (Matt. 5:9).

A missionary was preaching in the village market, and some of the people were laughing at him because he was not a very handsome man. He took it for a time, and then he said to the crowd, "It is true that I do not have beautiful hair, for I am almost bald. Nor do I have beautiful teeth, for they are really not mine; they were made by the dentist. I do not have a beautiful face, nor can I afford to wear beautiful clothes. But this I know: I have beautiful feet!" And he quoted the verse from Isaiah: "How beautiful upon the mountains are the feet of him that bringeth good tidings, that publisheth peace" (Isa. 52:7). Do you have beautiful feet?

# CHAPTER SIX
# I KNOW A SECRET
*Ephesians 3:1-13*

I was once a character witness at a child-custody trial. I was grateful that the case was being tried at a small rural county seat rather than in a big city, because it was my first experience on the witness stand. I have since learned that the location of the court makes little difference. All trials can be difficult and it is no fun to be a witness at any.

The prosecutor's first question caught me unawares, "Reverend, do you think that a man who has been in prison is fit to raise a child?"

I was supposed to answer "Yes" or "No," so the reply I gave did not make the judge too happy. "Well," I said slowly, stalling for time, "I guess it depends on the man. Some very famous people have been in jail and have made the world a better place because of their experiences—John Bunyan, for example, and the great Apostle Paul." I could have given other examples from the Bible, but I detected that my answer was not acceptable to the court.

Twice in this letter, Paul reminds his readers that he is a prisoner (Eph. 3:1; 4:1), and at the close he calls himself an "ambassador in bonds" (Eph. 6:20). No doubt the Ephesians were asking, "Why is Paul a prisoner in Rome? Why would God permit such a thing?" In this paragraph, Paul explains his situation and, in doing so, also explains one of the greatest truths in this letter, the "mystery" of the church. In the New Testament, a *mystery* is not something eerie or inscrutable, but rather "a truth that was hidden by God in times past and is now revealed to those who are in His family." A *mystery* is a "sacred secret" that is unknown to unbelievers, but understood and treasured by the people of God.

Paul explains the mystery—the Gentile believers are now united to the Jewish believers in one body, the church (Eph. 3:6). He had mentioned this new work of God, so his readers were familiar with the concept (Eph. 1:10; 2:11, 22). But now Paul explains the tremendous impact of this "sacred secret" that had so possessed his own life and ministry. Actually, this explanation is almost a parenthesis in the letter, for Paul begins this section with the intention of praying for his readers. Compare Ephesians 3:1 and 14. His use of the words "prisoner" and "Gentiles" leads him into this important explanation of the "mystery of the church," and in this explanation, Paul shows us that the "mystery" is important to four different groups of persons.

## It Was Important to Paul (Eph. 3:1-5)

The best way to grasp the importance of "the mystery" in Paul's life is to focus on the two descriptions he gives of himself in this section. He begins by calling himself "a prisoner" (Eph. 3:1), and then he calls himself "a minister" (Eph. 3:7). Paul was a prisoner because he believed in God's new program of uniting believing Jews and Gentiles into one body, the church. The orthodox Jews in Paul's day considered the Gentiles "dogs," but some of the Christian Jews did not have a much better attitude toward the Gentiles.

Paul was a leader in Jewish orthodoxy when Christ saved him (Gal. 1:11-24; Phil. 3:1-11); yet in the providence of God, he began his early ministry in a local church in Antioch that was composed of both Jews and Gentiles (Acts 11:19-26). When the council was held at Jerusalem to determine the status of believing Gentiles, Paul courageously defended the grace of God and the unity of the church (Acts 15; Gal. 2:1-10).

Paul knew from the very beginning of his Christian life that God had called him to take the Gospel to the Gentiles (Acts 9:15; 26:13-18), and he was not disobedient to that call. Wherever Paul ministered, he founded local churches composed of believing Jews and Gentiles, all "one in Christ Jesus" (Gal. 3:28).

Because Paul was the "apostle to the Gentiles" (Rom. 11:13; 15:15-16; Eph. 3:8; 1 Tim. 2:7), he was accused of being prejudiced against the Jews, particularly the Jewish believers in Jerusalem and Judea. The special offering Paul collected for the needy believers in Judea should have shown the goodwill that existed between these churches and the churches Paul founded (Rom. 15:25-33). Paul delivered the offering in person (Acts 21:17-19), and from all evidence, it was graciously received by the Judean Christians. Even though Paul took drastic steps to pacify the Jewish believers, there was a riot in the temple and Paul was arrested (Acts 21:30-33). Paul defended himself by giving his personal testimony, and the crowd listened to him until he got to the word "Gentiles" and then they

rioted again (Acts 22:22-23). The rest of the Book of Acts explains how Paul got from Jerusalem to Rome, "a prisoner of Jesus Christ for you Gentiles" (Eph. 3:1). Had Paul compromised his message and encouraged the selfish prejudices of the Jews he probably would have been released.

Paul was not only a "prisoner" because of "the mystery," but he was also a "minister." God gave him a "dispensation" (stewardship) that he might go to the Gentiles, not only with the Good News of salvation through Christ, but also with the message that Jews and Gentiles are now one in Christ. The word *dispensation* comes from two Greek words: *oikos*, meaning "house" and *nomos*, meaning "law." Our English word "economy" is derived directly from the Greek *oikonomia*, "the law of the house," or "a stewardship, a management." God has different ways of managing His program from age to age, and these different "stewardships" Bible students sometimes call "dispensations" (Eph. 1:9-10). God's principles do not change, but His methods of dealing with mankind do change over the course of history. "Distinguish the ages," wrote St. Augustine, "and the Scriptures harmonize."

God made Paul a steward of "the mystery" with the responsibility of sharing it with the Gentiles. It was not enough simply to win them to Christ and form them into local assemblies. He was also to teach them their wonderful position in Christ as members of the body, sharing God's grace equally with the Jews. This truth had not been revealed in the Old Testament Scriptures. It was revealed to the New Testament Apostles and prophets (see Eph. 4:11) by the Holy Spirit. God revealed it personally to Paul, and it was his responsibility to share it with the Gentile Christians. This was the "dispensation"—or stewardship—that God had given him. And because Paul was a faithful steward, he was now a prisoner in Rome. Like Joseph in the Old Testament, his faithful stewardship resulted in false arrest and imprisonment. But, in the end, it brought great glory to God and salvation to Jews and Gentiles.

## It Was Important to the Gentiles (Eph. 3:6-8)

In Ephesians 2:11-22, we discovered that Christ's work on the cross accomplished much more than the salvation of individual sinners. It reconciled Jews and Gentiles to each other and to God. It is this truth that Paul presents here, and you can imagine what exciting news it would be! The truth of "the mystery" reveals to believing Gentiles that they have a wonderful new relationship through Jesus Christ.

To begin with, they are fellow-heirs with the Jews and share in the spiritual riches God gave them because of His covenant with Abraham (Gal. 3:29). In Christ, being a Jew or a Gentile is neither an asset nor a liability, for together we share the riches of Christ. The Gentiles are also fellow-members of the body of Christ, the church. "There is one body" (Eph. 4:4). Our human birth determines our racial distinctions, but our spiritual birth unites us as members of the same body (1 Cor. 12:12-14). Christ is the Head of this body (Eph. 5:22-23), and each individual member shares in the ministry (Eph. 4:10-13). Finally, in their new relationship, the Gentiles are partakers of God's promises. Once they were outside the covenant, with no claims on the promises of God (Eph. 2:12); but now, in Christ, they share the promises of God with the believing Jews. In Romans 11:13-15, Paul explains that believing Gentiles share in the spiritual riches that God gave to Israel. But in Romans 11:1-12, Paul explains that God has not, because of the church, negated His promises to Israel. The church today shares in the spiritual riches of Israel, but one day God will restore His people and fulfill His promises concerning their land and their kingdom.

"The mystery" not only gives believing Gentiles a new relationship, it also reveals that there is a new power available to them (Eph. 3:7). This power is illustrated in the life of Paul. God saved him by grace and gave him a stewardship, a special ministry to the Gentiles. But God also gave Paul the power to accomplish this ministry. The word "working" here is *energeia* from which we get our word "energy." The word "power" is *dunamis* which gives us our words "dynamic" and "dynamite." Paul has already told us about this mighty power in Ephesians 1:19-23, and he will mention it again in Ephesians 3:20 and Ephesians 4:16. The mighty resurrection power of Christ is available to us for daily life and service.

Finally, there is available to the Gentiles new riches: "the unsearchable riches of Christ" (Eph. 3:8). Paul called them "exceeding riches" (Eph. 2:7) but here he describes them as "unfathomable." The words can also be translated "untraceable," which means that they are so vast you cannot discover their end. (Some students suggest that "untraceable" might also carry the idea that "the mystery" cannot be traced in the Old Testament since it was hidden by God.)

Are these riches available to every believer? Yes! In fact, Paul makes it clear that he himself had no special claim on God's wealth, for he considered himself "less than the least of all saints" (Eph. 3:8). The name *Paul* (Paulus) means "little" in Latin, and perhaps Paul bore this name because he realized how insignificant he really was (Acts 13:9). He calls himself "the least of the apostles" (1 Cor. 15:9), but at least he was an apostle, which is more than we can claim. Here he calls himself, not "the least of all saints," but "less than the least of all saints" (Eph. 3:8), and he later calls himself the "chief of sinners" (1 Tim. 1:15). Understanding the deep truths of God's Word does not give a man a big head; it gives him a broken and contrite heart.

## It Is Important to the Angels (Eph. 3:9-10)

Perhaps at this point, you are asking yourself the question, "Why did God keep His secret about the church hidden for so many centuries?" Certainly the Old Testament clearly states that God will save the Gentiles through Israel, but nowhere are we told that both Jews and Gentiles will form a new creation, the church, the body of Christ. It was this mystery that the Spirit revealed to Paul and other leaders in the early church, and that was so difficult for the Jews to accept.

Paul tells us that "the principalities and powers" are also involved in this great secret. God is "educating" the angels by means of the church! By "the principalities and powers," Paul means the angelic beings created by God, both good and evil (Eph. 1:21; 6:12; Col. 1:16; 2:15). Angels are created beings and are not omniscient. In fact, Peter indicates that during the Old Testament period, the angels were curious about God's plan of salvation then being worked out on earth (1 Peter 1:10-12). Certainly the angels rejoice at the repentance of a lost sinner (Luke 15:10); and Paul suggests that the angels watch the activities of the local assembly (1 Cor. 11:10). "We are made a spectacle unto the world, and to angels," Paul writes (1 Cor. 4:9).

What, then, do the angels learn from the church? "The manifold wisdom of God" (Eph.

3:10). Certainly the angels know about the power of God as seen in His creation. But the wisdom of God as seen in His new creation, the church, is something new to them. Unsaved men, including wise philosophers, look at God's plan of salvation and consider it "foolishness" (1 Cor. 1:18-31). But the angels watch the outworking of God's salvation, and they praise His wisdom. Paul calls it *manifold wisdom,* and this word carries the idea of "variegated" or "many-colored." This suggests the beauty and variety of God's wisdom in His great plan of salvation.

But there is another facet to this truth that must be explored. What are the *evil* angels learning from God's "mystery"? That their leader, Satan, does not have any wisdom! Satan knows the Bible, and he understood from the Old Testament Scriptures *that* the Saviour would come, *when* He would come, *how* He would come, and *where* He would come. Satan also understood *why* He would come, as far as redemption is concerned. But nowhere in the Old Testament would Satan find any prophecies concerning the church, "the mystery" of Jews and Gentiles united in one body! Satan could see unbelieving Jews rejecting their Messiah, and he could see Gentiles trusting the Messiah, but he could not see both believing Jews and Gentiles united in one body, seated with Christ in the heavenlies, and completely victorious over Satan! Had Satan known the far-reaching results of the Cross, no doubt he would have altered his plans accordingly.

God hid this great plan "from the beginning of the world," but now He wants "the mystery" to be known by His church. And this is why He made Paul a "steward" of this great truth. Ephesians 3:9 should read, "And to make all men see what is the stewardship of the mystery." Here is an amazing truth: Now *all believers* are to be faithful stewards of this great truth! This "sacred secret" that was so important to Paul, and to the Gentiles, and to angels, is now in *our* hands!

## It Should Be Important to Christians Today (Eph. 3:11-13)

When God saved Paul, He deposited with him the precious treasures of Gospel truth (1 Tim. 1:11). Paul in turn committed these truths to others, exhorting them to commit the truths to faithful men who would guard them and share them (2 Tim. 2:2). "O Timothy! Keep that which is committed to thy trust!" (1 Tim.

6:20) At the close of his life, Paul would say, to the glory of God, "I have kept the faith" (2 Tim. 4:7). During those apostolic days, the truths of the Gospel and "the mystery" were guarded, preached, and handed down to faithful men.

But a study of church history reveals that, one by one, many of the basic truths of the Word of God were lost during the centuries that followed. God had His faithful people—a minority—at all times, but many of the great truths of the Word were buried under man-made theology, tradition, and ritual. Then, God's Spirit began to open the eyes of seeking souls, and these great truths were unveiled again. Martin Luther championed justification by faith. Other spiritual leaders rediscovered the person and work of the Holy Spirit, the glorious truth of the return of Jesus Christ, and the joy of the victorious Christian life. In recent years, the truth of "the mystery" has again excited the hearts of God's people. We rejoice that we are "all one in Christ Jesus."

Most of us identify Napoleon Bonaparte as the would-be conqueror of Europe. But not many would name him as a patron of arts and sciences. Yet he was. In July 1798, Napoleon began to occupy Egypt, but by September 1801, he was forced to get out. Those three years meant failure as far as his military and political plans were concerned, but they meant success in one area that greatly interested him—archeology. For in August 1799, a Frenchman named Boussand discovered the Rosetta Stone about thirty miles from Alexandria. This discovery gave to archeologists the key to understanding Egyptian hieroglyphics. It opened the door to modern Egyptian studies.

"The mystery" is God's "Rosetta Stone." It is the key to what He promised in the Old Testament, what Christ did in the Gospels, what the early church did in the Book of Acts, what Paul and the other writers teach in the Epistles, and what God will do as recorded in the Book of Revelation. God's program today is not "the headship of Israel" (Deut. 28:1-13), but the headship of Christ over His church. We today are under a different "stewardship" from that of Moses and the prophets, and we must be careful not to confuse what God has clarified.

The reason many churches are weak and ineffective is because they do not understand what they have in Christ. And the cause of this is often spiritual leaders who are not good "stewards of the mystery." Because they do not "rightly divide the Word of truth" (2 Tim. 2:15), they confuse their people concerning their spiritual position in Christ, and they rob their people of the spiritual wealth in Christ.

This great truth concerning the church is not a divine afterthought. It is a part of God's eternal purpose in Christ (Eph. 3:11). To ignore this truth is to sin against the Father who planned it, the Son whose death made it possible, and the Spirit who today seeks to work in our lives to accomplish what God has planned. When you understand this truth, it gives you great confidence and faith (Eph. 3:12). When you know what God is doing in the world, and you work with Him, you can be sure that He will work *in* you and *for* you. All of His divine resources are available to those who sincerely want to do His will and help Him accomplish His purposes on earth.

The early church thought that the Gospel belonged to the Jews because it had come *through* them and *to* them first. Until Peter, by divine direction, went to the Gentiles in Acts 10, the Jewish believers thought that a Gentile had to become a Jew before he could become a Christian! God's Spirit gradually revealed to the churches that God was doing a new thing: He was calling out a people for His name from both the Jews and Gentiles (Acts 15:14). There are no national, racial, political, physical, or social distinctions in the church! "There is neither Jew nor Greek, there is neither bond nor free, there is neither male nor female; for ye are all one in Christ Jesus" (Gal. 3:28).

But an understanding of God's program in this present age not only gives the believer confidence toward God. It also gives him courage in the difficult circumstances of life. Paul's sufferings for the Gentiles would mean glory for the Gentiles. In the Old Testament age, when God's people obeyed, God blessed them materially, nationally, and physically (Deut. 28); and if they disobeyed, He withdrew these blessings. This is not the way He deals with the church today. Our blessings are spiritual, not material (Eph. 1:3); they have *all* been given to us completely in Christ. We appropriate them by faith; but if we disobey God, He does not revoke them. We simply lose the enjoyment and the enrichment of them. Paul was certainly a dedicated, Spirit-filled man; yet he was suffering as a prisoner. Paul made it clear that physical, material blessings are not always the experience of the

dedicated Christian (2 Cor. 4:7-12; 11:23–12:10).

I was driving to a preaching engagement, trying to follow a map I had found in the glove compartment of my car. (I am a very poor navigator, so my wife is usually the navigator in our family.) For some reason, I could not locate the interstate highway I needed, so I stopped to get directions at a filling station.

"You've got an ancient map there, Mister!" the attendant told me. "Here's the latest map. Follow it and you'll get where you are going." He was right. I followed the new map and arrived in plenty of time to preach.

People who do not understand God's "mystery" in His church are trying to make spiritual progress with the wrong map. Or, to change the figure, they are trying to build with the wrong blueprints. God's churches on this earth—the local assemblies—are not supposed to be either Gentile culture cliques or Jewish culture cliques. For a German church to refuse fellowship to a Swede is just as unscriptural as for a Jewish congregation to refuse a Gentile. God's church is not to be shackled by culture, class, or any other physical distinction. It is a spiritual entity that must submit to the headship of Jesus Christ in the power of the Spirit.

Yes, God had a "secret"—but God does not want it to be a secret anymore! If you understand your wonderful position in Christ, then live up to it—and share the blessing with others. This "secret" was important to Paul, to the Gentiles, and to the angels—and it ought to be important to you and me today.

# CHAPTER SEVEN
# GET YOUR HANDS ON YOUR WEALTH
*Ephesians 3:14-21*

This passage is the second of two prayers recorded in Ephesians, the first one being Ephesians 1:15-23. In the first prayer, the emphasis is on *enlightenment;* but in this prayer, the emphasis is on *enablement.* It is not so much a matter of *knowing* as *being*—laying our hands on what God has for us and by faith making it a vital part of our lives. Paul is saying, "I want you to get your hands on your wealth, realize how vast it is, and start to use it."

It is worth noting that both of these prayers, as well as the other prison prayers (Phil. 1:9-11; Col. 1:9-12), deal with the spiritual condition of the inner man, and not the material needs of the body. Certainly it is not wrong to pray for physical and material needs, but the emphasis in these petitions is on the spiritual. Paul knew that if the inner man is what he ought to be, the outer man will be taken care of in due time. Too many of our prayers focus only on physical and material needs and fail to lay hold of the deeper inner needs of the heart. It would do us good to use these prison prayers as our own, and ask God to help us in our inner person. That is where the greatest needs are.

### The Invocation (Eph. 3:14-15)
The first thing that strikes us is Paul's posture: "I bow my knees." (This must have been quite an experience for the Roman soldier chained to Paul!) The Bible nowhere commands any special posture for prayer. Abraham stood before the Lord when he prayed for Sodom (Gen. 18:22), and Solomon stood when he prayed to dedicate the temple (1 Kings 8:22). David "sat before the Lord" (1 Chron. 17:16) when he prayed about the future of his kingdom. And Jesus "fell on His face" when He prayed in Gethsemane (Matt. 26:39).

You have noticed, no doubt, the emphasis on spiritual posture in Ephesians. As lost sinners, we were buried in the graveyard (Eph. 2:1). But when we trusted Christ, He raised us from the dead and seated us with Christ in the heavenlies (Eph. 2:4-6). Because we are *seated* with Christ, we can *walk* so as to please Him (Eph. 4:1, 17; 5:2, 8, 15); and we can *stand* against the devil (Eph. 6:10-13). But the posture that links "sitting" with "walking" and "standing" is "bowing the knee." It is through prayer that we lay hold of God's riches that enable us to behave like Christians and battle like Christians. Whether we actually bow our knees is not the important thing; that we bow our hearts and wills to the Lord and ask Him for what we need is the vital matter.

Paul's prayer was addressed to "the Father of our Lord Jesus Christ." In the Bible, prayer is addressed to the Father, through the Son, and in the Spirit. This is the usual pattern,

though you do find petitions addressed to the Son, and possibly to the Spirit (1 Thes. 3:12-13). In Ephesians 1:3, Paul calls the Father "the God and Father of our Lord Jesus Christ." He was the "God . . . of our Lord Jesus Christ" when Jesus was here on earth, for as man, Jesus lived in total dependence on God. This title reminds us of Christ's humanity. But God is the "Father of our Lord Jesus Christ" because Jesus Christ is eternal God; so this title reminds us of His deity.

There is a sense, however, in which all men in general, and Christians in particular, share in the fatherhood of God. Paul states that "the whole family in heaven and earth is named" after the divine Father. That word *family* can be translated "fatherhood." Every fatherhood in heaven and on earth gets its origin and name from the Father. He is the great Original; every other fatherhood is but a copy. Adam is called "the son of God" (Luke 3:38), referring to his creation. Believers are the "sons of God" by rebirth (John 1:11-13; 1 John 3:1-2). All men are not children of God by nature. Instead, they are children of disobedience and children of wrath (Eph. 2:2-3). As Creator, God is the Father of each man; but as Saviour, He is only the Father of those who believe. There is no such thing in Scripture as the universal fatherhood of God that saves all men. "Ye must be born again" (John 3:7).

### The Petition (Eph. 3:16-19)
There are four requests in Paul's prayer, but they must not be looked on as isolated, individual petitions. These four requests are more like four parts to a telescope. One request leads into the next one, and so on. He prays that the inner man might have spiritual strength, which will, in turn, lead to a deeper experience with Christ. This deeper experience will enable them to "apprehend" (get hold of) God's great love, which will result in their being "filled unto all the fullness of God." So, then, Paul is praying for strength, depth, apprehension, and fullness.

***Strength (v. 16).*** The presence of the Holy Spirit in the life is evidence of salvation (Rom. 8:9); but the power of the Spirit is enablement for Christian living, and it is this power that Paul desires for his readers. "Ye shall receive power, when the Holy Spirit is come upon you" (Acts 1:8, literal translation). Jesus performed His ministry on earth in the power of the Spirit (Luke 4:1, 14; Acts

10:38), and this is the only resource we have for Christian living today. As you read the Book of Acts, you see the importance of the Holy Spirit in the life of the church, for there are some fifty-nine references to the Spirit in the book, or one fourth of the total references found in the New Testament. Someone has said, "If God took the Holy Spirit out of this world, most of what we Christians are doing would go right on—and nobody would know the difference!" Sad, but true.

The power of the Spirit is given to us "according to the riches of His glory" (Eph. 3:16). Christ returned to glory and sent the Spirit from heaven to indwell and empower His people. It is not necessary for us to "work something up." The power has to be sent down. How marvelous that God does not give the Spirit's power to us "out of His riches" but "according to"—which is a far greater thing. If I am a billionaire and I give you ten dollars, I have given you *out of* my riches; but if I give you a million dollars, I have given to you *according to* my riches. The first is a *portion;* the second is a *proportion.*

This power is available for "the inner man." This means the spiritual part of man where God dwells and works. The inner man of the lost sinner is dead (Eph. 2:1), but it becomes alive when Christ is invited in. The inner man can see (Ps. 119:18), hear (Matt. 13:9), taste (Ps. 34:8), and feel (Acts 17:27); and he must be "exercised" (1 Tim. 4:7-8). He also must be cleansed (Ps. 51:7) and fed (Matt. 4:4). The outer man is perishing, but the inner man can be renewed spiritually in spite of outward physical decay (2 Cor. 4:16-18). It is this inner power that makes him succeed.

What does it mean to have the Holy Spirit empower the inner man? It means that our spiritual faculties are controlled by God, and we are exercising them and growing in the Word (Heb. 5:12-14). It is only when we yield to the Spirit and let Him control the inner man that we succeed in living to the glory of God. This means feeding the inner man the Word of God, praying and worshiping, keeping clean, and exercising the senses by loving obedience.

**Depth (v. 17).** Paul uses three pictures here to convey this idea of spiritual depth, and the three pictures are hidden in the three verbs: "dwell," "rooted," and "grounded." The verb *dwell* literally means (and here I follow Dr. Kenneth Wuest) "to settle down and feel at home." Certainly Christ was already

resident in the hearts of the Ephesians, or else Paul would not have addressed them as "saints" in Ephesians 1:1. What Paul is praying for is a deeper experience between Christ and His people. He yearns for Christ to settle down and feel at home in their hearts—not a surface relationship, but an ever-deepening fellowship.

Abraham's life is an illustration of this truth. God was going to bless Abraham with a son, so the Lord Himself came down and visited Abraham's tent, and He brought two angels with Him. They came to the tent, they talked with Abraham, and they even ate a meal with him. They felt very much at home, because Abraham was a man of faith and obedience. But the three guests had another task. They had to investigate the sins of Sodom because God planned to destroy the cities of Sodom and Gomorrah. Lot, a believer, was living in Sodom, and God wanted to warn him to get out before the judgment could fall. But the Lord Himself did not go to Sodom. He sent the two angels (Gen. 18–19). The Lord did not feel at home in Lot's house the way He felt at home in Abraham's tent.

The verb *rooted* moves us into the plant world. The tree must get its roots deep into the soil if it is to have both nourishment and stability; and the Christian must have his spiritual roots deep into the love of God. Psalm 1:1-3 is a perfect description of this word, and Jeremiah 17:5-8 is a good commentary on it. One of the most important questions a Christian can ask himself is, "From what do I draw my nourishment and my stability?" If there is to be power in the Christian life, then there must be depth. The roots must go deeper and deeper into the love of Christ.

*Grounded* is an architectural term; it refers to the foundations on which we build. In the first two churches I pastored, we were privileged to construct new buildings, and in both projects it seemed we would never get out of the ground. In my second building program, we had to spend several thousand dollars taking soil tests because we were building over an old lake bed. For weeks, the men were laying out and pouring the footings. One day I complained to the architect, and he replied, "Pastor, the most important part of this building is the foundation. If you don't go deep, you can't go high." That sentence has been a sermon to me ever since.

The trials of life test the depth of our experience. If two roommates in college have a falling out, they may seek new roommates, for after all, living with a roommate is a passing experience. But if a husband and wife, who love each other, have a disagreement, the trial only deepens their love as they seek to solve the problems. The storm that blows reveals the strength of the roots. Jesus told the story about the two builders, one of whom did not go deep enough for his foundation (Matt. 7:24-29). Paul prayed that the believers might have a deeper experience with Christ, because only a deep experience could sustain them during the severe trials of life.

*Apprehension (vv. 18-19a).* The English words "comprehend" and "apprehend" both stem from the Latin word *prehendere* which means "to grasp." We say that a monkey has a "prehensile tail." That is, its tail is able to grasp a tree limb and hold on. Our word *comprehend* carries the idea of mentally grasping something; while *apprehend* suggests laying hold of it for yourself. In other words, it is possible to understand something but not really make it your own. Paul's concern is that we lay hold of the vast expanses of the love of God. He wants us to live in four dimensions. When God gave the land to Abraham, He told him to "walk through the land in the length of it and in the breadth of it" (Gen. 13:17). Abraham had to step out by faith and claim his inheritance. But we today have an inheritance in four dimensions: breadth, length, depth, and height. God's fourth dimension is love!

But there is a paradox here. Paul wants us to know personally the love of Christ "which passeth knowledge." There are dimensions, but they cannot be measured. "The love of Christ which passeth knowledge" parallels "the unsearchable riches of Christ" (Eph. 3:8). We are so rich in Christ that our riches cannot be calculated even with the most sophisticated computer.

Perhaps you saw the cartoon that depicted a man chatting with a boat salesman. In the beautiful showroom were yachts and cabin cruisers that glittered with elegance. In the caption, the salesman is saying to the customer: "Sir, if you have to ask how much they are, they are too expensive for you!"

No Christian ever has to worry about having inadequate spiritual resources to meet the demands of life. If he prays for spiritual strength and spiritual depth, he will be able to apprehend—get his hands on—all the resources of God's love and grace. "I can do all things through Christ which strengtheneth me" (Phil. 4:13). And what is the result of all of this?

*Fullness (v. 19b).* It is said that nature abhors a vacuum. This explains why air or water will automatically flow into an empty place. The *divine* nature abhors a vacuum. God wants us to experience His fullness. "Filled *unto* all the fullness of God" is the more accurate translation. The *means* of our fullness is the Holy Spirit (Eph. 5:18), and the *measure* of our fullness is God Himself (Eph. 4:11-16). It is tragic when Christians use the wrong measurements in examining their own spiritual lives. We like to measure ourselves by the weakest Christians that we know, and then boast, "Well, I'm better than they are." Paul tells us that the measure is Christ, and that we cannot boast about anything (nor should we). When we have reached *His* fullness, then we have reached the limit.

In one sense, the Christian is already "made full in Christ" (Col. 2:9-10, where "complete" means "filled full"). Positionally, we are complete in Him, but practically, we enjoy only the grace that we apprehend by faith. The resources are there. All we need do is accept them and enjoy them. Paul will have more to say about this fullness (Eph. 5:18-21), so we will reserve further comment until we reach that section.

## The Benediction (Eph. 3:20-21)

After contemplating such a marvelous spiritual experience, it is no wonder Paul bursts forth in a doxology, a fitting benediction to such a prayer. Note again the trinitarian emphasis in this benediction: Paul prays to God the Father, concerning the indwelling power of God the Spirit, made available through God the Son.

Perhaps the best way for us to grasp some of the greatness of this doxology is to look at it in outlined form:

Now unto Him that is
able to do *all*
*above* all
*abundantly* above all
*exceeding* abundantly above all

Paul seems to want to use every word possible to convey to us the vastness of God's power as found in Jesus Christ. He has ended each of the two previous chapters with praise to God for His great victory in Christ. He tells us that Christ's power is so great He arose from the dead and ascended *far above all* (Eph. 1:19-23). He teaches us that His power is so great He has reconciled Jews and Gentiles to each other, and to God; and that He is now building a temple to the eternal glory of God (Eph. 2:19-22). But in the paragraph before us, Paul shares the exciting truth that this *far above all* power is available to us! It is even "above all that we ask or think." In other words, the power of Christ, like the love of Christ, is beyond human understanding or measurement. And this is just the kind of power you and I need if we are to walk and war in victory.

The word "power" is again *dunamis,* which we met back in Ephesians 3:7; and "working" is *energeia* (energy) found in Ephesians 1:11, 19; 2:2; 3:7; and 4:16. Some power is dormant; it is available, but not being used, such as the power stored in a battery. But God's energy is effectual power—power at work in our lives. This power works *in* us, in the inner man (Eph. 3:16). Philippians 2:12-13 are parallel verses, so be sure to read them. It is the Holy Spirit who releases the resurrection power of Christ in our lives.

One winter day, I had an important engagement in Chicago, and the evening before the area was hit by a severe snowstorm. I did not have a garage, so my car was not only covered with snow, but heavy cakes of ice had formed on the fenders and bumpers. These ice cakes I simply kicked off, after I had swept off the car. I drove to the gas station to fill the tank. When I pushed the button on the dashboard to open the gas cap, it didn't work. No matter how hard or often I pushed, the cap stayed shut. The station attendant looked under the fender and discovered the problem. In kicking off the ice, I had broken the wire that connected the gas cap with the battery.

Apparently this is what has happened to many Christians. They have been cut off from their source of power. Unbelief, unconfessed sin, careless living, worldliness in action or attitude—all of these can rob us of power. And a Christian robbed of power cannot be used of God. "Without Me, ye can do nothing" (John 15:5).

Why does God share His power with us? So that we can build great churches for our own glory? So that we can boast of our own achievements? No! "To Him be glory in the church!" The Spirit of God was given to glorify the Son of God (John 16:14). The church on earth is here to glorify the Son of God. If our motive is to glorify God by building His church, then God will share His power with us. The power of the Spirit is not a luxury; it is a necessity.

But the amazing thing is that what we do in His power today will glorify Christ "throughout all ages, world without end" (Eph. 3:21). The church's greatest ministry is yet to come. What we do here and now is preparing us for the eternal ages, when we shall glorify Christ forever.

He is able to do all—*above* all—*abundantly* above all—*exceeding* abundantly above all!

Get your hands on your spiritual wealth by opening your heart to the Holy Spirit, and praying with Paul for strength for the inner man . . . for a new depth of love . . . for spiritual apprehension . . . and for spiritual fullness.

"Ye have not because ye ask not" (James 4:2).

# CHAPTER EIGHT
# LET'S WALK TOGETHER
*Ephesians 4:1-16*

All of Paul's letters contain a beautiful balance between doctrine and duty, and Ephesians is the perfect example. The first three chapters deal with doctrine, our riches in Christ, while the last three chapters explain duty, our responsibilities in Christ. The key word in this last half of the book is *walk* (Eph. 4:1, 17; 5:2, 8, 15), while the key idea in the first half is wealth. In these last three chapters, Paul admonishes us to walk in *unity* (Eph. 4:1-16), *purity* (Eph. 4:17–5:17), *harmony* (Eph. 5:18–6:9), and *victory* (Eph. 6:10-24).

These four "walks" perfectly parallel the basic doctrines Paul has taught us in the first three chapters.

Before we look at this section in detail, we must note two important words in Ephesians 4:1: *therefore* and *beseech.* The word *therefore* indicates that Paul is basing his exhortations to duty on the doctrines taught in the first three chapters. (Rom. 12:1-2 are parallel verses.) The Christian life is not based on ignorance but knowledge, and the better we understand

| Our Wealth | Our Walk |
|---|---|
| Called by grace to belong to His body (chap. 1) | Walk worthy of your calling—the unity of the Body (4:1-16) |
| Raised from the dead (2:1-10) | Put off the grave clothes (4:17–5:17); walk in purity |
| Reconciled (2:11-22) | Walk in harmony (5:18–6:9) |
| Christ's victory over Satan is the mystery (chap. 3) | Walk in victory (6:10-24) |

Bible doctrine, the easier it is to obey Bible duties. When people say, "Don't talk to me about doctrine—just let me live my Christian life!" they are revealing their ignorance of the way the Holy Spirit works in the life of the believer. "It makes no difference what you believe, just as long as you live right" is a similar confession of ignorance. It *does* make a difference what you believe, because what you believe determines how you behave!

The word *beseech* indicates that God, in love, urges us to live for His glory. He does not say, as He did to the Old Testament Jews, "If you obey Me, I will bless you." Rather, He says, "I have already blessed you—now, in response to My love and grace, obey Me." He has given us such a marvelous calling in Christ; now it is our responsibility to live up to that calling.

The main idea in these first sixteen verses is the unity of believers in Christ. This is simply the practical application of the doctrine taught in the first half of the letter: God is building a body, a temple. He has reconciled Jews and Gentiles to Himself in Christ. The oneness of believers in Christ is already a spiritual reality. Our responsibility is to guard, protect, and preserve that unity. To do this, we must understand four important facts.

### The Grace of Unity (Eph. 4:1-3)
Unity is not uniformity. Unity comes from within and is a spiritual grace, while uniformity is the result of pressure from without. Paul used the human body as a picture of Christian unity (1 Cor. 12), and he adapts the same illustration here in this section (Eph. 4:13-16).

Each part of the body is different from the other parts, yet all make up one body and work together.

If we are going to preserve the "unity of the Spirit," we must possess the necessary Christian graces, and there are seven of them listed here. The first is *lowliness,* or *humility.* Someone has said, "Humility is that grace that, when you know you have it, you have lost it." Humility means putting Christ first, others second, and self last. It means knowing ourselves, accepting ourselves, and being ourselves to the glory of God. God does not condemn you when you accept yourself and your gifts (Rom. 12:3). He just does not want us to think more *highly* of ourselves than we ought to—or *less highly* than we ought to.

*Meekness* is not weakness. It is power under control. Moses was a meek man (Num. 12:3), yet see the tremendous power he exercised. Jesus Christ was "meek and lowly in heart" (Matt. 11:29), yet He drove the money changers from the temple. In the Greek language, this word was used for a soothing medicine, a colt that had been broken, and a soft wind. In each case you have power, but that power is under control.

Allied with meekness is *long-suffering,* which literally means "long-tempered," the ability to endure discomfort without fighting back. This leads to the mentioning of *forbearance,* a grace that cannot be experienced apart from love. "Love suffereth long and is kind" (1 Cor. 13:4). Actually, Paul is describing some of the "fruit of the Spirit" (Gal. 5:22-23); for the "unity of the Spirit" (Eph. 4:3) is the result of the believer "walking in the Spirit" (Gal. 5:16).

The next grace that contributes to the unity of the Spirit is *endeavor.* Literally it reads "being eager to maintain, or guard, the unity of the Spirit." "It's great that you love each other," I once heard a seasoned saint say to a newly wedded couple, "but if you're going to be happy in marriage, you gotta work at it!" The verb used here is a present participle, which means we must constantly be endeavoring to maintain this unity. In fact, when we think the situation is the best, Satan will move in to wreck it. The spiritual unity of a home, a Sunday School class, or a church is the responsibility of each person involved, and the job never ends.

The final grace is *peace*—"the bond of peace." Read James 3:13–4:10 for the most vivid treatment of war and peace in the New

Testament. Note that the reason for war on the outside is war on the inside. If a believer cannot get along with God, he cannot get along with other believers. When "the peace of God" rules in our hearts, then we build unity (Col. 3:15).

### The Ground of Unity (Eph. 4:4-6)

Many people today attempt to unite Christians in a way that is not biblical. For example, they will say: "We are not interested in doctrines, but in love. Now, let's forget our doctrines and just love one another!" But Paul did not discuss spiritual unity in the first three chapters; he waited until he had laid the doctrinal foundation. While not all Christians agree on some minor matters of Christian doctrine, they all do agree on the foundation truths of the faith. Unity built on anything other than Bible truth is standing on a very shaky foundation. Paul names here the seven basic spiritual realities that unite all true Christians.

**One body.** This is, of course, the body of Christ in which each believer is a member, placed there at conversion by the Spirit of God (1 Cor. 12:12-31). The one body is the model for the many local bodies that God has established across the world. The fact that a person is a member of the one body does not excuse him from belonging to a local body, for it is there that he exercises his spiritual gifts and helps others to grow.

**One Spirit.** The same Holy Spirit indwells each believer, so that we belong to each other in the Lord. There are perhaps a dozen references to the Holy Spirit in Ephesians, because He is important to us in the living of the Christian life.

**One hope of your calling.** This refers to the return of the Lord to take His church to heaven. The Holy Spirit within is the assurance of this great promise (Eph. 1:13-14). Paul is suggesting here that the believer who realizes the existence of the one body, who walks in the Spirit, and who looks for the Lord's return, is going to be a peacemaker and not a troublemaker.

**One Lord.** This is our Lord Jesus Christ who died for us, lives for us, and one day will come for us. It is difficult to believe that two believers can claim to obey the same Lord, and yet not be able to walk together in unity. Someone asked Ghandi, the spiritual leader of India, "What is the greatest hindrance to Christianity in India?" He replied, "Christians." Acknowledging the lordship of Christ is a giant step toward spiritual unity among His people.

**One faith.** There is one settled body of truth deposited by Christ in His church, and this is "the faith." Jude calls it "the faith which was once delivered unto the saints" (Jude 3). The early Christians recognized a body of basic doctrine that they taught, guarded, and committed to others (2 Tim. 2:2). Christians may differ in some matters of interpretation and church practice; but all true Christians agree on "the faith"—and to depart from "the faith" is to bring about disunity within the body of Christ.

**One baptism.** Since Paul is here discussing the one body, this "one baptism" is probably the baptism of the Spirit, that act of the Spirit when He places the believing sinner into the body of Christ at conversion (1 Cor. 12:13). This is not an experience after conversion, nor is it an experience the believer should pray for or seek after. We are commanded to be filled with the Spirit (Eph. 5:18), but we are never commanded to be baptized with the Spirit, for we have already been baptized by the Spirit at conversion. As far as the one body is concerned, there is one baptism— the baptism of the Spirit. But as far as local bodies of believers are concerned, there are two baptisms: the baptism of the Spirit, and water baptism.

**One God and Father.** Paul likes to emphasize God as Father (Eph. 1:3, 17; 2:18; 3:14; 5:20). The marvelous oneness of believers in the family of God is evident here, for God is over all, and working through all, and in all. We are children in the same family, loving and serving the same Father, so we ought to be able to walk together in unity. Just as in an earthly family, the various members have to give and take in order to keep a loving unity in the home, so God's heavenly family must do the same. The "Lord's Prayer" opens with "Our Father"—not "My Father."

Paul is quite concerned that Christians not break the unity of the Spirit by agreeing with false doctrine (Rom. 16:17-20), and the Apostle John echoes this warning (2 John 6-11). The local church cannot believe in peace at any price, for God's wisdom is "first pure, then peaceable" (James 3:17). Purity of doctrine of itself does not produce spiritual unity, for there are churches that are sound in faith, but unsound when it comes to love. This is why Paul joins the two: "speaking the truth in love" (Eph. 4:15).

## The Gifts for Unity (Eph. 4:7-11)

Paul moves now from what all Christians have in common to how Christians differ from each other. He is discussing variety and individuality within the unity of the Spirit. God has given each believer at least one spiritual gift (1 Cor. 12:1-12), and this gift is to be used for the unifying and edifying (building up) of the body of Christ. We must make a distinction between "spiritual gifts" and natural abilities. When you were born into this world God gave you certain natural abilities, perhaps in mechanics, art, athletics, or music. In this regard, all men are not created equal, because some are smarter, or stronger, or more talented than others. But in the spiritual realm, each believer has at least one spiritual gift no matter what natural abilities he may or may not possess. A spiritual gift is a God-given ability to serve God and other Christians in such a way that Christ is glorified and believers are edified.

How does the believer discover and develop his gifts? By fellowshipping with other Christians in the local assembly. Gifts are not toys to play with. They are tools to build with. And if they are not used in love, they become weapons to fight with, which is what happened in the Corinthian church (1 Cor. 12–14). Christians are not to live in isolation, for after all, they are members of the same body.

Paul taught that Christ is the Giver of these gifts, through the Holy Spirit (Eph. 4:8-10). He ascended to heaven as Victor forevermore. The picture here is of a military conqueror leading his captives and sharing the spoil with his followers. Only in this case, the "captives" are not His enemies, but His own. Sinners who once were held captives by sin and Satan have now been taken captive by Christ. Even death itself is a defeated foe! When He came to earth, Christ experienced the depths of humiliation (Phil. 2:5-11), but when He ascended to heaven, He experienced the very highest exaltation possible. Paul quotes Psalm 68:18, applying to Jesus Christ a victory song written by David (Eph. 4:8).

There are three lists of spiritual gifts given in the New Testament: 1 Corinthians 12:4-11, 27-31; Romans 12:3-8; and Ephesians 4:11. Since these lists are not identical, it may be that Paul has not named all the gifts that are available. Paul wrote that some gifts are more important than others, but that all believers are needed if the body is to function normally (1 Cor. 14:5, 39). Paul named, not so much "gifts" as the gifted men God has placed in the church, and there are four of them.

**Apostles (v. 11a).** The word means "one who is sent with a commission." Jesus had many disciples, but He selected 12 Apostles (Matt. 10:1-4). A *disciple* is a "follower" or a "learner," but an *apostle* is a "divinely appointed representative." The Apostles were to give witness of the Resurrection (Acts 1:15-22), and therefore had to have seen the risen Christ personally (1 Cor. 9:1-2). There are no apostles today in the strictest New Testament sense. These men helped to lay the foundation of the church—"the foundation laid by the Apostles and prophets" (Eph. 2:20), and once the foundation was laid, they were no longer needed. God authenticated their ministry with special miracles (Heb. 2:1-4), so we should not demand these same miracles today. Of course, in a broad sense, all Christians have an apostolic ministry. "As My Father hath sent Me, even so send I you" (John 20:21). But we must not claim to be apostles.

**Prophets (v. 11b).** We commonly associate a prophet with predictions of future events, but this is not his primary function. A New Testament prophet is one who proclaims the Word of God (Acts 11:28; Eph. 3:5). Believers in the New Testament churches did not possess Bibles, nor was the New Testament written and completed. How, then, would these local assemblies discover God's will? His Spirit would share God's truth with those possessing the gift of prophecy. Paul suggests that the gift of prophecy had to do with understanding "all mysteries and all knowledge" (1 Cor. 13:2), meaning, of course, spiritual truths. The purpose of prophecy is "edification, encouragement, and consolation" (1 Cor. 14:3, literal translation). Christians today do not get their spiritual knowledge *immediately* from the Holy Spirit, but *mediately* through the Spirit teaching the Word. With the Apostles, the prophets had a foundational ministry in the early church and they are not needed today (Eph. 2:20).

**Evangelists (v. 11c).** "Bearers of the Good News." These men traveled from place to place to preach the Gospel and win the lost (Acts 8:26-40; 21:28). All ministers should "do the work of an evangelist," but this does not mean that all ministers are evangelists (2 Tim. 4:5). The Apostles and prophets laid the foundation of the church, and the evangelists built on it by winning the lost to Christ.

Of course, in the early church, every believer was a witness (Acts 2:41-47; 11:19-21), and so should we be witnesses today. But there are people also today who have the gift of evangelism. The fact that a believer may not possess this gift does not excuse him from being burdened for lost souls or witnessing to them.

**Pastors and teachers (v. 11d).** The fact that the word "some" is not repeated indicates that we have here one office with two ministries. *Pastor* means "shepherd," indicating that the local church is a flock of sheep (Acts 20:28), and it is his responsibility to feed and lead the flock (1 Peter 5:1-4, where "elder" is another name for "pastor"). He does this by means of the Word of God, the food that nourishes the sheep. The Word is the staff that guides and disciplines the sheep. The Word of God is the local church's protection and provision, and no amount of entertainment, good fellowship, or other religious substitutes can take its place.

## The Growth of Unity (Eph. 4:12-16)

Paul was looking at the church on two levels in this section. He saw the body of Christ, made up of all true believers, growing gradually until it reaches spiritual maturity, "the measure of the stature of the fullness of Christ." But he also saw the local body of believers ministering to each other, growing together, and thereby experiencing spiritual unity.

A free-lance missionary visited a pastor friend of mine asking for financial support. "What group are you associated with?" my friend asked.

The man replied, "I belong to the invisible church."

My friend then asked, "Well, what church are you a member of?"

Again he got the answer, "I belong to the invisible church!"

Getting a bit suspicious, my friend asked, "When does this invisible church meet? Who pastors it?"

The missionary then became incensed and said, "Well, your church here isn't the true church. I belong to the invisible church!"

My friend replied, "Well, here's some invisible money to help you minister to the invisible church!"

Now, my pastor friend was not denying the existence of the one body. Rather, he was affirming the fact that the *invisible church* (not a biblical term, but I will use it) ministers through *the visible church.*

The gifted leaders are supposed to "equip the saints unto the work of the ministry, unto the building up of the body of Christ" (literal translation). The saints do not call a pastor and pay him to do the work. They call him and follow his leadership as he, through the Word, equips them to do the job (2 Tim. 3:13-17). The members of the church grow by feeding on the Word and ministering to each other. The first evidence of spiritual growth is *Christlikeness.*

The second evidence is *stability.* The maturing Christian is not tossed about by every religious novelty that comes along. There are religious quacks waiting to kidnap God's children and get them into their false cults, but the maturing believer recognizes false doctrine and stays clear of it. The cultists do not try to win lost souls to Christ. They do not establish rescue missions in the slum areas of our cities, because they have no good news for the man on skid row. Instead, these false teachers try to capture immature Christians, and for this reason, most of the membership of the false cults comes from local churches, particularly churches that do not feed their people the Word of God.

The third evidence of maturity is *truth joined with love:* "Speaking the truth in love" (Eph. 4:15). It has well been said that truth without love is brutality, but love without truth is hypocrisy. Little children do not know how to blend truth and love. They think that if you love someone, you must shield him from the truth if knowing the truth will hurt him. It is a mark of maturity when we are able to share the truth with our fellow Christians, and do it in love. "Faithful are the wounds of a friend, but the kisses of an enemy are deceitful" (Prov. 27:6).

One more evidence of maturity is *cooperation* (Eph. 4:16). We realize that, as members of the one body and a local body, we belong to each other, we affect each other, and we need each other. Each believer, no matter how insignificant he may appear, has a ministry to other believers. The body grows as the individual members grow, and they grow as they feed on the Word and minister to each other. Note once again the emphasis on love: "forbearing one another in love" (Eph. 4:2); "speaking the truth in love" (Eph. 4:15); "the edifying of itself in love" (4:16). Love is the circulatory system of the body. It has been discovered that isolated, unloved babies do not grow properly and are especially suscepti-ble to disease, while babies who are loved and handled grow normally and are stronger. So it is with the children of God. An isolated Chris-tian cannot minister to others, nor can others minister to him, and it is impossible for the gifts to be ministered either way.

So, then, spiritual unity is not something we manufacture. It is something we already have in Christ, and we must protect and maintain it. Truth unites, but lies divide. Love unites, but selfishness divides. Therefore, "speaking the truth in love," let us equip one another and edify one another, that all of us may grow up to be more like Christ.

# CHAPTER NINE
# TAKE OFF THE
# GRAVECLOTHES!
## *Ephesians 4:17-32*

The Bible was written to be obeyed, and not simply studied, and this is why the words "therefore" and "wherefore" are repeated so often in the second half of Ephesians (4:1, 17, 25; 5:1, 7, 14, 17, 24). Paul was saying, "Here is what Christ has done for you. Now, in the light of this, here is what we ought to do for Christ." We are to be doers of the Word, and not hearers only (James 1:22). The fact that we have been called in Christ (Eph. 1:18) ought to motivate us to walk in unity (Eph. 4:1-16). And the fact that we have been raised from the dead (Eph. 2:1-10) should motivate us to walk in purity (Eph. 4:17–5:17), or, as Paul told the Romans, "walk in newness of life" (Rom. 6:4). We are alive in Christ, not dead in sins; therefore "put off the old man . . . and put on the new man (Eph. 4:22, 24). Take off the graveclothes and put on the grace-clothes!

## The Admonition (Eph. 4:17-19)
There are some negatives in the Christian life, and here is one of them: "Walk not as other Gentiles walk." The Christian is not to imitate the life of the unsaved people around him. They are "dead in trespasses and sins" (Eph. 2:1), while he has been raised from the dead

and been given eternal life in Christ. Paul ex-plains the differences between the saved and the unsaved.

To begin with, Christians *think* differently from unsaved people. Note the emphasis here on thinking: mind (Eph. 4:17, 23), understand-ing (Eph. 4:18), ignorance (Eph. 4:18), "learned Christ" (Eph. 4:20). Salvation begins with repentance, which is a change of mind. The whole outlook of a person changes when he trusts Christ, including his values, goals, and interpretation of life. What is wrong with the mind of the unsaved person? For one thing, his thinking is "vain" (futile). It leads to no substantial purpose. Since he does not know God, he cannot truly understand the world around him, nor can he understand him-self. The sad story is told in Romans 1:21-25. Our world today possesses a great deal of knowledge, but very little wisdom. Thoreau put it beautifully when he said that we have "improved means to unimproved ends."

The unsaved man's thinking is futile be-cause it is darkened. He thinks he is enlight-ened because he rejects the Bible and be-lieves the latest philosophies, when in reality he is in the dark. "Professing themselves to be wise, they become fools" (Rom. 1:22). But they think they are wise. Satan has blinded the minds of the unsaved (2 Cor. 4:3-6) be-cause he does not want them to see the truth in Jesus Christ. It is not simply that their eyes are blinded so they cannot see, but that their minds are darkened so that they cannot think straight about spiritual matters.

Of course, the unsaved man is dead be-cause of this spiritual ignorance. The truth and the life go together. If you believe God's truth, then you receive God's life. But you would think that the unbeliever would do his utmost to get out of his terrible spiritual plight. Alas, the hardness of his heart enslaves him. He is "past feeling" because he has so given himself over to sin that sin controls him. Read Romans 1:18-32 for a vivid expansion of these three brief verses.

The Christian cannot pattern himself after the unsaved person, because the Christian has experienced a miracle of being raised from the dead. His life is not futile, but purposeful. His mind is filled with the light of God's Word, and his heart with the fullness of God's life. He gives his body to God as an instrument of righteousness (Rom. 6:13), and not to sin for the satisfaction of his own selfish lusts. In ev-ery way, the believer is different from the unbeliever, and therefore the admonition: "Walk not."

## The Argument (Eph. 4:20-24)

Paul reinforced his admonition with an argument from the spiritual experience of his readers. Again the emphasis is on the mind, or the outlook, of the believer. "But ye have not so learned Christ" (Eph. 4:20). He did not say "learned about Christ," because it is possible to learn about Christ and never be saved. To "learn Christ" means to have a personal relationship to Christ so that you get to know Him better each day. I can learn about Sir Winston Churchill because I own many of his books and can secure books about his life. But I can never learn him because he is dead. Jesus Christ is alive! Therefore, I can "learn Christ" through a personal fellowship with Him.

This fellowship is based on the Word of God. I can be taught "the truth" as it is in Jesus Christ. The better I understand the Word of God, the better I know the Son of God, for the whole Bible is a revelation of the Lord Jesus Christ (Luke 24:27; John 5:39). The unsaved man is spiritually ignorant, while the Christian is intelligent in the things of the Word. And the unsaved man does not know Christ, while the believer grows in his personal knowledge of Christ day by day. We have believed the truth; we have received the life; therefore, we will walk "in the way" and not walk after the example of the unsaved world.

But this experience of salvation goes much deeper than this, for it has resulted in a whole new position before God. The old man (the former life) has been put away, and we can now walk in newness of life through Christ. Ephesians 4:22-24 is a summary of Romans 5–8, where Paul explained the believer's identification with Christ in death, burial, and resurrection. He also dealt with this in Ephesians 2:4-6, as well as in Colossians 3. As Christians, we have not simply changed our minds. We have totally changed our citizenship. We belong to God's "new creation" in Christ (2 Cor. 5:17), and therefore, the ideas and desires of the old creation no longer should control our lives.

The simplest illustration of this great truth is given in John 11, the resurrection of Lazarus. Our Lord's friend, Lazarus, had been in the grave four days when Jesus and His disciples arrived at Bethany, and even Martha admitted that, by now, the decaying body would smell (John 11:39). But Jesus spoke the word and Lazarus came forth alive, an illustration of John 5:24. Notice our Lord's next words, "Loose him, and let him go" (John 11:44). Take off the graveclothes! Lazarus no longer belonged to the old dominion of death, for he was now alive. Why go about wearing graveclothes? Take off the old and put on the new!

This was Paul's argument—you no longer belong to the old corruption of sin; you belong to the new creation in Christ. Take off the graveclothes! How do we do this? "Be renewed in the spirit of your mind" (Eph. 4:23). Conversion is a crisis that leads to a process. Through Christ, once and for all, we have been given a new position in His new creation, but day by day, we must by faith appropriate what He has given us. The Word of God renews the mind as we surrender our all to Him (Rom. 12:1-2). "Sanctify them through Thy truth: Thy Word is truth" (John 17:17). As the mind understands the truth of God's Word, it is gradually transformed by the Spirit, and this renewal leads to a changed life. Physically, you are what you eat, but spiritually, you are what you think. "As he thinketh in his heart, so is he" (Prov. 23:7). This is why it is important for us as Christians to spend time daily meditating on the Word, praying, and fellowshipping with Christ.

## The Application (Eph. 4:25-32)

Paul was not content to explain a principle and then leave it. He always applied it to the different areas of life that need to feel its power. Paul even dared to name sins. Five different sins are named in this section, and Paul told us to avoid them and he explained why.

*Lying (v. 25).* A lie is a statement that is contrary to fact, spoken with the intent to deceive. If I tell you it is noon, and then discover that my watch is wrong, I did not tell a lie. But if I gave you the wrong time so you would be late to a meeting and I would benefit from it, that would be a lie. Satan is a liar (John 8:44); and he wants us to believe that God is a liar. "Yea, hath God said?" (Gen. 3:1) Whenever we speak truth, the Spirit of God works, but whenever we tell a lie, Satan goes to work. We like to believe that we help people by lying to them, but such is not the case. We may not see the sad consequences immediately, but ultimately they will come. "Ye know that no lie is of the truth" (1 John 2:21). Hell is prepared for "whosoever loveth and maketh a lie" (Rev. 22:15). This does not mean that anybody who ever told a lie will go to hell, but rather that those whose lives are controlled by lies—they love lies and they make lies—are lost forever. The Christian's life is controlled by truth.

Note the reason Paul gave for telling the truth: We belong to each other in Christ. He urged us to build the body in love (Eph. 4:16) and he urged us to build the body in truth. "Speaking the truth in love" (Eph. 4:15). As "members one of another" we affect each other, and we cannot build each other apart from truth. The first sin that was judged in the early church was the sin of lying (Acts 5:1-11).

*Anger (vv. 26-27).* Anger is an emotional arousal caused by something that displeases us. In itself, anger is not a sin, because even God can be angry (Deut. 9:8, 20; Ps. 2:12). Several times in the Old Testament the phrase appears, "the anger of the Lord" (Num. 25:4; Jer. 4:8; 12:13). The holy anger of God is a part of His judgment against sin, as illustrated in our Lord's anger when He cleansed the temple (Matt. 21:12-13). The Bible often speaks of anger "being kindled" (Gen. 30:2; Deut. 6:15), as though anger can be compared to fire. Sometimes a man's anger smolders, and this we would call *malice;* but this same anger can suddenly burst forth and destroy, and this we would call *wrath.*

It is difficult for us to practice a truly holy anger or righteous indignation because our emotions are tainted by sin, and we do not have the same knowledge that God has in all matters. God sees everything clearly and knows everything completely, and we do not. The New Testament principle seems to be that the believer should be angry at sin but loving toward people. "Ye that love the Lord, hate evil" (Ps. 97:10).

It is possible to be angry and not sin, but if we do sin, we must settle the matter quickly and not let the sun go down on our wrath. "Agree with thine adversary quickly" (Matt. 5:25). "Go and tell him his fault between thee and him alone" (Matt. 18:15). The fire of anger, if not quenched by loving forgiveness, will spread and defile and destroy the work of God. According to Jesus, anger is the first step toward murder (Matt. 5:21-26), because anger gives the devil a foothold in our lives, and Satan is a murderer (John 8:44). Satan hates God and God's people, and when he finds a believer with the sparks of anger in his heart, he fans those sparks, adds fuel to the fire, and does a great deal of damage to God's

people and God's church. Both lying and anger "give peace to the devil" (Eph. 4:27).

When I was living in Chicago, one out of every thirty-five deaths was a murder, and most of these murders involved relatives and friends. They are what the law calls "crimes of passion." Two friends get into an argument (often while gambling), one of them gets angry, pulls a gun or knife, and kills his friend. Horace was right when he said, "Anger is momentary insanity."

A woman tried to defend her bad temper by saying, "I explode and then it's all over with."

"Yes," replied a friend, "just like a shotgun—but look at the damage that's left behind."

"Anyone can become angry," wrote Aristotle. "But to be angry with the right person, to the right degree, at the right time, for the right purpose, and in the right way—this is not easy."

Solomon has a good solution: "A soft answer turneth away wrath, but grievous words stir up anger" (Prov. 15:1).

*Stealing (v. 28).* "Thou shalt not steal" is one of the Ten Commandments, and when God gave that commandment, He instituted the right of private ownership of property. A man has the right to turn his strength into gain, and to keep that gain and use it as he sees fit. God gave numerous laws to the Jews for the protection of their property, and these principles have become a part of our law today. Stealing was particularly a sin of the slaves in Paul's day. Usually they were not well cared for and were always in need, and the law gave them almost no protection. When he wrote to Titus, Paul urged him to admonish the slaves not to "purloin" but to be faithful to their masters (Titus 2:10). But it was not only the slaves, but citizens in general, who were addicted to thievery, for Paul wrote to people in the Ephesian church who were gainfully employed (Eph. 4:28).

Just as Satan is a liar and a murderer, he is also a thief. "The thief cometh not, but for to steal, and to kill, and to destroy" (John 10:10). He turned Judas into a thief (John 12:6) and he would do the same to us if he could. When he tempted Eve, he led her to become a thief, for she took the fruit that was forbidden. And she, in turn, made Adam a thief. The first Adam was a thief and was cast out of Paradise, but the Last Adam, Christ, turned to a thief and said, "Today shalt thou be with Me in paradise" (Luke 23:43).

Paul added motive to the admonition. We should tell the truth because we are "members one of another." We should control our anger lest we "give place to the devil." We should work, and not steal, so that we might be able "to give to him that needeth." You would expect Paul to have said, "Let him work that he might take care of himself and not be tempted to steal." Instead, he lifted human labor to a much higher level. We work that we might be able to help others. If we steal, we hurt others; therefore, we should work that we might be able to help others. Even honest labor could become a selfish thing, and this Paul seeks to avoid. Of course, it was a fundamental rule in the early church that "if any would not work, neither should he eat" (2 Thes. 3:10). A lazy Christian robs himself, others, and God. Of course, Paul was not writing to believers who could not work because of handicaps, but with those who would not work.

Paul himself was an example of a hard worker, for while he was establishing local churches, he labored as a tentmaker. Every Jewish rabbi was taught a trade, for, said the rabbis, "If you do not teach your son a trade, you teach him to be a thief." The men that God called in the Scriptures were busy working when their call came. Moses was caring for sheep; Gideon was threshing wheat; David was minding his father's flock; and the first four disciples were either casting nets or mending them. Jesus Himself was a carpenter.

***Corrupt speech (v. 29).*** The mouth and heart are connected. "Out of the abundance of the heart, the mouth speaketh" (Matt. 12:34). We expect a change in speech when a person becomes a Christian. It is interesting to trace the word *mouth* through the Book of Romans and see how Christ makes a difference in a man's speech. The sinner's mouth is "full of cursing and bitterness" (Rom. 3:14); but when he trusts Christ, he gladly confesses with his mouth "Jesus Christ is Lord" (Rom. 10:9-10, NIV). As a condemned sinner, his mouth is stopped before the throne of God (Rom. 3:19); but as a believer, his mouth is opened to praise God (Rom. 15:6). Change the heart and you change the speech. Paul certainly knew the difference, for when he was an unsaved rabbi, he was "breathing out threatenings and slaughter against the disciples of the Lord" (Acts 9:1). But when he trusted Christ, a change took place: "Behold, he prayeth" (Acts 9:11). From "preying" to "praying" in one step of faith!

The word *corrupt*, used in Matthew 7:17-18, refers to rotten fruit. It means "that which is worthless, bad, or rotten." Our words do not have to be "dirty" to be worthless. Sometimes we go along with the crowd and try to impress people with the fact that we are not as puritanical as they think. Peter may have had this motive in mind when he was accused by the girl of being one of Christ's disciples. "Then began he to curse and to swear, saying, 'I know not the man' " (Matt. 26:74). The appetites of the old life sometimes show up when we permit "filthy communication" out of the mouth (Col. 3:8). Remember, before we were saved, we lived in spiritual death (Eph. 2:1-3) and, like Lazarus, our personal corruption produced an odor that was not pleasing to God. No wonder Paul wrote, "Their throat is an open sepulchre" (Rom. 3:13).

The remedy is to make sure the heart is full of blessing. So fill the heart with the love of Christ so that only truth and purity can come out of the mouth. Never have to say, "Now, take this with a grain of salt." Paul told us to put the salt of God's grace in everything we say. "Let your speech be always with grace, seasoned with salt" (Col. 4:6). And keep in mind that your words have power, either for good or evil. Paul tells us to speak in such a way that what we say will build up our hearers, and not tear them down. Our words should minister grace and help to draw others closer to Christ. Satan, of course, encourages speech that will tear people down and destroy the work of Christ. If you need to be reminded of the power of the tongue, read the third chapter of James.

***Bitterness (vv. 30-32).*** These verses warn us against several sins of the attitude and amplify what Paul wrote about anger. *Bitterness* refers to a settled hostility that poisons the whole inner man. Somebody does something we do not like, so we harbor ill will against him. "Husbands, love your wives and be not bitter against them" (Col. 3:19). Bitterness leads to wrath, which is the explosion on the outside of the feelings on the inside. Wrath and anger often lead to brawling (clamor) or blasphemy (evil speaking). The first is fighting with fists, the second is fighting with words. It is difficult to believe that Christians would act this way, but they do, and this is why Paul warned us, "Behold, how good and how pleasant it is for brethren to dwell together in unity" (Ps. 133:1).

A handsome elderly man stopped at my study one day and asked me if I would perform a wedding for him. I suggested that he bring the bride in so that we might chat together and get better acquainted, since I hesitate to marry strangers. "Before she comes in," he said, "let me explain this wedding to you. Both of us have been married before—to each other! Over thirty years ago, we got into an argument, I got mad, and we separated. Then we did a stupid thing and got a divorce. I guess we were both too proud to apologize. Well, all these years we've lived alone, and now we see how foolish we've been. Our bitterness has robbed us of the joys of life, and now we want to remarry and see if the Lord won't give us a few years of happiness before we die." Bitterness and anger, usually over trivial things, make havoc of homes, churches, and friendships.

Paul gives three reasons why we must avoid bitterness. First, *it grieves the Holy Spirit.* He lives within the Christian, and when the heart is filled with bitterness and anger, the Spirit grieves. We parents know just a little of this feeling when our children at home fight with each other. The Holy Spirit is happiest in an atmosphere of love, joy, and peace, for these are the "fruit of the Spirit" that He produces in our lives as we obey Him. The Holy Spirit cannot leave us, because He has sealed us until that day when Christ returns to take us home. We do not lose our salvation because of our sinful attitudes, but we certainly lose the joy of our salvation and the fullness of the Spirit's blessing.

Second, our sin *grieves God the Son,* who died for us. Third, it *grieves God the Father* who forgave us when we trusted Christ. Here Paul put his finger on the basic cause of a bitter attitude: We cannot forgive people. An unforgiving spirit is the devil's playground, and before long it becomes the Christian's battleground. If somebody hurts us, either deliberately or unintentionally, and we do not forgive him, then we begin to develop bitterness within, which hardens the heart. We should be tenderhearted and kind, but instead we are hardhearted and bitter. Actually, we are not hurting the person who hurt us; we are only hurting ourselves. Bitterness in the heart makes us treat others the way Satan treats them, when we should treat others the way God has treated us. In His gracious kindness, God has forgiven us, and we should forgive

others. We do not forgive for *our* sake (though we do get a blessing from it) or even for *their* sake, but for *Jesus'* sake. Learning how to forgive and forget is one of the secrets of a happy Christian life.

Review once again the motives for "walking in purity": We are members one of another; Satan wants to get a foothold in our lives; we ought to share with others; we ought to build one another up; and we ought not to grieve God. And, after all, we have been raised from the dead—so why wear the graveclothes? Jesus says of us as He said of Lazarus: "Loose him, and let him go!"

# CHAPTER TEN
# IMITATING OUR FATHER
*Ephesians 5:1-17*

The word "followers" in Ephesians 5:1 is the word *mimics,* so that the verse can be translated: "Be ye imitators of God as beloved children." This sets the theme for the section. Paul is simply arguing that children are like their parents, a fact that can be both encouraging and embarrassing to those of us who have children. Have you ever seen a child sitting in the front seat of an automobile, trying to drive like his father! Or walking behind him, pretending to mow the lawn? Or, sad to say, imitating Dad smoking a cigarette or taking a drink of alcohol? Children probably learn more by watching and imitating than any other way.

If we are the children of God, then we ought to imitate our Father. This is the basis for the three admonitions in this section. God is love (1 John 4:8); therefore, "walk in love" (Eph. 5:1-2). God is light (1 John 1:5); therefore, walk as children of light (Eph. 5:3-14). God is truth (1 John 5:6); therefore, walk in wisdom (Eph. 5:15-17). Of course, each of these "walks" is a part of Paul's exhortation to "walk in purity."

**Walk in Love (Eph. 5:1-2)**
This admonition ties in with the last two verses of the previous chapter where Paul has

warned us against bitterness and anger. It is tragic when these attitudes show up in the family of God. As a pastor, I have witnessed malice and bitterness in the lives of people as I have conducted funerals and even weddings. You would think that sharing the sorrow of losing a loved one, or sharing a joy of a marriage, would enable people to forgive past wrongs and try to get along with each other. But such is not the case. It takes a real love in the heart, for "charity [love] shall cover the multitude of sins" (1 Peter 4:8).

Paul gave several reasons why the Christian ought to walk in love.

**He is God's child.** Having been born again through faith in Christ, he is therefore one of the "partakers of the divine nature" (2 Peter 1:4); and since "God is love" it is logical that God's children will walk in love. When Paul encouraged his readers to "walk in love," he was not asking them to do something that was foreign to the Christian life; for we have received a new nature that wants to express itself in love. The old nature is basically selfish, and for this reason builds walls and declares war. But the new nature is loving, and therefore builds bridges and proclaims peace.

**He is God's beloved child.** "Be ye imitators of God as beloved children." Imagine, God speaks of us the same way He spoke of Jesus Christ: "This is My beloved Son" (Matt. 3:17). In fact, the Father loves us as He loves His Son (John 17:23). We are born into a loving relationship with the Father that ought to result in our showing love to Him by the way we live. What more could the Father do to express His love to us? Is it asking too much for us to "walk in love" to please Him?

**He was purchased with a great price.** "Greater love hath no man than this, that a man lay down his life for his friends" (John 15:13). But He laid down His life for His enemies (Rom. 5:10). Our love for Him is our response to His love for us. Paul compares Christ's sacrifice on the cross to the Old Testament "sweet-savor" sacrifices that were presented at the altar of the temple (Lev. 1:9, 13, 17; 2:9). The idea behind "sweet-savor" is simply that the sacrifice is well-pleasing to God. This does not suggest that God is pleased that sin demands death, and that His Son had to die to save lost sinners. Rather, it indicates that the death of Christ satisfies the holy law of God and therefore is acceptable and pleasing to the Father. The sweet-savor

offerings are described in Leviticus 1–3; the burnt offering, the meal offering, and the peace offering. The burnt offering pictures Christ's complete devotion to God; the meal offering, His perfection of character; and the peace offering, His making peace between sinners and God. Since the sin offering and the trespass offering (Lev. 4–5) picture Christ taking the place of the sinner, they are not considered "sweet-savor" offerings. Certainly nothing is beautiful about sin!

Paul begins with "walk in love" because love is the fundamental factor in the Christian life. If we walk in love, we will not disobey God or injure men because "he that loveth another hath fulfilled the law" (Rom. 13:8). The Holy Spirit puts this love in our hearts (Rom. 5:5).

**Walk As Children of Light (Eph. 5:3-14)**
Since "God is light" and we are imitating our Father, then we should walk in the light and have nothing to do with the darkness of sin. Paul gives three descriptions of believers that prove his point.

**We are saints (vv. 3-4).** That is, we are "set-apart ones" and no longer belong to the world of darkness around us. We have been "called out of darkness into His marvelous light" (1 Peter 2:9). It is beneath the dignity of a saint to indulge in the sins that belong to the world of darkness, some of which Paul names here. He warns us against the sexual sins (fornication, uncleanness) which were so prevalent in that day—and are prevalent today. Sad to say, these sins have invaded the homes of Christians and brought grief to local churches too. "Covetousness" may seem out of place next to fornication, but the two sins are but different expressions of the same basic weakness of fallen nature—uncontrolled appetite. The fornicator and the covetous person each desire to satisfy the appetite by taking what does not belong to them. "The lust of the flesh and the lust of the eyes" (1 John 2:16) would describe these two sins. "Let there not be even a hint of these sins!" said Paul.

In Ephesians 5:4 he warned against sins of the tongue, which, of course, are really sins of the heart. It is not difficult to see the relationship between the sins named in Ephesians 5:3 and those in Ephesians 5:4. People who have base appetites usually cultivate a base kind of speech and humor, and often people who want to commit sexual sins, or have committed them, enjoy jesting about them. Two indications of a person's character are what makes him laugh and what makes him weep. The saint of God sees nothing humorous in obscene language or jests. "Foolish talking" does not mean innocent humor but rather senseless conversation that cheapens the man and does not edify or minister grace to the hearers (Eph. 4:29). Paul is not condemning small talk because much conversation falls into that classification. He is condemning foolish talk that accomplishes no good purpose.

*Jesting* is a translation of a word that means "able to turn easily." This suggests a certain kind of conversationalist who can turn any statement into a coarse jest. The gift of wit is a blessing, but when it is attached to a filthy mind or a base motive, it becomes a curse. There are quick-witted people who can pollute any conversation with jests that are always inconvenient (out of place). How much better it is for us to be quick to give thanks! This is certainly the best way to give glory to God and keep the conversation pure.

A Christian woman attended an anniversary dinner in honor of a friend, not knowing that there would be a program of low comedy following the meal. The so-called comedian tried to entertain the crowd with coarse humor that degraded everything that the Christian guest held to be sacred and honorable. At one point in the program, the comedian's throat became dry. "Please bring me a glass of water," he called to a waiter.

At that point the Christian woman added, "And bring a toothbrush and a bar of soap with it!" To be sure, soap in the mouth will never cleanse the conversation, but she made her point.

Christians who have God's Word in their hearts (Col. 3:16) will always season their speech with salt (Col. 4:6); for grace in the heart means grace on the lips.

**We are kings (vv. 5-6).** When we trusted Christ, we entered into the kingdom of God (John 3:3); but we are also awaiting the full revelation of His kingdom when He returns (2 Tim. 4:1). Paul makes it clear that people who deliberately and persistently live in sin will not share in God's kingdom. "They which practice such things shall not inherit the kingdom of God" (Gal. 5:21, literal translation). "Whoremonger" is a translation of the Greek word *pornos,* from which we get our word *pornography,* and it means "one who practices fornication—illicit sex." The morally unclean and the covetous will join the fornicator in judgment. Paul equates covetousness with idolatry, for it is the worship of something other than God. These warnings deal with the habitual practice of sin, and not the occasional act of sin. David committed adultery, yet God forgave him and one day took him to heaven. Certainly David was disciplined for his sin, but he was not rejected by God.

In Paul's day, there were false Christians who argued that believers could live in sin and get away with it. These deceivers had many arguments to convince ignorant Christians that they could sin repeatedly and still enter God's kingdom. "You were saved by grace!" they argued. "Therefore go ahead and sin that God's grace might abound!" Paul answered that foolish argument in Romans 6. "Sin in the life of a believer is different from sin in the life of an unsaved person!" Yes—*it's worse!* God judges sin no matter where He finds it, and He does not want to find it in the life of one of His own children. I personally believe that no true Christian can ever be lost, but he will prove the reality of his faith by an obedient life.

There are many professors who are not possessors (Matt. 7:21-23). A Christian is not *sinless,* but he does *sin less*—and less—and less! The Christian is a king, and it is beneath his dignity to indulge in the practices of the lost world that is outside the kingdom of God.

**We are light (vv. 7-14).** This figure is the main thrust of the passage, for Paul was admonishing his readers to "walk as children of light." You will want to read 2 Corinthians 6:14–7:1 for a parallel passage that explains the contrasts that exist between the child of God and the unsaved person. Paul did not say that we were "in the darkness," but that we "were darkness." Now that we are saved, "what communion hath light with darkness?" After all, light produces fruit, but the works of darkness are unfruitful as far as spiritual things are concerned. "For the fruit of the Spirit [or "the light"] is in all goodness and righteousness and truth." It is impossible to be in darkness and light at the same time!

The light produces "goodness," one manifestation of the fruit of the Spirit (Gal. 5:22). Goodness is "love in action." Righteousness means rightness of character before God and rightness of actions before men. Both of these qualities are based on *truth,* which is conformity to the Word and will of God.

Jesus had much to say about light and darkness. "Let your light so shine before men, that they may see your good works, and glorify your Father which is in heaven" (Matt. 5:16). "Everyone that doeth evil hateth the light, neither cometh to the light, lest his deeds should be reproved. But he that doeth truth cometh to the light, that his deeds may be made manifest, that they are wrought in God" (John 3:20-21).

To "walk as children of light" means to live before the eyes of God, not hiding anything. It is relatively easy to hide things from other people because they cannot see our hearts and minds; but "all things are naked and opened unto the eyes of Him with whom we have to do" (Heb. 4:13). Every time I take a plane to a meeting, I must surrender myself and my luggage to a special inspection, and I am happy to do so, because this inspection helps to detect bombs. I have never been afraid to walk through the "detection tunnel" or have my luggage pass through the X-ray equipment, because I have nothing to hide.

An author asked Charles Spurgeon for permission to write his life story, and the great preacher replied, "You may write my life in the skies—I have nothing to hide!"

But walking "as children of light" also means revealing God's light in our daily lives. By our character and conduct, we bring God's light into a dark world. As God's lights, we help others find their way to Christ. The mind of the unsaved person is blinded by Satan (2 Cor. 4:3-4) and by sin (Eph. 4:17-19). Only as we witness and share Christ can the light enter in. Just as a healthy person can assist the sickly, so a child of God can lead the lost out of darkness into God's wonderful light.

Light reveals God; light produces fruit; but light also exposes what is wrong. No surgeon would willingly operate in darkness lest he made a false move and take a life. How could an artist paint a true picture in darkness? The light reveals the truth and exposes the true character of things. This explains why the unsaved person stays clear of the church and the Bible. God's light reveals his true character, and the exposure is not very complimentary. As we Christians walk in light, we refuse to fellowship with the darkness, and we expose the dark things of sin for what they really are.

"I am come a light into the world," said Jesus (John 12:46). He also said to His disciples, "Ye are the light of the world" (Matt. 5:14). When He was here on earth, the perfection of His character and conduct exposed the sinfulness of those around Him. This is one reason why the religious leaders hated Him and sought to destroy Him. "If I had not come and spoken unto them, they had not had sin, but now they have no cloak for their sin" (John 15:22). Just as a healthy person unconsciously exposes the handicaps and sicknesses of people he visits in a hospital, so the Christian exposes the darkness and sin around him just by living like a Christian. Paul tells us to live balanced lives—positively, to walk in the light; negatively, to denounce and expose the wickedness of those in the darkness. It is not enough simply to expose the wickedness of those in the darkness. It is not enough simply to expose sin. We must also bear fruit.

But Ephesians 5:12 gives us a caution. Be careful how you deal with the "unfruitful works of darkness." The motto today seems to be, "Tell it like it is!" And yet that can be a dangerous policy when it comes to exposing the filthy things of darkness, lest we unconsciously advertise and promote sin. Paul said, "It is a shame even to speak of those things" (Eph. 6:12). Some preachers enjoy reveling in the sensational, so much so that their sermons excite appetites and give to the innocent more information than they need. "But yet I would have you wise unto that which is good, and simple concerning evil" (Rom. 16:19).

I recall a friend in youth work who felt it necessary to read all that the teenagers were reading "in order to understand them better," and it so polluted his mind that he himself fell into sin. It is not necessary for the believer to perform an autopsy on a rotting corpse to expose its rottenness. All he has to do is turn on the light! "For whatsoever doth make manifest is light" (Eph. 5:13).

When you think of light, you think of waking up to a new day, and Paul presented this picture (Eph. 5:14), paraphrasing Isaiah 60:1. You have the same image in Romans 13:11-13 and 1 Thessalonians 5:1-10. That Easter morning, when Christ arose from the dead, was the dawning of a new day for the world. Christians are not sleeping in sin and death. We have been raised from the dead through faith in Him. The darkness of the graveyard is past, and we are now walking in the light of salvation. Salvation is the beginning of a new day, and we ought to live as those who belong to the light, not to the darkness. "Lazarus, come forth!"

The believer has no business in the darkness. He is a *saint,* which means he is a partaker "of the inheritance of the saints in light" (Col. 1:12). He is a *king,* because he has been delivered "from the power of darkness" and has been translated "into the kingdom of His dear Son" (Col. 1:13). He is "light in the Lord" (Eph. 5:8).

## Walk in Wisdom (Eph. 5:15-17)

*Circumspect* comes from two Latin words which mean "looking around." The Greek word carries the idea of precision and accuracy. "See that you walk carefully, with exactness" is the meaning. The opposite would be walking carelessly and without proper guidance and forethought. We cannot leave the Christian life to chance. We must make wise decisions and seek to do the will of God.

Ephesians 5:14-15 are related. Paul appeared to be saying, "Don't walk in your sleep! Wake up! Open your eyes! Make the most of the day!" It is sad to see many professed Christians "drift" through life, like sleepwalkers, who never really make the most of opportunities to live for Christ and serve Him. Paul presented several reasons why we should be accurate and careful in our walk.

*It is a mark of wisdom (v. 15).* Only a fool drifts with the wind and tide. A wise man marks out his course, sets his sails, and guides the rudder until he reaches his destination. When a man wants to build a house, he first draws his plans so he knows what he is doing. Yet, how many Christians plan their days so that they use their opportunities wisely? True, we cannot know what a day may bring forth (James 4:13-17). But it is also true that a planned life can better deal with unexpected events. Someone said, "When the pilot does not know what port he is heading for, no wind is the right wind."

*Life is short (v. 16a).* "Buying up the opportunity—taking advantage of it." An old Chinese adage says, "Opportunity has a forelock so you can seize it when you meet it. Once it is past, you cannot seize it again." Our English word *opportunity* comes from the Latin and means "toward the port." It suggests a ship taking advantage of the wind and tide to arrive safely in the harbor. The brevity of life is a strong argument for making the best use of the opportunities God gives us.

*The days are evil (v. 16b).* In Paul's time, this meant that Roman persecution was on the way (1 Peter 4:12-19). How foolish to waste opportunities to win the lost when soon those opportunities might be taken away by the advances of sin in society! If the days were evil when Paul wrote this letter, what must be their condition today?

*God has given us a mind (v. 17a).* "Understanding" suggests using our minds to discover and do the will of God. Too many Christians have the idea that discovering God's will is a mystical experience that rules out clear thinking. But this idea is wrong—and dangerous. We discover the will of God as He transforms the mind (Rom. 12:1-2); and this transformation is the result of the Word of God, prayer, meditation, and worship. If God gave you a mind, then He expects you to use it. This means that learning His will involves gathering facts, examining them, weighing them, and praying for His wisdom (James 1:5). God does not want us simply to *know* His will; He wants us to *understand* His will.

*God has a plan for our lives (v. 17b).* Paul alluded to this plan (Eph. 2:10). If God saved me, He has a purpose for my life, and I should discover that purpose and then guide my life accordingly. He reveals His plan through His Word (Col. 1:9-10), His Spirit in our hearts (Col. 3:15), and the working of circumstances (Rom. 8:28). The Christian can walk carefully and accurately because he knows what God wants him to do. Like the builder following the blueprint, he accomplishes what the architect planned.

This completes the section we have called "Walk in Purity." The emphasis is on the new life as contrasted with the old life, imitating God and not the evil world around us. In the next section, "Walk in Harmony," Paul deals with the relationships of life and shows how life in Christ can bring heaven to the home.

# CHAPTER ELEVEN
# HEAVEN IN YOUR HOME
*Ephesians 5:18-33*

W hen home is ruled according to God's Word," said Charles Haddon Spurgeon, "angels might be asked to stay with us, and they would not find themselves out of their element."

The trouble is that many homes are not governed by God's Word—even homes where the members are professing Christians—and the consequences are tragic. Instead of angels being guests in some homes, it seems that demons are the masters. Too many marriages end in the divorce court, and nobody knows how many husbands and wives are emotionally divorced even though they share the same address. The poet William Cowper called the home "the only bliss of Paradise that hast surviv'd the Fall," but too many homes are an outpost of hell instead of a parcel of paradise.

The answer is the Holy Spirit of God! It is only through the power of the Holy Spirit that we can walk in harmony as husbands and wives (Eph. 5:22-33), parents and children (Eph. 6:1-4), and employers and employees (Eph. 6:5-9). The unity of the people of God that Paul described (Eph. 4:1-16) must be translated into daily living if we are to enjoy the harmony that is a foretaste of heaven on earth.

"Be filled with the Spirit" is God's command, and He expects us to obey. The command is plural, so it applies to all Christians and not just to a select few. The verb is in the present tense—"keep on being filled"—so it is an experience we should enjoy constantly and not just on special occasions. And the verb is passive. We do not fill ourselves but permit the Spirit to fill us. The verb "fill" has nothing to do with contents or quantity, as though we are empty vessels that need a required amount of spiritual fuel to keep going. In the Bible, *filled* means "controlled by." "They . . . were filled with wrath" (Luke 4:28) means "they were controlled by wrath" and for that reason tried to kill Jesus. "The Jews were filled with envy" (Acts 13:45) means that the Jews were controlled by envy and opposed

the ministry of Paul and Barnabas. To be "filled with the Spirit" means to be constantly controlled by the Spirit in our mind, emotions, and will.

When a person trusts Christ as his Saviour, he is immediately baptized by the Spirit into the body of Christ (1 Cor. 12:13). Nowhere in the New Testament are we commanded to be baptized by the Spirit, because this is a once-for-all experience that takes place at conversion. When the Spirit came at Pentecost, the believers were baptized by the Spirit and thus the body of Christ was formed (Acts 1:4-5). But they were also "filled with the Spirit" (Acts 2:4), and it was this filling that gave them the power they needed to witness for Christ (Acts 1:8). In Acts 2, the Jewish believers were baptized by the Spirit, and in Acts 10 the Gentile believers had the same experience (Acts 10:44-48; 11:15-17). Thus the body of Christ was made up of Jews and Gentiles (Eph. 2:11-22). That historic baptism, in two stages, has never been repeated any more than Calvary has been repeated. But that baptism is made personal when the sinner trusts Christ and the Spirit enters in to make him a member of the body of Christ. The baptism of the Spirit means that I belong to Christ's body. The filling of the Spirit means that my body belongs to Christ.

We usually think of the power of the Spirit as necessary for preaching and witnessing, and this is true. (See Acts 4:8, 31; 6:3, 5; 7:55; 13:9. The Apostles experienced repeated fillings after that initial experience at Pentecost.) But Paul wrote that the Spirit's fullness is also needed in the home. If our homes are to be a heaven on earth, then we must be controlled by the Holy Spirit. But how can a person tell whether or not he is filled with the Spirit? Paul stated that there are three evidences of the fullness of the Spirit in the life of the believer: he is *joyful* (Eph. 5:19), *thankful* (Eph. 5:20), and *submissive* (Eph. 5:21-33). Paul said nothing about miracles or tongues, or other special manifestations. He stated that the home can be a heaven on earth if each family member is controlled by the Spirit, and is joyful, thankful, and submissive.

## Joyful (Eph. 5:19)

Joy is one of the fruit of the Spirit (Gal. 5:22). Christian joy is not a shallow emotion that, like a thermometer, rises and falls with the changing atmosphere of the home. Rather, Christian joy is a deep experience of adequacy and confidence in spite of the circumstances around us. The Christian can be joyful even in the midst of pain and suffering. This kind of joy is not a thermometer but a thermostat. Instead of rising and falling with the circumstances, it determines the spiritual temperature of the circumstances. Paul put it beautifully when he wrote, "I have learned in whatsoever state I am, therewith to be content" (Phil. 4:11).

To illustrate this joy, Paul used the familiar image of drunkenness: "Be not drunk with wine . . . but be filled with the Spirit" (Eph. 5:18). When the believers at Pentecost were filled with the Spirit, the crowd accused them of being drunk with new wine (Acts 2:13-15). There was such a joyfulness about them that the unbelievers could think of no better comparison. But some practical lessons can be learned from the contrasts. To begin with, the drunk is under the control of another force, since alcohol is actually a depressant. He feels a great sense of release—all his troubles are gone. He can "lick anybody in the house!" The drunk is not ashamed to express himself (though what he says and does is shameful), nor can he hide what is going on in his life.

Transfer this picture to the believer who is filled with the Spirit. God controls his life, and he experiences a deep joy he is not afraid to express to the glory of God. Of course, the drunk is really out of control, since the alcohol affects his brain, while the believer experiences a beautiful self-control that is really God in control. Self-control is among the fruit of the Spirit (Gal. 5:23). "The spirits of the prophets are subject to the prophets" (1 Cor. 14:32). The drunk makes a fool of himself, but the Spirit-filled Christian glorifies God and is willing to be a "fool for Christ's sake" (1 Cor. 4:10). The drunk calls attention to himself, while the Spirit-filled believer is a witness for Christ.

It is certainly not difficult to live or work with someone who is filled with the Spirit and joyful. He has a song in his heart and on his lips. The drunk often sings, but his songs only reveal the corruption in his heart. The Spirit-filled Christian's song comes from God, a song he could never sing apart from the Spirit's power. God even gives us songs in the night (Ps. 42:8). In spite of pain and shame, Paul and Silas were able to sing praises to God in the Philippian jail (Acts 16:25), and the result was the conversion of the jailer and his family.

What a happy time they all had that midnight hour—and they did not need to get drunk to enjoy it!

"Your neighborhood tavern is the friendliest place in town!" That slogan appeared in a headline of a special newspaper insert during "National Tavern Month," so I decided to test its veracity. I watched the newspapers for several weeks and cut out items that related to taverns—and all of them were connected with brawls and murders. The friendliest place in town! But this headline reminded me that people who drink together often experience a sympathy and conviviality. This fact is no argument for alcohol, but it does illustrate a point: Christians who are filled with the Holy Spirit enjoy being together and experience a sense of joyful oneness in the Lord. They do not need the false stimulants of the world. They have the Spirit of God—and He is all they need.

## Thankful (Eph. 5:20)

Someone defined the home as "the place where we are treated the best—and complain the most!" How true this is! "My father never talks to me unless he wants to bawl me out or ask about my grades," a teenager once told me. "After all, a guy needs some encouragement once in a while!" Marriage counselors tell us that "taking each other for granted" is one of the chief causes of marital problems. Being thankful to God for each other is a secret of a happy home, and it is the Holy Spirit who gives us the grace of thankfulness.

How does a grateful heart promote harmony in the home? For one thing, the sincerely grateful person realizes that he is enriched because of others, which is a mark of humility. The person who thinks the world owes him a living is never thankful for anything. He thinks he is doing others a favor by permitting them to serve him. The thankful heart is usually humble, a heart that gladly acknowledges God as the "Giver of every good and perfect gift" (James 1:17). Like Mary's gift to Jesus in John 12, gratitude fills the house with fragrance.

To be sure, all of us are grateful for some things at some special occasions; but Paul commanded his readers to be thankful for all things at all times. This exhortation in itself proves our need of the Spirit of God, because in our own strength we could never obey this commandment. Can we really be thankful in times of suffering, disappointment, and even bereavement? Keep in mind that Paul was a prisoner when he wrote those words, yet he was thankful for what God was doing in him and for him (Eph. 1:16; 5:4, 20; Phil. 1:3; Col. 1:3, 12; 2:7; 3:17; 4:2). When a Christian finds himself in a difficult situation, he should immediately give thanks to the Father, in the name of Jesus Christ, by the power of the Spirit, to keep his heart from complaining and fretting. The devil moves in when a Christian starts to complain, but thanksgiving in the Spirit defeats the devil and glorifies the Lord. "In everything give thanks: for this is the will of God in Christ Jesus concerning you" (1 Thes. 5:18).

The word *gratitude* comes from the same root word as *grace*. If we have experienced the grace of God, then we ought to be grateful for what God brings to us. *Thank* and *think* also come from the same root word. If we would think more, we would thank more.

## Submissive (Eph. 5:21-33)

Paul applied the principle of harmony to husbands and wives (Eph. 5:21-33), parents and children (Eph. 6:1-4), and masters and servants (Eph. 6:5-9); and he began with the admonition that each submit to the other (Eph. 5:21). Does this suggest that the children tell the parents what to do, or that the masters obey the servants? Of course not! *Submission* has nothing to do with the *order* of authority, but rather governs the *operation* of authority, how it is given and how it is received. Often Jesus tried to teach His disciples not to throw their weight around, or seek to become great at somebody else's expense. Unfortunately, they failed to learn the lesson, and even at the Last Supper they were arguing over who was the greatest (Luke 22:24-27). When Jesus washed their feet, He taught them that the greatest is the person who uses his authority to build up people and not, like the Pharisees, to build up his authority and make himself important. We are to esteem others "more important than ourselves" (Rom 12:10; Phil. 2:1-4). By nature, we want to promote ourselves, but the Holy Spirit enables us to submit ourselves.

As you study Paul's words to husbands and wives, remember that he was writing to believers. He was nowhere suggesting that women are inferior to men, or that all women must be in subjection to all men in every situation. The fact that he uses Christ and the church as his illustration is evidence that he has the Christian home in mind.

*Wives, submit yourselves (vv. 22-24).* He gives two reasons for this command: the lordship of Christ (Eph. 5:22) and the headship of the man in Christ (Eph. 5:23). When the Christian wife submits herself to Christ and lets Him be the Lord of her life, she will have no difficulty submitting to her husband. This does not mean that she becomes a slave, for the husband is also to submit to Christ. And if both are living under the lordship of Christ, there can be only harmony. Headship is not dictatorship. "Each for the other, both for the Lord." The Christian husband and wife should pray together and spend time in the Word, so that they might know God's will for their individual lives and for their home. Most of the marital conflicts I have dealt with as a pastor have stemmed from failure of the husband and or wife to submit to Christ, spend time in His Word, and seek to do His will each day.

This explains why a Christian should marry a Christian and not become "unequally yoked together" with an unbeliever (2 Cor. 6:14-18). If the Christian is submitted to Christ, he will not try to establish a home that disobeys the Word of God. Such a home invites civil war from the beginning. But something else is important. The Christian couple must be careful to submit to Christ's lordship even before they are married. Unless the couple prays together and sincerely seeks God's will in His Word, their marriage begins on a weak foundation. Sins committed before marriage ("We're Christians—we can get away with this!") have a way of causing problems after marriage. Certainly God is able to forgive, but something very precious is lost just the same. Dr. William Culbertson, former president of Moody Bible Institute, used to warn about "the sad consequences of forgiven sins," and engaged Christian couples need to take that warning to heart.

*Husbands, love your wives (vv. 25-33).* Paul had much more to say to the Christian husbands than to the wives. He set for them a very high standard: Love your wives "even as Christ also loved the church." Paul was lifting married love to the highest level possible, for he saw in the Christian home an illustration of the relationship between Christ and the church. God established marriage for many reasons. For one thing, it meets man's *emotional* needs. "It is not good that the man should be alone" (Gen. 2:18). Marriage also has a *social* purpose in the bearing of children to continue the race (Gen. 1:28). Paul indicated a *physical* purpose for marriage—to help man and woman fulfill the normal desires given them by God (1 Cor. 7:1-3). But in Ephesians 5, Paul indicated also a *spiritual* purpose in marriage, as the husband and wife experience with each other the submission and the love of Christ (Eph. 5:22-33).

If the husband makes Christ's love for the church the pattern for loving his wife, then he will love her *sacrificially* (Eph. 5:25). Christ gave Himself for the church; so the husband, in love, gives himself for his wife. Jacob so loved Rachel that he sacrificially worked fourteen years to win her. True Christian love "seeketh not her own" (1 Cor. 13:5)—it is not selfish. If a husband is submitted to Christ and filled with the Spirit, his sacrificial love will willingly pay a price that she might be able to serve Christ in the home and glorify Him.

The husband's love will also be a *sanctifying* love (Eph. 5:26-27). The word *sanctify* means "to set apart." In the marriage ceremony, the husband is set apart to belong to the wife, and the wife is set apart to belong to the husband. Any interference with this God-given arrangement is sin. Today, Christ is cleansing His church through the ministry of His Word (John 15:3; 17:17). The love of the husband for his wife ought to be cleansing her (and him) so that both are becoming more like Christ. Even their physical relationship should be so controlled by God that it becomes a means of spiritual enrichment as well as personal enjoyment (1 Cor. 7:3-5). The husband is not to "use" his wife for his own pleasure, but rather is to show the kind of love that is mutually rewarding and sanctifying. The marriage experience is one of constant growth when Christ is the Lord of the home. Love always enlarges and enriches, while selfishness does just the opposite.

The church today is not perfect; it has spots and wrinkles. Spots are caused by defilement on the outside, while wrinkles are caused by decay on the inside. Because the church becomes defiled by the world, it needs constant cleansing, and the Word of God is the cleansing agent. "Keep yourselves unspotted from the world" (James 1:27). Strictly speaking, there should be no wrinkles in the church, because wrinkles are evidence of old age and internal decay. As the church is nourished by the Word, these wrinkles ought to disappear. Like a beautiful bride, the church ought to be clean and youthful, which is possi-

ble through the Spirit of God using the Word of God. One day the church will be presented in heaven "a glorious church" at the coming of Jesus Christ (Jude 24).

The husband's love for his wife should be sacrificial and sanctifying, but it should also be *satisfying* (Eph. 5:28-30). In the marriage relationship, the husband and wife become "one flesh." Therefore, whatever each does to the other, he does to himself or herself. It is a mutually satisfying experience. The man who loves his wife is actually loving his own body, since he and his wife are one flesh. As he loves her, he is nourishing her. Just as love is the circulatory system of the body of Christ (Eph. 4:16), so love is the nourishment of the home. How many people have confessed, "I am starved for love." There should be no starvation for love in the Christian home, for the husband and wife should so love each other that their physical, emotional, and spiritual needs are met. If both are submitted to the Lord, and to each other, they will be so satisfied that they will not be tempted to look anywhere else for fulfillment.

Our Christian homes are to be pictures of Christ's relationship to His church. Each believer is a member of Christ's body, and each believer is to help nourish the body in love (Eph. 4:16). We are one with Christ. The church is His body and His bride, and the Christian home is a divinely ordained illustration of this relationship. This certainly makes marriage a serious matter.

Paul referred to the creation of Eve and the forming of the first home (Gen. 2:18-24). Adam had to give part of himself in order to get a bride, but Christ gave all of Himself to purchase His bride at the cross. God opened Adam's side, but sinful men pierced Christ's side. So united are a husband and wife that they are "one flesh." Their union is even closer than that of parents and children. The believer's union with Christ is even closer and, unlike human marriage, will last for all eternity. Paul closed with a final admonition that the husband love his wife and that the wife reverence (respect) her husband, all of which require the power of the Holy Spirit.

If Christian husbands and wives have the power of the Spirit to enable them, and the example of Christ to encourage them, why do too many Christian marriages fail? Somebody is out of the will of God. Just because two Christians know each other and get along together does not mean they are supposed to get married. In fact, not every believer is supposed to marry. It is sometimes God's will for a Christian to remain single (Matt. 19:12; 1 Cor. 7:7-9). It is wrong for a believer to marry an unbeliever, but it is also wrong for two Christians to marry out of the will of God.

But even if two Christians marry in the will of God, they must stay in God's will if their home is to be the creative fellowship God wants it to be. "The fruit of the Spirit is love" (Gal. 5:22), and unless both husband and wife are walking in the Spirit they cannot share the love of Christ, the love that is so beautifully described in 1 Corinthians 13. The root of most marital problems is sin, and the root of all sin is selfishness. Submission to Christ and to one another is the only way to overcome selfishness, for when we submit, the Holy Spirit can fill us and enable us to love one another in a sacrificial, sanctifying, satisfying way—the way Christ loves the church.

To experience the fullness of the Spirit a person must first possess the Spirit—be a Christian. Then there must be a sincere desire to glorify Christ, since this is why the Holy Spirit was given (John 16:14). We do not use the Holy Spirit; He uses us. There must be a deep thirst for God's fullness, a confession that we cannot do His will apart from His power. We must claim the promise of John 7:37-39: "If any man thirst, let him come unto Me and drink!" By faith yield yourself to Christ; by faith ask Him for the fullness of the Spirit. By faith receive. When you find yourself joyful, thankful, and submissive, you will know that God has answered.

One more important factor should be considered. The Spirit of God uses the Word of God to work in our lives. Read Colossians 3:16—4:1 and you will see a parallel to our Ephesians passage. And you will note that to be filled with the Word of God produces joy, thanksgiving, and submission. In other words, when you are controlled by the Word of God, you are filled with the Spirit of God. Not only husbands and wives, but all Christians need to spend time daily letting the Word of Christ dwell in them richly, for then the Spirit of God can work in our lives to make us joyful, thankful, and submissive. And this means heaven in the home—or wherever God may put us.

# CHAPTER TWELVE
# LIVING THE
# LORDSHIP OF CHRIST
*Ephesians 6:1-9*

After watching a television presentation about rebellious youth, a husband said to his wife, "What a mess! Where did our generation go wrong?" The wife calmly answered, "We had children."

It seems no matter where we look in modern society, we see antagonism, division, and rebellion. Husbands and wives are divorcing each other; children are rebelling against their parents; and employers and employees are seeking for new ways to avoid strikes and keep the machinery of industry running productively. We have tried education, legislation, and every other approach, but nothing seems to work. Paul's solution to the antagonisms in the home and in society was *regeneration*—a new heart from God and a new submission to Christ and to one another. God's great program is to "gather together in one all things in Christ" (Eph. 1:10). Paul indicated that this spiritual harmony begins in the lives of Christians who are submitted to the lordship of Christ.

In this section Paul admonished four groups of Christians about how they could have harmony in Christ.

### Christian Children (Eph. 6:1-3)
Paul did not tell the parents to admonish the children; he did it himself. Children were present in the assembly when this letter was read. Did they understand all that Paul wrote? Do *we* understand it all? Christian families attended the public worship together, and no doubt the parents explained the Word to the children when they were at home. He gave them four reasons why they should obey their parents.

***They are Christians ("in the Lord," v. 1a).*** This argument is an application of the theme of the entire section, which is "submitting yourselves one to another in the fear of God" (Eph. 5:21). When a person becomes a Christian, he is not released from normal obligations of life. If anything, his faith in Christ ought to make him a better child in the home.

To the Colossians Paul enforced his admonition with "for this is well pleasing unto the Lord" (Col. 3:20). Here is harmony in the home: the wife submits to the husband "as unto Christ"; the husband loves his wife "even as Christ also loved the church"; and the children obey "in the Lord."

***Obedience is right (v. 1b).*** There is an order in nature, ordained of God, that argues for the rightness of an action. Since the parents brought the child into the world, and since they have more knowledge and wisdom than the child, it is right that the child obey his parents. Even young animals are taught to obey. The "modern version" of Ephesians 6:1 would be, "Parents, obey your children, for this will keep them happy and bring peace to the home." But this is contrary to God's order in nature.

***Obedience is commanded (v. 2a).*** Here Paul cites the fifth commandment (Ex. 20:12; Deut. 5:16) and applies it to the New Testament believer. This does not mean that the Christian is "under the Law," for Christ has set us free from both the curse and the bondage of the Law (Gal. 3:13; 5:1). But the righteousness of the Law is still a revelation of the holiness of God, and the Holy Spirit enables us to practice that righteousness in our daily lives (Rom. 8:1-4). All of the Ten Commandments are repeated in the New Testament epistles for the Christian to observe except, "Remember the Sabbath Day to keep it holy." It is just as wrong for a New Testament Christian to dishonor his parents as it was for an Old Testament Jew.

To "honor" our parents means much more than simply to obey them. It means to show them respect and love, to care for them as long as they need us, and to seek to bring honor to them by the way we live. A young couple came to see me about getting married, and I asked if their parents agreed to the wedding. They looked at each other in embarrassment, then confessed, "We were hoping you wouldn't ask about that." I spent the next hour trying to convince them that their parents had a right to rejoice in this event, and that to exclude them would cause wounds that might never heal. "Even if they are not believers," I said, "they are your parents, and you owe them love and respect." They finally agreed, and the plans we made together made both families happy. Had we followed the couple's original plans, the two of them would have lost their testimony with their relatives, but, instead, they were able to give a good witness for Jesus Christ.

***Obedience brings blessing (vv. 2b-3).*** The fifth commandment has a promise attached to it: "That thy days may be long upon the land which the Lord thy God giveth thee" (Ex. 20:12). This promise originally applied to the Jews as they entered Canaan, but Paul applied it to believers today. He substituted "earth" for "land" and tells us that the Christian child who honors his parents can expect two blessings. It will be well with him, and he will live long on the earth. This does not mean that everyone who died young dishonored his parents. He was stating a principle: when children obey their parents in the Lord, they will escape a good deal of sin and danger and thus avoid the things that could threaten or shorten their lives. But life is not measured only by quantity of time. It is also measured by quality of experience. God enriches the life of the obedient child no matter how long he may live on the earth. Sin always robs us; obedience always enriches us.

So, the child must learn early to obey father and mother, not only because they are his parents, but also because God has commanded it to be so. Disobedience to parents is rebellion against God. The sad situation in homes today is the result of rejecting God's Word (Rom. 1:28-30; 2 Tim. 3:1-5). By nature, a child is selfish, but in the power of the Holy Spirit, a child can learn to obey his parents and glorify God.

## Christian Fathers (Eph. 6:4)
If left to themselves, children will be rebels, so it is necessary for the parents to train their children. Years ago, the then Duke of Windsor said, "Everything in the American home is controlled by switches—except the children!" The Bible records the sad results of parents neglecting their children, either by being bad examples to them or failing to discipline them properly. David pampered Absalom and set him a bad example, and the results were tragic. Eli failed to discipline his sons and they brought disgrace to his name and defeat to the nation of Israel. In his latter years, even Isaac pampered Esau, while his wife showed favoritism to Jacob; and the result was a divided home. Jacob was showing favoritism to Joseph when God providentially rescued the lad and made a man out of him in Egypt. Paul tells us that the father has several responsibilities toward his children.

**He must not provoke them.** In Paul's day, the father had supreme authority over the family. When a baby was born into a Roman family, for example, it was brought out and laid before the father. If he picked it up, it meant he was accepting it into the home. But if he did not pick it up, it meant the child was rejected. It could be sold, given away, or even killed by exposure. No doubt a father's love would overcome such monstrous acts, but these practices were legal in that day. Paul told the parents, "Don't use your authority to abuse the child, but to encourage and build the child." To the Colossians he wrote, "Fathers, provoke not your children to anger, lest they be discouraged" (Col. 3:21). So, the opposite of "provoke" is "encourage."

I was addressing a group of Christian students on the subject of prayer, and was pointing out that our Father in heaven is always available when we call. To illustrate it, I told them that the receptionist at our church office has a list of names prepared by me, and these people could get to me at any time, no matter what I was doing. Even if I was in a staff meeting, or in a counseling session, if any of these people phoned, she was to call me immediately. At the top of this list was my family. Even if the matter seems to me inconsequential, I want my family to know that I am available. After the service, one of the students said to me, "Would you adopt me? I can never get through to my father, and I need his encouragement so much!"

Fathers provoke their children and discourage them by saying one thing and doing another—by always blaming and never praising, by being inconsistent and unfair in discipline, and by showing favoritism in the home, by making promises and not keeping them, and by making light of problems that, to the children, are very important. Christian parents need the fullness of the Spirit so they can be sensitive to the needs and problems of their children.

**He must nurture them.** The text reads, "But nurture them in the discipline and admonition of the Lord." The verb translated "bring them up" is the same word that is translated "nourisheth" in Ephesians 5:29. The Christian husband is to nourish his wife and his children by sharing love and encouragement in the Lord. It is not enough to nurture the children physically by providing food, shelter, and clothing. He must also nurture them emotionally and spiritually. The development of the Boy Jesus is our example: "And Jesus increased in wisdom and stature, and in favor with God and man" (Luke 2:52). Here is balanced growth: intellectual, physical, spiritual, and social. Nowhere in the Bible is the training of children assigned to agencies outside the home, no matter how they might assist. God looks to the parents for the kind of training that the children need.

**He must discipline them.** The word "nurture" carries with it the idea of learning through discipline. It is translated "chastening" in Hebrews 12. Some modern psychologists oppose the old-fashioned idea of discipline, and many educators follow their philosophy. "Let the children express themselves!" they tell us. "If you discipline them, you may warp their characters." Yet discipline is a basic principle of life and an evidence of love. "Whom the Lord loveth, He chasteneth" (Heb. 12:6). "He that spareth him chasteneth him diligently" (Prov. 13:24, literal translation).

We must be sure, however, that we discipline our children in the right manner. To begin with, we must discipline in love and not in anger, lest we injure either the body or the spirit of the child, or possibly both. If we are not disciplined, we surely cannot discipline others, and "flying off the handle" never made either a better child or a better parent.

Also, our discipline must be fair and consistent. "My father would use a cannon to kill a mosquito!" a teenager once told me. "I either get away with murder, or get blamed for everything!" Consistent, loving discipline gives assurance to the child. He may not agree with us, but at least he knows that we care enough to build some protective walls around him until he can take care of himself.

"I never knew how far I could go," a wayward girl told me, "because my parents never cared enough to discipline me. I figured that if it wasn't important to them, why should it be important to me?"

**He must instruct and encourage them.** This is the meaning of the word "admonition." The father and mother not only use actions to raise the child, but also words. In the Book of Proverbs, for example, we have an inspired record of a father sharing wise counsel with his son. Our children do not always appreciate our counsel, but that does not eliminate the obligation we have to instruct and encourage them. Of course, our instruction must always be tied to the Word of God (see 2 Tim. 3:13-17).

When the Supreme Court handed down its ruling against required prayer in the public schools, the famous editorial cartoonist Herblock published a cartoon in the *Washington Post* showing an angry father waving a newspaper at his family and shouting, "What do they expect us to do—listen to the kids pray at home?" The answer is: Yes! Home is the place where the children ought to learn about the Lord and the Christian life. It is time that Christian parents stop "passing the buck" to Sunday School teachers and Christian day-school teachers, and start nurturing their children.

## Christian Servants (Eph. 6:5-8)

The word "servants" undoubtedly refers to Christian slaves, but we may certainly apply these words to the Christian employee today. There were probably 6 million slaves in the Roman Empire in that day, and slavery was an accepted institution. Nowhere in the New Testament is slavery *per se* attacked or condemned, though the overall thrust of the Gospel is against it. Paul's ministry was not to overthrow the Roman government or any of its institutions, but to preach the Gospel and win the lost to Christ. Certainly the results of his evangelism ultimately led to the overthrow of the Roman Empire, but that was not Paul's main motive. Just as the preaching of Wesley and Whitefield resulted in the abolition of slavery and child labor, the elevation of women, and the care of the needy, so Paul's ministry contributed to the death of slavery and the encouragement of freedom. However, he was careful not to confuse the social system with the spiritual order in the church (1 Cor. 7:20-24).

Paul admonished the servants to be obedient, with several good reasons. First, they were really serving Christ. True, they had "masters according to the flesh," but their true Master was in heaven (Eph. 6:9). The fact that an employee and his employer are both Christians is no excuse for either one to do less work. Rather, it is a good reason to be more faithful to each other. The employee should show proper respect for employer, and not try to take advantage of him. He should devote his full attention and energy to the job at hand ("singleness of heart"). The best way to be a witness on the job is to do a good day's work. The Christian worker will avoid "eye service"—working only when the boss is watching, or working extra hard when he is watching to give the impression he is doing a very good job.

The second reason is that doing a good job is the will of God. Christianity knows nothing of sacred and secular. A Christian can perform any good work as a ministry to Christ, to the glory of God. For this reason, the worker must do his job "from the heart," since he is serving Christ and doing the will of God. There were tasks assigned to these slaves that they detested, but they were to perform them just the same, so long as they were not disobeying the will of God. "Singleness of heart" and "doing the will of God from the heart" both indicate the importance of a right heart attitude on the job.

Paul's third argument is that they will be rewarded by the Lord (Eph. 6:8). In that day, slaves were treated like pieces of property, no matter how well educated they might be. An educated, cultured slave who became a Christian might receive even harsher treatment from his master because of his faith, but harsh treatment was not to keep him from doing his best (1 Peter 2:18-25). We are to serve Christ, not men. We shall receive our rewards from Christ, not from men.

## Christian Masters (Eph. 6:9)

The Christian faith does not bring about harmony by erasing social or cultural distinctions. Servants are still servants when they trust Christ, and masters are still masters. Rather, the Christian faith brings harmony by working in the heart. Christ gives us a new motivation, not a new organization. Both servant and master are serving the Lord and seeking to please Him, and in this way they are able to work together to the glory of God. What are the responsibilities of a Christian master (or employer) to his workers?

*He must seek their welfare.* "Do the same things unto them." If the employer expects the workers to do their best for him, he must do his best for them. The master must serve the Lord from his heart if he expects his servants to do the same. He must not exploit them.

One of the greatest examples of this in the Bible is Boaz in the Book of Ruth. He greeted his workers with, "The Lord be with you!" And they replied, "The Lord bless thee!" (Ruth 2:4) Boaz was sensitive to the needs of his workers and generous to the stranger, Ruth. His relationship with his workers was one of mutual respect and a desire to glorify the Lord. It is unfortunate when an employee says, "My boss is supposed to be a Christian, but you'd never know it!"

**He must not threaten.** Roman masters had the power and lawful authority to kill a slave who was rebellious, though few of them did so. Slaves cost too much money to destroy them. Paul suggested that the Christian master has a better way to encourage obedience and service than threats of punishment. The negative power of fear could result in the worker doing less instead of more, and this kind of motivation could not be continued over a long period of time. Far better was the positive motivation of "that which is just and equal" (Col. 4:1). Let a man share the results of his labor and he will work better and harder. Even the Old Testament gives this same counsel: "Thou shalt not rule over him with rigor, but shalt fear thy God" (Lev. 25:43).

**He must be submitted to the Lord.** "Your master also is in heaven" (Eph. 6:9). This is practicing the lordship of Christ. The wife submits to her own husband "as unto the Lord" (Eph. 5:22), and the husband loves the wife "as Christ also loved the church" (Eph. 5:25). Children obey their parents "in the Lord" (Eph. 6:1), and parents raise their children "in the nurture and admonition of the Lord" (Eph. 6:4). Servants are obedient "as unto Christ" (Eph. 6:5), and masters treat their servants as their "Master in heaven" would have them do. Each person, in submission to the Lord, has no problems submitting to those over him.

Jesus said the way to be a ruler is first to be a servant (Matt. 25:21). The person who is not under authority has no right to exercise authority. This explains why many of the great men of the Bible were first servants before God made them rulers: Joseph, Moses, Joshua, David, and Nehemiah are just a few examples. Even after a man becomes a leader, he must still lead by serving. An African proverb says, "The chief is servant of all." "And whosoever will be chief among you, let him be your servant" (Matt. 20:27).

A friend of mine was promoted to a place of executive leadership and, unfortunately, it went to his head. He enjoyed all of his executive privileges and more, and never lost an opportunity to remind his employees who was in charge. But he lost the respect of his workers, and production and efficiency went down so fast that the board had to replace him. Because my friend forgot that he had a "Master

in heaven," he failed to be a good "master on earth."

**He must not play favorites.** God is no respecter of persons. He will judge a master or a servant if he sins, or He will reward a master or a servant if he obeys (Eph. 6:8). A Christian employer cannot take privileges with God simply because of his position; nor should a Christian employer play favorites with those under his authority. Paul warned Timothy to "observe these things without preferring one before another, doing nothing by partiality" (1 Tim. 5:21). One of the fastest ways for a leader to divide his followers and lose their confidence is for the leader to play favorites and show partiality.

This closes the section we have called "Walk in Harmony." If we are filled with the Holy Spirit and are joyful, thankful, and submissive, then we can enjoy harmony in the relationships of life as we live and work with other Christians. We will also find it easier to work with and witness to the unbelievers who may disagree with us. The fruit of the Spirit is love, and love is the greatest adhesive in the world!

# CHAPTER THIRTEEN
# YOU'RE IN THE ARMY NOW!
*Ephesians 6:10-24*

Sooner or later every believer discovers that the Christian life is a battleground, not a playground, and that he faces an enemy who is much stronger than he is—apart from the Lord. That Paul should use the military to illustrate the believer's conflict with Satan is reasonable. He himself was chained to a Roman soldier (Eph. 6:20), and his readers were certainly familiar with soldiers and the equipment they used. In fact, military illustrations were favorites with Paul (2 Cor. 10:4; 1 Tim. 6:12; 2 Tim. 2:3; 4:7).

As Christians, we face three enemies: the world, the flesh, and the devil (Eph. 2:1-3). "The world" refers to the system around us that is opposed to God, that caters to "the lust of the flesh, and the lust of the eyes, and the pride of life" (1 John 2:15-17). "Society apart from God" is a simple, but accurate, definition of "the world." "The flesh" is the old nature that we inherited from Adam, a nature that is opposed to God and can do nothing spiritual to please God. By His death and resurrection, Christ overcame the world (John 16:33; Gal. 6:14), and the flesh (Rom. 6:1-6; Gal. 2:20), and the devil (Eph. 1:19-23). In other words, as believers, we do not fight *for* victory—we fight *from* victory! The Spirit of God enables us, by faith, to appropriate Christ's victory for ourselves.

In these closing verses of the letter, Paul discussed four topics so that his readers, by understanding and applying these truths, might walk in victory.

## The Enemy (Eph. 6:10-12)

The intelligence corps plays a vital part in warfare because it enables the officers to know and understand the enemy. Unless we know who the enemy is, where he is, and what he can do, we have a difficult time defeating him. Not only in Ephesians 6, but throughout the entire Bible, God instructs us about the enemy, so there is no reason for us to be caught off guard.

*The leader—the devil.* The enemy has many different names. *Devil* means "accuser," because he accuses God's people day and night before the throne of God (Rev. 12:7-11). *Satan* means "adversary," because he is the enemy of God. He is also called the tempter (Matt. 4:3), and the murderer and the liar (John 8:44). He is compared to a lion (1 Peter 5:8), a serpent (Gen. 3:1; Rev. 12:9), and an angel of light (2 Cor. 11:13-15), as well as "the god of this age" (2 Cor. 4:4, NIV).

Where did he come from, this spirit-creature that seeks to oppose God and defeat His work? Many students believe that in the original Creation, he was "Lucifer, son of the morning" (Isa. 14:12-15) and that he was cast down because of his pride and his desire to occupy God's throne. Many mysteries are connected with the origin of Satan, but what he is doing and where he is going are certainly no mystery! Since he is a created being, and not eternal (as God is), he is limited in his knowledge and activity. Unlike God, Satan is not all-knowing, all-powerful, or everywhere-present. Then how does he accomplish so much in so many different parts of the world?

The answer is in his organized helpers.

*Satan's helpers.* Paul called them "principalities . . . powers . . . rulers . . . spiritual wickedness in high places" (Eph. 6:12). Charles B. Williams translates it: "For our contest is not with human foes alone, but with the rulers, authorities, and cosmic powers of this dark world; that is, with the spirit forces of evil challenging us in the heavenly contest" (WMS). This suggests a definite army of demonic creatures that assist Satan in his attacks against believers. The Apostle John hinted that one third of the angels fell with Satan when he rebelled against God (Rev. 12:4), and Daniel wrote that Satan's angels struggle against God's angels for control of the affairs of nations (Dan. 10:13-20). A spiritual battle is going on in this world, and in the sphere of "the heavenlies," and you and I are a part of this battle. Knowing this makes "walking in victory" a vitally important thing to us—and to God.

The important point is that our battle is not against human beings. It is against spiritual powers. We are wasting our time fighting people when we ought to be fighting the devil who seeks to control people and make them oppose the work of God. During Paul's ministry in Ephesus, a riot took place that could have destroyed the church (Acts 19:21-41). It wasn't caused only by Demetrius and his associates, for behind them were Satan and his associates. Certainly Paul and the church prayed, and the opposition was silenced. The advice of the King of Syria to his soldiers can be applied to our spiritual battle: "Fight neither with small nor great, save only with the king" (1 Kings 22:31).

*Satan's abilities.* The admonitions Paul gave indicate that Satan is a strong enemy (Eph. 6:10-12), and that we need the power of God to be able to stand against him. Never underestimate the power of the devil. He is not compared to a lion and a dragon just for fun! The Book of Job tells what his power can do to a man's body, home, wealth, and friends. Jesus calls Satan a thief who comes "to steal, and to kill, and to destroy" (John 10:10). Not only is Satan strong, but he is also wise and subtle, and we fight against "the wiles of the devil." *Wiles* means "cunning, crafty arts, stratagems." The Christian cannot afford to be "ignorant of his devices" (2 Cor. 2:11). Some men are cunning and crafty and "lie in wait to receive" (Eph. 4:14), but behind them is the arch-deceiver, Satan. He masquerades as an angel of light (2 Cor. 11:14) and seeks to blind men's minds to the truth of God's Word. The fact that Paul uses the word "wrestle" indicates that we are involved in a hand-to-hand battle and are not mere spectators at a game. Satan wants to use our external enemy, the world, and our internal enemy, the flesh, to defeat us. His weapons and battle plans are formidable.

### The Equipment (Eph. 6:13-17)

Since we are fighting against enemies in the spirit world, we need special equipment both for offense and defense. God has provided the "whole armor" for us, and we dare not omit any part. Satan looks for that unguarded area where he can get a beachhead (Eph. 4:27). Paul commanded his readers to put on the armor, take the weapons, and withstand Satan, all of which we do by faith. Knowing that Christ has already conquered Satan, and that the spiritual armor and weapons are available, by faith we accept what God gives us and go out to meet the foe. The day is evil, and the enemy is evil, but "if God be for us, who can be against us?" (Rom. 8:31)

**The girdle of truth (v. 14a).** Satan is a liar (John 8:44), but the believer whose life is controlled by truth will defeat him. The girdle holds the other parts of the armor together, and truth is the integrating force in the life of the victorious Christian. A man of integrity, with a clear conscience, can face the enemy without fear. The girdle also held the sword. Unless we practice the truth, we cannot use the Word of truth. Once a lie gets into the life of a believer, everything begins to fall apart. For over a year, King David lied about his sin with Bathsheba, and nothing went right. Psalms 32 and 51 tell of the price he paid.

**The breastplace of righteousness (v. 14b.)** This piece of armor, made of metal plates or chains, covered the body from the neck to the waist, both front and back. It symbolizes the believer's righteousness in Christ (2 Cor. 5:21) as well as his righteous life in Christ (Eph. 4:24). Satan is the accuser, but he cannot accuse the believer who is living a godly life in the power of the Spirit. The life we live either fortifies us against Satan's attacks or makes it easier for him to defeat us (2 Cor. 6:1-10). When Satan accuses the Christian, it is the righteousness of Christ that assures the believer of his salvation. But our positional righteousness in Christ, without practical righteousness in the daily life, only

gives Satan opportunity to attack us.

**The shoes of the Gospel (v. 15).** The Roman soldier wore sandals with hobnails in the soles to give him better footing for the battle. If we are going to "stand" and "withstand," then we need the shoes of the Gospel. Because we have the peace with God (Rom. 5:1) that comes from the Gospel, we need not fear the attack of Satan or men. We must be at peace with God and with each other if we are to defeat the devil (James 4:1-7). But the shoes have another meaning. We must be prepared each day to share the Gospel of peace with a lost world. The most victorious Christian is a witnessing Christian. If we wear the shoes of the Gospel, then we have the "beautiful feet" mentioned in Isaiah 52:7 and Romans 10:15. Satan has declared war, but you and I are ambassadors of peace (2 Cor. 5:18-21); and, as such, we take the Gospel of peace wherever we go.

**The shield of faith (v. 16).** The shield was large, usually about four feet by two feet, made of wood, and covered with tough leather. As the soldier held it before him, it protected him from spears, arrows, and "fiery darts." The edges of these shields were so constructed that an entire line of soldiers could interlock shields and march into the enemy like a solid wall. This suggests that we Christians are not in the battle alone. The "faith" mentioned here is not saving faith, but rather living faith, a trust in the promises and the power of God. Faith is a defensive weapon which protects us from Satan's fiery darts. In Paul's day, arrows, dipped in some inflammable substance and ignited, were shot at the enemy. Satan shoots "fiery darts" at our hearts and minds: lies, blasphemous thoughts, hateful thoughts about others, doubts, and burning desires for sin. If we do not by faith quench these darts, they will light a fire within and we will disobey God. We never know when Satan will shoot a dart at us, so we must always walk by faith and use the shield of faith.

**The helmet of salvation (v. 17).** Satan wants to attack the mind, the way he defeated Eve (Gen. 3; 2 Cor. 11:1-3). The helmet refers to the mind controlled by God. It is too bad that many Christians have the idea that the intellect is not important, when in reality it plays a vital role in Christian growth, service, and victory. When God controls the mind, Satan cannot lead the believer astray. The Christian who studies his Bible and learns the meaning of Bible doctrines is not going to be led astray too easily. We need to be "taught by Him as the truth is in Jesus" (Eph. 4:21). We are to "grow in grace, and in the knowledge of our Lord and Saviour Jesus Christ" (2 Peter 3:18). Wherever Paul ministered, he taught the new converts the truths of the Word of God, and this helmet protected them from Satan's lies.

One Sunday afternoon, I visited a man who had been a deacon in a local church, but was at that time involved in a false cult. We sat at the table with open Bibles, and I tried to show him the truth of God's Word, but it seemed his mind was blinded by lies. "How did you happen to turn away from a Bible-preaching church and get involved in this belief?" I asked, and his reply stunned me.

"Preacher, I blame the church. I didn't know anything about the Bible, and they didn't teach me much more. I wanted to study the Bible, but nobody told me how. Then they made me a deacon, and I wasn't ready for it. It was too much for me. I heard this man preaching the Bible over the radio and it sounded as if he knew something. I started reading his magazine and studying his books, and now I'm convinced he's right."

What a tragedy that when his local church took him in, they failed to fit him with the helmet of salvation. Had they practiced the truth found in 2 Timothy 2:2, this man might not have been a casualty in the battle.

**The sword of the Spirit (v. 17b).** This sword is the offensive weapon God provides us. The Roman soldier wore on his girdle a short sword which was used for close-in fighting. Hebrews 4:12 compares the Word of God to a sword, because it is sharp and is able to pierce the inner man just as a material sword pierces the body. You and I were "cut to the heart" (Acts 2:37; 5:33) when the Word convicted us of our sins. Peter tried to use a sword to defend Jesus in the Garden (Luke 22:47-51); but he learned at Pentecost that the "sword of the Spirit" does a much better job. Moses also tried to conquer with a physical sword (Ex. 2:11-15), only to discover that God's Word alone was more than enough to defeat Egypt.

A material sword pierces the body, but the Word of God pierces the heart. The more you use a physical sword, the duller it becomes; but using God's Word only makes it sharper in our lives. A physical sword requires the hand of a soldier, but the sword of the Spirit has its own power, for it is "living and powerful" (Heb. 4:12). The Spirit wrote the Word, and the Spirit wields the Word as we take it by faith and use it. A physical sword wounds to hurt and kill, while the sword of the Spirit wounds to heal and give life. But when we use the sword against Satan, we are out to deal him a blow that will cripple him and keep him from hindering God's work.

When He was tempted by Satan in the wilderness, Christ used the sword of the Spirit and defeated the enemy. Three times Jesus said, "It is written" (Luke 4:1-13). Note that Satan can also quote the Word: "For it is written" (Luke 4:10), but he does not quote it completely. Satan tries to use the Word of God to confuse us, so it is important that we know every word that God has given us. "You can prove anything by the Bible," someone said. True—if you take verses out of context, leave out words, and apply verses to Christians today that do not really apply. The better you know the Word of God, the easier it will be for you to detect Satan's lies and reject his offers.

In one sense, the "whole armor of God" is a picture of Jesus Christ. Christ is the Truth (John 14:6), and He is our righteousness (2 Cor. 5:21) and our peace (Eph. 2:14). His faithfulness makes possible our faith (Gal. 2:20); He is our salvation (Luke 2:30); and He is the Word of God (John 1:1, 14). This means that when we trusted Christ, we received the armor. Paul told the Romans what to do with the armor (Rom. 13:11-14): wake up (Rom. 13:11), cast off sin, and "put on the armor of light" (Rom. 13:12). We do this by putting "on the Lord Jesus Christ" (Rom. 13:14). By faith, put on the armor and trust God for the victory. Once and for all, we have put on the armor at the moment of salvation. But there must be a daily appropriation. When King David put off his armor and returned to his palace, he was in greater danger than when he was on the battlefield (2 Sam. 11). We are never out of reach of Satan's devices, so we must never be without the whole armor of God.

## The Energy (Eph. 6:18-20)

Prayer is the energy that enables the Christian soldier to wear the armor and wield the sword. We cannot fight the battle in our own power, no matter how strong or talented we may think we are. When Amalek attacked Israel, Moses went to the mountaintop to pray, while Joshua used the sword down in the valley (Ex. 17:8-16). It took both to defeat Amalek—Moses' intercession on the mountain, and Joshua's use of the sword in the valley. Prayer is the power for victory, but not just any kind of prayer. Paul tells how to pray if we would defeat Satan.

**Pray always.** This obviously does not mean "always saying prayers." We are not heard for our "much speaking" (Matt. 6:7). "Pray without ceasing" (1 Thes. 5:17) says to us, "Always be in communion with the Lord. Keep the receiver off the hook!" Never have to say when you pray, "Lord, we come into Thy presence," because you never left His presence! A Christian must "pray always" because he is always subject to temptations and attacks of the devil. A surprise attack has defeated more than one believer who forgot to "pray without ceasing."

**Pray with all prayer.** There is more than one kind of praying: prayer, supplication, intercession, thanksgiving (Phil. 4:6; 1 Tim. 2:1). The believer who prays only to ask for things is missing out on blessings that come with intercessions and giving of thanks. In fact, thanksgiving is a great prayer weapon for defeating Satan. "Praise changes things" as much as "prayer changes things." Intercession for others can bring victory to our own lives. "And the Lord turned the captivity of Job when he prayed for his friends" (Job 42:10).

**Pray in the Spirit.** The Bible formula is that we pray to the Father, through the Son, and in the Spirit. Romans 8:26-27 tells us that only in the Spirit's power can we pray in the will of God. Otherwise, our praying could be selfish and out of the will of God. In the Old Testament tabernacle, there was a small golden altar standing before the veil, and here the priest burned the incense (Ex. 30:1-10; Luke 1:1-11). The incense is a picture of prayer. It had to be mixed according to God's plan and could not be counterfeited by man. The fire on the altar is a picture of the Holy Spirit, for it is He who takes our prayers and "ignites" them in the will of God. It is possible to pray fervently in the flesh and never get through to God. It is also possible to pray quietly in the Spirit and see God's hand do great things.

**Pray with your eyes open.** *Watching* means "keeping on the alert." The phrase "watch and pray" occurs often in the Bible. When Nehemiah was repairing the walls of Jerusalem, and the enemy was trying to stop the work, Nehemiah defeated the enemy by watching and praying. "Nevertheless we made our prayer unto our God, and set a watch" (Neh. 4:9). "Watch and pray" is the secret of victory over the world (Mark 13:33), the flesh (Mark 14:38), and the devil (Eph. 6:18). Peter went to sleep when he should have been praying, and the result was victory for Satan (Mark 14:29-31, 67-72). God expects us to use our God-given senses, led by the Spirit, so that we detect Satan when he is beginning to work.

**Keep on praying.** The word *perseverance* simply means "to stick to it and not quit." The early believers prayed this way (Acts 1:14; 2:42; 6:4); and we also should pray this way (Rom. 12:12). Perseverance in prayer does not mean we are trying to twist God's arm, but rather that we are deeply concerned and burdened and cannot rest until we get God's answer. As Robert Law puts it, "Prayer is not getting man's will done in heaven; it is getting God's will done on earth" (*Tests of Life*, [Grand Rapids: Baker, 1968]). Most of us quit praying just before God is about to give the victory. Not everybody is so constituted that he can sincerely spend a whole night in prayer, but all of us can persevere in prayer far more than we do. The early church prayed without ceasing when Peter was in prison and, at the last moment, God gave them their answer (Acts 12:1-19). Keep on praying until the Spirit stops you or the Father answers you. Just about the time you feel like quitting, God will give the answer.

**Pray for all the saints.** The Lord's Prayer begins with "Our Father"—not "My Father." We pray as part of a great family that is also talking to God, and we ought to pray for the other members of the family. Even Paul asked for the prayer support of the Ephesians—and he had been to the third heaven and back. If Paul needed the prayers of the saints, how much more do you and I need them! If my prayers help another believer defeat Satan, then that victory will help me too. Note that Paul did not ask them to pray for his comfort or safety, but for the effectiveness of his witness and ministry.

**The Encouragement (Eph. 6:21-24)**
We are not fighting the battle alone. There are other believers who stand with us in the fight, and we ought to be careful to encourage one another. Paul encouraged the Ephesians; Tychicus was an encouragement to Paul (Acts 20:4); and Paul was going to send Tychicus to

Ephesus to be an encouragement to them. Paul was not the kind of missionary who kept his affairs to himself. He wanted the people of God to know what God was doing, how their prayers were being answered, and what Satan was doing to oppose the work. His motive was not selfish. He was not trying to get something out of them.

What an encouragement it is to be a part of the family of God! Nowhere in the New Testament do we find an isolated believer. Christians are like sheep; they flock together. The church is an army and the soldiers need to stand together and fight together.

Note the words Paul uses as he closes this letter: peace—love—faith—grace! He was a prisoner of Rome, yet he was richer than the emperor. No matter what our circumstances may be, in Jesus Christ we are "blessed with all spiritual blessings"!

# PHILIPPIANS

## OUTLINE

Key theme: The joy of the Lord
Key verse: Philippians 3:1

I. **THE SINGLE MIND—chapter 1**
A. The fellowship of the Gospel—1:1-11
B. The furtherance of the Gospel—1:12-26
C. The faith of the Gospel—1:27-30

II. **THE SUBMISSIVE MIND—chapter 2**
A. The example of Christ—2:1-11
B. The example of Paul—2:12-18
C. The example of Timothy—2:19-24
D. The example of Epaphroditus—2:25-30

III. **THE SPIRITUAL MIND—chapter 3**
A. Paul's past—3:1-11
(the accountant—"I count")
B. Paul's present—3:12-16
(the athlete—"I press")
C. Paul's future—3:17-21
(the alien—"I look")

IV. **THE SECURE MIND—chapter 4**
A. God's peace—4:1-9
B. God's power—4:10-13
C. God's provision—4:14-23

## CONTENTS

# CHAPTER ONE
# HOW TO INCREASE YOUR JOY
*Philippians 1:1-11*

"How about coming over to the house for some fellowship?"

"What a golf game! Man, did we have great fellowship!"

"The fellowship at the retreat was just terrific!"

That word *fellowship* seems to mean many things to many different people. Perhaps, like a worn coin, it may be losing its true impression. If so, we had better take some steps to rescue it. After all, a good Bible word like *fellowship* needs to stay in circulation as long as possible.

In spite of his difficult circumstances as a prisoner in Rome, Paul is rejoicing. The secret of his joy is the *single mind;* he lives for Christ and the Gospel. (Christ is named eighteen times in Philippians 1, and the Gospel is mentioned six times.) "For to me to live is Christ, and to die is gain" (Phil. 1:21). But what really is "the single mind"? It is the attitude that says, "It makes no difference what happens to me, just as long as Christ is glorified and the Gospel shared with others." Paul rejoiced in spite of his circumstances, because his circumstances strengthened the *fellowship of the Gospel* (Phil. 1:1-11), promoted the *furtherance of the Gospel* (Phil. 1:12-26), and guarded the *faith of the Gospel* (Phil. 1:27-30).

The word *fellowship* simply means "to have in common." But true Christian fellowship is really much deeper than sharing coffee and pie, or even enjoying a golf game together. Too often what we think is "fellowship" is really only acquaintanceship or friendship. You cannot have fellowship with someone unless you have something in common; and for Christian fellowship, this means the possessing of eternal life within the heart. Unless a person has trusted Christ as his Saviour, he knows nothing of "the fellowship of the Gospel." In Philippians 2:1, Paul writes about "the fellowship of the Spirit," because when a person is born again he receives the gift of the Spirit (Rom. 8:9). There is also "the fellowship of His sufferings" (Phil. 3:10). When we share what we have with others, this is also

fellowship (Phil. 4:15, translated "communicate" in KJV).

So, true Christian fellowship is much more than having a name on a church roll or being present at a meeting. It is possible to be close to people physically and miles away from them spiritually. One of the sources of Christian joy is this fellowship that believers have in Jesus Christ. Paul was in Rome, his friends were miles away in Philippi, but their spiritual fellowship was real and satisfying. When you have the single mind, you will not complain about circumstances because you know that difficult circumstances will result in the strengthening of the fellowship of the Gospel.

Paul uses three thoughts in Philippians 1:1-11 that describe true Christian fellowship: I have you in my mind (Phil. 1:3-6), I have you in my heart (Phil. 1:7-8), I have you in my prayers (Phil. 1:9-11).

**I Have You in My Mind (Phil. 1:3-6)**
Isn't it remarkable that Paul is thinking of others and not of himself? As he awaits his trial in Rome, Paul's mind goes back to the believers in Philippi, and every recollection he has brings him joy. Read Acts 16; you may discover that some things happened to Paul at Philippi, the memory of which could produce sorrow. He was illegally arrested and beaten, was placed in the stocks, and was humiliated before the people. But even those memories brought joy to Paul, because it was through this suffering that the jailer found Christ! Paul recalled Lydia and her household, the poor slave girl who had been demon-possessed, and the other dear Christians at Philippi; and each recollection was a source of joy. (It is worth asking, "Am I the kind of Christian who brings joy to my pastor's mind when he thinks of me?")

It is possible that Philippians 1:5 is talking about their *financial* fellowship with Paul, a topic he picks up again in Philippians 4:14-19. The church at Philippi was the only church that entered into fellowship with Paul to help support his ministry. The "good work" of Philippians 1:6 may refer to the sharing of their means; it was started by the Lord and Paul was sure the Lord would continue it and complete it.

But we will not go astray if we apply these verses to the work of salvation and Christian living. We are not saved by our good works (Eph. 2:8-9). Salvation is the good work God does in us when we trust His Son. In Philippians 2:12-13 we are told that God continues to work in us through His Spirit. In other words, salvation includes a threefold work:

- the work God does *for* us—salvation;
- the work God does *in* us—sanctification;
- the work God does *through* us—service.

This work will continue until we see Christ, and then the work will be fulfilled. "We shall be like Him, for we shall see Him as He is" (1 John 3:2).

It was a source of joy to Paul to know that God was still working in the lives of his fellow-believers at Philippi. After all, this is the real basis for joyful Christian fellowship, to have God at work in our lives day by day.

"There seems to be friction in our home," a concerned wife said to a marriage counselor. "I really don't know what the trouble is."

"Friction is caused by one of two things," said the counselor, and to illustrate he picked up two blocks of wood from his desk. "If one block is moving and one is standing still, there's friction. Or, if both are moving but in opposite directions, there's friction. Now, which is it?"

"I'll have to admit that I've been going backward in my Christian life, and Joe has really been growing," the wife admitted. "What I need is to get back to fellowship with the Lord."

## I Have You in My Heart (Phil. 1:7-8)

Now we move a bit deeper, for it is possible to have others in our minds without really having them in our hearts. (Someone has observed that many people today would have to confess, "I have you *on my nerves!*") Paul's sincere love for his friends was something that could not be disguised or hidden.

Christian love is "the tie that binds." Love is the evidence of salvation: "We know that we have passed from death unto life, because we love the brethren" (1 John 3:14). It is the "spiritual lubrication" that keeps the machinery of life running smoothly. Have you noticed how often Paul uses the phrase "you all" as he writes? There are at least nine instances in this letter. He does not want to leave anyone out! (Some translations read, "You have me in your heart" in Phil. 1:7, but the basic truth is the same.)

How did Paul evidence his love for them? For one thing, he was suffering on their behalf. His bonds were proof of his love. He was "the prisoner of Jesus Christ for you Gentiles" (Eph. 3:1). Because of Paul's trial, Christianity was going to get a fair hearing before the officials of Rome. Since Philippi was a Roman colony, the decision would affect the believers there. Paul's love was not something he merely talked about; it was something he practiced. He considered his difficult circumstances an opportunity for defending and confirming the Gospel, and this would help his brethren everywhere.

But how can Christians learn to practice this kind of love? "I get along better with my unsaved neighbors than I do my saved relatives!" a man confided to his pastor. "Maybe it takes a diamond to cut a diamond, but I've just about had it!" Christian love is not something we work up; it is something that God does in us and through us. Paul longed for his friends "in the bowels [love] of Jesus Christ" (Phil. 1:8). It was not Paul's love channeled through Christ; it was Christ's love channeled through Paul. "God has poured out His love into our hearts by the Holy Spirit, whom He has given us" (Rom. 5:5, NIV). When we permit God to perform His "good work" in us, then we grow in our love for one another.

How can we tell that we are truly bound in love to other Christians? For one thing, we are concerned about them. The believers at Philippi were concerned about Paul and sent Epaphroditus to minister to him. Paul was also greatly concerned about his friends at Philippi, especially when Epaphroditus became ill and could not return right away (Phil. 2:25-28). "My little children, let us not love in word, neither in tongue; but in deed and in truth" (1 John 3:18).

Another evidence of Christian love is a willingness to forgive one another. "And above all things have fervent charity [love] among yourselves: for charity [love] shall cover the multitude of sins" (1 Peter 4:8).

"Tell us some of the blunders your wife has made," a radio quizmaster asked a contestant.

"I can't remember any," the man replied.

"Oh, surely you can remember something!" the announcer said.

"No, I really can't," said the contestant. "I love my wife very much, and I just don't remember things like that." First Corinthians 13:5 states that "love keeps no record of wrongs" (NIV).

Christians who practice love always experience joy; both come as a result of the presence of the same Holy Spirit. "The fruit of the Spirit is love, joy" (Gal. 5:22).

## I Have You in My Prayers (Phil. 1:9-11)

Paul found joy in his memories of the friends at Philippi and in his growing love for them. He also found joy in remembering them before the throne of grace in prayer. The high priest in the Old Testament wore a special garment, the ephod, over his heart. On it were twelve stones with the names of the twelve tribes of Israel engraved on them, a jewel for each tribe (Ex. 28:15-29). He carried the people over his heart in love, and so did Paul. Perhaps the deepest Christian fellowship and joy we can experience in this life is at the throne of grace, praying with and for one another.

This is a prayer for maturity, and Paul begins with *love*. After all, if our Christian love is what it ought to be, everything else should follow. He prays that they might experience *abounding* love and *discerning* love. Christian love is not blind! The heart and mind work together so that we have discerning love and loving discernment. Paul wants his friends to grow in discernment, in being able to "distinguish the things that differ."

The ability to distinguish is a mark of maturity. When a baby learns to speak, it may call every four-legged animal a "bow-wow." But then the child discovers that there are cats, white mice, cows, and other four-legged creatures. To a little child, one automobile is just like another, but not to a car-crazy teenager! He can spot the differences between models faster than his parents can even name the cars! One of the sure marks of maturity is discerning love.

Paul also prays that they might have mature Christian *character*, "sincere and without offense." The Greek word translated "sincere" may have several meanings. Some translate it "tested by sunlight." The sincere Christian is not afraid to "stand in the light!"

*Sincere* may also mean "to whirl in a sieve," suggesting the idea of a winnowing process that removes chaff. In both cases the truth is the same: Paul prays that his friends will have the kind of character that can pass the test. (Our English word *sincere* comes from a Latin word that means "unadulterated, pure, unmixed.")

Paul prays for them to have mature Christian love and character, "without offense till the day of Christ" (Phil. 1:10). This means that our lives do not cause others to stumble, and that they are ready for the Judgment Seat of Christ when He returns (see 2 Cor. 5:10; 1 John 2:28). Here are two good tests for us

to follow as we exercise spiritual discernment: (1) Will it make others stumble? (2) Will I be ashamed if Jesus should return?

Paul also prays that they might have mature Christian *service*. He wants them filled and fruitful (Phil. 1:11). He is not interested simply in "church activities," but in the kind of spiritual fruit that is produced when we are in fellowship with Christ. "Abide in Me, and I in you. As the branch cannot bear fruit of itself, except it abide in the vine; no more can ye, except ye abide in Me" (John 15:4). Too many Christians try to "produce results" in their own efforts instead of abiding in Christ and allowing His life to produce the fruit.

What is the "fruit" God wants to see from our lives? Certainly He wants the "fruit of the Spirit" (Gal. 5:22-23), Christian character that glorifies God. Paul compares winning lost souls to Christ to bearing fruit (Rom. 1:13), and he also names "holiness" as a spiritual fruit (Rom. 6:22). He exhorts us to be "fruitful in every good work" (Col. 1:10), and the writer to the Hebrews reminds us that our praise is the "fruit of the lips" (Heb. 13:15).

The fruit tree does not make a great deal of noise when it produces its crop; it merely allows the life within to work in a natural way, and fruit is the result. "He that abideth in Me, and I in him, the same bringeth forth much fruit: for without Me ye can do nothing" (John 15:5).

The difference between spiritual fruit and human "religious activity" is that the fruit brings glory to Jesus Christ. Whenever we do anything in our own strength, we have a tendency to boast about it. True spiritual fruit is so beautiful and wonderful that no man can claim credit for it; the glory must go to God alone.

This, then, is true Christian fellowship—a having-in-common that is much deeper than mere friendship. "I have you in my mind . . . I have you in my heart . . . I have you in my prayers." This is the kind of fellowship that produces joy, *and it is the single mind that produces this kind of fellowship!*

Jerry had to go to New York City for special surgery, and he hated to go. "Why can't we have it done at home?" he asked his doctor. "I don't know a soul in that big, unfriendly city!" But when he and his wife arrived at the hospital, there was a pastor to meet them and invite them to stay at his home until they got settled. The operation was serious, and the wait in the hospital was long and difficult; but the fellowship of the pastor and his wife brought a new joy to Jerry and his wife. They learned that circumstances need not rob us of joy if we will but permit these circumstances to strengthen the fellowship of the Gospel.

# CHAPTER TWO
# PIONEERS WANTED
*Philippians 1:12-26*

More than anything else, Paul's desire as a missionary was to preach the Gospel in Rome. The hub of the great Empire, Rome was the key city of its day. If Paul could conquer it for Christ, it would mean reaching millions with the message of salvation. It was critically important on Paul's agenda, for he said, "After I have been there [Jerusalem], I must also see Rome" (Acts 19:21). From Corinth he wrote, "So, as much as in me is, I am ready [eager] to preach the Gospel to you that are at Rome also" (Rom. 1:15).

Paul wanted to go to Rome as a preacher, but instead he went as *a prisoner!* He could have written a long letter about that experience alone. Instead, he sums it all up as "the things which happened unto me" (Phil. 1:12). The record of these things is given in Acts 21:17–28:31, and it begins with Paul's illegal arrest in the temple in Jerusalem. The Jews thought he had desecrated their temple by bringing in Gentiles, and the Romans thought he was an Egyptian renegade who was on their "most-wanted" list. Paul became the focal point of both political and religious plotting and remained a prisoner in Caesarea for two years. When he finally appealed to Caesar (which was the privilege of every Roman citizen), he was sent to Rome. En route, the ship was wrecked! The account of that storm and Paul's courage and faith is one of the most dramatic in the Bible (Acts 27). After three months of waiting on the Island of Malta, Paul finally embarked for Rome and the trial he had requested before Caesar.

To many, all of this would have looked like failure, but not to this man with a "single mind," concerned with sharing Christ and the Gospel. Paul did not find his joy in ideal circumstances; he found his joy in winning others to Christ. And if his circumstances promoted the furtherance of the Gospel, that was all that mattered! The word *furtherance* means "pioneer advance." It is a Greek military term referring to the army engineers who go before the troops to open the way into new territory. Instead of finding himself confined as a prisoner, Paul discovered that his circumstances really opened up new areas of ministry.

Everyone has heard of Charles Haddon Spurgeon, the famous British preacher, but few know the story of his wife, Susannah. Early in their married life, Mrs. Spurgeon became an invalid. It looked as though her only ministry would be encouraging her husband and praying for his work. But God gave her a burden to share her husband's books with pastors who were unable to purchase them. This burden soon led to the founding of the "Book Fund." As a work of faith, the "Book Fund" provided thousands of pastors with tools for their work. All this was supervised by Mrs. Spurgeon from her home. It was a pioneer ministry.

God still wants His children to take the Gospel into new areas. He wants us to be pioneers, and sometimes He arranges circumstances so that we can be nothing else but pioneers. In fact, that is how the Gospel originally came to Philippi! Paul had tried to enter other territory, but God had repeatedly shut the door (Acts 16:6-10). Paul wanted to take the message eastward into Asia, but God directed him to take it westward into Europe. What a difference it would have made in the history of mankind if Paul had been permitted to follow his plan!

God sometimes uses strange tools to help us pioneer the Gospel. In Paul's case, there were three tools that helped him take the Gospel even into the elite Praetorian Guard, Caesar's special troops: his *chains* (Phil. 1:12-14), his *critics* (Phil. 1:15-19), and his *crisis* (Phil. 1:20-26).

**Paul's Chains (Phil. 1:12-14)**
The same God who used Moses' rod, Gideon's pitchers, and David's sling, used Paul's chains. Little did the Romans realize that the chains they affixed to his wrists would *release* Paul instead of *bind* him! Even as he wrote during a later imprisonment, "I suffer trouble, as an evildoer, even unto bonds; but the Word of God is not bound" (2 Tim. 2:9). He did not complain about his chains; instead he conse-

crated them to God and asked God to use them for the pioneer advance of the Gospel. And God answered his prayers.

To begin with, these chains gave Paul *contact with the lost.* He was chained to a Roman soldier twenty-four hours a day! The shifts changed every six hours, which meant Paul could witness to at least four men each day! Imagine yourself as one of those soldiers, chained to a man who prayed "without ceasing," who was constantly interviewing people about their spiritual condition, and who was repeatedly writing letters to Christians and churches throughout the Empire! It was not long before some of these soldiers put their faith in Christ. Paul was able to get the Gospel into the elite Praetorian Guard, something he could not have done had he been a free man.

But the chains gave Paul contact with another group of people: the officials in Caesar's court. He was in Rome as an official prisoner, and his case was an important one. The Roman government was going to determine the official status of this new "Christian" sect. Was it merely another sect of the Jews? Or was it something new and possibly dangerous? Imagine how pleased Paul must have been knowing that the court officials were forced to study the doctrines of the Christian faith!

Sometimes God has to put "chains" on His people to get them to accomplish a "pioneer advance" that could never happen any other way. Young mothers may feel chained to the home as they care for their children, but God can use those "chains" to reach people with the message of salvation. Susannah Wesley was the mother of nineteen children, before the days of labor-saving devices and disposable diapers! Out of that large family came John and Charles Wesley, whose combined ministries shook the British Isles. At six weeks of age, Fanny Crosby was blinded, but even as a youngster she determined not to be confined by the chains of darkness. In time, she became a mighty force for God through her hymns and Gospel songs.

The secret is this: when you have the single mind, you look on your circumstances as God-given opportunities for the furtherance of the Gospel; and you rejoice at *what God is going to do* instead of complaining about *what God did not do.*

Paul's chains not only gave contact with the lost, but they also gave *courage to the saved.* Many of the believers in Rome took fresh courage when they saw Paul's faith and deter-

mination (Phil. 1:14). They were "much more bold to speak the word without fear." That word *speak* does not mean "preach." Rather, it means "everyday conversation." No doubt many of the Romans were discussing Paul's case, because such legal matters were of primary concern to this nation of lawmakers. And the Christians in Rome who were sympathetic to Paul took advantage of this conversation to say a good word for Jesus Christ. Discouragement has a way of spreading, but so does encouragement! Because of Paul's joyful attitude, the believers in Rome took fresh courage and witnessed boldly for Christ.

While recovering in the hospital from a serious auto accident, I received a letter from a total stranger who seemed to know just what to say to make my day brighter. In fact, I received several letters from him, and each one was better than the one before. When I was able to get around, I met him personally. I was amazed to discover that he was blind, a diabetic, handicapped because of a leg amputation (and since then the other leg has been removed), and that he lived with and cared for his elderly mother! If a man ever wore chains, this man did! But if a man ever was free to pioneer the Gospel, this man was! He was able to share Christ in high school assemblies, before service clubs, at the "Y," and before professional people in meetings that would have been closed to an ordained minister. My friend had the single mind; he lived for Christ and the Gospel. Consequently, he shared the joy of furthering the Gospel.

Our chains may not be as dramatic or difficult, but there is no reason why God cannot use them in the same way.

## Paul's Critics (Phil. 1:15-19)
It is hard to believe that anyone would oppose Paul, but there were believers in Rome doing just that. The churches there were divided. Some preached Christ sincerely, wanting to see people saved. Some preached Christ insincerely, wanting to make the situation more difficult for Paul. The latter group was using the Gospel to further their own selfish purposes. Perhaps they belonged to the "legalistic" wing of the church that opposed Paul's ministry to the Gentiles and his emphasis on the grace of God as opposed to obedience to the Jewish Law. Envy and strife go together, just as love and unity go together.

Paul uses an interesting word in Philippians 1:16—*contention.* It means "to canvass for office, to get people to support you." Paul's aim was to glorify Christ and get people to follow Him; his critics' aim was to promote themselves and win a following of their own. Instead of asking, "Have you trusted Christ?" they asked, "Whose side are you on—ours or Paul's?" Unfortunately, this kind of "religious politics" is still seen today. And the people who practice it need to realize that they are only hurting themselves.

When you have the single mind, you look on your critics as another opportunity for the furtherance of the Gospel. Like a faithful soldier, Paul was "set [appointed] for the defense of the Gospel" (Phil. 1:17). He was able to rejoice, not in the selfishness of his critics, but in the fact that *Christ was being preached!* There was no envy in Paul's heart. It mattered not that some were for him and some were against him. All that mattered was the preaching of the Gospel of Jesus Christ!

It is a matter of historic record that the two great English evangelists, John Wesley and George Whitefield, disagreed on doctrinal matters. Both of them were very successful, preaching to thousands of people and seeing multitudes come to Christ. It is reported that somebody asked Wesley if he expected to see Whitefield in heaven, and the evangelist replied, "No, I do not."

"Then you do not think Whitefield is a converted man?"

"Of course he is a converted man!" Wesley said. "But I do not expect to see him in heaven—because he will be so close to the throne of God and I so far away that I will not be able to see him!" Though he differed with his brother in some matters, Wesley did not have any envy in his heart, nor did he seek to oppose Whitefield's ministry.

Criticism is usually very hard to take, particularly when we are in difficult circumstances, as Paul was. How was the apostle able to rejoice even in the face of such diverse criticism? He possessed the single mind! Philippians 1:19 indicates that Paul expected his case to turn out victoriously ("to my salvation") because of the prayers of his friends and the supply of the Holy Spirit of God. The word *supply* gives us our English word *chorus.* Whenever a Greek city was going to put on a special festival, somebody had to pay for the singers and dancers. The donation called for had to be a lavish one, and so this word came to mean "to provide generously and lavishly." Paul was not depending on his own dwindling resources; he was depending on the generous resources of God, ministered by the Holy Spirit.

Paul shared in the pioneer advance of the Gospel in Rome through his chains and his critics; but he had a third tool that he used.

## Paul's Crisis (Phil. 1:20-26)

Because of Paul's chains, Christ was *known* (Phil. 1:13), and because of Paul's critics, Christ was *preached* (Phil. 1:18). But because of Paul's crisis, Christ was *magnified!* (Phil. 1:20) It was possible that Paul would be found a traitor to Rome and then executed. His preliminary trial had apparently gone in his favor. The final verdict, however, was yet to come. But Paul's body was not his own, and his only desire (because he had the single mind) was to magnify Christ in his body.

Does Christ need to be magnified? After all, how can a mere human being ever magnify the Son of God? Well, the stars are much bigger than the telescope, and yet the telescope magnifies them and brings them closer. The believer's body is to be a telescope that brings Jesus Christ close to people. To the average person, Christ is a misty figure in history who lived centuries ago. But as the unsaved watch the believer go through a crisis, they can see Jesus magnified and brought so much closer. To the Christian with the single mind, Christ is with us here and now.

The telescope brings distant things closer, and the microscope makes tiny things look big. To the unbeliever, Jesus is not very big. Other people and other things are far more important. But as the unbeliever watches the Christian go through a crisis experience, he ought to be able to see how big Jesus Christ really is. The believer's body is a "lens" that makes a "little Christ" look very big, and a "distant Christ" come very close.

Paul was not afraid of life or death! Either way, he wanted to magnify Christ in his body. No wonder he had joy!

Paul confesses that he is facing a difficult decision. To remain alive was necessary for the believers' benefit in Philippi, but to depart and be with Christ was far better. Paul decided that Christ would have him remain, not only for the "furtherance of the Gospel" (Phil. 1:12) but also for the "furtherance and joy of [their] faith" (Phil. 1:25). He wanted them to make some "pioneer advance" into new areas of spiritual growth. (By the way, Paul admonished Timothy, the young pastor, to be sure to pioneer new spiritual territory in his own life and ministry. See 1 Tim. 4:15, where "profiting" is our word "pioneer advance.")

What a man Paul is! He is willing to postpone going to heaven in order to help Christians grow, and he is willing to go to hell in order to win the lost to Christ! (Rom. 9:1-3)

Of course, death had no terrors for Paul. It simply meant "departing." This word was used by the soldiers; it meant "to take down your tent and move on." What a picture of Christian death! The "tent" we live in is taken down at death, and the spirit goes home to be with Christ in heaven. (Read 2 Cor. 5:1-8.) The sailors also used this word; it meant "to loosen a ship and set sail." Lord Tennyson used this figure of death in his famous poem "Crossing the Bar."

But *departure* was also a political term; it described the setting free of a prisoner. God's people are in bondage because of the limitations of the body and the temptations of the flesh, but death will free them. Or they will be freed at the return of Christ (Rom. 8:18-23) if that should come first. Finally, *departure* was a word used by the farmers; it meant "to unyoke the oxen." Paul had taken Christ's yoke, which is an easy yoke to bear (Matt. 11:28-30), but how many burdens he carried in his ministry! (If you need your memory refreshed, read 2 Cor. 11:22–12:10.) To depart to be with Christ would mean laying aside the burdens, his earthly work completed.

No matter how you look at it, nothing can steal a man's joy if he possesses the single mind! "For to me to live is Christ, and to die is gain" (Phil. 1:21). Maltbie Babcock, who wrote "This Is My Father's World," has said, "Life is what we are alive to." When my wife and I go shopping, I dread going to the yard goods department, but I often have to go because my wife enjoys looking at fabrics. If on the way to the yard goods section I spot the book department, I suddenly come alive! The thing that excites us and "turns us on" is the thing that really is "life" to us. In Paul's case, Christ was his life. Christ excited him and made his life worth living.

Philippians 1:21 becomes a valuable test of our lives. "For to me to live is _____ and to die is _____." Fill in the blanks yourself.

"For to me to live is *money* and to die is *to leave it all behind.*"

"For to me to live is *fame* and to die is *to be forgotten.*"

"For to me to live is *power* and to die is *to lose it all.*"

No, we must echo Paul's convictions if we are going to have joy in spite of circumstances, and if we are going to share in the furtherance of the Gospel. "For to me to live is *Christ,* and to die is *gain!*"

# CHAPTER THREE
# BATTLE STATIONS!
*Philippians 1:27-30*

The Christian life is not a playground; it is a battleground. We are *sons* in the family, enjoying the *fellowship* of the Gospel (Phil. 1:1-11); we are *servants* sharing in the *furtherance* of the Gospel (Phil. 1:12-26); but we are also *soldiers* defending the *faith* of the Gospel. And the believer with the single mind can have the joy of the Holy Spirit even in the midst of battle.

"The faith of the Gospel" is that body of divine truth given to the church. Jude calls it "the faith which was once delivered unto the saints" (Jude 3). Paul warns in 1 Timothy 4:1 that "in the latter times some shall depart from the faith." God committed this spiritual treasure to Paul (1 Tim. 1:11), and he in turn committed it to others, like Timothy (1 Tim. 6:20), whose responsibility was to commit this deposit to still others (2 Tim. 2:2). This is why the church must engage in a teaching ministry, so that each new generation of believers will know, appreciate, and use the great heritage of the faith.

But there is an enemy who is out to steal the treasure from God's people. Paul had met the enemy in Philippi, and he was now facing him in Rome. If Satan can only rob believers of their Christian faith, the doctrines that are distinctively theirs, then he can cripple and defeat the ministry of the Gospel. It is sad to hear people say, "I don't care what you believe, just so long as you live right." What we believe determines how we behave, and wrong belief ultimately means a wrong life. Each local church is but one generation short of potential extinction. No wonder Satan attacks our young people in particular, seeking to get them away from "the faith."

How can a group of Christians fight this enemy? "For the weapons of our warfare are not of the flesh" (2 Cor. 10:4, NASB). Peter took up a sword in the Garden, and Jesus rebuked him (John 18:10-11). We use spiritual weapons—the Word of God and prayer (Eph. 6:11-18; Heb. 4:12); and we must depend on the Holy Spirit to give us the power that we need. But an army must fight *together,* and this is why Paul sends these admonitions to his friends at Philippi. He is explaining in this paragraph that there are three essentials for victory in the battle to protect "the faith."

### Consistency (Phil. 1:27a)

The old English word *conversation,* of course, means *walk* and not *talk.* "Only conduct yourselves in a manner worthy of the Gospel of Christ" (NASB). The most important weapon against the enemy is not a stirring sermon or a powerful book; it is the consistent life of believers.

The verb Paul uses is related to our word *politics.* He is saying, "Behave the way citizens are supposed to behave." My wife and I were visiting in London and one day decided to go to the zoo. We boarded the bus and sat back to enjoy the ride; but it was impossible to enjoy it because of the loud, coarse conversation of the passengers at the front of the bus. Unfortunately, they were Americans; and we could see the Britishers around us raising their eyebrows and shaking their heads, as though to say, "Oh, yes, they're from America!" We were embarrassed, because we knew that these people did not really represent the best of American citizens.

Paul is suggesting that we Christians are the citizens of heaven, and while we are on earth we ought to behave like heaven's citizens. He brings this concept up again in Philippians 3:20. It would be a very meaningful expression to the people in Philippi because Philippi was a Roman colony, and its citizens were actually Roman citizens, protected by Roman law. The church of Jesus Christ is a colony of heaven on earth! And we ought to behave like the citizens of heaven.

"Am I conducting myself in a manner worthy of the Gospel?" is a good question for us to ask ourselves regularly. We should "walk . . . worthy of the calling" that we have in Christ (Eph. 4:1, NASB), which means walking "worthy of the Lord unto all pleasing" (Col. 1:10). We do not behave in order to go to heaven, as though we could be saved by our good works; but we behave because our names are already written in heaven, and our citizenship is in heaven.

It is worth remembering that the world around us knows only the Gospel that it sees in our lives.

> *You are writing a Gospel,*
> *A chapter each day,*
> *By the deeds that you do*
> *And the words that you say.*
> *Men read what you write,*
> *Whether faithful or true:*
> *Just what is the Gospel*
> *According to you?*
>
> (source unknown)

"The Gospel" is the Good News that Christ died for our sins, was buried, and rose again (1 Cor. 15:1-8). There is only one "Good News" of salvation; any other gospel is false (Gal. 1:6-10). The message of the Gospel is the Good News that sinners can become the children of God through faith in Jesus Christ, God's Son (John 3:16). To add anything to the Gospel is to deprive it of its power. We are not saved from our sins by faith in Christ *plus* something else; we are saved by faith in Christ *alone.*

"We have some neighbors who believe a false gospel," a church member told his pastor. "Do you have some literature I can give them?"

The pastor opened his Bible to 2 Corinthians 3:2, "You are our letter, written in our hearts, known and read by all men" (NASB). He said, "The best literature in the world is no substitute for your own life. Let them see Christ in your behavior and this will open up opportunities to share Christ's Gospel with them."

The greatest weapon against the devil is a godly life. And a local church that practices the truth, that "behaves what it believes," is going to defeat the enemy. This is the first essential for victory in this battle.

### Cooperation (Phil. 1:27b)

Paul now changes the illustration from politics to athletics. The word translated "striving together" gives us our English word "athletics." Paul pictures the church as a team, and he reminds them that it is teamwork that wins victories.

Keep in mind that there was division in the

church at Philippi. For one thing, two women were not getting along with each other (Phil. 4:2). Apparently the members of the fellowship were taking sides, as is often the case, and the resulting division was hindering the work of the church. The enemy is always happy to see internal divisions in a local ministry. "Divide and conquer!" is his motto, and too often he has his way. It is only as believers stand together that they can overcome the wicked one.

Throughout this letter, Paul uses an interesting device to emphasize the importance of unity. In the Greek language, the prefix *sun-* means "with, together," and when used with different words, strengthens the idea of unity. (It is somewhat like our prefix *co-.)* At least sixteen times, Paul uses this prefix in Philippians, and his readers could not have missed the message! In Philippians 1:27, the Greek word is *sunathleo*—"striving together as athletes."

Jerry was disgusted, and he decided to tell the coach how he felt. "There's no sense coming out for practice anymore," he complained. "Mike is the team—you don't need the rest of us."

Coach Gardner knew the trouble. "Look, Jerry, just because Mike gets many of the chances to shoot doesn't mean the rest of you guys aren't needed. Somebody has to set things up at the basket, and that's where you come in."

Sometimes a team has a "glory hound" who has to be in the spotlight and get all the praise. Usually he makes it difficult for the rest of the team. They aren't working equally together, but are working to make one person look good. It is this attitude that makes for defeat. Unfortunately, we have some "glory hounds" in the church. John had to deal with a man named Diotrephes because the man "loved to have the preeminence" (3 John 9). Even the Apostles James and John asked to have special thrones (Matt. 20:20-28). The important word is *together:* standing firmly together in one spirit, striving together against the enemy, and doing it with one mind and heart.

It would not be difficult to expand this idea of the local church as a team of athletes. Each person has his assigned place and job, and if each one is doing his job, it helps all the others. Not everybody can be captain or quarterback! The team has to follow the rules, and the Word of God is our "rule book." There is

one goal—to honor Christ and do His will. If we all work together, we can reach the goal, win the prize, and glorify the Lord. But the minute any one of us starts disobeying the rules, breaking training (the Christian life does demand discipline), or looking for glory, the teamwork disappears and division and competition take over.

In other words, Paul is reminding us again of the need for *the single mind.* There is joy in our lives, even as we battle the enemy, if we live for Christ and the Gospel and practice "Christian teamwork." To be sure, there are some people with whom we cannot cooperate (2 Cor. 6:14-18; Eph. 5:11); but there are many with whom we *can*—and should!

We are citizens of heaven and therefore should walk consistently. We are members of the same "team" and should work cooperatively. But there is a third essential for success as we face the enemy, and that is *confidence.*

## Confidence (Phil. 1:28-30)
"Don't be alarmed by your opponents!" The word Paul uses pictures a horse shying away from battle. To be sure, nobody blindly runs into a fight; but then, no true believer should deliberately avoid facing the enemy. In these verses, Paul gives us several encouragements that give us confidence in the battle.

First, *these battles prove that we are saved* (Phil. 1:29). We not only believe on Christ but also suffer for Christ. Paul calls this "the fellowship of His sufferings" (Phil. 3:10). For some reason, many new believers have the idea that trusting Christ means the end of their battles. In reality, it means the beginning of *new* battles. "In the world ye shall have tribulation" (John 16:33). "Yea, and all that will live godly in Christ Jesus shall suffer persecution" (2 Tim. 3:12).

But the presence of conflict is *a privilege;* we suffer "for His sake." In fact, Paul tells us that this conflict is "granted" to us—it is a gift! If we were suffering for ourselves, it would be no privilege; but because we are suffering for and with Christ, it is a high and holy honor. After all, He suffered for us, and a willingness to suffer for Him is the very least we can do to show our love and gratitude.

A third encouragement is this: *others are experiencing the same conflict* (Phil. 1:30). Satan wants us to think we are alone in the battle, that our difficulties are unique, but such is not the case. Paul reminds the Philippians that he is going through the same difficulties they are experiencing hundreds of miles from Rome! A change in geography is usually no solution to spiritual problems, because human nature is the same wherever you go, and the enemy is everywhere. Knowing that my fellow believers are also sharing in the battle is an encouragement for me to keep going and to pray for them as I pray for myself.

Actually, going through spiritual conflict is one way we have *to grow in Christ.* God gives us the strength we need to stand firm against the enemy, and this confidence is proof to him that he will lose and we are on the winning side (Phil. 1:28). The Philippians had seen Paul go through conflict when he was with them (read Acts 16:19ff), and they had witnessed his firmness in the Lord. The word "conflict" gives us our word "agony" *(agonia),* and is the same word that is used for Christ's struggle in the Garden (Luke 22:44). As we face the enemy and depend on the Lord, He gives us all that we need for the battle. When the enemy sees our God-given confidence, it makes him fear.

So, the single mind enables us to have joy in the midst of battle, because it produces in us consistency, cooperation, and confidence. We experience the joy of "spiritual teamwork" as we strive together for the faith of the Gospel.

# CHAPTER FOUR
# THE GREAT EXAMPLE
*Philippians 2:1-11*

People can rob us of our joy. Paul was facing his problems with people at Rome (Phil. 1:15-18) as well as with people in Philippi, and it was the latter who concerned him the most. When Epaphroditus brought a generous gift from the church in Philippi, and good news of the church's concern for Paul, he also brought the bad news of a possible division in the church family. Apparently there was a double threat to the unity of the church; false teachers coming in from without (Phil. 3:1-3) and disagreeing members within (Phil. 4:1-3). What Euodia ("fragrance") and Syntyche ("fortunate") were

debating about, Paul does not state. Perhaps they both wanted to be president of the missionary guild or the choir!

Paul knew what some church workers today do not know, that there is a difference between *unity* and *uniformity.* True spiritual unity comes from within; it is a matter of the heart. Uniformity is the result of pressure from without. This is why Paul opens this section appealing to the highest possible spiritual motives (Phil. 2:1-4). Since the believers at Philippi are "in Christ," this ought to encourage them to work toward unity and love, not division and rivalry. In a gracious way, Paul is saying to the church, "Your disagreements reveal that there is a spiritual problem in your fellowship. It isn't going to be solved by rules or threats; it's going to be solved when your hearts are right with Christ and with each other." Paul wanted them to see that the basic cause was *selfishness,* and the cause of selfishness is *pride.* There can be no joy in the life of the Christian who puts himself above others.

The secret of joy in spite of circumstances is *the single mind.* The secret of joy in spite of people is *the submissive mind.* The key verse is: "Let nothing be done through strife or vainglory; but in lowliness of mind let each esteem other better [more important] than themselves" (Phil. 2:3). In Philippians 1, it is "Christ first" and in Philippians 2 it is "others next." Paul the soul winner in Philippians 1 becomes Paul the servant in Philippians 2.

It is important that we understand what the Bible means by "humility." The humble person is not one who thinks meanly of himself; he simply does not think of himself at all! (I think Andrew Murray said that.) Humility is that grace that, when you know you have it, you have lost it. The truly humble person knows himself and accepts himself (Rom. 12:3). He yields himself to Christ to be a servant, to use what he is and has for the glory of God and the good of others. "Others" is the key idea in this chapter (Phil. 2:3-4); the believer's eyes are turned away from himself and focused on the needs of others.

The "submissive mind" does not mean that the believer is at the beck and call of everybody else or that he is a "religious doormat" for everybody to use! Some people try to purchase friends and maintain church unity by "giving in" to everybody else's whims and wishes. This is not what Paul is suggesting at all. The Scripture puts it perfectly: "ourselves your servants for Jesus' sake" (2 Cor. 4:5). If we have the single mind of Philippians 1, then we will have no problem with the submissive mind of Philippians 2.

Paul gives us four examples of the submissive mind: Jesus Christ (Phil. 2:1-11), Paul himself (Phil. 2:12-18), Timothy (Phil. 2:19-24), and Epaphroditus (Phil. 2:25-30). Of course, the great Example is Jesus, and Paul begins with Him. Jesus Christ illustrates the four characteristics of the person with the submissive mind.

## He Thinks of Others, Not Himself (Phil. 2:5-6)

The "mind" of Christ means the "attitude" Christ exhibited. "Your attitude should be the same as that of Christ Jesus" (Phil. 2:5, NIV). After all, outlook determines outcome. If the outlook is selfish, the actions will be devisive and destructive. James says the same thing (see James 4:1-10).

These verses in Philippians take us to eternity past. "Form of God" has nothing to do with shape or size. God is Spirit (John 4:24), and as such is not to be thought of in human terms. When the Bible refers to "the eyes of the Lord" or "the hand of the Lord," it is not claiming that God has a human shape. Rather, it is using human terms to describe divine attributes (the characteristics of God) and activities. The word "form" means "the outward expression of the inward nature." This means that in eternity past, *Jesus Christ was God.* In fact, Paul states that He was "equal with God." Other verses such as John 1:1-4; Colossians 1:15; and Hebrews 1:1-3 also state that Jesus Christ is God.

Certainly as God, Jesus Christ did not need anything! He had all the glory and praise of heaven. With the Father and the Spirit, He reigned over the universe. But Philippians 2:6 states an amazing fact: He did not consider His equality with God as "something selfishly to be held on to." Jesus did not think of Himself; He thought of others. His outlook (or attitude) was that of unselfish concern for others. This is "the mind of Christ," an attitude that says, "I cannot keep my privileges for myself, I must use them for others; and to do this, I will gladly lay them aside and pay whatever price is necessary."

A reporter was interviewing a successful job counselor who had placed hundreds of workers in their vocations quite happily. When asked the secret of his success, the man re-

plied: "If you want to find out what a worker is really like, don't give him responsibilities—give him *privileges.* Most people can handle responsibilities if you pay them enough, but it takes a real leader to handle privileges. A leader will use his privileges to help others and build the organization; a lesser man will use privileges to promote himself." Jesus used His heavenly privileges for the sake of others—for *our* sake.

It would be worthwhile to contrast Christ's attitude with that of Lucifer (Isa. 14:12-15) and Adam (Gen. 3:1-7). Many Bible students believe that the fall of Lucifer is a description of the fall of Satan. He once was the highest of the angelic beings, close to the throne of God (Ezek. 28:11-19), but he desired to be *on* the throne of God! Lucifer said, "I will!" but Jesus said, *"Thy* will." Lucifer was not satisfied to be a creature; he wanted to be the Creator! Jesus was the Creator, yet He willingly became man. Christ's humility is a rebuke to Satan's pride.

Lucifer was not satisfied to be a rebel himself; he invaded Eden and tempted man to be a rebel. Adam had all that he needed; he was actually the "king" of God's creation ("let them have dominion," Gen. 1:26). But Satan said, "Ye shall be as God!" Man deliberately grasped after something that was beyond his reach, and as a result plunged the whole human race into sin and death. Adam and Eve thought only of themselves; Jesus Christ thought of others.

We expect unsaved people to be selfish and grasping, but we do not expect this of Christians, who have experienced the love of Christ and the fellowship of the Spirit (Phil. 2:1-2). More than twenty times in the New Testament, God instructs us how to live with "one another." We are to prefer one another (Rom. 12:10), edify one another (1 Thes. 5:11), and bear each other's burdens (Gal. 6:2). We should not judge one another (Rom. 14:13) but rather admonish one another (Rom. 15:14). *Others* is the key word in the vocabulary of the Christian who exercises the submissive mind.

## He Serves (Phil. 2:7)

Thinking of "others" in an abstract sense only is insufficient; we must get down to the nitty-gritty of true service. A famous philosopher wrote glowing words about educating children but abandoned his own. It was easy for him to love children in the abstract, but when it came

74

down to practice, that was something else. Jesus thought of others *and became a servant!* Paul traces the steps in the humiliation of Christ: (1) He emptied Himself, laying aside the independent use of His own attributes as God; (2) He permanently became a human, in a sinless physical body; (3) He used that body to be a servant; (4) He took that body to the cross and willingly died.

What grace! From heaven to earth, from glory to shame, from Master to servant, from life to death, "even the death of the cross!" In the Old Testament Age, Christ had visited earth on occasion for some special ministry (Gen. 18 is a case in point), but these visits were temporary. When Christ was born at Bethlehem, He entered into a *permanent* union with humanity from which there could be no escape. He willingly humbled Himself that He might lift us up! Note that Paul uses the word "form" again in Philippians 2:7, "the outward expression of the inward nature." Jesus did not pretend to be a servant; He was not an actor playing a role. *He actually was a servant!* This was the true expression of His innermost nature. He was the God-Man, Deity and humanity united in one, and He came as a servant.

Have you noticed as you read the four Gospels that it is Jesus who serves others, not others who serve Jesus? He is at the beck and call of all kinds of people—fishermen, harlots, tax collectors, the sick, the sorrowing. "Even as the Son of man came not to be ministered unto, but to minister, and to give His life a ransom for many" (Matt. 20:28). In the Upper Room, when His disciples apparently refused to minister, Jesus arose, laid aside His outer garments, put on the long linen towel, and *washed their feet!* (John 13) He took the place of a menial slave! This was the submissive mind in action—and no wonder Jesus experienced such joy!

During the American Civil War, Gen. George B. McClellan was put in charge of the great Army of the Potomac, mainly because public opinion was on his side. He fancied himself to be a great military leader and enjoyed hearing the people call him "a young Napoleon." However, his performance was less than sensational. President Lincoln commissioned him General-in-Chief, hoping this would get some action; but still he procrastinated. One evening, Lincoln and two of his staff members went to visit McClellan, only to learn that he was at a wedding. The three

men sat down to wait, and an hour later the general arrived home. Without paying any attention to the President, McClellan went upstairs and did not return. Half an hour later, Lincoln sent the servant to tell McClellan that the men were waiting. The servant came back to report McClellan had gone to bed!

His associates angry, Lincoln merely got up and led the way home. "This is no time to be making points of etiquette and personal dignity," the President explained. "I would hold McClellan's horse if he will only bring us success." This attitude of humility was what helped to make Lincoln a great man and a great President. He was not thinking of himself; he was thinking of serving others. Service is the second mark of the submissive mind.

## He Sacrifices (Phil. 2:8)

Many people are willing to serve others *if* it does not cost them anything. But if there is a price to pay, they suddenly lose interest. Jesus "became obedient unto death, even the death of the cross" (Phil. 2:8). His was not the death of a martyr but the death of a Saviour. He willingly laid down His life for the sins of the world.

Dr. J.H. Jowett has said, "Ministry that costs nothing accomplishes nothing." If there is to be any blessing, there must be some "bleeding." At a religious festival in Brazil, a missionary was going from booth to booth, examining the wares. He saw a sign above one booth: "Cheap Crosses." He thought to himself, "That's what many Christians are looking for these days—cheap crosses. My Lord's cross was not cheap. Why should mine be?"

The person with the submissive mind does not avoid sacrifice. He lives for the glory of God and the good of others; and if paying a price will honor Christ and help others, he is willing to do it. This was Paul's attitude (Phil. 2:17), Timothy's (Phil. 2:20), and also Epaphroditus' (Phil. 2:30). Sacrifice and service go together if service is to be true Christian ministry.

In his book *Dedication and Leadership,* Douglas Hyde explains how the Communists succeed in their program. A member of the Communist Party himself for twenty years, Hyde understands their philosophy. He points out that the Communists never ask a man to do a "mean, little job." They always ask him boldly to undertake something that will cost him. They make big demands, and they get a ready response. Mr. Hyde calls "the willingness to sacrifice" one of the most important factors in the success of the Communist program. Even the youths in the movement are expected to study, serve, give, and obey, and this is what attracts and holds them.

A church council was planning the annual "Youth Sunday" program, and one of the members suggested that the teenagers serve as ushers, lead in prayer, bring special music. One of the teens stood up and said, "Quite frankly, we're tired of being asked to do little things. We'd like to do something difficult this year, and maybe keep it going all year long. The kids have talked and prayed about this, and we'd like to work with our trustees in remodeling that basement room so it can be used for a classroom. And we'd like to start visiting our elderly members each week and taking them cassettes of the services. And, if it's OK, we'd like to have a weekly witness on Sunday afternoons in the park. We hope this is OK with you."

He sat down, and the new youth pastor smiled to himself. He had privately challenged the teens to do something that would cost them—and they enthusiastically responded to the challenge. He knew that sacrifice is necessary if there is going to be true growth and ministry.

The test of the submissive mind is not just how much we are willing to take in terms of suffering, but how much we are willing to give in terms of sacrifice. One pastor complained that his men were changing the words of the hymn from "Take my life and let it be" to "Take my wife and let me be!" They were willing for others to make the sacrifices, but they were unwilling to sacrifice for others.

It is one of the paradoxes of the Christian life that the more we give, the more we receive; the more we sacrifice, the more God blesses. This is why the submissive mind leads to joy; it makes us more like Christ. This means sharing His joy as we also share in His sufferings. Of course, when love is the motive (Phil. 2:1), sacrifice is never measured or mentioned. The person who constantly talks about his sacrifices does not have the submissive mind.

Is it costing *you* anything to be a Christian?

## He Glorifies God (Phil. 2:9-11)

This, of course, is the great goal of all that we do—to glorify God. Paul warns us against "vainglory" in Philippians 2:3. The kind of rivalry that pits Christian against Christian and ministry against ministry is not spiritual, nor is it satisfying. It is vain, empty. Jesus humbled Himself for others, and God highly exalted Him; and the result of this exaltation is glory to God.

Our Lord's exaltation began with His resurrection. When men buried the body of Jesus, that was the last thing any human hands did to Him. From that point on, it was God who worked. Men had done their worst to the Saviour, but God exalted Him and honored Him. Men gave Him names of ridicule and slander, but the Father gave Him a glorious name! Just as in His humiliation He was given the name "Jesus" (Matt. 1:21), so in His exaltation He was given the name "Lord" (Phil. 2:11; see Acts 2:32-36). He arose from the dead and then returned in victory to heaven, ascending to the Father's throne.

His exaltation included sovereign authority over all creatures in heaven, on earth, and under the earth. All will bow to Him (see Isa. 45:23). It is likely that "under the earth" refers to the lost, since God's family is either in heaven or on earth (Eph. 3:14-15). One day all will bow before Him and confess that He is Lord. Of course, it is possible for people to bow and confess *today,* and receive His gift of salvation (Rom. 10:9-10). To bow before Him now means salvation; to bow before Him at the judgment means condemnation.

The whole purpose of Christ's humiliation and exaltation is the glory of God (Phil. 2:11). As Jesus faced the cross, the glory of the Father was uppermost in His mind, "Father, the hour is come; glorify Thy Son, that Thy Son also may glorify Thee" (John 17:1). In fact, He has given this glory to us (John 17:22), and one day we shall share it with Him in heaven (John 17:24; see Rom. 8:28-30). The work of salvation is much greater and grander than simply the salvation of a lost soul, as wonderful as that is. Our salvation has as its ultimate purpose the glory of God (Eph. 1:6, 12, 14).

The person with the submissive mind, as he lives for others, must expect sacrifice and service; but in the end, it is going to lead to glory. "Humble yourselves therefore under the mighty hand of God, that He may exalt you in due time" (1 Peter 5:6). Joseph suffered and served for thirteen years; but then God exalted him and made him the second ruler of Egypt. David was anointed king when he was but a youth. He experienced years of hardship and suffering, but at the right time, God exalted him as king of Israel.

The joy of the submissive mind comes not only from helping others, and sharing in the fellowship of Christ's sufferings (Phil. 3:10), but primarily from the knowledge that we are glorifying God. We are letting our light shine through our good works, and this glorifies the Father in heaven (Matt. 5:16). We may not see the glory today, but we shall see it when Jesus comes and rewards His faithful servants.

# CHAPTER FIVE
# THE INS AND OUTS
# OF CHRISTIAN LIVING
*Philippians 2:12-18*

F ew things are harder to put up with," wrote Mark Twain, "than the annoyance of a good example." Perhaps the thing most annoying about a good example is its inability to accomplish the same achievements in our own lives. Admiration for a great person can inspire us, but it cannot enable us. Unless the person can enter into our own lives and share his skills, we cannot attain to his heights of accomplishment. It takes more than an example on the outside; it takes power on the inside.

Paul has just presented Jesus Christ as our great Example in the exercise of the submissive mind. We read it, and we agree with it, *but how do we go about practicing it?* How could any mortal man ever hope to achieve what Jesus Christ achieved? It seems almost presumptuous to even try! Here we are, trying to develop humility, and we are exercising pride by daring to imitate the Lord Jesus Christ!

The problem is really not that difficult. Paul is not asking us to "reach for the stars," though the higher the goal the more we ought to achieve. Rather, he is setting before us the divine *pattern* for the submissive mind and the divine *power* to accomplish what God has commanded. "It is God which worketh in you" (Phil. 2:13). It is not by imitation, but by incarnation—"Christ liveth in me" (Gal. 2:20).

The Christian life is not a series of ups and downs. It is rather a process of "ins and outs." God works *in,* and we work *out.* We cultivate the submissive mind by responding to the divine provisions God makes available to us.

## There Is a Purpose to Achieve
## (Phil. 2:12, 14-16)

"Work out your own salvation" (Phil. 2:12) does not suggest, "Work *for* your own salvation." To begin with, Paul is writing to people who are already "saints" (Phil. 1:1), which means they have trusted Christ and have been set apart for Him. The verb "work out" carries the meaning of "work to full completion," such as working out a problem in mathematics. In Paul's day it was also used for "working a mine," that is, getting out of the mine all the valuable ore possible; or "working a field" so as to get the greatest harvest possible. The purpose God wants us to achieve is Christlikeness, "to be conformed to the image of His Son" (Rom. 8:29). There are problems in life, but God will help us to "work them out." Our lives have tremendous potential, like a mine or a field, and He wants to help us fulfill that potential.

Cindy did not seem very happy when she arrived home from college to spend the holiday with her family. Her parents noticed her unusual behavior but were wise enough to wait until she was ready to share her problem with them. It happened after dinner.

"Mother, Dad, I have something to tell you, and I'm afraid it's going to hurt you."

"Just tell us what's on your heart," her father said, "and we'll understand. We want to pray with you about it—whatever it is."

"Well, you know that all during high school I talked about becoming a nurse, mainly because Mom is a nurse and I guess you expected me to follow in her footsteps. But I can't go on. The Lord just doesn't want me to be a nurse!"

Her mother smiled and took Cindy's hand. "Dear, your father and I want God's will for your life. If you do anything else, we'll *all* be unhappy!"

Cindy had done the courageous thing; she had faced God's will and decided that she wanted to work out *her own salvation*—her own Christian life—and not what somebody else wanted her to do. One of the wonderful things about being a Christian is the knowledge that God has a plan for our lives (Eph.

2:10) and will help us to work it out for His glory. Our God is a God of infinite variety! No two flowers are the same, no two snowflakes are the same; why should two Christians be the same? All of us must be like Christ, *but we must also be ourselves.*

The phrase "work out your own salvation" probably has reference particularly to the special problems in the church at Philippi; but the statement also applies to the individual Christian. We are not to be "cheap imitations" of other people, especially "great Christians." We are to follow only what we see of Christ in their lives. "Be ye followers of me, even as I also am of Christ" (1 Cor. 11:1). Every "great saint" has feet of clay and ultimately may disappoint you, but Jesus Christ can never fail you.

In Philippians 2:14-15, Paul contrasts the life of the believer with the lives of those who live in the world. Unsaved people complain and find fault, but Christians rejoice. Society around us is "twisted and distorted," but the Christian stands straight because he measures his life by God's Word, the perfect standard. The world is dark, but Christians shine as bright lights. The world has nothing to offer, but the Christian holds out the Word of life, the message of salvation through faith in Christ. In other words, as we allow God to achieve this purpose in our lives, we become better witnesses in a world that desperately needs Christ. Apply these characteristics to Jesus and you will see that He lived a perfect life in an imperfect world.

It is important to note that this purpose is achieved "in the midst of a crooked and perverse generation" (Phil. 2:15). Paul does not admonish us to retreat from the world and go into a spiritual isolation ward. It is only as we are confronted with the needs and problems of real life that we can begin to become more like Christ. The Pharisees were so isolated and insulated from reality that they developed an artificial kind of self-righteousness that was totally unlike the righteousness God wanted them to have. Consequently, the Pharisees forced a religion of fear and bondage on the people (read Matt. 23), and they crucified Christ because He dared to oppose that kind of religion. It is not by leaving the world but by ministering to it that we see God's purpose fulfilled in our lives.

**There Is a Power to Receive (Phil. 2:13)**
The principle Paul lays down is this: God must work *in* us before He can work *through* us.

This principle is seen at work throughout the Bible in the lives of men like Moses, David, the Apostles, and others. God had a special purpose for each man to fulfill, and each man was unique and not an imitation of somebody else. For example, it took God forty years to bring Moses to the place where He could use him to lead the people of Israel. As Moses tended sheep during those forty years, God was working in him so that one day He might work through him. *God is more interested in the workman than in the work.* If the workman is what he ought to be, the work will be what it ought to be.

Too many Christians obey God only because of pressure on the outside, and not power on the inside. Paul warned the Philippians that not his presence with them but their desire to obey God and please Him was the important thing (Phil. 1:27; 2:12). They could not build their lives on Paul because he might not be with them very long. It is sad to see the way some ministries in the church weaken or fall apart because of a change in leadership. We have a tendency to please men, and to obey God only when others are watching. But when you surrender to the power of God within you, then obedience becomes a delight and not a battle.

The power that works in us is the power of the Holy Spirit of God (John 14:16-17, 26; Acts 1:8; 1 Cor. 6:19-20). Our English word *energy* comes from the word translated "worketh" in Philippians 2:13. It is God's divine energy at work in us and through us! The same Holy Spirit who empowered Christ when He was ministering on earth can empower us as well. But we must recognize the fact that the energy of the flesh (Rom. 7:5) and of the devil (Eph. 2:2; 2 Thes. 2:7) are also at work. Because of the death, resurrection, and ascension of Christ, God's divine energy is available to us (Eph. 1:18-23). The power is here, but how do we use it? What "tools" does God use, by His Spirit, to work in our lives? There are three "tools": the Word of God, prayer, and suffering.

*The Word of God.* "For this cause also thank we God without ceasing, because, when ye received the Word of God, which ye heard of us, ye received it not as the word of men, but as it is in truth, the Word of God, which effectually worketh also in you that believe" (1 Thes. 2:13). God's divine energy is released in our lives through His inspired Word. The same Word that spoke the universe into being can release divine power in our lives! But we have a responsibility to *appreciate* the Word, and not treat it the way we treat the words of men. The Word of God is unique: it is inspired, authoritative, and infallible. If we do not appreciate the Word, then God's power cannot energize our lives.

But we must also *appropriate* the Word—"receive it." This means much more than listening to it, or even reading and studying it. To "receive" God's Word means to welcome it and make it a part of our inner being. God's truth is to the spiritual man what food is to the physical man.

Finally, we must *apply* the Word; it works only in those "that believe." When we trust God's Word and act on it, then God's power is released in our lives. The angel's promise to Mary in Luke 1:37—"For with God nothing shall be impossible"—is translated "For no word from God shall be void of power" in the *American Standard Version* (1901). God's Word has the power of accomplishment in it, and faith releases that power.

We see this truth operating in the life of Jesus. He commanded the crippled man to stretch out his hand, and the very command gave him the power to obey and be healed (Matt. 12:13). He commanded Peter to walk to Him on the water, and the command enabled Peter to do so, as long as he exercised faith (Matt. 14:22-33). It is faith in God's promises that releases God's power. His commandments are His enablements. The Holy Spirit wrote down the promises for us in the Word, and He gives us the faith to lay hold of these promises. "For no matter how many promises God has made, they are 'Yes' in Christ. And so through Him the 'Amen' is spoken by us to the glory of God" (2 Cor. 1:20, NIV).

*Prayer.* So, if we want God's power working in us, we must spend time daily with the Word of God. But we must also pray, because *prayer* is the second "tool" God uses to work in the lives of His children. "Now unto Him that is able to do exceeding abundantly above all that we ask or think, according to the power that worketh in us" (Eph. 3:20). The Holy Spirit is closely related to the practice of prayer in our lives (Rom. 8:26-27; Zech. 12:10). The Book of Acts makes it clear that prayer is a divinely ordained source of spiritual power (Acts 1:14; 4:23-31; 12:5, 12), and the Word of God and prayer go together (Acts 6:4). Unless the Christian takes time for prayer, God cannot work in him and through him. In the Bible and in church history, the people God used were people who prayed.

*Suffering.* God's third "tool" is *suffering.* The Spirit of God works in a special way in the lives of those who suffer for the glory of Christ (1 Peter 4:12-19). The "fiery trial" has a way of burning away the dross and empowering the believer to serve Christ. Paul himself had experienced God's power in that Philippian jail when he was beaten and thrust into the stocks in the inner prison; for he was able to sing and praise God in spite of his suffering (Acts 16:19-33). His "fiery trial" also enabled him to forgive the jailer. It was not the earthquake that brought conviction to the man; the earthquake almost led him to suicide! It was Paul's encouraging word, "Don't do it! We are all here!" (TLB) This kind of love broke the man's heart, and he fell before Paul asking how to be saved.

The Word of God, prayer, and suffering are the three "tools" that God uses in our lives. Just as electricity must run through a conductor, so the Holy Spirit must work through the means God has provided. As the Christian reads the Word and prays, he becomes more like Christ; and the more he becomes like Christ, the more the unsaved world opposes him. This daily "fellowship of His sufferings" (Phil. 3:10) drives the believer back to the Word and prayer, so that all three "tools" work together to provide the spiritual power he needs to glorify Christ.

If we are to have the submissive mind, and the joy that goes with it, we must recognize that there is a purpose to achieve (God's plan for our lives), a power to receive (the Holy Spirit), and a promise to believe.

### There Is a Promise to Believe (Phil. 2:16-18)

What is this promise? *That joy comes from submission.* The world's philosophy is that joy comes from aggression: fight everybody to get what you want, and you will get it and be happy. The example of Jesus is proof enough that the world's philosophy is wrong. He never used a sword or any other weapon; yet He won the greatest battle in history—the battle against sin and death and hell. He defeated hatred by manifesting love; He overcame lies with truth. *Because He surrendered He was victorious!* And you and I must dare to believe His promise, "For whosoever exalteth himself shall be abased; and he that humbleth himself shall be exalted" (Luke 14:11). "How happy are the humble-minded, for the kingdom of heaven is theirs" (Matt. 5:3, PH).

There is a twofold joy that comes to the person who possesses and practices the submissive mind: a joy hereafter (Phil. 2:16) and a joy here and now (Phil. 2:17-18). In the day of Christ (see Phil. 1:6, 10), God is going to reward those who have been faithful to Him. "The joy of thy Lord" is going to be a part of that reward (Matt. 25:21). The faithful Christian will discover that his sufferings on earth have been transformed into glory in heaven! He will see that his work was not in vain (1 Cor. 15:58). It was this same kind of promise of future joy that helped our Saviour in His sufferings on the cross (Heb. 12:1-2).

But we do not have to wait for the return of Christ to start experiencing the joy of the submissive mind. That joy is a present reality (Phil. 2:17-18), and it comes through sacrifice and service. It is remarkable that in two verses that discuss sacrifice, Paul uses the words *joy* and *rejoice*—and repeats them! Most people would associate sorrow with suffering, but Paul sees suffering and sacrifice as doorways to a deeper joy in Christ.

In Philippians 2:17, Paul is comparing his experience of sacrifice to that of the priest pouring out the drink offering (Num. 15:1-10). It was possible that Paul's trial would go against him and he would be executed. But this did not rob Paul of his joy. His death would be a willing sacrifice, a priestly ministry, on behalf of Christ and His church; and this would give him joy. "Sacrifice and service" are marks of the submissive mind (Phil. 2:7-8, 21-22, 30), and the submissive mind experiences joy even in the midst of suffering.

It takes faith to exercise the submissive mind. We must believe that God's promises are true and that they are going to work in our lives just as they worked in Paul's life. God works *in* us through the Word, prayer, and suffering; and we work *out* in daily living and service. God fulfills His purposes in us as we receive and believe His Word. Life is not a series of disappointing "ups and downs." Rather, it is a sequence of delightful "ins and outs." God works in—we work out! The example comes from Christ, the energy comes from the Holy Spirit, and the result is—JOY!

# CHAPTER SIX
# A PRICELESS PAIR
*Philippians 2:19-30*

A reporter in San Bernardino, California arranged for a man to lie in the gutter on a busy street. Hundreds of people passed the man but not one stopped to help him or even show sympathy!

Newspapers across the country a few years ago told how thirty-eight people watched a man stalk a young lady and finally attack her—and none of the spectators even picked up a phone to call the police!

A couple of teenagers in Detroit discovered a woman in a telephone booth who had suffered a heart attack. They carried her to a nearby house and rang the bell, asking for help. The only reply they received was, "Get off my porch—and take her with you!"

A Kentucky doctor was driving down the highway to visit a patient when he saw an accident take place. He stopped and gave aid to the injured and then made his visit. One of the drivers he helped sued him!

Is it possible to be a "Good Samaritan" today? Must everybody harden his heart in order to protect himself? Perhaps "sacrifice and service" are ancient virtues that somehow do not fit into our so-called modern civilization. It is worth noting that even in Paul's day mutual concern was not a popular virtue. The Christians at Rome were not too interested in the problems at Philippi; Paul could not find *one person* among them willing to go to Philippi (Phil. 2:19-21). Times have not changed too much.

In this paragraph, Paul is still discussing the submissive mind. He has given us a *description* of the submissive mind in the example of Jesus Christ (Phil. 2:1-11). He has explained the *dynamics* of the submissive mind in his own experience (Phil. 2:12-18). Now he introduces us to two of his helpers in the ministry, Timothy and Epaphroditus, and he does this for a reason. He knows that his readers will be prone to say, "It is impossible for us to follow such examples as Christ and Paul! After all, Jesus is the very Son of God, and Paul is a chosen apostle who has had great spiritual experiences!" For this reason, Paul introduces us to two "ordinary saints," men who were not apostles or spectacular miracle workers.

He wants us to know that the submissive mind is not a luxury enjoyed by a chosen few; it is a necessity for Christian joy, and an opportunity for *all* believers.

### Timothy (Phil. 2:19-24)

Paul probably met Timothy on his first missionary journey (Acts 14:6ff), at which time, perhaps, the youth was converted (1 Cor. 4:17). Apparently, Timothy's mother and grandmother had been converted first (2 Tim. 1:3-5). He was the son of a Jewish mother and Gentile father, but Paul always considered the young man his own "dearly beloved son" in the faith (2 Tim. 1:2). When Paul returned to Derbe and Lystra while on his second journey, he enlisted young Timothy as one of his fellow laborers (Acts 16:1-4). In one sense, Timothy replaced John Mark, whom Paul had refused to take along on the journey because of Mark's previous abandonment of the cause (Acts 13:13; 15:36-41).

In Timothy's experience, we learn that the submissive mind is not something that suddenly, automatically appears in the life of the believer. Timothy had to develop and cultivate the "mind of Christ." It was not natural for him to be a servant; but, as he walked with the Lord and worked with Paul, he became the kind of servant that Paul could trust and God could bless. Notice the characteristics of this young man.

*He had a servant's mind (vv. 19-21).* To begin with, Timothy naturally cared for people and was concerned about their needs. He was not interested in "winning friends and influencing people"; he was genuinely interested in their physical and spiritual welfare. Paul was concerned about the church at Philippi and wanted to send someone to convey his concern and get the facts. There were certainly hundreds of Christians in Rome (Paul greets twenty-six of them by name in Rom. 16); yet not one of them was available to make the trip! "All seek their own, not the things which are Jesus Christ's" (Phil. 2:21). In a very real sense, all of us live either in Philippians 1:21 or Philippians 2:21!

But Timothy had a natural concern for the welfare of others; he had a servant's mind. It is too bad that the believers in Rome were so engrossed in themselves and their own internal wranglings (Phil. 1:15-16) that they had no time for the important work of the Lord. This is one of the tragedies of church problems; they divert time, energy, and concern away from the things that matter most. Timothy was not interested in promoting any party or supporting any divisive cause. He was interested only in the spiritual condition of God's people, and this concern was *natural* to him. How did this concern develop? The answer is in the next characteristic of this remarkable young man.

*He had a servant's training (v. 22).* Paul did not add Timothy to his "team" the very day the boy was saved. Paul was too wise to make an error like that. He left him behind to become a part of the church fellowship in Derbe and Lystra, and it was in that fellowship that Timothy grew in spiritual matters and learned how to serve the Lord. When Paul returned to that area a few years later, he was happy to discover that young Timothy "was well reported of the brethren" (Acts 16:2). Years later, Paul would write to Timothy about the importance of permitting new converts to grow before thrusting them into important places of ministry (1 Tim. 3:6-7).

A popular local nightclub performer visited a pastor and announced that he had been saved and wanted to serve the Lord. "What should I do next?" he asked.

"Well, I'd suggest you unite with a good church and start growing," the pastor replied. "Is your wife a Christian?"

"No, she isn't," the musician replied. "I hope to win her. But, do I have to wait? I mean, I'd like to do something for God right now."

"No, you don't have to wait to witness for the Lord," explained the pastor. "Get busy in a church, and use your talents for Christ."

"But you don't know who I am!" the man protested. "I'm a big performer—everybody knows me. I want to start my own organization, make records, and appear before big crowds!"

"If you go too far too fast," warned the pastor, "you may hurt yourself and your testimony. And the place to start winning people is right at home. God will open up places of service for you as He sees you are ready. Meanwhile, study the Bible and give yourself a chance to grow."

The man did not take the pastor's counsel. Instead, he set up a big organization and started out on his own. His "success" lasted less than a year. Not only did he lose his testimony because he was not strong enough to carry the heavy burdens, but his constant traveling alienated him from his wife and family. He drifted into a "fringe group" and disappeared from public ministry, a broken and bankrupt man.

"His branches went out farther than his roots went deep," the pastor said. "When that happens, you eventually topple."

Paul did not make this mistake with Timothy. He gave him time to get his roots down, and then he enlisted the young man to work with him on his missionary tours. He taught Timothy the Word and permitted him to watch the apostle in his ministry (2 Tim. 3:10-17). This was the way Jesus trained His disciples. He gave personal instruction balanced by on-the-job experience. Experience without teaching can lead to discouragement, and teaching without experience can lead to spiritual deadness. It takes both.

**He had a servant's reward (vv. 23-24).** Timothy knew the meaning of "sacrifice and service" (Phil. 2:17), but God rewarded him for his faithfulness. To begin with, Timothy had the joy of helping others. To be sure, there were hardships and difficulties, but there were also victories and blessings. Because Timothy was a "good and faithful servant," faithful over a few things, God rewarded him with "many things," and he entered into the joy of the submissive mind (Matt. 25:21). He had the joy of serving with the great Apostle Paul and assisting him in some of his most difficult assignments (1 Cor. 4:17ff; Timothy is mentioned at least twenty-four times in Paul's letters).

But perhaps the greatest reward God gave to Timothy was to choose him to be Paul's replacement when the great apostle was called home (see 2 Tim. 4:1-11). Paul himself wanted to go to Philippi, but had had to send Timothy in his place. But, what an honor! Timothy was not only Paul's son, and Paul's servant, but he became Paul's substitute! His name is held in high regard by Christians today, something that young Timothy never dreamed of when he was busy serving Christ.

The submissive mind is not the product of an hour's sermon, or a week's seminar, or even a year's service. The submissive mind grows in us as, like Timothy, we yield to the Lord and seek to serve others.

## Epaphroditus (Phil. 2:25-30)

Paul was a "Hebrew of the Hebrews"; Timothy was part Jew and part Gentile (Acts 16:1); and Epaphroditus was a full Gentile as far as we know. He was the member of the Philippian church who risked his health and life to carry their missionary offering to the apostle in Rome (Phil. 4:18). His name means "charming" and a charming Christian he is!

**He was a balanced Christian (v. 25).** Paul could not say enough about this man— "My brother, and companion in labor, and fellow-soldier." These three descriptions parallel what Paul wrote about the Gospel in the first chapter of this letter:

| | |
|---|---|
| "my brother"— | the "fellowship in the Gospel" (Phil. 1:5) |
| "my companion in labor"— | "the furtherance of the Gospel" (Phil. 1:12) |
| "my fellow-soldier"— | "the faith of the Gospel" (Phil. 1:27) |

Epaphroditus was a balanced Christian!

Balance is important in the Christian life. Some people emphasize "fellowship" so much that they forget the furtherance of the Gospel. Others are so involved in defending the "faith of the Gospel" that they neglect building fellowship with other believers. Epaphroditus did not fall into either of these traps. He was like Nehemiah, the man who rebuilt the walls of Jerusalem with his sword in one hand and his trowel in the other (Neh. 4:17). You cannot build with a sword nor battle with a trowel! It takes both to get the Lord's work accomplished.

Dr. H.A. Ironside used to tell about a group of believers who thought only of "fellowship." They had little concern for reaching the lost or for defending the faith against its enemies. In front of their meeting place they hung a sign: JESUS ONLY. But the wind blew away some of the letters, and the sign read—US ONLY. It was a perfect description of a group of people who were not balanced Christians.

**He was a burdened Christian (vv. 26-27, 30).** Like Timothy, Epaphroditus was concerned about others. To begin with, he was concerned about *Paul*. When he heard in Philippi that Paul was a prisoner in Rome, he volunteered to make that long, dangerous trip to Rome to stand at Paul's side and assist him. He carried the church's love gift with him, protecting it with his own life.

Our churches today need men and women who are burdened for missions and for those in difficult places of Christian service. "The problem in our churches," states one missionary leader, "is that we have too many spectators and not enough participants." Epaphroditus was not content simply to contribute to the offering. He gave *himself* to help carry the offering!

But this man was also burdened for *his own home church*. After arriving in Rome, he became very ill. In fact, he almost died. This delayed his return to Philippi, and the people there became concerned about him. But Epaphroditus was not burdened about himself; he was burdened over the people in Philippi *because they were worried about him!* This man lived in Philippians 1:21, not Philippians 2:21. Like Timothy, he had a natural concern for others. The phrase "full of heaviness" in Philippines 2:26 is the same description used of Christ in Gethsemane (Matt. 26:37). Like Christ, Epaphroditus knew the meaning of sacrifice and service (Phil. 2:30), which are two of the marks of the submissive mind.

**He was a blessed Christian (vv. 28-30).** What a tragedy it would be to go through life and not be a blessing to anyone! Epaphroditus was a blessing to Paul. He stood with him in his prison experience and did not permit even his own sickness to hinder his service. What times he and Paul must have had together! But he was also a blessing to his own church. Paul admonishes the church to honor him because of his sacrifice and service. (Christ gets the glory, but there is nothing wrong with the servant receiving honor. Read 1 Thes. 5:12-13.) There is no contradiction between Philippians 2:7 ("made Himself of no reputation") and Philippians 2:29 ("hold such in reputation"). Christ "emptied Himself" in His gracious act of humiliation, and God exalted Him. Epaphroditus sacrificed himself with no thought of reward, and Paul encouraged the church to hold him in honor to the glory of God.

He was a blessing to Paul and to his own church, and he is also a blessing to *us today!* He proves to us that the joyful life is the life of sacrifice and service, that the submissive mind really does work. He and Timothy together encourage us to submit ourselves to the Lord, and to one another, in the Spirit of Christ. Christ is the Pattern we follow. Paul shows us the power (Phil. 4:12-19); and Timothy and Epaphroditus are the proof that this mind really works.

Will you permit the Spirit to reproduce "the mind of Christ" in you?

# CHAPTER SEVEN
# LEARNING HOW TO COUNT
## *Philippians 3:1-11*

Circumstances and people can rob us of joy, but so can *things;* and it is this "thief" that Paul deals with in Philippians 3. It is important to see the total message of this chapter before examining it in detail, so perhaps the following outline will be helpful.

| *Vv. 1-11* | *Vv. 12-16* | *Vv. 17-21* |
|---|---|---|
| Paul's past | Paul's present | Paul's future |
| the accountant | the athlete | the alien |
| "I count" | "I press" | "I look" |
| new values | new vigor | new vision |

What Paul is describing is the "spiritual mind." In Philippians 3:18-19, he describes professed Christians who "mind earthly things," but then in Philippians 3:20 he describes the believer with the spiritual mind, who "minds heavenly things." You will recall that the city of Philippi was actually a Roman colony—a "Rome away from Rome." In the same sense, the people of God are a colony of heaven on earth. "Our citizenship is in heaven" (Phil. 3:20, NASB), and we look at earth from heaven's point of view. This is the spiritual mind.

It is easy for us to get wrapped up in "things," not only the tangible things that we can see, but also the intangibles such as reputation, fame, achievement. Paul writes about "what things were gain" to him (Phil. 3:7); he also mentions "things which are behind" and "things which are before" (Phil. 3:13). In Paul's case, some of these "things" were intangible, such as religious achievements (Gal. 1:14), a feeling of self-satisfaction, morality. We today can be snared both by tangibles and intangibles, and as a result lose our joy.

But even the tangible things are not in themselves sinful. God made things, and the Bible declares that these things are good (Gen. 1:31). God knows that we need certain things in order to live (Matt. 6:31-34). In fact, He "giveth us richly all things to enjoy"

(1 Tim. 6:17). But Jesus warns us that our lives do not consist in the abundance of the things that we possess (Luke 12:15). Quantity is no assurance of quality. Many people who have the things money can buy have lost the things that money cannot buy.

The key word in Philippians 3:1-11 is *count* (Phil. 3:7-8, 13). In the Greek, two different words are used, but the basic idea is the same: to evaluate, to assess. "The unexamined life is not worth living," said Socrates. Yet, few people sit down to weigh seriously the values that control their decisions and directions. Many people today are the slaves of "things," and as a result do not experience real Christian joy.

In Paul's case, the "things" he was living for before he knew Christ seemed to be very commendable: a righteous life, obedience to the Law, the defense of the religion of his fathers. But none of these things satisfied him or gave him acceptance with God.

Like most "religious" people today, Paul had enough morality to keep him out of trouble, but not enough righteousness to get him into heaven! It was not bad things that kept Paul away from Jesus—it was good things! He had to lose his "religion" to find salvation.

One day, Saul of Tarsus, the rabbi, met Jesus Christ, the Son of God, and on that day Saul's values changed (read Acts 9:1-31). When Saul opened his books to evaluate his wealth, he discovered that apart from Jesus Christ, everything he lived for was only refuse. He explains in this section that there are only two kinds of righteousness (or spiritual wealth)—works righteousness and faith righteousness—and only faith righteousness is acceptable to God.

## Works Righteousness (Phil. 3:1-6)

*The exhortation (vv. 1-3).* "Finally" at this point does not mean Paul is about to close the letter, because he keeps on going. The word means "For the rest," and introduces the new section. Paul's "finally" at Philippians 4:18 is the one that means "I am about to close." Paul has warned the believers at Philippi before, but now he warns them again. "Look out for dogs! Look out for the workers of evil! Look out for the mutilation!" To whom is he referring in this triple warning? The answer takes us back into the early history of the church.

From the very beginning, the Gospel came "to the Jew first" (see Acts 3:26; Rom. 1:16),

so that the first seven chapters of Acts deal only with Jewish believers or with Gentiles who were Jewish proselytes (Acts 2:10). In Acts 8:5-25, the message went to the Samaritans, but this did not cause too much of an upheaval since the Samaritans were at least partly Jewish. But when Peter went to the Gentiles in Acts 10, this created an uproar. Peter was called on the carpet to explain his activities (Acts 11). After all, the Gentiles in Acts 10 had become Christians *without first becoming Jews,* and this was a whole new thing for the church. Peter explained that it was God who had directed him to preach to the Gentiles, and the matter seemed to be settled.

But it was not settled for long. Paul was sent out by the Holy Spirit to minister especially to the Gentiles (Acts 13:1-3; 22:21). Peter had opened the door of faith to the Gentiles in Acts 10, and Paul followed his example on his first missionary journey (see Acts 14:26-28). It did not take long for the strict Jewish believers to oppose Paul's ministry and come to Antioch teaching that it was necessary for the Gentiles to submit to Jewish rules before they could be saved (Acts 15:1). This disagreement led to the Conference at Jerusalem that is described in Acts 15. The result of the conference was an approval of Paul's ministry and a victory for the Gospel of the grace of God. Gentiles did *not* have to become Jewish proselytes in order to become Christians!

But the dissenters were not content. Having failed in their opposition to Paul at Antioch and Jerusalem, they followed him wherever he went and tried to steal his converts and his churches. Bible students call this group of false teachers who try to mix Law and grace "Judaizers." The Epistle to the Galatians was written primarily to combat this false teaching. It is this group of "Judaizers" that Paul is referring to in Philippians 3:1-2. He uses three terms to describe them.

*"Dogs."* The orthodox Jew would call the Gentile a "dog," but here Paul calls orthodox Jews "dogs"! Paul is not just using names; he is comparing these false teachers to the dirty scavengers so contemptible to decent people. Like those dogs, these Judaizers snapped at Paul's heels and followed him from place to place "barking" their false doctrines. They were troublemakers and carriers of dangerous infection.

*"Evil workers."* These men taught that the sinner was saved by faith *plus* good works,

especially the works of the Law. But Paul states that their "good works" are really *evil* works because they are performed by the flesh (old nature) and not the Spirit, and they glorify the workers and not Jesus Christ. Ephesians 2:8-10 and Titus 3:3-7 make it clear that nobody can be saved by doing good works, even religious works. A Christian's good works are the result of his faith, not the basis for his salvation.

"*The mutilation.*" Here Paul uses a pun on the word "circumcision." The word translated "circumcision" literally means "a mutilation." The Judaizers taught that circumcision was essential to salvation (Acts 15:1; Gal. 6:12-18); but Paul states that circumcision of *itself* is only a mutilation! The true Christian has experienced a spiritual circumcision in Christ (Col. 2:11), and does not need any fleshly operations. Circumcision, baptism, the Lord's Supper, tithing, or any other religious practice cannot save a person from his sins. Only faith in Jesus Christ can do that.

In contrast to the false Christians, Paul describes the true Christians, the "true circumcision" (see Rom. 2:25-29 for a parallel).

*He worships God in the Spirit.* He does not depend on his own good works which are only of the flesh (see John 4:19-24).

*He boasts in Jesus Christ.* People who depend on religion are usually boasting about what they have done. The true Christian has nothing of which to boast (Eph. 2:8-10). His boast is only in Christ! In Luke 18:9-14, Jesus gives a parable that describes these two opposite attitudes.

*He has no confidence in the flesh.* The popular religious philosophy of today is, "The Lord helps those who help themselves." It was also popular in Paul's day, and it is just as wrong today as it was then. (By "the flesh" Paul means "the old nature" that we received at birth.) The Bible has nothing good to say about "flesh," and yet most people today depend entirely on what they themselves can do to please God. Flesh only corrupts God's way on earth (Gen. 6:12). It profits nothing as far as spiritual life is concerned (John 6:63). It has nothing good in it (Rom. 7:18). No wonder we should put no confidence in the flesh!

A lady was arguing with her pastor about this matter of faith and works. "I think that getting to heaven is like rowing a boat," she said. "One oar is faith, and the other is works. If you use both, you get there. If you use only one, you go around in circles."

"There is only one thing wrong with your illustration," replied the pastor. "Nobody is going to heaven *in a rowboat!*"

There is only one "good work" that takes the sinner to heaven: the finished work of Christ on the cross (John 17:1-4; 19:30; Heb. 10:11-14).

*The example (vv. 4-6).* Paul was not speaking from an ivory tower; he personally *knew* the futility of trying to attain salvation by means of good works. As a young student, he had sat at the feet of Gamaliel, the great rabbi (Acts 22:3). His career as a Jewish religious leader was a promising one (Gal. 1:13-14); and yet Paul gave it all up—to become a hated member of the "Christian sect" and a preacher of the Gospel! Actually, the Judaizers were compromising in order to avoid persecution (Gal. 6:12-13), while Paul was being true to Christ's message of grace and as a result was suffering persecution.

In this intensely autobiographical section, Paul examines his own life. He becomes an "auditor" who opens the books to see what wealth he has, and he discovers that *he is bankrupt!*

*Paul's relationship to the nation.* He was born into a pure Hebrew family and entered into a covenantal relationship when he was circumcised. He was not a proselyte, nor was he descended from Ishmael (Abraham's other son) or Esau (Isaac's other son). The Judaizers would understand Paul's reference to the tribe of Benjamin, because Benjamin and Joseph were Jacob's favorite sons. They were born to Rachel, Jacob's favorite wife. Israel's first king came from Benjamin, and this little tribe was faithful to David during the rebellion under Absalom. Paul's human heritage was something to be proud of! When measured by this standard, he passed with flying colors.

*Paul's relationship to the Law.* "As touching the Law, a Pharisee . . . touching the righteousness which is in the Law, blameless" (Phil. 3:5-6). To the Jews of Paul's day, a Pharisee had reached the very summit of religious experience, the highest ideal a Jew could ever hope to attain. If anybody was going to heaven, it was the Pharisee! He held to orthodox doctrine (see Acts 23:6-9) and tried to fulfill the religious duties faithfully (Luke 18:10-14). While we today are accustomed to use the word "Pharisee" as the equivalent of "hypocrite," this usage was not prevalent in Paul's day. Measured by the righteousness of the Law, Paul was blameless. He kept the

Law and the traditions perfectly.

*Paul's relationship to Israel's enemies.* But it is not enough to believe the truth; a man must also oppose lies. Paul defended his orthodox faith by persecuting the followers of "that pretender," Jesus (Matt. 27:62-66). He assisted at the stoning of Stephen (Acts 7:54-60), and after that he led the attack against the church in general (Acts 8:1-3). Even in later years, Paul admitted his role in persecuting the church (Acts 22:1-5; 26:1-11; see also 1 Tim. 1:12-16). Every Jew could boast of his own blood heritage (though he certainly could not take any credit for it). Some Jews could boast of their faithfulness to the Jewish religion. But Paul could boast of those things *plus* his zeal in persecuting the church.

At this point we might ask: "How could a sincere man like Saul of Tarsus be so wrong?" The answer is: *he was using the wrong measuring stick!* Like the rich young ruler (Mark 10:17-22) and the Pharisee in Christ's parable (Luke 18:10-14), Saul of Tarsus was looking at the *outside* and not the *inside*. He was comparing himself with standards set by men, not by God. As far as obeying *outwardly* the demands of the Law, Paul was a success, but he did not stop to consider the *inward sins* he was committing. In the Sermon on the Mount, Jesus makes it clear that there are sinful *attitudes* and *appetites* as well as sinful *actions* (Matt. 5:21-48).

When he looked at himself or looked at others, Saul of Tarsus considered himself to be righteous. But one day he saw himself as compared with Jesus Christ! It was then that he changed his evaluations and values, and abandoned "works righteousness" for the righteousness of Jesus Christ.

## Faith Righteousness (Phil. 3:7-11)

When Paul met Jesus Christ on the Damascus road (Acts 9), he trusted Him and became a child of God. It was an instantaneous miracle of the grace of God, the kind that still takes place today whenever sinners will admit their need and turn to the Saviour by faith. When Paul met Christ, he realized how futile were his good works and how sinful were his claims of righteousness. A wonderful transaction took place. Paul lost some things, but he gained much more than he lost!

*Paul's losses (v. 7).* To begin with, he lost whatever was *gain to him personally apart from God.* Certainly Paul had a great reputation as a scholar (Acts 26:24) and a religious leader. He was proud of his Jewish heritage and his religious achievements. All of these things were valuable to him; he could profit from them. He certainly had many friends who admired his zeal. But he measured these "treasures" against what Jesus Christ had to offer, and he realized that all he held dear was really nothing but "refuse" compared to what he had in Christ. His own "treasures" brought glory to him personally, but they did not bring glory to God. They were "gain" to him only, and as such, were selfish.

This does not mean that Paul repudiated his rich heritage as an orthodox Jew. As you read his letters and follow his ministry in the Book of Acts, you see how he valued both his Jewish blood and his Roman citizenship. Becoming a Christian did not make him *less* a Jew. In fact, it made him a *completed* Jew, a true child of Abraham both spiritually and physically (Gal. 3:6-9). Nor did he lower his standards of morality because he saw the shallowness of pharisaical religion. He accepted the *higher* standard of living—conformity to Jesus Christ (Rom. 12:1-2). When a person becomes a Christian, God takes away the bad, but He also takes the good and makes it better.

*Paul's gains (vv. 8-11).* Again we are reminded of Jim Elliot's words: "He is no fool to give what he cannot keep to gain what he cannot lose." This is what Paul experienced: he lost his religion and his reputation, but he gained far more than he lost.

*The knowledge of Christ (v. 8).* This means much more than knowledge *about* Christ, because Paul had that kind of historical information before he was saved. To "know Christ" means to have a personal relationship with Him through faith. It is this experience that Jesus mentions in John 17:3. You and I know *about* many people, even people who lived centuries ago, but we know personally very few. "Christianity *is* Christ." Salvation is knowing Him in a personal way.

*The righteousness of Christ (v. 9).* Righteousness was the great goal of Paul's life when he was a Pharisee, but it was a self-righteousness, a works righteousness, that he never really could attain. But when Paul trusted Christ, he lost his own self-righteousness and gained the righteousness of Christ. The technical word for this transaction is *imputation* (read Rom. 4:1-8 carefully). It means "to put to one's account." Paul looked at his own record and discovered that he was spiritually bankrupt. He looked at Christ's record and saw that He was perfect. When Paul trusted Christ, he saw God put Christ's righteousness *to his own account!* More than that, Paul discovered that his sins had been put on Christ's account on the cross (2 Cor. 5:21). And God promised Paul that He would never write his sins against him anymore. What a fantastic experience of God's grace!

Romans 9:30–10:13 is a parallel passage and you ought to read it carefully. What Paul says about the nation Israel was true in his own life before he was saved. And it is true in the lives of many religious people today; they refuse to abandon their own righteousness that they might receive the free gift of the righteousness of Christ. Many religious people will not even admit they *need* any righteousness. Like Saul of Tarsus, they are measuring themselves by themselves, or by the standards of the Ten Commandments, and they fail to see the *inwardness* of sin. Paul had to give up his religion to receive righteousness, but he did not consider it a sacrifice.

*The fellowship of Christ (vv. 10-11).* When he became a Christian, it was not the *end* for Paul, but the *beginning.* His experience with Christ was so tremendous that it transformed his life. And this experience continued in the years to follow. It was a *personal* experience ("That I may know Him") as Paul walked with Christ, prayed, obeyed His will, and sought to glorify His name. When he was living under Law, all Paul had was a set of rules. But now he had a Friend, a Master, a constant Companion! It was also a *powerful* experience ("and the power of His resurrection"), as the resurrection power of Christ went to work in Paul's life. "Christ liveth in me!" (Gal. 2:20) Read Ephesians 1:15-23 and 3:13-21 for Paul's estimate of the resurrection power of Christ and what it can do in your life.

It was also a *painful* experience ("and the fellowship of His sufferings"). Paul knew that it was a privilege to suffer for Christ (Phil. 1:29-30). In fact, suffering had been a part of his experience from the very beginning (Acts 9:16). As we grow in our knowledge of Christ and our experience of His power, we come under the attack of the enemy. Paul had been a persecutor at one time, but he learned what it means to be persecuted. But it was worth it! For walking with Christ was also a *practical* experience ("being made conformable unto His death"). Paul lived for Christ because he died to self (Rom. 6 explains this); he took up his cross daily and followed Him. The result of

this death was a spiritual resurrection (Phil. 3:11) that caused Paul to walk "in newness of life" (Rom. 6:4). Paul summarizes this whole experience in Galatians 2:20, so take time to read it.

Yes, Paul gained far more than he lost. In fact, the gains were so thrilling that Paul considered all other "things" nothing but garbage in comparison! No wonder he had joy—his life did not depend on the cheap "things" of the world but on the eternal values found in Christ. Paul had the "spiritual mind" and looked at the "things" of earth from heaven's point of view. People who live for "things" are never really happy, because they must constantly protect their treasures and worry lest they lose their value. Not so the believer with the spiritual mind; his treasures in Christ can never be stolen and they never lose their value.

Maybe now is a good time for you to become an accountant and evaluate in your life the "things" that matter most to you.

# CHAPTER EIGHT
# LET'S WIN THE RACE!
*Philippians 3:12-16*

Most people read biographies to satisfy their curiosity about great people, hoping also that they may discover the "secret" that made them great. I recall sitting in a grade school assembly program many years ago, listening to an aged doctor who promised to tell us the secret of his long, healthy life. (At one time he was a physician to the President of the United States. I've forgotten which one, but at that stage in my life, it seemed it must have been Washington or Jefferson.) All of us sat there with great expectation, hoping to learn the secret of a long life. At the climax of his address, the doctor told us, "Drink eight glasses of water a day!"

In Philippians 3, Paul is giving us his spiritual biography, his past (Phil. 3:1-11), his present (Phil. 3:12-16), and his future (Phil. 3:17-21). We have already met Paul "the accountant" who discovered new values when he met Jesus Christ. In this section we meet

Paul "the athlete" with his spiritual vigor, pressing toward the finish line in the Christian race. In the final section we will see Paul "the alien," having his citizenship in heaven and looking for the coming of Jesus Christ. In each of these experiences, Paul is exercising the *spiritual mind;* he is looking at things on earth from God's point of view. As a result, he is not upset by things behind him, around him, or before him—*things* do not rob him of his joy!

In his letters, Paul uses many illustrations from the world to communicate truth about the Christian life. Four are prominent: the military ("Put on the whole armor of God"), architecture ("You are the temple of God"), agriculture ("Whatsoever a man sows, that shall he also reap"), and athletics. In this paragraph, it is Paul the athlete. Bible students are not agreed as to the exact sport Paul is describing, whether the footrace or the chariot race. Either one will do, but my own preference is the chariot race. The Greek chariot, used in the Olympic Games and other events, was really only a small platform with a wheel on each side. The driver had very little to hold on to as he raced around the course. He had to lean forward and strain every nerve and muscle to maintain balance and control the horses. The verb "reaching forth" in Philippians 3:13 literally means "stretching as in a race."

It is important to note that Paul is not telling us how to be saved. If he were, it would be a picture of salvation by works or self-effort, and this would contradict what he wrote in the first eleven verses of Philippians 3. In order to participate in the Greek games, the athlete had to be a citizen. He did not run the race to gain his citizenship. In Philippians 3:20, Paul reminds us that "our conversation [citizenship] is in heaven." Because we are already the children of God through faith in Christ, we have the responsibility of "running the race" and achieving the goals God has set for us. This is a graphic picture of Philippians 2:12-13: "Work out your own salvation . . . for it is God which worketh in you." Each believer is on the track; each has a special lane in which to run; and each has a goal to achieve. If we reach the goal the way God has planned, then we receive a reward. If we fail, we lose the reward, but we do not lose our citizenship. (Read 1 Cor. 3:11-15 for the same idea, only using architecture as the symbol.)

All of us want to be "winning Christians" and fulfill the purposes for which we have been saved. What are the essentials for winning the race and one day receiving the reward that is promised?

### Dissatisfaction (Phil. 3:12-13a)

"Not as though I had already attained!" This is the statement of a great Christian who never permitted himself to be satisfied with his spiritual attainments. Obviously, Paul was satisfied with Jesus Christ (Phil. 3:10), but he was not satisfied with his Christian life. A sanctified dissatisfaction is the first essential to progress in the Christian race.

Harry came out of the manager's office with a look on his face dismal enough to wilt the roses on the secretary's desk.

"You didn't get fired?" she asked.

"No, it's not that bad. But he sure did lay into me about my sales record. I can't figure it out; for the past month I've been bringing in plenty of orders. I thought he'd compliment me, but instead he told me to get with it."

Later in the day, the secretary talked to her boss about Harry. The boss chuckled. "Harry is one of our best salesmen and I'd hate to lose him. But he has a tendency to rest on his laurels and be satisfied with his performance. If I didn't get him mad at me once a month, he'd never produce!"

Many Christians are self-satisfied because they compare their "running" with that of other Christians, usually those who are not making much progress. Had Paul compared himself with others, he would have been tempted to be proud and perhaps to let up a bit. After all, there were not too many believers in Paul's day who had experienced all that he had! But Paul did not compare himself with others; he compared himself *with himself* and with *Jesus Christ!* The dual use of the word "perfect" in Philippians 3:12 and 15 explains his thinking. He has not arrived yet at perfection (Phil. 3:12), but he is "perfect" [mature] (Phil. 3:15), and one mark of this maturity is the knowledge that he is *not* perfect! The mature Christian honestly evaluates himself and strives to do better.

Often in the Bible we are warned against a false estimate of our spiritual condition. The church at Sardis had "a name that thou livest, and art dead" (Rev. 3:1). They had reputation without reality. The church at Laodicea boasted that it was rich, when in God's sight it was "wretched, and miserable, and poor, and blind, and naked" (Rev. 3:17). In contrast to the Laodicean church, the believers at Smyrna thought they were poor when they were really rich! (Rev. 2:9) Samson thought he still had his old power, but in reality it had departed from him (Jud. 16:20).

Self-evaluation can be a dangerous thing, because we can err in two directions: (1) making ourselves *better* than we are, or (2) making ourselves *worse* than we really are. Paul had no illusions about himself; he still had to keep "pressing forward" in order to "lay hold of that for which Christ laid hold" of him. A divine dissatisfaction is essential for spiritual progress. "As the hart panteth after the water brooks, so panteth my soul after thee, O God. My soul thirsteth for God, for the living God" (Ps. 42:1-2).

### Devotion (Phil. 3:13b)
"One thing" is a phrase that is important to the Christian life. "One thing thou lackest," said Jesus to the self-righteous rich young ruler (Mark 10:21). "One thing is needful," He explained to busy Martha when she criticized her sister (Luke 10:42). "One thing I know!" exclaimed the man who had received his sight by the power of Christ (John 9:25). "One thing have I desired of the Lord, that will I seek after!" testified the psalmist (Ps. 27:4). Too many Christians are too involved in "many things," when the secret of progress is to concentrate on "one thing." It was this decision that was a turning point in D.L. Moody's life. Before the tragedy of the Chicago fire in 1871, Mr. Moody was involved in Sunday School promotion, Y.M.C.A. work, evangelistic meetings, and many other activities; but after the fire, he determined to devote himself exclusively to evangelism. "This one thing I do!" became a reality to him. As a result, millions of people heard the Gospel.

The believer must devote himself to "running the Christian race." No athlete succeeds by doing everything; he succeeds by *specializing*. There are those few athletes who seem proficient in many sports, but they are the exception. The winners are those who concentrate, who keep their eyes on the goal and let nothing distract them. They are devoted entirely to their calling. Like Nehemiah the wall-building governor, they reply to the distracting invitations, "I am doing a great work, so that I cannot come down!" (Neh. 6:3) "A double-minded man is unstable in all his ways" (James 1:8). Concentration is the secret of power. If a river is allowed to overflow its banks, the area around it becomes a swamp. But if that river is dammed and controlled, it becomes a source of power. It is wholly a matter of values and priorities, living for that which matters most.

### Direction (Phil. 3:13c)
The unsaved person is controlled by the past, but the Christian running the race looks toward the future. Imagine what would happen on the race course if the charioteers (or the runners) started looking behind them! It is bad enough for a plowman to look back (Luke 9:62), but for a charioteer to do so means a possible collision and serious injury.

We are accustomed to saying "past, present, future," but we should view time as flowing from the *future* into the *present* and then into the *past*. At least, the believer should be future-oriented, "forgetting those things which are behind." Please keep in mind that in Bible terminology, "to forget" does not mean "to fail to remember." Apart from senility, hypnosis, or a brain malfunction, no mature person can forget what has happened in the past. We may wish that we could erase certain bad memories, but we cannot. "To forget" in the Bible means "no longer to be influenced by or affected by." When God promises, "And their sins and iniquities will I remember no more" (Heb. 10:17), He is not suggesting that He will conveniently have a bad memory! This is impossible with God. What God is saying is, "I will no longer hold their sins against them. Their sins can no longer affect their standing with Me or influence My attitude toward them."

So, "forgetting those things which are behind" does not suggest an impossible feat of mental and psychological gymnastics by which we try to erase the sins and mistakes of the past. *It simply means that we break the power of the past by living for the future.* We cannot change the past, but we can change the *meaning* of the past. There were things in Paul's past that could have been weights to hold him back (1 Tim. 1:12-17), but they became inspirations to speed him ahead. The events did not change, but his understanding of them changed.

A good example of this principle is Joseph (Gen. 45:1-15). When he met his brothers the second time and revealed himself to them, he held no grudge against them. To be sure, they had mistreated him, but he saw the past from God's point of view. As a result he was unable to hold anything against his brothers. Joseph knew that God had a plan for his life—a race for him to run—and in fulfilling that plan and looking ahead, he broke the power of the past.

Too many Christians are shackled by regrets of the past. They are trying to run the race by looking backward! No wonder they stumble and fall and get in the way of other Christians! Some Christian runners are being distracted by the *successes* of the past, not the failures; and this is just as bad. "The things which are behind" must be set aside and "the things which are before" must take their place.

It is possible to have dissatisfaction, devotion, and direction, and still lose the race and the reward. There is a fourth essential.

## Determination (Phil. 3:14)

"I press!" This same verb is translated "I follow after" in Philippians 3:12, and it carries the idea of intense endeavor. The Greeks used it to describe a hunter eagerly pursuing his prey. A man does not become a winning athlete by listening to lectures, watching movies, reading books, or cheering at the games. He becomes a winning athlete by getting into the game and determining to win! The same zeal that Paul employed when he persecuted the church (Phil. 3:6), he displayed in serving Christ. Come to think of it, wouldn't it be wonderful if Christians put as much determination into their spiritual life as they do their golfing, fishing, or bowling?

There are two extremes to avoid here: (1) *"I* must do it all" and (2) *"God* must do it all!" The first describes the activist, the second the quietist, and both are heading for failure. "Let go and let God!" is a clever slogan, but it does not fully describe the process of Christian living. What quarterback would say to his team, "OK, men, just let go and let the coach do it all!" On the other hand, no quarterback would say, "Listen to me and forget what the coach says!" Both extremes are wrong.

The Christian runner with the spiritual mind realizes that God must work *in* him if he is going to win the race (Phil. 2:12-13). "Without Me ye can do nothing" (John 15:5). God works *in* us that He might work *through* us. As we apply ourselves to the things of the spiritual life, God is able to mature us and strengthen us for the race. "Exercise thyself rather unto godliness!" (1 Tim. 4:7-8) Some Christians are so busy "dying to self" that they never come back to life again to run the race! And others are so sure they can make it on their own that they never stop to read the Word, pray, or ask for the power of the Lord.

Toward what goal is the runner pressing with such spiritual determination? "The prize of the high [upward] calling of God in Christ Jesus" (Phil. 3:14). When he reaches the goal he will receive the reward! Again, Paul is not suggesting that we attain to heaven by our own efforts. He is simply saying that just as the athlete is rewarded for his performance, so the faithful believer will be crowned when Jesus Christ returns. (See 1 Cor. 9:24-27 for a parallel, and note that while only *one* athlete may receive a prize, *all* Christians may receive the reward. Furthermore, the laurel wreath of the Olympic Games will fade, but the crown Christ gives will never fade.) The important thing is that we reach the goal He has established for us. No matter how successful we may be in the eyes of men, we cannot be rewarded unless we "take hold of that for which Christ Jesus took hold of [us]" (Phil. 3:12, NIV).

## Discipline (Phil. 3:15-16)

It is not enough to run hard and win the race; the runner must also obey the rules. In the Greek games, the judges were very strict about this. Any infringement of the rules disqualified the athlete. He did not lose his citizenship (though he disgraced it), but he did lose his privilege to participate and win a prize. In Philippians 3:15-16, Paul emphasizes the importance of the Christian remembering the "spiritual rules" laid down in the Word.

One of the greatest athletes ever to come out of the United States was Jim Thorpe. At the 1912 Olympics at Stockholm, he won the pentathlon and the decathlon, and was undoubtedly the hero of the games. But the next year officials found that Thorpe had played semiprofessional baseball and therefore had forfeited his amateur standing. This meant that he had to return his gold medals and his trophy, and that his Olympic achievements were erased from the records. It was a high price to pay for breaking the rules. (Thorpe's medals were reinstated in 1985 by the Olympic Committee.)

This is what Paul has in mind in 1 Corinthians 9:24-27. "Any man who enters an athletic contest practices rigid self-control in training" (Phil. 3:25, WMS). If the athlete breaks training, he is disqualified; if he breaks the rules of the game, he is disqualified. "No contestant in the games is crowned, unless he competes according to the rules" (2 Tim. 2:5, WMS). The issue is not what *he* thinks or what the *spectators* think but what the judges say. One day each Christian will stand before the Judgment Seat of Christ (Rom. 14:10-12). The Greek word for "judgment seat" is *bema,* the very same word used to describe the place where the Olympic judges gave out the prizes! If we have disciplined ourselves to obey the rules, we shall receive a prize.

Bible history is filled with people who began the race with great success but failed at the end because they disregarded God's rules. They did not lose their salvation, but they did lose their rewards (1 Cor. 3:15). It happened to Lot (Gen. 19), Samson (Jud. 16), Saul (1 Sam. 28; 31), and Ananias and Sapphira (Acts 5). And it can happen to us! It is an exciting experience to run the race daily, "looking unto Jesus" (Heb. 12:1-2). It will be even more exciting when we experience that "upward calling" and Jesus returns to take us to heaven! Then we will stand before the *bema* to receive our rewards! It was this future prospect that motivated Paul, and it can also motivate us.

# CHAPTER NINE
# LIVING IN THE
# FUTURE TENSE
*Philippians 3:17-21*

How strange in a letter filled with joy to find Paul *weeping!* Perhaps he is weeping over himself and his difficult situation! No, he is a man with a *single mind,* and his circumstances do not discourage him. Is he weeping because of what some of the Roman Christians are doing to him? No, he has the *submissive mind* and will not permit people to rob him of his joy. These tears are not for himself at all; they are shed because of others. Because Paul has the *spiritual mind,* he is heartbroken over the way some professed Christians are living, people who "mind earthly things."

While we cannot be sure, it is likely that Philippians 3:18-19 describe the Judaizers and

their followers. Certainly Paul is writing about professed Christians and not people outside the church. The Judaizers were the "enemies of the cross of Christ" in that they added the Law of Moses to the work of redemption that Christ wrought on the cross. Their obedience to the Old Testament dietary laws would make a "god" out of the belly (see Col. 2:20-23); and their emphasis on circumcision would amount to glorying in that about which they ought to be ashamed (see Gal. 6:12-15). These men were not spiritually minded; they were earthly minded. They were holding on to earthly rituals and beliefs that God had given to Israel, and they were opposing the heavenly blessings that the Christian has in Christ (Eph. 1:3; 2:6; Col. 3:1-3).

The word "spiritual" has suffered as much abuse as the word "fellowship." Too many people think that a "spiritual Christian" is mystical, dreamy, impractical, and distant. When he prays, he shifts his voice into a sepulchral tone *in tremolo* and goes to great lengths to inform God of the things He already knows. Unfortunately, this kind of unctuous piety is a poor example of true spirituality. To be spiritually minded does not require one to be impractical and mystical. Quite the contrary, the spiritual mind makes the believer think more clearly and get things done more efficiently.

To be "spiritually minded" simply means to look at earth from heaven's point of view. "Give your heart to the heavenly things, not to the passing things of earth" (Col. 3:2, PH). "Practice occupying your minds with the things above, not with the things on earth" (Col. 3:2, WMS). D.L. Moody used to scold Christians for being "so heavenly minded they were no earthly good," and that exhortation still needs to be heeded. Christians have a dual citizenship—on earth and in heaven—and our citizenship in heaven ought to make us better people here on earth. The spiritually minded believer is not attracted by the "things" of this world. He makes his decisions on the basis of eternal values and not the passing fads of society. Lot chose the well-watered plain of Jordan because his values were worldly, and ultimately he lost everything. Moses refused the pleasures and treasures of Egypt because he had something infinitely more wonderful to live for (Heb. 11:24-26). "What shall it profit a man, if he shall gain the whole world, and lose his own soul?" (Mark 8:36)

"For our citizenship is in heaven" (Phil.

3:20, NASB). The Greek word translated "conversation" or "citizenship" is the word from which we get the English word "politics." It has to do with one's behavior as a citizen of a nation. Paul is encouraging us to have the spiritual mind, and he does this by pointing out the characteristics of the Christian whose citizenship is in heaven. Just as Philippi was a colony of Rome on foreign soil, so the church is a "colony of heaven" on earth.

## Our Names Are on Heaven's Record

The citizens of Philippi were privileged to be Roman citizens away from Rome. When a baby was born in Philippi, it was important that its name be registered on the legal records. When the lost sinner trusts Christ and becomes a citizen of heaven, his name is written in "the Book of Life" (Phil. 4:3).

Citizenship is important. When you travel to another country, it is essential that you have a passport that proves your citizenship. None of us wants to suffer the fate of Philip Nolan in the classic tale *The Man Without a Country*. Because he cursed the name of his country, Nolan was sentenced to live aboard ship and never again see his native land or even hear its name or news about its progress. For fifty-six years he was on an endless journey from ship to ship and sea to sea, and finally was buried at sea. He was a "man without a country."

The Christian's name is written in "the Book of Life," and this is what determines his final entrance into the heavenly country (Rev. 20:15). When you confess Christ on earth, He confesses your name in heaven (Matt. 10:32-33). Your name is written down in heaven (Luke 10:20) and it stands written forever. (The Greek verb "written" in Luke 10:20 is in the perfect tense: "it is once-for-all written and stands written.")

A friend in Washington, D.C., arranged for my oldest son and me to tour the White House. She told us to be at a certain gate at 8 o'clock in the morning and to be prepared to show evidence of who we were. David and I walked up to the gate, and the guard politely asked our names. We told him, showing our credentials. He said, "Yes, sir! Mr. Warren Wiersbe and David! You may enter!" We got into the White House because our names were written down on the proper list, and our names got on that list through the intercession of another. So it is with our entrance into heaven: because we have trusted Christ, our names are written down, and we will enter glory on His merits and intercession alone.

## We Speak Heaven's Language

Those who "mind earthly things" *talk* about earthly things. After all, what comes out of the mouth reveals what is in the heart (Matt. 12:34-37). The unsaved person does not understand the things of God's Spirit (1 Cor. 2:14-16), so how can he talk about them intelligently? The citizens of heaven understand spiritual things and enjoy discussing them and sharing them with one another.

"They are of the world: therefore speak they of the world, and the world heareth them. We are of God: he that knoweth God heareth us; he that is not of God heareth not us. Hereby know we the spirit of truth, and the spirit of error" (1 John 4:5-6).

But speaking heaven's language not only involves what we say, but also the way we say it. The spiritually minded Christian doesn't go around quoting Bible verses all day! But he is careful to speak in a manner that glorifies God. "Let your speech be alway with grace, seasoned with salt, that ye may know how ye ought to answer every man" (Col. 4:6). No believer ought ever to say, "Now take this with a grain of salt!" *Put the salt into your speech!* Salt prevents corruption. "Let no corrupt communication proceed out of your mouth, but that which is good to the use of edifying, that it may minister grace unto the hearers" (Eph. 4:29).

## We Obey Heaven's Laws

The citizens of Philippi were governed by Roman law, not Greek law, even though they were located hundreds of miles away from Rome. In fact, it was this policy that put Paul into jail when he first visited Philippi (Acts 16:16-24). Paul himself used his Roman citizenship to guarantee his protection under Roman law (Acts 16:35-40; 21:33-40; 22:24-30).

In Philippians 3:17, Paul warns the Philippian believers against imitating the wrong kind of citizens. "Be followers together of me." Of course, Paul was a follower of Christ, so his admonition is not egotistical! (1 Cor. 11:1) Paul knew himself to be an "alien" in this world, a "pilgrim and a stranger" (see 1 Peter 2:11). His life was governed by heaven's laws, and this is what made him different. He was concerned about others, not himself. He was interested in giving, not getting. His motive was love (2 Cor. 5:14), not hatred. By faith,

Paul obeyed the Word of God, knowing that one day he would be rewarded. Men might oppose him and persecute him now, but in that final day of reckoning, he would be the winner.

Sad to say, there are those today, like the Judaizers in Paul's day, who profess to be citizens of heaven, but whose lives do not show it. They may be zealous in their religious activities and even austere in their disciplines, but there is no evidence of the control of the Spirit of God in their lives. All that they do is energized by the flesh, and they get all the glory. It is bad enough that they are going astray, but they also lead other people astray. No wonder Paul wept over them.

### He Is Loyal to Heaven's Cause

The Cross of Jesus Christ is the theme of the Bible, the heart of the Gospel, and the chief source of praise in heaven (Rev. 5:8-10). The Cross is the proof of God's love for sinners (Rom. 5:8) and God's hatred for sin. The Cross condemns what the world values. It judges mankind and pronounces the true verdict: *Guilty!*

In what sense were the Judaizers the "enemies of the Cross of Christ"? For one thing, the Cross ended the Old Testament religion. When the veil of the temple was torn in two, God was announcing that the way to God was open through Christ (Heb. 10:19-25). When Jesus shouted, "It is finished!" He made one sacrifice for sins, and thus ended the whole sacrificial system (Heb. 10:1-14). By His death and resurrection, Jesus accomplished a "spiritual circumcision" that made ritual circumcision unnecessary (Col. 2:10-13). Everything that the Judaizers advocated had been eliminated by the death of Christ on the cross!

Furthermore, everything that they lived for was condemned by the Cross. Jesus had broken down the wall that stood between Jews and Gentiles (Eph. 2:14-16), and the Judaizers were rebuilding that wall! They were obeying "carnal [fleshly] ordinances" (Heb. 9:10), regulations that appealed to the flesh and were not directed by the Spirit. But the true believer crucifies the flesh (Gal. 5:24). He also crucifies the world (Gal. 6:14). Yet the Judaizers were minding "earthly things." It is the Cross that is central in the life of the believer. He does not glory in men, in religion, or in his own achievements; he glories in the Cross (Gal. 6:14).

Paul weeps because he knows the future of these men: "whose end is destruction" (Phil. 3:19). This word carries with it the idea of waste and "lostness." (It is translated "waste" in Mark 14:4.) Judas is called "the son of perdition," and this is the word used (John 17:12). A wasted life and an eternity of waste! In contrast, the true child of God, whose citizenship is in heaven, has a bright future.

### We Are Looking for Heaven's Lord

The Judaizers were living in the past tense, trying to get the Philippian believers to go back to Moses and the Law; but true Christians live in the future tense, anticipating the return of their Saviour (Phil. 3:20-21). As the *accountant* in Philippians 3:1-11, Paul discovered new *values*. As the *athlete* in Philippians 3:12-16, he displayed new *vigor*. Now as the *alien,* he experiences a new *vision:* "We look for the Saviour!" It is this anticipation of the coming of Christ that motivates the believer with the spiritual mind.

There is tremendous energy in the present power of a future hope. Because Abraham looked for a city, he was content to live in a tent (Heb. 11:13-16). Because Moses looked for the rewards of heaven, he was willing to forsake the treasures of earth (Heb. 11:24-26). Because of the "joy that was set before Him" (Heb. 12:2), Jesus was willing to endure the cross. The fact that Jesus Christ is returning is a powerful motive for dedicated living and devoted service *today.* "And every man that hath this hope in him purifieth himself, even as He is pure" (read 1 John 2:28–3:3).

The citizen of heaven, living on earth, is never discouraged because he knows that his Lord is one day going to return. He faithfully keeps on doing his job lest his Lord return and find him disobedient (Luke 12:40-48). The spiritually minded believer does not live for the things of this world; he anticipates the blessings of the world to come. This does not mean that he ignores or neglects his daily obligations; but it does mean that what he does today is governed by what Christ will do in the future.

Paul mentions particularly that the believer will receive a glorified body, like the body of Christ. Today we live in a "body of humiliation" (which is the meaning of the word translated "vile" in Phil. 3:21); but when we see Christ, we will receive a body of glory. It will happen in a moment, in the twinkling of an eye! (1 Cor. 15:42-53) At that moment, all the things of this world will be worthless to us—

just as they ought to be, relatively, today! If we are living in the future tense, then we will be exercising the spiritual mind and living for the things that really matter.

When Jesus returns, He will "subdue all things unto Himself" (Phil. 3:21b). That word "subdue" means "to arrange in ranks." Isn't that our problem today? *We do not arrange "things" in their proper order.* Our values are twisted. Consequently, our vigor is wasted on useless activities, and our vision is clouded so that the return of Christ is not a real motivating power in our lives. Living in the future tense means letting Christ arrange the "things" in life according to the proper rank. It means living "with eternity's values in view," and daring to believe God's promise that "he that doeth the will of God abideth forever" (1 John 2:17).

# CHAPTER TEN
# YOU DON'T HAVE TO WORRY!
*Philippians 4:1-9*

If anybody had an excuse for worrying, it was the Apostle Paul. His beloved Christian friends at Philippi were disagreeing with one another, and he was not there to help them. We have no idea what Euodia and Syntyche were disputing about, but whatever it was, it was bringing division into the church. Along with the potential division at Philippi, Paul had to face division among the believers at Rome (Phil. 1:14-17). Added to these burdens was the possibility of his own death! Yes, Paul had a good excuse to worry—*but he did not!* Instead, he took time to explain to us the secret of victory over worry.

What is worry? The Greek word translated "anxious" (careful) in Philippians 4:6 means "to be pulled in different directions." Our hopes pull us in one direction; our fears pull us the opposite direction; and we are pulled apart! The Old English root from which we get our word "worry" means "to strangle." If you have ever really worried, you know how it does strangle a person! In fact, worry has definite physical consequences: headaches,

neck pains, ulcers, even back pains. Worry affects our thinking, our digestion, and even our coordination.

From the spiritual point of view, worry is *wrong thinking* (the mind) and *wrong feeling* (the heart) about circumstances, people, and things. Worry is the greatest thief of joy. It is not enough for us, however, to tell ourselves to "quit worrying" because that will never capture the thief. Worry is an "inside job," and it takes more than good intentions to get the victory. The antidote to worry is the *secure mind:* "And the peace of God . . . shall keep [garrison, guard like a soldier] your hearts and minds through Christ Jesus" (Phil. 4:7). When you have the secure mind, the peace of God guards you (Phil. 4:7) and the God of peace guides you (Phil. 4:9). With that kind of protection—why worry?

If we are to conquer worry and experience the secure mind, we must meet the conditions that God has laid down. There are three: right praying (Phil. 4:6-7), right thinking (Phil. 4:8), and right living (Phil. 4:9).

**Right Praying (Phil. 4:6-7)**
Paul does not write, "Pray about it!" He is too wise to do that. He uses three different words to describe "right praying": *prayer, supplication,* and *thanksgiving.* "Right praying" involves all three. The word *prayer* is the general word for making requests known to the Lord. It carries the idea of adoration, devotion, and worship. Whenever we find ourselves worrying, our first action ought to be to get alone with God and worship Him. Adoration is what is needed. We must see the greatness and majesty of God! We must realize that He is big enough to solve our problems. Too often we rush into His presence and hastily tell Him our needs, when we ought to approach His throne calmly and in deepest reverence. The first step in "right praying" is *adoration.*

The second is *supplication,* an earnest sharing of our needs and problems. There is no place for halfhearted, insincere prayer! While we know we are not heard for our "much speaking" (Matt. 6:7-8), still we realize that our Father wants us to be earnest in our asking (Matt. 7:1-11). This is the way Jesus prayed in the Garden (Heb. 5:7), and while His closest disciples were sleeping, Jesus was sweating great drops of blood! Supplication is not a matter of carnal energy but of spiritual intensity (Rom. 15:30; Col. 4:12).

After adoration and supplication comes *appreciation*, giving thanks to God (see Eph. 5:20; Col. 3:15-17). Certainly the Father enjoys hearing His children say, "Thank You!" When Jesus healed ten lepers, only one of the ten returned to give thanks (Luke 17:11-19), and we wonder if the percentage is any higher today. We are eager to ask but slow to appreciate.

You will note that "right praying" is not something every Christian can do immediately, because "right praying" depends on the right kind of mind. This is why Paul's formula for peace is found at the *end* of Philippians and not at the *beginning*. If we have the *single mind* of Philippians 1 then we can give *adoration*. (How can a double-minded person ever praise God?) If we have the *submissive mind* of Philippians 2, we can come with *supplication*. (Would a person with a proud mind ask God for something?) If we have the *spiritual mind* of Philippians 3 we can show our *appreciation*. (A worldly minded person would not know that God had given him anything to appreciate!) In other words, we must practice Philippians 1, 2, and 3 if we are going to experience the *secure mind* of Philippians 4.

Paul counsels us to take "everything to God in prayer." "Don't worry about *anything*, but pray about *everything!*" is his admonition. We are prone to pray about the "big things" in life and forget to pray about the so-called "little things"—until they grow and become big things! Talking to God about *everything* that concerns us and Him is the first step toward victory over worry.

The result is that the "peace of God" guards the heart and the mind. You will remember that Paul was chained to a Roman soldier, guarded day and night. In like manner, "the peace of God" stands guard over the two areas that create worry—the heart (wrong feeling) and the mind (wrong thinking). When we give our hearts to Christ in salvation, we experience "peace with God" (Rom. 5:1); but the "peace of God" takes us a step farther into His blessings. This does not mean the absence of trials on the outside, but it does mean a quiet confidence within, regardless of circumstances, people, or things.

Daniel gives us a wonderful illustration of peace through prayer. When the king announced that none of his subjects was to pray to anyone except the king, Daniel went to his room, opened his windows, and prayed as before (Dan. 6:1-10). Note how Daniel prayed.

He "prayed, and gave thanks before his God" (Dan. 6:10) and he made supplication (Dan. 6:11). Prayer—supplication—thanksgiving! And the result was perfect peace *in the midst of difficulty!* Daniel was able to spend the night with the lions in perfect peace, while the king *in his palace* could not sleep (Dan. 6:18).

The first condition for the secure mind and victory over worry is right praying.

**Right Thinking (Phil. 4:8)**
Peace involves the heart *and the mind.* "Thou wilt keep him in perfect peace, whose mind is stayed on Thee: because he trusteth in Thee" (Isa. 26:3). Wrong thinking leads to wrong feeling, and before long the heart and mind are pulled apart and we are strangled by worry. We must realize that thoughts are real and powerful, even though they cannot be seen, weighed, or measured. We must bring "into captivity every thought to the obedience of Christ" (2 Cor. 10:5).

"Sow a thought, reap an action.
Sow an action, reap a habit.
Sow a habit, reap a character.
Sow a character, reap a destiny!"

Paul spells out in detail the things we ought to think about as Christians.

*Whatever is true.* Dr. Walter Cavert reported a survey on worry that indicated that only 8 percent of the things people worried about were legitimate matters of concern! The other 92 percent were either imaginary, never happened, or involved matters over which the people had no control anyway. Satan is the liar (John 8:44), and he wants to corrupt our minds with his lies (2 Cor. 11:3). "Yea, hath God said?" is the way he approaches us, just as he approached Eve (Gen. 3:1ff). The Holy Spirit controls our minds through truth (John 17:17; 1 John 5:6), but the devil tries to control them through lies. *Whenever we believe a lie, Satan takes over!*

*Whatever is honest and just.* This means "worthy of respect and right." There are many things that are not respectable, and Christians should not think about these things. This does not mean we hide our heads in the sand and avoid what is unpleasant and displeasing, but it does mean we do not focus our attention on dishonorable things and permit them to control our thoughts.

*Whatever is pure, lovely, and of good report.* "Pure" probably refers to moral purity, since the people then, as now, were constantly attacked by temptations to sexual impurity (Eph. 4:17-24; 5:8-12). "Lovely" means "beautiful, attractive." "Of good report" means "worth talking about, appealing." The believer must major on the high and noble thoughts, not the base thoughts of this corrupt world.

**Whatever possesses virtue and praise.** If it has *virtue,* it will motivate us to do better; and if it has *praise,* it is worth commending to others. No Christian can afford to waste "mind power" on thoughts that tear him down or that would tear others down if these thoughts were shared.

If you will compare this list to David's description of the Word of God in Psalm 19:7-9, you will see a parallel. The Christian who fills his heart and mind with God's Word will have a "built-in radar" for detecting wrong thoughts. "Great peace have they which love Thy Law" (Ps. 119:165). Right thinking is the result of daily meditation on the Word of God.

### Right Living (Phil. 4:9)

You cannot separate outward action and inward attitude. Sin always results in unrest (unless the conscience is seared), and purity ought to result in peace. "And the work of righteousness shall be peace; and the effect of righteousness quietness and peace" (Isa. 32:17). "But the wisdom that is from above is first pure, then peaceable" (James 3:17). Right living is a necessary condition for experiencing the peace of God.

Paul balances four activities: "learned and received" and "heard and seen." It is one thing to *learn* a truth, but quite another to *receive* it inwardly and make it a part of our inner man (see 1 Thes. 2:13). Facts in the head are not enough; we must also have truths in the heart. In Paul's ministry, he not only *taught* the Word but also *lived* it so that his listeners could see the truth in his life. Paul's experience ought to be our experience. We must learn the Word, receive it, hear it, and do it. "But be ye doers of the Word, and not hearers only" (James 1:22).

"The peace of God" is one test of whether or not we are in the will of God. "Let the peace that Christ can give keep on acting as umpire in your hearts" (Col. 3:15, WMS). If we are walking with the Lord, then the peace of God and the God of peace exercise their influence over our hearts. Whenever we disobey, we lose that peace and we know we have done something wrong. God's peace is the "umpire" that calls us "out"!

Right praying, right thinking, and right living: these are the conditions for having the secure mind and victory over worry. As Philippians 4 is the "peace chapter" of the New Testament, James 4 is the "war chapter." It begins with a question: "From whence come wars and fightings among you?" James explains the causes of war: *wrong praying* ("Ye ask, and receive not, because ye ask amiss," James 4:3), *wrong thinking* ("purify your hearts, ye double-minded," James 4:8), and *wrong living* ("know ye not that the friendship of the world is enmity with God?" James 4:4). There is no middle ground. Either we yield heart and mind to the Spirit of God and practice right praying, thinking, and living; or we yield to the flesh and find ourselves torn apart by worry.

There is no need to worry! And, worry is a sin! (Have you read Matt. 6:24-34 lately?) With the peace of God to guard us and the God of peace to guide us—*why worry?*

# CHAPTER ELEVEN
# THE SECRET
# OF CONTENTMENT
*Philippians 4:10-23*

"The trouble with him is that he's a thermometer and not a thermostat!"

This statement by one of his deacons aroused the pastor's curiosity. They were discussing possible board members, and Jim's name had come up.

"Pastor, it's like this," the deacon explained. "A thermometer doesn't change anything around it—it just registers the temperature. It's always going up and down. But a thermostat regulates the surroundings and changes them when they need to be changed. Jim is a thermometer—he lacks the power to change things. Instead, they change him!"

The Apostle Paul was a thermostat. Instead of having spiritual ups and downs as the situation changed, he went right on, steadily doing his work and serving Christ. His personal references at the close of this letter indicate that he was not the victim of circumstances but the victor over circumstances: "I can accept all things" (Phil. 4:11); "I can do all things" (Phil. 4:13); "I have all things" (Phil. 4:18). Paul did not have to be pampered to be content; he found his contentment in the spiritual resources abundantly provided by Christ.

Contentment is not complacency, nor is it a false peace based on ignorance. The complacent believer is unconcerned about others, while the contented Christian wants to share his blessings. Contentment is not escape from the battle, but rather an abiding peace and confidence in the midst of the battle. "I have learned, in whatsoever state I am, therewith to be content" (Phil. 4:11). Two words in that verse are vitally important—"learned" and "content."

The verb "learned" means "learned by experience." Paul's spiritual contentment was not something he had immediately after he was saved. He had to go through many difficult experiences of life in order to learn how to be content. The word "content" actually means "contained." It is a description of the man whose resources are within him so that he does not have to depend on substitutes without. The Greek word means "self-sufficient" and was a favorite word of the stoic philosophers. But the Christian is not sufficient in himself; he is sufficient in Christ. Because Christ lives within us, we are adequate for the demands of life.

In this chapter, Paul names three wonderful spiritual resources that make us adequate and give us contentment.

## The Overruling Providence of God (Phil. 4:10)

In this day of scientific achievement, we hear less and less about the providence of God. We sometimes get the idea that the world is a vast natural machine and that even God Himself cannot interrupt the wheels as they are turning. But the Word of God clearly teaches the providential workings of God in nature and in the lives of His people. The word "providence" comes from two Latin words: *pro,* meaning "before," and *video,* meaning "to see." God's providence simply means that God sees to it beforehand. It does not mean that God simply *knows* beforehand, because providence involves much more. It is the working of God in advance to arrange circumstances and situations for the fulfilling of His purposes.

The familiar story of Joseph and his brothers illustrates the meaning of providence (Gen. 37–50). Joseph's brothers envied him and sold him as a slave when he was only seventeen years old. He was taken to Egypt, and there God revealed that seven years of famine were coming after seven years of plenty. It was through Joseph's interpretation of Pharaoh's dreams that this fact was discovered. Because of that, Joseph was elevated to the position of second ruler in Egypt. After twenty years of separation, Joseph's brothers were reconciled to him, and they understood what the Lord had done.

"God did send me before you to preserve life!" said Joseph (Gen. 45:5). "But as for you, ye thought evil against me; but God meant it unto good" (Gen. 50:20). This is the providence of God: His hand ruling and overruling in the affairs of life. Paul experienced this divine providence in his life and ministry, and he was able to write, "And we know that all things work together for good to them that love God, to them that are the called according to His purpose" (Rom. 8:28). God in His providence had caused the church at Philippi to become concerned about Paul's needs, and it came at the very time Paul needed their love most! They had been concerned, but they had lacked the opportunity to help. Many Christians today have the opportunities, but they lack the concern!

Life is not a series of accidents; it is a series of appointments. "I will guide thee with Mine eye" (Ps. 32:8). Abraham called God "Jehovah-Jireh," meaning "the Lord will see to it" (Gen. 22:14). "And when He putteth forth His own sheep, He goeth before them" (John 10:4). This is the providence of God, a wonderful source of contentment.

## The Unfailing Power of God (Phil. 4:11-13)

Paul is quick to let his friends know that he is not complaining! His happiness does not depend on circumstances or things; his joy comes from something deeper, something apart from either poverty or prosperity. Most of us have learned how to "be abased," because when difficulties come we immediately run to the Lord! But few have learned how "to abound." Prosperity has done more damage to believers than has adversity. "I am rich, and increased with goods, and have need of nothing" (Rev. 3:17).

The word "instructed" in Philippians 4:12 is

not the same as "learned" in Philippians 4:11. "Instructed" means "initiated into the secret." This word was used by the pagan religions with reference to their "inner secrets." Through trial and testing, Paul was "initiated" into the wonderful secret of contentment in spite of poverty or prosperity. "I can do all things through Christ which strengtheneth me" (Phil. 4:13). It was the power of Christ within him that gave him spiritual contentment.

Fog had moved into O'Hare Field, the airport that serves Chicago, and my departure had been delayed. I was sitting in the terminal reading a book and quietly asking God to work out His plans for the trip. Near me was a gentleman waiting for the same plane, but he was pacing up and down like a caged lion, and the language he was using to describe the fog was making the atmosphere more dense! I thought to myself, "Here is a man without any inner resources." Later, he asked me how I could be so calm when the planes were all late, and I had the opportunity to share the Gospel with him.

While flying back to Chicago from upper New York via New York City, we had to stay in our holding pattern over Kennedy Airport for more than an hour. When the stewardess announced that we would be landing an hour late, a man across the aisle shouted, "Bring out the booze!" This was his only resource when things were going against him.

All of nature depends on hidden resources. The great trees send their roots down into the earth to draw up water and minerals. Rivers have their sources in the snow-capped mountains. The most important part of a tree is the part you cannot see, the root system, and the most important part of the Christian's life is the part that only God sees. Unless we draw on the deep resources of God by faith, we fail against the pressures of life. Paul depended on the power of Christ at work in his life (see Phil. 1:6, 21; 2:12-13; 3:10). "I can—through Christ!" was Paul's motto, and it can be our motto too.

"I am ready for anything through the strength of the One who lives within me," is the way J.B. Phillips translates Philippians 4:13. *The Living Bible* puts it this way: "I can do everything God asks me to with the help of Christ who gives me the strength and power." No matter which translation you prefer, they all say the same thing: the Christian has all the power *within* that he needs to be adequate for

the demands of life. We need only release this power by faith.

Every Christian ought to read *Hudson Taylor's Spiritual Secret,* by Dr. and Mrs. Howard Taylor, because it illustrates this principle of inner power in the life of a great missionary to China. For many years, Hudson Taylor worked hard and felt that he was trusting Christ to meet his needs, but somehow he had no joy or liberty in his ministry. Then a letter from a friend opened his eyes to the adequacy of Christ. "It is not by trusting my own faithfulness, but by looking away to the Faithful One!" he said. This was a turning point in his life. Moment by moment, he drew on the power of Christ for every responsibility of the day, and Christ's power carried him through.

Jesus teaches this same lesson in the sermon on the vine and branches in John 15. He is the Vine; we are the branches. A branch is good only for bearing fruit; otherwise you may as well burn it. The branch does not bear fruit through its own self-effort, but by drawing on the life of the Vine. "Without Me, ye can do nothing" (John 15:5). As the believer maintains his communion with Christ, the power of God is there to see him through. "I am self-sufficient in Christ's sufficiency" (Phil. 4:13, AMP).

The overruling providence of God and the unfailing power of God are two spiritual resources on which we can draw that we might be adequate for the tasks of life. But there is a third resource.

## The Unchanging Promise of God (Phil. 4:14-20)
Paul thanks the church at Philippi for their generous gift. He compares their giving to three very familiar things.

*A budding tree (v. 10).* The word "flourished" carries the idea of a flower or tree budding or blossoming. Often we go through "winter seasons" spiritually, but then the spring arrives and there is new life and blessing. The tree itself is not picked up and moved; the circumstances are not changed. The difference is *the new life within.*

*An investment (vv. 14-17).* Paul looked on their missionary gift as an investment that would pay them rich spiritual dividends. The word "communicate" is our familiar word "fellowship." The church entered into an arrangement of "giving and receiving"; the church gave *materially* to Paul, and received *spiritual-*

*ly* from the Lord. The Lord keeps the books and will never fail to pay one spiritual dividend! That church is poor that fails to share materially with others.

*A sacrifice (v. 18).* Paul looked on their gift as a spiritual sacrifice, laid on the altar to the glory of God. There are such things as "spiritual sacrifices" in the Christian life (see 1 Peter 2:5). We are to yield our bodies as spiritual sacrifices (Rom. 12:1-2), as well as the praise of our lips (Heb. 13:15). Good works are a sacrifice to the Lord (Heb. 13:16), and so are the lost souls that we are privileged to win to Christ (Rom. 15:16). Here, Paul sees the Philippian believers as priests, giving their offering as a sacrifice to the Lord. In the light of Malachi 1:6-14, we need to present the very finest that we have to the Lord.

But Paul does not see this gift as simply coming from Philippi. He sees it as the supply of his need from heaven. Paul's trust was in the Lord. There is an interesting contrast between Philippians 4:18 and 19. We might state it this way if we were to paraphrase Paul: "You met *my* need, and God is going to meet *your* need. You met *one* need that I have, but my God will meet *all* of your needs. You gave out of your *poverty*, but God will supply your needs out of His *riches* in glory!"

God has not promised to supply all our "greeds." When the child of God is in the will of God, serving for the glory of God, then he will have every need met. Hudson Taylor often said, "When God's work is done in God's way for God's glory, it will not lack for God's supply."

A young pastor came to a church that had been accustomed to raising its annual budget by means of suppers, bazaars, and the like. He told his officers he could not agree with their program. "Let's pray and ask God to meet every need," he suggested. "At the end of the month, pay all the bills and leave my salary till the last. If there isn't enough money for my salary, then I'm the one who suffers, and not the church. But I don't think anybody is going to suffer!" The officers were sure that both the pastor and the church would die, but such was not the case. Each month every bill was paid, and at the end of the year there was a surplus in the treasury for the first time in many years.

Contentment comes from adequate resources. Our resources are the providence of God, the power of God, and the promises of God. These resources made Paul sufficient for every demand of life, and they can make us sufficient too.

# CHAPTER TWELVE PUTTING PHILIPPIANS TO WORK

Now that you have completed your study of this exciting and practical letter, *don't lose what you have learned!* The best thing about Bible study isn't the learning but the *living.* So, here are a few suggestions for keeping the joy in your life.

*1. Surrender your mind to the Lord at the beginning of each day.* This is a part of dedication: "I beseech you therefore, brethren, by the mercies of God, that ye present your *bodies* a living sacrifice. . . . And be not conformed to this world: but be ye transformed by the renewing of your *mind,* that ye may prove what is that good, and acceptable, and perfect *will* of God" (Rom. 12:1-2). Give God your body, mind, and will—by faith—as you start each day.

*2. Let the Holy Spirit renew your mind through the Word.* Daily systematic reading of the Bible is a must if you are going to have victory and joy.

*3. As you pray, ask God to give you that day a single mind, a submissive mind, a spiritual mind, a secure mind.* As you contemplate the day's schedule, be sure that nothing you have planned robs you of the joy God wants you to have. Perhaps you must meet a person you don't especially like. Ask God to give you the submissive mind that you will need. Or, maybe you must go through a difficult experience. Then be sure you have the single mind, concerned with Christ and the Gospel, and not only with your own personal likes and dislikes.

*4. During the day, "mind your mind!"* If you find yourself losing your inner peace and joy, stop and take inventory. *Do I have the single mind? Did I just miss an opportunity to glorify Christ? Or was I a bit pushy, so that I lost the submissive mind?* If you discover you have sinned, then immediately confess it to the Lord (1 John 1:9). If possible, go back and remedy your mistake. If this cannot be done, ask God to give you another opportunity for witness.

5. *Guard the gates of your mind.* Remember Paul's admonition in Philippians 4:8: "Whatsoever things are true . . . honest . . . just . . . pure . . . lovely . . . of good report . . . think on these things." When an unkind or impure thought enters your mind, *deal with it instantly.* If you cultivate it, it will take root and grow—and rob you of your joy. Sometimes Satan will throw his "fiery darts" at you, and sometimes he will use other people to do it for him. One of the best ways to defeat the wrong kinds of thoughts is to fill your mind with Scripture; so take time to memorize the Word of God.

6. *Remember that your joy is not meant to be a selfish thing; it is God's way of glorifying Christ and helping others through you.* Jesus first, Others second, Yourself last; and the result is JOY.

# COLOSSIANS

## OUTLINE

**Key theme:** Jesus Christ is preeminent
**Key verse:** Colossians 1:18

I. **DOCTRINE: CHRIST'S PREEMINENCE DECLARED—chapter 1**
   A. In the Gospel message—1:1-12
   B. In redemption—1:13-14
   C. In Creation—1:15-17
   D. In the church—1:18-23
   E. In Paul's ministry—1:24-29

II. **DANGER: CHRIST'S PREEMINENCE DEFENDED—chapter 2**
   A. Beware of empty philosophies—2:1-10
   B. Beware of religious legalism—2:11-17
   C. Beware of man-made disciplines—2:18-23

III. **DUTY: CHRIST'S PREEMINENCE DEMONSTRATED—chapters 3–4**
   A. In person purity—3:1-11
   B. In Christian fellowship—13:12-17
   C. In the home—3:18-21
   D. In daily work—3:22–4:1
   E. In Christian witness—4:2-6
   F. In Christian service—4:7-18

## CONTENTS

# CHAPTER ONE
# FROM PAUL,
# WITH LOVE
## *Colossians 1:1-2*

Do the heavenly bodies have any influence over our lives? The millions of people who consult their horoscopes each day would say, "Yes!" In the United States, there are about 1,750 daily newspapers, and 1,220 of them carry astrological data!

Is there any relationship between diet and spiritual living?

Does God speak to us immediately, in our minds, or only through His Word, the Bible?

Do the Eastern religions have something to offer the evangelical Christian?

These questions sound very contemporary. Yet they are the very issues Paul dealt with in his magnificent Epistle to the Colossians. We need this important letter today just as they needed it back in A.D. 60 when Paul wrote it.

## The City
Colossae was one of three cities located about 100 miles inland from Ephesus. The other two cities were Laodicea and Hierapolis (Col. 4:13, 16). This area was a meeting point of East and West because an important trade route passed through there. At one time, all three cities were growing and prosperous, but gradually Colossae slipped into a second-rate position. It became what we would call a small town. Yet the church there was important enough to merit the attention of the Apostle Paul.

All kinds of philosophies mingled in this cosmopolitan area, and religious hucksters abounded. There was a large Jewish colony in Colossae, and there was also a constant influx of new ideas and doctrines from the East. It was fertile ground for religious speculations and heresies!

## The Church
Colossae probably would never have been mentioned in the New Testament had it not been for the church there. The city is never named in the Book of Acts because Paul did not start the Colossian church, nor did he ever visit it. Paul had *heard* of their faith (Col.

1:4, 9); but he had never seen these believers personally (Col. 2:1). Here was a church of unknown people, in a small town, receiving an inspired letter from the great Apostle Paul!

How did the Colossian church begin? It was the outgrowth of Paul's three-year ministry in Ephesus (Acts 19; 20:17-38). So effective was the witness of the church at Ephesus that "all they which dwelt in Asia heard the word of the Lord Jesus, both Jews and Greeks" (Acts 19:10). This would include people in Colossae, Laodicea, and Hierapolis.

When we examine the persons involved in the prison correspondence of Paul (see Eph., Phil., Col., Phile., and 2 Tim.), we can just about put the story together of how the Colossian church was founded. During Paul's ministry in Ephesus, at least two men from Colossae were brought to faith in Jesus Christ—Epaphras and Philemon (see Phile. 19). Epaphras apparently was one of the key founders of the church in Colossae, for he shared the Gospel with his friends there (Col. 1:7). He also had a ministry in the cities of Hierapolis and Laodicea (Col. 4:12-13).

Philemon had a church meeting in his home (Phile. 2). It is likely that Apphia and Archippus, mentioned in this verse, were respectively the wife and son of Philemon, and that Archippus was the pastor of the church (Col. 4:17).

There is a good lesson for us here: God does not always need an apostle, or a "full-time Christian worker" to get a ministry established. Nor does He need elaborate buildings and extensive organizations. Here were two laymen who were used of God to start ministries in at least three cities. It is God's plan that the Christians in the large urban areas like Ephesus reach out into the smaller towns and share the Gospel. Is *your* church helping to evangelize "small-town" mission fields?

The Colossian assembly was predominantly Gentile in its membership. The sins that Paul named (Col. 3:5-9) were commonly associated with the Gentiles, and his statement about the mystery applied more to the Gentiles than to the Jews (Col. 1:25-29). The church was probably about five years old when Paul wrote this letter.

## The Crisis
Why did Paul write this letter to the church in Colossae? Because a crisis had occurred that was about to destroy the ministry of the

church. By comparing the prison letters, we can arrive at the following reconstruction of events.

Paul was at that time a prisoner in Rome (Acts 21:17–28:31). He met a runaway slave named Onesimus who belonged to Philemon, one of the leaders of the church in Colossae. Paul led Onesimus to Christ. He then wrote his letter to Philemon, asking his friend to forgive Onesimus and receive him back as a brother in Christ.

About the same time, Epaphras showed up in Rome because he needed Paul's help. Some new doctrines were being taught in Colossae and were invading the church and creating problems. So Paul wrote this letter to the Colossians in order to refute these heretical teachings and establish the truth of the Gospel.

Epaphras remained with Paul in Rome (Col. 4:12-13). Onesimus and Tychicus carried Paul's epistles to their destinations: Ephesians 6:21; Colossians 4:7-9; and Philemon. Epaphras was called Paul's "fellow-prisoner," a title also given to Aristarchus (Col. 4:10; Phile. 23). This suggests that Epaphras *willingly* remained with Paul to assist him. Neither Aristarchus nor Epaphras was a prisoner because he broke the law and was arrested. They were Paul's willing companions, sacrificing their own comfort to help him.

What was the heresy that threatened the peace and purity of the Colossian church? It was a combination of Eastern philosophy and Jewish legalism, with elements of what Bible scholars call gnosticism (NOS-ti-cism). This term comes from the Greek word *gnosis* (KNOW-sis) which means "to know." (An *agnostic* is one who does not know.) The gnostics were the people who were "in the know" when it came to the deep things of God. They were the "spiritual aristocracy" in the church.

To begin with, this heresy promised people such a close union with God that they would achieve a "spiritual perfection." Spiritual fullness could be theirs only if they entered into the teachings and ceremonies prescribed. There was also a "full knowledge," a spiritual depth, that only the initiated could enjoy. This "wisdom" would release them from earthly things and put them in touch with heavenly things.

Of course, all of this teaching was but manmade philosophy based on traditions and not on divine truth (Col. 2:8). It grew out of the philosophical question, *Why is there evil in this world if creation was made by a holy God?* As these philosophers speculated and pondered, they came to the false conclusion that matter was evil. Their next false conclusion was that a holy God could not come into contact with evil matter, so there had to be a series of "emanations" from God to His creation. They believed in a powerful spirit world that used material things to attack mankind. They also held to a form of astrology, believing that angelic beings ruled heavenly bodies and influenced affairs on earth (see Col. 1:16; 2:10, 15).

Added to these Eastern speculations was a form of Jewish legalism. The teachers believed that the rite of circumcision was helpful in spiritual development (Col. 2:11). They taught that the Old Testament Law, especially the dietary laws, was also useful in attaining spiritual perfection (Col. 2:14-17). Definite rules and regulations told them what was evil and what was good (Col. 2:21).

Since to them matter was evil, they had to find some way to control their own human natures in this pursuit of perfection. Two different practices resulted. One school of thought held that the only way to conquer evil matter was by means of rigid discipline and asceticism (Col. 2:23). The other view taught that it was permissible to engage in all kinds of sin, since matter was evil anyway! It appears that the first opinion was the predominant one in Colossae.

It is easy to see how this kind of teaching undermined the very foundations of the Christian faith. To begin with, these heretics attacked the person and work of Jesus Christ. To them, He was merely one of God's many "emanations" and not the very Son of God, come in the flesh. The Incarnation means God *with us* (Matt. 1:23), but these false teachers claimed that God was keeping His distance from us! When we trust the Son of God, there is no need for intermediary beings between us and heaven!

In His work on the cross, Jesus Christ settled the sin question (Col. 1:20) and completely defeated all satanic forces (Col. 2:15). He put an end to the legal demands of the Law (Col. 2:14-17). In fact, Jesus Christ alone is the Preeminent One! (Col. 1:18; 3:11) All that the believer needs is Jesus!

Matter is not evil, and the human body is not evil. Each person is born with a fallen human nature that wants to control the body and use it for sin; but the body itself is not evil. If that were the case, Jesus Christ would never have come to earth in a human body. Nor would He have enjoyed the everyday blessings of life as He ministered on earth, such as attending wedding feasts and accepting invitations to dinner. Diets and disciplines can be good for one's health, but they have no power to develop true spirituality (Col. 2:20-23).

As for astrology and the influence of angels and heavenly bodies, Paul denounced this with vigor. On the cross, Jesus won a complete victory over all satanic powers (Col. 2:15). Christians do not need to turn to the rudiments of the world (Col. 2:8, 20). This word translated *rudiments* means "elemental beings" or "elementary principles." In this case, it refers to the beings that (according to the gnostics) controlled the heavenly bodies that in turn controlled events on earth. Believers who consult horoscopes substitute superstition for revelation and deny the person and work of Christ.

This false teaching was a deceptive combination of many things: Jewish legalism, Oriental philosophy, pagan astrology, mysticism, asceticism, and even a touch of Christianity. There was something for everybody, and this was what made it so dangerous. The false teachers claimed that they were not *denying* the Christian faith, but only lifting it to a higher level. They offered fullness and freedom, a satisfying life that solved all the problems that people face.

Do we have any of this heresy today? Yes, we do; and it is just as deceptive and dangerous! When we make Jesus Christ and the Christian revelation only *part* of a total religious system or philosophy, we cease to give Him the preeminence. When we strive for "spiritual perfection" or "spiritual fullness" by means of formulas, disciplines, or rituals, we go backward instead of forward. Christian believers must beware of mixing their Christian faith with such alluring things as yoga, transcendental meditation, Oriental mysticism, and the like. We must also beware of "deeper life" teachers who offer a system for victory and fullness that bypasses devotion to Jesus Christ. In all things, He must have the preeminence!

This heresy was in direct contrast to the teaching of Paul. It took a negative view of life: "God is far away, matter is evil, and demonic forces are constantly threatening us." The Christian faith teaches that God is near

us, that God made all things good (though they can be used for evil), and that Christ has delivered His people from the powers of darkness (Col. 1:13). This heresy turned the world into a frightful prison, while Jesus made it clear that the Father is at work in this world caring for His own. Finally, these false teachers tried to change people from the outside, by means of diets and disciplines. But true spiritual growth comes from within.

**The Correspondence**
With this background, we can now look at Paul's Letter to the Colossians and get an overview of what he has written. We know that his Epistle to the Ephesians was written and sent about the same time as his Colossian letter. Keeping this in mind, we can discover many parallels between these two letters. However, the emphasis in Ephesians is on the church, the body of Christ; but the emphasis in Colossians is on Christ, the Head of the body.

In this letter, Paul used the vocabulary of the false teachers, but he did not use their definitions. He used these words in their true Christian meaning. As we study Colossians, we will find words such as *fullness, perfect, complete.* all of which were used by the gnostic heretics. Over thirty times Paul used the little word *all.* He also wrote about *wisdom* which was a key term in the gnostic vocabulary; he had a great deal to say about angels and spirit powers too.

His main theme was *the preeminence of Jesus Christ* (Col. 1:18; 3:11). There is no need for us to worry about angelic mediators or spiritual emanations. God has sent His Son to die for us! Every person who believes on Jesus Christ is saved and is a part of His body, the church, of which He is the Head (Col. 1:18). We are united to Christ in a wonderful living relationship!

Furthermore, nothing need be added to this relationship, because each believer is "complete in Him" (Col. 2:10). All of God's fullness dwells in Christ (Col. 2:9), and we share that fullness! "For in Christ all the fullness of the Deity lives in bodily form, and you have been given fullness in Christ" (Col. 2:9-10, NIV).

While in an airport waiting for my plane to be called, I was approached by a young man who wanted to sell me a book. One look at the garish cover told me that the book was filled with Oriental myths and philosophies.

"I have a book here that meets all my

needs," I told the young man, and I reached into my briefcase and took out my Bible.

"Oh, we aren't against the Bible!" he assured me. "It's just that we have something more, and it makes our faith even better."

"Nobody can give me more than Jesus Christ has already given me," I replied. I turned to Colossians 2, but by that time the young man was hurrying down the corridor.

Sad to say, there are many Christians who actually believe that some person, religious system, or discipline can add something to their spiritual experience. But they already have everything they ever will need in the person and work of Jesus Christ.

Paul did not begin by attacking the false teachers and their doctrines. He began by exalting Jesus Christ and showing His preeminence in five areas: the Gospel message, redemption, Creation, the church, and Paul's own ministry. The people to whom Paul was writing had become Christians because of the Gospel message brought to them by Epaphras. If this message was wrong, then they were not saved at all!

Once he had established the preeminence of Christ, then Paul attacked the heretics on their own ground. In Colossians 2, Paul exposed the false origin of their teachings and showed how their teachings contradicted everything Paul taught about Jesus Christ. The believer who masters this chapter is not likely to be led astray by some alluring and enticing "new-and-improved brand of Christianity."

But Paul did not think his task completed when he had refuted the heretics, for he still had some important words for the church. In Colossians 3–4, Paul explained the greatest antidote to false teaching—*a godly life.* Those who say, "I don't care what you believe, just so long as you live a good life" are not thinking logically. *What we believe determines how we behave.* If we believe that matter is evil, we will use our bodies one way; but if we believe that our bodies are temples of the Holy Spirit, we will live accordingly.

Wrong doctrine always leads to wrong living. Right doctrine should lead to right living. In the two concluding chapters, Paul applied the preeminence of Christ to the daily affairs of life. If Christ is truly preeminent in our lives, then we will glorify Him by keeping pure, by enjoying fellowship with other saints, by loving each other at home and being faithful at work, and by seeking to witness for Christ and serve Him effectively. Unless doctrine

leads to duty, it is of no use to us.

Many Bible scholars have concluded that Colossians is the most profound letter Paul ever wrote. This must not keep us from reading and studying this wonderful letter. But we must be cautioned against a superficial approach to these chapters. Unless we depend on the Spirit of God to teach us, we will miss the truths God wants us to learn.

The church today desperately needs the message of Colossians. We live in a day when religious toleration is interpreted to mean "one religion is just as good as another." Some people try to take the best from various religious systems and manufacture their own private religion. To many people, Jesus Christ is only *one* of several great religious teachers, with no more authority than they. He may be prominent, but He is definitely not preeminent.

This is an age of "syncretism." People are trying to harmonize and unite many different schools of thought and come up with a superior religion. Our evangelical churches are in danger of diluting the faith in their loving attempt to understand the beliefs of others. Mysticism, legalism, Eastern religions, asceticism, and man-made philosophies are secretly creeping into churches. They are not denying Christ, but they are dethroning Him and robbing Him of His rightful place of preeminence.

As we study this exciting letter, we must heed Paul's warnings: "Lest any man should beguile you" (Col. 2:4), "Lest any man spoil you" (Col. 2:8), "Let no man therefore judge you!" (Col. 2:16)

# CHAPTER TWO
# MIRACLES
# AT COLOSSAE
*Colossians 1:3-8*

The famous Scottish preacher, Alexander Whyte, was known as an appreciator. He loved to write postcards to people, thanking them for some kindness or blessing they had brought to his life. Those messages often brought a touch of encouragement to a heart just when it was needed most. Appreciation is great medicine for the soul.

The Apostle Paul was a great encourager, and this epistle is a good example of the grace of thanksgiving. In this section (which is one long sentence in the original Greek), he gives thanks for what Christ has done in the lives of the Colossian Christians. But he also mentions thanksgiving in five other places in this letter: Colossians 1:12; 2:7; 3:15, 17; and 4:2. When you recall that Paul wrote this letter *in prison,* his attitude of thanksgiving is even more wonderful.

Like Paul, we should be grateful for what God is doing in the lives of others. As Christians, we are all members of one body (1 Cor. 12:12-13). If one member of the body is strengthened, this helps to strengthen the entire body. If one church experiences a revival touch from God, it will help all the churches. In this expression of thanksgiving, Paul traced the stages in the spiritual experience of the Colossian believers.

**They Heard the Gospel (Col. 1:5b-7)**
The Good News of the Gospel was not native to their city. It had to be brought to them; and in their case, Epaphras was the messenger. He was himself a citizen of Colossae (Col. 4:12-13), but he had come in contact with Paul and had been converted to Jesus Christ. This was probably during Paul's great three-year ministry in Ephesus (Acts 19:10).

Once Epaphras had been saved, he shared this thrilling news with his relatives and friends back home. Perhaps it would have been exciting for Epaphras to stay with Paul in Ephesus where so many wonderful things were taking place. But his first responsibility was to take the Gospel to his own home city (see Mark 5:19).

The Gospel is the Good News that Jesus Christ has solved the problem of sin through His death, burial, and resurrection. The word *Gospel* means "Good News." Unfortunately, some people witness as though the Gospel is the bad news of condemnation.

I recall one church officer who was more of a prosecuting attorney than a Christian witness. Though he constantly reproved people for their sins, he failed to share the Good News of forgiveness through faith in Christ.

But we can learn a lesson from him. In our witnessing, we should remember to emphasize the good news of the Gospel (see 1 Cor. 15:1-8). In this section in his Letter to the Colossians, Paul reviews the characteristics of this exciting Gospel message.

*It centers in a Person—Jesus Christ.* The theme of this epistle is the preeminence of Jesus Christ, and He is certainly preeminent in the Gospel. The false teachers who had invaded the fellowship in Colossae were trying to remove Jesus Christ from His place of preeminence; but to do this was to destroy the Gospel. It is *Christ* who died for us, and who arose again. The Gospel message does not center in a philosophy, a doctrine, or a religious system. It centers in Jesus Christ, the Son of God.

*It is the "Word of truth" (v. 5, NIV).* This means that it came from God and can be trusted. "Thy Word is truth" (John 17:17). There are many messages and ideas that can be called *true,* but only God's Word can be called *truth.* Satan is the liar; to believe his lies is to be led astray into death (John 8:44). Jesus is the Truth (John 14:6); when we trust Him, we experience life. Men have tried to destroy God's truth, but they have failed. The Word of truth still stands!

Everybody has faith in something. But faith is only as good as the object in which a person puts his trust. The jungle pagan worships a god of stone; the educated city pagan worships money or possessions or status. In both cases, faith is empty. The true Christian believer has faith in Jesus Christ, and that faith is based on the Word of truth. Any other kind of faith is but superstition—it cannot save.

*It is the message of God's grace (v. 6b).* Two words in the Christian vocabulary are often confused: *grace* and *mercy.* God in His grace gives me what I do not deserve. Yet God in His mercy does not give me what I do deserve. Grace is God's favor shown to undeserving sinners. The reason the Gospel is *good* news is because of grace: God is willing and able to save all who will trust Jesus Christ.

John Selden (1584–1654) was a leading historian and legal authority in England. He had a library of 8,000 volumes and was recognized for his learning. When he was dying, he said to Archbishop Ussher: "I have surveyed most of the learning that is among the sons of men, and my study is filled with books and manuscripts on various subjects. But at present, I cannot recollect any passage out of all my books and papers whereon I can rest my soul, save this from the sacred Scriptures: 'The grace of God that bringeth salvation hath appeared to all men' (Titus 2:11)."

*It is for the whole world (v. 6).* When I was a young pastor, one of my favorite preachers was Dr. Walter Wilson of Kansas City. He had a unique way of making old truths seem new and exciting. I once heard him quote John 3:16 and ask, "If you were to give a gift that would be suitable for the whole world, what would you give?"

He then listed several possibilities and showed how those gifts could not suit everybody: books (many people cannot read); foods (people eat different things in different parts of the world); clothing (climates are different); money (not every culture makes use of money). He came to the logical conclusion that only the Gospel, with its gift of eternal life, was suitable for the whole world; and he was right.

Paul said that the Gospel was bearing fruit in all the world. The Word of God is the only seed that can be planted anywhere in the world and bear fruit. The Gospel can be preached "to every creature which is under heaven" (Col. 1:23). Paul's emphasis was on "every man" (Col. 1:28). False teachers do not take their message to all the world. They go where the Gospel has already gone and try to lead believers astray. *They have no good news for lost sinners!*

If people are to be saved, they must hear the Gospel of Jesus Christ. And if they are to hear, we who are saved must carry the message. Are you doing your part?

**They Believed in Jesus Christ (Col. 1:4)**
It is possible to hear and not believe, even though the Word of God has the power to generate faith in those who hear (Rom. 10:17). Millions of people have heard the Good News of salvation and yet not believed. But those who believe in Jesus Christ receive from God the gift of eternal life (John 3:14-18).

We are not saved by faith *in faith.* There is a cult of "believism" today that promotes faith but has little to do with Jesus Christ. Even some popular songs carry the message of "faith in faith." The modern attitude is, "If you believe, you are safe." But the obvious question is, "Believe in *what?*" Their answer: "Just believe!"

Nor are we saved by faith *in a set of doctrines.* I have often told the story about the famous evangelist, George Whitefield, who was witnessing to a man. "What do you be-

lieve?" Whitefield asked. The man replied, "I believe what my church believes."

"And what does your church believe?" asked the evangelist.

"What I believe," replied the man.

Undaunted, Whitefield tried again and asked, "And what do you *both* believe?"

"Why, we both believe the same thing!" was the man's evasive reply.

Saving faith involves the mind, the emotions, and the will. With the mind we understand the truth of the Gospel, and with the heart we feel conviction and the need to be saved. But it is only when we exercise the will and commit ourselves to Christ that the process is complete. Faith is not mental assent to a body of doctrines, no matter how true those doctrines may be. Faith is not emotional concern. *Faith is commitment to Jesus Christ.*

When missionary John G. Paton was translating the Bible in the Outer Hebrides, he searched for the exact word to translate *believe.* Finally, he discovered it: the word meant "lean your whole weight upon." That is what saving faith is—leaning your whole weight upon Jesus Christ.

Saving faith is grounded in the Gospel (Col. 1:23). It is the Word of God that gives us assurance. As we grow in the Lord, our faith becomes steadfast (Col. 2:5) and established (Col. 2:7).

The false teachers who had come to Colossae tried to undermine the saints' faith in Christ and the Word. This same kind of undermining goes on today. Any religious teaching that dethrones Jesus Christ, or that makes salvation other than an experience of God's grace through faith, is either confused or antichristian and born of Satan.

One final thought: the experience of the believers in Colossae was so wonderful that people talked about it! Paul heard about it from Epaphras; the false teachers heard about it and decided to visit the Colossian assembly to see the remarkable change for themselves.

You cannot keep silent once you have experienced salvation in Jesus Christ. Is your Christian life the kind that encourages others and makes it easy for them to witness? Is your church fellowship so exciting that even the unsaved are taking notice?

**They Were Discipled (Col. 1:7)**
Epaphras did not simply lead the Colossians to Christ and then abandon them. He taught them the Word and sought to establish their

faith. The word translated "learned" in Colossians 1:7 is related to the word *disciple* in the Greek language. It is the same word Jesus used: "Learn of Me" (Matt. 11:29) or, in effect, "Become My disciple."

These new believers were in danger of turning from the truth and following the false teachers. Paul reminded them that it was Epaphras who led them to Christ, discipled them, and taught them the Word. The word *before* (Col. 1:5) probably means "before these false teachers appeared on the scene." Like the Colossians, we should beware of any religious leader who does not seek to win lost souls, but who devotes himself to "stealing sheep" from the flocks of others.

We should never forget that new Christians must be discipled. Just as the newborn baby needs loving care and protection till he can care for himself, so the new Christian needs discipling. The Great Commission does not stop with the salvation of the lost, for in that commission Jesus commanded us to teach converts the Word as well (Matt. 28:19-20). That is what the fellowship of the local church is all about. The New Testament does not teach the kind of "individual Christianity" that is so prevalent today—people who ignore the local church and who find all their spiritual food in books, radio, TV, or cassette tapes.

Epaphras was a faithful minister. He not only won people to Christ, but he taught them the Word and helped them to grow. He also prayed for them (Col. 4:12-13) that they might become mature in Jesus Christ. When danger threatened the members of the church, Epaphras went to Rome to get counsel from Paul. He loved his people and wanted to protect them from false doctrines that would destroy the fellowship and hinder their spiritual development.

The word *disciple* is found more than 260 times in the Gospels and Acts, and the verb translated, "to learn as a disciple" is found 25 times in the New Testament. In that day, a disciple was not simply a person who sat and listened to a teacher. He was someone who lived with the teacher and who learned by listening, looking, and living. Discipleship involved more than enrolling in a school and attending lectures. It meant total surrender to the teacher. It meant learning by living. Perhaps our modern-day medical students or trade apprentices come close to illustrating the meaning of discipleship.

But we who disciple other believers must be careful not to get in the way. We are not to make disciples *for ourselves,* but for Jesus Christ. We must relate people to Him so that they love and obey Him. Epaphras faithfully taught his people and related them to Jesus Christ, but the false teachers came in and tried to "draw away disciples." (For Paul's warning about this problem, see Acts 20:28-30.) Human nature has the tendency to want to follow men instead of God—to want "something new" instead of the basic foundational truths of the Gospel.

Now we come to the results of Epaphras' efforts.

### They Became Faithful in Christ (Col. 1:6, 8)

The Word of God is seed (Luke 8:11). This means the Word has life in it (Heb. 4:12). When it is planted in the heart, it can produce fruit. "All over the world this Gospel is producing fruit and growing" (Col. 1:6, NIV).

Near King's Cross station in London, England, there is a cemetery containing a unique grave, that of the agnostic Lady Ann Grimston. She is buried in a marble tomb, marked by a marble slab. Before she died, she said sarcastically to a friend, "I shall live again as surely as a tree will grow from my body."

An unbeliever, Lady Ann Grimston did not believe that there was life after death. However, *a tree did grow from her grave!* A tiny seed took root, and as it grew, it cracked the marble and even tore the metal railing out of the ground! There is life and power in a seed, and there is life and power in the Word of God.

When God's Word is planted and cultivated, it produces fruit. Faith, hope, and love are among the firstfruits in the spiritual harvest. These spiritual graces are among the evidences that a person has truly been born again (see Rom. 5:1-4; Eph. 1:13-15; 1 Thes. 1:3; Heb. 6:9-12; 1 Peter 1:3-9).

*Faith* comes through the hearing of God's Word (Rom. 10:17). Our Christian lives start with *saving* faith; but this is only the beginning. We learn to walk by faith (2 Cor. 5:7) and work by faith (1 Thes. 1:3). It is faith that gives power to prayer (Luke 17:5-6). Faith is a shield that protects us from Satan's fiery darts (Eph. 6:16).

*Love* is another evidence of true salvation, for the unsaved person is wrapped up mainly in himself (Eph. 2:1-3). The fact that these people loved *all* the saints was proof that God had changed them and given them eternal life.

Christian love is not a shallow feeling that we manufacture; it is the work of the Holy Spirit in our hearts (Rom. 5:5; Col. 1:8). It is worth noting that Colossians 1:8 is the only verse in the letter that mentions the Holy Spirit, and it is in connection with love.

This Spirit-given love was for "all the saints" (Col. 1:4) and not only for the people of their own fellowship. As Christians, we also need to realize the vastness of God's love and share it with all the saints (Eph. 3:17-19). Believers should be "knit together in love" (Col. 2:2) so that there will be a true spiritual unity to the glory of God. The bond that unites us is love (Col. 3:14). Uniformity is the result of compulsion from the outside; unity is the result of compassion on the inside.

*Hope* is also a characteristic of the believer. Unsaved people are without hope because they are without God (Eph. 2:11-12). Those outside of Christ have no hope (1 Thes. 4:13). In the Bible, hope does not mean "hope so." Our hope in Christ is as definite and assured as our faith in Christ. Because Christ is in us, we have the "hope of glory" (Col. 1:27).

The false teachers tried to unsettle the Colossian believers and move them away from the hope of the Gospel (Col. 1:23). But Paul made it clear that this hope is "laid up" for believers in heaven (Col. 1:5). The word translated "laid up" carries the meaning of "to be reserved, to be set aside for someone." It was used to refer to money laid up or hidden. The tense of the verb indicates that this hope has *once and for all* been reserved so that nothing can take it from us. Not only has this hope (our glorious inheritance in glory) been reserved for us, but we are being kept by God's power so that we can be sure of enjoying heaven one day (1 Peter 1:1-5). We are being guarded for glory!

What is the relationship between faith, hope, and love? Certainly the more we love someone, the more we will trust him. We do not trust a casual acquaintance to the same degree that we trust a confidential friend. As we come to know God better, we trust Him more and we love Him more. Love and faith encourage each other.

But hope also has a valuable contribution to make. Wherever there is a relationship of faith and love, there will be a growing hope. When a man and woman fall in love and learn to trust each other in that love, their future always becomes brighter. In fact, Paul taught that hope is a motivating power for love and for

faith: "The faith and love that spring from the hope that is stored up for you in heaven" (Col. 1:5, NIV).

The blessed hope of seeing Jesus Christ and going to heaven to be with Him is a powerful force in the Christian's life. When we realize the joy we shall have in heaven, it makes us love Him more. The fact that we *know* we shall be with Him in glory encourages us to trust Him more. Even the problems and trials here on earth do not move us away from that hope.

I have noticed that the prospect of a future happiness has a way of making people love one another more. Have you ever watched children just before Christmas or a family vacation? The bright promise of heaven encourages our faith and expands our love. Then faith and love work together to make the present more enjoyable and the future more exciting.

Divisions and dissensions among Christians are tragic. I am not suggesting that we all get together in a "super church," but I do feel that there could be more love and understanding among God's people. The fact that we are going to be together in heaven ought to encourage us to love each other on earth. This is one reason why Christ has already given us His glory within. "And the glory which Thou gavest Me I have given them; that they may be one, even as We are One" (John 17:22).

The hope of seeing Christ and going to heaven is not only a motivation for faith and love, but it is also a motivation for holy living. "And every man that hath this hope in Him purifieth himself, even as He is pure" (1 John 3:3). When I was a young Christian, an older friend warned me, "Don't be caught doing anything that would embarrass you if Jesus returned!" That is a rather negative view of the promise of heaven, even though it does have some merit. In fact, John warns us that if we do not abide in Christ (keep in fellowship with Him in obedience), we may be ashamed when He returns (1 John 2:28).

But there is a positive side to this truth. We should keep our lives clean so that when Jesus Christ *does* return, nothing will cloud our first meeting with Him. We will enter into the joy and glory of His presence with confidence and love! Peter called this a "rich welcome" into the everlasting kingdom (2 Peter 1:11, NIV).

The hope of heaven is also an encouragement in times of suffering (1 Peter 1:4-9). As believers, we have our share of suffering; but in the midst of trials, we can rejoice "with joy unspeakable and full of glory" (1 Peter 1:8). When unbelievers suffer, they get discouraged and they want to give up. But when Christians suffer, their faith can become stronger and their love can deepen because their hope shines brighter.

How do we know that we have this hope? The promise is given in "the Word of the truth of the Gospel" (Col. 1:5). We believers do not have to "work up" a good feeling of hope. God's unchanging Word assures us that our hope is secure in Christ. In fact, this hope is compared to an anchor (Heb. 6:19) that can never break or drift.

No wonder Paul was thankful for the believers in Colossae! God had given Paul "special miracles" at Ephesus (Acts 19:11). But no miracle is greater than the salvation of the lost sinner. Through the faithful witness of Epaphras, God performed miracles of grace in Colossae.

Have you experienced the miracle of salvation?

If you have, then keep growing and being fruitful for the Lord. The same Word that gave you life when you trusted Christ will continue to nourish that life and make you a faithful, fruitful Christian.

Are there any "Gospel miracles" of grace taking place where you live?

# CHAPTER THREE
# A PRISONER'S PRAYER
*Colossians 1:9-12*

The prayers in Paul's prison letters are certainly unique. To begin with, he prays for others and not for himself. The requests in his prayers center on *spiritual* blessings, not on material or physical matters. Of course, it is not wrong to pray about physical or material needs. But spiritual needs are vastly more important.

How would you pray for a group of people you had never seen? All that Paul knew about the believers in Colossae he learned from their faithful pastor, Epaphras. Paul knew of the false teaching that was threatening the church, so he centered his praying on that problem. In his prayer, Paul made three requests.

## He Prayed for Spiritual Intelligence (Col. 1:9)

The false teachers promised the Colossian believers that they would be "in the know" if they accepted the new doctrines. Words like *knowledge, wisdom,* and *spiritual understanding* were a part of their religious vocabulary; so Paul used these words in his prayer.

Satan is so deceptive! He likes to borrow Christian vocabulary, but he does not use the Christian dictionary! Long before the false teachers had adopted these terms, the words had been in the Christian vocabulary.

The phrase, *for this cause,* relates the prayer to what Paul had written in Colossians 1:6: "And knew the grace of God in truth." The report from Epaphras convinced Paul that these believers truly knew Christ and were born again. But there was much more to learn *from* Him and *about* Him! "You do not need a new spiritual experience," Paul was saying. "You only need to grow in the experience you have already had."

When a person is born into God's family by faith in Jesus Christ, he is born with all that he needs for growth and maturity. This is the theme of Colossians: "And you are complete in Him" (Col. 2:10). No other experience is needed than the new birth. "Do not look for something new," Paul warned the church. "Continue to grow in that which you received at the beginning" (author's paraphrase).

Every believer needs to have "the knowledge of His will." The Greek word translated "knowledge" in this verse carries the meaning of "full knowledge." There is always more to learn about God and His will for our lives. No Christian would ever dare to say that he had "arrived" and needed to learn nothing more. Like the college freshman who handed in a ten-page report on "The History of the Universe," that Christian would only declare his ignorance.

The will of God is an important part of a successful Christian life. God wants us to *know* His will (Acts 22:14) and *understand* it (Eph. 5:17). God is not a distant dictator who issues orders and never explains. Because we are His friends, we can know what He is doing and why He is doing it (John 15:13-15). As we study His Word and pray, we discover new and exciting truths about God's will for His people.

The word *filled* is a key word in Colossians. It was also a key word in the teachings of the false teachers who had invaded the Colossian church. Paul used it many times (see Col. 1:19, 25; 2:2, 9-10; 4:12, 17 [*complete* = "filled full"]). The word carries the idea of being fully equipped. It was used to describe a ship that was ready for a voyage. The believer has in Christ all that he needs for the voyage of life. "And you are complete in Him" (Col. 2:10). "And of His fullness have all we received" (John 1:16).

In the language of the New Testament, to be *filled* means to be "controlled by." When we are filled with anger, we are controlled by anger. To be "filled with the Spirit" (Eph. 5:18) means to be "controlled by the Spirit." Paul's prayer, then, is that these believers might be controlled by the full knowledge of God's will.

But how does this take place? How can believers grow in the full knowledge of God's will? Paul's closing words of Colossians 1:9 tell us: "By means of all wisdom and spiritual insight" (literal translation). *We understand the will of God through the Word of God.* The Holy Spirit teaches us as we submit to Him (John 14:26; 16:13). As we pray and sincerely seek God's truth, He gives us through the Spirit the wisdom and insight that we need (Eph. 1:17).

The *general* will of God for all His children is given clearly in the Bible. The *specific* will of God for any given situation must always agree with what He has already revealed in His Word. The better we know God's general will, the easier it will be to determine His specific guidance in daily life. Paul did not encourage the Colossians to seek visions or wait for voices. He prayed that they might get deeper into God's Word and thus have greater wisdom and insight concerning God's will. He wanted them to have "all wisdom"—not that they would know everything, but that they would have all the wisdom necessary for making decisions and living to please God.

Spiritual intelligence is the beginning of a successful, fruitful Christian life. God puts no premium on ignorance. I once heard a preacher say, "I didn't never go to school. I'm just a igerant Christian, and I'm glad I is!" A man does not have to go to school to gain spiritual intelligence; but neither should he magnify his "igerance."

Great men of God like Charles Spurgeon, G. Campbell Morgan, and H.A. Ironside never had the privilege of formal Bible training. But they were devoted students of the Word, learning its deeper truths through hours of study, meditation, and prayer. The first step toward fullness of life is spiritual intelligence—growing in the will of God by knowing the Word of God.

### He Prayed for Practical Obedience (Col. 1:10)

The false teachers in Colossae attracted people through their offer of "spiritual knowledge," but they did not relate this knowledge to life. In the Christian life, knowledge and obedience go together. There is no separation between *learning* and *living*. The wisdom about which Paul prayed was not simply a head knowledge of deep spiritual truths (see Col. 1:28; 2:3; 3:16; 4:5). True spiritual wisdom must affect the daily life. Wisdom and practical intelligence must go together (see Ex. 31:3; Deut. 4:6; 1 Cor. 1:19).

In my pastoral ministry, I have met people who have become intoxicated with "studying the deeper truths of the Bible." Usually they have been given a book or introduced to some teacher's tapes. Before long, they get so smart they become dumb! The "deeper truths" they discover only detour them from practical Christian living. Instead of getting burning hearts of devotion to Christ (Luke 24:32), they get big heads and start creating problems in their homes and churches. All Bible truths are practical, not theoretical. If we are growing in knowledge, we should also be growing in grace (2 Peter 3:18).

Two words summarize the practicality of the Christian life: *walk* and *work*. The sequence is important: first, wisdom; then walk; then work. I cannot work for God unless I am walking with Him; but I cannot walk with Him if I am ignorant of His will. The believer who spends time daily in the Word and prayer (Acts 6:4) will know God's will and be able to walk with Him and work for Him.

After all, our purpose in life is not to please ourselves, but to please the Lord. We should walk *worthy of our calling* (Eph. 4:1) and *worthy of the Gospel* (Phil. 1:27), which means we will walk *worthy of God* (1 Thes. 2:12). In short, we should walk to *please* God (1 Thes. 4:1).

It is not we who work for God; it is God who works in us and through us to produce the fruit of His grace (Phil. 2:12-13). Christian service is the result of Christian devotion. The work that we do is the outflow of the life that we live. It is by abiding in Christ that we can produce fruit (John 15:1ff).

God must make the worker before He can do the work. God spent thirteen years preparing Joseph for his ministry in Egypt, and eighty years preparing Moses to lead Israel. Jesus spent three years teaching His disciples how to bear fruit; and even the learned Apostle Paul needed a "postgraduate course" in Arabia before he could serve God with effectiveness. A newborn babe can cry and make its presence known, but it cannot work. A new Christian can witness for Christ and even win others—but he must be taught to walk and learn God's wisdom before he is placed in an office of responsible ministry.

God's wisdom reveals God's will. As we obey God's will in our walk, we can work for Him and bear fruit. We will not just occasionally serve God; we will be "fruitful in every good work" (Col. 1:10). But there is a blessed by-product of this experience: "increasing in the knowledge of God" (Col. 1:10). As we walk with God and work for God, we get to know Him better and better.

Our Christian lives desperately need *balance*. Certainly we get to know God better as we pray in our private rooms and as we meditate on His Word. But we also get to know Him as we walk in our daily lives and work to win others and help His people.

Worship and service are not competitive. They always go together. When He was ministering on earth, our Lord retired to pray—then He went out to serve. We need to avoid the extremes of impractical mysticism and fleshly enthusiasm. As we spend time with God, we get to understand Him and His will for our lives; and as we go out to obey Him, we learn more.

Practical obedience means pleasing God, serving Him, and getting to know Him better. Any doctrine that isolates the believer from the needs of the world around him is not spiritual doctrine. Evangelist D.L. Moody often said, "Every Bible should be bound in shoe-leather." Paul would agree.

Paul has prayed that we might have spiritual intelligence, and that this intelligence might result in practical obedience. But there is a third request that completes these first two; and without it, the Christian life could not be mature.

## He Prayed for Moral Excellence (Col. 1:11-12)

Wisdom and conduct should always be related to moral character. One of the great problems in our evangelical world today is the emphasis on "spiritual knowledge" and "Christian service," without connecting these important matters to personal character.

For example, some teachers and preachers claim to have God's wisdom—yet they lack love and kindness and the other basic qualities that make the Christian life beautiful and distinctive. Even some "soul-winning Christians" are so busy serving God that they cannot take time to check facts—so they publish lies about other Christians. For some months, I read a certain religious publication. But when I discovered that they had no "Letters to the Editor" column (except for praise), and that they never published a correction or apologized for an error, I stopped reading the magazine.

Knowledge, conduct, service, and character must always go together. We know God's will that we might obey it; and, in obeying it, we serve Him and grow in Christian character. While none of us is perfectly balanced in these four factors, we ought to strive for that balance.

It is God's energy that empowers us. Colossians 1:11 reads, in effect: "With all power being empowered according to the might of His glory." Paul used two different Greek words for God's energy: *dunamis* (from which we get our word "dynamite") means "inherent power"; and *kratos* means "manifested power," power that is put forth in action. The grace of our Christian lives is but a result of God's power at work in our lives. Spiritual growth and maturity can come only as we yield to God's power and permit Him to work in us.

We usually think of God's glorious power being revealed in great feats of daring—the Israelites crossing the Red Sea, David leading a victorious army, or Paul raising the dead. But the emphasis here is on Christian character: patience, long-suffering, joyfulness, and thanksgiving. The inner victories of the soul are just as great, if not greater, than the public victories recorded in the annals of history. For David to control his temper when he was being maligned by Shimei was a greater victory than his slaying of Goliath (2 Sam. 16:5-13). "He who is slow to anger is better than the mighty, and he who rules his spirit, than he who captures a city" (Prov. 16:32, NASB).

The word *patience* means "endurance when circumstances are difficult." It is the opposite of despondency. This word is never used in reference to God, for God does not face difficult circumstances. Nothing is impossible with God (Jer. 32:27).

Patience is an important characteristic of the maturing Christian life. If we do not learn to be patient, we are not likely to learn anything else. As believers, we are able to rejoice even in our tribulations, because we know that "tribulation brings about perseverance; and perseverance proven character; and proven character, hope" (Rom. 5:3-4, NASB).

We must never think that patience is complacency. Patience is *endurance in action.* It is not the Christian sitting in a rocking chair, waiting for God to do something. It is the soldier on the battlefield, keeping on when the going is tough. It is the runner on the race track, refusing to stop because he wants to win the race (Heb. 12:1).

Too many Christians have a tendency to quit when circumstances become difficult. The saintly Dr. V. Raymond Edman, late president of Wheaton College (Illinois), used to remind the students, "It is always too soon to quit."

I have often thought of that statement when I find myself in the midst of trying circumstances. It is not talent or training that guarantees victory: it is perseverance. "By perseverance the snail reached the ark," said Charles Spurgeon.

Along with patience, we need *long-suffering.* This word means "self-restraint" and is the opposite of revenge. Patience has to do primarily with circumstances, while long-suffering has to do with people. God is long-suffering toward people because of His love and grace (2 Peter 3:9). Long-suffering is one fruit of the Spirit (Gal. 5:22). It is among the "grace garments" that the believer should wear (Col. 3:12).

It is amazing how people can patiently endure trying circumstances, only to lose their tempers with a friend or loved one. Moses was patient during the contest with Pharaoh in Egypt. But he lost his temper with his own people and, as a result, forfeited his right to enter the Promised Land (Num. 20). "Like a city that is broken into and without walls is a man who has no control over his spirit" (Prov. 25:28, NASB).

Patience and long-suffering go together if we are growing spiritually. Paul listed them as the marks of the true minister of Jesus Christ

(2 Cor. 6:4-6). Certainly, Paul displayed these graces in his own life (2 Tim. 3:10). The great example of patience and long-suffering in the Old Testament is Job (James 5:10-11). In the New Testament, of course, it is Jesus Christ.

It is easy for God to perform miracles in the realms of the material or physical, because everything in creation obeys His command. Jesus could heal Malchus' ear, but He could not automatically change Peter's heart and remove the hatred and violence that was in it (Luke 22:50-51). God could bring water out of the rock, but He could not force Moses to be patient.

A pastor often visited a Christian young man who had been badly burned. The young man had to lie still for hours, and it was difficult for him to perform even the basic functions of life.

"I wish God would do a miracle and heal me," the young man said to his pastor one day.

"God is doing a miracle," the pastor replied, "but not the kind you are looking for. I have watched you grow in patience and kindness during these weeks. That, to me, is a greater miracle than the healing of your body."

God's power is evidenced in our lives not only in our patience and long-suffering, but also in our *joyfulness.* When circumstances are difficult, we should exhibit *joyful* patience; and when people are hard to live with, we should reveal *joyful* long-suffering. There is a kind of patience that "endures but does not enjoy." Paul prayed that the Colossian Christians might experience *joyful* patience and long-suffering.

We often use the words *joy* and *happiness* interchangeably, but a distinction should be made. Happiness often depends on happenings. If circumstances are encouraging and people are kind, we are happy. But joy is independent of both circumstances and people. The most joyful epistle Paul wrote was Philippians, and he wrote it from jail as he faced the possibility of being martyred for his faith.

Only God's Spirit working within us can give us joy in the midst of problem circumstances and problem people. "The fruit of the Spirit is . . . joy" (Gal. 5:22). Joy is not something that we ourselves "work up"; it is something the Spirit Himself "works in"—"joy in the Holy Spirit" (Rom. 14:17, NIV).

I can recall times in my life when all the circumstances around me pointed to difficulty and possible defeat. Yet my heart was filled with a spiritual joy that could only come from God. Sad to say, I also remember times (far too many!) when I gave in to the problems around me, and I lost both the joy and the victory.

The fourth evidence of God's power in our lives is *thankfulness*. Christians who are filled with the Holy Spirit will be joyful and thankful (Eph. 5:18-20). When we lose our joy, we start complaining and becoming critical.

The Colossian epistle is filled with thanksgiving. Paul gave thanks for the church in Colossae (Col. 1:3), and he prayed that they might grow in their own thanksgiving to God (Col. 1:12). The Christian life should abound with thanksgiving (Col. 2:7). One of the evidences of spiritual growth in our Bible study is thanksgiving (Col. 3:15-17). Our prayers should always include thanksgiving (Col. 4:2). The Christian who is filled with the Spirit, filled with the Word, and watching in prayer will prove it by his attitude of appreciation and thanksgiving to God.

Some people are appreciative by nature, but some are not; and it is these latter people who especially need God's power to express thanksgiving. We should remember that every good gift comes from God (James 1:17) and that He is (as the theologians put it) "the Source, Support, and End of all things." The very breath in our mouths is the free gift of God.

Years ago, Northwestern University in Evanston, Illinois had a life-saving squad that assisted passengers on the Lake Michigan boats. On September 8, 1860, a passenger boat, the *Lady Elgin*, floundered near Evanston, and a ministerial student, Edward Spencer, personally rescued seventeen persons. The exertion of that day permanently damaged his health and he was unable to train for the ministry. When he died some years later, it was noted that not one of the seventeen persons he had saved ever came to thank him.

Thankfulness is the opposite of selfishness. The selfish person says, "I *deserve* what comes to me! Other people *ought* to make me happy!" But the mature Christian realizes that life is a gift from God, and that the blessings of life come only from His bountiful hand.

Of course, the one blessing that ought to move us constantly to thanksgiving is that God has made us "meet [fit] to be partakers of the inheritance of the saints in light" (Col.

1:12). The word *fit* means "qualified": God has qualified us for heaven! And, while we are waiting for Christ to return, we enjoy our share of the spiritual inheritance that we have in Him (Eph. 1:11, 18-23).

In the Old Testament, God's people had an *earthly* inheritance, the land of Canaan. Christians today have a *spiritual* inheritance in Christ. Canaan is not a picture of heaven, for there will be no battles or defeats in heaven. Canaan is a picture of our *present* inheritance in Christ. We must claim our inheritance by faith as we step out on the promises of God (Josh. 1:1-9). Day by day, we claim our blessings; and this makes us even more thankful to the Lord.

As we review this marvelous prayer, we can see how penetrating it is. We need spiritual intelligence if we are going to live to please God. We also need practical obedience in our walk and work. But the result of all of this must be spiritual power in the inner man, power that leads to joyful patience and long-suffering, with thanksgiving.

Have you been praying this way lately?

# CHAPTER FOUR
# CROWN HIM
# LORD OF ALL!
## *Colossians 1:13-20*

The false teachers in Colossae, like the false teachers of our own day, would not *deny* the importance of Jesus Christ. They would simply *dethrone* Him, giving Him prominence but not preeminence. In their philosophy, Jesus Christ was but one of many "emanations" that proceeded from God and through which men could reach God. It was this claim that Paul refuted in this section.

Probably no paragraph in the New Testament contains more concentrated doctrine about Jesus Christ than this one. We can keep ourselves from going on a detour if we remember that Paul wrote to prove the preeminence of Christ, and he did so by using four unanswerable arguments.

### Christ Is the Saviour (Col. 1:13-14)

Man's greatest problem is sin—a problem that can never be solved by a philosopher or a religious teacher. Sinners need a Saviour. These two verses present a vivid picture of the four saving actions of Christ on our behalf.

*He delivered us (v. 13a).* This word means "rescued from danger." We could not deliver ourselves from the guilt and penalty of sin, but Jesus could and did deliver us. We were in danger of spending eternity apart from God. The sword of God's judgment was hanging over our heads!

But this deliverance involved something else: we were delivered from the authority of Satan and the powers of darkness. The gnostic false teachers believed in an organization of evil spirits that controlled the world (see Col. 1:16; 2:10, 15): angels, archangels, principalities, powers, virtues, dominions, and thrones. John Milton used these titles when describing Satan's forces in his classic *Paradise Lost.*

*He translated us (v. 13b).* This word was used to describe the deportation of a population from one country into another. History records the fact that Antiochus the Great transported at least 2,000 Jews from Babylonia to Colossae.

Jesus Christ did not release us from bondage, only to have us wander aimlessly. He moved us into His own kingdom of light and made us victors over Satan's kingdom of darkness. Earthly rulers transported the defeated people, but Jesus Christ transported the winners.

The phrase *His dear Son* can be translated "the Son of His love." At the baptism and transfiguration of Jesus Christ, the Father declared that Jesus was His "beloved Son" (Matt. 3:17; 17:5). This fact reminds us of the price the Father paid when He gave His Son for us. It also reminds us that His kingdom is a kingdom of love as well as a kingdom of light.

The experience of Israel in the Old Testament is an illustration of this spiritual experience; for God delivered them from the bondage of Egypt and took them into the Promised Land of their inheritance. God brings us out that He might bring us in.

*He redeemed us (v. 14a).* This word means "to release a prisoner by the payment of a ransom." Paul did not suggest that Jesus paid a ransom to Satan in order to rescue us from the kingdom of darkness. By His death and resurrection, Jesus met the holy demands of God's Law. Satan seeks to accuse us and imprison us because he knows we are guilty of breaking God's Law. But the ransom has been paid on Calvary, and through faith in Jesus Christ, we have been set free.

*He has forgiven us (v. 14b).* Redemption and forgiveness go together (Eph. 1:7). The word translated *forgiveness* means "to send away" or "to cancel a debt." Christ has not only set us free and transferred us to a new kingdom, but He has canceled every debt so that we cannot be enslaved again. Satan cannot find anything in the files that will indict us!

In recent years, the church has rediscovered the freedom of forgiveness. God's forgiveness of sinners is an act of His grace. We did not deserve to be forgiven, nor can we earn forgiveness. Knowing that we are forgiven makes it possible for us to fellowship with God, enjoy His grace, and seek to do His will. Forgiveness is not an excuse for sin; rather, it is an encouragement for obedience. And, because we have been forgiven, we can forgive others (Col. 3:13). The Parable of the Unforgiving Servant makes it clear that an unforgiving spirit always leads to bondage (Matt. 18:21-35).

Jesus Christ is preeminent in salvation. No other person could redeem us, forgive us, transfer us out of Satan's kingdom into God's kingdom, and do it wholly by grace. The phrase, "through His blood," reminds us of the cost of our salvation. Moses and the Israelites only had to shed the blood of a lamb to be delivered from Egypt. But Jesus had to shed His blood to deliver us from sin.

### Christ Is the Creator (Col. 1:15-17)

The false teachers were very confused about Creation. They taught that matter was evil, including the human body. They also taught that Jesus Christ did not have a real body since this would have put Him in contact with evil matter. The results of these false teachings were tragic, including extreme asceticism on the one hand and unbridled sin on the other. After all, if your body is sinful, you either try to enslave it or you enjoy it.

In this section, Paul explained the fourfold relationship of Jesus Christ to Creation.

*He existed before Creation (v. 15).* The term *firstborn* does not refer to time, but to place or status. Jesus Christ was not the first being created, since He Himself is the Creator of all things. *Firstborn* simply means "of first importance, of first rank." Solomon was certainly not born first of all of David's sons, yet he was named the firstborn (Ps. 89:27). *Firstborn of all Creation* means "prior to all Creation." Jesus Christ is not a created being; He is eternal God.

Paul used the word *image* to make this fact clear. It means "an exact representation and revelation." The writer to the Hebrews affirms that Jesus Christ is "the express image of His Person" (Heb. 1:3). Jesus was able to say, "He that hath seen Me, hath seen the Father" (John 14:9). In His essence, God is invisible; but Jesus Christ has revealed Him to us (John 1:18). Nature reveals the existence, power, and wisdom of God; but nature cannot reveal the very essence of God to us. It is only in Jesus Christ that the invisible God is revealed perfectly. Since no mere creature can perfectly reveal God, Jesus Christ must be God.

*He created all things (v. 16a).* Since Christ created all things, He Himself is uncreated. The word *for* that introduces this verse could be translated "because." Jesus Christ is the Firstborn of all *because* He created all things. It is no wonder that the winds and waves obeyed Him, and diseases and death fled from Him, for He is Master over all. "All things were made by Him" (John 1:3). This includes all things in heaven and earth, visible and invisible. All things are under His command.

*All things exist for Him (v. 16b).* Everything exists *in* Him, *for* Him, and *through* Him. Jesus Christ is the Sphere in which they exist, the Agent through which they came into being, and the One for whom they were made.

Paul's use of three different prepositions is one way of refuting the philosophy of the false teachers. For centuries, the Greek philosophers had taught that everything needed a primary cause, an instrumental cause, and a final cause. The primary cause is the plan, the instrumental cause the power, and the final cause the purpose. When it comes to Creation, Jesus Christ is the primary cause (He planned it), the instrumental cause (He produced it), and the final cause (He did it for His own pleasure).

If everything in creation exists *for* Him, then nothing can be evil of itself (except for Satan and fallen angels, even those God uses to accomplish His will). Gnostic regulations about using God's creation are all foolish (Col. 2:20-23). It also means that God's creation, even though under bondage to sin (Rom.

8:22), can be used for God's glory and enjoyed by God's people (1 Tim. 6:17).

*He holds all things together (v. 17).* "In Him all things hold together" (NIV). A guide took a group of people through an atomic laboratory and explained how all matter was composed of rapidly moving electric particles. The tourists studied models of molecules and were amazed to learn that matter is made up primarily of space. During the question period, one visitor asked, "If this is the way matter works, what holds it all together?" For that, the guide had no answer.

But the Christian has an answer: Jesus Christ! Because "He is before all things," He can hold all things together. Again, this is another affirmation that Jesus Christ is God. Only God exists before all of Creation, and only God can make Creation cohere. To make Jesus Christ less than God is to dethrone Him.

It used to bother me to sing the familiar song, "This Is My Father's World." I thought Satan and sin were in control of this world. I have since changed my mind, and now I sing the song with joy and victory. Jesus Christ made all things, He controls all things, and by Him all things hold together. Indeed, this *is* my Father's world!

## Christ Is the Head of the Church (Col. 1:18)

There are many images of the church in the New Testament, and the body is one of the most important (Rom. 12:4ff; 1 Cor. 12:14; Eph. 4:8-16). No denomination or local assembly can claim to be "the body of Christ," for that body is composed of *all* true believers. When a person trusts Christ, he is immediately baptized by the Holy Spirit into this body (1 Cor. 12:12-13). The baptism of the Spirit is not a postconversion experience—for it occurs the instant a person believes in Jesus Christ.

Each Christian is a member of this spiritual body, and Jesus Christ is the Head. In Greek usage, the word *head* meant "source" and "origin" as well as "leader, ruler." Jesus Christ is the Source of the church, His body, and the Leader. Paul called Him "the Beginning" which tells us that Jesus Christ has priority in time as far as His church is concerned. The term *beginning* can be translated "originator."

No matter which name you select, it will affirm the preeminence of Jesus Christ in the church. The church had its origin in Him, and today it has its operation in Him. As the Head of the church, Jesus Christ supplies it with life through His Spirit. He gives gifts to men, and then places these gifted people in His church that they might serve Him where they are needed. Through His Word, Jesus Christ nourishes and cleanses the church (Eph. 5:25-30).

No believer on earth is the head of the church. This position is reserved exclusively for Jesus Christ. Various religious leaders may have founded churches, or denominations; but only Jesus Christ is the Founder of the church which is His body. This church is composed of all true believers, and it was born at Pentecost. It was then that the Holy Spirit came and baptized the believers into one spiritual body.

The fact that there is "one body" in this world (Eph. 4:4) does not eliminate or minimize the need for *local* bodies of believers. The fact that I belong to the universal church does not release me from my responsibilities to the local church. I cannot minister to the whole church, but I can strengthen and build the church by ministering to God's people in a local assembly.

Jesus Christ is the Head of the church, and the Beginning of the church; and He is also the Firstborn from the dead. We saw this word *firstborn* in Colossians 1:15. Paul did not say that Jesus was the first person to be raised from the dead, for He was not. But He is the most important of all who have been raised from the dead; for without His resurrection, there could be no resurrection for others (1 Cor. 15:20ff).

It seems odd that Paul used the word *born* in connection with death, for the two concepts seem opposed to each other. But the tomb was a womb from which Christ came forth in victory, for death could not hold Him (Acts 2:24). The Son was begotten in resurrection glory (Ps. 2:7; Acts 13:33).

This brings us to the theme of this entire section: "That in all things He might have the preeminence" (Col. 1:18). This was God's purpose in making His Son the Saviour, Creator, and Head of the church. The word translated "preeminence" is used nowhere else in the New Testament. It is related to the word translated "firstborn," and it magnifies the unique position of Jesus Christ. "Christ is all, and in all" (Col. 3:11).

In 1893, the World's Columbian Exposition was held in Chicago, and more than 21 million people visited the exhibits. Among the features was a "World Parliament of Religions," with representatives of the world's religions, meeting to share their "best points" and perhaps come up with a new religion for the world.

Evangelist D.L. Moody saw this as a great opportunity for evangelism. He used churches, rented theaters, and even rented a circus tent (when the show was not on) to present the Gospel of Jesus Christ. His friends wanted Moody to attack the "Parliament of Religions," but he refused. "I am going to make Jesus Christ so attractive," he said, "that men will turn to Him." Moody knew that Jesus Christ was the preeminent Saviour, not just one of many "religious leaders" of history. The "Chicago Campaign" of 1893 was probably the greatest evangelistic endeavor in D.L. Moody's life, and thousands came to Christ.

But the false teachers of Colossae could never give Jesus Christ the place of preeminence; for, according to their philosophy, Jesus Christ was only one of many "emanations" from God. He was not the only way to God (John 14:6); rather, He was but one rung on the ladder! It has well been said, "If Jesus Christ is not Lord of all, He cannot be Lord at all."

We have now studied three arguments for the preeminence of Jesus Christ: He is the Saviour, He is the Creator, and He is the Head of the church. These arguments reveal His relationship with lost sinners, with the universe, and with believers. But what about His relationship with God the Father?

## He Is the Beloved of the Father (Col. 1:19-20)

Paul had already called Jesus Christ "His [God's] dear Son" (Col. 1:13). Those who have trusted Jesus Christ as their Saviour are "accepted in the Beloved" (Eph. 1:6). For this reason, God can call *us* His beloved (Col. 3:12).

Then Paul took a giant step forward in his argument, for he declared that "all fullness" dwelt in Jesus Christ! The word translated "fullness" is the Greek word *pleroma* (pronounced "play-RO-ma"). It was a technical term in the vocabulary of the gnostic false teachers. It meant "the sum total of all the divine power and attributes." We have already noted that Paul used this important word eight times in the Colossian letter, so he was meeting the false teachers on their own ground.

The word *dwell* is equally important. It means much more than merely "to reside." The form of the verb means "to be at home permanently." The late Dr. Kenneth S. Wuest, noted Greek expert, pointed out in his excellent commentary on Colossians that the verb indicates that this fullness was "not something added to His Being that was not natural to Him, but that it was part of His essential Being as part of His very constitution, and that permanently" *(Ephesians and Colossians in the Greek New Testament,* Eerdmans, p. 187).

The Father would not permanently give His *pleroma* to some created being. The fact that it "pleased the Father" to have His fullness in Christ is proof that Jesus Christ is God. "And of His [Christ's] fullness have all we received" (John 1:16). "For in Him [Jesus Christ] dwelleth all the fullness of the Godhead bodily" (Col. 2:9).

Because Jesus Christ is God, He is able to do what no mere man could ever do: reconcile lost sinners to a holy God. When the first man and woman sinned, they declared war on God; but God did not declare war on them. Instead, God sought Adam and Eve; and He provided a covering for their sins.

The natural mind of the unsaved sinner is at war with God (Rom. 8:7). The sinner may be sincere, religious, and even moral; but he is still at war with God.

How can a holy God ever be reconciled with sinful man? Can God lower His standards, close His eyes to sin, and compromise with man? If He did, the universe would fall to pieces! God must be consistent with Himself and maintain His own holy Law.

Perhaps man could somehow please God. But by nature, man is separated from God; and by his deeds, he is alienated from God (Col. 1:21). The sinner is "dead in trespasses and sins" (Eph. 2:1ff), and therefore is unable to do anything to save himself or to please God (Rom. 8:8).

If there is to be reconciliation between man and God, the initiative and action must come from God. It is *in Christ* that God was reconciled to man (2 Cor. 5:19). But it was not the incarnation of Christ that accomplished this reconciliation, nor was it His example as He lived among men. It was through His *death* that peace was made between God and man. He "made peace through the blood of His cross" (Col. 1:20).

Of course, the false teachers offered a kind of reconciliation between man and God. However, the reconciliation they offered was not complete or final. The angels and the "emanations" could in some way bring men closer to God, according to the gnostic teachers. But the reconciliation we have in Jesus Christ is perfect, complete, and final. More than that, the reconciliation in Christ *involves the whole universe!* He reconciles "all things unto Himself . . . things in earth, or things in heaven" (Col. 1:20).

However, we must not conclude wrongly that universal reconciliation is the same as universal salvation. "Universalism" is the teaching that all beings, including those who have rejected Jesus Christ, will one day be saved. This was not what Paul believed. "Universal restorationism" was not a part of Paul's theology, for he definitely taught that sinners needed to believe in Jesus Christ to be saved (2 Thes. 1).

Paul wrote that Christ solved the sin problem on the cross once and for all. This means that one day God can bring together in Christ all that belong to Him (Eph. 1:9-10). He will be able to glorify believers and punish unbelievers, *and do it justly,* because of Christ's death on the cross. No one—not even Satan—can accuse God of doing wrong, because sin has been effectively dealt with on the cross.

If Jesus Christ is only a man, or only an emanation from God, He cannot reconcile God and man. The only arbitrator who can bring God and man together is One who is *both God and Man Himself.* Contrary to what the gnostics taught, Jesus Christ was a true human being with a real body. He was God in human flesh (John 1:14). When He died on the cross, He met the just demands of the Law because He paid the penalty for man's sins (1 Peter 2:24). Reconciliation was completed on the cross (Rom. 5:11).

A man once came to see me because he had difficulties at home. He was not a very well-educated man and sometimes got his words confused. He told me that he and his wife were having "martial problems" when he meant to say "marital problems." (Later I found out that they really were "at war" with each other, so maybe he was right after all!) But the word that caught my attention was in this sentence: "Pastor, me and my wife need a recancellation."

He meant to say *reconciliation,* but the

word *recancellation* was not a bad choice. There can be peace and a reunion of those who are at war *only when sin has been cancelled.* As sinners before a righteous God, we need a "recancellation." Our sins were cancelled on the cross.

As we review this profound section (and this study has only scratched the surface), we notice several important truths.

First, Jesus Christ has taken care of *all things.* All things were created by Him and for Him. He existed before all things, and today He holds all things together. He has reconciled all things through the Cross. No wonder Paul declared that "in all things He might have the preeminence" (Col. 1:18).

Second, all that we need is Jesus Christ. We have all of God's fullness in Him, and we are "filled full" (complete) in Him (Col. 2:10). There is no need to add anything to the person or work of Jesus Christ. To add anything is to take away from His glory. To give Him prominence instead of preeminence is to dethrone Him.

Third, God is pleased when His Son, Jesus Christ, is honored and given preeminence. There are people who tell us they are Christians, but they ignore or deny Jesus Christ. "We worship the Father," they tell us, "and that is all that is necessary."

But Jesus made it clear that *the Son* is to be worshiped as well as the Father "that all may honor the Son just as they honor the Father. He who does not honor the Son does not honor the Father, who sent Him" (John 5:23-24, NIV).

The late Dr. M.R. DeHaan, noted radio Bible teacher, told about a preacher who was confronted by a cultist who rejected the deity of Jesus Christ.

"Jesus cannot be the eternal Son of God, for a father is always older than his son," the man argued. "If the Father is not eternal, then He is not God. If Jesus is His Son, then He is not eternal."

The preacher was ready with an answer. "The thing that makes a person a father is having a son. But if God is the *eternal* Father, then He must have an *eternal* Son! This means that Jesus Christ is eternal—and that He is God!"

Jesus Christ is the Saviour, the Creator, the Head of the church, and the Beloved of the Father. He is eternal God . . . and in Our lives He deserves to have the preeminence. Is Jesus Christ preeminent in your life?

# CHAPTER FIVE
# ONE MAN'S
# MINISTRY
## *Colossians 1:21–2:3*

If you received a letter from a man you had never met, a man who was a prisoner, accused of being a troublemaker, how would you respond?

The Colossian believers faced that exact problem. They knew that Paul had been instrumental in leading their pastor, Epaphras, to saving faith in Christ. They also knew that Epaphras had gone to Rome to consult with Paul and had not yet returned. The church members had received Paul's letter, brought to them by Tychicus and Onesimus. But the false teachers in Colossae had been discrediting Paul and causing doubts in the people's minds. "Why listen to a man who is a political prisoner?" they asked. "Can you trust him?"

Paul no doubt realized that this would be the situation, so he paused in the first part of this letter to give some words of explanation. He had been so wrapped up in exalting Jesus Christ that he had not shown any interest in writing about himself! In this section, Paul explained his three ministries.

### Sharing the Gospel (Col. 1:21-23)

Even though Paul had not personally evangelized Colossae, it was his ministry in Ephesus that led to the founding of the Colossian church. Paul was "made a minister" (Col. 1:25). A large part of his ministry consisted in preaching the Good News of salvation through faith in Jesus Christ. His was a ministry of reconciliation (2 Cor. 5:17-21). Paul reviewed for his readers their own spiritual experience.

***Their past alienation (v. 21a).*** The word translated *alienated* means "estranged." These Gentiles in Colossae were estranged from God and separated from the spiritual blessings of Israel (Eph. 2:11ff). The gods that they worshiped were false gods, and their religious rituals could not take care of their sin or guilt.

But this estrangement was not only a matter of Gentile position; it was also a matter of sinful practices and attitudes. The Gentiles were *enemies,* which means they were "actively hostile to God." Even though they had not received a divine law, such as God gave to Israel, these Gentiles knew the truth about God through creation and conscience (Rom. 1:18ff). They could not plead ignorance before the bar of God's justice.

The enmity of their minds led to wicked works. Both in attitude and action, they were at war with God. "Because the carnal mind [the mind of the unbeliever] is enmity against God" (Rom. 8:7). This explains why the unbeliever must repent—change his mind—before he can be saved.

### Their present reconciliation (vv. 21b-22).
They did not reconcile themselves to God; it was God who took the initiative in His love and grace. The Father sent the Son to die on a cross that sinners might be reconciled to God. Jesus died for us when we were "without strength" (Rom. 5:6) and could do nothing for ourselves. He died for us "while we were yet sinners" and "when we were enemies" (Rom. 5:8, 10).

Paul emphasized the physical body of Jesus Christ that was nailed to the cross. The false teachers denied the Incarnation and taught that Jesus Christ did not have a real human body. Their philosophy that all matter was evil made it necessary for them to draw this false conclusion. But the New Testament makes it clear that Jesus *did* have a fully human body, and that He bore our sins on that body on the cross (1 Peter 2:24).

The purpose of this reconciliation is *personal holiness*. God does not make peace (Col. 1:20) so that we can continue to be rebels! He has reconciled us to Himself so that we may share His life and His holiness. We are presented to God "holy and unblameable and unreproveable" (Col. 1:22).

The word *holy* is closely related to the word *saint*. Both of these words express the idea of "being set apart, being devoted to God." In the New Testament, saints are not dead people who during their lives performed miracles and never sinned. New Testament saints were living people who had trusted Jesus Christ. Paul wrote this letter to living saints (Col. 1:2).

*Unblameable* means "without blemish." The word was applied to the temple sacrifices which had to be without blemish. It is amazing that God looks at His children and sees no blemish on them! God chose us to be "holy and without blame" (Eph. 1:4).

*Unreproveable* means "free from accusation." Once we have been reconciled to God,

no charges can be brought against us (Rom. 8:31-34). Satan, the accuser of the brethren (Rev. 12:1-12), would like to hurl charges at us; but God will not accept them (see Zech. 3). People may have accusations to bring against us, but they cannot change our relationship with God.

The most important thing in our Christian lives is not how we look in our own sight, or in the sight of others (1 Cor. 4:1-4)—but how we look in God's sight. I recall counseling a Christian who was in the habit of reminding herself of her past sins and failures. She seemed to enjoy having other people criticize her. I kept reminding her of what she was *in God's sight*. Her constant emphasis on her failures denied the work that Jesus Christ had done for her on the cross. It took time, but eventually she accepted her wonderful new position in Christ and began to get victory over criticism and depression.

Paul's emphasis on our holy standing before God was certainly an attack on the false teachers, for they promised their followers a kind of "perfection" that nothing else could give. "You already have a perfect standing in Christ," Paul wrote, "so why seek for it anywhere else?"

### Their future glorification (v. 23).
"The hope of the Gospel" means that blessed hope of our Lord's return (Titus 2:13). Paul had already mentioned this hope: "The hope which is laid up for you in heaven" (Col. 1:5). Later in the chapter, he called it "the hope of glory" (Col. 1:27).

There was a time when these Gentile Colossians were without hope (Eph. 2:12). The reason? They were without God. But when they were reconciled to God, they were given a wonderful hope of glory. All of God's children will one day be with Christ in heaven (John 17:24). In fact, so secure is our future that Paul stated that we have *already been glorified!* (Rom. 8:30) All we are waiting for is the revelation of this glory when Jesus Christ returns (Rom. 8:17-19).

Paul's statement to the Colossians seems to cast a shadow on the assurance of our future glory (see Col. 1:23). Is it possible for a believer to lose his salvation? No, the *if* clause does not suggest doubt or lay down a condition by which we "keep up our salvation."

Paul used an architectural image in this verse—a house, firmly set on the foundation. The town of Colossae was located in a region known for earthquakes, and the word translated "moved away" can mean "earthquake stricken." Paul was saying, "If you are truly saved, and built on the solid foundation, Jesus Christ, then you will continue in the faith and nothing will move you. You have heard the Gospel and trusted Jesus Christ, and He has saved you."

In other words, we are not saved by continuing in the faith. But we continue in the faith and thus prove that we are saved. It behooves each professing Christian to test his own faith and examine his own heart to be sure he is a child of God (2 Cor. 13:5; 2 Peter 1:10ff).

## Suffering for the Gentiles (Col. 1:24-27)

Paul's enemies made much of the fact that the great apostle was a prisoner of Rome. The false teachers in Colossae probably ridiculed Paul and used this as a weapon to fight the truth of the Gospel. But Paul turned this weapon around and used it to defeat his enemies and to build a closer relationship with the church in Colossae.

*Paul's rejoicing (v. 24).* "Instead of being ashamed of my suffering, I am rejoicing in it!" How could anyone rejoice in suffering? To begin with, Paul was suffering because of Jesus Christ. It was "the fellowship of His sufferings" (Phil. 3:10). Like the early Apostles, Paul rejoiced that he was "counted worthy to suffer shame for His name" (Acts 5:41). A Christian should never suffer "as a thief or as an evildoer"; but it is an honor to "suffer as a Christian" (1 Peter 4:15-16). There is a special blessing and reward reserved for the faithful believer who suffers for the sake of Christ (Matt. 5:10-12).

Paul had a second cause for rejoicing in his suffering: he was suffering because of the Gentiles. Paul was the chosen apostle to the Gentiles (Eph. 3:1-13). In fact, he was a prisoner in Rome because of his love for the Gentiles. He was arrested in Jerusalem on false charges, and the Jews listened to his defense until he used the word *Gentiles* (see Acts 22:21ff). It was that word that infuriated them and drove them to ask for his execution. (The full account is given in Acts 21–28, and an exciting account it is.)

So the Gentile believers in Colossae had every reason to love Paul and be thankful for his special ministry to them. But there was a third cause for Paul's rejoicing: he was suffering for the sake of Christ's body, the church. There was a time when Paul had persecuted

the church and caused it to suffer. But now Paul devoted his life to the care of the church. Paul did not ask, as do some believers. "What will *I* get out of it?" Instead he asked, "How much will God let me put into it?" The fact that Paul was a prisoner did not stop him from ministering to the church.

It is important to note, however, that these sufferings had nothing to do with the sacrificial sufferings of Christ on the cross. Only the sinless Lamb of God could die for the sins of the world (John 1:29). Paul was "filling up in his turn the leftover parts of Christ's sufferings" (Col. 1:24, literal translation). The word *afflictions* refers to the "pressures" of life, the persecutions Paul endured. This word is never used in the New Testament for the sacrificial sufferings of Jesus Christ.

The sacrificial sufferings of Christ are over, but His body, the church, experiences suffering because of its stand for the faith. The Head of the church in heaven feels the sufferings that His people endure. ("Saul, Saul, why persecutest thou Me?" [Acts 9:4]) Paul was taking his turn in sharing these afflictions, and others would follow in his train. But Paul did not complain. "For as the sufferings of Christ abound in us, so our consolation also abounds by Christ" (2 Cor. 1:5).

*Paul's responsibility (vv. 25-27).* Had Paul compromised with the Jews and stopped ministering to the Gentiles, he could have been spared a great deal of suffering. But he could not abandon his calling just for personal safety and comfort. He had been made a minister by God; he had been given a "stewardship" (dispensation) and he had to be faithful to his calling (1 Cor. 4:2). It was not a matter of choice: he was called to fulfill the Word of God. This can mean, "I must preach the Word fully and not compromise any truth." It can also mean, "I am commissioned by God's Word and I must be faithful to discharge my office."

Paul's special message regarding the Gentiles had to do with what he called *the mystery.* To us today, a mystery is something eerie and perhaps frightening; but this was not the way the word was defined in Paul's day. The false teachers used this word to describe the inner secrets of their religions. A *mystery* is a "sacred secret," hidden in the past and now revealed by the Holy Spirit (see Eph. 3:1-13).

God called the nation of Israel to be His people, He gave them His Law (including the priesthood and sacrifices), and He gave them a wonderful land. He promised them a King who would one day establish a glorious kingdom and fulfill the many promises made to Abraham and David. The Old Testament prophets wrote about a Messiah who would suffer, and a Messiah who would reign. They could not explain the seeming contradiction (see 1 Peter 1:9-12). They did not understand that the Messiah first had to suffer before He could enter into glory (Luke 24:13-27).

Jesus Christ came to earth, was rejected by His people, and was crucified. He arose again and returned to heaven. Did this mean that God's promised kingdom for Israel was now abandoned? No, because God had initiated a new program—His *mystery*—that was not explained by the Old Testament prophets. The mystery is that today God is uniting Jews and Gentiles in the church (Eph. 2:11-22). When the church is completed, then Jesus Christ will return and take His people to heaven (1 Thes. 4:13-18). Then He will again deal with Israel as a nation and establish the promised kingdom (Acts 15:12-18).

Imagine what this message meant to the Gentiles. They were no longer excluded from the glory and riches of God's grace! During the Old Testament dispensation, a Gentile had to become a Jewish proselyte in order to share in the blessings of Israel. But in the new dispensation, Jews and Gentiles alike are saved by faith in Jesus Christ (Rom. 10:12-13). No wonder the Jewish false teachers opposed Paul. He dared to say, "There is no difference!"

We who have grown up in somewhat Christian surroundings have a tendency to take all of this for granted. But think of the excitement this message must have generated in a church composed of new believers who had no background in the church. Once they were outside the covenants of God, but now they were members of His family. Once they were living in spiritual ignorance and death, but now they were alive and sharing in the riches of God's wisdom in Christ. Once they had no hope, but now they had a glorious hope because Christ now lived within! It would be good for us today to recapture some of that "first love" excitement.

I was privileged to minister in Africa for three weeks, and there I was introduced to some of the finest Christians I have ever met. I taught the Word to over 500 national pastors in Kenya for almost a week, and each service was a challenge and blessing to me. Many of the pastors still had the marks of paganism

and idolatry on their bodies; yet their faces were aglow with the joy of the Lord. I went to Africa to minister to them, *but they ministered to me!* They reminded me not to take for granted the glorious riches I have in Jesus Christ.

## Striving for the Saints (Col. 1:28–2:3)
We have met Paul the preacher, sharing the Gospel and Paul the prisoner, suffering for the Gentiles.

Now we meet Paul the prayer-warrior, striving in prayer for the individual saints that they might mature in the faith. The words *striving* (Col. 1:29) and *conflict* (Col. 2:1) are athletic terms. They refer to the strenuous effort put forth by the runner to win the race. Our English word *agony* comes from this Greek word.

*Paul's instruction (v. 28a). Whom* refers, of course, to Jesus Christ. "For we preach not ourselves, but Christ Jesus the Lord" (2 Cor. 4:5). The false teachers exalted themselves and their great "spiritual" attainments. They preached a system of teaching, but Paul preached a Person. The gnostics preached philosophy and the empty traditions of men (Col. 2:8), but Paul proclaimed Jesus Christ. The false teachers had lists of rules and regulations (Col. 2:16, 20-21), but Paul presented Christ. What a difference in ministries!

Paul not only *preached* (the word means "to announce with authority as a herald"), but he also *warned*. While it is good to proclaim positive truth, it is also necessary to warn God's people against the lies of the enemy (Acts 20:31). In fact, God's people should be alert to warn one another (*admonish* in Col. 3:16, NIV). Paul considered himself a spiritual father to the local churches, and it was his duty to warn his children (1 Cor. 4:14).

But Paul was also a *teacher* of the truth. It is not enough to warn people; we must also teach them the positive truths of the Word of God. How far would we get in our travels if the highway signs told us where the roads were *not* going? Not very far! It is good to *win* a man to Christ, and then to *warn* him about the dangers ahead; but it is also important to *teach* that convert the basic truths of the Christian life.

Paul not only preached Christ, but he also "taught Christ," for in Christ are "all the treasures of wisdom and knowledge" (Col. 2:3). It was not necessary to introduce any new teaching, for all that a believer needs to know is related to Jesus Christ. "Teaching every man in all wisdom" was Paul's concern (Col. 1:28). Wisdom is the right use of knowledge. The false teachers promised to give people a "hidden wisdom" that would make them "spiritually elite." But all true spiritual wisdom is found only in Jesus Christ.

**Paul's intent (v. 28b; 2:2-3).** He wanted to present every believer "perfect in Christ Jesus." The word *perfect* was a favorite word with the gnostic teachers. It described the disciple who was no longer a novice, but who had matured and was fully instructed in the secrets of the religion. Paul used it to mean "complete, mature in Christ." This is the goal of all preaching, warning, and teaching.

What are the evidences of this spiritual maturity? Paul described them next (Col. 2:2).

*Encouragement*—"that their hearts might be comforted." Our English word *encourage* means "with heart." To encourage people is to give them new heart. Shallow sympathy usually makes people feel worse, but true spiritual encouragement makes them feel better. It brings out the best in people.

*Endearment*—"being knit together in love." The mature Christian loves the brethren and seeks to be a peacemaker, not a troublemaker. He is a part of spiritual unity in the church. An immature person is often selfish and causes division.

*Enrichment*—"unto all riches of the full assurance of understanding." Paul mentioned the riches of Christ earlier (Col. 1:27). Too many Christians are living like paupers when they could be living like kings. Mature Christians do not complain about what they don't have. Rather, they make use of the vast resources that they do have in Jesus Christ.

*Enlightenment*—"full assurance of understanding." The mature believer has assurance in his heart that he is a child of God. The spiritual knowledge that he has in Christ constantly enlightens him and directs him daily. I have often counseled believers who told me they lacked assurance of their salvation. Invariably, they have been neglecting God's Word and living in ignorance.

God wants us as His children to have "understanding" and "wisdom and knowledge" (Col. 2:2-3). The word translated "understanding" literally means "to place together." It is the ability to assess things. *Wisdom* implies the ability to defend what we understand. *Knowledge* suggests the ability to grasp truth.

All of these terms were also used by the gnostics.

**Paul's intercession (1:29–2:1).** "For this I labor to the point of exhaustion, agonizing" is a literal translation of the first part of Colossians 1:29. What a picture of prayer! So much of our praying is calm and comfortable, and yet Paul exerted his spiritual muscles the way a Greek runner would exert himself in the Olympic Games. He also taught Epaphras to pray the same way (Col. 4:12).

This does not mean that our prayers are more effective if we exert all kinds of fleshly energy. Nor does it mean that we must "wrestle with God" and wear Him out before He will meet our needs. Paul described a *spiritual* striving: it was *God's* power at work in his life. True prayer is directed to the Father (Matt. 6:9), through the Son (in His name, John 14:13-14), in the power of the Holy Spirit (Jude 20). When the Spirit is at work in our lives, then we can pray mightily in the will of God.

How does the Spirit assist us in our praying? For one thing, the Spirit teaches us the Word and shows us the will of God (John 16:13-15). Prayer is not our trying to change God's mind. It is learning what is the mind of God and asking accordingly (1 John 5:14-15). The Holy Spirit constantly intercedes for us even though we do not hear His voice (Rom. 8:26-27). He knows the Father's will and He helps us pray in that will.

There are times when we simply do not feel like praying—and that is when we must pray the most! The Spirit gives us divine energy for prayer, in spite of the way we feel. The resurrection power of Jesus Christ is made available to us (Eph. 3:20-21).

In these verses Paul explained his ministry, and in so doing, he silenced the accusations of the enemy. He also stirred the affections of the believers as they realized how much Paul had done for them.

All of us are not called to be apostles, but each one of us does have a God-given ministry. We can share the Gospel and be soul-winners. We can suffer for Christ and fulfill the ministry God has given us. We can strive in prayer for God's people and encourage them to mature. Paul took time to minister to *individuals;* note the repetition of "every man" in Colossians 1:28. If we minister to only a few believers, we are helping the whole church.

Are you fulfilling your God-given ministry?

# CHAPTER SIX
# SAINTS ALIVE—
# AND ALERT
*Colossians 2:4-15*

I recall a story about a pastor who was concerned about some unsavory businesses that had opened near a school. His protests finally led to a court case, and the defense attorney did all he could to embarrass the Gospel minister.

"Are you not a pastor?" the lawyer asked. "And doesn't the word *pastor* mean 'shepherd'?"

To this definition the minister agreed.

"Well, if you are a shepherd, why aren't you out taking care of the sheep?"

"Because today I'm fighting the wolves!" was the pastor's quick reply, and a good answer it was.

Knowing that there were enemies already attacking the church in Colossae, Paul offered encouragement. By heeding his admonitions, the Colossians would overcome their enemies.

## Keep Making Spiritual Progress
## (Col. 2:4-7)

In the Christian life, we never stand still: we either go forward or gradually slip backward. "Let us go on to maturity!" is the call we must obey (Heb. 6:1, literal translation). The Christian who is not making spiritual progress is an open target for the enemy to attack and destroy.

**The need for progress (v. 4).** Satan is deceptive. He wants to lead believers astray, and to do this, he uses deceptive words. The Greek term used here describes the persuasive arguments of a lawyer. Satan is a liar (John 8:44) and by his lies he leads believers into the wrong path. It is important that we exercise spiritual discernment, and that we continue to grow in our knowledge of spiritual truth.

**The nature of progress (vv. 5-7).** In order to emphasize his admonition, Paul used several vivid pictures to illustrate spiritual progress.

*The army (v. 5).* The words *order* and *steadfastness* are military terms. They describe an army that is solidly united against the enemy.

*Order* describes the arrangement of the army in ranks, with each soldier in his proper place. Not everybody can be a five-star general, but the general could never fight the battle alone. *Steadfastness* pictures the soldiers in battle formation, presenting a solid front to the enemy. Christians ought to make progress in discipline and obedience, just as soldiers on the battlefield.

*The pilgrim (v. 6).* The Christian life is compared to a pilgrimage, and believers must learn to walk. Paul had already encouraged his readers to "walk worthy of the Lord" (Col. 1:10), and later he used this image again (Col. 3:7; 4:5). In the Ephesian epistle, the companion letter to the Colossian epistle, Paul used the image at least seven times (Eph. 2:2, 10; 4:1, 17; 5:2, 8, 15).

We are to walk in Christ the same way we originally received Christ—*by faith*. The gnostic teachers wanted to introduce some "new truths" for Christian maturity, but Paul denounced them. "You started with Christ and you must continue with Christ," Paul wrote. "You started with faith and you must continue with faith. This is the only way to make spiritual progress."

*The tree (v. 7a). Rooted* is an agricultural word. The tense of the Greek word means "once and for all having been rooted." Christians are not to be tumbleweeds that have no roots and are blown about by "every wind of doctrine" (Eph. 4:14). Nor are they to be "transplants" that are repeatedly moved from soil to soil. Once we are rooted by faith in Christ, there is no need to change the soil! The roots draw up the nourishment so that the tree can grow. The roots also give strength and stability.

*The building (v. 7b). Built up* is an architectural term. It is in the present tense: "being built up." When we trust Christ to save us, we are put on the foundation; from then on, we grow in grace. The word *edify* that is found often in Paul's letters simply means "to build up." To make spiritual progress means to keep adding to the temple to the glory of God.

*The school (v. 7c).* It is the Word of God that builds and strengthens the Christian. Epaphras had faithfully taught the Colossian believers the truth of the Word (Col. 1:7). But the false teachers were undermining that doctrine. Today, Christians who study the Word become established in the faith. Satan has a difficult time deceiving the Bible-taught believer.

*The river (v. 7d).* The word *abounding* is often used by Paul. It suggests the picture of a river overflowing its banks. Our first experience in the Lord is that of drinking the water of life by faith, and He puts within us an artesian well of living water (John 4:10-14). But that artesian well should become a "river of living water" (John 7:37-39) that grows deeper and deeper. The image of the river flowing from the sanctuary (Ezek. 47) getting deeper as it flows, probably is what Paul had in mind. Sad to say, many of us are making no progress—our lives are shallow trickles instead of mighty rivers.

Again, Paul mentioned "thanksgiving" (see Col. 1:3, 12). A thankful spirit is a mark of Christian maturity. When a believer is abounding in thanksgiving, he is really making progress!

By reviewing these pictures of spiritual progress, we see how the growing Christian can easily defeat the enemy and not be led astray. If his spiritual roots are deep in Christ, he will not want any other soil. If Christ is his sure foundation, he has no need to move. If he is studying and growing in the Word, he will not be easily enticed by false doctrine. And if his heart is overflowing with thanksgiving, he will not even consider turning from the fullness he has in Christ. A grounded, growing, grateful believer will not be led astray.

## Watch Out for Spiritual Perils (Col. 2:8-10)

Paul continued the military image with this warning: "Beware lest any man carry you off as a captive" (literal translation). The false teachers did not go out and win the lost, no more than the cultists do today. They "kidnapped" converts from churches! Most of the people I have talked with who are members of antichristian cults were at one time associated with a Christian church of one denomination or another.

How is it possible for false teachers to capture people? The answer is simple: These "captives" are ignorant of the truths of the Word of God. They become fascinated by the philosophy and empty delusion of the false teachers. (This is not to say that *all* philosophy is wrong, because there is a Christian philosophy of life. The word simply means "to love wisdom.") When a person does not know the doctrines of the Christian faith, he can easily be captured by false religions.

This philosophy of the false teachers is "hollow and deceptive" (Col. 2:8, NIV) for several reasons. To begin with, it is the tradition of men and not the truth of God's Word. The word *tradition* means "that which is handed down"; and there is a true Christian tradition (1 Cor. 15:3ff; 2 Thes. 2:15; 3:6; 2 Tim. 2:2). The important thing about any teaching is its origin: Did it come from God or from man? The religious leaders in our Lord's day had their traditions and were very zealous to obey them and protect them (Matt. 15:1-20). Even the Apostle Paul, before he met the Lord, was "exceedingly zealous of the traditions" (Gal. 1:14).

If a new Christian from a distant mission field were to visit many of our churches, he would probably be astounded at the ideas and practices we have that cannot be supported by God's Word. Our man-made traditions are usually more important to us than the God-given doctrines of the Scriptures! While it is not wrong to have church traditions that remind us of our godly heritage, we must be careful not to make these traditions equal to the Word of God.

The false teachers' traditions were "hollow and deceptive" for another reason: they involved "the rudiments of the world." The Greek word translated "rudiments" basically means "one of a row or series." It had several meanings attached to it: (1) the elementary sounds or letters, the ABCs; (2) the basic elements of the universe, as in 2 Peter 3:10-12; (3) the basic elements of knowledge, the ABCs of some system, as in Hebrews 5:12. But in ancient Greece, this word also meant "the elemental spirits of the universe, the angels that influenced the heavenly bodies." It was one of the words in the vocabulary of the religious astrology of that day.

The gnostics believed that the angels and the heavenly bodies influenced people's lives. Paul's warnings to the Colossians about "new moon" and other religious practices determined by the calendar (Col. 2:16) may be related to this gnostic teaching, though the Jewish people also watched the calendar (Gal. 4:10). One thing is certain: such teachings about demons and angels were not a part of true Christian doctrine. If anything, such teachings were satanic.

The fact that this teaching is not after Christ is sufficient to warn us against horoscopes, astral charts, Ouija boards, and other spiritist practices. The whole zodiac system is contrary to the teaching of the Word of God.

The Christian who dabbles in mysticism and the occult is only asking for trouble.

Why follow empty philosophy when we have all fullness in Christ? This is like turning away from the satisfying river to drink at the dirty cisterns of the world (Jer. 2:13). Of course, the false teachers in Colossae did not ask the believers to forsake Christ. They asked them to make Christ a *part* of the new system. But this would only remove Him from His rightful place of preeminence.

So Paul gave the true and lasting antidote to all false teaching: "All fullness is in Christ, and you have been made full in Him. *Why, then, would you need anything else?*" (see Col. 2:9-10)

We have seen the word "fullness" *(pleroma)* before (Col. 1:19). It means "the sum total of all that God is, all of His being and attributes." This word was used by the gnostics, but they did not give it the same meaning as did Paul. To them, the *pleroma* was the source of all the "emanations" through which men could come to God. The highest point in gnostic religious experience was to share in the *pleroma*.

Of course, there are no emanations from God. The gulf between heaven and earth was bridged in the incarnation of Jesus Christ. He is declared to be "Emmanuel, God with us" (Matt. 1:23). Jesus Christ is the fullness of God, and that fullness dwells continually and permanently in Him *bodily*. Once again, Paul refuted the gnostic doctrine that matter was evil and that Jesus did not have a human body.

When Jesus Christ ascended to heaven, He went in a human body. It was a glorified body, to be sure, but it was real. After His resurrection, our Lord was careful to assure His disciples that He was the same Person in the same body; He was not a ghost or a spirit (see John 20:19-29). There is a glorified Man in heaven! The God-Man, Jesus Christ, embodies the fullness of God!

Now, the remarkable thing is this: *every believer shares that fullness!* "And you are complete in Him" (Col. 2:10). The tense of the Greek verb indicates that this fullness is a permanent experience. Dr. Kenneth Wuest's very literal *Expanded Translation* reads, "And you are in Him, having been completely filled full with the present result that you are in a state of fullness."

When a person is born again into the family of God, he is born complete in Christ. His spiritual growth is not by *addition*, but by *nu-*

*trition*. He grows from the inside out. Nothing needs to be added to Christ because He already is the very fullness of God. As the believer draws on Christ's fullness, he is "filled unto all the fullness of God" (Eph. 3:19). What more does he need?

Indeed, there are spiritual perils that the Christian faces. The fundamental test of any religious teaching is, "Where does it put Jesus Christ—His person and His work?" Does it rob Him of His fullness? Does it deny either His deity or His humanity? Does it affirm that the believer must have some "new experience" to supplement his experience with Christ? If so, that teaching is wrong and dangerous.

## Draw on Your Spiritual Provisions (Col. 2:11-15)

Remember that the false teaching that threatened the Colossian church was made up of several elements: Oriental mysticism, astrology, philosophy, and Jewish legalism. It is the latter element that Paul dealt with in this section of his letter. Apparently, the false teachers insisted that their converts submit to circumcision and obey the Old Testament Law.

Gnostic legalism was not quite the same as the brand of legalism practiced by the Judaizers whom Paul refuted in his Epistle to the Galatians. The Jewish teachers that Paul attacked in Galatians insisted that circumcision and obedience to the Law were necessary for salvation. (See Acts 15 for some background on this problem.) Gnostic legalism said that the Jewish Law would help the believers become more spiritual. If they were circumcised, and if they watched their diets and observed the holy days, then they would become part of the "spiritual elite" in the church. Unfortunately, we have people with similar ideas in our churches today.

Paul made it clear that the Christian is not subject in any way to the Old Testament legal system, *nor can it do him any good spiritually.* Jesus Christ *alone* is sufficient for our every spiritual need, for all of God's fullness is in Him. We are identified with Jesus Christ because He is the Head of the body (Col. 1:18) and we are the members of the body (1 Cor. 12:12-13). Paul explained our fourfold identification with Jesus Christ that makes it not only unnecessary, but sinful for us to get involved in any kind of legalism.

***Circumcised in Him (v. 11).*** Circumcision was a sign of God's covenant with the

Jewish people (Gen. 17:9-14). Though it was a physical operation, it had a spiritual significance. The trouble was that the Jewish people depended on the physical and not the spiritual. A mere physical operation could never convey spiritual grace (Rom. 2:25-29). Often in the Old Testament, God warned His people to turn from their sins and experience a *spiritual* circumcision of the heart (Deut. 10:16; 30:6; Jer. 4:4; 6:10; Ezek. 44:7). People make the same mistake today when they depend on some religious ritual to save them—such as baptism or the Lord's Supper.

It is not necessary for the believer to submit to circumcision, because he has already experienced a spiritual circumcision through his identification with Jesus Christ. But there is a contrast here between Jewish circumcision and the believer's spiritual circumcision in Christ:

| *Jews* | *Believers* |
|---|---|
| external surgery | internal—the heart |
| only a part of the body | the whole "body of sins" |
| done by hands | done without hands |
| no spiritual help in conquering sin | enables them to overcome sin |

When Jesus Christ died and rose again, He won a complete and final victory over sin. He not only died *for* our sins (salvation), but He "died *unto* sin" (sanctification; see Rom. 6:10ff). What the Law could not do, Jesus Christ accomplished for us. The old nature ("the body of the sins of the flesh") was put off—rendered inoperative—so that we need no longer be enslaved to its desires. The old sinful nature is not eradicated, for we can still sin (1 John 1:5–2:6). But the power has been broken as we yield to Christ and walk in the power of the Spirit.

**Alive in Him (vv. 12-13).** Here Paul used the illustration of baptism. Keep in mind that in the New Testament, the word *baptize* has both a literal and a figurative meaning. The literal meaning is "to dip, to immerse." The figurative meaning is "to be identified with." For example, the Jewish nation was "baptized unto Moses" when it went through the Red Sea (1 Cor. 10:1-2). There was no water involved in this baptism, because they went over on dry land. In this experience, the nation was identified with Moses.

Paul used the word *baptism* in a figurative sense in this section of his letter—for no amount of material water could bury a person with Christ or make him alive in Christ. Water

baptism by immersion is a picture of this spiritual experience. When a person is saved, he is immediately baptized by the Spirit into the body of Christ (1 Cor. 12:12-13) and identified with the Head, Jesus Christ. This identification means that *whatever happened to Christ also happened to us.* When He died, we died with Him. When He was buried, we were buried. When He arose again, we arose with Him—and we left the graveclothes of the old life behind (Col. 3:1-14).

All of this took place "through the faith of the operation of God" (Col. 2:12). It was the power of God that changed us, not the power of water. The Spirit of God identified us with Jesus Christ, and we were buried with Him, raised with Him, and made alive with Him! (The Greek verbs are very expressive: co-buried, co-raised, and co-made alive.) Because God raised His Son from the dead, we have eternal life.

The practical application is clear: since we are identified with Christ, and He is the fullness of God, *what more do we need?* We have experienced the energy of God through faith in Christ, so why turn to the deadness of the Law? God has forgiven us all our trespasses (Col. 2:13b) so that we have a perfect standing before Him.

**Free from the Law in Him (v. 14).** Jesus not only took our sins to the cross (1 Peter 2:24), but He also took the Law to the cross and nailed it there, forever out of the way. The Law was certainly against us, because it was impossible for us to meet its holy demands. Even though God never gave the Ten Commandments to the Gentiles, the righteous demands of the Law—God's holy standards—were "written in their hearts" (Rom. 2:12-16).

When He shed His blood for sinners, Jesus Christ canceled the huge debt that was against sinners because of their disobedience to God's holy Law. In Bible days, financial records were often kept on parchment, and the writing could be washed off. This is the picture Paul painted.

How could the holy God be just in canceling a debt? In this way His Son paid the full debt when He died on the cross. If a judge sets a man free who is guilty of a crime, the judge cheapens the law and leaves the injured party without restitution. God paid sin's debt when He gave His Son on the cross, and He upheld the holiness of His own Law.

But Jesus Christ did even more than cancel

the debt: He took the Law that condemned us and set it aside so that we are no longer under its dominion. We are "delivered from the Law" (Rom. 7:6). We "are not under the Law, but under grace" (Rom. 6:14). This does not mean that we are lawless, because the righteousness of the Law is fulfilled in us as we walk in the power of the Spirit (Rom. 8:4). Our relationship with Jesus Christ enables us to obey God out of love, not out of slavish fear.

**Victorious in Him (v. 15).** Jesus not only dealt with sin and the Law on the cross, but He also dealt with Satan. Speaking about His crucifixion, Jesus said, "Now is the judgment of this world; now shall the prince of this world be cast out" (John 12:31). The death of Christ on the cross looked like a great victory for Satan, but it turned out to be a great defeat from which Satan cannot recover.

Jesus had three great victories on the cross. First, He "disarmed the powers and authorities" (Col. 2:15, NIV), stripping Satan and his army of whatever weapons they held. Satan cannot harm the believer who will not harm himself. It is when we cease to watch and pray (as did Peter) that Satan can use his weapons against us.

Second, Jesus "made a public spectacle" (Col. 2:15, NIV) of the enemy, exposing Satan's deceit and vileness. In His death, resurrection, and ascension, Christ vindicated God and vanquished the devil.

His third victory is found in the word *triumph*. Whenever a Roman general won a great victory on foreign soil, took many captives and much loot, and gained new territory for Rome, he was honored by an official parade known as "the Roman triumph." Paul alluded to this practice in his Second Letter to the Corinthians (see 2 Cor. 2:14). Jesus Christ won a complete victory, and He returned to glory in a great triumphal procession (Eph. 4:8ff). In this, He disgraced and defeated Satan.

You and I share in His victory over the devil. We need not worry about the elemental forces that govern the planets and try to influence men's lives. The satanic armies of principalities and powers are defeated and disgraced! As we claim the victory of Christ, use the equipment He has provided for us (Eph. 6:10ff), and trust Him, we are free from the influence of the devil.

What a wonderful position and provision we have in Christ! Are we living up to it by faith?

# CHAPTER SEVEN
# BELIEVER, BEWARE!
## *Colossians 2:16-23*

From the flashing red signals at a railroad crossing to the skull and crossbones on a bottle of rubbing alcohol, warnings are a part of daily life. Children must be taught to heed warnings, and adults must be reminded not to get too accustomed to them. Warnings are a matter of life or death.

The spiritual life also has its dangers and its warnings. Moses warned the Israelites to beware of forgetting the Lord once they got settled in the Promised Land (Deut. 6:12). The Lord Jesus often used the word *beware* (Matt. 7:15; Mark 12:38; Luke 12:15).

Paul had already warned about the false teachers (Col. 2:8). In this section of his letter, Paul gave three warnings for us to heed if we are to enjoy our fullness in Jesus Christ.

**"Let No One Judge You" (Col. 2:16-17)**
This warning exposes the danger of the *legalism* of the gnostic teachers in Colossae. Their doctrines were a strange mixture of Oriental mysticism, Jewish legalism, and a smattering of philosophy and Christian teaching. Apparently, the Jewish legalism played a very important role. This is no surprise, because human nature thrives in "religious duties." The flesh is weak when it comes to doing spiritual things (Matt. 26:41), but it is very strong when it comes to practicing religious rules and regulations. Somehow, adhering to the religious routine inflates the ego and makes a person content in his self-righteousness. In discussing this problem, Paul presented three important truths.

**The basis for our freedom (v. 16a).** It is found in the word *therefore*, which relates this discussion to the previous verses. The basis for our freedom is the person and work of Jesus Christ. All the fullness of the Godhead dwells bodily in Him (Col. 2:9). On the cross, He canceled the debt and the dominion of the Law (Col. 2:14). As believers, we are under grace as a rule of life and not under Law (Rom. 6:14ff).

The believing Gentiles in Colossae never

were under the Law of Moses since that Law was given only to Israel (Rom. 9:4). It seems strange that, now that they were Christians, they would want to submit themselves to Jewish legalism! Paul had the same problem with the Gentiles in the churches of Galatia, and he refuted Jewish legalism in his letter to the Galatian believers (Gal. 3:1ff).

The person who judges a believer because that believer is not living under Jewish laws is really judging Jesus Christ. He is saying that Christ did not finish the work of salvation on the cross, and that we must add something to it. He is also saying that Jesus Christ is not sufficient for all the spiritual needs of the Christian. The false teachers in Colossae were claiming a "deeper spiritual life" for all who would practice the Law. Outwardly, their practices seemed to be spiritual; but in actual fact, these practices accomplished nothing spiritual.

*The bondage of legalism (v. 16).* Let no one tell you otherwise: legalism *is* bondage! Peter called it a "yoke upon the neck" (Acts 15:10). Paul used the same image when he warned the Galatians: "Stand fast therefore in the liberty wherewith Christ hath made us free, and be not entangled again with the yoke of bondage" (Gal. 5:1).

These legalistic regulations had to do with foods and with eating and drinking (partaking or abstaining). Under the Old Testament system, certain foods were classified as "clean" or "unclean" (see Lev. 11). But Jesus made it clear that, of *itself,* food was neutral. It was what came out of the heart that made a person spiritual or unspiritual (Matt. 15:1-20). Peter was reminded of this lesson again when he was on the housetop in Joppa (Acts 10:9ff) and when he was rebuked in Antioch by Paul (Gal. 2:11ff). "But food does not bring us near to God; we are no worse if we do not eat, and no better if we do" (1 Cor. 8:8, NIV).

It is likely that God's instructions about foods given through Moses had *physical* reasons behind them as well as spiritual. This point that Paul brings up is a different matter. If a man feels he is healthier for abstaining from certain foods, then he should abstain and care for his body. But he should not judge others who can eat that food, nor should he make it a test of spiritual living. Romans 14—15 is the key passage on this subject.

But the legalistic system not only involved diet; it also involved *days.* Once again, this was borrowed from the laws given through Moses. The Old Testament Jew was commanded to keep the weekly Sabbath, which was the seventh day of the week (Ex. 20:9-11). It is wrong to call Sunday "the Christian Sabbath" because it is not so designated in the New Testament. It is "the Lord's Day" (Rev. 1:10), the first day of the week (Acts 20:7; 1 Cor. 16:2), the day that commemorates the victorious resurrection of Jesus Christ from the dead (John 20:1, 19, 26).

The Jews also had their feast days (Lev. 25) and their special "new-moon" celebrations (see Isa. 1:13). Their religion was tied to the calendar. Now, all of this had its proper function under the old dispensation; but it was not meant to be a permanent part of the faith under the new dispensation (see John 1:17). The Law was a schoolmaster that helped to train and discipline Israel in the childhood of the nation, preparing the people for the coming of the Messiah. Now that Jesus had come, the schoolmaster was no longer needed to perform the same functions (Gal. 3:24—4:11).

Does this mean that the Old Testament Law has no ministry to New Testament Christians? Of course not! The Law still reveals the holiness of God, and in the Law Jesus Christ can be seen (Luke 24:27). "We know that the Law is good if a man uses it properly" (1 Tim. 1:8, NIV). The Law reveals sin and warns of the consequences of sin—but it has no power to prevent sin or redeem the sinner. Only grace can do that.

*The blessing of grace (v. 17).* The Law is but a shadow; but in Christ we have the reality, the substance. "The Law is only a shadow of the good things that are coming" (Heb. 10:1, NIV). Why go back into shadows when we have the reality in Jesus Christ? This is like trying to hug a shadow when the reality is at hand!

People who religiously observe diets and days give an outward semblance of spirituality, but these practices cannot change their hearts. Legalism is a popular thing because you can "measure" your spiritual life—and even brag about it! But this is a far cry from measuring up to Christ! (Eph. 4:13)

## "Let No Man Beguile You of Your Reward" (Col. 2:18-19)

The word translated *beguile* in the *King James Version* means "to declare unworthy of a prize." It is an athletic term: the umpire disqualifies the contestant because he has not obeyed the rules. The contestant does not cease to be a citizen of the land, but he forfeits the honor of winning a prize. A Christian who fails to obey God's directions does not lose his salvation. But he does lose the approval of the Lord and the rewards He has promised to those who are faithful (1 Cor. 3:8).

It is a gracious act of God that He has promised rewards to those who serve Him. Certainly He does not owe us anything! We ought to be so grateful that He has saved us from judgment that we would serve Him whether or not we received a reward. Most of God's servants probably obey Him out of love and devotion and never think about rewards. Just as there are degrees of punishment in hell (Matt. 23:14), so there will be degrees of glory in heaven—even though all believers will be like Christ in their glorified bodies. The old Puritan Thomas Watson said it perfectly: "Though every vessel of mercy shall be full [in heaven], yet one may hold more than another."

There is, then, the danger that our lives today will rob us of reward and glory tomorrow. The peril Paul had in mind here was Oriental *mysticism*, the belief that a person can have an immediate experience with the spiritual world, completely apart from the Word of God or the Holy Spirit. The false teachers in Colossae had visions and made contact with angels. In bypassing the Word of God and the Spirit of God, they were opening themselves to all kinds of demonic activity—because Satan knows how to give counterfeit experiences to people (2 Cor. 11:13-15).

The word translated "intruding" was a technical term used by the mystical religions of that day. It meant "to set foot in the inner shrine, to be fully initiated into the mysteries of the religion." No Christian has to go through any initiation ceremony to get into the presence of God. We may have "boldness to enter into the holiest by the blood of Jesus" (Heb. 10:19). We may "come boldly unto the throne of grace" (Heb. 4:16). And as for worshiping angels, *they are our servants!* The angels are "all ministering spirits, sent forth to minister for them who shall be heirs of salvation" (Heb. 1:14).

Of course, all of this mystical ceremony was wrapped up in a false humility that was actually an expression of pride. "I am not good enough to come directly to God," the gnostic would say, "so I will start with one of the angels."

Trying to reach God the Father through anyone or anything other than His Son, Jesus Christ, is idolatry. Jesus Christ is the one and only Mediator between God and man (John 14:6; 1 Tim. 2:5). The person who worships through angels or saints now in heaven does not prove his humility, for he is not submitting to the authority of God's Word. Actually, he reveals a subtle kind of pride that substitutes man-made traditions for the Word of God. "His unspiritual mind puffs him up with idle notions" (Col. 2:18, NIV).

True worship always humbles a person. The *mind* is awed by the greatness of God; the *heart* is filled with love for God; and the *will* is submitted to the purpose God has for the life. The gnostics, however, were interested primarily in "deeper spiritual knowledge," and they ignored God's truth. Their "inner secrets" gave them big heads, but not burning hearts or submissive wills. "Knowledge puffs up, but love builds up" (1 Cor. 8:1, NIV).

It is worth noting that a true spiritual experience with God leads to submission and service. When Job met the Lord he said, "I have heard of Thee by the hearing of the ear, but now mine eye seeth Thee. Wherefore I abhor myself, and repent in dust and ashes" (Job 42:5-6). Peter fell down before his Lord and said, "Depart from me; for I am a sinful man, O Lord" (Luke 5:8). Isaiah saw the Lord and confessed how sinful he was (Isa. 6); and when John saw the risen Christ, he fell at His feet like a dead man (Rev. 1:17).

The cheap familiarity with which some people approach God in prayer, or talk about Him in testimony or conversation sometimes borders on blasphemy. The saintly Bishop Westcott of Great Britain, author of many scholarly commentaries on various books of the Bible, once wrote: "Every year makes me tremble at the daring with which people speak of spiritual things."

Tragically, this "vain religion of the puffed-up fleshly mind" is but a mere substitute for true spiritual nourishment from Jesus Christ, the Head of the body, His church. This is one of several passages in the New Testament that pictures the church as the body of Christ (see Rom. 12:4ff; 1 Cor. 12–14; Eph. 4:4-16; Col. 1:18, 24). All of us, as believers, are members of the spiritual body, the church, because of the work of the Holy Spirit (1 Cor.

12:12-13). As Christians, we minister to one another in the body just as the various parts of the human body minister to each other (1 Cor. 12:14ff).

But if a believer does not draw on the spiritual nourishment that comes from Christ and other Christians, he becomes weak. The false teachers were not holding to the Head, and therefore they were spiritually undernourished; but *they* thought they were spiritual experts. Imagine thinking yourself a giant when in reality you are a pygmy!

The false teachers were anxious to win converts to their cause; but the spiritual body grows by *nutrition,* not by *addition.* Every member of Christ's body, including the "ligaments and sinews" (joints and bands), is important to the health and growth of the body. No matter what your spiritual gift may be, you are important to the church. In fact, some people who may not have spectacular public ministries are probably just as important behind the scenes as those out in public.

It is through worship, prayer, and the Word that we draw on the spiritual resources of Christ. All of us must be part of a local church where we can exercise our own spiritual gifts (Eph. 4:11-17). "Now to each one the manifestation of the Spirit is given for the common good" (1 Cor. 12:7, NIV). The New Testament says nothing of "isolated saints" outside of the local church.

But it is possible to be *in* a local church and not draw on the Head and the nourishment of the spiritual body. The false teachers in Colossae sought to introduce their teachings into the local assembly; and if they succeeded, they would have caused the spiritual nourishment to *decrease* instead of *increase.* Unless the members of the local assembly abide in Christ, yield to the Spirit, and obey the Word, they cannot experience the life of the Head, Jesus Christ.

There is a fascination with "religious mysticism" that attracts people. Learning mysteries, being initiated into the inner secrets, and having contact with the spirit world all seem exciting.

But these practices are soundly condemned by God. The true Christian glories in Christ, not in his own experience. He follows the Word, led by the Holy Spirit; and as he abides in Christ, he experiences blessing and fruitfulness. He seeks no other experience than that which relates him to the Head, Jesus Christ.

## "Let No One Enslave You!"
## (Col. 2:20-23)

Paul condemned legalism and mysticism; next he attacked and condemned *asceticism.* An ascetic practices rigorous self-denial and even self-mortification in order to become more spiritual. Ascetic practices were popular during the Middle Ages: wearing hair shirts next to the skin, sleeping on hard beds, whipping oneself, not speaking for days (maybe years), going without food or sleep, etc.

There is a definite relationship between legalism and asceticism, for the ascetic often subjects himself to rules and regulations: "Touch not, taste not, handle not" (Col. 2:21). Certain foods or practices are unholy and must be avoided. Other practices are holy and must never be neglected. The ascetic's entire life is wrapped up in a system of rules.

As Christians, we admit that physical discipline is needed in our lives. Some of us eat too much and are overweight. Some of us drink too much coffee or cola drinks and are nervous and upset. We believe that our bodies are temples of the Holy Spirit (1 Cor. 6:19-20), yet sometimes we do not care for our bodies as we should. "Physical training is of some value," Paul wrote (1 Tim. 4:8, NIV). Paul disciplined his own body and kept it under control (1 Cor. 9:27). So there is a place in our Christian lives for proper care of our bodies.

But the ascetic hopes to sanctify the soul by his discipline of the body, and it is this heresy that Paul attacked. Just as days and diets have no sanctifying value, neither does fleshly discipline. In this section Paul gave several arguments to warn the Christian against carnal religious asceticism.

*The Christian's spiritual position (v. 20).* Asceticism has to do with the rudiments of the world and not the riches of the kingdom. Earlier we saw the word *rudiments* and learned that it meant "the fundamentals or ABCs of something" (Col. 2:8). In this case, "the rudiments of the world" refers to rules and regulations about foods. As Christians, we are dead to all of this because of our union with Jesus Christ in death, burial, and resurrection (see Rom. 6; Col. 2:12-15). Though we are *in* the world physically, we are not *of* the world spiritually (John 17:15-16). We have been transferred into God's kingdom (Col. 1:13), and therefore we govern our lives by His laws and not the rules of men.

This is not to suggest that Christians are

lawless. A student in a Christian school once told me it was "unspiritual" for him to obey the rules! I reminded him that Christians always respect the authority of those over them (1 Peter 2:11ff), and that he knew the rules before he arrived on campus. If he did not like them, he should have stayed home! Paul was not counseling us to be rebels, but he was warning us not to think we are spiritual because we obey certain rules and regulations that pertain to the body.

**The futility of ascetic rules (vv. 21-22).** To begin with, these rules did not come from God; they were the inventions of men. God "giveth us richly all things to enjoy" (1 Tim. 6:17). Foods have been "created to be received with thanksgiving" (1 Tim. 4:3). But the "commandments and doctrines" of the false teachers replaced the inspired Word of God (see Mark 7:6-9). The doctrines were what the false teachers believed; the commandments were the regulations they gave in applying their doctrines to practical daily life.

God gave foods to be used, and they "perish with the using" (Col. 2:22). Jesus explained that food went into the stomach, not the heart (Mark 7:18ff). The man who refuses certain foods because they will defile him does not understand what either Jesus or Paul taught: "I know, and am persuaded by the Lord Jesus, that there is nothing unclean of itself" (Rom. 14:14).

Many of us are quick to criticize the ancient monks, the Oriental mystics, and the Hindu or Muslim fakirs; but we fail to see this same error in our own churches. While there are automatic connections between physical discipline and health, there is no connection between such discipline and holiness. If we deliberately abstain from some food or drink to keep from hurting a weaker Christian (Rom. 14:13ff), that is one thing. But we must not say that our abstinence makes us more spiritual than another brother who partakes of that food and gives thanks to God (Rom. 14:6).

**The deception of asceticism (v. 23).** The people who practice asceticism have a "reputation" for spirituality, but the product does not live up to the promotion. I am amazed at the way educated people in America flock to see and hear gurus and other Eastern spiritual leaders whose teachings cannot change the human heart. This "self-imposed worship" is not the true worship of God, which must be "in spirit and in truth" (John 4:24). Their humility is false, and their harsh disciplines accomplish nothing for the inner man.

While it is certainly better to exercise self-control than to yield to the physical appetites of the body, we must not think that such self-control is necessarily *spiritually* motivated. The ascetics of many non-Christian religions give evidence of remarkable self-control. The stoics and their ascetic philosophy were well known in Paul's day. Their adherents could duplicate any discipline that the gnostic teachers cared to present.

The power of Christ in the life of the believer does more than merely restrain the desires of the flesh: *it puts new desires within him.* Nature determines appetite. The Christian has the very nature of God within (2 Peter 1:4), and this means he has godly ambitions and desires. He does not need *law* on the outside to control his appetites because he has *life* on the inside! The harsh rules of the ascetics "lack any value in restraining sensual indulgence" (Col. 2:23, NIV). If anything, they eventually bring out the worst instead of the best. In the closing two chapters of this letter, Paul explained how the new life functions in the believer to give him purity and victory.

This section closes the second chapter of Colossians in which the emphasis was on *danger*. Paul defended the preeminence of Jesus Christ, and he refuted the false doctrines of legalism, mysticism, and asceticism. It now remains for us to believe what he wrote and practice these spiritual principles.

The answer to legalism is the spiritual reality we have in Christ. The answer to mysticism is the spiritual union with Christ, the Head of the church. The answer to asceticism is our position in Christ in death, burial, and resurrection.

We put all of this into daily practice as we fellowship with Christ through worship, the Word, and prayer. As we yield to the indwelling Spirit, we receive the power we need for daily living. It is in our fellowship with other believers that we contribute spiritually to the growth of the body, the church, and the other members of the body contribute to us. What a wonderful way to live!

Is Christ preeminent in your life? Are you drawing on His spiritual power, or depending on some man-made "religious" substitute?

# CHAPTER EIGHT
# HEAVEN
# ON EARTH
*Colossians 3:1-11*

In the final two chapters of Colossians, Paul moved into the practical application of the doctrines he had been teaching. After all, it does little good if Christians *declare* and *defend* the truth, but fail to *demonstrate* it in their lives. There are some Christians who will defend the truth at the drop of a hat, but their personal lives deny the doctrines they profess to love. "They profess that they know God, but in works they deny Him" (Titus 1:16).

We must keep in mind that the pagan religions of Paul's day said little or nothing about personal morality. A worshiper could bow before an idol, put his offering on the altar, and go back to live the same old life of sin. What a person believed had no direct relationship with how he behaved, and no one would condemn a person for his behavior.

But the Christian faith brought a whole new concept into pagan society: what we believe has a very definite connection with how we behave! After all, faith in Christ means being united to Christ; and if we share His life, we must follow His example. He cannot live in us by His Spirit and permit us to live in sin. Paul connected doctrine with duty in this section by giving his readers three instructions.

## Seek the Heavenly (Col. 3:1-4)
The emphasis is on the believer's relationship with Christ.

**We died with Christ (v. 3a).** The fullest explanation of this wonderful truth is found in Romans 6–8. Christ not only died *for* us (substitution), but we died *with* Him (identification). Christ not only died *for* sin, bearing its penalty; but He died *unto* sin, breaking its power. Because we are "in Christ" through the work of the Holy Spirit (1 Cor. 12:13), we died with Christ. This means that we can have victory over the old sin nature that wants to control us. "How shall we, that are dead to sin, live any longer therein?" (Rom. 6:2)

**We live in Christ (v. 4a).** Christ is our life. Eternal life is not some heavenly substance that God imparts when we, as sinners, trust the Saviour. Eternal life is Jesus Christ Himself. "He that hath the Son hath life; and he that hath not the Son of God hath not life" (1 John 5:12). We are dead and alive at the same time—dead to sin and alive in Christ.

Someone has said, "Life is what you are alive to." A child may come alive when you talk about a baseball game or an ice-cream cone. A teenager may come alive when you mention cars or dates. Paul wrote, "For to me to live is Christ" (Phil. 1:21). Christ was Paul's life and he was alive to anything that related to Christ. So should it be with every believer.

Years ago I heard a story about two sisters who enjoyed attending dances and wild parties. Then they were converted and found new life in Christ. They received an invitation to a party and sent their RSVP in these words: "We regret that we cannot attend because we recently died."

**We are raised with Christ (v. 1a).** It is possible to be alive and still live in the grave. During World War II, several Jewish refugees hid in a cemetery, and a baby was actually born in one of the graves. However, when Jesus gave us His life, He lifted us out of the grave and set us on the throne in heaven! Christ is seated at the right hand of God, and we are seated there "in Christ."

The word *if* does not suggest that Paul's readers might not have been "risen with Christ"; for all of us, as believers, are identified with Christ in death, burial, resurrection, and ascension. The word *since* gives the truer meaning of the word. Our exalted position in Christ is not a hypothetical thing, or a goal for which we strive. It is an accomplished fact.

**We are hidden in Christ (v. 3b).** We no longer belong to the world, but to Christ; and the sources of life that we enjoy come only from Him. "Hidden in Christ" means security and satisfaction. The eminent Greek scholar, Dr. A.T. Robertson, comments on this: "So here we are in Christ who is in God, and no burglar, not even Satan himself, can separate us from the love of God in Christ Jesus (Rom. 8:31-39)" *(Paul and the Intellectuals,* Broadman, p. 98).

The Christian life is a "hidden life" as far as the world is concerned, because the world does not know Christ (see 1 John 4:1-6). Our sphere of life is not this earth, but heaven; and the things that attract us and excite us belong to heaven, not to earth. This does not mean that we should ignore our earthly responsibilities. Rather it means that our motives and our strength come from heaven, not earth.

**We are glorified in Christ (v. 4b).** Christ is now seated at the Father's right hand, but one day He will come to take His people home (1 Thes. 4:13-18). When He does, we shall enter into eternal glory with Christ. When He is revealed in His glory, we shall also be revealed in glory. According to the Apostle Paul, *we have already been glorified!* (Rom. 8:30) This glory simply has not yet been revealed. Christ has already given us His glory (John 17:22), but the full revelation of the glory awaits the return of the Saviour (Rom. 8:17-25).

Now, in view of our wonderful identification with Christ, we have a great responsibility: "Seek those things which are above" (Col. 3:1). Through Christ's death, burial, resurrection, and ascension, we have been separated from the old life of this world, and we now belong to a new heavenly life.

But how do we "seek those things which are above"? The secret is found in Colossians 3:2: "Habitually set your mind—your attention—on things above, not on things on the earth" (literal translation). Our feet must be on earth, but our minds must be in heaven. This is not to suggest that (as D.L. Moody used to say) we become "so heavenly minded that we are no earthly good." It means that the practical everyday affairs of life get their direction from Christ in heaven. It means further that we look at earth from heaven's point of view.

While attending a convention in Washington, D.C., I watched a Senate committee hearing over television. I believe they were considering a new ambassador to the United Nations. The late Senator Hubert Humphrey was making a comment as I turned on the television set: "You must remember that in politics, how you stand depends on where you sit." He was referring, of course, to the political party seating arrangement in the Senate, but I immediately applied it to my position in Christ. How I stand—and walk—depends on where I sit; *and I am seated with Christ in the heavenlies!*

When the nation of Israel came to the border of the Promised Land, they refused to enter; and, because of their stubborn unbelief, they had to wander in the wilderness for forty years (see Num. 13–14). That whole generation, starting with the twenty-year-olds, died in the wilderness, except for Caleb and Joshua, the only two spies who believed God. How were Caleb and Joshua able to "get the victory" during those forty difficult years in the wilderness? *Their minds and hearts were in Canaan!* They knew they had an inheritance coming, and they lived in the light of that inheritance.

The Queen of England exercises certain powers and privileges because she sits on the throne. The President of the United States has privileges and powers because he sits behind the desk in the oval office of the White House. The believer is seated on the throne with Christ. We must constantly keep our affection and our attention fixed on the things of heaven, through the Word and prayer, as well as through worship and service. We can enjoy "days of heaven upon the earth" (Deut. 11:21) if we will keep our hearts and minds in the heavenlies.

## Slay the Earthly (Col. 3:5-9)

We turn now from the positive to the negative. There are some people who do not like the negative. "Give us positive doctrines!" they say. "Forget about negative warnings and admonitions!" But the negative warnings and commands grow out of the positive truths of Christian doctrine. This is why Paul wrote, "Mortify *therefore.*"

No amount of positive talk about health will cure a ruptured appendix. The doctor will have to "get negative" and take out the appendix. No amount of lecturing on beauty will produce a garden. The gardener has to pull weeds! The positive and the negative go together, and one without the other leads to imbalance.

The word *mortify* means "put to death." Because we have died with Christ (Col. 3:3), we have the spiritual power to slay the earthly, fleshly desires that want to control us. Paul called this "reckoning" ourselves to be dead to sin but alive in Christ (Rom. 6:11). Our Lord used the same idea when He said, "And if thy right eye offend thee, pluck it out" (Matt. 5:29-30).

Obviously, neither Paul nor Jesus was talking about *literal* surgery. Sin does not come from the eye, hand, or foot; it comes from the heart, the evil desires within. Centuries ago in England, if a pickpocket was convicted, his right hand was cut off. If he was convicted a second time, his left hand was amputated. One pickpocket lost both hands and continued his "trade" by using his teeth! Physical surgery can never change the heart.

Not only was Paul negative in this paragraph, but he also *named sins;* and some people do not like that. These sins belong to the old life and have no place in our new life in Christ. Furthermore, God's judgment falls on those who practice these sins; and God is no respecter of persons. God's wrath fell on the Gentile world because of these sins (Rom. 1:18ff), and His wrath will fall again. "Because of these, the wrath of God is coming," Paul warned (Col. 3:6, NIV).

*Fornication* refers to sexual immorality in general. *Uncleanness* means "lustful impurity that is connected with luxury and loose living." *Inordinate affection* describes a state of mind that excites sexual impurity. The person who cultivates this kind of appetite can always find opportunity to satisfy it. *Evil concupiscence* means "base, evil desires." It is clear that desires lead to deeds, appetites lead to actions. If we would purify our actions, then we must first purify our minds and hearts.

What we desire usually determines what we do. If I create in my children an appetite for candy, then I must satisfy that appetite. If they become overweight and unhealthy, then I must change their appetites, and I must teach them how to enjoy foods other than sweets. "Create in me a clean heart, O God" (Ps. 51:10) should be our prayer; for it is out of the heart that these evil desires come (Mark 7:21-23).

After he had named these sensual sins, Paul added, "and covetousness, which is idolatry" (Col. 3:5b). *Covetousness* is the sin of always wanting more, whether it be more things or more pleasures. The covetous person is never satisfied with what he has, and he is usually envious of what other people have. This is idolatry, for covetousness puts things in the place of God. "Thou shalt not covet" is the last of the Ten Commandments (Ex. 20:17). Yet this sin can make us break all of the other nine! A covetous person will dishonor God, take God's name in vain, lie, steal, and commit every other sin in order to satisfy his sinful desires.

Do believers in local churches commit such sins? Unfortunately, they sometimes do. Each of the New Testament epistles sent to local churches makes mention of these sins and warns against them. I am reminded of a pastor who preached a series of sermons against the sins of the saints. A member of his congregation challenged him one day and said that it would be better if the pastor preached those messages to the lost. "After all," said the church member, "sin in the life of a Christian is different from sin in the lives of other people."

"Yes" replied the pastor, *"it's worse!"*

After warning us against the sensual sins, Paul then pointed out the dangers of the social sins (Col. 3:8-9). Dr. G. Campbell Morgan called these "the sins in good standing." We are so accustomed to anger, critical attitudes, lying, and coarse humor among believers that we are no longer upset or convicted about these sins. We would be shocked to see a church member commit some sensual sin, but we will watch him lose his temper in a business meeting and call it "righteous indignation."

The picture here is that of a person changing clothes: "Put off . . . put on" (Col. 3:9-10). This relates to the resurrection of Jesus Christ (Col. 3:1); for when He arose from the dead, Jesus Christ left the graveclothes behind (John 20:1-10). He had entered into a glorious resurrection life and had no need for the graveclothes. Likewise, when Lazarus was raised from the dead, Jesus instructed the people to "loose him, and let him go" (John 11:44).

The graveclothes represent the old life with its sinful deeds. Now that we have new life in Christ, we must walk "in newness of life" by putting off the old deeds and desires (Rom. 6:4). We do this by practicing our position in Christ, by reckoning ourselves to be dead to the old and alive to the new.

Paul began with *anger, wrath, and malice*—sins of bad attitude toward others. The word *anger* is the same as the word *wrath* (Col. 3:6), referring there to the wrath of God. This word describes habitual attitudes, while *wrath* refers to the sudden outburst of anger. God has a right to be angry at sin and to judge it, because He is holy and just. In fact, there is a righteous anger against sin that ought to characterize the saints (Eph. 4:26). But none of us have the right to "play God" and pass final judgment on others by our attitudes. *Malice* is an attitude of ill will toward a person. If we have malice toward a person, we are sad when he is successful, and we rejoice when he has trouble. This is sinful.

*Blasphemy* describes speech that slanders others and tears them down. Often among Christians this kind of malicious gossip masquerades as a spiritual concern: "I would never tell you what I know about her, except that I know you'll want to pray about it." Evil speaking is caused by malice (1 Peter 2:1). If you have deep-seated ill will toward a person, you will use every opportunity to say something bad about him.

*Filthy communication* is just that: foul speech, coarse humor, obscene language. For some reason, some Christians think it is manly or contemporary to use this kind of speech. Low humor sometimes creeps into conversations. If someone says, "Now, take this with a grain of salt!" you can remind him of Colossians 4:6: "Let your speech be always with grace, seasoned with salt." Salt is a symbol of purity, and grace and purity go together.

The final sin Paul named was *lying* (Col. 3:9). He wrote this same warning to the believers in Ephesus (Eph. 4:25). Satan is the liar (John 8:44), while the Holy Spirit is the Spirit of Truth (John 14:17; 15:26). When a Christian lies, he is cooperating with Satan; when he speaks the truth in love (Eph. 4:15), he is cooperating with the Spirit of God.

A lie is any misrepresentation of the truth, *even if the words are accurate.* The tone of voice, the look on the face, or a gesture of the hand can alter the meaning of a sentence. So can the motive of the heart. If my watch is wrong and I give a friend the wrong time, that is not a lie. Lying involves the intent to deceive for the purpose of personal gain. An old proverb says, "Half a fact is a whole lie."

Bishop Warren A. Candler was preaching about the lies of Ananias and Sapphira (Acts 5), and asked the congregation, "If God still struck people dead for lying, where would I be?" The congregation snickered a bit, but the smiles disappeared when the Bishop shouted, "I'd be right here—*preaching to an empty church!*"

## Strengthen the Christly (Col. 3:10-11)

Because we are alive in Christ, we must seek the things that are above. And, because we died with Christ, we must put off the things that belong to the earthly life of past sin. The result is that we can become like Jesus Christ! God wants to renew us and make us into the image of His Son!

The Greek verbs translated *put off* and *put on* (Col. 3:9-10) indicate a once-for-all action. When we trust Christ, we put off the old life and put on the new. The old man has been buried, and the new man is now in control.

But the verb translated "renewed" is a present participle—"who is constantly being renewed." The *crisis* of salvation leads to the *process* of sanctification, becoming more like Jesus Christ.

The Greeks had two different words for *new.* The word *neos* meant "new in time." We use this word as an English prefix in such words as "neoorthodoxy" and "neoclassicism." The word *kainos* meant "new in quality, fresh." Sometimes the two words were used interchangeably in the New Testament, but there is still a fundamental difference.

The believer has once and for all put on the "new man" *(neos),* and, as a consequence, he is being renewed *(kainos).* There is a change in quality, for he is becoming like Jesus Christ. The "new Man" is Jesus Christ, the last Adam (1 Cor. 15:45), the Head of the new creation (2 Cor. 5:17).

How does this renewal come about? Through knowledge. The word *knowledge* was one of the key terms in the vocabulary of the gnostics. But their so-called spiritual knowledge could never change a person's life to make him like Christ. The better he gets to know Christ, the more he becomes like Him (Phil. 3:10).

Man was created in the image of God (Gen. 1:26-27). This involves man's personality (intellect, emotion, will) and man's spirituality (he is more than a body). When man sinned, this image of God was marred and ruined. Adam's children were born in the image of their father (Gen. 5:1, 3). In spite of the ravages of sin, man still bears the image of God (Gen. 9:6; James 3:9).

We were *formed* in God's image, and *deformed* from God's image by sin. But through Jesus Christ, we can be *transformed* into God's image! We must be renewed in the spirit of our minds (Eph. 4:23). As we grow in knowledge of the Word of God, we will be transformed by the Spirit of God to share in the glorious image of God (2 Cor. 3:18). God transforms us by the renewing of our minds (Rom. 12:2), and this involves the study of God's Word. It is the truth that sets us free from the old life (John 8:31-32).

God's purpose for us is that we be "conformed to the image of His Son" (Rom. 8:29). This refers to character, the spiritual quality of the inner man. When we see Jesus Christ, we shall be like Him and have glorified bodies (1 John 3:1-3); but while we are waiting for Him to return, we can become like Him and share His holy image. This is a process of constant renewing as the Spirit of God uses the Word of God.

Human distinctions and differences should be no barrier to holy living in the church. In Jesus Christ, all human distinctions disappear (Col. 3:11). In Christ, there are no nationalities ("neither Greek nor Jew"). There is no recognition of former religious differences ("circumcision nor uncircumcision"). The gnostics taught that circumcision was important to the spiritual life (Col. 2:11ff). But Paul made it clear that this traditional act of physical surgery gave no advantages in the spiritual life.

There are also no cultural differences in Christ ("barbarian, Scythian"). The Greeks considered all non-Greeks to be barbarians; and the Scythians were the lowest barbarians of all! Yet, in Jesus Christ, a person's cultural status is no advantage or disadvantage. Nor is his economic or political status ("bond or free"). Paul made it clear that a slave should try to get his freedom (1 Cor. 7:20-23), but he should not think he is handicapped *spiritually* because of his social position.

All of these human distinctions belong to the "old man" and not the "new man." In his Letter to the Galatians, Paul added, "There is neither male nor female," and thus erased even differences between the sexes. "Christ is all, and in all", was Paul's conclusion. "For ye are all one in Christ Jesus" (Gal. 3:28).

It is wrong to build the fellowship of the church on anything other than Jesus Christ, His person and His work. Ministries that are built on human distinctions, such as race, color, or social standing, are not biblical. One of the evidences of spiritual growth and the renewing of the mind is this willingness to receive and love all who sincerely know Christ and seek to glorify Him. The gnostic "super saints" were trying to isolate the Colossian believers from the rest of the church, and this was wrong. Even though *physically* we do not lose our national heritage when we become Christians, we do not use that heritage as a test of what is spiritual.

"Christ is all and in all" is the emphasis in this letter. "That in all things He might have the preeminence" (Col. 1:18). Because we are complete in Christ, we can look beyond the earthly differences that separate people and enjoy a spiritual unity in the Lord. The gnostic false teachers, like the false teachers today, tried to rob God's people of the rich-

ness of their oneness in Christ. Beware!

We are alive in Christ; therefore, we should seek the heavenly. We are dead in Christ; therefore, we should slay the earthly. We can become like Christ; therefore, we must strengthen the Christly and permit the Spirit to renew our minds, making us more into the image of God.

# CHAPTER NINE
# ALL DRESSED UP AND SOMEPLACE TO GO
*Colossians 3:12-17*

This section completes Paul's exhortation to the Christian to live a holy life. It continues the illustration of *garments:* "Put off . . . put on" (Col. 3:8-10). He exhorted his readers to put off the graveclothes of sin and the old life, and to put on the "graceclothes" of holiness and the new life in Christ.

The emphasis in this section is on *motives.* Why should we put off the old deeds and put on the qualities of the new life? Paul explained four motives that ought to encourage us to walk in newness of life (Rom. 6:4).

**The Grace of Christ (Col. 3:12-14)**
Grace is God's favor to undeserving sinners. Paul reminded the Colossians of what God's grace had done for them.

*God chose them (v. 12a).* The word *elect* means "chosen of God." God's words to Israel through Moses help us to understand the meaning of salvation by grace: "The Lord did not set His love upon you, nor choose you, because ye were more in number than any people; for ye were the fewest of all people. But because the Lord loved you . . . hath the Lord brought you out [of Egypt] with a mighty hand" (Deut. 7:7-8).

This miracle of divine election did not depend on anything that we are or that we have done; for God chose us in Christ "before the foundation of the world" (Eph. 1:4). If God saved a sinner on the basis of merit or works, nobody would be saved. It is all done through God's grace that it might all bring glory to God.

Of course, *election* is a "sacred secret" that belongs to God's children. It is not a doctrine that we believers explain to the unsaved. "The Lord knows them that are His" (2 Tim. 2:19), so we must leave the working out of His eternal purposes with Him. Our task is to share the Good News of the Gospel with a lost world.

*God set them apart (v. 12).* That is the meaning of the word holy. Because we have trusted Christ, we have been set apart from the world unto the Lord. We are not our own; we belong completely to Him (1 Cor. 6:19-20). Just as the marriage ceremony sets apart a man and a woman for each other exclusively, so salvation sets the believer apart exclusively for Jesus Christ. Would it not be a horrible thing, at the end of a wedding, to see the groom run off with the maid of honor? It is just as horrible to contemplate the Christian living for the world and the flesh.

*God loves them (v. 12).* When an unbeliever sins, he is a creature breaking the laws of the holy Creator and Judge. But when a Christian sins, he is a child of God breaking the loving heart of his Father. Love is the strongest motivating power in the world. As the believer grows in his love for God, he will grow in his desire to obey Him and walk in the newness of life that he has in Christ.

*God has forgiven them (vv. 13-14).* "Having forgiven you all trespasses" (Col. 2:13). God's forgiveness is complete and final; it is not conditional or partial. How is the holy God able to forgive us guilty sinners? Because of the sacrifice of Jesus Christ on the cross. God has forgiven us "for Christ's sake" (Eph. 4:32), and not for our own sake.

Chosen by God, set apart for God, loved by God, and forgiven by God. They all add up to GRACE! Now, because of these gracious blessings, the Christian has some solemn responsibilities before God. He must put on the beautiful graces of the Christian life. Paul named eight graces.

1. Put on . . . tender mercies (Col. 3:12). The Greek uses the term *bowels of compassion* because the Greek people located the deeper emotions in the intestinal area, while we locate them in the heart. As believers, we need to display tender feelings of compassion toward one another (see Phil. 2:1ff). This is not something that we turn on and off, like the TV set. It is a constant attitude of heart that makes us easy to live with.

2. Put on . . . kindness (Col. 3:12). We

have been saved because of God's kindness toward us through Jesus Christ (Eph. 2:7; Titus 3:4). We, in turn, ought to show kindness toward others. "Be ye kind one to another" (Eph. 4:32) is God's command.

One of the most beautiful pictures of kindness in the Bible is King David's treatment of the crippled prince, Mephibosheth (see 2 Samuel 9). David's desire was to show "the kindness of God" to King Saul's family because of his own love for Saul's son, Jonathan. The young man chosen was Mephibosheth, Jonathan's son, a poor cripple. If David had acted according to justice, he would have condemned Mephibosheth, for the man belonged to a condemned family. But David acted on the basis of love and grace.

David sought Mephibosheth and assured him not to be afraid. He invited Mephibosheth to live in the palace as a member of his family, and to eat at the king's bountiful table. This is the kindness of God! You and I have experienced an even greater kindness, for as Christians, we are God's children and shall live with Him in heaven forever!

3. Put on . . . humbleness of mind (Col. 3:12). The pagan world of Paul's day did not admire humility. Instead, they admired pride and domination. Jesus Christ is the greatest example of humbleness of mind (Phil. 2:1ff). Humility is not thinking poorly of oneself. Rather, it is having the proper estimate of oneself in the will of God (Rom. 12:3). The person with humbleness of mind thinks of others first and not of himself.

4. Put on . . . meekness (Col. 3:12). Meekness is not weakness; it is power under control. This word was used to describe a soothing wind, a healing medicine, and a colt that had been broken. In each instance, there is *power:* a wind can become a storm; too much medicine can kill; a horse can break loose. But this power is under control. The meek person does not have to fly off the handle because he has everything under control.

5. Put on . . . long-suffering (Col. 3:12). This word is literally "long-temper." The short-tempered person speaks and acts impulsively and lacks self-control. When a person is long-suffering, he can put up with provoking people or circumstances without retaliating. It is good to be able to get angry, for this is a sign of holy character. But it is wrong to get angry quickly at the wrong things and for the wrong reasons.

6. Put on . . . forbearance (Col. 3:13). This word literally means "to hold up" or "to hold back." God is forbearing toward sinners in that He holds back His judgment (Rom. 2:4; 3:25). Meekness, long-suffering, and forbearance go together.

7. Put on . . . forgiveness (Col. 3:13). This is the logical result of all that Paul has written so far in this section. It is not enough that the Christian must endure grief and provocation, and refuse to retaliate; he must also forgive the troublemaker. If he does not, then feelings of malice will develop in the heart; and these can lead to greater sins.

It is Christlike to forgive (Eph. 4:32), and forgiveness opens the heart to the fullness of the love of God. The very instant we have a complaint against another person, we should forgive him in our hearts. ("Family forgiveness" is another matter. We should go to the offender and seek to help him in love. See Matt. 18:15-35.)

8. Put on . . . love (Col. 3:14). This is the most important of the Christian virtues, and it acts like a "girdle" that ties all the other virtues together. All of the spiritual qualities Paul has named are aspects of true Christian love, as a reading of 1 Corinthians 13 will reveal. Love is the first of the fruit of the Spirit and the other virtues follow—joy (Col. 3:16), peace (Col. 3:15), long-suffering, gentleness, kindness, and meekness (Col. 3:12).

When love rules in our lives, it unites all these spiritual virtues so that there is beauty and harmony, indicating spiritual maturity. This harmony and maturity keep the life balanced and growing. The gnostic system could never do this.

### The Peace of Christ (Col. 3:15)

In this verse Paul turned from character to conduct. How can a Christian know when he is doing God's will? One answer is: the peace of Christ in the heart and in the church. When the believer loses his inner peace, he knows that he has in some way disobeyed God.

The word translated "rule" is an athletic term. It means "to preside at the games and distribute the prizes." Paul used a variation of this word in his Letter to the Colossians: "Let no one declare you unworthy of a prize" (literal translation, Col. 2:18). In the Greek games, there were judges (we would call them *umpires)* who rejected the contestants who were not qualified, and who disqualified those who broke the rules.

The peace of God is the "Umpire" in our believing hearts and our churches. When we obey the will of God, we have His peace within; but when we step out of His will (even unintentionally), we lose His peace.

We must beware, however, of a false peace in the heart. Jonah deliberately disobeyed God, yet he was able to go to sleep in the hold of a ship *in a storm!* "I had peace about it!" is not sufficient evidence that we are in the will of God. We must pray, surrender to His will, and seek His guidance in the Scriptures. The peace of heart *alone* is not always the peace of God.

Something else is involved: if we have peace in our hearts, we will be at peace with others in the church. We are called to one body, and our relationship in that body must be one of harmony and peace. If we are out of the will of God, we are certain to bring discord and disharmony to the church. Jonah thought he was at peace, when actually his sins created a storm!

When a Christian loses the peace of God, he begins to go off in directions that are out of the will of God. He turns to the things of the world and the flesh to compensate for his lack of peace within. He tries to escape, but he cannot escape *himself!* It is only when he confesses his sin, claims God's forgiveness, and does God's will that he experiences God's peace within.

When there is peace in the heart, there will be praise on the lips: "And be ye thankful" (Col. 3:15). The Christian out of God's will is never found giving sincere praise to God. When David covered up his sins, he lost his peace and his praise (Pss. 32; 51). When he confessed his sins, then his song returned.

### The Word of Christ (Col. 3:16)

This means, of course, the Word of God. The false teachers came to Colossae with man-made traditions, religious rules, and human philosophies. They tried to harmonize God's Word with their teachings, but they could not succeed. God's Word always magnifies Jesus Christ.

It was not the word of false teachers that brought salvation to the Colossians; it was the Word of the truth of the Gospel (Col. 1:5). This same Word gives us life and sustains and strengthens us (1 Peter 1:22–2:3).

The Word will transform our lives if we will but permit it to "dwell" in us richly. The word *dwell* means "to feel at home." If we have experienced the grace and the peace of Christ, then the Word of Christ will feel at home in our hearts. We will discover how rich the Word is with spiritual treasures that give value to our lives.

However, we must not think that Paul wrote this only to individual Christians; for he directed it to the entire church body. "Let the Word of Christ dwell among you" is a possible translation. As it dwells richly in each member of the church, it will dwell richly in the church fellowship.

There is a danger today, as there was in Paul's day, that local churches minimize the Word of God. There seems to be a lack of simple Bible teaching in Sunday School classes and pulpits. Far more interest is shown in movies, musical performances, and various entertainments than in God's Word. Many saved people cannot honestly say that God's Word dwells in their hearts richly because they do not take time to read, study, and memorize it.

There is (according to Paul) a definite relationship between our knowledge of the Bible and our expression of worship in song. One way we teach and encourage ourselves and others is through the singing of the Word of God. But if we do not know the Bible and understand it, we cannot honestly sing it from our hearts.

Perhaps this "poverty of Scripture" in our churches is one cause of the abundance of unbiblical songs that we have today. A singer has no more right to sing a lie than a preacher has to preach a lie. The great songs of the faith were, for the most part, written by believers who knew the doctrines of the Word of God. Many so-called "Christian songs" today are written by people with little or no knowledge of the Word of God. It is a dangerous thing to separate the praise of God from the Word of God.

Psalms were, of course, the songs taken from the Old Testament. For centuries, the churches in the English-speaking world sang only metrical versions of the Psalms. I am glad to see today a return to the singing of Scripture, especially the Psalms. Hymns were songs of praise to God written by believers but not taken from the Psalms. The church today has a rich heritage of hymnody which, I fear, is being neglected. Spiritual songs were expressions of Bible truth other than in psalms and hymns. When we sing a hymn, we address the Lord; when we sing a spiritual song, we address each other.

Paul described a local church worship service (1 Cor. 14:26; Col. 3:16). Note that the believer sings to *himself* as well as to the other believers and to the Lord. Our singing must be from our hearts and not just our lips. But if the Word of God is not in our hearts, we cannot sing from our hearts. This shows how important it is to know the Word of God, for it enriches our public and private worship of God.

Our singing must be with grace. This does not mean "singing in a gracious way," but singing because we have God's grace in our hearts. It takes grace to sing when we are in pain, or when circumstances seem to be against us. It certainly took grace for Paul and Silas to sing in that Philippian prison (Acts 16:22-25). Our singing must not be a display of fleshly talent; it must be a demonstration of the grace of God in our hearts.

Someone has said that a successful Christian life involves attention to three books: God's Book, the Bible; the pocketbook; and the hymn book. I agree. I often use a hymnal in my devotional time, to help express my praise to God. As a believer grows in his knowledge of the Word, he will want to grow in his expression of praise. He will learn to appreciate the great hymns of the church, the Gospel songs, and the spiritual songs that teach spiritual truths. To sing only the elementary songs of the faith is to rob himself of spiritual enrichment.

Before we leave this section, we should notice an important parallel with Ephesians 5:18–6:9. In his Letter to the Ephesians, Paul emphasized being filled with the Spirit; in his Letter to the Colossians, he emphasized being filled with the Word. *But the evidences of this spiritual fullness are the same!* How can we tell if a believer is filled with the Spirit? He is joyful, thankful, and submissive (Eph. 5:19-21); all of this shows up in his relationships in the home and on the job (Eph. 5:22–6:9). How can we tell if a believer is filled with the Word of God? He is joyful, thankful, and submissive (Col. 3:16–4:1).

### The Name of Christ (Col. 3:17)

In modern society, we pay little attention to names. But the ancient world held a man's name to be of utmost importance. Often, during Old Testament days, God changed a person's name because of some important experience or some new development.

As Christians, we bear the name of Christ. The word *Christian* is found only three times in the entire New Testament (Acts 11:26; 26:28; 1 Peter 4:16). The name was given originally as a term of contempt, but gradually it became a name of honor. The name of Christ, then, means *identification:* we belong to Jesus Christ.

But His name also means *authority.* A man's name signed to a check authorizes the withdrawal of money from the bank. The President's name signed to a bill makes it a law. In the same way, it is in the name of Jesus Christ that we have the authority to pray (John 14:13-14; 16:23-26). Because Jesus Christ is God, and He has died for us, we have authority in His name.

All that we say and do should be associated with the name of Jesus Christ. By our words and our works, we should glorify His name. If we permit anything into our lives that cannot be associated with the name of Jesus, then we are sinning. We must do and say everything on the authority of His name and for the honor of His name.

Bearing the name of Jesus is a great privilege, but it is also a tremendous responsibility. We suffer persecution because we bear His name (John 15:20-21). I have noticed in conversations that you can tell people you are a Baptist, Presbyterian, Lutheran, or even an atheist, and there will be little response. But if you tell people you are a Christian, and bring the name of Christ into the conversation, almost immediately there is some kind of response, and it is usually negative.

Every parent tries to teach his children to honor the family name. In just a few minutes, a person can disgrace a name that it has taken his ancestors years to build. For example, the Hebrew name *Judah* is a respected name; it means "praise." The New Testament equivalent is "Judas"—and who would name his son Judas?

Note that Paul again mentioned thanksgiving in this Colossian letter. Whatever we do in the name of Christ ought to be joined with thanksgiving. If we cannot give thanks, then we had better not do it or say it! This is the fifth of six references in Colossians to thanksgiving (Col. 1:3, 12; 2:7; 3:15, 17; 4:2). When we remember that Paul was a Roman prisoner when he wrote this letter, it makes this emphasis on thanksgiving that much more wonderful.

As we review these four spiritual motiva-tions for godly living, we are impressed with the centrality of Jesus Christ. We forgive be-cause Christ forgave us (Col. 3:13). It is the peace of Christ that should rule in our hearts (Col. 3:15). The Word of Christ should dwell in us richly (Col. 3:16). The name of Christ should be our identification and our authority. "Christ is all, and in all" (Col. 3:11).

Since we are united with Christ through the indwelling Holy Spirit, we have all the resources we need for holy living. But we must be spiritually motivated. Because we have experienced the grace of Christ, we want to live for Him. Because we have enjoyed the peace of Christ, we want to obey Him. We have been enriched by the Word of Christ, and ennobled by the name of Christ; therefore, we want to honor and glorify Him.

Can we desire any higher motivation?

# CHAPTER TEN
# A FAMILY AFFAIR
*Colossians 3:18–4:1*

Faith in Jesus Christ not only changes individuals; it also changes homes. In this section, Paul addressed himself to family members: husbands and wives, children, and household servants. It seems clear that these persons being addressed were believers since the apostle appealed to all of them to live to please Jesus Christ.

Something is radically wrong with homes today. The last report I saw indicated that in America there are now more broken homes than ever. Single-parent families are on the increase. Over half of all mothers are now working outside the home, and many of them have small children. The average American child from six to sixteen watches from twenty to twenty-four hours of television each week and is greatly influenced by what he sees. The "battered child" syndrome continues to increase, with from 2 to 4 million cases being reported annually, and many not reported at all.

The first institution God founded on earth was the home (Gen. 2:18-25; Matt. 19:1-6). As goes the home, so goes society and the nation. The breakdown of the home is a sign of the end times (2 Tim. 3:1-5). Centuries ago Confucius said, "The strength of a nation is derived from the integrity of its homes." One of the greatest things we can do as individuals is help to build godly Christian homes. Paul addressed the various members of the family and pointed out the factors that make for a strong and godly home.

### Husbands and Wives: Love and Submission (Col. 3:18-19)

Paul did not address the wives first because they were the neediest! The Gospel radically changed the position of women in the Roman world. It gave them a new freedom and stature that some of them were unable to handle, and for this reason Paul admonished them (similar admonitions are found in Eph. 5:18ff and 1 Peter 3:1ff).

We must not think of *submission* as "slavery" or "subjugation." The word comes from the military vocabulary and simply means "to arrange under rank." The fact that one soldier is a private and another is a colonel does not mean that one man is necessarily *better* than the other. It only means that they have different ranks.

God does all things "decently and in order" (1 Cor. 14:40). If He did not have a chain of command in society, we would have chaos. The fact that the woman is to submit to her husband does not suggest that the man is better than the woman. It only means that the man has the responsibility of headship and leadership in the home.

Headship is not dictatorship or lordship. It is loving leadership. In fact, both the husband and the wife must be submitted to the *Lord* and to *each other* (Eph. 5:21). It is a mutual respect under the lordship of Jesus Christ.

True spiritual submission is the secret of growth and fulfillment. When a Christian woman is submitted to the Lord and to her own husband, she experiences a release and fulfillment that she can have in no other way. This mutual love and submission creates an atmosphere of growth in the home that enables both the husband and the wife to become all that God wants them to be.

The fact that the Christian wife is "in the Lord" is not an excuse for selfish independence. Just the opposite is true, for her salvation makes it important that she obey the Word and submit to her husband. While it is true that in Jesus Christ "there is neither male nor female" (Gal. 3:28), it is also true that joyful submission is an evidence that the wife belongs to Jesus Christ.

However, the husband has the responsibility of loving his wife; and the word for "love" used here is *agape*—the sacrificing, serving love that Christ shares with His church. A marriage may begin with normal, human, romantic love, but it must grow deeper into the spiritual *agape* love that comes only from God. In the parallel passage (Eph. 5:18ff), Paul made it clear that the husband must love his wife "even as Christ loved the church." Jesus Christ gave His all for the church! He willingly died for us! The measure of a man's love for his wife is not seen only in gifts or words, but in acts of sacrifice and concern for her happiness and welfare.

Paul added a special word of warning for the husbands: "And be not bitter against them" (Col. 3:19). Husbands must be careful not to harbor ill will toward their wives because of something they did or did not do. A "root of bitterness" in a home can poison the marriage relationship and give Satan a foothold (Eph. 4:31; Heb. 12:15). The Christian husband and wife must be open and honest with each other and not hide their feelings or lie to one another. "Speaking the truth in love" (Eph. 4:15) is a good way to solve family differences. "Let not the sun go down upon your wrath" is a wise policy to follow if you want to have a happy home (Eph. 4:26).

A husband who truly loves his wife will not behave harshly or try to throw his weight around in the home. "Love is patient, love is kind. It does not envy, it does not boast, it is not proud. It is not rude, it is not self-seeking, it is not easily angered, it keeps no record of wrongs" (1 Cor. 13:4-5, NIV).

A wife really has little difficulty submitting to a husband who loves her. She knows he seeks the very best for her, and that he will not do anything to harm her. The husband's love for his wife is seen in his sacrifice for her, and the wife's love for her husband is seen in her submission to him. Where there are sacrifice and submission in an atmosphere of love, you will find a happy home.

A happy marriage does not come automatically; it is something that must be worked at all the time. As we walk with Christ in submission to Him, we have no problem submitting to one another and seeking to serve one another. But where there is selfishness, there will be conflict and division. If there is bitterness in the heart, there will eventually be trouble in the home.

Where do we get the power to love and to submit? From the Lord. If we are wearing the "graceclothes" described earlier (Col. 3:5-14), and if we have our hearts filled with the peace of Christ and the Word of Christ, then we will contribute to the joy and harmony of the home. If we live to please Christ first, others second, and ourselves last, we will build strong marriages and spiritual homes.

### Parents and Children: Encouragement and Obedience (Col. 3:20-21)

There were children in these Christian homes, and Paul addressed part of his letter to them. The normal result of marriage is the bearing of children, and fortunate are those children who are born into Christian homes where there is love and submission. "Be fruitful and multiply" was God's order to our first parents (Gen. 1:28), and this order was given before man sinned. The marriage relationship and the bearing of children are not sinful; rather, they are part of God's mandate to man. In the begetting and bearing of children, the husband and wife share in the creative activity of God.

A great deal is being said about the rights of children, and they *do* have rights. One of them is the right to be born. Another is the right to be born into a dedicated Christian home where they will be raised in the "nurture and admonition of the Lord" (Eph. 6:4). They have the right to have godly parents who will teach them the Word of God and discipline them in love.

John H. Starkey was a violent British criminal. He murdered his own wife, then was convicted for the crime and executed. The officials asked General William Booth, founder of the Salvation Army, to conduct Starkey's funeral. Booth faced as ugly and mean a crowd as he had ever seen in his life, but his first words stopped them and held them: "John H. Starkey never had a praying mother!"

Children have rights, but they also have responsibilities; and their foremost responsibility is to obey. They are to obey "in all things" and not simply in those things that please them. Will their parents ever ask them to do something that is wrong? Not if the parents are submitted to the Lord and to one another, and not if they love each other and their children.

The child who does not learn to obey his parents is not likely to grow up obeying *any*

authority. He will defy his teachers, the police, his employers, and anyone else who tries to exercise authority over him. The breakdown in authority in our society reflects the breakdown of authority in the home.

For the most part, children do not *create* problems; they *reveal* them. Parents who cannot discipline themselves cannot discipline their children. If a father and mother are not *under* authority themselves, they cannot *exercise* authority over others. It is only as parents submit to each other and to the Lord that they can exercise properly balanced spiritual and physical authority over their children.

The *measure* of the child's obedience is "all things"; and the *motive* is to please the Lord. It is possible to please the parents and not please the Lord, if the parents are not yielded to the Lord. The family that lives in an atmosphere of love and truth, that reads the Word of God, and that prays together will have an easier time discovering God's will and pleasing the Lord.

The word *fathers* in Colossians 3:21 could be translated "parents," as it is in Hebrews 11:23. Paul made it clear that parents must make it as easy as possible for children to obey. "Provoke not your children" (Col. 3:21) is a commandment to parents, and how often it is disobeyed! Too often, parents automatically say *no* when their children ask for something, when the parents should listen carefully and evaluate each request. Parents often change their minds and create problems for their children, sometimes by swinging from extreme permissiveness to extreme legalism.

Fathers and mothers should encourage their children, not discourage them. One of the most important things parents can do is spend time with their children. A survey in one town indicated that fathers spent only thirty-seven seconds a day with their small sons! It is an encouragement for children to know that their parents, as busy as they are, take time—*make* time—to be with them.

Parents also need to listen and be patient as their children talk to them. A listening ear and a loving heart always go together. "You took time to have me," a child said to her father, "but you won't take time to listen to me!" What an indictment!

Life is not easy for children, especially Christian children. Their problems might seem small to us, but they are quite large to them! Christian parents must listen carefully, share the feelings and frustrations of their children, pray with them, and seek to encourage them. Home ought to be the happiest and best place in all the world!

Discouraged children are fair prey for Satan and the world. When a child does not get "ego-strength" at home, he will seek it elsewhere. It is a pity that some Christian parents do not help their children develop their personalities, their gifts, and their skills. It is even worse when Christian parents compare one child with another and thereby set up unnecessary competition in the home.

Parents sometimes use their children as weapons for fighting against each other. Father will forbid Junior from doing something, but Mother will veto that order and give her approval. The poor child is caught between his parents, and before long he learns how to play both ends against the middle. The result is moral and spiritual tragedy.

If a home is truly Christian, it is a place of encouragement. In such a home, the child finds refuge from battles, and yet strength to fight the battles and carry the burdens of growing maturity. He finds a loving heart, a watching eye, a listening ear, and a helping hand. He does not want any other place— home meets his needs. In this kind of a home, it is natural for the child to trust Christ and want to live for Him.

### Masters and Servants: Honesty and Devotion (Col. 3:22—4:1)

Slavery was an established institution in Paul's day. There were 60 million of them, and many of them were well-educated people who carried great responsibilities in the homes of the wealthy. In many homes, the slaves helped to educate and discipline the children.

Why didn't the church of that day openly oppose slavery and seek to destroy it? For one thing, the church was a minority group that had no political power to change an institution that was built into the social order. Paul was careful to instruct Christian slaves to secure their freedom if they could (1 Cor. 7:21); but he did not advocate rebellion or the overthrow of the existing order.

Something should be noted: the purpose of the early church was to spread the Gospel and win souls, not to get involved in social action. Had the first Christians been branded as an antigovernment sect, they would have been greatly hindered in their soul-winning and their church expansion. While it is good and right for Christians to get involved in the promotion of honesty and morality in government and society, this concern must never replace the mandate to go into all the world and preach the Gospel (Mark 16:15).

You will remember that the Book of Colossians was one of three letters that came from Paul's Roman imprisonment; the other two were Ephesians and Philemon. Read Paul's little letter to Philemon and see his attitude toward slavery. Paul did not advise Philemon to treat his runaway slave severely, but to receive him as a brother even though he was still a slave. In fact, Onesimus, the slave, was one of the men who carried this letter to Colossae! (Col. 4:9)

A Christian servant owed complete obedience to his master as a ministry to the Lord. If a Christian servant had a believing master, that servant was not to take advantage of his master because they were brothers in the Lord. If anything, the servant strived to do a better job because he was a Christian. He showed singleness of heart and gave his full devotion to his master. His work was done heartily, not grudgingly, and as to the Lord and not to men. "Ye serve the Lord Christ" (Col. 3:24).

Single hearts and sincere hearts were necessary for Christian servants to please God and serve their masters acceptably. These instructions emphasized the *positive* side of obedience. Servants were to obey to please God, not just to avoid punishment. Even if the master did not commend them, they would have their reward from the Lord. In the same manner, if they disobeyed, the Lord would deal with them even if their master did not. God is no respecter of persons (Acts 10:34; Rom. 2:11; Eph. 6:9; James 2:1, 9).

In our society we do not have slaves. But these principles apply to any kind of honest employment. A Christian worker ought to be the best worker on the job. He ought to obey orders and not argue. He ought to serve Christ and not the boss only, and he ought to work whether anybody is watching or not. If he follows these principles, he will receive his reward from Christ even if his earthly master (his boss) does not recognize him or reward him.

I have a friend who, years ago, was fired from his job for working too hard. He was earning money to go to college, and he wanted to give the employer a good day's work each day. The trouble was, his zeal was showing up the laziness of some of the other employees—and they started fighting back. One of them falsely accused my friend of something, and he was fired. He lost his job but he kept his character, and the Lord rewarded him.

In today's complex, competitive world, it is sometimes difficult for a Christian to obey God and hold his job, or get a promotion. But he must obey God just the same and trust Him for what he needs. Unsaved fellow employees may take advantage of the Christian worker, but perhaps this can be an opportunity for the Christian to witness and back up his witness with his life. It is far more important to win a lost soul than to make a few extra dollars.

Just as the husbands and wives and parents and children have mutual and reciprocal responsibilities, so do masters and servants. Paul admonished the Christian masters to treat their servants with fairness and honesty. This would be a new idea to Roman masters because they considered their slaves as "things," and not people. Masters had almost total control over their slaves and could do with them whatever they pleased. Few unsaved Roman masters ever thought of treating their slaves with fairness, for slaves deserved nothing.

The Gospel did not immediately destroy slavery, but it did gradually change the relationship between slave and master. Social standards and pressures disagreed with Christian ideals, but the Christian master was to practice those ideals just the same. He was to treat his slave like a person and like a brother in Christ (Gal. 3:28). He was not to mistreat him; he was to deal with his slave justly and fairly. After all, the Christian slave was a free man in the Lord, and the master was a slave to Christ (1 Cor. 7:22). In the same way, our social and physical relationships must always be governed by our spiritual relationships.

As we review this very practical section of Colossians, we see once again the preeminence of Jesus Christ in our lives as believers. Christ must be the Head of the home. This series of admonitions is actually a practical application of Colossians 3:17: "And whatsoever ye do in word or deed, do all in the name of the Lord Jesus." It is by His power and authority that we should live in our daily relationships. If He is the preeminent One in our lives, then we will love each other, submit to each other, obey, and treat one another fairly in the Lord.

It would be well for us to review Ephesians 5:18–6:9 and note the parallels between that passage and the one we have just studied. This section of Ephesians emphasizes being filled with the Spirit, while the Letter to the Colossians emphasizes being filled with the Word; but the evidences are the same: joyful, thankful, and submissive living. To be filled with the Spirit means to be controlled by the Word.

The fullness of the Spirit and the fullness of the Word are needed in the home. If family members are controlled by the Spirit of God and the Word of God, they will be joyful, thankful, and submissive—and they will have little trouble getting along with each other. Christian employers and employees will treat each other fairly if they are filled with the Spirit and the Word.

The heart of every problem is the problem of the heart, and only God's Spirit and God's Word can change and control the heart.

Can the people who live with you detect that you are filled with the Spirit and the Word?

# CHAPTER ELEVEN
# TALK IS
# NOT CHEAP!
*Colossians 4:2-9*

Never underestimate the power of speech.

A judge says a few words, and a man's life is saved or condemned. A doctor speaks a few words, and a patient either rejoices ecstatically or gives up in despair. Whether the communication is oral or written, there is great power in words. I am told that for every word in Adolph Hitler's book *Mein Kampf,* 125 persons lost their lives in World War II.

The power of speech is a gift from God, and it must be used the way God ordains. In the Book of James, the tongue is compared to a bridle and a rudder, a fire and a poisonous animal, and a fruitful tree and a fountain (James 3). These three pairs of pictures teach us that the tongue has the power to direct, the power to destroy, and the power to delight. The tongue is but a little member in our bodies, but it can accomplish great things for good or for evil.

In this brief section, Paul pointed to four important ministries of speech.

### Praying (Col. 4:2-3a)

Prayer and worship are perhaps the highest uses of the gift of speech. Paul was not ashamed to ask his friends to pray for him. Even though he was an apostle, he needed prayer support for himself and his ministry. If a great Christian like Paul felt the need for prayer support, how much more do you and I need this kind of spiritual help! In these few words, Paul described the characteristics of a satisfying and spiritual prayer life.

First, our praying must be *faithful*. "Continue in prayer" (Col. 4:2). This means, "Be steadfast in your prayer life; be devoted; don't quit." This is the way the early church prayed (Acts 1:14; 2:46). Too many of us pray only occasionally—when we feel like it or when there is a crisis. "Pray without ceasing" is God's command to us (1 Thes. 5:17). This does not mean that we should walk around muttering prayers under our breath. Rather, it means we should be constantly in fellowship with God so that prayer is as normal to us as breathing.

This is not to suggest that God is reluctant to answer prayer and that we must "wear Him out" by our praying. Quite the opposite is true: God enjoys answering our prayers. But He sometimes delays the answer to increase our faith and devotion and to accomplish His purposes at the right time. God's delays are not always God's denials. As we continue in prayer, our own hearts are prepared for the answer God will give. We find ourselves growing in grace even before His answer comes.

Our praying must also be *watchful*. We must be awake and alert as we pray. The phrase "Watch and pray!" is used often in the Bible. It had its beginning in Bible history when Nehemiah was rebuilding the walls and gates of Jerusalem: "Nevertheless we made our prayer unto our God, and set a watch against them [the enemy] day and night" (Neh. 4:9). Jesus used the phrase (Mark 13:33; 14:38); Paul used it too (Eph. 6:18).

There is no power in dull, listless praying. If there is no fire on the altar, the incense will not rise to God (Ps. 141:2). Real praying demands spiritual energy and alertness, and this can come only from the Holy Spirit of God. Routine prayers are unanswered prayers.

Our praying should also be *thankful:* "Watch in the same with thanksgiving" (Col. 4:2). Thanksgiving is an important ingredient in successful praying (Phil. 4:6). If all we do is ask, and never thank God for His gifts, we are selfish. Sincere gratitude to God is one of the best ways to put fervor into our praying.

There is always so much to be thankful for! We have already noted the emphasis in Paul's Letter to the Colossians on thanksgiving (Col. 1:3, 12; 2:7; 3:15, 17; 4:2). When we recall that Paul was a prisoner when he wrote this letter, it makes this emphasis even more wonderful.

Finally, our praying ought to be *purposeful:* "Praying also for us" (Col. 4:3). Too often our prayers are vague and general. "Lord, bless the missionaries!" How much better it would be if we would pray for specific needs. By doing so, we would know when God answered and we could praise Him for it. Perhaps it is our lack of faith that causes us to pray generally instead of specifically.

It has well been said that the purpose of prayer is not to get man's will done in heaven, but to get God's will done on earth. Prayer is not telling God what to do or what to give. Prayer is asking God for that which He wants to do and give, according to His will (1 John 5:14-15). As we read the Word and fellowship with our Father, we discover His will and then boldly ask Him to do what He has planned. Richard Trench (1807–1886), archbishop of Dublin, said it perfectly: "Prayer is not overcoming God's reluctance; it is laying hold of His willingness."

Of course, it is possible to pray in our hearts and never use the gift of speech (1 Sam. 1:13); but we are using words even if we don't say them audibly. True prayer must first come from the heart, whether the words are spoken or not.

Study Paul's prison prayers (Phil. 1:9-11; Eph. 1:15-23; 3:14-21; Col. 1:9-12) for examples of prayer at its best.

### Proclaiming the Word (Col. 4:3b-4)

Paul did not ask for the prison doors to be opened, but that doors of ministry might be opened (1 Cor. 16:9; Acts 14:27). It was more important to Paul that he be a faithful minister than a free man. It is worth noting that in all of Paul's prison prayers, his concern was not for personal safety or material help, but for spiritual character and blessing.

Paul was in prison because of the "mystery of Christ" which related to the Gentiles (see Eph. 3:1-13). The mystery involved God's purpose for the Gentiles in relation to Israel; for in the church, Jews and Gentiles are one (Eph. 2:11-22). Read the account of Paul's arrest in the Jewish temple (Acts 21:18–22:30). Note that the Jews listened to Paul till he spoke the word *Gentiles* (Acts 22:21-22). It was Paul's concern for the Gentiles and his ministry to them that put him into prison.

Even among some believing Jews, there was a kind of bigotry that wanted to force the Gentiles into a lower position (Acts 15:1ff). This extreme legalistic party wanted the Gentiles to become Jews ceremonially before they could become Christians! Paul and Barnabas met this threat to the Gospel of grace head-on and the council decided in their favor. But the legalistic party continued to oppose Paul and his ministry. They did not want the Good News of the mystery of Christ to get to the Gentiles. They wanted to maintain their air of Jewish superiority.

How strange that Paul would want God to help him do the very thing that had caused his arrest! He had no intention of giving up his ministry or of changing his message. When John Bunyan was arrested for preaching illegally and put into prison, he was told that he would be released if he promised to stop preaching. "If I am out of prison today," he replied, "I will preach the Gospel again tomorrow, by the help of God."

How could Paul share the mystery of Christ when he was a prisoner? Paul's case was discussed by many people; Paul was also able to witness to the guards to whom he was chained (Phil. 1:12-18). Imagine being chained to the Apostle Paul! Through this witness, the Gospel was carried into parts of Rome that would have been inaccessible to Paul had he been a free man. There were even "saints in Caesar's household"! (Phil. 4:22)

The proclamation of the Gospel is empowered by prayer. The Spirit of God uses the Word of God as we come to the throne of grace and ask God for His blessing. We must never separate the Word of God from prayer because God has joined them together (Acts 6:4).

A visitor at Spurgeon's Tabernacle in London was being shown around the building by the pastor, Charles Spurgeon.

"Would you like to see the powerhouse of this ministry?" Spurgeon asked, as he showed the man into a lower auditorium. "It is here that we get our power, for while I am preaching upstairs, hundreds of my people are in this room praying." Is it any wonder that God blessed Spurgeon's preaching of the Word?

You, as a church member, can assist your pastor in the preaching of the Word by praying for him. Never say to your pastor, "Well, the least I can do is to pray for you." The *most* you can do is to pray! Pray for your pastor as he prepares the Word, studies, and meditates. Pray that the Holy Spirit will give deeper insights into the truths of the Word. Pray too that your pastor will practice the Word that he preaches so that it will be real in his own life. As he preaches the message, pray that the Spirit will give him freedom of utterance, and that the Word will reach into hearts and minds in a powerful way. (It wouldn't hurt to pray for other church leaders too.)

The proclaiming of the Word of God is a great privilege and a tremendous responsibility. You do not have to be an ordained preacher or a missionary to share God's Word. Even in your daily conversation you can drop the seed of the Word into hearts, and then pray that God will water that seed and bring forth fruit.

### Witnessing to the Lost (Col. 4:5-6)

"Them that are without" refers to those who are outside the family of God. Jesus made a distinction between His disciples and those who were outside (Mark 4:11). Paul also made this same distinction (1 Cor. 5:12-13). Those of us who are born again are the "spiritual insiders" because we belong to God's family and share His life.

However, as Christians, we must never have a sanctified superiority complex. We have a responsibility to witness to the lost around us and to seek to bring them into God's family. To begin with, we have the responsibility to *walk wisely* (Col. 4:5). *Walk* refers, of course, to our conduct in daily life. The unsaved outsiders watch us Christians and are very critical of us. There must be nothing in our lives that would jeopardize our testimony.

This story has often been told about Dr. Will H. Houghton, who pastored the Calvary Baptist Church in New York City and later served as president of Chicago's Moody Bible Institute till his death in 1946. When Dr. Houghton became pastor of the Baptist Tabernacle in Atlanta, a man in that city hired a private detective to follow Dr. Houghton and report on his conduct. After a few weeks, the detective was able to report to the man that Dr. Houghton's life matched his preaching. As a result, that man became a Christian.

What does it mean to "walk in wisdom"? For one thing, it means that we are careful not to say or do anything that would make it difficult to share the Gospel. It also means we must be alert to use the opportunities God gives us for personal witnessing. "Redeeming the time" means buying up the opportunity (Eph. 5:16). This is a commercial term and pictures the Christian as a faithful steward who knows an opportunity when he sees one. Just as a merchant seizes a bargain when he finds one, so a Christian seizes the opportunity to win a soul to Christ.

*Walking in wisdom* also includes doing our work, paying our bills, and keeping our promises. We must "walk honestly toward them that are without" (1 Thes. 4:12). A friend of mine went into a store to make a purchase for his church. The salesman asked, "Is _____ a member of your church?" My friend said that he was, and the salesman proceeded to tell him how much money that church member owed his store and how difficult it was to get anything from him. It would probably have been futile for my friend to witness to that clerk.

Christians in general and Christian leaders in particular must have "a good report of them which are without" (1 Tim. 3:7). When members of a church are calling a new pastor, they ought to investigate his testimony among his neighbors and the businessmen who know him. Even though unsaved people are in the dark spiritually (2 Cor. 4:3-4), they have a great deal of discernment when it comes to the things of this life (Luke 16:8). It is unfortunate when members of a church call a pastor who has not paid his bills and has left behind a bad witness to unsaved people.

It is not enough simply to walk wisely and carefully before unbelievers. We must also *talk* with them and share the Gospel message with them. But we must take care that our speech is controlled by *grace,* so that it points to Christ and glorifies the Lord. This means we must have grace in our hearts (Col. 3:16), because it is from the heart that the mouth speaks. With grace in our hearts and on our lips, we will be faithful witnesses and not judges or prosecuting attorneys!

The Lord Jesus Christ spoke with grace on His lips. "And all . . . wondered at the gracious words which proceeded out of His mouth" (Luke 4:22). Among the many statements about Jesus Christ in Psalm 45 (a messianic psalm) is this: "Grace is poured into Thy lips" (Ps. 45:2). Even when our Lord was dealing with sin, He spoke words of grace.

Our speech is supposed to "minister grace unto the hearers" (Eph. 4:29). But it cannot do that unless we have grace in our hearts and in our words. "Speaking the truth in love" (Eph. 4:15) is God's ideal for our conversation.

Why did Paul add "seasoned with salt"? (Col. 4:6) In that day, salt was used as a preservative as well as a seasoner. We should never say to anyone, "Now, take this with a grain of salt." *We* must put the salt into our speech to make sure it is pure and properly seasoned. "Let no corrupt communication proceed out of your mouth" (Eph. 4:29). Our speech must be pure.

Salt was also added to the sacrifices (Lev. 2:13). Perhaps Paul was suggesting that we look on our words as sacrifices offered to God, just as our words of praise are spiritual sacrifices (Heb. 13:15). It would no doubt help us to say the right things in the right manner if we remembered that our words are looked on as sacrifices to God.

It is unfortunate when a Christian speaks in a rude or coarse manner, particularly when the unsaved are listening. "Be ready always to give an answer to every man that asketh you a reason of the hope that is in you with meekness and fear" (1 Peter 3:15). Meekness is the opposite of harshness, and fear is the opposite of arrogance. There is no place in a Christian's conversation for a know-it-all attitude. While we need to have convictions and not compromise, we must also cultivate a gracious spirit of love.

The Christian's *walk* and *talk* must be in harmony with each other. Nothing will silence the lips like a careless life. When character, conduct, and conversation are all working together, it makes for a powerful witness.

### Sharing Burdens (Col. 4:7-9)

Paul did not spell out the details of his personal situation in this letter. He left it to his two spiritual brothers, Tychicus and Onesimus, to share the burdens with the church in Colossae. This is another wonderful ministry of speech: we can share our needs and burdens with others; then they can encourage and assist us.

When Paul left Ephesus, he was accompanied by seven other believers—among them, Tychicus (Acts 20:4). These men were helping Paul deliver the love offering from the Gentile churches to the poor saints in Judea (1 Cor. 16:1; 2 Cor. 8–9). It is possible that Tychicus and Trophimus were the two brethren Paul referred to in his Second Letter to the Corinthians (see 2 Cor. 8:19-24).

Tychicus shared Paul's Roman imprisonment and no doubt was helpful to him in many ways. Paul chose Tychicus and Onesimus to deliver the Ephesian letter (Eph. 6:21) and the Colossian letter (Col. 4:7-9). Of course, they also took the personal letter to Philemon. Paul instructed Tychicus to share with the Colossian Christians all the details of his situation there in Rome.

Paul's description of Tychicus reveals what a splendid Christian Tychicus really was. He was a *beloved brother,* willing to stay with Paul even though the situation was difficult. How encouraging it is to have a Christian at your side when everything seems to be against you!

Tychicus was also a *faithful minister.* His love revealed itself in action. He ministered *to* Paul, and he also ministered *for* Paul to assist him in his many obligations. Someone has said that the greatest ability in the world is dependability, and this is true. Paul could depend on Tychicus to get the job done.

Tychicus was also Paul's *fellow servant.* Though he was not an apostle himself, he was assisting Paul in his apostolic ministry. Paul and Tychicus worked together in the service of the Lord. Later, Paul was able to send Tychicus to Crete (Titus 3:12), and then to Ephesus (2 Tim. 4:12).

It was not easy for Tychicus to be associated with Paul, the prisoner; for Paul had many enemies. Nor was it easy for Tychicus to travel as he did, assisting Paul in his various tasks. Tychicus did not take the easy way, but rather the right way. Our churches today could use more members like Tychicus!

Paul also mentioned Onesimus ("one of you") who himself came from Colossae. He was the runaway slave who belonged to Philemon and who had been won to Christ through Paul's ministry in Rome. Paul sent Onesimus back to his master with a letter asking Philemon to receive him and forgive him. It is interesting to note that Paul also called Onesi-

mus *faithful* and *beloved.* Onesimus had been a believer only a short time, and yet he had already proved himself to Paul.

These two men had a dual ministry to perform: to encourage the Colossian Christians and to inform them about Paul's situation. Is it wrong for God's people to share information in this way? Of course not! Paul was not begging for money or asking for sympathy. He wanted the Colossian saints to know his situation so they could pray for him. While it is true that some Christian workers "use" circumstances selfishly to enlist support, this was not true of Paul. He simply wanted his friends in Colossae to know the facts and to support him in prayer.

In our home, we receive a number of missionary prayer letters. We read them and try to note the special burdens and needs. In my own private devotions, I use several prayer calendars that help me remember to pray about specific needs for different ministries. I appreciate knowing the facts so that I can intercede in a specific way. I also enjoy getting reports of how God has answered prayer, for this encourages my faith.

Praying, proclaiming the Word, witnessing, and sharing burdens—these are four wonderful ministries of speech. How much better it is to be involved in these ministries than to be using our tongues for gossip, malicious criticism, and other sinful purposes.

Let's make David's prayer our prayer: "Set a watch, O Lord, before my mouth; keep the door of my lips" (Ps. 141:3).

# CHAPTER TWELVE
# FRIENDS, ROMANS, COUNTRYMEN
## *Colossians 4:10-18*

Paul was not only a soul winner; he was a great friend-maker. If my count is correct, there are more than 100 different Christians (named and unnamed) associated with Paul in the Book of Acts and in his epistles. He named 26 different friends in Romans 16 alone!

It was customary in Paul's day to close each letter with personal greetings. Friends did not see one another that much, and letter service was very slow and limited. Of course, Paul's greetings were much more than social; they conveyed his genuine spiritual concern for his friends. In this closing section, Paul sent personal greetings to Colossae from six of his associates in the ministry: Aristarchus, John Mark, and Jesus Justus, all of whom were Jews; and Epaphras, Luke, and Demas, who were Gentiles. Paul then added special greetings to two church assemblies, with a special word to one of the pastors.

When we first read this list of names, we are probably not greatly moved. But when we get behind the scenes and discover the drama of these men's lives as they worked with Paul, the list becomes very exciting. We can categorize these men into three groups.

## The Men Who Stayed
## (Col. 4:10-11, 14a)

This group is made up of three Jews (Aristarchus, John Mark, Jesus Justus), and one Gentile (Luke). All of them were characterized by faithfulness to the Apostle Paul in his hour of special need. They were the men who stayed.

*Aristarchus (v. 10a).* This man was identified as Paul's fellow prisoner and fellow worker (Col. 4:11). Aristarchus was from Macedonia and was one of Paul's traveling companions (Acts 19:29). He was originally from Thessalonica (Acts 20:4) and willingly risked his life in that Ephesian riot (Acts 19:28-41). He sailed with Paul to Rome (Acts 27:2), which meant he also experienced the storm and shipwreck that Luke so graphically described in Acts 27.

Aristarchus stayed with Paul no matter what the circumstances were—a riot in Ephesus, a voyage, a storm, or even a prison. It is not likely that Aristarchus was an official Roman prisoner. "Fellow prisoner" probably means that Aristarchus shared Paul's confinement with him so that he could be a help and comfort to the apostle. He was a voluntary prisoner for the sake of Jesus Christ and the Gospel.

Paul could not have accomplished all that he did apart from the assistance of his friends. Aristarchus stands out as one of the greatest of Paul's helpers. He did not look for an easy task. He did not run when the going got tough. He suffered and labored with Paul.

*John Mark (v. 10b).* Mark, the writer of the second Gospel, played a very important part in the early history of the church. He too was a Jew, a native of Jerusalem where his mother, Mary, kept "open house" for the believers (Acts 12:12). John Mark was a cousin of Barnabas, the man who went with Paul on that first missionary journey (Acts 13:1-3). It is a good possibility that John Mark was led to faith in Christ through the ministry of Peter (1 Peter 5:13).

When Paul and Barnabas set out on that first missionary journey, they took John Mark with them as their assistant. He probably took care of the travel arrangements, supplies, etc. But when the going got tough, John Mark abandoned the preachers and returned home to Jerusalem (Acts 13:5-13).

Why John quit is not explained in Scripture. Perhaps he was afraid, for the group was about to move into dangerous territory. Perhaps he resented the fact that Paul was taking over the leadership of the mission and replacing his relative, Barnabas. Or maybe John Mark resented Paul's ministry to the Gentiles. Whatever the reason or excuse, he left them and returned home.

Later, when Paul and Barnabas wanted to go on a second journey, Paul refused to take John Mark along (Acts 15:36-41). Was Paul wrong in his assessment of this young man? Perhaps, but we cannot blame Paul for being cautious when John Mark had failed him in the past. Paul was not running a popular tour; he was seeking to win lost souls to Christ. No amount of danger or inconvenience could hinder Paul from reaching unbelievers with the Gospel. It was too bad that John Mark caused a division between Paul and Barnabas. However, we must admit that Paul did forgive John Mark and commend him: "Take Mark and bring him with thee: for he is profitable to me for the ministry" (2 Tim. 4:11).

Mark, Titus, and Timothy were young men who served as special representatives for the Apostle Paul. He could send them to churches that were having problems and trust them to help solve them. By the grace of God, John Mark had overcome his first failure and had become a valuable servant of God. He was even chosen to write the Gospel of Mark!

John Mark is an encouragement to everyone who has failed in his first attempts to serve God. He did not sit around and sulk. He got back into the ministry and proved himself faithful to the Lord and to the Apostle Paul. He was one of the men who stayed.

I might add that it is good to be a Barnabas and encourage younger Christians in the Lord.

Perhaps John Mark would have made it without the help of cousin Barnabas, but I doubt it. God used Barnabas to encourage John Mark and restore him to service again. Barnabas lived up to his name: "son of encouragement" (Acts 4:36, NIV).

***Jesus Justus (v. 11).*** Jesus Justus was a Jewish believer who served with Paul, but we know nothing about him. The name *Jesus* (Joshua) was a popular Jewish name, and it was not unusual for Jewish people to have a Roman name as well (Justus). John Mark is a case in point. Jesus Justus represents those faithful believers who serve God but whose deeds are not announced for the whole world to know. He was a fellow worker with Paul and a comfort to Paul, and that is all we know about him. However, the Lord has kept a faithful record of this man's life and ministry and will reward him accordingly.

***Luke (v. 14a).*** Luke was a very important man in the early church. He was a Gentile, yet he was chosen by God to write the Gospel of Luke and the Book of Acts. He is probably the only Gentile writer of any book of the Bible. He was also a physician, and was dearly loved by Paul. The profession of medicine had been perfected by the Greeks, and physicians were held in the highest regard. Even though Paul had the power to heal people, he traveled with a physician!

Luke joined Paul and his party at Troas (note the pronoun *we* in Acts 16:10). Luke traveled with Paul to Jerusalem (Acts 20:5ff) and was with him on the voyage to Rome (Acts 27:1ff). No doubt Luke's personal presence and his professional skill were a great encouragement to Paul during that very difficult time. While God can and does bring strength and healing in miraculous ways, He also uses the means provided in nature, such as medication. When my wife and I ministered to missionaries in Africa, a physician friend and his wife traveled with us; and we were grateful for their help.

Luke remained with Paul to the very end (see 2 Tim. 4:11). God used Luke to write the Book of Acts and to give us the inspired history of the early church and the ministry of Paul. Luke is a glowing example of the professional man who uses his skills in the service of the Lord and gives himself to go wherever God sends. He was a beloved Christian, a skillful physician, a devoted friend, and a careful historian—all wrapped up in one!

## The Man Who Prayed (Col. 4:12-13)

We met Epaphras at the beginning of this study, for he was the man who founded the church in Colossae (Col. 1:7-8). He had been led to Christ through Paul's ministry in Ephesus, and had returned home to share the Good News of salvation. It seems likely that Epaphras also founded the churches in Laodicea and Hierapolis (Col. 4:13). In our modern terms, Epaphras became a "home missionary."

What motivated Epaphras to share the Gospel? He was "a servant of Christ" (Col. 4:12). Paul called him "our dear fellow servant . . . a faithful minister of Christ" (Col. 1:7). Epaphras loved Jesus Christ and wanted to serve Him and share His message of salvation. But he did not do it alone. Epaphras also believed in the ministry of the local church, and in working with other saints. He was not just a "servant"; he was a *"fellow* servant."

I was chatting one day with a foreign mission executive about a mutual friend who had been forced to resign from his work on the field. "There was no problem with sin or anything like that," my friend explained. "His whole difficulty is that he is a loner. He can't work well with other people. On the mission field, it's a team effort or it's nothing."

One of the secrets of the ministry of Epaphras was his prayer life. Paul knew about this because Epaphras and Paul shared the same room, and when Epaphras prayed, Paul knew about it. What were the characteristics of this man's prayer life?

***He prayed constantly (v. 12—"always").*** He was a good example of Paul's admonition: "Continue in prayer" (Col. 4:2). Epaphras did not pray only when he felt like it, as do many Christians today. Nor did he pray when he was told to pray, or when the other believers prayed. He was constantly in prayer, seeking God's blessing.

***He prayed fervently (v. 12—"laboring fervently").*** The word used here means "agonizing." It is the same word used for our Lord's praying in the Garden (Luke 22:44). We get the impression that prayer was serious business with Epaphras! This Greek word was used to describe the athletes as they gave themselves fully to their sports. If church members today put as much concern and enthusiasm into their praying as they did into their baseball games or bowling, we would have revival!

***He prayed personally (v. 12—"for***

*you"*). Epaphras did not pray around the world for everybody in general and nobody in particular. He centered his intercession on the saints in Colossae, Laodicea, and Hierapolis. No doubt he mentioned some of them by name. Prayer for Epaphras was not an impersonal religious exercise, for he carried these people in his heart and prayed for them personally.

*He prayed definitely.* If you had asked Epaphras, "What are you praying for?" he could have told you. His great desire was that the believers in those three assemblies might mature in their Christian faith. Paul used four significant words to summarize the prayer of Epaphras, and these four words also summarize the message of the Book of Colossians: "perfect—complete—all—will."

Epaphras was concerned that these Christians know and do the will of God. But he wanted them to be involved in *all* the will of God, not just in part of it. (*All* is a key word in Colossians, used over thirty times.) He also wanted them to stand *perfect* and *complete* in God's will. The gnostic teachers offered these Christians "perfection and maturity," but they could not deliver the goods. Only in Jesus Christ can we have these blessings. "And ye are complete in Him," for only in Christ does the fullness of God dwell (Col. 2:9-10).

This request carries the thought of being mature and perfectly assured in the will of God, and parallels Paul's prayer burden (Col. 2:2). "Full assurance in the will of God" is a tremendous blessing! It is not necessary for the believer to drift in life. He can know God's will and enjoy it. As he learns God's will and lives it, he matures in the faith and experiences God's fullness.

*He prayed sacrificially (v. 13—"great zeal" or "much distress").* Real prayer is difficult. When Jesus prayed in the Garden, He sweat great drops of blood. Paul had "great conflict" (agony) as he prayed for the Colossians (2:1), and Epaphras also experienced "much distress." This does not mean that we must wrestle with God in order to get Him to answer. But it does mean that we must throw ourselves into our praying with zeal and concern. If there is no burden, there can be no blessing. To rephrase what John H. Jowett said about preaching: "Praying that costs nothing accomplishes nothing."

All of the men with Paul were named and commended in one way or another, but Epaphras was the only one commended for his prayer ministry. This does not mean that the other men did not pray; but it does suggest that prayer was his major interest and ministry. Epaphras was Paul's fellow prisoner (Phile. 23)—but even confinement could not keep him from entering the courts of heaven and praying for his brothers and sisters in the churches.

E.M. Bounds was a prayer-warrior of the last generation. He would often rise early in the morning and pray for many hours before he began the work of the day. His many books on prayer testify to the fact that Bounds, like Epaphras, knew how to agonize in prayer before God. (If you have never read *Power in Prayer* [Baker] by E.M. Bounds, by all means do so.)

I am impressed with the fact that Epaphras prayed for believers in three different cities. We are fortunate today if church members pray for their own pastor and church, let alone believers in other places! Perhaps one reason that revival tarries is because we do not pray fervently for one another.

## The Man Who Strayed (Col. 4:14b)

Demas is mentioned only three times in Paul's letters, and these three references tell a sad story. First he is called "Demas . . . my fellow laborer" and is linked with three good men—Mark, Aristarchus, and Luke (Phile. 24). Then he is simply called "Demas," and there is no special word of identification or commendation (Col. 4:14). But the third reference tells what became of Demas: "For Demas hath forsaken me, having loved this present world" (2 Tim. 4:10).

At one point in his life, John Mark had forsaken Paul; but he was reclaimed and restored. Demas forsook Paul and apparently was never reclaimed. His sin was that he loved this present world. The word *world* refers to the whole system of things that runs this world, or "society without God." In the first of his epistles, John the Apostle pointed out that the world entices the believer with "the lust of the flesh, the lust of the eyes, and the pride of life" (1 John 2:15-17). Which of these traps caught Demas, we do not know; perhaps he fell into all three.

But we do know that Christians today can succumb to the world just as Demas did. How easy it is to maintain a religious veneer, while all the time we are living for the things of this world. Demas thought that he could serve two masters, but eventually he had to make a decision; unfortunately, he made the wrong decision.

It must have hurt Paul greatly when Demas forsook him. It also hurt the work of the Lord, for there never has been a time when the laborers were many. This decision hurt Demas most of all, for he wasted his life in that which could never last. "He that doeth the will of God abideth forever" (1 John 2:17).

After conveying greetings from his friends and fellow servants, Paul himself sent greetings to the sister churches in Laodicea and Hierapolis. These people had never seen Paul (Col. 2:1), yet he was interested in them and concerned about their spiritual welfare.

### Final Greetings (Col. 4:15-18)
We know nothing about Nymphas, except that he had a church meeting in his house. (Some versions read *Nympha* and seem to indicate that this believer was a woman.) In the first centuries of the church, local assemblies met in private homes. Even today, many new local churches get their start this way. It was not until the Christian faith emerged from persecution into official government approval that church buildings were constructed. It really matters little where the assembly meets, so long as Jesus Christ is the center of the fellowship. (For other examples of "the church in the home," see Rom. 16:5 and 1 Cor. 16:19.)

Paul's great concern was that the Word of God be read and studied in these churches. The verb *read* means "to read aloud." There would not be copies of these letters for each member. It is a strong conviction of mine that we need to return to the public reading of the Word of God in many of our churches. "Give attendance to reading" (1 Tim. 4:13) means the public reading of God's Word.

It is worth noting that the various letters from Paul were good for *all* of these assemblies. In my ministry, I have shared God's Word in many different places and situations, and it has always reached the heart and met the need. Even in different cultures, God's Word has a message for the heart. God's Word does not have to be edited or changed to meet different problems in various situations, for it is always applicable.

What was "the epistle from Laodicea"? We do not know for sure. Some scholars think that the Epistle to the Ephesians was this missing letter, but this idea is pure speculation. The fact that this letter has been lost does not mean we are missing a part of God's

inspired Word. Some of Paul's correspondence with the church at Corinth has also been lost. God not only inspired His Word, but He providentially watched over it so that nothing would be lost that was supposed to be in that Word. Instead of wondering about what we do not have, we should be applying ourselves to what we do have!

When we compare Colossians 4:17 with Philemon 2, we get the impression that Archippus belonged to the family of Philemon. Possibly, he was Philemon's son and the pastor of the church that met in Philemon's house. We cannot prove this, of course, but it does seem a logical conclusion. This would make Apphia the wife of Philemon.

Paul's last words before his salutation are directed at Archippus as an encouragement to continue faithfully in his ministry. Was Archippus discouraged? Had the gnostic false teachers invaded his church and created problems for him? We do not know. But we do know that pastors of local churches face many problems and carry many burdens, and they often need a word of encouragement.

Paul reminded Archippus that his ministry was a gift from God, and that he was a steward of God who would one day have to give an account of his work. Since the Lord gave him his ministry, the Lord could also help him carry it out in the right way. Ministry is not something we do for God; it is something God does in and through us.

The word *fulfill* carries with it the idea that God has definite purposes for His servants to accomplish. He works in us and through us to complete those good works that He has prepared for us (see Eph. 2:10). Of course, *fulfill* also parallels the theme of Colossians—the fullness of Jesus Christ available to each believer. We are able to fulfill our ministries because we have been "filled full" through Jesus Christ.

Unless we make a practical application of Bible doctrine, our study is in vain. After reading this letter and studying it, we cannot help but see that we have in Jesus Christ all that we can ever want or need. All of God's fullness is in Jesus Christ and we have been made complete in Him. What an encouragement this must have been to Archippus! What an encouragement it should be to us today!

Paul usually dictated his letters to a secretary (see Rom. 16:22) and then signed his name at the end. He always added a sentence about the grace of God, for this was his "trademark" (see 2 Thes. 3:17-18). The combination of his signature and "grace" gave proof that the letter was authentic.

The New Testament contains many references to Paul's bonds and the fact that he was a prisoner (see Acts 20:23; 23:18, 29; 26:29; Phil. 1:7, 13-14, 16; 2 Tim. 1:8; 2:9; Phile. 10, 13; Eph. 3:1; 4:1). Why did Paul want them to remember his bonds? Primarily because those bonds were a reminder of his love for lost souls, especially the Gentiles. He was "the prisoner of Jesus Christ for you Gentiles" (Eph. 3:1). Paul's bonds were evidence of his obedience to the Lord and his willingness to pay any price so that the Gentiles might hear the Gospel.

Even today, there are devoted Christians who are in bonds because of their faithfulness to the Lord. We ought to remember them and pray for them. "Remember them that are in bonds, as bound with them" (Heb. 13:3).

As we come to the close of our study of this remarkable letter, we must remind ourselves that we are complete in Jesus Christ. We should beware of any teaching that claims to give us "something more" than we already have in Christ. All of God's fullness is in Him, and He has perfectly equipped us for the life that God wants us to live. We do not live and grow by *addition,* but by *appropriation.*

May the Lord help us to live as those who are complete in Christ.

# 1 THESSALONIANS

## OUTLINE

**Key theme:** The coming of Christ for the church
**Key verses:** 1 Thessalonians 5:9-10

## CONTENTS

# CHAPTER ONE
# A CHURCH
# IS BORN

A father took his son to a large city museum, thinking that the visit would entertain the boy. But for two hours the lad did nothing but sigh and complain. Finally in desperation he said to his father, "Dad, let's go someplace where *things are real!*"

Some people feel that way when they read the Bible. They think they are in a religious museum, looking at ancient artifacts that have no meaning for life in today's scientific world. *But they are wrong.* No book published has more meaning for our lives, and more relevance to our problems, than the Bible. No wonder William Lyon Phelps, for years called "Yale's most inspiring professor," said: "I believe a knowledge of the Bible without a college course is more valuable than a college course without a Bible."

Two of Paul's earliest letters are 1 and 2 Thessalonians. (It is possible that Galatians was written first.) These two letters were written to real people who were experiencing real problems in a world that was not friendly to their Christian faith. You and I can easily identify with these people because we live in a similar world and face many of the same problems. Once you understand the background, the burden, and the blessing of these two letters, you will see how up-to-date and practical they are.

## The Background

You can visit Thessalonica today, only the travel guide will call it Thessaloniki. (It used to be known as Salonika.) It is an important industrial and commercial city in modern Greece and is second to Athens in population. It served as an important Allied base during World War I. In World War II it was captured by the German army, and the Jewish population of about 60,000 persons was deported and exterminated.

It is an ancient city, originally named Therma from the many hot springs adjacent to it. In 315 B.C. it was renamed Thessalonica after the half sister of Alexander the Great. When Rome conquered Macedonia in 168 B.C., the city was made capital of that entire province. In Paul's day 200,000 people lived there, most of them Greeks, but also many Romans and a strong Jewish minority. Today it has a population of 300,000, and is one of the few cities that has survived from the New Testament era of apostolic ministry.

Dr. Luke explained how Paul came to Thessalonica and how the church was founded (Acts 17:1-15). Paul went to Macedonia in response to a "call" from a man in Macedonia who said, "Come over into Macedonia and help us" (Acts 16:9). Paul, Silas, Luke, and Timothy arrived first in Philippi where they led Lydia and her household to Christ and there established a church. Paul and Silas were arrested on false charges, beaten, and put into jail. But God delivered them and they were able to lead the jailer and his household to faith in Christ.

After encouraging the new believers, Paul and his friends left Philippi (though Luke probably stayed behind temporarily) and headed for the important city of Thessalonica. They bypassed Amphipolis and Apollonia (Acts 17:1), not because they had no burden for the people in those cities, but because Paul's policy was to minister in the large cities and then have the believers reach out into the smaller towns nearby. It is about 100 miles from Philippi to Thessalonica.

Paul's commission was to take the Gospel to the Gentiles (Acts 9:15; Eph. 3:1-12), but he always started his ministry among the Jews. The local synagogue was the place where the Old Testament Law was known and revered. Paul could get a sympathetic hearing in the synagogue, at least until persecution began. Furthermore, there were always many Gentile "God-fearers" in the synagogues, and through them Paul could begin a witness to the pagan Gentiles. Add to this Paul's great burden for the Jews (Rom. 9:1-3; 10:1), and the historical principle of "to the Jew first" (Rom. 1:16), and you can see why Paul and his associates began their work in the synagogue.

It is interesting to study the words Luke used to describe Paul's public ministry in the synagogue (Acts 17:2-3). *Reasoned* means "to discourse using questions and answers." Perhaps "dialogue" would be a good synonym. *Opening* simply means "explaining." Paul would read a portion of the Old Testament Scriptures and explain their meaning with reference to Jesus Christ and the Gospel. *Alleging* literally means "to lay beside." Paul put the Scriptures before them in an orderly manner, showing them how they harmonized. *Preach* means "to proclaim, to announce." Paul did not simply teach the Scriptures; he proclaimed Christ and urged his listeners to receive Him by faith.

We can learn much from Paul's approach to evangelism. He used the Word of God, and he declared the Son of God. He started where the people were and led them into the truth of the Gospel. (When Paul preached to Gentiles, he started with the God of Creation, since they had no knowledge of the Old Testament Scriptures. See Acts 14:8-18; 17:16ff.)

He ministered in the synagogue for three Sabbaths, and the Lord worked in power. Many people believed in Jesus Christ and were saved, including a number of high-ranking women. However, the unbelieving Jews began to oppose the work, and Paul and his helpers had to leave the city. They went forty miles to Berea and there had a good ministry; but the Jews from Thessalonica followed them and caused trouble. It was then that Paul left for Athens, and from there to Corinth.

How long did Paul minister in Thessalonica? Does the statement "three Sabbath days" (Acts 17:2) mean three weeks only, or that he preached *in the synagogue* only three weeks but continued in another place? We know that Paul was there long enough to receive two "home missions offerings" from the church in Philippi (Phil. 4:16). Also, Paul worked at his tentmaking trade to support himself (1 Thes. 2:9; 2 Thes. 3:6-15).

If Paul were there only three weeks, he certainly taught the new Christians a great deal of basic Bible doctrine. As we study these two letters, we will discover that almost every major doctrine of the Christian faith is mentioned.

Even though Paul's ministry in Thessalonica was not a long one, it was solid enough to leave behind a thriving church. When he left for Athens, Paul told Timothy and Silas to remain there and help the new church and then to join him later. When they did meet again, Paul sent Timothy back to Thessalonica to encourage the Christians and assure them of his love and concern. (He had tried to go back twice, but was hindered; 1 Thes. 2:17-18.) It was when Timothy rejoined Paul at Corinth and gave him the report on the new church that Paul wrote 1 Thessalonians. He wrote 2 Thessalonians just a short time later.

All of this background teaches us several helpful lessons. Obviously, *God uses people.* God did not send angels to evangelize Thessalonica; He sent a converted Jewish rabbi and his friends, including a young man who was part Jew, part Gentile. God still uses people—dedicated people who will obey His leading and share His message.

Here is a second lesson: the Gospel is still "the power of God unto salvation" (Rom. 1:16). It did not require years to set up a church in Thessalonica. God's power was effective in changing lives, and a church was founded in less than a month. Paul reminded them that the Gospel came to them not "in word only, but also in power in the Holy Spirit" (1 Thes. 1:5).

Finally, Satan still opposes the Gospel and persecutes God's people; *but persecution can be a means of growth.* As we study these two letters, we will see that God's Spirit strengthens and encourages suffering saints as they go through the difficulties of Christian life.

## The Burden

Why did Paul write these two letters? First, he wanted to assure his friends of his love and concern. After all, he left the city hastily at night, and he did not want them to think he had deserted them. Also, Paul's enemies were attacking his character and telling the new believers that their leader was really a greedy charlatan who preached religion in order to make money (1 Thes. 2). There were plenty of itinerant rogues in Greece who did just that, and some were spreading the word that Paul was one of them. In this letter, Paul assured his readers of his love for them and his honesty in ministering to them.

He had a second purpose in view: he wanted to ground them in the doctrines of the Christian faith, particularly with reference to Christ's return. It appears that the church was going through severe persecution, and this is always a time of temptation to compromise and give in to discouragement. By reminding them of the truths of the Christian faith and what God had done for them in Christ, Paul encouraged them to stand firm and maintain their strong witness.

He also encouraged them to live holy lives. Keep in mind that temptations to immorality were rife in the cities then, and that sexual sins were not condemned by most people. These letters emphasize purity of life—a concept that needs to be emphasized in our churches too.

The new Christians were confused about the return of Jesus Christ. Paul had told them that the Lord would return in the air and take them home, but some of their number had died. The bereaved ones wondered if their Christian dead would be included in the "catching up" of the church. Paul explained this in 1 Thessalonians 4:13-18.

But there was a second confusion. Because the persecutions were so intense, some of the believers thought that "the Day of the Lord" had arrived. (It is possible that a forged letter contributed to this confusion. See 2 Thes. 2:1-2.) Paul wrote 2 Thessalonians to explain this doctrine and to assure them that the Day of the Lord had not yet arrived.

Finally, in this letter, Paul sought to correct some weaknesses in the church. Some members were not respecting and honoring their spiritual leaders as they should (1 Thes. 5:12-13). Others were refusing to work, arguing that the soon-coming of the Lord made this the logical thing to do (2 Thes. 3:6ff). There was some confusion in their public services that also needed correcting (1 Thes. 5:19-21).

Confusion still exists about Bible prophecy, with radio and television preachers contradicting each other (and the Bible) and upsetting the saints. Is the coming of the Lord near? Must any signs take place before He can return? Will God's people have to go through the Day of the Lord (the Tribulation) before He can return? Paul answered these important questions in these two inspired letters.

And what about the matter of *practical holiness?* It is not easy for Christians to avoid the pollutions of the world. The sex promoters offer their wares at almost every newspaper stand and drugstore. Immorality and infidelity are common themes of radio and television programs as well as of popular music. The bad examples of famous people make it easier for young people to say, "Everybody is doing it!"

In addition to being more cautious in daily living, we also need more order and respect in our local churches. I have discovered that lack of respect for spiritual leadership is the main cause of church fights and splits. What Paul wrote in 1 Thessalonians 5:12-13 and 2 Thessalonians 3:6-15 is greatly needed today.

In all fairness to church officers, I realize that some pastors do not deserve to be followed. They are not spiritual; they do not pray; and they have no concern for the lost. They are merely using the ministry to make an easy living. A pastor must not *demand* respect; he must *command* respect, as did Paul, by his dedicated life and sacrificial ministry.

First Thessalonians is a letter from a spiritual father to his children. Paul pictured the church as a family (the word "brethren" or "brother" is used nineteen times in the first letter and nine times in the second), and he reminded them of what God did for them through his ministry.

The second letter was written to correct certain wrong ideas—and wrong practices—relating to the doctrine of the Lord's return.

We have seen the background of the letters, and the burden that motivated Paul to write them. We shall now consider the blessing of these letters and discover what they can mean to us.

## The Blessing

Each New Testament letter has a special message, or blessing, that is uniquely its own. Romans, for example, emphasizes the righteousness of God and shows that God is righteous in His dealings with both sinners and believers. First Corinthians focuses on the wisdom of God, and 2 Corinthians on the comfort of God. Galatians is the freedom letter and Philippians is the joy letter, while Ephesians stresses the wealth that we have in Christ Jesus.

What is the special blessing in the message of 1 and 2 Thessalonians? *It is the message of the return of Jesus Christ and how this vital doctrine can affect our lives and churches and make us more spiritual.* Every chapter in 1 Thessalonians ends with reference to the coming of Jesus Christ, and each reference relates the doctrine to a practical aspect of Christian living. Here is a summary:

1:10—salvation and assurance
2:19-20—soul-winning and service
3:11-13—stability in Christian living
4:13-18—strength in sorrow
5:23-24—sanctification of life

In other words, Paul did not look on this doctrine as a theory to be discussed, but as a truth to be lived. These letters encourage us to live "in the future tense" since Jesus could appear at any time. We are to practice the promise of His return in our manner of life.

Turning to 2 Thessalonians, we discover additional truth concerning future events and the church. Keep in mind that the second letter was written to correct the confusion regarding our Lord's return. Some believers thought the Day of the Lord (the time of

Tribulation) had arrived, and they wondered when the Lord would appear. Perhaps the best way to grasp the major messages of the two letters is by contrast:

| 1 Thessalonians | 2 Thessalonians |
|---|---|
| Christ comes in the air for His church (4:13-18) | Christ comes to the earth with His church (1:10) |
| A sudden secret rapture that can occur at any time | A crisis that is part of a predicted program |
| Can occur today | Can occur only after certain events happen |
| The Day of Christ | The Day of the Lord |

I realize that godly men differ in their interpretations of prophecy, particularly the matter of the church escaping or entering the time of Tribulation. My own position is that the church will be taken to heaven before the Tribulation, and then will return to the earth with the Lord to bring the Tribulation to a close (Rev. 19:11ff). I see 1 Thessalonians emphasizing the Rapture of the church and 2 Thessalonians, the revelation of the Lord with the church when He comes to judge.

However, the practical spiritual lessons of these truths should not be lost in debates over interpretations. I am encouraged to read what Dr. Leon Morris wrote in his excellent commentary on the Thessalonian epistles in *The New International Commentary* (Eerdmans, 1959), p. 152.

In his discussion of 1 Thessalonians 5:1-3, Dr. Morris faced the matter of whether believers will escape the Tribulation or be left on earth to pass through that terrible event. "The language of this chapter could be understood either way," he stated, and then affirmed his own position that the church will go through the Tribulation. Then he added: "But I fully recognize that other interpretations are possible, and suggest that it is not wise for any of us to condemn those who see such passages differently."

In other words, we can disagree without being disagreeable. My own conviction is that we shall be delivered from "the wrath to come" (1 Thes. 1:10; 5:9-10). I believe the Lord wants us to live in the constant expectation of His coming. I have studied carefully the excellent defenses of the other positions, and I respect the men who hold to them. But I must lovingly disagree with them.

Paul did not write these letters to stir up a debate. His desire was that these letters bless our lives and our churches. The doctrine of the Lord's return is not a toy to play with, or a weapon to fight with, but a tool to build with. Believers may disagree on some of the fine points of Bible prophecy, but we all believe that Jesus Christ is coming again to reward believers and judge the lost. And we must all live in the light of His coming.

Your study of these letters should give you assurance for the future, encouragement in witnessing and walking with the Lord, comfort in the loss of Christian loved ones, and stability in a world that is very unsure of itself.

# CHAPTER TWO
# WHAT EVERY CHURCH SHOULD BE
## *1 Thessalonians 1:1-10*

No doubt you have heard some preacher say, "If you ever find the perfect church, *please don't join it*. If you do, it won't be perfect anymore!"

Since local churches are made up of human beings, saved by God's grace, no church is perfect. But some churches are closer to the New Testament ideal than others. The church at Thessalonica was in that category. At least three times in this letter, Paul gave thanks for the church and the way it responded to his ministry (1 Thes. 1:2; 2:13; 3:9). Not every pastor can be that thankful.

What characteristics of this church made it so ideal and such a joy to Paul's heart?

**An Elect People (1 Thes. 1:1-4)**
The word *church* in 1 Thessalonians 1:1 means "a called-out people." Whenever you read about a call in the Bible, it indicates divine election—God is calling out a people from this world (Acts 15:13-18). Seven times in John 17, our Lord referred to believers as those whom the Father gave to Him out of the world (John 17:2, 6, 9, 11-12, 24). Paul stated that he knew the Thessalonians had

been chosen by God (1 Thes. 1:4).

The doctrine of divine election confuses some people and frightens others, yet neither response is justified. A seminary professor once told me, "Try to explain election, and you may lose your mind. But explain it away—and you may lose your soul!"

We will never understand the total concept of election this side of heaven. But we should not ignore this important doctrine that is taught throughout the Bible. Let's notice some obvious facts about divine election.

**Salvation begins with God.** "God hath from the beginning chosen you to salvation" (2 Thes. 2:13). "Ye have not chosen Me, but I have chosen you" (John 15:16). "He [the Father] hath chosen us in Him [Christ] before the foundation of the world" (Eph. 1:4). The entire plan of salvation was born in the heart of God long before man was created or the universe formed.

**Salvation involves God's love.** Paul called these saints "brethren beloved"—not only beloved by Paul (see 1 Thes. 2:17), but also beloved by God. God's love made Calvary possible (Rom. 5:8), and there Jesus Christ died for our sins. But it is not God's love that saves the sinner; it is God's grace. God in His grace gives us what we do not deserve, and God in His mercy does not give us what we do deserve. This explains why Paul often opened his letters with, "Grace be unto you, and peace, from God our Father, and the Lord Jesus Christ" (1 Thes. 1:1).

**Salvation involves faith.** "For by grace are ye saved through faith" (Eph. 2:8). Paul, Silas (Silvanus is the Roman spelling), and Timothy brought the Gospel to Thessalonica and preached in the power of God (1 Thes. 1:5). Some people who heard the message believed and turned from their vain idols to the true and living God (1 Thes. 1:9). The Spirit of God used the Word of God to generate faith (Rom. 10:17). Paul called this "sanctification of the Spirit and belief of the truth" (2 Thes. 2:13).

**Salvation involves the Trinity.** As you read this letter, you discover the doctrine of the Trinity. Christians believe in one God existing in three Persons: God the Father, and God the Son, and God the Holy Spirit. Keep in mind that all three Persons are involved in our salvation. This will help you escape dangerous extremes that either deny human responsibility or dilute divine sovereignty—for both are taught in the Bible.

As far as God the Father is concerned, I was saved when He chose me in Christ before the world began. As far as God the Son is concerned, I was saved when He died for me on the cross. As far as God the Holy Spirit is concerned, I was saved one Saturday night in May 1945, when I heard the Word and trusted Jesus Christ. At that moment, the entire plan fell together and I became a child of God. If you had asked me that night if I was one of the elect, I would have been speechless. At that time I knew nothing about election. But the Holy Spirit witnessed in my heart that I was a child of God.

**Salvation changes the life.** How did Paul know that these Thessalonians were elected of God? He saw a change in their lives. If you put 1 Thessalonians 1:3 next to 1 Thessalonians 1:9-10, You will get the picture:

| | |
|---|---|
| your work of faith | you turned to God from idols |
| your labor of love | to serve the living and true God |
| and patience of hope | to wait for His Son from heaven |

The person who claims to be one of God's elect, but whose life has not changed, is only fooling himself. *Those whom God chooses, He changes.* This does not mean they are perfect, but they are possessors of a new life that cannot be hidden.

Faith, hope, and love are the three cardinal virtues of the Christian life, and the three greatest evidences of salvation. *Faith* must always lead to works (James 2:14-26). It has been said, "We are not saved by faith plus works, but by a faith that works." If the Thessalonians had continued to worship their dead idols while professing faith in the living God, it would have proved that they were not among God's elect.

*Love* is also an evidence of salvation: "the love of God is shed abroad in our hearts by the Holy Ghost which is given unto us" (Rom. 5:5). We are "taught by God to love one another" (1 Thes. 4:9). We serve Christ because we love Him; this is the "labor of love" that Paul mentioned. "If ye love Me, keep My commandments" (John 14:15).

The third evidence of salvation is *hope*, waiting for Jesus Christ to return (1 Thes. 1:10). The return of Jesus Christ is the dominant theme of both of these Thessalonian letters. Unsaved people are not eagerly awaiting the Lord's return. In fact, when our Lord catches His church up into the air, unsaved people will be totally surprised (1 Thes. 5:1-11).

Faith, hope, and love are evidences of election. These spiritual qualities are bound together and can come only from God. For further evidence, see these passages: 1 Corinthians 13:13; Romans 5:1-5; Galatians 5:5-6; Colossians 1:4-5; Hebrews 6:10-12; 10:22-24; 1 Peter 1:21-22.

A local church must be composed of elect people, those who have been saved by the grace of God. One problem today is the presence, in the church family, of unbelievers whose names may be on the church roll, but not written in the Lamb's Book of Life. Every church member should examine his heart to determine whether he has truly been born again and belongs to God's elect.

## An Exemplary People (1 Thes. 1:5 7)

From the very inception of this church, Paul looked to them with joy and gratitude as Christians worthy of the name. They were examples in several areas of their lives.

**They received the Word (v. 5).** The Gospel came to them through the ministry of Paul and his associates. Many traveling preachers and philosophers in that day were only interested in making money from ignorant people. But the Holy Spirit used the Word in great power, and the Thessalonians responded by receiving both the message and the messengers. In spite of the persecution in Philippi, Paul and Silas had been "bold . . . to speak . . . the Gospel" (1 Thes. 2:2); and the people believed and were saved. They never lost that eagerness for the Word of God (1 Thes. 2:13).

**They followed their spiritual leaders (v. 6a).** The word "followers" is actually "imitators." These new believers not only accepted the message and the messengers, but they also imitated their lives. This led to severe persecution. It is important that young Christians respect spiritual leadership and learn from mature believers. Just as a newborn baby needs a family, so a newborn Christian needs the local church and the leaders there. "Obey them that have the [spiritual] rule over you, and submit yourselves: for they watch for your souls" (Heb. 13:17). It is not enough for us as mature believers to *win* souls; we must also *watch* for souls and encourage new

Christians to obey God's Word.

**They suffered for Christ (v. 6b).** In turning from idols to serve God, these believers angered their friends and relatives, and this led to persecution. No doubt some of them lost their jobs because of their new faith. Just as the Jewish unbelievers persecuted the believers in Judea, so the Gentile unbelievers persecuted the Thessalonian believers (1 Thes. 2:14-16). Faith is always tested, and persecution is one of the tests (Matt. 13:21; 2 Tim. 3:12).

**They encouraged other churches (v. 7).** Christians either encourage or discourage each other. This principle applies also to churches. Paul used the churches of Macedonia as a stimulus for the Corinthian church to give to the missionary offering (2 Cor. 8:1-8). Even though they were new believers, the Thessalonians set a good example that encouraged the surrounding assemblies. Churches must never compete with one another in a worldly manner, but they can "provoke unto love and to good works" (Heb. 10:24).

In every way, the church at Thessalonica was exemplary. The secret was found in their faith, hope, and love; for these are the spiritual motivators of the Christian life.

## An Enthusiastic People (1 Thes. 1:8)

Their "work of faith and labor of love" expressed itself in their sharing of the Gospel with others. They were both "receivers" (the Word came to them, 1 Thes. 1:5) and "transmitters" (the Word went out from them, 1 Thes. 1:8). Each believer and each local church must receive and transmit God's Word.

The verb *sounded out* actually means "to sound as a trumpet." But the Thessalonians were not "tooting their own horns" as did the Pharisees (Matt. 6:1-4). They were trumpeting forth the Good News of salvation, and their message had a clear and certain sound to it (1 Cor. 14:8). Wherever Paul went, the people told him about the faith of the Thessalonian believers.

It is the responsibility and privilege of each local church to share the message of salvation with the lost world. At the end of each of the four Gospels and at the beginning of the Book of Acts, there are commissions for the churches to obey (Matt. 28:18-20; Mark 16:15-16; Luke 24:46-49; John 20:21; Acts 1:8). Many congregations are content to pay a staff to do the witnessing and soul-winning. But in New Testament churches, the entire congregation was involved in sharing the Good News (Acts 2:44-47; 5:42).

A recent survey of church growth indicated that 70 to 80 percent of a church's growth is the result of friends witnessing to friends and relatives to relatives. While visitation evangelism and other methods of outreach help, the personal contact brings the harvest.

But election and evangelism go together. The person who says, "God will save those He wants to save and He doesn't need my help!" understands neither election nor evangelism. In the Bible, election always involves *responsibility*. God chose Israel and made them an elect nation so that they might witness to the Gentiles.

In the same way, God has chosen the church that we might be witnesses today. The fact that we are God's elect people does not excuse us from the task of evangelism. On the contrary, the doctrine of election is one of the greatest encouragements to evangelism.

Paul's experience at Corinth (Acts 18:1-11) is a perfect illustration of this truth. Corinth was a wicked city, and it was not easy to start a church there. The people were godless sinners (1 Cor. 6:9-11), but Paul preached the Word faithfully. When persecution arose from the Jewish unbelievers, Paul moved from the synagogue into the house of Justus. Then the Lord encouraged Paul: "Be not afraid, but speak, and hold not thy peace: for I am with thee, and no man shall set on thee to hurt thee: for I have much people in this city" (Acts 18:9-10). The fact that God had His elect in Corinth encouraged Paul to remain there for a year and a half.

If salvation were the work of man, we would have every right to be discouraged and quit. But salvation is the work of God, and He uses people to call out His elect. "He called you by our Gospel" (2 Thes. 2:14). The same God who ordains *the end* (the salvation of the lost) also ordains *the means* to the end (the preaching of the Gospel). There is no conflict between divine sovereignty and human responsibility, even though we cannot reconcile the two.

We need more churches today where the people are enthusiastic to share the message of salvation with others. As I write this, 2.4 billion people in our world have no visible witness of the Gospel in their midst, or no church body. In spite of the outreach of radio, televi-sion, and the printing press, we are losing ground in the work of reaching the lost. Are you an enthusiastic Christian? Is your church enthusiastic about witnessing?

### An Expectant People (1 Thes. 1:9-10)

Their *work of faith* made them an elect people, for they turned to God from their idols and trusted Jesus Christ. Their *labor of love* made them an exemplary and enthusiastic people as they lived the Word of God and shared the Gospel. Their *patience of hope* made them an expectant people, looking for their Saviour's return.

In these verses, Paul related the second coming of Christ to their salvation. Because they had trusted Christ, they looked for His return with joyful expectancy and knew that they would be delivered "from the wrath to come" (1 Thes. 1:10). Paul repeated this truth in 1 Thessalonians 5:9-10, and he amplified it again in 2 Thessalonians 1:5-10.

When they worshiped idols, the Thessalonians had no hope. But when they trusted "the living God," they had a living hope (see 1 Peter 1:2-3). Those of us who have been brought up in the Christian doctrine cannot understand the bondage of pagan idolatry. Before Paul came to them with the Gospel, these people were without hope and "without God in the world" (Eph. 2:12). Read Psalm 115 for a vivid description of what it is like to worship an idol.

Christians are "children of the living God" (Rom. 9:26). Their bodies are the "temples of the living God" (2 Cor. 6:16), indwelt by the "Spirit of the living God" (2 Cor. 3:3). The church is "the church of the living God" (1 Tim. 3:15); and for His church, God is preparing "the city of the living God" (Heb. 12:22). The living God has given us a living hope by raising His Son Jesus Christ from the dead.

Two aspects of the Lord's return must be distinguished. First, Jesus Christ will come in the air for His church (1 Thes. 4:13-18). This will usher in a period of Tribulation on the earth (1 Thes. 5:1-3). At the close of this period, He will return to the earth with His church (2 Thes. 1:5-10; Rev. 19:11-21), defeat His enemies, and then set up His kingdom (Rev. 20:1-6).

The word translated "wait" in 1 Thessalonians 1:10 means "to await someone with patience and confidence, expectantly." Waiting involves activity and endurance. Some of the

Thessalonian believers quit their work and became idle busybodies, arguing that the Lord was coming soon. But if we really believe the Lord is coming, we will prove our faith by keeping busy and obeying His Word. Our Lord's Parable of the Pounds (Luke 19:11-27) teaches that we must "occupy" (be busy; in this case, invest the money) till He returns.

Christians are waiting for Jesus Christ, and He may return at any time. We are not waiting for any "signs"; we are waiting for the Saviour. We are waiting for the redemption of the body (Rom. 8:23-25) and the hope of righteousness (Gal. 5:5). When Jesus Christ returns we shall receive new bodies (Phil. 3:20-21), and we shall be like Him (1 John 3:1-2). He will take us to the home He has prepared (John 14:1-6), and He will reward us for the service we have given in His name (Rom. 14:10-12).

A local church that truly lives in the expectation of seeing Jesus Christ at any time will be a vibrant and victorious group of people. Expecting the Lord's return is a great motivation for soul-winning (1 Thes. 2:19-20) and Christian stability (1 Thes. 3:11-13). It is a wonderful comfort in sorrow (1 Thes. 4:13-18) and a great encouragement for godly living (1 Thes. 5:23-24). It is tragic when churches forget this wonderful doctrine. It is even more tragic when churches believe it and preach it—but do not practice it.

Paul remembered how this church was born (1 Thes. 1:3), and he gave thanks for their spiritual characteristics: they were elect, exemplary, enthusiastic, and expectant. But churches are made up of individuals. When you and I speak of the church, we must never say "they." We should say "we." *We are the church!* This means that if you and I have these spiritual characteristics, our churches will become what God wants them to become. The result will be the winning of the lost and the glorifying of the Lord.

What every church should be is what every Christian should be: *elect* (born again), *exemplary* (imitating the right people), *enthusiastic* (sharing the Gospel with others), and *expectant* (daily looking for Jesus Christ to return).

Perhaps it is time for an inventory.

# CHAPTER THREE
# HELPING THE BABY GROW UP
## *1 Thessalonians 2:1-12*

Chapter 1 of 1 Thessalonians introduced us to Paul the evangelist. This chapter introduces us to Paul the pastor, for it explains how the great apostle cared for the new believers in the churches that he founded. Paul considered "the care of all the churches" (2 Cor. 11:28) a greater burden than all the sufferings and difficulties he experienced in his ministry (2 Cor. 11:23ff).

Just as God uses people to bring the Gospel to the lost, so He uses people to nurture the babes in Christ and help lead them to maturity. The church at Thessalonica was born through the faithful *preaching* of the apostle and his helpers, and the church was nurtured through the faithful *pastoring* that Paul and his friends gave to the infant church. This helped them stand strong in the midst of persecution.

In these verses, Paul reminded them of the kind of ministry he had as he taught and cared for the young church. Three pictures of his ministry emerge.

### The Faithful Steward (1 Thes. 2:1-6)
Paul had been "put in trust with the Gospel" (1 Thes. 2:4). It was not a message that he made up or that he received from men (Gal. 1:11-12). Paul looked on himself as a steward of God's message.

A steward owns nothing, but possesses and uses everything that belongs to his master. Joseph was a steward in the household of Potiphar (Gen. 39:1-6). He managed his master's affairs and used all his master's goods to promote his master's welfare. Every steward one day must give an account of his stewardship (Luke 16:1-2). If he is found unfaithful, he will suffer.

The message of the Gospel is a treasure God has entrusted to us. We must not bury it; we must invest it so it will multiply and produce "spiritual dividends" to God's glory. Some Christians think that the church's only responsibility is to protect the Gospel from those who would change it (Gal. 1:6-9). But we also must *share* the Gospel; otherwise, we are protecting it in vain.

Faithfulness is the most important quality a steward possesses (1 Cor. 4:1-2). He may not be popular in the eyes of men; but he dare not be unfaithful in the eyes of God. "Not as pleasing men, but God who trieth [testeth] our hearts" (1 Thes. 2:4). The Christian who "plays to the grandstands" will lose God's approval. When we see the characteristics of Paul's ministry as a steward, we understand what faithfulness means.

**The manner of his ministry (vv. 1-2).** Paul and Silas had been beaten and humiliated at Philippi; yet they came to Thessalonica and preached. Most of us would have taken a vacation or found an excuse not to minister. Paul was courageous—he was not a quitter. He had a "holy boldness" that was born of dedication to God. Like the other Apostles before him, Paul boldly proclaimed the Good News (Acts 4:13, 29, 31).

His preaching was "with much contention." This is an athletic term that means "a contest, a struggle." The Greek world was familiar with athletic contests, and Paul often used this idea to illustrate spiritual truths (1 Cor. 9:24-27; Phil. 3:13-14; 2 Tim. 4:7). He used this same word in Philippians 1:30 where he pictured the Christian life as an athletic contest that demanded dedication and energy. It had not been easy to start a church in Philippi, and it was not easy to start one in Thessalonica.

**The message of his ministry (v. 3a).** "For the appeal we make does not spring from error" (NIV). Here he assured them that his message was true. Six times in this letter he mentioned the Gospel. This message of Christ's death and resurrection (1 Cor. 15:1-6) is a true message and is the only true Gospel (Gal. 1:6-12). Paul received this Gospel from God, not from man. It is the only Good News that saves the lost sinner.

**The motive of his ministry (v. 3b).** He was not guilty of "uncleanness," for his motives were pure. It is possible to preach the right message with the wrong motives (Phil. 1:14-19). Unfortunately, some people in Paul's day used religion as a means for making money. Paul did not use the Gospel as "a cloak to cover his covetousness" (1 Thes. 2:5). He was open and honest in all his dealings, and he even worked at a trade to earn his own support (see 2 Thes. 3:8-10).

Paul was very sensitive about money matters. He did not want to give anyone a reason to accuse him of being a religious salesman

(1 Cor. 9:1-18). As an apostle, he had the privilege of receiving support. But he gave up that right in order to be free from any possible blame that would disgrace the ministry.

**The method of his ministry (vv. 3c-6).** Paul did not use guile or trickery to win converts. The word translated "guile" carries the idea of "baiting a hook." In other words, Paul did not trap people into being saved, the way a clever salesman traps people into buying his product. Spiritual witnessing and "Christian salesmanship" are different. Salvation does not lie at the end of a clever argument or a subtle presentation. It is the result of God's Word and the power of the Holy Spirit (1 Thes. 1:5).

Often we hear, "I don't care what your method is, just so long as your message is right." But some methods are unworthy of the Gospel. They are cheap, whereas the Gospel is a costly message that required the death of God's only Son. They are worldly and man centered, whereas the Gospel is a divine message centered in God's glory.

Paul's enemies in Thessalonica accused him of being a cheap peddler of this new message. They said that his only motive was to make money. In describing himself as a faithful steward, Paul answered these critics; *and Paul's readers knew that he told the truth.* (Trace that phrase "as ye know" in 1 Thes. 1:5; 2:1, 5, 11; 3:3-4; 4:2; 5:2.) Paul appealed to the witness of God (1 Thes. 2:5) and to their own witness. He had "a conscience void of offense toward God, and toward men" (Acts 24:16).

Paul abhorred flattery (1 Thes. 2:5). David also hated this sin. "They speak vanity everyone with his neighbor; with flattering lips and with a double heart do they speak" (Ps. 12:2).

I once read that a flatterer is a person who manipulates rather than communicates. A flatterer can use either truth or lies to achieve his unholy purpose, which is to control your decisions for his own profit.

Some people even flatter themselves. "For he flatters himself in his own eyes" (Ps. 36:2, RSV). This was the sin of Haman, that evil man in the Book of Esther. He was so interested in flattering himself that he even plotted to slaughter all the Jews to achieve that goal.

Some people try to flatter God. "Nevertheless they [Israel] did flatter Him [God] with their mouth, and they lied unto Him with their tongues" (Ps. 78:36). Flattery is another form of lying. It means saying one thing to God with our lips while our hearts are far from Him (Mark 7:6).

Some Christians try to win friends and influence people by appealing to their egos. A true ministry of the Gospel deals honestly (but lovingly) with sin and judgment and leaves the unbeliever with nothing to boast of in himself. Paul's method was as pure as his motive: he presented the Word of God in the power of the Spirit, and trusted God to work.

## The Loving Mother (1 Thes. 2:7-8)

The emphasis of the steward is *faithfulness;* the emphasis of the mother is *gentleness.* As an apostle, Paul was a man of authority; but he always used his authority in love. The babes in Christ sensed his tender loving care as he nurtured them. He was indeed like a loving mother who cared for her children.

It takes time and energy to care for children. Paul did not turn his converts over to baby-sitters; he made sacrifices and cared for them himself. He did not tell them to "read a book" as a substitute for his own personal ministry (though good Christian literature can help young believers to grow).

Paul had patience with the new Christians. Our four children are into adulthood now, but I can assure you that my wife and I needed a great deal of patience before they reached that state. (To even things up, our parents needed patience with us!) Children do not grow up instantly. They all experience growing pains and encounter problems as they mature. Paul's love for them made him patient, because love suffers long, and is kind (1 Cor. 13:4).

Paul also nourished them. First Thessalonians 2:7 can read "even as a nursing mother cherishes her own children." What is the lesson here? *A nursing mother imparts her own life to the child.* This is exactly what Paul wrote in 1 Thessalonians 2:8. You cannot be a nursing mother and turn your baby over to someone else. That baby must be in your arms, next to your heart.

The nursing mother eats the food and transforms it into milk for the baby. The mature Christian feeds on the Word of God and then shares its nourishment with the younger believers so they can grow (1 Peter 2:1-3). A nursing child can become ill through reaction to something the mother has eaten. The Christian who is feeding others must be careful not to feed on the wrong things himself.

Besides making sacrifices, having patience,

and giving nourishment, a mother also *protects* her child. It was this fact that enabled King Solomon to discover which woman was the real mother of the living child (1 Kings 3:16-28). Paul was willing to give not only the Gospel but his own life as well. His love for the Thessalonians was so great he would die for them if necessary.

But it is not easy to be a "nursing mother." Even Moses felt the burden of caring for God's people. "Was it I who conceived all this people? Was it I who brought them forth, that Thou shouldest say to me, 'Carry them in your bosom as a nurse carries a nursing infant, to the land which Thou didst swear to their fathers'?" (Num. 11:12, NASB) But if we do not nurse the new Christians on the milk of the Word, they can never mature to appreciate the meat of the Word (Heb. 5:10-14).

## The Concerned Father (1 Thes. 2:9-12)

Paul considered himself a "spiritual father" to the believers at Thessalonica, just as he did toward the saints at Corinth. "For if you were to have countless tutors in Christ, yet you would not have many fathers; for in Christ Jesus I became your father through the Gospel" (1 Cor. 4:15, NASB). The Spirit of God used the Word of God in Paul's ministry, and many people in Thessalonica were born again into the family of God.

But the father not only begets the children; he also cares for them. As he defended his own work against false accusations, Paul pointed out three of his duties as the spiritual father to the Thessalonicans.

*His work (v. 9).* The father works to support his family. Even though the Christians in Philippi sent financial help (Phil. 4:15-16), Paul still made tents and paid his own way. No one could accuse him of using his ministry for his own profit. Later on, Paul used this fact to shame the lazy Christians in the Thessalonican church (2 Thes. 3:6ff).

Paul used the words "labor and travail." J.B. Phillips translated these words "our struggles and hard work." "Toil and hardship" would be another translation. It was not easy to make tents and minister the Word at the same time. No wonder Paul toiled "night and day" (Acts 20:31). He toiled because he loved the believers and wanted to help them as much as possible. "For I seek not yours, but you: for the children ought not to lay up for the parents, but the parents for the children" (2 Cor. 12:14).

*His walk (v. 10).* Fathers must live so that they are good examples to their children. He could call the Thessalonican believers as witnesses that his life had been exemplary in every way. None of the members of the assembly could accuse Paul of being a poor example. Furthermore, God had witnessed Paul's life; and Paul was not afraid to call God as a witness that he had lived a dedicated life, while caring for the church family.

His life was holy. In the Greek, this means to "carefully fulfill the duties God gives to a person." Our word *pious* is close to it, if you think of piety at its best and not as some fake kind of religion. This same word is applied to the character of God in Revelation 15:4 and 16:5.

His life was also righteous. This refers to integrity, uprightness of character, and behavior. This is not the "righteousness of the Law" but the practical righteousness that God works out in our lives as we yield to Him (Phil. 3:4-10).

Paul's life was also unblamable. Literally, this word means "not able to find fault in." His enemies might accuse him, but no one could level any charge against Paul and prove it. Christians are supposed to be "blameless and harmless" as they live in this world (Phil. 2:15).

*His words (vv. 11-12).* A father must not only support the family by working, and teach the family by being a good example. He must also take time to speak to the family members. Paul knew the importance of teaching these new believers the truths that would help them grow in the Lord.

Paul dealt with each of the believers *personally.* "For you know that we dealt with each of you as a father deals with his own children" (1 Thes. 2:11, NIV). As busy as he was, Paul still had time for personal counseling with the members of the assembly. While it is good for church leaders to address the larger group, spending time with people on a one-to-one basis is also needed. Our Lord was never too busy to speak to individuals, even though He preached to great multitudes. To be sure, this is difficult and demanding work. But it is rewarding work that glorifies God.

Paul *encouraged* the new believers. This is what a father does with his children, for children are easily discouraged. New Christians need someone to encourage them in the Lord. The word *exhorting* in our *Authorized Version* means "to call to one's side, to encourage." It

does not mean that Paul scolded them. Rather, it means he encouraged them to go on with the Lord.

I once received a letter from a radio listener who thanked me for the encouragement of the messages she had heard. "When we go to church," she wrote, "all our pastor does is scold us and whip us. We really get tired of this. It's refreshing to hear some words of encouragement!"

Paul also *comforted* them. This word carries the same idea of "encouragement," with the emphasis on *activity.* Paul not only made them feel better, but he made them want to *do* better. A father must not pamper a child; rather, he must encourage the child to go right back and try over again. Christian encouragement must not become an anesthesia that puts us to sleep. It must be a stimulant that awakens us to do better.

Finally, Paul *charged* them. This word means that Paul "testified to them" out of his own experience with the Lord. It carries the idea of giving personal witness. Sometimes we go through difficulties so that we may share with new Christians what the Lord has done. God "comforts us in all our troubles, so that we can comfort those in any trouble with the comfort we ourselves have received from God" (2 Cor. 1:4, NIV).

We who are parents know that our children (especially teenagers) do not like to hear us say, "Now, back when I was a kid. . . ." But this is an important part of training a family. It is a wonderful thing when a "spiritual father" can encourage and help his "children" out of his own experience with the Lord. "Come, ye children, hearken unto me: I will teach you the fear of the Lord" (Ps. 34:11).

What was the purpose for this fatherly ministry to the believers? His aim was that his children might "walk worthy of God" (1 Thes. 2:12). Just as a father wants to be proud of his children, so the Lord wants to get glory through the lives of His children. "I was very glad to find some of your children walking in truth" (2 John 4, NASB). Paul ministered to them in such a personal way because he was teaching them how to walk.

Every child must learn how to walk. He must have good models to follow. Paul admonished them to walk "worthy of the Lord" (see Col. 1:10 and Phil. 1:27). We are to walk worthy of the calling we have in Christ Jesus (Eph. 4:1). God has called us; we are saved by grace. We are a part of His kingdom and glory. One day we shall enter the eternal kingdom and share His glory. This assurance ought to govern our lives and make us want to please the Lord.

The verb in 1 Thessalonians 2:12 is in the present tense: "who is continually calling you." God called us to salvation (2 Thes. 2:13-14), and He is constantly calling us to a life of holiness and obedience. "But as He which hath called you is holy, so be ye holy in all manner of conversation [behavior]; because it is written, 'Be ye holy, for I am holy' " (1 Peter 1:15-16).

This passage gives us a beautiful example of New Testament follow-up. Paul has shown us how to raise the babies. We must be faithful stewards, loving mothers, and concerned fathers. If we are not faithful to God, we may find ourselves becoming doting mothers and pampering fathers. Children need discipline as well as love. In fact, discipline is one evidence of love.

No wonder the church at Thessalonica prospered in spite of persecution, and shared the Gospel with others for miles around. They had been born right (1 Thes. 1) and nurtured right (1 Thes. 2). This is a good example for us to follow.

# CHAPTER FOUR
# GROWING PAINS
*1 Thessalonians 2:13-20*

It was not easy to be a Christian in Thessalonica where believers faced persecution and suffering. Their situation explains Paul's choice of words: *affliction* (1 Thes. 1:6; 3:3), which means "pressure from circumstances"; *suffered* (1 Thes. 2:14), the same word used for our Lord's sufferings; *persecuted* (1 Thes. 2:15), meaning "driven out and rejected"; *contrary* (1 Thes. 2:15), used of winds that blow against and hinder progress; and *hindered* (1 Thes. 2:18), which pictures a road so broken up that travel is blocked.

Yet in the midst of suffering, the Thessalonian Christians experienced joy. They received Paul's ministry of the Word "in much affliction, with joy of the Holy Spirit" (1 Thes. 1:6). Paul certainly was burdened for his brethren who were going through suffering, and yet he also had joy (1 Thes. 2:19-20). It was a fulfillment of our Lord's promise, "In the world ye shall have tribulation: but be of good cheer; I have overcome the world" (John 16:33).

Churches do experience "growing pains" as they seek to win the lost and glorify the Lord. We may not experience the same kind of political and religious persecution that the early Christians suffered (though in some parts of the world today the persecution is just as intense as it was then). Yet if we are living "godly in Christ Jesus," we will suffer for His sake (2 Tim. 3:12). In this paragraph, Paul explained the divine resources we have in times of suffering and persecution.

### God's Word within Us (1 Thes. 2:13)
The church has been founded on the Word of God (1 Thes. 1:6), the message of the Gospel of Jesus Christ. The same Word that brings us salvation also enables us to live for Christ and endure suffering for His sake. Paul was thankful that the saints in Thessalonica had the right spiritual attitudes toward the Word of God. This helped them endure in the hour of suffering.

*They appreciated the Word.* They did not receive it as the word of men; they received it as the Word of God. We must never treat the Bible as any other book, for the Bible is different in origin, character, content, and cost. The Bible is the Word of God. It was inspired by the Spirit of God (2 Tim. 3:16) and written by men of God who were used by the Spirit (2 Peter 1:20-21). God's Word is holy, pure, and perfect (Ps. 19:7-9). The Bible was written at great cost, not only to the writers, but to Jesus Christ who became Man that the Word of God might be given to us.

The way a Christian treats his Bible shows how he regards Jesus Christ. He is the living Word (John 1:1, 14), and the Bible is the written Word; but *in essence* they are the same. Both are bread (Matt. 4:4; John 6:48), light (Ps. 119:105; John 8:12), and truth (John 14:6; 17:17). The Holy Spirit gave birth to Jesus Christ through a holy woman (Luke 1:35), and He gave birth to the Bible through holy men of God (2 Peter 1:20-21). Jesus Christ is the eternal Son of God forever (Rom. 1:25), and the Word of God will live forever (Ps. 119:89; 1 Peter 1:23, 25).

It may be a personal prejudice, but I dislike

seeing a Bible on the floor or at the bottom of a stack of books. If I am carrying several books with my Bible, I try to remember to put the Bible on the top. If we appreciate the Bible as the inspired Word of God, then we will reveal this appreciation in our treatment of the Bible.

Would you rather have your Bible than *food?* Job said, "I have esteemed the words of His mouth more than my necessary food" (Job 23:12). God's Word is *bread* (Matt. 4:4), *milk* and *meat* (Heb. 5:11-14), and even *honey* (Ps. 119:103). Mary chose the Word, but her sister Martha got involved in making a meal (Luke 10:38-42). Mary got the blessing while Martha lost the victory.

Would you rather have God's Word than *money?* The believer who wrote Psalm 119 made it clear that God's Word meant more to him than "all riches" (Ps. 119:14), "thousands of gold and silver" (Ps. 119:72), "fine gold" (Ps. 119:127), and even "great spoil" (Ps. 119:162).

I recall a young couple I sought to help in one of my churches. They had a lovely little son, but they were very careless about attending church and Sunday School. The little boy was not getting the Christian training he needed. A visit to the home told me why: the father wanted more money and so he worked on Sundays to make double time. He did not *have* to work on the Lord's Day, but he wanted the money rather than God's Word. He earned more money, but he was never able to keep it. The little son became ill and the extra money went to doctors.

Would you rather have God's Word than *sleep?* "My eyes anticipate the night watches, that I may meditate on Thy Word" (Ps. 119:148, NASB). The Jews had three night watches: sunset to 10, 10 to 2, and 2 until dawn. The psalmist gave up sleep three times each night that he might spend time with the Word. But some Christians cannot get out of bed on Sunday morning to study the Word.

If we are going to be victorious in suffering, we must appreciate the Word. But there is a second attitude we must show toward the Bible.

***They appropriated the Word.*** Paul used two different words for "received": the first means simply "to accept from another," while the second means "to welcome." One means "the hearing of the ear," while the other means "the hearing of the heart." The believers at Thessalonica did not only *hear* the Word; they took it into their inner man and made it a part of their lives.

The Lord Jesus repeatedly warned people about the wrong kind of hearing, and His warnings are still needed. "Who hath ears to hear, let him hear" (Matt. 13:9). In other words, "Take heed that you hear." Use every opportunity you have to hear the Word of God.

But He gave another warning in Mark 4:24: "Take heed *what* ye hear." How often believers hear the Word of God in Sunday School and church, and then get in their cars, turn on the radio, and listen to programs that help erase the impressions made by the Word. When we visited church congregations in Great Britain, my wife and I were impressed with their practice of sitting down after the benediction. They meditated on the Word and allowed the Spirit to minister to them. This is far better than rushing out of church and joking with friends.

Our Lord's third warning is in Luke 8:18: "Take heed therefore *how* ye hear." Many people are careless hearers and cannot apply themselves to listen to the teaching of God's Word. These people have "itching ears" and want religious entertainment (2 Tim. 4:3). Some of them are "dull of hearing" (Heb. 5:11), too lazy to apply themselves and pay attention. One of these days our churches will be hungry because of a famine "for hearing the words of the Lord" (Amos 8:11). Too many churches have substituted entertainment for the preaching of God's Word, and many people no longer welcome the Word of God.

How do we appropriate the Word? By understanding it and receiving it into our hearts, and by meditating on it so that it becomes part of the inner man. Meditation is to the spiritual life what digestion is to the physical life. If you did not digest your food, you would die. It takes time to meditate, but it is the only way to appropriate the Word and grow.

***They applied the Word.*** They obeyed the Word by faith, and the Word went to work in their lives. It is not enough to appreciate the Bible, or even to appropriate the Bible. We must apply the Word in our lives and be hearers and doers of the Word (James 1:19-25).

The Word of God has in it the power to accomplish the will of God. "For nothing is impossible with God" (Luke 1:37, NIV). It has well been said, "God's commandments are

God's enablements." Jesus commanded the crippled man to stretch out his hand—the very thing the man could not do. Yet that word of command gave him the power to obey. He trusted the word, obeyed, and was made whole (Mark 3:1-5). When we believe God's Word and obey, He releases power—divine energy—that works in our lives to fulfill His purposes.

The Word of God within us is a great source of power in times of testing and suffering. If we appreciate the Word (the heart), appropriate the Word (the mind), and apply the Word (the will), then the whole person will be controlled by God's Word and He will give us the victory.

## God's People around Us
## (1 Thes. 2:14-16)

In my pastoral work, I often found that suffering people can become very self-centered and think that they are the only ones going through the furnace. Everyone goes through the normal human suffering such as sickness, pain, and bereavement. But I am referring to the suffering we endure *because we are Christians.*

Perhaps your family has disowned you because of your faith; or perhaps you have been bypassed for a promotion at work because you are a Christian. These experiences hurt, but they are not ours alone. Other Christians are going through the same trials, and many, in other parts of the world, face much greater difficulty.

Not only were the Thessalonian saints imitators of the Lord and of Paul (1 Thes. 1:6), but they also became imitators of the Jewish believers in their experience of persecution. The saints in Judea suffered at the hands of the Jews, and the saints in Thessalonica suffered at the hands of the Gentiles. But keep in mind that even this Gentile persecution was encouraged by the Jewish unbelievers (Acts 17:5, 13). Jesus promised that this would happen (John 15:18-27).

Was Paul giving evidence of "religious bigotry" when he accused the Jews of killing Jesus Christ and persecuting the Christians? No, he was simply stating a fact of history. Nowhere does the Bible accuse *all* Jews of what *a few Jews* did in Jerusalem and Judea when Christ was crucified and the church founded. The Romans also participated in the trial and death of Christ, and, for that matter, it was *our sins* that sent Him to the cross (Isa.

53:6). There is no place in the Christian faith for anti-Semitism. Paul himself loved his fellow Jews and sought to help them (Acts 24:17; Rom. 9:1-5).

God called Israel to be a blessing to all the world (Gen. 12:1-3; 22:18). Through Israel He gave the promises and the covenants, and the Word of God; and through Israel, Jesus Christ the Saviour came into the world. "Salvation is of the Jews" (John 4:22). The first Christians were Jews, as was Paul, the greatest Christian missionary.

Why, then, did the leaders of Israel officially reject Jesus Christ and persecute His followers? *They were only repeating the sins of their fathers.* Their ancestors had persecuted the prophets long before Jesus came to earth (Matt. 5:10-12). They could not see that their Law was only a temporary preparation for God's New Covenant of grace. By rejecting God's truth, they protected their man-made traditions (Mark 7:1-8). Our Lord's parable in Luke 20:9-19 explained their sinful attitudes.

The sad thing was that Israel was filling up their sins (1 Thes. 2:16) and storing up wrath for the day of judgment. This image is used in Genesis 15:16, and Jesus used it in His sermon against the Pharisees (Matt. 23:32). God patiently waits as sinners rebel against Him, and He watches as their measure of sin and judgment fills up. When the time is up, God's patience will end and judgment will fall.

In one sense, judgment had already fallen on Israel; for they were a scattered people, and their nation in Palestine was under Roman rule (see Deut. 28:15ff). But an even greater judgment was to fall in the future; for in A.D. 70 the Roman armies besieged Jerusalem, destroyed the city and the temple, and ended the period of God's patience with His people during the ministry of the Apostles (see Matt. 22:1-11). It is tragic but true that the righteous suffered because of the sins of the wicked.

Paul encouraged the suffering Christians by assuring them that their experiences were not new or isolated. Others had suffered before them and were even then suffering with them. The churches in Judea had not been exterminated by suffering; if anything, they had been purified and increased. But the persecutors were filling up the measure of wrath to be heaped on their heads. Saints have been saved to the uttermost (Heb. 7:25), but sinners will experience wrath to the uttermost (1 Thes. 2:16).

Here is one of the great values of the local church: we stand together in times of difficulty and encourage one another. It was when Elijah isolated himself from the other faithful Israelites that he became discouraged and wanted to quit. One reason Paul sent Timothy back to Thessalonica was to encourage the believers (1 Thes. 3:1-4). A lonely saint is very vulnerable to the attacks of Satan. We need each other in the battles of life.

**God's Glory before Us (1 Thes. 2:17-20)**
Paul was not ashamed to state his affection for the Thessalonian Christians. He felt as though he had been "orphaned" from them (1 Thes. 2:17) since he was their spiritual mother and father (1 Thes. 2:7, 11). Paul wanted to remain there longer to help ground them in the faith, but the enemy drove him out. However, his absence was only physical; he was still with them in heart (see Phil. 1:7).

Paul made every effort possible to return to them, though Satan was "breaking up the road and putting up obstacles" (literal meaning of "hindered" in 1 Thes. 2:18). Paul had the same kind of deep desire to be with them as Jesus had to be with His disciples before His death (Luke 22:15).

But Paul did not look back and give in to regret and remorse. Instead, he looked ahead and rejoiced. For the Christian, the best is yet to come. Paul looked ahead by faith and saw his friends in the presence of Jesus Christ in glory.

In times of trouble and testing, it is important that we take the long view of things. Paul lived in the future tense, as well as in the present. His actions were governed by what God would do in the future. He knew that Jesus Christ would return and reward him for his faithful ministry; and on that day, the saints from Thessalonica would bring glory to God and joy to Paul's heart. As the familiar song says, "It will be worth it all, when we see Jesus."

The fact that we shall one day stand at the Judgment Seat of Christ ought to motivate us to be faithful in spite of difficulties. We must remember that *faithfulness* is the important thing (1 Cor. 4:2). At the Judgment Seat of Christ, our works will be judged and rewards will be given (Rom. 14:10-12; 1 Cor. 4:1-5; 2 Cor. 5:9-10). In his letters, Paul often pictured these rewards as *crowns*. The word used signified the "victor's crown" at the races, not the royal crown of the king. It is the word *stephanos* from which we get the names Stephen and Stephanie.

Paul did not say that he would receive a crown, though this is suggested. He said that *the saints themselves* would be his crown when he met them at the Judgment Seat. To be sure, some of the believers in the church were not living as they should, and some were a burden to Paul. But when he looked ahead and saw them in glory, they brought joy to his heart.

This joy of greeting believers in heaven also brings with it a solemn warning: we will lose joy if we go to heaven empty-handed. The Christian who has not sincerely tried to win others to Christ will not experience this glory and joy when Jesus Christ returns. It is not enough to "wait for His Son" (1 Thes. 1:10). We must also witness for God and work for His Son, so that when we get to heaven, we will have trophies to present for His glory. There is a special joy and reward for the soul winner (Dan. 12:3).

There is also a crown for the believer who subdues his body and keeps it controlled for the glory of God (1 Cor. 9:24-27). Self-control is produced by the Spirit (Gal. 5:23). Since our bodies are God's temples, we must be careful not to defile them. The ultimate in giving the body to God is dying for His sake; and for this there is a crown (Rev. 2:10). Those who lovingly look for Christ's appearing will receive the "crown of righteousness" (2 Tim. 4:8). The faithful pastor can anticipate the "crown of glory" (1 Peter 5:4).

We must never look on future rewards as a means of showing up the other saints. Like the elders described in Revelation 4:4 (a picture of the glorified church), we will worship the Lord and lay our crowns at His feet (Rev. 4:10). After all, our work was done in his power and for His glory, so He deserves all the praise.

The fact that God promises rewards to us is another evidence of His grace. God could demand our service simply on the basis of all He has done for us. Our motive for serving Him is love. In His grace, He gives us rewards so that we may have something to give Him in return.

When the Christians at Thessalonica read this letter, it must have encouraged them tremendously. They were going through intense persecution and suffering, and perhaps some of them were tempted to give up.

"Don't give up!" Paul encouraged them.

"Lay hold of the spiritual resources you have in Jesus Christ. You have the Word of God within you, the people of God around you, and the glory of God before you. There is no need to give up."

# CHAPTER FIVE
# TAKE A STAND!
## 1 Thessalonians 3:1-13

Before a child can walk, he must learn to stand. Usually the father and mother teach the child to stand and then to walk. Paul was "spiritual parent" to these believers, but he had been forced to leave Thessalonica. How, then, could he help these young Christians learn to stand in the trials of life?

In the first two chapters, Paul explained how the church was born and nurtured. Now he dealt with the next step in maturity: how the church was to stand. The key word in this chapter is *establish* (1 Thes. 3:2, 13). The key thought is expressed in 1 Thessalonians 3:8: "For now we live, if ye stand fast in the Lord."

Paul explained three ministries that he performed to help these new Christians become firmly established.

**He Sent Them a Helper (1 Thes. 3:1-5)**
When Paul and his friends left Thessalonica, they went to Berea and ministered the Word. But the troublemakers from Thessalonica followed them and stirred up opposition. Paul left for Athens while Silas and Timothy remained at Berea (see Acts 17:10-15). Apparently, Timothy did join Paul in Athens (note the "we" in 1 Thes. 3:1-2), but Paul sent him back to Thessalonica to help the young church that was going through tribulations. Several important factors were involved in this move.

**Paul's concern (v. 1).** The "wherefore" that opens this chapter refers to 1 Thessalonians 2:17-20, where Paul expressed his great love for the believers. It was because of this love that he could not abandon them when they needed spiritual help. Paul was not only an evangelist; he was also a pastor. He knew that soul-winning was but one part of the com-

mission God gave him. These new believers must also be taught and established in the faith.

Instead, Paul chose to be left alone in Athens so that Timothy could return to Thessalonica and establish the saints. The word translated "left" in 1 Thessalonians 3:1 means "to leave loved ones at death." In 1 Thessalonians 2:17 he said that he felt "orphaned" from his friends in Thessalonica, and the Greek word can also mean "bereaved." Paul was not a "hireling shepherd" who abandoned the sheep when there was danger (John 10:12-13). To leave these new believers was like an experience of bereavement.

This is a good lesson for Christian workers today. Paul so loved the Thessalonican believers that he would have risked his own life to return to them. He so loved the saints at Philippi that he was willing to stay out of heaven in order to encourage them (Phil. 1:22-26). He wanted to give of himself and his resources for them, as a parent provides for loved children. "I will very gladly spend and be spent for you" (2 Cor. 12:15).

**Timothy's character (v. 2).** Not every believer is equipped to establish other Christians in the faith. Ideally, every Christian should be mature enough to help other Christians grow in the Lord and learn to stand on their own two feet. Unfortunately, some Christians are like those described in Hebrews 5:11-14. They have gone backward in their spiritual walk and have forgotten the basic truths of the Word. Instead of teaching others, they themselves need to be taught again. They are going through a second childhood spiritually.

Timothy was the ideal man to send to the church to help them stand firm. Timothy and Titus were Paul's "special agents" whom he used as troubleshooters whenever the churches had problems. Paul sent Timothy to Corinth to help straighten out the problems there (1 Cor. 16:10-11). He also planned to send Timothy to help the saints in Philippi (Phil. 2:19-23).

What kind of a person can help younger believers grow in the Lord? To begin with, *he must be a Christian himself*: "Timothy, our brother" (1 Thes. 3:2). We cannot lead another where we have not been ourselves, nor can we share that which we do not possess. Paul had led Timothy to faith in Christ (1 Tim. 1:2) so that he was truly a brother.

But Timothy was also *a minister*. This is

simply the Greek word for a servant. Our English word "deacon" comes from this word, *diakonos.* Timothy was not afraid to work. He had faithfully served with Paul (Phil. 2:22) and knew how to minister in the churches. It is a demanding thing to establish new Christians. They have many problems and often do not grow as fast as we think they should. Teaching them requires love and patience, and Timothy had these qualities.

Timothy was a good *team man;* he was a "fellow worker." He did not try to run the show himself and get people to follow him. To begin with, he was a fellow worker with God. It was God who worked in and through Timothy to accomplish His work (see 1 Cor. 3:9 and Phil. 2:13).

But Timothy was also a fellow worker with the other believers. He obeyed Paul and left Athens for Thessalonica. He returned to Paul in Corinth with news about the Thessalonican church. No wonder Paul wrote of him: "For I have no man like-minded, who will naturally care for your state" (Phil. 2:20).

*The church's conflict (vv. 3-5).* The trials and testings that come to our lives as Christians are not accidents—they are *appointments.* We must expect to "suffer for His sake" (Phil. 1:29). Persecution is not foreign to the believer (1 Peter 4:12ff), but a normal part of the Christian life. Paul had repeatedly told them this while he was with them. We must warn new believers that the way is not easy as they seek to live for Christ; otherwise, when trials come, these babes in Christ will be discouraged and defeated.

Of course, behind these persecutions is Satan, the enemy of the Christian (1 Thes. 3:5). He is the tempter, and he seeks to ruin our faith. Note the emphasis on *faith* in this chapter (1 Thes. 3:5-7, 10). As a roaring lion, Satan stalks believers; and we must resist him "steadfast in the faith" (1 Peter 5:8-9). When Satan tempted Eve, he began by weakening her faith in God: "Yea, hath God said?" (Gen. 3:1) As a serpent, Satan deceives (2 Cor. 11:3); as a lion, he devours (1 Peter 5:8). He will use any means to attack the Christian and weaken his faith in God.

The word "moved" in 1 Thessalonians 3 is interesting. It literally means "to wag the tail, to fawn over." The idea is that Satan often flatters the believer in order to lead him astray. Satan told Eve she would be like God if she ate of the tree, and she fell for his flattery. Satan is more dangerous when he flatters than when he frowns.

Timothy's task was to establish these believers and encourage (comfort) them in their faith. It is faith in God that keeps our feet on the ground when the enemy attacks. Without faith in God, we are defeated. "This is the victory that overcometh the world, even our faith" (1 John 5:4).

**He Wrote Them a Letter (1 Thes. 3:6-8)**
Timothy met Paul at Corinth (Acts 18:5) and gave him the glad news that things were going well at Thessalonica. The phrase "brought us good tidings" is the exact equivalent of "preaching the Good News of the Gospel." The report from Timothy was, to Paul, like hearing the Gospel.

Timothy reported that the new believers were standing firm in spite of persecution. They did not believe the lies that the enemy had told about Paul, but they still held him in the highest esteem in love.

Paul's response was to write them this letter. Paul wrote some letters which are not a part of the New Testament (1 Cor. 5:9), but the two letters to the Thessalonican church are a part of God's inspired Word.

This suggests that God's Word is one of the best tools for establishing new Christians in the faith. "So then, brothers, stand firm and hold to the teachings we passed on to you, whether by word of mouth or by letter" (2 Thes. 2:15, NIV). When Jesus was tempted by Satan, He used the Word of God to defeat him (Matt. 4:1-11). Paul admonished the Ephesian believers to take "the sword of the Spirit, which is the Word of God" (Eph. 6:17) in their battle against Satan and his demonic assistants.

The Bible is able to establish us because it is inspired of God (2 Tim. 3:16). It is not simply a book of religious ideas or good moral advice; it is the very Word of God. It is "profitable for doctrine, for reproof, for correction, for instruction in righteousness." It has well been said that *doctrine* tells us what is right, *reproof* tells us what is not right, *correction* tells us how to get right, and *instruction* tells us how to stay right.

First Thessalonians is saturated with Bible doctrines. Every major doctrine of the faith is touched on in these brief chapters. There are dozens of references to God the Father and Jesus Christ, and at least four references to the Holy Spirit (1 Thes. 1:5-6; 4:8; 5:19). In this epistle, Paul dealt with sin and salvation, the doctrine of the church, the work of the ministry, and especially the doctrine of the last things. Since Paul did not remain in Thessalonica very long, it is remarkable that he taught his converts so much.

Dr. R.W. Dale was pastor of Carr's Lane Congregational Church in England for nearly fifty years. He began a series of sermons on basic Bible doctrine, knowing that his members could not stand firm in their faith if they did not know what they believed or why they believed it. A fellow pastor said to Dr. Dale, "They will never take it." But Dale replied, "They will *have* to take it!" And they did, to the strengthening of the church.

When I became a Christian, churches did not have regular follow-up courses for new converts such as we have today. My "follow-up course" was a series of Bible studies from the Book of Hebrews, led by a gifted layman and taught in his living room. Much of what was taught was over my head as a new believer. But what I did learn grounded me in the Word and established me in the faith.

A working knowledge of the Bible is essential for spiritual growth and stability. God's Word is *food* to nourish us (Matt. 4:4), *light* to guide us (Ps. 119:105), and a *weapon* to defend us (Eph. 6:17) "Thus saith the Lord!" is our sure foundation. One reason God has established local churches is that believers might grow in the Word and, in turn, help others to grow (2 Tim. 2:2; Eph. 4:11-16).

Paul sent them a man, and that man established them in the Word. Paul ministered to them in a third way.

### He Prayed for Them (1 Thes. 3:9-13)

The Word of God and prayer should go together. The Prophet Samuel told the people of Israel, "God forbid that I should sin against the Lord in ceasing to pray for you: but I will teach you the good and the right way" (1 Sam. 12:23). Peter said, "But we [the Apostles] will give ourselves continually to prayer, and to the ministry of the Word" (Acts 6:4). Paul had this same emphasis: "And now, brethren, I commend you to God [prayer], and to the Word of His grace, which is able to build you up" (Acts 20:32).

Jesus prayed for His disciples, just as Paul prayed for the Thessalonican Christians, that their faith would not fail (Luke 22:31-32). I ministered for several weeks in Kenya and Zaire, and when I arrived home, I was more convinced than ever that the greatest need of missionaries and national churches is *prayer.* We must also pray for young Christians here at home. It is not enough to teach them Bible truth; we must also support them in our prayers.

Paul prayed for three specific requests. First, he prayed *that their faith might mature* (1 Thes. 3:10). Paul asked God to make it possible for him to minister to them personally, but God did not answer that request. Paul longed to see them again; he longed to minister to them and help bring their faith to maturity. The word translated "perfect" has the meaning of "adjust, equip, furnish." It is even used for the mending of nets (Mark 1:19). Our faith never reaches perfection; there is always need for adjustment and growth. We go "from faith to faith" (Rom. 1:17).

Abraham is a good illustration of this principle. God called him to the land of Canaan, and when he arrived, he discovered a famine. God permitted that famine so that Abraham's faith might be tested. Unfortunately, Abraham failed the test and went down to Egypt for help.

Each step of the way, God brought circumstances to bear on Abraham that forced him to trust God and grow in his faith. Faith is like a muscle: it gets stronger with use. Abraham had problems with his worldly nephew, Lot. He also had problems with his wife and her handmaid, Hagar. The ultimate test of faith came when God asked Abraham to sacrifice his beloved son, Isaac.

Faith that cannot be tested cannot be trusted. God tries our faith, not to destroy it, but to develop it. Had Abraham not learned to trust God in the famine, he could never have trusted Him in the other difficulties. Paul prayed that the suffering Christians in Thessalonica might grow in their faith, and God answered his prayer. Paul wrote in his second letter, "We are bound to thank God always for you, brethren . . . because that your faith groweth exceedingly" (2 Thes. 1:3).

Paul's second request was *that their love might abound* (1 Thes. 3:12). Times of suffering can be times of selfishness. Persecuted people often become very self-centered and demanding. What life does to us depends on what life finds in us; and nothing reveals the true inner man like the furnace of affliction. Some people build walls in times of trial, and shut themselves off. Others build bridges and draw closer to the Lord and His people. This was Paul's prayer for these believers, and

God answered it: "The charity of every one of you all toward each other aboundeth" (2 Thes. 1:3).

Our growing faith in God ought to result in a growing love for others. We are "taught of God to love one another" (1 Thes. 4:9), and some of these lessons are best learned in the school of suffering. Joseph suffered for thirteen years because of his brothers' envy and persecution. Yet he learned to love them in spite of their hatred. The Jewish legalists persecuted Paul from city to city, yet Paul so loved his people that he willingly would have died for them (Rom. 9:1-3).

When I counsel young couples in preparation for marriage, I often ask the man: "If your wife became paralyzed three weeks after you were married, do you love her enough to stay with her and care for her?" True love deepens in times of difficulty; shallow romance disappears when difficulties appear.

But true Christian love is shown not only to believers, but also "toward all men" (1 Thes. 3:12). We love one another, but we also love the lost and our enemies. Abounding love must not be bound. It must be free to expand and touch all men.

Paul's third request was for *holiness of life* (1 Thes. 3:13). Again, it is the return of Jesus Christ that motivates the believer to live a holy life. Our Lord's return is also a source of stability in the Christian life. Where there is stability, there can be sanctity; and where there is holiness, there is assurance. The two go together.

Notice that Paul's prayers for his friends were not careless or occasional. He prayed "night and day"; he prayed "exceedingly" which is the same word translated "exceeding abundantly" in Ephesians 3:20. True prayer is hard work. Epaphras must have learned from Paul how to pray for people: "always laboring fervently . . . that ye may stand perfect and complete in all the will of God" (Col. 4:12).

The entire Trinity is involved in this prayer. Paul addressed the Father and Son in 1 Thessalonians 3:11. In verse 12 "the Lord" may refer to the Holy Spirit, since "our Lord" at the end of 1 Thessalonians 3:13 certainly refers to Jesus Christ. If this is so, then this is the only prayer I know of in the New Testament directed to the Holy Spirit. The Bible pattern of prayer is: to the Father, through the Son, and in the Spirit. Since the Holy Spirit is the Sanctifier of the believer, and this is a prayer for holy living, the address is proper.

Paul ended 1 Thessalonians 2 with a reference to the place of the saints at the return of Christ, and he ended this chapter in the same way. He prayed that his converts might stand blameless and holy before God at Christ's return. Since all believers will be transformed to be like Christ when He returns (1 John 3:2), Paul could not be referring to our personal condition in heaven. He was referring to our lives here on earth as they will be reviewed at the Judgment Seat of Christ. We will never face our sins in heaven, for they are remembered against us no more (Rom. 8:1; Heb. 10:14-18). But our works will be tested, and you cannot separate conduct from character.

Paul's prayer teaches us how to pray not only for new believers, but for *all* believers. We should pray that their faith will mature, their love grow, and their character and conduct be holy and blameless before God. "And every man that hath this hope in Him [Christ] purifieth himself, even as He is pure" (1 John 3:3).

As we review this chapter, we see how important it is to care for new Christians. Leading someone to Christ is not enough. We must also lead him on in the Christian life and help him get established. If he is not established, he will fall when the winds of persecution start to blow. If he cannot stand, he will never learn to walk.

What shall we do? We can be an encouragement and stand at his side as he matures. We can share the Word of God. We can pray. This is what Paul did—and it worked.

# CHAPTER SIX
# HOW TO PLEASE YOUR FATHER
*1 Thessalonians 4:1-12*

Along with jogging, walking has become a popular exercise and outdoor sport. I often see individuals and entire families enjoying a walk in the park or in the forest preserves. When driving on the highway, I sometimes wave to "walking parties" heading for some distant rendezvous.

The Christian life can be compared to a walk. In fact, this is one of Paul's favorite pictures: "Walk worthy of the vocation wherewith ye are called" (Eph. 4:1); "walk not as other Gentiles walk" (Eph. 4:17); "walk in love" (Eph. 5:2); "walk as children of light" (Eph. 5:8).

The Christian life begins with a step of faith. But that step leads to a walk of faith, "For we walk by faith, not by sight" (2 Cor. 5:7). Walking suggests progress, and we must make progress in the Christian life (Phil. 3:13-16; Heb. 6:1). Walking also demands strength, and God has promised, "As thy days, so shall thy strength be" (Deut. 33:25).

But we must be sure to "walk in the light" for the enemy has put traps and detours to catch us (1 John 1:5-7). Of course, at the end of life's walk, we will step into the very presence of the Lord. "And Enoch walked with God, and he was not, for God took him" (Gen. 5:24).

Paul described a threefold walk for the Christian to follow.

## Walk in Holiness (1 Thes. 4:1-8)

The moral climate in the Roman Empire was not healthy. Immorality was a way of life, and, thanks to slavery, people had the leisure time to indulge in the latest pleasures. The Christian message of holy living was new to that culture, and it was not easy for these young believers to fight the temptations around them. Paul gave four reasons why they should live a holy life and abstain from sensual lusts.

*To please God (v. 1).* Everybody lives to please somebody. Many people live to please themselves. They have no sensitivity to the needs of others. "The soul of a journey," wrote William Hazlitt, "is liberty, perfect liberty, to think, feel, do just as one pleases." That advice may work for a vacation but it could never work in the everyday affairs of life. Christians cannot go through life pleasing only themselves (Rom. 15:1).

We must also be careful when it comes to pleasing others. It is possible to both please others and honor God, but it is also possible to dishonor God. "For if I yet pleased men, I should not be the servant of Christ" (Gal. 1:10). This had been Paul's attitude when he ministered in Thessalonica. "Even so we speak, not as pleasing men but God, who trieth our hearts" (1 Thes. 2:4).

Pleasing God ought to be the major motive of the Christian life. Children should live to please their father. The Holy Spirit works in our lives "both to will and to do of His good pleasure" (Phil. 2:13). Enoch walked with God, and before God called him to heaven, Enoch "had this testimony, that he pleased God" (Heb. 11:5). Jesus said, "I do always those things that please Him" (John 8:29).

Pleasing God means much more than simply doing God's will. It is possible to obey God and yet not please Him. Jonah is a case in point. He obeyed God and did what he was commanded, but his heart was not in it. God blessed His Word but He could not bless His servant. So Jonah sat outside the city of Nineveh angry with everybody, including the Lord! Our obedience should be "not with eyeservice, as men-pleasers, but as the servants of Christ, doing the will of God from the heart" (Eph. 6:6).

How do we know what pleases God? How do we know what pleases an earthly father? By listening to him and living with him. As we read the Word, and as we fellowship in worship and service, we get to know the heart of God; and this opens us up to the will of God.

*To obey God (vv. 2-3).* When he ministered in Thessalonica, Paul gave the believers the commandments of God regarding personal purity. The word *commandments* is a military term. It refers to orders handed down from superior officers. We are soldiers in God's army, and we must obey orders. "No one serving as a soldier gets involved in civilian affairs—he wants to please his commanding officer" (2 Tim. 2:4, NIV).

In 1 Thessalonians 4:3, Paul reminded these new believers that sexual immorality did not please God. God created sex, and He has the authority to govern its use. From the beginning, He established marriage as a sacred union between one man and one woman. God created sex both for the continuance of the race and for the pleasure of the marriage partners. "Marriage should be honored by all, and the marriage bed kept pure" (Heb. 13:4, NIV). God's commandments concerning sex are not for the purpose of robbing people of joy, but rather of protecting them that they might not lose their joy. "Thou shalt not commit adultery" builds a wall around marriage that makes the relationship not a prison, but a safe and beautiful garden.

We never have to seek to know the will of God in this matter; He has told us clearly. "Abstain from fornication" is His commandment, and no amount of liberal theology or modern philosophy can alter it. Throughout the Bible, God warns against sexual sin; and these warnings must be heeded. God's purpose is *our sanctification,* that we might live separated lives in purity of mind and body.

*To glorify God (vv. 4-5).* This is the positive side of God's commandment. Christians are supposed to be different from the unsaved. The Gentiles (unsaved) do not know God; therefore, they live ungodly lives. But we know God, and we are obligated to glorify Him in this world. "God's plan is to make you holy, and that entails first of all a clean break with sexual immorality" (1 Thes. 4:3, PH).

"Possess his vessel" in 1 Thessalonians 4:4 probably means "control his body," for our bodies are the vessels of God (see 2 Cor. 4:7; 2 Tim. 2:20-21). But it can also mean "learn to live with his own wife," for the wife is called "the weaker vessel" (1 Peter 3:7). I prefer the first interpretation, for Paul wrote to *all* Christians, not just the married ones. The Christian who commits sexual sin is sinning against his own body (1 Cor. 6:19-20), and he is robbing God of the glory He should receive through a believer's way of life.

This explains why God gives such demanding requirements for spiritual leadership in the church (1 Tim. 3). If spiritual leaders cannot rule in their own homes, how can they lead the church? If we glorify God in our bodies, then we can glorify Him in the body which is the church.

*To escape the judgment of God (vv. 6-8).* God is no respecter of persons; He must deal with His children when they sin (Col. 3:23-25). A church member criticized her pastor because he was preaching against sin in the lives of Christians. "After all," she said, "sin in the life of a believer is different from sin in the lives of unsaved people." "Yes," replied the pastor, *"it is worse."*

While it is true that the Christian is not under condemnation (John 5:24; Rom. 8:1), it is also true that he is not free from the harvest of sorrow that comes when we sow to the flesh (Gal. 6:7-8). When King David committed adultery, he tried to cover his sin, but God chastened him severely. (Read Pss. 32; 51 to see what he lost during those months.) When David confessed his sins, God forgave him; *but God could not change the consequences.* David reaped what he sowed, and it was a painful experience for him.

"But I am one of God's elect!" a Christian may argue. "I belong to Him, and He can never cast me out." Election is not an excuse for sin—it is an encouragement for holiness. "For God hath not called us unto uncleanness, but unto holiness" (1 Thes. 4:7). "But as He which hath called you is holy, so be ye holy" (1 Peter 1:15). The privilege of election also involves responsibilities of obedience (Deut. 7:6, 11).

A holy walk involves a right relationship with God the Father (who called us), God the Son (who died for us), and God the Spirit (who lives within us). It is the presence of the Holy Spirit that makes our body the temple of God (1 Cor. 6:19-20). Furthermore, it is by walking in the Spirit that we get victory over the lusts of the flesh (Gal. 5:16ff). To despise God's commandments is to invite the judgment of God and also to grieve the Spirit of God.

How does the Spirit of God help us live a clean life, free from sexual impurity? To begin with, He creates holy desires within us so that we have an appetite for God's pure Word (1 Peter 2:1-3) and not the polluted garbage of the flesh (Rom. 13:12-14). Also, He teaches us the Word and helps us to recall God's promises in times of temptation (John 14:26; Eph. 6:17). As we yield to the Spirit, He empowers us to walk in holiness and not be detoured into the lusts of the world and the flesh. The fruit of the Spirit overcomes the works of the flesh (Gal. 5:16-26).

Paul devoted a great deal of space to this theme of sexual purity because it was a critical problem in the church of that day. *It is also a critical problem in the church today.* For many people, marriage vows are no longer considered sacred, and divorce (even among believers) is no longer governed by the Word of God. There are "gay churches" where homosexuals and lesbians "love one another" and claim to be Christians. Premarital sex and "Christian pornography" are accepted parts of the religious landscape in many places. Yet God has said, "Walk in holiness."

## Walk in Harmony (1 Thes. 4:9-10)

The transition from *holiness* to *love* is not a difficult one. Paul made this transition in his prayer recorded in 1 Thessalonians 3:11-13. Just as God's love is a holy love, so our love for God and for one another ought to motivate us to holy living. The more we live like God, the more we will love one another. If a Christian really loves his brother, he will not sin against him (1 Thes. 4:6).

There are four basic words for "love" in the Greek language. *Eros* refers to physical love; it gives us our English word *erotic*. Eros love does not have to be sinful, but in Paul's day its main emphasis was sensual. This word is never used in the New Testament. Another word, *storge* (pronounced STOR-gay), refers to family love, the love of parents for their children. This word is also absent from our New Testament, although a related word is translated "kindly affectioned" in Romans 12:10.

The two words most used for love are *philia* (fil-E-uh) and *agape* (a-GA-pay). *Philia* love is the love of deep affection, such as in friendship or even marriage. But *agape* love is the love God shows toward us. It is not simply a love based on feeling; it is expressed in our wills. Agape love treats others as God would treat them, regardless of feelings or personal preferences.

The word *philadelphia* is translated "brotherly love." Because Christians belong to the same family, and have the same Father, they should love one another. In fact, we are "taught of God to love one another." God the Father taught us to love each other when He gave Christ to die for us on the cross. "We love, because He first loved us" (1 John 4:19, NIV). God the Son taught us to love one another when He said, "A new commandment I give unto you, that ye love one another" (John 13:34). And the Holy Spirit taught us to love one another when He poured out the love of God in our hearts (Rom. 5:5) when we trusted Christ.

Have you noticed that animals do *instinctively* what is necessary to keep them alive and safe? Fish do not attend classes to learn how to swim (even though they swim in schools), and birds by nature put out their wings and flap them in order to fly. It is *nature* that determines action. Because a fish has a fish's nature, it swims; because a hawk has a hawk's nature, it flies. And because a Christian has God's nature (2 Peter 1:4), he loves, because "God is love" (1 John 4:8).

Faith, hope, and love had been the distinctive characteristics of the Thessalonican Christians from the beginning (1 Thes. 1:3). Timothy had reported the good news of their love (1 Thes. 3:6), so Paul was not exhorting them to acquire something they did not already possess. He was encouraging them to get more of what they already enjoyed. You can never have too much Christian love. Paul had prayed that their love might "increase and abound" (1 Thes. 3:12); and God answered that prayer (see 2 Thes. 1:3).

How does God cause our love to "increase more and more"? By putting us into circumstances that force us to practice Christian love. Love is the "circulatory system" of the body of Christ, but if our spiritual muscles are not exercised, the circulation is impaired. The difficulties that we believers have *with one another* are opportunities for us to grow in our love. This explains why Christians who have had the most problems with each other often end up loving one another deeply, much to the amazement of the world.

### Walk in Honesty (1 Thes. 4:11-12)

The word in 1 Thessalonians 4:12 that is translated "honestly" in our *Authorized Version*, carries the meaning of "becomingly, in a seemly way." It is translated "decently" in 1 Corinthians 14:40, "Let all things be done decently and in order." The emphasis is on the believer's witness to those who are outside the Christian fellowship. "Them that are without" is a familiar description of unbelievers.

Christians not only have the obligation to love one another but also to be good testimonies to the people of the world. Paul's great concern was that the Thessalonican believers earn their own wages and not become freeloaders depending on the support of unbelievers. "Make it your ambition to lead a quiet life" (1 Thes. 4:11, NIV) seems like a paradox; if you are ambitious, your life will probably not be quiet. But the emphasis is on quietness of mind and heart, the inner peace that enables a man to be sufficient through faith in Christ. Paul did not want the saints running around creating problems as they earned their daily bread.

For the most part, the Greeks despised manual labor. Most of the work was done by slaves. Paul, of course, was a tentmaker; and he was careful in Thessalonica to set the example of hard work (see 1 Thes. 2:6; 2 Thes. 3:6ff). Unfortunately, some of the new believers in the church misunderstood the doctrine of Christ's return and gave up their jobs in order to wait for His coming. This meant that they were supported by other Christians, some of whom may not have had sufficient funds for their own families. It also meant that these fanatical people could not pay their bills, and therefore they lost their testimony with the unsaved merchants.

"My wife is going to have plastic surgery," a man said to his friend. "I'm taking away all of her credit cards!" How easy it is to purchase things we do not need with money we do not have, and then lose not only our credit, but also our good Christian witness. "If therefore you have not been faithful in the use of unrighteous mammon [money] who will entrust the true riches to you?" (Luke 16:11, NASB) Churches and Christians who defend their orthodoxy but do not pay their bills have no orthodoxy to defend.

"Mind your own business and work with your hands" (1 Thes. 4:11, NIV) was what Paul commanded them. Idle people spend their time interfering with the affairs of others and getting themselves and others into trouble. "We hear that some among you are idle. They are not busy; they are busybodies" (2 Thes. 3:11, NIV). "But let none of you suffer . . . as a busybody in other men's matters" (1 Peter 4:15).

Believers who are about the Father's business (Luke 2:49) do not have the time—or desire—to meddle in the affairs of others. Unfortunately, even a Bible class could become an opportunity for gossip ("so that you might pray more intelligently") and a substitute for true Christian service.

As believers, we must be careful in our relationships with "those that are without." It requires spiritual grace and wisdom to have contact without contamination and to be different without being judgmental and proud. "Walk in wisdom toward them that are without" (Col. 4:5). If we lack this spiritual wisdom, we will do more harm than good.

There are several good reasons why Christians should work, not the least of which is to provide for their own families (1 Tim. 5:8). If unsaved people have to work to pay their bills, why should Christians be exempt? We also work in order to be able to give to those who have need (Eph. 4:28); but "if any would not work, neither should he eat" (2 Thes. 3:10). Work is not a curse; it is a blessing. God gave Adam work to do in Paradise. It is the toil and sweat of work that belongs to the curse, and not the work itself (Gen. 2:15 and 3:17ff).

As we review this section, we see how practical the Christian walk really is. The obedient Christian will have *a holy life* by abstaining from sexual sin; *a harmonious life* by loving the brethren; and *an honest life* by working with his hands and not meddling in the affairs of others. When unsaved people see Christ magnified in this kind of a life, they will either oppose it with envy or desire to have it for themselves. Either way, God is glorified.

# CHAPTER SEVEN
# THE COMFORT OF HIS COMING
*1 Thessalonians 4:13-18*

The pagan world in Paul's day had no hope of life after death. A typical inscription on a grave demonstrates this fact:

> I was not
> I became
> I am not
> I care not

While some of the philosophers, such as Socrates, sought to prove happiness after death, the pagan world had no word of assurance.

The believers in Thessalonica were concerned about their loved ones who had died. What if the Lord should return? Would their deceased loved ones be handicapped in any way? Will those who are alive at His coming have an advantage over the believers who have died? In this paragraph, Paul answered their questions. He based his encouragement and comfort on five fundamental facts.

## Revelation: We Have God's Truth (1 Thes. 4:13, 15a)

How can mortal man penetrate beyond the grave and find assurance and peace for his own heart? From Old Testament days till the present, mankind has tried to solve the riddle of death and the afterlife. Philosophers have wrestled with the question of immortality. Spiritists have tried to communicate with those who have gone beyond.

In our modern world, scientists have investigated the experiences of people who claimed to have died and returned to life again. They have also studied occult phenomena, hoping to find a clue to the mystery of life after death.

Paul solved the problem when he wrote,

"For this we say unto you by the Word of the Lord" (1 Thes. 4:15). We Christians need not wonder about death or life after death, for we have a revelation from God in His Word. Why substitute human speculation for divine revelation?

It is important to note that the revelation concerning death and the afterlife was not given all at one time. Many cults use verses from the Psalms and Ecclesiastes to "prove" their false doctrines. These verses seem to teach that the grave is the end, or that the soul "sleeps" till the resurrection. We must keep in mind that God's revelation was *gradual* and *progressive,* and that it climaxed in the coming of Christ "who abolished death, and brought life and immortality to light through the Gospel" (2 Tim. 1:10, NASB). We look to Christ and the New Testament for the complete revelation concerning death.

God gave Paul a special revelation concerning the resurrection and the return of Christ (see 1 Cor. 15:51-54). What Paul taught agreed with what Jesus taught (John 5:24-29; 11:21-27). And God's revelation is based on the historic fact of Christ's resurrection. Since our Saviour has conquered death, we need not fear death or the future (1 Cor. 15:12ff). The authority of God's Word gives us the assurance and comfort we need.

### Return: Christ Is Coming Again
### (1 Thes. 4:14-15)

We have noted the emphasis on the return of Christ in the Thessalonian letters. Paul related Christ's return to salvation (1 Thes. 1:9-10), service (1 Thes. 2:19-20), and stability (1 Thes. 3:11-13). In this paragraph, he related it to sorrow, and he showed how the doctrine of Christ's return can comfort the brokenhearted.

Paul applied the word *sleep* to those believers who died. Jesus used the same expression (John 11:11-13). Paul was careful to state that Jesus *died;* the word *sleep* is not applied to His experience. It is because He died that we need not fear death.

However, Paul did not say that the *soul* went to sleep at death. He made it clear that the soul of the believer went to be with the Lord: "them also which sleep in Jesus will God bring with Him" (1 Thes. 4:14). He cannot bring them when He returns unless they are with Him. It is not the soul that sleeps; *it is the body.* The Bible definition of death is given in James 2:26—"For as the body without the

spirit is dead." At death, the spirit leaves the body, and the body goes to sleep and no longer functions. The soul-spirit goes to be with the Lord, if the person has trusted Jesus Christ. "Absent from the body, and . . . present with the Lord" (2 Cor. 5:8).

The fact of our Lord's return is comfort to us in bereavement, because we know that He will bring with Him His people who have "died in the Lord." I recall stating to a friend, "I hear you lost your wife. I'm very sorry." He replied, "No, I didn't lose her. You can't lose something when you know where it is—*and I know where she is!*" On the authority of the Word of God, we also know what will happen: Jesus Christ will one day return and bring His people with Him.

When will this event occur? Nobody knows, and it is wrong to set dates. The fact that Paul used the pronoun *we* in 1 Thessalonians 4:15, 17 suggests that he expected to be alive when the Lord returned. Theologians call this the doctrine of the imminent return of Christ. *Imminent* means that it can happen at any moment. As Christians, we do not look for signs, nor must any special events transpire before the Lord can return. These great events will take place "in a moment, in the twinkling of an eye" (1 Cor. 15:52).

Jesus Christ will return *in the air,* and this is where we shall meet Him (1 Thes. 4:17). Suddenly, millions of people will vanish! One summer a church camp staff staged an elaborate "rapture" while the camp director was off the grounds. When he returned, everybody was missing, clothing was on the ground as though people had "passed through" it, a motorboat was circling on the lake without pilot or passengers, and everything in the kitchen was functioning without a cook. A carefully timed phone call from town ("Hey, what's happening? Everybody's missing over here!") only added to the effect. "I've got to admit," said the director, "it really shook me for a minute." Just think of what effect this event will have on a lost world!

Whether we Christians live or die, we have nothing to fear because Jesus will come either *with us* or *for us!* The fact of His return is a comfort to our hearts.

### Resurrection: The Christian Dead
### Will Rise (1 Thes. 4:15-16)

When Paul preached the doctrine of the resurrection to the Athenian philosophers, most of them mocked him (Acts 17:32). To the

Greeks, *being rid of the body* was their great hope. Why would any man want to have his body resurrected? Furthermore, *how* could his body be resurrected, when the elements of the body would decay and become a part of the earth? To them, the doctrine of resurrection was foolish and impossible.

When Jesus Christ returns in thc air, He will issue the "shout of command" and the "dead in Christ shall rise first" (1 Thes. 4:16). This does not mean that He will put the elements of the body together again, for resurrection is not "reconstruction." Paul argued for the resurrection in 1 Corinthians 15:35ff. He pointed out that the resurrection of the human body is like the growing of a plant from a seed. The flower is not the identical seed that was planted, yet there is continuity from seed to plant. Christians shall receive glorified bodies, like the glorified body of Christ (Phil. 3:20-21; 1 Cor. 15:47-58). The dead body is the "seed" that is planted in the ground; the resurrection body is the "flower" that comes from that seed.

Passages like John 5:28-29 and Revelation 20:1-6 indicate that there are *two* resurrections in the future. When Jesus Christ returns in the air, He will call to Himself only those who are saved through faith in Him. This is called "the first resurrection" or "the resurrection of life." At the end of time, just before God ushers in the new heaven and earth, there will be another resurrection. This is called "the second resurrection" or "the resurrection of judgment." Between these two events, I believe that the Tribulation on earth and the 1,000-year-kingdom will occur.

In Paul's day, the Pharisees believed in the resurrection of the dead, but the Sadducees did not (Acts 23:8). Jesus taught the doctrine of the resurrection and silenced the Sadducees (Matt. 22:23-33). The Old Testament Scriptures taught this doctrine (Job 14:13-15; 19:23-27; Ps. 16:9-11; Dan. 12:2). The fact that Jesus arose from the dead proves that there is a resurrection.

Three unique sounds will be involved in this event: the Lord's shout, the sound of the trumpet, and the voice of the archangel. Jesus Christ will give "a shout of command," just as He did outside the tomb of Lazarus (John 11:43). Those "in the graves shall hear His voice" (John 5:28).

First Corinthians 15:52 also relates His return to the sound of a trumpet. The Jewish people were familiar with trumpets, because trumpets were used to declare war, to announce special times and seasons, and to gather the people for a journey (see Num. 10). In the Roman Empire, trumpets were used to announce the arrival of a great person. When God gave the Law to Israel, the event was preceded by a trumpet blast (Ex. 19:18-20).

Why "the voice of the archangel"? The only archangel who is named in the Bible is Michael (Jude 9), who apparently has a special ministry to Israel (Dan. 10:21; Rev. 12:7) According to Daniel 10:13, there is more than one archangel; so we cannot be sure that it will be Michael's voice. At any rate, the angelic hosts will share in the victory shout when Jesus Christ comes.

The Christian doctrine of resurrection assures us that death is not the end. The grave is not the end. The body goes to sleep, but the soul goes to be with the Lord (Phil. 1:20-24). When the Lord returns, He will bring the soul with Him, will raise the body in glory, and will unite body and soul into one being to share His glory forever. This leads us to the fourth fact that gives us comfort and assurance in the face of death.

**Rapture: Living Believers Caught Up (1 Thes. 4:17)**
The word *rapture* is not used in this section, but that is the literal meaning of "caught up." The Latin word *rapto* means "to seize, to carry off"; and from it we get our English word "rapture."

I once heard the Greek scholar, Dr. Kenneth S. Wuest, preach on this passage and explain the various meanings of the Greek word that is translated "caught up" in 1 Thessalonians 4:17. Each of these meanings adds a special truth to the doctrine of our Lord's return.

*"To catch away speedily."* This is the translation in Acts 8:39, where the Spirit "caught away Philip" after he had led the Ethiopian to Christ. When the Lord returns in the air, we who are alive will be caught away quickly, in the twinkling of an eye. This means we should live each moment in the expectation of our Lord's return, lest He come and find us out of His will (1 John 3:1-3).

*"To seize by force."* See John 6:15. Does this suggest that Satan and his armies will try to keep us from leaving the earth? I trust it does not suggest that some of the saints will be so attached to the world that they must

literally be dragged away. Like Lot being delivered from Sodom, they will be scarcely saved (Gen. 19:16).

*"To claim for one's own self."* This views the Rapture from our Lord's point of view as He comes to claim His bride.

*"To move to a new place."* Paul used this word when he described his visit to heaven (2 Cor. 12:1-4). Jesus Christ has gone to prepare a home for us (John 14:1-6), and when He comes, He will take us to that glorious place. We are pilgrims and strangers in this world. Our true citizenship is in heaven (Phil. 3:20-21).

*"To rescue from danger."* See Acts 23:10. This suggests that the church will be taken home *before* the time of Tribulation that will come to the world from God. First Thessalonians 1:10; 5:9 seem to state this clearly.

Will the unsaved world be aware of what is happening? Will they hear the shout, the voice, and the trumpet? First Corinthians 15:52 indicates that this will happen so suddenly that it will be over in the twinkling of an eye. Since the shout, voice, and trumpet apply to God's people, there is no reason to believe that the unsaved masses will hear them. If they do, they will hear sounds without meanings (see John 12:27-30). Millions of people will vanish instantly, and no doubt there will be chaos and great concern. Except for those who know the Bible teaching, the world will wonder at what has happened.

## Reunion: Christians Forever with the Lord (1 Thes. 4:17-18)

You and I shall meet the Lord in the air, in person, when He comes for us. The Greek word translated "meet" carries the idea of meeting a royal person or an important person. We have walked with Christ by faith here on earth, but in the air we shall "see Him as He is" and become like Him (1 John 3:1-2). What a meeting that will be!

It will be a *glorious* meeting, because we shall have glorified bodies. When He was here on earth, Jesus prayed that we might one day see His glory and share in it (John 17:22-24). The suffering that we endure today will be transformed into glory when He returns (Rom. 8:17-19; 2 Cor. 4:17-18).

It will be an *everlasting* meeting, for we shall be "forever with the Lord." This was His promise: "I will come again, and receive you unto Myself; that where I am, there ye may be also" (John 14:3). The goal of redemption is not just to rescue us from judgment, but to relate us to Christ.

Our meeting with the Lord will also be a time of *reckoning*. This is called "the Judgment Seat of Christ" (Rom. 14:10; 2 Cor. 5:10). The Greek word *bema,* which is translated "judgment seat," referred to the place where the Olympic judges awarded crowns to the winners. Our works will be judged and rewards will be given (1 Cor. 3:8-15).

The Judgment Seat of Christ must not be confused with the White Throne Judgment described in Revelation 20:11-15. You may contrast these two important events as follows:

| Judgment Seat of Christ | White Throne Judgment |
|---|---|
| Only believers | Only unbelievers |
| Immediately after the Rapture | After the thousand-year kingdom |
| Determines rewards for service | Determines amount of judgment |

We will not only meet our Lord Jesus Christ at the Rapture, but will also be reunited with our believing friends and loved ones who have died. "Together with them" is a great statement of encouragement. Death is the great separator, but Jesus Christ is the great Reconciler.

The Bible does not reveal all the details of this reunion. When Jesus raised the widow's son from the dead, He tenderly "delivered him to his mother" (Luke 7:15). This suggests that our Lord will have the happy ministry of reuniting broken families and friendships.

On the Mount of Transfiguration, the three disciples knew and recognized Moses and Elijah (Matt. 17:1-5). Certainly, the saints will know each other in glory, including believers we have never met. "For now we see through a glass, darkly; but then face to face: now I know in part; but then shall I know even as also I am known" (1 Cor. 13:12).

In the next chapter, we will see how Paul related this doctrine of the return of Christ to the unsaved. But it would be good for us now to examine our own hearts to see if we are ready to meet the Lord. One mark of a true Christian is his eager looking for the coming of Jesus Christ (1 Thes. 1:10). As we grow in the Lord, we not only *look for* His appearing, but we *love* His appearing (2 Tim. 4:8). Because we have this hope in Him, we keep our lives pure so that we may not be ashamed at His coming (1 John 2:28–3:3).

Robert Murray McCheyne, the godly Presbyterian preacher, used to ask people: "Do you think Jesus Christ will return today?" Most of them would reply, "No, not today." Then McCheyne would say, "Then, my friend, you had better be ready; for He is coming at such an hour as ye think not" (Luke 12:40).

Death is a fact of life. The only way we can escape death is to be alive when the Lord Jesus Christ returns. Death is not an accident; it is an appointment: "It is appointed unto men once to die, but after this the judgment" (Heb. 9:27). If you should die today, *where would your soul go?*

I once saw a quaint inscription on a gravestone in an old British cemetery not far from Windsor Castle. It read:

Pause, my friend, as you walk by;
As you are now, so once was I.
As I am now, so you will be.
Prepare, my friend, to follow me!

I heard about a visitor who read that epitaph and added these lines:

To follow you is not my intent,
Until I know which way you went!

We Christians have wonderful assurance and hope, because of the resurrection of Jesus Christ and His promised return.

Do you have that hope today?

Which way are *you* going?

# CHAPTER EIGHT
# DON'T WALK IN YOUR SLEEP!
## *1 Thessalonians 5:1-11*

Jesus Christ both unites and divides. Those who have trusted Him as Saviour are united in Christ as God's children. We are members of His body and "all one in Christ Jesus" (Gal. 3:28). When Jesus Christ returns in the air, we shall be "caught up together" (1 Thes. 4:17) never to be separated again.

But Christ is also a divider. "So there was a division among the people because of Him" (John 7:43; 9:16; 10:19). Faith in Jesus Christ not only unites us to other believers; it also separates us spiritually from the rest of the world. Jesus said, "They are not of the world, even as I am not of the world" (John 17:16). There is a difference between believers who are looking for the Lord's return and the people of the world; it is this theme that Paul developed in this section.

His purpose was to encourage the believers to live holy lives in the midst of their pagan surroundings. He did this by pointing out the contrasts between believers and unbelievers.

## Knowledge and Ignorance
## (1 Thes. 5:1-2)

Three phrases in these verses need careful consideration.

*"Times and seasons."* This phrase is found only three times in the Bible, and refers primarily to God's plans for Israel. This is the way Daniel stated it when God gave him understanding of the king's dream (Dan. 2:21). Our Lord's use of the phrase in Acts 1:7 indicates that times and seasons relate primarily to Israel.

God has a definite plan for the nations of the world (Acts 17:26), and Israel is the key nation. Dr. A.T. Pierson used to say, "History is His story." (Quite a contrast to Napoleon's definition: "History is a set of lies agreed upon.") God has ordained times and seasons for the nations on earth, particularly Israel; and all of this will culminate in a terrible time called "the Day of the Lord."

*"The Day of the Lord."* In the Bible, the word *day* can refer to a twenty-four-hour period, or to a longer time during which God accomplishes some special purpose. In Genesis 2:3 the word means twenty-four hours, but in Genesis 2:4 it describes the entire week of Creation.

The Day of the Lord is that time when God will judge the world and punish the nations. At the same time, God will prepare Israel for the return of Jesus Christ to the earth to establish His kingdom. Read Amos 5:18ff; Joel 2:1ff; Zephaniah 1:14-18; and Isaiah 2:12-21 for a description of this great period.

Another term for this period is "the time of Jacob's trouble" (Jer. 30:7). Many prophetic students also call it the Tribulation and point to Revelation 6–19 as the Scripture that most vividly describes this event.

*"Thief in the night."* Our Lord used this image in His own teaching (Matt. 24:42-43; Luke 12:35-40). It describes the suddenness and the surprise involved in the coming of the Day of the Lord. In Revelation 3:3; 16:15, He used this image to warn believers not to be caught napping. Since we do not know when the Lord will return for His people, we must live in a constant attitude of watching and waiting, while we are busy working and witnessing.

Now we can put these three concepts together and discover what Paul wanted to teach his troubled friends in Thessalonica. He had already told them about the coming of Christ for the church, the event described in 1 Thessalonians 4:13-18. He had told them that there would be a period of intense suffering and Tribulation on the earth following this Rapture of the church. These "times and seasons" that relate to Israel and the nations do not apply to the church or affect the truth of the Lord's coming for the church. He may come at any time, and this will usher in the Day of the Lord.

Paul explained more about the Day of the Lord in his second letter to the Thessalonians, so we will save these details for a later chapter. His emphasis here was simply that the believers were "in the know" while the unbelievers were living in ignorance of God's plan. The suddenness of these events will reveal to the world its ignorance of divine truth.

## Expectancy and Surprise (1 Thes. 5:3-5)

The unsaved world will be enjoying a time of false peace and security just before these cataclysmic events occur. Note carefully the contrast between "they" and "you" (or "us") throughout this entire section, "they" referring to the unsaved. *They* will say, "Peace and safety!" but *we* will say, "Jesus is coming, and judgment is coming!"

The world is caught by surprise because men will not hear God's Word or heed God's warning. God warned that the Flood was coming, yet only eight people believed and were saved (1 Peter 3:20). Lot warned his family that the city would be destroyed, but they would not listen (Gen. 19:12-14). Jesus warned His generation that Jerusalem would be destroyed (Luke 21:19ff), and this warning enabled believers to escape; but many others perished in the siege.

In fact, Jesus used the Flood and the overthrow of Sodom and Gomorrah as examples (Matt. 24:37-39; Luke 17:26-30). People in those days were going about their regular daily activities—eating, drinking, getting married—and never considering that judgment was around the corner.

Well-meaning people have tried to set dates for our Lord's return, only to be embarrassed by their failures. However, it is possible to expect His coming without setting a specific time. No "signs" must be fulfilled before He can return for His church.

Christians are "sons of the light" and therefore are not "in the dark" when it comes to future events. Unbelievers ridicule the idea of Christ's return. "Knowing this first, that there shall come in the last days scoffers, walking after their own lusts, and saying, 'Where is the promise of His coming?' " (2 Peter 3:3-4)

Nearly twenty centuries have come and gone since our Lord gave the promise of His return, and He has not returned yet. This does not mean that God does not keep His promises. It simply means that God does not follow our calendar. "One day is with the Lord as a thousand years, and a thousand years as one day" (2 Peter 3:8).

Paul compared the coming judgment to "travail upon a woman with child" (1 Thes. 5:3). Even with our modern medical skills, birth pangs are very real and very painful. They accompany the muscle contractions that enable the mother to give birth to the baby. The Prophet Isaiah used this same picture when he described the coming "Day of the Lord" (Isa. 13:6-13). The early part of this Day of the Lord was called "the beginning of sorrows" by the Lord Jesus (Matt. 24:8); and the Greek word translated "sorrows" actually means "birth pangs."

What truth do Isaiah, Jesus, and Paul teach us? The truth that out of the Day of the Lord will come the birth of the kingdom. When God's judgments are finished, God's Son will return "with power and great glory" (Matt. 24:30). Paul described this event in his second Letter to the Thessalonian Christians.

*Live expectantly.* This does not mean putting on a white sheet and sitting atop a mountain. That is the very attitude God condemned (Acts 1:10-11). But it does mean living in the light of His return, realizing that our works will be judged and that our opportunities for service on earth will end. It means to live "with eternity's values in view."

There is a difference between being ready to go to heaven and being ready to meet the

Lord. Anyone who has sincerely trusted Christ for salvation is ready to go to heaven. Christ's sacrifice on the cross has taken care of that. But to be ready to meet the Lord at the Judgment Seat of Christ is quite another matter. Scripture indicates that some believers will not be happy to see Jesus Christ! "And now, little children, abide in Him; that when He shall appear, we may have confidence, and not be ashamed before Him at His coming" (1 John 2:28).

Having been a pastor for many years, I have had the sad experience of seeing believers deliberately disobey the Word of God. I recall one young lady who stubbornly chose to marry an unsaved man. When I tried to help her from the Bible, she said, "I don't care what you say. I don't care what the Bible says. I'm going to get married!" In the light of Hebrews 13:17, will she be happy at the Judgment Seat of Christ?

Believers who live in the expectation of the Lord's return will certainly enjoy a better life than Christians who compromise with the world. At the end of each chapter in this letter, Paul pointed out the practical results of living expectantly. Take time now to review those verses and to examine your heart.

## Soberness and Drunkenness
## (1 Thes. 5:6-8)

To be sober-minded means to be alert, to live with your eyes open, to be sane and steady. To make the contrast more vivid, Paul pictured two groups of people: one group was drunk and asleep, while the other group was awake and alert. Danger was coming, but the drunken sleepers were unaware of it. The alert crowd was ready and unafraid.

Since we are "sons of the day" we should not live as those who belong to the darkness. "The night is far spent, the day is at hand: let us therefore cast off the works of darkness, and let us put on the armor of light. Let us walk honestly, as in the day; not in rioting and drunkenness, not in chambering [immorality] and wantonness [indecency], not in strife and envying" (Rom. 13:12-13).

In other words, because "the day" is approaching, it is time to wake up, clean up, and dress up. And when we dress up, we had better put on "the breastplate of faith and love: and for a helmet, the hope of salvation" (1 Thes. 5:8). Only the "armor of light" (Rom. 13:12) will adequately protect us in these last days before our Lord returns.

The sober-minded believer has a calm, sane outlook on life. He is not complacent, but neither is he frustrated and afraid. He hears the tragic news of the day, yet he does not lose heart. He experiences the difficulties of life, but he does not give up. He knows his future is secure in God's hands, so he lives each day creatively, calmly, and obediently. Outlook determines outcome; and when your outlook is the *uplook,* then your outcome is secure.

But the unsaved people of the world are not alert. They are like drunken men, living in a false paradise and enjoying a false security. When the Holy Spirit filled the first Christians at Pentecost, the unsaved people accused the Christians of being drunk (Acts 2:13). In reality, it is the unsaved who are living like drunken men. The sword of God's wrath hangs over the world; yet people live godless lives, empty lives, and rarely if ever give any thought to eternal matters.

We have met faith, hope, and love before (1 Thes. 1:3). Here they are described as armor to protect us in this evil world. Faith and love are like a breastplate that covers the heart: faith toward God, and love toward God's people. Hope is a sturdy helmet that protects the mind. The unsaved fix their minds on the things of this world, while dedicated believers set their attention on things above (Col. 3:1-3).

*Hope of salvation* does not mean the hope that at last we will be saved. A person can *know today* that he is saved and going to heaven. Paul knew that the Thessalonian believers were saved (1 Thes. 1:4), and he was certain that he and they would meet Christ in the air (1 Thes. 4:17). The person who confidently says, "I know I am saved!" is not exhibiting pride; he is demonstrating faith in God's Word. First John was written to help us know that we are saved (1 John 5:9-13).

*Hope of salvation* means "the hope that salvation gives to us." There are actually three tenses to salvation: (1) *past*—I have been saved from the guilt and penalty of sin; (2) *present*—I am being saved from the power and pollution of sin; (3) *future*—I shall be saved from the very presence of sin when Christ returns. The blessed hope of our Lord's return is the "hope of salvation." Unsaved people are without hope (Eph. 2:12). This helps explain why they live as they do: "Eat, drink, and be merry, for tomorrow we die!"

Paul repeated the word *sleep* several times in these verses to describe the attitude of the lost world. In the previous paragraph (1 Thes. 4:13-18) Paul used the word to describe the death of the believer. The body goes to sleep and the spirit goes to be with the Lord. But in this section, sleep does not mean death. It means moral indifference and carelessness about spiritual things. Jesus used the word *sleep* with this meaning in Mark 13:32-37.

Doctors tell us that some people are "morning people" while others are "evening people." That is, some people are wide awake before the alarm clock rings. They hit the floor running, and never have to yawn or throw cold water in their faces. Others (like myself) wake up slowly—first one eye, then the other—and then gradually shift gears as they move into the day. When it comes to the return of our Lord, we must all be "morning people"— awake, alert, sober, and ready for the dawning of that wonderful new day.

But, for the unsaved crowd, reveling in its drunkenness, the coming of Jesus Christ will mean the end of light and the beginning of eternal darkness.

## Salvation and Judgment
## (1 Thes. 5:9-11)

Believers do not have to fear future judgment because it is not part of God's appointed plan for us. Will Christians go through the Day of the Lord, that awful period of judgment that God will send on the earth? I think not, and verses like 1 Thessalonians 1:10; 5:9 seem to support this. Christians have always gone through tribulation, since this is a part of dedicated Christian living (John 15:18-27; 16:33). But they will not go through *the* Tribulation that is appointed for the godless world.

I realize that good and godly students of the Word disagree on this matter, and I will not make it a test of fellowship or spirituality. But I do believe that the church will be raptured to heaven prior to the Tribulation period. Let me share the reasons that have convinced me.

*The nature of the church.* The church is the body of Christ, and He is the Head (Col. 2:17-19). When He died for us on the cross, He bore for us all the divine judgment necessary for our salvation. He has promised that we shall never taste any of God's wrath (John 5:24). The Day of the Lord is a day of God's wrath, and it seems unjust and unnecessary that the church should experience it.

*The nature of the Tribulation.* This is the time when God will judge the Gentile nations and also purge Israel and prepare her for the coming of her Messiah. The "earth-dwellers" will taste of God's wrath (Rev. 3:10) and not those whose citizenship is in heaven (Phil. 3:20). God will judge the earth-dwellers for their iniquity (Isa. 26:20-21). But He has already judged believers' sins on the cross.

*The promise of Christ's imminent return.* The word *imminent* means "ready to happen." Nothing has to occur for Christ to return, except the calling out of the last person who will be saved and complete the body of Christ. If our Lord did not return for us until the end of the Tribulation period, then we would know *when* He was coming; for the sequence, signs, and times are all spelled out in Revelation 6–19. It is worth noting that the word *church* is not used in Revelation from 4:1 to 22:13. Also notice that Paul lived in the expectation of seeing Christ, for he used the pronouns *we* and *us* in discussing this doctrine (1 Thes. 4:13–5:11). The Apostle John had this same attitude. He closed his book with the prayer, "Even so, come, Lord Jesus" (Rev. 22:20).

*The course of the seven churches in Revelation 2–3.* Many Bible students believe the Lord selected these seven churches to illustrate the spiritual course of church history. Ephesus would be the church of the Apostles; Smyrna would be the persecuted church of the early centuries. The last church, Laodicea, represents the apostate church of the last days.

This suggests that the Philadelphia church (Rev. 3:7-13) pictures the weak but faithful church of the period just before Christ returns. It is an evangelistic church with great opportunities and open doors. It is the church that proclaims the soon-coming of Christ ("Thou has kept the word of My patience," Rev. 3:10), and to it He has promised deliverance from the day of judgment: "I also will keep thee from the hour of temptation, which shall come upon all the world, to try them that dwell upon the earth" (Rev. 3:10). This promise parallels the promise of 1 Thessalonians 5:9.

*The order of events in 2 Thessalonians 2.* Notice that the order Paul uses harmonizes with the order indicated in other prophetic Scriptures.

Paul connected the return of Christ with the redemption He purchased for us on the cross. We are "bought with a price." We are His bride, and He will come to claim us for Himself before He sends judgment on the earth.

Remember that Christ died for us that we might live *through* Him (1 John 4:9), *for* Him (2 Cor. 5:15), and *with* Him (1 Thes. 5:10). Whether we live or die ("wake or sleep"), we are the Lord's and we shall live with Him.

We must never permit the study of prophecy to become purely academic, or a source of tension or argument. Paul closed this section with the practical application of the prophetic Scriptures: *encouragement* and *edification.* The fact that we will meet our loved ones again and forever be with the Lord is a source of encouragement (1 Thes. 4:18); and the fact that we will not endure God's wrath during the Day of the Lord is another source of encouragement (1 Thes. 5:11). The first is positive, and the second is negative, and both are comforting.

The truth of our Lord's imminent return encourages us to keep clean (1 John 3:1-3) and to do faithfully whatever work He has assigned to us (Luke 12:41-48). It also encourages us to attend church and love the brethren (Heb. 10:25). Knowing that we shall be with the Lord strengthens us in the difficulties of life (2 Cor. 5:1-8) and motivates us to win the lost (2 Cor. 5:9-21).

Many believers have such a comfortable situation here on earth that they rarely think about going to heaven and meeting the Lord. They forget that they must one day stand at the Judgment Seat of Christ. It helps to hold us up and build us up when we recall that Jesus is coming again.

If you have never trusted Him, then your future is judgment. You needn't be ignorant, for God's Word gives you the truth. You needn't be unprepared, for today you can trust Christ and be born again. Why should you live for the cheap sinful experiences of the world when you can enjoy the riches of salvation in Christ?

If you are not saved, then you have an appointment with judgment. And it may come sooner than you expect, for it is "appointed unto men once to die, but after this the judgment" (Heb. 9:27). Why not make an "appointment" with Christ, meet Him personally, and trust Him to save you? "For whosoever shall call upon the name of the Lord shall be saved" (Rom. 10:13).

# CHAPTER NINE
# IT'S ALL IN THE FAMILY
## *1 Thessalonians 5:12-28*

Paul's favorite name for believers was *brethren*. He used it at least sixty times in his letters; and in the two Thessalonian Epistles, he used it twenty-seven times. Paul saw the local church as a family. Each member was born again by the Spirit of God and possessed God's nature (1 Peter 1:22-25; 2 Peter 1:3-4). They all were part of God's family.

It is tragic when believers neglect or ignore the local church. No family is perfect and no local church is perfect; but without a family to protect him and provide for him, a child would suffer and die. The child of God needs the church family if he is to grow, develop his gifts, and serve God.

What are the essentials for a happy, thriving church family? How can we make our local churches more spiritual to the glory of God? In this closing section, Paul discussed these matters.

**Family Leadership (1 Thes. 5:12-13)**
Without leadership, a family falls apart. The father is the head of the home; the mother stands with him in love and cooperation. The children are to obey their parents. This is the order God has laid down, and for us to disturb this order is to ask for serious trouble.

According to Martin L. Gross in his book, *The Psychological Society,* more than 60,000 guidance workers and 7,000 school psychologists work in our American public education system; and many of them function as substitute parents. Many students need counseling, but no professional worker can take the place of a loving, faithful father or mother.

When our oldest son entered high school, he met his assigned counselor. "Now, if you have any problems, feel free to come to me," the counselor said. Our son replied, "If I have any problems, I'll talk to my father!" He was not being disrespectful or unappreciative of the counselor, but he was giving expression of a basic principle: children need the leadership and guidance that only parents can give.

God has ordained leadership for the local

church. It is true that we are "all one in Christ Jesus" (Gal. 3:28); but it is also true that the Head of the church has given gifts to people, and then given these people to the churches to exercise His will (Eph. 4:7-16). Just as the flock needs a shepherd (1 Peter 5:1-5), so the family needs a leader.

What responsibilities do the brethren have toward their spiritual leaders?

*Accept them.* They are God's gifts to the church. They have spiritual authority from the Lord and we should accept them in the Lord. They are not dictators, but leaders and examples. As they follow the Lord, we must follow them.

*Appreciate them.* That is the meaning of the exhortation "know them who labor among you" (1 Thes. 5:12). There is nothing wrong with honoring faithful servants of God, so long as God gets the glory. Spiritual leadership is a great responsibility and a difficult task. It is not easy to serve as a pastor, elder, deacon, or other spiritual leader. The battles and burdens are many, and sometimes the encouragements are few. It is dangerous when a church family takes their leaders for granted and fails to pray for them, work with them, and encourage them.

*Love them.* As brothers, the leaders are "among us"; and as leaders, they are "over us in the Lord." This could be a very strained relationship apart from true Christian love. For a pastor to be "among" and "over" at the same time demands grace and the power of the Spirit. If he gets out of balance, his ministry will be weakened and possibly destroyed. Some church members want their pastor to be a buddy, but this weakens his authority. On the other hand, if he emphasizes *only* his authority, he could become a selfish dictator.

*Obey them.* "Obey them that have the rule over you, and submit yourselves" (Heb. 13:17). When God's servant, led by God's Spirit, calls us to obey God's Word, then we must obey. This does not mean that every spiritual leader is always right in everything. Abraham, Moses, David, and even Peter made mistakes in their words and deeds. A wise pastor knows he is made of clay and admits when he is wrong or when he needs expert counsel. In my own ministry, I have benefited tremendously from the counsel and help of experienced laymen whose knowledge in many areas was far greater than mine.

But, in spite of their limitations, God's spiritual leaders should be respected and obeyed—unless it is obvious that they are out of God's will. As the spiritual leaders of the church meet together, plan, pray, and seek and follow God's will, we can be sure that God will rule and overrule in the decisions they make.

The result of the church family following the spiritual leaders will be peace and harmony in the church: "And be at peace among yourselves" (1 Thes. 5:13). Whenever you find division and dissension in a local church, it is usually because of selfishness and sin on the part of the leaders, or the members, or both. James 4:1-3 makes it clear that selfishness on the inside leads to strife on the outside. It is only as we submit to one another in the Lord that we can enjoy His blessing, and peace in the family.

But the leaders alone cannot do all of the work of the ministry; so Paul added a second essential.

## Family Partnership (1 Thes. 5:14-16)

In recent years, churches have rediscovered what we are calling "body-life." This is a scriptural concept, though it does not define all that is involved in the ministry of the local church, since there are other pictures of the church besides that of the body. Body-life refers to the ministry of each Christian to the others, just as the various members of the human body minister to one another to maintain health and life.

Family members must learn to minister to each other. The older members teach the younger members (see Titus 2:3-5) and encourage them when they are in difficulty. While ministering at a summer Bible conference, my wife and I met a lovely Christian couple who had nine children. It was a delight to see how the older children helped the younger ones, and how the parents were relieved of minor tasks and able to enjoy their leisure time.

According to Ephesians 4:12, the spiritual leaders in the church are supposed to equip the members to do the work of the ministry. In most churches, the members pay the leaders to do the work of the ministry; and the leaders cannot do it all. Consequently, the work begins to weaken and die, and everybody blames the preacher.

Paul named some special family members who need personal help.

*The unruly (v. 14a).* This word means "careless, out of line." It was applied to a soldier who would not keep rank but insisted on marching his own way. While the loving atmosphere of the family encourages individual development, there are some things we all must do in the same way. If we do not have rules and standards in the family, we have chaos. Paul dealt with this problem again when he wrote his second Epistle to the Thessalonians (2 Thes. 3:6, 11), so apparently this first admonition did not impress them.

Rules and traditions in a family must never be so overemphasized that creativity is stifled. As a parent, it is a joy to see each child blossom out with his or her own personality, talents, and ambitions. But it is a sorrow to see a child rebel against the rules, abandon the traditions and standards, and think that this kind of lifestyle shows freedom and maturity. This kind of attitude in the church family causes arguments and splits.

**The feebleminded (v. 14b).** This term has nothing to do with mentality. The literal translation of the Greek word is "little-souled, fainthearted." These are the quitters in the church family. They always look on the dark side of things and give up when the going is tough. In families where there are three or more children, usually one of them is a quitter. Every church family has its share of quitters too.

These people need to be encouraged, which is the meaning of the word translated "comfort" in the *King James Version.* It is also found in 1 Thessalonians 2:11. The Greek word is made up of two words: *para,* near; and *muthos,* speech. Instead of scolding the fainthearted from a distance, we must get close to them and speak tenderly. We must teach the "little-souled" that the trials of life will help to enlarge them and make them stronger in the faith.

**The weak (v. 14c).** "Hold fast to the weak!" is the literal translation. "Don't let them fall!" But who are these weak believers? Certainly, Paul did not mean people who were weak physically, since he was dealing with the spiritual ministry in the church. No, he was referring to those who were "weak in the faith" and had not grown strong in the Lord (Rom. 14:1–15:3).

Usually, the weak Christians were afraid of their liberty in Christ. They lived by rules and regulations. In the Roman assemblies, the weak Christians would not eat meat, and they held to the Jewish system of holy days. They were severe in their judgment of the mature saints who enjoyed all foods and all days.

We have the strong and the weak in our church families today, just as in our natural families we have children who mature faster than others. How should we handle them? *With patient, reassuring love.* It is unfair and unwise to compare one child with another, for each one matures in his own time and his own way. We must "take hold" of these weaker believers and help them stand and walk in the Lord.

This kind of personal ministry is not easy, and so Paul added some wise counsel to encourage us.

**Be patient (v. 14d).** It takes patience to raise a family. That weaker member who demands much help may one day be a choice leader, so never give up. A pastor friend and I were chatting after I had spoken at a service in his church, when a red-headed boy about ten years old came running past us, heading up the center aisle. "Have you ever noticed," remarked my friend, "that the biggest scamps in the Sunday School usually turn out to be pastors or missionaries?" Patience!

**Watch your motives (v. 15).** Often as we minister to others, they reject us and even oppose us. Often they show no appreciation. But we should always serve in love, and be ready to forgive. "Never pay back evil for evil to anyone. Respect what is right in the sight of all men. If possible, so far as it depends on you, be at peace with all men. Never take your own revenge, beloved, but leave room for the wrath of God, for it is written, 'Vengeance is Mine, I will repay, says the Lord. But if your enemy is hungry, feed him, and if he is thirsty, give him a drink; for in so doing you will heap burning coals upon his head.' Do not be overcome by evil, but overcome evil with good" (Rom. 12:17-21, NASB).

If your motive is a desire for appreciation and praise, you may be disappointed. If your motive is "ourselves your servants for Jesus' sake" (2 Cor. 4:5), you will never be disappointed.

**Be joyful (v. 16).** Joy takes the burden out of service. "The joy of the Lord is your strength" (Neh. 8:10). God loves a cheerful servant as well as a cheerful giver. Every church family has its Doubting Thomas or its Gloomy Gus. To see them and listen to them is like witnessing an autopsy, or diving into a cold lake on a winter's day. God wants His family to be happy, and that means that each member must contribute to the joy.

The four spiritual characteristics Paul mentioned are part of the fruit of the Spirit named in Galatians 5:22—love (1 Thes. 5:13), joy (1 Thes. 5:16), peace (1 Thes. 5:13), and long-suffering (1 Thes. 5:14). We cannot manufacture these spiritual qualities; they only come as we yield to the Spirit and permit Him to control us.

Family partnership is vital to the health and growth of the church. Are you bearing your share of the burdens, or are you merely a spectator who watches the others do the job?

### Family Worship (1 Thes. 5:17-28)

Worship is the most important activity of a local church family. Ministry must flow out of worship, otherwise it becomes busy activity without power and without heart. There may be "results," but they will not glorify God or really last. Many church services lack an emphasis on true worship and are more like religious entertainments, catering to the appetites of the congregation.

Paul named the various elements that make up the worship ministry of the church.

*Prayer (v. 17).* Prayer was important in the early church (1 Cor. 11:1-6; Acts 1:13-14; 4:23ff). It was a high and holy experience when the church united in prayer. Today we "call someone to lead in prayer," and we have no idea whether that believer is even in fellowship with God. In some churches, there are two or three people who monopolize the prayer meeting. If we are led by the Spirit (Jude 20), we will experience unity and freedom in our praying, and God will answer.

"Pray without ceasing" does not mean we must always be mumbling prayers. The word means "constantly recurring," not continuously occurring. We are to "keep the receiver off the hook" and be in touch with God so that our praying is part of a long conversation that is not broken. God knows the desires of the heart (Ps. 37:4), and He responds to those desires even when our voice is silent. See Psalms 10:17; 21:2.

*Praise (v. 18).* Thanksgiving is also a vital element of worship. We use "psalms and hymns and spiritual songs" (Eph. 5:19) to express our love and gratitude to the Lord. As we grow in our application of the Word of God, we must also grow in our expression of praise, for the two go together (Col. 3:16). If a local church is "growing in grace" the members will want to learn new hymns in order to give praise to God. If the heart and head do not keep pace with each other, Christian worship becomes either juvenile or hypocritical.

*The Word of God (vv. 19-21).* Apart from God's Word, we have no certain revelation from the Lord. Worship that ignores the Bible is not spiritual. There may be emotion—and even commotion—but unless there is *spiritual truth,* the Holy Spirit is not at work. The three admonitions in these verses go together and help us understand how the Holy Spirit works in Christian worship.

The early church did not have a completed Bible as we do. The Holy Spirit gave the gift of prophecy to certain members of the church and would speak the message through them. When I preach in a church service, I preach the truth *mediately* by means of the Bible. These early prophets preached the truth *immediately* as they were moved by the Holy Spirit. Their spiritual knowledge was given to them by the Spirit, and often they spoke in a tongue. This is why the three gifts of prophecy, tongues, and knowledge are grouped together in 1 Corinthians 13.

Of course, there are dangers in this kind of ministry, because Satan (or the flesh) could seek to counterfeit a message from God, and thus lead the church astray. If the church restrained the speakers, they might be guilty of quenching the Spirit. If they believed all that was spoken, they might be obeying false spirits. The answer was to "prove all things." There must be a discerning of the spirits (1 Cor. 12:10; 1 John 4:1-4). Paul gave specific rules for this in 1 Corinthians 14:29-33.

Today, we have a completed revelation in the Word of God and there is no need for prophets. The Apostles and prophets helped lay the foundation of the church (Eph. 2:20) and have now passed from the scene. The only "prophetic ministry" we have is in the preaching and teaching of the Word of God.

In using the word *quench,* Paul pictured the Spirit of God as fire (see Isa. 4:4; Acts 2:3; Rev. 4:5). Fire speaks of purity, power, light, warmth, and (if necessary) destruction. When the Holy Spirit is at work in our lives and churches, we have a warmth of love in our hearts, light for our minds, and energy for our wills. He "melts us together" so that there is harmony and cooperation; and He purifies us so that we put away sin.

The fire of the Spirit must not go out on the altar of our hearts; we must maintain that devotion to Christ that motivates and energizes our lives.

"Stir up the gift of God which is in thee," Paul wrote to Timothy (2 Tim. 1:6), and the verb means "stir the fire again into life." Apparently Timothy had been neglecting this gift (1 Tim. 4:14) and had to be reminded. The believer, and the local assembly, must avoid extremes: the legalist and formalist would put the fire out, while the fanatic would permit the fire to burn everything up.

It is important that we permit the Spirit of God to teach us the Word of God when we meet to worship. "Sharing" is good if you have something relevant to share from the Word; but I have listened to some "sharing meetings" that were not only unspiritual, but antispiritual. "Apt to teach" requires that we be "apt to learn." Beware of a false spirit that can lead you and your church astray. Follow the Word of God and prove all things.

**Godly living (vv. 22-24).** The purpose of worship is that we might become more like Christ in character and conduct. The greatest definition of worship I ever read was given by William Temple, a late Archbishop of Canterbury: "For to worship is to quicken the conscience by the holiness of God, to feed the mind with the truth of God, to purge the imagination by the beauty of God, to open up the heart to the love of God, to devote the will to the purpose of God."

Paul emphasized balance in Christian living: the negative—"Abstain from all appearance of evil" (1 Thes. 5:22) and the positive—"And the very God of peace sanctify you" (1 Thes. 5:23). Some churches only preach the negative, and this leads to lives and ministries that are out of balance. *Sanctify* simply means "set apart for God's exclusive use." There is *positional* sanctification (Heb. 10:10); we have once and for all been set apart for God. There is also *practical* sanctification (2 Cor. 7:1), a daily dealing with our sins and a growth in holiness. All of this will culminate in *perfect* sanctification (1 John 3:2), when we see Christ and become eternally like Him. Expecting to see Jesus Christ is a great motivation for holy living.

**Christian fellowship (vv. 25-28).** After the corporate worship is ended, the saints minister to one another. They greet one another and seek to encourage. I have been in churches where the congregation escaped like rats leaving a sinking ship. Fellowship is a part of worship.

The "holy kiss" was not a sensual thing. Usually the men kissed the men, and the women kissed the women (see Rom. 16:16; 1 Cor. 16:20; 1 Peter 5:14). Often when ministering on mission fields, I have had the saints greet me in this way; and I have never been offended or suspicious. J.B. Phillips in his paraphrase solves the problem by saying, "Give a handshake all around among the brotherhood."

Paul ended with another reminder that the Word of God is the important thing in the local church. The Word must govern our conduct and guide our lives. We are to read the Word personally, but we also need to hear the Word in the fellowship of the local church, for the one experience helps balance the other.

# 2 THESSALONIANS

## OUTLINE

**Key theme:** The church and the Day of the Lord
**Key verses:** 2 Thessalonians 2:1-2

### I. ENCOURAGEMENT IN SUFFERING—chapter 1
A. Praise—1:1-4
B. Promise—1:5-10
C. Prayer—1:11-12

### II. ENLIGHTENMENT IN TEACHING—chapter 2
A. How the man of sin appears—2:1-7
B. How the Son of God appears—2:8-12
C. How the child of God should live—2:13-17

### III. ENABLEMENT IN LIVING—chapter 3
A. Obey the Word—3:1-6
B. Follow our example—3:7-9
C. Discipline the unruly—3:10-15
D. Closing benediction—3:16-18

## CONTENTS

# CHAPTER ONE
# NO REST
# FOR THE WICKED
*2 Thessalonians 1:1-12*

The Christians in Thessalonica were grateful to God for Paul's first letter, but it did not immediately solve all their problems. In fact, the persecution grew worse and some believers thought they were living in the time of the Tribulation. Then a letter arrived claiming to be from Paul, stating that the Day of the Lord was actually present. Needless to say, the assembly was confused and frightened by this prospect.

Some of the believers concluded that since the Lord's coming was so near, they ought to quit their jobs and spend their time waiting for Him. This meant that the other members were under an extra burden to care for them. Satan was working overtime; as the lion, he was seeking to devour (1 Peter 5:7-8), and as the serpent, he was seeking to deceive (2 Cor. 11:3).

It was in response to these needs that Paul wrote his second letter. He began with their most pressing need, the persecution they were experiencing because of their faith. In this first chapter, Paul shared three encouragements with his suffering friends.

## The Encouragement of Praise
## (2 Thes. 1:1-4)
After greeting his friends, Paul launched into a statement of praise to God for what He had been accomplishing in their lives. Paul was practicing his own admonition, "In everything give thanks" (1 Thes. 5:18). You cannot help but notice Paul's repeated thanksgivings in these two letters (1 Thes. 1:2; 2:13, 3:9; 2 Thes. 1:3; 2:13). Not only does *prayer* change people and situations, but so does *praise*.

Once I was teaching a series of lessons in a church about Satan's devices to defeat Christians. One of these devices is suffering, as in the case of Job. If Satan can put us into difficult circumstances, he may be able to weaken our faith.

"One of the best weapons for fighting Satan is praise," I told my morning class. "In spite of his pain, Job was able to say, 'Blessed be the name of the Lord!' So, the next time things go wrong and you are tempted to get impatient, turn to God and give thanks."

That evening, just before the class started, a lady rushed up to me and said, "It works! It works!" And then she told me about her afternoon and all that had happened. Her story was so unbelievable that I would have doubted it, had I not known her character. "But in it all I gave thanks," she told me, "and God gave me the grace and strength I needed. It works. Praise works!"

No doubt the Thessalonian believers did not consider themselves to be very spiritual as they suffered, but Paul detected what God was doing among them. You and I are the worst ones to evaluate our own lives. Many times others can see the spiritual improvement when you and I miss it completely. For what blessings did Paul give thanks and thereby encourage his friends?

**Their faith was growing (v. 3a).** A faith that cannot be tested cannot be trusted. New believers must expect their faith to be tried, because this is the way God proves whether or not their decision is genuine. Faith, like a muscle, must be exercised to grow stronger. Tribulation and persecution are God's ways to strengthen our faith.

One of my favorite books is *Hudson Taylor's Spiritual Secret*, by Dr. and Mrs. Howard Taylor. In it you read how Hudson Taylor's faith in God grew from that first day he determined to live by faith in God alone. He learned to trust God for his salary, especially when his busy employer forgot to pay him. He learned to trust God for daily needs; and, as his faith was tested, he grew in faith and was able to trust God for His supply for an entire missionary organization. Sometimes it seemed that God had forgotten, but Taylor continued to pray and trust, and God answered.

An easy life can lead to a shallow faith. The great men and women of faith in Hebrews 11 all suffered in one way or another, or faced tremendous obstacles, so that their faith could grow. Paul had prayed for the believers in Thessalonica, that their faith might be perfected (1 Thes. 3:10); and now he thanked God for answered prayer.

**Their love was abounding (v. 3b).** Again, this was an answer to Paul's previous prayer (1 Thes. 3:12). Suffering can make us selfish; but when suffering is mixed with grace and faith, it produces love. It is "faith which worketh by love" (Gal. 5:6). When Christians suffer, their faith reaches *upward* to God, and their love reaches *outward* to their fellow believers.

Thoreau once described a city as a place where many people are "lonely together." Residents of a high-rise apartment can be suffering greatly and the people in the next apartment know nothing about it. Our modern world can promote spiritual and emotional isolation and insulation, even to the point of our watching others suffer without really caring.

But for the Christian, suffering can help to produce abounding love. "Behold, how they love one another!" was the confession of the pagan world as it beheld the miracle of Christian fellowship. The early believers were only obeying the commandment of their Lord, "Love one another." Their own suffering did not prevent them from sharing love with others who were suffering.

*Their patience was increasing (v. 4).* Perhaps "perseverance" would be the best translation of this Greek word. "Tribulation works out endurance" (Rom. 5:3, literal translation). You do not become patient and persevering by reading a book (even this one) or listening to a lecture. *You have to suffer.*

What were these believers enduring? Paul used several words to describe their situation: *persecutions,* which means "attacks from without," or "trials"; *tribulations,* which literally means "pressures," or afflictions that result from the trials; and *trouble* (2 Thes. 1:7), which means "to be pressed into a narrow place." No matter how we look at it, the Thessalonican Christians were not having an easy time.

But God never wastes suffering. Trials work *for* us, not *against* us (2 Cor. 4:15-18; James 1:1-5). If we trust God and yield to Him, then trials will produce patience and maturity in our lives. If we rebel and fight our circumstances, then we will remain immature and impatient. God permits trials that He might build character into our lives. He can grow a mushroom overnight, but it takes many years—and many storms—to build a mighty oak.

*Their testimony was helping others (v. 4a).* "Therefore, among God's churches we boast about your perseverance and faith" (2 Thes. 1:4, NIV). Not only can suffering help us to grow, but we can then help others to grow. God encourages us that we may encourage others (2 Cor. 1:4-5). We are not to be cisterns that receive and keep, but channels that receive and share.

The word translated "faith" in 2 Thessalonians 1:3-4, can be translated "faithfulness." Actually, the two go together; we reveal our faith in God by our faithfulness of life. The Thessalonians were faithful to the Lord and to one another, in spite of the troubles they endured. When a person in difficulty forsakes the Lord and the church, he shows that either he has never been born again, or that his spiritual life is very weak. A true Christian who is growing will be faithful, come what may.

During World War II, when enemy armies invaded North Africa, the missionaries had to flee; and there was great concern over the churches left behind. But when the war ended and the missionaries returned, they discovered strong, thriving churches. The sufferings of war purified the church and helped strengthen the faith of the true believers. What an encouragement this was to the churches of the free world.

Paul had every reason to praise God and give thanks for what God was doing in the lives of these young Christians. But did you notice that one element was missing—hope? "Faith, hope, and love" had characterized these believers from the beginning (1 Thes. 1:3); but Paul gave thanks only for their faith and love. Why? Apparently they were confused about their hope. This leads us to the second encouragement.

## The Encouragement of Promise (2 Thes. 1:5-10)

No matter how difficult their present circumstances may have been, the Thessalonican believers had a secure and glorious future. In fact, their sufferings were evidence, "a manifest token," that God was righteous, working out His great plan for them. We are prone to think that suffering proves that God does not care, when just the opposite is true. Furthermore, the way we act in times of trial proves to others that God is at work. (See Phil. 1:28-30 for another example of this principle.)

Three experiences are involved in the promises of God for His people.

*Reward (v. 5).* "You will be counted worthy of the kingdom of God, for which you are suffering" (NIV). This was one of God's purposes in permitting their suffering. It does not suggest that their suffering earned them the right to go to heaven, because we know that they were saved through faith in Christ (1 Thes. 1). The little word "also" indicated that this worthiness related both to their present experience and their future entrance into God's glorious kingdom. You find the same idea in 1 Peter 1:3-9.

One day Jesus Christ will turn the tables and the wicked will suffer while the believers are rewarded. Our Lord never promised us that life here would be easy; in fact, He taught that we would have to face difficulties and fight battles. But He also promised a future reward for all who were faithful to Him (Matt. 5:10-12).

**Recompense (vv. 6, 7b-9).** God will recompense affliction to the lost, but rest to the saved. To *recompense* means "to repay." Certainly, the wicked who persecute the godly do not always receive their just payment in this life. In fact, the apparent prosperity of the wicked and difficulty of the godly have posed a problem for many of God's people (see Ps. 73; Jer. 12:1; Hab. 1). Why live a godly life if your only experience is that of suffering?

As Christians, we must live for eternity and not just for the present. In fact, living "with eternity's values in view" is what makes our Christian life meaningful today. We walk by faith, and not by sight.

This brings to mind the story of the two farmers, one a believer and the other an atheist. When harvest season came, the atheist taunted his believing neighbor because apparently God had not blessed him too much. The atheist's family had not been sick, his fields were rich with harvest, and he was sure to make a lot of money.

"I thought you said it paid to believe in God and be a Christian," said the atheist.

"It does pay," replied the Christian. "But God doesn't always pay His people in September."

What kind of a future does the unbeliever face? Look at the dramatic words Paul used to describe it: tribulation, vengeance, flaming fire, punishment, and everlasting destruction. The Christ-rejecting world will receive from God exactly what it gave to God's people! When God recompenses, He pays in kind; for there is a law of compensation that operates in human history.

Pharaoh tried to drown all the male babies born to the Jews, and his own army was drowned in the Red Sea. Haman plotted to wipe out the Jews, and he and his own sons were wiped out. The advisers of King Darius forced him to arrest Daniel and throw him into a lions' den, but later they themselves were thrown to the lions. The unbelieving Jewish leaders who sacrificed Christ in order to save the nation (see John 11:49-53) in a few years saw their city destroyed and their nation scattered.

It is a *righteous* thing for God to judge sin and condemn sinners. A holy God cannot leave sin unjudged. People who say, "I cannot believe that a loving God would judge sinners and send people to hell" understand neither the holiness of God nor the awfulness of sin. While it is true that "God is love" (1 John 4:8), it is also true that "God is light" (1 John 1:5), and in His holiness He must deal with sin.

A Christian doctor had tried to witness to a very moral woman who belonged to a church that denied the need for salvation and the reality of future judgment. "God loves me too much to condemn me," the patient would reply. "I cannot believe that God would make such a place as a lake of fire."

The woman became ill and the diagnosis was cancer. An operation was necessary. "I wonder if I really should operate," the doctor said to her in her hospital room. "I really love you too much to cut into you and give you pain."

"Doctor," said the patient, "if you really loved me, you would do everything possible to save me. How can you permit this awful thing to remain in my body?"

It was easy then for him to explain that what cancer is to the body, sin is to the world; and both must be dealt with radically and completely. Just as a physician cannot love health without hating disease and dealing with it, so God cannot love righteousness without hating sin and judging it.

The word *vengeance* must not be confused with *revenge*. The purpose of vengeance is to satisfy God's holy law; the purpose of revenge is to pacify a personal grudge. God does not hold a grudge against lost sinners. Quite the contrary, He sent His Son to die for them, and He pleads with them to return to Him. But if sinners prefer to "know not God, and . . . obey not the Gospel" (2 Thes. 1:8), there is nothing left for God to do but judge them.

This judgment will take place when Jesus Christ returns to the earth with His church and His angels (2 Thes. 1:7). This is not the same event described by Paul in 1 Thessalonians 4:13-18. We may contrast these two events:

| 1 Thessalonians 4:13-18 | 2 Thessalonians 1 |
|---|---|
| Christ returns in the air | Christ returns to the earth |
| He comes secretly *for* the church | He comes openly *with* the church |
| Believers escape the Tribulation | Unbelievers experience Tribulation, judgment |
| Occurs at an undisclosed time | Occurs at the end of the Tribulation period, the Day of the Lord |

**Rest (vv. 7a, 10).** God will recompense tribulation to the lost, but rest to the saved. I believe that the first phrase in 2 Thessalonians 1:7 should be treated as a parenthesis: "to recompense tribulation to them that trouble you (and to you who are troubled, rest with us) when the Lord Jesus shall be revealed." The saints receive their rest when the Lord returns in the air and catches us up to be with Him.

The word *rest* means "relief, release, not under pressure." It is the opposite of "tribulation." The word describes the releasing of a bowstring. In this life, God's people are pressured, "pressed out of measure" (2 Cor. 1:8), and under the burdens of trial and persecution. But when we see Christ, we will be released. We need not fear fiery wrath and judgment (1 Thes. 1:10; 5:9), for God has already judged our sins at Calvary.

What kind of future is there for the lost? They face punishment and eternal judgment (2 Thes. 1:9), while the saved shall enjoy the rest and glories of heaven. The lost shall be separated from God, while the saved "shall see His face" (Rev. 22:4). Some cultists have tried to dilute the meaning of "everlasting destruction," saying it means either temporary suffering or total annihilation; but both ideas are false. The phrase means "eternal judgment," no matter how men try to twist it or avoid it (see Matt. 25:41).

Paul encouraged his friends with praise and promise; and he had a third encouragement.

## The Encouragement of Prayer (2 Thes. 1:11-12)

Paul prayed for his converts (1 Thes. 1:2; 3:10). His "wherefore" in 2 Thessalonians 1:11 means, "And because of all I have just said"—the return of Christ to be glorified in the saints, and to judge the lost. The future prospect of glory motivated the apostle to pray for the saints. We must never neglect a present responsibility because of a future hope. On the contrary, the future hope must encourage us to be faithful today.

There were three concerns in Paul's prayer.

**Their worthiness (v. 11a).** In 2 Thessalonians 1:5, Paul had stated that he wanted them to be worthy of the kingdom when they entered glory in the future. But here he emphasized their present situation. God's calling was in grace and love, and Paul desired that they might live up to that calling (see 2 Thes. 2:13-14).

Trials do not make a person; they reveal what a person is made of. When our faith is tried, we are revealing our worth (1 Peter 1:6-9). God certainly knows our hearts even before we are tried, but *we do not know our own hearts.* And others do not know what we are worth. We need to pray that God will build our worth and make us more valuable Christians because of the trials we have endured.

**Their walk (v. 11b).** "That by His power He may fulfill every good purpose of yours and every act prompted by your faith" (NIV). Character must lead to conduct. Paul prayed that they might have a resolute will, empowered by God, to do what He wanted them to do. Obedience and service do not spring from human talent and efforts, but from God's power as we trust Him.

Paul had linked faith with *love* (2 Thes. 1:3) and *endurance* (2 Thes. 1:4), and here he linked it with *power.* If we believe God, we will receive His power in our lives. We cannot be victorious in tribulations if we only trust ourselves; but we can be victorious through trusting Him.

When I travel, I carry an electric razor that can store up the energy and run for perhaps two hours without any outside source of power. It is especially useful when I visit the mission fields.

While preaching for a week at a summer conference, I noticed that my razor was losing power. In fact, one morning it operated so slowly that I was convinced it was broken. Then by evening, it had picked up speed again. A few minutes investigation revealed the problem: I had plugged the razor into a socket that was controlled by a wall switch. When my wife had the desk lamp on, my razor was storing up power; when the light was off, the razor received no power.

That incident taught me a spiritual lesson: it is easy (by force of habit) to trust a source of power without checking to see if the switch is on. Paul was praying that his friends might "have the switch on" and, by their faith, receive the power needed to endure suffering and glorify God.

**Their witness (v. 12).** Jesus Christ will be glorified in His saints when they return with Him (2 Thes. 1:10); but He should also be glorified in our lives today. Unbelievers blaspheme His name (1 Peter 4:12ff), but believers bless His name and seek to glorify it. The amazing thing is that the believer who glorifies Christ is likewise glorified *in Christ*, "glorified in you, and you in Him" (NIV).

How can this be done? "According to the grace of our God and Lord Jesus Christ" (2 Thes. 1:12). Grace and glory go together, as do suffering and glory (see Pss. 45:2-3; 84:11; Rom. 5:2; 2 Cor. 8:19; 1 Peter 5:10). As we receive His grace, we reveal His glory.

" 'There is no peace,' saith the Lord, 'unto the wicked' " (Isa. 48:22). No rest for the wicked! But there is rest for those who trust Christ and seek to live for His glory. For the Christian, the best is yet to come. We know that "the sufferings of this present time are not worthy to be compared with the glory which shall be revealed in us" (Rom. 8:18).

# CHAPTER TWO
# GOD'S TIMETABLE
*2 Thessalonians 2:1-12*

The purpose of Bible prophecy is not for us to make a calendar, but to build character. Paul emphasized this fact in both of his Thessalonian letters, and our Lord warned us not to set dates for His coming (Matt. 24:36, 42). Date-setters are usually upsetters, and that is exactly what happened in the Thessalonican assembly.

Someone had deceived the believers into thinking they were already living in the Day of the Lord. The teaching probably first came through a "prophetic utterance" in one of their meetings, and then it was further enhanced by a letter claiming to come from Paul himself.

The believers were instantly shaken by this teaching, and continued to be deeply troubled. Had God changed His program? Had not Paul promised them deliverance from the Tribulation? (see 1 Thes. 1:10; 5:9)

To calm their hearts and stabilize their faith, Paul explained that they were not in the Day of the Lord. The reason was simple: that Day could not arrive till certain other events had taken place. Paul then stated for them the prophetic events that make up God's timetable.

## The Rapture of the Church
## (2 Thes. 2:1, 6-7)
Paul appealed to them to "calm down" on the basis of the truth he had taught them in his first letter: the Lord would return and catch up His own to meet Him in the air (1 Thes. 4:13-18). This is "the coming of our Lord Jesus Christ and . . . our gathering together unto Him" (2 Thes. 2:1). Not two separated events, but one great event that will occur suddenly and without warning.

Once the church is out of the world, Satan and his forces will unfold their program. The Day of the Lord is the period that follows the Rapture of the church. It will be a time of Tribulation for the people on earth: Satan and his hosts will be working on earth, and God will send righteous judgments from heaven. Revelation 6–19 describes this period for us.

Why is Satan unable to reveal his "man of sin" sooner? Because God is restraining the forces of evil in the world today. Satan cannot do whatever he wants to do, whenever he pleases. Our sovereign Lord is able to make even the wrath of man to praise Him, and "the remainder of wrath shalt Thou restrain" (Ps. 76:10). In 2 Thessalonians 2:6-7, Paul mentioned a restraining force that even today is helping keep everything on schedule.

Who or what is this restrainer? Paul told the Thessalonicans when he was teaching them personally, but he did not put this information in either of his letters. This restrainer is now at work in the world and will continue to work till it (or he) is "taken out of the midst" (literal translation of 2 Thes. 2:7b).

Notice that in 2 Thessalonians 2:6 Paul referred to this restrainer in the neuter gender ("what restraineth"), while in 2 Thessalonians 2:7, he used the masculine gender ("he who now hindereth"). The restrainer is a person who is today "in the midst," but will one day be "taken out of the midst."

Many Bible students identify this restrainer as the Holy Spirit of God. Certainly, He is "in the midst" of God's program today, working through the church to accomplish God's purposes. When the church is raptured, the Holy Spirit will not be taken *out of the world* (otherwise nobody could be saved during the Tribulation), but He will be taken *out of the midst* to allow Satan and his forces to go to work. The Holy Spirit will certainly be present on the earth during the Day of the Lord, but He will not be restraining the forces of evil as He is today.

In spite of its weakness and seeming failure, never underestimate the importance of the church in the world. People who criticize the church do not realize that the presence of the people of God in this world gives unsaved people opportunity to be saved. The presence of the church is delaying the coming of judgment. Lot was not a dedicated man, but his presence in Sodom held back the wrath of God (Gen. 19:12-29).

There are two programs at work in the world today: God's program of salvation, and Satan's program of sin, "the mystery of iniquity." God has a timetable for His program, and nothing Satan does can change that timetable. Just as there was a "fullness of the time" for the coming of Christ (Gal. 4:4), so there is a "fullness of the time" for the appearance of Antichrist; and nothing will be off schedule. Once the restraining ministry of the Spirit of God has ended, the next event can take place.

### The Revelation of Antichrist
### (2 Thes. 2:3-5, 8a)

Paul did not use the term *Antichrist* in his letter. This term is used in the New Testament only by John (1 John 2:18, 22; 4:3; 2 John 7). But this is the name we use to identify the last great world dictator whom Paul designated as "that man of sin," "the son of perdition" (2 Thes. 2:3), and "that lawless one" (2 Thes. 2:8, literal translation).

Satan has been at war with God ever since he, as Lucifer, rebelled against God and tried to capture God's throne (Isa. 14:12-15). He tempted Eve in the Garden and, through her, caused Adam to fall (Gen. 3). In Genesis 3:15, God declared war on Satan and his family ("seed") and promised the coming of the Redeemer who would finally and completely defeat Satan.

The Greek prefix *anti* has two meanings: *against*, and *instead of*. Satan not only opposes Christ, but he wants to be worshiped and obeyed *instead of* Christ. Satan has always wanted to be worshiped and served as God (Isa. 14:14; Luke 4:5-8). He will one day produce his masterpiece, the Antichrist, who will cause the world to worship Satan and believe Satan's lies.

Paul had explained all of this to the believers in Thessalonica, referring them, no doubt, to the relevant Scriptures in the Old Testament. We are fortunate to have the entire Bible to study, so we can get the total picture of Antichrist and his career. Prophetic students may not agree on every detail; but the main facts, when they are related, give us the following description of Antichrist in the last days.

*The peacemaker (Rev. 6:1-2).* Certainly, this man will be on the scene before the Rapture of the church. He will be a peaceful political leader who unites ten nations of Europe into a strong power bloc (see Rev. 17:12-13). The rider on the white horse imitates Christ (Rev. 19:11ff). He goes forth to conquer peacefully: he has a bow, but no arrows. He will bring a brief time of peace to the world (1 Thes. 5:1-3) before the storm of the Day of the Lord breaks loose.

*The protector (Dan. 9:24-27).* We cannot examine the exciting details of this prophecy, but it is important to note several facts. First, the prophecy applies to Israel, Jerusalem, and the temple, and not to the church. Second, it announces the time when Messiah will come and accomplish certain purposes for the Jewish people. The word *week* refers to a period of 7 years; 70 weeks are equal to 490 years. Note that these 490 years are divided into three parts: 7 weeks or 49 years, during which the city would be rebuilt; 62 weeks or 434 years, at the end of which time Messiah would come and be cut off; 1 week or 7 years, during which a "prince" would have a covenant with Israel.

Notice that *two princes* are involved in this prophecy: Christ, Messiah the Prince (Dan. 9:25), and Antichrist, "the prince that shall come" (Dan. 9:26). "The people of the prince that shall come" are the Romans; for it was they who destroyed the city and the temple in A.D. 70. The coming Antichrist will belong to a nation that was part of the old Roman Empire.

Finally, note that there is a parenthesis between the sixty-ninth and the seventieth week. We are now living in that parenthesis. The sixty-ninth week ended with the ministry of Christ. The seventieth week will start with the arrival of Antichrist. He will make a covenant with Israel to protect her and permit her to rebuild her temple. This covenant will be for seven years. *He will temporarily solve the Middle East crisis.* Israel will rebuild her temple in peaceful times. It is the signing of this covenant, not the Rapture of the church, that signals the start of Daniel's seventieth week, that seven-year period known as the Day of the Lord.

*The peace-breaker (Dan. 9:27).* After three and one-half years, Antichrist will break his covenant with the Jews *and take over their temple.* This was what Paul termed "the falling away" (2 Thes. 2:3b). A better translation would be "the rebellion, the apostasy." Not simply *a* rebellion, but *the* rebellion. Up to this point, Antichrist has been a peacemaking leader of ten European nations, obligated to protect Israel. But now he reveals his true character by taking over the Jewish temple and demanding that the world worship him (see Rev. 13).

Since Antichrist will be energized by Satan, it is no surprise that he will seek worship; for Satan has always wanted the worship of the world. There have been various "apostasies" in church history, when groups have turned away from God's truth; but this final rebellion will be the greatest of all. The man of sin will oppose everything that belongs to any other religion, true or false. He will organize a world church that will, by worshiping him, worship Satan.

Our Lord predicted this apostasy; He called it "the abomination of desolation" (Matt. 24:15), a clear reference to Daniel 9:27. The world will wonder at this great leader who, with Satan's power, will perform signs and wonders and deceive the nations.

*The persecutor (Rev. 13:15-17).* Most prophetic students agree that the abomination of desolation will occur three and one-half years after the Antichrist makes his covenant with the Jews. (Dan. 9:27—"in the midst of the week" or three and one-half years.) This will usher in a period of intense persecution and Tribulation. Jesus said, "For then shall be great Tribulation" (Matt. 24:21). Satan will vent his wrath against Israel. He will so control the world's economic system that citizens must bear "the mark of the beast" to be able to buy and sell (Rev. 13:16-17).

People often ask, "Will anybody be saved during the seven-year period?" The answer is,

yes! Revelation 7:1-8 states that 144,000 Jews will be saved (probably as was the Apostle Paul, by a dramatic vision of Christ) and will carry the Gospel to the nations. The Apostle John described a great multitude of Gentiles who will come out of the great Tribulation (Rev. 7:9-17) as converted people. Even though the Holy Spirit will be "out of the midst" as the restraining power, He will still work with redeeming power.

However, it will cost dearly to trust Christ and live for Him during that time. Believers will refuse to bow down to the beast's image and will be slain. They will refuse to wear his mark and thus be unable to get jobs or make purchases. It will be quite a contrast to our situation now when even famous people admit that they are "born again."

*The prisoner (Rev. 19:11-21).* Keep in mind that God has a timetable. Satan will not be permitted to control the world forever. Jesus Christ will return "in power and great glory" and take Antichrist and his associates prisoner—and also Satan—and cast them into the bottomless pit (Rev. 20:1-3). This will be the climax of the great Battle of Armageddon (Rev. 16:16) during which the nations of the world unite with Satan to fight Jesus Christ. This leads to our next event.

## The Return of Jesus Christ
## (2 Thes. 2:8-12)

This is His return to the earth in glory and judgment, the event described in 2 Thessalonians 1:5-10 and Revelation 19:11ff. It will occur at the end of the seven-year Tribulation period when the "mystery of iniquity" (Satan's evil program) will have ended with the Battle of Armageddon. It is important that we distinguish His Rapture of the church from His return to the earth. The first event is secret, as the church is caught up to meet Him in the air. The second event is public, when the church returns with Him to defeat Satan and his hosts.

*His judgment of Antichrist (vv. 8-9).* Nobody on earth will be able to overcome the Antichrist and his forces, for he is energized by Satan. "Who is like unto the beast? Who is able to make war with him?" (Rev. 13:4) Satan will enable his false messiah to perform "power and signs and lying wonders" (2 Thes. 2:9). This, of course, is in imitation of Jesus Christ who performed "miracles and wonders and signs" (Acts 2:22).

Satan has always been an imitator. There

are false Christians in the world who are really children of the devil (Matt. 13:38; 2 Cor. 11:26). He has false ministers (2 Cor. 11:13ff) who preach a false gospel (Gal. 1:6-9). There is even a "synagogue of Satan" (Rev. 2:9), which means a gathering of people who think they are worshiping God but who are really worshiping the devil (1 Cor. 10:19-21). These false Christians have a counterfeit righteousness that is not the saving righteousness of Christ (Rom. 10:1-3; Phil. 3:4-10). They have a false assurance of salvation that will prove useless when they face judgment (Matt. 7:15-29).

During the Apostolic Age, miracles were given to verify the message (Heb. 2:1-4). God's chosen Apostles used miracles as their credential to prove they were sent by God (2 Cor. 12:12). However, miracles *alone* never prove that a man is sent from God: his message and his character must also be considered. John the Baptist was "a man sent from God" (John 1:6), yet "John did no miracle" (John 10:41).

Satan can perform miracles that seem to rival those of the Lord. This is how he opposed Moses in the court of Pharaoh (Ex. 7:8-12, 20-22, 8:5-7). In the final judgment, some people who performed miracles *in the name of Jesus* will be rejected by the Lord because they were never saved (Matt. 7:21-23). Judas performed miracles, yet he was never born again (John 6:66-71; 13:11, 18).

The purpose of God's miracles was to lead people to the truth; the purpose of Antichrist's miracles will be to lead people to believe his lies. Paul called them "lying wonders" (2 Thes. 2:9), not because the miracles are not real, but because they persuade people to believe Satan's lies. The world would not long follow a leader who practiced cheap trickery (see Rev. 13:13-14).

When Jesus Christ returns, He will judge Antichrist by "the spirit of His mouth . . . and the brightness of His coming" (2 Thes. 2:8). The verbs "consume" and "destroy" do not mean annihilate; for Revelation 20:10 indicates that Satan and his associates will be tormented in the lake of fire forever. You could translate this statement: "whom the Lord Jesus will overthrow with the breath of His mouth, and bring an end to his operations by the outshining of His presence."

As the coming of the Lord for His church draws near, Satan's operations in this world will intensify (read 1 Tim. 4; 2 Tim. 3). Since Satan is a liar, we must resist him through the truth of God's Word (Eph. 6:17). It was this sword that our Lord used when He defeated Satan in the wilderness (Matt. 4:1-11). Satan is a liar and a murderer (John 8:44). God gives life through His truth; Satan slays with his lies. We are encouraged to know that one day Jesus Christ will completely overthrow Satan and his system.

***His judgment of the unsaved (vv. 10-12).*** We have noted that a great number of Jews and Gentiles will be saved during the seven-year Tribulation period. But the vast majority of the world's population will be lost. Many will die in the terrible judgments that God will send on earth (see Rev. 6:7-8; 8:11; 9:18; 11:13). Others will perish in judgment when Jesus Christ returns and separates the saved from the lost (Matt. 25:31-46).

It is important to note that these people did have opportunity to believe and be saved. God has no delight in judging the lost (Ezek. 33:11). God is "not willing that any should perish, but that all should come to repentance" (2 Peter 3:9). These people will be judged and will suffer forever because they would not receive and believe the truth. In fact, their hearts will be so evil that they will not even have any *love* for the truth. Those who love lies and make lies will be excluded from the heavenly city (Rev. 22:15) and sent to the lake of fire.

In this paragraph, Paul taught a sobering truth: a person can so resist the truth that he finally becomes deluded and has to believe a lie. There can be no neutral ground: either we believe the truth or we believe a lie. To reject the truth means to receive the lie.

Does this mean that God is to blame for a man's rejection of Christ? No more than God was to blame for Pharaoh's spiritual condition when Moses was bringing the plagues on Egypt. Pharaoh heard God's Word and saw God's wonders, yet he refused to bow to God's will. Pharaoh occasionally relented and gave lip service to God's will; but he always resisted in the end and refused to obey God. He hardened his heart so that he could not believe the truth, and this led to God's final judgment of the land of Egypt.

Second Thessalonians 2:11 reads literally, "That they should believe *the* lie." What is "the lie"? Satan is the liar and has foisted many deceptions on the human race. But there is one "lie" that, from the beginning, has led people astray. Satan first spoke it to Eve:

"You shall be as God!" *The lie* is the idea that man is his own God and therefore can do whatever he pleases and better himself by his own human efforts. The process is described in Romans 1:18ff. Note especially Romans 1:25: "Who exchanged the truth of God for the lie, and worshiped and served the creature rather than the Creator" (literal translation).

All of which means that Satan appeals to man's pride. It was pride that turned Lucifer into Satan (Isa. 14:12-15; Ezek. 28:11-18). It is pride that traps men into doing Satan's will in this world (see 2 Tim. 2:24-26).

A friend told me about a church officer on the mission field who was causing great problems in the church. Whenever the missionary was in the village, the officer lived a godly life; but no sooner did the missionary leave than the man began to behave as though he were controlled by Satan. Finally the missionary and several church leaders confronted the man in the name of Jesus Christ, and they discovered the truth: Satan was using pride to control the officer's life.

"When I was ordained an elder," the man explained, "I heard a voice say to me, 'Now you are somebody important.' I yielded to that voice, and Satan took over in my life." He confessed his sin, the church prayed, and God delivered him.

"Now you are somebody important!" "Worship and serve the creature rather than the Creator." This is Satan's lie, and I fear it is what rules the world today. God originally made man in His own image. Today, man is making God in his own image.

The people Christ will judge not only do not love the truth, but they have "pleasure in unrighteousness" (2 Thes. 2:12). Read Psalm 50:16-21 for one description of this kind of person, and also Psalm 52. The chief priests actually were *glad* when Judas promised to help them kill Christ (Mark 14:10-11). I mentioned before that this process of believing the lie is described in Romans 1. The closing verse of that section (Rom. 1:32) states this truth clearly: "Who knowing the judgment of God, that they which commit such things are worthy of death, not only do the same, but have pleasure in them that do them."

Does this mean that those who have heard the Gospel before the Rapture of the church cannot be saved after the Rapture? Not necessarily. If that were true, then our witness to the lost is condemning them, should Christ return. However, it does mean that no lost sinner can afford to treat God's truth carelessly or reject God's Son repeatedly. The human heart becomes harder each time the sinner rejects God's truth; and this makes it easier to believe Satan's lies.

How much better it is to follow the example of the Thessalonican believers who received the Word of God "not as the word of men, but as it is in truth, the Word of God" (1 Thes. 2:13). They received the truth and were saved.

Have you received the truth?

# CHAPTER THREE
# NOTHING BUT THE TRUTH
*2 Thessalonians 2:13–3:5*

Paul was a balanced Christian who had a balanced ministry; and we see evidence of this as he brought his letter to a close. He moved from prophecy to practical Christian living. He turned from the negative (Satan's lies) to the positive (God's truth), and from warning to thanksgiving and prayer.

We desperately need balanced ministries today. I have attended Bible conferences where the only emphasis was on what Christ *will do* with the Jews in the future, to the total neglect of what He *wants to do* with the church in the present. We must never permit the study of prophecy to be an escape from responsibility today.

Paul's emphasis was on the truth of God's Word, in contrast to Satan's great lie which Paul discussed in the previous section. Every believer has four responsibilities to God's truth.

**Believe the Truth (2 Thes. 2:13-14)**
We have noted Paul's repeated thanksgiving in his letters to this church (1 Thes. 1:2; 2:13; 3:9; 2 Thes. 1:3; 2:13). He gave thanks for the way they responded to God's work in their lives. In these two verses, Paul reviewed the stages in their salvation experience.

***God loved them (v. 13a).*** Whatever God

does for the lost world springs from His eternal love. We must never conceive of His great plan of salvation as an impersonal machine. His salvation is rooted and grounded in His love (John 3:16). God proved this love at the cross where Jesus Christ died for the sins of the world (Rom. 5:8).

**God chose them (v. 13b).** It is not love alone that saves us, for God loves the whole world, and yet the whole world is not saved. Love reveals itself in *grace* and *mercy*. God in His grace gives us through Christ what we do not deserve, and God in His mercy does not give what we do deserve—but He gave that to Christ! We dare not explain away God's election of sinners (1 Thes. 1:4; Eph. 1:4; 1 Peter 1:2).

**God set them apart (v. 13c).** The word *sanctify* means "to set apart." There is a progressive sanctification that makes us more like Jesus Christ (1 Thes. 5:23). But the sanctification Paul mentioned here refers to the Spirit's work in leading the unbeliever to faith in Christ. "Elect according to the foreknowledge of God the Father, through sanctification of the Spirit" (1 Peter 1:2). It is the work of the Holy Spirit to bring conviction to the sinner (John 16:7-11). Though I did not realize it at the time, as I look back I can see how the Spirit led in bringing me to faith in Christ; and this is the experience of every believer.

**God called them (v. 14).** The same God who ordained the end (salvation) also ordained the means to the end ("belief of the truth"). The person who says, "God already has His elect, so there is no need for us to pray, witness, and send out missionaries" does not understand divine election. The greatest encouragement to evangelism is the knowledge that God has His people who have been prepared to respond to His Word (read Acts 18:1-11).

In order for God to fulfill His eternal plan, He sent Paul, Silas, and Timothy to Thessalonica to preach the Word of God. What was ordained *in eternity* was accomplished *in time*. God used human instruments to bring the Gospel to the lost; and by trusting Christ, these people proved their "election of God" (1 Thes. 1:4). The call of God went out to the whole city, but it was effective only in those who believed the truth and trusted Christ.

It is dangerous to engage in idle speculation about divine sovereignty and human responsibility. Both are taught in the Bible. We know that "salvation is of the Lord" (Jonah 2:9), and

that lost sinners can never save themselves. We must admit that there are *mysteries* to our salvation; but we can rejoice that there are *certainties* on which we can rest. We must not use the doctrine of election to divide the church or disturb the weak, but to glorify the Lord.

**God gave them glory (v. 14b).** What began in eternity past reaches its climax in eternity future: we share in the glory of God (John 17:24; Rom. 8:29-30). What begins with grace always leads to glory. This is quite a contrast to the future assigned to the lost (2 Thes. 1:8-10). Believers already possess God's glory within (John 17:22; note the past tense in Rom. 8:30—"glorified"). We are awaiting Christ's return, and then the glory shall be revealed (Rom. 8:17-19; 2 Thes. 1:10).

When sinners believe God's truth, God saves them. When they believe Satan's lie, and reject the love of the truth, they cannot be saved (2 Thes. 2:10-12). Being neutral about God's truth is a dangerous thing. It has tragic eternal consequences.

## Guard the Truth (2 Thes. 2:15)

Paul had told them about the *future* rebellion against the truth (2 Thes. 2:3), the great apostasy headed by the Antichrist. But he also warned in his letters that there was a *present* danger, and that the church must guard God's truth and not turn from it. There are repeated warnings about this in the New Testament: 1 John 2:18-24; 4:1-3; 2 Peter 2; 1 Timothy 4; and 2 Timothy 3, to name only a few.

God works in this world through the truth of His Word, and Satan opposes this truth by substituting his lies. Human nature is prone to believe a lie and resist the truth. Satan accomplishes his best work through people in so-called Christian institutions (churches, schools, etc.) who do not believe God's truth. They have "a form of godliness" but have never experienced the power of God's saving truth.

When Paul used the word *traditions*, he was not referring to man-made religious ideas that are not based on the Word of God. Our Lord rejected man's religious traditions (Mark 7:1-13). Paul warned against them in Colossians 2:8. It is sad to see religious people argue over man's traditions and, at the same time, reject the simple truth of the Word of God.

The word *tradition* simply means "that which is handed down from one person to another." The truth of the Gospel began as an oral message proclaimed by Christ and the Apostles. Later, this truth was written down by the inspiration of the Holy Spirit, and it became Holy Scripture (see 2 Tim. 3:12-17; 2 Peter 2:16-21). God's truth was not invented by men: it was handed down from God to man (1 Cor. 15:1-6; Gal. 1:11-12) and each generation of believers had guarded this truth and passed it on to others (2 Tim. 2:2).

Paul stated clearly the believers' dual responsibility in guarding the truth: "stand fast, and hold the traditions" (2 Thes. 2:15). *Stand fast* means, "Do not move away from the truth of the Gospel" (see 1 Cor. 16:13; Col. 1:23). When my wife and I visited the Tower of London and saw the royal jewels, we noticed that the crowd was kept moving, but the guards stood still. They were constantly watching the visitors and nothing could move them from their appointed places. You and I are helping to guard the "precious faith" and we must not be moved by the wiles of Satan or the praises of men.

If we *stand*, then we can *hold*. This word means "to hold fast, to hold firmly." It is related to a Greek word that means "strength, might, power." We are not to hold God's truth in a careless way, but grasp it firmly with power and never let it slip from us. Each generation of Christians must receive the truth from others, guard it, and make sure it is kept intact for the next generation.

It is not easy to *stand* or *hold*, because forces around us want to move us from the faith. Satan knows how to use lies to oppose God's truth, and he seeks to do this *within the fellowship* (Acts 20:28-32). Sometimes faithful believers must refuse the fellowship of those who have rejected the faith (Rom. 16:17-20; 2 Cor. 6:14–7:1; 1 Tim. 6:3-5; 2 John 7-10).

Let me sum this up with two words of caution. First, "the faith" that has been handed down to us must not be confused with man's interpretations and ideas. The Pharisees made their own interpretations as sacred as the Word of God (Mark 7:7-9). The basic doctrines of God's Word are held by all evangelical believers, but not all believers agree on minor matters of interpretation (especially in the area of prophecy) or matters of church order. It is dangerous to make man's ideas a test of fellowship or spirituality.

Second, we must not embalm the truth so that it loses its life and power. We are to be like faithful householders who bring out of

God's treasury of truth "things new and old" (Matt. 13:52). There is yet more truth to be found in God's Word, and we must not think that we know it all. The Word is like seed (Luke 8:11), and when seed is sown, it produces plants, fruit, *and more seed*. While it is good to "tell the old, old story" it is also good to let the Spirit teach us new truths from the Word, and to make new applications of old truths.

## Practice the Truth (2 Thes. 2:16-17)

It is not enough to believe the truth and guard it; we must also practice it. If we hear the Word, but do not obey it, we are only fooling ourselves (James 1:22-25).

These two verses record Paul's desire and prayer for his friends: he wanted God to *encourage* them ("comfort your hearts") and *establish* them ("stablish you") "in every good word and work." Both of these words are prominent in the Thessalonian letters.

When Paul was with them, he *encouraged* them individually as a father does his children (1 Thes. 2:11). He sent Timothy to encourage them (1 Thes. 3:2), and Paul himself was greatly encouraged with Timothy's report of their faithfulness (1 Thes. 3:7).

Paul encouraged them to walk to please God (1 Thes. 4:1), and to grow in their love for others (1 Thes. 4:10). He taught them about the Rapture of the church in order that they might encourage each other (1 Thes. 4:18). To calm their fears, he explained the Day of the Lord to them (1 Thes. 5:11). In addition to his teaching, he urged them to minister to each other (1 Thes. 5:18).

*Establishment* in the Lord is also an important theme. Paul sent Timothy back to Thessalonica that he might establish them in their faith (1 Thes. 3:2); and Paul prayed that God might establish them (1 Thes. 3:13). The child must be taught to stand before he can learn to walk or run.

It is God who establishes, but He uses people to accomplish His work. A great need in our churches is for Christians who will take time to establish the younger believers. Group Bible studies are very valuable, as are the public meetings of the church; but individual discipling is also important. Paul encouraged the Thessalonian believers on a one-to-one basis, and we should follow his example.

Paul was concerned about two aspects of their Christian life: their *word* and their *work*, their *saying* and their *doing*. If our walk contradicts our words, we lose our testimony. Our "walk" and our "talk" must agree; good works and good words must come from the same yielded heart.

We are not saved by good works (Eph. 2:8-10; Titus 3:3-7); but good works are the evidence of salvation (Titus 2:11-15). It is not enough to depend on good words; the words must be backed up by the deeds (1 John 3:18). It must be a steady practice, not an occasional one. We must be *established* in our words and works.

How is this possible? Only God can do it by His grace; and this is what Paul desired for his friends. God has given us eternal encouragement and good hope through His grace. Notice that Paul's words united the Lord Jesus Christ and God the Father in such a way that he affirmed the deity of Christ. The two names for God in 2 Thessalonians 2:16 are governed by a *singular* verb, not a plural, which means they are equal. He used the same construction in 1 Thessalonians 3:11, again affirming the equality of the Son with the Father.

Too many Christians today emphasize *guarding* the truth, but downplay *living* the truth. One of the best ways to guard the truth is to put it into practice. It is good to be defenders of the faith, but we must not forget to be demonstrators of the faith. Lazarus did not have to give lectures on the resurrection. People had only to look at him and they believed (John 12:9-11).

### Share the Truth (2 Thes. 3:1-5)

A sequence of responsibilities is logical. Learning and living must go together. If we believe the truth, it changes our lives. We guard the truth and practice it so that we can share it with others. We cannot share what we do not believe (unless we want to be hypocrites); and we can best share that which we have practiced ourselves.

God's Word is alive (Heb. 4:12); we must let it move freely. Paul alluded here to Psalm 147:15—"He sent forth His commandment upon earth: His word runneth very swiftly." God's servants may be bound, but God's Word cannot be bound (2 Tim. 2:9). As we practice the truth and pray for the ministry of the truth, God's Word will have freedom to run and accomplish God's purposes in the world.

The Word of God is glorified in the lives of those who share it and those who receive it.

This was Paul's experience in Antioch of Pisidia: "And when the Gentiles heard this [that they could be saved], they were glad, and glorified the word of the Lord: and as many as were ordained to eternal life believed. And the Word of the Lord was published [spread abroad] throughout all the region" (Acts 13:48-49).

Too much Christian work these days is accomplished by human plans and promotion, and not by the Word of God. We trust our programs and do not publish the Word of God. The universe was created, and is sustained, by the Word of God (Heb. 11:3). Surely His Word can accomplish His work in this world. But the preaching of the Word in the pulpit has too often been replaced by the entertainment of the world on the platform. Dr. Donald Coggan, Archbishop of Canterbury, has said of Christian pastors: "It is their task to feed the sheep—not to entertain the goats."

It has been my experience in three pastorates that God's Word will accomplish God's work. When the sheep are fed, they will flock together in love, reproduce, follow the shepherd—and they can be "fleeced" and will love it. It is when the sheep are hungry that they start biting each other, becoming sick, and wandering away. When the Word of God does the work, then God gets the glory. My good friend Dr. Bob Cook used to remind us, "If you can explain what is going on, then God isn't doing it!"

Of course, there is always opposition to the Word and work of God. Paul asked his friends to pray that he might be delivered from unbelieving men who were evil and wicked. Just as the Spirit uses dedicated people to share the Word, Satan uses wicked people to oppose the Word. The evil one enjoys using Christian believers to oppose the work of God. He spoke through Peter (Matt. 16:21-23), and he worked through Ananias and Sapphira (Acts 5:1-11).

Paul had confidence that his readers would not yield to Satan, but would permit the faithful Lord to establish them and guard them from the evil one (literal meaning of 2 Thes. 3:3). We cannot have confidence in ourselves, but we can have confidence in God for ourselves and for others.

It is not enough that the pastor or church officers alone share the Word; each Christian must be a part of this vital ministry. The word *command* that Paul used in 2 Thessalonians 3:4 means "a military order passed down from a superior officer." He used this word in 1 Thessalonians 4:2; and he repeated it in 2 Thessalonians 3:4, 6, 10, 12. Christ is the Captain of our salvation; we are His soldiers (2 Tim. 2:3-4). In a battle, it is not enough for only the officers to fight; every man must do his duty. This is also true in the work of the local church.

What if an army were run with the same lack of obedience, order, and discipline that we often see in the local church? It would never win the war. If soldiers attended drill whenever they felt like it, they would never be equipped to face the enemy. If the recruits disobeyed their officers' orders the way some church members disobey the Word of God, they would be court-martialed.

A soldier obeys primarily out of loyalty and fear. But a Christian has much higher motives for obedience: God's love and Christ's return (2 Thes. 3:5). "If ye love Me, keep My commandments" (John 14:15). A commanding officer does not require his men to love him; but if they do, they will respect and obey him with greater diligence. The history of warfare records heroic deeds done by men who loved their leaders and willingly died for them. Our Saviour loved us and died for us. Can we not obey Him?

He is coming for us. This has been the theme of Paul's two Letters to the Thessalonians, and he related this truth to everyday practical living. As God's soldiers, we must be sharing the Word, for He will one day return and ask for an accounting of our lives. Do we "love His appearing"? (2 Tim. 4:8) Will we "be ashamed before Him at His coming"? (1 John 2:28)

Here, then, are four great responsibilities for us to fulfill: believe the truth, guard the truth, practice the truth, and share the truth. If we fulfill these duties, we will experience joy and power in our lives, and growth and blessing in our churches.

# CHAPTER FOUR
# ORDER IN THE CHURCH
## *2 Thessalonians 3:6-18*

When problems are not solved, they grow and become worse. A sliver left in the finger can become infected and cause a toxic condition so serious that surgery may become necessary. If you tell your doctor that you stepped on a rusty nail, he will immediately give you a tetanus shot, even though the wound may appear insignificant to you.

Church problems are like physical problems: if left unsolved, they grow and become worse, and they infect more people. The local church is a body; and what germs are to the physical body, sin is to the spiritual body. When Paul wrote his first letter to the Thessalonican church, he warned the idle busybodies to get to work (1 Thes. 4:11). He admonished the church leaders to "warn them that are unruly" (1 Thes. 5:14). The word *unruly* means "a soldier out of rank." Apparently these troublemakers did not repent, because Paul devoted the rest of his second letter to this problem.

What was the problem? Some members of the assembly had misinterpreted Paul's teachings about the return of Christ, left their jobs, and were living off the generosity of the church. They were idle while others were working. Yet they expected the church to support them. It is possible that this group of lazy saints was the source of the false teaching Paul mentioned in 2 Thessalonians 2:2. They were also spreading gossip about people in the church. They had time on their hands and gossip on their lips, but they defended themselves by arguing, "The Lord is coming soon!"

Misinterpretations and misapplications of the truths of God's Word can cause endless trouble. History records the foolishness of people who set dates, sold their possessions, and sat on mountains waiting for the Lord to return. Any teaching that encourages us to disobey another divine teaching is not Bible teaching.

The Pharisees figured out a way to rob their parents and yet obey the fifth commandment:

And He [Jesus] said to them, "Rightly did Isaiah prophesy of you hypocrites, as it is written, 'This people honors Me with their lips, but their heart is far away from Me. But in vain do they worship Me, teaching as doctrines the precepts of men.' Neglecting the commandment of God, you hold to the tradition of men." He was also saying to them, "You nicely set aside the commandment of God in order to keep your tradition. For Moses said, 'Honor your father and your mother;' and 'He who speaks evil of father or mother, let him be put to death'; but you say, 'If a man says to his father or his mother, anything of mine you might have been helped by is Corban (that is to say, given to God),' you no longer permit him to do anything for his father or his mother; thus invalidating the Word of God by your tradition which you have handed down; and you do many such things like that" (Mark 7:6-13, NASB).

Paul expected the whole church to work together in solving this problem. The church in love must deal with its own members and seek to help each one obey God. To assist them in this task, Paul gave four motives to encourage the careless believers to turn from their sins and start earning their own bread.

### The Exhortation of the Word
### (2 Thes. 3:6)

Paul had used this powerful word *command* in his first Thessalonian letter (1 Thes. 4:2, 11); and we met it earlier in this chapter (2 Thes. 3:4). He used it again in 2 Thessalonians 3:10, 12. The word means "a military order handed down from a superior officer." Paul considered the church to be like an army; and if the army does not obey the orders, there can be no order. Unfortunately, some of the saints were "out of rank" ("unruly" in 1 Thes. 5:14, and "disorderly" in 2 Thes. 3:6-7 and 11).

What authority did Paul have to issue this command, "If any is not willing to work, neither should he eat"? (2 Thes. 3:10, literal translation) He had the authority of the name of the Lord Jesus Christ. At least twenty times in the Thessalonian letters, Paul used this complete title of the Saviour. *Jesus* means "Saviour" and is His human name (Matt. 1:21). *Christ* is His divine title; it means "Messiah—the Anointed One." Other persons could use the name Jesus (the Hebrew form is "Joshua"); and other persons could claim to be anointed, such as prophets, priests, and kings. But the two names, Jesus Christ, are further defined by the name *LORD*, "Jehovah God."

In the four Gospels and the Book of Acts, our Lord is often called Jesus; but this single name is used very infrequently in the rest of the New Testament. That it is *occasionally* used should restrain us from criticizing those who call their Saviour "Jesus"; but that its use is found mainly during His ministry on earth should encourage us to address Him, and speak of Him with His name of exaltation—Lord Jesus Christ (Phil. 2:11). We no longer know "Christ after the flesh" (2 Cor. 5:16), but as the exalted Son of God and "Head over all things to the church." His lordship includes our work and money management.

What does the Bible teach about manual (or mental) labor? For one thing, labor was a part of man's life *before* sin entered the scene. God gave Adam the job of dressing and guarding the Garden (Gen. 2:15). Though sin turned labor into almost hopeless toil (Gen. 3:17-19), it must never be thought that the necessity for work is a result of sin. Man needs work for the fulfillment of his own person. God created him to work.

Have you noticed that God called people who were busy at work? Moses was caring for sheep (Ex. 3). Joshua was Moses' servant before he became Moses' successor (Ex. 33:11). Gideon was threshing wheat when God called him (Jud. 6:11ff), and David was caring for his father's sheep (1 Sam. 16:11ff). Our Lord called four fishermen to serve as His disciples, and He Himself had worked as a carpenter. Paul was a tentmaker (Acts 18:1-3) and used his trade to support his own ministry.

The Jews honored honest labor and required all their rabbis to have a trade. But the Greeks despised manual labor and left it to their slaves. This Greek influence, plus their wrong ideas about the doctrine of the Lord's return, led these believers into an unchristian way of life.

Paul recognized the fact that some people could not work, perhaps because of physical handicaps or family responsibilities. This is why he phrased the statement as he did: "If any man *is not willing* to work." It was not a question of *ability* but *willingness*. When a believer cannot work and is in need, it is the privilege and duty of the church to help him (James 2:14-17; 1 John 3:16-18).

The exhortation of the Word should have

motivated these lazy believers to work; but Paul added a second motivation.

### The Example of the Apostle
### (2 Thes. 3:7-10)

As an apostle, Paul had the right to expect financial support; but he deliberately gave up this right that he might be an example to the young believers (see 1 Cor. 9:6-14). In this attitude, Paul proved himself to be a mature Christian leader. Selfish leaders use people to build up their support, and they are always claiming their rights. A truly dedicated leader will use his rights to build up the people, and will lay aside his rights and privileges for the sake of others.

He had referred to his example in labor in his previous letter (1 Thes. 2:9). His readers knew that Paul and his associates had not taken any support from the infant church. Instead, they had set the example of meeting their own needs and also helping to meet the needs of others. "You ought to imitate us," he admonished his readers.

The greatest influence is that of godly living and sacrifice. A Christian leader may appeal to the authority of the Word; but if he cannot point also to his own example of obedience, his people will not listen. This is the difference between *authority* and *stature*. A leader earns stature as he obeys the Word and serves His people in the will of God. Authority comes from position; stature comes from practice and example. Stature earns the leader the right to exercise authority.

Every Christian worker has the right to support from the church as he serves the Lord (Luke 10:7; Gal. 6:6; 1 Tim. 5:17-18). We must not use Paul's example as an excuse not to support God's servants. But any servant of God has the privilege of setting aside that right to the glory of God. Paul did this so that he might be an example to the young believers in Thessalonica.

Paul's policy not only encouraged the new believers but also silenced the accusers. In every city there were itinerant teachers who "peddled their wares" for what they could earn. Paul did not want to be classified with them. Nor did he want any unsaved person to say, "Paul preaches only to make money." As he stated in 1 Corinthians 9, Paul wanted to make the Gospel "free of charge"; he would not permit money to hinder the winning of lost souls.

Needless to say, the careless attitude of these believers was affecting the church; so Paul added yet a third motive for their obedience.

### The Encouragement of the Church
### (2 Thes. 3:11-15)

Second Thessalonians 3:13 is the key: "And you, brothers, do not lose heart doing good!" (literal translation) The faithful Christians were discouraged by the conduct of the careless saints who refused to work. "If *they* don't have to work, why should *we?*" was their argument; and Paul nipped it in the bud.

Sin in the life of a believer always affects the rest of the church. As members of His body, we belong to each other and we affect each other. The bad example of a few saints can destroy the devotion, and hinder the service, of the rest of the church.

Paul named the sins of this group. To begin with, they were "disorderly," or out of order, out of rank. They were disobeying orders, and this brought confusion and division to the assembly. Further, they were "busybodies," not busy workers. The Greek word for "busybody" literally means "to be working around"; that is, busy but "fooling around" and not accomplishing anything. First Timothy 5:13 suggests that busybodies meddle in matters that do not belong to them.

Almost every culture has its saying about idleness. The Romans said, "By doing nothing, men learn to do evil." Isaac Watts wrote: "For Satan finds some mischief still, for idle hands to do." The Jewish rabbis taught, "He who does not teach his son a trade, teaches him to be a thief."

Instead of noisily running around, these people should "with quietness . . . work, and eat their own bread." Their false views about the return of Christ had worked them into a pitch of excitement. "Your overemotional attitude is wrong," warned Paul. "Settle down and get to work." Work is a great antidote to unbalanced speculation and unthinking activity.

But suppose these saints did *not* obey God's Word and go to work? What then should the church do? Paul had already taken the first step when he exhorted them in his first letter (1 Thes. 5:14) and warned them that they were wrong. But they had still persisted in their unruly behavior. He now warned them again in his second letter, and then added a further step: if these believers did not obey, the members of the church should personally discipline them.

The subject of church discipline is not discussed much these days. In many churches, once a person is baptized and becomes a member of a local church, he is pretty much left to himself. If he commits some gross public sin, he will probably be dealt with by the pastor or the board; but the total church family will not begin to minister to him or exercise discipline over him.

What is church discipline? For one thing, it is *not* the pastor and official board acting like evangelical policemen to trap a sinning saint and kick him out of the church. No doubt there are churches that have such dictatorial leaders, but this is not what Paul had in mind. Church discipline is to the church member what family discipline is to a child: it is an exercise of, and evidence of, correcting love. When a parent disciplines his child, he is not a judge punishing a criminal; he is a loving father seeking to make his child a better person.

There are various levels of church discipline that must be distinguished.

**Personal differences between Christians (Matt. 18:15-18; Phil. 4:1-3).** If a brother or sister sins against me (either deliberately or unknowingly), I should go to that person privately and seek to get the matter settled. Only if the person refuses to settle the matter should I bring anyone else in; and the problem must not go to the church family until every other means has been exhausted.

In my pastoral ministry, I have seen many problems of this type. The big mistake Christians make when another believer wrongs them is in telling the pastor or other members, and not going to the person directly. Another mistake is in trying to win an argument instead of trying to win the sinning brother.

**Doctrinal error.** Determine first of all why the person is teaching wrong doctrine. Perhaps it is because of ignorance and lack of Bible knowledge. In that case, patiently teach him the truth (2 Tim. 2:23-26). If he persists, rebuke him (Titus 1:10-14). Paul had to do this to Peter (Gal. 2:11ff). If the error continues, avoid him (Rom. 16:17-18), and then separate yourself from him (2 Tim. 2:18ff; 2 John 9ff).

**A believer overtaken by sin (Gal. 6:1-3).** Even the great Apostle Peter denied the Lord. And David yielded to lust and committed adultery. When a Christian is caught in known sin, the spiritual members of the church must seek to restore him with gentle-

ness and love. The word *restore* here means "to set a broken bone"—and that takes tenderness and patience. Too often the church quickly passes judgment on a believer who has sinned, and the damage done causes problems for years to come.

**A repeating troublemaker (Titus 3:10).** The word *heretic* does not refer to doctrinal error, but to a proud attitude of one who gets people to "take sides" in the church. The Greek word means "to make a choice." This leads to divisions and cliques in the local church (see Gal. 5:20 where *heresies* ought to be translated "sects, parties"). There is hardly a church that does not have its parties *for* or *against* anything—the pastor, the building program, even the color of the kitchen walls. Usually these "heretics" are people who like to be important; they want a following. Often they have deep emotional problems that Satan can use to create spiritual problems in the church. Perhaps they are frustrated at home or on the job; or perhaps they have, in the past, been hurt by some pastor or church.

These "factious people" should be given two official warnings. If they repeat their sin of dividing the church, they should be given a third warning and rejected. "Warn a divisive person once, and then warn him a second time. After that, have nothing to do with him. You may be sure that such a man is warped and sinful; he is self-condemned" (Titus 3:10-11, NIV).

It is my conviction that such people should not hold office in the church. It is also my conviction that, if they leave the church "in a huff," they should be restored to fellowship only twice. The third time—they are out!

**Open immorality (1 Cor. 5).** The church must mourn over the sinner (the same word is used for mourning over the dead) and seek to bring him to repentance. If he refuses, the church collectively should dismiss him (1 Cor. 5:13, where the Greek word means "expel"). If he repents, he must be forgiven and restored to fellowship in the church (2 Cor. 2:6-11).

In the case of the "lazy saints," Paul told the believers to exhort them, warn them, and if they did not repent, withdraw intimate fellowship from them. This probably meant that these believers were not permitted to share in the Lord's Supper, and that the church members would not invite them to their homes. Second Thessalonians 3:14 does *not* apply to every case of discipline. It applies only to the matter of saints not working for a living.

"Have no company" literally means "do not get mixed up with"; the same word is used in 1 Corinthians 5:9. There is a difference between acquaintanceship, friendship, and fellowship; for fellowship means "to have in common." For obedient saints to treat disobedient Christians with the same friendship they show to other dedicated saints is to give approval to their sins.

However, Paul (knowing the tendency of human nature to go to extremes) cautioned them not to treat the offenders like enemies. "They are still your brothers in Christ," he added. Lot was out of fellowship with God and Abraham because he lived in Sodom; yet Abraham rescued Lot from the enemy because Lot was his brother (Gen. 14, and note especially v. 14). It requires much patience, love, and grace to help an erring brother; and this is why Paul added a final motive for earning a living.

### The Enablement of the Lord
### (2 Thes. 3:16-18)

No believer can say, "I am not able to obey God's Word and go to work," because God has made every provision for us to obey Him. He is the Lord of peace. If He is the Lord of our lives, then we will have peace in our own hearts, and we will help to encourage peace in our church fellowship.

If there is trouble in the church, it is because there is trouble in somebody's heart. If Christ is Lord, then there is peace in the heart. If there is war in the heart, then Jesus Christ is not Lord (see James 4:1-10).

I recall a Sunday School class that was in a constant state of confusion and competition. We would just get matters settled down for a few weeks when the volcano would erupt again. After much prayer and examination, we discovered that one class member wanted to be the teacher. She was proud of her own spiritual attainments and felt she could do a better job than the devoted lady who was teaching the class.

Even though this class member never openly attacked or criticized the teacher, her attitudes and the things she did *not* say sowed seeds of discord in the fellowship. When this problem was dealt with, the Lord of peace took over in the class, and God began to bless.

Not only does God's peace enable us to obey Him, but so does His presence: "The Lord be with you all!" He never leaves us or forsakes us; He is with us to the end of the age (Matt. 28:20; Heb. 13:5).

Finally, Paul reminded them of God's grace. "The grace of our Lord Jesus Christ be with you all" (2 Thes. 3:18) was Paul's official signature to his letters. He mentioned this because of the counterfeit letter they had received (2 Thes. 2:2). If we depend on the grace of God, we can do His will to the glory of God. "My grace is sufficient for thee" (2 Cor. 12:9).

The soldier who is out of rank and disobedient of the Lord's command proves that he is not surrendered to his Master. Church problems are individual problems, and they must be solved individually. God wants order in the church. "Let all things be done decently and in order" (1 Cor. 14:40).

Are you a part of the peace of the church or part of a war in the church?

Let's do what Joshua did and fall at the feet of the Captain of the Hosts of the Lord, that He might enable us to win the victory (Josh. 5:13-15), and fulfill His purposes for His people.

# 1 TIMOTHY

## OUTLINE

**Key theme:** How to manage the ministry of the local church
**Key verse:** 1 Timothy 3:15

### I. THE CHURCH AND ITS MESSAGE—chapter 1
A. Teaching sound doctrine—1:1-11
B. Proclaiming the Gospel—1:12-17
C. Defending the faith—1:18-20

### II. THE CHURCH AND ITS MEMBERS—chapters 2–3
A. Praying men—2:1-8
B. Submitting women—2:9-15
C. Qualified pastors—3:1-7
D. Qualified deacons—3:8-13
E. Behaving believers—3:14-16

### III. THE CHURCH AND ITS MINISTER—chapter 4
A. A good minister, preaching the Word—4:1-6
B. A godly minister, practicing the Word—4:7-12
C. A growing minister, progressing in the Word—4:13-16

### IV. THE CHURCH AND ITS MINISTRY—chapters 5–6
A. To older members—5:1-2
B. To older widows—5:3-10
C. To younger widows—5:11-16
D. To church officers—5:17-25
E. To servants (slaves)—6:1-2
F. To false teachers—6:3-10
G. To the pastor—6:11-16, 20-21
H. To the rich—6:17-19

## CONTENTS

# CHAPTER ONE
# STAY ON THE JOB
*1 Timothy 1*

Men wanted for hazardous journey, small wages, bitter cold, long months of complete darkness, constant danger, safe return doubtful. Honor and recognition in case of success."

That advertisement appeared in a London newspaper and *thousands of men responded!* It was signed by the noted Arctic explorer, Sir Ernest Shackleton, and that was what made the difference.

If Jesus Christ had advertised for workers, the announcement might have read something like this:

"Men and women wanted for difficult task of helping to build My church. You will often be misunderstood, even by those working with you. You will face constant attack from an invisible enemy. You may not see the results of your labor, and your full reward will not come till after all your work is completed. It may cost you your home, your ambitions, even your life."

In spite of the demands that He makes, Jesus Christ receives the "applications" of many who gladly give their all for Him. He is certainly the greatest Master for whom anyone could work, and the task of building His church is certainly the greatest challenge to which a believer could give his life.

Timothy was one young man who responded to Christ's call to help build His church. He was one of the Apostle Paul's special assistants. Along with Titus, Timothy tackled some of the tough assignments in the churches that Paul had founded. Timothy was brought up in a religious home (2 Tim. 1:5) and had been led to faith in Christ by Paul himself. This explains why Paul called Timothy "my own [genuine] son in the faith" (1 Tim. 1:2).

Timothy was born of mixed parentage: his mother was a Jewess, his father a Greek. He was so devoted to Christ that his local church leaders recommended him to Paul, and Paul added him to his "missionary staff" (Acts 16:1-5). Paul often reminded Timothy that he was chosen for this ministry (1 Tim. 1:18; 4:14). Timothy was faithful to the Lord (1 Cor. 4:17)

and had a deep concern for God's people (Phil. 2:20-22).

But in spite of his calling, his close association with Paul, and his spiritual gifts, Timothy was easily discouraged. The last time Paul had been with Timothy, he had encouraged him to stay on at Ephesus and finish his work (1 Tim. 1:3). Apparently Timothy had physical problems (1 Tim. 5:23) as well as periods of discouragement; and you get the impression that some of the church members were not giving their pastor the proper respect as God's servant (1 Tim. 4:12; 2 Tim. 2:6-8).

Ephesus would not be the easiest place to pastor a church. (Are there any "easy places"? I doubt it.) The city was devoted to the worship of Diana, the patroness of the sexual instinct. Her lascivious images helped promote sexual immorality of all kinds (see Acts 19). Paul had done a great work in Ephesus during his three-year ministry, so "all they which dwelt in [the province of] Asia heard the word of the Lord Jesus" (Acts 19:10). It was not easy for Timothy to follow a man like Paul! Of course, Satan had his workers in the city; for wherever there are spiritual opportunities there are also satanic obstacles (1 Cor. 16:8-9).

Paul wrote the letter we call 1 Timothy to encourage Timothy, to explain how a local church should be managed, and to enforce his own authority as a servant of God. In 1 Timothy 1 Paul explained the three responsibilities of a pastor and people in a local church.

## Teach Sound Doctrine (1 Tim. 1:1-11)

From the very greeting of the letter, Paul affirmed his authority as a servant of Jesus Christ. Those who were giving Timothy trouble needed to remember that their pastor was there because God had put him there, for Paul's authority was given by God. Paul was an "apostle," one whom God sent with a special commission. His apostleship came by "commandment" from Jesus Christ. This word means "a royal commission." Both Paul and Timothy were sent by the King of kings!

Jesus Christ is not only Lord, but He is our "Saviour," a title used ten times in the Pastoral Epistles (1 Tim. 1:1; 2:3; 4:10; 2 Tim. 1:10; Titus 1:3-4; 2:10, 13; 3:4, 6). To discouraged Timothy, the title "our hope" (1 Tim. 1:1) was a real boost. Paul wrote the same encouragement to Titus (Titus 1:2; 2:13; 3:7). Knowing that Jesus Christ is coming for us encourages us to serve Him faithfully.

One reason Christian workers must stay on the job is that false teachers are busy trying to capture Christians. There were teachers of false doctrines in Paul's day just as there are today, and we must take them seriously. These false teachers have no good news for lost sinners. They seek instead to lead Christians astray and capture them for their causes.

Paul used military language to help Timothy and his people see the seriousness of the problem (1 Tim. 1:3). *Charge* means "to give strict orders from a superior officer." Paul used this word (sometimes translated "commandment" and "command" in KJV) eight times in his two letters to Timothy (1 Tim. 1:3, 5, 18; 4:11; 5:7; 6:13, 17; 2 Tim. 4:1). He was conveying this idea: "Timothy, you are not only a pastor of the church in a difficult city. You are also a Christian soldier under orders from the King. Now pass these orders along to the soldiers in your church!"

What was the order? "Do not teach different doctrines from those taught by Paul!" In the original text there are thirty-two references to "doctrine," "teach," "teacher," "teaches," and "teaching" in the three Pastoral Epistles. In the early church, the believers were taught the Word of God and the meanings of basic Christian doctrines. In many churches today, the pulpit and choir loft are places for entertainment, not enlightenment and enrichment.

God had committed the truth of the Word to Paul (1 Tim. 1:11), and Paul had committed it to Timothy (1 Tim. 6:20). It was Timothy's responsibility to guard the faith (2 Tim. 1:14) and to pass it along to faithful people (2 Tim. 2:2).

Paul identified the false teaching as "fables and endless genealogies" (1 Tim. 1:4). Titus faced the same kind of false teaching in Crete (Titus 1:14; 3:9). The false teachers were using the Old Testament Law, and especially the genealogies, to manufacture all kinds of novelties; and these new doctrines were leading people astray. The false teachers were raising questions, not answering them. They were not promoting "God's saving plan" ("godly edifying," 1 Tim. 1:4), but were leading people away from the truth. Instead of producing love, purity, a good conscience, and sincere faith, these novel doctrines were causing division, hypocrisy, and all sorts of problems.

Paul used the word "conscience(s)" twenty-one times in his letters, and six of these references are in the Pastoral Epistles (1 Tim. 1:5, 19; 3:9; 4:2; 2 Tim. 1:3; Titus 1:15). The word "conscience" means "to know with." Conscience is the inner judge that accuses us when we have done wrong and approves when we have done right (Rom. 2:14-15). It is possible to sin against the conscience so that it becomes "defiled" (Titus 1:15). Repeated sinning hardens the conscience so that it becomes "seared" like scar tissue (1 Tim. 4:2).

It is tragic when professed Christians get off course because they refuse "healthy doctrine" ("sound doctrine," 1 Tim. 1:10). Paul also calls it "the doctrine . . . according to godliness" (1 Tim. 6:3), "sound words" (2 Tim. 1:13), "sound doctrine" (2 Tim. 4:3; Titus 1:9; 2:1), "faith" (Titus 1:13; 2:2), and "sound speech" (Titus 2:8). But many prefer the "vain jangling" (1 Tim. 1:6) of those who teach novelties rather than the pure Word of God that produces holiness in lives. It is unfortunate today that we not only have "vain jangling" ("meaningless talk," NIV) in teaching and preaching, but also in music. Far too many songs not only teach *no* doctrine, but many even teach *false* doctrines. A singer has no more right to sing a lie than a teacher has to teach a lie.

The reason for this false doctrine was a misuse of the Old Testament Law. These false teachers did not understand the content or the purpose of God's Law. They were leading believers out of the liberty of grace (Gal. 5:1ff) into the bondage of legalism, a tragedy that still occurs today. The flesh (our old nature) loves religious legalism because rules and regulations enable a person to *appear* holy without really having to change his heart.

Paul listed fourteen kinds of people who were condemned by the Law (1 Tim. 1:9-10). This is one of several such lists in the New Testament (see Mark 7:20-23; Rom. 1:18-32; Gal. 5:19-21). The lawful use of the Law is to expose, restrain, and convict the lawless. The Law cannot save lost sinners (Gal. 2:21; 3:21-29); it can only reveal their need for a Saviour. When a sinner believes on Jesus Christ, he is freed from the curse of the Law (Gal. 3:10-14); and the righteous demands of the Law are met by the indwelling Holy Spirit as a believer yields to God (Rom. 8:1-4).

Paul (1 Tim. 1:9-10) centered particularly on five of the Ten Commandments in Exodus 20:

No. 5—*"Honor thy father and thy moth-er"*—"murderers of the fathers and . . . mothers."

No. 6—*"Thou shalt not kill [murder]"*—"murderers of fathers and . . . mothers . . . manslayers."

No. 7—*"Thou shalt not commit adul-tery"*—"whoremongers [fornica-tors] . . . them that defile them-selves with mankind [sodom-ites]."

No. 8—*"Thou shalt not steal"*—"men-stealers [kidnappers]."

No. 9—*"Thou shalt not bear false wit-ness"*—"liars . . . perjured per-sons."

It is the "glorious Gospel" that saves lost sinners. Paul had experienced the power of the Gospel (Rom. 1:16), and he had been en-trusted with the ministry of the Gospel (1 Thes. 2:4). Law and Gospel go together, for the Law without the Gospel is diagnosis without remedy; but the Gospel without Law is only the Good News of salvation for people who don't believe they need it because they have never heard the bad news of judgment. The Law is not Gospel, but the Gospel is not lawless (Rom. 3:20-31).

## Proclaim the Gospel (1 Tim. 1:12-17)

The mention of "the Gospel of the glory of the blessed God" (1 Tim. 1:11, literal translation) moved Paul to share his own personal testi-mony. He was "Exhibit A" to prove that the Gospel of the grace of God really works. When you read Paul's testimony (see also Acts 9:1-22; 22:1-21; 26:9-18), you begin to grasp the wonder of God's grace and His sav-ing power.

***What Paul used to be (v. 13a).*** He was a *blasphemer* because he denied the deity of Jesus Christ and forced others to deny it. He was a *persecutor* who used physical power to try to destroy the church. "Murderous threats" were the very breath of his life (Acts 9:1, NIV). He persecuted the Christian church (1 Cor. 15:9) and then discovered that he was actually laying hands on Jesus Christ, the Messiah! (Acts 9:4) During this period of his life, Paul consented to the stoning of Stephen and made havoc of the church (Acts 8:1-4). Paul was *injurious*, a word that means "proud and insolent." A modern equivalent might be "bully." It conveys the idea of a haughty man "throwing his weight around" in violence. But the basic causes of his godless behavior were "ignorance" and "unbelief." Even though Saul of Tarsus was a brilliant man and well educated (Acts 22:3; Gal. 1:13-14), his mind was blinded from the truth (1 Cor. 2:14; 2 Cor. 4:3-4). He was a reli-gious man, yet he was not headed for heaven! It was not until he put faith in Jesus Christ that he was saved (Phil. 3:1-11).

***How Paul was saved (vv. 13b-15).*** How could the holy God ever save and forgive such a self-righteous sinner? The key words are "mercy" and "grace." God in His mercy did not give Paul what he did deserve; instead God in His grace gave Paul what he did not deserve. Grace and mercy are God's love in action, God's love *paying a price* to save lost sinners. It is not God's love alone that saves us, for God loves the whole world (John 3:16). It is by grace that we are saved (Eph. 2:8-9) because God is rich in mercy (Eph. 2:4) and grace (Eph. 2:7).

What did Paul's "ignorance" have to do with his salvation? Is ignorance an excuse before God? Of course not! The fact of his ignorance is related to a special Jewish law (Lev. 5:15-19; Num. 15:22-31). If a person sinned know-ingly "with a high hand" in Israel, he was cut off from the people. But if he sinned in igno-rance, he was permitted to bring the proper sacrifices to atone for his sins. Jesus recog-nized this principle when He prayed on the cross, "Father, forgive them, for they know not what they do" (Luke 23:34). Their igno-rance did not save them, nor did Christ's prayer save them; but the combination of the two postponed God's judgment, giving them an opportunity to be saved.

Paul stated that it took "exceedingly abun-dant" grace to save him! Paul liked to use the Greek prefix *huper* (meaning "an exceeding abundant amount"), and he often attached it to words in his letters. You might translate some of these as "superincrease of faith" (2 Thes. 1:3); "superabounding power" (Eph. 1:19); "superconqueror" (Rom. 8:37). This same prefix has come into the English language as *hyper*. We speak of "hyperactive" children and "hypersensitive" people.

Paul makes it clear that this salvation is not for him only, but for all who receive Jesus Christ (1 Tim. 1:15). If Jesus could save Saul of Tarsus, the *chief* of sinners, then He can save anybody! We admire Paul's humility, and we note that he considered himself to be the "least of the apostles" (1 Cor. 15:9) and the "least of all saints" (Eph. 3:8). Notice that

Paul did not write "of whom I *was* chief" but "of whom I *am* chief."

***What Paul became (vv. 12, 16).*** The grace of God turned the persecutor into a preacher, and the murderer into a minister and a missionary! So dramatic was the change in Paul's life that the Jerusalem church suspected that it was a trick, and they had a hard time accepting him (Acts 9:26-31). God gave Paul his ministry; he did not get it from Peter or the other Apostles (Gal. 1:11-24). He was called and commissioned by the risen Christ in heaven.

God saw that Paul was faithful, and so He entrusted the Gospel to him. Even as an unbelieving and Gospel-ignorant Jewish leader, Paul had maintained a good conscience and he lived up to the light that he had. So often those who are intensely wrong as lost sinners become intensely right as Christians and are greatly used of God to win souls. God not only *entrusted* the Gospel to Paul, but He *enabled* Paul to minister that Gospel (1 Cor. 15:10; Phil. 4:13). When someone obeys God's call to serve, God always equips and enables that person.

But Paul not only became a minister; he also became *an example* (1 Tim. 1:16). In what sense is Paul an example to lost sinners who believe on Christ? None of us has had the same experience that Paul had on the Damascus road (Acts 9). We did not see a light, fall to the ground, and hear Jesus speak from heaven. But Paul is a pattern ("type") to all lost sinners, for he was the chief of sinners! He is proof that the grace of God can change *any* sinner!

But there is a special application of this to today's people of Israel, Paul's countrymen, for whom he had a special burden (Rom. 9:1-5; 10:1-3). The people of Israel, like unconverted Saul of Tarsus, are religious, self-righteous, blind to their own Law and its message of the Messiah, and unwilling to believe. One day, Israel shall see Jesus Christ even as Paul saw Him; and the nation shall be saved. "They shall look upon Me whom they have pierced" (Zech. 12:10). This may be one reason why Paul said he was "born out of due time" (1 Cor. 15:8), for his experience of seeing the risen Christ came at the beginning of this Church Age and not at its end (Matt. 24:29ff).

Paul gave a third responsibility for the local church to fulfill besides teaching sound doctrine and proclaiming the Gospel.

## Defend the Faith (1 Tim. 1:18-20)

Again, Paul used military language to enforce his statement, for the word "charge" (1 Tim. 1:18) means "an urgent command handed down from a superior officer" (1 Tim. 1:3). Paul also reminded Timothy that God had chosen him for his ministry. Apparently some of the prophets in the local assemblies had been led by the Spirit to select Timothy for service (see Acts 13:1-3 for an example of this procedure).

It was not easy to serve God in pagan Ephesus, but Timothy was a man under orders, and he had to obey. The soldier's task is to "please him who hath chosen him to be a soldier" (2 Tim. 2:4), and not to please himself. Furthermore, Timothy was there by divine appointment: God had chosen him and sent him. It was this fact that could give him assurance in difficult days. If you are God's servant, called by the Spirit, obeying His will, then you can "stay with it" and finish the work. These assurances enabled Timothy to war the good warfare.

Paul changed the illustration from army to navy (1 Tim. 1:19). He warned Timothy that the only way to succeed was to hold fast to "faith and a good conscience." It is not enough to proclaim the faith with our lips; we must practice the faith in our daily lives. One man said of his hypocritical pastor, "He is such a good preacher, he should never get out of the pulpit; but he is such a poor Christian, he should never get into the pulpit!"

A good conscience is important to a good warfare and a good ministry. The magazine editor H.L. Mencken defined conscience as "the inner voice which warns us that somebody may be looking." But a man with a good conscience will do the will of God in spite of who is watching or what people may say. Like Martin Luther, he will say, "Here I stand; I can do no other, so help me God!"

Professed Christians who "make shipwreck" of their faith do so by sinning against their consciences. Bad doctrine usually starts with bad conduct, and usually with secret sin. Hymenaeus and Alexander deliberately rejected their good consciences in order to defend their ungodly lives. Paul did not tell us exactly what they did, except that their sin involved "blaspheming" in some way. Hymenaeus said that the resurrection was already past (2 Tim. 2:16-18). Alexander was a popular name in that day, so we cannot be sure that the man named in Paul's next letter to Timothy

(2 Tim. 4:14) is the same man; but if he is, no doubt he withstood Paul by teaching false doctrine.

"Delivered unto Satan" (1 Tim. 1:20) implies an apostolic discipline (see 1 Cor. 5:5) and disassociation from the local church. The verb "learn" (1 Tim. 1:20) means "to learn by discipline." When a Christian refuses to repent, the local fellowship should exercise discipline, excluding him from the protective fellowship of the saints, making him vulnerable to the attacks of Satan. The fellowship of the local church, in obedience to the will of God, gives a believer spiritual protection. Satan has to ask God for permission to attack a believer (see Job 1–2; Luke 22:31-34).

Each local church is in a constant battle against the forces of evil. There are false prophets and false teachers, as well as false christs. Satan is the originator of false doctrines, for he is a liar from the beginning (John 8:44). It is not enough for a local church to teach sound doctrine and to proclaim the Gospel. The church must also defend the faith by exposing lies and opposing the doctrines of demons (1 Tim. 4:1).

It is important that our ministry be balanced. Some churches only preach the Gospel and seldom teach their converts the truths of the Christian life. Other churches are only opposing false doctrine; they have no positive ministry. We must be teachers of healthy doctrine ("sound doctrine," 1 Tim. 1:10) or the believers will not grow. We must preach the Gospel and keep winning the lost to Christ. And we must defend the faith against those who would corrupt the church with false doctrine and godless living. It is a constant battle, but it must be carried on.

Timothy must have been greatly helped and encouraged when he read this first section of Paul's letter. God had called Timothy, equipped him, and put him into his place of ministry. Timothy's job was not to run all over Ephesus, being involved in a multitude of tasks. His job was to care for the church by winning the lost, teaching the saved, and defending the faith. Any task that did not relate to these ministries would have to be abandoned. One reason some local churches are having problems is that the pastors and spiritual leaders are involved in too many extracurricular activities and are not doing the tasks God has called them to do.

It might be a good idea for our churches to take a spiritual inventory!

# CHAPTER TWO
# SERVICE—OR CIRCUS?
## *1 Timothy 2*

L et all things be done decently and in order" (1 Cor. 14:40) is a basic principle for the conduct of the ministry of the church. Apparently, young Timothy was having some problems applying this principle to the assemblies in Ephesus. The public worship services were losing their order and effectiveness because both the men and the women members of the church were disobeying God's Word.

"The church is an organism," a pastor told me, "so we shouldn't put too much emphasis on organization. We should allow the Spirit to have freedom."

"But if an organism is *disorganized*," I quickly reminded him, "it will die. Yes, I agree that we must permit the Spirit to have freedom, but even the Holy Spirit is not free to disobey the Word of God."

Often, what we think is the "freedom of the Spirit" are the carnal ideas of some Christian who is not walking in the Spirit. Eventually this "freedom" becomes anarchy, and the Spirit grieves as a church gradually moves away from the standards of God's Word.

To counteract this tendency, Paul exhorted the men and women in the church and reminded them of their spiritual responsibilities.

### The Men—Praying (1 Tim. 2:1-8)
*The priority of prayer (v. 1a).* "First of all" indicates that prayer is most important in the public worship of the church. It is sad to see how prayer has lost importance in many churches. "If I announce a banquet," a pastor said, "people will come out of the woodwork to attend. But if I announce a prayer meeting, I'm lucky if the ushers show up!" Not only have the special meetings for prayer lost stature in most local churches, but even prayer *in the public services* is greatly minimized. Many pastors spend more time on the announcements than they do in prayer!

The late Peter Deyneka, Sr., my good friend and founder of the Slavic Gospel Association, often reminded me: "Much prayer, much power! No prayer, no power!" Prayer was as much a part of the apostolic ministry as preaching the Word (Acts 6:4). Yet some pastors spend hours preparing their sermons, but never prepare their public prayers. Consequently, their prayers are routine, humdrum, and repetitious. I am not suggesting that a pastor write out every word and read it, but that he think through what he will pray about. This will keep "the pastoral prayer" from becoming dull and a mere repetition of what was "prayed" the previous week.

But the church members also need to be prepared to pray. Our hearts must be right with God and with each other. We must really want to pray, and not pray simply to please people (as did the Pharisees, Matt. 6:5), or to fulfill a religious duty. When a local church ceases to depend on prayer, God ceases to bless its ministry.

**The variety of prayer (v. 1b).** There are at least seven different Greek nouns for "prayer," and four of them are used here. *Supplications* carries the idea of "offering a request for a felt need."

*Prayers* is the commonest term for this activity, and it emphasizes the sacredness of prayer. We are praying *to God;* prayer is an act of worship, not just an expression of our wants and needs. There should be reverence in our hearts as we pray to God.

*Intercessions* is best translated "petitions." This same word is translated "prayer" in 1 Timothy 4:5, where it refers to blessing the food we eat. (It is rather obvious that we do not *intercede* for our food in the usual sense of that word.) The basic meaning is "to draw near to a person and converse confidently with him." It suggests that we enjoy fellowship with God so that we have confidence in Him as we pray.

*Giving of thanks* is definitely a part of worship and prayer. We not only give thanks for answers to prayer, but for who God is and what He does for us in His grace. We should not simply add our thanksgiving to the end of a selfish prayer! Thanksgiving should be an important ingredient in all of our prayers. In fact, sometimes we need to imitate David and present to God *only* thanksgiving with no petitions at all! (see Ps. 103)

"Prayer and supplication [petition] with thanksgiving" are a part of Paul's formula for God's peace in our hearts (Phil. 4:6). It is worth noting that Daniel, the great prayer-warrior, practiced this kind of praying (Dan. 6:10-11).

**The objects of prayer (vv. 1c-2).** "All men" makes it clear that no person on earth is outside the influence of believing prayer. (We have no examples of exhortations that say we should pray for the dead. If we should pray for the dead, Paul certainly had a good opportunity to tell us in this section of his letter.) This means we should pray for the unsaved and the saved, for people near us and people far away, for enemies as well as friends. Unfortunately, the Pharisees did not have this universal outlook in their prayers, for they centered their attention primarily on Israel.

Paul urged the church to especially pray for those in authority. Godless Emperor Nero was on the throne at that time, and yet the believers were supposed to pray for him! Even when we cannot respect men or women in authority, we must respect their offices and pray for them. In fact, it is for our own good that we do so: "that we may live peaceful and quiet lives in all godliness and holiness" (1 Tim. 2:2b, NIV). The early church was always subject to opposition and persecution, so it was wise to pray for those in authority. "Quiet" refers to circumstances around us, while "peaceful" refers to a calm attitude within us. The results should be lives that are godly and honorable.

To be sure, Paul has not named all the persons we can and should pray for, since "all men" covers the matter fully. We can't pray for everybody in the world by name, but we certainly ought to pray for those we know and know about. Why? Because it's a good thing to do and because it pleases God.

**The reasons for prayer (vv. 3-4).** The word "good" is a key word in Paul's pastoral epistles (1 Tim. 1:8, 18; 2:3; 3:1, 7, 13; 4:4, 6; 5:4, 10, 25; 6:12-13, 18-19; 2 Tim. 1:14; 2:3; 4:7; Titus 2:7, 14; 3:8, 14). The Greek word emphasizes the idea of something being intrinsically good, not just good in its effects. "Fair" and "beautiful" are synonyms. Certainly prayer of itself is a goodly practice, and brings with it many good benefits.

But prayer is also pleasing to the Lord. It pleases the Father when His children pray as He has commanded them to. The Pharisees prayed in order to be praised by men (Matt. 6:5) or to impress other worshipers (Luke 18:9-14). True Christians pray in order to please God. This suggests that we must pray in the will of God, because it certainly does not please the Father when we pray selfishly (James 4:1-10; 1 John 5:14-15). It's often said that the purpose of prayer is not to get man's will done in heaven, but to get God's will done on earth.

What is God's will? The salvation of lost souls, for one thing. We can pray for "all men" because it is God's will that "all men" come to the knowledge of salvation through faith in Jesus Christ. God loved the world (John 3:16) and Christ died for the whole world (1 John 2:2; 4:14). Jesus died on the cross that He might draw "all men" to salvation (John 12:32). This does not mean all people without *exception,* for certainly the whole world is not going to be saved. It means all people without *distinction*—Jews and Gentiles, rich and poor, religious and pagan.

If God doesn't want anyone to perish, then why are so many lost? God is long-suffering with lost sinners, even delaying His judgment that they might come to Christ (2 Peter 3:9). But salvation depends on a "knowledge of the truth" (1 Tim. 2:4). Not everyone has heard the truth of the Gospel, and many who have heard have rejected it. We cannot explain the mystery of God's sovereignty and man's responsibility (see John 6:37), but realize that both are taught in the Bible and are harmonized in God's great plan of salvation. We do know that prayer is an important part of God's program for reaching a lost world. We have the responsibility of praying for lost souls (Rom. 10:1) and making ourselves available to share the Gospel with others.

**The basis for prayer (vv. 5-7).** Many believers do not realize that prayer is based on the work of Jesus Christ as Saviour and Mediator. As the God-Man, Jesus Christ is the perfect Mediator between the holy God and His failing children. One of Job's complaints had to do with the absence of a mediator who could take his message to the throne of God. "There is no umpire between us, who may lay his hand upon us both" (Job 9:33, NASB).

Since there is only one God, there is need for only one Mediator; and that Mediator is Jesus Christ. *No other person can qualify.* Jesus Christ is both God and man, and, therefore, can be the "umpire" between God and man. In His perfect life and substitutionary death, He met the just demands of God's holy law. He was the "ransom for all." The word *ransom* means "a price paid to free a slave." His death was "on behalf of all." Though the death of Christ is efficient only for those who trust Him, it is sufficient for the sins of the whole world. Jesus said that He came "to give His life a ransom for many" (Matt. 20:28).

Christ died for "all men," and God is willing for "all men to be saved." How does this Good News get out to a sinful world? God calls and ordains messengers who take the Gospel to lost sinners. Paul was such a messenger: he was a *preacher* (the herald of the King), an *apostle* (one sent with a special commission), and a *teacher.* The same God who ordains *the end* (the salvation of the lost) also ordains *the means to the end:* prayer and preaching of the Word. This Good News is not for the Jews only, but also for the Gentiles.

If the basis for prayer is the sacrificial work of Jesus Christ on the cross, then prayer is a most important activity in a church. Not to pray is to slight the cross! To pray only for ourselves is to deny the worldwide outreach of the cross. To ignore lost souls is to ignore the cross. "All men" [people] is the key to this paragraph: We pray for "all" because Christ died for "all" and it is God's will that "all" be saved. We must give ourselves to God to be a part of His worldwide program to reach people before it is too late.

**The attitude in prayer (v. 8).** Paul stated definitely that "men" should pray in the local assembly. Both men and women prayed in the early church (1 Cor. 11:4-5), but the emphasis here is on the men. It is common to find women's prayer meetings, but not often do we find men's prayer meetings. If the men do not pray, the local church will not have dedicated leaders to oversee its ministry.

It was customary for Jewish men to pray with their arms extended and their hands open to heaven. Our traditional posture of bowing the head, folding the hands, and closing the eyes is nowhere found or commanded in Scripture. Actually, there are many prayer postures found in the Bible: standing with outstretched hands (1 Kings 8:22); kneeling (Dan. 6:10); standing (Luke 18:11); sitting (2 Sam. 7:18); bowing the head (Gen. 24:26); lifting the eyes (John 17:1); falling on the ground (Gen. 17:3). The important thing is not the posture of the body but the posture of the heart.

Paul stated three essentials for effective prayer, and the first was "holy hands." Obviously this means a holy life. "Clean hands" was symbolic of a blameless life (2 Sam. 22:21; Ps. 24:4). If we have sin in our lives, we cannot pray and expect God to answer (Ps. 66:18).

"Without wrath" is the second essential, and requires that we be on good terms with one another. "Without anger" might be a better translation. A person who is constantly having trouble with other believers, who is a troublemaker rather than a peacemaker, cannot pray and get answers from God.

"Doubting" suggests that we must pray *in faith*, but the word really means "disputing." When we have anger in the heart, we often have open disagreements with others. Christians should learn to disagree without being disagreeable. We should "do all things without murmurings and disputings" (Phil. 2:14).

Effective praying, then, demands that I be in a right relationship with God ("holy hands") and with my fellow believers ("without murmurings and disputings"). Jesus taught the same truth (Mark 11:24-26). If we spent more time *preparing* to pray and getting our hearts right before God, our prayers would be more effective.

## The Women—Submitting
## (1 Tim. 2:9-15)

In these days of "Women's Lib" and other feminist movements, the word "submission" makes some people see red. Some well-meaning writers have even accused Paul of being a "crusty old bachelor" who was antiwomen. Those of us who hold to the inspiration and authority of the Word of God know that Paul's teachings came from God and not from himself. If we have a problem with what the Bible says about women in the church, the issue is not with Paul (or Peter—see 1 Peter 3:1-7), but with the Lord who gave the Word (2 Tim. 3:16-17).

The word translated "subjection" in 1 Timothy 2:11 is translated "submitting" and "submit" in Ephesians 5:21-22 and Colossians 3:18. It literally means "to rank under." Anyone who has served in the armed forces knows that "rank" has to do with order and authority, not with value or ability. A colonel is higher in rank than a private, but that does not necessarily mean that the colonel is a better man than the private. It only means that the colonel has a higher rank and, therefore, more authority.

"Let all things be done decently and in order" (1 Cor. 14:40) is a principle God follows in His creation. Just as an army would be in confusion if there were no levels of author-

ity, so society would be in chaos without submission. Children should submit to their parents because God has given parents the authority to train their children and discipline them in love. Employees should submit to employers and obey them (Eph. 6:5-8, where the immediate reference is to household slaves, but the application can be made to workers today). Citizens should submit to government authorities, even if the authorities are not Christians (Rom. 13; 1 Peter 2:13-20).

Submission is not subjugation. Submission is recognizing God's order in the home and the church, and joyfully obeying it. When a Christian wife joyfully submits to the Lord and to her own husband, it should bring out the best in her. (For this to happen, the husband must love his wife and use God's order as a tool to build with, not a weapon to fight with—Eph. 5:18-33.) Submission is the key to spiritual growth and ministry: husbands should be submitted to the Lord, Christians should submit to each other (Eph. 5:21), and wives should be submitted to the Lord and to their husbands.

The emphasis in this section (1 Tim. 2:9-15) is on the place of women in the local church. Paul admonished these believing women to give evidence of their submission in several ways.

*Modest dress (v. 9).* The contrast here is between the artificial glamour of the world and the true beauty of a godly life. Paul did not forbid the use of jewelry or lovely clothes, but rather the excessive use of them as substitutes for the true beauty of "a meek and quiet spirit" (see 1 Peter 3:1-6). A woman who depends only on externals will soon run out of ammunition! She may attract attention, but she will not win lasting affection. Perhaps the latest fashion fads were tempting the women in the church at Ephesus, and Paul had to remind Timothy to warn the women not to get trapped.

The word translated "modest" (1 Tim. 2:9) simply means "decent and orderly." It is related to the Greek word from which we get the English word "cosmetic." A woman's clothing should be decent, orderly, and in good taste. "Shamefacedness" literally means "modesty, the avoidance of extremes." A woman who possesses this quality is ashamed to go beyond the bounds of what is decent and proper. "Sobriety" comes from a Greek word that means "having a sound mind and good sense." It describes an inner self-control—a spiritual "radar" that tells a person what is good and proper.

Ephesus was a wealthy commercial city, and some women there competed against each other for attention and popularity. In that day expensive hairdos arrayed with costly jewelry were an accepted way to get to the top socially. Paul admonished the Christian women to major on the "inner person," the true beauty that only Christ can give. He did not forbid the use of nice clothing or ornaments. He urged balance and propriety, with the emphasis on modesty and holy character.

"It's getting harder and harder for a Christian woman to find the right kind of clothes!" a church member complained to me one summer. "I refuse to wear the kind of swimsuits they're selling! I simply won't go swimming. Whatever happened to old-fashioned modesty?"

*Godly works (v. 10).* Paul did not suggest that good works are a substitute for clothing! Rather, he was contrasting the "cheapness" of expensive clothes and jewelry with the true values of godly character and Christian service. "Godliness" is another key word in Paul's pastoral letters (1 Tim. 2:2, 10; 3:16; 4:7-8; 6:3, 5-6, 11; 2 Tim. 3:5; Titus 1:1). Glamour can be partially applied on the outside, but godliness must come from within.

We must never underestimate the important place that godly women played in the ministry of the church. The Gospel message had a tremendous impact on them because it affirmed their value before God and their equality in the body of Christ (Gal. 3:28). Women had a low place in the Roman world, but the Gospel changed that.

There were devoted women who ministered to Jesus in the days of His earthly ministry (Luke 8:1-3). They were present at His crucifixion and burial, and it was a woman who first heralded the glorious news of His resurrection. In the Book of Acts we meet Dorcas (Acts 9:36ff), Lydia (Acts 16:14ff), Priscilla (Acts 18:1-3), and godly women in the Berean and Thessalonian churches (Acts 17:4, 12). Paul greeted at least eight women in Romans 16; and Phebe, who carried the Roman epistle to its destination, was a deaconess in a local church (Rom. 16:1). Many believing women won their husbands to the Lord and then opened their homes for Christian ministry.

*Quiet learning (v. 11).* "Silence" is an unfortunate translation because it gives the impression that believing women were never to open their mouths in the assembly. This is the same word that is translated "peaceable" in 1 Timothy 2:2. Some of the women abused their newfound freedom in Christ and created disturbances in the services by interrupting. It is this problem that Paul addressed in this admonition. It appears that women were in danger of upsetting the church by trying to "enjoy" their freedom. Paul wrote a similar admonition to the church in Corinth (1 Cor. 14:34), though this admonition may apply primarily to speaking in tongues.

*Respecting authority (vv. 12-15).* Women *are* permitted to teach. Older women should teach the younger women (Titus 2:3-4). Timothy was taught at home by his mother and grandmother (2 Tim. 1:5; 3:15). But in their teaching ministry, they must not "lord it over" men. There is nothing wrong with a godly woman instructing a man in private (Acts 18:24-28); but she must not assume authority in the church and try to take the place of a man. She should exercise "quietness" and help keep order in the church.

Paul gave several arguments to back up this admonition that the Christian men in the church should be the spiritual leaders. The first is an argument from *Creation:* Adam was formed first, and then Eve (1 Tim. 2:12-13). (Paul used this same argument in 1 Cor. 11:1-10.) We must keep in mind that *priority* does not mean *superiority.* Man and woman were both created by God and in God's image. The issue is only authority: man was created first.

The second argument has to do with man's fall into sin. Satan deceived the woman into sinning (Gen. 3:1ff; 2 Cor. 11:3); the man sinned with his eyes wide open. Because Adam rejected the God-given order, he listened to his wife, disobeyed God, and brought sin and death into the world. The submission of wives to their own husbands is a part of the original Creation. The disorder we have in society today results from a violation of that God-given order.

I do not think Paul suggested that women are more gullible than men and thus more easily deceived; for experience proves that both men and women are deceived by Satan. On one occasion, Abraham listened to his wife and got into trouble (Gen. 16). Later on, she gave him counsel and God told him to obey it (Gen. 21). In my own pastoral ministry, I have benefited greatly from the encouragement and counsel of godly women; but I have tried not to let them usurp authority in the church. In fact, the godly women I have known have no desire to "run" things in the church.

The creation of humans and their fall both seem to put the woman in an inferior position, but she does have a ministry from God (1 Tim. 2:15). There was probably a close relationship in Paul's mind between what he wrote here and what Moses wrote in Genesis 3:16—the promise of the Saviour who would be "made of a woman" (Gal 4:4). It was through a woman that the Saviour came into the world. (Keep in mind that Jesus had an earthly mother but not an earthly father—Matt. 1:18ff; Luke 1:34-35.)

But Paul teaches a practical lesson (1 Tim. 2:15). He promised that the woman would "be kept safe through childbirth" (NIV) if "they" (both husband and wife) continued in sincere dedication to the Lord.

Does this mean that Christian mothers will never die in childbirth? History and experience both tell us that they do. God has His purposes, and His ways are far above our thoughts (Isa. 55:8-9). Paul laid down a general principle that encouraged the believing women of that day. Their ministry was not to "run" the church, but to care for the home and bear children to the glory of God (1 Tim. 5:14). Their home congregation would give them abundant opportunities for teaching the Word and ministering to the saints (see Rom. 16:1-6).

Godly women do have an important ministry in the local assembly, even though they are not called to be teachers of the Word in a pastoral sense. If all is done "decently and in order," then God will bless.

# CHAPTER THREE
# FOLLOW THE LEADERS
*1 Timothy 3*

Everything rises or falls with leadership, whether it be a family or a local church. The Holy Spirit imparts gifts to believers for ministry in the local church, and among those gifts are "pastors and teachers" (Eph. 4:11) and "helps" and "governments" ("administration," 1 Cor. 12:28, NIV). As we noted before, even though the church is an organism, it must be organized or it will die. Leadership is a part of spiritual organization.

In this section, Paul described the bishop, the deacon, and the church itself. By understanding these three descriptions, we shall be able to give better leadership to the ministry of the church.

## The Pastor (1 Tim. 3:1-7)

According to the New Testament, the terms "bishop," "pastor," and "elder" are synonymous. *Bishop* means "overseer," and the elders had the responsibility of overseeing the work of the church (Acts 20:17, 28; 1 Peter 5:1-3). "Elder" is the translation of the Greek word *presbutes,* which means "an old man." Paul used the word *presbytery* in 1 Timothy 4:14, referring not to a denomination, but to the "eldership" of the assembly that ordained Timothy. Elders and bishops (two names for the same office, Titus 1:5, 7) were mature people with spiritual wisdom and experience. Finally, "pastor" means "shepherd," one who leads and cares for the flock of God.

When you compare the qualifications given here for bishops with those given for elders in Titus 1:5-9, you quickly see that the same office is in view. Church organization was quite simple in apostolic days: There were pastors (elders, bishops) and deacons (Phil. 1:1). It seems that there was a plurality of elders overseeing the work of each church, some involved in "ruling" (organization and government), others in teaching (1 Tim. 5:17).

But these men had to be qualified. It was good for a growing believer to aspire to the office of bishop, but the best way to achieve it was to develop Christian character and meet the following requirements. To become an elder/bishop was a serious decision, one not treated lightly in the early church. Paul gave sixteen qualifications for a man to meet if he expected to serve as an elder/bishop/pastor.

*Blameless (v. 2a).* This word literally means "nothing to hold upon"; that is, there must be nothing in his life that Satan or the unsaved can take hold of to criticize or attack the church. No man living is sinless, but we must strive to be blameless, or "above reproach" (NIV).

*The husband of one wife (v. 2b).* All of the qualifying adjectives in this passage are masculine. While there is ample scope for feminine ministry in a local assembly, the office of elder is not given to women. However, a pastor's homelife is very important, and especially his marital status. (This same requirement applies to deacons, according to 1 Tim. 3:12.) It means that a pastor must not be divorced and remarried. Paul was certainly not referring to polygamy, since no church member, let alone a pastor, would be accepted if he had more than one wife. Nor is he referring to remarriage after the death of the wife; for why would a pastor be prohibited from marrying again, in the light of Genesis 2:18 and 1 Timothy 4:3? Certainly the members of the church who had lost mates could marry again; so why penalize the pastor?

It's clear that a man's ability to manage his own marriage and home indicate ability to oversee a local church (1 Tim. 3:4-5). A pastor who has been divorced opens himself and the church to criticism from outsiders, and it is not likely that people with marital difficulties would consult a man who could not keep his own marriage together. I see no reason why *dedicated* Christians who have been divorced and remarried cannot serve in other offices in the church, but they are disqualified from being elders or deacons.

**Vigilant (v. 2c).** This means "temperate" or "sober." "Temperate in all things" (2 Tim. 4:5, literal translation). Or "keep your head in all situations" (NIV). A pastor needs to exercise sober, sensible judgment in all things.

**Sober (v. 2d).** He must have a serious attitude and be in earnest about his work. This does not mean he has no sense of humor, or that he is always solemn and somber. Rather it suggests that he knows the value of things and does not cheapen the ministry or the Gospel message by foolish behavior.

**Of good behavior (v. 2e).** "Orderly" would be a good translation. The pastor should be organized in his thinking and his living, as well as in his teaching and preaching. It is the same Greek word that is translated "modest" in 1 Timothy 2:9, referring to women's clothing.

**Given to hospitality (v. 2f).** Literally, "loving the stranger." This was an important ministry in the early church when traveling believers would need places to stay (Rom. 12:13; Heb. 13:2; 3 John 5-8). But even today, a pastor and wife who are hospitable are a great help to the fellowship of a local church.

**Apt to teach (v. 2g).** Teaching the Word

of God is one of an elder's main ministries. In fact, many scholars believe that "pastors and teachers" in Ephesians 4:11 refer to one person but to two functions. A pastor is automatically a teacher (2 Tim. 2:2, 24). Phillips Brooks, famous American bishop of the 1800s, said, "Apt to teach—it is not something to which one comes by accident or by any sudden burst of fiery zeal." A pastor must be a careful student of the Word of God, and of all that assists him in knowing and teaching that Word. The pastor who is lazy in his study is a disgrace in the pulpit.

**Not given to wine (v. 3a).** The word describes a person who sits long with the cup and thus drinks to excess. The fact that Paul advised Timothy to use wine for medicinal purposes (1 Tim. 5:23) indicates that total abstinence was not demanded of believers. Sad to say, some of the members of the Corinthian church got drunk, even at the love feast that accompanied the Lord's Supper (1 Cor. 11:21). The Jewish people diluted their wine with water to make sure it was not too strong. It was a well-known fact that water was not pure in those days, so that weak wine taken in moderation would have been healthier to drink.

However, there is a vast difference between the cultural use of wine in Bible days and supporting the alcohol industry of today. Paul's admonition and example in Romans 14 (especially Rom. 14:21) would apply today in a special way. A godly pastor would certainly want to give the best example and not be an excuse for sin in the life of some weaker brother.

**No striker (v. 3b).** "Not contentious, not looking for a fight." Charles Spurgeon told his Pastor's College students, "Don't go about the world with your fist doubled up for fighting, carrying a theological revolver in the leg of your trousers."

**Not greedy of filthy lucre (v. 3c).** Paul will have more to say about money in 1 Timothy 6:3ff. It is possible to use the ministry as an easy way to make money, if a man has no conscience or integrity. (Not that pastors are paid that much in most churches!) Covetous pastors always have "deals" going on outside their churches, and these activities erode their character and hinder their ministry. Pastors should "not [work] for filthy lucre" (1 Peter 5:2).

**Patient (v. 3d).** "Gentle" is a better translation. The pastor must listen to people and be able to take criticism without reacting. He should permit others to serve God in the church without dictating to them.

*Not a brawler (v. 3e).* Pastors must be peacemakers, not troublemakers. This does not mean they must compromise their convictions, but that they must "disagree" without being "disagreeable." Short tempers do not make for long ministries.

*Not covetous (v. 3f).* You can covet many things besides money: popularity, a large ministry that makes you famous, denominational advancement, etc. This word centers mainly on money.

*A godly family (vv. 4-5).* This does not mean that a pastor must be married, or, if married, must have children. However, marriage and a family are probably in the will of God for most pastors. If a man's own children cannot obey and respect him, then his church is not likely to respect and obey his leadership. For Christians, the church and the home are one. We should oversee both of them with love, truth, and discipline. The pastor cannot be one thing at home and something else in church. If he is, his children will detect it, and there will be problems. The words "rule" and "ruleth" in 1 Timothy 3:4-5 mean "to preside over, to govern," and suggest that a pastor is the one who directs the business of the church. (Not as a dictator, of course, but as a loving shepherd—1 Peter 5:3.) The word translated "take care of" in 1 Timothy 3:5 suggests a personal ministry to the needs of the church. It is used in the Parable of the Good Samaritan to describe the care given to the injured man (Luke 10:34-35).

*Not a novice (v. 6).* "Novice" literally means "one newly planted," referring to a young Christian. Age is no guarantee of maturity, but it is good for a man to give himself time for study and growth before he accepts a church. Some men mature faster than others, of course. Satan enjoys seeing a youthful pastor succeed and get proud; then Satan can tear down all that has been built up.

*A good testimony outside the church (v. 7).* Does he pay his bills? Does he have a good reputation among unsaved people with whom he does business? (see Col. 4:5 and 1 Thes. 4:12)

No pastor ever feels that he is all he ought to be, and his people need to pray for him constantly. It is not easy to serve as a pastor/elder, but it is much easier if your character is all God wants it to be.

## The Deacon (1 Tim. 3:8-13)

The English word *deacon* is a transliteration of the Greek word *diakonos*, which simply means "servant." It is likely that the origin of the deacons is recorded in Acts 6. The first deacons were appointed to be assistants to the Apostles. In a local church today deacons relieve the pastors/elders of other tasks so that they may concentrate on the ministry of the Word, prayer, and spiritual oversight.

Even though deacons are not given the authority of elders, they still must meet certain qualifications. Many faithful deacons have been made elders after they proved themselves.

*Grave (v. 8a).* A deacon should be worthy of respect, a man of Christian character worth imitating. A deacon should take his responsibilities seriously and *use* the office, not just *fill* it.

*Not double-tongued (v. 8b).* He does not tell tales from house to house; he is not a gossip. He does not say one thing to one member and something entirely opposite to another member. You can depend on what he says.

*Not given to much wine (v. 8c).* We have discussed this in our comments on 1 Timothy 3:3.

*Not greedy of filthy lucre (v. 8d).* Deacons handle offerings and distribute money to needy people in the church. It may be tempting to steal or to use funds in selfish ways. Finance committees in churches need to have a spiritual attitude toward money.

*Doctrinally sound (v. 9).* The word *mystery* means "truth once hidden but now revealed by God." The great doctrines of the faith are hidden to those outside the faith, but they can be understood by those who trust the Lord. Deacons must understand Christian doctrine and obey it with a good conscience. It is not enough to sit in meetings and decide how to "run the church." They must base their decisions on the Word of God, and they must back up their decisions with godly lives.

I have noticed that some church officers know their church constitutions better than they know the Word of God. While it is good to have bylaws and regulations that help maintain order, it is important to manage the affairs of a church on the basis of the Word of God. The Scriptures were the "constitution" of the early church! A deacon who does not know the Bible is an obstacle to progress in a local assembly.

A pastor friend of mine, now home with the Lord, took a church that was a split from another church and constantly at war with itself. From what he told me, their business meetings were something to behold! The church constitution was revered almost as much as the Bible. The people called it "the green book." My friend began to teach the people the Word of God, and the Spirit began to make changes in lives. But the enemy went to work and stirred up some officers to defy their pastor in a meeting.

"You aren't following the green book!" they said.

My friend lifted his Bible high and asked, "Are we going to obey the Word of God, or a green book written by men?" This was a turning point in the church, and then God blessed with wonderful growth and power.

A deacon who does not *know* the Word of God cannot manage the affairs of the church of God. A deacon who does not *live* the Word of God, but has a "defiled conscience," cannot manage the church of God. Simply because a church member is popular, successful in business, or generous in his giving does not mean he is qualified to serve as a deacon.

**Tested and proved (v. 10).** This implies watching their lives and seeing how they conduct themselves. In most churches, a new member or a new Christian may begin serving God in visitation, ushering, helping in Sunday School, and numerous other ways. This is the principle in Matthew 25:21: "Thou hast been faithful over a few things; I will make thee ruler over many things."

It is worth noting that quite a few leaders mentioned in the Bible were first tested as servants. Joseph was a servant in Egypt for thirteen years before he became a second ruler in the land. Moses cared for sheep for forty years before God called him. Joshua was Moses' servant before he became Moses' successor. David was tending his father's sheep when Samuel anointed him king of Israel. Even our Lord Jesus came as a servant and labored as a carpenter; and the Apostle Paul was a tentmaker. First a servant, then a ruler.

It always weakens the testimony of a local church when a member who has not been proved is made an officer of the church. "Maybe Jim will attend church more if we make him a deacon," is a statement that shows ignorance both of Jim and of the Word of God. *An untested Christian is an unprepared Christian.* He will probably do more harm than good if you give him an office in the church.

**Godly homes (vv. 11-12).** The deacon's wife is a part of his ministry, for godliness must begin at home. The deacons must not be men who have been divorced and remarried. Their wives must be Christians, women who are serious about the ministry, not given to slanderous talk (literally "not devils," for the word *devil* means "slanderer, false accuser"), and faithful in all that they do. It is sad to see the damage that is done to a local church when the wives of elders or deacons gossip and slander others.

Some students think that 1 Timothy 3:11 refers, not to the wives of deacons, but to another order of ministers—the deaconesses. Many churches do have deaconesses who assist with the women's work, in baptisms, in fellowship times, etc. Phebe was a deaconess from the church at Cenchrea (Rom. 16:1, where the word is *diakonon*). Perhaps in some of the churches, the wives of the deacons did serve as deaconesses. We thank God for the ministry of godly women in the local church, whether they hold offices or not! It is not necessary to hold an office to have a ministry or exercise a gift.

**A willingness to work (v. 13).** He is to *use* the office, not just *fill* it. The Greek word translated "degree" means "rank (as in the army), a base, a step, or rung on a ladder." What an encouragement to a faithful deacon! God will "promote" him spiritually and give him more and more respect among the saints, which means greater opportunity for ministry. A faithful deacon has a good standing before God and men, and can be used of God to build the church. He has a spiritual boldness that makes for effective ministry.

Certainly a part of this blessing could include the possibility of a "spiritual promotion." What a joy it is to a pastor to see deacons become elders, and then to see some of the elders called into pastoral ministry on a full-time basis. (It should be remembered that, in the New Testament churches, the elders were called from out of their own local congregations. They were not usually imported from other places.)

It is a serious matter to serve the local church. Each of us must search his own heart to be certain that he is qualified by the grace of God.

## The Believers (1 Tim. 3:14-16)

Elders, deacons, and church members need to be reminded of what a local church is. In this brief paragraph, Paul gave three pictures of the church.

**The house of God (v. 15a).** God's church is a family, so "household" might be a better translation. One of Paul's favorite words is "brethren" (see 1 Tim. 4:6). When a sinner believes in Jesus Christ as Saviour, he immediately is born again into God's family (John 1:11-13; 1 Peter 1:22-25). Paul advised young Timothy to treat the members of the local church as he would treat the members of his own family (1 Tim. 5:1-2).

Because the local church is a family, it must be fed; and the only diet that will nourish the people is the Word of God. It is our bread (Matt. 4:4), milk and meat (1 Cor. 3:1-2; Heb. 5:12-14), and honey (Ps. 119:103). A pastor must take time to nourish himself so that he might nourish others (1 Tim. 4:6). A church does not grow by addition, but by nutrition (Eph. 4:11-16). It is tragic to see the way some pastors waste their time (and their church's time) all week long and then have nothing nourishing to give the people on the Lord's Day.

Like a family, a church needs discipline in love. Children who are not disciplined become rebels and tyrants. The spiritual leaders of the assembly should exercise discipline (1 Cor. 4:18–5:13; 2 Cor. 2:6-11). Sometimes the children need rebuke; other times the discipline must be more severe.

Children also need encouragement and example (1 Thes. 2:7-12). Spiritual leaders must have the gentleness of a nursing mother and the strength of a loving father.

**The assembly (v. 15b).** The word *church* is a translation of the Greek word *ekklēsia* (ek-klay-SEE-a), which means "assembly." It referred to the political assemblies in the Greek cities (Acts 19:29, 32) where business was transacted by qualified citizens. But it is used about 100 times in the New Testament to refer to local churches, assemblies of believers. The Greek word means "those called out." (It is used in Acts 7:38 to describe the nation of Israel, called out of Egypt; but Israel was not a "church" in the New Testament sense.)

Paul wanted young Timothy to know how to "conduct himself" as a leader of a local assembly. The Pastoral Epistles are guidebooks for conduct of a local church. Scores of books have been published in recent years, purporting to tell us how to start, build, and increase a local church; and some of them contain good counsel. However, the best counsel for managing a local church is found in these three inspired letters. The young pastor in his first church, as well as the seasoned veteran in the ministry, should saturate himself with the teachings Paul shared with Timothy and Titus.

There are many different kinds of "assemblies," but the church is the assembly of the living God. Because it is God's assembly, He has the right to tell us how it ought to be governed. The church has been purchased with the blood of God's Son (Acts 20:28); therefore, we must be careful how we conduct ourselves. Church officers must not become religious dictators who abuse the people in order to achieve their own selfish ends (1 Peter 5:3-5; 3 John 9-12).

**The pillar and ground of the truth (vv. 15c-16).** This is an architectural image which would mean much to Timothy at Ephesus, for the great temple of Diana had 127 pillars. The word *ground* suggests a *bulwark* or a *stay*. The local church is built on Jesus Christ the Truth (John 14:6; 1 Cor. 3:9-15); but the local church is also itself a pillar and bulwark for the truth.

It is likely that the *pillar* aspect of the church's ministry relates primarily to displaying the truth of the Word, much as a statue is put on a pedestal so all can see it. We must hold "forth the Word of life" so the world can see it (Phil. 2:16). The local church puts Jesus Christ on display in the lives of faithful members.

As a *bulwark*, the church protects the truth and makes sure it does not fall (for elsewhere "truth is fallen in the street, and equity cannot enter"—Isa. 59:14). When local churches turn away from the truth (1 Tim. 4:1ff) and compromise in their ministry, then the enemy makes progress. Sometimes church leaders must take a militant stand against sin and apostasy. This does not make them popular, but it does please the Lord.

The main truth to which a church should bear witness is the person and work of Jesus Christ (1 Tim. 3:16—it is probable that this verse is quoted from an early Christian hymn). Jesus Christ was God *manifest in the flesh*, not only at His birth, but during His entire earthly ministry (John 14:1-9). Though His own people as a nation rejected Him, Jesus Christ was *vindicated in the Spirit;* for the Spirit empowered Him to do miracles and even to raise Himself from the dead (Rom.

1:4). The very presence of the Spirit in the world is itself a judgment on the world (John 16:7-11).

*Seen of angels* suggests the many times that the elect angels were associated with the life and ministry of our Lord. (The word *angelos,* translated "angels," also means "messengers." See James 2:25. Perhaps Paul was referring to the chosen messengers who witnessed the resurrected Christ.) However, Christ did not die for angels, but for lost sinners; and so He was *preached unto the nations.* This reminds us of the commissions the Lord gave to His church to carry the Gospel to the ends of the earth, where He is *believed on in the world.* At the Ascension, He was *received up in glory* (Acts 1:2, 22); and He will return one day to take His church to share that glory.

What an exciting challenge it is for your local church to witness of Jesus Christ to lost sinners at home and around the world!

# CHAPTER FOUR
# HOW TO BE A MAN OF GOD
*1 Timothy 4*

If you were to write a job description for your pastor, what would it contain? How would it compare with the description he might write? A pastor preaches regularly, performs weddings and other Christian services, visits the sick, and counsels the distressed. But what *is* his ministry, and what kind of person must he be to fulfill his God-given ministry?

In this section of his letter to Timothy, Paul emphasized the character and the work of the minister himself; and he listed three qualities that a minister must possess if he is to be successful in serving God.

## A Good Minister, Preaching the Word (1 Tim. 4:1-6)

Paul had warned the Ephesian elders that false teachers would invade the church (Acts 20:28-31); and now they had arrived. The Holy Spirit had spoken in specific terms about these teachers, and the prophecy was starting to be fulfilled in Paul's time. Certainly it is fulfilled in our own time! We can recognize false teachers by the description Paul gave in this paragraph.

**They are energized by Satan (v. 1a).** This is the only place where demons are mentioned in the Pastoral Epistles. Just as there is a "mystery of godliness" concerning Christ (1 Tim. 3:16), so there is a "mystery of iniquity" that surrounds Satan and his work (2 Thes. 2:7). Satan is an imitator (2 Cor. 11:13-15); he has his own ministers and doctrines, and seeks to deceive God's people and lead them astray (2 Cor. 11:3). The first test of any religious doctrine is what it says about Jesus Christ (1 John 4:1-6).

It comes as a shock to some people that Satan uses professed Christians *in the church* to accomplish his work. But Satan once used Peter to try to lead Jesus on a wrong path (Matt. 16:21-23), and he used Ananias and Sapphira to try to deceive the church at Jerusalem (Acts 5). Paul warned that false teachers would arise *from within the church* (Acts 20:30).

**They lead people astray (v. 1b).** Their goal is to seduce people and get them to depart from the faith. This is the word *apostasy,* and it is defined as "a willful turning away from the truth of the Christian faith." These false teachers do not try to build up the church or relate people to the Lord Jesus Christ in a deeper way. Instead they want to get disciples to follow them and join their groups and promote their programs. This is one difference between a true church and a religious cult: A true church seeks to win converts to Jesus Christ and to build them spiritually; conversely, a cult proselytizes, steals converts from others, and makes them servants (even slaves!) of the leaders of the cult. However, not all apostates are in cults; some of them are in churches *and pulpits,* teaching false doctrine and leading people astray.

**They are hypocrites (v. 2).** "Ye shall know them by their fruits" (Matt. 7:15-20). These false teachers preach one thing but practice another. They tell their disciples what to do, but they do not do it themselves. Satan works "by means of the hypocrisy of liars" (1 Tim. 4:2, literal translation). One of the marks of a true servant of God is his honesty and integrity: He practices what he preaches. This does not mean he is sinlessly perfect, but that he sincerely seeks to obey the Word of God. He tries to maintain a good conscience (see 1 Tim. 1:5, 19; 3:9).

The word *seared* means "cauterized." Just as a person's flesh can be "branded" so that it becomes hard and without feeling, so a person's conscience can be deadened. Whenever we affirm with our lips something that we deny with our lives (whether people know it or not), we deaden our consciences just a little more. Jesus made it clear that it is not religious talk or even performing miracles that qualifies a person for heaven, but doing God's will in everyday life (Matt. 7:21-29).

An apostate is not just wrong doctrinally; he is wrong morally. His personal life became wrong before his doctrines were changed. In fact, it is likely that he changed his teachings so that he could continue his sinful living and pacify his conscience. *Believing* and *behaving* always go together.

**They deny God's Word (vv. 3-5).** The false teachers in Ephesus combined Jewish legalism with Eastern asceticism. You find Paul dealing with this same false doctrine in his Letter to the Colossians (Col. 2:8-23 especially). For one thing, the false teachers taught that an unmarried life was more spiritual than a married life, which is contrary to Scripture. "It is not good that the man should be alone" are God's own words (Gen. 2:18). Jesus put His seal of approval on marriage (Matt. 19:1-9), though He pointed out that not everybody is supposed to marry (Matt. 19:10-12). Paul also affirmed the biblical basis for marriage (1 Cor. 7:1-24), teaching that each person should follow the will of God in the matter.

Beware of any religious teaching that tampers with God's institution of marriage. And beware of any teaching that tampers with God's creation. The false teachers who were infecting the Ephesian church taught that certain foods were taboo; if you ate them, you were not spiritual. The fact that God called His own Creation "good" (Gen. 1:10, 12, 18, 21, 25) did not interest these teachers. Their authority to dictate diets gave them power over their converts.

Those who "believe and know the truth" are not impressed with the do's and don'ts of the legalists. Jesus stated that all foods are clean (Mark 7:14-23). He taught this lesson again to Peter (Acts 10), and reaffirmed it through Paul (1 Cor. 10:23-33). A person may not be able to eat certain foods for physical reasons (an allergy, for example); but no food is to be rejected for spiritual reasons. We should not, however, use our freedom to eat and drink to destroy weaker Christians (Rom. 14:13-23). The food we eat is sanctified (set apart, devoted to God) when we pray and give thanks; so the Word of God and prayer turn even an ordinary meal into a spiritual service for God's glory (1 Cor. 10:31).

The emphasis in a minister's life should be on "the Word of God and prayer" (1 Tim. 4:5). It is tragic when a church keeps its pastors so busy with menial tasks that they have hardly any time for God's Word and prayer (Acts 6:1-7). Paul reminded young Timothy of his great responsibility to study, teach, and preach the Scriptures, and to spend time in prayer. As a "good minister" he must be "nourished up in the words of faith" (1 Tim. 4:6). Timothy had certain responsibilities in the light of this growing apostasy:

**Teach the church the truth (v. 6a).** God's people need to be warned about false doctrine and religious apostasy. A minister must not major on these subjects, because he is obligated to teach "all the counsel of God" (Acts 20:27); but neither should he ignore them. As we travel the streets and highways, we see two kinds of signs: those that tell us where we are going ("Boston 45 miles") and those that warn us of possible dangers ("Bridge Out!"). A pastor must teach positive doctrine so that people will know what they believe and where they are going. But he must also expose false doctrine so that people will not be seduced and led astray.

**He must nourish himself in the Word (v. 6b).** Of course, *every* Christian ought to feed daily on the Word (Jer. 15:16; Matt. 4:4; 1 Peter 2:2); but it is especially important that a pastor grow in the Word. It is by daily studying the "good doctrine" and meditating on the Word that he grows in the Lord and is able to lead the church.

The "good minister" preaches the Word that he himself feeds on day by day. But it is not enough to preach the Word; he must also practice it.

## A Godly Minister, Practicing the Word (1 Tim. 4:7-12)

Paul shifted to an athletic illustration at this point in his letter. Just as a Greek or Roman athlete had to refuse certain things, eat the right food, and do the right exercises, so a Christian should practice "spiritual exercise." If a Christian puts as much energy and discipline into his spiritual life as an athlete does into his game, the Christian grows faster and accomplishes much more for God. Paul discussed in this section three levels of life.

**The bad—"profane and old wives' fables" (v. 7a).** These are, of course, the false teachings and traditions of the apostates. These doctrines have no basis in Scripture; in fact, they contradict the Word of God. They are the kind of teachings that silly people would discuss, not dedicated men and women of the Word! No doubt these teachings involved the false doctrines just named (1 Tim. 4:2-3). Paul also warned Titus about "Jewish fables" (Titus 1:14). Paul warned Timothy about these same "fables" in his second letter (2 Tim. 4:4).

A believer cannot rediscover new doctrines. Paul admonished Timothy to remain true to "the good doctrine which you have closely followed up to now" (1 Tim. 4:6b, literal translation). He warned him not to "give heed to fables and endless genealogies" (1 Tim. 1:4). While a pastor must know what the enemy is teaching, he must not be influenced by it. A chemist may handle and study poisons, but he does not permit them to get into his system.

**The temporary—"bodily exercise" (vv. 7-8).** Again, this is an athletic image. Certainly we ought to care for our bodies, and exercise is a part of that care. Our bodies are God's temples, to be used for His glory (1 Cor. 6:19-20), and His tools for His service (Rom. 12:1-2). But bodily exercise benefits us only during this life; godly exercise is profitable now and for eternity. Paul did not ask Timothy to choose between the two; I think God expects us to practice both. A healthy body can be used of God, but we must major on holiness.

**The eternal—"godliness" (vv. 7-12).** Phillips Brooks said, "The great purpose of life—the shaping of character by truth." Godly character and conduct are far more important than golf trophies or home-run records, though it is possible for a person to have both. Paul challenged Timothy to be as devoted to godliness as an athlete is to his sport. We are living and laboring for eternity.

Paul used two similar athletic images in writing to the Corinthians (1 Cor. 9:24-27), emphasizing the disciplines necessary for godly living. As an athlete must control his body and obey the rules, so a Christian must make his body his servant and not his master. When

I see high school football squads and baseball teams going through their calisthenics under the hot summer sun, I am reminded that there are spiritual exercises that I ought to be doing (Heb. 5:14). Prayer, meditation, self-examination, fellowship, service, sacrifice, submission to the will of others, witness—all of these can assist me, through the Spirit, to become a more godly person.

Spiritual exercise is not easy; we must "labor and suffer reproach" (1 Tim. 4:10a). "For this we labor and strive" (NIV). The word translated "strive" is an athletic word from which we get our English word *agonize*. It is the picture of an athlete straining and giving his best to win. A Christian who wants to excel must really work at it, by the grace of God and to the glory of God.

But exercising ourselves in godly living is not only profitable for us; it is also profitable for others (1 Tim. 4:11-12). It enables us to be good examples, so that we encourage others. Paul named several areas of life in which you and I should be examples.

"In word" (1 Tim. 4:12) implies that our speech should always be honest and loving, "speaking the truth in love" (Eph. 4:15).

"In conduct" (the KJV's "conversation" means "walk," not "talk") suggests that our lives are to be controlled by the Word of God. We must not be like the hypocrites Paul described to Titus (Titus 1:16): "They profess that they know God; but in works they deny Him."

"In love" (charity) points to the motivation of our lives. We do not obey God to be applauded by men (Matt. 6:1ff), but because we love God and love God's people.

("In spirit" is not in many manuscripts, but it would describe the inner enthusiasm and excitement of a child of God.)

"In faith" implies that we trust God and are faithful to Him. Faith and love often go together (1 Tim. 1:14; 2:15; 6:11; 2 Tim. 1:13; 2:22). Faith always leads to faithfulness.

"In purity" is important as we live in this present evil world. Ephesus was a center for sexual impurity, and the young man Timothy was faced with temptations. He must have a chaste relationship to the women in the church (1 Tim. 5:2) and keep himself pure in mind, heart, and body.

But godly living not only helps *us* and *other believers;* it also has its influence on *the lost.* Paul reminded pastor Timothy that Jesus Christ is the Saviour (1 Tim. 4:10), and it is the believer's task to share that Good News with the lost. In effect he wrote, "We Christians have fixed our hope in the living God, but the lost have no hope and do not know the living God. All that many of them know are the dead idols that can never save them."

The title "Saviour of all men" does not imply that everybody will be saved (universalism), or that God saves people in spite of themselves; for Paul added "specially of those that believe." It is faith that saves one's soul (Eph. 2:8-10). Since God "will have all men to be saved" (1 Tim. 2:4), and since Christ "gave Himself a ransom for all" (1 Tim. 2:6), then *any* lost sinner can trust Christ and be saved. Christ is "the Saviour of all men," so nobody need despair.

Timothy should not fear to practice the Word of God and apply it to the life of the church, for this Word is "a faithful saying and worthy of all acceptation" (1 Tim. 4:9). These faithful sayings made up a summary of truth for the early church (see 1 Tim. 1:15; 3:1; 2 Tim. 2:11; Titus 3:8). The fact that Timothy was a young man (the word then applied to a person from youth to forty) should not deter him from practicing the Word. In fact, he was to "command" these things, and this is our military word "charge" (1 Tim. 1:3). The local church is a unit in God's spiritual army, and its leaders are to pass God's orders along to the people with authority and conviction.

## A Growing Minister, Progressing in the Word (1 Tim. 4:13-16)

The key thought in this section is "that thy profiting may appear to all" (1 Tim. 4:15). The word *profiting* ("progress," NIV) is a Greek military term; it means "pioneer advance." It describes the soldiers who go ahead of the troops, clear away the obstacles, and make it possible for others to follow. As a godly pastor, Timothy was to grow spiritually so that the whole church could see his spiritual progress and imitate it.

No pastor can lead his people where he has not been himself. "Such as I have, give I thee" is a basic principle of life and ministry (Acts 3:6). The pastor (or church member) who is not growing is actually going backward, for it is impossible to stand still in the Christian life. In his living, teaching, preaching, and leading, the minister must give evidence of spiritual growth. But what are factors that make spiritual progress possible?

*Emphasize God's Word (v. 13).* "Give attendance to" means "devote yourself to, be absorbed in." Ministering the Word was not something Timothy was to do after he had done other things; it was to be the most important thing he did. *Reading* means the public reading of Scripture in the local assembly. The Jewish people always had the reading of the Law and the Prophets in their synagogues, and this practice carried over into Christian churches. Jesus read the Scriptures in the synagogue at Nazareth (Luke 4:16ff), and Paul often read the lessons when he visited a synagogue (Acts 13:15).

In my itinerant ministry, I have noted that many churches have dispensed with the public reading of God's Word; and I am disappointed. They have time for "special music" and endless announcements, but there is no time for the reading of the Bible. The pastor may read a text before he preaches, but that is a different thing. Every local church ought to have a schedule of Bible readings for the public services. It is commanded by Scripture that we read God's Word in the public assemblies. (I might add that those who read the Word publicly ought to prepare themselves privately. Nobody should be asked "at the last minute" to read the Scriptures publicly. The Bible deserves the best we can give.)

*Exhortation* (1 Tim. 4:13) literally means "encouragement" and suggests the applying of the Word to the lives of the people. The pastor was to read the Word, explain it, and apply it. *Doctrine* means "teaching," and is a major emphasis in the pastoral letters. There are at least twenty-two references to "teaching" or "doctrine" in these thirteen chapters.

"Apt to teach" is one of the qualifications of a minister (1 Tim. 3:2); and it has been correctly said, "Apt to teach implies apt to learn." A growing minister (or church member) must be a student of the Word. Before he teaches others he must teach himself (Rom. 2:21). His spiritual progress is an example to his flock and an encouragement to others.

*Use your spiritual gifts (v. 14).* So much has been written in recent years about spiritual gifts that we have almost forgotten the *graces* of the Spirit (Gal. 5:22-23). The word *gift* is the Greek word *charisma.* It simply means "a gracious gift from God." (The world uses the word *charisma* to describe a person with magnetic personality and commanding appearance.) *Every Christian* has the gift of the Spirit (Rom. 8:9) and at least one gift from the Spirit (1 Cor. 12:1-11). The gift of the Spirit, and the gifts from the Spirit, are bestowed by God at the moment of conversion (see 1 Cor. 12:13ff).

However, when God calls a believer into a special place of ministry, He can (and often does) impart a spiritual gift for that task. When Timothy was ordained by the elders ("presbytery"), he received an enabling gift from God when the elders laid hands on him. But for some reason, Timothy had neglected to cultivate this gift which was so necessary to his spiritual progress and ministry. In fact, Paul had to admonish him in his second letter, "Stir up the gift of God, which is in thee by the putting on of my hands" (2 Tim. 1:6).

It is encouraging to know that the God who calls us also equips us to do His work. We have nothing in ourselves that enables us to serve Him; the ministry must all come from God (1 Cor. 15:9-10; Phil. 4:13; 1 Tim. 1:12). However, we must not be passive; we must cultivate God's gifts, use them, and develop them in the ministry of the local church and wherever God puts us.

*Devote yourself fully to Christ (v. 15).* "Meditate" carried the idea of "be in them, give yourself totally to them." Timothy's spiritual life and ministry were to be the absorbing, controlling things in his life, not merely sidelines that he occasionally practiced. There can be no real pioneer advance in one's ministry without total dedication to the task. "No man can serve two masters" (Matt. 6:24).

While I do not want to sound critical, I must confess that I am disturbed by the fact that too many pastors and Christian workers divide their time and interest between the church and some sideline. It may be real estate, trips to the Holy Land, politics, civic duties, even denominational service. Their own spiritual lives suffer, and their churches suffer, because these men are not devoting themselves wholly to their ministry. "This one thing I do" was Paul's controlling motive, and it ought to be ours too (Phil. 3:13). "A double-minded man is unstable in all his ways" (James 1:8).

*Take spiritual inventory (v. 16).* Examine your own heart in the light of the Word of God. Note that Paul put "thyself" ahead of "the doctrine." Paul had given this same warning to the Ephesian elders in his farewell message: "Take heed therefore unto yourselves" (Acts 20:28). A servant of God can be so busy helping others that he neglects himself and his own spiritual walk.

The great American evangelist of the 1800s, Charles Finney, used to preach on this text. He titled his sermon "Preacher, Save Thyself!" That sermon is needed today, for we are seeing people having to leave the ministry because their lives have not kept up with their profession. Moral problems, divorces, and other kinds of shameful conduct have destroyed many of God's servants. "Let him that thinketh he standeth take heed lest he fall" (1 Cor. 10:12).

The building up of the saved and the winning of the lost are the purposes for our ministry, to the glory of God. But God must work *in* us before He can effectively work *through* us (Phil. 2:12-13). As good ministers, we preach the Word; as godly ministers, we practice the Word; as growing ministers, we progress in the Word.

# CHAPTER FIVE
# ORDER IN THE CHURCH!
*1 Timothy 5*

The first problem the early church faced was also a modern one: A group of church members was neglected by the ministering staff (Acts 6). I once heard a certain pastor described as "a man who is invisible during the week and incomprehensible on Sunday." Again, somebody in his congregation was feeling neglected.

Then Paul instructed Timothy how to minister to specific groups in his church.

**The Older Members (1 Tim. 5:1-2)**
Paul admonished Timothy to minister to the various kinds of people in the church, and not to show partiality (1 Tim. 5:21). Since Timothy was a younger man, he might be tempted to ignore the older members; so Paul urged him to love and serve all of the people, regardless of their ages. The church is a family: Treat the older members like your mother and father, and the younger members like your brothers and sisters.

## The Old Widows (1 Tim. 5:3-10)

From the beginning of its ministry, the church had a concern for believing widows (Acts 6:1; 9:39). Of course, the nation of Israel had sought to care for widows; and God had given special legislation to protect them (Deut. 10:18; 24:17; Isa. 1:17). God's special care for the widows is a recurring theme in Scripture (Deut. 14:29; Ps. 94:6; Mal. 3:5). It was only right that the local church show compassion to these women who were in need.

However, the church must be careful not to waste its resources on people who really are not in need. Whether we like to admit it or not, there are individuals and entire families that "milk" local churches, while they themselves refuse to work or to use their own resources wisely. As long as they can get handouts from the church, why bother to go to work?

Paul listed the qualifications a widow must meet if she is to be supported by the church.

*Without human support (vv. 5a, 8, "desolate").* If a widow had relatives they should care for her so that the church might use its money to care for others who have no help. If her own children were dead, then her grandchildren (the KJV translates them "nephews" in 1 Tim. 5:4) should accept the responsibility. When you recall that society in that day did not have the kind of institutions we have today—pensions, Social Security, retirement homes, etc.—you can see how important family care really was. Of course, the presence of such institutions *today* does not relieve any family of its loving obligations. "Honor thy father and thy mother" is still in the Bible (Ex. 20:12; Eph. 6:1-3).

Suppose a relative is unwilling to help support his loved one? "He . . . is worse than an unbeliever!" was Paul's judgment (1 Tim. 5:8, NIV; also see v. 16). A missionary friend of mine, now with the Lord, came home from the field to care for her sick and elderly parents. She was severely criticized by some of her associates ("We should love God more than father and mother!"), but she remained faithful to the end. Then she returned to the field for years of fruitful service, knowing she had obeyed God. After all, we love God by loving His people; and He has a special concern for the elderly, the widows, and the orphans.

*A believer with a faithful testimony (vv. 5b-7).* The church could not care for *all* the widows in the city, but it should care for believers who are a part of the fellowship. We should "do good unto all . . . especially unto them who are of the household of faith" (Gal. 6:10). A widow the church helps should not be a self-indulgent person, seeking pleasure, but a godly woman who hopes in God and has a ministry of intercession and prayer. See Luke 2:36-37 for an example of a godly widow.

It has been my experience in three different pastorates that godly widows are "spiritual powerhouses" in the church. They are the backbone of the prayer meetings. They give themselves to visitation, and they swell the ranks of teachers in the Sunday School. It has also been my experience that, if a widow is *not* godly, she can be a great problem to the church. She will demand attention, complain about what the younger people do, and often "hang on the telephone" and gossip. (Of course, it is not really "gossip." She only wants her friends to be able to "pray more intelligently" about these matters!) Paul made it clear (1 Tim. 5:7) that church-helped widows must be "blameless"—irreproachable.

*At least sixty years old (v. 9a).* A woman of this age was not likely to get remarried in that day, though sixty is not considered that "old" today. Perhaps the verb "taken into the number" gives us a clue. It literally means "to be enrolled and put on the list." The word was used for the enrollment of soldiers. The early church had an official list of the names of qualified widows, and we get the impression that these "enlisted" women ministered to the congregation in various ways. (Remember Dorcas and her widow friends, Acts 9:36-43?) Paul probably would have told us if they had been officially ordained as deaconesses.

*A good marriage record (v. 9b).* We have met this same requirement before, for bishops (1 Tim. 3:2) and for deacons (1 Tim. 3:12). The implication is that the widow was not a divorced woman. Since younger widows were advised to remarry (1 Tim. 5:14), this stipulation cannot refer to a woman who had a temporary second marriage after the death of her husband. Faithfulness to one's marriage vows is very important in the eyes of God.

*A witness of good works (v. 10).* If a person is faithfully serving God, the light will shine and others will see it and glorify God (Matt. 5:16). "Brought up children" can refer either to a widow's own children or the reference may be to orphans who needed a home. If it refers to her own children, then they would have to have died; otherwise the church would not support her. It is likely that the reference here is to the practice of rescuing abandoned children and raising them to know the Lord.

Hospitality is another factor, for this was an important ministry in those days when travel was dangerous and safe places to sleep were scarce. The washing of feet does not refer to a special ritual, but to the common practice of washing a guest's feet when he arrived in the home (Luke 7:44). It was not beneath this woman's dignity to take the place of a humble servant.

"Relieved the afflicted" could cover many kinds of ministry to the needy: feeding the hungry, caring for the sick, encouraging the sorrowing, etc. Every pastor gives thanks for godly women who minister to the material and physical needs in the church. These widows were cared for by the church, but they, in turn, helped to care for the church.

### The Younger Widows (1 Tim. 5:11-16)

The younger widows would technically be women under sixty years of age, but no doubt Paul had much younger women in mind. It was not likely that a fifty-nine-year-old woman would "bear children" if she remarried! (1 Tim. 5:14) The dangers of travel, the ravages of disease, war, and a host of other things could rob a young wife of her husband. But Paul forbade Timothy to enroll the younger widows and put them under the care of the church.

*The reasons for refusing them (vv. 11-14a).* Because of their age, younger widows are naturally attracted to men and want to marry again. What is so bad about that? Paul seems to imply (1 Tim. 5:12) that each of the widows enrolled pledged herself to remain a widow and serve the Lord in the church. This pledge must not be interpreted as a "vow of celibacy," nor should we look on this group of ministering widows as a "special monastic order." There seemed to be an agreement between the widows and the church that they would remain widows and serve the Lord.

There is another possible interpretation: These younger widows, if supported by the church, would have opportunities to "live it up" and find other husbands, most likely unbelievers. By marrying unbelievers, they would be casting off their first faith. However, I prefer the first explanation.

Paul does make it clear (1 Tim. 5:13) that younger widows, if cared for by the church, would have time on their hands and get involved in sinful activities. They would get in the habit of being idle instead of being useful. They would gad about from house to house and indulge in gossip and be busybodies. There is a definite connection between idleness and sin.

Paul warned Timothy against using the "charity" ministry of the church to encourage people to be idle. The church certainly ought to assist those who really need help, but it must not subsidize sin. As a pastor, I have had to make decisions in these matters, and sometimes it is not easy.

*Requirements for younger widows (vv. 14b-16).* Moving from the negative, Paul listed the positive things he wanted the younger widows to do to be accepted and approved in the church. He wanted the younger widows to marry and have families. While not every person is supposed to get married, marriage is natural for most people who have been married before. Why remain in lonely widowhood if there was yet opportunity for a husband and a family? Of course, all of this would have to be "in the Lord" (1 Cor. 7:39).

"Be fruitful and multiply" was God's mandate to our first parents (Gen. 1:28), so the normal result of marriage is a family. Those today who refuse to have children because of the "awfulness of the times" should check out how difficult the times were in Paul's day! If *Christians* do not have children and raise them to live for God, who will?

"Guide the house" (1 Tim. 5:14) literally means "rule the house." The wife should manage the affairs of the household, and her husband should trust her to do so (Prov. 31:10-31). Of course, marriage is a partnership; but each partner has a special sphere of responsibility. Few men can do in a home what a woman can do. Whenever my wife was ill, or caring for our babies, and I had to manage some of the affairs of the home, I discovered quickly that I was out of my sphere of ministry!

The result of all this is a good testimony that silences the accusers. Satan (the adversary) is always alert to an opportunity to invade and destroy a Christian home. The word *occasion* is a military term that means "a base of operations." A Christian wife who is not doing her job at home gives Satan a beachhead for his operations, and the results are tragic. While there are times when a Christian wife and mother may have to work outside the home, it must not destroy her ministry in the home. The wife who works simply to get luxuries may discover too late that she has lost some necessities. It may be all right to have what money can buy *if* you do not lose what money cannot buy.

How Christian wives and mothers manage their homes can be a testimony to those outside the church. Just as a pastor is to have a good reputation with outsiders (1 Tim. 3:7), and the servants are not to bring reproach on God's Word (1 Tim. 6:1), so the wives are to have a good witness. Women may not be able to be elders of the church, but they can minister for the Lord right in their own homes. (See Titus 2:4-5 for an additional emphasis on this vital ministry.)

Paul then summarized the principle of each family caring for the needs of its own members (1 Tim. 5:16). Paul did not tell them *how* these widows should be relieved—giving them a regular dole, taking them into a home, giving them employment, etc. Each local assembly would have to decide this according to the needs of individual cases.

How does this principle apply to Christians today? Certainly we must honor our parents and grandparents and seek to provide for them if they have needs. Not every Christian family is able to take in another member, and not every widow wants to live with her children. Where there is sickness or handicap, professional care is necessary, and perhaps this cannot be given in a home. Each family must decide what God's will is in the matter, and no decision is easy. The important thing is that believers show love and concern and do all they can to help each other.

## Church Officers (1 Tim. 5:17-25)

The instructions in this section deal primarily with the elders, but the principles also apply to a pastor's relationship with any officer in his church. It is a wonderful thing when the elders and deacons (and other officers) work together in harmony and love. It is tragic when a pastor tries to become a spiritual dictator (1 Peter 5:3), or when an officer tries to be a preeminent "big shot" (3 John 9-10).

Apparently Timothy was having some problems with the elders of the church at Ephesus. He was a young man and still had much to learn. Ephesus was not an easy place to minister. Furthermore, Timothy had followed Paul as overseer of the church, and Paul would not be an easy man to follow! Paul's farewell address to the Ephesian elders (Acts 20) shows how hard he had worked and how faithful he had been, and how much the elders loved Paul (Acts 20:36-38). In spite of the fact that Paul had personally sent Timothy to Ephesus, the young man was having a hard time.

This situation may be the reason for Paul's instruction about wine (1 Tim. 5:23). Did Timothy have stomach trouble? Was he ill because of his many responsibilities and problems? Or had he tried to follow the ideas of some ascetics (1 Tim. 4:1-5), only to discover that his diet was making him worse instead of better? We do not know the answers to all these questions; we can only read between the lines. It is worth noting that Paul's mention of wine here is not an endorsement of the entire alcohol industry. Using wine for medicinal reasons is not an encouragement for social drinking. As we have seen, though the Bible does not demand total abstinence, it does denounce drunkenness.

Paul counseled Timothy in his relationship to the elders by discussing three topics:

***Paying the elders (vv. 17-18).*** In the early church, instead of one pastor, several elders ministered to the people. These men would devote themselves full-time to the work of the Lord, and, therefore, they deserved some kind of remuneration. In most congregations today, the elders are laymen who have other vocations, but who assist in the work of the church. Usually the pastoral staff are the only full-time workers in the church. (Of course, there are also secretaries, custodians, etc., but Paul was not writing about them.)

There were two kinds of elders in the church: *ruling elders* who supervised the work of the congregation; and *teaching elders* who taught the Word of God. These elders were chosen from the congregation on the basis of God's call, the Spirit's equipping, and the witness and work of the men themselves. After they were chosen, they were ordained and set apart for this ministry (Acts 14:23; 20:17, 28; Titus 1:5).

The local church needs both ruling and teaching. The Spirit gives the gifts of "helps" and "governments" to the church (1 Cor. 12:28). If a church is not organized, there will be wasted effort, money, and opportunities. If spiritually minded leaders do not supervise the various ministries of the local church, there will be chaos instead of order. However, this supervision must not be dictatorial. You do not manage the work of a local church in the same manner as you do a grocery store or a manufacturing plant. While a church should follow good business principles, it is not a business. The ruthless way some church leaders have pushed people around is a disgrace to the Gospel.

But ruling without teaching would accomplish very little. The local church grows through the ministry of the Word of God (Eph. 4:11ff). You cannot rule over babies! Unless the believers are fed, cleansed, and strengthened by the Word, they will be weak and useless and will only create problems.

Paul told Timothy to be sure that the leaders were paid adequately, on the basis of their ministries. He quoted an Old Testament law to prove his point (Deut. 25:4). (The best commentary on this is 1 Cor. 9:7-14.) Then Paul added a statement from our Lord Jesus Christ: "The laborer deserves his wages" (Luke 10:7, NIV). This was a common saying in that day, but Paul equated the words of Christ with Old Testament Scripture!

If pastors are faithful in feeding and leading the people, then the church ought to be faithful and pay them adequately. "Double honor" (1 Tim. 5:17) can be translated "generous pay." (The word *honor* is used as in "honorarium.") It is God's plan that the needs of His servants be met by their local churches; and He will bless churches that are faithful to His servants. If a church is not faithful, and its pastor's needs are not met, it is a poor testimony; and God has ways of dealing with the situation. He can provide through other means, but then the church misses the blessing; or He may move His servant elsewhere.

The other side of the coin is this: A pastor must never minister simply to earn money (see 1 Tim. 3:3). To "negotiate" with churches, or to canvass around looking for a place with a bigger salary is not in the will of God. Nor is it right for a pastor to bring into his sermons his own financial needs, hoping to arouse some support from the finance committee!

**Disciplining the elders (vv. 19-21).** Church discipline usually goes to one of two extremes. Either there is no discipline at all, and the church languishes because of disobedience and sin. Or the church officers become evangelical policemen who hold a kangaroo court and violate many of the Bible's spiritual principles.

The disciplining of church *members* is explained in Matthew 18:15-18; Romans 16:17-18; 1 Corinthians 5; 2 Corinthians 2:6-11; Galatians 6:1-3; 2 Thessalonians 3:6-16; 2 Timothy 2:23-26; Titus 3:10; and 2 John 9-11.

Paul in this passage (1 Tim. 5:19-21) discussed the disciplining of church *leaders*. It is sad when a church member must be disciplined, but it is even sadder when a spiritual leader fails and must be disciplined; for leaders, when they fall, have a way of affecting others.

The purpose of discipline is restoration, not revenge. Our purpose must be to save the offender, not to drive him away. Our attitude must be one of love and tenderness (Gal. 6:1-3). In fact the verb *restore* that Paul used in Galatians 6:1 means "to set a broken bone." Think of the patience and tenderness involved in that procedure!

Paul's first caution to Timothy was to *be sure of his facts,* and the way to do that is to have witnesses (1 Tim. 5:19). This principle is also stated in Deuteronomy 19:15; Matthew 18:16; and 2 Corinthians 13:1. I think a dual application of the principle is suggested here. First, those who make any accusation against a pastor must be able to support it with witnesses. Rumor and suspicion are not adequate grounds for discipline. Second, when an accusation is made, witnesses ought to be present. In other words, the accused has the right to face his accuser in the presence of witnesses.

A church member approached me at a church dinner one evening, and began to accuse me of ruining the church. She had all sorts of miscellaneous bits of gossip, none of which was true. As soon as she started her tirade, I asked two of the officers standing nearby to witness what she was saying. Of course, she immediately stopped talking and marched defiantly away.

It is sad when churches disobey the Word and listen to rumors, lies, and gossip. Many a godly pastor has been defeated in his life and ministry in this way, and some have even resigned from the ministry. "Where there's smoke, there's fire" may be a good slogan for a volunteer fire department, but it does not apply to local churches. "Where there's smoke, there's fire" could possibly mean that somebody's tongue has been "set on fire of hell!" (James 3:6)

Paul's second caution was that Timothy do everything openly and aboveboard. The under-the-counter politics of city hall have no place in a church. "In secret have I said nothing," said Jesus (John 18:20). If an officer *is* guilty, then he should be rebuked before all the other leaders (1 Tim. 5:20). He should be given opportunity to repent, and if he does he should be forgiven (2 Cor. 2:6-11). Once he is forgiven, the matter is settled and should never be brought up again.

Paul's third caution (1 Tim. 5:21) is that Timothy obey the Word no matter what his personal feelings might be. He should act without prejudice *against* or partiality *for* the accused officer. There are no seniority rights in a local church; each member has the same standing before God and His Word. To show either prejudice or partiality is to make the situation even worse.

**Selecting and ordaining the elders (vv. 22-25).** Only God knows the hearts of everyone (Acts 1:24). The church needs spiritual wisdom and guidance in selecting its officers. It is dangerous to impulsively place a new Christian or a new church member in a place of spiritual responsibility. Some people's sins are clearly seen; others are able to cover their sins, though their sins pursue them (1 Tim. 5:24). The good works of dedicated believers ought to be evident, even though they do not serve in order to be seen by people (1 Tim. 5:25).

In other words, the church must carefully investigate the lives of potential leaders to make sure that there is nothing seriously wrong. To ordain elders with sin in their lives is to partake of those sins! If simply saying "Good-bye" (God be with you) to a heretic makes us partakers of his evil deeds (2 John 10-11), then how much guiltier are we if we ordain people whose lives are not right with God?

No pastor or church member is perfect, but that should not hinder us from striving for perfection. The ministry of a local church rises and falls with its leadership. Godly leadership means God's blessing, and that is what we want and need.

# CHAPTER SIX
# ORDERS FROM HEADQUARTERS
*1 Timothy 6*

This chapter continues Paul's advice to Timothy on ministering to the various kinds of believers in the church.

The atmosphere is military, for Paul used words that belong to the army: "Fight the good fight of faith" (1 Tim. 6:12). "I give thee charge" (1 Tim. 6:13, which is the same military term used in 1:3). "Charge them that are rich" (1 Tim. 6:17). "O Timothy, keep [guard] that which is committed to thy trust" (1 Tim. 6:20). In other words, you might say Paul was the general, giving Timothy orders from the Lord, the Commander in Chief.

D.L. Moody did not want his soloist, Ira Sankey, to use "Onward, Christian Soldiers" in their evangelistic campaigns. Moody felt that the church he saw was very *un*like an army. If the average military man on our side in World War II had behaved toward his superiors and their orders the way the average Christian behaves toward the Lord, we probably would have lost the war! Instead of "Onward, Christian Soldiers," someone has suggested that perhaps we ought to sing "Backward, Christian Soldiers."

Paul instructed Timothy how to minister to four more groups in the church, and also how to keep his own life in the will of God.

## Christian Slaves (1 Tim. 6:1-2)

Some historians have estimated that half of the population of the Roman Empire was composed of slaves. Many of these people were educated and cultured, but legally they were not considered persons at all. The Gospel message of salvation and freedom in Christ appealed to the slaves, and many of them became believers. (The word translated "servant" in the KJV New Testament usually means "slave.") When slaves were able to get away from their household duties, they would fellowship in local assemblies where being a slave was not a handicap (Gal. 3:28).

But there was a problem: Some slaves used their newfound freedom in Christ as an excuse to disobey, if not defy, their masters. They needed to learn that their spiritual freedom in Christ did not alter their social position, even though they were accepted graciously into the fellowship of the church.

**Slaves with unbelieving masters (v. 1).** No Christian master would consider his slaves "under the yoke," but would treat them with love and respect (Col. 4:1; Phile. 16). For a slave to rebel against an unsaved master would bring disgrace on the Gospel. "The name of God" and His doctrine would be blasphemed (Rom. 2:24). This is one reason Paul and the early missionaries did not go around preaching against the sinful institution of slavery. Such a practice would have branded the church as a militant group trying to undermine the social order, and the progress of the Gospel would have been greatly hindered.

**Slaves with believing masters (v. 2).** The danger here is that a Christian slave might take advantage of his master because both are saved. "My master is my brother!" a slave might argue. "Since we are equal, he has no right to tell me what to do!" This attitude would create serious problems both in the homes and in the churches.

Paul gave three reasons why Christian slaves should show respect for their believing masters and not take advantage of them. The most obvious reason is: *Their masters are Christians* ("faithful" = believing). How can one believer take advantage of another believer? Second, *their masters are beloved.* Love does not rebel or look for opportunities to escape responsibility. Finally, *both master and servant benefit from obedience* ("partakers of the benefit" can apply to both of them). There is a mutual blessing when Christians serve each other in the will of God.

I recall counseling a young lady who resigned from a secular job to go to work in a Christian organization. She had been there about a month and was completely disillusioned.

"I thought it was going to be heaven on earth," she complained. "Instead, there are nothing but problems."

"Are you working just as hard for your Christian boss as you did for your other boss?" I asked. The look on her face gave me the answer. "Try working harder," I advised, "and show him real respect. Just because all of you in the office are saved doesn't mean you can do less than your best." She took my advice and her problems cleared up.

## False Teachers (1 Tim. 6:3-10)

Paul had opened this letter with warnings about false teachers (1 Tim. 1:3ff), and had even refuted some of their dangerous teachings (1 Tim. 4:1ff). The spiritual leaders in the local church must constantly oversee what is being taught because it is easy for false doctrines to slip in (Acts 20:28-32). A pastor I know discovered a Sunday School teacher who was sharing his "visions" instead of teaching God's Word!

**The marks of these false teachers (vv. 3-5a).** The first mark is that they refused to adhere to "the sound instruction of our Lord Jesus Christ and to godly teaching" (1 Tim. 6:3, NIV). This teaching is godly and it promotes godliness. Isaiah's first test of any teacher was, "To the Law and to the testimony: if they speak not according to this word, it is because there is no light in them" (Isa. 8:20). It is important that a church "hold fast the form of sound [healthy] words" (2 Tim. 1:13).

A second mark is the teacher's own attitude. Instead of being humble, a false teacher is proud; yet he has nothing to be proud about because he does not know anything (1 Tim. 6:4; also 1:7).

A believer who understands the Word will have a burning heart, not a big head (Luke 24:32; and see Dan. 9:1-20). This "conceited attitude" causes a teacher to argue about minor matters concerning "words" (1 Tim. 6:3). Instead of feeding on the "wholesome words of . . . Christ," you might say he gets sick about questions. The word *doting* (1 Tim. 6:4) means "filled with a morbid desire, sick." The result of such unspiritual teaching is "envy, quarreling, malicious talk, evil suspicions, and constant friction" (1 Tim. 6:4b-5a, NIV).

The tragedy of all this is that the people are "robbed of the truth" (1 Tim. 6:5, NIV) while they think they are discovering the truth! They think that the weekly arguments in their meetings, during which they exchange their ignorance, are a means of growing in grace; meanwhile the result is a *loss* of character, not an improvement.

**The motive for their teaching (vv. 5b-10).** These false teachers supposed "that godliness is a way of financial gain" (literal translation). "Godliness" here (1 Tim. 6:5) means "the profession of Christian faith" and not true holy living in the power of the Spirit. They used their religious profession as a means to make money. What they did was not a true ministry; it was just a religious business.

Paul was always careful not to use his calling and ministry as a means of making money. In fact, he even refused support from the Corinthian church so that no one could accuse him of greed (1 Cor. 9:15-19). He never used his preaching as "a cloak of covetousness" (1 Thes. 2:5). What a tragedy it is today to see the religious racketeers who prey on gullible people, promising them help while taking away their money.

To warn Timothy—and us—about the dangers of covetousness, Paul shared four facts:

*Wealth does not bring contentment (v. 6).* The word *contentment* means "an inner sufficiency that keeps us at peace in spite of outward circumstances." Paul used this same word later. "For I have learned, in whatsoever state I am, therewith to be content" (Phil. 4:11). True contentment comes from godliness in the heart, not wealth in the hand. A person who depends on material things for peace and assurance will never be satisfied, for material things have a way of losing their appeal. It is the wealthy people, not the poor people, who go to psychiatrists and who are more apt to try to commit suicide.

*Wealth is not lasting (v. 7).* I like to translate this verse: "We brought nothing into this world because we can carry nothing out" (see Job 1:21). When someone's spirit leaves his body at death, it can take nothing with it because, when that person came into the world at birth, he brought nothing with him. Whatever wealth we amass goes to the government, our heirs, and perhaps charity and the church. We always know the answer to the question, "How much did he leave?" *Everything!*

*Our basic needs are easily met (v. 8).* Food and "covering" (clothing and shelter) are basic needs; if we lose them, we lose the ability to secure other things. A miser without food would starve to death counting his money. I am reminded of the simple-living Quaker who was watching his new neighbor move in, with all of the furnishings and expensive "toys" that "successful people" collect. The Quaker finally went over to his new neighbor and said, "Neighbor, if ever thou dost need anything, come to see me, and I will tell thee how to get along without it." Henry David Thoreau, the naturalist of the 1800s, reminded us that a man is wealthy in proportion to the number of things he can afford to do without.

The economic and energy crises that the world faces will probably be used by God to encourage people to simplify their lives. Too many of us know the "price of everything and the value of nothing." We are so glutted with luxuries that we have forgotten how to enjoy our necessities.

*The desire for wealth leads to sin (vv. 9-10).* "They that *will be* rich," is the accurate translation. It describes a person who has to have more and more material things in order to be happy and feel successful. But riches are a trap; they lead to bondage, not freedom. Instead of giving satisfaction, riches create additional lusts (desires); and these must be satisfied. Instead of providing help and health, an excess of material things hurts and wounds. The result Paul described very vividly: "Harmful desires . . . plunge men into ruin and destruction" (1 Tim. 6:9, NIV). It is the picture of a man drowning! He trusted his wealth and "sailed along," but the storm came and he sank.

It is a dangerous thing to use religion as a cover-up for acquiring wealth. God's laborer is certainly worthy of his hire (1 Tim. 5:17-18), but his motive for laboring must not be money. That would make him a "hireling," and not a true shepherd (John 10:11-14). We should not ask, "How much will I get?" but rather "How much can I give?"

## The Pastor Himself
## (1 Tim. 6:11-16, 20-21)

While caring for the needs of his people, Timothy needed to care for himself as well. "Take heed unto thyself" (1 Tim. 4:16) was one of Paul's admonitions. The phrase "But thou" (1 Tim. 6:11) indicates a contrast between Timothy and the false teachers. They were men of the world, but he was a "man of God." This special designation was also given to Moses (Deut. 33:1), Samuel (1 Sam. 9:6), Elijah (1 Kings 17:18), and David (Neh. 12:24); so Timothy was in good company.

Paul gave four admonitions to Timothy that, if obeyed, would assure him success in his ministry and a continued testimony as "a man of God."

*Flee (v. 11a).* There are times when running away is a mark of cowardice. "Should such a man as I flee?" asked Nehemiah (Neh. 6:11). But there are other times when fleeing is a mark of wisdom and a means of victory. Joseph fled when he was tempted by his master's wife (Gen. 39:12), and David fled when King Saul tried to kill him (1 Sam. 19:10). The word "flee" that Paul used here did not refer to literal running, but to Timothy's *separating himself* from the sins of the false teachers. This echoes the admonition in 1 Timothy 6:5: *"From such withdraw thyself."*

Not all unity is good, and not all division is bad. There are times when a servant of God should take a stand against false doctrine and godless practices, and separate himself from them. He must be sure, however, that he acts on the basis of biblical conviction and not because of a personal prejudice or a carnal party spirit.

*Follow (v. 11b).* Separation without positive growth becomes isolation. We must cultivate these graces of the Spirit in our lives, or else we will be known only for what we oppose rather than for what we propose. "Righteousness" means "personal integrity."

"Godliness" means "practical piety." The first has to do with character; the second, with conduct.

"Faith" might better be translated "faithfulness." It has well been said that the greatest ability is dependability.

"Love" is the *agape* love that sacrifices for the sake of others. It seeks to give, not to gain.

"Patience" carries the idea of "endurance," sticking to it when the going is tough. It is not a complacency that waits, but a courage that continues in hard places.

"Meekness" is not weakness, but instead is "power under control." Courageous endurance without meekness could make a person a tyrant. Perhaps "gentleness" expresses the meaning best.

*Fight (vv. 12-16).* The verb means "keep on fighting!" It is a word from which we get our English word *agonize,* and it applies both to athletes and to soldiers. It described a person straining and giving his best to win the prize or win the battle. Near the end of his own life, Paul wrote, "I have fought a good fight" (2 Tim. 4:7).

This "fight," however, is not between believers; it is between a person of God and the enemy around him. He is fighting to defend the faith, that body of truth deposited with the church (see 1 Tim. 6:20). Like Nehemiah of old, Christians today need to have a trowel in one hand for building, and a sword in the other hand for battling (Neh. 4:17). It is sad when some Christians spend so much time fighting the enemy that they have no time do to their work and build the church. On the other hand,

if we do not stand guard and oppose the enemy, what we have built could be taken from us.

What is it that encourages us in the battle? We have "eternal life" and need to take hold of it and let it work in our experience. We have been called by God, and this assures us of victory. We have made our public profession of faith in Christ, and others in the church stand with us.

Another encouragement in our battle is the witness of Jesus Christ our Saviour. He "witnessed a good confession" (1 Tim. 6:13) before Pontius Pilate and did not relent before the enemy. He knew that God the Father was with Him and watching over Him, and that He would be raised from the dead. It is "God who makes all things alive" (literal translation), who is caring for us, so we need not fear. Timothy's natural timidity might want to make him shrink from the battle. But all he had to do was remember Jesus Christ and His bold confession, and this would encourage him.

Paul gave Timothy military orders: "I give thee charge" (1 Tim. 6:13, also 1:3). He was to guard the commandment and obey it. Why? Because one day the Commander would appear and he would have to report on his assignment! The only way he could be ready would be to obey orders "without spot or blame" (1 Tim. 6:14, NIV).

The Greek word translated "appearing" (1 Tim. 6:14) gives us our English word *epiphany* which means "a glorious manifestation." In Paul's day, the word was used in the myths to describe the appearing of a god, especially to deliver someone from trouble. Paul used it of the first coming of Jesus Christ (2 Tim. 1:10) and of His return (2 Tim. 4:1, 8). We do not know when Christ will come again, but it will be "in His own time" (1 Tim. 6:15, NIV) and He knows the schedule. Our task is to be faithful every day and abide in Him (1 John 2:28).

The subject of 1 Timothy 6:16 is God, the God and Father of our Lord Jesus Christ. He is the *only* Ruler, though others may take the title. "Potentate" (1 Tim. 6:15) comes from a word that means "power." The kings and rulers of the earth may think they have power and authority, but God is sovereign over all (see Ps. 2).

"King of kings, and Lord of lords" (1 Tim. 6:15) makes us think of Jesus Christ (Rev. 17:14; 19:16); but here the title is applied to God the Father. Jesus Christ, of course, reveals the Father to us; so He can justly claim this title.

"Immortality" (1 Tim. 6:16) means "not subject to death." Man is subject to death, but God is not. Only God has immortality as an essential and inherent part of His being. He is "immortal, invisible, the only wise God" (1 Tim. 1:17). Because God is not subject to death, He is Life and the Giver of life. He is incorruptible and not subject to decay or change. In this life, believers are in mortal bodies; but when Jesus Christ returns, we shall share His immortality (1 Cor. 15:50-58).

Keep in mind that Paul explained all these truths about God in order to encourage Timothy to "fight the good fight of faith" and not give up. We need not fear life because God is the Ruler of all; and we need not fear death because He shares immortality with us.

Timothy lived in the godless city of Ephesus, but God dwells in glorious light. "And the sight of the glory of the Lord was like devouring fire" (Ex. 24:17). "Who coverest Thyself with light as with a garment" (Ps. 104:2). John's description of heaven emphasized the glory of God that gives light to the city (Rev. 21:11, 23-24; 22:5). Of course, light is a symbol of holiness (1 John 1:5-7). God dwells apart from sin, and God is glorious in His holiness.

It is impossible for a sinful human to approach the holy God. It is only through Jesus Christ that we can be accepted into His presence. Jacob saw God in one of His Old Testament appearances on earth (Gen. 32:30); and God allowed Moses to see some of His glory (Ex. 33:18-23). "No man hath seen God at any time" (John 1:18) refers to seeing God *in His essence*, His spiritual nature. We can only see manifestations of this essence, as in the person of Jesus Christ.

Why did Paul write so much about the person and glory of God? Probably as a warning against the "emperor cult" that existed in the Roman Empire. It was customary to acknowledge regularly, "Caesar is Lord!" Of course, Christians would say "Jesus Christ is Lord!" Only God has "honor and power everlasting" (1 Tim. 6:16b). If Timothy was going to fight the good fight of faith, he had to decide that Jesus Christ *alone* was worthy of worship and complete devotion.

*Be faithful (vv. 20-21).* God had committed the truth to Paul (1 Tim. 1:11), and Paul had committed it to Timothy. It was Timothy's responsibility to guard the deposit and

then pass it along to others who would, in turn, continue to pass it on (2 Tim. 2:2). This is God's way of protecting the truth and spreading it around the world. We are stewards of the doctrines of the faith, and God expects us to be faithful in sharing His Good News.

The word *science* (1 Tim. 6:20) does not refer to the kind of technology we know today by that name. "*Knowledge* falsely so called" is a better translation. Paul referred here to the teachings of a heretical group called "gnostics" who claimed to have a "special spiritual knowledge." (The Greek word for "knowledge" is *gnosis,* pronounced NO-sis. An "agnostic" is one who does not know. A gnostic is one who claimed to know a great deal.)

There is no need to go into detail here about the heretical claims of the gnostics. Paul's letter to the Colossians was written to counteract them. They claimed to have "special spiritual knowledge" from visions and other experiences. They also claimed to find "hidden truths" in the Old Testament Scriptures, especially the genealogies. They considered matter to be evil, and they taught that a series of "emanations" connected God with man. Jesus Christ, they said, was only the greatest of these emanations.

The gnostics actually had a doctrine that was a strange mixture of Christianity, Oriental mysticism, Greek philosophy, and Jewish legalism. Like many of the Eastern cults we see today, it offered "something for everybody." But Paul summarized all that they taught in one devastating phrase: "profane and vain babblings." Phillips translates it "the godless mixture of contradictory notions."

Why should Timothy avoid these teachings? Because some who got involved in them "wandered from the faith" (1 Tim. 6:21, NIV). Not only will wrong motives (a desire for money) cause a person to wander from the faith (1 Tim. 6:10), but so will wrong teachings. These lies work their way into a person's mind and heart gradually, and before he realizes it, he is wandering off the path of truth.

### The Rich (1 Tim. 6:17-19)

Paul had already written about the danger of the love of money, but he added a special "charge" for Timothy to give to the rich. We may not think that this charge applies to us, but it does. After all, our standard of living today would certainly make us "rich" in the eyes of Timothy's congregation!

**Be humble (v. 17a).** If wealth makes a person proud, then he understands neither himself nor his wealth. "But thou shalt remember the Lord thy God; for it is He that gives thee power to get wealth" (Deut. 8:18). We are not owners; we are stewards. If we have wealth, it is by the goodness of God and not because of any special merits on our part. The possessing of material wealth ought to humble a person and cause him to glorify God, not himself.

It possible to be "rich in the world [age]" (1 Tim. 6:17) and be poor in the next. It is also possible to be poor in this world and rich in the next. Jesus talked about both (Luke 16:19-31). But a believer can be rich in this world and also rich in the next if he uses what he has to honor God (Matt. 6:19-34). In fact, a person who is poor in this world can use even his limited means to glorify God, and discover great reward in the next world.

**Trust God, not wealth (v. 17b).** The rich farmer in our Lord's parable (Luke 12:13-21) thought that his wealth meant security, when really it was an evidence of insecurity. He was not really trusting God. Riches are uncertain, not only in their value (which changes constantly), but also in their durability. Thieves can steal wealth, investments can drop in value, and the ravages of time can ruin houses and cars. If God gives us wealth, we should trust Him, the Giver, and not the gifts.

**Enjoy what God gives you (v. 17c).** Yes, the word *enjoy* is in the Bible! In fact, one of the recurring themes in Ecclesiastes is, "Enjoy the blessings of life now, because life will end one day" (Ecc. 2:24; 3:12-15, 22; 5:18-20; 9:7-10; 11:9-10). This is not sinful "hedonism," living for the pleasures of life. It is simply enjoying all that God gives us for His glory.

**Employ what God gives you (vv. 18-19).** We should use our wealth to do good to others; we should share; we should put our money to work. When we do, we enrich ourselves spiritually, and we make investments for the future (see Luke 16:1-13). "That they may lay hold on eternal life" (1 Tim. 6:19) does not suggest that these people are not saved. "That they may lay hold on the life that is real" would express it perfectly. Riches can lure a person into a make-believe world of shallow pleasure. But riches *plus God's will* can introduce a person to life that is real and ministry that is lasting.

Paul's final sentence was not for Timothy alone, because the pronoun is plural: "Grace be with all of you." Paul had the entire church in mind when he wrote this letter, and certainly all of the elders, not just Timothy. As leader of the church, Timothy needed to heed the word of the apostle; but all of his church members had a responsibility to hear and obey as well.

And so do we today.

# 2 TIMOTHY

## OUTLINE

**Key theme:** Preparation for the ministry in the last days
**Key verses:** 2 Timothy 1:13-14

### I. THE PASTORAL APPEAL—
chapter 1
- A. Courageous enthusiasm—1:1-7
- B. Shameless suffering—1:8-12
- C. Spiritual loyalty—1:13-18

### II. THE PRACTICAL APPEAL—
chapter 2
- A. The steward—2:1-2
- B. The soldier—2:3-4, 8-13
- C. The athlete—2:5
- D. The farmer—2:6-7
- E. The workman—2:14-18
- F. The vessel—2:19-22
- G. The servant—2:23-26

### III. THE PROPHETIC APPEAL—
chapter 3
- A. Turn away from the false—3:1-9
- B. Follow those who are true—3:10-12
- C. Continue in God's Word—3:13-17

### IV. THE PERSONAL APPEAL—
chapter 4
- A. Preach the Word—4:1-4
- B. Fulfill your ministry—4:5-8
- C. Be diligent and faithful—4:9-22

## CONTENTS

# CHAPTER ONE
# CHRISTIANS
# COURAGEOUS!
*2 Timothy 1*

When Paul wrote the letter we know as 2 Timothy, his situation had changed drastically. He was now a prisoner in Rome and was facing certain death (2 Tim. 4:6). For one reason or another, almost all of Paul's associates in the ministry were gone and only Luke was at the apostle's side to assist him (2 Tim. 4:11). It was a dark hour indeed.

But Paul's great concern was not for himself; it was for Timothy and the success of the Gospel ministry. As in his First Letter to Timothy, Paul encouraged his beloved colleague to be faithful. As we have learned, Timothy was timid, suffered from physical ailments, and was tempted to let other people take advantage of him and not assert his authority as a pastor.

Paul sent Tychicus to replace Timothy at Ephesus so that Timothy might join Paul at Rome (2 Tim. 4:9, 12). God would soon move Paul off the scene, and Timothy would take his place and continue to give spiritual leadership to the churches. It would not be an easy task, but Timothy could succeed with the Lord's help. In his first chapter, Paul gave Timothy three essentials that he must possess to have success.

**Courageous Enthusiasm (2 Tim. 1:1-7)**
The ministry of the Gospel is no place for a "timid soul" who lacks enthusiasm. In fact, courageous enthusiasm is essential for success in *any* kind of work. Paul compared this attitude to stirring up a fire into full flame (2 Tim. 1:6). We must not conclude that Timothy was backslidden or lacked spiritual fire. Rather, Paul was encouraging his associate to keep the fire burning brightly so that it might generate spiritual power in his life. Paul gave Timothy four encouragements.

*Paul's love (vv. 1-2).* "Timothy, my dearly beloved son" is much stronger than "Timothy, my own son in the faith" (1 Tim. 1:2). It is not that Paul loved Timothy less when he wrote that first letter, but that Paul was now expressing it more. As Paul's life

drew to a close, he realized in a deeper way how dear Timothy was to him.

Paul's own circumstances were difficult, and yet he was greatly encouraged. For one thing, he was Christ's ambassador ("apostle"); and he knew that his Master would care for him. Whatever happened to him was in the hands of God, so there was no need to fear. Furthermore, Paul had "the promise of life" in Jesus Christ, and Christ had defeated death (2 Tim. 1:10). No wonder Paul was able to extend to Timothy "grace, mercy, and peace." (It is worth noting that Paul added "mercy" to his greetings when he wrote to the pastors—1 Tim. 1:2; 2 Tim. 1:2; Titus 1:4. Paul knew that pastors need mercy!)

*Paul's prayers (vv. 3-4).* What an encouragement to know that the great apostle was praying for him! Paul, who knew Timothy's weaknesses and problems, was able to pray definitely and with a real burden on his heart. His praying was not routine; it was done with compassion and concern. Knowing that he would soon die, Paul was anxious that Timothy join him at Rome for those last days of fellowship and ministry. This would bring joy to Paul's heart.

We must not assume that Paul tried to defend his evil actions before his conversion by claiming he did it all with "a pure conscience." After all, he was guilty of causing terror among Christians, forcing people to blaspheme by denying Christ, and agreeing to the murder of Stephen! It is true that Paul thought he was serving God (see John 16:2), and that he was in spiritual ignorance (1 Tim. 1:13), but these facts cannot guarantee a pure conscience.

Paul had known God from his earliest years because he was "an Hebrew of the Hebrews" (Phil. 3:5). His ancestors had given him the orthodox Jewish faith. But when he met Jesus Christ, Paul realized that his Jewish faith was but preparation for the fulfillment Christ gave him in Christianity. He did not serve God with a pure conscience "from his forefathers," as the *King James Version* says. Rather, he heard about the true God from his forefathers; and *now* he was serving that God with a pure conscience. The fact that he had a pure conscience helped give power to his prayers.

*Paul's confidence in Timothy (v. 5).* Paul did not think that Timothy's tears were evidence of failure or insincerity. Paul was sure that Timothy's faith was genuine, and that this faith would see him through in spite of the troubles he was facing. Apparently

Lois, Timothy's grandmother, was the first one in the family won to Christ; then his mother, Eunice, was converted. Timothy's father was a Greek (Acts 16:1), so Eunice had not practiced the orthodox Jewish faith. However, Timothy's mother and grandmother had seen to it that he was taught the Scriptures (2 Tim. 3:15); and this was great preparation for the hearing of the Gospel. When Paul came to Lystra on his first missionary journey, that was probably the occasion for Timothy's conversion. When Paul returned on his second journey, he enlisted Timothy into Christian service.

Paul had watched Timothy's life and service during those years they were together. He was certain that Timothy's faith was genuine. In fact, Timothy's heritage was a great one; for he was reared in a godly home, trained by a wonderful apostle, and given marvelous opportunities for serving the Lord.

**God's gift to Timothy (vv. 6-7).** Paul reminded Timothy of the time God called him into service and the local church ordained him. Paul had laid his hands on Timothy (1 Tim. 4:14). Through Paul, God had imparted to Timothy the spiritual gift he needed for his ministry. The laying on of hands was a common practice in apostolic days (Acts 6:6; 13:3), but no believer today has the same authority and privileges that the Apostles did. Today, when we lay hands on people for the ministry, it is a symbolic act and does not necessarily impart any special spiritual gifts to them.

It is the Holy Spirit who enables us to serve God, and through Him we can overcome fear and weakness. The word *fear* in 2 Timothy 1:7 means "timidity, cowardice." The Holy Spirit gives us power for witness and for service (Acts 1:8). It is futile for us to try to serve God without the power of the Holy Spirit. Talent, training, and experience cannot take the place of the power of the Spirit.

The Holy Spirit also gives us love. If we have love for lost souls and for the people of God, we will be able to endure suffering and accomplish the work of God. Selfishness leads to fear because, if we are selfish, we are interested only in what we will get out of serving God, and we will be afraid of losing prestige, power, or money. True Christian love, energized by the Spirit (Rom. 5:5), enables us to sacrifice for others and not be afraid. The Spirit gives love (Gal. 5:22).

He is also the One who gives self-control ("a sound mind"). This word is related to the words *sober* and *sobriety* that we often meet in the pastoral letters (1 Tim. 2:9, 15; Titus 1:8; 2:2, 4, 6, 12). "Self-discipline" is a better translation of "sound mind" (2 Tim. 1:7). It describes a person who is sensibly minded and balanced, who has his life under control. The *Amplified Version* reads, "calm and well-balanced mind and discipline and self-control."

Timothy did not need any new spiritual ingredients in his life; all he had to do was "stir up" what he already had. Paul had written in his first letter, "Neglect not the gift that is in thee" (1 Tim. 4:14). Now he added, "Stir up—stir into flame—the gift of God." The Holy Spirit does not leave us when we fail (John 14:16); but He cannot fill us, empower us, and use us if we neglect our spiritual lives. It is possible to grieve the Spirit (Eph. 4:30) and quench the Spirit (1 Thes. 5:19).

Timothy had every reason to be encouraged and to have spiritual enthusiasm in his ministry. Paul loved him and prayed for him. His experiences in life had been preparation for his ministry, and Paul was confident of the genuineness of Timothy's faith. The Spirit within him would give all the power needed for ministry. What more could he want?

## Shameless Suffering (2 Tim. 1:8-12)

"Not ashamed" is a key idea in this chapter: Paul was not ashamed (2 Tim. 1:12); he admonished Timothy not to be ashamed (2 Tim. 1:8); and he reported that Onesiphorus was not ashamed of Paul's chain (2 Tim. 1:16).

**Be not ashamed of the Lord's testimony (vv. 8-10).** Timothy's natural timidity might make it easy for him to avoid circumstances that demanded witness and involved suffering. Once again, Paul gave his associate needed encouragement.

*God gives us power (v. 8).* By nature, none of us enjoys suffering. Even our Lord prayed, "Father, if Thou be willing, remove this cup from Me" (Luke 22:42); and Paul prayed three times for God to remove his painful thorn in the flesh (2 Cor. 12:7-8). But suffering may well be a part of a faithful Christian life. Christians should not suffer because they have done wrong (1 Peter 2:20; 3:17); rather, they sometimes suffer because they have done right and served God. When we suffer for doing good, then we are sharing Christ's sufferings (Phil. 3:10) and suffering on behalf of the whole church (Col. 1:24).

Years ago, I read about a Christian who

was in prison because of his faith. He was to be burned at the stake, and he was certain he would never be able to endure the suffering. One night, he experimented with pain by putting his little finger into the candle flame. It hurt, and he immediately withdrew it. "I will disgrace my Lord," he said to himself. "I cannot bear the pain." But when the hour came for him to die, he praised God and gave a noble witness for Jesus Christ. God gave him the power *when he needed it,* and not before.

*God has called us by His grace (v. 9).* We are part of a great eternal plan that God determined "before the world began." God knows the end from the beginning. He has purposes for His people to accomplish for His glory. Suffering is a part of His plan. Jesus Christ suffered in the will of God here on earth, and all those who trust in Him will also suffer.

The emphasis in this verse is on *grace.* God saved us; we did not save ourselves (Eph. 2:8-9; Titus 3:5). He called us, not on the basis of our good works, but wholly on the basis of His grace. It is His purposes that we are to fulfill; and if these purposes include suffering, then we can accept it by faith and know that God's will is best. This is not fatalism. It is confidence in the wise plan of our gracious Heavenly Father.

All of this grace was given to us in Jesus Christ. We could not earn it; we did not merit it. This is the grace of God!

*Christ has defeated death (v. 10).* When we are timid it is because we are afraid. Of what are we afraid? Suffering and possible death? Paul himself was facing death as he dictated this letter. But Jesus Christ has defeated our last enemy, death! By His own death and resurrection, Christ has "abolished death" (made it inoperative, taken out the sting). "O death, where is thy sting? O grave, where is thy victory?" (1 Cor. 15:55)

Christ was not only the Destroyer of death (see Heb. 2:14-15), but He was also the Revealer of life and immortality. In the Old Testament the doctrines of eternal life, death, resurrection, and the eternal state were in the shadows. Here and there you find glimpses of light; but for the most part, the picture is dark. But then Jesus Christ shone His light on death and the grave. Through the Gospel, He has given us assurance of eternal life, resurrection, and the hope of heaven.

Religious groups that teach "soul sleep" and other strange doctrines usually get their ideas from the Psalms and Ecclesiastes. Instead of allowing the clear light of the New Testament to shine on the Old, they look at the New through the shadows of the Old! If you turn your back on the light of the Gospel, you will only cast another shadow and make the scene darker.

"Immortality" (2 Tim. 1:10, KJV) means "incorruptibility," and refers to the resurrection body. The present body is corruptible; it dies and decays. But the glorified body we shall have when we see Christ will not be subject to decay or death (1 Cor. 15:49-58; Phil. 3:21). In fact, the heavenly inheritance that we share will be "incorruptible and undefiled, and [one] that fadeth not away" (1 Peter 1:4).

**Be not ashamed of the Lord's prisoner *(vv. 11-12).*** Though a prisoner, Paul was still bearing witness for the Gospel of Jesus Christ. Sad to say, the people in Ephesus had deserted Paul in his time of need (2 Tim. 1:15). Many of them could have come to Rome to witness on Paul's behalf, but they did not. They were even ashamed to be identified with the apostle! It would have made Timothy's ministry in Ephesus (and in the surrounding cities; see 2 Tim. 4:13) much easier if he had gone along with the crowd; but Paul admonished him to remain true. He gave four reasons why Timothy should not be ashamed of his association with Paul, the prisoner.

*Paul was called by God (v. 11).* Jesus Christ had met Paul on the Damascus road (Acts 9) and had personally called him into the ministry. Paul was a *herald* ("preacher") of the Gospel. In ancient times, a "herald" was the official messenger of the king or emperor, and his message was treated with great respect. The fact that professed believers in Asia were rejecting Paul did not change his calling or his message.

Paul was not only a herald; he was also *an apostle, "one sent with a commission."* Not every Christian was an apostle of Jesus Christ, for a person had to meet certain qualifications and be chosen by the Lord personally, or through His Spirit (see Acts 1:15-26; 1 Cor. 9:1; 2 Cor. 12:12). An apostle represented Jesus Christ. To reject an apostle was to reject the Lord.

*Paul was a teacher of the Gentiles.* This meant that he shepherded local churches. It was this word *Gentiles* that put him into prison in Rome the first time (Acts 22:21ff). The Gentile believers in Asia should have shown their appreciation of Paul by rallying to his support, for after all, it was Paul who brought them the Good News of salvation. But instead they were ashamed of him and tried not to get involved.

*Paul was confident in Christ (v. 12).* Paul was not ashamed! Why? Because he knew that Christ was faithful and would keep him. Note his emphasis on the person of Christ: "I know *whom* I have believed." Salvation is not the result of believing certain doctrines, though doctrines are important. A sinner is saved because he believes in a Person—Jesus Christ the Saviour. Paul had deposited his soul in the care and keeping of the Saviour, and Paul was sure that Jesus Christ would faithfully guard that deposit. What difference did it make to Paul what happened on any certain day? What really mattered is what will happen on "that day" when Jesus Christ rewards His servants (see 2 Tim. 1:18; 4:8).

In these difficult days, it is important that we stand true to Christ and be willing to suffer for Him and not be ashamed. We may not be put into prison, as was Paul; but we suffer in other ways: the loss of friends, being bypassed for a promotion, loss of customers, being snubbed by people, etc. It is also important that we stand by God's servants who are suffering for righteousness' sake.

### Spiritual Loyalty (2 Tim. 1:13-18)
Throughout the centuries God's work has been done by men and women who stood steadfast in their hours of trial. It would have been convenient for them to have compromised, but they stood firm. Paul was such a man, and he encouraged Timothy to follow his example in a twofold loyalty.

*Be loyal to God's Word (vv. 13-14).* God had given the deposit of spiritual truth to Paul (1 Tim. 1:11), and he had given it to Timothy (1 Tim. 6:20). It was now Timothy's solemn responsibility to "hold fast" (2 Tim. 1:13) and "guard" (2 Tim. 1:14, NIV) the precious deposit of Christian truth, and to pass it along to others (2 Tim. 2:2).

The word *form* (2 Tim. 1:13) means "a pattern, an architect's sketch." There was a definite outline of doctrine in the early church, a standard by which teaching was tested. If Timothy changed this outline or abandoned it, then he would have nothing by which to test other teachers and preachers. We today need to hold fast to what Paul taught for the same reason.

However, note that Timothy's orthodoxy was to be tempered with "faith and love."

"Speaking the truth in love" (Eph. 4:15) is the divine pattern. How easy it is to become pugnacious in our desire to defend the faith, or a witch-hunter who creates problems.

It was the Holy Spirit who committed the truth to Timothy, and He would help him guard it. Apart from the ministry of the Spirit, we are in the dark when it comes to understanding the Word of God. It is He who must teach us (John 16:13) and enable us to guard the truth and share it with others.

From the beginning of human history, Satan has opposed God's Word. "Yea, hath God said?" was Satan's first word to mankind (Gen. 3:1), and he continues to ask that question. Throughout the history of the church, the Word of God has been attacked, often by people *within* the church; yet it still stands today. Why? Because dedicated men and women have (like Paul and Timothy) guarded the deposit and faithfully handed it to a new generation of Christians. When a church or any other Christian organization goes liberal, it usually starts with a weakening of their leaders' convictions about the Word of God.

*Be loyal to God's servant (vv. 15-18).* The province of Asia in that day comprised the Roman districts of Lydia, Mysia, Caria, and Phrygia. Paul was forbidden to minister in this area on his second missionary journey (Acts 16:6); but on his third journey, he stayed nearly three years in Ephesus, the capital of Asia, and evangelized the entire area (Acts 19; 20:31). The seven churches of Asia were all in this area (Rev. 1:4, 11).

We do not know who Phygelus and Hermogenes (2 Tim. 1:15) were. It is likely that they were leaders in the church who opposed Paul and would not come to his defense in Rome. You would think that the Asian believers would have stood by Paul; but, instead, they were ashamed of him and at the same time (whether they knew it or not) ashamed of Christ (see 2 Tim. 4:16).

It was certainly a dark hour for Paul. Demas had forsaken him (2 Tim. 4:10). His other associates had been sent to distant places of ministry. False doctrines were spreading in the church (2 Tim. 2:17-18). How Paul would have loved to be free to preach the Word and defend the faith—but he was in a Roman prison. It was up to Timothy to get the job done.

But there was one man who dared to leave Ephesus and come to Rome to assist Paul—Onesiphorus. His name means "profit-bearing," and he certainly was a profitable friend to Paul. It is possible that he was a deacon in the church at Ephesus ("ministered" in 2 Tim. 1:18 comes from the word that gives us "deacon"). During Paul's ministry at Ephesus, Onesiphorus was a faithful minister, along with his household. Since Timothy had pastored the Ephesian church, he would know this choice saint.

Let me add here that every pastor is thankful for those faithful members who assist him in the work of the Lord. My wife and I have found choice saints in each of the three churches we have served—people whose homes were open to us (and they didn't tell the whole church we were there!), whose hearts felt our burdens and needs, and whose prayers sustained us in difficult times. These believers minister behind the scenes, but the Lord will reward them openly "in that day" (2 Tim. 1:18).

Onesiphorus traveled from Ephesus to Rome and diligently looked for Paul so he might minister to the prisoner's needs. It seemed difficult for him to find his former pastor (2 Tim. 1:17). Perhaps some of the Roman Christians were still opposed to Paul as they had been during his first imprisonment (see Phil. 1:12-17). Perhaps the Roman officials were not cooperative and did not want their choice prisoner to receive any help. In his first imprisonment, Paul was in his own house (Acts 28:30); but now he was in a Roman prison under careful guard.

But Onesiphorus persisted! He located Paul and risked his own life to stand with him and assist him. Some students believe that Onesiphorus was also arrested and possibly executed. They base this on the fact that Paul greeted the "household of Onesiphorus" in 2 Timothy 4:19, but not the man himself. Also, Paul asked for *present* mercies for the household, but *future* mercies for Onesiphorus (2 Tim. 1:16, 18).

But the problem is this: If Onesiphorus was dead, then Paul prayed for the dead (2 Tim. 1:18); and we have no authorization in the Bible to pray for the dead.

We have no proof that Onesiphorus was dead when Paul wrote this letter. The fact that Paul asked God to bless the man's household, but that he did not mention the man, simply means that at the time Onesiphorus was not with his household. "When he *was* in Rome" (2 Tim. 1:17) suggests that, at that writing, Onesiphorus was not in Rome.

Therefore, he was somewhere between Rome and Ephesus; so Paul prayed for him and his household. There was no need to greet Onesiphorus, for Paul had just spent much time with him; so Paul only greeted his household.

Onesiphorus was not ashamed of Paul's chain. The apostle was manacled to a Roman soldier twenty-four hours a day. Onesiphorus could have invented many excuses for staying in Ephesus. But instead he made the dangerous journey to Rome and ministered to Paul. "He often refreshed me" was Paul's description of this man's ministry. The Greek word means "to cool again." "Bracing me like fresh air" is the way the *Amplified Bible* translated it. How we thank God for Christians who are "a breath of fresh air" in our hours of trial!

Were it not for Paul's letter, we would never know that Onesiphorus had served Paul and the church. But the Lord knew and will reward him "on that day."

The essentials for a successful ministry have not changed: courageous enthusiasm, shameless suffering, and spiritual loyalty.

# CHAPTER TWO
# GETTING THE
# PICTURE
*2 Timothy 2*

While attending a convention, I noticed a man wearing two name badges. When I asked him why, he replied, "Oh, I'm having an identity crisis!"

Paul did not want Timothy to have an identity crisis, so he carefully explained what a pastor is and does. (Of course, the same principles apply to all Christians.) Paul represented seven pictures of the Christian minister.

### The Steward (2 Tim. 2:1-2)
The ministry is not something we get for ourselves and keep to ourselves. We are stewards of the spiritual treasure God has given us. It is our responsibility to guard the deposit and then invest it in the lives of others. They, in turn, are to share the Word with the next generation of believers.

It is important that we get our original treasure from the Word of God, and not from the ideas and philosophies of men. We do not test modern teachers by their popularity, education, or skill. We test them by the Word of God, and particularly the doctrines of grace as given by Paul. It is not we who examine Paul to see if he is right; it is Paul who examines us!

It takes strength to teach the Word of God. We must dig out of the rich mines of Scripture the "gold, silver, precious stones" that are hidden there (see Prov. 2:1-10; 3:13-15; 8:10-21; 1 Cor. 3:10-23). This strength can only come from God's grace. The secret of Paul's great ministry was the grace of God (1 Cor. 15:10).

The ability to study, understand, and teach the Word of God is a gift of God's grace. "Apt to teach" is one of God's requirements for the pastor (1 Tim. 3:2; 2 Tim. 2:24). "Apt to teach" implies apt to learn; so a steward must also be a diligent student of the Word of God.

### The Soldier (2 Tim. 2:3-4, 8-13)

Paul often used military illustrations in his letters. This is not surprising since he lived in a military state and was in prison himself. He described in these verses the characteristics of a "good soldier of Jesus Christ."

*He endures hardship (v. 3).* Many people have the idea that the ministry is a soft job. Preachers are often the butt of jokes that suggest they are lazy and should be ashamed of accepting their salaries. But a dedicated Christian minister is in a battle that requires spiritual endurance (see Eph. 6:10ff).

*He avoids worldly entanglements (v. 4).* He is totally committed to his Commanding Officer, the One who enlisted him. In our case, this is Jesus Christ. I recall a story about a Civil War soldier who happened to be a watchmaker. One day the bugle sounded and the men were told to break camp. "But I can't go now!" the soldier complained. "I have a dozen watches to repair!"

It is sometimes necessary for a pastor, or a pastor's wife, to be employed because their church is not able to support them. This is a sacrifice on their part and an investment in the work. But a pastor who is fully supported should not get involved in sidelines that divide his interest and weaken his ministry. I have met pastors who spend more time on their real estate ventures than on their churches. Our purpose is to please the Lord, not ourselves.

*He magnifies Jesus Christ (vv. 8-9).* "Remember Jesus Christ!" is the way this phrase should be translated. It sounds almost like a war cry, like "Remember the Alamo!" or "Remember Pearl Harbor!" Jesus is the Captain of our salvation (Heb. 2:10), and our purpose is to bring honor and glory to Him. What an encouragement Jesus Christ is to a suffering Christian soldier! For He died and rose again, proving that suffering leads to glory, and that seeming defeat leads to victory. Jesus was treated as an evildoer, and His soldiers will be treated the same way.

The best way to magnify Christ is through the ministry of the Word. Paul was bound, but God's Word cannot be bound. "His Word runneth very swiftly" (Ps. 147:15). "The Word of God grew and multiplied" (Acts 12:24).

*He thinks of the whole army (v. 10).* "The elect" are God's people, chosen by His grace and called by His Spirit (2 Thes. 2:13-14). Paul not only suffered for the Lord's sake, but he also suffered for the sake of the church. There were yet many people to reach with the Gospel, and Paul wanted to help reach them. A soldier who thinks only of himself is disloyal and undependable.

*He trusts his Commanding Officer (vv. 11-13).* This "faithful saying" is probably part of an early statement of faith recited by believers. (For other "faithful sayings" in the pastoral letters, see 1 Tim. 1:15; 4:9; and Titus 3:8.) It is faith in Jesus Christ that gives us victory (1 John 5:4). We do not fear the enemies, for He has already conquered them. Through our identification with Christ in death, burial, and resurrection, we have won the victory (see Rom. 6).

What a pair of paradoxes! Death leads to life! Suffering leads to reigning in glory! We have nothing to fear! The important thing is that we not "disown" our Lord; for if we disown Him here, He will disown us before the Father (Matt. 10:33). In that great "roll call" in glory, when the "medals" are given out, we will lose our reward if we disown His name.

But Paul makes it clear (2 Tim. 2:13) that even our own doubt and unbelief cannot change Him: "He abideth faithful; He cannot deny Himself." We do not put faith in our faith or in our feelings because they will change and fail. We put our faith in Christ. The great missionary, J. Hudson Taylor, often said, "It is not by trying to be faithful, but in looking to the Faithful One, that we win the victory."

## The Athlete (2 Tim. 2:5)

Paul sometimes used athletic illustrations in his writings—wrestling, boxing, running, and exercising. The Greeks and the Romans were enthusiastic about sports, and the Olympic and Isthmian games were important events to them. Paul had already urged Timothy to exercise like an athlete (1 Tim. 4:7-8). Now Paul admonished him to obey the rules.

A person who strives as an athlete to win a game and get a crown must be careful to obey all the rules of the game. In the Greek games in particular, the judges were most careful about enforcing the rules. Each competitor had to be a citizen of his nation, with a good reputation. In his preparations for the event, he had to follow specific standards. If an athlete was found defective in any matter, he was disqualified from competing. If, after he had competed and won, he was found to have broken some rule, he then lost his crown. Jim Thorpe, a great American athlete, lost his Olympic medals because he participated in sports in a way that broke an Olympic rule.

From the human point of view, Paul was a loser. There was nobody in the grandstands cheering him, for "all they which are in Asia" had turned away from him (2 Tim. 1:15). He was in prison, suffering as an evildoer. Yet, *Paul was a winner!* He had kept the rules laid down in the Word of God, and one day he would get his reward from Jesus Christ. Paul was saying to young Timothy, "The important thing is that you obey the Word of God, no matter what people may say. You are not running the race to please people or to get fame. You are running to please Jesus Christ."

## The Farmer (2 Tim. 2:6-7)

This is another favorite image found in Paul's letters. Paul once compared the local church to a cultivated field in which all the believers worked together (1 Cor. 3:5-9). Each Christian has his particular task to perform—plowing, sowing, watering, or harvesting—but it is God alone who gives the increase.

Several practical truths are found in this image of the farmer and field. For one thing, *a farmer has to work.* If you leave a field to itself, it will produce mostly weeds. Solomon had this truth in mind when he wrote about the field of the sluggard (Prov. 24:30-34). Real ministry is hard work, and a pastor (and church members) ought to work in their spiritual field as diligently as a farmer works in his field. Pastors do not punch clocks, but they ought to be up in the morning and at their work just as if God blew a whistle for them.

*A farmer needs patience.* "See how the farmer waits for the land to yield its valuable crop and how patient he is for the fall and spring rains" (James 5:7, NIV). A pastor friend of mine often reminds me, "The harvest is not the end of the meeting—it is the end of the age."

*A farmer deserves his share of the harvest.* "The hardworking farmer should be the first to receive a share of the crops" (2 Tim. 2:6, NIV). Paul is stating here that a faithful pastor ought to be supported by his church. The same idea is found in 1 Corinthians 9:7, where Paul used a soldier, a farmer, and a herdsman to prove his point: "The laborer is worthy of his reward" (1 Tim. 5:18). Paul deliberately gave up his right to ask for support so that nobody could accuse him of using the Gospel for personal gain (1 Cor. 9:14ff). But this policy is not required for all of God's servants.

As a local church grows and progresses, the people ought to faithfully increase their support of their pastors and other staff members. "If we have sown spiritual seed among you, is it too much if we reap a material harvest from you?" (1 Cor. 9:11, NIV) It is sad to see the way some local churches waste money and fail to care for their own laborers. God will honor a church that honors His faithful servants.

Something else is true in this image of the farmer: The spiritual leaders who share the Word with the people are the first ones to enjoy its blessings. The preacher and the teacher always get more out of the sermon or lesson than do the hearers because they put much more into it. They also get great joy out of seeing planted seeds bear fruit in the lives of others. Farming is hard work, and it can have many disappointments; but the rewards are worth it.

## The Workman (2 Tim. 2:14-18)

The word *study* (2 Tim. 2:15) has nothing to do with books and teachers. It means "to be diligent, be zealous." It is translated in this way in 2 Timothy 4:9, 21, and also in Titus 3:12. The emphasis in this paragraph is that the workman needs to be diligent in his labors so that he will not be ashamed when his work is inspected. "Rightly dividing" means "cutting straight" and can be applied to many different tasks: plowing a straight furrow, cutting a straight board, sewing a straight seam.

The pastor is a workman in God's Word. The Word is a treasure that the steward must guard and invest. It is the soldier's sword and the farmer's seed. But it is also the workman's tool for building, measuring, and repairing God's people. The preacher and teacher who use the Word correctly will build their church the way God wants it to be built. But a sloppy worker will handle God's Word deceitfully in order to make it say what he wants it to say (2 Cor. 4:2). When God tests our ministries in His local churches, some of it, sad to say, will become ashes (1 Cor. 3:10ff).

An approved worker diligently studies the Word and seeks to apply it to his own life. An ashamed worker wastes his time with other "religious duties" and has little or nothing to give his class or congregation. An approved worker does not waste his time arguing about "words to no profit" (2 Tim. 2:14) because he knows that such arguing only undermines God's work (see 1 Tim. 6:4; Titus 3:9).

An approved workman will shun "godless chatter" (2 Tim. 2:16, NIV; and see 1 Tim. 6:20), because he knows it only leads to more ungodliness. I fear that some "sharing times" do more harm than good as well-meaning people exchange their "spiritual ignorance."

An approved workman knows that false doctrine is dangerous, and he will oppose it. Paul compared it to gangrene (2 Tim. 2:17). Much as gangrene spreads, infects, and kills other tissue, so false doctrine spreads and infects the body of believers, the church. This infection must be exposed and removed. Only the "sound [healthy] doctrine" of the Word of God can keep a church healthy and growing.

Paul named two men who were false teachers, and he also identified their error. It is likely that the Hymenaeus named here (2 Tim. 2:17) is the same man named in 1 Timothy 1:20. We know nothing about his associate, Philetus. Both of them "wandered from the truth" by teaching that the resurrection had already taken place. Perhaps they taught that salvation is resurrection in a spiritual sense, so a believer must not expect a physical resurrection. But the denial of a physical resurrection is a serious thing (see 1 Cor. 15:12ff), for it involves the resurrection of Christ and the completion of God's plan of salvation for His people. No wonder these false teachers were able to "overthrow the faith of some" (2 Tim. 2:18). The Resurrection is a foundational truth of the Gospel.

Each of us as God's workman will be either

*approved* or *ashamed*. The word *approved* means "one who has been tested and found acceptable." The word was used for testing and approving metals. Each trial that we go through forces us to study the Word to find God's will. As we rightly use the Word, we succeed in overcoming our trials, and we are approved by God. Martin Luther once said that prayer, study, and suffering make a pastor; and this is true. We cannot be approved unless we are tested.

What does it mean to be "ashamed"? Certainly it means that such a workman's work is below standard and cannot be accepted. It means loss of reward. In fact, in Paul's day, a builder was fined if he failed to follow the specifications. When the Lord judges our works, it will be revealed whether we as workmen have handled the Word of God honestly and carefully. Some who are now first will end up last!

### The Vessel (2 Tim. 2:19-22)

In this illustration, Paul described a "great house," which is the professing church. The *foundation* of the house is safe and secure because God's seal is on it. (In the Bible, a seal is a mark of ownership and security. No one would dare break a Roman seal.) Paul quoted Moses: "The Lord knoweth them that are His" (Num. 16:5). This refers to the Godward aspect of the Christian life: God chose us who trust Him as His elect (see 2 Tim. 2:10).

But there is also a manward aspect of the Christian life: "Let everyone that nameth the name of Christ depart from iniquity" (2 Tim. 2:19). This refers back to Numbers 16:26, where the Lord warned the people to get away from the tents of Korah and the rebels. In other words, those who are the elect of God prove it by living godly lives. We are chosen in Christ "that we should be holy and without blame" (Eph. 1:4).

This great house not only has a solid foundation that is sealed, but it also has vessels (utensils of various kinds) for performing household functions. Paul divides the utensils into two categories: those of honor (gold and silver) and those of dishonor (wood and clay). He is not distinguishing between kinds of Christians, but rather is making a distinction between true teachers of the Word and the false teachers he described (2 Tim. 2:16-18). A faithful pastor is like a gold or silver vessel that brings honor to Jesus Christ. The head of a house displays his costliest and most beautiful utensils and gets honor from them. I remember the first time I viewed the crown jewels of England in the Tower of London, along with the priceless table vessels and utensils. I was overwhelmed with their glory and beauty. That is the kind of beauty God gives to his servants who faithfully handle the Word of God.

False teachers are not valuable; they are like wood and clay. They are utensils to dishonor, no matter how popular they may be today. Wood and clay will not survive the test of fire. It is worth noting that the name *Timothy* comes from two Greek words which together mean "God-honoring." Paul was encouraging Timothy to live up to his name!

The important thing is that the honorable vessels not be contaminated by the dishonorable ones. The word "these" (2 Tim. 2:21) refers to the vessels of dishonor (2 Tim. 2:20). Paul is admonishing Timothy to separate himself from false teachers. If he does, then God will honor him, set him apart, and equip him for service. "Useful to the Master" (2 Tim. 2:21, NIV)—what a tremendous honor that is! A useful human vessel of honor does not get involved in the popular things of the world, even the "religious world." He must remain holy, and this means he must be separated from everything that would defile him.

This includes the sins of the flesh as well (2 Tim. 2:22). Paul used a similar admonition in 1 Timothy 6:11-12—"Flee . . . follow . . . fight." True Bible separation is balanced: we flee sin, but we follow after righteousness. If we are not balanced, then we will be isolated instead of separated. In fact, God's man Paul commands us to fellowship "with them that call on the Lord out of a pure heart" (2 Tim. 2:22). After all, this is the purpose of the ministry of the Word (1 Tim. 1:5). It is sad when true believers are isolated because of a false view of separation.

For God to be able to use us as vessels, we must be empty, clean, and available. He will take us and fill us and use us for His glory. But if we are filled with sin or defiled by disobedience, He will first have to purge us; and that might not be an enjoyable experience. In the "great house" of the professing church, there are true believers and false. We must exercise spiritual discernment and be careful that we are vessels sanctified unto honor.

## The Servant (2 Tim. 2:23-26)

"Servant" (2 Tim. 2:24) is the Greek word *doulos* which means "slave." So Paul called himself "a slave of Jesus Christ" (Rom. 1:1; Phil. 1:1). A slave had no will of his own; he was totally under the command of his master. Once, we Christians were the slaves of sin, but now we are the slaves of God (Rom. 6:16ff). Like the servant in Old Testament days, we say, "I love my master . . . I will not go out free" (Ex. 21:5).

God's slave does not have an easy time teaching the Word. Satan opposes him and tries to trap his listeners (2 Tim. 2:26). Also, some people are just naturally difficult to teach. They enjoy "foolish and stupid arguments" (2 Tim. 2:23, NIV) and have no desire to feed on the nourishing Word of God. Until you have experienced it, you have no idea how difficult it is to impart spiritual truth to some people.

How easy it would be to ignore them! But then Satan would get them. Paul admonished Timothy to avoid the arguments that create strifes, but not to ignore the people. He must not argue or fight. He must be patient and gentle, teaching the Word of God in meekness. It is not enough just to expose error and refute it; we must also teach positive truths and establish the saints in faith.

A servant of God must instruct those who oppose him, for this is the only way he can rescue them from Satan's captivity. Satan is a liar (John 8:44). He captures people by his lying promises, as he did Eve (see Gen. 3; 2 Cor. 11:3). A servant's purpose is not to win arguments but to win souls. He wants to see deceived persons brought to repentance ("I was wrong—I have changed my mind") and the acknowledging of the truth.

The word *recover* (2 Tim. 2:26) describes a man coming out of a drunken stupor. Satan makes people drunk with his lies, and the servant's task is to sober them up and rescue them. The last phrase in 2 Timothy 2:26 can be interpreted three ways: (1) they are delivered from the snare of the devil who took them captive to do his will; (2) they are taken captive by God's servant to do God's will; (3) they are delivered out of the snare of the devil, who took them captive, to do God's will. I prefer the third interpretation.

As you survey these seven aspects of the work of the ministry, you can see how important and how demanding a work it is. The ministry is no place for a loafer because it demands discipline and work. It is no place for a shirker because there are enemies to fight and tasks to be completed.

Church members need to pray for their pastors and encourage them in the work of the Lord. Church officers should faithfully do their work so that the pastors can devote themselves to their own ministry (see Acts 6:1-7). Churches should provide enough financial support for the ministers so that they can fully devote themselves to the work of the ministry.

In other words, ministers and members should labor together in the work of the Lord.

# CHAPTER THREE
# WHAT TO DO BEFORE IT ENDS
*2 Timothy 3*

The emphasis in this chapter is on *knowledge* and *responsibility*. Paul informed Timothy about the character of the last days, and then instructed him how to respond. Action must be based on knowledge. Too many Christians are like the pilot who informed his passengers, "We are lost, but we are making very good time."

"These last days" began with the ministry of Jesus Christ (Heb. 1:1-2) and will continue until He returns. They are called the "last days" because in them God is completing His purposes for His people. Because our Lord has delayed His return, some people scoff at the promise of His coming (2 Peter 3:3ff); but He will come as He promised.

Within this period of "last days" there will be "times" (seasons) of different kinds; but as the "times" draw to a close, they will become perilous. This word means "dangerous, hard to deal with, savage." This is the same Greek word that is used to describe the two violent demoniacs of Gadara (Matt. 8:28). This suggests that the violence of the last times will be energized by demons (1 Tim. 4:1).

There is no doubt that these characteristics started to appear in Paul's day, and now they have increased in intensity. It is not simply that we have more people in the world, or

better news coverage. It appears that evil is deeper and of greater intensity, and that it is being accepted and promoted by society in a bolder way. It is not that we have small pockets of rebellion here and there. All of society seems to be in ferment and rebellion. We are indeed in "terrible times" (2 Tim. 3:1, NIV).

Paul gave Timothy three instructions to obey in order that his ministry might be effective during perilous times.

## Turn Away from the False (2 Tim. 3:1-9)

"From such turn away" (2 Tim. 3:5b). A faithful believer should have nothing to do with the people Paul described in this section. It is important to note that these people operate *under the guise of religion:* "Having a form of godliness, but denying the power thereof" (2 Tim. 3:5). They are "religious" but rebellious! Paul discussed three facts about these people.

*Their characteristics (vv. 2-5).* At least eighteen different characteristics are listed here, and Paul probably could have listed more. There is an emphasis on *love:* "lovers of their own selves," lovers of money ("covetous"), "lovers of pleasures more than lovers of God." The heart of every problem is a problem in the heart. God commands us to love Him supremely, and our neighbors as ourselves (Matt. 22:34-40); but if we love ourselves supremely, we will not love God *or* our neighbors.

In this universe there is God, and there are people and things. We should worship God, love people, and use things. But if we start worshiping ourselves, we will ignore God and start loving things and using people. This is the formula for a miserable life; yet it characterizes many people today. The worldwide craving for *things* is just one evidence that people's hearts have turned away from God.

Of course, if someone loves and worships himself, the result will be *pride.* "Ye shall be as gods" was Satan's offer to Eve (Gen. 3:5), and the result was that people "changed the truth of God into a lie, and worshiped and served the creature more than [rather than] the Creator" (Rom. 1:25). Man became his own god! The creature is now the creator! "Boasters, proud [arrogant], blasphemers [given to contemptuous and bitter words]" (2 Tim. 3:2).

"Disobedient to parents" suggests that this apostasy reaches into the family. Children are "unthankful" and do not appreciate what their parents have done for them. They are "unholy" in their attitude toward their parents. "Honor thy father and thy mother" is not widely taught or respected.

The phrase "without natural affection" is the translation of one word that describes "family love." The family is under attack these days, and, as go its families, so goes the nation.

In place of the natural love that God has put into men and women and families, today we have a good deal of *un*natural love which God has condemned (see Rom. 1:18-27; 1 Cor. 6:9-10). It is confusion, and God will judge it (Rom. 1:28-32).

Not only in homes, but out in society and the business world, the characteristics of these perilous times may be seen. "Trucebreakers" (2 Tim. 3:3) describes people who will not try to agree. They are unyielding and irreconcilable and must have their own way.

In order to defend their position, they become "slanderers" ["false accusers," KJV] and try to tear down the reputations of others. Unfortunately, some of this activity goes on even among professed Christians. "Christian leaders" accuse one another in the pages of their publications.

"Incontinent" means "without self-control." The motto of our society today is "Do your own thing and enjoy it!" Sad to say, some of the children born to these people do not always enjoy it because they are deformed or handicapped as the result of drugs, alcohol, or venereal diseases.

This lack of self-control reveals itself in a number of ways. "Fierce" means "untamed, brutal." When these people cannot have their way, they become much like savage beasts. Instead of honoring what is good, they despise what is good and honor what is evil. In society today the standards of right and wrong have been twisted, if not destroyed. "Woe unto them that call evil good and good evil," cried Isaiah the prophet (Isa. 5:20).

"Traitors" (2 Tim. 3:4) describes people who betray others and cannot be trusted. Neither friendship nor partnership makes any difference to them; they lie and break their promises whenever doing so helps them get their own way.

"Heady" means "reckless, rash, acting without careful thought." Paul did not condemn honest adventure, but foolish endeavor.

"High-minded" does not describe a person with lofty thoughts. Rather, it means a person who is "puffed up" with his importance. "Conceited" is a good synonym.

"Lovers of pleasures more than lovers of God" does not suggest that we must choose between pleasure and God; for when we live for God, we enjoy the greatest pleasures (Ps. 16:11). The choice is between *loving* pleasure or loving God. If we love God, we will also enjoy fullness of life here and forever; but the pleasures of sin can only last for a brief time (Heb. 11:25). No one can deny that we live in a pleasure-mad world; but these pleasures too often are just shallow entertainment and escape; they are not enrichment and true enjoyment.

Paul stated that these people he has just described would consider themselves religious! "Having a form of godliness" (2 Tim. 3:5) suggests an outward appearance of religion, not true Christian faith; for they have never experienced the power of God in their lives. Form without force. Religion without reality.

***Their converts (vv. 6-7).*** The fact that Paul described "silly ['weak-willed,' NIV] women" does not suggest that all women are like this, or that men are not vulnerable to the wiles of false teachers. In Paul's day, women were especially susceptible to this kind of experience since they had a low status in society. Whether men or women, people who fall for this false religious system have the same characteristics.

They are *burdened with guilt* and looking for some escape from bondage and fear. They find themselves unable to control their various desires ("divers lusts," KJV). The emphasis here may be on sexual problems. Finally, they are always searching for truth, trying this approach and that; yet they are never able to be satisfied. This kind of person is fair game for the cultists and the religious racketeers.

These false religious leaders take advantage of the problems people have, and promise them quick and easy solutions. They "worm their way in" and soon control people's lives. It is not long before these leaders grab their followers' loyalty, money, and service. And their "converts" are worse off than they were before. They still have their problems, but they have been duped into thinking that all is well.

And, remember: All of this underhanded activity is done in the name of religion! No wonder Paul told Timothy, "From such turn away."

***Their religious leaders (vv. 8-9).*** Read
Exodus 7–9 for the record of the contest between Moses and the Egyptian magicians.
Tradition says that the magicians were Jannes
and Jambres, two men mentioned by Paul
(2 Tim. 3:8). These men opposed Moses *by
imitating what he did.* When Aaron's rod
turned into a serpent, the magicians cast
down their rods and they turned into serpents. Moses turned the water into blood, and
the magicians followed with the same miracle.
When Moses brought up all the frogs, the
magicians duplicated the miracle. But when it
came to the miracle of the lice, the magicians
could not imitate it (Ex. 8:16-19).

Satan is an imitator; what God does, Satan
counterfeits. The religious leaders in the last
days will have a counterfeit faith, and their
purpose is to promote a lie and resist the
truth of God's Word. They deny the authority
of the Bible and substitute human wisdom and
philosophy. In their attempt to be "modern,"
they deny the reality of sin and people's need
for salvation. "Reprobate" is the word Paul
used to describe them. This means "tested
and found counterfeit."

Jannes and Jambres were finally exposed
and made fools of by the judgments of God.
This will also happen to the leaders of false
religions in the last days. When God's judgments fall, the true character of these counterfeits will be revealed to everyone.

## Follow Those Who Are True
## (2 Tim. 3:10-12)
Paul turned from the false leaders to remind
Timothy that he (Paul) had been a faithful ser-
vant of God. It is important in these difficult
days that we follow the right spiritual leaders.
What are their characteristics?

***Their lives are open for all to see (v.
10a).*** Paul had nothing to hide. Like his Master, he could say, "In secret have I said nothing" (John 18:20). "My manner of life from my
youth . . . know all the Jews," Paul had told
Agrippa (Acts 26:4). Timothy had lived and
labored with Paul and knew the man well. Paul
had not hidden behind extravagant claims or
religious propaganda.

***They teach true doctrine (v. 10b).*** "My
doctrine" in Paul's case meant the true faith,
the Gospel of Jesus Christ. No matter how
appealing a preacher may be, if he does not
preach the truth of God's Word, he does not
deserve our support. On radio and TV today,
we have a great deal of "pseudo-Christianity"

which is a mixture of psychology, success motivation, and personality cults, with a little bit
of Bible thrown in to make it look religious.
Beware!

***They practice what they preach (v.
10c).*** Paul's "manner of life" backed up his
messages. He did not preach sacrifice and live
in luxury. He gave to others far more than he
received from them. He stood up for the truth
even when it meant losing friends and, in the
end, losing his life. Paul was a servant, not a
celebrity.

***Their purpose is to glorify God (v.
10d).*** There was never a question about
Paul's "purpose" in ministry: He wanted to do
God's will and finish the work God gave him to
do (Acts 20:24; Phil. 1:21). The Apostle Paul
was a man of "faith" who trusted God to meet
his needs. He was a man of "long-suffering"
who bore up under people's attacks. He was a
man of *love* ("charity") who willingly gave himself to serve others.

The word *patience* at the end of 2 Timothy
3:10 means "endurance, the ability to stick
with it when the going gets tough."

***They are willing to suffer (vv. 11-12).***
Paul did not ask others to suffer for him; *he
suffered for others.* The fact that he was persecuted from city to city was proof that he was
living a godly life. Some people today have the
idea that godliness means *escaping* persecution, when just the opposite is true.

I wonder how Paul would match up with
today's concept of a Christian leader. He
would probably fail miserably. If he applied for
service with a modern mission board, would
he be accepted? He had a prison record; he
had a physical affliction; he stirred up problems in just about every place he visited. He
was poor, and he did not cater to the rich. Yet
God used him, and we are being blessed today because Paul was faithful.

## Continue in God's Word
## (2 Tim. 3:13-17)
The only way to defeat Satan's lies is with
God's truth. "Thus saith the Lord!" is the final
answer to every question. Evil men and deceivers are going to get worse and worse.
They will deceive more and more. Why? Because they are being deceived by Satan! In
these last days, there will be more deception
and imitation; and the only way a believer will
be able to tell the true from the false is by
knowing the Word of God.

Timothy had been taught the Word of God

from the time he was a child. Some people are prone to say, "Well, I needed the Bible when I was younger; but I can do without it now that I'm older." How wrong they are! Adults need the guidance of the Word far more than children do because adults face more temptations and make more decisions. Timothy's grandmother and mother had faithfully taught him the Old Testament Scriptures. (The word *whom* in 2 Tim. 3:14 is plural, referring to these women; see 2 Tim. 1:5.) Timothy was to continue in what he had been taught. We never outgrow the Word of God.

This is a good place to admonish Christian parents to teach their children the Bible. In our home, my wife and I used Kenneth Taylor's *Bible Stories with Pictures for Little Eyes;* in fact, we wore out two copies! What a joy it was to see our older children who had learned to read share the stories with the younger ones and help them answer the questions. Little by little, the children graduated to older Bible storybooks and then to Bibles of their own. We were fortunate that our Sunday School included a Bible memory program. As soon as your child is born, surround him with the Word of God and prayer. You will not have this opportunity after he grows up.

In this paragraph, Paul made some important statements about the Scriptures:

**They are the Holy Scriptures (v. 15a).** "The sacred letters" is a literal translation. The suggestion is that young Timothy learned his Hebrew alphabet by spelling his way through the Old Testament Scriptures. The word for *holy* means "consecrated for sacred use." The Bible is different from every other book—even books about the Bible—because it has been set apart by God for special sacred uses. We must treat the Bible as the special book it is.

The way we treat the Bible shows others how much or how little we respect it. While I don't want to become a crank in this matter, I must confess that I hate to see a Bible on the floor. When we are carrying a Bible and other books, the Bible should be on the top. There is a difference between properly marking a Bible as we study and defacing it by careless marking. I have seen people put a cup of coffee on a Bible! Paul gives us the right attitude toward the Word of God (1 Thes. 2:13).

**The Scriptures lead us to salvation (v. 15b).** We are not saved by believing the Bible (see John 5:39), but by trusting the Christ who is revealed in the Bible. Satan knows the

Bible but he is not saved. Timothy was raised on the Holy Scriptures in a godly home. Yet it was not until Paul led him to Christ that he was saved.

What is the relationship of the Bible to salvation? To begin with, the Bible reveals our need for salvation. It is a mirror that shows us how filthy we are in God's sight. The Bible explains that every lost sinner is condemned *now* (John 3:18-21) and needs a Saviour *now.* It also makes it clear that a lost sinner cannot save himself.

But the Bible also reveals God's wonderful plan of salvation: Christ died for our sins! If we trust Him, He will save us (John 3:16-18). The Bible also helps give us the assurance of our salvation (see 1 John 5:9-13). Then the Bible becomes our spiritual food to nourish us that we might grow in grace and serve Christ. It is our sword for fighting Satan and overcoming temptation.

**The Scriptures are true and dependable (v. 16a).** "All Scripture is God-breathed" (NIV). The doctrine of the inspiration of Scripture is vitally important, and a doctrine that Satan has attacked from the beginning ("Yea, hath God said?" [Gen. 3:1]). It is inconceivable that God would give His people a book they could not trust. He is the God of truth (Deut. 32:4); Jesus is "the truth" (John 14:6); and the "Spirit is truth" (1 John 5:6). Jesus said of the Scriptures, "Thy Word is truth" (John 17:17).

The Holy Spirit of God used men of God to write the Word of God (2 Peter 1:20-21). The Spirit did not erase the natural characteristics of the writers. In fact, God in His providence prepared the writers for the task of writing the Scriptures. Each writer has his own distinctive style and vocabulary. Each book of the Bible grew out of a special set of circumstances. In His preparation of men, in His guiding of history, and in His working through the Spirit, God brought about the miracle of the Scriptures.

We must not think of "inspiration" the way the world thinks when it says, "Shakespeare was certainly an inspired writer." What we mean by biblical *inspiration* is the supernatural influence of the Holy Spirit on the Bible's writers, which guaranteed that what they wrote was accurate and trustworthy. *Revelation* means the communicating of truth to man by God; *inspiration* has to do with the *recording* of this communication in a way that is dependable.

Whatever the Bible says about itself, man, God, life, death, history, science, and every other subject is true. This does not mean that every statement in the Bible is true, because the Bible records the lies of men and of Satan. *But the record is true.*

**The Scriptures are profitable (v. 16b).** They are profitable for *doctrine* (what is right), for *reproof* (what is not right), for *correction* (how to get right), and for *instruction in righteousness* (how to stay right). A Christian who studies the Bible and applies what he learns will grow in holiness and avoid many pitfalls in this world.

**The Scriptures equip us for service (v. 17).** Earlier Paul had called Timothy a "man of God" (1 Tim. 6:11); but here Paul states that *any* Christian can become a person "of God." How? By studying the Word of God, obeying it, and letting it control his life. It is worth noting that all of the "men of God" named in Scripture—including Moses, Samuel, Elijah, Elisha, David, and Timothy—were men who were devoted to God's Word.

Two words in this verse are especially important: "perfect" and "furnished." The word translated "perfect" means "complete, in fit shape, in fit condition." It does not begin to suggest sinless perfection. Rather, it implies being fitted for use.

"Furnished" has a similar meaning: "equipped for service." In other words, the Word of God furnishes and equips a believer so that he can live a life that pleases God and do the work God wants him to do. The better we know the Word, the better we are able to live and work for God.

The purpose of Bible study is *not* just to understand doctrines or to be able to defend the faith, as important as these things are. The ultimate purpose is the equipping of the believers who read it. It is the Word of God that equips God's people to do the work of God.

The times are not going to get better, but we Christians can become better people, even in bad times. We must separate ourselves from that which is false, devote ourselves to that which is true, and continue in our study of the Word of God. Then God can equip us for ministry in these difficult days, and we will have the joy of seeing others come to a knowledge of the truth.

# CHAPTER FOUR
# LAST WORDS
## *2 Timothy 4*

A great person's last words are significant. They are a window that helps us to look into his heart, or a measure that helps us evaluate his life. In this chapter, we have Paul's last words to Timothy and to the church.

It is interesting that Paul expressed no regrets as he came to the end. He even forgave those who made his situation difficult (2 Tim. 4:16). More than seventeen people are referred to in this chapter, which shows that Paul was a friend-maker as well as a soul winner. Though his own days were numbered, Paul thought of others.

The apostle gave three final admonitions to Timothy, and he backed each of them up with a reason.

### Preach the Word! (2 Tim. 4:1-4)

"I charge thee" should read "I solemnly witness." This was a serious moment, and Paul wanted Timothy to sense the importance of it. It was serious, not only because Paul was facing death, but even more because both Paul and Timothy would be judged one day when Jesus Christ appeared. It would do us all good to occasionally reflect on the fact that one day we will face God and our works will be judged.

For one thing, this realization would encourage us to do our work carefully and faithfully. It would also deliver us from the fear of man; for, after all, our final Judge is God. Finally, the realization that God will one day judge our works encourages us to keep going even when we face difficulties. We are serving Him, not ourselves.

"Preach the Word!" is the main responsibility that Paul shared in this section. Everything else he said is related to this. The word "preach" means "to preach like a herald." In Paul's day, a ruler had a special herald who made announcements to the people. He was commissioned by the ruler to make his announcements in a loud, clear voice so everyone could hear. He was not an ambassador with the privilege of negotiating; he was a messenger with a proclamation to be heard and heeded. Not to heed the ruler's messenger was serious; to abuse the messenger was even worse.

Timothy was to herald God's Word with the authority of heaven behind him. The Word of God is what both sinners and saints need. It is a pity that many churches have substituted other things for the preaching of the Word, things that may be good in their place, but that are bad when they replace the proclamation of the Word. In my own pastoral ministry, I have seen what the preaching of the Word can do in churches and in individual lives; and I affirm that *nothing can take its place.*

Timothy should be diligent and alert to use every opportunity to preach the Word, when it is favorable and even when it is not favorable. *It is easy to make excuses when we ought to be making opportunities.* Paul himself always found an opportunity to share the Word, whether it was in the temple courts, on a stormy sea, or even in prison. "He that observeth the wind shall not sow; and he that regardeth the clouds shall not reap" (Ecc. 11:4). Stop making excuses and get to work!

Preaching must be marked by three elements: conviction, warning, and appeal ("reprove, rebuke, exhort"). To quote an old rule of preachers, "He should afflict the comfortable and comfort the afflicted." If there is conviction but no remedy, we add to people's burdens. And if we encourage those who ought to be rebuked, we are assisting them to sin. Biblical preaching must be balanced.

God's speaker must be patient as he preaches the Word. He will not always see immediate results. He must be patient with those who oppose his preaching. Above all else, *he must preach doctrine.* He must not simply tell Bible stories, relate interesting illustrations, or read a verse and then forget it. *True preaching is the explanation and application of Bible doctrine. Anything else is just religious speechmaking.*

Paul gave the responsibility—"preach the Word" (2 Tim. 4:2)—and he also gave the reason (2 Tim. 4:3-4). The time would come (and it has been here for a long time!) when most people would not want the "healthy doctrine" of the Word of God. They would have carnal desires for religious novelties. Because of their "itching ears" they would accumulate teachers who would satisfy their cravings for things that disagree with God's truths. The fact that a preacher has a large congregation is not always a sign that he is preaching the truth. In fact, it may be evidence that he is tickling people's "itching ears" and giving them what they *want* to hear instead of what they *need* to hear.

It is but a short step from "itching ears" to turning one's ears away from the truth. Once people have rejected the truth, they turn to fables (myths). It is not likely that man-made fables will convict them of sin or make them want to repent! The result is a congregation of comfortable, professing Christians, listening to a comfortable, religious talk that contains no Bible doctrine. These people become the prey of every false cult because their lives lack a foundation in the Word of God. It is a recognized fact that most cultists were formerly members of churches.

Note the emphasis on Scripture: "Preach the Word . . . with . . . doctrine. . . . They will not endure sound doctrine . . . they shall turn away their ears from the truth" (2 Tim. 4:2-4). This emphasis on sound (healthy) doctrine runs through all three of Paul's Pastoral Epistles, and this emphasis is surely needed today.

### Fulfill Your Ministry (2 Tim. 4:5-8)

"Make full proof of thy ministry" means "fulfill whatever God wants you to do." Timothy's ministry would not be exactly like Paul's, but it would be important to the cause of Christ. No God-directed ministry is small or unimportant. In this final chapter, Paul named some co-laborers about whom we know nothing; yet they too had a ministry to fulfill.

A young preacher once complained to Charles Spurgeon, the famous British preacher of the 1800s, that he did not have as big a church as he deserved.

"How many do you preach to?" Spurgeon asked.

"Oh, about 100," the man replied.

Solemnly Spurgeon said, "That will be enough to give account for on the day of judgment."

We do not measure the fulfillment of a ministry only on the basis of statistics or on what people see. We realize that faithfulness is important and that God sees the heart. This was why Timothy had to be "sober in all things" (2 Tim. 4:5, NASB) and carry on his ministry with seriousness of purpose. (We have met this word "sober" many times in these letters.)

Timothy was not only a preacher; he was also a soldier (2 Tim. 2:3-4) who would have to "endure afflictions" (2 Tim. 4:5). He had seen Paul go through sufferings on more than one occasion (2 Cor. 6:1-10; 2 Tim. 3:10-12). Most of Timothy's sufferings would come from the "religious crowd" that did not want to hear the truth. It was the "religious crowd" that crucified Christ and that persecuted Paul and had him arrested.

"Do the work of an evangelist" (2 Tim. 4:5) would remind Timothy that all of his ministry must have soul-winning at its heart. This does not mean that every sermon should be a "sawdust trail, hellfire-and-brimstone" message, because the saints need feeding as well. But it does mean that a preacher, no matter what he is preaching, should keep the lost souls in mind. This burden for the lost should characterize a pastor's private ministry as well. (See Acts 20:17-21 for a description of a balanced ministry.)

God has given special men to the church as evangelists (Acts 21:8; Eph. 4:11); but this does not absolve a pastor from his soul-winning responsibility. Not every preacher has the same gifts, but every preacher can share the same burden and proclaim the same saving message. A friend of mine went to hear a famous preacher, and I asked him how the message was. He replied, "There wasn't enough Gospel in it to save a flea!"

Paul gave the reason behind the responsibility (2 Tim. 4:6 8): He was about to move off the scene and Timothy would have to take his place. In this beautiful paragraph of personal testimony, you find Paul looking in three different directions.

**He looked around (v. 6).** Paul realized that his time was short. He was on trial in Rome and had been through the first hearing (2 Tim. 4:17). But Paul knew that the end was near. However, he did not tremble at the prospect of death! The two words "offered" and "departure" (2 Tim. 4:6) tell us of his faith and confidence. "Offered" means "poured out on the altar as a drink-offering." He used the same picture in Philippians 2:7-8. In effect Paul was saying, "Caesar is not going to kill me. I am going to give my life as a sacrifice to Jesus Christ. I have been a living sacrifice, serving Him since the day I was saved. Now I will complete that sacrifice by laying down my life for Him."

The word *departure* (2 Tim. 4:6) is a beautiful word that has many meanings. It means "to hoist anchor and set sail." Paul looked on death as a release from the world, an opportunity to "set sail" into eternity. The word also means "to take down a tent." This parallels 2 Corinthians 5:1-8, where Paul compared the death of believers to the taking down of a tent (tabernacle), in order to receive a permanent, glorified body ("house not made with hands"— a glorified body, not a "mansion" in heaven).

*Departure* also has the meaning of "loosing a prisoner." Paul was facing release, not execution! "The unyoking of an ox" is another meaning of this word. Paul had been in hard service for many years. Now his Master would unyoke him and promote him to higher service.

**Paul looked back (v. 7).** He summed up his life and ministry. Two of the images here are athletic: like a determined wrestler or boxer, he had fought a good fight; and, like a runner, he had finished his lifelong race victoriously. He had kept the rules and deserved a prize (see Acts 20:24; Phil. 3:13-14). The third image is that of a steward who had faithfully guarded his boss' deposit: "I have kept the faith" (2 Tim. 4:7). Paul used this image often in his pastoral letters.

It is heartening to be able to look back and have no regrets. Paul was not always popular, nor was he usually comfortable; but he remained faithful. That is what really counted.

**Paul looked ahead (v. 8).** A Greek or Roman athlete who was a winner was rewarded by the crowds and usually got a laurel wreath or a garland of oak leaves. The word for "crown" is *stephanos*—the victor's crown; we get our name Stephen from this word. (The kingly crown is *diadema*, from which we get "diadem.") However, Paul would not be given a fading crown of leaves; his would be a crown of righteousness that would never fade.

Jesus Christ is the "righteous Judge" who always judges correctly. Paul's judges in Rome were not righteous. If they were, they would have released him. How many times Paul had been tried in one court after another, yet now he faced his last Judge—his Lord and Saviour Jesus Christ. When you are ready to face the Lord, you need not fear the judgment of men.

The crown of righteousness is God's reward for a faithful and righteous life; and our incentive for faithfulness and holiness is the promise of the Lord's appearing. Because Paul loved His appearing and looked for it, he lived righteously and served faithfully. This is why Paul used the return of Jesus Christ as a basis for his admonitions in this chapter (see 2 Tim. 4:1).

We are not called to be apostles; yet we can win the same crown that Paul won. If we love Christ's appearing, live in obedience to His will, and do the work He has called us to do, we will be crowned.

## Be Diligent and Faithful (2 Tim. 4:9-22)

"Hurry and get here!" is the meaning of the admonition to Timothy (2 Tim. 4:9). Tychicus would take Timothy's place in Ephesus (2 Tim. 4:12). As Timothy hurried to Rome, he could stop in Troas and get the cloak, books, and parchments (2 Tim. 4:13). Paul probably left them there in his haste to depart. It is touching to see that, in his closing days on earth, Paul wanted his dear "son in the faith" at his side. But he was also practical: he needed his cloak for warmth, and he wanted his books for study. The "books" would be papyrus scrolls, perhaps of the Old Testament Scriptures; and the "parchments" would be books made from the skins of animals. We do not know what these "parchments" were, but we are not surprised that a scholar such as Paul wanted material for study and writing.

Before he ended the letter, Paul urged Timothy to "come before winter" (2 Tim. 4:21). Why? All the ships would be in port during the winter since it would be too dangerous for sailing. If Timothy waited too long, he would miss his opportunity to travel to Paul; and then it would be too late.

Why should Timothy be diligent and faithful? Look at 2 Timothy 4:10, which gives part of the answer: Some in Paul's circle were not faithful, and he could not depend on them. Demas is named only three times in the New Testament; yet these three citations tell a sad story of failure. Paul listed Demas along with Mark and Luke as one of his "fellow laborers" (Phile. 24). Then he is simply called "Demas" (Col. 4:14). Here (2 Tim. 4:10) it is, "Demas hath forsaken me."

Paul gave the reason: Demas "loved this present world." He had, as a believer, "tasted . . . the powers of the world to come" (Heb. 6:5); but he preferred "this present evil world" (Gal. 1:4). In his *Pilgrim's Progress,* John Bunyan pictured Demas as the keeper of a silver mine at the Hill Lucre. Perhaps it was the love of money that enticed Demas back into the world. It must have broken Paul's heart to see Demas fail so shamefully; yet it can happen to any believer. Perhaps this explains why Paul had so much to say about riches in his pastoral letters.

Another reason why Paul wanted Timothy in Rome was that his next hearing was coming up and only Luke was with him. The believers in Rome and Ephesus who could have stood with Paul had failed him (2 Tim. 4:16); but Paul knew that Timothy would not fail him. Of course, the Lord had not failed Paul either! (2 Tim. 4:17) The Lord had promised to stay with Paul, and He had kept His promise.

When Paul had been discouraged in Corinth, the Lord came to him and encouraged him (Acts 18:9-11). After he had been arrested in Jerusalem, Paul again was visited by the Lord and encouraged (Acts 23:11). During that terrible storm, when Paul was on board ship, the Lord had again given him strength and courage (Acts 27:22ff). Now, in that horrible Roman prison, Paul again experienced the strengthening presence of the Lord, who had promised, "I will never leave thee, nor forsake thee" (Heb. 13:5).

But note that Paul's concern was not for his own safety or comfort. It was the preaching of the Word so that Gentiles might be saved. It was Paul's special calling to minister to the Gentiles (see Eph. 3); and he was not ashamed of the Gospel, even in the great city of Rome (Rom. 1:16).

What a man! His friends forsake him, and he prays that God will forgive them. His enemies try him, and he looks for opportunities to tell them how to be saved! What a difference it makes when the Holy Spirit controls your life.

"I was delivered out of the mouth of the lion" (2 Tim. 4:17). Who or what is this "lion"? It cannot mean a literal lion because Paul was a Roman citizen and, if convicted, he could not be thrown to the lions. Instead, he would be executed by being beheaded. Was "the lion" the Emperor Nero? Probably not. If he had been delivered from Nero, then this meant he was acquitted; yet, he had only had a preliminary first hearing. The lion is a symbol of Satan (1 Peter 5:8). Perhaps Paul was referring to some scheme of the devil to defeat him and hinder the work of the Gospel. To be "saved from the lion's mouth" was a proverbial saying which meant "to be delivered from great danger" (Ps. 22:21).

But for a Christian, there are things even more dangerous than suffering and death. Sin, for example. This is what Paul had in mind (2 Tim. 4:18). He was confident that the Lord would deliver him from "every evil work" and take him to the heavenly kingdom. Paul's greatest fear was not of death; it was that he might deny his Lord or do something else that would disgrace God's name. Paul was certain that the time had come for his permanent departure (2 Tim. 4:6). He wanted to end his life-race well and be free from any disobedience.

It is heartening to see how many people are named in the closing part of this last letter Paul wrote. I believe that there are at least 100 different men and women named in Acts and Paul's letters, as a part of his circle of friends and fellow laborers. Paul could not do the job by himself. It is a great man who enlists others to help get the job done, and who lets them share in the greatness of the work.

*Luke* (2 Tim. 4:11) is the "beloved physician" who traveled with Paul (Col. 4:14). He is author of the Gospel of Luke and the Book of Acts. (Notice the "we" sections in Acts, the eyewitness reports of Dr. Luke.) Paul probably dictated this letter (2 Tim.) to Luke. Being a doctor, Luke must have appreciated Paul's reference to gangrene (2 Tim. 2:17, NIV).

*Crescens* (2 Tim. 4:10) was sent by Paul to Galatia. We know nothing about him, nor do we really need to know. He was another faithful laborer who assisted Paul in an hour of great need.

*Titus* (2 Tim. 4:10) was Paul's close associate and, along with Timothy, a trusted "troubleshooter." Paul had left Titus in Crete to straighten out the problems in the churches there (Titus 1:5). As we study Paul's letter to Titus, we get better acquainted with this choice servant of God. Titus had met Paul at Nicopolis during that period between Paul's arrests (Titus 3:12). Now Paul had summoned him to Rome and sent him to Dalmatia (our modern Yugoslavia).

*Mark* (2 Tim. 4:11) was a cousin of Barnabas, Paul's first partner in missionary service (Acts 13:1-3). His mother was a noted Christian in Jerusalem (Acts 12:5, 12). Unfortunately, John Mark failed on that first missionary journey (Acts 13:5, 13). Paul refused to take Mark on the second trip, and this led to a falling-out between Paul and Barnabas (Acts 15:36-41). However, Paul now admitted that John Mark was a valuable worker; and he wanted Mark with him in Rome. How good it is to know that one failure in Christian service need not make one's whole life a failure.

*Tychicus* (2 Tim. 4:12) was a believer from the province of Asia (Acts 20:4) who willingly accompanied Paul and probably ministered as a personal servant to the apostle. He was with Paul during his first imprisonment (Eph. 6:21-22; Col. 4:7-8). Paul sent Tychicus to Crete to relieve Titus (Titus 3:12). Now he was sending him to Ephesus to relieve Timothy. What a blessing it is to have people who can replace others! A relief pitcher may not get all the glory, but he may help win the game!

*Carpus* (2 Tim. 4:13) lived at Troas and gave Paul hospitality. Paul must have departed in a hurry (was he being sought for arrest?) because he left his cloak and books behind. However, Carpus was a faithful brother; he would guard them until somebody picked them up to take to Paul. Even such so-called menial tasks are ministries for the Lord.

Is *Alexander the coppersmith* (2 Tim. 4:14) the same Alexander mentioned in 1 Timothy 1:20? Nobody knows, and there is no value in conjecturing. The name was common, but it is possible that this heretic went to Rome to make things difficult for Paul. Satan has his workers too. By the way, Paul's words, "The Lord reward him according to his works" (2 Tim. 4:14), are not a prayer of judgment, for this would be contrary to Jesus' teaching (Matt. 5:43-48). "The Lord *will* reward him" is a better translation.

*Prisca* (or Priscilla) *and Aquila* (2 Tim. 4:19) were a husband-and-wife team that assisted Paul in many ways (see Acts 18:1-3, 24-28; Rom. 16:3-4; 1 Cor. 16:19). Now they were in Ephesus helping Timothy with his ministry. It is wonderful when God's people do their work regardless of who their leader is.

*Onesiphorus* (2 Tim. 4:19) and his household we met in 2 Timothy 1.

*Erastus* (2 Tim. 4:20) might be the treasurer of Corinth (Rom. 16:23); and he might be the same man who ministered with Timothy in Macedonia (Acts 19:22).

*Trophimus* (2 Tim. 4:20) from Ephesus was a friend of Tychicus (Acts 20:4), and the man whose presence with Paul helped to incite that riot in Jerusalem (Acts 21:28-29). He had been serving at Miletus, but now he was ill. Why did Paul not heal him? Apparently not every sick person is supposed to be miraculously healed.

The other people mentioned (2 Tim. 4:21) are unknown to us, but certainly not to the Lord.

"Grace be with you" (2 Tim. 4:22) was Paul's personal farewell, used at the end of his letters as a "trademark" that the letter was not a forgery.

The Bible does not record the final days of Paul. Tradition tells us that he was found guilty and sentenced to die. He was probably taken outside the city and beheaded.

But Timothy and the other devoted believers carried on the work! As John Wesley used to say, "God buries His workmen, but His work goes on." You and I must be faithful so that (if the Lord does not return soon) future generations may hear the Gospel and have the opportunity to be saved.

# TITUS

## OUTLINE

**Key theme:** Christians should maintain good works
**Key verse:** Titus 3:8

### I. CHURCH ORGANIZATION— chapter 1
A. Preach God's Word—1:1-4
B. Ordain qualified leaders—1:5-9
C. Silence false teachers—1:10-16

### II. CHRISTIAN OBLIGATION— chapters 2–3
A. Older saints—2:1-4a
B. Younger saints—2:4b-8
C. Christian slaves—2:9-15
D. Christians as citizens—3:1-8
E. Problem people—3:9-11
F. Conclusion—3:12-15

## CONTENTS

# CHAPTER ONE
# OUR MAN IN CRETE
*Titus 1*

While Timothy was laboring in metropolitan Ephesus, Titus had his hands full on the island of Crete. Titus was a Greek believer (Gal. 2:3) who had served Paul well on special assignments to the church in Corinth (2 Cor. 7:13-14; 8:6, 16, 23; 12:18). Apparently Titus had been won to Christ through Paul's personal ministry (Titus 1:4) as Timothy had been (1 Tim. 1:2). "As for Titus," Paul wrote, "he is my partner and fellow worker among you" (2 Cor. 8:23, NIV).

But the people on the island of Crete were not the easiest to work with, and Titus became somewhat discouraged. Like Timothy, he was probably a young man. But unlike Timothy, he was not given to timidity and physical ailments. Paul had been with Titus on Crete and had left him there to correct the things that were wrong. Since Jews from Crete were present at Pentecost (Acts 2:11), it is possible that they had carried the Gospel to their native land.

Titus had his share of problems! The churches needed qualified leaders, and the various groups in the churches needed shepherding. One group of false teachers was trying to mix Jewish law with the Gospel of grace (Titus 1:10, 14), while some of the Gentile believers were abusing the message of grace and turning it into license (Titus 2:11-15). By nature, the people of Crete were not easy to work with (Titus 1:12-13), and Titus needed extraordinary patience and love. It would have been easy for Titus to have "heard God's call to go elsewhere," but he stuck it out and finished his work.

As you read and study this letter, you will discover that it is a condensed version of Paul's first letter to Timothy. In this first chapter, Paul reminded Titus of three responsibilities he had to fulfill.

**Preach God's Word (Titus 1:1-4)**
In this rather lengthy greeting, Paul emphasized the importance of the Word of God. Four times he used the Greek preposition *kata,* the root meaning of which is "down." But in this context, *kata* helps us see the relationship between the ministry and the Word of God. Consider the four phrases.

*"According to the faith of God's elect" (v. 1a).* Paul's ministry was governed by the Word of God. He was "a slave of God" (the only place Paul used this phrase) and "a messenger sent on a special commission" by Jesus Christ. But the purpose of his ministry was to share the faith, that body of truth contained in the Word of God. "God's elect" are those who have trusted Jesus Christ as their Saviour (Eph. 1:4; 1 Peter 1:1-5).

*"The truth which is after [according to] godliness" (vv. 1b-2).* "Godliness" is an important concept in this letter, just as it was in 1 Timothy, even though the actual word is used only once. But the repetition of "good works" emphasizes the point (Titus 1:16; 2:7, 14; 3:1, 5, 8, 14). The truth of the Gospel changes a life from ungodliness (Titus 2:12) to holy living. Sad to say, there were people in the churches on Crete, like some church members today, who professed to be saved, but whose lives denied their profession (Titus 1:12).

This faith in Jesus Christ not only saves us *today* and makes our lives godly, but it also gives us hope for *the future* (Titus 1:2). We have assurance for the future because of God's promises, and God cannot lie (see Num. 23:19). We are born again "unto a living hope" (1 Peter 1:3, NIV) because we have trusted the living Christ. We believers have eternal life now (John 3:16; 1 John 5:11-12); but when Jesus Christ returns, we will enjoy eternal life in an even greater way.

*"According to the commandment of God" (v. 3).* God reveals His message through preaching. This does not mean the act of proclaiming the Word, but rather the *content* of the message. "It pleased God by the foolishness of preaching [the message of the Cross] to save them that believe" (1 Cor. 1:21). This Word of the Gospel was committed to Paul (see 1 Tim. 1:11), and he had committed it to Titus. This ministry was according to the commandment of God and was not given by men (Gal. 1:10-12).

As in 1 Timothy, the title *Saviour* is often repeated in Titus (1:3-4; 2:10, 13; 3:4, 6). The God-given written Word reveals the Saviour, because a Saviour is what sinners need. God's grace brings salvation, not condemnation (Titus 2:11). Jesus could have come to earth as a Judge, but He chose to come as a Saviour (Luke 2:10-11).

*"After the common faith" (v. 4).* The word *common* means "to have in common." This faith is the possession of all of God's people and not just a selected few. Christians in different denominational groups may wear different labels, but all who possess the same saving faith share "the common salvation" (Jude 3). There was a definite body of truth deposited in the church, "the faith that was once for all entrusted to the saints" (Jude 3, NIV). Any departure from this "common faith" is false teaching and must not be tolerated in the church.

As you review these four statements, you can see that Paul related everything in his ministry to the Word of God. His calling and his preaching depended on faith in Christ. He wanted Titus to grasp this fact and to make the Word of God a priority in his ministry. Throughout all three of the Pastoral Epistles there is an emphasis on teaching the Word of God. Local churches ought to be "Bible schools" where the Word of God is taught systematically and in a practical way.

## Ordain Qualified Leaders (Titus 1:5-9)

One reason Paul had left Titus on the island of Crete was that he might organize the local assemblies and "set in order" the things that were lacking. That phrase is a medical term; it was applied to the setting of a crooked limb. Titus was not the spiritual dictator of the island, but he was Paul's official apostolic representative with authority to work. It had been Paul's policy to ordain elders in the churches he had established (Acts 14:23), but he had not been able to stay in Crete long enough to accomplish this task.

Several of the qualifications listed here (Titus 1:6-8) have already been discussed in our study of 1 Timothy 3:2-3: "blameless, the husband of one wife . . . not given to wine, no striker [not violent], not given to filthy lucre . . . a lover of hospitality . . . sober." The fact that these standards applied to Christians on the island of Crete as well as to those in the city of Ephesus proves that God's measure for leaders does not fluctuate. A big-city church and a small-town church both need godly people in places of leadership.

Now, consider nine additional qualifications.

*"Having faithful children" (v. 6b).* *Faithful* means "believing." The bishop's children should be Christians. After all, if a servant of God cannot win his own children to Christ, what success can he expect with out-

siders? This is the same principle Paul emphasized to Timothy (1 Tim. 3:5)—Christian living and Christian service must begin at home. The children in an elder's home must not only be saved, but must be good examples of obedience and dedication. To be accused of "riot" [wild living] or disobedience ["unruly," unable to be ruled] would disqualify their father from the eldership. This applies, of course, to children still at home, under the authority of their father.

Too often, new Christians feel a call to the ministry and want to be ordained before they have had a chance to establish their families in the faith. If the children are small, the problem is not too great; but mature children go through a tremendous shock when all of a sudden their household becomes "religious"! A wise father first wins his own family to Christ and gives them a chance to grow before he pulls up stakes and moves to Bible school. We would have fewer casualties in the ministry if this policy were followed more often.

*"The steward of God" (v. 7a).* A steward does not own but manages all that his master puts into his hands. Perhaps the most famous steward in the Bible is Joseph, who had complete control over all of Potiphar's business (Gen. 39:1-9). The most important characteristic of a steward is *faithfulness* (Matt. 25:21; 1 Cor. 4:1-2). He must use what his master gives him for the good and glory of his master, and not for himself personally (see Luke 16:1-13).

The elder must never say, "This is mine!" All that he has comes from God (John 3:27) and must be used for God. His time, possessions, ambitions, and talents are all loaned to him by the Lord; and he must be faithful to use them to honor God and build the church. Of course, *all* Christians ought to be faithful stewards, and not the pastors only!

*"Not self-willed" (v. 7b).* An elder must not be "overbearing" (NIV), a person always pushing to have his own way. While church members ought to respect and follow the leadership of the elders, they should be certain that it is leadership and not dictatorship. A self-willed pastor is arrogant, will not take his people's suggestions and criticisms, and makes sure he always gets his own way.

*"Not soon angry" (v. 7c).* He must not have a quick temper. There is a righteous anger against sin (Eph. 4:26), but much of our anger is unrighteous and directed against people. A righteous man ought to get angry when

wrongs are done. Someone has said, "Temper is such a wonderful thing that it's a shame to lose it." Wise counsel, indeed.

*"A lover of good men" (v. 8a).* "One who loves what is good" (NIV) is an alternate translation, and this would include good men. But it also includes good books, good music, good causes, and many other good things. A man is a good man because he has a good heart and surrounds himself with good things. It is difficult to believe that a dedicated servant of God would deliberately associate with things that are bad for him and his family.

*"Just" (v. 8b).* "Upright" is a good translation. He should be a man of integrity who sticks by his word and who practices what he preaches. His conduct is righteous.

*"Holy" (v. 8c).* "Unstained" gives the idea. "Be ye holy, for I am holy" (1 Peter 1:16). The root meaning of *holy* is "different." Christians are different from lost sinners because Christians are new creations by the grace of God (2 Cor. 5:17).

*"Temperate" (v. 8d).* "Self-controlled" is the meaning, and it applies to a man's appetites and actions. "Disciplined" is a synonym. A pastor must discipline his time so that he gets his work done. He must discipline his desires, especially when well-meaning members try to stuff him with coffee and cake! He must keep his mind and body under control, as he yields to the Holy Spirit (Gal. 5:23, where *temperance* means "self-control").

*"Holding fast the faithful Word" (v. 9).* The word *faithful* was a favorite with Paul (see 1 Tim. 1:15; 4:9; 2 Tim. 2:11; Titus 3:8). God's Word is trustworthy because God cannot lie (Titus 1:2). Because the Word is faithful, those who teach and preach the Word should be faithful. Again, Paul used the term *sound* doctrine which we have already met in 1 Timothy 1:10. It means "healthy doctrine" that promotes spiritual growth.

So the elders have a twofold ministry of God's Word: (1) building up the church with "healthy" doctrine, and (2) refuting the false teachers who spread unhealthy doctrine. The naive church member who says, "We don't want doctrine; just give us helpful devotional thoughts!" does not know what he is saying. Apart from the truth (and this means Bible doctrine), there can be no spiritual help or health.

The mentioning of those who oppose true doctrine led Paul to give the third responsibility that Titus was to fulfill.

**Silence False Teachers (Titus 1:10-16)**
It did not take long for false teachers to arise in the early church. Wherever God sows the truth, Satan quickly shows up to sow lies. Titus faced an enemy similar to that described in 1 Timothy—a mixture of Jewish legalism, man-made traditions, and mysticism. Paul gave three facts about these false teachers.

*What they were personally.* Paul had nothing good to say about them! They would not submit to God's Word or to the authority of God's servant, for they were *unruly.* "Rebellious" would be a good translation. Beware of teachers who will not put themselves under authority.

They were *vain talkers.* What they said impressed people, but it had no content or substance. When you "boiled it down," it was just so much hot air. Furthermore, they excelled in *talking,* not in *doing.* They could tell others what to do, but they did not do it themselves. Note especially Titus 1:16.

The great tragedy was that they *deceived* people by their false doctrines. They claimed to be teaching truth, but they were peddlers of error. Because they themselves were deceived by Satan, they deceived others, "teaching things they ought not to teach" (Titus 1:11, NIV).

They were *carnal* and *worldly:* "liars, evil brutes, lazy gluttons" (Titus 1:12, NIV). What an indictment! Instead of living for the beautiful things of the spiritual life, they lived for their own appetites. Paul's adjectives are arresting. These men were not just "beasts," but *"evil* beasts"; they were not just "gluttons," but *"lazy* gluttons." They were celebrities, not servants. They "lived it up" at the expense of their followers, and (true to human nature), *their followers loved it!*

Paul summed up their character in Titus 1:16. They were "abominable," which means "detestable, disgusting." Christians with good spiritual sense would be completely disgusted with the character and conduct of these teachers, and would never follow them. "Disobedient" means "they cannot and will not be persuaded." Their minds have been made up and they will not face the truth. "Reprobate" literally means "not able to pass the test." God does not use them because they have been proved unfit. This same Greek word is translated "castaway" in 1 Corinthians 9:27. There it is in an athletic context and means "disqualified."

Having described what these teachers

were, Paul then shared a second fact.

**What they did.** The picture was clear: These false teachers told lies from house to house and thus upset the faith of the people. Whole families were affected by their unhealthy doctrines. For one thing, they were teaching Jewish legalism ("they of the circumcision," Titus 1:10; see 3:9) which Paul rejected. They were also teaching "Jewish fables" (Titus 1:14), which probably described their fanciful interpretations of the genealogies in the Old Testament (1 Tim. 1:4).

It never ceases to amaze me what some people get out of the Scriptures! I was once on a telephone talk program on a Chicago radio station, discussing Bible prophecy. A man phoned in and tried to take over the program by proclaiming his strange interpretations of Daniel's prophecies. He rejected the clear explanation given in the Bible and was very upset with me when I refused to agree with his fanciful ideas.

Dr. David Cooper used to say, "When the plain sense of Scripture makes good sense, seek no other sense." There is no need to find "deeper meanings" to the plain teachings of the Word of God. Such an approach to the Bible enables a "student" to find anything he is looking for!

Since the early church assemblies usually met in private homes, it is easy to understand how "whole houses" (Titus 1:11) could be upset by false teachers. People today who have Bible study classes in their homes must be careful lest visitors come in with strange doctrines. There are sects and cults that look for these classes and plant their agents just for the purpose of winning converts, so we must be careful.

**Why they did it.** Their main motive was to make money "for filthy lucre's sake" (Titus 1:11). They were not ministering to the church; they were using religion to fill their own pockets. This explains why Paul said that "not given to filthy lucre" was one requirement for an elder. A true servant of God does not minister for personal gain; he ministers to help others grow in the faith.

But behind this covetousness was another problem: Their minds and consciences had been defiled (Titus 1:15). This is what happens when a person lives a double life: Outwardly, he commands respect; but inwardly, he deteriorates. No one can serve two masters. These deceivers' love for money caused them to teach false doctrine and live false lives, and the result was a defiled conscience *that did not convict them*. This is one step closer to that "seared conscience" that Paul wrote about (1 Tim. 4:2).

Titus 1:15 is one of those verses that some ignorant people try to use to defend their ungodly practices. "To the pure, all things are pure" is used to excuse all sorts of sin. I recall warning a teenager about the kind of literature he was reading, and his defense was, "Beauty is in the eye of the beholder. Your heart must be filthy if you see sin in what I'm reading. After all, 'To the pure, all things are pure.' "

To begin with, Paul was refuting the false teaching of these legalists with reference to *foods*. They were teaching that Jewish dietary laws still applied to Christian believers (see 1 Tim. 4:3-5). If you ate forbidden food, you defiled yourself; but if you refused that food, you became holier.

"It is just the opposite," Paul argued. "These teachers have defiled minds and consciences. Therefore, when they look at these innocent foods, they see sin, because sin has defiled their vision. But those of us who have pure minds and consciences know that all foods are clean. It is not the foods which are defiling the teachers; it is the teachers who are defiling the foods!"

But this principle must not be applied to things that we know are evil. The difference, for example, between great art and pornography is more than "in the eye of the beholder." A great artist does not exploit the human body for base gain. For a believer to indulge in sinful, erotic experiences and claim that they were pure because his heart was pure, is to use the Word of God to excuse sin. The application Paul made was to food, and we must be careful to keep it there.

Having shared these three facts about these false teachers, Paul added one further matter.

**What Titus was to do.** He was not to stand quietly by and let them take over! First, he was to "exhort and to convince" them by means of "sound doctrine" (Titus 1:9). The only weapon against Satan's lies is God's truth. "Thus saith the Lord!" is the end of every argument.

Titus was to stop their mouths (Titus 1:11) and prevent them from teaching and spreading false doctrines. He was to "rebuke them sharply" (Titus 1:13). Paul would give this same counsel to Timothy in his final letter: "Reprove, rebuke, exhort with all long-suffering and doctrine" (2 Tim. 4:2).

Paul's purpose, of course, was to convince these teachers and get them to be "sound in the faith" (Titus 1:13). But while he is doing this, he must protect the church from their false teachings. False doctrine is like yeast: it enters secretly, it grows quickly, and permeates completely (Gal. 5:9). The best time to attack false doctrine is at the beginning, before it has a chance to spread.

The attitude of some church members is, "It makes no difference what you believe, just as long as you believe something." Paul would not agree with that foolish philosophy. It makes all the difference between life and death whether or not you believe the truth of the Word or believe lies. You can choose what you want to believe, but you cannot change the consequences.

"And ye shall know the truth," said Jesus Christ, "and the truth shall make you free" (John 8:32).

# CHAPTER TWO
# HOW TO HAVE
# A HEALTHY CHURCH
*Titus 2–3*

In contrast to the false teachers, Titus was to "speak the things which belong to healthy doctrine" (Titus 2:1, literal translation). What germs are to a physical body, false teaching is to a spiritual body, the church. In the verses that make up this section, you will find a blending of doctrinal teaching and practical admonition, for the two must go together. Paul discussed several different areas of ministry in the local church.

## The Older Saints (Titus 2:1-4a)
How easy it would be for a younger man like Titus to misunderstand or even neglect the older members of his congregation.

"I want a church of young people!" a pastor once said to me, forgetting that one day he would be old himself. A church needs both the old and the young, and they should minister to one another. The grace of God enables us to bridge the generation gap in the church. One way to do this is for all members, young and old, to live up the standards that God has set for our lives.

The older men were to be *sober,* which means "to be temperate in the use of wine." Old men with time on their hands could linger too long over the cup.

*Grave* means "dignified," but it does not suggest a solemn person who never laughs. There is a dignity to old age that produces respect, and this respect gives an older saint authority. How I thank God for the venerable saints who have assisted me in my own pastoral ministry! When they stood to speak, the whole church listened and took heed.

*Temperate* describes an attitude of mind that leads to prudence and self-control in life. It is the opposite of frivolity and carelessness that are based on ignorance. It is translated "sober" in Titus 1:8 and 2:4, 6, and 12, and "discreet" in 2:5. Seriousness of life and purpose are important in the Christian life, and especially to older saints who cannot afford to waste time, for their time is short.

*Sound in faith, in love, in patience* all go together. The older men should know what they believe, and their doctrinal convictions should accord with God's Word. For a knowledge of Bible doctrine is no substitute for the other necessary virtues, such as love for the brethren and patience in the trials of life. In fact, a right faith in God's Word should encourage a believer in love and endurance.

Possibly the word *likewise* in Titus 2:3 means that the older women were to have the same qualities as the older men, plus the additional ones listed. The deportment (behavior) of these older women must always reflect holiness. They must not be slanderers ("false accusers"—the Greek word is "devils," which means "slanderers"), picking up gossip and spreading it. They must also be temperate in their use of wine.

When it comes to the older women, Paul's emphasis is on *teaching:* "teachers of good things." Experienced, godly women are usually excellent teachers. The word *teach* in Titus 2:4 is related to the word translated "temperate" in Titus 2:2, and probably should be translated, "that they may train by making sober-minded." It is not only that the older women should show the younger mothers how to keep house, but that they put within their hearts and minds the right spiritual and mental attitudes.

One of the strongest forces for spiritual

ministry in the local church lies with the older believers. Those who are retired have time for service. It is good to see that many local churches have organized and mobilized these important people. In my own ministry, I have been greatly helped by senior saints who knew how to pray, teach the Word, visit, troubleshoot, and help build the church.

### The Younger Saints (Titus 2:4b-8)

The godly older women have the responsibility of teaching the younger women how to be successful wives, mothers, and housekeepers; and the younger women have the responsibility of listening and obeying. The Christian home was a totally new thing, and young women saved out of paganism would have to get accustomed to a whole new set of priorities and privileges. Those who had unsaved husbands would need special encouragement.

The greatest priority in a home should be love. If a wife loved her husband and her children, she was well on the way to making the marriage and the home a success. In our Western society, a man and a woman fall in love and then get married; but in the East, marriages were less romantic. Often the two got married and then had to learn to love each other. (Eph. 5:18-33 is probably the best Scripture for a husband and wife who really want to love each other in the will of God.)

Surely a mother loves her children! Yes, this is a natural instinct; but this instinct needs to be controlled. I once heard a "modern mother" say, "I love my child too much to spank her." In reality, she had a selfish love for herself and did not really love the child. "He who spares the rod hates his son, but he who loves him is careful to discipline him" (Prov. 13:24, NIV). While it was usually the father who disciplined the children in Eastern homes, the mother could not escape being a part of the procedure, or else a child would run to its mother for protection.

"To be discreet" (Titus 2:5) is our familiar word sober-minded again ("temperate" in Titus 2:2). Outlook determines outcome; and if a person is not thinking rightly, he will not act properly. A woman needs a correct and disciplined outlook on her ministry in the home. "Self-controlled" is the idea contained in this word. If parents do not discipline themselves, they can never discipline their children.

"Chaste" means "pure of mind and heart." A Christian wife is true to her husband in mind and heart as well as in action.

"Keepers at home" does not suggest that her home is a prison where she must be kept! "Caring for the home" is the idea. "Guide the house," Paul wrote (1 Tim. 5:14). The wise husband allows his wife to manage the affairs of the household, for this is her ministry.

"Good" (Titus 2:5) can be translated "kind." She does not rule her household with an iron hand, but practices "the law of kindness" (Prov. 31:26).

While the wife is "busy at home" (NIV), it is the husband who is the leader in the home; so the wife must be obedient. But where there is love (Titus 2:4) there is little problem with obedience. And where the desire is to glorify God, there is no difficulty that cannot be worked out.

"That the Word of God be not blasphemed" is a good motive for cooperation and obedience at home. It is sad to see the way family problems, and even divorces, among Christians cause unsaved people to sneer at the Bible.

Titus was to let older women minister to younger women, lest he get himself into a difficult situation. But he was to be an example to the younger men with whom he would easily identify. Exhortation and example were to be his tools for building them up in the faith (Titus 2:6-7). He was to exhort them to be self-controlled, for there were many temptations to sin.

But Paul wrote more about Titus the *example* than he did about Titus the *exhorter!* A pastor preaches best by his life. He must constantly be a good example in all things. Whatever the pastor wants his church to be, he must first be himself. "For they say, and do not" was our Lord's indictment against the Pharisees (Matt. 23:3). This is hypocrisy.

The Greek word *tupos* ("pattern," Titus 2:7) gives us our English word *type*. The word originally meant "an impression made by a die." Titus was to live so that his life would be like a "spiritual die" that would impress itself on others. This involved good works, sound doctrine, a seriousness of attitude, and sound speech that no one—not even the enemy—could condemn. Whether we like it or not, there are "contrary" people who are always looking for a fight. A pastor's speech should be such that he stands without rebuke.

It is not easy to pastor a church. You do not punch a clock; yet you are always on duty. You must be careful to practice what you preach; you must be the same man in and out of the pulpit. Hypocrisy in speech or conduct will ruin a man's ministry. No pastor is perfect, just as no church member is perfect; but he must strive to be the best example possible. A church will never rise any higher than its leadership.

## Christian Slaves (Titus 2:9-15)

Paul usually had a word concerning the slaves (see Eph. 6:5-9; 1 Tim. 6:1-2). We are glad for this word to Titus because Paul backed it up with one of the greatest statements about salvation found in the New Testament. Paul always linked doctrine and duty.

Paul warned these Christian slaves about three common sins they must avoid (Titus 2:9-10). First, *disobedience.* They were to obey their masters and seek to please them, which meant going the extra mile. It is possible to obey, but not "from the heart" (Eph. 6:6). It is possible to do a job grudgingly. Some unsaved masters would not be thoughtful and would overwork their slaves.

The second sin was *talking back* ("answering again," Titus 2:9). While a slave would not carry this too far (his master might severely discipline him), he could argue with his master since the master probably knew less about the job than the slave did. The slave could also "gripe" about his master to others on the job. This would certainly be a poor testimony for a Christian slave.

Christian slaves were also to avoid the sin of *stealing* ("purloining"). This was the sin Onesimus probably committed against Philemon (see Phile. 18). It would be easy for a slave to pilfer little items and sell them, and then report that they had been broken or lost.

There are no slaves in our society today, but there are employees. Christian workers must obey orders and not talk back. They must not steal from their employers. Millions of dollars are lost each year by employers whose workers steal from them, everything from paper clips and pencils to office machines and vehicles. "They owe it to me!" is no excuse. Neither is, "Well, I've earned it!"

Paul gave a good reason why Christian workers should be trustworthy ("showing all good fidelity"): This will "embellish with honor" the Word of God (WUEST). When we serve faithfully, we "beautify the Bible" and make the Christian message attractive to unbelievers. When Paul addressed the slaves in Timothy's church (1 Tim. 6:1), he used a negative motive: "that the name of God and His

doctrine be not blasphemed." But the positive motive, to make God's message attractive, and the negative motive, to keep God's teaching from being slandered, ought to control our lives.

Here (Titus 2:11) Paul expanded the meaning of "Saviour" (Titus 2:10) by explaining what was involved in this salvation that we have through Jesus Christ. The emphasis is on *grace*—God's lavish favor on undeserving sinners. Paul pointed out three wonderful ministries of the grace of God (Titus 2:11-14).

***Grace redeems us (vv. 11, 14a).*** People could not save themselves. God's grace had to bring salvation to lost mankind. This salvation was not discovered by sinners; it appeared to them via the life, death, and resurrection of Jesus Christ. God in His grace sent His Son to redeem those in the bondage of sin. This salvation is for "all men" who receive it (see 1 Tim. 2:4-6). There is a universal need, and God provided a universal remedy for all who will believe.

Paul explained this salvation further (Titus 2:14). Christ "gave Himself for us," which means that He became our substitute. "Who His own self bare our sins in His own body on the tree" (1 Peter 2:24). The word *redeem* means "to set free by paying a price." We were all slaves of sin (Titus 3:3) and could not set ourselves free; but Jesus Christ gave Himself as the ransom for our sins. By His death, He met the just demands of God's holy law, so that God in His grace could forgive and free those who believe on Christ.

We have been redeemed "from all iniquity," which means that sin should no longer master our lives. (Remember that the context of this passage is Paul's counsel to *slaves.* They knew the meaning of "redeem.") "Iniquity" means "lawlessness." In our unsaved condition, we were rebels against God's law; but now all of that has been changed. This led Paul to the second ministry of the grace of God.

***Grace reforms us (vv. 12, 14b).*** Salvation is not only a change in position (set free from the slavery of sin), but it is also a change in attitude, appetite, ambition, and action. The same grace that redeems us also reforms our lives and makes us godly. "Teaching" has the idea of "disciplining." We are disciplined by God's grace, trained to be the kind of people that glorify Him.

Godly living involves both the negative and the positive. We deny "ungodliness [whatever is unlike God] and worldly lusts" (see 1 John 2:15-17). The verb means that we do it once and for all. It is a settled matter. Then, we work on the positive. "Sober" is our familiar word for "self-control, prudence, restraint" (see Titus 2:2). This emphasizes the believer's relationship to himself, while "righteously" deals with his relationships with other people. "Godly" speaks of the Christian's relationship to the Lord, though the qualities must not be separated.

Christians live "in this present age" (NIV), but they do not live *like* it or *for* it. Christ has redeemed us from this evil age (Gal. 1:4), and we must not be conformed to it (Rom. 12:1-2). Neither should we walk according to its standards (Eph. 2:2). We have tasted the powers of "the coming age" (Heb. 6:5, NIV), and we should not desire to cultivate the present age with its shallowness and godlessness.

Grace reforms us because God purifies us and makes us His own special possession (Titus 2:14b). This process of purification is called "sanctification," and its goal is to make the believer more like Jesus Christ (Rom. 8:29). Sanctification is not only separation from sin, but it is also devotion to God (2 Cor. 6:14–7:1). "Peculiar" does not mean "odd" or "strange." It means "a special people for God's own possession" (see Deut. 14:2; 26:18).

**Grace rewards us (v. 13).** We are looking for Jesus Christ to return; this is our only hope and glory. This verse boldly affirms that Jesus Christ is God, for there is only one article in the Greek: "the great God and our Saviour." Paul did not go into detail about the events surrounding the return of Christ. Believers should always be expecting His return and live like those who will see Him face-to-face.

### Christians as Citizens (Titus 3:1-8)

Christians were often looked on with suspicion in the Roman Empire because their conduct was so different and they met in private meetings for worship (see 1 Peter 2:11-25; 3:13–4:5). It was important that they be good citizens without compromising the faith. Their pagan neighbors might disobey the law but Christians must submit to the authority of the state (see Rom. 13). "Ready to every good work" (Titus 3:1) means "cooperating in those matters that involve the whole community." Our heavenly citizenship (Phil. 3:20) does not absolve us from responsibilities as citizens on earth.

The believer should not have a bad attitude toward the government and show it by slanderous accusations and pugnacious actions. The word *gentle* (Titus 3:2) means "an attitude of moderation, a sweet reasonableness." Christians with this quality do not insist on the letter of the law, but are willing to compromise where no moral issue is at stake.

Again, Paul linked duty to doctrine. "Don't be too critical of your pagan neighbors," he wrote. "Just remember what you were before God saved you!" Titus 3:3 needs little explanation; we know what it means from our own experience.

What a difference "the kindness and love of God" (Titus 3:4) made! If you want a beautiful illustration of "the kindness of God," read 2 Samuel and note David's treatment of Mephibosheth, a little lame prince. Because Mephibosheth was a part of Saul's family, he expected to be slain. But David, in kindness, spared him and treated him as one of his own sons at the palace table.

Salvation came not only because of God's kindness and love, but also because of His mercy (Titus 3:5). We did not save ourselves; "He saved us." How did He do it? Through the miracle of the new birth, the work of the Holy Spirit of God. I do not think that "washing" here refers to baptism because, in New Testament times, people were baptized *after* they were saved, and not in order to be saved (see Acts 10:43-48). "Washing" here means "bathed all over." When a sinner trusts Christ, he is cleansed from all his sins, and he is made "a new person" by the indwelling Holy Spirit.

Paul related this same cleansing experience to the Word of God (Eph. 5:26). Salvation comes to a sinner when he trusts Christ, when the Spirit of God uses the Word of God to bring about the new birth. We are born of the *Spirit* (John 3:5-6, where "water" refers to physical birth, which Nicodemus had mentioned earlier, John 3:4) and of the *Word* (1 Peter 1:23-25). "Which" in Titus 3:6 ought to be "whom," referring to the Holy Spirit who is given to us at conversion (Acts 2:38; Rom. 5:5; 8:9).

Not only have we who are Christians been washed and made new in Christ, but we have also been *justified* (Titus 3:7). This wonderful doctrine is discussed in detail in Romans 3:21–8:39. Justification is the gracious act of God whereby He declares a believing sinner righteous because of the finished work of Christ on the cross. God puts to our account the righteousness of His Son, so that we can be condemned no more. Not only does He forget our sins, but He forgets that we were even sinners!

What is the result of this kindness, love, mercy, and grace? Hope! We are heirs of God! This means that today we can draw on His riches; and when He comes, we will share His wealth and His kingdom forever. This hope ties in with Titus 2:13: "Looking for that blessed hope." But there is something more involved: We should live godly lives and be "careful to maintain good works" (Titus 3:8). The only evidence the unsaved world has that we belong to God is our godly lives.

"Good works" do not necessarily mean religious works or church work. It is fine to work at church, sing in the choir, and hold an office; but it is also good to serve our unsaved neighbors, to be helpful in the community, and to have a reputation for assisting those in need. Baby-sitting to relieve a harassed young mother is just as much a spiritual work as passing out a Gospel tract. The best way a local church has to witness to the lost is through the sacrificial service of its members.

### Problem People (Titus 3:9-11)

We wish we did not have "problem people" in our churches; but wherever there are people, there can be problems. In this case, Paul warned Titus to avoid people who like to argue about the unimportant things of the faith. I recall being approached by a young man after a Bible lesson and getting involved with him in all sorts of hypothetical questions of doctrine. "Now, if this were true . . . if that were true . . ." was about all he could say. I was very inexperienced at the time; I should have ignored him in a gracious way. As it was, I missed the opportunity to talk with several sincere people who had personal problems and wanted help. I have learned that professed Christians who like to argue about the Bible are usually covering up some sin in their lives, are very insecure, and are usually unhappy at work or at home.

But there is another kind of problem person we should deal with: the "heretic." This word means "one who makes a choice, a person who causes divisions." This is a self-willed person who thinks he is right, and who goes from person to person in the church, forcing people to make a choice. "Are you for *me* or for the pastor?" This is a work of the flesh (see Gal. 5:20). Such a person should be admonished at least twice, and then rejected.

How do we apply this in a local church? Let me suggest one way. If a church member goes about trying to get a following, and then gets angry and leaves the church, let him go. If he comes back (maybe the other churches don't want him either), and if he shows a repentant attitude, receive him back. If he repeats this behavior (and they usually do), receive him back the second time. But if he does it a third time, do not receive him back into the fellowship of the church (Titus 3:10). Why not? "Such a man is warped in character, keeps on sinning, and has condemned himself" (Titus 3:11, literal translation). If more churches would follow this principle, we would have fewer "church tramps" who cause problems in various churches.

### Conclusion (Titus 3:12-15)

In the closing verses, Paul conveyed some personal information to Titus, and reminded him of the main theme of the letter: Insist that God's people "learn to devote themselves to doing what is good, in order that they may provide for daily necessities and not live unproductive lives" (Titus 3:14, NIV).

We know nothing about Artemas; Tychicus we met in Acts 20:4. He was with Paul in his first Roman imprisonment and carried the epistles from Paul to the Ephesians (Eph. 6:21), the Colossians (Col. 4:7-8), and to Philemon (cf. Col. 4:7-9 with Phile. 10). Either Artemas or Tychicus would replace Titus on Crete, and then Titus was to join Paul at Nicopolis.

It is possible that Zenas and Apollos (see Acts 18:24ff; Titus 3:13) carried this letter to Titus. Paul had sent them on a mission and Titus was to aid them all he could.

Paul ended the letter to Titus with a variation of his usual benediction (see 2 Thes. 3:17-18): "Grace be with you all."

Grace—and good works! They go together!

# PHILEMON

## OUTLINE

**Key theme:** Christian forgiveness
**Key verses:** Philemon 15-16

**I. APPRECIATION—1-7—
"I thank my God"**
   A. Paul's love—1-3
   B. Paul's thanksgiving—4 5, 7
   C. Paul's prayer—6

**II. APPEAL—8-16—"I beseech thee"**
   A. Philemon's character—8-9
   B. Onesimus' conversion—10-14
   C. God's providence  15-16

**III. ASSURANCE—17-25—
"I will repay"**
   A. Paul's partnership—17-19
   B. Paul's confidence—20-22
   C. Paul's greetings—23-25

## CONTENTS

# CHAPTER ONE
# A TALE OF TWO CITIES
*Philemon 1-25*

Paul was a prisoner in Rome, his friend Philemon was in Colossae, and the human link between them was a runaway slave named Onesimus. The details are not clear, but it appears that Onesimus robbed his master and then fled to Rome, hoping to be swallowed up in the crowded metropolis. But, in the providence of God, he met Paul and was converted!

Now what? Perhaps Onesimus should remain with Paul, who needed all the assistance he could get. But what about the slave's responsibilities to his master back in Colossae? The law permitted a master to execute a rebellious slave, but Philemon was a Christian. If he forgave Onesimus, what would the other masters (and slaves) think? If he punished him, how would it affect his testimony? What a dilemma!

Along with the Epistle to the Colossians, this letter probably was carried to Colossae by Tychicus and Onesimus (Col. 4:7-9). In it, we see Paul in three important roles as he tried to help Philemon solve his problems. At the same time, we see a beautiful picture of what the Father has done for us in Jesus Christ. Martin Luther said, "All of us are Onesimuses!" and he was right.

## Paul, the Beloved Friend (Phile. 1-7)

Paul had not founded the church in Colossae, nor had he visited it (Col. 1:1-8; 2:1). It is likely that the church started as a result of his ministry in Ephesus (Acts 19:10, 20, 26) and that Epaphras was the founding pastor (Phile. 23). The church met in the home of Philemon and Apphia, his wife. Some people assume that Archippus was their son, but this is not certain. He may have been the elder who took the place of Epaphras who had gone to Rome to help Paul. If this is true, then it would explain Paul's strong admonition to Archippus in Colossians 4:17, a letter written to the whole church.

In his greeting, Paul expressed his deep love for his Christian friends, and he reminded them that he was a prisoner for Jesus Christ (see also Phile. 9-10, 13, 23). Timothy was included in the greeting, though the burden of the letter was from the heart of Paul to the heart of Philemon. Paul's ministry was a "team" operation, and he often included the names of his associates when he wrote his letters. He liked to use the term "fellow worker" (see Rom. 16:3, 9, 21; 1 Cor. 3:9; Phil. 2:25; 4:3; Col. 4:11).

The New Testament churches met in homes (Rom. 16:5, 23; 1 Cor. 16:19), and perhaps the church in Philemon's house was one of two assemblies in Colossae (Col. 4:15). Paul had won Philemon to faith in Christ (see Phile. 19), and Philemon became a blessing to other Christians (Phile. 7).

It was customary for Paul to open his letters with words of thanks and praise to God. (Galatians is an exception.) In his thanksgiving, Paul described his friend as a man of love and faith, both toward Jesus Christ and God's people. His love was practical: he "refreshed" the saints through his words and work.

Paul told Philemon that he was praying for him and asking God to make his witness effective ("the sharing of your faith") so that others would trust Christ. He also prayed that his friend would have a deeper understanding of all that he had in Jesus Christ. After all, the better we know Christ and experience His blessings, the more we want to share these blessings with others.

## Paul, the Beseeching Intercessor (Phile. 8-16)

Estimates suggest that there were 60 million slaves in the Roman Empire, men and women who were treated like pieces of merchandise to buy and sell. A familiar proverb was "So many slaves, just so many enemies!" The average slave sold for 500 denarii (one denarius was a day's wage for a common laborer), while the educated and skilled slaves were priced as high as 50,000 denarii. A master could free a slave, or a slave could buy his freedom if he could raise the money (Acts 22:28).

If a slave ran away, the master would register the name and description with the officials, and the slave would be on the "wanted" list. Any free citizen who found a runaway slave could assume custody and even intercede with the owner. The slave was not automatically returned to the owner, nor was he automatically sentenced to death. While it is true that some masters were cruel (one man threw his slave into a pool of man-eating fish!), many of them were reasonable and humane. After all, a slave was an expensive and useful piece of personal property, and it would cost the owner to lose him.

As Paul interceded for Onesimus, he presented five strong appeals. He began with Philemon's reputation as a man who brought blessing to others. The word *wherefore* in Philemon 8 carries the meaning of "accordingly." Since Philemon was a "refreshing" believer, Paul wanted to give him an opportunity to refresh the apostle's heart! Philemon had been a great blessing to many saints, and now he could be a blessing to one of his own slaves who had just been saved!

Paul might have used apostolic authority and ordered his friend to obey, but he preferred to appeal in Christian love (Phile. 9). See how tactfully Paul reminded Philemon of his own personal situation: "Paul the aged, and now also a prisoner of Jesus Christ" (Phile. 9). Who could turn down the request of a suffering saint like Paul! He was perhaps sixty years old at this time, but that was a good age for men in that day. Along with Philemon's gracious character and Christian love, Paul's third appeal was the conversion of Onesimus (Phile. 10). Onesimus was no longer "just a slave"; he was now Paul's son in the faith and Philemon's Christian brother! In Jesus Christ, there is "neither bond nor free" (Gal. 3:28). This does not mean that his conversion altered Onesimus' legal position as a slave, or that it canceled his debt to the law or to his master. However, it did mean that Onesimus had a new standing before God and before God's people, and Philemon had to take this into consideration.

The fourth appeal was that Onesimus was valuable to Paul in his ministry in Rome (Phile. 11-14). The name *Onesimus* means "profitable," so there is a play on words in Philemon 11. (The name *Philemon* means "affectionate" or "one who is kind." If the slave was expected to live up to his name, then what about the master?) Paul loved Onesimus and would have kept him in Rome as a fellow worker, but he did not want to tell Philemon what to do. Voluntary sacrifice and service, motivated by love, is what the Lord wants from His children.

The fifth appeal relates to the providence of God (Phile. 15-16). Paul was not dogmatic ("perhaps") as he made this telling point: as Christians, we must believe that God is in control of even the most difficult experiences of life. God permitted Onesimus to go to Rome that he might meet Paul and become a believer. (Certainly Philemon and his family had witnessed to the slave and prayed for him.) Onesimus departed so he could come back. He was gone a short time so that he and his master might be together forever. He left for Rome a slave, but he would return to Colossae a brother. How gracious God was to rule and overrule in these affairs!

As you review these five appeals, you can see how Paul tenderly convinced his friend Philemon that he should receive his disobedient slave and forgive him. But it would not be easy for Philemon to do this. If he was too easy on Onesimus, it might influence other slaves to "become Christians" and want to influence their masters. However, if he was too hard on the man, it might affect Philemon's testimony and ministry in Colossae.

At this point, Paul offered the perfect solution. It was a costly solution as far as the apostle was concerned, but he was willing to pay the price.

## Paul, the Burdened Partner (Phile. 17-25)

The word translated "partner" is *koinonia*, which means "to have in common." It is translated "communication" in Philemon 6, which means "fellowship." Paul volunteered to become a "business partner" with Philemon and help him solve the problem with Onesimus. He made two suggestions: "Receive him as myself," and "Put that [whatever he stole from you] on my account."

As Philemon's new "partner," Paul could not leave Rome and go to Colossae, *but he could send Onesimus as his personal representative.* "The way you treat Onesimus is the way you treat me," said the apostle. "He is to me as my own heart" (Phile. 12).

This is to me an illustration of what Jesus Christ has done for us as believers. God's people are so identified with Jesus Christ that God receives them as He receives His Son! We are "accepted in the Beloved" (Eph. 1:6) and clothed in His righteousness (2 Cor. 5:21). We certainly cannot approach God with any merit of our own, but God must receive us when we come to Him "in Jesus Christ." The word *receive* in Philemon 17 means "to receive into one's family circle." Imagine a slave entering his master's family! But imagine a guilty sinner entering *God's* family!

Paul did not suggest that Philemon ignore the slave's crimes and forget about the debt

Onesimus owed. Rather, Paul offered to pay the debt himself. "Put it on my account—I will repay it!" The language in Philemon 19 sounds like a legal promissory note of that time. This was Paul's assurance to his friend that the debt would be paid.

It takes more than love to solve the problem; *love must pay a price.* God does not save us by His love, for though He loves the whole world, the whole world is not saved. God saves sinners by His grace (Eph. 2:8-9), *and grace is love that pays a price.* God in His holiness could not ignore the debt that we owe, for God must be faithful to His own Law. *So He paid the debt for us!*

Theologians call this "the doctrine of imputation." (To *impute* means "to put it on account.") When Jesus Christ died on the cross, my sins were put on His account; and He was treated the way I should have been treated. When I trusted Him as my Saviour, His righteousness was put on my account; and now God accepts me in Jesus Christ. Jesus said to the Father, "He no longer owes You a debt because I paid it fully on the cross. Receive him as You would receive Me. Let him come into the family circle!"

However, we must keep in mind that there is a difference between being *accepted in Christ* and *acceptable to Christ.* Anyone who trusts Jesus Christ for salvation is *accepted* in Him (Rom. 4:1-4). But the believer must strive with God's help to be *acceptable* to the Lord in his daily life (Rom. 12:2; 14:18; 2 Cor. 5:9; Heb. 12:28, NIV). The Father wants to look at those who are in His Son and say of them as He said of Jesus, "I am well pleased!"

Philemon 19 suggests that it was Paul who led Philemon to faith in Christ. Paul used this special relationship to encourage his friend to receive Onesimus. Philemon and Onesimus were not only spiritual brothers in the Lord, but they had the same "spiritual father"—Paul! (see Phile. 10 and 1 Cor. 4:15)

Was Paul hinting in Philemon 21 that Philemon should do even more and *free* Onesimus? For that matter, why did he not come right out and *condemn* slavery? This letter certainly would have been the ideal place to do it. Paul did not "condemn" slavery in this letter or in any of his letters, though he often had a word of admonition for slaves and their masters (Eph. 6:5-9; Col. 3:22–4:1; 1 Tim. 6:1-2; Titus 2:9-10). In fact, he encouraged Christian slaves to obtain their freedom if they could (1 Cor. 7:21-24).

During the American Civil War, both sides used the same Bible to "prove" their cases for or against slavery. One of the popular arguments was, "If slavery is so wrong, why did Jesus and the Apostles say nothing against it? Paul gave instructions to *regulate* slavery, but he did not condemn it."

One of the best explanations was given by Alexander Maclaren in his commentary on Colossians in *The Expositor's Bible* (Eerdmans, 1940; vol. VI, p. 301):

First, the message of Christianity is primarily to individuals, and only secondarily to society. It leaves the units whom it has influenced to influence the mass. Second, it acts on spiritual and moral sentiment, and only afterwards and consequently on deeds or institutions. Third, it hates violence, and trusts wholly to enlightened conscience. So it meddles directly with no political or social arrangements, but lays down principles which will profoundly affect these, and leaves them to soak into the general mind.

Had the early Christians begun an open crusade against slavery, they would have been crushed by the opposition, and the message of the Gospel would have become confused with a social and political program. Think of how difficult it was for people to overcome slavery in England and America, and those two nations had general education and the Christian religion to help prepare the way. Think also of the struggles in the modern Civil Rights movement *even within the church.* If the battle for freedom was difficult for us to win in the nineteenth and twentieth centuries, what would the struggle have been like back in the *first* century?

Christians are the salt of the earth and the light of the world (Matt. 5:13-16), and their spiritual influence must be felt in society to the glory of God. God used Joseph in Egypt, Esther and Nehemiah in Persia, and Daniel in Babylon; and throughout church history, there have been believers in political offices who have faithfully served the Lord. But Christians in the Roman Empire could not work through local democratic political structures as we can today, so they really had no political power to bring about change. The change had to come from within, even though it took centuries for slavery to end.

Paul closed the letter with his usual personal requests and greetings. He fully expected to be released and to visit Philemon and Apphia in Colossae ("you" in Phile. 22 is plural). Even this fact would encourage Philemon to follow Paul's instructions, for he certainly would not want to be ashamed when he met the apostle face-to-face.

As we have seen, Epaphras was probably the pastor of the church; and he had gone to Rome to assist Paul. Whether he was a "voluntary prisoner" for Paul's sake, or whether he had actually been arrested by the Romans, we do not know. We must commend him for his dedication to Christ and to Paul.

John Mark was with Paul (Col. 4:10), the young man who failed Paul on his first missionary journey (Acts 12:12, 25; 15:36-41). Paul had forgiven Mark and was grateful for his faithful ministry (see 2 Tim. 4:11).

Aristarchus was from Thessalonica and accompanied Paul to Jerusalem and then to Rome (Acts 19:29; 27:2). Demas is mentioned three times in Paul's letters: "Demas . . . my fellow worker" (Phile. 24), "Demas" (Col. 4:14), "Demas hath forsaken me, having loved this present world" (2 Tim. 4:10). John Mark failed but was restored. Demas seemed to be doing well but then he fell.

Luke, of course, was the beloved physician (Col. 4:14) who accompanied Paul, ministered to him, and eventually wrote the Gospel of Luke and the Book of Acts.

Paul's benediction was his "official signature" for his letters (2 Thes. 3:17-18), and it magnified the grace of God. After all, it was the grace of Jesus Christ that made our salvation possible (Eph. 2:1-10). It was He who said, "Charge that to My account! Receive them as You would receive Me!"

# HEBREWS

## OUTLINE

**Key theme:** Press on to maturity
**Key verse:** Hebrews 6:1

I. A SUPERIOR PERSON—
   CHRIST—chapters 1–6
   A. Better than the prophets—1:1-3
   B. Better than the angels—1:4–2:18
   *(Exhortation:* drifting from the
   Word, 2:1-4)
   C. Better than Moses—3:1–4:13
   *(Exhortation:* doubting the
   Word, 3:7–4:13)
   D. Better than Aaron—4:14–6:20
   *(Exhortation:* dullness toward
   the Word, 5:11–6:20)

II. A SUPERIOR PRIESTHOOD—
    MELCHIZEDEK—chapters 7–10
    A. A superior order—7
    B. A superior covenant—8
    C. A superior sanctuary—9
    D. A superior sacrifice—10
    *(Exhortation:* despising the
    Word—10:26-39

III. A SUPERIOR PRINCIPLE—
     FAITH—chapters 11–13
     A. The great examples of faith—11
     B. The endurance of faith—
     chastening—12
     *(Exhortation:* defying the
     Word—12:14-29
     C. Closing practical exhortations—13

## CONTENTS

# CHAPTER ONE
# IS ANYBODY
# LISTENING?
*Hebrews 1:1-3*

A man from Leeds, England visited his doctor to have his hearing checked. The doctor removed the man's hearing aid, and the patient's hearing immediately improved! He had been wearing the device *in the wrong ear* for over 20 years!

I once asked a pastor friend, "Do you have a deaf ministry in your church?" He replied, "There are times when I think the whole church needs a deaf ministry—they just don't seem to hear me."

There is a difference between *listening* and really *hearing.* Jesus often cried, "He who has ears to hear, let him hear!" This statement suggests that it takes more than physical ears to hear the voice of God. It also requires a receptive heart. "Today, if ye will hear His voice, harden not your hearts" (Heb. 3:7-8).

Many people have avoided the Epistle to the Hebrews and, consequently, have robbed themselves of practical spiritual help. Some have avoided this book because they are "afraid of it." The "warnings" in Hebrews have made them uneasy. Others have avoided this book because they think it is "too difficult" for the average Bible student. To be sure, there are some profound truths in Hebrews, and no preacher or teacher would dare to claim that he knows them all! But the general message of the book is clear and there is no reason why you and I should not understand and profit from it.

Perhaps the best way to begin our study is to notice five characteristics of the Epistle to the Hebrews.

## It Is a Book of Evaluation

The word *better* is used thirteen times in this book as the writer shows the superiority of Jesus Christ and His salvation over the Hebrew system of religion. Christ is "better than the angels" (Heb. 1:4). He brought in "a better hope" (Heb. 7:19) because He is the Mediator of "a better covenant, which was established on better promises" (Heb. 8:6).

Another word that is repeated in this book is *perfect;* in the original Greek it is used four-teen times. It means a perfect standing before God. This perfection could never be accomplished by the levitical priesthood (Heb. 7:11) or by the Law (Heb. 7:19), nor could the blood of animal sacrifices achieve it (Heb. 10:1). Jesus Christ gave Himself as one offering for sin, and by this He has "perfected forever them that are sanctified" (Heb. 10:14).

So the writer is contrasting the Old Testament system of Law with the New Testament ministry of grace. He is making it clear that the Jewish religious system was temporary and that it could not bring in the eternal "better things" that are found in Jesus Christ.

*Eternal* is a third word that is important to the message of Hebrews. Christ is the "author of eternal salvation" (Heb. 5:9). Through His death, He "obtained eternal redemption" (Heb. 9:12) and He shares with believers "the promise of eternal inheritance" (Heb. 9:15). His throne is forever (Heb. 1:8) and He is a priest forever (Heb. 5:6; 6:20; 7:17, 21). "Jesus Christ, the same yesterday, and today, and forever" (Heb. 13:8).

When you combine these three important words, you discover that Jesus Christ and the Christian life He gives us are *better* because these blessings are *eternal* and they give us a *perfect* standing before God. The religious system under the Mosaic Law was imperfect because it could not accomplish a once-for-all redemption that was eternal.

But why did the writer ask his readers to evaluate their faith and what Jesus Christ had to offer them? Because they were going through difficult times and were being tempted to go back to the Jewish religion. The temple was still standing when this book was written, and all the priestly ceremonies were still being carried on daily. How easy it would have been for these Jewish believers to escape persecution by going back into the old Mosaic system which they had known before.

These people were "second generation believers," having been won to Christ by those who had known Jesus Christ during His ministry on earth (Heb. 2:3). They were true believers (Heb. 3:1) and not mere professors. They had been persecuted because of their faith (Heb. 10:32-34; 12:4; 13:13-14), and yet they had faithfully ministered to the needs of others who had suffered (Heb. 6:10). But they were being seduced by teachers of false doctrine (Heb. 13:9), and they were in danger of forgetting the true Word that their first leaders, now dead, had taught them (Heb. 13:7).

The tragic thing about these believers is that they were at a standstill spiritually and in danger of going backward (Heb. 5:12ff). Some of them had even forsaken the regular worship services (Heb. 10:25) and were not making spiritual progress (Heb. 6:1). In the Christian life, if you do not go forward, you go backward; there is no permanent standing still.

"How can you go back into your former religion?" the writer asked them. "Just take time to evaluate what you have in Jesus Christ. He is better than anything you ever had under the Law."

The Book of Hebrews exalts the person and the work of Jesus Christ, the Son of God. When you realize all that you have in and through Him, you have no desire for anyone else or anything else!

### It Is a Book of Exhortation
The writer calls this epistle "the word of exhortation" (Heb. 13:22). The Greek word translated "exhortation" simply means "encouragement." It is translated "comfort" in Romans 15:4, and "consolation" in 2 Corinthians 1:5-7; 7:7. This word is related to the Greek word translated "Comforter" in John 14:16, referring to the Holy Spirit. The Epistle to the Hebrews was not written to frighten people, but to encourage people. We are commanded to "encourage one another daily" (Heb. 3:13, NIV). It reminds us that we have "strong encouragement" in Jesus Christ (Heb. 6:18, NASB).

At this point we must answer the usual question: "But what about those five terrible warnings found in Hebrews?"

To begin with, these five passages are not really "warnings." Three basic words are translated "warn" in the New Testament, and the only one used in Hebrews is translated "admonished" in Hebrews 8:5 (KJV, where it refers to Moses) and "spake" in Hebrews 12:25. Only in Hebrews 11:7 is it translated "warned," where it refers to Noah "being warned of God." I think that the best description of the five so-called warning passages is the one given in Hebrews 13:22—"exhortation" (KJV), or "encouragement" (BERK). This does not minimize the seriousness of these five sections of the book, but it does help us grasp their purpose: to encourage us to trust God and heed His Word.

The Epistle to the Hebrews opens with an important declaration: "God . . . has spoken to us in His Son" (Heb. 1:1-2, NASB). Near the close of the book, the writer states: "See to it that you do not refuse Him who is speaking" (Heb. 12:25, NASB). In other words, the theme of Hebrews seems to be: "God has spoken; we have His Word. What are we doing about it?"

With this truth in mind, we can now better understand the significance of those five "problem passages" in Hebrews. Each of these passages encourages us to heed God's Word ("God . . . has spoken") by pointing out the sad spiritual consequences that result if we do not. Let me list these passages for you and explain their sequence in the Book of Hebrews. I think you will see how they all hang together and present one message: *heed God's word.*

*Drifting* from the Word—2:1-4 (neglect)
*Doubting* the Word—3:7–4:13 (hard heart)
*Dullness* toward the Word—5:11–6:20 (sluggishness)
*Despising* the Word—10:26-39 (willfulness)
*Defying* the Word—12:14-29 (refusing to hear)

If we do not listen to God's Word and really *hear* it, we will start to *drift*. Neglect always leads to drifting, in things material and physical as well as spiritual. As we drift from the Word, we start to *doubt* the Word; because *faith* comes by hearing the Word of God (Rom. 10:17). We start to get hard hearts, and this leads to spiritual sluggishness which produces *dullness* toward the Word. We become "dull of hearing"—lazy listeners! This leads to a *despiteful* attitude toward the Word to the extent that we willfully *disobey* God; and this gradually develops into a *defiant* attitude—we almost "dare" God to do anything!

Now what does God do while this spiritual regression is going on? He keeps speaking to us, encouraging us to get back to the Word. If we fail to listen and obey, then He begins to chasten us. This chastening process is the theme of Hebrews 12, the climactic chapter in the epistle. "The Lord shall judge *His people*" (Heb. 10:30, italics mine). God does not allow His children to become "spoiled brats" by permitting them to willfully defy His Word. He always chastens in love.

These five exhortations are addressed to

people who are truly born again. Their purpose is to get the readers to pay close attention to God's Word. While there is some stern language in some of these passages, it is my understanding that none of these exhortations "threatens" the reader by suggesting that he may "lose his salvation." If he persists in defying God's Word, he may lose *his life* ("Shall we not much rather be in subjection unto the Father of spirits, and live?"—Heb. 12:9). The inference is that if we do not submit, we might die. "There is a sin unto death" (1 John 5:16). But if the Epistle to the Hebrews teaches anything, it teaches the assurance of eternal life in a living High Priest who can never die (Heb. 7:22-28).

Some students try to explain away the "problem" of "losing your salvation" or "apostasy" by claiming that the readers were not truly born again, but were only "professors" of Christian faith. However, the way the writer addresses them would eliminate that approach; for he called them "holy brethren, partakers of the heavenly calling" (Heb. 3:1). He told them that they had a High Priest in heaven (Heb. 4:14), which he would not have written if they were lost. They had been "made partakers of the Holy Spirit" (Heb. 6:4). The admonitions in Hebrews 10:19-25 would be meaningless if addressed to unsaved people.

The Epistle to the Hebrews is a book of evaluation, proving that Jesus Christ is better than anything the Law of Moses has to offer. The epistle is also a book of exhortation, urging its readers to hear and heed the Word of God, lest they regress spiritually and experience the chastening hand of God.

### It Is a Book of Examination

As you study this book, you will find yourself asking: "What am I *really* trusting? Am I trusting the Word of God, or am I trusting the things of this world that are shaking and ready to fall away?"

This letter was written to believers at a strategic time in history. The temple was still standing and the sacrifices were still being offered. But in a few years, both the city and the temple would be destroyed. The Jewish nation would be scattered, and this would include Jewish believers in Jesus Christ. The ages were colliding! God was "shaking" the order of things (Heb. 12:25-29). He wanted His people to have their feet on the solid foundation of faith; He did not want them to trust in things that would vanish.

I believe that the church today is living in similar circumstances. Everything around us is shaking and changing. People are discovering that they have been depending on the "scaffolding" and not on the solid foundation. Even God's people have gotten so caught up in this world's system that their confidence is not in the Lord, but in money, buildings, programs, and other passing material things. As God continues to "shake" society, the scaffolding will fall away; and God's people will discover that their only confidence must be in the Word of God.

God wants our hearts to be "established with grace" (Heb. 13:9). That word "established" is used, in one form or another, eight times in Hebrews. It means: "to be solidly grounded, to stand firm on your feet." It carries the idea of strength, reliability, confirmation, permanence. This, I think, is the key message of Hebrews: "You can be secure while everything around you is falling apart!" We have a "kingdom which cannot be moved" (Heb. 12:28). God's Word is steadfast (Heb. 2:2) and so is the hope we have in Him (Heb. 6:19).

Of course, there is no security for a person who has never trusted Jesus Christ as his own Saviour from sin. Nor is there security to those who have made a "lip profession" but whose lives do not give evidence of true salvation (Matt. 7:21-27; Titus 1:16). Christ saves "to the uttermost" (i.e., "eternally") only those who have come to God through faith in Him (Heb. 7:25).

I like to tell congregations the story about the conductor who got on the train, began to take tickets, and told the first passenger whose ticket he took, "Sir, you're on the wrong train." When he looked at the next ticket, he told that passenger the same thing.

"But the brakeman told me to get on this train," the passenger protested.

"I'll double-check," said the conductor. He did and discovered that *he* was on the wrong train!

I fear there are many people who have a false faith, who have not really heard and heeded God's Word. Sometimes they are so busy telling everybody else what to do that they fail to examine their own situations. The Epistle to the Hebrews is a book of examination: it helps you discover where your faith really is.

### It Is a Book of Expectation

The focus in this book is on the future. The writer informs us that he is speaking about "the world to come" (Heb. 2:5), a time when believers will reign with Christ. Jesus Christ is "heir of all things" (Heb. 1:2) and we share the "promise of eternal inheritance" (Heb. 9:15). Like the patriarchs lauded in Hebrews 11, we are looking for that future city of God (Heb. 11:10-16, 26).

Like these great men and women of faith, we today should be "strangers and pilgrims on the earth" (Heb. 11:13). This is one reason why God is shaking everything around us. *He wants us to turn loose from the things of this world and stop depending on them.* He wants us to center our attention on the world to come. This does *not* mean that we become so heavenly minded that we're no earthly good. Rather it means that we "hang loose" as far as this world is concerned, and start living for the eternal values of the world to come.

Abraham and Lot, his nephew, illustrate these two different attitudes (Gen. 13–14). Abraham was a wealthy man who could have lived in an expensive house in any location that he chose. But he was first of all God's servant, a pilgrim and a stranger; and this meant living in tents. Lot chose to abandon the pilgrim life and move into the evil city of Sodom. Which of these two men had true security? It would appear that Lot was safer in the city than Abraham was in his tents on the plain. But Lot became a prisoner of war! And Abraham had to rescue him.

Instead of heeding God's warning, Lot went back into the city; and when God destroyed Sodom and Gomorrah, Lot lost everything (Gen. 19). Lot was a saved man (2 Peter 2:7), but he trusted in the things of this world instead of trusting the Word of God. Lot forfeited the permanent because he depended on and lived for the immediate.

Martyred missionary Jim Elliot said it best: "He is no fool to give what he cannot keep, to gain what he cannot lose."

You and I as God's children have been promised a future reward. As with Abraham and Moses of old, the decisions we make today will determine the rewards tomorrow. More than this, our decisions should be motivated by the expectation of receiving rewards. Abraham obeyed God *because* "he looked for a city" (Heb. 11:10). Moses forsook the treasures and the pleasures of Egypt *because* "he had respect unto the recompense of the re-

ward" (Heb. 11:26). These great men and women (Heb. 11:31, 35) of faith "lived in the future tense" and thus were able to overcome the temptations of the world and the flesh.

In fact, it was this same attitude of faith that carried our Lord Jesus Christ through the agony of the cross: "Jesus . . . for the joy that was set before Him endured the cross, despising the shame" (Heb. 12:2). The emphasis in the Epistle to the Hebrews is: "Don't live for what the world will promise you today! Live for what God has promised you in the future! Be a stranger and a pilgrim on this earth! Walk by faith, not by sight!"

This letter is not a diet for "spiritual babes" who want to be spoon-fed and coddled (Heb. 5:11-14). In this letter you will find "strong meat" that demands some "spiritual molars" for chewing and enjoying. The emphasis in Hebrews is not on what Christ did on the earth (the "milk"), but what He is now doing in heaven (the "meat" of the Word). He is the great High Priest who *enables us* by giving us grace (Heb. 4:14-16). He is also the Great Shepherd of the sheep who *equips us* to do His will (Heb. 13:20-21). He is working *in us* to accomplish His purposes. What a thrill it is for us to be a part of such a marvelous ministry!

Dr. A.W. Tozer used to remind us, "Every man must choose his world." True believers have "tasted the good Word of God, and the powers of the world [age] to come" (Heb. 6:5); this should mean we have no interest in or appetite for the present sinful world system. Abraham chose the right world and became the father of the faithful. Lot chose the wrong world and became the father of the enemies of God's people (Gen. 19:30-38). Abraham became the friend of God (2 Chron. 20:7), but Lot became the friend of the world—and lost everything. Lot was "saved, yet so as by fire" (1 Cor. 3:15) and lost his reward.

### It Is a Book of Exaltation

The Epistle to the Hebrews exalts the person and the work of our Lord Jesus Christ. The first three verses set this high and holy theme which is maintained throughout the entire book. Their immediate purpose is to prove that Jesus Christ is superior to the prophets, men who were held in the highest esteem by the Jewish people.

*In His person,* Christ is superior to the prophets. To begin with, He is the very Son of God and not merely a man called by God. The author makes it clear that Jesus Christ is God (Heb. 1:3), for his description could never be applied to mortal man. "Brightness of His glory" refers to the shekinah glory of God that dwelt in the tabernacle and temple. (See Ex. 40:34-38 and 1 Kings 8:10. The word *Shekinah* is a transliteration of a Hebrew word that means "to dwell.") Christ is to the Father what the rays of the sun are to the sun. He is the radiance of God's glory. As it is impossible to separate the rays from the sun, it is also impossible to separate Christ's glory from the nature of God.

"Express image" (Heb. 1:3) carries the idea of "the exact imprint." Our English word *character* comes from the Greek word translated "image." Literally, Jesus Christ is "the exact representation of the very substance of God" (see Col. 2:9). Only Jesus could honestly say, "He that hath seen Me hath seen the Father" (John 14:9). When you see Christ, you see the glory of God (John 1:14).

*In His work,* Christ is also superior to the prophets. To begin with, He is the Creator of the universe; for by Him, God "made the worlds" (Heb. 1:2). Not only did Christ create all things by His Word (John 1:1-5), but He also upholds all things by that same powerful Word (Heb. 1:3). "And He is before all things, and by Him all things consist [hold together]" (Col. 1:17).

The word "upholding" (Heb. 1:3) does not mean "holding up," as though the universe is a burden on the back of Jesus. It means "holding and carrying from one place to another." He is the God of Creation and the God of providence who guides this universe to its divinely ordained destiny.

He is also the superior Prophet who declares God's Word. The contrast between Christ, the Prophet, and the other prophets, is easy to see:

| *Christ* | *The Prophets* |
|---|---|
| God the Son | Men called by God |
| One Son | Many prophets |
| A final and complete message | A fragmentary and incomplete message |

Of course, both the Old Testament and the Gospel revelation came from God; but Jesus Christ was God's "last word" as far as revelation is concerned. Christ is the source, center, and end of everything that God has to say.

But Jesus Christ has a ministry as *Priest,* and this reveals His greatness. By Himself He "purged our sins" (Heb. 1:3). This aspect of His ministry will be explained in detail in Hebrews 7–10.

Finally, Jesus Christ reigns as *King* (Heb. 1:3). He has sat down, for His work is finished; and He has sat down "on the right hand of the Majesty on high," the place of honor. This proves that He is equal with God the Father, for no mere created being could ever sit at God's right hand.

Creator, Prophet, Priest, and King—Jesus Christ is superior to all of the prophets and servants of God who have ever appeared on the sacred pages of the Scriptures. It is no wonder that the Father said, at the hour of Christ's transfiguration, "This is My beloved Son, in whom I am well pleased; hear ye Him" (Matt. 17:5). Two of the greatest prophets were there with Jesus—Moses and Elijah; but Christ is superior to them.

As we study Hebrews together, we must keep in mind that our purpose is not to get lost in curious doctrinal details. Nor is our purpose to attack or defend some pet doctrine. Our purpose is to hear God speak in Jesus Christ, and to heed that Word. We want to echo the prayer of the Greeks: "Sir, we would see Jesus" (John 12:21). If our purpose is to know Christ better and exalt Him more, then whatever differences we may have in our understanding of the book will be forgotten in our worship of Him.

# CHAPTER TWO
# GREATER THAN ANGELS
*Hebrews 1:4–2:18*

Angels were most important in the Jewish religion, primarily because thousands of angels assisted in the giving of the Law at Mount Sinai. This fact is stated in Deuteronomy 33:2 (where "saints" in KJV means "holy ones" or "angels"); Psalm 68:17; Acts 7:53; and Galatians 3:19. Since the theme of Hebrews is the superiority of Christ and His salvation to the

Law of Moses, the writer would have to deal with the important subject of angels.

This long section on angels is divided into three sections. First, there is an *affirmation* (Heb. 1:4-14) of the superiority of Christ to the angels. The proof presented consists of seven quotations from the Old Testament. Second, there is en *exhortation* (Heb. 2:1-4) that the readers (and this includes us) pay earnest heed to the Word God has given through His Son. Finally, there is an *explanation* (Heb. 2:5-18) as to how Christ, with a human body, could still be superior to angels who are spirits.

### Affirmation: Christ Is Superior to the Angels (Heb. 1:4-14)

This section is comprised of seven quotations from the Old Testament, all of which prove the superiority of Christ to the angels. Scholars tell us that the writer quoted from the Greek version of the Hebrew Old Testament, known as the Septuagint. (The word *Septuagint* is a Greek word that means "seventy." Tradition claims that seventy men translated the Hebrew Old Testament into the Greek. The abbreviation for Septuagint is LXX, Roman numerals for seventy.) However, the same Holy Spirit who inspired the Scriptures has the right to quote and restate the truth as He sees fit.

Let us note the affirmations that are made about our Lord Jesus Christ, and the quotations that are cited to support them.

*He is the Son (vv. 4-5).* The "more excellent name" that Jesus possesses is "Son." While the angels *collectively* may be termed "the sons of God" (Job 1:6), no angel would be given this title *individually*. It belongs uniquely to our Lord Jesus Christ. The first quotation is from Psalm 2:7: "Thou art My Son, this day have I begotten Thee." Paul pinpointed the time of this "begetting": the resurrection of Jesus Christ (Acts 13:33). From eternity, Jesus Christ was God the Son. He humbled Himself and became Man (see Phil. 2:5-6). In His resurrection, however, He glorified that humanity received from the Father and received back the eternal glory He had veiled (John 17:1, 5). The Resurrection declares: "Jesus is God's Son!" (Rom. 1:4)

The second quotation is from 2 Samuel 7:14. The immediate application in David's experience was to his son, Solomon, whom God would love and discipline as a son (see Ps. 89:27). But the ultimate application is to Jesus

Christ, the "greater than Solomon" (Matt. 12:42).

*He is the Firstborn who receives worship (v. 6).* The term "firstborn" in the Bible does not always mean "born first." God made Solomon the firstborn (Ps. 89:27) even though Solomon is listed *tenth* in the official genealogy (1 Chron. 3:1-5). The title is one of rank and honor, for the firstborn receives the inheritance and the special blessing. Christ is the "Firstborn of all creation" (Col. 1:15, NASB) because He created all things; and He is the highest of all who came back from the dead (Col. 1:18). When He came into the world, the angels worshiped Him (quoted from Deut. 32:43 in the LXX: "Heavens, rejoice with Him, let the sons of God pay Him homage!"). God commanded them to do so, which proves that Jesus Christ is God; for none of God's angels would worship a mere creature.

*He is served by the angels (v. 7).* This is a quotation from Psalm 104:4. The Hebrew and Greek words for "spirit" are also translated "wind." Angels are created spirits; they have no bodies, though they can assume human forms when ministering on earth. Angels sometimes served our Lord when He was on earth (Matt. 4:11; Luke 22:43), and they serve Him and us now.

*He is God enthroned and anointed (vv. 8-9).* In some false cults this quotation from Psalm 45:6-7 is translated, "Thy divine throne," because cultists dislike this strong affirmation that Jesus Christ is God. But the translation must stand: "Thy throne, O God, is forever and ever." Angels minister *before* the throne; they do not *sit* on the throne. One of the main teachings of Psalm 110 is that Jesus Christ, God's Anointed (Messiah, Christ), is now enthroned in glory. Jesus Himself referred to this important psalm (Mark 12:35-37; 14:62), and Peter used it on the Day of Pentecost (Acts 2:34-36). Our Lord has not yet entered into His earthly kingdom, but He has been enthroned in glory (Eph. 1:20).

When Christ ascended and entered the heavenly glory, He was anointed for His heavenly ministry with "the oil of gladness" (Heb. 1:9). This probably refers to Psalm 16:11, which Peter referred to at Pentecost: "Thou shalt make Me full of joy with Thy countenance" (Acts 2:28). What a joyful scene that must have been! Psalm 45 is a wedding psalm, and our Lord today is the heavenly Bridegroom who experiences "the joy that was set before Him" (Heb. 12:2). Angels praise Him, but they cannot share that position or that joy. Our Lord's throne is forever, which means He is eternal God.

**He is the eternal Creator (vv. 10-12).** This long quotation comes from Psalm 102:25-27. The angels did not found the earth, for they too are a part of creation. Jesus Christ is the Creator, and one day He will do away with the old creation and bring in a new creation. Everything around us changes, but He will never change. He is "the same yesterday, and today, and forever" (Heb. 13:8). Creation is like an old garment which will one day be discarded in favor of a new one.

**Christ is the Sovereign; angels are the servants (vv. 13-14).** Again, the writer quotes Psalm 110:1. The fact that Jesus Christ is now at the Father's right hand (the place of honor) is mentioned many times in the New Testament (see Matt. 22:43-44; 26:64; Mark 16:19; Acts 2:33-34; Rom. 8:34; Col. 3:1; Heb. 1:3, 13; 8:1; 10:12; 12:2; 1 Peter 3:22). Angels are the ministering spirits who serve the Lord seated on the throne. But they also minister to us who are the "heirs of salvation" through faith in Christ. The angels today are serving us!

It would be impossible to do away with the evidence presented in these quotations. Jesus Christ is greater than the angels, and this means He is also greater than the Law which they helped deliver to the people of Israel.

## Admonition: Heed the Word and Don't Drift (Heb. 2:1-4)

This is the first of the five admonitions found in Hebrews. Their purpose is to encourage all readers to pay attention to God's Word and obey it. We have already noted that these admonitions become stronger as we progress through the book, from *drifting* from God's Word to *defying* God's Word (Heb. 12:14-29). We also noted that God does not sit idly by and permit His children to rebel against Him. He will continue to speak and, when necessary, He chastens His own.

The admonition is written to believers, for the writer includes himself when he writes "we." The danger here is that of *neglecting our salvation*. Please note that the author did not write "rejecting" but "neglecting." He is not encouraging sinners to become Christians; rather, he is encouraging Christians to pay attention to the great salvation they have received from the Lord.

"Lest . . . we should let them slip" (Heb. 2:1) might better be translated "lest we drift away from them." Later (Heb. 6:19), the writer uses the illustration of an anchor to show how confident we can be in the promises of God. More spiritual problems are caused by neglect than perhaps by any other failure on our part. We neglect God's Word, prayer, worship with God's people (see Heb. 10:25), and other opportunities for spiritual growth, and as a result, we start to drift. The anchor does not move; we do.

During the Old Testament days, people who did not heed the Word were sometimes punished. That Word was given through angels, so how much greater responsibility do we have today who have received the Word from the Son of God! In Hebrews 2:2, "transgression" refers to sins of commission, while "disobedience" suggests sins of omission.

I have often told the story of the pastor who preached a series of sermons on "the sins of the saints." He was reprimanded by a member of the church. "After all," said the member, "sin in the life of a Christian is different from sin in the lives of other people."

"Yes," replied the pastor, "it's worse!"

We have the idea that believers today "under grace" can escape the chastening hand of God that was so evident "under Law." But to whom much is given, much shall be required. Not only have we received the Word from the Son of God, but that Word has been confirmed by apostolic miracles (Heb. 2:4). The phrase "signs and wonders" is found eleven times in the New Testament. Here it refers to the miracles that witnessed to the Word and gave confirmation that it was true. These miracles were performed by the Apostles (see Mark 16:17-20; Acts 2:43). Today we have the completed Word of God; so there is no need for these apostolic miracles. God now bears witness through His Spirit using the Word (Rom. 8:16; 1 John 5:1-13). The Spirit also gives spiritual gifts to God's people so that they may minister in the church (1 Cor. 12; Eph. 4:11ff).

Too many Christians today take the Word of God for granted and neglect it. In my pastoral ministry, I have discovered that neglect of the Word of God and prayer, publicly and privately, is the cause of most "spiritual drifting." I need not multiply examples because every believer knows that this is true. He has either experienced this "drifting" or has seen it in the lives of others.

The next time you sing "Come, Thou Fount of Every Blessing," recall that the composer, Robert Robinson, was converted under the mighty preaching of George Whitefield, but that later he drifted from the Lord, He had been greatly used as a pastor, but neglect of spiritual things led him astray. In an attempt to find peace, he began to travel. During one of his journeys, he met a young woman who was evidently very spiritually minded.

"What do you think of this hymn I have been reading?" she asked Robinson, handing him the book. *It was his own hymn!* He tried to avoid her question but it was hopeless, for the Lord was speaking to him. Finally, he broke down and confessed who he was and how he had been living away from the Lord.

"But these 'streams of mercy' are still flowing," the woman assured him; and through her encouragement, Robinson was restored to fellowship with the Lord.

It is easy to drift with the current, but it is difficult to return against the stream. Our salvation is a "great salvation," purchased at a great price. It brings with it great promises and blessings, and it leads to a great inheritance in glory. How can we neglect it?

### Explanation: Why Jesus Christ Is Not Inferior Because of His Humanity (Heb. 2:5-18)

The fact that angels are "ministering spirits" without human bodies would seem to give them an advantage over Jesus Christ who had a human body while He ministered on earth. (Today He has a glorified body that knows no limitations.) The writer gave four reasons that explain why our Lord's humanity was neither a handicap nor a mark of inferiority.

*His humanity enabled Him to regain man's lost dominion (vv. 5-9).* The quotation here is from Psalm 8:4-6, and you will want to read that entire psalm carefully. When God created the first man and woman, He gave them dominion over His Creation (Gen. 1:26-31). David marveled that God would share His power and glory with feeble man! Man was created "a little lower than the angels" (and therefore inferior to them), but man was given privileges far higher than the angels. God never promised the angels that they would reign in "the world to come" (Heb. 2:5).

But we have a serious problem here, for it is obvious that man today is *not* exercising dominion over creation. Certainly man cannot control the fish, fowl, or animals. In fact, man has a hard time controlling himself! "But now we see not yet all things put under him" (Heb. 2:8).

"But we see Jesus!" (Heb. 2:9) He is God's answer to man's dilemma. Jesus Christ became man that He might suffer and die for man's sin and restore the dominion that was lost because of sin. When our Lord was here on earth, He exercised that lost dominion. He had dominion over the fish (see Matt. 17:24-27; Luke 5:1-11; John 21:1-11), over the fowl (Luke 22:34, 60), and over the wild beasts (Mark 1:12-13), and the domesticated beasts (Mark 11:1-7). As the last Adam (1 Cor. 15:45), Jesus Christ regained man's lost dominion. Today, everything is under His feet (Eph. 1:20-23).

Man was "crowned . . . with glory and honor" (Heb. 2:7, NASB), but he lost his crown and became the slave of sin. Jesus Christ has regained that "glory and honor" (Heb. 2:9), and believers today share His kingly dominion (Rev. 1:5-6). One day, when He establishes His kingdom, we shall reign with Him in glory and honor. Jesus Christ did all of this for us— for lost sinners—because of "the grace of God" (Heb. 2:9). If He had not become man, He could not have died and "taste[d] death [experienced death] for every man" (Heb. 2:9). It is true that angels cannot die; but it is also true that angels cannot save lost sinners and restore man's lost dominion.

*His humanity enabled Him to bring many sons to glory (vv. 10-13).* Christ is not only the Last Adam, but He is also the Captain of salvation. That word *Captain* literally means "pioneer—one who opens the way for others to follow." Christ gave up His glory to become man. He regained His glory when He arose and ascended to heaven. Now He shares that glory with all who trust Him for salvation (John 17:22-24). He is bringing many sons and daughters to glory!

Christ is united to us, and we are united to Him: we are spiritually one. In fact, we are His "brethren" (Heb. 2:12). The writer quotes Psalm 22:22—a messianic psalm—in which Christ refers to His church as His brethren. This means we and the Son of God share the same nature and belong to the same family! What a marvel of God's grace!

The writer of Hebrews also quoted Isaiah 8:17-18 from the LXX. The immediate reference, of course, is to the Prophet Isaiah and his unique sons who were given significant names (see Isa. 7:3; 8:1-4). But the ultimate reference is to Jesus Christ. Not only are believers His brethren, but we are also His children: "Behold I and the children which God hath given Me" (Heb. 2:13). If Jesus Christ had not come to earth and become man, He could not take us from earth to share in His glory. The Incarnation, Crucifixion, and Resurrection must go together. They all lead to glory.

One phrase in Hebrews 2:10 ought to be discussed before we move on: "Make the Captain of their salvation perfect through sufferings." This statement does not suggest that Jesus Christ was imperfect when He was here on earth. The word translated "perfect" means "complete, effective, adequate." Jesus could not have become an adequate Saviour and High Priest had He not become Man and suffered and died.

*His humanity enabled Him to disarm Satan and deliver us from death (vv. 14-16).* Angels cannot die. Jesus did not come to save angels (note Heb. 2:16); He came to save humans. This meant that He had to take on Himself flesh and blood and become a Man. Only then could He die and through His death defeat Satan. The word "destroy" does not mean "annihilate," for it is obvious that Satan is still alive and busy. The word means "render inoperative, make of none effect." Satan is not destroyed, but he is disarmed.

In what sense did Satan have the power of death? The final authority of death is in the hands of our God (Deut. 32:39; Matt. 10:28; Rev. 1:18). Satan can do only that which is permitted by God (Job 1:12; 2:6). But because Satan is the author of sin (John 8:44), and sin brings death (Rom. 6:23), in this sense Satan exercises power in the realm of death. Jesus called him a murderer (John 8:44). Satan uses the fear of death as a terrible weapon to gain control over the lives of people. His kingdom is one of darkness and death (Col. 1:13). We who trust in Jesus Christ have once and for all been delivered from Satan's authority and from the terrible fear of death. The death, burial, and resurrection of Christ have given us victory! (1 Cor. 15:55-58)

Jesus Christ did not take on Himself the nature of angels in order to save the fallen angels (2 Peter 2:4; Rev. 12:7-9). Instead, He stooped lower than the angels to become Man! And not just "man" in general; but He became a Jew, a part of the "seed of Abra-ham" (Heb. 2:16). The Jews were a despised and hated race, and yet our Lord became a Jew.

*His humanity enables Him to be a sympathetic High Priest to His people (vv. 17-18).* Being pure spirits who have never suffered, the angels cannot identify with us in our weaknesses and needs. But Jesus can! While He was here on earth, Jesus was "made like unto His brethren" in that He experienced the sinless infirmities of human nature. He knew what it was to be a helpless baby, a growing child, a maturing adolescent. He knew the experiences of weariness, hunger, and thirst (John 4:6-8). He knew what it was to be despised and rejected, to be lied about and falsely accused. He experienced physical suffering and death. All of this was a part of His "training" for His heavenly ministry as High Priest.

If you want an example of a man who was *not* a merciful and faithful high priest, then read the account about Eli (1 Sam. 2:27-36). Here was a high priest who did not even lead his own sons into a faithful walk with God. Eli even accused brokenhearted Hannah of being drunk! (1 Sam. 1:9-18)

Jesus Christ is both merciful and faithful: He is merciful toward people and faithful toward God. He can never fail in His priestly ministries. He made the necessary sacrifice for our sins so that we might be reconciled to God. He did not need to make a sacrifice for Himself, because He is sinless.

But what happens when we who have been saved are tempted to sin? He stands ready to help us! He was tempted when He was on earth, but no temptation ever conquered Him. Because He has defeated every enemy, He is able to give us the grace that we need to overcome temptation. The word "succour" (Heb. 2:18) literally means "to run to the cry of a child." It means "to bring help when it is needed." Angels are able to *serve* us (Heb. 1:14), but they are not able to *succour* us in our times of temptation. Only Jesus Christ can do that, and He can do it because He became a man and suffered and died.

It might be good at this point to explain the difference between our Lord's ministry as High Priest and His ministry as Advocate (1 John 2:1). As our High Priest, our Lord is able to give us grace to keep us from sinning when we are tempted. If we do sin, then He as our Advocate represents us before the throne of God and forgives us when we sincerely confess our sins to Him (1 John 1:5–2:2). Both of these ministries are involved in His present work of intercession; and it is this intercessory ministry that is the guarantee of our eternal salvation (note that in Heb. 7:25 it is *"to* the uttermost"—i.e., eternally— and not *"from* the uttermost").

As you review this section, you cannot help but be amazed at the grace and wisdom of God. From a human point of view, it would seem foolish for God to become Man; yet it was this very act of grace that made possible our salvation and all that goes with it. When Jesus Christ became Man, He did not become inferior to the angels, for in His human body He accomplished something that angels could never accomplish. At the same time, He made it possible for us to share in His glory!

He is not ashamed to call us His brothers and sisters.

Are we ashamed to call Him "Lord"?

# CHAPTER THREE
# GREATER THAN MOSES
*Hebrews 3:1–4:13*

Next to Abraham, Moses was undoubtedly the man most greatly revered by the Jewish people. To go back to the Law meant to go back to Moses, and the recipients of this Letter to the Hebrews were sorely tempted to do just that. It was important that the writer convince his readers that Jesus Christ is greater than Moses, for the entire system of Jewish religion came through Moses. In this section, we learn that Jesus Christ is superior to Moses in at least three respects.

### Christ Is Greater in His Person (Heb. 3:1-2)
The twofold description of the readers makes it clear that they were converted people. "Holy brethren" could only be applied to people in the family of God, set apart by the grace of God. That the writer was referring to people in the church, the body of Christ, is clear from his use of the phrase "partakers of the

heavenly calling." No unconverted Jew or Gentile could ever claim that blessing! The word translated "partakers" here is translated "partners" in Luke 5:7, where it describes the relationship of four men in the fishing business: they were in it together.

True Christians not only share in a heavenly calling, but they also share in Jesus Christ (Heb. 3:14). Through the Holy Spirit, we are "members of His body, of His flesh, and of His bones" (Eph. 5:30). True believers are also "partakers of the Holy Spirit" (Heb. 6:4). "Now if any man have not the Spirit of Christ, he is none of His" (Rom. 8:9). Because we are God's children, we also partake in God's loving chastening (Heb. 12:8). Not to be chastened is evidence that a person is not one of God's children.

Because these people were holy brothers and sisters, and partakers of a heavenly calling, they were able to give a "confession" of their faith in Jesus Christ. The word simply means "to say the same thing." All true Christians "say the same thing" when it comes to their experience of salvation. Twice in this epistle, the writer exhorted the readers to hold fast to this confession (Heb. 4:14; 10:23, NASB). It was this same confession that they were "strangers and pilgrims" on the earth that characterized men and women of faith in the ages past (Heb. 11:13).

It was not Moses who did all of this for the people addressed in this epistle; it was Jesus Christ! The writer did not exhort them to consider Moses, but to consider Christ. The word means "to consider *carefully,* to understand fully." This is no quick glance at Jesus Christ! It is a careful consideration of who He is and what He has done.

That Christ is superior to Moses in His person is an obvious fact. Moses was a mere man, called to be a prophet and leader, while Jesus Christ is the Son of God sent by the Father into the world. The title *apostle* means "one sent with a commission." Moses was called and commissioned by God, but Jesus Christ was *sent* as God's "last Word" to sinful man. You may want to read some of the verses in the Gospel of John where Jesus is referred to as "sent from God" (John 3:17, 34; 5:36, 38; 6:29, 57; 7:29; 8:42; 10:36; 11:42; 17:3; and note also 13:3).

Jesus Christ is not only the Apostle, but He is also the High Priest. Moses was a prophet who on occasion served as a priest (see Ps. 99:6), but he was never a high priest. That title belonged to his brother Aaron. In fact, Jesus Christ has the title "great High Priest" (Heb. 4:14).

As the Apostle, Jesus Christ represented God to men; and as the High Priest, He now represents men to God in heaven. Moses, of course, fulfilled similar ministries, for he taught Israel God's truth and he prayed for Israel when he met God on the mount (see Ex. 32:30-32). Moses was primarily the prophet of Law, while Jesus Christ is the Messenger of God's grace (see John 1:17). Moses helped prepare the way for the coming of the Saviour to the earth.

However, the writer of Hebrews notes that Moses and Jesus Christ were *both* faithful in the work God gave them to do. Moses was not sinless, as was Jesus Christ, but he was faithful and obeyed God's will (Num. 12:7). This would be an encouragement to those first-century Jewish believers to remain faithful to Christ, even in the midst of the tough trials they were experiencing. Instead of going back to Moses, they should *imitate* Moses and be faithful in their calling.

### Christ Is Greater in His Ministry (Heb. 3:3-6)

The word "house" is used six times in these verses. It refers to the people of God, not to a material building. Moses ministered to Israel, the people of God under the Old Covenant. Today, Christ ministers to His church, the people of God under the New Covenant ("whose house are we," Heb. 3:6). You find an illustration of this dual use of "house" in 2 Samuel 7. David wanted to build a temple for God, a house in which God could dwell. But God told David that He would build David's house (household, family) and make a covenant with David's descendants.

The contrast between Moses and Christ is clear: Moses was a *servant in the house,* while Jesus Christ is a *Son over the house.* Moses was a member of the household, but Jesus *built* the house! By the way, the truth in these verses is a powerful argument for the deity of Jesus Christ. If God built all things, and Jesus Christ built God's house, then Jesus Christ must be God.

There is another factor in Christ's superiority over Moses: the Prophet Moses spoke about things to come, but Jesus Christ brought the fulfillment of these things (Heb. 3:6). Moses ministered "in the shadows," as it were (see Heb. 8:5 and 10:1), while Jesus

Christ brought the full and final light of the Gospel of the grace of God.

The Greek word translated "servant" (Heb. 3:5) is not the usual New Testament word for servant or slave. This word carries the meaning of "a voluntary servant who acts because of affection." In the New Testament, it is used only of Moses. At the beginning of his ministry, Moses was a bit hesitant and resisted God's call. But once he surrendered, he obeyed out of a heart of love and devotion.

The "if" clause (Heb. 3:6) needs to be understood in the light of the total context, which is Moses leading Israel out of Egypt and to the Promised Land. The writer is not suggesting that we, as Christians, must keep ourselves saved. This would contradict the major theme of the book, which is the finished work of Christ and His heavenly ministry guaranteeing our eternal salvation (Heb. 7:14ff). Rather, the writer is affirming that those who hold fast their confidence and hope are proving that they are truly born again.

The word "confidence" literally means "freedom of speech, openness." When you are free to speak, then there is no fear and you have confidence. A believer can come with boldness (same word as "confidence") to the throne of grace (Heb. 4:16) with openness and freedom and not be afraid. We have this boldness because of the shed blood of Jesus Christ (Heb. 10:19). Therefore, we should not cast away our confidence, no matter what the circumstances might be. We should not have confidence in ourselves, because we are too prone to fail; but we should have confidence in Jesus Christ who never fails.

Because of this confidence in Christ and this confession of Christ, we can experience joy and hope (Heb. 3:6). The writer exhorted these suffering saints to *enjoy* their spiritual experience and not simply *endure* it. Jesus Christ is the beloved Son over His house, and He will care for each member of the family. He is the faithful High Priest who provides all the grace we need for each demand of life. As the Great Shepherd of the sheep (Heb. 13:19-20), Jesus Christ is using the experiences in His people's lives to equip them for service that will glorify His name.

In other words, those who have trusted Christ *prove* this confession by their steadfastness, confidence, and joyful hope. They are not burdened by the past or threatened by the present, but are "living in the future tense" as they await the "blessed hope" of their Lord's return. It is this "heavenly calling" that motivates the believers to keep on living for the Saviour even when the going is tough.

The wandering of Israel in the wilderness is a major topic in this section. Two men in that nation—Caleb and Joshua—illustrate the attitude described in Hebrews 3:6. Everybody else in Israel over the age of twenty was to die in the wilderness and never enter the Promised Land (see Num. 14:26-38). But Caleb and Joshua believed God and God honored their faith. For forty years, Caleb and Joshua watched their friends and relatives die; but those two men of faith had confidence in God's Word that they would one day enter Canaan. While others were experiencing sorrow and death, Caleb and Joshua rejoiced in confident hope. As believers, we know that God is taking us to heaven, and we should reveal the same kind of joyful confidence and hope.

### Christ Is Greater in the Rest He Gives (Heb. 3:7—4:13)

This long section is the second of the five exhortations in this epistle. In the first exhortation (Heb. 2:1-4), the writer pointed out the danger of *drifting* from the Word because of neglect. In this exhortation, he explains the danger of *doubting* and *disbelieving* the Word because of hardness of heart. It is important that we understand the background of this section, which is the Exodus of Israel from Egypt and their experiences of unbelief in the wilderness.

To begin with, we must understand that there are spiritual lessons in the geography of Israel's experiences. The nation's bondage in Egypt is an illustration of a sinner's bondage in this world. Much as Israel was delivered from Egypt by the blood of lambs and the power of God, so a sinner who believes on Christ is delivered from the bondage of sin (Col. 1:13-14). Jesus Christ is "the Lamb of God" whose death and resurrection have made our deliverance from sin a reality.

It was not God's will that Israel remain either in Egypt or in the wilderness. His desire was that the people enter their glorious inheritance in the land of Canaan. But when Israel got to the border of their inheritance, they delayed because they doubted the promise of God (Num. 13–14). "We are not able" wept the ten spies and the people. "We *are* able with God's help!" said Moses, Joshua, and Caleb. Because the people went backward in unbelief instead of forward by faith, they missed their inheritance and died in the wilderness. It was the new generation that possessed the land and entered into their rest.

What does Canaan represent to us as Christians today? It represents our spiritual inheritance in Christ (Eph. 1:3, 11, 15-23). It is unfortunate that some of our hymns and Gospel songs use Canaan as a picture of heaven, and "crossing the Jordan" as a picture of death. Since Canaan was a place of battles, and even of defeats, it is not a good illustration of heaven! Israel had to cross the river by faith (a picture of the believer as he dies to self and the world, Rom. 6) and claim the inheritance by faith. They had to "step out by faith" (Josh. 1:3) and claim the land for themselves, just as believers today must do.

Now we can understand what the wilderness wanderings represent: the experiences of believers who will not claim their spiritual inheritance in Christ, who doubt God's Word and live in restless unbelief. To be sure, God is with them, as He was with Israel; but they do not enjoy the fullness of God's blessing. They are "out of Egypt" but they are not yet "in Canaan."

With this background, we can now better understand one of the key words in this section—*rest* (Heb. 3:11, 18; 4:1, 3-5, 8-11). The writer mentioned two different "rests" found in Old Testament history: (1) *God's Sabbath rest*, when He ceased from His Creation activities (Gen. 2:2; Heb. 4:4); (2) *Israel's rest in Canaan* (Deut. 12:9; Josh. 21:43-45; Heb. 3:11). But he saw in these "rests" illustrations of the spiritual experiences of believers today. The Sabbath rest is a picture of our rest in Christ through salvation (Heb. 4:3; see Matt. 11:28). The Canaan rest is a picture of our present rest as we claim our inheritance in Christ (Heb. 4:11-13; note the emphasis on the Word of God). The first is the rest of salvation; the second is the rest of submission.

But there is a third rest that enters into the discussion, that *future rest* that all believers will enjoy with God. "There remaineth, therefore, a rest to the people of God" (Heb. 4:9). This word for rest is the Greek word *sabbatismos*—"a keeping of a Sabbath"—and this is the only place in the New Testament where this word is used. When the saints enter heaven, it will be like sharing God's great Sabbath rest, with all labors and battles ended (Rev. 14:13).

We may diagram these rests in this way:

| Past | Present | Future |
|------|---------|--------|
| God's Sabbath rest | Salvation rest | Heaven |
| Israel's Canaan rest | Submission rest (victory in Christ) | |

With this background of Israel's history and the "rests" involved, we may now examine the passage itself. The writer gives a three-fold admonition.

**Let us take heed (vv. 7-19).** Take heed to what? To the sad history of the nation of Israel and the important lesson it teaches. The writer quotes from Psalm 95:7-11, which records God's response to Israel's tragic spiritual condition. God had delivered His people from Egypt and had cared for them, revealing His power in many signs and wonders. Israel saw all of this and benefited from it, but the experience did not bring them closer to God or make them trust Him more. All that God did for them did not benefit them spiritually. In fact, just the opposite took place: they hardened their hearts against God! They put God to the test and He did not fail them; yet they failed Him.

The heart of every problem is a problem in the heart. The people of Israel (except Moses, Joshua, and Caleb) erred in their hearts (Heb. 3:10), which means that their hearts wandered from God and His Word. They also had evil hearts of unbelief (Heb. 3:12); they did not believe that God would give them victory in Canaan. They had seen God perform great signs in Egypt. Yet they doubted He was adequate for the challenge of Canaan.

When a person has an *erring* heart and a *disbelieving* heart, the result will also be a *hard* heart. This is a heart that is insensitive to the Word and work of God. So hard was the heart of Israel that the people even wanted to return to Egypt! Imagine wanting to exchange their freedom under God for slavery in Egypt! Of course, all this history spoke to the hearts of the readers of this letter because they were in danger of "going back" themselves.

God's judgment fell on Israel in the wilderness at Kadesh Barnea. That entire generation was condemned to die, and only the new generation would enter the land. God said, "They shall not enter into My rest" (Heb. 3:11). But what message does this bring to a believer today? No believer today, Jew or Gentile, could go back into the Mosaic legal system since the temple is gone and there is no priesthood. But every believer is tempted to give up his confession of Christ and go back into the world system's life of compromise and bondage. This is especially true during times of persecution and suffering. The fires of persecution have always purified the church because suffering separates true believers from the counterfeit. True believers are willing to suffer for Christ and they hold firmly to their convictions and their confession of faith (see Heb. 3:6, 14). We are not saved by holding to our confession. The fact that we hold to our confession is proof that we are God's true children.

It is important that we take heed and recognize the spiritual dangers that exist. But it is also important that we encourage each other to be faithful to the Lord (Heb. 3:13). We get the impression that some of these believers addressed were careless about their fellowship in the local assembly (see Heb. 10:23-25). Christians belong to each other and need each other. Moses, Caleb, and Joshua did try to encourage Israel when the nation refused to enter Canaan, but the people would not listen.

It is clear from this section that God was grieved with Israel during the entire forty years they wandered in the wilderness. The Jews had not been out of Egypt long when they began to provoke God (Ex. 16:1ff). After He supplied bread for them, they complained about a lack of water (Ex. 17:1-7). Moses called that place "Massah and Meribah" which means "provocation and trial." These same words are used in Hebrews 3:10.

The sin of Israel is stated in Hebrews 3:12—"departing from the living God." The Greek word gives us our English word "apostasy." This is the only place this word is used in Hebrews. Does "apostasy" mean abandoning one's faith and therefore being condemned forever? That does not fit into this context. Israel departed from the living God by refusing God's will for their lives and stubbornly wanting to go their own way back to Egypt. God did not permit them to return to Egypt. Rather, He disciplined them in the wilderness. God did not allow His people to return to bondage.

The emphasis in Hebrews is that true believers have an eternal salvation because they trust a living Saviour who constantly intercedes for them. But the writer is careful to point out that this confidence is no excuse for sin. God disciplines His children. Remember that Canaan is not a picture of heaven, but of the believer's present spiritual inheritance in Christ. Believers who doubt God's Word and rebel against Him do not miss heaven, but they do miss out on the blessings of their inheritance today, and they must suffer the chastening of God.

**Let us fear (vv. 1-8).** Believers today may enter and enjoy their spiritual inheritance in Christ. We must be careful lest we fail to believe God's Word, for it is only as the Word is "mixed with faith" that it can accomplish its purposes. The argument in this section is given in several propositions: (1) God finished His work and rested, so that His rest has been available since Creation. (2) The Jews failed to enter into their rest. (3) Many years later (Ps. 95), God said that a rest was still available. That "today" is still here! This means that Joshua did not lead Israel into the true rest, because a rest still remains. (Note that the name "Jesus" in Heb. 4:8, KJV, ought to be "Joshua." "Jesus" is the Greek form of "Joshua.")

The Canaan rest for Israel is a picture of the spiritual rest we find in Christ when we surrender to Him. When we come to Christ by faith, we find *salvation* rest (Matt. 11:28). When we yield and learn of Him and obey Him by faith, we enjoy *submission* rest (Matt. 11:29-30). The first is "peace with God" (Rom. 5:1); the second is the "peace of God" (Phil. 4:6-8). It is by believing that we enter into rest (Heb. 4:3); it is by obeying God by faith and surrendering to His will that the rest enters into us.

**Let us labor (vv. 9-13).** "Give diligence" is a good translation of this admonition. Diligence is the opposite of "drifting" (Heb. 2:1-3). How do we give diligence? By paying close attention to the Word of God. Israel did not believe God's Word, so the rebels fell in the wilderness. "So then faith cometh by hearing, and hearing by the Word of God" (Rom. 10:17).

In comparing the Word of God to a sword, the writer is not suggesting that God uses His Word to slaughter the saints! It is true that the Word cuts the heart of sinners with conviction (Acts 5:33; 7:54), and that the Word defeats Satan (Eph. 6:17). The Greek word translated "sword" means "a short sword or dagger." The emphasis is on the power of the Word to penetrate and expose the inner heart of man. The Word is a "discerner" or "critic."

The Israelites criticized God's Word instead of allowing the Word to judge them. Consequently, they lost their inheritance.

Of course, God sees our hearts (Heb. 4:13); but we do not always know what is there (Jer. 17:9). God uses the Word to enable us to see the sin and unbelief in our own hearts. The Word *exposes* our hearts; and then, if we trust God, the Word *enables* our hearts to obey God and claim His promises. This is why each believer should be diligent to apply himself to hear and heed God's Word. In the Word we see God, and we also see how God sees us. We see ourselves as we really are. This experience enables us to be honest with God, to trust His will, and to obey Him.

All of this is possible because of the finished work of Jesus Christ. (The two "He's" in Heb. 4:10 refer to Jesus Christ.) God rested when He finished the work of Creation. God's Son rested when He completed the work of the new creation. We may enter into His rest by trusting His Word and obeying His will. We can do this as we listen to His Word, understand it, trust it, and obey it. Only in this way can we claim our inheritance in Christ.

Before Joshua conquered Jericho, he went out to survey the situation; and he met the Lord Jesus Christ (Josh. 5:13-15). Joshua discovered that he was second in command! The Lord had a sword in His hand, and Joshua fell at His feet in complete submission. It was this action in private that gave Joshua his public victory.

We too claim our spiritual inheritance by surrendering to Him and trusting His Word. We must beware of an evil heart of unbelief.

# CHAPTER FOUR
# GREATER THAN AARON THE HIGH PRIEST
*Hebrews 4:14–5:10*

Moses did not lead the people of Israel into the promised rest; in fact, he himself was forbidden to enter the land. Joshua led them into their *physical* rest, but not into the promised *spiritual* rest (see Heb. 4:8). But what about Aaron, the first high priest? Is it possible that the Aaronic priesthood, with all of its sacrifices and ceremonies, could bring a troubled soul into rest?

The Hebrew Christians who received this letter were sorely tempted to return to the religion of their fathers. After all, any Jew could travel to Jerusalem and *see* the temple and the priests ministering at the altar. Here was something real, visible, concrete. When a person is going through persecution, as these Hebrew Christians were, it is much easier to walk by sight than by faith. Some of us have doubted the Lord under much less provocation than these people were enduring.

The central theme of Hebrews is the priesthood of Jesus Christ, what He is now doing in heaven on behalf of His people. Is the high priestly ministry of Christ superior to that of Aaron and his successors? Yes, it is; and the writer proves his assertion by presenting four arguments.

## Jesus Christ Has a Superior Title (Heb. 4:14-16)

"Seeing then that we have a GREAT High Priest" (Heb. 4:14, emphasis mine). Aaron was a "high priest," but Jesus Christ is the GREAT High Priest. No Old Testament priest could assume that title. But in what does our Lord's greatness consist?

To begin with, Jesus Christ is both God and Man. He is "Jesus, the Son of God." The name "Jesus" means "Saviour" and identifies His humanity and His ministry on earth. "Son of God" affirms His deity and the fact that He is God. In His unique person, Jesus Christ unites Deity and humanity, so that He can bring people to God and bring to people all that God has for them.

Not only in His *person*, but also in His *position* Jesus Christ is great. Aaron and his successors ministered in the tabernacle and temple precincts, once a year entering the holy of holies. But Jesus Christ has "passed through the heavens" (Heb. 4:14, literal translation). When He ascended to the Father, Jesus Christ passed through the atmospheric heavens and the planetary heavens into the third heaven where God dwells (2 Cor. 12:2). How much better is it to have a High Priest who ministers in a heavenly tabernacle than in an earthly one!

But there is another aspect to Christ's position: not only is He in heaven, but He is *enthroned*. His throne is "the throne of grace" (Heb. 4:16). The mercy seat on the ark of the covenant was God's throne in Israel (Ex. 25:17-22), but it could never be called "a throne of grace." Grace does not veil itself from the people. Grace does not hide itself in a tent.

Furthermore, the common people were not permitted to enter the holy precincts of the tabernacle and the temple, and the priests got only as far as the veil. The high priest alone went beyond the veil, and only on the Day of Atonement (Lev. 16). But *every believer* in Christ is invited, and is even encouraged, to "come boldly unto the throne of grace"! What a great throne it is because our Great High Priest is ministering there.

Jesus Christ, our Great High Priest, is enthroned in heaven. Something else makes Him great: He is ministering mercy and grace to those who come for help. *Mercy* means that God does not give us what we do deserve; *grace* means that He gives us what we do not deserve. No Old Testament high priest could minister mercy and grace in quite the same way. When an Israelite was tempted, he could not easily run to the high priest for help; and he certainly could not enter the holy of holies for God's help. But as believers in Jesus Christ, we can run to our High Priest at any time, in any circumstance, and find the help that we need.

Now because of the superiority of Jesus Christ, the Great High Priest, over Aaron, two important conclusions can be drawn. First, there is no need in giving up our profession just because we are going through testing and trial (Heb. 4:14). The word translated "profession" means "confession." These Hebrew Christians were tempted to give up their confession of faith in Christ and their confidence in Him (see Heb. 3:6, 14). It was not a matter of giving up their salvation, since salvation through Christ is eternal (Heb. 5:9). It was a matter of their public confession of faith. By returning to the Old Testament system, they would be telling everyone that they had no faith in Christ (see Gal. 2:11-21). This kind of unbelief would only bring reproach to Christ's name.

After all, the great purpose of salvation is the glory of God (see Eph. 1:6, 12, 14). It was the glory of God that so concerned Moses when Israel broke God's Law and made the golden calf (Ex. 32). God offered to destroy the nation and to begin a new one from Moses, but Moses refused the offer. Instead Moses interceded for Israel on the basis of God's glory and God's promise; and God spared the people, even though He disciplined them for their sin (Ex. 32:11-13).

The second conclusion is this: there is no need to go back because we can come boldly into the presence of God and get the help we need (Heb. 4:16). No trial is too great, no temptation is too strong, but that Jesus Christ can give us the mercy and grace that we need, when we need it. "But He is so far away!" we may argue. "And He is the perfect Son of God! What can He know about the problems of weak sinners like us?"

But that is a part of His greatness! When He was ministering on earth in a human body, He experienced all that we experience, *and even more.* After all, a sinless person would feel temptations and trials in a much greater way than you and I could ever feel them. Christ was tempted, yet He did not sin; and He is able to help us when we are tempted. If we fail to hold fast our confession, we are not proving that Jesus Christ has failed. We are only telling the world that *we failed* to draw on His grace and mercy when it was freely available to us.

## Jesus Christ Has a Superior Ordination (Heb. 5:1, 4-6)

When I became pastor of the Calvary Baptist Church in Covington, Kentucky, it was necessary for me to go to the city hall and be bonded. Otherwise, I would not have the authority to perform marriages. I had to show my ordination certificate and prove that I was indeed ministering at the church.

One day I received a frantic phone call from one of our members. Some Christian friends were being married the next day by a relative

from Michigan, and they discovered that he was not authorized to perform the ceremony! Could I help them? The visiting pastor could read the ceremony as well as I could, and he knew the couple better than I did; but he lacked the authority to minister.

No man could appoint himself as a priest, let alone as *high* priest. King Saul invaded the priesthood and lost his kingdom (1 Sam. 13). Korah and his fellow rebels tried to make themselves priests, and God judged them (Num. 16). When King Uzziah tried to enter the temple and burn incense, God smote him with leprosy (2 Chron. 26:16-21).

Aaron was chosen by God to be the high priest, and he was duly ordained and installed in office (Ex. 28). He was chosen *from* men to minister *for* men. His main task was at the altar: to offer the sacrifices God had appointed (see Heb. 8:3-4; 9:14). Unless the sacrifices were offered in the right place, by the right person, they were not accepted by God.

The very existence of a priesthood and a system of sacrifices gave evidence that man is estranged from God. It was an act of grace on God's part that He instituted the whole levitical system. Today, that system is fulfilled in the ministry of Jesus Christ. He is both the sacrifice and the High Priest who ministers to God's people on the basis of His once-for-all offering on the cross.

The subject of ordination stated in Hebrews 5:1 is further developed in Hebrews 5:5-6. Jesus Christ did not appoint Himself as High Priest. He was appointed by God the Father. The quotation in Hebrews 5:5 is from Psalm 2:7. This psalm was already quoted in Hebrews 1:5 to prove that Jesus Christ is the Son of God. But the emphasis in Hebrews 5:5 is on the priesthood of Jesus Christ, not on His deity. What significance, then, does this quotation have for the argument?

The answer to that question is in Acts 13:33-34, where the Apostle Paul quoted Psalm 2:7 and explained what it means. The phrase, "Today have I begotten Thee," does not refer to the birth of Christ at Bethlehem, but to *His resurrection from the dead.* The Son of God was "begotten" into a glorious new life in His resurrection! He ascended to heaven in a glorified body to become our High Priest at the throne of grace. When Aaron was ordained to the priesthood, he offered the sacrifices of animals. But Jesus Christ, to become our High Priest, offered the sacrifice of Himself—and then arose from the dead!

But God the Father not only said, "Thou art My Son" in Psalm 2:7; He also said, "Thou art a Priest forever after the order of Melchizedek" (Heb. 5:6, quoted from Ps. 110:4). This psalm was also quoted earlier in Hebrews (1:13) to affirm Jesus Christ's final victory over all His enemies. When Aaron was ordained, God did not speak directly to him and declare his priesthood. But the Father did make this special declaration concerning His Son.

Two factors make Christ's priesthood unique and, therefore, His ordination greater. First, He is a High Priest *forever*. No Old Testament priest ministered forever because each priest died and relinquished the office to his successor. The word "forever" is an important one in this epistle. At least six times the writer affirms that Christ's high priesthood is forever (Heb. 5:6; 6:20; 7:17, 21, 24, 28). And, since He is a Priest forever, He gives His people salvation forever (Heb. 7:23-28).

The second factor that makes Christ's ordination unique is that He belongs to *a different order* from the Old Testament priests. They belonged to the order of Aaron; He belongs to the order of Melchizedek. This is a key concept in Hebrews, so we must take time to examine and understand it.

Melchizedek is mentioned in only two places in the entire Old Testament—Genesis 14:17-24 and Psalm 110:4. His name means "King of Righteousness," and he was also "King of Salem [peace]." But the fascinating thing about Melchizedek is that he was *both a priest and a king!* King Uzziah wanted to be both a priest and a king, and God judged him. Only in Jesus Christ and in pre-Law Melchizedek were these two offices combined. Jesus Christ is a High Priest *on a throne!*

The reason Jesus Christ can be "a Priest forever" is that He belongs to the "order of Melchizedek." As far as the Old Testament record is concerned, Melchizedek did not die (see Heb. 7:1-3). Of course, because he was a real man, he did die at some time; but the record is not given to us. So Melchizedek becomes a picture of our Lord Jesus Christ who is a *Priest* forever.

But Melchizedek also pictures our Lord as a *heavenly* High Priest. Jesus Christ could never have served as a priest when He was on earth because He did not belong to the tribe of Levi. Jesus was born of the seed of David, the tribe of Judah. He became the sacrifice on earth that He might become the High Priest in

heaven. All of these truths will be developed in Hebrews 7–10, but they are introduced here.

### Jesus Christ Reveals a Superior Sympathy (Heb. 5:2, 7-8)

Every Old Testament high priest had to minister to people who were "ignorant, and . . . out of the way [wayward]" (Heb. 5:2). God made no provision but judgment for high-handed sins of rebellion (see Ex. 21:12-14; Num. 15:27-31). But He did make provision when people sinned through ignorance or weakness. An Old Testament priest could identify with the sinners, since he himself was a sinner. In fact, on the Day of Atonement, the high priest had to offer a sacrifice *for himself* before he could offer one for the nation! (Lev. 16; Heb. 9:7)

You would think that one sinner would have compassion for another sinner, but this is not always the case. Sin makes a person selfish. Sin can blind us to the hurts of others. Sin can harden our hearts and make us judgmental instead of sympathetic. Remember how heartbroken Hannah, who was praying for a son, was accused by high priest Eli of being drunk? (1 Sam. 1:9-18) And when King David was confronted with a story of a rich man's sin, he had no sympathy for him, even though David himself was a worse sinner (2 Sam. 12).

No, it is the spiritually minded person with a clean heart who sympathizes with a sinner and seeks to help him (see Gal. 6:1). Because we are so sinful, we have a hard time helping other sinners; but because Jesus is perfect, He is able to meet our needs after we sin.

Our Lord was prepared for His high priestly ministry during His days of ministry on earth (Heb. 5:7-8). The phrase, "In the days of His flesh," means, "In the days when He was on earth in a human body." From birth to death, our Lord experienced the sinless infirmities of human nature. He knew what it was to grow and mature (Luke 2:52). He experienced hunger and thirst, as well as weariness (John 4:6-8, 31). He also faced temptations to sin (Matt. 4:1-11) and persecutions from the hands of sinful men.

How could the Son of God "learn obedience"? In the same way any son must learn obedience: by the experiences of life. We must remember that our Lord, in His earthly walk, lived by faith in the Father's will. As God, He needed to learn nothing. But as the Son of God come in human flesh, He had to experience that which His people would experience, so that He might be able to minister as their High Priest. He did not need to learn *how* to obey because it would be impossible for God to be disobedient. Rather, as the God-Man in human flesh, He had to learn what was involved in obedience. In this way, He identified with us.

This preparation involved the experience of death. The writer of Hebrews (5:7) focuses on our Lord's experience in the Garden of Gethsemane (Matt. 26:36-46). As He faced the Cross, it was not the physical suffering that burdened Jesus, but the fact that He would be made sin and separated from His Father. Other servants of God have faced death and not expressed such great emotion; but no other servant ever bore on his body the sins of the whole world.

In His Gethsemane prayer, our Lord did not oppose the Father, but prayed, "Not My will, but Thine, be done" (Luke 22:42). He was not praying to be spared *from* death, but to be saved *out of death.* He was praying for resurrection from the dead, and God answered that prayer. He had prophesied His own death and had made it clear that He was laying down His life of His own free will. This ties in with the quotation from Psalm 2:7, cited in Hebrews 5:5, that promised His resurrection from the dead.

The writer of Hebrews states that Jesus' prayer "was heard" (Heb. 5:7), that is, answered by the Father. Since He *did* die on the cross, this could not have been what He was praying about; for if the Father had answered, the Son would not have been crucified. He did not pray to be saved *from* death, but *out of death;* and God answered His prayer by raising Him from the dead.

No one else ever died the kind of death that Jesus died. He was made sin for us (2 Cor. 5:21; 1 Peter 2:24). Men have died because of their own sins, but only Jesus died for the sins of a whole world. He experienced the ultimate in suffering and, therefore, He is able to sympathize with His people when they are suffering. The readers of this epistle were going through difficult times, but they had "not yet resisted unto blood" (Heb. 12:4). Their goods had been seized and they had been ridiculed (Heb. 10:32-34), but they had not been crucified and forsaken by the Father.

No matter what trials we meet, Jesus Christ is able to understand our needs and help us. We need never doubt His ability to sympathize and strengthen. It is also worth noting that sometimes God puts *us* through difficulties that we might better understand the needs of others, and become able to encourage them (see 2 Cor. 1:8ff).

When Charles Haddon Spurgeon was a young preacher in London, his successful ministry aroused the envy of some of the clergy; and they attacked him with various kinds of slander and gossip. His sermons were called "trashy," and he was called "an actor" and "a pulpit buffoon." Even after his ministry was established, Spurgeon was lied about in the press (including the *religious* press); and this was bound to discourage him.

After one particularly scurrilous report in the press, Spurgeon fell before the Lord and prayed, "O Lord Jesus, Thou didst make Thyself of no reputation for me. I willingly lay my reputation down for Thy sake." From that time on, Spurgeon had peace in his heart. He knew that his Great High Priest understood his need and would give him the grace that he needed for each hour.

## Jesus Christ Offered a Superior Sacrifice (Heb. 5:3, 9-10)

This topic has already been touched on, and the writer of Hebrews discusses it in detail in Hebrews 9-10. Two important matters are involved.

The first is that Jesus Christ did not need to offer any sacrifices for Himself. On the annual Day of Atonement, the high priest first had to sacrifice for himself; and then he could offer the sacrifices for his nation (Lev. 16). Since Jesus is the sinless Son of God, there was no need for Him to sacrifice for Himself. He was in perfect fellowship with the Father and needed no cleansing.

The second matter is that our Lord's sacrifice was once and for all, whereas the Old Testament sacrifices had to be repeated. Furthermore, those sacrifices could only *cover* sins; they could never *cleanse* sins. It required the sacrifice of the spotless Lamb of God for sin to be cleansed and removed.

Because He is the sinless, eternal Son of God, and because He offered a perfect sacrifice, Jesus Christ is the "Author of eternal salvation" (Heb. 5:9). No Old Testament priest could offer *eternal* salvation to anyone, but that is exactly what we have in Jesus Christ. The phrase "being made perfect" does not suggest that Jesus was imperfect! The word means "made complete"; we described it in our study of Hebrews 2:10. By means of His earthly sufferings, Jesus Christ was equipped for His heavenly ministry as our High Priest. He is able to save, keep, and strengthen His people.

Does the phrase "them that obey Him" (Heb. 5:9) suggest that, if we do not obey Him, we may lose that eternal salvation? To "obey God" is the same as "to trust God," as "them that obey Him" is a description of those who have put their faith in Jesus Christ. "A great company of the priests were obedient to the faith" (Acts 6:7). "But they have not all obeyed the Gospel" (Rom. 10:16). "Ye have purified your souls in obeying the truth" (1 Peter 1:22). Once we have put our faith in Jesus Christ, and thus obeyed His call, we experience His eternal salvation.

It is difficult to resist the four arguments presented in this section. We must conclude with the writer that Jesus Christ the great High Priest is superior to Aaron. It would be foolish for anyone to return to the inferiorities of the old Law when he could enjoy the superiorities of Jesus Christ. Then why were these Hebrew believers tempted to go back into legalism? *Because they were not going on to maturity in Christ!* For this reason the writer paused to exhort them to grow up in the Lord; and that is the theme for our next chapter.

# CHAPTER FIVE
# PILGRIMS SHOULD MAKE PROGRESS
*Hebrews 5:11–6:20*

We do not want you to become lazy, but to imitate those who through faith and patience inherit what has been promised" (Heb. 6:12, NIV).

This verse summarizes the main message of this difficult (and often misunderstood) section of the epistle. Israel wanted to go back to Egypt; and, as a result, a whole generation failed to inherit what God had promised. They were safely delivered out of Egypt, but they never enjoyed the promised rest in Canaan. We believers today can make the same mistake.

If you keep in mind that the emphasis in this section is on *making spiritual progress,* you will steer safely through misinterpretations that could create problems. In this section, the writer deals with three topics that relate to spiritual progress.

## The Marks of Spiritual Immaturity (Heb. 5:11-14)

The writer is about to begin his explanation of the heavenly priesthood of Christ, but he is not sure his readers are ready for what he has to teach. The problem is not that he is a dull teacher, but that they are dull hearers! The word translated "dull" in Hebrews 5:11 is translated "slothful" in Hebrews 6:12. It refers to a condition of spiritual apathy and laziness that prevents spiritual development.

What, then, are the marks of spiritual immaturity?

*Dullness toward the Word (v. 11).* These believers started on their "backward journey" by *drifting from the Word* (Heb. 2:1-4), and then *doubting the Word* (Heb. 3:7–4:13). As a result, they were now "dull of hearing"; that is, unable to listen to the Word, receive it, and act on it. They did not have the attitude of the Thessalonians: "For this cause also thank we God without ceasing, because, when ye received the Word of God which ye heard of us, ye received it not as the word of men, but as it is in truth, the Word of God, which effectually worketh also in you that believe" (1 Thes. 2:13).

One of the first symptoms of spiritual regression, or backsliding, is a dullness toward the Bible. Sunday School class is dull, the preaching is dull, anything spiritual is dull. The problem is usually not with the Sunday School teacher or the pastor, but with the believer himself.

*Inability to share (v. 12a).* The ability to share spiritual truth with others is a mark of maturity. Not all Christians have the gift of teaching, but all can share what they learn from the Word. One of the hardest lessons children must learn is the lesson of sharing. The recipients of this letter had been saved long enough to be able to share God's truth with others. But, instead of helping others to grow, these Hebrew Christians were in need of learning *again* the simple teachings of the Christian life. They were experiencing a second childhood!

*A "baby food" diet (vv. 12b-13).* Milk is predigested food, and it is specially suited to babies. But only those who have teeth can enjoy meat. The writer defines the "milk" as "the first principles of the oracles of God" (Heb. 5:12). The "meat" of the Word is the teaching about our Lord's ministry *now* in heaven as our High Priest. The writer wanted to give this "meat" to them, but they were not ready for it.

The "milk" of the Word refers to what Jesus Christ did on earth—His birth, life, teaching, death, burial, and resurrection. The "meat" of the Word refers to what Jesus Christ is now doing in heaven. We begin the Christian life on the basis of His finished work on earth. We grow in the Christian life on the basis of His unfinished work in heaven.

Of course, even the maturest adult never outgrows milk. As believers, we can still learn much from our Lord's work on earth. *But we must not stop there!* We must make spiritual progress, and we can do this only if we learn about Christ's priestly ministry for us in heaven. (See Heb. 13:20-21 for a summary of what the Lord wants to do for His people now.)

*Unskillful in using the Word (v. 14).* As we grow in the Word, we learn to use it in daily life. As we apply the Word, we exercise our "spiritual senses" and develop spiritual discernment. It is a characteristic of little children that they lack discernment. A baby will put anything into its mouth. An immature believer will listen to any preacher on the radio or television and not be able to identify whether or not he is true to the Scriptures.

Just as our physical bodies have senses without which we could not function, so our inner "spiritual man" has "spiritual senses." For example: "O taste and see that the Lord is good" (Ps. 34:8). "But blessed are your eyes, for they see; and your ears, for they hear" (Matt. 13:16). As we feed on the Word of God and apply it in daily life, our inner "spiritual senses" get their exercise and become strong and keen. Paul called this process exercising ourselves unto godliness (1 Tim. 4:7-8).

The ability to discern good and evil is a vital part of Christian maturity. The nation of Israel in Moses' day lacked this discernment and failed to claim its promised inheritance. The readers of this letter were in danger of making the same mistake. It is impossible to stand still in the Christian life: we either go forward and claim God's blessing, or we go backward and wander about aimlessly.

I once heard a preacher say, "Most Christians are 'betweeners.' "

"What do you mean by that?" I asked.

"They are between Egypt and Canaan—out of the place of danger, but not yet into the place of rest and rich inheritance," he replied. "They are between Good Friday and Easter Sunday—saved by the blood but not yet enjoying newness of resurrection life."

Are *you* a "betweener"?

## The Call to Spiritual Maturity
## (Heb. 6:1-12)

No one can escape coming into the world as a baby because that is the only way to get here! But it is tragic when a baby fails to mature. No matter how much parents and grandparents love to hold and cuddle a baby, it is their great desire that the baby grow up and enjoy a full life as a mature adult. God has the same desire for His children. That is why He calls to us, "Go on to maturity!" (Heb. 6:1, NIV)

*It is a call to spiritual progress (vv. 1-3).* If we are going to make progress, we have to leave the childhood things behind and go forward in spiritual growth. Hebrews 6:1 literally reads, "Therefore, having left [once and for all] the elementary lessons [the ABCs] of the teaching of Christ." When I was in kindergarten, the teacher taught us our ABCs. (We didn't have television to teach us in those days.) You learn your ABCs so that you might read words, sentences, books—in fact, anything in literature. But you do not keep learning the basics. You use the basics to go on to better things.

The phrase, "Let us go on," should be translated, "Let us be carried forward." It is God who enables us to progress as we yield to Him, receive His Word, and act on it. A baby does not "grow himself." He grows as he eats, sleeps, exercises, and permits his body to function. Nature, as ordained by God, carries the baby along day after day, and gradually he matures into an adult. It is normal for Christians to grow; it is abnormal for them to have arrested growth.

The writer lists six foundational truths of the Christian life, all of which, by the way, are also foundational to the Jewish faith. After all, our Christian faith is based on the Jewish faith and is a fulfillment of it. "Salvation is of the Jews" (John 4:22). If the readers of this epistle went back to Judaism in order to escape persecution, they would only be abandoning the perfect for the imperfect, the mature for the immature.

The first two items (repentance and faith) are *Godward* and mark the initiation of the spiritual life. To repent means to change one's mind. It is not simply a "bad feeling about sin," because that could be regret or remorse. It is changing one's mind about sin to the point of turning from it. Once a sinner has repented (and this itself is a gift from God, Acts 5:31; 11:18), then he is able to exercise faith in God. Repentance and faith go together (Acts 20:21).

The next two items (baptisms and laying on of hands) have to do with a person's relationship to *the local assembly of believers.* In the New Testament, a person who repented and trusted Christ was baptized and became a part of a local church (Acts 2:41-47). The word "baptisms" in Hebrews 6:2 is plural and can be translated "washings" (Heb. 9:10). While water itself can never cleanse sin (1 Peter 3:21), baptism is a symbol of spiritual cleansing ("Get up, be baptized, and wash your sins away, calling on His name"—Acts 22:16, NIV) as well as our identification with Christ in death, burial, and resurrection (Rom. 6:1-4). The "laying on of hands" (Heb. 6:2) symbolized the sharing of some blessing (Luke 24:50; Acts 19:6) or the setting apart of a person for ministry (1 Tim. 4:14).

The last two items, the resurrection of the dead (Acts 24:14-15) and the final judgment (Acts 17:30-31), have to do with *the future.* Both orthodox Jews and Christians believe in these doctrines. The Old Testament teaches a general resurrection, but does not make the doctrine clear. The New Testament teaches a resurrection of the saved and also a resurrection of the lost (John 5:24-29; Rev. 20:4-6, 12-15).

The lesson of the paragraph (Heb. 6:1-3) is clear: "You have laid the foundation. You know your ABCs. Now move forward! Let God carry you along to maturity!"

**This progress does not affect salvation (vv. 4-6).** These verses, along with the exhortation in Hebrews 10:26-39, have given people cause for worry and concern, mainly because these verses have been misunderstood and misapplied. I have received long-distance phone calls from upset people who have misread this passage and convinced themselves (or been convinced by Satan) that they were hopelessly lost and had committed some unpardonable sin. While I do not want to give a false assurance to any professed Christian who is not truly born again, neither do I want to cause some true believer to stumble and miss God's best.

Bible students over the years have come up with several approaches to this serious passage. One view is that the writer is warning us against the sin of apostasy, willfully turning one's back on Jesus Christ and returning to the old life. According to them, such a person would be lost forever. I have several problems with this interpretation. To begin with, the Greek word *apostasia* is not used in this passage. The verb for "fall away" (Heb. 6:6) is *parapipto,* which literally means "to fall alongside." Second, we always interpret the obscure by the obvious. There are many verses in Scripture that assure the true believer that he can never be lost. In fact, one of the greatest arguments for security is the last section of this chapter! (Heb. 6:13-20; see also John 5:24; 10:26-30; Rom. 8:28-39)

Those who teach that we can lose our salvation also teach that such a person can be restored. But this passage (Heb. 6:4-6) teaches just the opposite! If you omit the intervening clauses, the statement reads: "For it is impossible . . . to renew them again to repentance." In other words, *if* this refers to apostasy, once a saved person turns his back on Christ, he *cannot* be restored to salvation. He is lost forever.

Others claim that the people addressed were not true believers. They had cooperated with the Holy Spirit up to a point, but were not actually born again. Well, let's examine the description of these people and see if they possessed true salvation.

They were "enlightened" (Heb. 6:4). The "once" means "enlightened once and for all." The way this same verb is used in Hebrews 10:32 indicates an experience of true salvation (see 2 Cor. 4:4-6).

They "tasted of the heavenly gift" (Heb. 6:4b), and "tasted the good Word of God, and the powers of the world [age] to come" (Heb. 6:5). To claim that these people "tasted but did not eat" is to base interpretation on one meaning of an English word. God permitted His Son to "taste death for every man" (Heb. 2:9). Surely Jesus Christ did not simply *sample* death on the cross! "Taste" carries the idea of "experience." These Hebrew believers had experienced the gift of salvation, the Word of God, and the power of God. Doesn't this describe authentic salvation?

They "were made partakers of the Holy Spirit" (Heb. 6:4c). To suggest that they only went along with the Holy Spirit to a certain extent is to ignore the simple meaning of the verb. It means "to become sharers." These same people were not only "sharers of the Holy Spirit," but also "sharers of the heavenly calling" (Heb. 3:1) and "sharers of Christ" (Heb. 3:14).

In view of these facts, I have concluded that the people addressed were true believers, not mere professors. Furthermore, how could *unsaved* people ever disgrace Jesus Christ and put Him to open shame?

A third view is that this sin (whatever it is) could be committed only by Hebrew Christians in the first century, while the temple services were still going on. If so, then why did the writer connect this exhortation with the *heavenly* priesthood of our Lord and the importance of spiritual maturity? If what he wrote about cannot happen today, what is the motivation behind the exhortation? It all seems futile to me if we limit these verses to first-century Jewish believers.

Then what is the writer trying to say to us? It is probable that he is describing a *hypothetical case* to prove his point that a true believer cannot lose his salvation. His statement in Hebrews 6:9 seems to support this interpretation: "Even though we speak like this, dear friends, we are confident of better things in your case" (NIV). His argument runs like this:

"Let's suppose that you do not go on to maturity. Does this mean that you will go back to condemnation, that you will lose your salvation? Impossible! If you *could* lose your salvation, it would be impossible to get it back again; and this would disgrace Jesus Christ. He would have to be crucified again for you, and this could never happen."

In Hebrews 6:4, the writer changed the pronouns from "we" and "us" to "those." This change also suggests that he had a hypothetical case in mind.

However, there is another possible interpretation that does not require a hypothetical case. You should note that the words "crucify" and "put" in Hebrews 6:6 are, in the Greek, present participles: "while they *are crucifying* . . . and while they *are putting* Him to an open shame." The writer did not say that these people could *never* be brought to repentance. He said that they could not be brought to repentance *while they were treating Jesus Christ in such a shameful way.* Once they stop

disgracing Jesus Christ in this way, they can be brought to repentance and renew their fellowship with God.

Whatever approach you take, please keep in mind that the writer's purpose was not to frighten the readers but to assure them. If he had wanted to frighten them, he would have named whatever sin (or sins) would have caused them to disgrace Jesus Christ; but he did not do so. In fact, he avoided the word *apostasy* and used instead "to fall by the wayside" (see Gal. 6:1 for a similar word).

Christians *can* "sin unto death" (1 Cor. 11:30-32; 1 John 5:16-17). This is God's chastening, a theme the writer of Hebrews will take up in Hebrews 12.

***This progress results in fruitfulness (vv. 7-10).*** This illustration of a field reminds us of our Lord's Parable of the Sower (Matt. 13:1-9, 18-23), as well as Paul's teaching about the fire testing our works (1 Cor. 3:6-23). A field proves its worth by bearing fruit; and a true believer, as he makes spiritual progress, bears fruit for God's glory. Note that the "thorns and briars" are burned, not the field. God never curses His own!

The crop of God's blessing pictured in Hebrews 6:7 is called "things that accompany salvation" in Hebrews 6:9. Not every believer bears the same *amount* of fruit ("some an hundredfold, some sixty, some thirty," Matt. 13:23); but every believer bears the same *kind* of fruit as proof that he is a child of God (Matt. 7:15-20). This is the fruit of Christian character and conduct (Gal. 5:22-26) produced by the Spirit as we mature in Christ.

The writer listed some of the fruit that he knew had been produced in their lives (Heb. 6:10): because of their love, they had worked and labored for the Lord; they had ministered to other saints; and they were still ministering (see 1 Thes. 1:3-10; Rev. 2:2). These are some of the "things that accompany salvation."

But he was concerned lest they rest on their achievements and not press on to full maturity and the enjoyment of God's rich inheritance.

***This progress demands diligent effort (vv. 11-12).*** While it is true that it is God who "carries us along" to maturity (Heb. 6:1, 3), it is also true that the believer must do his part. We must not be lazy ("slothful," the same word as "dull" in Heb. 5:11) but apply ourselves to the spiritual resources God has given us. We have the promises from God.

We should exercise faith and patience and claim these promises for ourselves! Like Caleb and Joshua, we must believe God's promise and want to go in and claim the land! The illustration of the farm (Heb. 6:7-8), and the admonition to be diligent, always remind me of Solomon's warning (Prov. 24:30-34). Read it—*and heed it!*

## The Basis for Spiritual Security (Heb. 6:13-20)

Lest anyone should misinterpret his exhortation to spiritual maturity, the writer ended this section with a tremendous argument for the assurance of salvation. All of us Christians are not making the spiritual progress we should, but we need never fear that God will condemn us. The writer gave three arguments for the certain salvation of true believers.

*God's promise (vv. 13-15).* God's main promise to Abraham is recorded in Genesis 22:16-17. In spite of Abraham's failures and sins, God kept His promise and Isaac was born. Many of God's promises do not depend on our character but on His faithfulness. The phrase "patiently endured" (Heb. 6:15) is the exact opposite of "slothful" (Heb. 6:12). The readers of this letter were about to give up; their endurance was running out (see Heb. 12:1-2). "You will obtain and enjoy what God has promised if you diligently apply yourself to the development of your spiritual life," is what the writer stated.

We Christians today have more of God's promises than did Abraham! What is keeping us from making spiritual progress? *We do not apply ourselves by faith.* To return to the illustration of the farm, the farmer does not reap a harvest by sitting on the porch looking at the seed. He must get busy and plow, plant, weed, cultivate, and perhaps water the soil. The believer who neglects church fellowship, ignores his Bible, and forgets to pray is not going to reap much of a harvest.

*God's oath (vv. 16-18).* God not only gave Abraham a promise, but He also confirmed that promise with an oath. When a witness takes an oath in court, he is confronted with the words "so help me God." We call on the greater to witness for the lesser. None is greater than God, so He swore by Himself! But God did not do this only for Abraham. He has also given His promise and oath to "the heirs of promise" (Heb. 6:17). Abraham and his descendants are the first of these heirs (see Heb. 11:9), but all believers are included

as "Abraham's [spiritual] seed" (Gal. 3:29). So our assurance of salvation is guaranteed by God's promise and God's oath, "two immutable [unchangeable] things" (Heb. 6:18). We have "strong consolation" (or "great encouragement") concerning the hope set before us! Hebrews is a book of *en*couragement, not *dis*couragement!

The phrase "fled for refuge" (Heb. 6:18) suggests the Old Testament "cities of refuge" described in Numbers 35:9ff and Joshua 20. God appointed six cities, three on each side of the Jordan, into which a man could flee if he had accidentally killed someone. The elders of the city would investigate the case. If they determined that it was indeed manslaughter and not murder, they would permit the man to live in the city until the death of the high priest. Then he could return to his home. The members of the slain man's family could not avenge themselves so long as the man remained in the city.

We have fled to Jesus Christ, and He is our eternal refuge. As our High Priest, He will never die (Heb. 7:23-25); and we have eternal salvation. No avenger can touch us, because He has already died and arisen from the dead.

*God's Son (vv. 19-20).* Our hope in Christ is like an anchor for the soul. The anchor was a popular symbol in the early church. At least sixty-six pictures of anchors have been found in the catacombs. The Greek stoic philosopher Epictetus wrote: "One must not tie a ship to a single anchor, nor life to a single hope." Christians have but one anchor—Jesus Christ our hope (Col. 1:5, 1 Tim. 1:1).

However, this spiritual anchor is different from material anchors on ships. For one thing, we are anchored *upward*—to heaven—not downward. We are anchored, not to stand still, but to *move ahead!* Our anchor is "sure"—it cannot break—and "steadfast"—it cannot slip. No earthly anchor can give that kind of security!

The writer then clinches the argument: this Saviour is our "forerunner" who has gone ahead to heaven so that we may one day follow! (Heb. 6:20) The Old Testament high priest was *not* a "forerunner" because nobody could follow him into the holy of holies. But Jesus Christ has gone to heaven so that one day we may follow.

Dr. H.A. Ironside has suggested that the two phrases "within the veil" (Heb. 6:19) and "without the camp" (Heb. 13:13) summarize the Epistle to the Hebrews. Jesus Christ is "within the veil" as our High Priest. We can therefore come boldly to His throne and receive all the help that we need. But we must not be "secret saints." We must be willing to identify with Christ in His rejection and go "without the camp, bearing His reproach" (Heb. 13:13). The Hebrew believers who received this letter were tempted to compromise to avoid that reproach. However, if we live "within the veil," we shall have no trouble going "without the camp."

Regardless of what approach you take to the exhortation in this section, be sure to lay hold of the main lesson: believers must go on to maturity, and God has made it possible for us to do so. If we start to *drift from the Word* (Heb. 2:1-4), then we will also start to *doubt the Word* (Heb. 3:7—4:13). Before long, we will get *dull toward the Word* (Heb. 5:11—6:20) and become lazy believers. The best way to keep from drifting is—*to lay hold of the anchor!*

Anchored heavenward! How much more secure can you be?

# CHAPTER SIX
# MYSTERIOUS
# MELCHIZEDEK
*Hebrews 7*

Ever since a city librarian introduced me to the Sherlock Holmes stories many years ago, I have been a reader of good detective fiction. Of course, I always try to solve the mystery before I get to the final chapter, and sometimes I succeed. This much I have learned: never overlook *any* character in the story, even the most incidental. He or she may be the criminal.

If you were asked to name the most important people in the Old Testament, I doubt that Melchizedek's name would be on your list. He appeared once, in Genesis 14:17-24; and he was referred to once more, in Psalm 110:4. You could hardly call this "top billing." But the Holy Spirit reached back into the Old Testament and used those two passages to present a most important truth: the priesthood of Jesus Christ is superior to that of Aaron be-

cause "the order of Melchizedek" is superior to "the order of Levi."

Chapter 7 of Hebrews introduces the second main section, as we have outlined it: *A superior Priesthood* (Heb. 7–10). In Hebrews 7, the writer argued that Christ's priesthood, like Melchizedek's, is superior in its *order*. In Hebrews 8, the emphasis is on Christ's better *covenant;* in Hebrews 9, it is His better *sanctuary;* and Hebrews 10 concludes the section by arguing for Christ's better *sacrifice*.

The Jewish nation was accustomed to the priesthood of the tribe of Levi. This tribe was chosen by God to serve in the tabernacle (Ex. 29; Num. 18). Aaron was the first high priest, appointed by God. In spite of their many failures, the priests had served God for centuries; but now the writer has affirmed that their priesthood has ended! To defend this statement, and to prove that the order of Melchizedek is superior to that of Aaron, he presents three arguments.

## The Historical Argument: Melchizedek and Abraham (Heb. 7:1-10)

The record of the event discussed is in Genesis 14:17-24, so take time to read it. The writer of our epistle wanted us to note several facts about this mysterious man, Melchizedek.

**He was both king and priest (v. 1).** We have noted already that, in the Old Testament economy, the throne and the altar were separated. Those persons who attempted to invade the priests' office were judged by God. But here is a man who had *both* offices—king and priest! Aaron never had that privilege. And it is important to note that Melchizedek was not a "counterfeit" priest: he was the "priest of the Most High God" (see Gen. 14:18, 22). His ministry was legitimate.

**His name is significant (v. 2b).** In the Bible, names and their meanings are often important. We name our children today without much consideration for what their names mean, but this was not the case in Bible days. Sometimes a great spiritual crisis was the occasion for changing a person's name (see Gen. 32:24-32; John 1:35-42). The name *Melchizedek* means "king of righteousness" in the Hebrew language. The word *Salem* means "peace" (the Hebrew word *shalom),* so that Melchizedek is "king of peace" as well as "king of righteousness."

"Righteousness" and "peace" are often found together in Scripture. "And the work of righteousness shall be peace; and the effect of righteousness quietness and assurance forever" (Isa. 32:17), "Mercy and truth are met together; righteousness and peace have kissed each other" (Ps. 85:10). "In his days shall the righteous flourish; and abundance of peace so long as the moon endureth" (Ps. 72:7). "But the wisdom that is from above is first pure, then peaceable. . . . And the fruit of righteousness is sown in peace of them that make peace" (James 3:17-18). Of course, God's purpose for His people is that they bear "the peaceable fruit of righteousness" (Heb. 12:10-11).

True peace can be experienced only on the basis of righteousness. If we want to enjoy "peace with God" we must be "justified [declared righteous] by faith" (Rom. 5:1). Man cannot produce righteousness by keeping the Old Testament Law (Gal. 2:21). It is only through the work of Jesus Christ on the cross that righteousness and peace could have "kissed each other."

**He received tithes from Abraham (v. 2a).** This important fact is explained in Hebrews 7:4-10. The word "tithe" means "one tenth." Under the Jewish Law, the Jews were commanded to give God one tenth of their crops, herds, and flocks (Lev. 27:30-32). These tithes were brought to the Levites (Num. 18:21ff) at the tabernacle and later at the temple (Deut. 12:5ff). If the trip was too long for transporting grain, fruit, or animals, the tithe could be converted into money (Deut. 14:22-27).

Tithing, however, did not originate with Moses. Abraham practiced tithing long before the Law was given. In fact, archeologists have discovered that other nations also tithed in that day; so the practice is an ancient one.

**His family history is different (v. 3).** Melchizedek was a man (see Heb. 7:4), so he had to have had a mother and a father. But there is no *record* of his genealogy ("descent") in the Old Testament; and this is significant because most great persons in the Old Testament have their ancestry identified. It was especially important that the priests be able to prove their ancestry (see Ezra 2:61-63; Neh. 7:63-65). Here the writer of Hebrews uses an argument from silence, but it is a valid one.

Melchizedek was not an angel or some superhuman creature; nor was he an Old Testament appearance of Jesus Christ. He was a real man, a real king, and a real priest in a real city. But *as far as the record is concerned*, he was not born, nor did he die. In this way, he

is a picture of the Lord Jesus Christ, the eternal Son of God. Though Jesus Christ did die, Calvary was not the end; for He arose from the dead and today lives in "the power of an endless life" (Heb. 7:16). Since there is no account of Melchizedek's death, as far as the record is concerned, it seems that Melchizedek is still serving as a priest and king. This is another way in which he is like the eternal Son of God.

The application is clear: neither Aaron nor any of his descendants could claim to be "without genealogy" (Heb. 7:3, NASB). They could not claim to have an endless ministry. Nor could they claim to be both kings and priests, like Jesus Christ.

**He had authority to receive tithes and to bless Abraham (vv. 4-10).** The greatness of Melchizedek is seen in the fact that Abraham gave him tithes from the loot of a miniwar. Abraham acknowledged the authority of Melchizedek. Furthermore, Melchizedek blessed Abraham in a special way; and "the less is blessed of the better" (Heb. 7:7). In giving Melchizedek tithes and in receiving his blessing, Abraham affirmed the greatness of this king-priest.

But how does this relate to Aaron? In an interesting way: Aaron and the tribe of Levi were "in the loins" of Abraham, yet unborn! So, when their father, Abraham, acknowledged the greatness of Melchizedek, the tribe of Levi was also involved. The Jewish people believe strongly in "racial solidarity," and this is one example of it. The paying of the tithes involved not just the patriarch Abraham, but also the unborn generations in his loins.

Since Jesus Christ came "of the seed of Abraham" (Heb. 2:16), does this mean that He too was a part of this experience? No, because Jesus Christ is the eternal Son of God. His identification with Abraham was for "the days of His flesh" (Heb. 5:7). Since Christ existed before Abraham (John 8:58), He could not have been "in Abraham" as were Aaron and his family.

## The Doctrinal Argument: Christ and Aaron (Heb. 7:11-25)

In this section, the writer took his argument one step further. Not only is Melchizedek *greater than* Aaron, but Melchizedek has *replaced Aaron!* It is no longer "the order of Aaron" or "the order of Levi." It is forever "the order of Melchizedek." Why would God effect such a radical change?

*Because both the priesthood and the Law were imperfect (vv. 11-14).* The words translated "perfect" and "perfection" are key words in this epistle (Heb. 2:10; 5:9; 6:1; 7:11, 19; 9:9; 10:1, 14). They essentially mean "completed, fulfilled." The Old Testament priests could not by their ministry complete the work of God in the heart of a worshiper. "For the Law made nothing perfect" (Heb. 7:19). The animal sacrifices could not give any worshiper a perfect standing before God (Heb. 10:1-3). The Mosaic system of divine Law was not a permanent system. It was "added" to serve as a "schoolmaster" to prepare the way for the coming of Christ (Gal. 3:19–4:7).

Since the priests received their authority from the Old Testament Law (Heb. 7:28), and since the priesthood has been changed, there has also been a change in that Law. The President of the United States cannot proclaim himself King of the United States because U.S. law makes no provision for a king. First, the law would have to be changed.

The Law of Moses made no provision for a priesthood from the tribe of Judah (Heb. 7:14). Since our High Priest *is* from the tribe of Judah, according to His human ancestry, then there must have been a change in Moses' Law. There has been! The entire system of Old Testament Law has been fulfilled in Jesus Christ and has been taken out of the way (Col. 2:13-14). The believer has been set free from the Law (Gal. 5:1-6) and is dead to the Law (Rom. 7:1-4).

This new arrangement does not suggest that a Christian has the right to be lawless. "Free from the Law" does not mean "free to sin." Rather, it means that we are free to do the will of God. We obey, not because of outward compulsion, but because of inward constraint (2 Cor. 5:14; Eph. 6:6). The indwelling Holy Spirit enables us to fulfill the "righteousness of the Law" as we yield to Him (Rom. 8:1-4).

*Because, being imperfect, the priesthood and the Law could not continue forever (vv. 15-19).* The word "another" in Hebrews 7:15 means "another of a different kind." The levitical priests were made priests by the authority of a temporary and imperfect Law. Jesus Christ was made Priest by a declaration of God. Because the Law was "weak and useless" (Heb. 7:18, NIV), it could not continue forever. But because Jesus Christ is the eternal Son of God, He lives by "the pow-

er of an endless life" (Heb. 7:16). What a contrast between the profitless Law and an endless life!

Since Jesus Christ is Priest *forever,* and since He has a nature to match that eternal priesthood, He can never be replaced. The annulling (Heb. 7:18, "disannulling") of the Law meant the abolishing of the priesthood. But nobody can annul "the power of an endless life"! The logic holds: Jesus Christ is a Priest forever.

The writer kept in mind the temptation his readers were facing to go back into the old temple system. This is why he reminded them (Heb. 7:19) that Jesus Christ has accomplished what the Law could never accomplish: He brought in a better hope, and He enables us to draw near to God. To go back to Judaism would mean losing the enjoyment of their fellowship with God through Christ. The only hope Judaism had was the coming of Christ, and that blessing these believers already had.

*Because God's oath cannot be broken (vv. 20-22).* No priest in the order of Aaron was ever ordained and established on the basis of God's personal oath. The Aaronic priests ministered "after the law of a carnal [physical] commandment" (Heb. 7:16). Their moral or spiritual fitness was not examined. The important thing was that a priest belonged to the right tribe and met the right physical and ceremonial requirements (Lev. 21:16-24).

Jesus Christ's heavenly priesthood was established on the basis of His work on the cross, His character (Heb. 2:10; 5:5-10), and the oath of God. "Thou art a Priest forever after the order of Melchizedek" (Heb. 7:21; Ps. 110:4). Note the introduction to the statement: "The Lord swore and will not repent [change His mind]." The matter is finally settled and it cannot be changed.

The presence of this oath gives to the priesthood of our Lord a greater degree of permanence and assurance. Jesus Christ is the "surety of a better testament [covenant]" (Heb. 7:22). The word "surety" means "one who guarantees that the terms of an agreement will be carried out." Judah was willing to be the surety for Benjamin, to guarantee to their father that the boy would return home safely (Gen. 43:1-14). Paul was willing to be the surety for the slave Onesimus (Phile. 18-19). Perhaps the nearest equivalent we have today is a bondsman who posts bail for someone under indictment and guarantees that the indicted person will appear in court and stand trial.

As the Mediator between God and man (1 Tim. 2:5), Jesus Christ is God's great Surety. Our risen and ever-living Saviour guarantees that the terms of God's covenant will be fulfilled completely. God will not abandon His people. But our Lord not only guarantees *to us* that God will fulfill the promises. As our Representative *to God,* He perfectly meets the terms of the agreement on our behalf. We of ourselves could never meet the terms; but because we have trusted Him, He has saved us and He has guaranteed that He will keep us.

In Hebrews 7:22, we have the first occurrence of a very important word in Hebrews—"testament." This word, which is usually translated "covenant," is used twenty-one times in the letter, and it is the equivalent of "last will and testament." We will examine the word more closely in our study of Hebrews 8.

The writer has given three reasons why God changed the order of the priesthood from that of Aaron to that of Melchizedek: (1) the priesthood and the Law were imperfect; (2) being imperfect, they could not continue forever; (3) God had sworn by His oath that the new order would be established. Then the writer of this letter to the Hebrews closed this section with a fourth reason.

**Because, being men, the priests died (vv. 23-25).** Not only was the priesthood imperfect, but it was also interrupted by death. There were *many* high priests because no one priest could live forever. In contrast, the church has *one* High Priest, Jesus the Son of God, who lives forever! An unchanging priest means an unchangeable priesthood, and this means security and confidence for God's people. "Jesus Christ, the same yesterday, today, and forever" (Heb. 13:8). "Thou art a Priest forever" (Ps. 110:4).

Occasionally we read a story in the newspaper about the illegal handling of a will. Perhaps some unscrupulous relative or business partner managed to get his hands on a will and use it for his own selfish purposes. But this could never happen to our Lord's "last will and testament" in His blood. He wrote the will and then died to make it take effect. But He arose from the dead and ascended to heaven, and there He is "probating" His own will!

The fact that the *unchanging* Christ continues as High Priest means, logically, that there is an "unchangeable priesthood" (Heb. 7:24). The Greek word translated "unchangeable"

carries the idea of "valid and unalterable." The word was used at the end of legal contracts. Our Lord's priesthood in heaven is "valid and unalterable." Because it is, we can have confidence in the midst of this shaking, changing world.

What is the conclusion of the matter? It is stated in Hebrews 7:25: "Wherefore [because He is the ever-living, unchanging High Priest], He is able also to save them to the uttermost [completely, forever] that come unto God by Him, seeing He ever liveth to make intercession for them." It is unfortunate that this verse is often read, "He is able to save *from* the uttermost" instead of "*to* the uttermost." To be sure, it is true that Christ can save any sinner from any condition; but that is not the import of the verse. The emphasis is on the fact that He saves completely, forever, all who put their faith in Him. Because He is our High Priest forever, He can save forever.

The basis for this completed salvation is the heavenly intercession of the Saviour. The word translated "make intercession" simply means "to meet, to approach, to appeal, to make petition." We must not imagine that God the Father is angry with us so that God the Son must constantly appeal to Him not to judge us! The Father and the Son are in total agreement in the plan of salvation (Heb. 13:20-21). Neither should we imagine our Lord Jesus uttering prayers on our behalf in heaven, or repeatedly "offering His blood" as a sacrifice. That work was completed on the cross once and for all.

Intercession involves our Lord's representation of His people at the throne of God. Through Christ, believers are able to draw near to God in prayer and also to offer spiritual sacrifices to God (Heb. 4:14-16; 1 Peter 2:5). It has well been said that Christ's life in heaven is His prayer for us. It is what He *is* that determines what He *does.*

In reviewing the reasoning found in this long section (Heb. 7:11-25), we are impressed with the logic of the writer. Jesus Christ's priesthood after the order of Melchizedek is superior to that of Aaron and has replaced it. Both the historical argument and the doctrinal argument are sound. But the writer adds a third argument.

**The Practical Argument: Christ and the Believer (Heb. 7:26-28)**

No matter how devoted and obedient the Aaronic priests were, they could not always meet the needs of all the people. But Jesus Christ perfectly meets all of our needs. "For such an High Priest became us" means "He was suited to us; He meets our needs completely." The emphasis here is on His sinlessness. Being perfect, He is able to exercise a perfect ministry for His people. Because of their sins, some of the Old Testament priests not only were unable to serve the people, but actually abused them. This could never happen with Jesus Christ and His people.

The Old Testament priests were "set apart" for their ministry, so in that sense they were "holy." But they were not always holy in character. They were sinners like the people to whom they ministered. "Harmless" (Heb. 7:26) means "blameless." No Jewish priest could claim this distinction. "Undefiled" means "unstained." Again, only Jesus Christ can claim these characteristics. When He was ministering on earth, our Lord was a friend of publicans and sinners (Matt. 9:10; 11:19), but His contact with them did not defile His character or His conduct. There was contact without contamination. He was not isolated; He was separated. Today, He is "separate from sinners" because of His position ("made higher than the heavens"); but He is not separated from the people to whom He ministers. He is always available to us at His throne of grace.

Another proof of His sinlessness is the fact that our Lord never had to offer sacrifices for His own cleansing, as did the priests. On the *annual* Day of Atonement, the high priest first had to sacrifice for himself before he could sacrifice for the people (Lev. 16). There were also *daily* sacrifices offered as a part of the temple ritual; and, if a priest had sinned, he had to bring a sacrifice for his own cleansing (Ex. 29:38-46; Lev. 4:3ff). But Jesus Christ offered just one sacrifice for our sins and settled the matter forever (see Heb. 9:23-28).

This is the kind of High Priest we need! We are prone to sin daily, even hourly; and we need to be able to turn to Him for spiritual help. As our High Priest, Jesus Christ gives us the grace and mercy that *we need not to sin*. But if we do sin, He is our Advocate at God's throne (1 John 2:1-2). If we confess our sins to Him, He forgives us and restores us (1 John 1:9).

The application is obvious: why turn away from such an adequate High Priest? What more can you find in any other person? The men who served under the Law of Moses had human infirmities and weaknesses, and they often failed. Our heavenly High Priest has been "consecrated [perfected] forevermore" (Heb. 7:28) and there is no spot or blemish in Him. Such a High Priest "suits us perfectly"!

Are you availing yourself of His gracious ministry?

# CHAPTER SEVEN
# THE BETTER COVENANT
*Hebrews 8*

I once spoke at a meeting of religious broadcasters at which a friend of mine was to provide the ministry of music. He is a superb pianist with a gift for interpreting Christian music, and I have always enjoyed listening to him. But that day my heart went out to him in sympathy, because the motel had given the most deteriorated and derelict piano I have ever seen. It must have been donated by a local wrecking company. My friend did his best, but it would have been much better had he been playing a decent instrument.

Jesus Christ is God's superior Priest; but is there anything that can minimize this superiority? Nothing! For He ministers on the basis of a better covenant (Heb. 8), in a better sanctuary (Heb. 9), and because of a better sacrifice (Heb. 10). It is the better covenant that is the theme of this chapter. The writer presented three evidences for the superiority of this covenant.

## It Is Ministered by a Superior High Priest (Heb. 8:1-2)

Is the writer arguing in circles? First he shows the superiority of Christ, and then says, "Since He is superior, the covenant He ministers must be a superior covenant." No, this is not reasoning in a circle; for the conclusion is logical. A superior priest could never minister on the basis of an inferior covenant. To change the illustration, the most gifted lawyer can do very little if the will he is probating is inadequate. It is unthinkable that our Lord would minister on the basis of an inferior "last will and testament."

"This is the sum" simply means, "This is the main point and the climax of my discussion." He then presented several "summary arguments" to prove that our Lord is indeed a superior High Priest.

**His moral adequacy (v. 1).** "We have *such* an High Priest" [italics mine]. This statement refers us back to Hebrews 7:22-28. "For *such an high priest* became us [was suited to us]" (Heb. 7:26). The fact that Jesus Christ is morally perfect and yet identified with us in our needs and temptations makes Him superior to any other priest, past or present. Those of his readers who wanted to go back into the Old Testament priesthood would have to leave this *suitable* High Priest.

**His finished work (v. 1).** Today our Lord is *seated* because His work is completed. There were no chairs in the Old Testament tabernacle because the work of the priests was never finished. Each repeated sacrifice was only a reminder that *none* of the sacrifices ever provided a finished salvation. The blood of animals did not wash away sin or cleanse the guilty conscience; it only covered sin until that day when Jesus Christ died to take away the sin of the world (John 1:29).

**His enthronement (v. 1).** Jesus Christ is not just "seated." It is *where* He is seated that adds glory to His person and His work. He is seated on the throne in heaven at the right hand of the Father. This great truth was introduced early in this epistle (Heb. 1:3), and it will be mentioned again (Heb. 10:12; 12:2). This enthronement was the fulfillment of the Father's promise to the Son: "Sit Thou at My right hand, until I make Thine enemies Thy footstool" (Ps. 110:1). Not only did the high priest of Israel never sit down in the tabernacle, but he never sat down *on a throne.* Only a priest "after the order of Melchizedek" could be enthroned, for Melchizedek was both king and priest (Heb. 7:1).

**His supreme exaltation (vv. 1-2).** He is "in the heavens." Jesus Christ, in His ascension and exaltation, "passed through the heavens" (Heb. 4:14, NASB). He is now exalted as high as anyone could be (Eph. 1:20-23; Phil. 2:5-11). The fact that He ministers in a *heavenly* sanctuary is important to the argument presented in this chapter.

As we review these four "summary arguments," we can see how logical it is that our Lord ministers on the basis of a superior cov-

enant. Can you conceive of a high priest who is perfect morally, ministering on the basis of a covenant that could not change human hearts? Could a priest who has *finished* his work minister from a covenant that could finish nothing? Can we conceive of a king-priest in the highest heaven being limited by an Old Covenant that made nothing perfect? (Heb. 7:19) The conclusion seems reasonable: the presence of a superior High Priest in heaven demands a superior covenant if He is to minister effectively to God's people.

**It Is Ministered in a Better Place (Heb. 8:3-5)**

In this paragraph, the writer expanded on the marvelous truth that Jesus Christ today ministers in the heavenly sanctuary. The reason for this discussion is not difficult to determine. His readers knew that there was a real temple in Jerusalem, and that in the temple there were priests offering gifts and sacrifices. How easy it would be to go back into the traditional Mosaic system! After all, how do we *know* that the Lord Jesus is ministering in a sanctuary? Has anyone actually seen Him in His high priestly work?

Good questions—and there are good answers!

**The logical answer (v. 3).** It has already been determined that Jesus Christ is a High Priest. But all high priests serve others; the title is not honorary. Each Old Testament high priest was appointed "to offer gifts and sacrifices"; therefore, Jesus Christ must offer gifts and sacrifices (see Heb. 5:1; 7:27). But these sacrifices must not be offered just anywhere; they must be offered in God's appointed place (Deut. 12:13-14). That appointed place is the sanctuary. The conclusion is logical: if Jesus Christ is a High Priest who offers gifts and sacrifices, then He must have a sanctuary in which He ministers. Since He is in heaven, that sanctuary must be in heaven.

We must not, however, get the impression that our Lord is offering sacrifices in heaven that correspond to the Old Testament sacrifices. The word "somewhat" in Hebrews 8:3 is in the singular, and the phrase "to offer" is in a Greek tense that implies "offer once and for all." On the cross, He offered Himself as the one sacrifice for sin forever (Heb. 9:24-28). In other words, our Lord is "a living sacrifice" in heaven. He is not offering Himself over and over because that is unnecessary.

**The genealogical answer (v. 4).** We

have met this truth before in Hebrews 7:11-14. As far as His human ancestry is concerned, our Lord came from the tribe of Judah. God had promised that the Messiah would come from the kingly tribe of Judah (Gen. 49:8-10). But the priests had to come from the tribe of Levi. Therefore, if Jesus Christ were still on earth, He could not function as a priest. But He can serve as High Priest in *heaven* because there the order of Melchizedek governs the ministry, not the order of Aaron.

Again, the argument is sound. David predicted that Jesus Christ would be a Priest (Ps. 110:4). Jesus' earthly birth into the tribe of Judah would not permit Him to be an earthly priest; therefore, He must be a Priest in heaven. He would not be accepted in the earthly sanctuary, so He must be serving in the heavenly sanctuary.

*The typological answer (v. 5).* A "type" is an Old Testament picture of a New Testament truth. Each type is identified as such in the New Testament, so we must not try to make every Old Testament person or event into a type. The word "pattern" in this verse is the Greek word *tupos*, from which we get our English word "type."

The priests then serving in the temple were actually serving in a sanctuary that was a copy ("example") of the heavenly sanctuary. The quotation is from Exodus 25:40, where it refers obliquely to a heavenly sanctuary. Moses saw this pattern on the mount and duplicated its essentials in the earthly tabernacle. This does not mean that the heavenly tabernacle is made up of skins and fabrics. It is the basic pattern and meaning of the sanctuary that is emphasized here. The true sanctuary is in heaven; the tabernacle and temple were but imitations or copies of the true.

This is a telling argument for remaining faithful to Jesus Christ and not going back into Judaism. The earthly priesthood and sanctuary seemed quite real and stable, and yet they were but *copies* of the true! The Old Testament system was but shadows (see Col. 2:17). The Law was but a "shadow of good things to come" (Heb. 10:1); the true and full light came in Jesus Christ. So why go back into the shadows?

In the Book of Revelation, where the heavenly scene is described, we can find parallels to the Old Testament tabernacle. John states that there is a temple of God in heaven (Rev. 11:19). Of course, there will be no temple in the eternal state, because the entire city of God will be a temple (Rev. 21:22). For example, there is a brazen altar (Rev. 6:9-11) as well as an altar of incense (Rev. 8:3-5). The "sea of glass" (Rev. 4:6) reminds us of the laver, and the seven lamps of fire (Rev. 4:5) suggest the seven-branched lampstand in the tabernacle.

Since Jesus Christ is ministering in the original sanctuary, and not the copy, He is ministering in a better place. Why fellowship with priests who are serving in a *copied* sanctuary when you can fellowship with Christ in the original heavenly sanctuary? It would be like trying to live on the blueprint instead of in the building itself!

The writer has now given us two evidences of the superiority of the New Covenant: it is ministered by a superior Priest, Jesus Christ; and it is ministered in a superior place, heaven itself. He devoted the remainder of this section to the third evidence.

## It Is Founded on Better Promises (Heb. 8:6-13)

Moses was the mediator (go-between) of the Old Covenant in the giving of the Law (Gal. 3:19-20). The people of Israel were so frightened at Mount Sinai that they begged Moses to speak to them so that they would not have to hear God speak (Ex. 20:18-21). Sad to say, this fear of God did not last long; for the people soon disobeyed the very Law they promised to keep. The Mediator of the New Covenant is Jesus Christ, and He is the only Mediator (1 Tim. 2:5). Christ's ministry as Mediator is more excellent than that of the Old Testament priests because it is based on a better covenant; *and His covenant is founded on better promises.*

The "better covenant" that is referred to in this paragraph was announced by the Prophet Jeremiah (Jer. 31:31-34). The promise was given in a prophecy that assured the Jews of future restoration. Jeremiah ministered during the closing years of the nation's history, before Judah went into Babylonian Captivity. At a time when the nation's future seemed completely destroyed, God gave the promise of restoration and blessing.

Before our Lord went to Calvary, He celebrated the Passover with His disciples in the Upper Room. At that supper, He instituted what we call "the Lord's Supper." He said, taking the cup, "This cup is the new testament [covenant] in My blood, which is shed for you" (Mark 14:22-24; Luke 22:20). The Apostle Paul quoted these words and applied them to the church (1 Cor. 11:23-27). The writer of Hebrews states clearly that Jesus Christ *now* "is the Mediator of the New Covenant" (Heb. 9:15) and repeats it (Heb. 12:24).

What, then, is the relationship between this New Covenant *promised* to Israel, but today *experienced* by the church? Or, to state it another way, how can God promise these blessings to the Jews and then turn around and give them to the church?

Some Bible students solve the problem by concluding that the church is "spiritual Israel" and that the New Covenant promises therefore belong to "Abraham's spiritual seed" today. That believers today are the "spiritual seed" of Abraham is clear from Galatians 3:13-29; but this is not the same as saying that the church is "spiritual Israel." The promise quoted in Hebrews 8:8 specifically names "the house of Israel and . . . the house of Judah." Once we are permitted to make such plain words as "Israel" and "Judah" mean something else, there is no end to how we might interpret the Bible!

Other students believe that this "New Covenant" has no present fulfillment in the church, but that it will be fulfilled only when the Jews are regathered and the kingdom is established at our Lord's return to earth in glory. But then we have the problem of explaining Hebrews 9:15 and 12:24, verses that state that Jesus Christ is *today* the Mediator of the New Covenant. To affirm that there are *two* "new covenants," one for Israel and one for the church, is to create more questions!

Perhaps the solution is found in God's principle of "to the Jew first" (Rom. 1:16). God did promise a New Covenant for His people, but the blessings of this covenant are wrapped up in God's Son, Jesus Christ. He is the Mediator of the New Covenant. When Jesus began His ministry on earth, He went to His own people first (Matt. 15:24). When He sent out His disciples, He sent them only to Israel (Matt. 10:5-6). When He commissioned the church to witness, He instructed them to begin in Jerusalem (Luke 24:46-48; Acts 1:8). Peter's message at Pentecost was addressed only to Jews and to Gentiles who were Jewish proselytes (see Acts 2:14, 22, 36). In his second recorded sermon, Peter clearly stated that the Good News of the Gospel would go to the Jews first (Acts 3:25-26).

But the nation rejected the message and the messengers. While it is true that thousands of individuals trusted Christ and were saved, it is also true that most of the nation rejected the Word, and that the religious leaders opposed the ministry of the church. One result was the stoning of Stephen (Acts 7). But what was God's response? The Gospel moved from Jerusalem and Judea into Samaria (Acts 8), and then to the Gentiles (Acts 10).

The church today is made up of regenerated Jews and Gentiles who are one body in Christ (Eph. 2:11-22; Gal. 3:27-29). All who are "in Christ" share in the New Covenant which was purchased on the cross. Today the blessings of the New Covenant are applied to individuals. When Jesus comes in glory to redeem Israel, then the blessings of the New Covenant will be applied to that beleaguered nation. Read all of Jeremiah 31 to see what God has planned for Israel, His people.

Before we examine the "better promises" of the New Covenant, we must settle another matter. We must not conclude that the existence of the New Covenant means that the Old Covenant was wrong or that the Law has no ministry today. Both covenants were given by God. Both covenants were given for people's good. Both covenants had blessings attached to them. If Israel had obeyed the terms of the Old Covenant, God would have blessed them and they would have been ready for the coming of their Messiah. Paul pointed out that the Old Covenant had its share of glory (2 Cor. 3:7-11). We must not criticize the Old Covenant or minimize it.

Even though the New Covenant of grace brings with it freedom from the Law of Moses (Gal. 5:1), it does not bring freedom to disobey God and sin. God still desires that the "righteousness of the Law" should be fulfilled in us through the ministry of the Holy Spirit (Rom. 8:1-4). There is a lawful use of the Law (1 Tim. 1:8-11).

Now we are ready to consider the "better promises" that belong to the New Covenant.

***The promise of God's grace (vv. 7-9).*** The emphasis in the New Covenant is on God's "I will." The nation of Israel at Sinai said, "All the words which the Lord hath said will we do" (Ex. 24:3). But they did not obey God's words. It is one thing to *say,* "We will!" and quite another thing to do it. But the New Covenant does not depend on man's faithfulness to God but on God's faithful promise to man. The writer of Hebrews affirms God's "I will" on behalf of those who trust Jesus Christ

(Heb. 8:10). In fact, God's "I will" is stated three times in that one verse and six times in Hebrews 8:8-12.

God led Israel out of Egypt the way a father would take a child by the hand and lead him. God gave Israel His holy Law for their own good, to separate them from the other nations and to protect them from the sinful practices of the heathen. But the nation failed; "they continued not in My covenant" (Heb. 8:9). God's responses to Israel's disobedience were to discipline them repeatedly and finally to send them into captivity.

God did not find fault with His covenant but with His people. "Wherefore, the Law is holy, and the commandment holy, and just, and good" (Rom. 7:12). The problem is not with the Law, but with our sinful natures, for by ourselves we cannot keep God's Law, The Law "made nothing perfect" (Heb. 7:19) because it could not change any human heart. Only God's grace can do that.

The New Covenant is *wholly* of God's grace; no sinner can become a part of this New Covenant without faith in Jesus Christ. Grace and faith go together just as the Law and works go together (Rom. 11:6). The Law says, "The man that doeth them [the things written in the Law] shall live in them" (Gal. 3:12). But grace says, "The work is done— believe and live!"

**The promise of internal change (v. 10).** The Law of Moses could *declare* God's holy standard, but it could never *provide* the power needed for obedience. Sinful people need a new heart and a new disposition within; and this is just what the New Covenant provides. (For a parallel passage, see Ezek. 36:26-27.) When a sinner trusts Christ, he receives a divine nature within (2 Peter 1:1-4). This divine nature creates a desire to love and obey God. By nature, sinful people are hateful and disobedient (Titus 3:3-7); but the new nature gives each believer both the desire and the dynamic for a godly life.

The Law was external; God's demands were written on tablets of stone. But the New Covenant makes it possible for God's Word to be written on human minds and hearts (2 Cor. 3:1-3). God's grace makes possible an internal transformation that makes a surrendered believer more and more like Jesus Christ (2 Cor. 3:18).

It is unfortunate that many Christians think they are saved by grace but must then fulfill their Christian life according to the Old Testament Law. They want the New Covenant for salvation but the Old Covenant for sanctification. The Apostle Paul had a phrase to describe this condition: "fallen from grace" (Gal. 5:4). Not "fallen from salvation," but fallen from the sphere of God's blessing through grace. We do not become holy people by trying to obey God's Law in our own power. It is by yielding to the Holy Spirit within that we fulfill the righteousness of the Law (Rom. 8:1-4); and this is wholly of grace.

**The promise of forgiveness for all (vv. 11-12).** There is no forgiveness under the Law because the Law was not given for that purpose. "Therefore by the deeds of the Law there shall no flesh be justified in His sight; for by the Law is knowledge of sin" (Rom. 3:20). The Law could not promise forgiveness to Israel, let alone to all mankind. It is only through the sacrifice of Jesus Christ that forgiveness is possible to all who will call on Him. The Old Testament sacrifices brought a *remembrance* of sins, not a *remission* of sins (Heb. 10:1-3, 18).

Hebrews 8:11 quotes Jeremiah 31:34. It refers to that day when Israel shall be reunited with Judah (Heb. 8:8) and shall rejoice in the promised kingdom (Jer. 31:1-14). In that day, there will be no need to share the Gospel with others because everyone will know the Lord personally. However, until that day, it is both our privilege and our responsibility to share the Gospel message with a lost world.

What does it mean that God remembers our sins and iniquities no more? (Heb. 8:12) This important statement is quoted again in Hebrews 10:16-17. Does it mean that our all-knowing God can actually *forget* what we have done? If God forgot anything, He would cease to be God! The phrase "remember no more" means "hold against us no more." God recalls what we have done, but He does not hold it against us. He deals with us on the basis of grace and mercy, not law and merit. Once sin has been forgiven, it is never brought before us again. The matter is settled eternally.

As a pastor in counseling ministry I have often heard people say, "Well, I can forgive— but I cannot forget!"

"Of course you can't forget," I usually reply. "The more you try to put this thing out of your mind, the more you will remember it. But that isn't what it means to forget." Then I go on to explain that "to forget" means "not to hold it against the person who has wronged us." We may remember what others have done, but we treat them *as though they never did it.*

How is this possible? It is possible because of the cross, for there God treated His Son *as though He had done it!* Our experience of forgiveness from God makes it possible for us to forgive others.

***The promise of eternal blessing (v. 13).*** The Old Covenant was still governing the nation of Israel at the time this epistle was written. The temple was standing and the priests were offering their appointed sacrifices. Devout Jews probably thought that their Christian friends were foolish to abandon such a "solid religion" for a faith that was seemingly intangible. What the unbelieving Jews did not realize was that their "solid religion" had grown old and was about to vanish away. In A.D. 70 the city of Jerusalem and the temple were destroyed by the Romans, and the Jews have not had a temple or a priesthood to serve them ever since (see Hosea 3:4).

However, the New Covenant brings eternal blessing. Jesus Christ is the Author of "eternal salvation" (Heb. 5:9) and "eternal redemption" (Heb. 9:12). The New Covenant can never get old and disappear. The Greek word translated "new" means "new in quality," not "new in time." This New Covenant is of such quality that it will never need to be replaced!

Yes, our Lord *is* ministering on the basis of a better covenant, a New Covenant that makes us partakers of the new nature and the wonderful new life that only Christ can give.

# CHAPTER EIGHT
# THE SUPERIOR SANCTUARY
*Hebrews 9*

The Christian is a citizen of two worlds, the earthly and the heavenly. He must render to Caesar the things that are Caesar's and to God the things that are God's (Matt. 22:21). Because he is a citizen of two worlds, he must learn how to walk by faith in a world that is governed by sight. Like Moses, a believer must

see the invisible if he is to overcome the pull of the world (Heb. 11:24-27). Practical man says, "Seeing is believing!" But the man of faith replies, "Believing is seeing!"

This principle of faith must apply to our relationship to the heavenly sanctuary. We have never seen this sanctuary. Yet we believe what the Bible tells us about it. We realize that God is not worshiped today in temples made with hands (Acts 7:46-50). There is no special place on earth where God dwells (see Isa. 57:15; 66:1-2; John 4:19-24). We may call a local church building a "house of God," but we know that God does not live there. The building is dedicated to God and His service, but it is not His dwelling place.

Hebrews 9 presents a detailed contrast between the Old Covenant sanctuary (the tabernacle) and the New Covenant heavenly sanctuary where Jesus Christ now ministers. This contrast makes it clear that the New Covenant sanctuary is superior.

## The Inferior Old Covenant Sanctuary (Heb. 9:1-10)
Hebrews reminds readers that the regulations and practices in the tabernacle were ordained of God. If there was any inferiority in the tabernacle service, it was not because God had not established the ritual. While the Old Covenant was in force, the ministry of the priests was ordained of God and perfectly proper.

What was it, then, that made the tabernacle inferior? There are five answers to that question.

***It was an earthly sanctuary (v. 1).*** This means it was made by man (Heb. 9:11) and pitched by man (Heb. 8:2). The Jewish people generously brought their gifts to Moses, and from these materials the tabernacle was constructed. Then God gave spiritual wisdom and skill to Bezalel and Oholiab to do the intricate work of making the various parts of the tabernacle and its furnishings (see Ex. 35–36). After the construction was completed, the sanctuary was put in place and dedicated to God (Ex. 40). Even though the glory of God moved into the sanctuary, it was still an earthly building, constructed by humans out of earthly materials.

Being an earthly building, it had several weaknesses. For one thing, it would need a certain amount of repair. Also, it was limited geographically: if it was pitched in one place, it could not be in another place. It had to be dismantled and the various parts carried from place to place. Furthermore, it belonged to the nation of Israel and not to the whole world.

*It was a type of something greater (vv. 2-5).* The writer listed the various parts and furnishings of the tabernacle because each of these carried a spiritual meaning. They were "patterns of things in the heavens" (Heb. 9:23). The diagram gives a general picture of the tabernacle.

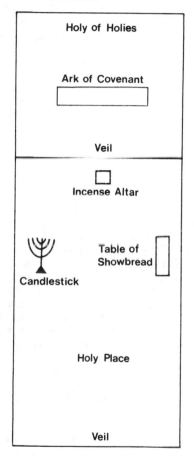

The phrases "the first" (Heb. 9:2) and "the second" (Heb. 9:7) refer to the first and second divisions of the tabernacle. The first was called the holy place and the second the holy of holies. Each of these divisions had its own furnishings, and each piece of furniture had its own special meaning.

In the holy place stood the seven-branched golden candlestick (Ex. 25:31-40; 27:20-21; 37:17-24). "Lampstand" would be a better term to use, because the light was produced by the burning of wicks in oil, not by the use

of candles. Since there were no windows in the tabernacle, this lampstand provided the necessary light for the priests' ministry in the holy place. The nation of Israel was supposed to be a light to the nations (Isa. 42:6; 49:6). Jesus Christ is the "Light of the world" (John 8:12), and believers are to shine as lights in the world (Phil. 2:14-15).

There was also a table in the holy place with twelve loaves of bread on it. It was called the table of showbread (Ex. 25:23-30; 37:10-16; Lev. 24:5-9). Each Sabbath, the priests would remove the old loaves and put fresh loaves on the table; and the old loaves would be eaten. These loaves were called "the bread of presence" and the table was called "the table of presence." Only the priests could eat this bread, and they were required to eat it in the sanctuary. It reminded the twelve tribes of God's presence that sustained them. It also speaks to us today of Jesus Christ, the "Bread of Life" given to the whole world (John 6).

The golden altar stood in the holy place just in front of the veil that divided the two parts of the tabernacle. The word translated "censer" (a device for burning incense) (Heb. 9:4) should be "altar." The golden altar did not stand in the holy of holies, but its ministry *pertained* to the holy of holies. In what way? On the annual Day of Atonement, the high priest used coals from this altar to burn incense before the mercy seat within the veil (Lev. 16:12-14). Moses (Ex. 40:5) relates the golden altar to the ark of the covenant, and so does the author of 1 Kings (1 Kings 6:22). Each morning and evening, a priest burned incense on this altar. David suggests that it is a picture of prayer ascending to God (Ps. 141:2). It can be a reminder that Jesus Christ intercedes for us (Rom. 8:33-34). For details about this incense altar, see Exodus 30:1-10; 37:25-29. The incense itself is described in Exodus 30:34-35.

The holy of holies contained only the ark of the covenant, a wooden chest three feet, nine inches long; two feet, three inches wide; and two feet, three inches high. On the top of this chest was a beautiful "mercy seat" made of gold, with a cherub at each end. This was the throne of God in the tabernacle (Ex. 25:10-22; Pss. 80:1; 99:1). On the Day of Atonement, the blood was sprinkled on this mercy seat to cover the tables of Law within the ark. God did not look at the broken Law; He saw the blood. Christ is our "mercy seat" ("propitiation" in 1 John 2:2; Rom. 3:25). But His blood does not just cover sin; it takes away sin.

No doubt many spiritual truths are wrapped up in these pieces of furniture, and all of them are of value. But the most important truth is this: all of this was *symbolism* and not the spiritual *reality*. It was this fact that made the tabernacle of the Old Covenant inferior.

**It was inaccessible to the people (vv. 6-7).** We must not get the idea that the Jews assembled in the tabernacle for worship. The priests and Levites were permitted into the tabernacle precincts, but not the people from the other tribes. Furthermore, though the priests ministered in the holy place day after day, only the high priest entered the holy of holies, and that only once a year. When he did, he had to offer a sacrifice for his own sins as well as for the sins of the people. In contrast, the heavenly tabernacle is open to all of the people of God, and at all times! (Heb. 10:19-25)

**It was temporary (v. 8).** The fact that the outer court ("first tabernacle," Heb. 9:6) was standing was proof that God's work of salvation for man had not yet been completed. The outer court stood between the people and the holy of holies! As long as the priests were ministering in the holy place, the way had not yet been opened into the presence of God. But when Jesus died on the cross, the veil of the temple was torn from top to bottom (Matt. 27:50-51) and the way was opened into the holy of holies. There was no longer any more need for either the holy place or the holy of holies, for now believing sinners could come into the presence of God.

**Its ministry was external, not internal (vv. 9-10).** The sacrifices offered and the blood applied to the mercy seat could never change the heart or the conscience of a worshiper. All of the ceremonies associated with the tabernacle had to do with ceremonial purity, not moral purity. They were "carnal ordinances" that pertained to the outer man but that could not change the inner man.

### The Superior Heavenly Sanctuary (Heb. 9:11-28)

The five deficiencies of the Old Covenant sanctuary are matched with the five superiorities of the New Covenant sanctuary. In every way, the present sanctuary is superior.

**It is heavenly (v. 11).** The writer has emphasized this fact before, because he has wanted his readers to focus their attention on the things of heaven and not on the things of earth. Some things on earth (including the beautiful Jewish temple) would soon be destroyed; but the heavenly realities would endure forever.

The Old Covenant tabernacle was made by the hands of men (Ex. 35:30-35). The New Covenant sanctuary was not made with hands. "Not of this building" (Heb. 9:11) means "not of this creation." The tabernacle of Moses was made with materials that belong to this creation. The heavenly tabernacle needed no such materials (Heb. 9:24). Since the heavenly tabernacle does not belong to this creation, it is free from the ravages of time.

The "good things to come" had already arrived! All that was foreshadowed by type in the tabernacle was now reality because of Christ's priestly ministry in heaven. The tabernacle was patterned after the sanctuary in heaven, but today we no longer need the pattern. We have the eternal reality!

**Its ministry is effective to deal with sin (vv. 12-15).** We have here a series of contrasts that show again the superiority of the heavenly ministry.

*Animal sacrifices and Christ's sacrifice (v. 12).* The writer will discuss the inferiority of animal sacrifices in Hebrews 10, but here he begins to lay the foundation. We need no proof that the blood of Jesus Christ is far superior to that of animal sacrifices. How can the blood of *animals* ever solve the problem of *humans'* sins? Jesus Christ became a Man that He might be able to die for people's sins. His death was voluntary; it is doubtful that any Old Testament sacrifice volunteered for the job! An animal's blood was carried by the high priest into the holy of holies, but Jesus Christ presented *Himself* in the presence of God as the final and complete sacrifice for sins. Of course, the animal sacrifices were repeated, while Jesus Christ offered Himself but once. Finally, no animal sacrifices ever purchased "eternal redemption." Their blood could only "cover" sin until the time when Christ's blood would "take away sin" (John 1:29). We have "eternal redemption." It is not conditioned on our merit or good works; it is secured once and for all by the finished work of Jesus Christ.

*Ceremonial cleansing and conscience cleansing (vv. 13-14).* The Old Covenant rituals could not change a person's heart. This is not to say that a worshiper did not have a spiritual experience if his heart trusted God, but it does mean that the emphasis was on the external ceremonial cleansing. So long as the worshiper obeyed the prescribed regulations, he was declared clean. It was "the purifying of the flesh" but not the cleansing of the conscience. (For "the ashes of an heifer," see Num. 19.)

We learned from Hebrews 8 that the ministry of the New Covenant is *internal*. "I will put My laws into their mind, and write them in their hearts" (Heb. 8:10). This work is done by the Holy Spirit of God (2 Cor. 3:1-3). But the Spirit could not dwell within us if Jesus Christ had not paid for our sins. Cleansing our consciences cannot be done by some external ceremony; it demands an internal power. Because Jesus Christ is "without spot [blemish]" He was able to offer the perfect sacrifice.

*Temporary blessings and eternal blessings (v. 15).* The blessings under the Old Covenant depended on the obedience of God's people. If they obeyed God, He blessed them; but if they disobeyed, He withheld His blessings. Not only were the blessings temporary, but they were primarily *temporal*—rain, bumper crops, protection from enemies and sickness, etc. Israel's Canaan inheritance involved material blessings. Our eternal inheritance is primarily spiritual in nature (Eph. 1:3). Note that the emphasis is on *eternal*—"eternal redemption" (Heb. 9:12) and "eternal inheritance" (Heb. 9:15). A believer can have confidence because all that he has in Christ is eternal.

This verse (Heb. 9:15) makes it clear that there was no final and complete redemption under the Old Covenant. Those transgressions were *covered* by the blood of the many sacrifices, but not *cleansed* until the sacrifice of Jesus Christ on the cross (Rom. 3:24-26). Since Christ has accomplished an eternal redemption, we are able to share in an eternal inheritance.

As we review these three contrasts, we can easily see that the ministry of Christ is effective to deal with our sins. His finished work on earth and His unfinished work of intercession in heaven are sufficient and efficient.

**Its ministry is based on a costly sacrifice (vv. 16-23).** The word "covenant" not only means "an agreement," but it also carries the idea of "a last will and testament." If a man writes his will, that will is not in force until he dies. It was necessary for Jesus Christ to die so that the terms of the New Covenant might be enforced. "This cup is the new testament [covenant, will] in My blood, which is shed for you" (Luke 22:20).

Even the Old Covenant was established on the basis of blood. Hebrews 9:19-21 is taken from Exodus 24:3-8, the account of the ratifying of the Old Covenant by Moses and the people of Israel. The book of the Law was sprinkled with blood, and so were the people and the tabernacle and its furnishings. It must have been a solemn occasion.

Not only was blood used at the *beginning* of the ministry of the Old Covenant, but it was used in the *regular* administration of the tabernacle service. Under the Old Covenant, people and objects were purified by blood, water, or fire (Num. 31:21-24). This was, of course, *ceremonial* purification; it meant that the persons and objects were now acceptable to God. The purification did not alter the nature of the person or object. God's principle is that blood must be shed before sin can be forgiven (Lev. 17:11).

Since God has ordained that remission of sins is through the *shedding* of blood, and since purification comes through the *sprinkling* of blood, it is necessary that blood be shed and applied if the New Covenant is to be in force. The "patterns" (the Old Covenant tabernacle) were purified by the sprinkling of the blood. But the "originals" were also purified! The blood of Jesus Christ not only purifies the conscience of the believer (Heb. 9:14), but also purified the "heavenly things" (Heb. 9:23, NASB).

How could the heavenly sanctuary ever become defiled? We can understand how the *earthly* sanctuary could be defiled since it was used by sinful men. Each year, on the great Day of Atonement, the tabernacle was purified through the sprinkling of blood (Lev. 16:12-19). But how could a heavenly sanctuary ever become defiled? Certainly nothing in heaven is defiled in a literal sense, for sin cannot pollute the sanctuary of God. But, for that matter, nothing in the earthly tabernacle was *literally* defiled by sin. It all had to do with people's relationships to God. The blood sprinkled on a piece of furniture did not change the nature of that piece, *but it changed God's relationship to it.* God could enter into communion with people because of the sprinkled blood.

Through Jesus Christ, we who are sinners can enter into the holy of holies in the heavenly sanctuary (Heb. 10:19-22). Physically, of course, we are on earth; but spiritually, we are communing with God in the heavenly holy of holies. In order for God to receive us into this heavenly fellowship, the blood of Jesus Christ *had to be applied.* We enter into God's presence "by the blood of Jesus" (Heb. 10:19).

Now we can summarize the writer's discussion. The Old Covenant was established by blood, and so was the New Covenant. But the New Covenant was established on the basis of a better sacrifice, applied in a better place! The patterns (types) were purified by the blood of animals, but the original sanctuary was purified by the blood of the Son of God. This was a far more costly sacrifice.

*Its ministry represents fulfillment (v. 24).* The New Covenant Christian has *reality!* We are not depending on a high priest on earth who annually visits the holy of holies in a temporary sanctuary. We depend on the heavenly High Priest who has entered once and for all into the eternal sanctuary. There He represents us before God, *and He always will.*

Beware of trusting anything for your spiritual life that is "made with hands" (Heb. 9:24). It will not last. The tabernacle was replaced by Solomon's temple, and that temple was destroyed by the Babylonians. When the Jews returned to their land after the Captivity, they rebuilt their temple; and King Herod, in later years, expanded and embellished it. But the Romans destroyed that temple, and it has never been rebuilt. Furthermore, since the genealogical records have been lost or destroyed, the Jews are not certain who can minister as priests. These things that are "made with hands" are perishable, but the things "not made with hands" are eternal.

*Its ministry is final and complete (vv. 25-28).* There can be nothing incomplete or temporary about our Lord's ministry in heaven. The writer pointed out again the obvious contrasts between the Old Covenant ministry and the New Covenant ministry.

| Old Covenant | New Covenant |
|---|---|
| Repeated sacrifices | One sacrifice |
| The blood of others | His own blood |
| Covering sin | Putting away sin |
| For Israel only | For all sinners |
| Left the holy of holies | Entered heaven and remains there |
| Came out to bless the people | Will come to take His people to heaven |

In short, the work of Christ is a completed work, final and eternal. On the basis of His completed work, He is ministering now in heaven on our behalf.

Did you notice that the word "appear" is used three times in Hebrews 9:24-28? These three uses give us a summary of our Lord's work. He *has appeared* to put away sin by dying on the cross (Heb. 9:26). He *is appearing* now in heaven for us (Heb. 9:24). One day, He *shall appear* to take Christians home (Heb. 9:28). These "three tenses of salvation" are all based on His finished work.

After reading this chapter, the Hebrew Christians who received this letter had to realize that there is no middle ground. They had to make a choice between the earthly or the heavenly, the temporary or the eternal, the incomplete or the complete. *Why not return to the temple but also practice the Christian faith?* Why not "the best of both worlds"? Because that would be compromising and refusing to go "without the camp, bearing His reproach" (Heb. 13:13). So there is no middle way.

The believer's sanctuary is in heaven. His Father is in heaven and his Saviour is in heaven. His citizenship is in heaven (Phil. 3:20) and his treasures should be in heaven (Matt. 6:19ff). And his hope is in heaven. The true believer walks by faith, not by sight. No matter what may happen on earth, a believer can be confident because everything is settled in heaven.

# CHAPTER NINE
# THE SUPERIOR SACRIFICE
*Hebrews 10*

A teenage boy, whose mother was away on a visit, found himself with time on his hands. He decided to read a book from the family library. His mother was a devout Christian, so the boy knew there would be a sermon at the beginning and an application at the end of the book, but there would also be some interesting stories in between.

While reading the book, he came across the phrase "the finished work of Christ." It struck him with unusual power. "The finished work of Christ."

"Why does the author use this expression?" he asked himself. "Why not say the atoning or the propitiatory work of Christ?" (You see, he knew all the biblical terms. He just did not know the Saviour!) Then the words, "It is finished," flashed into his mind, and he realized afresh that the work of salvation was accomplished.

"If the whole work was finished and the whole debt paid, what is there left for me to do?" He knew the answer and fell to his knees to receive the Saviour and full forgiveness of sins. That is how J. Hudson Taylor, founder of the China Inland Mission, was saved.

The tenth chapter of Hebrews emphasizes the perfect sacrifice of Jesus Christ, in contrast with the imperfect sacrifices that were offered under the Old Covenant. Our Lord's superior priesthood belongs to a better order—Melchizedek's and not Aaron's. It functions on the basis of a better covenant—the New Covenant—and in a better sanctuary, in heaven. But all of this depends on the better sacrifice, which is the theme of this chapter.

The writer presented three benefits that explain why the sacrifice of Jesus Christ is superior to the Old Covenant sacrifices.

## Christ's Sacrifice Takes Away Sin (Heb. 10:1-10)

Sin, of course, is man's greatest problem. No matter what kind of religion a man has, if it cannot deal with sin, it is of no value. By nature, man is a sinner; and by choice, he proves that his nature is sinful. It has well been said, "We are not sinners because we sin. We sin because we are sinners."

*The need for a better sacrifice (vv. 1-4).* Why were the Old Covenant sacrifices inferior? After all, they were ordained by the Lord; and they were in force for hundreds of years. While it is true that at times the Jewish people permitted these sacrifices to become empty rituals (Isa. 1:11-15), it is also true that many sincere people brought their offerings to God and were blessed.

The very *nature* of the Old Covenant sacrifices made them inferior. The Law was only "a shadow of good things to come" and not the reality itself. The sacrificial system was a type or picture of the work our Lord would accomplish on the cross. This meant that the system was temporary, and therefore could accomplish nothing permanent. The very repetition of the sacrifices day after day, and the

Day of Atonement year after year, pointed out the entire system's weakness.

Animal sacrifices could never completely deal with human guilt. God did promise forgiveness to believing worshipers (Lev. 4:20, 26, 31, 35), but this was a judicial forgiveness and not the removal of guilt from people's hearts. People lacked that inward witness of full and final forgiveness. They could not claim, "I have no more consciousness of sins." If those worshipers had been "once purged [from guilt of sin]" they would never again have had to offer another sacrifice.

So the annual Day of Atonement did not accomplish "remission of sin" but only "reminder of sin." The annual repetition of the ceremony was evidence that the previous year's sacrifices had not done the job. True, the nation's sins were *covered;* but they were not *cleansed.* Nor did the people have God's inward witness of forgiveness and acceptance.

Yes, there was a desperate need for a better sacrifice because the blood of bulls and of goats could not take away sins. It could cover sin and postpone judgment; but it could never effect a once-and-for-all redemption. Only the better sacrifice of the Son of God could do that.

*The provision of the better sacrifice (vv. 5-9).* It was God who provided the sacrifice and not man. The quotation is from Psalm 40:6-8, and it is applied to Jesus Christ in His incarnation ("when He cometh into the world"). The quotation makes it clear that Jesus Christ is the fulfillment of the Old Covenant sacrifices.

The word *sacrifice* refers to any of the animal sacrifices. *Offering* covers the meal offerings and the drink offerings. The burnt offering and sin offering are mentioned (Heb. 10:5, 8). The trespass offering would be covered in the word *sacrifice* (Heb. 10:5). Each of these offerings typified the sacrifice of Christ and revealed some aspect of His work on the cross (see Lev. 1–7).

The phrase, "a body hast Thou prepared Me" (Heb. 10:5), is not found in the original quotation. Psalm 40:6 reads, "Mine ears hast Thou opened." The writer of Hebrews was quoting from the Septuagint, the Greek translation of the Old Testament. How do we explain this variation? Some connect "Mine ears hast Thou opened" with Exodus 21:1-6, a passage that describes the actions of a master whose servant did not want to be set free. The master bored a hole through the ear lobe of the servant, which was a sign that the servant preferred to remain with his master. The idea is that our Lord was like a willing servant who had His ears bored.

The problem with that explanation is that only *one* ear was bored, while the verse (Ps. 40:6) speaks of *both* ears. Furthermore, the verb used in Exodus 21 means "to pierce," while the verb in Psalm 40:6 means "to dig." Our Lord was a servant, but it is not likely that the writer had this in mind. Probably "opened ears" signified a readiness to hear and obey the will of God (see Isa. 50:4-6). God gave His Son a prepared body that the Son might serve God and fulfill His will on earth. Our Lord often referred to this truth (John 4:34; 5:30; 6:38; 17:4).

Of course, the same Holy Spirit who inspired Psalm 40 has the right to amplify and interpret His Word in Hebrews 10. "Opened ears" indicates a body ready for service.

Twice in this paragraph, the writer stated that God "had no pleasure" in the Old Covenant sacrifices (see Heb. 10:6, 8). This does not suggest that the old sacrifices were wrong, or that sincere worshipers received no benefit from obeying God's Law. It only means that God had no delight in sacrifices as such, apart from the obedient hearts of the worshipers. No amount of sacrifices could substitute for obedience (1 Sam. 15:22, Ps. 51:16-17; Isa. 1:11, 19; Jer. 6:19-20; Hosea 6:6; Amos 5:20-21).

Jesus came to do the Father's will. This will is the New Covenant that has replaced the Old Covenant. Through His death and resurrection, Jesus Christ has taken away the first covenant and established the second. The readers of this epistle called Hebrews would get the message: why go back to a covenant that has been taken away? Why go back to sacrifices that are inferior?

**The effectiveness of the better sacrifice (v. 10).** Believers have been set apart ("sanctified") by the offering of Christ's body once for all. No Old Covenant sacrifice could do that. An Old Covenant worshiper had to be purified from ceremonial defilement repeatedly. But a New Covenant saint is set apart finally and completely.

## Christ's Sacrifice Need Not Be Repeated (Heb. 10:11-18)

Again the writer contrasted the Old Covenant high priest with Jesus Christ, our Great High Priest. The fact that Jesus *sat down* after He ascended to the Father is proof that His work was completed (Heb. 1:3, 13; 8:1). The ministry of the priests in the tabernacle and temple was *never done* and *never different:* they offered the same sacrifices day after day. This constant repetition was proof that their sacrifices did not take away sins. What tens of thousands of animal sacrifices could not accomplish, Jesus accomplished with *one sacrifice forever!*

The phrase "sat down" refers us again to Psalm 110:1: "Sit Thou at My right hand, until I make Thine enemies Thy footstool." Christ is in the place of exaltation and victory. When He returns, He shall overcome every enemy and establish His righteous kingdom. Those who have trusted Him need not fear, for they have been "perfected forever" (Heb. 10:14). Believers are "complete in Him" (Col. 2:10). We have a perfect standing before God because of the finished work of Jesus Christ.

How do we know *personally* that we have this perfect standing before God? Because of the witness of the Holy Spirit through the Word (Heb. 10:15-18). The witness of the Spirit is based on the work of the Son and is given through the words of Scripture. The writer (Heb. 10:16-17) quoted Jeremiah 31:33-34, part of a passage he'd also quoted in Hebrews 8:7-12. The Old Covenant worshiper could not say that he had "no more consciousness of sins" (Heb. 10:2). But the New Covenant believer *can* say that his sins and iniquities are remembered *no more*. There is "no more offering for sin" (Heb. 10:18) and no more remembrance of sin!

I once shared a conference with a fine Christian psychiatrist whose lectures were very true to the Word. "The trouble with psychiatry," he told me, "is that it can only deal with symptoms. A psychiatrist can remove a patient's *feelings* of guilt, but he cannot remove the guilt. It's like a trucker loosening a fender on his truck so he won't hear the motor knock. A patient can end up feeling better, but have *two* problems instead of one!"

When a sinner trusts Christ, his sins are all forgiven, the guilt is gone, and the matter is completely settled forever.

## Christ's Sacrifice Opens the Way to God (Heb. 10:19-39)

No Old Covenant worshiper would have been bold enough to try to enter the holy of holies in the tabernacle. Even the high priest entered the holy of holies only once a year. The thick veil that separated the holy place from the holy of holies was a barrier between people and God. Only the death of Christ could tear that veil (Mark 15:38) and open the way into the *heavenly* sanctuary where God dwells.

*A gracious invitation (vv. 19-25).* "Let us draw near. . . . Let us hold fast . . . Let us consider one another." This threefold invitation hinges on our boldness to enter into the holiest. And this boldness ("freedom of speech") rests on the finished work of the Saviour. On the Day of Atonement, the high priest could not enter the holy of holies unless he had the blood of the sacrifice (Heb. 9:7). But our entrance into God's presence is not because of an animal's blood, but because of Christ's shed blood.

This open way into God's presence is "new" (recent, fresh) and not a part of the Old Covenant that "waxeth [grows] old [and] is ready to vanish away" (Heb. 8:13). It is "living" because Christ "ever liveth to make intercession" for us (Heb. 7:25). Christ is the new and living way! We come to God through Him, our High Priest over the house of God (the church, see Heb. 3:6). When His flesh was torn on the cross, and His life sacrificed, God tore the veil in the temple. This symbolized the new and living way now opened for all who believe.

On the basis of these assurances—that we have boldness to enter because we have a living High Priest—we have an "open invitation" to enter the presence of God. The Old Covenant high priest *visited* the holy of holies once a year, but we are invited to *dwell in the presence of God* every moment of each day. What a tremendous privilege! Consider what is involved in this threefold invitation.

*Let us draw near (v. 22).* Of course, we must prepare ourselves spiritually to fellowship with God. The Old Testament priest had to go through various washings and the applying of blood on the Day of Atonement (Lev. 16). Also, during the regular daily ministry, the priests had to wash at the laver before they entered the holy place (Ex. 30:18-21). The New Testament Christian must come to God with a pure heart and a clean conscience. Fellowship with God demands purity (1 John 1:5–2:2).

*Let us hold fast (v. 23).* The readers of this epistle were being tempted to forsake their confession of Jesus Christ by going back to the Old Covenant worship. The writer did not exhort them to hold on to their salvation, be-

cause their security was in Christ and not in themselves (Heb. 7:25). Rather, he invited them to hold fast "the profession [confession] of . . . hope." (There is no manuscript evidence for the word "faith." The Greek word is "hope.")

We have noted in our study of Hebrews that there is an emphasis on the glorious hope of the believer. God is "bringing many sons unto glory" (Heb. 2:10). Believers are "partakers of the heavenly calling" (Heb. 3:1) and therefore can rejoice in hope (Heb. 3:6). *Hope* is one of the main themes of Hebrews 6 (vv. 11-12, 18-20). We are looking for Christ to return (Heb. 9:28) and we are seeking that city that is yet to come (Heb. 13:14).

When a believer has his hope fixed on Christ, and relies on the faithfulness of God, then he will not waver. Instead of looking back (as the Jews so often did), we should look ahead to the coming of the Lord.

*Let us consider one another (vv. 24-25).* Fellowship with God must never become selfish. We must also fellowship with other Christians in the local assembly. Apparently, some of the wavering believers had been absenting themselves from the church fellowship. It is interesting to note that the emphasis here is not on what a believer *gets from* the assembly, but rather on what he can *contribute to* the assembly. Faithfulness in church attendance encourages others and provokes them to love and good works. One of the strong motives for faithfulness is the soon coming of Jesus Christ. In fact, the only other place the word translated "assembling" (Heb. 10:25) is used in the New Testament is in 2 Thessalonians 2:1, where it's translated "gathering" and deals with the coming of Christ.

The three great Christian virtues are evidenced here: *faith* (Heb. 10:22), *hope* (Heb. 10:23), and *love* (Heb. 10:24). They are the fruit of our fellowship with God in His heavenly sanctuary.

*A solemn exhortation (vv. 26-31).* This is the fourth of the five exhortations found in Hebrews. It is written to believers and follows in sequence with the other exhortations. The believer who begins to *drift* from the Word (Heb. 2:1-4) will soon start to *doubt* the Word (Heb. 3:7–4:13). Soon, he will become *dull* toward the Word (Heb. 5:11–6:20) and become "lazy" in his spiritual life. This will result in *despising* the Word, which is the theme of this exhortation.

The evidence of this "despising" is willful

sin. The tense of the verb indicates that Hebrews 10:26 should read, "For if we willfully *go on sinning.*" This exhortation is not dealing with one particular act of sin, but with an attitude that leads to repeated disobedience. Under the Old Covenant, there were no sacrifices for deliberate and willful sins (Ex. 21:12-14; Num. 15:27-31). Presumptuous sinners who despised Moses' Law and broke it were executed (Deut. 17:1-7). This explains why David prayed as he did in Psalm 51. Because he deliberately sinned "with a high hand," he should have been slain; but he cried out for God's mercy. David knew that even a multitude of sacrifices could not save him. All he could offer was the sacrifice of a broken heart (Ps. 51:16-17).

How does an arrogant attitude affect a believer's relationship with God? It is as though he trods Jesus Christ underfoot, cheapens the precious blood that saved him ("an unholy thing" [Heb. 10:29] = "a common thing"), and insults the Holy Spirit. This is just the opposite of the exhortation given in Hebrews 10:19-25! Instead of having a bold profession of faith, hope, and love, a backslidden believer so lives that his actions and attitudes bring disgrace to the name of Christ and the church.

What can this kind of a Christian expect from God? He can expect severe discipline. (Chastening is the theme of Heb. 12.) There is no need to "water down" words such as "judgment and fiery indignation" (Heb. 10:27), or "sorer punishment" (Heb. 10:29). We have already seen from the history of Israel that hardly anybody who was saved out of Egypt by the blood of the lamb entered into the promised inheritance. Nearly all of them died in the wilderness. "There is a sin unto death" (1 John 5:16). Some of the Corinthian believers were disciplined and their lives taken because of their presumptuous sins (1 Cor. 11:30, where "sleep" means "died").

God does not always take the life of a rebellious believer, but He always deals with him. "Vengeance belongeth unto Me" was spoken to Israel, God's people. "The Lord shall judge His people!" (Heb. 10:30, quoted from Deut. 32:35) "It is a fearful thing to fall into the hands of the living God" (Heb. 10:31).

The major theme of Hebrews is "God has spoken—how are you responding to His Word?" When the nation of Israel refused to believe and obey His Word, God chastened them. Paul used this fact to warn the Corinthians against presumptuous sins (1 Cor. 10:1-

12). Note that the examples given in this passage involve people who died because of their willful sins. When we study the subject of "chastening" in Hebrews 12, we will get greater insight into this awesome aspect of God's dealings with His children.

In stating that this exhortation applies to believers today, but that it does not involve loss of salvation, I am not suggesting that chastening is unimportant. On the contrary, it is important that every Christian obey God and please the Father in all things. Dr. William Culbertson, late president of the Moody Bible Institute, used to warn us about "the sad consequences of *forgiven sins.*" God forgave David's sins, but David suffered the sad consequences for years afterward (2 Sam. 12:7-15). David had "despised the commandment of the Lord" (2 Sam. 12:9) and God dealt with him.

What should a believer do who has drifted away into spiritual doubt and dullness and is deliberately despising God's Word? He should turn to God for mercy and forgiveness. There is no other sacrifice for sin, but the sacrifice Christ made is sufficient for all our sins. It is a fearful thing to fall into the Lord's hands for chastening, but it is a wonderful thing to fall into His hands for cleansing and restoration. David said, "Let me fall now into the hand of the Lord; for very great are His mercies" (1 Chron. 21:13).

*An encouraging confirmation (vv. 32-39).* Lest any of his readers should misinterpret his exhortation, the writer followed it with words of encouragement and confirmation. His readers had given every evidence that they were true Christians. He did not expect *them* to despise God's Word and experience the chastening of God! In fact, as in Hebrews 6, the writer shifted the pronouns from "we" in Hebrews 10:26 to "he" in Hebrews 10:29 and "them" in Hebrews 10:39.

The readers had been willing to suffer reproach and persecution, even to the spoiling of their goods. When they were not being persecuted themselves, they courageously identified with the other Christians who were in danger, even to the point of sharing their bonds (imprisonment). At that time, they had great confidence and hope; but now they were in danger of casting away that confidence and going back into their old religion.

The secret of victory was in their *faith* and *patience* ("courageous endurance"). We have met this combination of graces in Hebrews 6:12, 15. It is here that the writer introduced the "text" around which Hebrews is written: "The just shall live by faith" (Heb. 10:38). The quotation is from Habakkuk 2:4, and it is also used in Romans 1:17; Galatians 3:11. Romans emphasizes "the just," Galatians deals with "shall live," and Hebrews centers on "by faith." We are not just *saved* from our sin by faith; we also must *live* by faith. This is the theme of Hebrews 11–13.

The believer who lives by faith will "go on to perfection" (Heb. 6:1). But the believer who lives by sight will "draw back unto perdition" (Heb. 10:39). What is "perdition" in this context? The Greek word translated "perdition" is used about twenty times in the New Testament and is translated by different words: "perish" (Acts 8:20), "die" (Acts 25:16), "destruction" (Rom. 9:22), and "waste" (Matt. 26:8). The word *can* mean eternal judgment, but it need not in *every* instance. I personally believe that "waste" is the best translation for this word in Hebrews 10:39. A believer who does not walk by faith goes back into the old ways and wastes his life.

"The saving of the soul" is the opposite of "waste." To walk by faith means to obey God's Word and live for Jesus Christ. We lose our lives for His sake—but we save them! (see Matt. 16:25-27) In my own pastoral ministry, I have met people who turned their backs on God's will and (like Israel) spent years "wandering in the wilderness" of waste.

But we can be confident! As we walk by faith, our Great High Priest will guide us and perfect us!

# CHAPTER TEN
# FAITH—THE GREATEST POWER IN THE WORLD
*Hebrews 11*

This chapter introduces the final section of the epistle (Heb. 11–13) which I have called "A Superior Principle—Faith." The fact that Christ is a superior Person (Heb. 1–6) and that He exercises a superior Priesthood (Heb. 7–10)

ought to encourage us to put our trust in Him. The readers of this epistle were being tempted to go back into Judaism and put their faith in Moses. Their confidence was in the visible things of this world, not the invisible realities of God. Instead of going on to perfection (maturity), they were going "back to perdition [waste]" (Heb. 6:1; 10:39).

In Hebrews 11 all Christians are called to live by faith. In it, the writer discusses two important topics relating to faith.

**The Description of Faith (Heb. 11:1-3)**
This is not a definition of faith but a description of what faith does and how it works. True Bible faith is not blind optimism or a manufactured "hope-so" feeling. Neither is it an intellectual assent to a doctrine. It is certainly not believing in spite of evidence! That would be superstition.

*True Bible faith is confident obedience to God's Word in spite of circumstances and consequences.* Read that last sentence again and let it soak into your mind and heart.

This faith operates quite simply. God speaks and we hear His Word. We trust His Word and act on it no matter what the circumstances are or what the consequences may be. The circumstances may be impossible, and the consequences frightening and unknown; but we obey God's Word just the same and believe Him to do what is right and what is best.

The unsaved world does not understand true Bible faith, probably because it sees so little faith in action in the church today. The cynical editor H.L. Mencken defined faith as "illogical belief in the occurrence of the impossible." The world fails to realize that faith is only as good as its object, and the object of our faith is *God.* Faith is not some "feeling" that we manufacture. It is our total response to what God has revealed in His Word.

Three words in Hebrews 11:1-3 summarize what true Bible faith is: *substance, evidence,* and *witness.* The word translated "substance" means literally "to stand under, to support." Faith is to a Christian what a foundation is to a house: it gives confidence and assurance that he will stand. So you might say, "Faith is the confidence of things hoped for." When a believer has faith, it is God's way of giving him confidence and assurance that what is promised will be experienced.

The word *evidence* simply means "conviction." This is the inward conviction from God that what He has promised, He will perform. The presence of God-given faith in one's heart is conviction enough that He will keep His Word.

*Witness* (KJV, "obtained a good report") is an important word in Hebrews 11. It occurs not only in verse 2, but twice in verse 4, once in verse 5, and once in verse 39. The summary in Hebrews 12:1 calls this list of men and women "so great a cloud of witnesses." They are witnesses to us because God witnessed to them. In each example cited, God gave witness to that person's faith. This witness was His divine approval on their lives and ministries.

The writer of Hebrews makes it clear that faith is a very practical thing (Heb. 11:3), in spite of what unbelievers say. Faith enables us to understand what God does. Faith enables us to see what others cannot see (note Heb. 11:7, 13, 27). As a result, faith enables us to do what others cannot do! People laughed at these great men and women when they stepped out by faith, but God was with them and enabled them to succeed to His glory. Dr. J. Oswald Sanders put it perfectly: "Faith enables the believing soul to treat the future as present and the invisible as seen."

The best way to grow in faith is to walk with the faithful. The remainder of this chapter is devoted to a summary of the lives and labors of great men and women of faith found in the Old Testament. In each instance, you will find the same elements of faith: (1) God spoke to them through His Word; (2) their inner selves were stirred in different ways; (3) they obeyed God; (4) He bore witness about them.

## The Demonstration of Faith (Heb. 11:4-40)

*Abel—faith worshiping (v. 4).* The background story is in Genesis 4:1-10. Abel was a righteous man because of faith (Matt. 23:35). God had revealed to Adam and his descendants the true way of worship, and Abel obeyed God by faith. In fact, his obedience cost him his life. Cain was not a child of God (1 John 3:12) because he did not have faith. He was religious but not righteous. Abel speaks to us today as the first martyr of the faith.

*Enoch—faith walking (vv. 5-6).* Our faith in God grows as we fellowship with God. We must have both the *desire* to please Him and the *diligence* to seek Him. Prayer, medi-

tating on the Word, worship, discipline—all of these help us in our walk with God. Enoch walked with God in the wicked world, before the Flood came; he was able to keep his life pure. Enoch was taken to heaven one day ("translated" = "carried across") and seen no more. Abel died a violent death, but Enoch never died. God has a diffcrent plan for each one who trusts Him. Some see in the translation of Enoch a picture of the Rapture of the church when Jesus Christ returns (1 Thes. 4:13-18).

*Noah—faith working (v. 7).* Noah's faith involved the whole person: his *mind* was warned of God; his *heart* was moved with fear; and his *will* acted on what God told him. Since nobody at that time had ever seen a flood (or perhaps even a rainstorm), Noah's actions must have generated a great deal of interest and probably ridicule as well. Noah's faith influenced his whole family and they were saved. It also condemned the whole world, for his faith revealed their unbelief. Events proved that Noah was right! Jesus used this experience to warn people to be ready for His return (Matt. 24:36-42). In Noah's day, the people were involved in innocent everyday activities and completely ignored Noah's witness (2 Peter 2:5).

*The patriarchs—faith waiting (vv. 8-22).* The emphasis in this section is on the promise of God and His plans for the nation of Israel (Heb. 11:9, 11, 13, 17). The nation began with the call of Abraham. God promised Abraham and Sarah a son, but they had to wait twenty-five years for the fulfillment of the promise. Their son Isaac became the father of Jacob and Esau, and it was Jacob who really built the nation through the birth of his twelve sons. Joseph saved the nation *in* the land of Egypt, and Moses would later deliver them *from* Egypt.

Waiting is, for me, one of the most difficult disciplines of life. Yet true faith is able to wait for the fulfillment of God's purposes *in God's time*. But, while we are waiting, we must also be obeying. "By faith Abraham . . . obeyed" (Heb. 11:8). He obeyed when *he did not know where he was going* (Heb. 11:8-10). He lived in tents because he was a stranger and pilgrim in the world and had to be ready to move whenever God spoke. Christians today are also strangers and pilgrims (1 Peter 1:1; 2:11). Abraham had his eyes on the heavenly city and lived "in the future tense."

He also obeyed when *he did not know how*

*God's will would be accomplished* (Heb. 11:11-12). Both Abraham and Sarah were too old to have children. Yet they both believed that God would do the miracle (Rom. 4:13-25). Unbelief asks, "How *can* this be?" (Luke 1:18-20) Faith asks, "How *shall* this be?" (Luke 1:34-37)

Abraham believed and obeyed God when *he did not know when God would fulfill His promises* (Heb. 11:13-16). None of the patriarchs saw the complete fulfillment of God's promises, but they saw from "afar off" what God was doing. Dr. George Morrison, a great Scottish preacher, once said, "The important thing is not what we live in, but what we look for." These men and women of faith lived in tents, but they knew a heavenly city awaited them. God always fulfills His promises to His believing people, either immediately or ultimately.

Finally, Abraham obeyed God by faith when *he did not know why God was so working* (Heb. 11:17-19). Why would God want Abraham to sacrifice his son when it was the Lord who gave him that son? All of a future nation's promises were wrapped up in Isaac. The tests of faith become more difficult as we walk with God, yet the rewards are more wonderful! And we must not ignore the obedient faith of Isaac.

In Abraham, Isaac, Jacob, and Joseph, we have four generations of faith. These men sometimes failed, but basically they were men of faith. They were not perfect, but they were devoted to God and trusted His Word. Isaac passed the promises and the blessings along to Jacob (Gen. 27), and Jacob shared them with his twelve sons (Gen. 48–49). Jacob was a pilgrim, for even as he was dying he leaned on his pilgrim staff.

The faith of Joseph was certainly remarkable. After the way his family treated him, you would think he would have abandoned his faith; but instead, it grew stronger. Even the ungodly influence of Egypt did not weaken his trust in God. Joseph did not use his family, his job, or his circumstances as an excuse for unbelief. *Joseph knew what he believed*—that God would one day deliver his people from Egypt (Gen. 50:24-26). *Joseph also knew where he belonged*—in Canaan, not in Egypt; so he made them promise to carry his remains out of Egypt at the Exodus. They did! (see Ex. 13:19 and Josh. 24:32)

We have to admire the faith of the patriarchs. They did not have a complete Bible, and yet their faith was strong. They handed God's promises down from one generation to another. In spite of their failures and testings, these men and women believed God and He bore witness to their faith. How much more faith you and I should have!

*Moses—faith warring (vv. 23-29).* Moses was fortunate to have believing parents. For them to hide their baby son from the authorities was certainly an act of faith. The account is given in Exodus 2:1-10. Moses' parents were named Amram and Jochebed (Ex. 6:20). Though godly parents cannot pass on their faith as they do family traits, they can certainly create an atmosphere of faith at home and be examples to their children. A home should be the first school of faith for a child.

Three great themes relating to faith are seen in the life of Moses. First, *the refusal of faith* (Heb. 11:24-25). As the adopted son of the Egyptian princess, Moses could have led an easy life in the palace. But his faith moved him to refuse that kind of life. He chose to identify with God's suffering people. True faith causes a believer to hold the right values and make the right decisions. The phrase "pleasures of sin" does not refer only to lust and other gross sins. The phrase describes a way of life that we today would call "successful"—position, prestige, power, wealth, and freedom from problems.

Moses' refusal of faith led *to the reproach of faith* (Heb. 11:26a). The mayor of a large American city moved into a dangerous and decayed housing project to demonstrate the problems and needs of the minorities. But she also kept her fashionable apartment and eventually moved out of the slum. We commend her for her courage but we have to admire Moses even more. He left the palace *and never went back to the old life!* He identified with the Jewish slaves! Men and women of faith often have to bear reproach and suffering. The Apostles suffered for their faith. Believers today behind the Iron Curtain know what it is to bear reproach. If reproach is an evidence of true faith, we wonder how much true faith there is in our own country today!

Finally, there is *the reward of faith* (Heb. 11:26b-29). God always rewards true faith—if not immediately, at least ultimately. Over against "the treasures in Egypt" Moses saw the "recompense of the reward." As Dr. Vance Havner said, "Moses chose the imperishable, saw the invisible, and did the impossible." Moses' faith enabled him to face Pharaoh unafraid, and to trust God to deal with the enemy. The endurance of Moses was not a natural gift, for by nature Moses was hesitant and retiring. This endurance and courage came as the reward of his faith.

The faith of Moses was rewarded with deliverance for him and his people. (See Ex. 11–13 for the exciting Passover account.) Faith brings us *out* (Heb. 11:28), takes us *through* (Heb. 11:29), and brings us *in* (Heb. 11:30). When we trust God, we get what God can do; but when we trust ourselves, we get only what weak people can do. The experience of Moses is proof that true biblical faith means obeying God in spite of circumstances and in spite of consequences.

If you and I had been writing this chapter, the next section would be *Faith Wandering*— but there is no mention of Israel's failure and forty years of wasted time. Why? Because that was an experience of *unbelief,* not faith! The writer did use this experience in Hebrews 3 and 4 as an illustration of doubting the Word. But nowhere in Hebrews 11 will you find a record of *any* failure because of unbelief. Faith records only the victories.

### Joshua and Rahab—faith winning (vv. 30-31).
The account of the conquest of Jericho is found in Joshua 2–6. Joshua was Moses' successor as leader of Israel, and he succeeded because he trusted the same God that Moses had trusted. God changes His workmen but He does not change His principles of operation. He blesses faith and He judges unbelief.

From a human point of view, Jericho was an impossible city to conquer. However, Joshua's first act of faith was not the defeat of the city, but the crossing of the Jordan River. By faith, the nation crossed the river just as the previous generation had crossed the Red Sea. This was a witness and a warning to the Canaanite nations that Israel was marching forward by the power of God.

Rahab was a harlot, an unlikely person to put faith in the true God of Israel! *She was saved by grace,* because the other inhabitants of the city were marked out for death. God in His mercy and grace permitted Rahab to live. But *she was saved by faith.* What she knew about God is recorded in Joshua 2:8-14. She knew that Jehovah had delivered Israel from Egypt and that He had opened the Red Sea. But that was forty years before! She also knew God had defeated the other nations during Israel's wilderness wanderings. "For the

Lord your God, He is God in heaven above, and in earth beneath" (Josh. 2:11). That was her testimony of faith, and God honored it.

*She was saved unto good works.* True faith must always show itself in good works (James 2:20-26). She protected the spies, put the cord in the window as directed (Josh. 2:15-21), apparently won her family to the true faith (Josh. 2:13; 6:25), and in every way obeyed the Lord. Not only was Rahab delivered from judgment, but she became a part of the nation of Israel. She married Salmon and gave birth to Boaz who was an ancestor of King David (Matt. 1:4-6). Imagine a pagan harlot becoming a part of the ancestry of Jesus Christ! That is what faith can do!

Rahab is certainly a rebuke to unsaved people who give excuses for not trusting Christ. "I don't know very much about the Bible" is an excuse I often hear. Rahab knew very little spiritual truth, but she acted on what she did know. "I am too bad to be saved!" is another excuse. But Rahab was a condemned heathen harlot! Another excuse is, "What will my family think?" Rahab's first concern was *saving* her family, not opposing them. She stands as one of the great women of faith in the Bible.

### Various heroes of faith (vv. 32-40).
Faith can operate in the life of any person who will dare to listen to God's Word and surrender to God's will. What a variety of personalities we have here! Gideon was a frightened farmer whose faith did not grow strong right away (Jud. 6:11–7:25). Barak won a resounding victory over Sisera, but he needed Deborah the prophetess as his helper to assure him (see Jud. 4:1–5:31). Both Gideon and Barak are encouragements to us who falter in our faith.

The story of Samson is familiar (Jud. 13–16). We would not call Samson a godly man, for he yielded to his fleshly appetites. He was a Nazarite, which meant he was dedicated to God and was never to cut his hair or partake of the fruit of the vine. (A Nazarite should not be confused with a Nazarene, a resident of Nazareth.) Samson did trust God to help and deliver him and, in the end, Samson was willing to give his life to defeat the enemy. However, we must not conclude that believers today can expect to lead double lives and still enjoy God's blessing.

Jephthah's story is fascinating (Jud. 11:1–12:7). It is unlikely that he sacrificed his only daughter as a burnt offering, for this was forbidden in Israel. Probably he dedicated her to the Lord on the basis of the "law of vows" (Lev. 27), dedicating her to perpetual virginity (Jud. 11:34-40).

It is not possible for us to examine each example of faith, and even the writer of Hebrews stopped citing names after he mentioned David and Samuel, who were certainly great men of faith. There are examples in the Old Testament of men and women who won the victories referred to in Hebrews 11:33-35. David certainly subdued kingdoms and wrought righteousness. Daniel's faith "stopped the mouths of lions" (Dan. 6), and the three Hebrew children overcame the power of the fiery furnace (Dan. 3:23-28). The women of faith mentioned in Hebrews 11:35 have their stories given in 1 Kings 17:17-24 and 2 Kings 4:18-37.

The transition in Hebrews 11:35 is important: not all men and women of faith experienced miraculous deliverance. Some were tortured and died! The word translated "others" in Hebrews 11:36 means "others of a different kind." These "others" had faith, but God did not see fit to deal with them in the same way he dealt with Moses, Gideon, and David.

While making a hospital visit, I found a patient lying in bed weeping. "What's the matter?" I asked. Her reply was to hand me a book that she had that day received in the mail. It was on "divine healing" and "the power of faith." Some anonymous person had written on the flyleaf, "Read this book—it will give you faith to be healed." The patient happened to be a dedicated Christian who trusted God even in the midst of suffering. But her anonymous correspondent thought that *all* people with faith should be delivered miraculously.

I have personally experienced God's miracle touch on my body when others were sure I would die. I know that God can heal. But I also know that God *does not have to heal* in order to prove that I have faith. The writer of Hebrews (11:36-38) records the fact that many unknown men and women of faith *were not delivered* from difficult circumstances; yet God honored their faith. In fact, it takes more faith to *endure* than it does to *escape*. Like the three Hebrew children, we should trust God and obey Him *even if He does not deliver us* (Dan. 3:16-18).

Man's estimate of these heroes of faith was a low one; so men persecuted them, arrested them, tortured them, and in some cases, killed them. But God's estimate is entirely different. He said that the world was not worthy of these people! The Apostle Paul is a good illustration of this truth. Festus said that Paul was out of his mind (Acts 26:24). The Jews said Paul was not fit to live (Acts 22:22). Paul himself said he was treated like "the filth of the world . . . the offscouring of all things" (1 Cor. 4:13). Yet Paul was God's chosen vessel, probably the greatest Christian who ever lived!

Faith enables us to turn from the approval of the world and seek only the approval of God. If God is glorified by delivering His people, He will do it. If He sees fit to be glorified by *not* delivering His people, then He will do that. But we must never conclude that the absence of deliverance means a lack of faith on the part of God's children.

Faith looks to the future, for that is where the greatest rewards are found. The people named in this chapter (and those unnamed) did not receive "the promises" (what was promised, Heb. 11:13) but they had God's witness to their faith that one day they would be rewarded. God's purpose involves Old Testament saints as well as New Testament saints! One day all of us shall share that heavenly city that true saints look for by faith.

We today should give thanks for these saints of old, for they were faithful during difficult times, and yet *we* are the ones who have received the "better blessing." They saw some of these blessings afar off (see John 8:56), but we enjoy them today through Jesus Christ. If the saints of old had not trusted God and obeyed His will, Israel would have perished and the Messiah would not have been born.

"Without faith it is impossible to please God" (Heb. 11:6). But this kind of faith grows as we listen to His Word (Rom. 10:17) and fellowship in worship and prayer. Faith is possible to all kinds of believers in all kinds of situations. It is not a luxury for a few "elite saints." It is a necessity for all of God's people.

Lord, increase our faith!

# CHAPTER ELEVEN
# STAY IN THE RUNNING!
*Hebrews 12*

If the Apostle Paul were alive today, he would probably read the sports pages of the newspaper and follow the progress of various teams and athletes. Why? Because several athletic references in his letters indicate his interest in sports. Of course, both the Greeks and the Romans were keenly interested in athletic contests, not only for their physical well-being, but also for the honor of their towns and countries. It was a patriotic thing to be a good athlete and to bring glory to your country.

The writer of Hebrews combined these two themes of athletics and citizenship in this important twelfth chapter. The atmosphere is that of the footraces in the arena. We can see the runners laying aside their training weights and striving to run their races successfully. Some get weary and faint, while others endure to the end and win the prize. First the writer pictures the race (Heb. 12:1-13), and then emphasizes citizenship in the heavenly city (Heb. 12:14-29). In the minds of his readers, these two themes would go together; for no one could take part in the official games unless he was a citizen of the nation.

The one theme that runs through this chapter is *endurance* (Heb. 12:1 ["patience"], 2-3, 7; also see 10:32, 36 ["patience"]). The Jewish believers who received this letter were getting weary and wanted to give up; but the writer encouraged them to keep moving forward in their Christian lives, like runners on a track (see Phil. 3:12-14). He pointed out three divine resources that encourage a Christian to keep going when the situation is difficult.

## The Example of the Son of God
(Heb. 12:1-4)
When I was in junior high school, I had a coach who felt it his duty to make an athlete out of me. Everybody in my class could have told him he was wasting his time, because I was the worst athlete in the class—perhaps in the school! I entered a city-wide school competition, running the low hurdles. I knocked down six hurdles, fractured my left ankle, and immediately abandoned my sports career. (Shortly after, the coach enlisted in the army. I may have driven him to it.)

Coach Walker used several techniques to get me to do my best. "Other students have done it, and so can you!" was one of his encouragements. "Just think of what it will do for you physically!" was another. "Now, watch the other kids—see how they do it!" was a third. As I reflect on this experience, I am amazed to discover that these same three approaches are used in this paragraph, to encourage us in the Christian race.

***Look around at the winners!*** *(v. 1a)* The "great . . . cloud [assembly, mass] of witnesses" was introduced to us in Hebrews 11. They are the heroes of the faith. It is not suggested here that these men and women now in heaven are watching us as we run the race, like people seated in a stadium. The word "witnesses" does not mean "spectators." Our English word "martyr" comes directly from the Greek word translated "witness." These people are not witnessing what we are doing; rather, they are bearing witness *to us* that God can see us through. God bore witness to them (Heb. 11:2, 4-5, 39) and they are bearing witness now to us.

"I rarely read the Old Testament, except for Psalms and Proverbs," a believer once told me.

"Then you are missing a great deal of spiritual help," I replied. I asked him to open to Romans 15:4 and read the verse aloud.

"For whatsoever things were written aforetime were written for our learning, that we through patience and comfort of the Scriptures might have hope."

I then explained that "patience" means "endurance," and that "comfort" means "encouragement." One of the best ways to develop endurance and encouragement is to get to know the godly men and women of the Old Testament who ran the race and won. If you are having problems with your family, read about Joseph. If you think your job is too big for you, study the life of Moses. If you are tempted to retaliate, see how David handled this problem.

***Look at yourself!*** *(v. 1b)* Athletes used to wear training weights to help them prepare for the events. No athlete would actually participate wearing the weights because they would slow him down. (The modern analogy is a baseball player who swings a bat with a heavy metal collar on it before he steps to the plate.) Too much weight would tax one's endurance.

What are the "weights" that we should remove so that we might win the race? Everything that hinders our progress. They might even be "good things" in the eyes of others. A winning athlete does not choose between the good and the bad; he chooses between the better and the best.

We should also get rid of "the sin that so easily entangles" (Heb. 12:1, NIV). While he does not name any specific sin, the writer was probably referring to the sin of unbelief. It was unbelief that kept Israel out of the Promised Land, and it is unbelief that hinders us from entering into our spiritual inheritance in Christ. The phrase "by faith" (or "through faith") is used twenty-one times in Hebrews 11, indicating that it is faith in Christ that enables us to endure.

***Look at Jesus Christ! (vv. 2-4)*** He is "the author [originator] and finisher of our faith." It was in "looking to Him" that we were saved, for *to look* means "to trust." When the dying Jews looked to the uplifted serpent, they were healed; and this is an illustration of our salvation through faith in Christ (Num. 21:4-9; John 3:14-16). "Looking unto Jesus" describes an *attitude* of faith and not just a single act.

When our Lord was here on earth, He lived by faith. The mystery of His divine and human natures is too profound for us to understand fully, but we do know that He had to trust His Father in heaven as He lived day by day. The writer of Hebrews quoted our Lord saying, "I will put My trust in Him" (Heb. 2:13). (The quotation is from Isa. 8:17.) The fact that Jesus *prayed* is evidence that He lived by faith.

Our Lord endured far more than did any of the heroes of faith named in Hebrews 11, and therefore He is a perfect example for us to follow. *He endured the cross!* This involved shame, suffering, the "contradiction [opposition]" of sinners, and even temporary rejection by the Father. On the cross He suffered for *all* the sins of *all* the world! Yet He endured and finished the work the Father gave Him to do (John 17:4). Though the readers of Hebrews had suffered persecution, they had not yet "resisted unto blood" (Heb. 12:4). None of them was yet a martyr. But in Jesus' battle against sin, He shed His own blood.

What was it that enabled our Lord to endure the cross? Please keep in mind that, during His ministry on earth, our Lord did not use His divine powers for His own personal needs. Satan tempted Him to do this (Matt. 4:1-4), but Jesus refused. It was our Lord's *faith* that enabled Him to endure. He kept the eye of faith on "the joy that was set before Him." From Psalm 16:8-10, He knew that He would come out of the tomb alive. (Peter referred to this messianic psalm in his sermon at Pentecost, Acts 2:24-33.) In that psalm (16:11) David speaks about "fullness of joy" in the presence of the Father. Also, from Psalm 110:1, 4, Jesus knew that He would be exalted to heaven in glory. (Peter also quoted this psalm—Acts 2:34-36.) So "the joy that was set before Him" would include Jesus' completing the Father's will, His resurrection and exaltation, and His joy in presenting believers to the Father in glory (Jude 24).

Throughout this epistle, the writer emphasized the importance of the *future hope*. His readers were prone to *look back* and want to *go back*, but he encouraged them to follow Christ's example and *look ahead* by faith. The heroes of faith named in the previous chapter lived for the future, and this enabled them to endure (Heb. 11:10, 14-16, 24-27). Like Peter, when we get our eyes of faith off the Saviour, we start to sink (Matt. 14:22-33).

Since Christ is the "author and finisher of our faith," trusting Him releases His power in our lives. I could try to follow the example of some great athlete for years and still be a failure. But if, in my younger days, that athlete could have entered into my life and shared his know-how and ability with me, that would have made me a winner. Christ is both the exemplar *and the enabler!* As we see Him in the Word and yield to His Spirit, He increases our faith and enables us to run the race.

**The Assurance of the Love of God (Heb. 12:5-13)**

The key word in this section is *chastening*. It is a Greek word that means "child training, instruction, discipline." A Greek boy was expected to "work out" in the gymnasium until he reached his maturity. It was a part of his preparation for adult life. The writer viewed the trials of the Christian life as spiritual discipline that could help a believer mature. Instead of trying to escape the difficulties of life, we should rather be "exercised" by them so that we might grow (Heb. 12:11).

When we are suffering, it is easy to think that God does not love us. So the writer gave three proofs that chastening comes from the Father's heart of love.

**The Scriptures (vv. 5-6).** The quotation is from Proverbs 3:11-12, a statement that his readers had known but had forgotten. (This is one of the sad consequences of getting "dull" toward the Word; see Heb. 5:11-12.) This quotation (IIeb. 12:5-6) is an "exhortation," which literally means "encouragement." Because they forgot the Word, they lost their encouragement and were ready to give up!

The key words in this quotation are "son," "children," and "sons." These words are used six times in Hebrews 12:5-8. They refer to *adult sons* and not little children. (The word "children" in Heb. 12:5 should be "sons.") A parent who would repeatedly chasten an *infant* child would be considered a monster. God deals with us as *adult* sons because we have been adopted and given an adult standing in His family (see Rom. 8:14-18; Gal. 4:1-7). The fact that the Father chastens us is proof that we are maturing, and it is the means by which we can mature even more.

Chastening is the evidence of the Father's love. Satan wants us to believe that the difficulties of life are proof that God does *not* love us, but just the opposite is true. Sometimes God's chastening is seen in His *rebukes* from the Word or from circumstances. At other times He shows His love by *punishing* ("the Lord . . . scourgeth") us with some physical suffering. Whatever the experience, we can be sure that His chastening hand is controlled by His loving heart. The Father does not want us to be pampered babies; He wants us to become mature adult sons and daughters who can be trusted with the responsibilities of life.

**Personal experience (vv. 7-11).** All of us had a father and, if this father was faithful, he had to discipline us. If a child is left to himself, he grows up to become a selfish tyrant. The point the writer made (Heb. 12:7-8) is that a father chastens *only his own sons,* and this is proof that they *are* his children. We may feel like spanking the neighbors' children (and our neighbors may feel like spanking ours), but we cannot do it. God's chastening is proof that we are indeed His children!

I have met in my ministry people who professed to be saved, but for some reason they never experienced any chastening. If they disobeyed, they seemed to get away with it. If I resisted God's will and did not experience His loving chastening, I would be afraid that I was not saved! All true children of God receive His chastening. All others who claim to be saved, but who escape chastening, are nothing but counterfeits—illegitimate children.

Why do good earthly fathers correct their kids? So that their offspring might show them reverence (respect) and obey what they command. This is why the Heavenly Father corrects us: He wants us to reverence Him and obey His will. A child who does not learn subjection to authority will never become a useful, mature adult. Any of God's children who rebel against His authority are in danger of death! "Shall we not much rather be in subjection unto the Father of spirits, and live?" (Heb. 12:9) The suggestion is that, if we do not submit, *we might not live.* "There is a sin unto death" (1 John 5:16).

We can see now how this twelfth chapter relates to the five exhortations in Hebrews. As a Christian drifts from the Word and backslides, the Father chastens him to bring him back to the place of submission and obedience. (If God does not chasten, that person is not truly born again.) If a believer *persists* in resisting God's will, God may permit his life to be taken. Rather than allow His child to ruin his life further, and disgrace the Father's name, God might permit him to die. God killed thousands of rebellious Jews in the wilderness (1 Cor. 10:1-12). Why should He spare us? Certainly this kind of chastening is not His usual approach, but it is possible; and we had better show Him reverence and fear. He chastens us for our profit so that we might share His holy character.

**The blessed results (vv. 11-13).** No chastening at the time is pleasant either to the father or to his son, but the benefits are profitable. I am sure that few children believe it when their parents say, "This hurts me more that it hurts you." But it is true just the same. The Father does not enjoy having to discipline His children, but the benefits afterward make the chastening an evidence of His love.

What are some of the benefits? For one thing, there is "the peaceable fruit of righteousness." Instead of continuing to sin, the child strives to do what is right. There is also peace instead of war—"the peaceable fruit of righteousness." The rebellion has ceased and the child is in a loving fellowship with the Father. Chastening also encourages a child to *exercise* in spiritual matters—the Word of God, prayer, meditation, witnessing, etc. All of this leads to a new *joy.* Paul describes it: "righteousness and peace and joy in the Holy

Spirit" (Rom. 14:17).

Of course, the important thing is how God's child responds to chastening. He can despise it or faint under it (Heb. 12:5), both of which are wrong. He should show reverence to the Father by submitting to His will (Heb. 12:9), using the experience to exercise himself spiritually (Heb. 12:11; 1 Tim. 4:7-8). Hebrews 12:12-13 sound like a coach's orders to his team! Lift up your hands! Strengthen those knees! (Isa. 35:3) Get those lazy feet on the track! (Prov. 4:26) On your mark, get set, GO!

The example of God's Son, and the assurance of God's love, certainly should encourage us to endure in the difficult Christian race. But there is a third resource.

### The Enablement of God's Grace (Heb. 12:14-29)

As we run the Christian race, what is our goal? The writer explained the goal in Hebrews 12:14: *Peace* with all men, and *holiness* before the Lord. (Remember "the *peaceable* fruit of *righteousness,*" Heb. 12:11.) These two goals remind us of our Lord's high priestly ministry—King of *peace* and King of *righteousness* (Heb. 7:1-2). It requires diligence to run the race successfully lest we "fail of the grace of God" (Heb. 12:15). God's grace does not fail, but we can fail to take advantage of His grace. At the end of the chapter, there is another emphasis on grace (Heb. 12:28).

In this section, the writer encouraged his readers to depend on the grace of God by urging them to look by faith in three directions.

*Look back—the bad example of Esau (vv. 15-17).* Esau certainly failed to act on God's grace. The account is given in Genesis 25:27-34; 27:30-45. Esau was "a profane person," which means "a common person, one who lives for the world and not God." (Our English word literally means "outside the temple," or not belonging to God.) Esau despised his birthright and sold it to Jacob, and he missed the blessing because it was given to Jacob. (It was supposed to go to Jacob anyway, but it was wrong for Jacob to use trickery to get it. See Gen. 25:19-26.) Afterward, Esau tried to get Isaac to change his mind, but it was too late. Even Esau's tears availed nothing.

What sins will rob us of the enabling of God's grace? These verses tell us: lack of spiritual diligence, bitterness against others

(see Deut. 29:18), sexual immorality, and living for the world and the flesh. Some people have the idea that a "profane person" is blasphemous and filthy; but Esau was a congenial fellow, a good hunter, and a man who loved his father. He would have made a fine neighbor—but he was not interested in the things of God.

God's grace does not fail, but we can fail to depend on God's grace. Esau is a warning to us not to live for lesser things.

*Look up—the glory of the heavenly city (vv. 18-24).* The writer of Hebrews contrasts Mt. Sinai and the giving of the Law with the heavenly Mt. Zion and the blessings of grace in the church (see Ex. 19:10-25; 20:18-21; Deut. 4:10-24). He describes the solemnity and even the terror that were involved in the giving of the Law (Heb. 12:18-21). The people were afraid to hear God's voice, and even Moses feared and trembled! God set boundaries around the mount, and even if an animal trespassed, it was slain with a spear ("dart"). Of course, God had to impress on His people the seriousness of His Law, just as we must with our own children. This was the infancy of the nation, and children can understand reward and punishment.

What a relief it is to move from Mt. Sinai to Mt. Zion! Mt. Sinai represents the Old Covenant of Law, and Mt. Zion represents the New Covenant of grace in Jesus Christ (see Gal. 4:19-31). The heavenly city is God's Mt. Zion (see Pss. 2; 110:1-2, 4). This is the city that the patriarchs were looking for by faith (Heb. 11:10, 14-17). The earthly Jerusalem was about to be destroyed by the Romans, but the heavenly Jerusalem would endure forever.

He described the "citizens" that make up the population of this city. Innumerable angels are there. The church is there, for believers have their citizenship in heaven (Phil. 3:20) and their names are written in heaven (Luke 10:20). "Firstborn" is a title of dignity and rank. Esau was actually Isaac's firstborn, but he rejected his privileges and lost his blessing and birthright.

God is there, of course, and so are the Old Testament saints ("spirits of just men made perfect"). Jesus Christ the Mediator is there, the One who shed His blood for us. We learned that Abel is still speaking (Heb. 11:4); and here we discover that Christ's blood speaks "better things than that of Abel" (Heb. 12:24). Abel's blood spoke from the earth and cried for justice (Gen. 4:10), while Christ's blood speaks from heaven and announces mercy for sinners. Abel's blood made Cain feel guilty (and rightly so) and drove him away in despair (Gen. 4:13-15); but Christ's blood frees us from guilt and has opened the way into the presence of God. Were it not for the blood of the New Covenant, we could not enter this heavenly city!

"Why is there so little preaching and teaching about heaven?" a friend asked me. And then he gave his own answer, which is probably correct. "I guess we have it so good on earth, we just don't think about heaven."

When the days are difficult and we are having a hard time enduring, that is when we should look up and contemplate the glories of heaven. Moses "endured, as seeing Him who is invisible" (Heb. 11:27). The patriarchs endured as they looked ahead to the city God was preparing for them. One way to lay hold of God's grace is to look ahead by faith to the wonderful future He has prepared for us.

***Look ahead—the unshakable kingdom*** *(vv. 25-29).* God is speaking to us today through His Word and His providential workings in the world. We had better listen! If God shook things at Sinai and those who refused to hear were judged, how much more responsible are we today who have experienced the blessings of the New Covenant! God today *is* shaking things. (Have you read the newspapers lately?) He wants to tear down the "scaffolding" and reveal the unshakable realities that are eternal. Alas, too many people (including Christians) are building their lives on things that can shake.

The "shaking" quotation is from Haggai 2:6 and refers to that time when the Lord shall return and fill His house with glory. As events draw nearer to that time, we shall see more shaking in this world. But a Christian can be confident, for he shall receive an unshakable kingdom. In fact, he is a part of God's kingdom today.

What shall we do as we live in a shaking world? Listen to God speak and obey Him. Receive grace day by day to serve Him "with reverence and godly fear." Do not be distracted or frightened by the tremendous changes going on around you. Keep running the race with endurance. Keep looking to Jesus Christ. Remember that your Father loves you. And draw on God's enabling grace.

While others are being frightened, you can be confident!

# CHAPTER TWELVE
# PARDON ME, YOUR FAITH IS SHOWING
*Hebrews 13*

As you read this last chapter in Hebrews, you get the impression that the writer had a great deal of miscellaneous matter to discuss and saved it till the end. In Hebrews 12, we were rejoicing on Mt. Zion; and now we are discussing such everyday topics as hospitality, marriage, church officers, and who was the last one to be released from jail.

But in the Bible, there is no division between doctrine and duty, revelation and responsibility. The two always go together. The emphasis in this last section of the book is on *living by faith.* The writer presented the great *examples* of faith in Hebrews 11, and the *encouragements* to faith in Hebrews 12. In Hebrews 13, he presented the *evidences* of faith that should appear in our lives if we are really walking by faith and not by sight. There are four such evidences.

## Enjoying Spiritual Fellowship (Heb. 13:1-6)
The *basis* for this fellowship is brotherly love. As Christians, these Hebrew people no doubt had been rejected by their friends and families. But the deepest kind of fellowship is not based on race or family relationship; it is based on the spiritual life we have in Christ. A church fellowship based on anything other than love for Christ and for one another simply will not last. For other references to "brotherly love" see Romans 12:10; 1 Thessalonians 4:9-10; 1 Peter 1:22; and 2 Peter 1:7.

Where there is true Christian love, there will also be *hospitality* (Heb. 13:2). This was an important ministry in the early church because persecution drove many believers away from their homes. Also, there were traveling ministers who needed places to stay (3 John 5-8). Many poor saints could not afford to stay in an inn; and since the churches met in homes (Rom. 16:5), it was natural for a visitor to just stay with his host. Pastors are supposed to be lovers of hospitality (Titus 1:8); but all saints should be "given to hospitality" (Rom. 12:13).

Moses (Gen. 18) gives the story of Abraham showing generous hospitality to Jesus Christ and two of His angels. Abraham did not know who they were when he welcomed them; it was only later that he discovered the identities of his illustrious guests. You and I may not entertain angels in a literal sense (though it is possible); but *any* stranger could turn out to be a messenger of blessing to us. (The word "angel" simply means "messenger.") Often we have had guests in our home who have turned out to be messengers of God's blessings.

Love also expresses itself in *concern* (Heb. 13:3). It was not unusual for Christians to be arrested and imprisoned for their faith. To identify with these prisoners might be dangerous; yet Christ's love demanded a ministry to them. To minister to a Christian prisoner in the name of Christ is to minister to Christ Himself (Matt. 25:36, 40). In our free country we are not arrested for our religious beliefs; but in other parts of the world, believers suffer for their faith. How we need to pray for them and share with them as the Lord enables us!

*The home* is the first place where Christian love should be practiced (Heb. 13:4). A Christian home begins with a Christian marriage in the will of God. This means loyalty and purity. Sex outside of marriage is sinful and destructive. Sex within the protective bonds of marriage can be enriching and glorifying to God. Fornication is committed by unmarried persons and adultery by married persons. (However, in the New Testament, the term "fornication" can refer to many kinds of sexual sins. See Acts 15:20 and 1 Cor. 6:18.)

How does God judge fornicators and adulterers? Sometimes they are judged in their own bodies (Rom. 1:24-27). Certainly they will be judged at the final judgment (Rev. 21:8; 22:15). Believers who commit these sins certainly may be forgiven, but they will lose rewards in heaven (Eph. 5:5ff). David was forgiven, but he suffered the consequences of his adultery for years to come; and he suffered in the hardest way: through his own children.

In these days, when sexual sins are paraded as entertainment in movies and on television, the church needs to take a stand for the purity of the marriage bond. A dedicated Christian home is the nearest thing to heaven on earth, and it starts with a Christian marriage.

If we love God and others as we should, then we will have a right relationship to *material things* (Heb. 13:5-6). Times of suffering can either be times of selfishness or times of service. It is not easy to take "joyfully the spoiling of your goods" (Heb. 10:34). But with the economic and ecological problems in our world today, comfortable Christians may soon find themselves doing without some luxuries that they now consider necessities.

A Christian couple was ministering to believers in Eastern Europe, behind the Iron Curtain. The couple had brought in Christian literature, blankets, and other necessary items. At the church gathering, the couple assured the believers that Christians in America were praying for believers in Eastern Europe.

"We are happy for that," one believer replied, "but we feel that Christians in America need more prayer than we do, We here in Eastern Europe are suffering, but you in America are very comfortable; and it is always harder to be a good Christian when you are comfortable."

The word *covetousness* literally means "love of money"; but it can be applied to a love for *more* of anything. Someone asked millionaire Bernard Baruch, "How much money does it take for a rich man to be satisfied?" Baruch replied, "Just a million more than he has." Covetousness is the desire for more, whether we need it or not.

Contentment cannot come from material things, for they can never satisfy the heart. Only God can do that. "Watch out! Be on your guard against all kinds of greed; a man's life does not consist in the abundance of his possessions" (Luke 12:15, NIV). When we have God, we have all that we need. The material things of life can decay or be stolen, but *God* will never leave us or forsake us. This promise was made to Joshua when he succeeded Moses (Deut. 31:7-8; Josh. 1:5, 9); and it is fulfilled to us in Jesus Christ (Matt. 28:20; Acts 18:9-10).

The affirmation of faith in Hebrews 13:6 comes from Psalm 118:6. This is a messianic psalm and is fulfilled in Jesus Christ, so we may claim this promise for ourselves. It was a source of great peace to the early Christians to know that they were safe from the fear of man, for no man could do anything to them apart from God's will. Men might take their goods, but God would meet their needs.

A woman said to evangelist D.L. Moody, "I have found a promise that helps me when I am afraid. It is Psalm 56:3—'What time I am afraid, I will trust in Thee.' "

Mr. Moody replied, "I have a better promise than that! Isaiah 12:2—'I will trust and not be afraid.' "

Both promises are true and each has its own application. The important thing is that we know Jesus Christ as our Lord and Helper, and that we not put our trust in material things. Contented Christians are people with priorities, and material things are not high on their priority lists.

## Submitting to Spiritual Leadership (Heb. 13:7-9, 17, 24)

Three times the writer used the designation, "Them that have the rule over you." The phrase refers to the spiritual leaders of the local assemblies. The church is an organism, but it is also an organization. If an organism is not organized, it will die! Wherever Paul went, he founded local churches and ordained qualified believers to lead them (Acts 14:23; Titus 1:5). "Saints . . . bishops [elders], and deacons" (Phil. 1:1) summarize the membership and leadership of the New Testament churches.

Each Christian has three responsibilities toward the spiritual leaders in his local church.

*Remember them (vv. 7-9).* The word "remember" may suggest that these leaders were dead, perhaps martyred, and should not be forgotten. How easy it is to forget the courageous Christians of the past whose labors and sacrifices make it possible for us to minister today. But while we do not worship people or give them the glory, it is certainly right to honor them for their faithful work (1 Thes. 5:12-13).

These leaders probably had led the readers to Christ because the leaders had spoken the Word to them. When you recall that few Christians then had copies of the Scriptures, you can see the importance of this personal ministry of the Word. Today, we can read the Bible for ourselves, listen to radio or television sermons, and even listen to cassettes. We are in danger of taking the Word for granted.

The believers could no longer hear their departed leaders speak, but they could imitate their faith and consider its outcome, or "end." This could refer to their deaths, suggesting that some of them were martyred. However, I believe that "the outcome of their way of life" (Heb. 13:7, NASB) is given in Hebrews

13:8—"Jesus Christ, the same yesterday, and today, and forever." Their lives pointed to Christ! Church leaders may come and go, but Jesus Christ remains the same; and it is Christ who is the center of our faith.

After I had announced my resignation from a church I had been pastoring for several years, one of the members said to me, "I don't see how I'm going to make it without you! I depend so much on you for my spiritual help!"

My reply shocked him. "Then the sooner I leave, the sooner you can start depending on the Lord. Never build your life on any servant of God. Build your life on Jesus Christ. He never changes."

Of course, there is always the danger of being "carried about with divers [various] and strange doctrines" (Heb. 13:9). The purpose of spiritual ministry is to establish God's people in grace, so they will not be blown around by dangerous doctrines (Eph. 4:11-14). Some recipients of the Letter to the Hebrews were considering going back to Jewish laws that governed foods. The writer warned them that these dietary regulations would not profit them spiritually because they never profited the Jews spiritually! The dietary laws impressed people as being spiritual, but they were only shadows of the reality that we have in Christ (read Col. 2:16-23 carefully).

When local churches change pastors, there is a tendency also to change doctrines or doctrinal emphases. We must be careful not to go beyond the Word of God. We must also be careful not to change the spiritual foundation of the church. It is unfortunate that there is not more doctrinal preaching today because Bible doctrine is the source of strength and growth in the church.

*Obey them (v. 17).* When a servant of God is in the will of God, teaching the Word of God, the people of God should submit and obey. This does not mean that pastors should be dictators. "Neither [be] lords over God's heritage" (1 Peter 5:3). Some church members have a flippant attitude toward pastoral authority, and this is dangerous. One day every pastor will have to give an account of his ministry to the Lord, and he wants to be able to do it with joy. A disobedient Christian will find on that day that the results of disobedience are unprofitable, not for the pastor, but for himself.

Quite frankly, it is much easier to "win souls" than it is to "watch for souls" (see

Ezek. 3:16-21). The larger a church grows, the more difficult it becomes to care for the sheep. Sad to say, there are some ministers whose only work is to preach and "run the program"; they have no desire to minister to the souls placed in their care. Some are even "hirelings" who work only for money, and who run away when danger is near (John 10:11-14). However, when a shepherd is faithful to watch for souls, it is important that the sheep obey him.

**Greet them (v. 24).** The Jews used to greet each other with "Shalom—peace!" The Greeks often greeted one another with "Grace!" Paul combined these two and greeted the saints with, "Grace and peace be unto you!" (1 Cor. 1:3; 2 Cor. 1:2; and all his epistles except 1 and 2 Timothy and Titus. When Paul wrote to pastors, he greeted them with, "Grace, *mercy,* and peace." I wonder why?)

Of course, the writer of the Hebrew epistle was sending his personal greetings to the leaders of the church; but this is a good example for all of us to follow. *Every Christian should be on speaking terms with his pastor.* Never allow any "root of bitterness" to grow up in your heart (Heb. 12:15) because it will only poison you and hurt the whole church.

While it is true that each member of a local body has an important ministry to perform, it is also true that God has ordained spiritual leaders in the church. I have been privileged to preach in many churches in America, and I have noticed that where the people permit the pastors (elders) to lead, there is usually blessing and growth. I am not talking about high-handed, egotistical dictatorship, but true spiritual leadership. This is God's pattern for the church.

### Sharing in Spiritual Worship (Heb. 13:10-16, 18-19)

While it is true that a New Covenant Christian is not involved in the ceremonies and furnishings of an earthly tabernacle or temple, it is not true that he is deprived of the blessings that they typify. A Jew under the Old Covenant could point to the temple, but a Christian has a heavenly sanctuary that can never be destroyed. The Jews were proud of the city of Jerusalem; but a Christian has an eternal city, the New Jerusalem. For each of an Old Testament believer's temporary earthly items, a New Covenant believer has a heavenly and eternal counterpart.

"We have an altar" (Heb. 13:10) does not suggest a material altar on earth, for that would contradict the whole message of the epistle. In the Old Testament sanctuary, the brazen altar was the place for offering blood sacrifices, and the golden altar before the veil was the place for burning incense, a picture of prayer ascending to God (Ps. 141:2). A New Covenant Christian's altar is Jesus Christ; for it is *through Him* that we offer our "spiritual sacrifices" to God (Heb. 13:15; 1 Peter 2:5). We may set aside places in our church buildings and call them altars; but they are really not altars in the biblical sense. Why? Because Christ's sacrifice has already been made, once and for all; and the gifts that we bring to God are acceptable, not because of any earthly altar, but because of a heavenly altar, Jesus Christ.

The emphasis in this section is on separation from dead religion and identification with the Lord Jesus Christ in His reproach. The image comes from the Day of Atonement. The sin offering was taken outside the camp and burned completely (Lev. 16:27). Jesus Christ, our perfect sin offering, suffered and died "outside the gate" of Jerusalem. All true Christians must go out to Him, spiritually speaking, to the place of reproach and rejection. "Why stay in Jerusalem when it is not your city?" asked the writer. "Why identify with the Old Covenant Law when it has been done away with in Christ?"

The readers of this epistle were looking for a way to continue as Christians while escaping the persecution that would come from unbelieving Jews. "It cannot be done," the writer stated in so many words. "Jerusalem is doomed. Get out of the Jewish religious system and identify with the Saviour who died for you." There can be no room for compromise.

The writer named two of the "spiritual sacrifices" that we offer as Christians (Heb. 13:15-16). Note that the word "spiritual" is not in contrast to "material," because material gifts can be accepted as spiritual sacrifices (see Phil. 4:10-20). The word "spiritual" means "spiritual in character, to be used by the Spirit for spiritual purposes." A believer's body, presented to God, is a spiritual sacrifice (Rom. 12:1-2).

The first spiritual sacrifice is *continual praise to God* (Heb. 13:15). The words of praise from our lips, coming from our hearts, is like beautiful fruit laid on the altar. How easy it is for suffering saints to complain, but how important it is for them to give thanks to God.

The second spiritual sacrifice is *good works of sharing* (Heb. 13:16). This would certainly include the hospitality mentioned in Hebrews 13:2, as well as the ministry to prisoners in Hebrews 13:3. "Doing good" can cover a multitude of ministries: sharing food with the needy; transporting people to and from church or other places; sharing money; perhaps just being a helpful neighbor. I once had the privilege of seeing a man come to Christ because I helped him mow his lawn after his own mower broke.

Next the writer emphasizes the importance of *prayer* (Heb. 13:18-19). He was unable to visit the readers personally, but he did want their prayer help. It is possible that some of his enemies had lied about him, so he affirms his honesty and integrity. We do not know for certain who the writer was. Many think it was Paul. The reference to Timothy in Hebrews 13:23 would suggest Paul, as would also the "benediction of grace" in Hebrews 13:25 (see 2 Thes. 3:17-18). Some scholars have suggested that Peter referred to Paul's authorship of Hebrews (2 Peter 3:15-16); but that statement could also be applied to things Paul wrote in Romans. We do not know the name of the human writer of this book, nor is it important that we do.

## Experiencing Spiritual Lordship (Heb. 13:20-21)

This benediction seems to gather together the major themes of Hebrews: peace, the resurrected Christ, the blood, the covenant, spiritual perfection (maturity), God's work in the believer. As the Good Shepherd, Jesus Christ *died* for the sheep (John 10:11). As the Great Shepherd, He *lives* for the sheep in heaven today, working on their behalf. As the Chief Shepherd, He will *come for the sheep* at His return (1 Peter 5:4). Our Shepherd cares for His own in the past, present, and future. He is the same yesterday, today, and forever!

Our Great High Priest is also our Great Shepherd. When He was on earth, He worked *for* us when He completed the great work of redemption (John 17:4). Now that He is in heaven, He is working *in us* to mature us in His will and bring us to a place of spiritual perfection. We will never reach that place until He returns (1 John 2:28–3:3); but while we are waiting, we are told to continue to grow.

The phrase "make you perfect" (Heb.

13:21) is the translation of one Greek word, *katartidzo*. This is an unfamiliar word to us, but it was familiar to the people who received this letter. The doctors knew it because it meant "to set a broken bone." To fishermen it meant "to mend a broken net" (see Matt. 4:21). To sailors it meant "to outfit a ship for a voyage." To soldiers it meant "to equip an army for battle."

Our Saviour in heaven wants to equip us for life on earth. Tenderly, He wants to set the "broken bones" in our lives so that we might walk straight and run our life-races successfully. He wants to repair the breaks in the nets so that we might catch fish and win souls. He wants to equip us for battle and outfit us so that we will not be battered in the storms of life. In brief, He wants to mature us so that He can work *in* us and *through* us that which pleases Him and accomplishes His will.

How does He equip us? By tracing this word *katartidzo* in the New Testament, we can discover the tools that God uses to mature and equip His children. He uses the Word of God (2 Tim. 3:16-17) and prayer (1 Thes. 3:10) in the fellowship of the local church (Eph. 4:11-12). He also uses individual believers to equip us and mend us (Gal. 6:1). Finally, He uses suffering to perfect His children (1 Peter 5:10), and this relates to what we learned from Hebrews 12 about chastening.

What a difference it would make in our lives if we would turn Hebrews 13:20-21 into a personal prayer each day. "Lord, make me perfect in every good work to do Thy will. Work in me that which is well-pleasing in Thy sight. Do it through Jesus Christ and may He receive the glory."

The basis for this marvelous work is "the blood of the everlasting covenant" (Heb. 13:20). This is the New Covenant that was discussed in Hebrews 8, a covenant based on the sacrifice discussed in Hebrews 10. Because this New Covenant was a part of God's eternal plan of salvation, and because it guarantees everlasting life, it is called "the everlasting covenant." But apart from the death of Jesus Christ, we can share in none of the blessings named in this profound benediction.

The "Amen" at the end of the benediction closed the body of the epistle. All that remained was for the writer to add a few words of greeting and personal information.

He had written a long letter, and in it he had dealt with some profound and difficult doctrines; so he encouraged his readers to "bear with [suffer]" this letter of encouragement. This seems like a long letter to us, but he felt it was just a "few words." No doubt some members of the congregation responded negatively to this letter, while others received it and acted on it. Paul (1 Thes. 2:13) tells us how we should respond to God's Word. Read the verse carefully—and practice it.

What Timothy's relationship to the group was, we do not know. He was a prominent minister in that day and most of the Christians would either know him or know about him. These personal touches remind us that God is interested in individuals and not just in groups of people.

"They of Italy salute you" (Heb. 13:24) could mean that the writer was in Italy at the time, or that saints from Italy were with him and wanted to send their greetings.

These personal references at the end of the letter raise questions that we cannot answer now. But the total impact of Hebrews answers the important question, "How can I stand firm in a world that is shaking all around me?" The answer: know the superior Person, Jesus Christ; trust His superior priesthood; and live by the superior principle of faith. Build your life on the things of heaven that will never shake.

Be confident! Jesus Christ saves to the uttermost!

# JAMES

## OUTLINE

**Key theme:** Spiritual maturity
**Key verse:** James 1:4

The Marks of the Mature Christian:

**I. HE IS PATIENT IN TESTING—chapter 1**
  A. Trials on the outside—1:1-12
  B. Temptations on the inside—1:13-27

**II. HE PRACTICES THE TRUTH—chapter 2**
  A. Faith and love—2:1-13
  B. Faith and works—2:14-26

**III. HE HAS POWER OVER HIS TONGUE—chapter 3**
  A. Exhortation—3:1-2
  B. Illustrations—3:3-12
  C. Application—3:13-18

**IV. HE IS A PEACEMAKER, NOT A TROUBLEMAKER—chapter 4**
  A. Three wars—4:1-3
  B. Three enemies—4:4-7
  C. Three admonitions—4:8-17

**V. HE IS PRAYERFUL IN TROUBLES—chapter 5**
  A. Economic troubles—5:1-9
  B. Physical troubles—5:10-16
  C. National troubles—5:17-18
  D. Church troubles—5:19-20

## CONTENTS

# CHAPTER ONE
# TIME TO
# GROW UP
*James 1:1*

Beginning a study of a book of the Bible is something like preparing for a trip: you like to know where you are going and what you can expect to see. When my wife and I were getting ready for our first visit to Great Britain, we spent many hours reading travel books and poring over maps. When we arrived there, we enjoyed the visit much more because we knew what we were looking for and how to find it.

Perhaps the best way to launch a study of the Epistle of James is to answer four important questions.

**Who Was James?**
"James, a servant of God and of the Lord Jesus Christ" (James 1:1a) is the way he introduced himself. It was a popular name, a form of the great Old Testament name Jacob. There were several men who bore this name in New Testament history.

*James, the son of Zebedee and brother of John.* He was one of the most prominent to bear the name. He was a fisherman called by Christ to follow and become a disciple (Matt. 4:17-22). He and his brother John were nicknamed by Christ "sons of thunder" because of their impulsiveness (Mark 3:17; Luke 9:51-56). James was the first of the disciples to give his life for Christ. He was killed by Herod in A.D. 44 (Acts 12:1-2).

*James, the son of Alphaeus.* He was another of the disciples (Matt. 10:3; Acts 1:13), but very little is known about him. Matthew (Levi) is also identified as "the son of Alphaeus" (Mark 2:14), and some students conjecture that the two men might have been brothers. There is no indication that this James wrote the letter we are about to study.

*James, the father of Judas the disciple.* He is an even more obscure man (Luke 6:16, KJV, where "brother" ought to be "father"). This Judas was called "the son of James" to distinguish him from Judas Iscariot.

*James, the brother of our Lord.* He seems to be the most likely candidate for author of this letter. He does not identify himself

in this way; humbly, he calls himself "a servant of God and of the Lord Jesus Christ." That Jesus had brothers and sisters is stated in Matthew 13:55-56 and Mark 6:3, and one of His brothers was named James. (By "brother," of course, I mean half-brother. Joseph was not our Lord's father since He was conceived by the Holy Spirit of God.)

James and the other brothers did not believe in Jesus during His earthly ministry (Mark 3:31-35; John 7:1-5). Yet we find our Lord's brethren in the Upper Room praying with the disciples (Acts 1:14). What effected the change from unbelief to faith? First Corinthians 15:7 indicates that Jesus appeared to James after His resurrection! This convinced James that Jesus truly was the Saviour, and he, in turn, shared this knowledge about Jesus to the other brothers.

James became the leader of the church in Jerusalem. Paul called him "a pillar," in Galatians 2:9. It was James who moderated the church conference described in Acts 15. When Peter was delivered from prison, he sent a special message to James (Acts 12:17); and when Paul visited Jerusalem, it was to James that he brought greetings and the special "love offering" from the Gentiles (Acts 21:18-19).

We have no record in the Bible, but tradition tells us that James was martyred in A.D. 62. The story is that the Pharisees in Jerusalem so hated James' testimony for Christ that they had him cast down from the temple and then beaten to death with clubs. The story also relates that James died, as did his Saviour, praying for his murderers, "Father, forgive them, for they know not what they do."

What kind of a man was James? He must have been a deeply spiritual man to gain the leadership of the Jerusalem church in so short a time. His stature is seen in Acts 15, where he was able to permit all the factions to express themselves, and then bring peace by drawing a conclusion based on the Word of God. Paul, in 1 Corinthians 9:5, suggested that he was a married man. Again, tradition tells us that he was a man of prayer, and this explains the emphasis on prayer in his letter. It was said that he prayed so much, his knees were as hard as a camel's!

James was a Jew, reared in the tradition of the Law of Moses; and his Jewish legalism stands out in his letter. (Note also Acts 21:18ff, where James asked Paul to help him pacify the Christian legalists in the Jerusalem church.) There are over fifty imperatives in the Epistle of James. James did not suggest—he commanded! He quoted the Old Testament only five times, but there are many allusions to Old Testament passages in the letter.

While still an unbeliever, James must have paid attention to what Jesus taught; in his letter there are numerous allusions to our Lord's sayings, particularly the Sermon on the Mount. Compare these passages:

James 1:2—Matthew 5:10-12
James 1:4—Matthew 5:48
James 1:5—Matthew 7:7-12
James 1:22—Matthew 7:21-27
James 4:11-12—Matthew 7:1-5
James 5:1-3—Matthew 6:19-21

Keep in mind that James led the church in Jerusalem during a very difficult time. It was a time of transition, and such times are always upsetting and demanding. There were many Christian Jews in Jerusalem who still held to the Old Testament Law (Acts 21:20). The temple and its services were still in operation, and the full light of the Gospel of God's grace had not yet dawned. We who have read Romans, Galatians, and Hebrews might be prone to judge these early believers; but we must not. They were saved people, but they were still in the shadows of the Law, moving out into the bright light of God's grace. While there may have been differences in degrees of spiritual knowledge and experience, there was no competition between Paul and those who directed the Jerusalem church (Gal. 2:1-10).

### To Whom Did James Write?

"To the twelve tribes which are scattered abroad, greeting" (James 1:1b). James wrote to Jews living outside the land of Palestine. The term "twelve tribes" can only mean the people of Israel, the Jewish nation (Acts 26:7). The fact that many Jews lived outside their Promised Land is evidence of the spiritual decline of the nation. God had to scatter them (Deut. 4:25ff). When Peter addressed that huge Jewish congregation at Pentecost, he spoke to men from many different nations (Acts 2:9-11).

James sent his letter to *Christian* Jews. At least nineteen times he addressed them as "brethren," indicating not only "brothers in the flesh" (fellow Jews), but also "brothers in the Lord." James was very clear on the doctrine of the new birth (James 1:18). There are times when James also addressed wicked men who were not in the fellowship (the rich, for example, in James 5:1-6); but he did so in

order to teach and encourage the saved Jews to whom he sent the letter.

The word *scattered* in James 1:1 is an interesting one. It means "in the dispersion." The term *the dispersion* was used to identify the Jews living outside the land of Palestine. But the Greek word carries the idea of "scattering seed." When the Jewish believers were scattered in that first wave of persecution (Acts 8:1, 4), it was really the sowing of seed in many places; and much of that seed bore fruit (Acts 11:19ff).

Christian Jews scattered throughout the Roman Empire would have needs and problems of their own. Being Jews, they would be rejected by the Gentiles; and being *Christian* Jews, they would be rejected by their own countrymen. This letter indicates that most of these believers were poor, and some of them were being oppressed by the rich.

### Why Did James Write?

Each New Testament letter has its own special theme, purpose, and destination. Paul wrote the Book of Romans to prepare the Roman Christians for his intended visit. First Corinthians was sent to the church at Corinth to help correct certain problems. Galatians was written to a group of churches to warn them against legalism and false teaching.

As you read the Epistle of James, you discover that these Jewish Christians were having some problems in their personal lives and in their church fellowship. For one thing, they were going through difficult testings. They were also facing temptations to sin. Some of the believers were catering to the rich, while others were being robbed by the rich. Church members were competing for offices in the church, particularly teaching offices.

One of the major problems in the church was a failure on the part of many to live what they professed to believe. Furthermore, the tongue was a serious problem, even to the point of creating wars and divisions in the assembly. Worldliness was another problem. Some of the members were disobeying God's Word and were sick physically because of it; and some were straying away from the Lord and the church.

As we review this list of problems, does it appear to be much different from the problems that beset the average local church today? Do we not have in our churches people who are suffering for one reason or another? Do we not have members who talk one way, but walk another way? Is not worldliness a serious problem? Are there not Christians who cannot control their tongues? It seems that James is dealing with very up-to-date matters!

But James was not discussing an array of miscellaneous problems. All of these problems had a common cause: *spiritual immaturity.* These Christians simply were not growing up. This gives us a hint as to the basic theme of this letter: *the marks of maturity in the Christian life.* James used the word *perfect* several times, a word that means "mature, complete" (see James 1:4, 17, 25; 2:22; 3:2). By "a perfect man" (James 3:2) James did not mean a sinless man, but rather one who is mature, balanced, grown-up.

Spiritual maturity is one of the greatest needs in churches today. Too many churches are playpens for babies instead of workshops for adults. The members are not mature enough to eat the solid spiritual food that they need, so they have to be fed on milk (Heb. 5:11-14). Just look at the problems James dealt with and you can see that each of them is characteristic of little children:

Impatience in difficulties—1:1-4

Talking but not living the truth—2:14ff

No control of the tongue—3:1ff

Fighting and coveting—4:1ff

Collecting material "toys"—5:1ff

After over a quarter century of ministry, I am convinced that spiritual immaturity is the number one problem in our churches. God is looking for mature men and women to carry on His work, and sometimes all He can find are little children who cannot even get along with each other.

The five chapters of this letter suggest the five marks of the mature Christian (see outline).

Of course, this is but one approach to this letter; there are other ways to study it. As the chapters are examined, spiritual maturity and how it may be attained will be emphasized.

The Epistle of James logically follows the Epistle to the Hebrews, for one of the major themes of Hebrews is *spiritual perfection.* The word *perfect* is found in Hebrews at least fourteen times. The key verse is Hebrews 6:1— "Let us go on unto perfection" meaning, "spiritual maturity." The writer of Hebrews explained the perfect salvation to be had in Christ. James exhorted his readers to build on this perfect salvation and grow into maturity.

Without the perfect work of Christ there could be no perfecting of the believers.

## How Can We Get the Most Out of This Study?

Since the theme is spiritual maturity, we must begin by examining our own hearts to see where we are in the Christian life.

First of all, it is essential that we have been born again. Apart from spiritual birth there can be no spiritual maturity. James mentioned the new birth early in his letter: "Of His own will begat He us with the Word of truth" (James 1:18). The parallel to this is 1 Peter 1:23— "Being born again, not of corruptible seed, but of incorruptible, by the Word of God, which liveth and abideth forever."

Just as a human baby has two parents, so a spiritual baby has two parents—the Word of God and the Spirit of God. We have already quoted two verses that mention the Word of God. John 3:5-6 mentions the Spirit of God. (It is my conviction that "born of water" here refers to physical birth. All babies are "born of water." Nicodemus thought in terms of physical birth in John 3:5.)

How, then, is a person "born again"? The Spirit of God takes the Word of God and generates new life within the heart of the sinner who believes on Jesus Christ. It is a miracle. The Spirit uses the Word to convict the sinner, and then to reveal the Saviour. We are saved by faith (Eph. 2:8-9) and faith comes from the Word of God (Rom. 10:17).

If we have been born again, there is a second essential for getting the most out of what James has written: we must honestly examine our lives in the light of God's Word. James compares the Bible to a mirror (James 1:22ff). As we study the Word, we are looking into the divine mirror and seeing ourselves as we really are. But James warns us that we must be honest about what we see and not merely glance at the image and walk away.

Perhaps you heard about the primitive savage who looked into a mirror for the first time. He was so shocked at what he saw that he broke the mirror! Many Christians make the same mistake: they criticize the preacher or the lesson, when they ought to be judging themselves.

This leads to a third essential: we must obey what God teaches us, no matter what the cost. We must be "doers of the Word and not hearers only" (James 1:22). It is easy to attend a Bible study, share the lesson, and discuss it; but it is much more difficult to go out into life in the workaday world and practice what we have learned. The blessing does not come in *studying* the Word, but in *doing* the Word. Unless we are willing to obey, the Lord is not obligated to teach us (John 7:17).

The fourth essential is that we be prepared for some extra trials and testings. Whenever we are serious about spiritual growth, the enemy gets serious about opposing us. Perhaps you feel a need for more patience. Then be prepared for more trials, because "tribulation worketh patience" (Rom. 5:3). The real examinations in Bible study come in the school of life, not in the classroom.

I read recently about a man who was burdened to grow in his patience. He knew he was immature in that area of his life, and he wanted to grow up. He sincerely prayed, "Lord, help me to grow in patience. I want to have more self-control in this area of my life." That morning, he missed his train to work and spent the next fifty minutes pacing the platform and complaining of his plight. As the next train to the city arrived, the man realized how stupid he had been. "The Lord gave me nearly an hour to grow in my patience, and all I did was practice my impatience!" he said to himself.

There may come a time in this study when you decide that continuing is too dangerous. Satan may turn on the heat and make things so difficult for you that you will want to retreat. *Don't do it!* When that time arrives, you will be on the verge of a new and wonderful blessing in your own life, a thrilling new step of maturity. Even if Satan does turn on the heat, your Father in heaven keeps His almighty hand on the thermostat!

Even physical maturity is not always an easy, pleasant experience. The teenager walking that difficult bridge from childhood to adulthood has his frustrations and failures; but if he keeps on going (and growing), he eventually enters a wonderful life of maturity. Christian growth is not automatic, as is physical growth. Christian maturity is something we must work at constantly. So don't give up! There is travail in birth, and there is also travail in maturity (Gal. 4:19).

Finally, we must measure our spiritual growth by the Word of God. We should not measure ourselves by other Christians, but by the Word of God and the Son of God (Eph. 4:13). At the close of this book, a dozen questions are listed based on James, that may help

in a personal evaluation. Feel free to turn to them at any time, because regular examinations are good for spiritual health.

Not everyone who grows old, grows up. There is a difference between age and maturity. Just because a Christian has been saved for ten or twenty years does not guarantee that he is mature in the Lord. Mature Christians are happy Christians, useful Christians, Christians who help to encourage others and to build their local church. As we study James together, with God's help we will learn together and mature together.

# CHAPTER TWO
# TURNING TRIALS INTO TRIUMPHS
*James 1:2-12*

Perhaps you have seen the bumper sticker that reads: "When life hands you a lemon, make lemonade!" It is easier to smile at that statement than to practice it, but the basic philosophy is sound. In fact, it is biblical. Throughout the Bible are people who turned defeat into victory and trial into triumph. Instead of being victims, they became victors.

James tells us that we can have this same experience today. No matter what the trials may be on the outside (James 1:1-12) or the temptations on the inside (James 1:13-27), through faith in Christ we can experience victory. The result of this victory is spiritual maturity.

If we are going to turn trials into triumphs, we must obey four imperatives: *count* (James 1:2), *know* (James 1:3), *let* (James 1:4, 9-11), and *ask* (James 1:5-8). Or, to put it another way, there are four essentials for victory in trials: a joyful attitude, an understanding mind, a surrendered will, and a heart that wants to believe.

### Count—a Joyful Attitude (James 1:2)
Outlook determines outcome, and attitude determines action. God tells us to *expect trials*. It is not *"if* you fall into various testings" but *"when* you fall into various testings." The believer who expects his Christian life to be easy

is in for a shock. Jesus warned His disciples, "In the world ye shall have tribulation" (John 16:33). Paul told his converts that "we must through much tribulation enter into the kingdom of God" (Acts 14:22).

Because we are God's "scattered people" and not God's "sheltered people," we must experience trials. We cannot always expect everything to go our way. Some trials come simply because we are human—sickness, accidents, disappointments, even seeming tragedies. Other trials come because we are Christians. Peter emphasizes this in his first letter: "Beloved, think it not strange concerning the fiery trial which is to try you, as though some strange thing happened unto you" (1 Peter 4:12). Satan fights us, the world opposes us, and this makes for a life of battle.

The phrase "fall into" does not suggest a stupid accident. Translate it "encounter, come across." A Christian certainly should not manufacture trials. The Greek word translated "divers" means "various, varicolored." Peter uses the same word in 1 Peter 1:6—"Ye are in heaviness through manifold temptations." The trials of life are not all alike; they are like variegated yarn that the weaver uses to make a beautiful rug. God arranges and mixes the colors and experiences of life. The final product is a beautiful thing for His glory.

My wife and I once visited a world-famous weaver and watched his men and women work on the looms. I noticed that the undersides of the rugs were not very beautiful: the patterns were obscure and the loose ends of yarn dangled. "Don't judge the worker or the work by looking at the wrong side," our guide told us. In the same way, we are looking at the wrong side of life; only the Lord sees the finished pattern. Let's not judge Him or His work from what we see today. His work is not finished yet!

The key word is *count.* It is a financial term, and it means "to evaluate." Paul used it several times in Philippians 3. When Paul became a Christian, he evaluated his life and set new goals and priorities. Things that were once important to him became "garbage" in the light of his experience with Christ. When we face the trials of life, we must evaluate them in the light of what God is doing for us.

This explains why the dedicated Christian can have joy in the midst of trials: *he lives for the things that matter most.* Even our Lord was able to endure the cross because of "the joy that was set before Him" (Heb. 12:2), the

joy of returning to heaven and one day sharing His glory with His church.

Our values determine our evaluations. If we value comfort more than character, then trials will upset us. If we value the material and physical more than the spiritual, we will not be able to "count it all joy." If we live only for the present and forget the future, then trials will make us bitter, not better. Job had the right outlook when he said, "But He knoweth the way that I take: when He hath tried me, I shall come forth as gold" (Job 23:10).

So, when trials come, immediately give thanks to the Lord and adopt a joyful attitude. Do not pretend; do not try self-hypnosis; simply look at trials through the eyes of faith. Outlook determines outcome; to *end* with joy, *begin* with joy.

"But how," we may ask, "is it possible to rejoice in the midst of trials?" The second imperative explains this.

### Know—an Understanding Mind (James 1:3)

What do Christians know that makes it easier to face trials and benefit from them?

***Faith is always tested.*** When God called Abraham to live by faith, He tested him in order to increase his faith. God always tests us to bring out the *best;* Satan tempts us to bring out the worst. The testing of our faith proves that we are truly born again.

***Testing works for us, not against us.*** The word *trying* can be translated "approval." Again, Peter helps us understand it better: "That the trial of your faith, being much more precious than of gold that perisheth" (1 Peter 1:7). A gold prospector brings his ore sample into the assayer's office to be tested. The sample itself may not be worth more than a few dollars, but the *approval*—the official statement about the ore—is worth millions! It assures the prospector that he has a gold mine. God's approval of our faith is precious, because it assures us that our faith is genuine.

Trials work *for* the believer, not *against* him. Paul said, "And we know that all things work together for good" (Rom. 8:28); and, "For our light affliction, which is but for a moment, worketh for us a far more exceeding and eternal weight of glory" (2 Cor. 4:17).

***Trials rightly used help us to mature.*** What does God want to produce in our lives? Patience, endurance, and the ability to keep going when things are tough. "We glory in tribulations also: knowing that tribulation worketh patience; and patience, experience; and experience, hope" (Rom. 5:3-4). In the Bible, *patience* is not a passive acceptance of circumstances. It is a courageous perseverance in the face of suffering and difficulty.

Immature people are always impatient; mature people are patient and persistent. Impatience and unbelief usually go together, just as faith and patience do. "Be . . . followers of them who through faith and patience inherit the promises" (Heb. 6:12). "For ye have need of patience, that, after ye have done the will of God, ye might receive the promise" (Heb. 10:36). "He that believeth shall not make haste" (Isa. 28:16).

God wants to make us patient because that is the key to every other blessing. The little child who does not learn patience will not learn much of anything else. When the believer learns to wait on the Lord, then God can do great things for him. Abraham ran ahead of the Lord, married Hagar, and brought great sorrow into his home (Gen. 16). Moses ran ahead of God, murdered a man, and had to spend forty years with the sheep to learn patience (Ex. 2:11ff). Peter almost killed a man in his impatience (John 18:10-11).

The only way the Lord can develop patience and character in our lives is through trials. Endurance cannot be attained by reading a book (even this one), listening to a sermon, or even praying a prayer. We must go through the difficulties of life, trust God, and obey Him. The result will be patience and character. Knowing this, we can face trials joyfully. We know what trials will do in us and for us, and we know that the end result will bring glory to God.

This fact explains why studying the Bible helps us grow in patience (Rom. 15:4). As we read about Abraham, Joseph, Moses, David, and even our Lord, we realize that God has a purpose in trials. God fulfills His purposes as we trust Him. There is no substitute for an understanding mind. Satan can defeat the ignorant believer, but he cannot overcome the Christian who knows his Bible and understands the purposes of God.

## Let—a Surrendered Will
## (James 1:4, 9-12)

God cannot build our character without our cooperation. If we resist Him, then He chastens us into submission. But if we submit to Him, then He can accomplish His work. He is not satisfied with a halfway job. God wants a perfect work; He wants a finished product that is mature and complete.

God's goal for our lives is maturity. It would be a tragedy if our children remained little babies. We enjoy watching them mature, even though maturity brings dangers as well as delights. Many Christians shelter themselves from the trials of life, and as a result, never grow up. God wants the "little children" to become "young men," and the "young men" He wants to become "fathers" (1 John 2:12-14).

Paul outlined three works that are involved in a complete Christian life (Eph. 2:8-10). First, there is the work God does *for us,* which is salvation. Jesus Christ completed this work on the cross. If we trust Him, He will save us. Second, there is the work God does *in us:* "For we are His workmanship." This work is known as *sanctification:* God builds our character and we become more like Jesus Christ, "conformed to the image of His Son" (Rom. 8:29). The third work is what God does *through us*—service. We are "created in Christ Jesus unto good works."

God builds character before He calls to service. He must work *in* us before He can work *through* us. God spent twenty-five years working in Abraham before He could give him his promised son. God worked thirteen years in Joseph's life, putting him into "various testings" before He could put him on the throne of Egypt. He spent eighty years preparing Moses for forty years of service. Our Lord took three years training His disciples, building their character.

But God cannot work in us without our consent. There must be a surrendered will. The mature person does not argue with God's will; instead, he accepts it willingly and obeys it joyfully. "Doing the will of God from the heart" (Eph. 6:6). If we try to go through trials without surrendered wills, we will end up more like immature children than mature adults.

Jonah is an illustration of this. God commanded Jonah to preach to the Gentiles at Nineveh, and he refused. God chastened Jonah before the prophet accepted his commission. But Jonah did not obey God from the heart. He did not grow in this experience. How do we know? Because in the last chapter of Jonah, the prophet is acting like a spoiled child! He is sitting outside the city pouting, hoping that God will send judgment. He is impatient with the sun, the wind, the gourd, the worm, and with God.

One difficult stage of maturing is *weaning*. A child being weaned is sure that his mother no longer loves him and that everything is against him. Actually, weaning is a step toward maturity and liberty. It is good for the child! Sometimes God has to wean His children away from their childish toys and immature attitudes. David pictured this in Psalm 131: "Surely I have behaved and quieted myself, as a child that is weaned of his mother: my soul is even as a weaned child" (Ps. 131:2). God uses trials to wean us away from childish things; but if we do not surrender to Him, we will become even more immature.

In James 1:9-11, James applies this principle to two different kinds of Christians: the poor and the rich. Apparently, money and social status were real problems among these people (see James 2:1-7, 15-16; 4:1-3, 13-17; 5:1-8). *God's testings have a way of leveling us.* When testing comes to the poor man, he lets God have His way and rejoices that he possesses spiritual riches that cannot be taken from him. When testing comes to the rich man, he also lets God have His way, and he rejoices that his riches in Christ cannot wither or fade away. In other words, it is not your material resources that take you through the testings of life; it is your spiritual resources.

We have three imperatives from James so far: *count*—a joyful attitude; *know*—an understanding heart; *let*—a surrendered will. He gives a fourth.

**Ask—a Believing Heart (James 1:5-8)**
The people to whom James wrote had problems with their praying (James 4:1-3; 5:13-18). When we are going through God-ordained difficulties, what should we pray about? James gives the answer: ask God for *wisdom*.

James has a great deal to say about wisdom (James 1:5; 3:13-18). The Jewish people were lovers of wisdom, as the Book of Proverbs gives evidence. Someone has said that knowledge is the ability to take things apart, while wisdom is the ability to put them together. Wisdom is the right use of knowledge. All of us know people who are educated fools: they have brilliant academic records, but they cannot make the simplest decisions in life. I once met a gifted professor on a seminary campus, and he was wearing two hats!

Why do we need wisdom when we are going through trials? Why not ask for strength, or grace, or even deliverance? For this rea-

son: *we need wisdom so we will not waste the opportunities God is giving us to mature.* Wisdom helps us understand how to use these circumstances for our good and God's glory.

An associate of mine, a gifted secretary, was going through great trials. She had had a stroke, her husband had gone blind, and then he had to be taken to the hospital where (we were sure) he would die. I saw her in church one Sunday and assured her that I was praying for her.

"What are you asking God to do?" she asked, and her question startled me.

"I'm asking God to help you and strengthen you," I replied.

"I appreciate that," she said, "but pray about one more thing. Pray that I'll have the wisdom not to waste all of this!"

She knew the meaning of James 1:5.

James not only explained *what* to ask for (wisdom), but he also described *how* to ask. We are to ask in faith. We do not have to be afraid, for God is anxious to answer, and He will never scold us! "He giveth more grace" (James 4:6). He also gives more and more wisdom. The greatest enemy to answered prayer is unbelief.

James compares the doubting believer to the waves of the sea, up one minute and down the next. While vacationing in Hawaii, I learned that you cannot trust the waves. I was sitting on a rock by the ocean, watching the waves and enjoying the sunshine. I heard a sound behind me, turned to see who was approaching, and instantly was drenched by a huge wave! Never turn your back on the waves—they are down, then they are up.

This is the experience of the "double-minded man." Faith says, "Yes!" but unbelief says, "No!" Then doubt comes along and says "Yes!" one minute and "No!" the next. It was doubt that made Peter sink in the waves as he was walking to Jesus (Matt. 14:22-33). Jesus asked him, "O thou of little faith, wherefore didst thou doubt?" When Peter started his walk of faith, he kept his eyes on Christ. But when he was distracted by the wind and waves, he ceased to walk by faith; and he began to sink. He was double-minded, and he almost drowned.

Many Christians live like corks on the waves: up one minute, down the next; tossed back and forth. This kind of experience is evidence of immaturity. Paul used a similar idea in Ephesians 4:14—"That we henceforth be no more children, tossed to and fro, and carried about with every wind of doctrine, by the sleight of men, and cunning craftiness, whereby they lie in wait to deceive." If we have believing and united hearts, we can ask in faith and God will give the wisdom we need. Instability and immaturity go together.

James closed this section with a beatitude: "Blessed is the man that endureth temptation" (James 1:12). He started (James 1:2) and ended with joy. Outlook determines outcome. This beatitude is a great encouragement because it promises a crown to those who patiently endure trials. Paul often used athletic illustrations in his letters, and James does so here. He is not saying that the sinner is saved by enduring trials. He is saying that the believer is rewarded by enduring trials.

How is he rewarded? First, by growth in Christian character. This is more important than anything else. He is rewarded also by bringing glory to God and by being granted a crown of life when Jesus Christ returns. First the cross, then the crown. First the suffering, then the glory. God does not help us by removing the tests, but by making the tests work for us. Satan wants to use the tests to tear us down, but God uses them to build us up.

In James 1:12, James used a very important word, *love*. We would expect him to write, "the crown of life, which the Lord hath promised to them that trust Him" or "that obey Him." Why did James use *love?* Because love is the spiritual motivation behind every imperative in this section.

Why do we have a joyful attitude as we face trials? Because we love God, and He loves us, and He will not harm us. Why do we have an understanding mind? Because He loves us and has shared His truth with us, and we love Him in return. Why do we have a surrendered will? Because we love Him. Where there is love, there is surrender and obedience. Why do we have a believing heart? Because love and faith go together. When you love someone, you trust him, and you do not hesitate to ask him for help.

Love is the spiritual force behind the imperatives James gives us. If we love God, we will have no problem counting, knowing, letting, and asking. But there is another factor involved: love keeps us faithful to the Lord. The double-minded person (James 1:8) is like an unfaithful husband or wife: he wants to love both God and the world. James admonished, "Purify your hearts, ye double-minded!"

(James 4:8) The Greek word translated *purify* literally means "make chaste." The picture is that of an unfaithful lover.

Let's go back to the weaning. The child who loves his mother, and who is sure that his mother loves him, will be able to get through the weaning and start to grow up. The Christian who loves God, and who knows that God loves him, will not fall apart when God permits trials to come. *He is secure in God's love.* He is not double-minded, trying to love both God and the world. Lot was double-minded; when trials came, he failed miserably. Abraham was the friend of God; he loved God and trusted Him. When trials came, Abraham triumphed and matured in the faith.

God's purpose in trials is maturity. "Let patience have her perfect work, that ye may be perfect and entire, wanting nothing." The Charles B. Williams translation says it graphically: "But you must let your endurance come to its perfect product so that you may be fully developed and perfectly equipped."

If that is what you want, then in love to Christ, count, know, let, and ask.

# CHAPTER THREE
# HOW TO HANDLE TEMPTATION
*James 1:13-18*

The mature person is patient in trials. Sometimes the trials are testings on the outside, and sometimes they are temptations on the inside. Trials may be tests sent by God, or they may be temptations sent by Satan and encouraged by our own fallen nature. It is this second aspect of trials—temptations on the inside—that James dealt with in this section.

We may ask, "Why did James connect the two? What is the relationship between testings without and temptations within?" Simply this: if we are not careful, the testings on the outside may become temptations on the inside. When our circumstances are difficult, we may find ourselves complaining against God, questioning His love, and resisting His will. At this point, Satan provides us with an opportunity to escape the difficulty. This opportunity is a temptation.

There are many illustrations of this truth found in the Bible. Abraham arrived in Canaan and discovered a famine there. He was not able to care for his flocks and herds. This trial was an opportunity to prove God; but Abraham turned it into a temptation and went down to Egypt. God had to chasten Abraham to bring him back to the place of obedience and blessing.

While Israel was wandering in the wilderness, the nation often turned testings into temptations and tempted the Lord. No sooner had they been delivered from Egypt than their water supply vanished and they had to march for three days without water. When they did find water, it was so bitter they could not drink it. Immediately they began to murmur and blame God. They turned their testing into a temptation, and they failed.

Certainly, God does not want us to yield to temptation, yet neither can He spare us the experience of temptation. We are not God's *sheltered* people; we are God's *scattered* people. If we are to mature, we must face testings and temptations. There are three facts that we must consider if we are to overcome temptation.

## Consider God's Judgment (James 1:13-16)

This is a negative approach, but it is an important one. James said, "Look ahead and see where sin ends—death!" Do not blame God for temptation. He is too holy to be tempted, and He is too loving to tempt others. God does test us, as He did Abraham (Gen. 22); but He does not and cannot tempt us. It is we who turn occasions of testing into temptations.

A temptation is an opportunity to accomplish a good thing in a bad way, out of the will of God. Is it wrong to want to pass an examination? Of course not; but if you cheat to pass it, then you have sinned. The temptation to cheat is an opportunity to accomplish a good thing (passing the examination) in a bad way. It is not wrong to eat; but if you consider stealing the food, you are tempting yourself.

We think of sin as a single act, but God sees it as a process. Adam committed one act of sin, and yet that one act brought sin, death, and judgment on the whole human race. James described this process of sin in four stages.

*Desire (v. 14).* The word *lust* means any kind of desire, and not necessarily sexual passions. The normal desires of life were given to us by God and, of themselves, are not sinful. Without these desires, we could not function. Unless we felt hunger and thirst, we would never eat and drink, and we would die. Without fatigue, the body would never rest and would eventually wear out. Sex is a normal desire; without it the human race could not continue.

It is when we want to satisfy these desires in ways outside God's will that we get into trouble. Eating is normal; gluttony is sin. Sleep is normal; laziness is sin. "Marriage is honorable in all, and the bed undefiled; but whoremongers and adulterers God will judge" (Heb. 13:4).

Some people try to become "spiritual" by denying these normal desires, or by seeking to suppress them; but this only makes them less than human. These fundamental desires of life are the steam in the boiler that makes the machinery go. Turn off the steam and you have no power. Let the steam go its own way and you have destruction. The secret is in *constant control.* These desires must be our servants and not our masters; and this we can do through Jesus Christ.

*Deception (v. 14).* No temptation appears as temptation; it always seems more alluring than it really is. James used two illustrations from the world of sports to prove his point. *Drawn away* carries with it the idea of the baiting of a trap; and *enticed* in the original Greek means "to bait a hook." The hunter and the fisherman have to use bait to attract and catch their prey. No animal is deliberately going to step into a trap and no fish will knowingly bite at a naked hook. The idea is to *hide* the trap and the hook.

Temptation always carries with it some bait that appeals to our natural desires. The bait not only attracts us, but it also hides the fact that yielding to the desire will eventually bring sorrow and punishment. It is the bait that is the exciting thing. Lot would never have moved toward Sodom had he not seen the "well-watered plains of Jordan" (Gen. 13:10ff). When David looked on his neighbor's wife, he would never have committed adultery had he seen the tragic consequences: the death of a baby (Bathsheba's son), the murder of a brave soldier (Uriah), the violation of a daughter (Tamar). *The bait keeps us from seeing the consequences of sin.*

When Jesus was tempted by Satan, He always dealt with the temptation on the basis of the Word of God. Three times He said, "It is written." From the human point of view, turning stones into bread to satisfy hunger is a sensible thing to do; but not from God's point of view. When you know the Bible, you can detect the bait and deal with it decisively. This is what it means to walk by faith and not by sight.

**Disobedience (v. 15).** We have moved from the emotions (desire) and the *intellect* (deception) to the *will.* James changed the picture from hunting and fishing to the birth of a baby. Desire conceives a method for taking the bait. The will approves and acts; and the result is sin. Whether we feel it or not, we are hooked and trapped. The baby is born, and just wait until it matures!

Christian living is a matter of the will, not the feelings. I often hear believers say, "I don't feel like reading the Bible." Or, "I don't feel like attending prayer meeting." Children operate on the basis of feeling, but adults operate on the basis of will. *They act because it is right, no matter how they feel.* This explains why immature Christians easily fall into temptation: they let their feelings make the decisions. The more you exercise your will in saying a decisive no to temptation, the more God will take control of your life. "For it is God which worketh in you both to will and to do of His good pleasure" (Phil. 2:13).

**Death (v. 15).** Disobedience gives birth to death, not life. It may take years for the sin to mature, but when it does, the result will be death. If we will only believe God's Word and see this final tragedy, it will encourage us not to yield to temptation. God has erected this barrier because He loves us. "Have I any pleasure at all that the wicked should die?" (Ezek. 18:23)

These four stages in temptation and sin are perfectly depicted in the first sin recorded in the Bible in Genesis 3.

The serpent used *desire* to interest Eve: "For God doth know that in the day ye eat thereof, then your eyes shall be opened, and ye shall be as gods, knowing good and evil" (Gen. 3:5). Is there anything wrong with gaining knowledge? Is there anything wrong with eating food? Eve saw that "the tree was good for food" (Gen. 3:6), and her desire was aroused.

Paul described the deception of Eve in 2 Corinthians 11:3. "But I fear, lest by any means, as the serpent beguiled Eve through his subtlety, so your minds should be corrupted from the simplicity that is in Christ." Satan is the deceiver, and he seeks to deceive the mind. The bait that he used with Eve was the fact that the forbidden tree was good and pleasant, and that eating of it would make her wise. She saw the bait but forgot the Lord's warning: "In the day that thou eatest thereof thou shalt surely die" (Gen. 2:17).

Eve disobeyed God by taking the fruit of the tree and eating it. Then she shared it with her husband, and he disobeyed God. Because Adam was not deceived, but sinned with his eyes wide open, it is his sin that plunged the human race into tragedy (read Rom. 5:12-21; 1 Tim. 2:12-15).

Both Adam and Eve experienced immediate spiritual death (separation from God), and ultimate physical death. All men die because of Adam (1 Cor. 15:21-22). The person who dies without Jesus Christ will experience eternal death, the lake of fire (Rev. 20:11-15).

Whenever you are faced with temptation, get your eyes off the bait and look ahead to see the consequences of sin: *the judgment of God.* "For the wages of sin is death" (Rom. 6:23).

**Consider God's Goodness (James 1:17)**
One of the enemy's tricks is to convince us that our Father is holding out on us, that He does not really love us and care for us. When Satan approached Eve, he suggested that if God really loved her, He would permit her to eat of the forbidden tree. When Satan tempted Jesus, he raised the question of hunger. "If Your Father loves You, why are You hungry?"

The goodness of God is a great barrier against yielding to temptation. Since God is good, we do not need any other person (including Satan) to meet our needs. It is better to be hungry *in* the will of God than full *outside* the will of God. Once we start to doubt God's goodness, we will be attracted to Satan's offers; and the natural desires within will reach out for his bait. Moses warned Israel not to forget God's goodness when they began to enjoy the blessings of the Promised Land (Deut. 6:10-15). We need this warning today.

James presented four facts about the goodness of God.

***God gives only good gifts.*** Everything good in this world comes from God. If it did not come from God, it is not good. If it comes from God, it must be good, even if we do not see the goodness in it immediately. Paul's thorn in the flesh was given to him by God and it seemed to be a strange gift; yet it became a tremendous blessing to him (2 Cor. 12:1-10).

**The way God gives is good.** We can translate the second clause "and every act of giving." It is possible for someone to give us a gift in a manner that is less than loving. The value of a gift can be diminished by the way it is given to us. But when God gives us a blessing, He does it in a loving, gracious manner. *What* He gives and *how* He gives are both good.

**He gives constantly.** "Cometh down" is a present participle: "it keeps on coming down." God does not give occasionally; He gives constantly. Even when we do not see His gifts, He is sending them. How do we know this? Because He tells us so and we believe His Word.

**God does not change.** There are no shadows with the Father of Lights. It is impossible for God to change. He cannot change for the worse because He is holy; He cannot change for the better because He is already perfect. The light of the sun varies as the earth changes, but the sun itself is still shining. If shadows come between us and the Father, He did not cause them. He is the unchanging God. This means that we should never question His love or doubt His goodness when difficulties come or temptations appear.

If King David had remembered the goodness of the Lord, he would not have taken Bathsheba and committed those terrible sins. At least this is what Nathan the prophet told the king. "Thus saith the Lord God of Israel, 'I anointed thee king over Israel, and I delivered thee out of the hand of Saul; and I gave thee thy master's house, and thy master's wives into thy bosom, and gave thee the house of Israel and of Judah; and if that had been too little, I would moreover have given unto thee such and such things' " (2 Sam. 12:7-8). Note the repetition of the word *give* in this brief statement. God had been good to David, yet David forgot God's goodness and took the bait.

The first barrier against temptation is a negative one: the judgment of God. This second barrier is positive: the goodness of God. A fear of God is a healthy attitude, but the love of God must balance it. We can obey Him because He may chasten us; or we can obey Him because He has already been so generous to us, and because we love Him for it.

It was this positive attitude that helped to keep Joseph from sinning when he was tempted by his master's wife (Gen. 39:7ff). "Behold, with me around, my master does not concern himself with anything in the house, and he has put all that he owns in my charge. There is no one greater in this house than I, and he has withheld nothing from me except you, because you are his wife. How then could I do this great evil, and sin against God?" (Gen. 39:8-9, NASB) Joseph knew that all these blessings had come from God. It was the goodness of God, through the hands of his employer, that restrained him in the hour of temptation.

God's gifts are always better than Satan's bargains. Satan never gives any gifts, because you end up *paying for them dearly.* "It is the blessing of the Lord that makes rich, and He adds no sorrow to it" (Prov. 10:22, NASB). Achan forgot the warning of God and the goodness of God, saw the forbidden wealth, coveted it, and took it. He became rich, but the sorrow that followed turned his riches into poverty (Josh. 7).

The next time you are tempted, meditate on the goodness of God in your life. If you think you need something, wait on the Lord to provide it. Never toy with the devil's bait. One purpose for temptation is to teach us patience. David was tempted twice to kill King Saul and hasten his own coronation, but he resisted the temptation and waited for God's time.

### Consider God's Divine Nature Within (James 1:18)

In the first barrier, God says, "Look ahead and beware of judgment." In the second barrier, He says, "Look around and see how good I have been to you." But with this third barrier, God says, "Look within and realize that you have been born from above and possess the divine nature."

James used birth as a picture of desire leading to sin and death (James 1:15). He also used it to explain how we can enjoy victory over temptation and sin. The Apostle John used a similar approach in 1 John 3:9, where "his seed" refers to the divine life and nature within the believer. Note the characteristics of this birth.

**It is divine.** Nicodemus thought he had to

reenter his mother's womb to be born again, but he was wrong. This birth is not of the flesh: it is from above (John 3:1-7). It is the work of God. Just as we did not generate our own human birth, we cannot generate our own spiritual birth. When we put our faith in Jesus Christ, it was God who performed the miracle.

*It is gracious.* We did not earn it or deserve it; God gave us spiritual birth because of His own grace and will. "Which were born, not of blood [human descent], nor of the will of the flesh [human efforts], nor of the will of man [human assistance], but of God" (John 1:13). No one can be born again because of his relatives, his resolutions, or his religion. The new birth is the work of God.

*It is through God's Word.* Just as human birth requires two parents, so divine birth has two parents: the Word of God and the Spirit of God. "That which is born of the flesh is flesh; and that which is born of the Spirit is spirit" (John 3:6). "Being born again, not of corruptible seed, but of incorruptible, by the Word of God, which liveth and abideth forever" (1 Peter 1:23). The Spirit of God uses the Word of God to bring about the miracle of the new birth. Since the Word of God is "living and powerful" (Heb. 4:12) it can generate life in the heart of the sinner who trusts Christ; and that life is God's life.

*It is the finest birth possible.* We are "a kind of firstfruits of His creatures," James wrote to Jewish believers, and the word *firstfruits* would be meaningful to them. The Old Testament Jews brought the firstfruits to the Lord as the expression of their devotion and obedience. "Honor the Lord with thy substance, and with the firstfruits of all thine increase" (Prov. 3:9). Of all the creatures God has in this universe, Christians are the very highest and the finest! We share God's nature. For this reason, it is beneath our dignity to accept Satan's bait or to desire sinful things. A higher birth must mean a higher life.

By granting us a new birth, God declares that He cannot accept the old birth. Throughout the Bible, God rejects the firstborn and accepts the secondborn. He accepted Abel, not Cain; Isaac, not Ishmael; Jacob, not Esau. He rejects your first birth (no matter how noble it might have been in the eyes of men), and He announces that you need a second birth.

It is this experience of the new birth that helps us overcome temptation. If we let the old nature (from the first birth) take over, we will fail. We received our old nature (the flesh) from Adam, and he was a failure. But if we yield to the new nature, we will succeed; for that new nature comes from Christ, and He is the Victor.

A Sunday School child explained the matter in simple terms. "Two men live in my heart: the old Adam and Jesus. When temptation knocks at the door, somebody has to answer. If I let Adam answer, I will sin; *so I send Jesus to answer.* He always wins!"

Of course, this new nature must be fed the Word of God daily, that it might be strong to fight the battle. Just as the Holy Spirit used the Word of God to give you spiritual birth, He uses the Word to give you spiritual strength. "Man shall not live by bread alone, but by every word that proceedeth out of the mouth of God" (Matt. 4:4).

No matter what excuses we make, we have no one to blame for sin but ourselves. Our own desires lead us into temptation and sin. God is not to blame. But God has erected these three barriers to keep us from sin. If we heed the barriers, we will win a crown (James 1:12). If we break through the barriers, we will find a coffin (James 1:15). Which will it be?

# CHAPTER FOUR
# QUIT KIDDING YOURSELF
## *James 1:19-27*

The emphasis in this section is on the dangers of self-deception: "deceiving your own selves" (James 1:22); "deceiveth his own heart" (James 1:26). If a Christian sins because Satan deceives him, that is one thing. But if he deceives himself, that is a far more serious matter.

Many people are deceiving themselves into thinking they are saved when they are not. "Many will say to me in that day, 'Lord, Lord, have we not prophesied in Thy name? and in Thy name have cast out devils? and in Thy name done many wonderful works?' And then will I profess unto them, 'I never knew you:

depart from Me, ye that work iniquity.' " (Matt. 7:22-23).

But there are true believers who are fooling themselves concerning their Christian walk. They think they are spiritual when they are not. It is a mark of maturity when a person faces himself honestly, knows himself, and admits his needs. It is the immature person who pretends, "I am rich, and increased with goods, and have need of nothing" (Rev. 3:17).

Spiritual reality results from the proper relationship to God through His Word. God's Word is truth (John 17:17), and if we are rightly related to God's truth, we cannot be dishonest or hypocritical. In these verses, James stated that we have three responsibilities toward God's Word; and if we fulfill these responsibilities, we will have an honest walk with God and men.

## Receive the Word (James 1:19-21)

James calls God's Word "the engrafted word" (James 1:21), which means "the implanted word." Borrowing from our Lord's Parable of the Sower (Matt. 13:1-9, 18-23), he compares God's Word to seed and the human heart to soil. In His parable, Jesus described four kinds of hearts: *the hard heart,* which did not understand or receive the Word and therefore bore no fruit; *the shallow heart,* which was very emotional but had no depth, and bore no fruit; *the crowded heart,* which lacked repentance and permitted sin to crowd out the Word; and *the fruitful heart,* which received the Word, allowed it to take root, and produced a harvest of fruit.

The final test of salvation is fruit. This means a changed life, Christian character and conduct, and ministry to others in the glory of God. This fruit might be winning souls to Christ (Rom. 1:16), growing in holy living (Rom. 6:22), sharing our material possessions (Rom. 15:28), spiritual character (Gal. 5:22-23), good works (Col. 1:10), and even praising the Lord (Heb. 13:15). Religious works may be manufactured, but they do not have life in them, nor do they bring glory to God. Real fruit has in it the seed for more fruit, so that the harvest continues to grow fruit, more fruit, much fruit (John 15:1-5).

But the Word of God cannot work in our lives unless we receive it in the right way. Jesus not only said, "Take heed what ye hear" (Mark 4:24), but He also said, "Take heed how ye hear" (Luke 8:18). Too many people are in that tragic condition in which "hearing they hear not, neither do they understand" (Matt. 13:13). They attend Bible classes and church services but never seem to grow. Is it the fault of the teacher or the preacher? Perhaps, but it may also be the fault of the hearer. It is possible to be "dull of hearing" (Heb. 5:11) because of decay of the spiritual life.

If the seed of the Word is to be planted in our hearts, then we must obey the instructions James gives us.

*Swift to hear (v. 19a).* "Who hath ears to hear, let him hear!" (Matt. 13:9) "So then faith cometh by hearing, and hearing by the Word of God" (Rom. 10:17). Just as the servant is quick to hear his master's voice, and the mother to hear her baby's smallest cry, so the believer should be quick to hear what God has to say.

There is a beautiful illustration of this truth in the life of King David (2 Sam. 23:14-17). David was hiding from the Philistines who were in possession of Bethlehem. He yearned for a drink of the cool water from the well in Bethlehem, a well that he had often visited in his boyhood and youth. He did not issue an order to his men; he simply said to himself, "Oh, that one would give me drink of the water of the well of Bethlehem, which is by the gate" (2 Sam. 23:15). Three of his mighty men heard their king sigh for the water, and they risked their lives to secure the water and bring it to him. They were "swift to hear."

*Slow to speak (v. 19b).* We have two ears and one mouth, which ought to remind us to listen more than we speak. Too many times we argue with God's Word, if not audibly, at least in our hearts and minds. "He that refraineth his lips is wise" (Prov. 10:19). "He that hath knowledge spareth his words" (Prov. 17:27). Instead of being slow to speak, the lawyer in Luke 10:29 argued with Jesus by asking, "And who is my neighbor?" In the early church, the services were informal; and often the listeners would debate with the speaker. There were even fightings and wars among the brethren James was writing to (James 4:1).

*Slow to wrath (v. 19c).* Do not get angry at God or His Word. "He that is slow to wrath is of great understanding: but he that is hasty of spirit exalteth folly" (Prov. 14:29). When the Prophet Nathan told King David the story about "the stolen ewe lamb," the king became angry, but at the wrong person. "Thou art the man," said Nathan, and David then confessed, "I have sinned" (2 Sam. 12). In the Garden,

Peter was slow to hear, swift to speak, and swift to anger—and he almost killed a man with the sword. Many church fights are the result of short tempers and hasty words. There is a godly anger against sin (Eph. 4:26); and if we love the Lord, we must hate sin (Ps. 97:10). But man's anger does not produce God's righteousness (James 1:20). In fact, anger is just the opposite of the patience God wants to produce in our lives as we mature in Christ (James 1:3-4).

I once saw a poster that read, "Temper is such a valuable thing, it is a shame to lose it!" It is temper that helps to give steel its strength. The person who cannot get angry at sin does not have much strength to fight it. James warns us against getting angry at God's Word because it reveals our sins to us. Like the man who broke the mirror because he disliked the image in it, people rebel against God's Word because it tells the truth about them and their sinfulness.

*A prepared heart (v. 21).* James saw the human heart as a garden; if left to itself, the soil would produce only weeds. He urged us to "pull out the weeds" and prepare the soil for the "implanted Word of God." The phrase "superfluity of naughtiness" gives the picture of a garden overgrown with weeds that cannot be controlled. It is foolish to try to receive God's Word into an unprepared heart.

How do we prepare the soil of our hearts for God's Word? First, by confessing our sins and asking the Father to forgive us (1 John 1:9). Then, by meditating on God's love and grace and asking Him to "plow up" any hardness in our hearts, "Break up your fallow ground, and sow not among thorns" (Jer. 4:3). Finally, we must have an attitude of "meekness" (James 1:21). Meekness is the opposite of "wrath" in James 1:19-20. When you receive the Word with meekness, you accept it, do not argue with it, and honor it as the Word of God. You do not try to twist it to conform it to your thinking.

If we do not receive the implanted Word, then we are deceiving ourselves. Christians who like to argue various "points of view" may be only fooling themselves. They think that their "discussions" are promoting spiritual growth, when in reality they may only be cultivating the weeds.

**Practice the Word (James 1:22-25)**
It is not enough to hear the Word; we must do it. Many people have the mistaken idea that hearing a good sermon or Bible study is what makes them grow and get God's blessing. It is not the hearing but *the doing* that brings the blessing. Too many Christians mark their Bibles, but their Bibles never mark them! If you think you are spiritual because you hear the Word, then you are only kidding yourself.

In the previous paragraph, James compared the Word to seed; but in this paragraph, he compared it to a mirror. There are two other references in the Bible to God's Word as a mirror; and when you put all three together, you discover three ministries of the Word of God as a mirror.

*Examination (vv. 23-25).* This is the main purpose for owning a mirror, to be able to see yourself and make yourself look as clean and neat as possible. As we look into the mirror of God's Word, we see ourselves as we really are. James mentions several mistakes people make as they look into God's mirror.

First, *they merely glance at themselves.* They do not carefully study themselves as they read the Word. Many sincere believers read a chapter of the Bible each day, but it is only a religious exercise and they fail to profit from it personally. Their conscience would bother them if they did not have their daily reading, when actually their conscience should bother them *because they read the Word carelessly.* A cursory reading of the Bible will never reveal our deepest needs. It is the difference between a candid photo and an X ray.

The second mistake is that *they forget what they see.* If they were looking deeply enough into their hearts, what they would see would be unforgettable! We tend to smile at the "extremes" of people back in the days of the great revivals, but perhaps we could use some of that conviction. John Wesley wrote about a preaching service: "One before me dropped as dead, and presently a second, and a third. Five others sunk down in half an hour, most of whom were in violent agonies" *(Wesley's Journal* for June 22, 1739). Before we consign these people to some psychological limbo, remember how saints in the Bible responded to the true knowledge of their own hearts. Isaiah cried, "Woe is me! for I am undone!" (Isa. 6:5) Peter cried, "Depart from me, for I am a sinful man, O Lord!" (Luke 5:8) Job was the most righteous man on earth in his day, yet he confessed, "I abhor myself, and repent in dust and ashes" (Job 42:6).

Mistake number three is: *they fail to obey what the Word tells them to do.* They think that *hearing* is the same as *doing,* and it is not. We Christians enjoy substituting *reading* for *doing,* or even *talking* for *doing.* We hold endless committee meetings and conferences about topics like evangelism and church growth, and think we have made progress. While there is certainly nothing wrong with conferences and committee meetings, they are sinful if they are a substitute for service.

If we are to use God's mirror profitably, then we must gaze into it carefully and with serious intent (James 1:25). No quick glances will do. We must examine our own hearts and lives in the light of God's Word. This requires time, attention, and sincere devotion. Five minutes with God each day will never accomplish a deep spiritual examination.

I have been fortunate with the doctors who have cared for me through the years, and I owe a great deal to them. Each of them has possessed two qualities that I have appreciated: they have spent time with me and have not been in a hurry, and they have always told me the truth. When Jesus, the Great Physician (Matt. 9:12), examines us, He uses His Word; and He wants us to give Him sufficient time to do the job well. Perhaps one reason we glance into the Word instead of gaze into the Word is that we are afraid of what we might see.

After seeing ourselves, we must remember what we are and what God says, and we must *do the Word.* The blessing comes in the doing, not in the reading of the Word. "This man shall be blessed in his doing" (James 1:25, literal translation). The emphasis in James is on the practice of the Word. We are to *continue* after reading the Word (James 1:25; see Acts 1:14; 2:42, 46; 13:43; 14:22; 26:22 for examples of this in the early church).

Why does James call the Word of God "the perfect law of liberty"? (James 1:25) Because when we obey it, God sets us free. "And I will walk at liberty: for I seek Thy precepts" (Ps. 119:45). "Whosoever committeth sin is the servant of sin" (John 8:34). "If ye continue in My Word, then are ye My disciples indeed; and ye shall know the truth, and the truth shall make you free" (John 8:31-32).

But *examination* is but the first ministry of the mirror of the Word. There is a second ministry.

**Restoration (Ex. 38:8).** When he built the tabernacle, Moses took the metal looking glasses of the women and from them made the laver. The laver was a huge basin that stood between the brazen altar of sacrifice and the holy place. (Read Ex. 30:17-21 for details.) The basin was filled with water, and the priests washed their hands and feet at the laver before they entered the holy place to minister.

Water for washing is a picture of the Word of God in its cleansing power. "Now ye are clean through the Word which I have spoken unto you" (John 15:3). The church is sanctified and cleansed "with the washing of water by the Word" (Eph. 5:26). When the sinner trusts Christ, he is once and for all washed clean (1 Cor. 6:9-11; Titus 3:4-6). But as the believer walks in this world, his hands and feet are defiled, and he needs cleansing (John 13:1-11).

The mirror of the Word not only examines us and reveals our sins, but it helps to cleanse us as well. It gives us the promise of cleansing (1 John 1:9) and, as we meditate on it, it cleanses the heart and the mind from spiritual defilement. It is the blood of Christ that cleanses the guilt, but the water of the Word helps to wash away the defilement.

Nathan's experience with David in 2 Samuel 12 helps to illustrate this truth. Nathan told David the story about the stolen ewe lamb, and David became angry at the sin described. "Thou art the man," said the prophet, and he held up the mirror of the Word for David to see himself. The result was confession and repentance: "I have sinned against the Lord!" The mirror of the Word did its work of examination.

But Nathan did not stop there. He also used the Word for *restoration.* "The Lord also hath put away thy sin; thou shalt not die" (2 Sam. 12:13). Here was the assurance of forgiveness and cleansing, and it came from the Word. David visited the laver and washed his hands and feet.

If we stop with examination and restoration, we will miss the full benefit of the mirror ministry of the Word. There is a third ministry.

**Transformation (2 Cor. 3:18).** After the Lord restores us, He wants to change us so that we will grow in grace and not commit that sin again. Too many Christians confess their sins, and claim forgiveness, but never grow spiritually to conquer self and sin.

Second Corinthians 3 is a discussion of the contrasts between the Old Covenant ministry of Law and the New Covenant ministry of grace. The Law is external, written on tables of stone; but salvation means that God's Word is written on the heart. The Old Covenant ministry condemned and killed; but the New Covenant ministry brings forgiveness and life. The glory of the Law gradually disappeared, but the glory of God's grace becomes brighter and brighter. The Law was temporary, but the New Covenant of grace is eternal.

Paul's illustration of this truth is Moses and his veil. When Moses came down from the mount, where he met God, his face was shining (Ex. 34:29-35). He did not want the Jews to see this glory fading away, so he put on a veil to hide it. When he returned to the mount, he took off the veil. When Jesus died, He rent the veil in the temple and removed the veil between men and God. The Old Testament prophet wore a veil to hide the fading of the glory. The New Testament believer has an unveiled face, and the glory gets greater and greater!

You may explain 2 Corinthians 3:18 in this way: "When the child of God looks into the Word of God [the glass, the mirror], he sees the Son of God, and he is transformed by the Spirit of God to share in the glory of God!" The word *changed* in the Greek gives us our English word "metamorphosis"—a change on the outside that comes from the inside. When an ugly worm turns into a beautiful butterfly, this is metamorphosis. When a believer spends time looking into the Word and seeing Christ, he is transformed: the glory on the inside is revealed on the outside.

It is this word that is translated "transfigured" in Matthew 17:2. The glory of Christ on the mount was not reflected; it was radiated from within. You will find the same word in Romans 12:2, "Be ye transformed by the renewing of your mind." As we meditate on the Word, the Spirit renews the mind and reveals the glory of God. We do not become spiritual Christians overnight. It is a process, the work of the Spirit of God through the mirror of the Word of God.

The important thing is that we hide nothing. Take off the veil! "Search me, O God, and know my heart: try me, and know my thoughts: and see if there be any wicked way in me, and lead me in the way everlasting" (Ps. 139:23-24). "If we say that we have no sin, we deceive ourselves, and the truth is not in us" (1 John 1:8).

Our first responsibility is to receive the Word. Then, we must practice the Word; otherwise we are deceiving ourselves. This leads to a third responsibility.

## Share the Word (James 1:26-27)

The word translated "religion" means "the outward practice, the service of a god." It is used only five times in the entire New Testament (James 1:26-27; Acts 26:5; and Col. 2:18, where it is translated "worshiping"). Pure religion has nothing to do with ceremonies, temples, or special days. Pure religion means practicing God's Word and sharing it with others, through speech, service, and separation from the world.

*Speech (v. 26).* There are many references to speech in this letter, giving the impression that the tongue was a serious problem in the assembly (see James 1:19; 2:12; 3:1-3, 14-18; 4:11-12). It is the tongue that reveals the heart (Matt. 12:34-35); if the heart is right, the speech will be right. A controlled tongue means a controlled body (James 3:1ff).

*Service (v. 27a).* After we have seen ourselves and Christ in the mirror of the Word, we must see others and their needs. Isaiah first saw the Lord, then himself, and then the people to whom he would minister (Isa. 6:1-8). Words are no substitute for deeds of love (James 2:14-18; 1 John 3:11-18). God does not want us to pay for others to minister as a substitute for our own personal service!

*Separation from the world (v. 27b).* By "the world" James means "society without God." Satan is the prince of this world (John 14:30), and the lost are the children of this world (Luke 16:8). As the children of God, we are *in* the world physically but not *of* the world spiritually (John 17:11-16). We are sent *into* the world to win others to Christ (John 17:18). It is only as we maintain our separation from the world that we can serve others.

The world wants to "spot" the Christian and start to defile him. First, there is "friendship of the world" (James 4:4), which can lead to a love for the world (1 John 2:15-17). If we are not careful, we will become conformed to this world (Rom. 12:1-2), and the result is being condemned with the world (1 Cor. 11:32). This does not suggest that we lose our salvation, but that we lose all we have lived for. Lot is an illustration of this principle. First he pitched his tent toward Sodom, and then moved into Sodom. Before long, Sodom moved into him and he lost his testimony even with his own family. When judgment fell on

Sodom, Lot lost everything. It was Abraham, the separated believer, the friend of God, who had a greater ministry to the people than did Lot, the friend of the world. It is not necessary for the Christian to get involved with the world to have a ministry to the world. Jesus was "unspotted" (1 Peter 1:19), and yet He was the friend of publicans and sinners. The best way to minister to the needs of the world is to be pure from the defilement of the world.

# CHAPTER FIVE
# RICH MAN, POOR MAN
*James 2:1-13*

Not only is the mature Christian patient in testing (James 1), but he also practices the truth. This is the theme of James 2. Immature people talk about their beliefs, but the mature person lives his faith. Hearing God's Word (James 1:22-25) and talking about God's Word can never substitute for doing God's Word.

Every believer has some statement of faith or personal expression of what he believes. Most churches have such statements and members are asked to subscribe to the statement and practice it. Most churches also have a "covenant" that they read publicly, often when they observe the Lord's Supper. Statements of faith and church covenants are good and useful, but they are not substitutes for doing God's will. As a pastor, I have heard believers read the church covenant and then come to a business meeting and act in ways completely contrary to the covenant.

James wanted to help us practice God's Word, so he gave us a simple test. He sent two visitors to a church service, a rich man and a poor man; and he watched to see how they were treated. *The way we behave toward people indicates what we really believe about God!* We cannot—and dare not—separate *human* relationships from *divine* fellowship. "If a man say, 'I love God,' and hateth his brother, he is a liar: for he that loveth not his brother whom he hath seen, how can he love God whom he hath not seen?" (1 John 4:20)

In this section, James examines four basic Christian doctrines in the light of the way we treat other people.

## The Deity of Christ (James 2:1-4)

"My brothers, don't hold the faith of our Lord Jesus Christ, the Lord of Glory, by showing favoritism" (literal translation). Jewish people in that day coveted recognition and honor, and vied with one another for praise. Our Lord's parables in Luke 14:7-14 deal with the problem, and also His denunciation of the Pharisees in Matthew 23.

We have this same problem with us today. Pyramid climbers are among us, not only in politics, industry, and society, but also in the church. Almost every church has its cliques, and often, new Christians find it difficult to get in. Some church members use their offices to enhance their own images of importance. Many of the believers James wrote to were trying to seize spiritual offices, and James had to warn them (James 3:1).

*Jesus did not respect persons.* Even His enemies admitted, "You aren't swayed by men, because You pay no attention to who they are" (Matt. 22:16, NIV). Our Lord did not look at the outward appearance; He looked at the heart. He was not impressed with riches or social status. The poor widow who gave her mite was greater in His eyes than the rich Pharisee who boastfully gave his large donation. Furthermore, He saw the potential in the lives of sinners. In Simon, He saw a rock. In Matthew, the publican, He saw a faithful disciple who would one day write one of the four Gospels. The disciples were amazed to see Jesus talking with the sinful woman at the well of Sychar, but Jesus saw in her an instrument for reaping a great harvest.

We are prone to judge people by their past, not their future. When Saul of Tarsus was converted, the church in Jerusalem was afraid to receive him! It took Barnabas, who believed in Saul's conversion, to break down the walls (Acts 9:26-28). We are also prone to judge by outward appearance rather than by the inner attitude of the heart. We do not enjoy sitting with certain people in church because they "are not our kind of people." Jesus was the Friend of sinners, though He disapproved of their sins. It was not compromise, but compassion, that caused Him to welcome them, and when they trusted Him, forgive them.

*Jesus was despised and rejected.* This fact was prophesied in Isaiah 53:1-3. He was "the poor man" who was rejected by the self-righteous nation. Unlike the foxes and the birds, He had no home. He grew up in the despised city of Nazareth in a home that knew the feeling of poverty. Had you and I met Him while He was ministering on earth, we would have seen nothing physically or materially that would attract us.

Yet, *He is the very glory of God!* In the Old Testament, God's glory dwelled first in the tabernacle (Ex. 40:34-38), and then in the temple (1 Kings 8:10-11). When Jesus came to earth, God's glory resided in Him (John 1:14). Today, the glory of God dwells in the believer individually (1 Cor. 6:19-20), and the church collectively (Eph. 2:21-22).

The religious experts in Christ's day judged Him by their human standards, and they rejected Him. He came from the wrong city, Nazareth of Galilee. He was not a graduate of their accepted schools. He did not have the official approval of the people in power. He had no wealth. His followers were a nondescript mob and included publicans and sinners. *Yet He was the very glory of God!* No wonder Jesus warned the religious leaders, "Stop judging by mere appearances, and make a right judgment" (John 7:24, NIV).

Sad to say, we often make the same mistakes. When visitors come into our churches, we tend to judge them on what we see outwardly rather than what they are inwardly. Dress, color of skin, fashion, and other superficial things carry more weight than the fruit of the Spirit that may be manifest in their lives. We cater to the rich because we hope to get something out of them, and we avoid the poor because they embarrass us. Jesus did not do this, and He cannot approve of it.

How do we practice the deity of Christ in our human relationships? It is really quite simple: *look at everyone through the eyes of Christ.* If the visitor is a Christian, we can accept him because *Christ lives in him.* If he is not a Christian, we can receive him because *Christ died for him.* It is Christ who is the link between us and others, and He is a link of love. The basis for relationship with others is the person and work of Jesus Christ. Any other basis is not going to work. Furthermore, God can use even the most unlikely person to bring glory to His name. He used Peter and Zaccheus and John Mark, and He can use that poor man whom we might reject.

## The Grace of God (James 2:5-7)

The emphasis here is on God's *choosing,* and this involves the grace of God. If salvation were on the basis of merit, it would not be by grace. Grace implies God's sovereign choice of those who cannot earn and do not deserve His salvation (Eph. 1:4-7; 2:8-10). God saves us completely on the basis of the work of Christ on the cross and not because of anything that we are or have.

God ignores *national* differences (Acts 10:34). The Jewish believers were shocked when Peter went to the Gentile household of Cornelius, preached to the Gentiles, and even ate with them. The topic of the first church council was, "Must a Gentile become a Jew to become a Christian?" (Acts 15) The answer the Holy Spirit gave them was, "No!" In the sight of God, there is no difference between Jew and Gentile when it comes to condemnation (Rom. 2:6-16) or salvation (Rom. 10:1-13).

God also ignores *social* differences. Masters and slaves (Eph. 6:9) and rich and poor are alike to Him. James teaches us that the grace of God makes the rich man poor, because he cannot depend on his wealth; and it makes the poor man rich, because he inherits the riches of grace in Christ. (Review James 1:9-11.) "The Lord maketh poor, and maketh rich: He bringeth low, and lifteth up. He raiseth up the poor out of the dust, and lifteth up the beggar from the dunghill, to set them among princes, and to make them inherit the throne of glory" (1 Sam. 2:7-8).

From the human point of view, God chooses the poor instead of the rich. "For ye see your calling, brethren, how that not many wise men after the flesh, not many mighty, not many noble, are called: but God hath chosen the foolish things of the world to confound the wise; and God hath chosen the weak things of the world to confound the things which are mighty" (1 Cor. 1:26-27). The poor of this world become rich in faith; as sons of God, they inherit the wealth of the kingdom.

It is possible to be poor in this world and rich in the next, or rich in this world and poor in the next (1 Tim. 6:17-18). Or, you could be poor both in this world and the next, or rich in this world and the next. It all depends on what you do with Christ and the material wealth He has given you. God promises the kingdom to "those that love Him" (James 2:5), not to those who love this world and its riches.

James gave a stern rebuke in James 2:6-7.

"When you despise the poor man, you are behaving like the unsaved rich people." In that day, it was easy for rich persons to exploit the poor, influence decisions at court, and make themselves richer. Unfortunately, we have the same sins being committed today; and these sins blaspheme the very name of Christ. Our Lord was poor, and He too was the victim of injustice perpetrated by the wealthy leaders of His day.

The doctrine of God's grace, if we really believe it, forces us to relate to people on the basis of God's plan and not on the basis of human merit or social status. A "class church" is not a church that magnifies the grace of God. When He died, Jesus broke down the wall that separated Jews and Gentiles (Eph. 2:11-22). But in His birth and life, Jesus broke down the walls between rich and poor, young and old, educated and uneducated. It is wrong for us to build those walls again; we cannot rebuild them if we believe in the grace of God.

### The Word of God (James 2:8-11)

In recent years, believers have waged battles over the inspiration and authority of the Word of God. Certainly, it is a good thing to defend the truth of God's Word, but we must never forget that *our lives and ministries are the best defense.* D.L. Moody often said, "Every Bible should be bound in shoe leather!"

James reached back into the Old Testament for one of God's laws, "Thou shalt love thy neighbor as thyself" (Lev. 19:18). In His Parable of the Good Samaritan, Jesus told us that our neighbor is anyone who needs our help (Luke 10:25-37). It is not a matter of geography, but opportunity. The important question is not, "Who is my neighbor?" but "To whom can I be a neighbor?"

Why is "love thy neighbor" called "the royal law"? For one thing, it was given by the King. God the Father gave it in the Law, and God the Son reaffirmed it to His disciples (John 13:34). God the Spirit fills our hearts with God's love and expects us to share it with others (Rom. 5:5). True believers are "taught of God to love one another" (1 Thes. 4:9).

But "love thy neighbor" is the royal law for a second reason: *it rules all the other laws.* "Love is the fulfilling of the Law" (Rom. 13:10). There would be no need for the thousands of complex laws if each citizen truly loved his neighbors.

But the main reason why this is the royal law is that *obeying it makes you a king.* Hatred makes a person a slave, but love sets us free from selfishness and enables us to reign like kings. Love enables us to obey the Word of God and treat people as God commands us to do. We obey His Law, not out of fear, but out of love.

Showing respect of persons can lead a person into disobeying all of God's Law. Take any of the Ten Commandments and you will find ways of breaking it if you respect a person's social or financial status. Respect of persons could make you lie, for example. It could lead to idolatry (getting money out of the rich), or even mistreatment of one's parents. Once we start acting on the basis of respecting persons and rejecting God's Word, we are heading for trouble. And we need not break *all* of God's Law to be guilty. There is only one Lawgiver, and all of His Laws are from His mind and heart. If I disobey one law, I am capable of disobeying all of them; and by rebelling, I have already done so.

Christian love does not mean that I must *like* a person and agree with him on everything. I may not like his vocabulary or his habits, and I may not want him for an intimate friend. *Christian love means treating others the way God has treated me.* It is an act of the will, not an emotion that I try to manufacture. The motive is to glorify God. The means is the power of the Spirit within ("for the fruit of the Spirit is love"). As I act in love toward another, I may find myself drawn more and more to him, and I may see in him (through Christ) qualities that before were hidden to me.

Also, Christian love does not leave the person where it finds him. Love should help the poor man do better; love should help the rich man make better use of his God-given resources. Love always builds up (1 Cor. 8:1); hatred always tears down.

We only believe as much of the Bible as we practice. If we fail to obey the most important word—"love thy neighbor as thyself"—then we will not do any good with the lesser matters of the Word. It was a glaring fault in the Pharisees that they were careful about the minor matters and careless about the fundamentals (Matt. 23:23). They broke the very Law they thought they were defending!

### The Judgment of God (James 2:12-13)

Every orthodox statement of faith ends with a statement about the return of Jesus Christ and the final judgment. Not all Christians agree as to the details of these future events, but the certainty of them none denies. Nor would any deny the importance of a final judgment. Both Jesus (John 5:24) and Paul (Rom. 8:1) assured us that Christian believers will never be judged for their sins; but our works will be judged and rewarded (Rom. 14:10-13; 2 Cor. 5:9-10).

**Our words will be judged.** Note the words spoken to the two visitors in James 2:3. What we say to people, and how we say it, will come up before God. Even our careless words will be judged (Matt. 12:36). Of course, the words we speak come from the heart; so when God judges the words, He is examining the heart (Matt. 12:34-37). Jesus emphasized caution when speaking in some of His warnings in the Sermon on the Mount (Matt. 5:21-26, 33-37; 7:1-5, 21-23).

**Our deeds will be judged.** Read Colossians 3:22-25 for additional insight. It is true that God remembers our sins against us no more (Jer. 31:34; Heb. 10:17); *but our sins affect our character and works.* We cannot sin lightly and serve faithfully. God forgives our sins when we confess them to Him, but He cannot change their consequences.

**Our attitudes will be judged (v. 13).** James contrasted two attitudes: showing mercy to others, and refusing to show mercy. If we have been merciful toward others, God can be merciful toward us. However, we must not twist this truth into a lie. It does not mean that we *earn* mercy by showing mercy, because it is impossible to earn mercy. If it is earned, it is not mercy! Nor does it mean that we should "be soft on sin" and never judge it in the lives of others. "I don't condemn anybody," a man once told me, "and God won't condemn me." How wrong he was!

Mercy and justice both come from God, so they are not competitors. Where God finds repentance and faith, He is able to show mercy; where He finds rebellion and unbelief, He must administer justice. It is the heart of the sinner that determines the treatment he gets. Our Lord's parable in Matthew 18:21-35 illustrates the truth. The parable is not illustrating salvation, but forgiveness between fellow servants. If we forgive our brothers, then we have the kind of heart that is open toward the forgiveness of God.

We shall be judged "by the Law of liberty." Why does James use this title for God's Law? For one thing, when we obey God's Law, it frees us from sin and enables us to walk in liberty (Ps. 119:45). Also, *law prepares us for*

*liberty.* A child must be under rules and regulations because he is not mature enough to handle the decisions and demands of life. He is given *outward discipline* so that he might develop *inward discipline,* and one day be free of rules.

Liberty does not mean license. License (doing whatever I want to do) is the worst kind of bondage. Liberty means the freedom to be all that I can be in Jesus Christ. License is confinement; liberty is fulfillment.

Finally, the Word is called "the Law of liberty" because God sees our hearts and knows what we would have done had we been free to do so. The Christian student who obeys only because the school has rules is not really maturing. What will he do when he leaves the school? God's Word can change our hearts and give us the desire to do God's will, so that we obey from inward compulsion and not outward constraint.

There is one obvious message to this section: our beliefs should control our behavior. If we really believe that Jesus is the Son of God, and that God is gracious, His Word is true, and one day He will judge us, then our conduct will reveal our convictions. Before we attack those who do not have orthodox doctrine, we must be sure that we practice the doctrines we defend. Jonah had wonderful theology, but he hated people and was angry with God (Jonah 4).

One of the tests of the reality of our faith is how we treat other people. Can we pass the test?

# CHAPTER SIX
# FALSE FAITH
*James 2:14-26*

Faith is a key doctrine in the Christian life. The sinner is saved by faith (Eph. 2:8-9), and the believer must walk by faith (2 Cor. 5:7). Without faith it is impossible to please God (Heb. 11:6); and whatever we do apart from faith is sin (Rom. 14:23).

Someone has said that faith is not "believing in spite of evidence, but obeying in spite of consequence." When you read Hebrews 11, you meet men and women who acted on

God's Word, no matter what price they had to pay. Faith is not some kind of nebulous feeling that we work up; faith is confidence that God's Word is true, and conviction that acting on that Word will bring His blessing.

In this paragraph, James discussed the relationship between faith and works. This is an important discussion, for if we are wrong in this matter, we jeopardize our eternal salvation. What kind of faith really saves a person? Is it necessary to perform good works in order to be saved? How can a person tell whether or not he is exercising true saving faith? James answers these questions by explaining to us that there are three kinds of faith, only one of which is true saving faith.

## Dead Faith (James 2:14-17)

Even in the early church there were those who claimed they had saving faith, yet did not possess salvation. Wherever there is the true, you will find the counterfeit. Jesus warned, "Not every one that saith unto Me, 'Lord, Lord,' shall enter into the kingdom of heaven; but he that doeth the will of My Father which is in heaven" (Matt. 7:21).

People with dead faith substitute words for deeds. They know the correct vocabulary for prayer and testimony, and can even quote the right verses from the Bible; but their walk does not measure up to their talk. They think that their words are as good as works, and they are wrong.

James gave a simple illustration. A poor believer came into a fellowship, without proper clothing and in need of food. The person with dead faith noticed the visitor and saw his needs, but he did not do anything to meet the needs. All he did was say a few pious words! "Go, I wish you well; keep warm and well fed" (James 2:16, NIV). But the visitor went away just as hungry and naked as he came in!

Food and clothing are basic needs of every human being, whether he is saved or unsaved. "And having food and raiment let us be therewith content" (1 Tim. 6:8). "Therefore take no thought, saying, 'What shall we eat?' or, 'What shall we drink?' or, 'Wherewithal shall we be clothed?' . . . for your Heavenly Father knoweth that ye have need of all these things" (Matt. 6:31-32). Jacob included these basic needs in his prayer to God: "If God will be with me . . . and will give me bread to eat, and raiment to put on" (Gen. 28:20).

As believers, we have an obligation to help meet the needs of people, no matter who they may be. "As we have therefore opportunity, let us do good unto all men, especially unto them who are of the household of faith" (Gal. 6:10). "Inasmuch as ye have done it unto one of the least of these My brethren, ye have done it unto Me" (Matt. 25:40).

To help a person in need is an expression of love, and faith works by love (Gal. 5:6). The Apostle John emphasized this aspect of good works. "If anyone has material possessions and sees his brother in need but has no pity on him, how can the love of God be in him? Dear children, let us not love with words or tongue but with actions and truth" (1 John 3:17-18, NIV). The priest and Levite in the Parable of the Good Samaritan each had religious training, but neither of them paused to assist the dying man at the side of the road (Luke 10:25-37). Each of them would *defend* his faith, yet neither *demonstrated* that faith in loving works.

The question in James 2:14 should read, "Can *that kind of faith* save him?" What kind? The kind of faith that is never seen in practical works. The answer is no! Any declaration of faith that does not result in a changed life and good works is a false declaration. That kind of faith is dead faith. "Even so faith, if it hath not works, is dead, being alone" (James 2:17). The great theologian, John Calvin, wrote, "It is faith alone that justifies, but faith that justifies can never be alone." The word *alone* in James 2:17 simply means "by itself." True saving faith can never be by itself: it always brings life, and life produces good works.

The person with dead faith has only an intellectual experience. In his mind, he knows the doctrines of salvation, but he has never submitted himself to God and trusted Christ for salvation. He knows the right words, but he does not back up his words with his works. Faith in Christ brings life (John 3:16), and where there is life there must be growth and fruit. Three times in this paragraph, James warns us that "faith without works is dead" (James 2:17, 20, 26).

Beware of a mere intellectual faith. No man can come to Christ by faith and remain the same any more than he can come into contact with a 220-volt wire and remain the same. "He that hath the Son hath life; and he that hath not the Son of God hath not life" (1 John 5:12). Dead faith is not saving faith. Dead faith is counterfeit faith and lulls the person into a false confidence of eternal life.

## Demonic Faith (James 2:18-19)

James wanted to shock his complacent readers, so he used demons as his illustration. In recent years the church has rediscovered the reality and activity of demons. When our Lord was ministering on earth, He often cast out demons; and He gave that power to His disciples. Paul often confronted demonic forces in his ministry; and in Ephesians 6:10-20, he admonished the early Christians to claim God's protection and defeat the spiritual forces of wickedness.

It comes as a shock to people that demons have faith! What do they believe? For one thing, they believe in the existence of God; they are neither atheists nor agnostics. They also believe in the deity of Christ. Whenever they met Christ when He was on earth, they bore witness to His sonship (Mark 3:11-12). They believe in the existence of a place of punishment (Luke 8:31); and they also recognize Jesus Christ as the Judge (Mark 5:1-13). They submit to the power of His Word.

"Hear, O Israel! The Lord our God is one Lord!" (Deut. 6:4) This was the daily affirmation of faith of the godly Jew. "You believe that there is one God. Good! Even the demons believe that—and shudder" (James 2:19, NIV). The man with dead faith was touched only in his intellect; but the demons are touched *also in their emotions.* They believe and tremble.

But it is not a saving experience to believe and tremble. A person can be enlightened in his mind and even stirred in his heart and be lost forever. True saving faith involves something more, something that can be seen and recognized: a changed life. "Show me thy faith without thy works," challenged James, "and I will show thee my faith by my works" (James 2:18).

How could a person show his faith without works? Can a dead sinner perform good works? Impossible! When you trust Christ, you are "created in Christ Jesus unto good works, which God hath before ordained that we should walk in them" (Eph. 2:10). Being a Christian involves trusting Christ and living for Christ; you *receive* the life, then you *reveal* the life. Faith that is barren is not saving faith. The Greek word translated "dead" in James 2:20 carries the meaning of "barren or idle," like money drawing no interest.

James has introduced us to two kinds of faith that can never save the sinner: dead faith (the intellect alone), and demonic faith (the intellect and the emotions). He closes this section by describing the only kind of faith that can save the sinner—dynamic faith.

## Dynamic Faith (James 2:20-26)

Dynamic faith is faith that is real, faith that has power, faith that results in a changed life.

James *described* this true saving faith. To begin with, dynamic saving faith is *based on the Word of God.* We receive our spiritual rebirth through God's Word (James 1:18). We receive the Word and this saves us (James 1:21). "So then faith cometh by hearing, and hearing by the Word of God" (Rom. 10:17). James used Abraham and Rahab as illustrations of dynamic saving faith, since both of them heard and received the message of God through His Word.

Faith is only as good as its object. The man in the jungle bows before an idol of stone and trusts it to help him, but he receives no help. No matter how much faith a person may generate, if it is not directed at the right object, it will accomplish nothing. "I believe" may be the testimony of many sincere people, but the big question is, "In whom do you believe? What do you believe?" We are not saved by *faith in faith;* we are saved by faith in Christ as revealed in His Word.

Dynamic faith is based on God's Word, and *it involves the whole man.* Dead faith touches only the intellect; demonic faith involves both the mind and the emotions; but dynamic faith involves the will. The whole person plays a part in true saving faith. The mind understands the truth; the heart desires the truth; and the will acts upon the truth. The men and women of faith named in Hebrews 11 were people of action: God spoke and they obeyed. Again, "Faith is not believing in spite of evidence; faith is obeying in spite of consequence."

True saving faith *leads to action.* Dynamic faith is not intellectual contemplation or emotional consternation; it leads to obedience on the part of the will. And this obedience is not an isolated event: it continues throughout the whole life. It leads to works.

Many different kinds of works are named in the New Testament. "The works of the Law" (Gal. 2:16) relate to the sinner's attempt to please God by obeying the Law of Moses. Of course, it is impossible for a sinner to be saved through the works of the Law. "The works of the flesh" (Gal. 5:19) are done by unsaved people who live for the things of the old nature. There are also "wicked works"

(Col. 1:21) and "dead works" (Heb. 9:14). Where there is dynamic faith—saving faith— you will always find good works.

James then *illustrated* his doctrine in the lives of two well-known Bible persons: Abraham and Rahab. You could not find two more different persons! Abraham was a Jew; Rahab was a Gentile. Abraham was a godly man, but Rahab was a sinful woman, a harlot. Abraham was the friend of God, while Rahab belonged to the enemies of God. What did they have in common? Both exercised saving faith in God.

You will want to read Genesis 15 and 22 to get the background facts for this illustration. God called Abraham out of Ur of the Chaldees to lead him into Canaan and to make out of him the great nation of Israel. It was through Israel that God would bring the Saviour into the world. Abraham's salvation experience is recorded in Genesis 15. At night, God showed His servant the stars and gave him a promise, "So shall thy seed [descendants] be!" How did Abraham respond? "And he believed in the Lord, and He [the Lord] counted it to him for righteousness" (Gen. 15:5-6).

The word *counted* is a legal or financial term; it means "to put to one's account." As a sinner, Abraham's spiritual bankbook was empty. He was bankrupt! But he trusted God, and God put *righteous* on Abraham's account. Abraham did not work for this righteousness; he received it as a gift from God. He was declared righteous by faith. He was justified by faith (read Rom. 4).

Justification is an important doctrine in the Bible. Justification is the act of God whereby He declares the believing sinner righteous on the basis of Christ's finished work on the cross. It is not a process; it is an act. It is not something the sinner does; it is something God does for the sinner when he trusts Christ. It is a once-for-all event. It never changes.

How can you tell if a person is justified by faith if this transaction takes place between the sinner and God privately? Abraham's example answers that important question: the justified person has a changed life and obeys God's will. His faith is demonstrated by his works.

James used another event in Abraham's life, an event that took place many years after Abraham's conversion. This event is the offering up of Isaac on the altar (Gen. 22). Abraham was not saved by obeying God's difficult command. His obedience proved that he al-ready was saved. "You see that his faith and his actions were working together, and his faith was made complete by what he did" (James 2:22, NIV). There is a perfect relationship between faith and works. As someone has expressed it, "Abraham was not saved by faith plus works, but by a faith that works."

How was Abraham "justified by works" (James 2:21) when he had already been "justified by faith"? (see Rom. 4) By faith, he was justified *before God* and his righteousness declared; by works he was justified *before men* and his righteousness demonstrated. It is true that no humans actually saw Abraham put his son on the altar, but the inspired record in Genesis 22 enables us to see the event and witness Abraham's faith demonstrated by his works.

D.L. Moody often said, "Every Bible should be bound in shoe leather." He did not say that because he had been a successful shoe salesman; he said it because he was a dedicated Christian. Dynamic faith obeys God and proves itself in daily life and works. Alas, we still have church members today who fit the description given in Titus, "They profess that they know God, but in works they deny Him" (Titus 1:16). Paul also writes, "This is a faithful saying, and these things I will that thou affirm constantly, that they which have believed in God might be careful to maintain good works" (Titus 3:8).

His second illustration is Rahab, and the background for her is found in Joshua 2 and 6. Israel was about to invade their Promised Land and take the city of Jericho. Joshua sent spies into the city to get the lay of the land. There they met Rahab, a harlot, who protected them and affirmed that she believed in what God had said and what God was going to do. When the men departed, they promised to save her and her family when the city was taken; and this they did.

It is an exciting story. But in it is one of the Bible's great examples of saving faith (see Heb. 11:31). Rahab heard the Word and knew that her city was condemned. This truth affected her and her fellow citizens so that their hearts melted within them (Josh. 2:11). Rahab responded with her mind and her emotions; but she also responded with her will: *she did something about it.* She risked her own life to protect the Jewish spies, and she further risked her life by sharing the good news of deliverance with the members of her family. The Hebrew word translated "harlot" in Joshua 2 can also have the wider meaning of "an innkeeper." Rahab ran a guest house, so it was normal for the spies to go there. The Greek word "harlot" in James 2:25 definitely means an immoral person. This is also the meaning in Hebrews 11:31. Matthew 1:5 indicates she married into Israel and became an ancestress of our Lord. What grace! Rahab is one of the first soul winners in the Bible, and you cannot help but compare her with the "bad Samaritan" in John 4.

Rahab could have had *dead* faith, a mere intellectual experience. Or she could have had *demonic* faith, her mind enlightened and her emotions stirred. But she exercised *dynamic* faith: her mind knew the truth, her heart was stirred by the truth, and her will acted on the truth. She proved her faith by her works.

When you realize the small amount of information Rahab had, you can see how truly marvelous her faith really was. Today we have the full revelation of God through His Word and His Son. We live on the other side of Calvary, and we have the Holy Spirit to convict and to teach us the Word. "For unto whomsoever much is given, of him shall be much required" (Luke 12:48). Her faith is an indictment against the unbelief of sinners today.

James 2 emphasized that the mature Christian practices the truth. He does not merely hold to ancient doctrines; he practices those doctrines in his everyday life. His faith is not the dead faith of the intellectuals, or the demonic faith of the fallen spirits. It is the dynamic faith of men like Abraham and women like Rahab, faith that changes a life and goes to work for God.

It is important that each professing Christian examine his own heart and life and make sure that he possesses true saving faith, dynamic faith. "Examine yourselves, whether ye be in the faith; prove your own selves" (2 Cor. 13:5a). Satan is the great deceiver; one of his devices is imitation. If he can convince a person that counterfeit faith is true faith, he has that person in his power.

Here are some questions we can ask ourselves as we examine our hearts:

1. Was there a time when I honestly realized I was a sinner and admitted this to myself and to God?

2. Was there a time when my heart stirred me to flee from the wrath to come? Have I ever seriously been exercised over my sins?

3. Do I truly understand the Gospel, that Christ died for my sins and arose again? Do I understand and confess that I cannot save myself?

4. Did I sincerely repent of my sins and turn from them? Or do I secretly love sin and want to enjoy it?

5. Have I trusted Christ and Christ alone for my salvation? Do I enjoy a living relationship with Him through the Word and in the Spirit?

6. Has there been a change in my life? Do I maintain good works, or are my works occasional and weak? Do I seek to grow in the things of the Lord? Can others tell that I have been with Jesus?

7. Do I have a desire to share Christ with others? Or am I ashamed of Him?

8. Do I enjoy the fellowship of God's people? Is worship a delight to me?

9. Am I ready for the Lord's return? Or will I be ashamed when He comes for me?

To be sure, not every Christian has the same personal experience; and there are degrees of sanctification. But for the most part, the preceding spiritual inventory can assist a person in determining his true standing before God.

"Search me, O Lord, and know my heart: try me, and know my thoughts: and see if there be any wicked way in me, and lead me in the way everlasting" (Ps. 139:23-24).

# CHAPTER SEVEN
# THE WORLD'S SMALLEST BUT LARGEST TROUBLEMAKER
## *James 3:1-12*

James has explained to us two characteristics of the mature Christian: he is patient in trouble (James 1) and he practices the truth (James 2). In this section, he shares the third characteristic of the mature believer: he has power over his tongue.

A pastor friend told me about a member of his church who was a notorious gossip. She would "hang on the phone" most of the day, sharing tidbits with any and all who would listen.

She came to the pastor one day and said, "Pastor, the Lord has convicted me of my sin of gossip. My tongue is getting me and others into trouble."

My friend knew she was not sincere because she had gone through that routine before. Guardedly he asked, "Well, what do you plan to do?"

"I want to put my tongue on the altar," she replied with pious fervor.

Calmly my friend replied, "There isn't an altar big enough," and he left her to think it over.

The Christians that James wrote to were apparently having serious problems with their tongues. James had warned them to be "swift to hear, slow to speak, slow to wrath" (James 1:19). The believer who does not bridle his tongue is not truly religious (James 1:26). We must speak and act as though we were already facing Christ in judgment (James 2:12). When you read passages like James 4:1, 11-12, you get the impression that this assembly must have had some interesting meetings!

The power of speech is one of the greatest powers God has given us. With the tongue, man can praise God, pray, preach the Word, and lead the lost to Christ. What a privilege! But with that same tongue he can tell lies that could ruin a man's reputation or break a person's heart. The ability to speak words is the ability to influence others and accomplish tremendous tasks; and yet we take this ability for granted.

In order to impress on us the importance of controlled speech, and the great consequences of our words, James gave us six pictures of the tongue: the bit, the rudder, fire, a poisonous animal, a fountain, and a fig tree. You can put these six pictures into three meaningful classifications that reveal the three powers of the tongue.

**Power to Direct: the Bit and Rudder (James 3:1-4)**
Apparently, everybody in the assembly wanted to teach and be a spiritual leader, for James had to warn them: "Not many of you should act as teachers, my brothers" (James 3:1, NIV). Perhaps they were impressed with the authority and prestige of the office, and forgot about the tremendous responsibility *and accountability!* Those who teach the Word

face the stricter judgment. Teachers must use their tongue to share God's truth, and it is easy to commit sins of the tongue. Furthermore, teachers must practice what they teach; otherwise, their teaching is hypocrisy. Think of the damage that can be done by a teacher who is unprepared, or whose spiritual life is not up to par.

But teachers are not the only ones who are tempted and sin; every Christian must admit that "we all stumble in many ways" (James 3:2, NIV). And sins of the tongue seem to head the list. The person who is able to discipline his tongue gives evidence that he can control his whole body. He proves that he is a mature (perfect) man.

Is James making a mistake by connecting sins of the tongue with sins committed by "the whole body"? No, because *words* usually lead to *deeds.* During World War II we were accustomed to seeing posters that read LOOSE LIPS SINK SHIPS! But loose lips also wreck lives. A person makes an unguarded statement and suddenly finds himself involved in a fight. His tongue has forced the rest of his body to defend itself.

In selecting the bit and the rudder ("helm" in James 3:4 means "rudder"), James presented two items that are small of themselves, yet exercise great power, just like the tongue. A small bit enables the rider to control the great horse, and a small rudder enables the pilot to steer the huge ship. The tongue is a small member in the body, and yet it has the power to accomplish great things.

Both the bit and the rudder must overcome contrary forces. The bit must overcome the wild nature of the horse, and the rudder must fight the winds and currents that would drive the ship off its course. The human tongue also must overcome contrary forces. We have an old nature that wants to control us and make us sin. There are circumstances around us that would make us say things we ought not to say. Sin on the inside and pressures on the outside are seeking to get control of the tongue.

This means that both the bit and the rudder must be under the control of a strong hand. The expert horseman keeps the mighty power of his steed under control, and the experienced pilot courageously steers the ship through the storm. When Jesus Christ controls the tongue, then we need not fear saying the wrong things—or even saying the right things in a wrong way! "Death and life are in the power of the tongue," warned Solomon (Prov. 18:21). No wonder David prayed, "Set a watch, O Lord, before my mouth; keep the door of my lips. Incline not my heart to any evil thing" (Ps. 141:3-4). David knew that *the heart* is the key to right speech. "Out of the abundance of the heart the mouth speaketh" (Matt. 12:34). When Jesus Christ is the Lord of the heart, then He is Lord of the lips too.

The bit and rudder have the power to direct, which means *they affect the lives of others.* A runaway horse or a shipwreck could mean injury or death to pedestrians or passengers. The words we speak affect the lives of others. A judge says "Guilty!" or "Not Guilty!" and those words affect the destiny of the prisoner, his family, and his friends. The President of the United States speaks a few words and signs some papers and the nation is at war. Even a simple yes or no from the lips of a parent can greatly affect the direction of a child's life.

Never underestimate the guidance you give by the words you speak or do not speak. Jesus spoke to a woman at a well, and her life and the lives of her neighbors experienced a miraculous change (John 4). Peter preached at Pentecost and 3,000 souls came to salvation through faith in Christ (Acts 2).

On April 21, 1855, Edward Kimball went into a Boston shoe store and led young Dwight L. Moody to Christ. The result: one of history's greatest evangelists, a man whose ministry still continues. The tongue has the power to direct others to the right choices.

It would do us all good to read frequently the Book of Proverbs, and to note especially the many references to speech. "A soft answer turneth away wrath: but grievous words stir up anger" (Prov. 15:1). "Lying lips are an abomination to the Lord" (Prov. 12:22). "In the multitude of words there wanteth not sin: but he that refraineth his lips is wise" (Prov. 10:19). Yes, the tongue is like a bit and a rudder: it has the power to direct. How important it is that our tongues direct people in the right way!

## Power to Destroy: the Fire and Animal (James 3:5-8)

I was visiting the used bookstores along Charing Cross Road in London, and I remarked to a clerk that there were not as many stores as I expected. "There's a reason for that," he replied. "One night during World War II, the incendiary bombs hit and the fires destroyed at least a million books!"

On another occasion, a friend was taking my wife and me on a tour of the beautiful forests in California, and we came to an ugly section that was burned out. Not only was the face of nature scarred, but millions of dollars of valuable timber had been wiped out. "Somebody's lit cigarette," my friend commented as we drove past the blackened earth.

A fire can begin with just a small spark, but it can grow to destroy a city. A fire reportedly started in the O'Leary barn in Chicago at 8:30 P.M., October 8, 1871; and because that fire spread, over 100,000 people were left homeless, 17,500 buildings were destroyed, and 300 people died. It cost the city over $400 million.

Our words can start fires. "Where no wood is, there the fire goeth out: so where there is no talebearer, the strife ceaseth. As coals are to burning coals, and wood to fire; so is a contentious man to kindle strife" (Prov. 26:20-21). In some churches, there are members or officers who cannot control their tongues, and the result is destruction. Let them move out of town or be replaced in office, and a beautiful spirit of harmony and love takes over.

Like a fire, the tongue can "heat things up." David wrote: "I said, 'I will take heed to my ways, that I sin not with my tongue.' . . . My heart was hot within me, while I was musing the fire burned; then spake I with my tongue" (Ps. 39:1, 3). Have you ever had that experience? Of course you have! A hot head and a hot heart can lead to burning words that later we will regret. David had a temper, and he had to have God's help in controlling it. No wonder Solomon wrote, "He who restrains his word has knowledge, and he who has a cool spirit is a man of understanding" (Prov. 17:27, NASB). "He who is slow to anger has great understanding, but he who is quick-tempered exalts folly" (Prov. 14:29, NASB).

Fire not only starts small and grows, and creates heat; it also defiles. A friend of mine suffered a fire in the basement of his house, and the smoke and fire damage so soiled the upstairs of the house that the family had to move out while the house was redecorated. Fiery words can defile a home, a Sunday School class, a church. The only thing that can wash away that defilement is the blood of Jesus Christ.

Fire burns and hurts, and our words can burn and hurt. One of the sorrows our Lord had to bear when He was here on earth was the way His enemies talked about Him. They called Him a "man gluttonous and a winebibber" (Matt. 11:19) because He graciously accepted invitations to dine with people the Pharisees did not like. When He performed miracles, they said He was in league with Satan. Even when He was dying on the cross, His enemies could not let Him alone but threw vicious taunts into His face.

Fire spreads, and the more fuel you give it, the faster and farther it will spread. The tongue "setteth on fire the course of nature" (James 3:6), or "sets the whole course of his life on fire" (NIV). James suggests that all of life is connected like a wheel, and therefore we cannot keep things from spreading. A person's entire life can be injured or destroyed by the tongue. Time does not correct the sins of the tongue. We may confess our sins of speech, but the fire keeps on spreading.

As it spreads, fire destroys; and the words we speak have the power to destroy. For every word in Hitler's book, *Mein Kampf,* 125 lives were lost in World War II. Our own words may not have caused wars or wrecked cities, but they can break hearts and ruin reputations. They can also destroy souls by sending them into eternity without Christ. How important it is for us to let our speech "be always full of grace, seasoned with salt" (Col. 4:6, NIV).

Not only is the tongue like a fire, but it is also like a dangerous animal. It is restless and cannot be ruled (unruly), and it seeks its prey and then pounces and kills. My wife and I once drove through a safari park, admiring the animals as they moved about in their natural habitat. But there were warning signs posted all over the park: DO NOT LEAVE YOUR CAR! DO NOT OPEN YOUR WINDOWS! Those "peaceful animals" were capable of doing great damage, and even killing.

Some animals are poisonous, and some tongues spread poison. The deceptive thing about poison is that it works secretly and slowly, and then kills. How many times has some malicious person injected a bit of poison into the conversation, hoping it would spread and finally get to the person he or she wanted to hurt? As a pastor, I have seen poisonous tongues do great damage to individuals, families, classes, and entire churches. Would you turn hungry lions or angry snakes loose in your Sunday morning service? Of course not! But unruly tongues accomplish the same results.

James reminds us that animals can be tamed; and, for that matter, fire can be tamed. When you tame an animal, you get a worker instead of a destroyer. When you control fire, you generate power. The tongue cannot be tamed by man, but it can be tamed by God. Your tongue need not be "set on fire of hell" (James 3:6). Like the Apostles at Pentecost, it can be set on fire from heaven! If God lights the fire and controls it, then the tongue can be a mighty tool for the winning of the lost and the building up of the church. The important thing, of course, is the heart; for it is "out of the abundance of the heart that the mouth speaketh" (Matt. 12:34). If the heart is filled with hatred, Satan will light the fire. But if the heart is filled with love, God will light the fire.

### Power to Delight: the Fountain and Tree (James 3:9-12)

The fountain, of course, provides the cool water that man needs to stay alive. In Oriental countries, the presence of a freshwater fountain is a great blessing to a village. Man needs water not only for drinking, but also for washing, cooking, farming, and a host of other activities so necessary to life.

"The words of a man's mouth are as deep waters, and the wellspring of wisdom as a flowing brook" (Prov. 18:4). "The mouth of a righteous man is a well of life" (Prov. 10:11). "The law of the wise is a fountain of life, to depart from the snares of death" (Prov. 13:14). These verses parallel what James has written and underscore the importance of our words.

Water is life-giving, and our words can give life. However, if water is not controlled, it brings death and destruction. The famous Johnstown, Pennsylvania flood of 1889 took 2,200 lives and destroyed $10 million in property. "Death and life are in the power of the tongue" (Prov. 18:21).

However, when we bend over a fountain for a drink of cool water, we rarely think of floods. We think only of the precious gift of refreshment that comes with a drink of water. We could not be healthy without water. "There is that speaketh like the piercings of a sword: but the tongue of the wise is health" (Prov. 12:18). Paul's prayer was that he might "refresh" the saints in Rome when he came to them (Rom. 15:32). He often named Christians who had refreshed him (1 Cor. 16:18; Phile. 7, 20).

Water also cleanses. There was a laver in the Old Testament tabernacle and temple, provided for the cleansing of the priests' hands and feet. God's Word is the spiritual water that cleanses us (John 15:3; Eph. 5:26-27). But our words to others can also help to cleanse and sanctify them. Our words ought to be like that river described in Ezekiel 47 that brought life to everything it touched.

The tongue is also delightful because it is like a tree. In Bible lands, trees are vitally important to the economy: they help to hold down the soil; they provide beauty and shade; and they bear fruit. Our words can help to shelter and encourage a weary traveler, and can help to feed a hungry soul. "The lips of the righteous feed many" (Prov. 10:21). Jesus said, "The words that I speak unto you, they are spirit, and they are life" (John 6:63). As we share His Word with others, we feed them and encourage them along the way.

The most important thing about a tree is the root system. If the roots do not go down deep, the tree will not grow in a healthy manner. If we are rooted in the things of the Lord, then our words will be the fruit of our fellowship with Him. We will be like that "blessed man" in Psalm 1 and produce fruit in due season. One reason our Lord was able to say the right words at the right times was because He communed with His Father and heard from heaven each day. Listen to His testimony:

"The Lord hath given Me the tongue of the learned, that I should know how to speak a word in season to him that is weary: He wakeneth morning by morning, He wakeneth Mine ear to hear as the learned" (Isa. 50:4). "And in the morning, rising up a great while before day, He went out, and departed into a solitary place, and there prayed" (Mark 1:35).

If you and I are going to have tongues that delight, then we must meet with the Lord each day and learn from Him. We must get our "spiritual roots" deep into His Word. We must pray and meditate and permit the Spirit of God to fill our hearts with God's love and truth.

But James issued a warning: a fountain cannot give forth two kinds of water, and a tree cannot bear two different kinds of fruit. We expect the fountain to flow with sweet water at all times, and we expect the fig tree to bear figs and the olive tree to bear olives. Nature reproduces after its kind.

If the tongue is inconsistent, there is something radically wrong with the heart. I heard about a professing Christian who got angry on the job and let loose with some oaths. Embarrassed, he turned to his partner and said, "I don't know why I said that. It really isn't in me." His partner wisely replied, "It had to be in you or it couldn't have come out of you." When Peter was out of fellowship with Christ, he uttered some oaths; but he went out and wept bitterly and confessed his sins.

The tongue that blesses the Father, and then turns around and curses men made in God's image, is in desperate need of spiritual medicine! How easy it is to sing the hymns during the worship service, then after the service, get into the family car and argue and fight all the way home! "My brethren, these things ought not so to be."

The problem, of course, is not the tongue; it is the heart. It is easy to have "bitter envying and strife" in our hearts (James 3:14). "But those things which proceed out of the mouth come forth from the heart; and they defile the man" (Matt. 15:18). "Keep thy heart with all diligence, for out of it are the issues of life" (Prov. 4:23). As we fill our hearts with God's Word, and yield to the Holy Spirit, He can use us to bring delight to others, and we will be refreshing fountains and trees.

As I close this chapter, let me suggest that you start using the "Twelve Words That Can Transform Your Life." If you use these words *and sincerely mean what you say from your heart,* you will find that God will use you to be a blessing and encouragement to others. There are only twelve of them, but they work.

*"Please" and "Thank you."* When you use these three words, you are treating others like people and not things. You are showing appreciation.

*"I'm sorry."* These two words have a way of breaking down walls and building bridges.

*"I love you."* Too many people read "romance" into these words, but they go much deeper than that. As Christians, we should love the brethren and even love our enemies. "I love you" is a statement that can carry tremendous power.

*"I'm praying for you."* And be sure that you are. When you talk to God about people, then you can talk to people about God. Our private praying for people helps us in our public meeting with people. Of course, we never

say "I'm praying for you" in a boastful way, as though we are more spiritual than others. We say it in an encouraging way, to let others know that we care enough for them to meet them at the throne of grace.

Yes, the smallest but largest troublemaker in all the world is the tongue. But it does not have to be a troublemaker! God can use our tongues to direct others into the way of life, and to delight them in the trials of life. The tongue is a little member, but it has great power.

Give God your tongue and your heart each day and ask Him to use you to be a blessing to others.

# CHAPTER EIGHT
# WHERE TO
# GET WISDOM
*James 3:13-18*

W isdom was an important thing to Jewish people. They realized that it was not enough to have knowledge; you had to have wisdom to be able to use that knowledge correctly. All of us know people who are very intelligent, perhaps almost geniuses, and yet who seemingly are unable to carry out the simplest tasks of life. They can run computers but they cannot manage their own lives! "Wisdom is the principal thing; therefore get wisdom" (Prov. 4:7).

James continued to exhort the people in the assembly who wanted to be teachers of the Word (James 3:1). It is not enough simply to stand before the people and say words; *you must have something to say*. This is where spiritual wisdom comes in. Knowledge enables us to take things apart, but wisdom enables us to put things together and relate God's truth to daily life. All of us have heard preachers and teachers who say many good things, but who somehow miss the heart of God's message and fail to relate truth to everyday life. It is this kind of "knowledge without wisdom" that James is writing about. He is contrasting true wisdom and false wisdom in three different aspects.

## Contrast in Origins (James 3:15, 17a)

The true wisdom comes from above, but the false wisdom comes from below. In other words, there is a "heavenly wisdom" that comes from God, and there is a "man-made wisdom" that does not come from God. Whatever does not come from God is destined to fail, no matter how successful it may seem at the time.

The Bible contains many examples of the folly of man's wisdom. The building of the Tower of Babel seemed like a wise enterprise, but it ended in failure and confusion (Gen. 11:1-9). It seemed wise for Abraham to go to Egypt when famine came to Canaan, but the results proved otherwise (Gen. 12:10-20). King Saul thought it was wise to put his own armor on young David for the lad's battle with Goliath, but God's plan was otherwise (1 Sam. 17:38ff). The disciples thought it was wise to dismiss the great crowd and let them find their own food; but Jesus took a few loaves and fishes and fed the multitude. The Roman "experts" in Acts 27 thought it was wise to leave port and set sail for Rome, even though Paul disagreed; and the storm that followed proved that Paul's wisdom was better than their expert counsel. They lived to regret it, but they lived!

What is the origin of man's wisdom? "This wisdom descendeth not from above, but is earthly, sensual, devilish" (James 3:15). The believer has three enemies: the world, the flesh, and the devil (Eph. 2:1-3). These enemies are suggested by the terms "earthly, sensual, devilish."

There is a "wisdom of this world" (1 Cor. 1:20-21). Do not confuse the world's *knowledge* and the world's *wisdom*. Certainly, there is a great deal of knowledge in this world, and we all benefit from it; but there is not much wisdom. Man unlocks the secrets of the universe, but he does not know what to do with them. Almost everything he discovers or devises turns against him. Over a century ago, Henry David Thoreau warned that we had "improved means to unimproved ends."

Whenever I ride a bus or elevated train in the city, I often think of the man in Boston who was entertaining a famous Chinese scholar. He met his Oriental friend at the train station and rushed him to the subway. As they ran through the subway station, the host panted to his guest, "If we run and catch this next train, we will save three minutes!" To which the patient Chinese philosopher replied, "And what significant thing shall we do with the three minutes we are saving?"

The world by its wisdom knew not God, and in its wisdom rejects the very Gospel of God. "For the preaching of the Cross is to them that perish foolishness" (1 Cor. 1:18). Any person enamored with the wisdom of this world ought to read the first two chapters of 1 Corinthians and notice how much Paul has to say about God's wisdom and man's wisdom. Man's wisdom is foolishness to God (1 Cor. 1:20), and God's wisdom is foolishness to man (1 Cor. 2:14). Man's wisdom comes from reason, while God's wisdom comes from revelation. Man's worldly wisdom will come to nothing (1 Cor. 1:19), while God's wisdom will endure forever.

Because the world has turned from God, it has lost its wisdom. Every increase in man's knowledge only magnifies the problems. "The fear of the Lord is the beginning of wisdom; and the knowledge of the holy is understanding" (Prov. 9:10). "There is no fear of God before their eyes" (Rom. 3:18).

But this false wisdom has another source: it is "sensual," that is, it is "natural." The Greek word is *psukikos*, which comes from the Greek word *psuke* meaning "life," or "soul." Our English word "psychology" is derived from it. In 1 Corinthians 2:14; 15:44, 46, *psukikos* is translated "natural," referring to the opposite of "spiritual." In Jude 19 it is translated "sensual." The main idea seems to be that of man's fallen nature as opposed to the new nature given by God. There is a wisdom that gets its origin in man's nature totally apart from the Spirit of God.

But this "wisdom that is from beneath" is also "devilish." Perhaps the best translation is *demonic*. Beginning with Genesis 3, where Satan successfully deceived Eve, and continuing through the entire Bible, there is a "wisdom of Satan" at work, fighting against the wisdom of God. Satan convinced Eve that she would be like God. He told her that the tree would make her wise. Ever since that event, people have continued to believe Satan's lies and have tried to become their own gods (Rom. 1:18-25). Satan is cunning; he is the old serpent! He has wisdom that will confound and confuse you if you do not know the wisdom of God.

In contrast to the wisdom that is earthly, sensual, and devilish, James describes a "wisdom that is from above" (James 3:17). "Every good gift and every perfect gift is from above" (James 1:17). The Christian looks up to heaven for all that he needs. His citizenship is in heaven (Phil. 3:20), just as his Father is in heaven (Matt. 6:9). His treasures are in heaven, not on earth (Matt. 6:19ff). He was born from above (John 3:1-7) when he trusted Jesus Christ. The believer's home is in heaven (John 14:1-6) and his hope is in heaven. He sets his affection and attention on things above, not on earthly things (Col. 3:1-4).

What is the Christian's wisdom? Does he look to the philosophies of this world? No! To begin with, Jesus Christ is our wisdom (1 Cor. 1:24, 30). In Jesus Christ "are hid all the treasures of wisdom and knowledge" (Col. 2:3). The first step toward true wisdom is the receiving of Jesus Christ as Saviour.

The Word of God is also our wisdom. "Behold, I have taught you statutes and judgments. . . . Keep therefore and do them; for this is your wisdom and your understanding in the sight of the nations" (Deut. 4:5-6). The Scriptures are able to make us "wise unto salvation" (2 Tim. 3:15).

James 1:5 indicates that we find wisdom through believing prayer. "If any of you lack wisdom, let him ask of God." The Holy Spirit of God is "the Spirit of wisdom and revelation" (Eph. 1:17) and He directs us in the wisest paths as we trust the Word and pray.

The origin of true spiritual wisdom is God. To get your wisdom from any other source is to ask for trouble. There is no need to get the counterfeit wisdom of the world, the wisdom that caters to the flesh and accomplishes the work of the devil. Get your wisdom from God!

**Contrast in Operations
(James 3:13-14, 17)**
The wisdom from above, God's wisdom, operates in a different way from the wisdom that is "earthly, sensual, devilish." Since they originate from radically different sources, they must operate in opposite ways.

What are the evidences of false wisdom?

*Envy (v. 14a).* This word carries the meaning of selfish ambition and zeal. It ties in with James 3:1, where James warned them not to be ambitious for spiritual offices. The wisdom of the world says, "Promote yourself. You're as good as the other candidates, maybe better! The wheel that squeaks the loudest gets the grease." Sad to say, there is a great deal of selfish, carnal promotion among God's people. Even the Apostles argued over who was the greatest in the kingdom.

It is easy to go on an ego trip under the guise of spiritual zeal. The Pharisees used their religious activities to promote the praise of men (Matt. 6:1-18). We ought to be zealous in the things of the Lord, but we must be sure that our motives are right. The wisdom of this world exalts man and robs God of glory. In 1 Corinthians 1:17ff, Paul discussed the wisdom of God and the wisdom of this world, and he explained why God works as He does: "That no flesh should glory in His presence" (1 Cor. 1:29). He concluded the section with the admonition, "He that glorieth, let him glory in the Lord" (1 Cor. 1:31).

Is our zeal for the Lord spiritual or carnal? Do we rejoice when others succeed, or do we have secret envy and criticism? Do we feel burdened when others fail, or are we glad? When the wisdom of the world gets into the church, there is a great deal of fleshly promotion and human glorification. Beware!

*Strife (v. 14b).* This word means "party spirit." It was used by the Greeks to describe a politician out canvassing for votes. The world's wisdom says, "Get all the support you can! Ask the people in the church if they are for you or against you!" Of course, this spirit of self-seeking only creates rivalry and division in the church. "Let nothing be done through strife or vainglory; but in lowliness of mind let each esteem other better than [more important than] themselves" (Phil. 2:3).

*Boasting (v. 14c).* Pride loves to boast, and nothing is prouder than the wisdom of men. There is a way to report blessings so that God gets the glory, but there is also an approach that gives men the praise. It is tragic to see mutual admiration societies among God's people. In 2 Corinthians 10, when Paul was forced to boast about his ministry, he was careful to give God the glory. "Of course, we shouldn't dare include ourselves in the same class as those who write their own testimonials, or even to compare ourselves with them! All they are doing, of course, is to measure themselves by their own standards or by comparisons within their own circle, and that doesn't make for accurate estimation, you may be sure" (2 Cor. 10:12, PH).

When God's wisdom is at work, there is a sense of humility and submission, and you want God to get all the glory. You have no desire to compare yourself with any other Christian, because you see only Christ—and compared with Him, all of us still have a long way to go!

*Deceit (v. 14d).* "Lie not against the truth." The sequence is not difficult to understand. First, there is selfish ambition that leads to party spirit and rivalry. In order to "win the election" we must resort to boasting; *and boasting usually involves lies!* A man's life is not read in his press releases; it is read by the Lord in his heart. "Therefore judge nothing before the time, until the Lord come, who both will bring to light the hidden things of darkness, and will make manifest the counsels of the hearts: and then shall every man have praise of God" (1 Cor. 4:5).

What a relief it is to turn to the evidences of true spiritual wisdom.

*Meekness (v. 13).* Meekness is not weakness; it is power under control. The meek person does not selfishly assert himself. The Greek word was used for a horse that had been broken so that his power was under control. The meek person seeks only the glory of God and does not cater to the praises of men. Meekness is a fruit of the Spirit (Gal. 5:23); it cannot be manufactured by man. There is a false humility that some people mistake for meekness, but it is only counterfeit.

The phrase, "meekness of wisdom," is an interesting one (James 3:3). Meekness is the right use of power, and wisdom is the right use of knowledge. They go together. The truly wise person will show in his daily life *(conversation* means "behavior") that he is a child of God. Attitude and action go together.

*Purity (v. 17a).* "First pure" indicates the importance of holiness. God is holy; therefore the wisdom from above is pure. The idea behind this word is "chaste, free from defilement." James used it again in James 4:8— "purify your hearts," or, "make chaste your hearts." God's wisdom leads to purity of life. Man's wisdom may lead to sin. There is a spiritual purity that results in a chaste relationship with the Lord (2 Cor. 11:3); and there is a worldliness that makes the person a spiritual adulterer (James 4:4).

*Peace (v. 17b).* Man's wisdom leads to competition, rivalry, and war (James 4:1-2); but God's wisdom leads to peace. It is a peace based on holiness, not on compromise. God never has "peace at any price." The peace of the church is not more important than the purity of the church. If the church is pure, devoted to God, then there will be peace. "And the work of righteousness shall be peace, and the effect of righteousness quietness and assurance forever" (Isa. 32:17). The church can never have peace by sweeping sins under the rug and pretending they are not there. Man's wisdom says, "Cover up sin! Keep things together!" God's wisdom says, "Confess sin and My peace will keep things together!"

**Gentleness (v. 17c).** Matthew Arnold liked to call this "sweet reasonableness." It carries the meaning of moderation without compromise, gentleness without weakness. The gentle person does not deliberately cause fights, but neither does he compromise the truth in order to keep peace. Carl Sandburg described Abraham Lincoln as a man of "velvet steel." That is a good description of gentleness.

**Compliance (v. 17d).** God's wisdom makes the believer agreeable and easy to live with and work with. Man's wisdom makes a person hard and stubborn. The compliant person is willing to hear all sides of a question, but he does not compromise his own convictions. He can disagree without being disagreeable. He is "swift to hear, slow to speak, slow to wrath" (James 1:19). Many people think that stubbornness is conviction, and they must have their own way. When God's wisdom is at work, there is a willingness to listen, think, pray, and obey whatever God reveals. "Yielding to persuasion" is another translation of this word.

**Mercy (v. 17e).** To be "full" of something means to be "controlled by." The person who follows God's wisdom is controlled by mercy. "Be ye therefore merciful, as your Father also is merciful" (Luke 6:36). God in His grace gives us what we do not deserve, and in His mercy He does not give us what we do deserve. Our Lord's Parable of the Good Samaritan illustrates the meaning of mercy (Luke 10:25-37). For a Samaritan to care for a Jewish stranger was an act of mercy. He could gain nothing from it, except the blessing that comes from doing the will of God; and the victim could not pay him back. That is mercy.

**Good fruits (v. 17f).** People who are faithful are fruitful. God's wisdom does not make a life empty; it makes it full. The Spirit produces fruit to the glory of God (see John 15:1-16). The lawyer in Luke 10:25-37 was willing to *discuss* the subject of neighborliness, but he was unwilling to be a neighbor and help someone else. God's wisdom is practical; it changes the life and produces good works to the glory of God.

**Decisiveness (v. 17g).** The word sug-gests singleness of mind and is the opposite of "wavering" (James 1:6). When you lean on the world's wisdom, you are pressured from one side and then another to change your mind or take a new viewpoint. When you have God's wisdom, you need not waver; you can be decisive and not be afraid. Wisdom from above brings strength from above.

**Sincerity (v. 17h).** The Greek word translated *hypocrite* in our New Testament means "one who wears a mask, an actor." When man's wisdom is at work, there may be insincerity and pretense. When God's wisdom is at work, there is openness and honesty, "speaking the truth in love" (Eph. 4:15). Wherever you find God's people pretending and hiding, you can be sure the wisdom of this world is governing their ministry. "Religious politics" is an abomination to God. "Faith is living without scheming."

There is quite a contrast between the operation of God's wisdom and the operation of the wisdom of this world. It would be profitable for church officers and leaders to evaluate their own lives and their ministries in the light of what James has written. While the local church is an organization, it cannot depend on the "Madison Avenue" methods that make secular businesses succeed. God's ways and God's thoughts are far above us! "Now we have received, not the spirit of the world, but the Spirit which is of God; that we might know the things that are freely given to us of God" (1 Cor. 2:12).

**Contrast in Outcomes (James 3:16, 18)**
Origin determines outcome. Worldly wisdom will produce worldly results; spiritual wisdom will give spiritual results.

**Worldly wisdom produces trouble (v. 16).** Envy, strife, confusion, evil works. It does not appear that God was at work in that assembly. In James 4, James would deal with the "wars and fightings" among the believers. Wrong thinking produces wrong living. One reason the world is in such a mess is because men have refused to accept the wisdom of God.

The word translated "confusion" means "disorder that comes from instability." It is related to "unstable" in James 1:8 and "unruly" in James 3:8. Read 2 Corinthians 12:20 and you will get a description of a church that is confused. Jesus used this word to describe the convulsions of the world in the last days (Luke 21:9).

Jealousy, competition, party spirit—all of these contribute to confusion. The Tower of Babel in Genesis 11 is a good illustration of this fact. From man's point of view, the building of the tower was a wise thing; but from God's viewpoint, the project was stupid and sinful. The result? Confusion. Even today, we use the word "babel" to mean "confusion."

Confusion sets the stage for "every evil work" (James 3:16). *Evil* here means "worthless, of no account." It reminds us of the "wood, hay, stubble" of 1 Corinthians 3:12. A ministry operating in the wisdom of this world may appear to be great and successful, but in the day of judgment it may burn up. "Therefore judge nothing before the time" (1 Cor. 4:5). The church at Smyrna thought it was poor, but the Lord said it was rich; while the "rich church" at Laodicea was declared to be poor (Rev. 2:9; 3:14-22).

The most important thing we can do in our local churches is measure our ministries by the Word of God, not by the wisdom of men. The many battles among Christians, the church splits, the absence of purity and peace, all suggest that something is wrong. Perhaps that "something" is the absence of the wisdom of God.

**God's wisdom produces blessing (v. 18).** James returned to that word, *fruit*. There is a vast difference between man-made results and God-given fruit. Fruit is the product of life, and fruit has in it *the seeds for more fruit*. Usually it is the *seed* that is sown, but here it is the *fruit* that is sown. As we share the fruit of God with others, they are fed and satisfied, and they in turn bear fruit.

The Christian life is a life of sowing and reaping. For that matter, *every* life is a life of sowing and reaping, and we reap just what we sow. The Christian who obeys God's wisdom sows righteousness, not sin; he sows peace, not war. The life we live enables the Lord to bring righteousness and peace into the lives of others.

What we *are* is what we live, and what we live is what we sow. What we sow determines what we reap. If we live in God's wisdom, we sow righteousness and peace, and we reap God's blessing. If we live in man's worldly wisdom, we sow sin and war, and we reap "confusion and every evil work."

It is a serious thing to be a troublemaker in God's family. One of the sins that God hates is that of sowing "discord among brethren" (read Prov. 6:16-19). Lot followed the world's wisdom and brought trouble to the camp of Abraham; but Abraham followed God's wisdom and brought peace. Lot's decision led to "good-for-nothing works," and everything he lived for went up in smoke at the destruction of Sodom and Gomorrah. Abraham's decision, in the wisdom of God, led to blessings for his own household and ultimately for the whole world (read Gen. 13).

"Happy is the man that findeth wisdom, and the man that getteth understanding" (Prov. 3:13).

# CHAPTER NINE
# HOW TO
# END WARS
*James 4:1-12*

Have you ever heard of "The War of the Whiskers" or "The War of the Oaken Bucket"? How about "The War of Jenkins' Ear"? These were actual wars fought between nations, and you can read about them in most history books.

War is a fact of life, in spite of treaties, world peace organizations, and the threat of atomic bombs. Not only are there wars between nations, but there are wars of one kind or another on almost every level of life—even "gas wars" among filling station operators!

James discussed this important theme of war in this paragraph, and he explained that there are three wars going on in the world. He also told how these wars could be stopped.

## At War with Each Other
## (James 4:1a, 11-12)
"What causes fights and quarrels among you?" (NIV) Among Christians! "Behold, how good and how pleasant it is for brethren to dwell together in unity" (Ps. 133:1). Surely *brethren* should live together in love and harmony, yet often they do not. Lot caused a quarrel with his Uncle Abraham (Gen. 13). Absalom created a war for his father David (2 Sam. 13–18). Even the disciples created problems for the Lord when they argued over who was the greatest in the kingdom (Luke 9:46-48).

When you examine some of the early churches, you discover that they had their share of disagreements. The members of the Corinthian church were competing with each other in the public meetings, and even suing each other in court (1 Cor. 6:1-8; 14:23-40). The Galatian believers were "biting and devouring" one another (Gal. 5:15). Paul had to admonish the Ephesians to cultivate spiritual unity (Eph. 4:1-16); and even his beloved church at Philippi had problems: two women could not get along with each other (Phil. 4:1-3).

James mentioned several different kinds of disagreements among the saints.

*Class wars (2:1-9).* Here is that age-long rivalry between the rich and the poor. The rich man gets the attention, the poor man is ignored. The rich man is honored, the poor man is disgraced. How tragic it is when local churches get their values confused and cater to the rich while they ignore, or even reject, the poor. If fellowship in a church depends on such external things as clothing and economic status, then the church is out of the will of God.

*Employment wars (5:1-6).* Again, it is the rich man who has the power to control and hurt the poor man. Laborers do not get their wages, or they do not get their fair wages. In spite of our modern labor movement and federal legislation, there are still many people who cannot get a good job, or whose income is less than adequate for the work they are doing.

*Church fights (1:19-20; 3:13-18).* Apparently, the believers James wrote to were at war with each other over positions in the church, many of them wanting to be teachers and leaders. When they studied the Word, the result was not edification, but strife and arguments. Each person thought that his ideas were the only right ideas and his ways the only right ways. Selfish ambition ruled their meetings, not spiritual submission.

*Personal wars (4:11-12).* The saints were speaking evil of one another and judging one another. Here, again, we see the wrong use of the tongue. Christians are to speak "the truth in love" (Eph. 4:15); they are not to speak evil in a spirit of rivalry and criticism. If the truth about a brother is harmful, then we should cover it in love and not repeat it (1 Peter 4:8). If he has sinned, we should go to him personally and try to win him back (Matt. 18:15-19; Gal. 6:1-2).

James was not forbidding us to use discrimination or even to evaluate people. Christians need to have discernment (Phil. 1:9-10), but they must not act like God in passing judgment. We must first examine our own lives, and then try to help others (Matt. 7:1-5). We never know all the facts in a case, and we certainly never know the motives that are at work in men's hearts. To speak evil of a brother and to judge a brother on the basis of partial evidence and (probably) unkind motives is to sin against him and against God. We are not called to be judges; God is the only Judge. He is patient and understanding; His judgments are just and holy; we can leave the matter with Him.

It is unfortunate that the saints are at war with each other, leader against leader, church against church, fellowship against fellowship. The world watches these religious wars and says, "Behold, how they hate one another!" No wonder Jesus prayed, "That they all may be one; as Thou, Father, art in Me, and I in Thee, that they also may be one in Us; that the world may believe that Thou hast sent Me" (John 17:21).

But, why are we at war with one another? We belong to the same family; we trust the same Saviour; we are indwelt by the same Holy Spirit—and yet we fight one another. Why? James answered this question by explaining the second war that is going on.

## At War with Ourselves (James 4:1b-3)

"What causes fights and quarrels among you? Don't they come from your desires that battle within you?" (James 4:1, NIV) The war in the heart is helping to cause the wars in the church! "But if ye have bitter envying and strife in your hearts, glory not, and lie not against the truth. . . . For where envying and strife is, there is confusion and every evil work" (James 3:14, 16).

The essence of sin is selfishness. Eve disobeyed God because she wanted to eat of the tree and become wise like God. Abraham lied about his wife because he selfishly wanted to save his own life (Gen. 12:10-20). Achan caused defeat to Israel because he selfishly took some forbidden loot from the ruins of Jericho (Josh. 7). "We have turned every one to his own way" (Isa. 53:6).

Often we veil our religious quarrels under the disguise of "spirituality." We are like Miriam and Aaron who complained about Moses' wife, but who really were envious of Moses' authority (Num. 12). Or we imitate James and John who asked for special thrones in the kingdom, when what we really want is recognition today (Mark 10:35-45). In both of these instances, the result of selfish desire was chastening and division among God's people. Miriam's sin halted the progress of Israel for a whole week!

Selfish desires are dangerous things. They lead to *wrong actions* ("ye kill, ye fight and war," James 4:2), and they even lead to *wrong praying* ("When you ask, you do not receive, because you ask with wrong motives, that you may spend what you get on your pleasures," James 4:3, NIV). When our praying is wrong, our whole Christian life is wrong. It has well been said that the purpose of prayer is not to get man's will done in heaven, but to get God's will done on earth.

"Thou shalt not covet" is the last of God's Ten Commandments, but its violation can make us break all of the other nine! Covetousness can make a person murder, tell lies, dishonor his parents, commit adultery, and in one way or another violate all of God's moral law. Selfish living and selfish praying always lead to war. If there is war on the inside, there will ultimately be war on the outside.

People who are at war with themselves because of selfish desires are always unhappy people. They never enjoy life. Instead of being thankful for the blessings they do have, they complain about the blessings they do not have. They cannot get along with other people because they are always envying others for what they have and do. They are always looking for that "magic something" that will change their lives, when the real problem is within their own hearts.

Sometimes we use prayer as a cloak to hide our true desires. "But I prayed about it!" can be one of the biggest excuses a Christian can use. Instead of seeking God's will, we tell God what He is supposed to do; and we get angry at Him if He does not obey. This anger at God eventually spills over and we get angry at God's people. More than one church split has been caused by saints who take out their frustrations with God on the members of the church. Many a church or family problem would be solved if people would only look into their own hearts and see the battles raging there.

God made us a unity; mind, emotions, and will should work together. James stated the reason we are at war with ourselves and, consequently, with each other.

## At War with God (James 4:4-10)

The root cause of every war, internal and external, is rebellion against God. At the beginning of Creation, you behold perfect harmony; but sin came into the world, and this led to conflict. Sin is lawlessness (1 John 3:4), and lawlessness is rebellion against God.

How does a believer declare war against God? By being friendly with God's enemies. James names three enemies that we must not fraternize with if we want to be at peace with God.

*The world (v. 4).* By the "world," James means, of course, human society apart from God. The whole system of things in this society of ours is anti-Christ and anti-God. Abraham was the friend of God (James 2:23); Lot was the friend of the world. Lot ended up in a war, and Abraham had to rescue him (Gen. 14).

A Christian gets involved with the world *gradually,* as I pointed out in chapter 4 of this study. First, there is "the friendship of the world" (James 4:4). This results in being "spotted" by the world (James 1:27) so that areas of our lives meet with the approval of the world. Friendship leads to loving the world (1 John 2:15-17), and this makes it easy to conform to the world (Rom. 12:2). The sad result is being condemned with the world (1 Cor. 11:32), our souls saved "yet as by fire" (1 Cor. 3:11-15).

Friendship with the world is compared to adultery. The believer is "married to Christ" (Rom. 7:4) and ought to be faithful to Him. The Jewish Christians who read this letter would understand this picture of "spiritual adultery" because the Prophets Ezekiel, Jeremiah, and Hosea used it when rebuking Judah for her sins (see Jer. 3:1-5; Ezek. 23; Hosea 1–2). By adopting the sinful ways of the other nations, and by worshiping their gods, the nation of Judah committed adultery against her God.

The world is the enemy of God, and whoever wills to be a friend of the world cannot be the friend of God. Neither can he be if he lives for the flesh, for this is the second enemy James named.

*The flesh (vv. 1, 5).* By "the flesh" is meant the old nature that we inherited from Adam, that is prone to sin. The flesh is not the body. The body is not sinful; the body is neutral. The Spirit may use the body to glorify God, or the flesh may use the body to serve sin. When a sinner yields to Christ, he receives a new nature within, but the old nature is neither removed nor reformed. For this reason, there is a battle within: "For the sinful nature desires what is contrary to the Spirit, and the Spirit what is contrary to the sinful nature. They are in conflict with each other so that you do not do what you want" (Gal. 5:17, NIV). This is what James terms "your lusts that are in your members" (James 4:1).

Living for the flesh means grieving the Holy Spirit of God who lives in us. "Or do you think Scripture says without reason that the Spirit He caused to live in us longs jealously?" (James 4:5, NIV, margin) Just as the world is the enemy of God the Father, so the flesh is the enemy of God the Holy Spirit. There is a holy, loving jealousy that a husband and wife have over each other, and rightly so. The Spirit within jealously guards our relationship to God, and the Spirit is grieved when we sin against God's love.

Living to please the old nature means to declare war against God. "The carnal mind is enmity against God" (Rom. 8:7). To allow the flesh to control the mind is to lose the blessing of fellowship with God. Abraham had a spiritual mind; he walked with God and enjoyed peace. Lot had a carnal mind; he disobeyed God and experienced war. "For to be carnally minded is death, but to be spiritually minded is life and peace" (Rom. 8:6).

**The devil (vv. 6-7).** The world is in conflict with the Father; the flesh fights against the Holy Spirit; and the devil opposes the Son of God. Pride is Satan's great sin, and it is one of his chief weapons in his warfare against the saint and the Saviour. God wants us to be humble; Satan wants us to be proud. "Ye shall be as God," Satan promised Eve, and she believed him. A new Christian must not be put into places of spiritual leadership "lest being lifted up with pride he fall into the condemnation of the devil" (1 Tim. 3:6).

God wants us to depend on His grace ("But He giveth more grace"), while the devil wants us to depend on ourselves. Satan is the author of all "do-it-yourself" spiritual enterprises. He enjoys inflating the ego and encouraging the believer to do it his own way. In spite of Jesus' warnings about Satan's plans, Peter fell into the snare, pulled out his sword, and tried to accomplish God's will in his own way. What a mess he made of things!

One of the problems in our churches today is that we have too many celebrities and not enough servants. Christian workers are promoted so much that there is very little place left for God's glory. Man has nothing to be proud of in himself. There dwells no good thing in us (Rom. 7:18); but when we trust Christ, He puts that "good thing" in us that makes us His children (2 Tim. 1:6, 14).

Here, then, are three enemies that want to turn us away from God: the world, the flesh, and the devil. These enemies are left over from our old life of sin (Eph. 2:1-3). Christ has delivered us from them, but they still attack us. How can we overcome them? How can we be the friends of God and the enemies of the world, the flesh, and the devil? James gives us three instructions to follow if we would enjoy peace instead of war.

**Submit to God (v. 7).** This word is a military term that means "get into your proper rank." When a buck private acts like the general, there is going to be trouble! Unconditional surrender is the only way to complete victory. If there is any area of the life kept back from God, there will always be battles. This explains why uncommitted Christians cannot live with themselves or with other people.

"Neither give place to the devil," cautions Paul in Ephesians 4:27. Satan needs a foothold in our lives if he is going to fight against God; and *we give him that foothold.* The way to resist the devil is to submit to God.

After King David committed adultery with Bathsheba, and killed her husband, he hid his sins for almost a year. There was war between him and God, and David had declared it. Read Psalms 32 and 51 to discover the high price David paid to be at war with God. When he finally submitted to God, David experienced peace and joy. This too he recorded in Psalms 32 and 51. Submission is an act of the will; it is saying, "Not my will but Thine be done."

**Draw near to God (v. 8).** How do we do this? By confessing our sins and asking for His cleansing. "Cleanse your hands, ye sinners; and purify your hearts, ye double-minded." The Greek word translated *purify* means "make chaste." This parallels the idea of "spiritual adultery" in James 4:4.

Dr. A.W. Tozer has a profound essay in one of his books, entitled, "Nearness Is Likeness." The more we are like God, the nearer we are to God. I may be sitting in my living room with my Siamese cat on my lap, and my wife may be twenty feet away in the kitchen; yet I am nearer to my wife than to the cat because the cat is unlike me. We have very little in common.

God graciously draws near to us when we deal with the sin in our lives that keeps Him at a distance. He will not share us with anyone else; He must have complete control. The double-minded Christian can never be close to God. Again, Abraham and Lot come to mind. Abraham "drew near" and talked to God about Sodom (Gen. 18:23ff), while Lot moved into Sodom and lost the blessing of God.

**Humble yourselves before God (vv. 9-10).** It is possible to submit outwardly and yet not be humbled inwardly. God hates the sin of pride (Prov. 6:16-17), and He will chasten the proud believer until he is humbled. We have a tendency to treat sin too lightly, even to laugh about it ("let your laughter be turned into mourning"). But sin is serious, and one mark of true humility is facing the seriousness of sin and dealing with our disobedience. "A broken and a contrite heart, O God, Thou wilt not despise" (Ps. 51:17).

Sometimes we hear a believer pray, "O Lord, humble me!" That is a dangerous thing to pray. Far better that we humble ourselves before God, confess our sins, weep over them, and turn from them. "To this man will I look, even to him that is poor and of a contrite spirit, and trembleth at My Word" (Isa. 66:2). "The Lord is nigh unto them that are of a broken heart; and saveth such as be of a contrite spirit" (Ps. 34:18).

If we obey these three instructions, then God will draw near, cleanse us, and forgive us; *and the wars will cease!* We will not be at war with God, so we will not be at war with ourselves. This means we will not be at war with others. "And the work of righteousness shall be peace; and the effect of righteousness quietness and assurance forever" (Isa. 32:17).

Put the government of your life on His shoulders, and let Him become the Prince of Peace in your life (Isa. 9:6).

# CHAPTER TEN
# PLAN AHEAD
*James 4:13-17*

J ames began chapter 4 talking about war with God, and he ends it talking about the will of God. But the two themes are related: when a believer is out of the will of God, he becomes a troublemaker and not a peacemaker.

Lot moved into Sodom and brought trouble to his family. David committed adultery and brought trouble to his family and his kingdom. Jonah disobeyed God and almost sent a shipload of heathen sailors into a watery grave. In each case, there was a wrong attitude toward the will of God.

That God would have a plan for each of our lives is an obvious truth. He is a God of *wisdom* and knows what ought to happen and when it should occur. And, as a God of *love,* He must desire the very best for His children. Too many Christians look on the will of God as bitter medicine they must take, instead of seeing it as the gracious evidence of the love of God.

"I would give my life to the Lord, but I'm afraid," a perplexed teenager told me at a church youth conference.

"What are you afraid of?" I asked.

"I'm afraid God will ask me to do something dangerous!"

"The dangerous life is not *in* the will of God," I replied, "but *out of* the will of God. The safest place in the world is right where God wants you."

I was going through a difficult time in my own ministry some years ago, questioning the will of God. While on vacation, I was reading the Book of Psalms, asking God to give me some assurance and encouragement. Psalm 33:11 was the answer to that prayer: "The counsel of the Lord standeth forever; the thoughts of His heart to all generations."

"The *will* of God comes from the *heart* of God," I said to myself. "His will is the expression of His love, so I don't have to be afraid!" It was a turning point in my life to discover the blessing of loving and living the will of God.

In this section of his letter, James pointed out three attitudes toward the will of God. Of course, only one of them is the correct one, the one that every Christian ought to cultivate.

## Ignoring God's Will (James 4:13-14, 16)

Perhaps James was addressing the wealthy merchants in the assembly. They might have discussed their business deals and boasted about their plans. There is no evidence that they sought the will of God or prayed about their decisions. They measured success in life by how many times they got their own way and accomplished what they had planned.

But James presented four arguments that revealed the foolishness of ignoring the will of God.

*The complexity of life (v. 13).* Think of all that is involved in life: today, tomorrow, buying, selling, getting gain, losing, going here, going there. Life is made up of people and places, activities and goals, days and years; and each of us must make many crucial decisions day after day.

Apart from the will of God, life is a mystery. When you know Jesus Christ as your Saviour, and seek to do His will, then life starts to make sense. Even the physical world around you takes on new meaning. There is a simplicity and unity to your life that makes for poise and confidence. You are no longer living in a mysterious, threatening universe. You can sing, "This is my Father's world!"

*The uncertainty of life (v. 14a).* This statement is based on Proverbs 27:1—"Boast not thyself of tomorrow; for thou knowest not what a day may bring forth." These businessmen were making plans for a whole year when they could not even see ahead into *one day!* See how confident they were: "We will go. We will stay a year. We will buy and sell and make a profit."

Their attitude reminds us of the farmer in the parable of Jesus in Luke 12:16-21. The man had a bumper crop; his barns were too small; so he decided to build bigger barns and have greater security for the future. "And I will say to my soul, 'Soul, thou hast much goods laid up for many years; take thine ease, eat, drink, and be merry' " (Luke 12:19).

What was God's reply to this man's boasting? "Thou fool, this night thy soul shall be required of thee" (Luke 12:20). Life is not uncertain to God, but it is uncertain to us. Only when we are in His will can we be confident of tomorrow, for we know that He is leading us.

*The brevity of life (v. 14b).* This is one of the repeated themes of Scripture. To us, life seems long and we measure it in years; but in comparison to eternity, life is but a vapor. James borrowed that figure from the Book of Job where you find many pictures of the brevity of life.

"My days are swifter than a weaver's shuttle" (Job 7:6). "The cloud is consumed and vanisheth away" (Job 7:9). "Our days upon earth are a shadow" (Job 8:9). "Now my days are swifter than a post" (Job 9:25), referring to the royal couriers that hastened in their missions. "They are passed away as the swift ships: as the eagle that hasteth to the prey" (Job 9:26). "Man that is born of a woman is of few days, and full of trouble. He cometh forth like a flower, and is cut down: he fleeth also as a shadow, and continueth not" (Job 14:1-2).

We count our *years* at each birthday, but God tells us to number our *days* (Ps. 90:12). After all, we live a day at a time, and those days rush by quickly the older we grow.

Since life is so brief, we cannot afford merely to "spend our lives"; and we certainly do not want to "waste our lives." We must *invest our lives* in those things that are eternal.

God reveals His will in His Word, and yet most people ignore the Bible. In the Bible, God gives precepts, principles, and promises that can guide us in every area of life. Knowing and obeying the Word of God is the surest way to success (Josh. 1:8; Ps. 1:3).

*The frailty of man (v. 16).* "As it is, you boast and brag. All such boasting is evil" (NIV). Man's boasting only covers up man's weakness. "Man proposes but God disposes," wrote Thomas à Kempis. Solomon said it first: "The lot is cast into the lap: but the whole disposing thereof is of the Lord" (Prov. 16:33). Man cannot control future events. He has neither the wisdom to *see* the future nor the power to *control* the future. For him to boast is sin; it is making himself God.

How foolish it is for people to ignore the will of God. It is like going through the dark jungles without a map, or over the stormy seas without a compass. When we visited Mammoth Cave in Kentucky, I was impressed with the maze of tunnels and the dense darkness when the lights were turned off. When we got to the "Pulpit Rock," the man in charge of the tour gave a five-word sermon from it: "Stay close to your guide." Good counsel indeed!

## Disobeying God's Will (James 4:17)

These people *know* the will of God but choose to disobey it. This attitude expresses even more pride than does the first; for the person says to God, "I know what You want me to do, but I prefer not to do it. I really know more about this than You do!" "For it had been better for them not to have known the way of righteousness, than, after they have known it, to turn from the holy commandment delivered unto them" (2 Peter 2:21).

Why do people who know the will of God deliberately disobey it? I have already suggested one reason: pride. Man likes to boast that he is the "master of his fate, the captain of his soul." Man has accomplished so many marvelous things that he thinks he can do anything.

Another reason is man's ignorance of the nature of God's will. He acts as though the will of God is something he can accept or reject. In reality, the will of God is not an option; it is an obligation. We cannot "take it or leave it." Because He is the Creator and we are the creatures, we must obey Him. Because He is the Saviour and Lord, and we are His children and servants, we must obey Him. To treat the will of God lightly is to invite the chastening of God in our lives.

Many people have the mistaken idea that the will of God is a formula for misery. Just the opposite is true! It is *disobeying* the Lord's will that leads to misery. The Bible, and human experience, are both witnesses to this truth. And even if a disobedient Christian seems to escape difficulty in this life, what will he say when he faces the Lord? "And that servant which knew his lord's will, and prepared not himself, neither did according to his will, shall be beaten with many stripes. But he that knew not, and did commit things worthy of stripes, shall be beaten with few stripes" (Luke 12:47-48).

What happens to Christians who deliberately disobey the known will of God? They are chastened by their loving Father until they submit (Heb. 12:5-11). If a professed believer is not chastened, it is evidence that he has never truly been born again but is a counterfeit. God's chastening is an evidence of His love, not His hatred. Just as we earthly fathers spank our children to help them respect our will and obey, so our Heavenly Father chastens His own. Though chastening is hard to take, it has a comforting truth of sonship with it.

But there is also the danger of losing heavenly rewards. In 1 Corinthians 9:24-27, Paul compared the believer to a runner in the Greek races. In order to qualify for a crown, he had to obey the rules of the game. If any contestant was found to have disobeyed the rules, he was disqualified and humiliated. The word "castaway" in 1 Corinthians 9:27 does not refer to the loss of salvation, but the loss of reward. "Disqualified" would be a good translation.

Disobeying God's will today may not seem a serious thing, but it will appear very serious when the Lord returns and examines our works (Col. 3:22-25).

## Obeying God's Will (James 4:15)

"If the Lord will" is not just a statement on a believer's lips: it is the constant attitude of his heart. "My food," said Jesus, "is to do the will of Him who sent Me and to finish His work" (John 4:34). Often in his letters, Paul referred to the will of God as he shared his plans with his friends (Rom. 1:10; 15:32; 1 Cor. 4:19; 16:7). Paul did not consider the will of God a chain that shackled him; rather, it was a key that opened doors and set him free.

Everything in this universe operates according to laws. If we cooperate with these laws and obey them, then the universe works *with* us. But if we fight these laws and disobey them, the universe will work *against* us. For example, certain laws govern flight. The engineer who obeys those laws in designing and building the plane, and the pilot who obeys those laws in flying the plane, will both have the joy of seeing the great machine operate perfectly. But if they disobey the basic laws that govern flight, the result will be a crash and the loss of life and money.

God's will for our lives is comparable to the laws He has built within the universe, with this exception: those laws are general, but the will He has planned for our lives is specifically designed for us. No two lives are planned according to the same pattern.

To be sure, there are some things that must be true of all Christians. It is God's will that we yield ourselves to Him (2 Cor. 8:5). It is God's will that we avoid sexual immorality (1 Thes. 4:3). All Christians should rejoice, pray, and thank God (1 Thes. 5:16-18). Every commandment in the Bible addressed to believers is part of the will of God, and must be obeyed. But God does not call each of us to the same work in life, or to exercise the same gifts and ministry. The will of God is "tailor-made" for each of us!

It is important that we have the right attitude toward the will of God. Some people think God's will is a cold, impersonal machine. God starts it going and it is up to us to keep it functioning smoothly. If we disobey Him in some way, the machine grinds to a halt, and we are out of God's will for the rest of our lives.

God's will is not a cold, impersonal machine. You do not determine God's will in some mechanical way, like getting a soft drink out of a "pop" machine. *The will of God is a living relationship between God and the believer.* This relationship is not *destroyed* when the believer disobeys, for the Father still deals with His child, even if He must chasten.

Rather than looking at the will of God as a cold, impersonal machine, I prefer to see it as a warm, growing, living body. If something goes wrong with my body, I don't die: the other parts of the body compensate for it until I get that organ working properly again. There is pain; there is also weakness; but there is not necessarily death.

When you and I get out of God's will, it is not the end of everything. We suffer, to be sure; but when God cannot rule, He overrules. Just as the body compensates for the malfunctioning of one part, so God adjusts things to bring us back into His will. You see this illustrated clearly in the lives of Abraham and Jonah.

The believer's relationship to the will of God is a growing experience. First, we should *know His will* (Acts 22:14). The will of God is not difficult to discover. If we are willing to obey, He is willing to reveal (John 7:17). It has been said that "obedience is the organ of spiritual knowledge." This is true. God does not reveal His will to the curious or the careless, but to those who are ready and willing to obey Him.

But we must not stop with merely knowing *some* of God's will. God wants us to be "filled with the knowledge of His will and all wisdom and spiritual understanding" (Col. 1:9). It is wrong to want to know God's will about some matters and ignore His will in other matters. Everything in our lives is important to God, and He has a plan for each detail.

God wants us to *understand His will* (Eph. 5:17). This is where spiritual wisdom comes in. A child can *know* the will of his father, but he may not *understand* his will. The child knows the "what" but not the "why." As the

"friends" of Jesus Christ, we have the privilege of knowing why God does what He does (John 15:15). "He made known His ways unto Moses, His acts unto the Children of Israel" (Ps. 103:7). The Israelites knew *what* God was doing, but Moses understood *why* He was doing it.

We must also *prove God's will* (Rom. 12:2). The Greek verb means "to prove by experience." We learn to determine the will of God by working at it. The more we obey, the easier it is to discover what God wants us to do. It is something like learning to swim or play a musical instrument. You eventually "get the feel" of what you are doing, and it becomes second nature to you.

People who keep asking, "How do I determine God's will for my life?" may be announcing to everybody that they have never really tried to do God's will. You start with the thing you know you ought to do, and you do that. Then God opens the way for the next step. You prove by experience what the will of God is. We learn both from successes and failures. "Take My yoke upon you, and learn of Me" (Matt. 11:29). The yoke suggests doing things together, putting into practice what God has taught you.

Finally, we must *do God's will from the heart* (Eph. 6:6). Jonah knew the will of God, and (after a spanking) did the will of God; but he did not do it from his heart. Jonah 4 indicates that the angry prophet did not love the Lord, nor did he love the people of Nineveh. He merely did God's will to keep from getting another spanking!

What Paul said about giving can also be applied to living: "not grudgingly, or of necessity, for God loveth a cheerful giver" (2 Cor. 9:7). *Grudgingly* means "reluctantly, painfully." They get absolutely no joy out of doing God's will. *Of necessity* means "under compulsion." These people obey because they have to, not because they want to. Their heart is not in it.

The secret of a happy life is to delight in duty. When duty becomes delight, then burdens become blessings. "Thy statutes have been my songs in the house of my pilgrimage" (Ps. 119:54). When we love God, then His statutes become songs, and we enjoy serving Him. When we serve God grudgingly, or because we have to, we may accomplish His work but we ourselves will miss the blessing. It will be toil, not ministry. But when we do God's will from the heart, we are enriched, no matter how difficult the task might have been.

We must never think that a failure in knowing or doing God's will permanently affects our relationship with the Lord. We can confess our sins and receive His forgiveness (1 John 1:9). We can learn from the mistakes. The important thing is a heart that loves God and wants sincerely to do His will and glorify His name.

What are the benefits of doing the will of God? For one thing, you enjoy a deeper fellowship with Jesus Christ (Mark 3:35). You have the privilege of knowing God's truth (John 7:17) and seeing your prayers answered (1 John 5:14-15). There is an eternal quality to the life and works of the one who does the will of God (1 John 2:15-17). Certainly, there is the expectation of reward at the return of Jesus Christ (Matt. 25:34).

Which of these three attitudes do you have toward the will of God? Do you totally ignore God's will as you make your daily plans and decisions? Or, do you know God's will and yet refuse to obey it? Each attitude is wrong and can only bring sorrow and ruin to the life of the person who holds it.

But the Christian who knows, loves, and obeys the will of God will enjoy God's blessing. His life may not be easier, but it will be holier and happier. His very food will be the will of God (John 4:34); it will be the joy and delight of his heart (Ps. 40:8).

# CHAPTER ELEVEN
# MONEY TALKS
*James 5:1-6*

If money talks," said a popular comedian, "all it ever says to me is good-bye!"

But money was not saying "good-bye" to the men James addressed in this section of his letter. These men were rich, and their riches were sinful. They were using their wealth for selfish purposes, and were persecuting the poor in the process.

One of the themes that runs through James 5 is *trouble*. We meet poor people deprived of their wages (James 5:4), as well as people who are physically afflicted (James 5:13-16), and spiritually backslidden (James 5:19-20). A

second theme that James introduced is *prayer*. The poor laborers cry out to God (James 5:4). The sick and afflicted should pray (James 5:13-16). He cited Elijah as an example of one who believed in prayer (James 5:17-18).

When you join these two themes, you arrive at the fifth mark of the mature Christian: *he is prayerful in troubles.* Instead of giving up when troubles come, the mature believer turns to God in prayer and seeks divine help. The immature person trusts in his own experience and skill, or else turns to others for help. While it is true that God often meets our needs through the hands of other people, this aid must be the result of prayer.

James did not say it was a sin to be rich. After all, Abraham was a wealthy man, yet he walked with God, and was greatly used of God to bless the whole world. James was concerned about the selfishness of the rich, and advised them to "weep and howl." He gave three reasons for his exhortation.

## The Way They Got Their Wealth
## (James 5:4, 6a)

The Bible does not discourage the acquiring of wealth. In the Law of Moses, specific rules are laid down for getting and securing wealth. The Jews in Canaan owned their own property, worked it, and benefited from the produce. In several of His parables, Jesus indicated His respect for personal property and private gain. There is nothing in the Epistles that contradicts the right of private ownership and profit.

What the Bible does condemn is acquiring wealth by illegal means or for illegal purposes. The Prophet Amos thundered a message of judgment against the wealthy upper crust who robbed the poor and used their stolen wealth for selfish luxuries. Isaiah and Jeremiah also exposed the selfishness of the rich and warned that judgment was coming. It is in this spirit that James wrote. He gave two illustrations of how the rich acquired their wealth.

*Holding back wages (v. 4).* Laborers were hired and paid by the day and did not have any legal contracts with their employers. The Parable of the Laborers in Matthew 20:1-16 gives some idea of the system in that day. In the Law, God gave definite instructions concerning the laboring man in order to protect him from the oppressive employer.

"You shall not oppress a hired servant who is poor and needy, whether he is one of your countrymen or one of your aliens who is in your land in your towns. You shall give him his wages on his day before the sun sets, for he is poor and sets his heart on it; so that he may not cry against you to the Lord and it become sin in you" (Deut. 24:14-15, NASB).

"You shall not oppress your neighbor, nor rob him. The wages of a hired man are not to remain with you all night until morning" (Lev. 19:13, NASB).

"Woe to him that buildeth his house by unrighteousness, and his chambers by wrong; that useth his neighbor's service without wages, and giveth him not for his work" (Jer. 22:13).

These rich men had hired the laborers and promised to pay them a specific amount. The men had completed their work but had not been paid. The tense of the verb "kept back" in the original Greek indicates that the laborers *never will get their salaries.*

"Thou shalt not steal" is still the law of God, and it is a law He will enforce. As Christians, it behooves us to be faithful to pay our bills. As a pastor, I find myself embarrassed when unsaved men tell me about Christians who owe them money and apparently have no intention of paying.

I recall meeting a doctor friend while I was visiting in the hospital. "How are things going?" I asked, and he replied, "Oh, I guess things are OK."

"I pray for you," I told him, wanting to be an encouragement.

"I appreciate that," he replied. "But while you're at it, pray for all the people who owe me money. It'd help if they would pay up!"

***Controlling the courts (v. 6a).*** It is often the case that those who have wealth also have political power and can get what they want. "What is the Golden Rule?" asked a character in a comic strip. His friend answered, "Whoever has the gold makes the rules!" James asked, "Do not the rich men oppress you and draw you before the judgment seats?" (James 2:6)

When the name *Watergate* is mentioned, nobody thinks of a beautiful hotel. That word reminds us of an ugly episode in American history that led to the revelation of lies and the resignation of the President of the United States. Each side accused the other of obstructing justice and manipulating the laws.

When God established Israel in her land, He gave the people a system of courts (see Deut. 17:8-13). He warned the judges not to be greedy (Ex. 18:21). They were not to be partial to the rich or the poor (Lev. 19:15). No

judge was to tolerate perjury (Deut. 19:16-21). Bribery was condemned by the Lord (Isa. 33:15; Micah 3:11; 7:3). The Prophet Amos denounced the judges in his day who took bribes and "fixed" cases (Amos 5:12, 15).

The courts in James' day were apparently easy to control if you had enough money. The poor workers could not afford expensive lawsuits, so they were beaten down every time. The workers had the just cause, but they were not given justice. Instead, they were abused and ruined. ("Killed" should probably be taken in a figurative way, as in James 4:2, though it is possible that the rich men could so oppress the poor that the poor would die.) The poor man did not resist the rich man because he had no weapons with which to fight. All he could do was call on the Lord for justice.

The Bible warns us against the securing of wealth by illegal means. God owns all wealth (Ps. 50:10); He permits us to be stewards of His wealth for His glory. "Wealth obtained by fraud dwindles, but the one who gathers by labor increases it" (Prov. 13:11, NASB). It is "the hand of the diligent that makes rich" (Prov. 10:4). "Do not weary yourself to gain wealth" (Prov. 23:4). We must put God first in our lives, and He will see to it that we always have all that we need (Matt. 6:33).

## The Way the Rich Used Their Wealth (James 5:3-5)

It is bad enough to gain wealth in a sinful way, but to use that wealth in sinful ways just makes the sin greater.

***They stored it up (v. 3).*** Of course, there is nothing sinful about saving. "For the children ought not to lay up for the parents, but the parents for the children" (2 Cor. 12:14). "But if any provide not for his own, and specially for those of his own house, he hath denied the faith, and is worse than an infidel" (1 Tim. 5:8). "Then you ought to have put my money in the bank, and on my arrival I would have received my money back with interest" (Matt. 25:27, NASB).

But it is wrong to store up wealth when you owe money to your employees. These rich men were hoarding grain, gold, and garments. They thought that they were rich because they had these possessions. Instead of laying up treasures in heaven by using their wealth for God's glory (Matt. 6:19ff), they were selfishly guarding it for their own security and pleasure. Not more than ten years after James wrote this letter, Jerusalem fell to the Romans, and all this accumulated wealth was taken.

What did Jesus mean by "laying up treasures in heaven"? Did He mean we should "sell everything and give to the poor" as He instructed the rich young ruler? I think not. He spoke that way to the rich ruler because covetousness was the young man's besetting sin, and Jesus wanted to expose it. To lay up treasures in heaven means to use all that we have as stewards of God's wealth. You and I may *possess* many things, but we do not *own* them. God is the Owner of everything, and we are His stewards.

What we possess and use are merely things, apart from the will of God. When we yield to His will and use what He gives us to serve Him, then things become treasures and we are investing in eternity. What we do on earth is recorded in heaven, and God keeps the books and pays the interest.

What a tragedy it is to see people "heap up treasures for the last days" instead of "laying up treasures in heaven." The Bible does not discourage saving, or even investing; but it does condemn hoarding.

**They kept others from benefiting from it (v. 4).** By fraudulent means, the rich men robbed the poor. The rich men were not using their own wealth, but they would not pay their laborers and permit them to use the wealth. Perhaps they were waiting for salaries to go down.

Since we are stewards of God's wealth, we have certain responsibilities toward our Master. We must be faithful to use what He gives us for the good of others and the glory of God. "Moreover, it is required in stewards, that a man be found faithful" (1 Cor. 4:2). Joseph was a faithful steward in Potiphar's house, and Potiphar prospered. There are ways that we can use God's wealth to help others.

**They lived in luxury (v. 5).** "You have lived in high style on the earth!" (James 5:5, literal translation) Luxury is waste, and waste is sin.

A magazine advertisement told of the shopping spree of an oil-rich sultan. He purchased nineteen Cadillacs, one for each of his nineteen wives, and paid extra to have the cars lengthened. He also bought two Porsches, six Mercedes, a $40,000 speedboat and a truck for hauling it. Add to the list sixteen refrigerators, $47,000 worth of women's luggage, two Florida grapefruit trees, two reclining chairs, and one slot machine. His total bill was $1.5 million, and he had to pay another $194,500 to have everything delivered. Talk about living in luxury!

All of us are grateful for the good things of life, and we would certainly not want to return to primitive conditions. But we recognize the fact that there is a point of diminishing returns. "Tell me what thou dost need," said the Quaker to his neighbor, "and I will tell thee how to get along without it." Jesus said, "Beware and be on your guard against every form of greed; for not even when one has an abundance does his life consist of his possessions" (Luke 12:15, NASB). These rich men James addressed were feeding themselves on their riches and starving to death. The Greek word pictures cattle being fattened for the slaughter.

There is a great difference between enjoying what God has given us (1 Tim. 6:17) and living extravagantly on what we have withheld from others. Even if what we have has been earned lawfully and in the will of God, we must not waste it on selfish living. There are too many needs to be met.

Luxury has a way of ruining character. It is a form of self-indulgence. If you match character with wealth, you can produce much good; but if you match self-indulgence with wealth, the result is sin. The rich man Jesus described in Luke 16:19-31 would have felt right at home with the rich men James wrote to!

## What Their Riches Will Do
## (James 5:1-4)

The rich thought they had it made because of their wealth, but God thought otherwise. "Howl for your miseries that shall come upon you" (James 5:1). James described the consequences of misusing riches.

**Riches will vanish (vv. 2-3a).** Grain will rot ("corrupted" in James 5:2); gold will rust; and garments will become moth-eaten. Nothing material in this world will last forever. The seeds of death and decay are found in all of creation.

It is a great mistake to think there is security in wealth. Paul wrote, "Instruct those who are rich in this present world not to be conceited, or to fix their hope on the uncertainty of riches" (1 Tim. 6:17). Riches are uncertain. The money market fluctuates from hour to hour, and so does the stock market. Actually, gold does not rust the way iron does; but the idea is the same: the gold is losing its value. Add to this the fact that life is brief, and we cannot take wealth with us, and you can see how foolish it is to live for the things of this world. God said to the rich man, "Thou fool, this night thy soul shall be required of thee: then whose shall those things be, which thou hast provided?" (Luke 12:20)

**Misused riches erode character (v. 3).** "Their corrosion . . . will eat your flesh like fire" (James 5:3, NIV). This is a present judgment: the poison of wealth has infected them and they are being eaten alive. Of itself, money is not sinful; it is neutral. But "the love of money is the root of all evil" (1 Tim. 6:10). "Thou shalt not covet" is the last of the Ten Commandments, but it is the most dangerous. Covetousness will make a person break all the other nine commandments.

Abraham was a rich man, but he maintained his faith and character. When Lot became rich, it ruined his character and ultimately ruined his family. It is good to have riches in your hand provided they do not get into your heart. "If riches increase, set not your heart upon them" (Ps. 62:10). "A good name is rather to be chosen than great riches, and loving favor rather than silver and gold" (Prov. 22:1)

**Judgment is a certainty (vv. 3, 5).** James not only saw a *present* judgment (their wealth decaying, their character eroding), but also a *future* judgment before God. Jesus Christ will be the Judge (James 5:9), and His judgment will be righteous.

Note the witnesses that God will call on that day of judgment. First, the rich men's *wealth* will witness against them (James 5:3). Their rotten grain, rusted gold and silver, and moth-eaten garments will bear witness of the selfishness of their hearts. There is a bit of irony here: the rich men saved their wealth to help them, but their hoarded riches will only testify against them.

The *wages* they held back will also witness against them in court (James 5:4a). Money talks! These stolen salaries cry out to God for justice and judgment. God heard Abel's blood cry out from the ground (Gen. 4:10), and He hears this stolen money cry out too.

The *workers* will also testify against them (James 5:4). There will be no opportunities for the rich to bribe the witnesses or the Judge. God hears the cries of His oppressed people and He will judge righteously.

This judgment is a serious thing. The lost will stand before Christ at the Great White Throne (Rev. 20:11-15). The saved will stand before the Judgment Seat of Christ (Rom. 14:10-12; 2 Cor. 5:9-10). God will not judge our *sins,* because they have already been judged on the cross; but He will judge our *works* and our ministry. If we have been faithful in serving and glorifying Him, we will receive a reward; if we have been unfaithful, we shall lose our reward but not our salvation (1 Cor. 3:1-15).

**The loss of a precious opportunity (v. 3).** "The last days" indicates that James believed that the coming of the Lord was near (see James 5:8-9). We must "buy up the opportunity" (Eph. 5:16, literal translation) and work while it is day (John 9:4). Think of the good that could have been accomplished with that hoarded wealth. There were poor people in that congregation who could have been helped (James 2:1-6). There were workers who deserved their wages. Sad to say, in a few years the Jewish nation was defeated and scattered, and Jerusalem destroyed.

It is good to have the things that money can buy, provided you also have the things that money cannot buy. What good is a $500,000 house if there is no home? Or a million-dollar diamond ring if there is no love? James did not condemn riches or rich people; he condemned the wrong use of riches, and rich people who use their wealth as a weapon and not as a tool with which to build.

It is possible to be "poor in this world" (James 2:5) and yet rich in the next world. It is also possible to be "rich in this world" (1 Tim. 6:17) and poor in the next world. The return of Jesus Christ will make some people poor and others rich, depending on the spiritual condition of their hearts. "For where your treasure is, there will your heart be also" (Matt. 6:21).

What we keep, we lose. What we give to God, we keep, and He adds interest to it. A famous preacher, known for his long sermons, was asked to give the annual "charity sermon" for the poor. It was suggested that if he preached too long, the congregation might not give as much as they should.

The preacher read his text from Proverbs 19:17—"He that hath pity upon the poor lendeth unto the Lord; and that which he hath given will He pay him again." His sermon indeed was brief:

"If you like the terms, then put down your money."

Yes, money talks. What will it say to you at the last judgment?

# CHAPTER TWELVE
# THE POWER
# OF PATIENCE
*James 5:7-12*

James was still addressing the suffering saints when he wrote, "Be patient." This was his counsel at the beginning of his letter (James 1:1-5), and his counsel as his letter came to a close. God is not going to right all the wrongs in this world until Jesus Christ returns, and we believers must patiently endure—and expect.

Three times James reminds us of the coming of the Lord (James 5:7-9). This is the "blessed hope" of the Christian (Titus 2:13). We do not expect to have everything easy and comfortable in this present life. "In the world ye shall have tribulation" (John 16:33). Paul reminded his converts that "we must through much tribulation enter into the kingdom of God" (Acts 14:22). We must patiently endure hardships and heartaches until Jesus returns.

James used two different words for patience. In James 5:7-8, 10 it was the word "long-tempered." The words "endure" and "patience" in James 5:11 literally mean "to remain under" and speak of endurance under great stress. *Patience* means "to stay put and stand fast when you'd like to run away." Many Greek scholars think that "long-suffering" refers to patience with respect to persons, while "endurance" refers to patience with respect to conditions or situations.

But the question we must answer is: How can we as Christians experience this kind of patient endurance as we wait for the Lord to return? To answer that question (and need), James gave three encouraging examples of patient endurance.

### The Farmer (James 5:7-9)
If a man is impatient, then he had better not become a farmer. No crop appears overnight (except perhaps a crop of weeds), and no farmer has control over the weather. Too much rain can cause the crop to rot, and too much sun can burn it up. An early frost can kill the crop. How long-suffering the farmer must be with the weather!

He must also have patience with the seed and the crop, for it takes time for plants to grow. Jewish farmers would plow and sow in what to us are the autumn months. The "early rain" would soften the soil. The "latter rain" would come in the early spring (our February–March) and help to mature the harvest. The farmer had to wait many weeks for his seed to produce fruit.

Why did he willingly wait so long? Because the fruit is "precious" (James 5:7). The harvest is worth waiting for. "In due season we shall reap, if we faint not" (Gal. 6:9). "For the earth produces crops by itself; first the blade, then the head, then the mature grain in the head. But when the crop permits, he immediately puts in the sickle, because the harvest has come" (Mark 4:28-29, NASB).

James pictured the Christian as a "spiritual farmer" looking for a spiritual harvest. "Be ye also patient, stablish your hearts" (James 5:8). Our hearts are the soil, and the "seed is the Word of God" (Luke 8:11). There are seasons to the spiritual life just as there are seasons to the soil. Sometimes, our hearts become cold and "wintry," and the Lord has to "plow them up" before He can plant the seed (Jer. 4:3). He sends the sunshine and the rains of His goodness to water and nurture the seeds planted; but we must be patient to wait for the harvest.

Here, then, is a secret of endurance when the going is tough: *God is producing a harvest in our lives.* He wants the "fruit of the Spirit" to grow (Gal. 5:22-23), and the only way He can do it is through trials and troubles. Instead of growing impatient with God and with ourselves, we must yield to the Lord and permit the fruit to grow. We are "spiritual farmers" looking for a harvest.

You can enjoy this kind of a harvest only if your heart is *established* (James 5:8). One of the purposes of the spiritual ministry of the local church is to establish the heart (Rom. 1:11). Paul sent Timothy to Thessalonica to establish the young Christians in their faith (1 Thes. 3:1-3); and Paul also prayed for them that they might be established (1 Thes. 3:10-13). The ministry of the Word of God and prayer are important if the heart is going to be established. A heart that is not established cannot bear fruit.

Keep in mind that the farmer does not stand around doing nothing: he is constantly at work as he looks toward the harvest. James did not tell these suffering believers to put on white robes, climb a hill, and wait for Jesus to return. "Keep working and waiting" was his admonition. "Blessed is that servant, whom his Lord when He cometh shall find so doing" (Luke 12:43).

Nor does the farmer get into fights with his neighbors. One of the usual marks of farmers is their willingness to help one another. Nobody on the farm has time or energy for disputes with the neighbors. James must have had this in mind when he added, "Don't grumble against each other, brothers, or you will be judged" (James 5:9, NIV). Impatience with God often leads to impatience with God's people, and this is a sin we must avoid. If we start using the sickles on each other, we will miss the harvest!

### The Prophets (James 5:10)

A Jewish congregation would understand this simple reference that James made to the Old Testament prophets. In His Sermon on the Mount, Jesus also used the prophets as an example of victory over persecution (Matt. 5:10-12). What encouragements do we receive from their example?

For one thing, they were in the will of God, yet they suffered. They were preaching "in the name of the Lord," yet they were persecuted. Satan tells the faithful Christian that his suffering is the result of sin or unfaithfulness; and yet his suffering might well be *because of faithfulness!* "Yea, and all that will live godly in Christ Jesus shall suffer persecution" (2 Tim. 3:12). We must never think that obedience automatically produces ease and pleasure. Our Lord was obedient, and it led to a cross!

The prophets encourage us by reminding us that God cares for us when we go through sufferings for His sake. Elijah announced to wicked King Ahab that there would be a drought in the land for three and one half years; and Elijah himself had to suffer in that drought. But God cared for him, and God gave him victory over the evil priests of Baal. It has been said, "The will of God will never lead you where the grace of God cannot keep you."

Many of the prophets had to endure great trials and sufferings, not only at the hands of unbelievers, but at the hands of professed believers. Jeremiah was arrested as a traitor and even thrown into an abandoned well to die. God fed Jeremiah and protected him throughout that terrible siege of Jerusalem, even though at times it looked as though the prophet was going to be killed. Both Ezekiel and Daniel had their share of hardships, but the Lord delivered them. And even those who were not delivered, who died for the faith, received that special reward for those who are true to Him.

Why is it that those who "speak in the name of the Lord" often must endure difficult trials? It is so that their lives might back up their messages. The impact of a faithful, godly life carries much power. We need to remind ourselves that our patience in times of suffering is a testimony to others around us.

But have not many faithful Christians suffered and died without any notice or recognition? Yes, but when Jesus returns, these "obscure heroes" will receive their rewards. The prophets were killed and buried, but today their names are honored. When our Lord comes again, He will bring His reward with Him (Rev. 22:12).

This example that James used from the Old Testament prophets ought to encourage us to spend more time in the Bible, getting acquainted with these heroes of faith. "For everything that was written in the past was written to teach us, so that through endurance and the encouragement of the Scriptures we might have hope" (Rom. 15:4, NIV). The better we know the Bible, the more God can encourage us in the difficult experiences of life. The important thing is that, like the farmer, we keep working, and, like the prophets, we keep witnessing, no matter how trying the circumstances may be.

### Job (James 5:11-12)

"As you know, we consider blessed those who have persevered" (James 5:11, NIV). But you cannot persevere unless there is a trial in your life. There can be no victories without battles; there can be no peaks without valleys. If you want the blessing, you must be prepared to carry the burden and fight the battle.

I once heard a young Christian pray, "O Lord, please teach me the deep truths of Thy Word! I want to be lifted up to the heavens to hear and see the wonderful things that are there!" It was a sincere prayer, but the young man did not realize what he was praying. Paul went to the third heaven and learned things too marvelous for words; and as a result, *God had to give Paul a thorn in the flesh to keep him humble* (2 Cor. 12:1-10). God has to balance privileges with responsibilities, blessings with burdens, or else you and I will become spoiled, pampered children.

When do "blessings" come? In the midst of

trials we may experience God's blessings, as did the three Hebrew children in the fiery furnace (Dan. 3); but James taught that there is a blessing *after we have endured*. His example was Job.

The Book of Job is a long book, and the chapters are filled with speeches that, to the Western mind, seem long and tedious. In the first three chapters you have *Job's distress:* he loses his wealth, his family (except for his wife, and she told him to commit suicide), and his health. In Job 4–31 we read *Job's defense,* as he debates with his three friends and answers their false accusations. Job 38–42 present *Job's deliverance:* first God humbles Job, and then He honors Job and gives him twice as much as he had before.

In studying the experience of Job, it is important to remember that *Job did not know what was going on "behind the scenes" between God and Satan.* Job's friends accused him of being a sinner and a hypocrite. "There must be some terrible sin in your life," they argued, "or God would never have permitted this suffering." Job disagreed with them and maintained his innocence (but not perfection) during the entire conversation. The friends were wrong: God had no cause against Job (Job 2:3), and in the end, God rebuked the friends for telling lies about Job (Job 42:7).

It is difficult to find a greater example of suffering than Job. Circumstances were against him, for he lost his wealth and his health. He also lost his beloved children. His wife was against him, for she said, "Curse God and die" (Job 2:9). His friends were against him, for they accused him of being a hypocrite, deserving of the judgment of God. And it seemed like God was against him! When Job cried out for answers to his questions, there was no reply from heaven.

Yet, Job endured. Satan predicted that Job would get impatient with God and abandon his faith, but that did not happen. It is true that Job questioned God's will, but Job did not forsake his faith in the Lord. "Though He slay me, I will hope in Him. Nevertheless, I will argue my ways before Him" (Job 13:15, NASB). Job was so sure of God's perfections that he persisted in arguing with Him, even though he did not understand all that God was doing. That is endurance.

God made a covenant with Israel that He would bless them if they would obey His Laws (see Deut. 11). This led to the idea that, if you were wealthy and comfortable, you were blessed of God; but if you were suffering and poor, you were cursed of God. Sad to say, many people have that same erroneous idea today. When Jesus said it was difficult for a rich man to enter heaven, the disciples were shocked. "Who then can be saved?" they asked (Matt. 19:23-26). "The rich are especially blessed of God," they were saying. "If *they* can't make it, nobody can!"

The Book of Job refutes that idea; for Job was a righteous man, *and yet he suffered.* God found no evil in him, and even Satan could not find any. Job's friends could not prove their accusations. Job teaches us that God has higher purposes in suffering than the punishing of sin. Job's experience paved the way for Jesus, the perfect Son of God who suffered, not for His own sins, but for the sins of the world.

In Job's case, what was "the end [purpose] of the Lord"? *To reveal Himself as full of pity and tender mercy.* Certainly, there were other results from Job's experience, for God never wastes the sufferings of His saints. Job met God in a new and deeper way (Job 42:1-6), and, after that, Job received greater blessings from the Lord.

"But if God is so merciful," someone may argue, "why didn't He protect Job from all that suffering to begin with?" To be sure, there are mysteries to God's working that our finite minds cannot fathom; but this we know: God was glorified and Job was purified through this difficult experience. If there is nothing to endure, you cannot learn endurance.

What did Job's story mean to the believers James wrote to, and what does it mean to us today? It means that some of the trials of life are caused directly by satanic opposition. God permits Satan to try His children, but He always limits the extent of the enemy's power (Job 1:12; 2:6). When you find yourself in the fire, remember that God keeps His gracious hand on the thermostat! "But He knoweth the way that I take: when He hath tried me, I shall come forth as gold" (Job 23:10).

Satan wants us to get impatient with God, for an impatient Christian is a powerful weapon in the devil's hands. You will recall from our study of James 1 that Moses' impatience robbed him of a trip to the Holy Land; Abraham's impatience led to the birth of Ishmael, the enemy of the Jews; and Peter's impatience almost made him a murderer. When Satan attacks us, it is easy for us to get impatient and run ahead of God and lose God's blessing as a result.

What is the answer? "My grace is sufficient for thee!" (2 Cor. 12:7-9) Paul's thorn in the flesh was a "messenger of Satan." Paul could have fought it, given up under it, or tried to deny that the thorn existed; but he did not. Instead, he trusted God for the grace he needed; and he turned Satan's weapon into a tool for the building up of his own spiritual life.

When you find yourself in the furnace, go to the throne of grace and receive from the Lord all the grace you need to endure (Heb. 4:14-16). Remind yourself that the Lord has a gracious purpose in all of this suffering, and that He will work out His purposes in His time and for His glory. You are not a robot caught in the jaws of fate. You are a loving child of God, privileged to be a part of a wonderful plan. There is a difference!

The exhortation in James 5:12 seems out of place; for what does "speaking oaths" have to do with the problem of suffering? If you have ever suffered, you know the answer: it is easy to say things you do not mean, and even make bargains with God, when you are going through difficulties. Go back to Job for an example. The patriarch said, "Naked came I out of my mother's womb, and naked shall I return thither: the Lord gave, and the Lord hath taken away; blessed be the name of the Lord. In all this Job sinned not, nor charged God foolishly" (Job 1:21-22). Job did curse the day he was born (Job 3:1ff), but he never cursed God or spoke with a foolish oath. Neither did he try to bargain with God.

Surely James is reminding us of our Lord's teaching in the Sermon on the Mount (Matt. 5:34-37). The Jews were great ones for using various oaths to back up their statements. They were careful, however, not to use the name of God in their oaths, lest they blaspheme God. So, they would swear by heaven, or earth, or Jerusalem, or even by their own heads! But Jesus taught that it is impossible to avoid God in such oaths. Heaven is His throne, earth is His footstool, and Jerusalem is the "city of the great King." As for swearing by your head, what good is it? "Thou canst not make one hair black or white" (Matt. 5:36)—or even keep one hair on your head.

It is a basic principle that true Christian character requires few words. The person who must use many words (including oaths) to convince us has something wrong with his character and must bolster this weakness by using words. If you are a true Christian, with integrity, then all you have to say is yes or no and people will believe you. Jesus warns us that anything more than this is from the evil one.

One of the purposes of suffering is the building of character. Certainly Job was a better man for having gone through the furnace. (James explained this process to us, James 1:2-12.) If words are a test of character, then oaths would indicate that there is yet work to be done. When Peter poured out those oaths in the courtyard (Matt. 26:71), he was giving evidence that his character was still in need of a transformation.

As you review this section, you can see the practicality of it. James wanted to encourage us to be patient in times of suffering. Like the farmer, we are waiting for a spiritual harvest, for fruit that will glorify God. Like the prophets, we look for opportunities for witness, to share the truth of God. And, like Job, we wait for the Lord to fulfill His loving purpose, knowing that He will never cause His children to suffer needlessly. And, like Job, we shall have a clearer vision of the Lord and come to know Him better for having been in the furnace of affliction.

"Be patient, for the coming of the Lord draweth nigh!"

# CHAPTER THIRTEEN
# LET US PRAY
*James 5:13-20*

The gift of speech is a marvelous blessing, if it is used to the glory of God. As we have seen, James had a great deal to say about the tongue; and this chapter is no exception. He mentioned some of the lowest uses of the tongue: complaining (James 5:9) and swearing (James 5:12). But he also named some of the highest uses of the tongue: proclaiming God's Word (James 5:10) and praying and praising God (James 5:13).

Prayer is certainly a high and holy privilege. To think that, as God's children, we can come freely and boldly to His throne and share with Him our needs! Seven times in this section James mentioned prayer. The mature Christian is prayerful in the troubles of life. Instead of complaining about his situation, he talks to God about it; and God hears and answers his prayers. "Taking it to the Lord in prayer" is certainly a mark of spiritual maturity.

In this section, James encourages us to pray by describing four situations in which God answers prayer.

## Prayer for the Suffering (James 5:13)

The word *afflicted* means "suffering in difficult circumstances." The phrase "in trouble" is a good translation. Paul used this word to describe the circumstances he was in as he suffered for the Gospel's sake (2 Tim. 2:9). As God's people go through life, they often must endure difficulties that are not the results of sin or the chastening of God.

What should we do when we find ourselves in such trying circumstances? We must not grumble and criticize the saints who are having an easier time of it (James 5:9); nor should we blame the Lord. We should pray, asking God for the wisdom we need to understand the situation and use it to His glory (James 1:5).

Prayer can remove affliction, if that is God's will. But prayer can also give us the grace we need to endure troubles and use them to accomplish God's perfect will. *God can transform troubles into triumphs.* "He giveth more grace" (James 4:6). Paul prayed that God might change his circumstances, but instead, God gave Paul the grace he needed to turn his weakness into strength (2 Cor. 12:7-10). Our Lord prayed in Gethsemane that the cup might be removed, and it was not; yet the Father gave Him the strength He needed to go to the cross and die for our sins.

James indicated that everybody does not go through troubles at the same time: "Is any merry? Let him sing psalms" (James 5:13). God balances our lives and gives us hours of suffering and days of singing. The mature Christian knows how to sing *while he is suffering.* (Anybody can sing after the trouble has passed.) God is able to give "songs in the night" (Job 35:10). He did this for Paul and Silas when they were suffering in that Philippian jail. "And at midnight Paul and Silas prayed, and sang praises unto God" (Acts 16:25).

Praying and singing were important elements in worship in the early church, and they should be important to us. Our singing ought to be an expression of our inner spiritual life. The believer's praise should be intelligent (1 Cor. 14:15) and not just the mouthing of words or ideas that mean nothing to him. It should come from the heart (Eph. 5:19) and be motivated by the Holy Spirit (Eph. 5:18). Christian singing must be based on the Word of God (Col. 3:16) and not simply on the clever ideas of men. If a song is not biblical, it is not acceptable to God.

## Prayer for the Sick (James 5:14-16)

I do not think that James gave us a blanket formula for healing the sick. In the churches I have pastored, the elders and I have prayed for the sick, and sometimes God has given healing. But other times, He has not seen fit to heal the person. I recall two cases within one week of each other: the one lady was restored in an almost miraculous way, but the other one had to enter the hospital for surgery, and eventually the Lord called her home.

What are the special characteristics of this case that James is describing?

*The person is sick because of sin (vv. 15b-16).* The Greek text says, "If he has been constantly sinning." This parallels 1 Corinthians 11:30, "For this cause many are weak and sickly among you, and many sleep" (have died). James has described a church member who is sick because he is being disciplined by God. This explains why the elders of the assembly are called: the man cannot go to church to confess his sins, so he asks the spiritual leaders to come to him. The leaders would be in charge of the discipline of the congregation.

*The person confesses his sins (v. 16).* In the early church, the believers practiced church discipline. First Corinthians 5 is a good example. Paul told the believers at Corinth to dismiss the sinning member from the assembly until he repented of his sins and made things right. The little word "therefore" belongs in James 5:16—"Confess your sins therefore to one another, and pray for one another, that you may be healed" (literal translation). The word *faults* in the *Authorized Version* gives the impression that the man's deeds were not too evil; they were only faults. But it is the word *hamartia* that James used, and this word means "sin." It is the same word used in James 1:15, where the subject is definitely sin.

*The person is healed by "the prayer of faith" (v. 15).* It is not the anointing that heals, but the praying. The Greek word translated "anointing" is a medicinal term; it could be translated "massaging." This may be an indication that James suggests using available means for healing along with asking the Lord for His divine touch. God can heal with or without means; in each case, it is God who does the healing.

But what is "the prayer of faith" that heals the sick? The answer is in 1 John 5:14-15— "And this is the confidence that we have in Him, that, if we ask anything according to His will, He heareth us: and if we know that He hear us, whatsoever we ask, we know that we have the petitions that we desired of Him." The "prayer of faith" is a prayer offered *when you know the will of God.* The elders would seek the mind of God in the matter, and then pray according to His will.

As I visit the sick among my congregation, I do not always know how to pray for them. (Paul had the same problem; read Rom. 8:26.) Is it God's will to heal? Is God planning to call His child home? I do not know; therefore, I must pray, "If it is Your will, heal Your child." Those who claim that God heals every case, and that it is not His will for His children to be sick, are denying both Scripture and experience. But where we have the inner conviction from the Word and the Spirit that it is God's will to heal, then we can pray "the prayer of faith" and expect God to work.

Keep in mind that it is not one individual who is praying: it is the body of elders—spiritual men of God—who seek God's will and pray. James does not instruct the believer to send for a faith healer. The matter is in the hands of the leaders of the local church.

There are some practical lessons from this section that we must not overlook. For one thing, disobedience to God can lead to sickness. This was David's experience when he tried to hide his sins (Ps. 32). Second, sin affects the whole church. We can never sin alone, for sin has a way of growing and infecting others. This man had to confess his sins to the church because he had sinned against the church. Third, there is healing (physical and spiritual) when sin is dealt with. "He that covereth his sins shall not prosper: but whoso confesseth and forsaketh them shall find mercy" (Prov. 28:13). James wrote, "Make it a habit to confess your sins to each other" (literal translation). Do not hide sin or delay confession.

The "confessing" that James wrote about is done among the saints. He was not suggesting confessing our sins to a preacher or priest. We confess our sins first of all to the Lord (1 John 1:9), but we must also confess them to those who have been affected by them. *We must never confess sin beyond the circle of that sin's influence.* Private sin requires private confession; public sin requires public confession. It is wrong for Christians to "hang dirty wash in public," for such "confessing" might do more harm than the original sin.

**Prayer for the Nation (James 5:17-18)**
James cited Elijah as an example of a "righteous man" whose prayers released power. "The prayer of a righteous man is powerful and effective" (James 5:16, NIV).

The background of this incident is found in 1 Kings 17–18. Wicked King Ahab and Jezebel, his queen, had led Israel away from the Lord and into the worship of Baal. God punished the nation by holding back the rain that they needed (see Deut. 28:12, 23). For three and one half years, the heavens were as brass and the earth unable to produce the crops so necessary for life.

Then Elijah challenged the priests of Baal on Mt. Carmel. All day long the priests cried out to their god, but no answer came. At the time of the evening sacrifice, Elijah repaired the altar and prepared the sacrifice. He prayed but once, and fire came from heaven to consume the sacrifice. He had proven that Jehovah was the true God.

But the nation still needed rain. Elijah went to the top of Carmel and fell down before the Lord in prayer. He prayed and sent his servant seven times to see if there was evidence of rain; and the seventh time his servant saw a little cloud. Before long, there was a great rain, and the nation was saved.

Do we need "showers of blessing" today? We certainly do!

"But Elijah was a special prophet of God," we might argue. "We can expect God to answer his prayers in a wonderful way."

"Elijah was a man just like us," stated James (5:17, NIV). He was not perfect; in fact, right after his victory on Mt. Carmel, Elijah became afraid and discouraged and ran away. But he was a "righteous man," that is, obedient to the Lord and trusting Him. God's promises of answered prayer are for all His children, not just for ones we may call the spiritual elite.

Elijah prayed in faith, for God told him He would send the rain (1 Kings 18:1). "Prayer," said Robert Law, "is not getting man's will done in heaven. It's getting God's will done on earth." You cannot separate the Word of God and prayer, for in His Word He gives us the promises that we claim when we pray.

Elijah was not only believing in his praying, but he was persistent. "He prayed . . . and he prayed again" (James 5:17-18). On Mt. Carmel, Elijah continued to pray for rain until his servant reported "a cloud the size of a man's hand." Too many times we fail to get what God promises because we stop praying. It is true that we are not heard "for our much praying" (Matt. 6:7); but there is a difference between vain repetitions and true believing persistence in prayer. Our Lord prayed three times in the Garden, and Paul prayed three times that his thorn in the flesh might be taken from him.

Elijah was determined and concerned in his praying. "He prayed earnestly" (James 5:17, NIV). The literal Greek reads "and he prayed in prayer." Many people do not pray in their prayers. They just lazily say religious words, and their hearts are not in their prayers.

A church member was "praying around the world" in a prayer meeting, and one of the men present was growing tired of the speech. Finally the man cried out, "Ask Him something!" That is what prayer is all about: "Ask Him something!"

Prayer power is the greatest power in the world today. "Tremendous power is made available through a good man's earnest prayer" (James 5:16, PH). History shows how mankind has progressed from manpower to horsepower, and then to dynamite and TNT, and now to atomic power.

But greater than atomic power is prayer power. Elijah prayed for his nation, and God answered prayer. We need to pray for our nation today, that God will bring conviction and revival, and that "showers of blessing" will come to the land. One of the first responsibilities of the local church is to pray for government leaders (1 Tim. 2:1-3).

**Prayer for the Straying (James 5:19-20)**
While James did not specifically name prayer in these verses, the implication is there. If we pray for the afflicted and the sick, surely we must pray for the brother who wanders from the truth.

These verses deal with our ministry to a fellow believer who strays from the truth and gets into sin. The verb *err* means "to wan-der," and suggests a gradual moving away from the will of God. The Old Testament term for this is "backsliding." Sad to say, we see this tragedy occurring in our churches regularly. Sometimes a brother is "overtaken in a fault" (Gal. 6:1); but usually the sin is the result of slow, gradual spiritual decline.

Such a condition is, of course, very dangerous. It is dangerous to the offender because he may be disciplined by the Lord (Heb. 12). He also faces the danger of committing "sin unto death" (1 John 5:16-17). God disciplined the sinning members of the Corinthian church, even to the point of taking some of them to heaven (1 Cor. 11:30).

But this backsliding is also dangerous to the church. A wandering offender can influence others and lead them astray. "One sinner destroys much good" (Ecc. 9:18, NASB). This is why the spiritual members of the church must step in and help the man who has wandered away.

The *origin of this problem* is found in the statement "wander from the truth" (James 5:19). The *truth* means, of course, the Word of God. "Thy Word is truth" (John 17:17). Unless the believer stays close to the truth, he will start to drift away. "For this reason we must pay much closer attention to what we have heard, lest we drift away from it" (Heb. 2:1, NASB). Jesus warned Peter that Satan was at hand to tempt him, and Peter refused to believe the Word. He even argued with the Lord! When he should have been praying, Peter was sleeping. No wonder he denied three times.

The *outcome* of this wandering is "sin" and possible "death" (James 5:20). The sinner here is a believer, not an unbeliever; and sin in the life of a Christian is worse than sin in the life of an unbeliever. We expect unsaved people to sin, but God expects His children to obey His Word.

What are we to do when we see a fellow believer wandering from the truth? We should pray for him, to be sure; but we must also seek to help him. He needs to be "converted"—turned back into the right path again. Do believers need to be converted? Yes, they do! Jesus said to Peter, "When thou art converted, strengthen thy brethren" (Luke 22:32).

It is important that we seek to win the lost, but it is also important to win the saved. If a brother has sinned against us, we should talk to him privately and seek to settle the matter. If he listens, then we have gained our brother

(Matt. 18:15). That word *gained* means "won." It is the same word translated "get gain" in James 4:13. It is important to win the saved as well as the lost.

If we are going to help an erring brother, we must have an attitude of love, for "love shall cover the multitude of sins" (1 Peter 4:8). Both James and Peter learned this principle from Proverbs 10:12—"Hate stirreth up strife: but love covereth all sins."

This does not mean that love "sweeps the dirt under the carpet." Where there is love, there must also be truth ("speaking the truth in love" says Paul in Eph. 4:15); and where there is truth, there is honest confession of sin and cleansing from God. Love not only helps the offender to face his sins and deal with them, but love also assures the offender that those sins, once forgiven, are remembered no more.

While the basic interpretation of these verses is as I have explained, the application can be made to the lost sinner. After all, if a straying brother needs to be restored, how much more does a lost sinner need to be brought to the Saviour. If the wandering believer loses his life, he at least goes to heaven; but the lost sinner is condemned to an eternal hell.

"Seeking the lost" is a common Bible picture of soul-winning. In Luke 15, Jesus pictures the lost sheep, the lost coin, and the lost son, all of whom needed to be found and brought back to where they belonged. Our Lord also compared winning souls to catching fish (Mark 1:17). Peter caught one fish individually with his hook (Matt. 17:24-27), but he also worked with his helpers and used the nets to catch many fish at one time. There is a place for both personal and collective evangelism.

Proverbs 11:30 compares evangelism to hunting: "He that catcheth souls is wise" (literal translation). Sin is out to catch and kill (James 1:13-15), but we ought to be out to catch and make alive.

The soul winner is also an ambassador of peace (2 Cor. 5:20). God has not declared war on this world; He has declared peace! One day He will declare war, and judgment will fall.

Both Zechariah 3:2 and Jude 23 picture the soul winner as a fireman, pulling brands out of the burning. John Wesley applied Zechariah 3:2 to himself, for when he was but a child, he was pulled from a burning house when it looked as though it was too late. Sometimes we must take risks of love to snatch people from the fires of judgment.

Jesus compared evangelism to sowing and reaping (John 4:34-38) and Paul used the same illustration (1 Cor. 3:6-9). There are seasons of sowing and seasons of reaping; and many people are needed for the work. We are "laborers together with God" (1 Cor. 3:9). Both the sower and the reaper will receive their rewards, for there is no competition in the Lord's fields.

This brings us to the end of our study of James. His emphasis has been spiritual maturity. This would be a good time for us to examine our own hearts to see how mature we really are. Here are a few questions to assist you:

1. Am I becoming more and more patient in the testings of life?

2. Do I play with temptation or resist it from the start?

3. Do I find joy in obeying the Word of God, or do I merely study it and learn it?

4. Are there any prejudices that shackle me?

5. Am I able to control my tongue?

6. Am I a peacemaker rather than a troublemaker? Do people come to me for spiritual wisdom?

7. Am I a friend of God or a friend of the world?

8. Do I make plans without considering the will of God?

9. Am I selfish when it comes to money? Am I unfaithful in the paying of my bills?

10. Do I naturally depend on prayer when I find myself in some kind of trouble?

11. Am I the kind of person others seek for prayer support?

12. What is my attitude toward the wandering brother? Do I criticize and gossip, or do I seek to restore him in love?

Don't just grow old—grow up!

# 1 PETER

## OUTLINE

**Key theme:** God's grace and the living hope
**Key verses:** 1 Peter 1:3; 5:12

### I. GOD'S GRACE AND SALVATION—1:1–2:10
A. Live in hope—1:1-12
B. Live in holiness—1:13-21
C. Live in harmony—1:22–2:10

### II. GOD'S GRACE AND SUBMISSION—2:11–3:12
A. Submit to authorities—2:11-17
B. Submit to masters—2:18-25
C. Submit in the home—3:1-7
D. Submit in the church—3:8-12

### III. GOD'S GRACE AND SUFFERING—3:13–5:11
A. Make Jesus Christ Lord—3:13-22
B. Have Christ's attitude—4:1-11
C. Glorify Christ's name—4:12-19
D. Look for Christ's return—5:1-6
E. Depend on Christ's grace—5:7-14

## CONTENTS

# CHAPTER ONE
# WHERE THERE'S CHRIST, THERE'S HOPE
*1 Peter 1:1; 5:12-14*

"W hile there's life, there's hope!" That ancient Roman saying is still quoted today and, like most adages, it has an element of truth but no guarantee of certainty. It is not the *fact* of life that determines hope, but the *faith* of life. A Christian believer has a "living hope" (1 Peter 1:3, NASB) because his faith and hope are in God (1 Peter 1:21). This "living hope" is the major theme of Peter's first letter. He is saying to all believers, "Be hopeful!"

Before we study the details of this fascinating letter, let's get acquainted with the man who wrote it, the people to whom he sent it, and the particular situation that prompted him to write.

**The Writer (1 Peter 1:1)**
He identified himself as "Peter, an apostle of Jesus Christ" (1 Peter 1:1). Some liberals have questioned whether a common fisherman could have penned this letter, especially since Peter and John were both called "unlearned and ignorant men" (Acts 4:13). However, this phrase only means "laymen without formal schooling"; that is, they were not professional religious leaders. We must never underestimate the training Peter had for three years with the Lord Jesus, nor should we minimize the work of the Holy Spirit in his life. Peter is a perfect illustration of the truth expressed in 1 Corinthians 1:26-31.

His given name was Simon, but Jesus changed it to Peter, which means "a stone" (John 1:35-42). The Aramaic equivalent of "Peter" is "Cephas," so Peter was a man with three names. Nearly fifty times in the New Testament, he is called "Simon"; and often he is called "Simon Peter." Perhaps the two names suggest a Christian's two natures: an old nature (Simon) that is prone to fail, and a new nature (Peter) that can give victory. As Simon, he was only another human piece of clay; but Jesus Christ made a rock out of him! Peter and Paul were the two leading apos-

tles in the early church. Paul was assigned especially to minister to the Gentiles, and Peter to the Jews (Gal. 2:1-10). The Lord had commanded Peter to strengthen his brethren (Luke 22:32) and to tend the flock (John 21:15-17; also see 1 Peter 5:1-4), and the writing of this letter was a part of that ministry. Peter told his readers that this was a letter of encouragement and personal witness (1 Peter 5:12). Some writings are manufactured out of books, the way freshmen students write term papers; but this letter grew out of a life lived to the glory of God. A number of events in Peter's life are woven into the fabric of this epistle.

This letter is also associated with Silas (Silvanus, 1 Peter 5:12). He was one of the "chief men" in the early church (Acts 15:22) and a prophet (Acts 15:32). This means that he communicated God's messages to the congregations as he was directed by the Holy Spirit (see 1 Cor. 14). The Apostles and prophets worked together to lay the foundation of the church (Eph. 2:20); and, once that foundation was laid, they passed off the scene. There are no apostles and prophets *in the New Testament sense* in the church today.

It is interesting that Silas was associated with Peter's ministry, because originally he went with Paul as a replacement for Barnabas (Acts 15:36-41). Peter also mentioned John Mark (1 Peter 5:13) whose failure on the mission field helped to cause the rupture between Paul and Barnabas. Peter had led Mark to faith in Christ ("Mark, my son") and certainly would maintain a concern for him. No doubt one of the early assemblies met in John Mark's home in Jerusalem (Acts 12:12). In the end, Paul forgave and accepted Mark as a valued helper in the work (2 Tim. 4:11).

Peter indicated that he wrote this letter "at Babylon" (1 Peter 5:13) where there was an assembly of believers. There is no evidence either from church history or tradition that Peter ministered in ancient Babylon which, at that time, did have a large community of Jews. There was another town called "Babylon" in Egypt, but we have no proof that Peter ever visited it. "Babylon" is probably another name for the city of Rome, and we do have reason to believe that Peter ministered in Rome and was probably martyred there. Rome is called "Babylon" in Revelation 17:5 and 18:10. It was not unusual for persecuted believers during those days to write or speak in "code."

In saying this, however, we must not assign

more to Peter than is due him. He did *not* found the church in Rome nor serve as its first bishop. It was Paul's policy not to minister where any other apostle had gone (Rom. 15:20); so Paul would not have ministered in Rome had Peter arrived there first. Peter probably arrived in Rome after Paul was released from his first imprisonment, about the year A.D. 62. First Peter was written about the year 63. Paul was martyred about 64, and perhaps that same year, or shortly after, Peter laid down his life for Christ.

### The Recipients (1 Peter 1:1)

Peter called them "strangers" (1 Peter 1:1), which means "resident aliens, sojourners." They are called "strangers and pilgrims" in 1 Peter 2:11. These people were citizens of heaven through faith in Christ (Phil. 3:20), and therefore were not permanent residents on earth. Like Abraham, they had their eyes of faith centered on the future city of God (Heb. 11:8-16). They were in the world, but not of the world (John 17:16).

Because Christians are "strangers" in the world, they are considered to be "strange" in the eyes of the world (1 Peter 4:4). Christians have standards and values different from those of the world, and this gives opportunity both for witness and for warfare. We will discover in this epistle that some of the readers were experiencing suffering because of their different lifestyle.

These believers were a "scattered" people as well as a "strange" people. The word translated "scattered" *(diaspora)* was a technical term for the Jews who lived outside of Palestine. It is used this way in John 7:35 and James 1:1. However, Peter's use of this word does not imply that he was writing only to Jewish Christians, because some statements in his letter suggest that some of his readers were converted out of Gentile paganism (1 Peter 1:14, 18; 2:9-10; 4:1-4). There was undoubtedly a mixture of both Jews and Gentiles in the churches that received this letter. We will notice a number of Old Testament references and allusions in these chapters.

These Christians were scattered in five different parts of the Roman Empire, all of them in northern Asia Minor (modern Turkey). The Holy Spirit did not permit Paul to minister in Bithynia (Acts 16:7), so he did not begin this work. There were Jews at Pentecost from Pontus and Cappadocia (Acts 2:9), and perhaps they carried the Gospel to their neighboring province. Possibly Jewish believers who had been under Peter's ministry in other places had migrated to towns in these provinces. People were "on the move" in those days, and dedicated believers shared the Word wherever they went (Acts 8:4).

The important thing for us to know about these "scattered strangers" is that they were going through a time of suffering and persecution. At least fifteen times in this letter, Peter referred to suffering; and he used eight different Greek words to do so. Some of these Christians were suffering because they were living godly lives and doing what was good and right (1 Peter 2:19-23; 3:14-18; 4:1-4, 15-19). Others were suffering reproach for the name of Christ (1 Peter 4:14) and being railed at by unsaved people (1 Peter 3:9-10). Peter wrote to encourage them to be good witnesses to their persecutors, and to remember that their suffering would lead to glory (1 Peter 1:6-7; 4:13-14; 5:10).

But Peter had another purpose in mind. He knew that a "fiery trial" was about to begin—official persecution from the Roman Empire (1 Peter 4:12). When the church began in Jerusalem, it was looked on as a "sect" of the traditional Jewish faith. The first Christians were Jews, and they met in the temple precincts. The Roman government took no official action against the Christians since the Jewish religion was accepted and approved. But when it became clear that Christianity was not a "sect" of Judaism, Rome had to take official steps.

Several events occurred that helped to precipitate this "fiery trial." To begin with, Paul had defended the Christian faith before the official court in Rome (Phil. 1:12-24). He had been released but then was arrested again. This second defense failed, and he was martyred (2 Tim. 4:16-18). Second, the deranged Emperor, Nero, blamed the fire of Rome (July A.D. 64) on the Christians, using them as a scapegoat. Peter was probably in Rome about that time and was slain by Nero, who had also killed Paul. Nero's persecution of Christians was local at first, but it probably spread. At any rate, Peter wanted to prepare the churches.

We must not get the idea that all Christians in every part of the Empire were going through the same trials to the same degree at the same time. It varied from place to place, though suffering and opposition were pretty general (1 Peter 5:9). Nero introduced official persecution of the church and other emperors followed his example in later years. Peter's letter must have been a tremendous help to Christians who suffered during the reigns of Trajan (98–117), Hadrian (117–138), and Diocletian (284–305). Christians in the world today may yet learn the value of Peter's letter when their own "fiery trials" of persecution begin. While I personally believe that the church will not go through *the* Tribulation, I do believe that these latter days will bring much suffering and persecution to the people of God.

It is possible that Silas was the bearer of this letter to the believers in the provinces, and also the secretary who wrote the epistle.

## The Message (1 Peter 5:12)

First Peter is a letter of encouragement (1 Peter 5:12). We have noted that the theme of *suffering* runs throughout the letter, but so also does the theme of *glory* (see 1 Peter 1:7-8, 11, 21; 2:12; 4:11-16; 5:1, 4, 10-11). One of the encouragements that Peter gives suffering saints is the assurance that their suffering will one day be transformed into glory (1 Peter 1:6-7; 4:13-14; 5:10). This is possible only because the Saviour suffered for us and then entered into His glory (1 Peter 1:11; 5:1). The sufferings of Christ are mentioned often in this letter (1 Peter 1:11; 3:18; 4:1, 13; 5:1).

Peter is preeminently the apostle of *hope*, as Paul is the apostle of *faith* and John of *love*. As believers, we have a "living hope" because we trust a living Christ (1 Peter 1:3). This hope enables us to keep our minds under control and "hope to the end" (1 Peter 1:13) when Jesus shall return. We must not be ashamed of our hope but be ready to explain and defend it (1 Peter 3:15). Like Sarah, Christian wives can hope in God (1 Peter 3:5, where "trusted" should be translated "hoped"). Since suffering brings glory, and because Jesus is coming again, we can indeed be hopeful!

But suffering does not *automatically* bring glory to God and blessing to God's people. Some believers have fainted and fallen in times of trial and have brought shame to the name of Christ. It is only when we depend on the grace of God that we can glorify God in times of suffering. Peter also emphasized God's grace in this letter. "I have written to you briefly, encouraging you and testifying that this is the true grace of God. Stand fast in it" (1 Peter 5:12, NIV).

The word "grace" is used in every chapter of 1 Peter: 1:2, 10, 13; 2:19 ("thankworthy"), 20 ("acceptable"); 3:7; 4:10; 5:5, 10, 12. Grace is God's generous favor to undeserving sinners and needy saints. When we depend on God's grace, we can endure suffering and turn trials into triumphs. It is grace alone that saves us (Eph. 2:8-10). God's grace can give us strength in times of trial (2 Cor. 12:1-10). Grace enables us to serve God in spite of difficulties (1 Cor. 15:9-10). Whatever begins with God's grace will always lead to glory (Ps. 84:11; 1 Peter 5:10).

As we study 1 Peter, we will see how the three themes of suffering, grace, and glory unite to form an encouraging message for believers experiencing times of trial and persecution. These themes are summarized in 1 Peter 5:10, a verse we would do well to memorize.

The cynical editor and writer H.L. Mencken once defined hope as "a pathological belief in the occurrence of the impossible." But that definition does not agree with the New Testament meaning of the word. True Christian hope is more than "hope so." It is confident assurance of future glory and blessing.

An Old Testament believer called God "the Hope of Israel" (Jer. 14:8). A New Testament believer affirms that Jesus Christ is his hope (1 Tim. 1:1; see Col. 1:27). The unsaved sinner is "without hope" (Eph. 2:12); and if he dies without Christ, he will be hopeless forever. The Italian poet, Dante, in his *Divine Comedy,* put this inscription over the world of the dead: "Abandon all hope, you who enter here!"

This confident hope gives us the encouragement and enablement we need for daily living. It does not put us in a rocking chair where we complacently await the return of Jesus Christ. Instead, it puts us in the marketplace, on the battlefield, where we keep on going when the burdens are heavy and the battles are hard. Hope is not a sedative; it is a shot of adrenaline, a blood transfusion. Like an anchor, our hope in Christ stabilizes us in the storms of life (Heb. 6:18-19); but unlike an anchor, our hope moves us forward, it does not hold us back.

It is not difficult to follow Peter's train of thought. Everything begins with salvation, our personal relationship to God through Jesus Christ. If we know Christ as Saviour, then we have hope! If we have hope, then we can walk in holiness and in harmony. There should be no problem submitting to those around us in society, the home, and the church family. Salvation and submission are preparation for suffering; but if we focus on Christ, we can overcome and God will transform suffering into glory.

# CHAPTER TWO
# IT'S GLORY
# ALL THE WAY!
*1 Peter 1:2-12*

On a balmy summer day, my wife and I visited one of the world's most famous cemeteries located at Stoke Poges, a little village not far from Windsor Castle in England. On this site Thomas Gray penned his famous "Elegy Written in a Country Churchyard," a poem most of us had to read at one time or another in school.

As we stood quietly in the midst of ancient graves, one stanza of that poem came to mind:

> The boast of heraldry, the pomp of power,
> And all that beauty, all that wealth e'er
> gave,
> Awaits alike the inevitable hour,
> The paths of glory lead but to the grave.

Man's glory simply does not last, but God's glory is eternal; and He has deigned to share that glory with us! In this first section of his letter, Peter shared four wonderful discoveries that he had made about the glory of God.

## Christians Are Born for Glory
## (1 Peter 1:2-4)

Because of the death and resurrection of Jesus Christ, believers have been "begotten again" to a living hope, and that hope includes the glory of God. But, what do we mean by "the glory of God"?

The glory of God means the sum total of all that God is and does. "Glory" is not a separate attribute or characteristic of God, such as His holiness, wisdom, or mercy. Everything that God is and does is characterized by glory.

He is glorious in wisdom and power, so that everything He thinks and does is marked by glory. He reveals His glory in creation (Ps. 19), in His dealings with the people of Israel, and especially in His plan of salvation for lost sinners.

When we were born the first time, we were not born for glory. "For all flesh is like grass, and all the glory of man like the flower of grass" (1 Peter 1:24, quoted from Isa. 40:6). Whatever feeble glory man has will eventually fade and disappear; but the glory of the Lord is eternal. The works of man done for the glory of God will last and be rewarded (1 John 2:17). But the selfish human achievements of sinners will one day vanish to be seen no more. One reason that we have encyclopedias is so that we can learn about the famous people who are now forgotten!

Peter gave two descriptions to help us better understand this wonderful truth about glory.

*A Christian's birth described (vv. 2-3).* This miracle all began with God: we were chosen by the Father (Eph. 1:3-4). This took place in the deep counsels of eternity, and we knew nothing about it until it was revealed to us in the Word of God. This election was not based on anything we had done, because we were not even on the scene. Nor was it based on anything God saw that we would be or do. God's election was based wholly on His grace and love. We cannot explain it (Rom. 11:33-36), but we can rejoice in it.

"Foreknowledge" does not suggest that God merely knew ahead of time that we would believe, and therefore He chose us. This would raise the question, "Who or what made us decide for Christ?" and would take our salvation completely out of God's hands. In the Bible, *to foreknow* means "to set one's love on a person or persons in a personal way." It is used this way in Amos 3:2: "You only have I known of all the families of the earth." God set His electing love on the nation of Israel. Other verses that use "know" in this special sense are Psalm 1:6; Matthew 7:23; John 10:14, 27; and 1 Corinthians 8:3.

But the plan of salvation includes more than the Father's electing love; it also includes the work of the Spirit in convicting the sinner and bringing him to faith in Christ. The best commentary on this is 2 Thessalonians 2:13-14. Also, the Son of God had to die on the cross for our sins, or there could be no salvation. We have been chosen by the Father, purchased by the Son, and set apart by the Spirit. It takes all three if there is to be a true experience of salvation.

As far as God the Father is concerned, I was saved when He chose me in Christ before the foundation of the world. As far as the Son is concerned, I was saved when He died for me on the cross. But as far as the Spirit is concerned, I was saved one night in May 1945 when I heard the Gospel and received Christ. Then it all came together, but it took all three Persons of the Godhead to bring me to salvation. If we separate these ministries, we will either deny divine sovereignty or human responsibility; and that would lead to heresy.

Peter does not deny man's part in God's plan to save sinners. In 1 Peter 1:23 he emphasizes the fact that the Gospel was preached to these people, and that they heard it and believed (see also 1 Peter 1:12). Peter's own example at Pentecost is proof that we do not "leave it all with God" and never urge lost sinners to come to Christ (Acts 2:37-40). The same God who ordains the end—our salvation—also ordains *the means to the end*—the preaching of the Gospel of the grace of God.

*A Christian's hope described (vv. 3-4).* To begin with, it is *a living hope* because it is grounded on the living Word of God (1 Peter 1:23), and was made possible by the living Son of God who arose from the dead. A "living hope" is one that has life in it and therefore can give life to us. Because it has life, it grows and becomes greater and more beautiful as time goes on. Time destroys most hopes; they fade and then die. But the passing of time only makes a Christian's hope that much more glorious.

Peter called this hope *an inheritance* (1 Peter 1:4). As the children of the King, we share His inheritance in glory (Rom. 8:17-18; Eph. 1:9-12). We are included in Christ's last will and testament, and we share the glory with Him (John 17:22-24).

Note the description of this inheritance, for it is totally unlike any earthly inheritance. For one thing, it is *incorruptible*, which means that nothing can ruin it. Because it is *undefiled*, it cannot be stained or cheapened in any way. It will never grow old because it is eternal; it cannot wear out, nor can it disappoint us in any way.

In 1 Peter 1:5 and 9, this inheritance is called "salvation." The believer is already saved through faith in Christ (Eph. 2:8-9), but the completion of that salvation awaits the re-

turn of the Saviour. Then we shall have new bodies and enter into a new environment, the heavenly city. In 1 Peter 1:7, Peter called this hope "the appearing of Jesus Christ." Paul called this "the blessed hope" (Titus 2:13).

What a thrilling thing it is to know that we were born for glory! When we were born again, we exchanged the passing glory of man for the eternal glory of God!

## Christians Are Kept for Glory
## (1 Peter 1:5)

Not only is the glory being "reserved" for us, but we are being kept for the glory! In my travels, I have sometimes gone to a hotel or motel, only to discover that the reservations have been confused or cancelled. This will not happen to us when we arrive in heaven, for our future home and inheritance are guaranteed and reserved.

"But suppose *we* don't make it?" a timid saint might ask. But we will; for all believers are being "kept by the power of God." The word translated "kept" is a military word that means "guarded, shielded." The tense of the verb reveals that we are *constantly* being guarded by God, assuring us that we shall safely arrive in heaven. This same word is used to describe the soldiers guarding Damascus when Paul made his escape (2 Cor. 11:32). See also Jude 24-25 and Romans 8:28-39.

Believers are not kept by their own power, but by the power of God. Our faith in Christ has so united us to Him that His power now guards us and guides us. We are not kept by our strength, but by His faithfulness. How long will He guard us? Until Jesus Christ returns and we will share in the full revelation of His great salvation. This same truth is repeated in 1 Peter 1:9.

It is encouraging to know that we are "guarded for glory." According to Romans 8:30, we have *already* been glorified. All that awaits is the public revelation of this glory (Rom. 8:18-23). If any believer were lost, it would rob God of His glory. God is so certain that we will be in heaven that He has already given us His glory as the assurance (John 17:24; Eph. 1:13-14).

The assurance of heaven is a great help to us today. As Dr. James M. Gray expressed it in one of his songs, "Who can mind the journey, when the road leads home?" If suffering today means glory tomorrow, then suffering becomes a blessing to us. The unsaved have their "glory" now, but it will be followed by eternal suffering *away from the glory of God* (2 Thes. 1:3-10). In the light of this, ponder 2 Corinthians 4:7-18—and rejoice!

## Christians Are Being Prepared for Glory (1 Peter 1:6-7)

We must keep in mind that all God plans and performs here is preparation for what He has in store for us in heaven. He is preparing us for the life and service yet to come. Nobody yet knows all that is in store for us in heaven; but this we do know: life today is a school in which God trains us for our future ministry in eternity. This explains the presence of trials in our lives: they are some of God's tools and textbooks in the school of Christian experience.

Peter used the word "trials" rather than "tribulations" or "persecutions," because he was dealing with the *general* problems that Christians face as they are surrounded by unbelievers. He shared several facts about trials.

*Trials meet needs.* The phrase "if need be" indicates that there are special times when God knows that we need to go through trials. Sometimes trials discipline us when we have disobeyed God's will (Ps. 119:67). At other times, trials prepare us for spiritual growth, or even help to prevent us from sinning (2 Cor. 12:1-9). We do not always know the need being met, but we can trust God to know and to do what is best.

*Trials are varied.* Peter used the word "manifold," which literally means "variegated, many-colored." He used the same word to describe God's grace in 1 Peter 4:10. No matter what "color" our day may be—a "blue" Monday or a "gray" Tuesday—God has grace sufficient to meet the need. We must not think that because we have overcome one kind of trial that we will automatically "win them all." Trials are varied, and God matches the trial to our strengths and needs.

*Trials are not easy.* Peter did not suggest that we take a careless attitude toward trials, because this would be deceitful. Trials produce what he called "heaviness." The word means "to experience grief or pain." It is used to describe our Lord in Gethsemane (Matt. 26:37), and the sorrow of saints at the death of loved ones (1 Thes. 4:13). To deny that our trials are painful is to make them even worse. Christians must accept the fact that there are difficult experiences in life and not put on a brave front just to appear "more spiritual."

*Trials are controlled by God.* They do not last forever; they are "for a season." When God permits His children to go through the furnace, He keeps His eye on the clock and His hand on the thermostat. If we rebel, He may have to reset the clock; but if we submit, He will not permit us to suffer one minute too long. The important thing is that we learn the lesson He wants to teach us and that we bring glory to Him alone.

Peter illustrated this truth by referring to the goldsmith. No goldsmith would deliberately waste the precious ore. He would put it into the smelting furnace long enough to remove the cheap impurities; then he would pour it out and make from it a beautiful article of value. It has been said that the Eastern goldsmith kept the metal in the furnace until he could see his face reflected in it. So our Lord keeps us in the furnace of suffering until we reflect the glory and beauty of Jesus Christ.

The important point is that this glory is not fully revealed until Jesus returns for His church. Our trying experiences today are preparing us for glory tomorrow. When we see Jesus Christ, we will bring "praise and honor and glory" to Him if we have been faithful in the sufferings of this life (see Rom. 8:17-18). This explains why Peter associated *rejoicing* with *suffering*. While we may not be able to rejoice as we look *around* in our trials, we can rejoice as we look *ahead*. The word "this" in 1 Peter 1:6 (NASB) refers back to the "salvation" (the return of Christ) mentioned in 1 Peter 1:5.

Just as the assayer tests the gold to see if it is pure gold or counterfeit, so the trials of life test our faith to prove its sincerity. A faith that cannot be tested cannot be trusted! Too many professing Christians have a "false faith" and this will be revealed in the trials of life. The seed that fell on shallow soil produced rootless plants, and the plants died when the sun came up (see Matt. 13:1-9, 18-23). The sun in the parable represents "tribulation or persecution." The person who abandons "his faith" when the going gets tough is only proving that he really had no faith at all.

The patriarch Job went through many painful trials, all of them with God's approval; and yet he understood somewhat of this truth about the refiner's fire. "But He knoweth the way that I take; when He hath tried me, I shall come forth as gold" (Job 23:10). And he did!

It is encouraging to know that we are born for glory, kept for glory, and being prepared for glory. But the fourth discovery Peter shared with his readers is perhaps the most exciting of all.

## Christians Can Enjoy the Glory Now (1 Peter 1:8-12)

The Christian philosophy of life is not "pie in the sky by and by." It carries with it a *present* dynamic that can turn suffering into glory *today*. Peter gave four directions for enjoying the glory now, even in the midst of trials.

*Love Christ (v. 8).* Our love for Christ is not based on physical sight, because we have not seen Him. It is based on our spiritual relationship with Him and what the Word has taught us about Him. The Holy Spirit has poured out God's love into our hearts (Rom. 5:5), and we return that love to Him. When you find yourself in some trial, and you hurt, immediately lift your heart to Christ in true love and worship. Why? Because this will take the poison out of the experience and replace it with healing medicine.

Satan wants to use life's trials to bring out the worst in us, but God wants to bring out the best in us. If we love ourselves more than we love Christ, then we will not experience any of the glory *now*. The fire will *burn* us, not *purify* us.

*Trust Christ (v. 8).* We must live by faith and not by sight. An elderly lady fell and broke her leg while attending a summer Bible conference. She said to the pastor who visited her, "I know the Lord led me to the conference. But I don't see why this had to happen! And I don't see any good coming from it." Wisely, the pastor replied, "Romans 8:28 doesn't say that we *see* all things working together for good. It says that we *know* it."

Faith means surrendering all to God and obeying His Word in spite of circumstances and consequences. Love and faith go together: when you love someone, you trust him. And faith and love together help to strengthen hope; for where you find faith and love, you will find confidence for the future.

How can we grow in faith during times of testing and suffering? The same way we grow in faith when things seem to be going well: by feeding on the Word of God (Rom. 10:17). Our fellowship with Christ through His Word not only strengthens our faith, but it also deepens our love. It is a basic principle of Christian living that we spend much time in the Word when God is testing us and Satan is tempting us.

*Rejoice in Christ (v. 8).* You may not be able to rejoice *over* the circumstances, but you can rejoice *in* them by centering your heart and mind on Jesus Christ. Each experience of trial helps us learn something new and wonderful about our Saviour. Abraham discovered new truths about the Lord on the mount where he offered his son (Gen. 22). The three Hebrew children discovered His nearness when they went through the fiery furnace (Dan. 3). Paul learned the sufficiency of His grace when he suffered with a thorn in the flesh (2 Cor. 12).

Note that the joy He produces is "unspeakable and full of glory." This joy is so deep and so wonderful that we cannot even express it. Words fail us! Peter had seen some of the glory on the Mount of Transfiguration where Jesus discussed with Moses and Elijah His own impending suffering and death (Luke 9:28-36).

*Receive from Christ (vv. 9-12).* "Believing . . . receiving" is God's way of meeting our needs. If we love Him, trust Him, and rejoice in Him, then we can receive from Him all that we need to turn trials into triumphs. First Peter 1:9 can be translated, "For you are receiving the consummation of your faith, that is, the final salvation of your souls." In other words, we can experience *today* some of that future glory. Charles Spurgeon used to say, "Little faith will take your soul to heaven, but great faith will bring heaven to your soul." It is not enough that we long for heaven during times of suffering, for anybody can do that. What Peter urged his readers to do was exercise love, faith, and rejoicing, so that they might experience some of the glory of heaven in the midst of suffering *now*.

The amazing thing is that this "salvation" we are awaiting—the return of Christ—was a part of God's great plan for us from eternity. The Old Testament prophets wrote about this salvation and studied closely what God revealed to them. They saw the sufferings of the Messiah, and also the glory that would follow; but they could not fully understand the connection between the two. In fact, in some of the prophecies, the Messiah's sufferings and glory are blended in one verse or paragraph.

When Jesus came to earth, the Jewish teachers were awaiting a conquering Messiah who would defeat Israel's enemies and establish the glorious kingdom promised to David. Even His own disciples were not clear about the need for His death on the cross (Matt. 16:13-28). They were still inquiring about the Jewish kingdom even after His resurrection (Acts 1:1-8). If the *disciples* were not clear about God's program, certainly the Old Testament *prophets* could be excused!

God told the prophets that they were ministering for a *future* generation. Between the suffering of Messiah and His return in glory comes what we call "the age of the church." The truth about the church was a hidden "mystery" in the Old Testament period (Eph. 3:1-13). The Old Testament believers looked ahead by faith and saw, as it were, two mountain peaks: Mount Calvary, where Messiah suffered and died (Isa. 53), and Mount Olivet, where He will return in glory (Zech. 14:4). They could not see the "valley" in between, the present age of the church.

Even the angels are interested in what God is doing in and through His church! Read 1 Corinthians 4:9 and Ephesians 3:10 for further information on how God is "educating" the angels through the church.

If the Old Testament prophets searched so diligently into the truths of salvation, and yet had so little to go on, how much more ought we to search into this subject, now that we have a complete Word from God! The same Holy Spirit who taught the prophets and, through them, wrote the Word of God, can teach us the truths in it (John 16:12-15).

Furthermore, we can learn these truths from the Old Testament as well as from the New Testament. You can find Christ in every part of the Old Testament Scriptures (Luke 24:25-27). What a delight it is to meet Christ in the Old Testament Law, the types, the Psalms, and the writings of the prophets. In times of trial, you can turn to the Bible, both the Old and New Testaments, and find all that you need for encouragement and enlightenment.

Yes, for Christians, it is glory all the way! When we trusted Christ, we were born for glory. We are being kept for glory. As we obey Him and experience trials, we are being prepared for glory. When we love Him, trust Him, and rejoice in Him, we experience the glory here and now.

Joy unspeakable and full of glory!

# CHAPTER THREE
# STAYING CLEAN IN A POLLUTED WORLD
## *1 Peter 1:13-21*

In the first section of this chapter, Peter emphasized *walking in hope;* but now his emphasis is *walking in holiness.* The two go together, for "every man that hath this hope in him purifieth himself, even as He is pure" (1 John 3:3).

The root meaning of the word translated *holy* is "different." A holy person is not an odd person, but a different person. His life has a quality about it that is different. His present "lifestyle" is not only different from his past way of life, but it is different from the "lifestyles" of the unbelievers around him. A Christian's life of holiness appears strange to the lost (1 Peter 4:4), but it is not strange to other believers.

However, it is not easy to live in this world and maintain a holy walk. The anti-God atmosphere around us that the Bible calls "the world" is always pressing against us, trying to force us to conform. In this paragraph, Peter presented to his readers five spiritual incentives to encourage them (and us) to maintain a different lifestyle, a holy walk in a polluted world.

### The Glory of God (1 Peter 1:13)
"The revelation of Jesus Christ" is another expression for the "living hope" and "the appearing of Jesus Christ." Christians live in the future tense; their present actions and decisions are governed by this future hope. Just as an engaged couple makes all their plans in the light of that future wedding, so Christians today live with the expectation of seeing Jesus Christ.

"Gird up the loins of your mind" simply means, "Pull your thoughts together! Have a disciplined mind!" The image is that of a robed man, tucking his skirts under the belt, so he can be free to run. When you center your thoughts on the return of Christ, and live accordingly, you escape the many worldly things that would encumber your mind and hinder your spiritual progress. Peter may have borrowed the idea from the Passover supper, because later in this section he identifies Christ as the Lamb (1 Peter 1:19). The Jews at Passover were supposed to eat the meal in haste, ready to move (Ex. 12:11).

Outlook determines outcome; attitude determines action. A Christian who is looking for the glory of God has a greater motivation for present obedience than a Christian who ignores the Lord's return. The contrast is illustrated in the lives of Abraham and Lot (Gen. 12–13; Heb. 11:8-16). Abraham had his eyes of faith on that heavenly city, so he had no interest in the world's real estate. But Lot, who had tasted the pleasures of the world in Egypt, gradually moved toward Sodom. Abraham brought blessing to his home, but Lot brought judgment. Outlook determined outcome.

Not only should we have a disciplined mind, but we should also have a *sober* mind. The word means "to be calm, steady, controlled; to weigh matters." Unfortunately some people get "carried away" with prophetic studies and lose their spiritual balance. The fact that Christ is coming should encourage us to be calm and collected (1 Peter 4:7). The fact that Satan is on the prowl is another reason to be sober-minded (1 Peter 5:8). Anyone whose mind becomes undisciplined, and whose life "falls apart" because of prophetic studies, is giving evidence that he does not really understand Bible prophecy.

We should also have an *optimistic* mind. "Hope to the end" means "set your hope fully." Have a hopeful outlook! A friend of mine sent me a note one day that read: "When the *out*look is gloomy, try the *up*look!" Good advice, indeed! It has to be dark for the stars to appear.

The result of this spiritual mind-set is that a believer experiences the grace of God in his life. To be sure, we will experience grace when we see Jesus Christ; but we can also experience grace today as we look for Him to return. We have been saved by grace and we depend moment by moment on God's grace (1 Peter 1:10). Looking for Christ to return strengthens our faith and hope in difficult days, and this imparts to us more of the grace of God. Titus 2:10-13 is another passage that shows the relationship between grace and the coming of Jesus Christ.

**The Holiness of God (1 Peter 1:14-15)**
The argument here is logical and simple. Children inherit the nature of their parents. God is holy; therefore, as His children, we should live holy lives. We are "partakers of the divine nature" (2 Peter 1:4) and ought to reveal that nature in godly living.

Peter reminded his readers of what they were before they trusted Christ. They had been *children of disobedience* (Eph. 2:1-3), but now they were to be obedient children. True salvation always results in obedience (Rom. 1:5; 1 Peter 1:2). They had also been *imitators of the world*, "fashioning themselves" after the standards and pleasures of the world. Romans 12:2 translates this same word as "conformed to this world." Unsaved people tell us that they want to be "free and different"; yet they all imitate one another!

The cause of all this is *ignorance* that leads to *indulgence*. Unsaved people lack spiritual intelligence, and this causes them to give themselves to all kinds of fleshly and worldly indulgences (see Acts 17:30; Eph. 4:17ff). Since we were born with a fallen nature, it was natural for us to live sinful lives. Nature determines appetites and actions. A dog and a cat behave differently because they have different natures.

We would still be in that sad sinful plight were it not for the grace of God. He called us! One day, Jesus called to Peter and his friends and said, "Come, follow Me . . . and I will make you fishers of men" (Mark 1:17, NIV). They responded by faith to His call, and this completely changed their lives.

Perhaps this explains why Peter used the word "called" so often in this letter. We are called to be holy (1 Peter 1:15). We are called "out of darkness into His marvelous light" (1 Peter 2:9). We are called to suffer and follow Christ's example of meekness (1 Peter 2:21). In the midst of persecution, we are called "to inherit a blessing" (1 Peter 3:9). Best of all, we are called to "His eternal glory" (1 Peter 5:10). God called us before we called on Him for salvation. It is all wholly of grace.

But God's gracious election of sinners to become saints always involves responsibility, and not just privilege. He has chosen us in Christ "that we should be holy and without blame before Him" (Eph. 1:4). God has called us to Himself, and He is holy; therefore, we should be holy. Peter quoted from the Old Testament Law to back up his admonition (Lev. 11:44-45; 19:2; 20:7, 26).

God's holiness is an essential part of His nature. "God is light, and in Him is no darkness at all" (1 John 1:5). Any holiness that we have in character and conduct must be derived from Him. Basically, to be *sanctified* means to be "set apart for God's exclusive use and pleasure." It involves separation from that which is unclean and complete devotion to God (2 Cor. 6:14–7:1). We are to be holy "in all manner of conversation [behavior]," so that everything we do reflects the holiness of God.

To a dedicated believer, there is no such thing as "secular" and "sacred." All of life is holy as we live to glorify God. Even such ordinary activities as eating and drinking can be done to the glory of God (1 Cor. 10:31). If something cannot be done to the glory of God, then we can be sure it must be out of the will of God.

### The Word of God (1 Peter 1:16)
"It is written!" is a statement that carries great authority for the believer. Our Lord used the Word of God to defeat Satan, and so may we (Matt. 4:1-11; see Eph. 6:17). But the Word of God is not only a sword for battle; it is also a light to guide us in this dark world (Ps. 119:105; 2 Peter 1:19), food that strengthens us (Matt. 4:4; 1 Peter 2:2), and water that washes us (Eph. 5:25-27).

The Word of God has a sanctifying ministry in the lives of dedicated believers (John 17:17). Those who delight in God's Word, meditate on it, and seek to obey it will experience God's direction and blessing in their lives (Ps. 1:1-3). The Word reveals God's mind, so we should *learn* it; God's heart, so we should *love* it; God's will, so we should *live* it. Our whole being—mind, will, and heart—should be controlled by the Word of God.

Peter quoted from the Book of Leviticus, "Ye shall be holy; for I am holy" (Lev. 11:44). Does this mean that the Old Testament Law is authoritative today for New Testament Christians? Keep in mind that the early Christians did not even have the New Testament. The only Word of God they possessed was the Old Testament, and God used that Word to direct and nurture them. Believers today are not under the ceremonial laws given to Israel; however, even in these laws we see moral and spiritual principles revealed. Nine of the Ten Commandments are repeated in the Epistles, so we must obey them. (The Sabbath commandment was given especially to Israel and does not apply to us today. See Rom. 14:1-9.) As we read and study the Old Testament, we will learn much about God's character and working, and we will see truths pictured in types and symbols.

The first step toward keeping clean in a filthy world is to ask, "What does the Bible say?" In the Scriptures, we will find precepts, principles, promises, and persons to guide us in today's decisions. If we are really willing to obey God, He will show us His truth (John 7:17). While God's methods of working may change from age to age, His character remains the same and His spiritual principles never vary. We do not study the Bible just to get to know the Bible. We study the Bible that we might get to know God better. Too many earnest Bible students are content with outlines and explanations, and do not really get to know God. It is good to know the Word of God, but this should help us better know the God of the Word.

### The Judgment of God (1 Peter 1:17)
As God's children, we need to be serious about sin and about holy living. Our Heavenly Father is a holy (John 17:11) and righteous Father (John 17:25). He will not compromise with sin. He is merciful and forgiving, but He is also a loving disciplinarian who cannot permit His children to enjoy sin. After all, it was sin that sent His Son to the cross. If we call God "Father," then we should reflect His nature.

What is this judgment that Peter wrote about? It is the judgment of a believer's works. It has nothing to do with salvation, except that salvation ought to produce good works (Titus 1:16; 2:7, 12). When we trusted Christ, God forgave our sins and declared us righteous in His Son (Rom. 5:1-10; 8:1-4; Col. 2:13). Our sins have already been judged on the cross (1 Peter 2:24), and therefore they cannot be held against us (Heb. 10:10-18).

But when the Lord returns, there will be a time of judgment called "the Judgment Seat of Christ" (Rom. 14:10-12; 2 Cor. 5:9-10). Each of us will give an account of his works, and each will receive the appropriate reward. This is a "family judgment," the Father dealing with His beloved children. The Greek word translated *judgeth* carries the meaning "to judge in order to find something good." God will search into the motives for our ministry; He will examine our hearts. But He assures us that His purpose is to glorify Himself in our lives and ministries, "and then shall every man have praise of God" (1 Cor. 4:5). What an encouragement!

God will give us many gifts and privileges,

as we grow in the Christian life; but He will never give us the privilege to disobey and sin. He never pampers His children or indulges them. He is no respecter of persons. He "shows no partiality and accepts no bribes" (Deut. 10:17, NIV). "For God does not show favoritism" (Rom. 2:11, NIV). Years of obedience cannot purchase an hour of disobedience. If one of His children disobeys, God must chasten (Heb. 12:1-13). But when His child obeys and serves Him in love, He notes that and prepares the proper reward.

Peter reminded his readers that they were only "sojourners" on earth. Life was too short to waste in disobedience and sin (see 1 Peter 4:1-6). It was when Lot stopped being a sojourner, and became a resident in Sodom, that he lost his consecration and his testimony. Everything he lived for went up in smoke! Keep reminding yourself that you are a "stranger and pilgrim" in this world (1 Peter 1:1; 2:11).

In view of the fact that the Father lovingly disciplines His children today, and will judge their works in the future, we ought to cultivate an attitude of godly fear. This is not the cringing fear of a slave before a master, but the loving reverence of a child before his father. It is not fear of judgment (1 John 4:18), but a fear of disappointing Him or sinning against His love. It is "godly fear" (2 Cor. 7:1), a sober reverence for the Father.

I sometimes feel that there is today an increase in carelessness, even flippancy, in the way we talk about God or talk to God. Nearly a century ago, Bishop B.F. Westcott said, "Every year makes me tremble at the daring with which people speak of spiritual things." The godly bishop should hear what is said today! A worldly actress calls God "the Man upstairs." A baseball player calls Him "the great Yankee in the sky." An Old Testament Jew so feared God that he would not even pronounce His holy name, yet we today speak of God with carelessness and irreverence. In our public praying, we sometimes get so familiar that other people wonder whether we are trying to express our requests or impress the listeners with our nearness to God!

### The Love of God (1 Peter 1:18-21)
This is the highest motive for holy living. In this paragraph, Peter reminded his readers of their salvation experience, a reminder that all of us regularly need. This is one reason our Lord established the Lord's Supper, so that regularly His people would remember that He died for them. Note the reminders that Peter gave.

He reminded them of *what they were*. To begin with, they were slaves who needed to be set free. The word *redeemed* is, to us, a theological term; but it carried a special meaning to people in the first-century Roman Empire. There were probably 60 million slaves in the Empire! Many slaves became Christians and fellowshipped in the local assemblies. A slave could purchase his own freedom, if he could collect sufficient funds; or his master could sell him to someone who would pay the price and set him free. Redemption was a precious thing in that day.

We must never forget the slavery of sin (Titus 3:3). Moses urged Israel to remember that they had been slaves in Egypt (Deut. 5:15; 16:12; 24:18, 22). The generation that died in the wilderness forgot the bondage of Egypt and wanted to go back!

Not only did we have a life of slavery, but it was also a life of *emptiness*. Peter called it "the empty way of life handed down to you from your forefathers" (1 Peter 1:18, NIV), and he described it more specifically in 1 Peter 4:1-4. At the time, these people thought their lives were "full" and "happy," when they were really empty and miserable. Unsaved people today are blindly living on substitutes.

While ministering in Canada, I met a woman who told me she had been converted early in life but had drifted into a "society life" that was exciting and satisfied her ego. One day, she was driving to a card party and happened to tune in a Christian radio broadcast. At that very moment, the speaker said, "Some of you women know more about cards than you do your Bible!" Those words arrested her. God spoke to her heart, she went back home, and from that hour her life was dedicated fully to God. She saw the futility and vanity of a life spent out of the will of God.

Peter not only reminded them of what they were, but he also reminded them *of what Christ did*. He shed His precious blood to purchase us out of the slavery of sin and set us free forever. *To redeem* means "to set free by paying a price." A slave could be freed with the payment of money, but no amount of money can set a lost sinner free. Only the blood of Jesus Christ can redeem us.

Peter was a witness of Christ's sufferings (1 Peter 5:1) and mentioned His sacrificial death often in this letter (1 Peter 2:21ff; 3:18; 4:1, 13; 5:1). In calling Christ "a Lamb,"

Peter was reminding his readers of an Old Testament teaching that was important in the early church, and that ought to be important to us today. It is the doctrine of substitution: an innocent victim giving his life for the guilty.

The doctrine of sacrifice begins in Genesis 3, when God killed animals that He might clothe Adam and Eve. A ram died for Isaac (Gen. 22:13) and the Passover lamb was slain for each Jewish household (Ex. 12). Messiah was presented as an innocent Lamb in Isaiah 53. Isaac asked the question, "Where is the lamb?" (Gen. 22:7) and John the Baptist answered it when he pointed to Jesus and said, "Behold the Lamb of God, which taketh away the sin of the world" (John 1:29). In heaven, the redeemed and the angels sing, "Worthy is the Lamb!" (Rev. 5:11-14)

Peter made it clear that Christ's death was an appointment, not an accident; for it was ordained by God before the foundation of the world (Acts 2:23). From the human perspective, our Lord was cruelly murdered; but from the divine perspective, He laid down His life for sinners (John 10:17-18). But He was raised from the dead! Now, anyone who trusts Him will be saved for eternity.

When you and I meditate on the sacrifice of Christ for us, certainly we should want to obey God and live holy lives for His glory. When only a young lady, Frances Ridley Havergal saw a picture of the crucified Christ with this caption under it: "I did this for thee. What hast thou done for Me?" Quickly, she wrote a poem, but was dissatisfied with it and threw it into the fireplace. The paper came out unharmed! Later, at her father's suggestion, she published the poem, and today we sing it.

> I gave My life for thee,
> My precious blood I shed;
> That thou might ransomed be,
> And quickened from the dead.
> I gave, I gave, My life for thee,
> What hast thou given for Me?

A good question, indeed! I trust we can give a good answer to the Lord.

# CHAPTER FOUR
# CHRISTIAN TOGETHERNESS
## 1 Peter 1:22–2:10

One of the painful facts of life is that the people of God do not always get along with each other. You would think that those who walk in *hope* and *holiness* would be able to walk in *harmony*, but this is not always true. From God's divine point of view, there is only one body (see Eph. 4:4-6); but what we see with human eyes is a church divided and sometimes at war. There is today a desperate need for spiritual unity.

In this section of his letter, Peter emphasized spiritual unity by presenting four vivid pictures of the church.

### We Are Children in the Same Family (1 Peter 1:22–2:3)
When you consider the implications of this fact, you will be encouraged to build and maintain unity among God's people.

*We have experienced the same birth (vv. 23-25).* The only way to enter God's spiritual family is by a spiritual birth, through faith in Jesus Christ (John 3:1-16). Just as there are two parents in physical birth, so there are two parents in spiritual birth: the Spirit of God (John 3:5-6) and the Word of God (1 Peter 1:23). The new birth gives to us a new nature (2 Peter 1:4) as well as a new and living hope (1 Peter 1:3).

Our first birth was a birth of "flesh," and the flesh is corruptible. Whatever is born of flesh is destined to die and decay. This explains why mankind cannot hold civilization together: it is all based on human flesh and is destined to fall apart. Like the beautiful flowers of spring, man's works look successful for a time, but then they start to decay and die. All the way from the Tower of Babel in Genesis 11, to "Babylon the Great" in Revelation 17–18, man's great attempts at unity are destined to fail.

If we try to build unity in the church on the basis of our first birth, we will fail; but if we build unity on the basis of the new birth, it will succeed. Each believer has the same Holy Spirit dwelling within (Rom. 8:9). We call on the same Father (1 Peter 1:17) and share His divine nature. We trust the same Word, and that Word will never decay or disappear. We have trusted the same Gospel and have been born of the same Spirit. The *externals* of the flesh that could divide us mean nothing when compared with the *eternals* of the Spirit that unite us.

**We express the same love (v. 22).** Peter used two different words for love: *philadelphia*, which is "brotherly love," and *agape*, which is godlike sacrificial love. It is important that we share both kinds of love. We share brotherly love because we are brothers and sisters in Christ and have likenesses. We share *agape* love because we belong to God and therefore can overlook differences.

By nature, all of us are selfish; so it took a miracle of God to give us this love. Because we "obeyed the truth through the Spirit," God purified our souls and poured His love into our hearts (Rom. 5:5). Love for the brethren is an evidence that we truly have been born of God (1 John 4:7-21). Now we are "obedient children" (1 Peter 1:14) who no longer want to live in the selfish desires of the old life.

It is tragic when people try to "manufacture" love, because the product is obviously cheap and artificial. "The words of his mouth were smoother than butter, but war was in his heart: his words were softer than oil, yet were they drawn swords" (Ps. 55:21). The love that we share with each other, and with a lost world, must be generated by the Spirit of God. It is a *constant* power in our lives, and not something that we turn on and off like a radio.

Not only is this love a spiritual love, but it is a *sincere* love ("unfeigned"). We love "with a pure heart." Our motive is not to get but to give. There is a kind of "success psychology" popular today that enables a person to subtly manipulate others in order to get what he wants. If our love is sincere and from a pure heart, we could never "use people" for our own advantage.

This love is also a *fervent* love, and this is an athletic term that means "striving with all of one's energy." Love is something we have to work at, just as an Olympic contestant has to work at his particular skills. Christian love is not a feeling; it is a matter of the will. We show love to others when we treat them the same way God treats us. God forgives us, so we forgive others. God is kind to us, so we are kind to others. It is not a matter of *feeling* but of *willing,* and this is something we must constantly work at if we are to succeed.

We have two wonderful "assistants" to help us: the Word of God and the Spirit of God. The same truth that we trusted and obeyed to become God's children also nurtures and empowers us. *It is impossible to love the truth and hate the brethren.* The Spirit of God produces the "fruit of the Spirit" in our lives, and the first of these is love (Gal. 5:22-23). If we are filled with the Word of God (Col. 3:16ff) and the Spirit of God (Eph. 5:18ff), we will manifest the love of God in our daily experiences.

**We enjoy the same nourishment (vv. 1-3).** God's Word *has* life, *gives* life, and *nourishes* life. We should have appetites for the Word just like hungry newborn babes! We should want the *pure* Word, unadulterated, because this alone can help us grow. When I was a child, I did not like to drink milk (and my father worked for the Borden Dairy!), so my mother used to add various syrups and powders to make my milk tastier. None of them really ever worked. It is sad when Christians have no appetite for God's Word, but must be "fed" religious entertainment instead. As we grow, we discover that the Word is milk for babes, but also strong meat for the mature (1 Cor. 3:1-4; Heb. 5:11-14). It is also bread (Matt. 4:4) and honey (Ps. 119:103).

Sometimes children have no appetite because they have been eating the wrong things. Peter warned his readers to "lay aside" certain wrong attitudes of heart that would hinder their appetite and spiritual growth. "Malice" means wickedness in general. "Guile" is craftiness, using devious words and actions to get what we want. Of course, if we are guilty of malice and guile, we will try to hide it; and this produces "hypocrisies." Often the cause of ill will is *envy,* and one result of envy is *evil speaking,* conversation that tears the other person down. If these attitudes and actions are in our lives, we will lose our appetite for the pure word of God. If we stop feeding on the Word, we stop growing, and we stop enjoying ("tasting") the grace that we find in the Lord. When Christians are growing in the Word, they are peacemakers, not troublemakers, and they promote the unity of the church.

## We Are Stones in the Same Building (1 Peter 2:4-8)

There is only one Saviour, Jesus Christ, and only one spiritual building, the church. Jesus

Christ is the chief cornerstone of the church (Eph. 2:20), binding the building together. Whether we agree with each other or not, all true Christians belong to each other as stones in God's building.

Peter gave a full description of Jesus Christ, the stone. He is a *living* stone because He was raised from the dead in victory. He is the *chosen* stone of the Father, and He is *precious.* Peter quoted Isaiah 28:16 and Psalm 118:22 in his description and pointed out that Jesus Christ, though chosen by God, was rejected by men. He was not the kind of Messiah they were expecting, so they stumbled over Him. Jesus referred to this same Scripture when He debated with the Jewish leaders (Matt. 21:42ff; see Ps. 118:22). Though rejected by men, Jesus Christ was exalted by God!

The real cause of this Jewish stumbling was their refusal to submit to the Word (1 Peter 2.8). Had they believed and obeyed the Word, they would have received their Messiah and been saved. Of course, people today still stumble over Christ and His cross (1 Cor. 1:18ff). Those who believe on Christ "shall not be confounded [ashamed]."

In His first mention of the church, Jesus compared it to a building: "I will build My church" (Matt. 16:18). Believers are living stones in His building. Each time someone trusts Christ, another stone is quarried out of the pit of sin and cemented by grace into the building. It may look to us that the church on earth is a pile of rubble and ruins, but God sees the total structure as it grows (Eph. 2:19-22). What a privilege we have to be a part of His church, "an habitation of God through the Spirit."

Peter wrote this letter to believers living in five different provinces, yet he said that they all belonged to *one* "spiritual house." There is a unity of God's people that transcends all local and individual assemblies and fellowships. We belong to each other because we belong to Christ. This does not mean that doctrinal and denominational distinctives are wrong, because each local church must be fully persuaded by the Spirit. But it does mean that we must not permit our differences to destroy the spiritual unity we have in Christ. We ought to be mature enough to disagree without in any sense becoming disagreeable.

A contractor in Michigan was building a house and the construction of the first floor went smoothly. But when they started on the second floor, they had nothing but trouble.

None of the materials from the lumberyard would fit properly. Then they discovered the reason: they were working with two different sets of blueprints! Once they got rid of the old set, everything went well and they built a lovely house.

Too often, Christians hinder the building of the church because they are following the wrong plans. When Solomon built his temple, his workmen followed the plans so carefully that everything fit together on the construction site (1 Kings 6:7). If all of us would follow God's blueprints given in His Word, we would be able to work together without discord and build His church for His glory.

## We Are Priests in the Same Temple (1 Peter 2:5, 9)

We are a "holy priesthood" and a "royal priesthood." This corresponds to the heavenly priesthood of our Lord, for He is both King and Priest (see Heb. 7). In the Old Testament, no king in Israel served as a priest; and the one king who tried was judged by God (2 Chron. 26:16-21). Our Lord's heavenly throne is a throne of grace from which we may obtain by faith all that we need to live for Him and serve Him (Heb. 4:14-16).

In the Old Testament period, God's people *had* a priesthood; but today, God's people *are* a priesthood. Each individual believer has the privilege of coming into the presence of God (Heb. 10:19-25). We do not come to God through any person on earth, but only through the one Mediator, Jesus Christ (1 Tim. 2:1-8). Because He is alive in glory, interceding for us, we can minister as holy priests.

This means that our lives should be lived as though we were priests in a temple. It is indeed a privilege to serve as a priest. No man in Israel could serve at the altar, or enter the tabernacle or temple holy places, except those born into the tribe of Levi and consecrated to God for service. Each priest and Levite had different ministries to perform, yet they were together under the high priest, serving to glorify God. As God's priests today, we must work together at the direction of our Great High Priest. Each ministry that we perform for His glory is a service to God.

Peter mentioned especially the privilege of offering "spiritual sacrifices." Christians today do not bring animal sacrifices as did the Old Testament worshipers; but we do have our own sacrifices to present to God. We ought to give *our bodies* to Him as living sacrifices

(Rom. 12:1-2), as well as the *praise* of our lips (Heb. 13:15) and the *good works* we do for others (Heb. 13:16). The *money* and other material things we share with others in God's service is also a spiritual sacrifice (Phil. 4:10-20). Even the *people* we win to Christ are sacrifices for His glory (Rom. 15:16). We offer these sacrifices through Jesus Christ, for only then are they acceptable with God. If we do any of this for our own pleasure or glory, then it will not be accepted as a spiritual sacrifice.

God wanted His people Israel to become "a kingdom of priests" (Ex. 19:6), a spiritual influence for godliness; but Israel failed Him. Instead of being a positive influence on the godless nations around them, Israel imitated those nations and adopted their practices. God had to discipline His people many times for their idolatry, but they still persisted in sin. Today, Israel has no temple or priesthood.

It is important that we, as God's priests, maintain our separated position in this world. We must not be isolated, because the world needs our influence and witness; but we must not permit the world to infect us or change us. Separation is not isolation; it is contact without contamination.

The fact that each individual believer can go to God personally and offer spiritual sacrifices should not encourage selfishness or "individualism" on our part. We are priests *together*, serving the same High Priest, ministering in the same spiritual temple. The fact that there is but *one* High Priest and heavenly Mediator indicates unity among the people of God. While we must maintain our personal walk with God, we must not do it at the expense of other Christians by ignoring or neglecting them.

Several social scientists have written books dealing with what they call the "me complex" in modern society. The emphasis today is on taking care of yourself and forgetting about others. This same attitude has crept into the church, as I see it. Too much modern church music centers on the individual and ignores the fellowship of the church. Many books and sermons focus on *personal* experience to the neglect of ministry to the whole body. I realize that the individual must care for himself if he is to help others, but there must be balance.

## We Are Citizens of the Same Nation (1 Peter 2:9-10)

The description of the church in these verses parallels God's description of Israel, in Exodus 19:5-6 and Deuteronomy 7:6. In contrast to the disobedient and rebellious nation of Israel, God's people today are His chosen and holy nation. This does not suggest that God is through with Israel, for I believe He will fulfill His promises and His covenants and establish the promised kingdom. But it does mean that the church today is to God and the world what Israel was meant to be.

We are a *chosen generation,* which immediately speaks of the grace of God. God did not choose Israel because they were a great people, but because He loved them (Deut. 7:7-8). God has chosen us purely because of His love and grace. "You did not choose Me, but I chose you" (John 15:16, NIV).

We are a *holy nation.* We have been set apart to belong exclusively to God. Our citizenship is in heaven (Phil. 3:20), so we obey heaven's laws and seek to please heaven's Lord. Israel forgot that she was a holy nation and began to break down the walls of separation that made her special and distinct. God commanded them to put a "difference between holy and unholy, and between unclean and clean" (Lev. 10:10); but they ignored the differences and disobeyed God.

We are the *people of God.* In our unsaved condition, we were not God's people, because we belonged to Satan and the world (Eph. 2:1-3, 11-19). Now that we have trusted Christ, we are a part of God's people. We are a "people of His own special possession," because He purchased us with the blood of His own Son (Acts 20:28).

All of these privileges carry with them one big responsibility: revealing the praises of God to a lost world. The verb translated "show forth" means "to tell out, to advertise." Because the world is "in the dark," people do not know the "excellencies" of God; but they should see them in our lives. Each citizen of heaven is a living "advertisement" for the virtues of God and the blessings of the Christian life. Our lives should radiate the "marvelous light" into which God has graciously called us.

After all, we have obtained mercy from God! Were it not for His mercy, we would be lost and on the way to eternal judgment! God reminded Israel many times that He had delivered them from the bondage of Egypt that they might glorify and serve Him, but the nation soon forgot and the people drifted back into their sinful ways. We are God's chosen people only because of His mercy, and it behooves us to be faithful to Him.

We are living in enemy territory, and the enemy is constantly watching us, looking for opportunities to move in and take over. As citizens of heaven, we must be united. We must present to the world a united demonstration of what the grace and mercy of God can do. As I write these words, the newspapers are reporting "dissensions" among the men who serve with the President of the United States. These men are not presenting a united front, and the nation is a bit uneasy. I wonder what the unsaved people think when they see the citizens of heaven and servants of God fighting among themselves.

Each of these four pictures emphasizes the importance of unity and harmony. We belong to one family of God and share the same divine nature. We are living stones in one building and priests serving in one temple. We are citizens of the same heavenly homeland. It is Jesus Christ who is the source and center of this unity. If we center our attention and affection on Him, we will walk and work together; if we focus on ourselves, we will only cause division.

Unity does not eliminate diversity. Not all children in a family are alike, nor are all the stones in a building identical. In fact, it is diversity that gives beauty and richness to a family or building. The absence of diversity is not *unity;* it is *uniformity,* and uniformity is dull. It is fine when the choir sings in unison, but I prefer that they sing in harmony.

Christians can differ and still get along. All who cherish the "one faith" and who seek to honor the "one Lord" can love each other and walk together (Eph. 4:1-6). God may call us into different ministries, or to use different methods, but we can still love each other and seek to present a united witness to the world.

After all, one day all of us will be together in heaven (John 17:24); so it might be a good idea if we learned to love each other down here!

St. Augustine said it perfectly: "In essentials, unity. In nonessentials, liberty. In all things, charity."

# CHAPTER FIVE
# SOMEBODY'S WATCHING YOU!
## *1 Peter 2:11-25*

The central section of Peter's letter (1 Peter 2:11–3:12) emphasizes *submission* in the life of a believer. This is certainly not a popular topic in this day of lawlessness and the quest for "personal fulfillment," but it is an important one. Peter applied the theme of submission to the life of a believer as a citizen (1 Peter 2:11-17), a worker (1 Peter 2:18-25), a marriage partner (1 Peter 3:1-7), and a member of the Christian assembly (1 Peter 3:8-12).

Submission does not mean slavery or subjugation but simply the recognition of God's authority in our lives. God has established the home, human government, and the church, and He has the right to tell us how these institutions should be run. God wants each of us to exercise authority; but before we can *exercise* authority, we must be *under* authority. Satan's offer to our first parents was freedom without authority, but they ended up losing both freedom and authority. The Prodigal Son found his freedom when he yielded to his father's will.

Peter shared with his readers three excellent motives for submitting to authority and thus living dedicated, obedient Christian lives.

### For the Sake of the Lost
### (1 Peter 2:11-12)
As Christians, we must constantly remind ourselves *who we are;* and Peter did this in 1 Peter 2:11. To begin with, we are *God's dearly beloved children.* Eight times in his two epistles, Peter reminded his readers of God's love for them (1 Peter 2:11; 4:12; 2 Peter 1:7; 3:1, 8, 14-15, 17). In ourselves, there is nothing that God can love; but He loves us because of Jesus Christ. "This is My beloved Son, in whom I am well pleased" (2 Peter 1:17). Because of our faith in Jesus Christ, we are "accepted in the beloved" (Eph. 1:6).

Our "love relationship" to Jesus Christ ought to be motivation enough for us to live godly lives in this godless world. "If ye love Me, keep My commandments" (John 14:15). There is something deeper than obedience because of duty, and that is obedience because of devotion. "If a man love Me, he will keep My words" (John 14:23).

Not only are we God's beloved children, but we are also "strangers [sojourners] and pilgrims" in this world. We are "resident aliens" who have our citizenship in another country—heaven. Like the patriarchs of old, we are temporary in this life, traveling toward the heavenly city (Heb. 11:8-16). If you have ever lived in a foreign land, you know that the citizens watch you and are prone to find things to criticize. (In all fairness, we must confess that sometimes we are critical of foreigners in our own country.) Some years ago, a bestselling novel called *The Ugly American* depicted the struggles of an American as he tried to meet the needs of a foreign people, and still maintain his credibility with his fellow Americans, who, unfortunately, completely misunderstood the situation.

We are also *soldiers involved in a spiritual battle*. There are sinful desires that war against us and want to defeat us (see Gal. 5:16-26). Our real battle is not with people around us, but with passions within us. D.L. Moody said, "I have more trouble with D.L. Moody than with any man I know." If we yield to these sinful appetites, then we will start living like the unsaved around us, and will become ineffective witnesses. The word translated "war" carries the idea of "a military campaign." We do not win one battle, and the war is over! It is a constant warfare, and we must be on our guard.

Most of all, we are *witnesses to the lost around us*. The word "Gentiles" here has nothing to do with race, since it is a synonym for "unsaved people" (1 Cor. 5:1; 12:2; 3 John 7). Unsaved people are watching us, speaking against us (1 Peter 3:16; 4:4), and looking for excuses to reject the Gospel.

If we are going to witness to the lost people around us, we must live "honest" lives. This word implies much more than telling the truth and doing what is right. It carries with it the idea of beauty, comeliness, that which is admirable and honorable. To use a cliché of the '60s, we must be "beautiful people" in the best sense of the word.

We do not witness only with our lips; we must back up our "talk" with our "walk." There should be nothing in our conduct that will give the unsaved ammunition to attack Christ and the Gospel. Our good works must back up our good words. Jesus said this in

Matthew 5:16, and the entire Bible echoes this truth.

During my many years of ministry, I have seen the powerful impact Christians can make on the lost when they combine a godly life with a loving witness. I remember many instances of some wonderful conversions simply because dedicated Christians let their lights shine. On the other hand, I recall with grief some lost persons who rejected the Word because of the inconsistent lives of professed believers.

Peter encouraged his readers to bear witness to the lost, by word and deed, so that one day God might visit them and save them. "The day of visitation" could mean that day when Christ returns and every tongue will confess that He is Lord. But I think the "visitation" Peter mentioned here is the time when God visits lost sinners and saves them by His grace. The word is used in this sense in Luke 19:44. When these people do trust Christ, they will glorify God and give thanks because we were faithful to witness to them even when they made life difficult for us.

In the summer of 1805, a number of Indian chiefs and warriors met in council at Buffalo Creek, New York to hear a presentation of the Christian message by a Mr. Cram from the Boston Missionary Society. After the sermon, a response was given by Red Jacket, one of the leading chiefs. Among other things, the chief said:

"Brother, you say that there is but one way to worship and serve the Great Spirit. If there is but one religion, why do you white people differ so much about it? Why not all agree, as you can all read the Book?

"Brother, we are told that you have been preaching to the white people in this place. These people are our neighbors. We are acquainted with them. We will wait a little while and see what effect your preaching has upon them. If we find it does them good, makes them honest and less disposed to cheat Indians, we will then consider again of what you have said."

## For the Lord's Sake (1 Peter 2:13-17)

Of course, *everything* we do should be for the glory of the Lord and the good of His kingdom! But Peter was careful to point out that Christians in society are representatives of Jesus Christ. It is our responsibility to "advertise God's virtues" (1 Peter 2:9, author's translation). This is especially true when it comes to our relationship to government and people in authority.

As Christian citizens, we should submit to the authority vested in human government. The word translated "ordinance" in our *Authorized Version* simply means "creation or institution." It does not refer to each individual law, but to the institutions that make and enforce the laws. It is possible to submit to the institutions and still disobey the laws.

For example, when Daniel and his three friends refused to obey the king's dietary regulations, they disobeyed the law; but the *way* that they did it proved that they honored the king and respected the authorities (Dan. 1). They were not rebels; they were careful not to embarrass the official in charge or get him into trouble; and yet they stood their ground. They glorified God and, at the same time, honored the authority of the king.

Peter and the other Apostles faced a similar challenge shortly after Pentecost (Acts 4–5). The Jewish council commanded them to stop preaching in the name of Jesus, but Peter and his associates refused to obey (see Acts 4:19; 5:29). They did not cause a rebellion or in any way question or deny the authority of the council. They submitted to the institution but they refused to stop preaching. They showed respect to their leaders even though these men were opposed to the Gospel.

It is important that we respect the office even though we cannot respect the man or woman in the office. As much as possible, we should seek to cooperate with the government and obey the law; but we must never allow the law to make us violate our conscience or disobey God's Word. Unfortunately, some zealous but ignorant Christians use these differences as opportunities for conflict and loud sermons about "freedom" and "separation of church and state."

When a local church constructs and furnishes a building, there is a local code that must be obeyed. (I have been through several building programs and I know!) The government has no right to control the pulpit or the business meeting, but it has every right to control matters that relate to safety and operation. If the law requires a certain number of exits, or fire extinguishers, or emergency lights, the church must comply. The state is not persecuting when it sets up the code, nor is the church compromising when it obeys the code. But I know some overly zealous saints who have disgraced the name of the Lord by

their attitudes and actions relating to these matters.

Peter named the offices we are to respect. "The king" meant "the emperor." In democratic nations, we have a president or premier. Peter did not criticize the Roman government or suggest that it be overthrown. God's church has been able to live and grow in all kinds of political systems. The "governors" are those under the supreme authority who administer the laws and execute justice. Ideally, they should punish those who do evil and praise those who do good. This ideal was not always reached in Peter's day (see Acts 24:24-27), nor is it reached in our own. Again, we must remind ourselves to respect the office even if we cannot respect the officer.

Two phrases are important: "the will of God" (1 Peter 2:15) and "the servants of God" (1 Peter 2:16). When we do something in the will of God and as the servants of God, then we are doing it "for the Lord's sake." God has willed that we silence the critics by doing good, not by opposing the authority. The word "silence" in 1 Peter 2:15 is literally "muzzle," as though the pagan critics were like a pack of yelping, snapping dogs!

Someone may argue, "But, as Christians, are we not free?" Yes, we are free in Christ; but we must never use our freedom for ourselves. We must always use it for others. Sad to say, there are "religious racketeers" who prey on ignorant people and use "religion" to veil their evil actions. A true Christian submits himself to authority because he is first of all submitted to Christ. He uses his freedom as a tool to build with and not as a weapon to fight with. A good example of this attitude is Nehemiah, who willingly gave up his own rights that he might help his people and restore the walls of Jerusalem.

If we are sincerely submitted to authority "for the Lord's sake," then we will show honor to all who deserve it. We may not agree with their politics or their practices, but we must respect their position (see Rom. 13). We will also "love the brotherhood," meaning, of course, the people of God in the church. This is a recurring theme in this letter (1 Peter 1:22; 3:8; 4:8; 5:14). One way we show love to the brethren is by submitting to the authority of the "powers that be," for we are bound together with one another in our Christian witness.

"Fear God" and "honor the king" go together, since "the powers that be are ordained of God" (Rom. 13:1). Solomon had the same counsel: "My son, fear thou the Lord and the king" (Prov. 24:21). We honor the king because we do fear the Lord. It is worth noting that the tenses of these verbs indicate that we should *constantly* maintain these attitudes. "Keep loving the brotherhood! Keep fearing God! Keep honoring the king!"

As Christians, we must exercise discernment in our relationship to human government. There are times when the right thing is to set aside our own privileges, and there are other times when *using* our citizenship is the right thing. Paul was willing to suffer personally in Philippi (Acts 16:16-24), but he was unwilling to "sneak out of town" like a criminal (Acts 16:35-40). When he was arrested on false charges, Paul used his citizenship to protect himself (Acts 22:22-29) and to insist on a fair trial before Caesar (Acts 25:1-12).

### For Our Own Sake (1 Peter 2:18-25)

In this paragraph Peter addressed the Christian slaves in the congregations, and again he stressed the importance of submission. Some newly converted slaves thought that their spiritual freedom also guaranteed personal and political freedom, and they created problems for themselves and the churches. Paul dealt with this problem in 1 Corinthians 7:20-24, and also touched on it in his letter to his friend Philemon. The Gospel eventually overthrew the Roman Empire and the terrible institution of slavery, even though the early church did not preach against either one.

There are no Christian slaves today, at least in the New Testament sense; but what Peter wrote does have application to employees. We are to be submissive to those who are over us, whether they are kind or unkind to us. Christian employees must never take advantage of Christian employers. Each worker should do a good day's work and honestly earn his pay.

Sometimes a Christian employee may be wronged by an unbelieving coworker or supervisor. For conscience' sake, he must "take it" even though he is not in the wrong. A Christian's relationship to God is far more important than his relationship to men. "For this is grace [thankworthy]" to bear reproach when you are innocent (see Matt. 5:10-12). Anybody, including an unbeliever, can "take it patiently" when he is in the wrong! It takes a dedicated Christian to "take it" when he is in the right. "This is grace [acceptable] with

God." God can give us the grace to submit and "take it" and in this way glorify God.

Of course, the human tendency is to fight back and to demand our rights. But that is the natural response of the unsaved person, and we must do much more than they do (Luke 6:32-34). Anybody can fight back; it takes a Spirit-filled Christian to submit and let God fight his battles (Rom. 12:16-21).

In the Bible, duty is always connected with doctrine. When Paul wrote to the slaves, he related his admonitions to the doctrine of the grace of God (Titus 2:9-15). Peter connected his counsels to the example of Jesus Christ, God's "Suffering Servant" (1 Peter 2:21-25; see Isa. 52:13–53:12). Peter had learned in his own experience that God's people *serve through suffering*. At first, Peter had opposed Christ's suffering on the cross (Matt. 16:21ff); but then he learned the important lesson that we lead by serving and serve by suffering. He also learned that this kind of suffering always leads to glory!

Peter encouraged these suffering slaves by presenting three "pictures" of Jesus Christ.

***He is our Example in His life (vv. 21-23).*** All that Jesus did on earth, as recorded in the four Gospels, is a perfect example for us to follow. But He is especially our example in the way He responded to suffering. In spite of the fact that He was sinless in both word and deed, He suffered at the hands of the authorities. This connects, of course, to Peter's words in 1 Peter 2:19-20. We wonder how he would have responded in the same circumstances! The fact that Peter used his sword in the Garden suggests that he might have fought rather than submitted to the will of God.

Jesus proved that a person could be in the will of God, be greatly loved by God, and still suffer unjustly. There is a shallow brand of popular theology today that claims that Christians will *not* suffer if they are in the will of God. Those who promote such ideas have not meditated much on the Cross.

Our Lord's humility and submission were not an evidence of weakness, but of power. Jesus could have summoned the armies of heaven to rescue Him! His words to Pilate in John 18:33-38 are proof that He was in complete command of the situation. It was Pilate who was on trial, not Jesus! Jesus had committed Himself to the Father, and the Father always judges righteously.

We are not saved by following Christ's example, because each of us would stumble over 1 Peter 2:22: "who did no sin." Sinners need a Saviour, not an Example. But after a person is saved, he will want to "follow closely upon His steps" (literal translation) and imitate the example of Christ.

**He is our Substitute in His death (v. 24).** He died as the sinner's Substitute. This entire section reflects that great "Servant Chapter," Isaiah 53, especially Isaiah 53:5-7, but also verses 9 and 12. Jesus did not die as a martyr; He died as a Saviour, a sinless Substitute. The word translated "bare" means "to carry as a sacrifice." The Jewish people did not crucify criminals; they stoned them to death. But if the victim was especially evil, his dead body was hung on a tree until evening, as a mark of shame (Deut. 21:23). Jesus died on a tree—a cross—and bore the curse of the Law (Gal. 3:13).

The paradoxes of the cross never cease to amaze us. Christ was wounded that we might be healed. He died that we might live. We died with Him, and thus we are "dead to sin" (Rom. 6) so that we might "live unto righteousness." The healing Peter mentioned in 1 Peter 2:24 is not physical healing, but rather the spiritual healing of the soul (Ps. 103:3). One day, when we have glorified bodies, all sicknesses will be gone; but meanwhile, even some of God's choicest servants may have physical afflictions (see Phil. 2:25-30; 2 Cor. 12:1ff).

It is not Jesus the Example or the Teacher who saves us, but Jesus the spotless Lamb of God who takes away the sins of the world (John 1:29).

**He is our Watchful Shepherd in heaven (v. 25).** In the Old Testament, the sheep died for the shepherd; but at Calvary, the Shepherd died for the sheep (John 10). Every lost sinner is like a sheep gone astray: ignorant, lost, wandering, in danger, away from the place of safety, and unable to help himself. The Shepherd went out to search for the lost sheep (Luke 15:1-7). He died for the sheep!

Now that we have been returned to the fold and are safely in His care, He watches over us lest we stray and get into sin. The word *bishop* simply means "one who watches over, who oversees." Just as the elder-bishop oversees the flock of God, the local church (1 Peter 5:2), so the Saviour in glory watches over His sheep to protect them and perfect them (Heb. 13:20-21).

Here, then, is the wonderful truth Peter

wanted to share: as we live godly lives and submit in times of suffering, we are following Christ's example *and becoming more like Him.* We submit and obey, not only for the sake of lost souls and for the Lord's sake, but also for our own sake, that we might grow spiritually and become more like Christ.

The unsaved world is watching us, but the Shepherd in heaven is also watching over us; so we have nothing to fear. We can submit to Him and know that He will work everything together for our good and His glory.

# CHAPTER SIX
# WEDLOCK OR
# DEADLOCK?
## *1 Peter 3:1-7*

A strange situation exists in society today. We have more readily available information about sex and marriage than ever before; yet we have more marital problems and divorces. Obviously something is wrong. It is not sufficient to say that God is needed in these homes, because even many *Christian* marriages are falling apart.

The fact that a man and a woman are both saved is no guarantee that their marriage will succeed. Marriage is something that we have to work at; success is not automatic. And when one marriage partner is not a Christian, that can make matters even more difficult. Peter addressed this section of his letter to Christian wives who had unsaved husbands, telling them how to win their mates to Christ. Then he added some important admonitions for Christian husbands.

No matter what your marital status may be, you can learn from Peter the essentials for a happy and successful marriage.

**The Example of Christ
(1 Peter 3:1a, 7a)**
The phrases "in the same manner" and "in like manner" refer us back to Peter's discussion of the example of Jesus Christ (1 Peter 2:21-25). Just as Jesus was submissive and obedient to God's will, so a Christian husband and wife should follow His example.

Much of our learning in life comes by way of imitation. Grandparents have a delightful time watching their grandchildren "pick up" new skills and words as they grow up. If we imitate the best models, we will become better people and better achievers; but if we imitate the wrong models, it will cripple our lives and possibly ruin our characters. The "role models" that we follow influence us in every area of life.

While standing in the checkout line in a supermarket, I overheard two women discussing the latest Hollywood scandal that was featured on the front page of a newspaper displayed on the counter. As I listened (and I could not *help* but hear them!), I thought: "How foolish to worry about the sinful lives of matinee idols. Why clutter up your mind with such trash? Why not get acquainted with decent people and learn from their lives?" A few days later, I overheard a conversation about the marital problems on a certain television "soap serial," and the same thoughts came to me.

When Christian couples try to imitate the world and get their standards from Hollywood instead of from heaven, there will be trouble in the home. But if both partners will imitate Jesus Christ in His submission and obedience, and His desire to serve others, then there will be triumph and joy in the home. A psychiatrist friend of mine states that the best thing a Christian husband can do is pattern himself after Jesus Christ. In Christ we see a beautiful blending of strength and tenderness, and that is what it takes to be a successful husband.

Peter also pointed to Sarah as a model for Christian wives to follow. To be sure, Sarah was not perfect; but she proved to be a good helpmeet to Abraham, and she is one of the few women named in Hebrews 11. I once made a pastoral visit to a woman who said she had marital problems, and I noticed a number of "movie fan club magazines" in the magazine rack. After listening to the woman's problems, I concluded that she needed to follow some Bible examples and models and get her mind off of the worldly examples.

We cannot follow Christ's example unless we first know Him as our Saviour, and then submit to Him as our Lord. We must spend time with Him each day, meditating on the Word and praying; and a Christian husband and wife must pray together and seek to encourage each other in the faith.

## Submission (1 Peter 3:1-6)

Twice in this paragraph Peter reminded Christian wives that they were to be submissive to their husbands (1 Peter 3:1, 5). The word translated "subjection" is a military term that means "to place under rank." God has a place for everything; He has ordained various levels of authority (see 1 Peter 2:13-14). He has ordained that the husband be the head of the home (Eph. 5:21ff) and that, as he submits to Christ, his wife should submit to him. Headship is not dictatorship, but the loving exercise of divine authority under the lordship of Jesus Christ.

Peter gave three reasons why a Christian wife should submit to her husband, even if the husband (as in this case) is not saved.

***Submission is an obligation (v. 1a).*** God has commanded it because, in His wisdom, He knows that this is the best arrangement for a happy, fulfilling marriage. Subjection does not mean that the wife is inferior to the husband. In fact, in 1 Peter 3:7, Peter made it clear that the husband and wife are "heirs together." The man and woman are made by the same Creator out of the same basic material, and both are made in God's image. God gave dominion to both Adam and Eve (Gen. 1:28), and in Jesus Christ Christian mates are one (Gal. 3:28).

Submission has to do with order and authority, not evaluation. For example, the slaves in the average Roman household were superior in many ways to their masters, but they still had to be under authority. The buck private in the army may be a better person than the five-star general, but he is still a buck private. Even Christ Himself became a servant and submitted to God's will. There is nothing degrading about submitting to authority or accepting God's order. If anything, it is the first step toward fulfillment. And Ephesians 5:21 makes it clear that *both* husband and wife must first be submitted to Jesus Christ.

Husbands and wives must be partners, not competitors. After a wedding ceremony, I often privately say to the bride and groom, "Now, remember, from now on it's no longer *mine* or *yours*, but *ours*." This explains why Christians must always marry other Christians, for a believer cannot enter into any kind of deep "oneness" with an unbeliever (2 Cor. 6:14-18).

***Submission is an opportunity (vv. 1b-2).*** An opportunity for what? To win an unsaved husband to Christ. God not only *com-*

*mands* submission, but He *uses* it as a powerful spiritual influence in a home. This does not mean that a Christian wife "gives in" to her unsaved husband in order to subtly manipulate him and get him to do what she desires. This kind of selfish psychological persuasion ought never to be found in a Christian's heart or home.

An unsaved husband will not be converted by preaching or nagging in the home. The phrase "without the word" does not mean "without the Word of God," because salvation comes through the Word (John 5:24). It means "without talk, without a lot of speaking." Christian wives who preach at their husbands only drive them farther from the Lord. I know one zealous wife who used to keep religious radio programs on all evening, usually very loud, so that her unsaved husband would "hear the truth." She only made it easier for him to leave home and spend his evenings with his friends.

It is the character and conduct of the wife that will win the lost husband—not arguments, but such attitudes as submission, understanding, love, kindness, patience. These qualities are not manufactured; they are the fruit of the Spirit that come when we are submitted to Christ and to one another. A Christian wife with "purity and reverence" will reveal in her life "the praises" of God (1 Peter 2:9) and influence her husband to trust Christ.

One of the greatest examples of a godly wife and mother in church history is Monica, the mother of the famous St. Augustine. God used Monica's witness and prayers to win both her son and her husband to Christ, though her husband was not converted until shortly before his death. Augustine wrote in his *Confessions,* "She served him as her lord; and did her diligence to win him unto Thee . . . preaching Thee unto him by her conversation [behavior]; by which Thou ornamentest her, making her reverently amiable unto her husband."

In a Christian home, we must minister to each other. A Christian husband must minister to his wife and help to "beautify her" in the Lord (Eph. 5:25-30). A Christian wife must encourage her husband and help him grow strong in the Lord. Parents and children must share burdens and blessings and seek to maintain an atmosphere of spiritual excitement and growth in the home. If there are unsaved people in the home, they will be won to Christ more by what they see in our lives and rela-tionships than by what they hear in our witness.

***Submission is an ornament (vv. 3-6).*** The word translated "adorning" is *kosmos* in the Greek, and gives us our English words "cosmos" (the ordered universe) and "cosmetic." It is the opposite of *chaos.* Peter warned the Christian wife not to major on external decorations but on internal character. Roman women were captivated by the latest fashions of the day, and competed with each other in dress and hairdos. It was not unusual for the women to have elaborate *coiffures,* studded with gold and silver combs and even jewels. They wore elaborate and expensive garments, all for the purpose of impressing each other.

A Christian wife with an unsaved husband might think that she must imitate the world if she is going to win her mate; but just the opposite is true. Glamour is artificial and external; true beauty is real and internal. Glamour is something a person can put on and take off, but true beauty is always present. Glamour is corruptible; it decays and fades. True beauty from the heart grows more wonderful as the years pass. A Christian woman who cultivates the beauty of the inner person will not have to depend on cheap externals. God is concerned about values, not prices.

Of course, this does not mean that a wife should neglect herself and not try to be up-to-date in her apparel. It simply means that she is not *majoring* on being a "fashion plate" just to "keep up with the crowd." Any husband is proud of a wife who is attractive, but that beauty must come from the heart, not the store. We are not *of* this world, but we must not look as though we came from *out of* this world!

Peter did not forbid the wearing of jewelry any more than the wearing of apparel. The word "wearing" in 1 Peter 3:3 means "the putting around," and refers to a gaudy display of jewelry. It is possible to wear jewelry and still honor God, and we must not judge one another in this matter.

Peter closed this section by pointing to Sarah as an example of a godly, submissive wife. Read Genesis 18 for the background. Christian wives today would probably embarrass their husbands if they called them "lord," but their attitudes ought to be such that they could call them "lord" and people would believe it. The believing wife who submits to Christ and to her husband, and who cultivates a "meek and quiet spirit" will never have to be afraid. (The "fear" in this verse means "terror," while in 1 Peter 3:2 it means "reverence.") God will watch over her even when her unsaved mate creates problems and difficulties for her.

### Consideration (1 Peter 3:7)

Why did Peter devote more space to instructing the wives than the husbands? Because the Christian wives were experiencing a whole new situation and needed guidance. In general, women were kept down in the Roman Empire, and their new freedom in Christ created new problems and challenges. Furthermore, many of them had unsaved husbands and needed extra encouragement and enlightenment.

As Peter wrote to the Christian husbands, he reminded them of four areas of responsibility in their relationship with their mates.

*Physical—"dwell with them."* This implies much more than sharing the same address. Marriage is fundamentally a physical relationship: "They two shall be one flesh" (Eph. 5:31). Of course, Christian mates enjoy a deeper spiritual relationship, but the two go together (1 Cor. 7:1-5). A truly spiritual husband will fulfill his marital duties and love his wife.

The husband must make time to be home with his wife. Christian workers and church officers who get too busy running around solving other people's problems, may end up creating problems of their own at home. One survey revealed that the average husband and wife had thirty-seven minutes a week together in actual communication! Is it any wonder that marriages fall apart after the children grow up and leave home? The husband and wife are left alone—to live with strangers!

"Dwell with them" also suggests that the husband provide for the physical and material needs of the home. While it is not wrong for a wife to have a job or career, her first responsibility is to care for the home (Titus 2:4-5). It is the husband who should provide (1 Tim. 5:8).

*Intellectual—"according to knowledge."* Somebody asked Mrs. Albert Einstein if she understood Dr. Einstein's theory of relativity, and she replied, "No, but I understand the Doctor." In my premarital counseling as a pastor, I often gave the couple pads of paper and asked them to write down the three things each one thinks the other enjoys doing

the most. Usually, the prospective bride made her list immediately; the man would sit and ponder. And usually the girl was right but the man wrong! What a beginning for a marriage!

It is amazing that two married people can live together and not really know each other! Ignorance is dangerous in any area of life, but it is especially dangerous in marriage. A Christian husband needs to know his wife's moods, feelings, needs, fears, and hopes. He needs to "listen with his heart" and share meaningful communication with her. There must be in the home such a protective atmosphere of love and submission that the husband and wife can disagree and still be happy together.

"Speaking the truth in love" is the solution to the communications problem (Eph. 4:15). It has well been said that love without truth is hypocrisy, and truth without love is brutality. We need both truth and love if we are to grow in our understanding of one another. How can a husband show consideration for his wife if he does not understand her needs or problems? To say, "I never knew you felt that way!" is to confess that, at some point, one mate excommunicated the other. When either mate is afraid to be open and honest about a matter, then he or she is building walls and not bridges.

*Emotional—"giving honor unto the wife."* Chivalry may be dead, but every husband must be a "knight in shining armor" who treats his wife like a princess. (By the way, the name Sarah means "princess.") Peter did not suggest that a wife is "the weaker vessel" mentally, morally, or spiritually, but rather physically. There are exceptions, of course, but generally speaking, the man is the stronger of the two when it comes to physical accomplishments. The husband should treat his wife like an expensive, beautiful, fragile vase, in which is a precious treasure.

When a young couple starts dating, the boy is courteous and thoughtful. After they get engaged, he shows even more courtesy and always acts like a gentleman. Sad to say, soon after they get married, many a husband forgets to be kind and gentlemanly and starts taking his wife for granted. He forgets that happiness in a home is made up of many *little* things, including the small courtesies of life.

Big resentments often grow out of small hurts. Husbands and wives need to be honest with each other, admit hurts, and seek for forgiveness and healing. "Giving honor unto the wife" does not mean "giving in to the wife." A husband can disagree with his wife and still respect and honor her. As the spiritual leader in the home, the husband must sometimes make decisions that are not popular; but he can still act with courtesy and respect.

"Giving honor" means that the husband respects his wife's feelings, thinking, and desires. He may not agree with her ideas, but he respects them. Often God balances a marriage so that the husband needs what the wife has in her personality, and she likewise needs his good qualities. An impulsive husband often has a patient wife, and this helps to keep him out of trouble!

The husband must be the "thermostat" in the home, setting the emotional and spiritual temperature. The wife often is the "thermometer," letting him know what that temperature is! Both are necessary. The husband who is sensitive to his wife's feelings will not only make her happy, but will also grow himself and help his children live in a home that honors God.

*Spiritual—"that your prayers be not hindered."* Peter assumed that husbands and wives would pray together. Often, they do not; and this is the reason for much failure and unhappiness. If unconverted people can have happy homes *without prayer* (and they do), how much happier Christian homes would be *with prayer!* In fact, it is the prayer life of a couple that indicates how things are going in the home. If something is wrong, their prayers will be hindered.

A husband and wife need to have their own private, individual prayer time each day. They also need to pray together and to have a time of "family devotion." How this is organized will change from home to home, and even from time to time as the children grow up and schedules change. The Word of God and prayer are basic to a happy, holy home (Acts 6:4).

A husband and wife are "heirs together." If the wife shows submission and the husband consideration, and if both submit to Christ and follow His example, then they will have an enriching experience in their marriage. If not, they will miss God's best and rob each other of blessing and growth. "The grace of life" may refer to children, who certainly are a heritage from God (Ps. 127:3); but even childless couples can enjoy spiritual riches if they will obey Peter's admonitions.

It might be good if husbands and wives occasionally took inventory of their marriages.

Here are some questions, based on what Peter wrote.

1. Are we partners or competitors?
2. Are we helping each other become more spiritual?
3. Are we depending on the externals or the eternals? The artificial or the real?
4. Do we understand each other better?
5. Are we sensitive to each other's feelings and ideas, or taking each other for granted?
6. Are we seeing God answer our prayers?
7. Are we enriched because of our marriage, or robbing each other of God's blessing?

Honest answers to these questions might make a difference!

# CHAPTER SEVEN
# PREPARING
# FOR THE BEST!
*1 Peter 3:8-17*

A devoted pastor was facing serious surgery, and a friend visited him in the hospital to pray with him. "An interesting thing happened today," the pastor told him. "One of the nurses looked at my chart and said, 'Well, I guess you're preparing for the worst!' I smiled at her and said, 'No, I'm preparing for the best. I'm a Christian, and God has promised to work all things together for good.' Boy, did she drop that chart and leave this room in a hurry!"

Peter wrote this letter to prepare Christians for a "fiery trial" of persecution, yet his approach was optimistic and positive. "Prepare for the best!" was his message. In this section, he gave them three instructions to follow if they would experience the best blessings in the worst times.

### Cultivate Christian Love
### (1 Peter 3:8-12)

We have noted that love is a recurring theme in Peter's letters, not only God's love for us, but also our love for others. Peter had to learn this important lesson himself, and he had a hard time learning it! How patient Jesus had to be with him!

We should begin with *love for God's people* (1 Peter 3:8). The word "finally" means "to sum it all up." Just as the whole of the Law is summed up in love (Rom. 13:8-10), so the whole of human relationships is fulfilled in love. This applies to every Christian and to every area of life.

This love is evidenced by a *unity of mind* (see Phil. 2:1-11). Unity does not mean uniformity; it means cooperation in the midst of diversity. The members of the body work together in unity, even though they are all different. Christians may differ on *how* things are to be done, but they must agree on *what* is to be done and *why*. A man criticized D.L. Moody's methods of evangelism, and Moody said, "Well, I'm always ready for improvement. What are *your* methods?" The man confessed that he had none! "Then I'll stick to my own," said Moody. Whatever methods we may use, we must seek to honor Christ, win the lost, and build the church. Some methods are definitely not scriptural, but there is plenty of room for variety in the church.

Another evidence of love is *compassion*, a sincere "feeling for and with" the needs of others. Our English word "sympathy" comes from this word. We dare not get hardhearted toward each other. We must share both joys and trials (Rom. 12:15). The basis for this is the fact that we are brethren in the same family (see 1 Peter 1:22; 2:17; 4:8; 5:14). We are "taught of God to love one another" (1 Thes. 4:9).

Love reveals itself in *pity*, a tenderness of heart toward others. In the Roman Empire, this was not a quality that was admired; but the Christian message changed all of that. Today, we are deluged with so much bad news that it is easy for us to get insulated and unfeeling. We need to cultivate compassion, and actively show others that we are concerned.

"Be courteous" involves much more than acting like a lady or gentleman. "Be humble-minded" is a good translation; and, after all, humility is the foundation for courtesy, for the humble person puts others ahead of himself.

Not only should we love God's people, but we should also *love our enemies* (1 Peter 3:9). The recipients of this letter were experiencing a certain amount of personal persecution because they were doing the will of God. Peter warned them that *official* persecution was just around the corner, so they had better prepare. The church today had better prepare, because difficult times are ahead.

As Christians, we can live on one of three levels. We can return evil for good, which is the satanic level. We can return good for good and evil for evil, which is the human level. Or, we can return good for evil, which is the divine level. Jesus is the perfect example of this latter approach (1 Peter 2:21-23). As God's loving children, we must do more than give "an eye for an eye, and a tooth for a tooth" (Matt. 5:38-48), which is the basis for *justice*. We must operate on the basis of *mercy*, for that is the way God deals with us.

This admonition must have meant much to Peter himself, because he once tried to fight Christ's enemies with a sword (Luke 22:47-53). When he was an unconverted rabbi, Paul used every means possible to oppose the church; but when he became a Christian, Paul never used human weapons to fight God's battles (Rom. 12:17-21; 2 Cor. 10:1-6). When Peter and the Apostles were persecuted, they depended on prayer and God's power, not on their own wisdom or strength (see Acts 4:23ff).

We must always be reminded of our *calling* as Christians, for this will help us love our enemies and do them good when they treat us badly. We are called to "inherit a blessing." The persecutions we experience on earth today only add to our blessed inheritance of glory in heaven someday (Matt. 5:10-12). But we also inherit a blessing *today* when we treat our enemies with love and mercy. By sharing a blessing with them, we receive a blessing ourselves! Persecution can be a time of spiritual enrichment for a believer. The saints and martyrs in church history all bear witness to this fact.

We should love one another, love our enemies, and *love life* (1 Peter 3:10-12). The news of impending persecution should not cause a believer to give up on life. What may appear to be "bad days" to the world can be "good days" for a Christian, if he will only meet certain conditions.

First, *we must deliberately decide to love life.* This is an act of the will: "He who wills to love life." It is an attitude of faith that sees the best in every situation. It is the opposite of the pessimistic attitude expressed in Ecclesiastes 2:17: "Therefore I hated life . . . for all is vanity and vexation of spirit." We can decide to *endure* life and make it a burden, *escape* life as though we were running from a battle, or *enjoy* life because we know God is in control. Peter was not suggesting some kind of unrealistic psychological gymnastics that refused to face facts. Rather, he was urging his readers to take a positive approach to life and *by faith* make the most of every situation.

Second, *we must control our tongues.* Many of the problems of life are caused by the wrong words, spoken in the wrong spirit. Every Christian should read James 3 regularly and pray Psalm 141:3 daily. How well Peter knew the sad consequences of hasty speech! There is no place for lies in the life of a saint.

Third, *we must do good and hate evil.* We need both the positive and the negative. The Old English word "eschew" means more than just "avoid." It means "to avoid something because you despise and loathe it." It is not enough for us to avoid sin because sin is wrong; we ought to shun it because we hate it.

Finally, *we must seek and pursue peace.* "Blessed are the peacemakers: for they shall be called the children of God" (Matt. 5:9). If we go out and seek trouble, we will find it; but if we seek peace, we can find it as well. This does not mean "peace at any price," because righteousness must always be the basis for peace (James 3:13-18). It simply means that a Christian exercises moderation as he relates to people and does not create problems because he wants to have his own way. "If it be possible, as much as lieth in you, live peaceably with all men" (Rom. 12:18). Sometimes it is not possible! See Romans 14:19 where we are also admonished to *work hard* to achieve peace. It does not come automatically.

"But what if our enemies take advantage of us?" a persecuted Christian might ask. "We may be seeking peace, but they are seeking war!" Peter gave them the assurance that God's eyes are on His people and His ears open to their prayers. (Peter learned that lesson when he tried to walk on the water without looking to Jesus—Matt. 14:22-33.) We must trust God to protect and provide, for He alone can defeat our enemies (Rom. 12:17-21).

Peter quoted these statements from Psalm 34:12-15, so it would be profitable for you to read the entire psalm. It describes what God means by "good days." They are not necessarily days free from problems, for the psalmist wrote about fears (Ps. 34:4), troubles (Ps. 34:6, 17), afflictions (Ps. 34:19), and even a broken heart (Ps. 34:18). A "good day" for the believer who "loves life" is not one in which he is pampered and sheltered, but one in which he experiences God's help and blessing *because of* life's problems and trials. It is a

day in which he magnifies the Lord (Ps. 34:1-3), experiences answers to prayer (Ps. 34:4-7), tastes the goodness of God (Ps. 34:8), and senses the nearness of God (Ps. 34:18).

The next time you think you are having a "bad day," and you hate life, read Psalm 34 and you may discover you are really having a "good day" to the glory of God!

## Practice the Lordship of Christ (1 Peter 3:13-15)

These verses introduce the third main section of 1 Peter—God's grace in suffering. They introduce the important spiritual principle that the fear of the Lord conquers every other fear. Peter quoted Isaiah 8:13-14 to back up his admonition: "But in your hearts set apart Christ as Lord" (1 Peter 3:15, NIV).

The setting of the Isaiah quotation is significant. Ahaz, King of Judah, faced a crisis because of an impending invasion by the Assyrian army. The kings of Israel and Syria wanted Ahaz to join them in an alliance, but Ahaz refused; so Israel and Syria threatened to invade Judah! Behind the scenes, Ahaz confederated himself with Assyria! The Prophet Isaiah warned him against ungodly alliances and urged him to trust God for deliverance. "Sanctify the Lord of hosts [armies] Himself; and let Him be your fear, and let Him be your dread" (Isa. 8:13).

As Christians, we are faced with crises, and we are tempted to give in to our fears and make the wrong decisions. But if we "sanctify Christ as Lord" in our hearts, we need never fear men or circumstances. Our enemies might *hurt* us, but they cannot *harm* us. Only we can harm ourselves if we fail to trust God. Generally speaking, people do not oppose us if we do good; but even if they do, it is better to suffer for righteousness' sake than to compromise our testimony. Peter discussed this theme in detail in 1 Peter 4:12-19.

Instead of experiencing fear as we face the enemy, we can experience blessing, if Jesus Christ is Lord in our hearts. The word "happy" in 1 Peter 3:14 is the same as "blessed" in Matthew 5:10ff. This is a part of the "joy unspeakable and full of glory" (1 Peter 1:8).

When Jesus Christ is Lord of our lives, each crisis becomes an opportunity for witness. We are "ready always to give an answer." Our English word *apology* comes from the Greek word translated "answer," but it does not mean "to say I am sorry." Rather, it means "a defense presented in court." "Apologetics" is the branch of theology that deals with the defense of the faith. Every Christian should be able to give a reasoned defense of his hope in Christ, *especially in hopeless situations*. A crisis creates the opportunity for witness when a believer behaves with faith and hope, because the unbelievers will then sit up and take notice.

This witness must be given "with meekness and fear [respect]" and not with arrogance and a know-it-all attitude. We are witnesses, not prosecuting attorneys! We must also be sure that our lives back up our defense. Peter did not suggest that Christians argue with lost people, but rather that we present to the unsaved an account of what we believe and why we believe it, in a loving manner. The purpose is not to win an argument but to win lost souls to Christ.

What does it mean to "sanctify Christ as Lord" in our hearts? It means to turn everything over to Him, and to live only to please Him and glorify Him. It means to fear displeasing Him rather than fear what men might do to us. How wonderfully this approach simplifies our lives! It is Matthew 6:33 and Romans 12:1-2 combined into a daily attitude of faith that obeys God's Word in spite of consequences. It means being satisfied with nothing less than the will of God in our lives (John 4:31-34). One evidence that Jesus Christ is Lord in our lives is the readiness with which we witness to others about Him and seek to win them to Christ.

### Maintain a Good Conscience (1 Peter 3:16-17)

Our word "conscience" comes from two Latin words: *con,* meaning "with," and *scio,* meaning "to know." The conscience is that internal judge that witnesses to us, that enables us to "know with," either approving our actions or accusing (see Rom. 2:14-15). Conscience may be compared to a window that lets in the light of God's truth. If we persist in disobeying, the window gets dirtier and dirtier, until the light cannot enter. This leads to a "defiled conscience" (Titus 1:15). A "seared conscience" is one that has been so sinned against that it no longer is sensitive to what is right and wrong (1 Tim. 4:2). It is even possible for the conscience to be so poisoned that it approves things that are bad and accuses when the person does good! This the Bible calls "an evil conscience" (Heb. 10:22). A criminal feels guilty if he "squeals" on his friends, but happy if he succeeds in his crime!

Conscience depends on knowledge, the "light" coming through the window. As a believer studies the Word, he better understands the will of God, and his conscience becomes more sensitive to right and wrong. A "good conscience" is one that accuses when we think or do wrong and approves when we do right. It takes "exercise" to keep the conscience strong and pure (Acts 24:16). If we do not grow in spiritual knowledge and obedience, we have a "weak conscience" that is upset very easily by trifles (1 Cor. 8).

How does a good conscience help a believer in times of trial and opposition? For one thing, it fortifies him with courage because he knows he is right with God and men, so that he need not be afraid. Inscribed on Martin Luther's monument at Worms, Germany are his courageous words spoken before the church council on April 18, 1521: "Here I stand; I can do no other. God help me. Amen." His conscience, bound to God's Word, gave him the courage to defy the whole established church!

A good conscience also gives us peace in our hearts; and when we have peace within, we can face battles without. The restlessness of an uneasy conscience divides the heart and drains the strength of a person, so that he is unable to function at his best. How can we boldly witness for Christ if conscience is witnessing against us?

A good conscience removes from us the fear of what other people may know about us, say against us, or do to us. When Christ is Lord and we fear only God, we need not fear the threats, opinions, or actions of our enemies. "The Lord is on my side; I will not fear: what can man do unto me?" (Ps. 118:6) It was in this matter that Peter failed when he feared the enemy and denied the Lord.

Peter made it clear that conscience *alone* is not the test of what is right or wrong. A person can be involved in either "welldoing" or "evildoing." For a person to disobey God's Word and claim it is right simply because his conscience does not convict him, is to admit that something is radically wrong with his conscience. Conscience is a safe guide only when the Word of God is the teacher.

More and more, Christians in today's society are going to be accused and lied about. Our personal standards are not those of the unsaved world. As a rule, Christians do not *create* problems; they *reveal* them. Let a born-again person start to work in an office, or move into a college dormitory, and in a short time there will be problems. Christians are lights in this dark world (Phil. 2:15), and they reveal "the unfruitful works of darkness" (Eph. 5:11).

When Joseph began to serve as steward in Potiphar's house, and refused to sin, he was falsely accused and thrown into prison. The government officials in Babylon schemed to get Daniel in trouble because his life and work were a witness against them. Our Lord Jesus Christ by His very life on earth revealed the sinful hearts and deeds of people, and this is why they crucified Him (see John 15:18-25). "Yea, and all that will live godly in Christ Jesus shall suffer persecution" (2 Tim. 3:12).

If we are to maintain a good conscience, we must deal with sin in our lives and confess it immediately (1 John 1:9). We must "keep the window clean." We must also spend time in the Word of God and "let in the light." A strong conscience is the result of obedience based on knowledge, and a strong conscience makes for a strong Christian witness to the lost. It also gives us strength in times of persecution and difficulty.

No Christian should ever suffer because of evildoing, and no Christian should be surprised if he suffers for welldoing. Our world is so mixed up that people "call evil good, and good evil" and "put darkness for light, and light for darkness" (Isa. 5:20). The religious leaders of Jesus' day called Him "a malefactor," which means "a person who does evil things" (John 18:29-30). How wrong people can be!

As times of difficulty come to the church, we must cultivate Christian love; for we will need one another's help and encouragement as never before. We must also maintain a good conscience, because a good conscience makes for a strong backbone and a courageous witness. The secret is to practice the lordship of Jesus Christ. If we fear God, we need not fear men. "Shame arises from the fear of men," said Samuel Johnson. "Conscience, from the fear of God."

# CHAPTER EIGHT
# LEARNING FROM NOAH
## *1 Peter 3:18-22*

A pastor was teaching a Bible study on Matthew 16, explaining the many interpretations of our Lord's words to Peter, "Thou art Peter, and upon this rock I will build My church" (Matt. 16:18). Afterward, a woman said to him, "Pastor, I'll bet if Jesus had known all the trouble those words would cause, He would never have said them!"

When Peter wrote this section of his letter, he had no idea that it would be classified as one of the most difficult portions of the New Testament. Good and godly interpreters have wrestled with these verses, debated and disagreed, and have not always left behind a great deal of spiritual help. We may not be able to solve all the problems found in this section, but we do want to get the practical help that Peter gave to encourage Christians in difficult days.

The section presents three different ministries. If we understand these ministries, we will be better able to suffer in the will of God and glorify Christ.

**The Ministry of Christ (1 Peter 3:18-22)**
Everything else in this paragraph is incidental to what Peter had to say about Jesus Christ. This material is parallel to what Peter wrote in 1 Peter 2:21ff. Peter presented Jesus Christ as the perfect example of one who suffered unjustly, and yet obeyed God.

*The death of Christ (v. 18).* In 1 Peter 3:17, Peter wrote about suffering for well-doing rather than for evil-doing; and then he gave the example of Jesus Christ. Jesus was the "just One" (Acts 3:14), and yet He was treated unjustly. Why? That He might die for the unjust ones and bring them to God! He died as a substitute (1 Peter 2:24), and He died only once (Heb. 9:24-28). In other words, Jesus suffered for well-doing; He did not die because of His own sins, for He had none (1 Peter 2:22).

The phrase "bring us to God" is a technical term that means "gain audience at court." Because of the work of Christ on the cross, we now have an open access to God (Eph. 2:18; 3:12). We may come boldly to His throne! (Heb. 10:19ff) We also have access to His marvelous grace to meet our daily needs (Rom. 5:2). When the veil of the temple was torn, it symbolized the new and open way to God through Jesus Christ.

**The proclamation of Christ (vv. 19-20).** The phrase "made alive by the Spirit" (KJV, SCO) creates a problem for us. In the Greek manuscripts, there were no capital letters; so we have no authority to write "Spirit" rather than "spirit." Greek scholars tell us that the end of 1 Peter 3:18 should read: "Being put to death with reference to the flesh, but made alive with reference to the spirit." The contrast is between flesh and spirit, as in Matthew 26:41 and Romans 1:3-4, and not between Christ's flesh and the Holy Spirit.

Our Lord had a real body (Matt. 26:26), soul (John 12:27), and spirit (Luke 23:46). He was not God inhabiting a man; He was the true God-Man. When He died, He yielded His spirit to the Father (Luke 23:46; see James 2:26). However, it seems evident that, if He was "made alive in the spirit," at some point His spirit must have died. It was probably when He was made sin for us and was forsaken by the Father (Mark 15:34; 2 Cor. 5:21). The phrase "quickened in [with reference to] the spirit" cannot mean resurrection, because resurrection has to do with *the body.*

So on the cross, our Lord suffered and died. His body was put to death, and His spirit died when He was made sin. But His spirit was made alive and He yielded it to the Father. Then according to Peter, sometime between His death and His resurrection Jesus made a special proclamation to "the spirits in prison." This raises two questions: Who were these "spirits" that He visited? What did He proclaim to them?

Those who say that these "spirits in prison" were the spirits of lost sinners in hell, to whom Jesus brought the good news of salvation, have some real problems to solve. To begin with, Peter referred to people as "souls" and not "spirits" (1 Peter 3:20). In the New Testament, the word "spirits" is used to describe angels or demons, not human beings; and 1 Peter 3:22 seems to argue for this meaning. Furthermore, nowhere in the Bible are we told that Jesus visited hell. Acts 2:31 states that He went to "hades" (NASB), but "hades" is not hell. The word "hades" refers to the realm of the unbelieving dead, a tempo-

rary place where they await the resurrection. Read Revelation 20:11-15 in the *New American Standard Bible* or the *New International Version* and you will see the important distinction. Hell is the permanent and final place of judgment for the lost. Hades is the temporary place. When a Christian dies, he goes to neither place, but to heaven to be with Christ (Phil. 1:20-24).

Our Lord yielded His spirit to the Father, died, and at some time between death and resurrection, visited the realm of the dead where He delivered a message to spirit beings (probably fallen angels; see Jude 6) who were somehow related to the period before the Flood. First Peter 3:20 makes this clear. The word translated "preached" simply means "to announce as a herald, to proclaim." It is not the word that means "to preach the Gospel" that Peter used in 1 Peter 1:12 and 4:6. Peter did not tell us *what* Jesus proclaimed to these imprisoned spirits, but it could not be a message of redemption since angels cannot be saved (Heb. 2:16). It was probably a declaration of victory over Satan and his hosts (see Col. 2:15; 1 Peter 3:22).

How these spirits were related to the pre-Flood era, Peter did not explain. Some students believe that "the sons of God" named in Genesis 6:1-4 were fallen angels who cohabited with women and produced a race of giants, but I cannot accept this interpretation. The *good* angels who did not fall are called "sons of God," but not the fallen angels (Job 1:6; 2:1, and note that Satan is distinguished from the "sons of God"). The world before the Flood was unbelievably wicked, and no doubt these spirits had much to do with it (see Gen. 6:5-13; Rom. 1:18ff).

**The resurrection of Christ (v. 21).** Since death comes when the spirit leaves the body (James 2:26), then resurrection involves the spirit *returning* to the body (Luke 8:55). The Father raised Jesus from the dead (Rom. 6:4; 8:11), but the Son also had authority to raise Himself (John 10:17-18). It was a miracle! It is because of His resurrection that Christians have the "living hope" (1 Peter 1:3-4). We shall see later how the resurrection of Christ relates to the experience of Noah.

We must never minimize the importance of the resurrection of Jesus Christ. It declares that He is God (Rom. 1:4), that the work of salvation is completed and accepted by the Father (Rom. 4:25), and that death has been conquered (1 Thes. 4:13-18; Rev. 1:17-18).

The Gospel message includes the Resurrection (1 Cor. 15:1-4), for a dead Saviour can save nobody. It is the risen Christ who gives us the power we need on a daily basis for life and service (Gal. 2:20).

*The ascension of Christ (v. 22).* Forty days after His resurrection, our Lord ascended to heaven to sit at the right hand of the Father, the place of exaltation (Ps. 110:1; Acts 2:34-36; Phil. 2:5-11; Heb. 12:1-3). Believers are seated with Him in the heavenlies (Eph. 2:4-6), and through Him we are able to "reign in life" (Rom. 5:17). He is ministering to the church as High Priest (Heb. 4:14-16; 7:25) and Advocate (1 John 1:9–2:2). He is preparing a place for His people (John 14:1-6) and will one day come to receive them to Himself.

But the main point Peter wanted to emphasize was Christ's complete victory over all "angels and authorities and powers" (1 Peter 3:22), referring to the evil hosts of Satan (Eph. 6:10-12; Col. 2:15). The unfallen angels were *always* subject to Him. As Christians, we do not fight *for* victory, but *from* victory—the mighty victory that our Lord Jesus Christ won for us in His death, resurrection, and ascension.

## The Ministry of Noah

The patriarch Noah was held in very high regard among Jewish people in Peter's day, and also among Christians. He was linked with Daniel and Job, two great men, in Ezekiel 14:19-20; and there are many references to the Flood in both the Psalms and the Prophets. Jesus referred to Noah in His prophetic sermon (Matt. 24:37-39; see Luke 17:26-27), and Peter mentioned him in his second letter (2 Peter 2:5; see 3:6). He is named with the heroes of faith in Hebrews 11:7.

What relationship did Peter see between his readers and the ministry of Noah? For one thing, Noah was a "preacher of righteousness" (2 Peter 2:5) during a very difficult time in history. In fact, he walked with God and preached God's truth for 120 years (Gen. 6:3), and during that time was certainly laughed at and opposed. The early Christians knew that Jesus had promised that, before His return, the world would become like the "days of Noah" (Matt. 24:37-39); and they were expecting Him soon (2 Peter 3:1-3). As they saw society decay around them, and persecution begin, they would think of our Lord's words.

Noah was a man of faith who kept doing the will of God even when he seemed to be a failure. This would certainly be an encouragement to Peter's readers. If we measured faithfulness by results, then Noah would get a very low grade. Yet God ranked him very high!

But there is another connection: Peter saw in the Flood a picture (type) of a Christian's experience of baptism. No matter what mode of baptism you may accept, it is certain that the early church practiced immersion. It is a picture of our Lord's death, burial, and resurrection. Many people today do not take baptism seriously, but it was a serious matter in the early church. Baptism meant a clean break with the past, and this could include separation from a convert's family, friends, and job. Candidates for baptism were interrogated carefully, for their submission in baptism was a step of consecration, and not just an "initiation rite" to "join the church."

The Flood pictures death, burial, and resurrection. The waters buried the earth in judgment, but they also lifted Noah and his family up to safety. The early church saw in the ark a picture of salvation. Noah and his family were saved by faith because they believed God and entered into the ark of safety. So sinners are saved by faith when they trust Christ and become one with Him.

When Peter wrote that Noah and his family were "saved by water," he was careful to explain that this illustration does not imply salvation by baptism. Baptism is a "figure" of that which does save us, namely, "the resurrection of Jesus Christ" (1 Peter 3:21). Water on the body, or the body placed in water, cannot remove the stains of sin. Only the blood of Jesus Christ can do that (1 John 1:7–2:2). However, baptism does save us from one thing: a bad conscience. Peter had already told his readers that a good conscience was important to a successful witness (see 1 Peter 3:16), and a part of that "good conscience" is being faithful to our commitment to Christ as expressed in baptism.

The word *answer* in 1 Peter 3:21 is a legal term meaning "a pledge, a demand." When a person was signing a contract, he would be asked, "Do you pledge to obey and fulfill the terms of this contract?" His answer had to be, "Yes, I do," or he could not sign. When converts were prepared for baptism, they would be asked if they intended to obey God and serve Him, and to break with their sinful past.

If they had reservations in their hearts, or deliberately lied, they would not have a good conscience if, under pressure of persecution, they denied the Lord. (Peter knew something about that!) So, Peter reminded them of their baptismal testimony to encourage them to be true to Christ.

It may be worth noting that the chronology of the Flood is closely related to our Lord's day of resurrection. Noah's ark rested on Ararat on the seventeenth day of the seventh month (Gen. 8:4). The Jewish *civil* year started with October; the religious year started with the Passover in April (Ex. 12:1-2), but that was not instituted until Moses' time. The seventh month from October is April. Our Lord was crucified on the fourteenth day, Passover (Ex. 12:6), and resurrected after three days. This takes us to the seventeenth day of the month, the date on which the ark rested on Mt. Ararat. So, the illustration of Noah relates closely to Peter's emphasis on the resurrection of the Saviour.

There is a sense in which our Lord's experience on the cross was a baptism of judgment, not unlike the Flood. He referred to His sufferings as a baptism (Matt. 20:22; Luke 12:50). He also used Jonah to illustrate His experience of death, burial, and resurrection (Matt. 12:38-41). Jesus could certainly have quoted Jonah 2:3 to describe His own experience: "All Thy billows and Thy waves passed over me."

### The Ministry of Christians Today

It is easy to agree on the main lessons Peter was sharing with his readers, lessons which we need today.

First of all, *Christians must expect opposition.* As the coming of Christ draws near, our welldoing will incite the anger and attacks of godless people. Jesus lived a perfect life on earth, and yet He was crucified like a common criminal. If the just One who did no sin was treated cruelly, what right do we who are imperfect have to escape suffering? We must be careful, however, that we suffer because of welldoing, for righteousness' sake, and not because we have disobeyed.

A second lesson is that *Christians must serve God by faith and not trust in results.* Noah served God and kept only seven people from the Flood; yet God honored him. From those seven people, we take courage! Jesus appeared a total failure when He died on the cross, yet His death was a supreme victory.

His cause today may seem to fail, but He will accomplish His purposes in this world. The harvest is not the end of a meeting; it is the end of the age.

Third, *we can be encouraged because we are identified with Christ's victory.* This is pictured in baptism, and the doctrine is explained in Romans 6. It is the baptism of the Spirit that identifies a believer with Christ (1 Cor. 12:12-13), and this is pictured in water baptism. It is through the Spirit's power that we live for Christ and witness for Him (Acts 1:8). The opposition of men is energized by Satan, and Christ has already defeated these principalities and powers. He has "all authority in heaven and on earth" (Matt. 28:18, NIV), and therefore we can go forth with confidence and victory.

Another practical lesson is that *our baptism is important.* It identifies us with Christ and gives witness that we have broken with the old life (see 1 Peter 4:1-4) and will, by His help, live a new life. The act of baptism is a pledge to God that we shall obey Him. To use Peter's illustration, we are agreeing to the terms of the contract. To take baptism lightly is to sin against God. Some people make too much of baptism by teaching that it is a means of salvation, while others minimize it. Both are wrong. If a believer is to have a good conscience, he must obey God.

Having said this, I want to make it clear that Christians must not make baptism a test of fellowship or of spirituality. There are dedicated believers who disagree on these matters, and we respect them. When General William Booth founded the Salvation Army, he determined not to make it "another church," so he eliminated the ordinances. There are Christian groups, such as the Quakers, who, because of conscience or doctrinal interpretation, do not practice baptism. I have stated my position, but I do not want to give the impression that I make this position a test of anything. "Let us therefore follow after the things which make for peace, and things wherewith one may edify another" (Rom. 14:19). "Let every man be fully persuaded in his own mind" (Rom. 14:5).

The important thing is that each Christian avow devotion to Christ and make it a definite act of commitment. Most Christians do this in baptism, but even the act of baptism can be minimized or forgotten. It is in taking up our cross daily that we prove we are true followers of Jesus Christ.

Finally, *Jesus Christ is the only Saviour, and the lost world needs to hear His Gospel.* Some people try to use this complex passage of Scripture to prove a "second chance for salvation after death." Our interpretation of "spirits in prison" seems to prove that these were angelic beings, and not the souls of the dead. But even if these "spirits" were those of unsaved people, this passage says nothing about their salvation. And why would Jesus offer salvation (if He did) *only to sinners from Noah's day?* And why did Peter use the verb "proclaim as a herald" instead of the usual word for preaching the Gospel?

Hebrews 9:27 makes it clear that death ends the opportunity for salvation. This is why the church needs to get concerned about evangelism and missions, because people are dying who have never even heard the Good News of salvation, let alone had the opportunity to reject it. It does us no good to quibble about differing interpretations of a difficult passage of Scripture, if what we *do* believe does not motivate us to want to share the Gospel with others.

Peter made it clear that difficult days give us multiplied opportunities for witness.

Are we taking advantage of our opportunities?

# CHAPTER NINE
# THE REST
# OF YOUR TIME
*1 Peter 4:1-11*

My wife and I were in Nairobi where I would be ministering to several hundred national pastors at an Africa Inland Mission conference. We were very excited about the conference even though we were a bit weary from the long air journey. We could hardly wait to get started, and the leader of the conference detected our impatience.

"You are in Africa now," he said to me in a fatherly fashion, "and the first thing you want to do is to put away your watch."

In the days that followed, as we ministered in Kenya and Zaire, we learned the wisdom of his words. Unfortunately, when we returned to the States, we found ourselves caught up again in the clockwork prison of deadlines and schedules.

Peter had a great deal to say about *time* (1 Peter 1:5, 11, 17, 20; 4:2-3, 17; 5:6). Certainly the awareness of his own impending martyrdom had something to do with this emphasis (John 21:15-19; 2 Peter 1:12ff). If a person really believes in eternity, then he will make the best use of time. If we are convinced that Jesus is coming, then we will want to live prepared lives. Whether Jesus comes first, or death comes first, we want to make "the rest of the time" count for eternity.

And we can! Peter described four attitudes that a Christian can cultivate in his lifetime ("the rest of his time") if he desires to make his life all that God wants it to be.

### A Militant Attitude toward Sin (1 Peter 4:1-3)

The picture is that of a soldier who puts on his equipment and arms himself for battle. Our attitudes are weapons, and weak or wrong attitudes will lead us to defeat. Outlook determines outcome, and a believer must have the right attitudes if he is to live a right life.

A friend and I met at a restaurant to have lunch. It was one of those places where the lights are low, and you need a miner's helmet to find your table. We had been seated several minutes before we started looking at the menu, and I remarked that I was amazed how easily I could read it. "Yes," said my friend, "it doesn't take us long to get accustomed to the darkness."

There is a sermon in that sentence: It is easy for Christians to get accustomed to sin. Instead of having a militant attitude that hates and opposes it, we gradually get used to sin, sometimes without even realizing it. The one thing that will destroy "the rest of our time" is sin. A believer living in sin is a terrible weapon in the hands of Satan. Peter presented several arguments to convince us to oppose sin in our lives.

***Think of what sin did to Jesus (v. 1).*** He had to *suffer* because of sin (see 1 Peter 2:21; 3:18). How can we enjoy that which made Jesus suffer and die on the cross? If a vicious criminal stabbed your child to death, would you preserve that knife in a glass case on your mantle? I doubt it. You would never want to see that knife again.

Our Lord came to earth to deal with sin and

to conquer it forever. He dealt with the ignorance of sin by teaching the truth and by living it before men's eyes. He dealt with the consequences of sin by healing and forgiving; and, on the cross, He dealt the final deathblow to sin itself. He was armed, as it were, with a militant attitude toward sin, even though He had great compassion for lost sinners.

Our goal in life is to "cease from sin." We will not reach this goal until we die, or are called home when the Lord returns; but this should not keep us from striving (1 John 2:28–3:9). Peter did not say that suffering *of itself* would cause a person to stop sinning. Pharaoh in Egypt went through great suffering in the plagues, and yet he sinned even more! I have visited suffering people who cursed God and grew more and more bitter because of their pain.

Suffering, *plus Christ in our lives,* can help us have victory over sin. But the central idea here seems to be the same truth taught in Romans 6: We are identified with Christ in His suffering and death, and therefore can have victory over sin. As we yield ourselves to God, and have the same attitude toward sin that Jesus had, we can overcome the old life and manifest the new life.

***Enjoy the will of God (v. 2).*** The contrast is between the desires of men and the will of God. Our longtime friends cannot understand the change in our lives, and they want us to return to the same "excess of riot" that we used to enjoy. But the will of God is so much better! If we do the will of God, then we will *invest* "the rest of our time" in that which is lasting and satisfying; but if we give in to the world around us, we will *waste* "the rest of our time" and regret it when we stand before Jesus.

The will of God is not a burden that the Father places on us. Rather it is the divine enjoyment and enablement that makes all burdens light. The will of God comes from the heart of God (Ps. 33:11) and therefore is an expression of the love of God. We may not always understand what He is doing, but we know that He is doing what is best for us. We do not live on explanations; we live on promises.

***Remember what you were before you met Christ (v. 3).*** There are times when looking back at your past life would be wrong, because Satan could use those memories to discourage you. But God urged Israel to remember that they had once been slaves in Egypt (Deut. 5:15). Paul remembered that he had been a persecutor of believers (1 Tim. 1:12ff), and this encouraged him to do even more for Christ. We sometimes forget the bondage of sin and remember only the passing pleasures of sin.

"The will of the Gentiles" means "the will of the unsaved world" (see 1 Peter 2:12). Lost sinners imitate each other as they conform to the fashions of this world (Rom. 12:2; Eph. 3:1-3). "Lasciviousness" and "lusts" describe all kinds of evil appetites and not just sexual sins. "Revelings and banquetings" refer to pagan orgies where the wine flowed freely. Of course, all of this could be a part of pagan worship, since "religious prostitution" was an accepted thing. Even though these practices were forbidden by law ("abominable" = illegal), they were often practiced in secret.

We may not have been guilty of such gross sins in our preconversion days, but we were still sinners—and our sins helped to crucify Christ. How foolish to go back to that kind of life!

### A Patient Attitude toward the Lost (1 Peter 4:4-6)

Unsaved people do not understand the radical change that their friends experience when they trust Christ and become children of God. They do not think it strange when people wreck their bodies, destroy their homes, and ruin their lives by running from one sin to another! But let a drunkard become sober, or an immoral person pure, and the family thinks he has lost his mind! Festus told Paul, "You are out of your mind!" (Acts 26:24, NASB) and people even thought the same thing of our Lord (Mark 3:21).

We must be patient toward the lost, even though we do not agree with their lifestyles or participate in their sins. After all, unsaved people are blind to spiritual truth (2 Cor. 4:3-4) and dead to spiritual enjoyment (Eph. 2:1). In fact, our contact with the lost is important *to them* since we are the bearers of the truth that they need. When unsaved friends attack us, this is our opportunity to witness to them (1 Peter 3:15).

The unsaved may judge us, but one day, God will judge them. Instead of arguing with them, we should pray for them, knowing that the final judgment is with God. This was the attitude that Jesus took (2:23), and also the Apostle Paul (2 Tim. 2:24-26).

We must not interpret 1 Peter 4:6 apart

from the context of suffering; otherwise, we will get the idea that there is a second chance for salvation after death. Peter was reminding his readers of the Christians who had been martyred for their faith. They had been falsely judged by men, but now, in the presence of God, they received their true judgment. "Them that are dead" means "them that are *now* dead" at the time Peter was writing. The Gospel is preached only to the living (1 Peter 1:25) because there is no opportunity for salvation after death (Heb. 9:27).

Unsaved friends may speak evil of us and even oppose us, but the final Judge is God. We may sacrifice our lives in the midst of persecution, but God will honor and reward us. We must fear God and not men (1 Peter 3:13-17; see Matt. 10:24-33). While we are in these human bodies ("in the flesh"), we are judged by human standards. One day, we shall be with the Lord ("in the spirit") and receive the true and final judgment.

## An Expectant Attitude toward Christ (1 Peter 4:7)

Christians in the early church expected Jesus to return in their lifetime (Rom. 13:12; 1 John 2:18). The fact that He did not return does not invalidate His promise (2 Peter 3; Rev. 22:20). No matter what interpretation we give to the prophetic Scriptures, we must all live in expectancy. The important thing is that we shall see the Lord one day and stand before Him. How we live and serve today will determine how we are judged and rewarded on that day.

This attitude of expectancy must not turn us into lazy dreamers (2 Thes. 3:6ff) or zealous fanatics. Peter gave "ten commandments" to his readers to keep them in balance as far as the Lord's return was concerned:

1. Be sober—v. 7
2. Watch unto prayer—v. 7
3. Have fervent love—v. 8
4. Use hospitality—v. 9
5. Minister your spiritual gifts—vv. 10-11
6. Think it not strange—v. 12
7. Rejoice—v. 13
8. Do not be ashamed—vv. 15-16
9. Glorify God—vv. 16-18
10. Commit yourself to God—v. 19

The phrase "be sober" means "be sober-minded, keep your mind steady and clear." Perhaps a modern equivalent would be "keep cool." It was a warning against wild thinking about prophecy that could lead to an unbalanced life and ministry. Often we hear of sincere people who go "off balance" because of an unbiblical emphasis on prophecy or a misinterpretation of prophecy. There are people who set dates for Christ's return, contrary to His warning (Matt. 25:13; see Acts 1:6-8); or they claim to know the name of the beast of Revelation 13. I have books in my library, written by sincere and godly men, in which all sorts of claims are made, only to the embarrassment of the writers.

The opposite of "be sober-minded" is "frenzy, madness." It is the Greek word *mania,* which has come into our English vocabulary via psychology. If we are sober-minded, we will be intellectually sound and not off on a tangent because of some "new" interpretation of the Scriptures. We will also face things realistically and be free from delusions. The sober-minded saint will have a purposeful life and not be drifting, and he will exercise restraint and not be impulsive. He will have "sound judgment" not only about doctrinal matters, but also about the practical affairs of life.

Ten times in the Pastoral Epistles, Paul admonished people to "be sober-minded." It is one of the qualifications for pastors (1 Tim. 3:2) and for the members of the church (Titus 2:1-6). In a world that is susceptible to wild thinking, the church must be sober-minded.

Early in my ministry, I gave a message on prophecy that sought to explain everything. I have since filed away that outline and will probably never look at it (except when I need to be humbled). A pastor friend who suffered through my message said to me after the service, "Brother, you must be on the planning committee for the return of Christ!" I got his point, but he made it even more pertinent when he said quietly, "I've moved from the planning committee to the welcoming committee."

I am not suggesting that we not study prophecy, or that we become timid about sharing our interpretations. What I am suggesting is that we not allow ourselves to get out of balance because of an abuse of prophecy. There is a practical application to the prophetic Scriptures. Peter's emphasis on hope and the glory of God ought to encourage us to be faithful *today* in whatever work God has given us to do (see Luke 12:31-48).

If you want to make the best use of "the rest of your time," live in the light of the return of Jesus Christ. All Christians may not agree on the details of the event, but we can agree on the demands of the experience. We shall stand before the Lord! Read Romans 14:10-23 and 2 Corinthians 5:1-21 for the practical meaning of this.

If we are sober-minded, we will "watch unto prayer." If our prayer life is confused, it is because the mind is confused. Dr. Kenneth Wuest, in his translation, shows the important relationship between the two: "Be calm and collected in spirit with a view to giving yourself to prayer." The word "watch" carries with it the idea of alertness and self-control. It is the opposite of being drunk or asleep (1 Thes. 5:6-8). This admonition had special meaning to Peter, because he went to sleep when he should have been "watching unto prayer" (Mark 14:37-40).

You find the phrase "watch and pray" often in the *Authorized Version* of the New Testament (Mark 13:33; 14:38; Eph. 6:18; Col. 4:2). It simply means to "be alert in our praying, to be controlled." There is no place in the Christian life for lazy, listless routine praying. We must have an alert attitude and be on guard, just like the workers in Nehemiah's day (Neh. 4:9).

An expectant attitude toward Christ's return involves a serious, balanced mind and an alert, awake prayer life. The test of our commitment to the doctrine of Christ's return is not our ability to draw charts or discern signs, but our thinking and praying. If our thinking and praying are right, our living should be right.

## A Fervent Attitude toward the Saints (1 Peter 4:8-11)

If we really look for the return of Christ, then we shall think of others and properly relate to them. Love for the saints is important, "above [before] all things." Love is the badge of a believer in this world (John 13:34-35). Especially in times of testing and persecution, Christians need to love one another and be united in heart.

This love should be "fervent." The word pictures an athlete straining to reach the goal. It speaks of eagerness and intensity. Christian love is something we have to work at, just the way an athlete works on his skills. It is not a matter of emotional feeling, though that is included, but of dedicated will. Christian love means that we treat others the way God treats us, obeying His commandments in the

Word. It is even possible to love people that we do not like!

Christian love is forgiving. Peter quoted from Proverbs 10:12—"Hatred stirreth up strifes: but love covereth all sins." This verse is alluded to in James 5:20 and 1 Corinthians 13:4 and 7. Love does not *condone* sin; for, if we love somebody, we will be grieved to see him sin and hurt himself and others. Rather, love *covers* sin in that love motivates us to hide the sin from others and not spread it abroad. Where there is hatred, there is malice; and malice causes a person to want to tear down the reputation of his enemy. This leads to gossip and slander (Prov. 11:13; 17:9; see 1 Peter 2:1). Sometimes we try to make our gossip sound "spiritual" by telling people things "so they might pray more intelligently."

No one can hide his sins from God, but believers ought to try, in love, to cover each other's sins at least from the eyes of the unsaved. After all, if the unsaved crowd finds ammunition for persecuting us because of our *good* words and works (1 Peter 2:19-20; 3:14), what would they do if they knew the *bad* things that Christians say and do!

Genesis 9:18-27 gives us a beautiful illustration of this principle. Noah got drunk and shamefully uncovered himself. His son Ham saw his father's shame and told the matter to the family. In loving concern, Ham's two brothers covered their father and his shame. It should not be too difficult for us to cover the sins of others; after all, Jesus Christ died that *our* sins might be washed away.

Our Christian love should not only be fervent and forgiving, but it should also be practical. We should share our homes with others in generous (and uncomplaining) hospitality, and we should use our spiritual gifts in ministry to one another. In New Testament times hospitality was an important thing, because there were few inns and poor Christians could not afford to stay at them anyway. Persecuted saints in particular would need places to stay where they could be assisted and encouraged.

Hospitality is a virtue that is commanded and commended throughout the Scriptures. Moses included it in the Law (Ex. 22:21; Deut. 14:28-29). Jesus enjoyed hospitality when He was on earth, and so did the Apostles in their ministry (Acts 28:7; Phile. 22). Human hospitality is a reflection of God's hospitality to us (Luke 14:16ff). Christian leaders in particular should be "given to hospitality"

(1 Tim. 3:2; Titus 1:8).

Abraham was hospitable to three strangers, and discovered that he had entertained the Lord and two angels (Gen. 18; Heb. 13:2). We help to promote the truth when we open our homes to God's servants (3 John 5-8). In fact, when we share with others, we share with Christ (Matt. 25:35, 43). We should not open our homes to others just so that others will invite us over (Luke 14:12-14). We should do it to glorify the Lord.

In my own itinerant ministry, I have often had the joy of staying in Christian homes. I have appreciated the kindness and (in some cases) sacrifice of dear saints who loved Christ and wanted to share with others. My wife and I have made new friends in many countries, and our children have been blessed, because we have both enjoyed and practiced Christian hospitality.

Finally, Christian love must result in service. Each Christian has at least one spiritual gift that he must use to the glory of God and the building up of the church (see Rom. 12:1-13; 1 Cor. 12; Eph. 4:1-16). We are stewards. God has entrusted these gifts to us that we might use them for the good of His church. He even gives us the spiritual ability to develop our gifts and be faithful servants of the church.

There are speaking gifts and there are serving gifts, and both are important to the church. Not everybody is a teacher or preacher, though all can be witnesses for Christ. There are those "behind-the-scenes" ministries that help to make the public ministries possible. God gives us the gifts, the abilities, and the opportunities to use the gifts, and He alone must get the glory.

The phrase "oracles of God" in 1 Peter 4:11 does not suggest that everything a preacher or teacher says today is God's truth, because human speakers are fallible. In the early church, there were prophets who had the special gift of uttering God's Word, but we do not have this gift today since the Word of God has been completed. Whoever shares God's Word must be careful about what he says and how he says it, and all must conform to the written Word of God.

While on our way home from the African trip I mentioned at the beginning of this chapter, we were delayed in London by a typical English fog. London is one of my favorite places, so I was not disturbed a bit! But the delay gave my wife and me the opportunity to show London to a couple who were traveling with us. Imagine trying to see that marvelous city in one day!

We had to make the most of the time—and we did! Our friends saw many exciting sites in the city.

How long is "the rest of your time"? Only God knows.

Don't waste it! Invest it by doing the will of God.

# CHAPTER TEN
# FACTS ABOUT
# FURNACES
*1 Peter 4:12-19*

Every Christian who lives a godly life experiences a certain amount of persecution. On the job, in school, in the neighborhood, perhaps even in the family, there are people who resist the truth and oppose the Gospel of Christ. No matter what a believer says or does, these people find fault and criticize. Peter dealt with this kind of "normal persecution" in the previous part of his letter.

But in this section, Peter explained about a special kind of persecution—a "fiery trial"—that was about to overtake the entire church. It would not be occasional personal persecution from those around them, but *official* persecution from those above them. Thus far, Christianity had been tolerated by Rome because it was considered a "sect" of Judaism, and the Jews were permitted to worship freely. That attitude would change and the fires of persecution would be ignited, first by Nero, and then by the emperors that followed.

Peter gave the believers four instructions to follow in the light of the coming "fiery trial."

**Expect Suffering (1 Peter 4:12)**
Persecution is not something that is alien to the Christian life. Throughout history the people of God have suffered at the hands of the unbelieving world. Christians are different from unbelievers (2 Cor. 6:14-18), and this different kind of life produces a different kind of lifestyle. Much of what goes on in the world

depends on lies, pride, pleasure, and the desire to "get more." A dedicated Christian builds his life on truth, humility, holiness, and the desire to glorify God.

This conflict is illustrated throughout the Bible. Cain was a religious man, yet he hated his brother and killed him (Gen. 4:1-8). The world does not persecute "religious people," but it does persecute righteous people. Why Cain killed Abel is explained in 1 John 3:12: "Because his own works were evil, and his brother's righteous." The Pharisees and Jewish leaders were religious people, yet they crucified Christ and persecuted the early church. "But beware of men," Jesus warned His disciples, "for they will deliver you up to the councils, and they will scourge you in their synagogues" (Matt. 10:17). Imagine scourging the servants of God in the very house of God!

God declared war on Satan after the Fall of man (Gen. 3:15), and Satan has been attacking God through His people ever since. Christians are "strangers and pilgrims" in an alien world where Satan is the god and prince (John 14:30; 2 Cor. 4:3-4). Whatever glorifies God will anger the enemy, and he will attack. For believers, persecution is not a strange thing. The *absence* of satanic opposition would be strange!

Jesus explained to His disciples that they should expect opposition and persecution from the world (John 15:17–16:4). But He also gave them an encouraging promise: "In the world ye shall have tribulation: but be of good cheer; I have overcome the world" (John 16:33). It was through His death on the cross of Calvary, plus His resurrection, that He overcame sin and the world (John 12:23-33; see Gal. 6:14).

The image of "fire" is often applied to testing or persecution even in modern conversation. "He is really going through the fire," is a typical statement to describe someone experiencing personal difficulties. In the Old Testament, fire was a symbol of the holiness of God and the presence of God. The fire on the altar consumed the sacrifice (Heb. 12:28-29). But Peter saw in the image of fire *a refining process* rather than a divine judgment (see Job 23:10; 1 Peter 1:7).

It is important to note that not all of the difficulties of life are necessarily fiery trials. There are some difficulties that are simply a part of human life and almost everybody experiences them. Unfortunately, there are some difficulties that we bring on ourselves because of disobedience and sin. Peter mentioned these in 1 Peter 2:18-20 and 3:13-17. The fiery trial he mentioned in 1 Peter 4:12 comes because we are faithful to God and stand up for that which is right. It is because we bear the name of Christ that the lost world attacks us. Christ told His disciples that people would persecute them, as they had Him, because their persecutors did not know God (John 15:20-21).

The word "happened" is important; it means "to go together." Persecution and trials do not just "happen," in the sense of being accidents. They are a part of God's plan, and He is in control. They are a part of Romans 8:28 and will work out for good if we let God have His way.

## Rejoice in Suffering (1 Peter 4:13-14)

Literally, Peter wrote, "Be constantly rejoicing!" In fact, he mentioned joy in one form or another *four times* in these two verses! "Rejoice . . . be glad also with exceeding joy. . . . Happy are ye!" The world cannot understand how difficult circumstances can produce exceeding joy, because the world has never experienced the grace of God (see 2 Cor. 8:1-5). Peter named several privileges that we share that encourage us to rejoice in the midst of the fiery trial.

*Our suffering means fellowship with Christ (v. 13).* It is an honor and a privilege to suffer *with* Christ and be treated by the world the way it treated Him. "The fellowship of His sufferings" is a gift from God (Phil. 1:29; 3:10). Not every believer grows to the point where God can trust him with this kind of experience, so we ought to rejoice when the privilege comes to us. "And they [the Apostles] departed from the presence of the council, rejoicing that they were counted worthy to suffer shame for His name" (Acts 5:41).

Christ is with us in the furnace of persecution (Isa. 41:10; 43:2). When the three Hebrew children were cast into the fiery furnace, they discovered they were not alone (Dan. 3:23-25). The Lord was with Paul in all of his trials (Acts 23:11; 27:21-25; 2 Tim. 4:9-18), and He promises to be with us "to the end of the age" (Matt. 28:20, NASB). In fact, when sinners persecute us, they are really persecuting Jesus Christ (Acts 9:4).

*Our suffering means glory in the future (v. 13).* "Suffering" and "glory" are twin truths that are woven into the fabric of

Peter's letter. The world believes that the *absence* of suffering means glory, but a Christian's outlook is different. The trial of our faith today is the assurance of glory when Jesus returns (1 Peter 1:7-8). This was the experience of our Lord (1 Peter 5:1), and it shall also be our experience.

But it is necessary to understand that God is not going to *replace* suffering with glory; rather He will *transform* suffering into glory. Jesus used the illustration of a woman giving birth (John 16:20-22). The same baby that gave her pain also gave her joy. The pain was *transformed* into joy by the birth of the baby. The thorn in the flesh that gave Paul difficulty also gave him power and glory (2 Cor. 12:7-10). The cross that gave Jesus shame and pain also brought power and glory.

Mature people know that life includes some "postponed pleasures." We pay a price *today* in order to have enjoyments in the *future*. The piano student may not enjoy practicing scales by the hour, but he looks forward to the pleasure of playing beautiful music one day. The athlete may not enjoy exercising and practicing his skills, but he looks forward to winning the game by doing his best. Christians have something even better: our very sufferings will one day be transformed into glory, and we will be "glad also with exceeding joy" (see Rom. 8:17; 2 Tim. 3:11).

*Our suffering brings to us the ministry of the Holy Spirit (v. 14).* He is the Spirit of glory and He has a special ministry to those who suffer for the glory of Jesus Christ. This verse can be translated "for the presence of the glory, even the Spirit, rests on you." The reference is to the Shekinah glory of God that dwelt in the tabernacle and in the temple (Ex. 40:34; 1 Kings 8:10-11). When the people stoned Stephen, he saw Jesus in heaven and experienced God's glory (Acts 6:15; 7:54-60). This is the "joy unspeakable and full of glory" that Peter wrote about in 1 Peter 1:7-8.

In other words, suffering Christians do not have to wait for heaven in order to experience His glory. Through the Holy Spirit, *they can have the glory now.* This explains how martyrs could sing praises to God while bound in the midst of blazing fires. It also explains how persecuted Christians (and there are many in today's world) can go to prison and to death without complaining or resisting their captors.

*Our suffering enables us to glorify His name (v. 14).* We suffer because of His name (John 15:21). You can tell your unsaved friends that you are Baptist, a Presbyterian, a Methodist, or even an agnostic, and there will be no opposition; but tell them you are *a Christian*—bring Christ's name into the conversation—and things will start to happen. Our authority is in the name of Jesus, and Satan hates that name. Every time we are reproached for the name of Christ, we have the opportunity to bring glory to that name. The world may speak against His name, but we will so speak and live that His name will be honored and God will be pleased.

The word "Christian" is found only three times in the entire New Testament (1 Peter 4:16; Acts 11:26; 26:28). The name was originally given by the enemies of the church as a term of reproach; but in time, it became an honored name. Of course, in today's world, the word "Christian" means to most people the opposite of "pagan." But the word carries the idea of "a Christ one, belonging to Christ." Certainly it is a privilege to bear the name and to suffer for His name's sake (Acts 5:41).

Polycarp was the Bishop of Smyrna about the middle of the second century. He was arrested for his faith and threatened with death if he did not recant. "Eighty and six years have I served Him," the saintly Bishop replied, "and He never did me any injury. How can I blaspheme my King and my Saviour?"

"I have respect for your age," said the Roman officer. "Simply say, 'Away with the atheists!' and be set free." By "the atheists" he meant the Christians who would not acknowledge that Caesar was "lord."

The old man pointed to the crowd of Roman pagans surrounding him, and cried, "Away with the atheists!" He was burned at the stake and in his martyrdom brought glory to the name of Jesus Christ.

### Examine Your Life (1 Peter 4:15-18)

In the furnace of persecution and suffering, we often have more light by which we can examine our lives and ministries. The fiery trial is a refining process, by which God removes the dross and purifies us. One day, a fiery judgment will overtake the whole world (2 Peter 3:7-16). Meanwhile, God's judgment begins "at the house of God," the church (1 Peter 2:5). This truth ought to motivate us to be as pure and obedient as possible (see Ezek. 9 for an Old Testament illustration of this truth).

There are several questions we should ask

ourselves as we examine our own lives.

*Why am I suffering? (v. 15)* We noted before that not all suffering is a "fiery trial" from the Lord. If a professed Christian breaks the law and gets into trouble, or becomes a meddler into other people's lives, then he *ought* to suffer! The fact that we are Christians is not a guarantee that we escape the normal consequences of our misdeeds. We may not be guilty of murder (though anger can be the same as murder in the heart, Matt. 5:21-26), but what about stealing, or meddling? When Abraham, David, Peter, and other Bible "greats" disobeyed God, they suffered for it; so, who are we that we should escape? Let's be sure we are suffering because we are Christians and not because we are criminals.

*Am I ashamed, or glorifying Christ? (v. 16)* This statement must have reminded Peter of his own denial of Christ (Luke 22:54-62). Jesus Christ is not ashamed of us (Heb. 2:11)—though many times He surely could be! The Father is not ashamed to be called our God (Heb. 11:16). On the cross Jesus Christ despised shame for us (Heb. 12:2), so surely we can bear reproach for Him and not be ashamed. The warning in Mark 8:38 is worth pondering.

"Not be ashamed" is negative; "glorify God" is positive. It takes both for a balanced witness. If we seek to glorify God, then we will not be ashamed of the name of Jesus Christ. It was this determination not to be ashamed that encouraged Paul when he went to Rome (Rom. 1:16), when he suffered in Rome (Phil. 1:20-21), and when he faced martyrdom in Rome (2 Tim. 1:12).

*Am I seeking to win the lost? (vv. 17-18)* Note the words that Peter used to describe the lost: "Them that obey not the Gospel. . . . the ungodly and the sinner." The argument of this verse is clear: If God sends a "fiery trial" to His own children, and they are saved "with difficulty," what will happen to lost sinners when God's fiery judgment falls?

When a believer suffers, he experiences glory and knows that there will be greater glory in the future. But a sinner who causes that suffering is only filling up the measure of God's wrath more and more (Matt. 23:29-33). Instead of being concerned only about ourselves, we need to be concerned about the lost sinners around us. Our present "fiery trial" is nothing compared with the "flaming fire" that shall punish the lost when Jesus returns in judgment (2 Thes. 1:7-10). The idea is expressed in Proverbs 11:31—"If the righteous receive their due on earth, how much more the ungodly and the sinner!" (NIV)

The phrase *scarcely be saved* means "saved with difficulty," but it does not suggest that God is too weak to save us. The reference is probably to Genesis 19:15-26, when God sought to rescue Lot from Sodom before the city was destroyed. God was able—but Lot was unwilling! He lingered, argued with the angels, and finally had to be taken by the hand and dragged out of the city! Lot was "saved as by fire" and everything he lived for went up in smoke (see 1 Cor. 3:9-15).

Times of persecution are times of opportunity for a loving witness to those who persecute us (see Matt. 5:10-12, 43-48). It was not the earthquake that brought that Philippian jailer to Christ, because that frightened him into almost committing suicide! No, it was Paul's loving concern for him that brought the jailer to faith in Christ. As Christians, we do not seek for vengeance on those who have hurt us. Rather, we pray for them and seek to lead them to Jesus Christ.

**Commit Yourself to God (1 Peter 4:19)** When we are suffering in the will of God, we can commit ourselves into the care of God. Everything else that we do as Christians depends on this. The word is a banking term; it means "to deposit for safekeeping" (see 2 Tim. 1:12). Of course, when you deposit your life in God's bank, you always receive eternal dividends on your investment.

This picture reminds us that we are valuable to God. He made us, redeemed us, lives in us, guards, and protects us. I saw a savings and loan association advertisement in the newspaper, reaffirming the financial stability of the firm and the backing of the Federal Deposit Insurance Corporation. In days of financial unsteadiness, such assurances are necessary to depositors. But when you "deposit" your life with God, you have nothing to fear; for He is able to keep you.

This commitment is not a single action but a constant attitude. "Be constantly committing" is the force of the admonition. How do we do this? "By means of welldoing." As we return good for evil and do good even though we suffer for it, we are committing ourselves to God so that He can care for us. This commitment involves every area of our lives and every hour of our lives.

If we really have hope, and believe that Jesus is coming again, then we will obey His Word and start laying up treasures and glory in heaven. Unsaved people have a present that is controlled by their past, but Christians have a present that is controlled by the future (Phil. 3:12-21). In our very serving, we are committing ourselves to God and making investments for the future.

There is a striking illustration of this truth in Jeremiah 32. The Prophet Jeremiah had been telling the people that one day their situation would change and they would be restored to their land. But at that time, the Babylonian army occupied the land and was about to take Jerusalem. Jeremiah's cousin, Hanamel, gave Jeremiah an option to purchase the family land *which was now occupied by enemy soldiers.* The prophet had to "put his money where his mouth is." And he did it! As an act of faith, he purchased the land and became, no doubt, the laughingstock of the people in Jerusalem. But God honored his faith because Jeremiah lived according to the Word that he preached.

Why did Peter refer to God as "a faithful Creator" rather than "a faithful Judge" or even "a faithful Saviour"? Because God the Creator meets the needs of His people (Matt. 6:24-34). It is the Creator who provides food and clothing to persecuted Christians, and who protects them in times of danger. When the early church was persecuted, they met together for prayer and addressed the Lord as the "God, which has made heaven, and earth, and the sea, and all that in them is" (Acts 4:24). They prayed to the Creator!

Our Heavenly Father is "the Lord of heaven and earth" (Matt. 11:25). With that kind of a Father, we have no need to worry! He is the *faithful* Creator, and His faithfulness will not fail.

Before God pours out His wrath on this evil world, a "fiery trial" will come to God's church, to unite and purify it, that it might be a strong witness to the lost. There is nothing for us to fear if we are suffering in the will of God. Our faithful Father-Creator will victoriously see us through!

# CHAPTER ELEVEN
# HOW TO BE
# A GOOD SHEPHERD
## *1 Peter 5:1-4*

Times of persecution demand that God's people have adequate spiritual leadership. If judgment is to begin at God's house (1 Peter 4:17), then that house had better be in order, or it will fall apart! This explains why Peter wrote this special message to the leaders of the church, to encourage them to do their work faithfully. Leaders who run away in times of difficulty are only proving that they are hirelings and not true shepherds (John 10:12-14).

The New Testament assemblies were organized under the leadership of elders and deacons (1 Tim. 3). The words "elder" and "bishop" refer to the same office (Acts 20:17, 28). The word "bishop" is often translated "overseer" (see 1 Peter 5:2, and note that this title is applied to Christ in 1 Peter 2:25). "Elder" refers to the maturity of the officer, and "bishop" to the responsibility of the office. The word "pastor" (which means "shepherd") is another title for this same office (Eph. 4:11). The elders were appointed to office (Acts 14:23, where the verb "ordain" means "to appoint by the raising of hands"). Apparently each congregation had the privilege of voting on qualified men.

Peter was concerned that the leadership in the local churches be at its best. When the fiery trial would come, the believers in the assemblies would look to their elders for encouragement and direction. What are the personal qualities that make for a successful pastor?

## A Vital Personal Experience with Christ (1 Peter 5:1)

Peter did not introduce himself in this letter as an apostle or a great spiritual leader, but simply as another elder. However, he did mention the fact that he had personally witnessed Christ's sufferings (see Matt. 26:36ff). The Greek word translated "witness" gives us our English word "martyr." We think of a "martyr" only as one who gives his life for Christ, and Peter did that; but basically, a "martyr" is a witness who tells what he has seen and heard.

It is interesting to read 1 Peter 5 in the light of Peter's personal experiences with Christ. First Peter 5:1 takes us to Gethsemane and Calvary. "The glory that shall be revealed" reminds us of Peter's experience with Christ on the Mount of Transfiguration (Matt. 17:1-5; 2 Peter 1:15-18). The emphasis in 1 Peter 5:2 on the shepherd and the sheep certainly brings to mind John 10 and our Lord's admonition to Peter in John 21:15-17.

The warning in 1 Peter 5:3 about "lording it over" the saints reminds us of Christ's lesson about true greatness in Luke 22:24-30, as well as the other times that He taught His disciples about humility and service. The phrase in 1 Peter 5:5, "Be clothed with humility," takes us back to the Upper Room where Jesus put on the towel and washed the disciples' feet (John 13:1-17).

The warning about Satan in 1 Peter 5:8 parallels our Lord's warning to Peter that Satan was going to "sift" him and the other Apostles (Luke 22:31). Peter did not heed that warning, and he ended up denying his Lord three times.

It is interesting to note that the verb "make you perfect" (1 Peter 5:10) is translated "mending their nets" in Matthew 4:21, the account of the call of the four fishermen into the Lord's service.

In other words, Peter wrote these words, inspired by the Spirit of God, out of his own personal experience with Jesus Christ. He had a vital and growing relationship with Christ, and this made it possible for him to minister effectively to God's people.

The pastor of the local assembly must be a man who walks with God and who is growing in his spiritual life. Paul admonished young Timothy: "Be diligent in these matters; give yourself wholly to them, so that everyone may see your progress" (1 Tim. 4:15, NIV). The word "progress" in the original means "pioneer advance." The elders must constantly be moving into new territories of study, achievement, and ministry. If the leaders of the church are not moving forward, the church will not move forward.

"We love our pastor," a fine church member said to me during a conference, "but we get tired of the same thing all the time. He repeats himself and doesn't seem to know that there are other books in the Bible besides Psalms and Revelation." That man needed to become a "spiritual pioneer" and move into new territory, so that he might lead his people into new blessings and challenges.

Sometimes God permits trials to come to a church so that the people will be *forced* to grow and discover new truths and new opportunities. Certainly Peter grew in his spiritual experience as he suffered for Christ in the city of Jerusalem. He was not perfect by any means; in fact, Paul had to rebuke him once for inconsistency (Gal. 2:11-21). But Peter was yielded to Christ and willing to learn all that God had for him.

If I have any counsel for God's shepherds today, it is this: cultivate a growing relationship with Jesus Christ, and share what He gives you with your people. That way, you will grow, and they will grow with you.

## A Loving Concern for God's Sheep (1 Peter 5:2-3)

The image of the flock is often used in the Bible, and it is a very instructive one (see Pss. 23; 100; Isa. 40:11; Luke 15:4-6; John 10; Acts 20:28; Heb. 13:20-21; 1 Peter 2:25; Rev. 7:17). We were once stray sheep, wandering toward ruin; but the Good Shepherd found us and restored us to the fold.

Sheep are clean animals, unlike dogs and pigs (2 Peter 2:20-22). Sheep tend to flock together, and God's people need to be together. Sheep are notoriously ignorant and prone to wander away if they do not follow the shepherd. Sheep are defenseless, for the most part, and need their shepherd to protect them (Ps. 23:4).

Sheep are very useful animals. Jewish shepherds tended their sheep, not for the meat (which would have been costly) but for the wool, milk, and lambs. God's people should be useful to Him and certainly ought to "reproduce" themselves by bringing others to Christ. Sheep were used for the sacrifices, and we ought to be "living sacrifices," doing the will of God (Rom. 12:1-2).

Peter reminded the shepherd-elders of their God-given responsibilities.

*Feed the flock of God (v. 2).* The word *feed* means "shepherd, care for." The shepherd had many tasks to perform in caring for the flock. He had to protect the sheep from thieves and marauders, and the pastor must protect God's people from those who want to spoil the flock (Acts 20:28-35). Sometimes the sheep do not like it when their shepherd rebukes or warns them, but this ministry is for their own good.

A faithful shepherd not only protected his

flock, but he also led them from pasture to pasture so that they might be adequately fed. The shepherd always went before the flock and searched out the land so that there would be nothing there to harm his flock. He would check for snakes, pits, poisonous plants, and dangerous animals. How important it is for pastors to lead their people into the green pastures of the Word of God so that they might feed themselves and grow.

Sometimes it was necessary for a shepherd to seek out a wayward sheep and give it personal attention. Some pastors today are interested only in the crowds; they have no time for individuals. Jesus preached to great multitudes, but He took time to chat with Nicodemus (John 3), the woman at the well (John 4), and others who had spiritual needs. Paul ministered to people *personally* in Thessalonica (1 Thes. 2:11) and loved them dearly.

If a sheep is too rebellious, the shepherd may have to discipline him in some way. If a sheep has a special need, the shepherd might carry it in his arms, next to his heart. At the close of each day, the faithful shepherd would examine each sheep to see if it needed special attention. He would anoint the bruises with healing oil, and remove the briars from the wool. A good shepherd would know each of his sheep by name and would understand the special traits of each one.

It is not an easy thing to be a faithful shepherd of God's sheep! It is a task that never ends and that demands the supernatural power of God if it is to be done correctly. What makes it even more challenging is the fact that the flock is not the shepherd's; it is God's. I sometimes hear pastors say, "Well, at *my* church . . ." and I know what they mean; but strictly speaking, it is *God's* flock, purchased by the precious blood of His Son (Acts 20:28). We pastors must be careful how we minister to *God's* sheep, because one day we will have to give an account of our ministry. But the sheep will also one day give an account of how they have obeyed their spiritual leaders (Heb. 13:17), so both shepherds and sheep have a great responsibility to each other.

**Take the oversight (v. 2).** The word *bishop* means "overseer, one who looks over for the purpose of leading." You will notice that the shepherd is both "among" and "over," and this can create problems if the sheep do not understand. Because he is one of the sheep, the pastor is "among" the members of the flock. But because he is called to be a leader, the pastor is "over" the flock. Some people try to emphasize the "among" relationship and refuse to follow the authority of the shepherd. Others want to put the pastor on a pedestal and make him a "super saint" who never mixes with the people.

The effective pastor needs both relationships. He must be "among" his people so that he can get to know them, their needs and problems; and he needs to be "over" his people so he can lead them and help them solve their problems. There must be no conflict between *pastoring* and *preaching,* because they are both ministries of a faithful Shepherd. The preacher needs to be a pastor so he can apply the Word to the needs of the people. The pastor needs to be a preacher so that he can have authority when he shares in their daily needs and problems. The pastor is not a religious lecturer who weekly passes along information about the Bible. He is a shepherd who knows his people and seeks to help them through the Word.

Being the spiritual leader of a flock has its dangers, and Peter pointed out some of the sins that the elders must avoid. The first was *laziness*—"not by constraint but willingly." His ministry must not be a job that he has to perform. He should do God's will from his heart (Eph. 6:6). Dr. George W. Truett was pastor of First Baptist Church in Dallas, Texas for nearly fifty years. Often he was asked to accept other positions, and he refused, saying, "I have sought and found a pastor's heart." When a man has a pastor's heart, he loves the sheep and serves them because he *wants* to, not because he *has* to.

If a man has no conscience, the ministry is a good place to be lazy. Church members rarely ask what their pastor is doing with his time, and he can "borrow" sermons from other preachers and use them as his own. I met one pastor who spent most of his week on the golf course; then on Saturday he listened to tapes of other preachers and used their sermons on Sunday. He seems to be getting away with it, but what will he say when he meets the Chief Shepherd?

Next to laziness, the shepherd must beware of *covetousness*—"not for filthy lucre, but of a ready mind." It is perfectly proper for the church to pay the pastor (1 Cor. 9; 1 Tim. 5:17-18), and they ought to be as fair and generous as possible. But making money must not be the main motive for his ministry. Paul stresses this in his qualifications for an elder:

"not greedy of filthy lucre" (1 Tim. 3:3); "not given to filthy lucre" (Titus 1:7). He must not be a lover of money nor devote himself to pursuing money.

Because of family or church situations, some pastors have to engage in outside employment. Paul was a tentmaker, so there is no disgrace in "moonlighting." But, as soon as possible, the members of the church ought to relieve their pastor of outside employment so he can devote himself fully to the ministry of the Word. Pastors need to beware of getting involved in money-making schemes that detour them from their ministry. "No one serving as a soldier gets involved in civilian affairs—he wants to please his commanding officer" (2 Tim. 2:4, NIV).

The phrase "a ready mind" means "an eager mind." It is the same word Paul used in Romans 1:15—"I am so eager to preach the Gospel" (NIV). It means a willingness to serve because of a readiness and an eagerness within the heart. This is the difference between a true shepherd and a hireling: a hireling works because he is paid for it, but a shepherd works because he loves the sheep and has a heart devoted to them. Read Acts 20:17-38 for a description of the heart and ministry of a true shepherd.

*Be an example to the flock (v. 3).* The contrast is between *dictatorship* and *leadership.* You cannot drive sheep; you must go before them and lead them. It has been well said that the church needs leaders who serve and servants who lead. A Christian leader said to me, "The trouble today is that we have too many celebrities and not enough servants."

It is by being an example that the shepherd solves the tension between being "among" the sheep and "over" the sheep. People are willing to follow a leader who practices what he preaches and gives them a good example to imitate. I know of a church that was constantly having financial problems, and no one could understand why. After the pastor left, it was discovered that he had not himself contributed to the work of the church but had preached sermons telling others to contribute. We cannot lead people where we have not been ourselves.

Peter was not changing the image when he called the church "God's heritage." The people of God are certainly His priceless possession (Deut. 32:9; Ps. 33:12). This word means "to be chosen by lot," as the dividing up of land (Num. 26:55). Each elder has his

own flock to care for, but the sheep all belong to the one flock of which Jesus Christ is the Chief Shepherd. The Lord assigns His workers to the places of His choosing, and we must all be submissive to Him. There is no competition in the work of God when you are serving in the will of God. Therefore, nobody has to act important and "lord it over" God's people. Pastors are to be "overseers" and not "overlords."

## A Desire to Please Christ Alone
## (1 Peter 5:4)
Since this is the epistle of hope, Peter brought in once again the promise of the Lord's return. His coming is an encouragement in suffering (1 Peter 1:7-8) and a motivation for faithful service. If a pastor ministers to please himself, or to please people, he will have a disappointing and difficult ministry. "It must be hard to keep all these people happy," a visitor said to me after a church service. "I don't even try to keep them happy," I replied with a smile. "I try to please the Lord, and I let Him take care of the rest."

Jesus Christ is the *Good* Shepherd who died for the sheep (John 10:11), the *Great* Shepherd who lives for the sheep (Heb. 13:20-21), and the *Chief* Shepherd who comes for the sheep (1 Peter 5:4). As the Chief Shepherd, He alone can assess a man's ministry and give him the proper reward. Some who appear to be first may end up last when the Lord examines each man's ministry.

One summer day, I stood amid the ruins of a church near Anwoth in Scotland. The building at one time seated perhaps 150 people. By modern standards, it would not have been a successful church. But the man who pastored that flock was the saintly Samuel Rutherford, whose *Letters of Samuel Rutherford* is a spiritual classic. His ministry continues, though today his church building is in ruins. The Chief Shepherd has rewarded him for his faithful labors, which included a great deal of persecution and physical suffering.

There were several kinds of "crowns" in those days. The one Peter mentioned was the athlete's crown, usually a garland of leaves or flowers that would quickly fade away. The faithful pastor's crown is a crown of glory, a perfect reward for an *inheritance* that will never fade away (1 Peter 1:4).

Today a Christian worker may labor for many different kinds of rewards. Some work hard to build personal empires; others strive for the applause of men; still others seek promotion in their denomination. All of these things will fade one day. The only reward we ought to strive for is the "Well done!" of the Saviour and the unfading crown of glory that goes with it. What a joy it will be to place the crown at His feet (Rev. 4:10) and acknowledge that all we did was because of His grace and power (1 Cor. 15:10; 1 Peter 4:11). We will have no desire for personal glory when we see Jesus Christ face-to-face.

Everything in the local church rises or falls with leadership. No matter how large or small a fellowship might be, the leaders must be Christians, each with a vital personal relationship with Christ, a loving concern for their people, and a real desire to please Jesus Christ.

We lead by serving, and we serve by suffering.

This is the way Jesus did it, and this is the only way that truly glorifies Him.

# CHAPTER TWELVE
# FROM GRACE
# TO GLORY!
## *1 Peter 5:5-14*

When World War II was being fought, I was a junior high school student, and the fighting seemed very far away from our northern Indiana city. But then the city began to organize Civil Defense units in each neighborhood, and officials appointed my father an assistant block captain. Often I went with him to watch the training films and listen to the speakers. (The best part of the evening was stopping for an ice cream cone!) But, no matter how many films we watched, we somehow didn't feel that our neighborhood was in danger of being bombed. Our philosophy was, "It can't happen here."

Peter knew that a "fiery trial" was about to occur, and he wanted the entire church family to be prepared. As he closed his letter, Peter gave the church three important admonitions to obey if they were to glorify God in this difficult experience.

## Be Humble (1 Peter 5:5-7)

He had already admonished the saints to be submissive to government authorities (1 Peter 2:13-17), the slaves to submit to their masters (1 Peter 2:18-25), and the wives to submit to their husbands (1 Peter 3:1-7). Now he commanded all of the believers to submit to God and to each other.

The younger believers should submit to the older believers, not only out of respect for their age, but also out of respect for their spiritual maturity. Not every "senior saint" is a mature Christian, of course, because quantity of years is no guarantee of quality of experience. This is not to suggest that the older church members "run the church" and never listen to the younger members! Too often there is a generation war in the church, with the older people resisting change, and the younger people resisting the older people!

The solution is twofold: (1) all believers, young and old, should submit to each other; (2) all should submit to God. "Be clothed with humility" is the answer to the problem. Just as Jesus laid aside His outer garments and put on a towel to become a servant, so each of us should have a servant's attitude and minister to each other. True humility is described in Philippians 2:1-11 Humility is not demeaning ourselves and thinking poorly of ourselves. It is simply not thinking of ourselves at all!

We can never be submissive to each other until we are first submissive to God. Peter quoted Proverbs 3:34 to defend his point, a verse that is also quoted in James 4:6. It takes grace to submit to another believer, but God can give that grace *if* we humble ourselves before Him.

God resists the proud because God hates the sin of pride (Prov. 6:16-17; 8:13). It was pride that turned Lucifer into Satan (Isa. 14:12-15). It was pride—a desire to be like God—that stirred Eve to take the forbidden fruit. "The pride of life" is an evidence of worldliness (1 John 2:16). The only antidote to pride is the grace of God, and we receive that grace when we yield ourselves to Him. The evidence of that grace is that we yield to one another.

Submission is an act of faith. We are trusting God to direct in our lives and to work out His purposes in His time. After all, there is a danger in submitting to others; they might take advantage of us—but not if we trust God and if we are submitted to one another! A person who is truly yielded to God, and who wants to serve his fellow Christians, would not even think of taking advantage of someone else, saved or unsaved. The "mighty hand of God" that directs our lives can also direct in the lives of others.

The key, of course, is the phrase "in due time." God never exalts anyone until that person is ready for it. First the cross, then the crown; first the suffering, then the glory. Moses was under God's hand for forty years before God sent him to deliver the Jews from Egypt. Joseph was under God's hand for at least thirteen years before God lifted him to the throne. One of the evidences of our pride is our impatience with God, and one reason for suffering is that we might learn patience (James 1:1-6). Here Peter was referring to words he heard the Master say: "For whosoever exalteth himself shall be abased; and he that humbleth himself shall be exalted" (Luke 14:11).

One of the benefits of this kind of relationship with God is the privilege of letting Him take care of our burdens. Unless we meet the conditions laid down in 1 Peter 5:5-6, we cannot claim the wonderful promise of 1 Peter 5:7. The word translated "care" means "anxiety, the state of being pulled apart." When circumstances are difficult, it is easy for us to be anxious and worried; but if we are, we will miss God's blessing and become poor witnesses to the lost. We need His inward peace if we are going to triumph in the fiery trial and bring glory to His name. Dr. George Morrison said, "God does not make His children carefree in order that they be careless."

According to 1 Peter 5:7, we must *once and for all* give all of our cares—past, present, and future—to the Lord. We must not hand them to Him piecemeal, keeping those cares that we think we can handle ourselves. If we keep "the little cares" for ourselves, they will soon become big problems! Each time a new burden arises, we must by faith remind the Lord (and ourselves) that we have already turned it over to Him.

If anybody knew from experience that God cares for His own, it was Peter! When you read the four Gospels, you discover that Peter shared in some wonderful miracles. Jesus healed Peter's mother-in-law (Mark 1:29-31), gave him a great catch of fish (Luke 5:1-11), helped him pay his temple tax (Matt. 17:24-27), helped him walk on the water (Matt. 14:22-33), repaired the damage he did to the ear of Malchus (Luke 22:50-51; John 18:10-11), and even delivered Peter from prison (Acts 12).

How does God show His love and care for us when we give our cares to Him? I believe that He performs four wonderful ministries on our behalf. (1) He gives us the courage to face our cares honestly and not run away (Isa. 41:10). (2) He gives us the wisdom to understand the situation (James 1:5). (3) He gives us the strength to do what we must do (Phil. 4:13). And (4) He gives us the faith to trust Him to do the rest (Ps. 37:5).

Some people give God their burdens and expect Him to do everything! It is important that we let Him work *in* us as well as work *for* us, so that we will be prepared when the answer comes. "Cast thy burden upon the Lord, and He shall sustain thee" (Ps. 55:22).

## Be Watchful (1 Peter 5:8-9)

One reason we have cares is because we have an enemy. As the serpent, Satan deceives (2 Cor. 11:3); and as the lion, Satan devours. The word "Satan" means "adversary," and the word "devil" means "the accuser, the slanderer." The recipients of this letter had already experienced the attacks of the slanderer (1 Peter 4:4, 14), and now they would meet "the lion" in their fiery trial. Peter gave them several practical instructions to help them get victory over their adversary.

*Respect him—he is dangerous.* Since I have no mechanical ability, I admire people who can build and repair things. During a church building program, I was watching an electrician install a complex control panel. I said to the man, "It just amazes me how you fellows can calmly work on those lines with all of that power there. How do you do it?" The electrician smiled and said, "Well, the first thing you have to do is respect it. Then you can handle it."

Satan is a dangerous enemy. He is a serpent who can bite us when we least expect it. He is a destroyer (Rev. 12:11; *Abaddon* and *Apollyon* both mean "destruction") and an accuser (Zech. 3:1-5; Rev. 12:9-11). He has great power and intelligence, and a host of demons who assist him in his attacks against God's people (Eph. 6:10ff). He is a formidable enemy; we must never joke about him, ignore him, or underestimate his ability. We must "be sober" and have our minds under control when it comes to our conflict with Satan.

A part of this soberness includes not blaming everything on the devil. Some people see a demon behind every bush and blame Satan for their headaches, flat tires, and high rent. While it is true that Satan can inflict physical sickness and pain (Luke 13:16; and the Book of Job), we have no biblical authority for casting out "demons of headache" or "demons of backache." One lady phoned me long distance to inform me that Satan had caused her to shrink seven and a half inches. While I have great respect for the wiles and powers of the devil, I still feel we must get our information about him from the Bible and not from our own interpretation of experiences.

*Recognize him—he is a great pretender (John 8:44; 2 Cor. 11:13-15).* Because he is a subtle foe, we must "be vigilant" and always on guard. His strategy is to counterfeit whatever God does. According to the Parable of the Tares, wherever God plants a true Christian, Satan seeks to plant a counterfeit (Matt. 13:24-30, 36-43). He would deceive us were it not for the Word of God and the Spirit of God (1 John 2:18-27). The better we know God's Word, the keener our spiritual senses will be to detect Satan at work. We must be able to "try the spirits" and know the true from the false (1 John 4:1-6).

*Resist him.* This means that we take our stand on the Word of God and refuse to be moved. Ephesians 6:10-13 instructs us to "stand . . . withstand . . . stand." Unless we stand, we cannot withstand. Our weapons are the Word of God and prayer (Eph. 6:17-18) and our protection is the complete armor God has provided. We resist him "in the faith," that is, our faith in God. Just as David took his stand against Goliath, and trusted in the name of Jehovah, so we take our stand against Satan in the victorious name of Jesus Christ.

A word of caution here: never discuss things with Satan or his associates. Eve made this mistake, and we all know the sad consequences. Also, never try to fight Satan in your own way. Resist him the way Jesus did, with the Word of God (Matt. 4:1-11). Never get the idea that you are the only one going through these battles, because "your brethren that are in the world" are facing the same trials. We must pray for one another and encourage each other in the Lord. And we must remember that our personal victories will help others, just as their victories will help us.

Had Peter obeyed these three instructions the night Jesus was arrested, he would not have gone to sleep in the Garden of Gethsem-

ane, attacked Malchus, or denied the Lord. He did not take the Lord's warning seriously; in fact, he argued with Him! Nor did he recognize Satan when the adversary inflated his ego with pride, told him he did not have to "watch and pray," and then incited him to use his sword. Had Peter listened to the Lord and resisted the enemy, he would have escaped all those failures.

Both Peter and James give us the same formula for success: "Submit yourselves therefore to God. Resist the devil, and he will flee from you" (James 4:7). Before we can stand before Satan, we must bow before God. Peter resisted the Lord and ended up submitting to Satan!

## Be Hopeful (1 Peter 5:10-14)

Peter closed on a positive note and reminded his readers that God knew what He was doing and was in complete control. No matter how difficult the fiery trial may become, a Christian always has hope. Peter gave several reasons for this hopeful attitude.

*We have God's grace.* Our salvation is because of His grace (1 Peter 1:10). He called us before we called on Him (1 Peter 1:2). We have "tasted that the Lord is gracious" (1 Peter 2:3), so we are not afraid of anything that He purposes for us. His grace is "manifold" (1 Peter 4:10) and meets every situation of life. As we submit to Him, He gives us the grace that we need. In fact, He is "the God of all grace." He has grace to help in every time of need (Heb. 4:16). "He giveth more grace" (James 4:6), and we must stand in that grace (1 Peter 5:12; see Rom. 5:2).

*We know we are going to glory.* He has "called us unto His eternal glory by Christ Jesus." This is the wonderful inheritance into which we were born (1 Peter 1:4). Whatever begins with God's grace will always lead to God's glory (Ps. 84:11). If we depend on God's grace when we suffer, that suffering will result in glory (1 Peter 4:13-16). The road may be difficult, but it leads to glory, and that is all that really counts.

*Our present suffering is only for a while.* Our various trials are only "for a season" (1 Peter 1:6), but the glory that results is *eternal.* Paul had this same thought in mind when he wrote 2 Corinthians 4:17— "These little troubles (which are really so transitory) are winning for us a permanent, glorious, and solid reward out of all proportion to our pain" (PH).

*We know that our trials are building Christian character.* The Greek word translated "make you perfect" means "to equip, to adjust, to fit together." It is translated "mending nets" in Matthew 4:21. God has several tools which He uses to equip His people for life and service, and suffering is one of them. The Word of God is another tool (2 Tim. 3:16-17, where *thoroughly furnished* means "fully equipped"). He also uses the fellowship and ministry of the church (Eph. 4:11-16). Our Saviour in heaven is perfecting His children so that they will do His will and His work (Heb. 13:20-21).

Peter used three words to describe the kind of character God wants us to have.

*Establish* means "to fix firmly, to set fast." Christians must not be unsteady in their stand for Christ. Our hearts need to be established (1 Thes. 3:13; James 5:8), and this is accomplished by God's truth (2 Peter 1:12). The believer who is established will not be moved by persecution, or led away by false doctrine (2 Peter 3:17).

*Strengthen* means just that: God's strength given to us to meet the demands of life. What good is it to stand on a firm foundation if we do not have power to act?

*Settle* is the translation of a word that means "to lay a foundation." It is used this way in Hebrews 1:10. The house founded on the rock withstood the storm (Matt. 7:24-27). A believer who is equipped by God will "continue in the faith grounded and settled" (Col. 1:23). He will not be "tossed to and fro, and carried about with every wind of doctrine" (Eph. 4:14).

When an unbeliever goes through suffering, he loses his hope; but for a believer, suffering only increases his hope. "Not only so, but we also rejoice in our sufferings, because we know that suffering produces perseverance; perseverance, character; and character, hope" (Rom. 5:3-4, NIV). God builds character and brightens hope when a believer trusts Him and depends on His grace. The result is that God receives the glory forever and ever.

We have already considered 1 Peter 5:12-13 in our introductory chapter.

Paul always ended his letters with a benediction of grace (2 Thes. 3:17-18). Peter closed this epistle with a benediction of peace. He opened the letter with a greeting of peace (1 Peter 1:2), so the entire epistle points to "God's peace" from beginning to end. What a wonderful way to end a letter that announced the coming of a fiery trial!

Four times in the New Testament we will find the admonition about "a holy kiss" (Rom. 16:16; 1 Cor. 16:20; 2 Cor. 13:12; and 1 Thes. 5:26). Peter called it "a kiss of love." Keep in mind that the men kissed the men and the women kissed the women. It was a standard form of greeting or farewell in that part of the world at that time, just as it is in many Latin countries today. How wonderful that Christian slaves and masters would so greet each other "in Jesus Christ"!

Peter has given to us a precious letter that encourages us to hope in the Lord no matter how trying the times may be. Down through the centuries, the church has experienced various fiery trials, and yet Satan has not been able to destroy it. The church today is facing a fiery trial, and we must be prepared.

But, whatever may come, Peter is still saying to each of us—BE HOPEFUL! The glory is soon to come!

# 2 PETER

## OUTLINE

**Key theme:** Spiritual knowledge
**Key verse:** 2 Peter 1:3

## CONTENTS

# CHAPTER ONE
# KNOWING AND
# GROWING
*2 Peter 1:1-11*

If anybody in the early church knew the importance of being alert, it was the Apostle Peter. He had a tendency in his early years to feel overconfident when danger was near and to overlook the Master's warnings. He rushed ahead when he should have waited; he slept when he should have prayed; he talked when he should have listened. He was a courageous, but careless, Christian.

But he learned his lesson, and he wants to help us learn it too. In his first epistle, Peter emphasized the grace of God (1 Peter 5:12), but in this second letter, his emphasis is on the knowledge of God. The word *know* or *knowledge* is used at least thirteen times in this short epistle. The word does not mean a mere intellectual understanding of some truth, though that is included. It means a living participation in the truth in the sense that our Lord used it in John 17:3—"This is life eternal, that they might *know* Thee the only true God, and Jesus Christ, whom Thou hast sent" (italics mine).

Peter opened his letter with a description of the Christian life. Before he described the counterfeits, he described the true believers. The best way to detect falsehood is to understand the characteristics of the truth. Peter made three important affirmations about the true Christian life.

## The Christian Life Begins with Faith (2 Peter 1:1-4)

Peter called it "like precious faith." It means that our standing with the Lord today is the same as that of the Apostles centuries ago. They had no special advantage over us simply because they were privileged to walk with Christ, see Him with their own eyes, and share in His miracles. It is not necessary to see the Lord with our human eyes in order to love Him, trust Him, and share His glory (1 Peter 1:8).

***This faith is in a person (vv. 1-2).*** That Person is Jesus Christ, the Son of God, the Saviour. From the very outset of his letter,

Peter affirmed the deity of Jesus Christ. "God" and "our Saviour" are not two different Persons; they describe one Person, Jesus Christ. Paul used a similar expression in Titus 2:10 and 3:4.

Peter reminded his readers that Jesus Christ is the Saviour by repeating this exalted title in 2 Peter 1:11; 2:20; 3:2, 18. A *savior* is "one who brings salvation," and the word *salvation* was familiar to the people of that day. In their vocabulary, it meant "deliverance from trouble," particularly "deliverance from the enemy." It also carried the idea of "health and safety." A physician was looked on as a savior because he helped deliver the body from pain and limitations. A victorious general was a savior because he delivered the people from defeat. Even a wise official was a savior because he kept the nation in order and delivered it from confusion and decay.

It requires little insight to see how the title "Saviour" applies to our Lord Jesus Christ. He is, indeed, the Great Physician who heals the heart from the sickness of sin. He is the victorious Conqueror who has defeated our enemies—sin, death, Satan, and hell—and is leading us in triumph (2 Cor. 2:14ff). He is "God and our Saviour" (2 Peter 1:1), "our Lord and Saviour" (2 Peter 1:11), and "the Lord and Saviour" (2 Peter 2:20). In order to be our Saviour, He had to give His life on the cross and die for the sins of the world.

Our Lord Jesus Christ has three "spiritual commodities" that can be secured from nobody else: righteousness, grace, and peace. When you trust Him as your Saviour, His righteousness becomes your righteousness and you are given a right standing before God (2 Cor. 5:21). You could never *earn* this righteousness; it is the gift of God to those who believe. "Not by works of righteousness which we have done, but according to His mercy He saved us" (Titus 3:5).

*Grace* is God's favor to the undeserving. God in His mercy does not give us what we do deserve; God in His grace gives us what we don't deserve. Our God is "the God of all grace" (1 Peter 5:10), and He channels that grace to us through Jesus Christ (John 1:16).

The result of this experience is *peace,* peace *with* God (Rom. 5:1) and the peace *of* God (Phil. 4:6-7). In fact, God's grace and peace are "multiplied" toward us as we walk with Him and trust His promises.

***This faith involves God's power (v. 3).*** The Christian life begins with saving faith,

faith in the person of Jesus Christ. But when you know Jesus Christ personally, you also experience God's power, and this power produces "life and godliness." The unsaved sinner is dead (Eph. 2:1-3) and only Christ can raise him from the dead (John 5:24). When Jesus raised Lazarus from the dead, He said, "Loose him, and let him go" (John 11:44). Get rid of the graveclothes!

When you are born into the family of God by faith in Christ, you are born complete. God gives you everything you will ever need "for life and godliness." Nothing has to be added! "And ye are complete in Him" (Col. 2:10). The false teachers claimed that they had a "special doctrine" that would add something to the lives of Peter's readers, but Peter knew that *nothing could be added.* Just as a normal baby is born with all the "equipment" he needs for life and only needs to grow, so the Christian has all that is needed and only needs to grow. God never has to call back any of His "models" because something is lacking or faulty.

Just as a baby has a definite genetic structure that determines how he will grow, so the believer is "genetically structured" to experience "glory and virtue." One day he will be like the Lord Jesus Christ (Rom. 8:29; 1 John 3:2). We have been "called . . . to His eternal glory" (1 Peter 5:10), and we shall share that glory when Jesus Christ returns and takes His people to heaven.

But we are also "called . . . to virtue." We have been saved so that we might "show forth the praises [virtues] of Him who hath called [us] out of darkness into His marvelous light" (1 Peter 2:9). We should not wait until we get to heaven to become like Jesus Christ! In our character and conduct, we should reveal His beauty and grace today.

*This faith involves God's promises (v. 4).* God has not only given us all that we need for life and godliness, but He has also given us His Word to enable us to develop this life and godliness. These promises are *great* because they come from a great God and they lead to a great life. They are *precious* because their value is beyond calculation. If we lost the Word of God, there would be no way to replace it. Peter must have liked the word *precious,* for he wrote about the "precious faith" (2 Peter 1:1; cf. 1 Peter 1:7), the "precious promises" (2 Peter 1:4), the "precious blood" (1 Peter 1:19), the precious stone (1 Peter 2:4, 6), and the precious Saviour (1 Peter 2:7).

When the sinner believes on Jesus Christ, the Spirit of God uses the Word of God to impart the life and nature of God within. A baby shares the nature of its parents, and a person born of God shares the divine nature of God. The lost sinner is dead, but the Christian is alive because he shares the divine nature. The lost sinner is decaying because of his corrupt nature, but the Christian can experience a dynamic life of godliness because he has God's divine nature within. Mankind is under the bondage of corruption (Rom. 8:21), but the believer shares the freedom and growth that is a part of possessing the divine nature.

Nature determines *appetite.* The pig wants slop and the dog will even eat its own vomit (2 Peter 2:22), but the sheep desires green pastures. Nature also determines *behavior.* An eagle flies because it has an eagle's nature and a dolphin swims because that is the nature of the dolphin. Nature determines *environment:* squirrels climb trees, moles burrow underground, and trout swim in the water. Nature also determines *association:* lions travel in prides, sheep in flocks, and fish in schools.

If nature determines appetite, and we have God's nature within, then we ought to have an appetite for that which is pure and holy. Our behavior ought to be like that of the Father, and we ought to live in the kind of "spiritual environment" that is suited to our nature. We ought to associate with that which is true to our nature (see 2 Cor. 6:14ff). The only normal, fruit-bearing life for the child of God is a *godly* life.

Because we possess this divine nature, we have "completely escaped" the defilement and decay in this present evil world. If we feed the new nature the nourishment of the Word, then we will have little interest in the garbage of the world. But if we "make provision for the flesh" (Rom. 13:14), our sinful nature will lust after the "old sins" (2 Peter 1:9) and we will disobey God. Godly living is the result of cultivating the new nature within.

## Faith Results in Spiritual Growth (2 Peter 1:5-7)

Where there is life, there must be growth. The new birth is not the end; it is the beginning. God gives His children all that they need to live godly lives, but His children must apply themselves and be diligent to use the "means of grace" He has provided. *Spiritual growth is not automatic.* It requires cooperation with

God and the application of spiritual diligence and discipline. "Work out your own salvation. . . . For it is God which worketh in you" (Phil. 2:12-13).

Peter listed seven characteristics of the godly life, but we must not think of them as seven beads on a string or even seven stages of development. The word translated "add" really means "to supply generously." In other words, we develop one quality as we exercise another quality. These graces relate to each other the way the branch relates to the trunk and the twigs to the branch. Like the "fruit of the Spirit" (Gal. 5:22-23), these qualities grow out of life and out of a vital relationship with Jesus Christ. It is not enough for the Christian to "let go and let God," as though spiritual growth were God's work alone. Literally, Peter wrote, "Make every effort to bring alongside." The Father and the child must work together.

The first quality of character Peter listed was *virtue.* We met this word in 2 Peter 1:3, and it basically means "excellence." To the Greek philosophers, it meant "the fulfillment of a thing." When anything in nature fulfills its purpose, that is "virtue—moral excellence." The word was also used to describe the power of the gods to do heroic deeds. The land that produces crops is "excellent" because it is fulfilling its purpose. The tool that works correctly is "excellent" because it is doing what a tool is supposed to do.

A Christian is supposed to glorify God because he has God's nature within; so, when he does this, he shows "excellence" because he is fulfilling his purpose in life. True virtue in the Christian life is not "polishing" human qualities, no matter how fine they may be, but producing *divine* qualities that make the person more like Jesus Christ.

Faith helps us develop virtue, and virtue helps us develop *knowledge* (2 Peter 1:5). The word translated "knowledge" in 2 Peter 1:2-3 means "full knowledge" or "knowledge that is growing." The word used here suggests *practical* knowledge or discernment. It refers to the ability to handle life successfully. It is the opposite of being "so heavenly minded as to be of no earthly good!" This kind of knowledge does not come automatically. It comes from obedience to the will of God (John 7:17). In the Christian life, you must not separate the heart and the mind, character and knowledge.

*Temperance* is the next quality on Peter's list of spiritual virtues, and it means self-control. "He that is slow to anger is better than the mighty; and he that ruleth his spirit than he that taketh a city" (Prov. 16:32). "He that hath no rule over his own spirit is like a city that is broken down and without walls" (Prov. 25:28). Paul in his letters often compared the Christian to an athlete who must exercise and discipline himself if he ever hopes to win the prize (1 Cor. 9:24-27; Phil. 3:12-16; 1 Tim. 4:7-8).

*Patience* is the ability to endure when circumstances are difficult. Self-control has to do with handling the *pleasures* of life, while patience relates primarily to the *pressures* and *problems* of life. (The ability to endure problem people is "long-suffering.") Often, the person who "gives in" to pleasures is not disciplined enough to handle pressures either, so he "gives up."

Patience is not something that develops automatically; we must work at it. James 1:2-8 gives us the right approach. We must expect trials to come, because without trials we could never learn patience. We must, by faith, let our trials work *for* us and not against us, because we know that God is at work in our trials. If we need wisdom in making decisions, God will grant that wisdom if we ask Him. Nobody enjoys trials, but we do enjoy the confidence we can have in trials that God is at work, causing everything to work together for our good and His glory.

*Godliness* simply means "God-likeness." In the original Greek, this word meant "to worship well." It described the man who was right in his relationship with God and with his fellowman. Perhaps the words *reverence* and *piety* come closer to defining this term. It is that quality of character that makes a person distinctive. He lives above the petty things of life, the passions and pressures that control the lives of others. He seeks to do the will of God and, as he does, he seeks the welfare of others.

We must never get the idea that godliness is an impractical thing, because it is intensely practical. The godly person makes the kinds of decisions that are right and noble. He does not take an easy path simply to avoid either pain or trial. He does what is right because it is right and because it is the will of God.

*Brotherly kindness* (*philadelphia* in the Greek) is a virtue that Peter must have acquired the hard way, for the disciples of our Lord often debated and disagreed with one another. If we love Jesus Christ, we must also love the brethren. We should practice an "unfeigned [sincere] love of the brethren" (1 Peter 1:22) and not just pretend that we love them. "Let brotherly love continue" (Heb. 13:1). "Be kindly affectioned one to another with brotherly love" (Rom. 12:10). The fact that we love our brothers and sisters in Christ is one evidence that we have been born of God (1 John 5:1-2).

But there is more to Christian growth than brotherly love; we must also have the sacrificial love that our Lord displayed when He went to the cross. The kind of love ("charity") spoken of in 2 Peter 1:7 is *agape* love, the kind of love that God shows toward lost sinners. This is the love that is described in 1 Corinthians 13, the love that the Holy Spirit produces in our hearts as we walk in the Spirit (Rom. 5:5; Gal. 5:22). When we have *brotherly* love, we love because of our likenesses to others; but with *agape* love, we love in spite of the differences we have.

It is impossible for fallen human nature to manufacture these seven qualities of Christian character. They must be produced by the Spirit of God. To be sure, there are unsaved people who possess amazing self-control and endurance, but these virtues point to *them* and not to the Lord. *They* get the glory. When God produces the beautiful nature of His Son in a Christian, it is God who receives the praise and glory.

Because we have the divine nature, we can grow spiritually and develop this kind of Christian character. It is through the power of God and the precious promises of God that this growth takes place. The divine "genetic structure" is already there: God wants us to be "conformed to the image of His Son" (Rom. 8:29). The life within will reproduce that image if we but diligently cooperate with God and use the means He has lavishly given us.

And the amazing thing is this: as the image of Christ is reproduced in us, the process does not destroy our own personalities. We still remain uniquely ourselves!

One of the dangers in the church today is imitation. People have a tendency to become like their pastor, or like a church leader, or perhaps like some "famous Christian." As they do this, they destroy their own uniqueness while failing to become like Jesus Christ. They lose both ways! Just as each child in a family resembles his parents and yet is different, so each child in God's family comes more

and more to resemble Jesus Christ and yet is different. Parents don't duplicate themselves, they reproduce themselves; and wise parents permit their children to be themselves.

## Spiritual Growth Brings Practical Results (2 Peter 1:8-11)

How can the believer be certain that he is growing spiritually? Peter gave three evidences of true spiritual growth.

*Fruitfulness (v. 8).* Christian character is an end in itself, but it is also a means to an end. The more we become like Jesus Christ, the more the Spirit can use us in witness and service. The believer who is not growing is idle ("barren") and unfruitful. His knowledge of Jesus Christ is producing nothing practical in his life. The word translated "idle" also means "ineffective." The people who fail to grow usually fail in everything else!

Some of the most effective Christians I have known are people without dramatic talents and special abilities, or even exciting personalities; yet God has used them in a marvelous way. Why? Because they are becoming more and more like Jesus Christ. They have the kind of character and conduct that God can trust with blessing. They are fruitful because they are faithful; they are effective because they are growing in their Christian experience.

These beautiful qualities of character do exist "within us" because we possess the divine nature. We must cultivate them so that they increase and produce fruit in and through our lives.

*Vision (v. 9).* Nutritionists tell us that diet can certainly affect vision and this is especially true in the spiritual realm. The unsaved person is in the dark because Satan has blinded his mind (2 Cor. 4:3-4). A person has to be born again before his eyes are opened and he can see the kingdom of God (John 3:3). But after our eyes are opened, it is important that we increase our vision and see all that God wants us to see. The phrase *cannot see afar off* is the translation of a word that means "shortsighted." It is the picture of somebody closing or squinting his eyes, unable to see at a distance.

There are some Christians who see only their own church, or their own denomination, but who fail to see the greatness of God's family around the world. Some believers see the needs at home but have no vision for a lost world. Someone asked Phillips Brooks what he would do to revive a dead church, and he replied, "I would preach a missionary sermon and take up a collection!" Jesus admonished His disciples, "Lift up your eyes, and look on the fields; for they are white already to harvest" (John 4:35).

Some congregations today are like the church at Laodicea: they are proud that they are "rich and increased with goods, and have need of nothing," and do not realize that they are "wretched, and miserable, and poor, and blind, and naked" (Rev. 3:17). It is a tragedy to be "spiritually nearsighted," but it is even a greater tragedy to be blind!

If we forget what God has done for us, we will not be excited to share Christ with others. Through the blood of Jesus Christ we have been purged and forgiven! God has opened our eyes! Let's not forget what He has done! Rather, let's cultivate gratitude in our hearts and sharpen our spiritual vision. Life is too brief and the needs of the world too great for God's people to be walking around with their eyes closed!

**Security (vv. 10-11).** If you walk around with your eyes closed, you will stumble! But the growing Christian walks with confidence because he knows he is secure in Christ. It is not our profession of faith that guarantees that we are saved; it is our progression in the faith that gives us that assurance. The person who claims to be a child of God but whose character and conduct give no evidence of spiritual growth is deceiving himself and heading for judgment.

Peter pointed out that "calling" and "election" go together. The same God who *elects* His people also ordains the means to *call* them. The two must go together, as Paul wrote to the Thessalonians: "God hath from the beginning chosen you to salvation. . . . Whereunto He called you by our Gospel" (2 Thes. 2:13-14). We do not preach election to unsaved people; we preach the Gospel. But God uses that Gospel to call sinners to repentance, and then those sinners discover that they were chosen by God!

Peter also pointed out that election is no excuse for spiritual immaturity or for lack of effort in the Christian life. Some believers say, "What is going to be is going to be. There is nothing we can do." But Peter admonishes us to "be diligent." This means "make every effort." (He used this same verb in 2 Peter 1:5.) While it is true that God must work in us before we can do His will (Phil. 2:12-13), it is

also true that we must *be willing* for God to work, and we must cooperate with Him. Divine election must never be an excuse for human laziness.

The Christian who is sure of his election and calling will never "stumble" but will prove by a consistent life that he is truly a child of God. He will not always be on the mountaintop, but he will always be climbing higher. If we do "these things" (the things listed in 2 Peter 1:5-7, cf. v. 8), if we display Christian growth and character in our daily lives, then we can be sure we are converted and will one day be in heaven.

In fact, the growing Christian can look forward to "an abundant entrance" into the eternal kingdom! The Greeks used this phrase to describe the welcome given Olympic winners when they returned home. Every believer will arrive in heaven, but some will have a more glorious welcome than others. Alas, some believers "shall be saved, yet so as by fire" (1 Cor. 3:15).

The word *ministered* in 2 Peter 1:11 is the same as the word *add* in 2 Peter 1:5, and is the translation of a Greek word that means "to bear the expenses of a chorus." When the Greek theatrical groups presented their dramas, somebody had to underwrite the expenses, which were very great. The word came to mean "to make lavish provision." If we make lavish provision to grow spiritually (2 Peter 1:5), then God will make lavish provision for us when we enter heaven!

Just think of the blessings that the growing Christian enjoys: fruitfulness, vision, security—and heaven's best! All this and heaven too!

The Christian life begins with faith, but that faith must lead to spiritual growth—unless it is dead faith. But dead faith is not saving faith (James 2:14-26). Faith leads to growth and growth leads to practical results in life and service. People who have this kind of Christian experience are not likely to fall prey to apostate false teachers.

# CHAPTER TWO
# WAKE UP AND REMEMBER!
*2 Peter 1:12-21*

The best defense against false teaching is true living. A church filled with growing Christians, vibrant in their faith, is not likely to fall prey to apostates with their counterfeit Christianity. But this Christian living must be based on the authoritative Word of God. False teachers find it easy to seduce people who do not know their Bible but who are desirous of "experiences" with the Lord. It is a dangerous thing to build on subjective experience alone and ignore objective revelation.

Peter discussed Christian experience in the first half of 2 Peter 1, and in the last half he discussed the revelation we have in the Word of God. His purpose is to show the importance of knowing God's Word and relying on it completely. The Christian who knows what he believes and why he believes it will rarely be seduced by the false teachers and their devious doctrines.

Peter underscores the dependability and durability of the Word of God by contrasting Scripture with men, experiences, and the world.

## Men Die, but the Word Lives
## (2 Peter 1:12-15)
Through their preaching and teaching, the Apostles and New Testament prophets laid the foundation of the church (Eph. 2:20) and we in later generations are building on that foundation. However, the men were not the foundation; Jesus Christ is the Foundation (1 Cor. 3:11). He is also the chief Cornerstone that ties the building together (Eph. 2:20). If the church is to last, it cannot be built on mere men. It must be built on the Son of God.

Our Lord had told Peter when he would die and how he would die. "When thou shalt be old, thou shalt stretch forth thy hands, and another shall gird thee, and carry thee whither thou wouldest not" (John 21:18). This explains why, shortly after Pentecost, Peter was able to sleep in prison the night before he was scheduled to be killed; he knew that Herod

could not take his life (Acts 12:1ff). Tradition says that Peter was crucified in Rome. Like all of God's faithful servants, Peter was immortal until his work was done.

There were at least three motives behind Peter's ministry as he wrote this letter. The first was *obedience to Christ's command.* "I will not be negligent" (2 Peter 1:12). "When thou art converted," Jesus had said to Peter, "strengthen thy brethren" (Luke 22:32). Peter knew that he had a ministry to fulfill.

His second motive was simply that this reminder was *the right thing to do.* "I think it meet," he wrote, which simply means, "I think it is right and suitable." It is always right to stir up the saints and remind them of the Word of God!

His third motive is wrapped up in the word *endeavor* in 2 Peter 1:15. It is the same word that is translated *diligence* in 2 Peter 1:5 and 10. It means "to hasten to do something, to be zealous in doing it." Peter knew that he would soon die, so he wanted to take care of his spiritual responsibilities before it was too late. You and I do not know when we will die, so we had better start being diligent today!

What was it that Peter wanted to accomplish? The answer is found in the word that is repeated in 2 Peter 1:12-13 and 15—*remembrance.* Peter wanted to impress his readers' minds with the Word of God so that they would never forget it! "I think it meet . . . to stir you up by putting you in remembrance" (2 Peter 1:13). The verb *stir you up* means "to awaken, to arouse." This same word is used to describe a storm on the Sea of Galilee! (John 6:18) Peter knew that our minds have a tendency to get accustomed to truth and then to take it for granted. We forget what we ought to remember, and we remember what we ought to forget!

The readers of this letter knew the truth and were even "established" in it (2 Peter 1:12), but that was no guarantee they would always remember the truth and apply it. One reason the Holy Spirit was given to the church was to remind believers of the lessons already learned (John 14:26). In my own radio ministry, I have received letters from listeners who get upset when I repeat something. In my reply, I often refer them to what Paul wrote in Philippians 3:1—"To write the same things to you, to me indeed is not grievous, but for you it is safe." Our Lord often repeated Himself as He taught the people, and He was the Master Teacher.

Peter knew that he was going to die, so he wanted to leave behind something that would never die—the written Word of God. His two epistles became a part of the inspired Scriptures, and they have been ministering to the saints for centuries. Men die, but the Word of God lives on!

It is possible that Peter was also alluding to the Gospel of Mark. Most Bible scholars believe that the Spirit used Peter to give John Mark some of the data for his book (see 1 Peter 5:13). One of the church fathers, Papias, said that Mark was "Peter's disciple and interpreter."

The church of Jesus Christ is always one generation away from extinction. If there were no dependable written revelation, we would have to depend on word-of-mouth tradition. If you have ever played the party game "Gossip," you know how a simple sentence can be radically changed when passed from one person to another! We do not depend on the traditions of dead men; we depend on the truth of the living Word. Men die, but the Word lives forever.

If we did not have a dependable written revelation, the church would be at the mercy of men's memories. People who pride themselves on having good memories should sit on the witness stand in a courtroom! It is amazing that three perfectly honest witnesses can, with good conscience, give three different accounts of an automobile accident! Our memories are defective and selective. We usually remember what we want to remember, and often we distort even that.

Fortunately, we can depend on the written Word of God. "It is written" and it stands written forever. We can be saved through this living Word (1 Peter 1:23-25), nurtured by it (1 Peter 2:2), and guided and protected as we trust and obey.

### Experiences Fade, but the Word Remains (2 Peter 1:16-18)

The focus in this paragraph is on the transfiguration of Jesus Christ. The experience is recorded by Matthew (17:1ff), Mark (9:2-8), and Luke (9:28-36); yet none of those writers actually participated in it! Peter was there when it happened! In fact, the very words that he used in this section (2 Peter 1:12-18) remind us of his experience on the Mount of Transfiguration. He used the word *tabernacle* twice (2 Peter 1:13-14), and this suggests Peter's words, "Let us make here three taberna-

cles" (Matt. 17:4). In 2 Peter 1:15, he used the word *decease*, which is "exodus" in the Greek and is used in Luke 9:31. Jesus did not consider His death on the cross a defeat; rather, it was an "exodus"—He would deliver His people from bondage the way Moses delivered Israel from Egypt! Peter wrote of his own death as an "exodus," a release from bondage.

Note the repetition of the pronoun *we* in 2 Peter 1:16-19. It refers to Peter, James, and John—the only Apostles with the Lord on the Mount of Transfiguration. (John referred to this experience in John 1:14—"We beheld His glory.") These three men had to keep silent about their experience until after the Lord was raised from the dead (Matt. 17:9); then they told the other believers what had happened on the mountain.

What was the significance of the Transfiguration? For one thing, it confirmed Peter's testimony about Jesus Christ (Matt. 16:13-16). Peter saw the Son in His glory, and he heard the Father speak from heaven, "This is My beloved Son, in whom I am well pleased" (2 Peter 1:17). First we put our faith in Christ and confess Him, and then He gives us wonderful confirmation.

The Transfiguration also had a special significance for Jesus Christ, who was nearing Calvary. It was the Father's way of strengthening His Son for that terrible ordeal of being the sacrifice for the sins of the world. The Law and the Prophets (Moses and Elijah) pointed to His ministry, and now He would fulfill those Scriptures. The Father spoke from heaven and assured the Son of His love and approval. The Transfiguration was proof that suffering leads to glory when we are in the will of God.

But there is a third message, and it has to do with the promised kingdom. In all three Gospels where the account of the Transfiguration is recorded, it is introduced with a statement about the kingdom of God (Matt. 16:28; Mark 9:1; Luke 9:27). Jesus promised that, before they died, some of the disciples would see the kingdom of God in power! This took place on the Mount of Transfiguration when our Lord revealed His glory. It was a word of assurance to the disciples, who could not understand our Lord's teaching about the Cross. If He were to die, what would happen to the promised kingdom that He had been preaching about all those months?

Now we can understand why Peter used

this event in his letter: he was refuting the false teachings of the apostates that the kingdom of God would never come (2 Peter 3:3ff). These false teachers denied the promise of Christ's coming! In the place of God's promises, these counterfeits put "cunningly devised fables" (2 Peter 1:16) that robbed the believers of their blessed hope.

The word *fables* means "myths," manufactured stories that have no basis in fact. The Greek and Roman world abounded in stories about the gods, mere human speculations that tried to explain the world and its origin. No matter how interesting these myths might be, the Christian is not to heed them (1 Tim. 1:4), but refuse them (1 Tim. 4:7). Paul warned Timothy that the time would come in the church when professed Christians would not want to hear true doctrine, but would "turn away their ears from the truth, and . . . be turned unto fables [myths]" (2 Tim. 4:4). Paul also warned Titus about "Jewish fables [myths]" (Titus 1:14), so even some of the Jews had abandoned their sacred Scriptures and accepted man-made substitutes.

Peter wrote a summary of what he saw and heard on the Mount of Transfiguration. He saw Jesus Christ robed in majestic glory, and therefore witnessed a demonstration of the "power and coming" of the Lord Jesus Christ. When Jesus Christ came to earth at Bethlehem, He did not display His glory openly. To be sure, He revealed His glory in His miracles (John 2:11), but even this was primarily for the sake of His disciples. His face did not shine, nor did He have a halo over His head. "He hath no form nor comeliness; and when we shall see Him, there is no beauty that we should desire Him" (Isa. 53:2).

Peter not only saw Christ's glory, but he heard the Father's voice "from the magnificent glory." Witnesses are people who tell accurately what they have seen and heard (Acts 4:20), and Peter was a faithful witness. Is Jesus Christ of Nazareth the Son of God? Yes, He is! How do we know? The Father said so!

You and I were not eyewitnesses of the Transfiguration. Peter was there, and he faithfully recorded his experience for us in the letter that he wrote, inspired by the Spirit of God. Experiences fade, but the Word of God remains! Experiences are subjective, but the Word of God is objective. Experiences may be interpreted in different ways by different participants, but the Word of God gives one clear message. What we remember about our ex-

periences can be unconsciously distorted, but the Word of God remains the same and abides forever.

When we study 2 Peter 2, we will discover that apostate teachers try to turn people away from the Word of God and into "deeper experiences" that are contrary to the Word. These false teachers use "feigned words" instead of God's inspired Word (2 Peter 2:3), and they teach "damnable heresies" (2 Peter 2:1). In other words, this is really a matter of life and death! If a person believes the truth, he will live; if he believes lies, he will die. It is the difference between salvation and condemnation.

By reminding his readers of the Transfiguration, Peter affirmed several important doctrines of the Christian faith. He affirmed that Jesus Christ is indeed the Son of God. The test of any religion is, "What do you say about Jesus Christ?" If a religious teacher denies the deity of Christ, then he is a false teacher (1 John 2:18-29; 4:1-6).

But the person of Jesus Christ is only one test; we must also ask, "And what is the work of Jesus Christ? Why did He come and what did He do?" Again, the Transfiguration gives us the answer; for Moses and Elijah "appeared in glory, and spake of His decease [exodus] which He should accomplish at Jerusalem" (Luke 9:31). His death was not simply an example, as some liberal theologians want us to believe; it was an exodus, an accomplishment. He accomplished something on the cross—the redemption of lost sinners!

The Transfiguration was also affirmation of the truth of the Scriptures. Moses represented the Law; Elijah represented the Prophets; both pointed to Jesus Christ (Heb. 1:1-3). He fulfilled the Law and the Prophets (Luke 24:27). We believe the Bible because Jesus believed the Bible and said it was the Word of God. Those who question the truth and authority of the Scriptures are not arguing with Moses, Elijah, or Peter, but with the Lord Jesus Christ.

This event also affirmed the reality of God's kingdom. We who have a completed Bible can look back and understand the progressive lessons that Jesus gave His disciples about the Cross and the kingdom, but at that time those twelve men were very confused. They did not understand the relationship between His suffering and His glory (Peter's first epistle discusses this theme) and the church and the kingdom. At the Transfiguration, our Lord made it clear to His followers that His suffering *would lead to glory* and that the cross would ultimately result in the crown.

There was also a very practical lesson that Peter, James, and John needed to learn, because each of these would also suffer. James was the first of the apostles to die (Acts 12:1-2). John lived a long life but it led to exile and suffering (Rev. 1:9). Peter suffered for the Lord during his ministry, and then laid down his life just as the Lord had prophesied. On the Mount of Transfiguration, Peter, James, and John learned that suffering and glory go together, and that the Father's special love and approval are given to those who are willing to suffer for the sake of the Lord. We need this same lesson today.

Peter could not share his experience with us, but he could share the record of that experience so that we could have it permanently in the Word of God. It is not necessary for us to try to duplicate these experiences; in fact, such attempts would be dangerous, for the devil could give us a counterfeit experience that could lead us astray.

Remember Peter's wonderful news at the beginning of this letter: "like precious faith." This means that our faith gives us "an equal standing" with the Apostles! They did not travel first-class and leave us to travel second-class! "Like precious faith *with us*" is what he wrote (italics mine). We were not on the Mount of Transfiguration, but we can still benefit from that experience as we meditate on it and permit the Spirit of God to reveal the glories of Jesus Christ.

We have learned two important truths as we have seen these contrasts: men die, but the Word lives, and experiences fade, but the Word remains. Peter added a third contrast.

## The World Darkens, but the Word Shines (2 Peter 1:19-21)

In some respects, the world is getting better. I thank God for the advances in medicine, transportation, and communication. I can speak to more people in one radio program than the Apostles preached to in their entire lifetimes. I can write books that can be spread abroad and even translated into different languages. In areas of scientific achievement, the world has made great progress. But the human heart is still wicked, and all of our improvements in means have not improved our lives. Medical science enables people to live longer, but there is no guarantee they will live

better. Modern means of communication only enable lies to travel faster! And jet planes enable us to get places faster, but we do not have better places to go!

We should not be surprised that our world is engulfed in spiritual darkness. In the Sermon on the Mount our Lord warned that there would be counterfeits who would invade the church with their false doctrines (Matt. 7:13-29). Paul gave a similar warning to the elders of Ephesus (Acts 20:28-35), and he gave further warnings when he wrote his epistles (Rom. 16:17-20; 2 Cor. 11:1-15; Gal. 1:1-9; Phil. 3:17-21; Col. 2; 1 Tim. 4; 2 Tim. 3-4). Even John, the great "apostle of love," warned about antichristian teachers who would seek to destroy the church (1 John 2:18-29; 4:1-6).

In other words, the Apostles did not expect the world to get better and better either morally or spiritually. They all warned the church that false teachers would invade the local churches, introduce false doctrines, and lead many people astray. The world would get darker and darker; but as it did, the Word of God would shine brighter and brighter.

Peter made three affirmations about this Word.

*It is the sure Word (v. 19a).* Peter was not suggesting that the Bible is more certain than the experience he had on the Mount of Transfiguration. His experience was real and true, and the record in the Bible is dependable. As we have seen, the Transfiguration was a demonstration of the promise given in the prophetic Word; and this promise now has added certainty because of what Peter experienced. The Transfiguration experience corroborated the prophetic promises. The apostates would attempt to discredit the promise of His coming (2 Peter 3:3ff), but the Scriptures were sure. For, after all, the promise of the kingdom was reaffirmed by Moses, Elijah, the Son of God, and the Father! And the Holy Spirit wrote the record for the church to read!

"The testimony of the Lord is sure" (Ps. 19:7). "Thy testimonies are very sure" (Ps. 93:5). "All His commandments are sure" (Ps. 111:7). "Therefore I esteem all Thy precepts concerning all things to be right; and I hate every false way" (Ps. 119:128).

It is interesting to put together 2 Peter 1:16 and 19: "For we have not followed cunningly devised fables. . . . We have also a more sure word of prophecy." As I travel, I often meet zealous cultists in airports, all of whom want me to buy their books. I always refuse because I have the sure Word of God and have no need for the religious fables of men. " 'What is the chaff to the wheat?' saith the Lord" (Jer. 23:28).

But one day I found one of those books, left behind in the men's room, so I decided to take it with me and read it. How anybody could believe such foolish fables is more than I can understand. The book claimed to be based on the Bible, but the writer so twisted the Scriptures that the verses quoted ended up meaning only what he wanted them to mean. Cunningly devised fables! Yet there was spiritual death between those covers to anyone who would believe those lies.

***It is the shining Word (v. 19b).*** Peter called the world "a dark place," and the word he used means "murky." It is the picture of a dank cellar or a dismal swamp. Human history began in a lovely Garden, but that Garden today is a murky swamp. What you see when you look at this world system is an indication of the spiritual condition of your heart. We still see beauty in God's creation, but we see no beauty in what mankind is doing with God's creation. Peter did not see this world as a Garden of Eden, nor should we.

God is light and His Word is light. "Thy Word is a lamp unto my feet, and a light unto my path" (Ps. 119:105). When Jesus Christ began His ministry, "the people which sat in darkness saw great light" (Matt. 4:16). His coming into this world was the dawning of a new day (Luke 1:78). We Christians are the light of the world (Matt. 5:14-16), and it is our privilege and responsibility to hold forth the Word of life—God's light—so that men might see the way and be saved (Phil. 2:14-16).

As believers, we must heed this Word and govern our lives by what it says. For unbelievers, things will get darker and darker, until they end up in eternal darkness; but God's people are looking for the return of Jesus Christ and the dawning of the new day of glory. The false teachers scoffed at the idea of Christ's return and the dawning of a new day, but Peter affirmed the truth of the sure Word of God. "But the Day of the Lord will come as a thief in the night" (2 Peter 3:10).

Before the day dawns, the "day star" (or morning star) shines brightly as the herald of the dawn. To the church, Jesus Christ is "the Bright and Morning Star" (Rev. 22:16). The promise of His coming shines brightly, no matter how dark the day may be (see Num. 24:17). He is also the "Sun of Righteousness," who will bring healing to believers but judgment to unbelievers (Mal. 4:1-2). How thankful we ought to be for God's sure and shining Word, and how we ought to heed it in these dark days!

***It is the Spirit-given Word (vv. 20-21).*** This is one of two important Scriptures affirming the divine inspiration of the Word of God. The other is 2 Timothy 3:14-17. Peter affirmed that the Scriptures were not written by men who used their own ideas and words, but by men of God who were "moved by the Holy Spirit." The word translated *moved* means "to be carried along, as a ship is carried by the wind." The Scriptures are "God-breathed"; they are not the inventions of men.

Again, Peter was refuting the doctrines of the apostates. They taught with "feigned words" (2 Peter 2:3) and twisted the Scriptures to make them mean something else (2 Peter 3:16). They denied the promise of Christ's coming (2 Peter 3:3-4), and thus denied the very prophetic Scriptures.

Since the Spirit gave the Word, only the Spirit can teach the Word and interpret it accurately (see 1 Cor. 2:14-15). Of course, every false teacher claims that he is "led by the Spirit," but his handling of the Word of God soon exposes him. Since the Bible did not come by the will of man, it cannot be understood by the will of man. Even religious Nicodemus, a leading teacher among the Jews, was ignorant of the most essential doctrines of the Word of God (John 3:10-12).

In 2 Peter 1:20, Peter was not prohibiting the private study of the Bible. Some religious groups have taught that only the "spiritual leaders" may interpret Scripture, and they have used this verse as their defense. But Peter was not writing primarily about the interpretation of Scripture, but the origin of Scripture: it came by the Holy Spirit through holy men of God. And since it came by the Spirit, it must be taught by the Spirit.

The word translated "private" simply means "one's own" or "its own." The suggestion is, since all Scripture is inspired by the Spirit it must all "hang together" and no one Scripture should be divorced from the others. You can use the Bible to prove almost anything if you isolate verses from their proper context, which is exactly the approach the false teachers use. Peter stated that the witness of the Apostles confirmed the witness of the prophetic Word; there is one message with no contradiction. Therefore, the only way these false teachers can "prove" their heretical doctrines is by misusing the Word of God. Isolated texts, apart from contexts, become pretexts.

The Word of God was written to common people, not to theological professors. The writers assumed that common people could read it, understand it, and apply it, led by the same Holy Spirit who inspired it. The humble individual believer can learn about God as he reads and meditates on the Word of God; he does not need the "experts" to show him truth. However, this does not deny the ministry of teachers in the church (Eph. 4:11), special people who have a gift for explaining and applying the Scriptures. Nor does it deny the "collective wisdom" of the church as, over the ages, these doctrines have been defined and refined. Teachers and creeds have their place, but they must not usurp the authority of the Word over the conscience of the individual believer.

Until the day dawns, we must be sure that the love for His coming is like a shining star in our hearts (2 Peter 1:19). Unless we love His appearing, we will not look for His appearing; and it is the Word that keeps that expectation bright.

Men die, but the Word lives. Experiences fade, but the Word remains. The world grows darker, but the prophetic light shines brighter. The believer who builds his life on the Word of God and who looks for the coming of the Saviour is not likely to be led astray by false teachers. He will be taught by the Spirit and grounded on the sure Word of God.

Peter's message is, "Wake up—and remember!" A sleeping church is the devil's playground. It is while men slept that the enemy came in and sowed the tares (Matt. 13:24ff).

"Be alert!" is the Apostle's message. "Wake up and remember!"

# CHAPTER THREE
# BEWARE OF COUNTERFEITS
## *2 Peter 2:1-9*

One of the most successful rackets in the world today is that of selling "fake art." Even some of the finest galleries and private collections have been invaded by paintings that are clever counterfeits of the great masters. Publishers have also had their share of hoaxes, purchasing "genuine" manuscripts that weren't so genuine after all.

But counterfeits are nothing new. Satan is the "great imitator" (2 Cor. 11:13-15), and he has been hard at work ever since he deceived Eve in the Garden (Gen. 3:1-7; 2 Cor. 11:1-4). He has false Christians (Matt. 13:38; John 8:44), a false gospel (Gal. 1:6-9), and even a false righteousness (Rom. 9:30–10:4). One day, he will present to the world a false Christ (2 Thes. 2).

The nation Israel was constantly being led astray by false prophets. Elijah had to contend with the prophets of Baal, but they promoted a pagan religion. It was the *Jewish* false prophets who did the most damage, for they claimed to speak for Jehovah God. Both Jeremiah and Ezekiel exposed this counterfeit ministry, but the people followed the pseudo-prophets just the same. Why? Because the religion of the false prophets was easy, comfortable, and popular. The fact that the false prophets preached a false peace did not worry the people (Jer. 6:14). That was the message they wanted to hear!

The Apostles and prophets laid the foundation for the church and then passed from the scene (Eph. 2:20). This is why Peter wrote about false *teachers,* rather than false prophets, because there are still teachers in the church. It is not likely that church members would listen to a "prophet," but they would listen to a teacher of the Word. Satan always uses the approach that will succeed.

In order to warn us to be alert, Peter presented three aspects of this subject of false teachers in the church.

### The False Teachers Described
### (2 Peter 2:1-3)

This is not a very pretty picture! When you read the Epistle of Jude, you will find him using similar language, and vivid language it is. Peter knew that the truth of God's Word and the false doctrines of the heretics simply could not coexist. There could be no compromise on his part, any more than a surgeon could compromise with a cancerous tumor in a patient's body.

*Deception (v. 1a).* This theme runs throughout the entire chapter. To begin with, these teachers' message is false; Peter called what they taught "destructive heresies." The word *heresy* originally meant simply "to make a choice," but then it came to mean "a sect, a party." Promoting a party spirit in a church is one of the works of the flesh (Gal. 5:20). Whenever a church member says to another member, "Are you on my side or the pastor's side?" he is promoting a party spirit and causing division. A false teacher forces you to make a choice between his doctrines and the doctrines of the true Christian faith.

Not only was their message false, but their methods were false. Instead of openly declaring what they believed, they came into the church under false colors and gave the impression that they were true to the Christian faith. "They secretly bring in alongside" is the literal translation. They do not throw out the truth immediately; they simply lay their false teachings alongside the truth and give the impression that they believe the fundamentals of the faith. Before long, they remove the true doctrine and leave their false doctrine in its place.

In 2 Peter 2:3, Peter pointed out that the false teachers used "feigned words." The Greek word is *plastos,* from which we get our English word *plastic.* Plastic words! Words that can be twisted to mean anything you want them to mean! The false teachers use our vocabulary, but they do not use our dictionary. They talk about "salvation," "inspiration," and the great words of the Christian faith, but they do not mean what we mean. Immature and untaught believers hear these preachers or read their books and think that these men are sound in the faith, but they are not.

Satan is a liar and his ministers are liars. They use the Bible, not to enlighten, but to deceive. They follow the same pattern Satan followed when he deceived Eve (Gen. 3:1-6).

First, he questioned God's Word—"Yea, hath God said?" Then he denied God's Word—"Ye shall not surely die." Finally, he substituted his own lie—"Ye shall be as gods."

Keep in mind that these apostate teachers are not innocently ignorant of the Word, as was Apollos (Acts 18:24-28). They know the truth but they deliberately reject it. I read about a liberal pastor who was asked to read a paper at a ministerial conference on "Paul's views of justification." He read a paper that superbly presented the truth of the Gospel and justification by faith.

"I didn't know you believed that," a friend said to him after the meeting.

"I don't believe it," the liberal pastor replied. "They didn't ask me for *my* views of justification. They asked for Paul's!"

*Denial (v. 1b).* False teachers are better known for what they deny than what they affirm. They deny the inspiration of the Bible, the sinfulness of man, the sacrificial death of Jesus Christ on the cross, salvation by faith alone, and even the reality of eternal judgment. They especially deny the deity of Jesus Christ, for they know that if they can do away with His deity they can destroy the entire body of Christian truth. Christianity is Christ, and if He is not what He claims to be, there is no Christian faith.

It must be made clear that these false teachers are unsaved. They are compared to dogs and pigs, not to sheep (2 Peter 2:22). Jude describes these same people, and in Jude 19 he clearly states, "having not the Spirit." If a person does not have the Spirit of God within, he is not a child of God (Rom. 8:9). He may pretend to be saved and even become a member or an officer in a fundamental church, but eventually he will deny the Lord.

In what sense were these people "bought" by the Lord? While it is true that Jesus Christ died for the church (Eph. 5:25), it is also true that He died for the sins of the whole world (1 John 2:2). He is the merchant who purchased the whole field (the world) that He might acquire the treasure in it (Matt. 13:44). When it comes to *application,* our Lord's atonement is limited to those who believe. But when it comes to *efficacy,* His death is sufficient for the whole world. He purchased even those who reject Him and deny Him! This makes their condemnation even greater.

Even good and godly Christians may disagree on fine points of doctrine, but they all agree on the person and work of Jesus Christ.

He is the Son of God and God the Son. He is the only Saviour. To deny this is to condemn your own soul.

**Sensuality (v. 2).** *Pernicious ways* simply means "licentious conduct." Jude accused the false teachers of "turning the grace of God into lasciviousness" (Jude 4). Now we understand why they deny the truths of the Christian faith: they want to satisfy their own lusts and do it under the guise of religion. The false prophets in Jeremiah's day were guilty of the same sins (Jer. 23:14, 32).

The fact that *many* follow the evil example of their conduct is proof that people would rather follow the false than the true, the sensual rather than the spiritual. These false teachers are very successful in their ministry! They have glowing statistics to report and crowds gather to hear them! But statistics are not proof of authenticity. The broad way that leads to destruction is crowded (Matt. 7:13-14). Many will claim to be true servants of Christ, but will be rejected on the last day (Matt. 7:21-23).

What happens to their followers? For one thing, they bring disgrace to the name of Christ. The Christian faith gets a bad name because of their filthy lives. "They profess that they know God; but in works they deny Him, being abominable, and disobedient, and unto every good work reprobate" (Titus 1:16). "For the name of God is blasphemed among the Gentiles through you" (Rom. 2:24). Few things hinder the cause of Christ like the bad reputations of professing Christians who are members of orthodox churches.

**Greed (v. 3).** False teachers are interested in one thing: making money. They exploit ("make merchandise of") ignorant people and use their religion as "a cloak of covetousness" (1 Thes. 2:5). Our Lord was a poor Man, and so were the Apostles; yet they gave of themselves to minister to others. These false prophets are rich men who cleverly get others to minister to them! Micah described these false prophets in his day: "Her leaders pronounce judgment for a bribe, her priests instruct for a price, and her prophets divine for money" (Micah 3:11, NASB). Certainly the laborer is worthy of his hire (Luke 10:7), but his motives for ministry had better go beyond money. It has often been said that immorality, love of money, and pride have been the ruin of many people. These false teachers were guilty of all three!

They use their "plastic words" as well as "great swelling words" (2 Peter 2:18) to fascinate and influence their victims. They flatter sinners and tell them the kind of ego-building words that they want to hear (see the contrast in 1 Thes. 2:5). They will scratch the itching ears of people who reject the truth of the Bible and turn to fables (2 Tim. 4:1-4). Religion can be a tremendous tool for exploiting weak people, and these false teachers use religion just to get what they can. They are not ministers; they are merchandisers.

The true minister of Jesus Christ has nothing to hide: his life and ministry are an open book. He preaches the truth in love and does not twist the Scriptures to support his own selfish ideas. He does not flatter the rich or minister only to make money. Paul described the true minister in 2 Corinthians 4:2—"But [we] have renounced the hidden things of dishonesty, not walking in craftiness, nor handling the Word of God deceitfully; but by manifestation of the truth commending ourselves to every man's conscience in the sight of God." Contrast that description with what Peter wrote in this chapter, and with what Jude wrote, and you will see the difference. How we need to be alert and refuse to support ministries that exploit people and deny the Saviour.

## The False Teachers Destroyed (2 Peter 2:3-6, 9b)

Peter saw no hope for these apostates; their doom was sealed. His attitude was different from that of "tolerant" religious people today who say, "Well, they may not agree with us, but there are many roads to heaven." Peter made it clear that these false teachers had "forsaken the right way" (2 Peter 2:15), which simply means they were going the *wrong* way! Their judgment was sure, even though it had not yet come. The trial was over, but the sentence had not yet been executed. It would not linger or slumber, Peter affirmed; it would come in due time.

In this section, Peter proved that judgment finally does come, no matter how secure the sinner might feel. He used three examples to verify this truth (see also Jude 6-8).

**The fallen angels (v. 4).** We wish we knew more about the creation of the angels and the fall of Lucifer and his host, but most of these details are shrouded in mystery. Many Bible students believe that Isaiah 14:12-15 describes the fall of Lucifer, the highest of the angels. Some students feel that Ezekiel 28:11-

19 also deals with the same topic. It would appear that Lucifer was God's deputy, in charge of the angelic hosts, but that his pride made him grasp after the very throne of God. (John Milton imaginatively portrayed this in the famous poem, *Paradise Lost.*) Revelation 12:4 suggests that perhaps one third of the angels fell with Lucifer, who became Satan, the adversary of God.

Where are these fallen angels now? We know that Satan is free and at work in the world (1 Peter 5:8), and that he has an army of demonic powers assisting him (Eph. 6:10-12), who are probably some of the fallen angels. But Peter said that some of the angels were confined to Tartarus ("hell"), which is a Greek word for the underworld. Tartarus may be a special section of hell where these angels are chained in pits of darkness, awaiting the final judgment. It is not necessary to debate the hidden mysteries of this verse in order to get the main message: God judges rebellion and will not spare those who reject His will. If God judged the angels, who in many respects are higher than men, then certainly He will judge rebellious men.

**The old world (v. 5).** Genesis 6:3 indicates that God waited 120 years before He sent the Flood. All during that time, Noah ministered as a "herald" of God's righteousness. If you want to read a description of the world before the Flood, read Romans 1:18ff. Gentile civilization had become so corrupt that it was necessary for God to wipe the earth clean. He saved only eight people, Noah and his family, because they had faith in God (Heb. 11:7).

But nobody believed Noah's message! Jesus made it clear that people were enjoying their normal lives up to the very day that Noah and his family entered the ark! (Luke 17:26-27) No doubt there were plenty of "experts" who laughed at Noah and assured the people that a rainstorm was out of the question. Had anybody ever seen one? The apostates in Peter's day used that same argument to "prove" that the Day of the Lord would not come (2 Peter 3:3ff).

When you compare our world with Noah's world, you see some frightening parallels. The population was multiplying (Gen. 6:1), and the world was filled with wickedness (Gen. 6:5) and violence (Gen. 6:11, 13). Lawlessness abounded. True believers were a minority, and nobody paid any attention to them! But the Flood came and the entire population of the world was destroyed. God does indeed judge those who reject His truth.

***Sodom and Gomorrah (vv. 6, 9b).*** The record is given in Genesis 18–19, and God's opinion of the people of these cities is found in Genesis 13:13—"But the men of Sodom were wicked and sinners before the Lord exceedingly." Peter said they were "ungodly," and Jude said they were given to "fornication and going after strange flesh" (Jude 7). The men of Sodom practiced filthy behavior and unlawful deeds (2 Peter 2:7-8). Since the Law of Moses had not yet been given, the word *unlawful* cannot refer to some Jewish law. In what sense were their filthy deeds "unlawful"? They were contrary to nature (see Rom. 1:24-27). The flagrant sin of Sodom and the other cities was unnatural sex, sodomy, or homosexual behavior, a sin that is clearly condemned in Scripture (Lev. 18:22; Rom. 1:24-27; 1 Cor. 6:9).

In spite of Abraham's intercessory prayer (Gen. 18:22ff) and Lot's last minute warning, the people of Sodom perished in fire and brimstone. Again, up to the very minute that Lot left the city, the people were confident that everything was safe; but then the fire fell (Luke 17:28-29). God did not spare them, nor will He spare sinners today who willfully reject His truth and deny His Son. God buried Sodom and Gomorrah, probably under the Dead Sea. They are examples to sinners today to beware the wrath to come.

Having cited these three examples of certain judgment, Peter then applied the lesson to the subject at hand, *the false teachers* (2 Peter 2:9b). God has reserved the unjust for special punishment on that day of judgment. The false teachers may seem successful (for "many" follow them), but in the end, they will be condemned. Their judgment is being prepared now ("lingereth not," 2 Peter 2:3), and what is prepared will be reserved and applied on the last day.

What a contrast between the false teachers and the true children of God! We have an inheritance reserved for us (1 Peter 1:4) because Jesus Christ is preparing a home for us in heaven (John 14:1-6). We are not looking for judgment, but for the coming of the Lord to take His people home to glory! "For God hath not appointed us to wrath, but to obtain salvation by our Lord Jesus Christ" (1 Thes. 5:9).

Peter next turned his attention to the believers themselves. How could they stay true to the Lord in such a wicked world?

## The True Believers Delivered
## (2 Peter 2:5-9a)

Peter's purpose was not just to denounce the apostates; he also wanted to encourage the true believers. He once again reached back into the Old Testament and cited two examples of deliverance.

*Noah (v. 5).* This man of faith experienced a twofold deliverance. First, God delivered him from the pollutions of the world around him. For 120 years, Noah faithfully proclaimed the Word of God to people who would not believe it. He and his family were surrounded by moral and spiritual darkness, yet they kept their lights shining. God did not protect Noah and his family by isolating them from the world, but by enabling them to remain pure in the midst of corruption. Through Jesus Christ, we too have "escaped the corruption that is in the world through lust" (2 Peter 1:4).

Our Lord petitioned the Heavenly Father, "I pray not that Thou shouldest take them out of the world, but that Thou shouldest keep them from the evil" (John 17:15). Imagine Noah and his wife raising a family in a world so wicked that they could have no believing friends! Yet God found believing wives for their three sons, and God guarded this home from the pollutions of the world.

But God also delivered Noah and his family from the judgment of the world. The flood waters that brought condemnation to the world only lifted Noah and his household up above the judgment. They were secure in the ark of safety. In his first epistle, Peter had seen in the ark a type of our salvation in Jesus Christ (1 Peter 3:20-22). The world, as it were, was "buried" in the baptism of the Flood, but Noah was lifted up, a picture of resurrection and salvation.

Certainly Peter was assuring his readers that, when the great day of judgment does come, they will be kept safe. Jesus Christ is our "ark of safety." He delivers us from the wrath to come (1 Thes. 1:10). God has promised that the earth will never again be judged by water, but there is coming a judgment of fire (2 Peter 3:10ff). But those who have trusted Christ will never face judgment (John 5:24), because He bore their judgment on the cross.

*Lot (vv. 6-9a).* Abraham took his nephew, Lot, with him when he left Ur and went to the land of Canaan, but Lot proved to be more of a problem than a blessing. When Abraham, in a lapse of faith, went down to Egypt, Lot went with him and got a taste of "the world" (Gen. 12:10–13:1). As Lot became richer, he had to separate from Abraham, and this removed him from his uncle's godly influence. What a privilege Lot had to walk with Abraham who walked with God! And yet, how Lot wasted his privileges.

When Lot had to choose a new area for his home, he measured it by what he had seen in Egypt (Gen. 13:10). Abraham took Lot out of Egypt, but he could not take Egypt out of Lot. Lot "pitched his tent toward Sodom" (Gen. 13:12), and then finally moved into Sodom (Gen. 14:12). God even used a local war to try to get Lot out of Sodom, but he went right back. That is where his heart was.

It is difficult for us to understand Lot. Peter made it clear that Lot was saved ("just Lot . . . that righteous man"), and yet we wonder what he was doing in such a wicked place as Sodom. If we understand Genesis 19 correctly, Lot had at least four daughters, two of whom had married men of Sodom. All the while Lot lived in Sodom, his soul was "tortured" and "greatly troubled" by the filthy conduct of the people. Perhaps he thought he could change them. If so, he failed miserably.

God enabled Lot and his family to remain unpolluted, even though they were living in the midst of a cesspool of iniquity. God also rescued Lot and two of his daughters before the judgment fell on Sodom and the other cities of the plain (Gen. 19). Lot was not rescued because of any merit on his part. He was rescued because he was a believer and because his Uncle Abraham had prayed for him. Abraham outside of Sodom had more influence than Lot inside the city. Lot even lost his testimony to his own family, for his married daughters and their husbands laughed at his warning, and his wife disobeyed God and was killed.

Lot *chose* to live in Sodom and could have avoided the filthy influence of the place, but many people today really have no choice and must live surrounded by the pollutions of the world. Think of the Christian slaves who had to serve godless masters, or Christian wives married to unsaved husbands, or believing children with unsaved parents. Christian employees working in offices or factories are forced to see and hear things that can easily stain the mind and heart. Peter assured his readers and us that God knows how to "be delivering the godly out of testing and temptation" (2 Peter 2:9, WUEST) so that we may live victoriously.

He also is able to rescue us from judgment. In Noah's case, it was a judgment of water, but in Lot's case it was a judgment of fire. The cities of the plain were caught in a violent overthrow as the area became a vast furnace of fire and brimstone. This certainly would parallel Peter's warning about the coming judgment of fire (2 Peter 3:10ff).

Peter was not pointing to Lot as an example of separated living, but rather as an example of one whom God rescued from pollution and condemnation. In a sense, Lot was even rescued against his will, because the angels had to grasp him by the hand and pull him out of the city (Gen. 19:16). Lot had entered Sodom, and then Sodom had entered Lot, and he found it difficult to leave.

Our Lord used both Noah and Lot to warn us to be prepared for His return (Luke 17:26-37). The people in Sodom were enjoying their regular pleasures, careless of the fact that judgment was coming; when it came, they were unprepared. "Wherefore, beloved, seeing that ye look for such things, be diligent that ye may be found of Him in peace, without spot, and blameless" (1 Peter 3:14).

But the same God who delivers the godly also reserves the ungodly for judgment. It has well been said that if God spares today's cities from judgment, He will have to apologize to Sodom and Gomorrah. Why is God's judgment lingering? Because God "is long-suffering . . . not willing that any should perish, but that all should come to repentance" (2 Peter 3:9). Society in Noah's day had 120 years in which to repent and believe, yet they rejected the truth. Though Lot's example and testimony were weak, he at least represented the truth; yet his immoral neighbors wanted nothing to do with God.

Our present age is not only like "the days of Noah," but it is also like "the days of Lot." Many believers have abandoned the place of separation and are compromising with the world. The professing church has but a weak testimony to the world and sinners do not really believe that judgment is coming. Society is full of immorality, especially the kind of sin for which Sodom was famous. It appears as though God is slumbering, unconcerned about the way rebellious sinners have polluted His world. But one day the fire will fall; then it will be too late.

God's people, as weak as they are, will be delivered from judgment by the grace and mercy of God. God could not judge Sodom until Lot and his family were out of the city. Likewise, it is my belief that God will not send wrath on this world until He takes His own people out and home to heaven. "For God hath not appointed us to wrath, but to obtain salvation by our Lord Jesus Christ, who died for us, that, whether we wake or sleep [live or die], we should live together with Him" (1 Thes. 5:9-10).

One day soon, the fire will fall. Are you ready?

# CHAPTER FOUR
# MARKED MEN
## *2 Peter 2:10-16*

Peter is not yet finished with the apostates! Unlike some believers today, Peter was disturbed by the inroads the false teachers were making into the churches. He knew that their approach was subtle but their teachings were fatal, and he wanted to warn the churches about them.

Remember, however, that Peter opened this letter with positive teaching about salvation, Christian growth, and the dependability of the Word of God. He had a balanced ministry, and it is important that we maintain that balance today. When Charles Spurgeon started his magazine, he named it *The Sword and Trowel,* alluding to the workers in the Book of Nehemiah, who kept their swords in one hand and their tools in the other as they were repairing the walls of Jerusalem.

Some people have a purely negative ministry and never build anything. They are too busy fighting the enemy! Others claim to be "positive," but they never defend what they have built. Peter knew that it was not enough only to attack the apostates; he also had to give solid teaching to the believers in the churches.

In this section of his letter, Peter condemned the apostates for three specific sins.

**Their Reviling (2 Peter 2:10-12)**
The picture here is of proud people who try to build themselves up while they try to tear down everybody else. They show no respect

for authority and are not afraid to attack and defame people in high positions.

God has established authority in this world, and when we resist authority, we are resisting God (Rom. 13:1ff). Parents are to have authority over their children (Eph. 6:1-4) and employers over their employees (Eph. 6:5-8). As citizens, we Christians should pray for those in authority (1 Tim. 2:1-4), show respect to them (1 Peter 2:11-17), and seek to glorify God in our behavior. As members of a local assembly, we should honor those who have the spiritual rule over us and seek to encourage them in their ministry (Heb. 13:7, 17; 1 Peter 5:1-6).

Human government is, in one sense, God's gift to help maintain order in the world, so that the church may minister the Word and win the lost to Christ (1 Tim. 2:1-8). We should pray daily for those in authority so that they might exercise that authority in the will of God. It is a serious thing for a Christian to oppose the law, and he must be sure he is in the will of God when he does it. He should also do it in a manner that glorifies Christ, so that innocent people (including unsaved government employees) might not be made to suffer.

**The reason for their reviling (v. 10).** One word gives the reason: *flesh.* The depraved nature of man does not want to submit to any kind of authority. "Do your own thing!" is its insistent message, and many people follow it. In recent years, there has been an epidemic of books that encourage people to succeed at any cost, even to the extent of hurting or intimidating others. The important thing, according to these books, is to take care of yourself—"number one"—and to use other people as tools for the achievement of your own selfish goals.

Man's fallen nature encourages pride. When the ego is at stake, these apostates will stop at nothing in order to promote and protect themselves. Their attitude is completely opposite that of our Lord who willingly emptied Himself to become a servant, and then died as a sacrifice for our sins (see Phil. 2). These men that Peter described were *presumptuous,* which means they were "very daring and bold" in the way they spoke about those in positions of dignity. There is a boldness that is heroic, but there is also a boldness that is satanic.

These men were also *self-willed,* which means they "lived to please only themselves." They were arrogant and would even defy God

to get what they wanted! Proverbs 21:24 describes them perfectly. While outwardly, they appeared to serve God and minister to the people, *inwardly* they fed their own egos and feathered their own nests.

In their arrogance, "they are not afraid to speak evil of dignities [glorious ones]." While the immediate reference is probably to "exalted ones" in places of authority, the angels may also be in view here, since in the next verse Peter referred to the angels. These apostates revile even the angels! And they do not even tremble when they do it! They are so secure in their pride, that they even dare God to judge them.

**The seriousness of their reviling (v. 11).** The angels are reviled by the apostates, but the apostates are not reviled by the angels! Even the angels, though greater in strength and power, will not intrude into a sphere that is not their own. The angels remember the rebellion of Lucifer and know how serious it is to revolt against God's authority. If God judged the rebellious angels, how much more will He judge rebellious men!

The suggestion here is that the godly angels do not even speak against the *fallen* angels. They have left all judgment to the Lord. We will learn more about this when we study Jude, for he mentions this matter of the angels in Jude 8-9.

Speaking evil of others is a great sin, and the people of God must avoid it. We may not respect the people in office, but we must respect the office, for all authority is God-given. Those who revile government officials in the name of Christ ought to read and ponder Titus 3:1-2—"Remind them to be subject to rulers, to authorities, to be obedient, to be ready for every good deed, to malign no one, to be uncontentious, gentle, showing every consideration for all men" (NASB).

When Daniel refused the king's food, he did it in a gracious way that did not get his guard into trouble (Dan. 1). Even when the Apostles refused to obey the Sanhedrin's order that they stop preaching in the name of Jesus, they acted like gentlemen. They respected the authority even though they disobeyed the order. It is when the flesh goes to work that pride enters in, and then we use our tongues as weapons instead of tools. "The words of his mouth are iniquity and deceit: he hath left off to be wise, and to do good" (Ps. 36:3).

**The judgment of their reviling (v. 12).** Peter compared these false teachers to "unreasoning animals" (NASB) whose only destiny is to be slaughtered! At the end of this chapter, they are pictured as pigs and dogs! Animals have life, but they live purely by instinct. They lack the finer sensibilities that humans possess. Jesus warned us not to waste precious things on unappreciative brute beasts (Matt. 7:6).

I once made a pastoral visit at a home where a death had occurred, and even before I made it up the stairs to the door, a huge dog began to bark and carry on as though I were there to rob everybody. I ignored his threats because I knew he was acting purely on instinct. He was making a lot of noise about something he knew nothing about! His master had to take him to the basement before it was safe for me to enter the home and minister to the bereaved family.

So with these apostates: they make a lot of noise about things they know nothing about! The Phillips translation of 2 Peter 2:12 says they "scoff at things outside their own experience." The *New International Version* reads, "But these men blaspheme in matters they do not understand." Whenever her pupils were noisy in class, one of my teachers used to say, "Empty barrels make the most noise!" And so they do!

It is sad when the media concentrates on the "big mouths" of the false teachers instead of the "still small voice" of the Lord as He ministers through those who are true to Him. It is sadder still when innocent people become fascinated by these "great swelling words of vanity" (2 Peter 2:18) and cannot discern between truth and propaganda. The truth of the Word of God leads to salvation, but the arrogant words of the apostates lead only to condemnation.

These "brute beasts" are destined for destruction, a truth Peter mentioned often in 2 Peter 2 (vv. 3-4, 9, 12, 17, 20). As they seek to destroy the faith, they themselves shall be destroyed. They will be "corrupted in their own corruption." Their very nature will drag them down into destruction, like the pig returning to the mire and the dog to its vomit (2 Peter 2:22). Unfortunately, before that event takes place, these people can do a great deal of moral and spiritual damage.

### Their Reveling (2 Peter 2:13-14a)

The words translated "riot" and "sporting" carry the meaning of "sensual reveling." They also contain the idea of luxury, softness, and extravagance. At the expense of those who support them (2 Peter 2:3), the apostates enjoy luxurious living. In our own society, there are those who plead for funds for their "ministries," yet live in expensive houses, drive luxury cars, and wear costly clothes. When we remember that Jesus became poor in order to make us rich, their garish lifestyle seems out of step with New Testament Christianity.

Not only do they deceive others, but they even deceive themselves! They can "prove" from the Bible that their lifestyle is right. In ancient times, it was expected that people would revel at night, but these people dared to revel in the daytime, so convinced were they of their practices. A person can become so accustomed to his vices that he sees them as virtues.

If they kept their way of life out of the church, we would not have to be as concerned—but they are a part of the fellowship! They were even sharing in the "love feasts" that the early church used to enjoy in connection with the celebration of the Lord's Supper (1 Cor. 11:20-34). It was a time when the poorer believers could enjoy a decent meal because of the generosity of the Christians who were better off economically. But the apostates only used the "love feast" as a time for displaying their wealth and impressing ignorant people who lacked discernment.

Instead of bringing blessing to the fellowship, these false teachers were "spots" and "blemishes" that defiled the assembly. Somehow their behavior at the feasts defiled others and brought disgrace to the name of the Lord. It is the Word of God that helps to remove the spots and blemishes (Eph. 5:27), but these teachers do not minister the truth of the Word. They twist Scripture to make it say what they want it to say (2 Peter 3:16).

This "unconscious defilement" is a deadly thing. The Pharisees were also guilty of it (Matt. 23:25-28). False doctrine inevitably leads to false living, and false living then encourages false doctrine. The apostate must "adjust" God's Word or change his way of life, and he is not about to change his lifestyle! So, wherever he goes, he secretly defiles people and makes it easier for them to sin. It is possible to go to a church fellowship and be defiled!

Certainly our churches need to exercise authority and practice discipline. Christian love does not mean that we tolerate every false doctrine and every so-called "lifestyle." The

Bible makes it clear that some things are right and some things are wrong. No Christian whose belief and behavior are contrary to the Word of God should be permitted to share in the Lord's Supper or to have a spiritual ministry in the church. His defiling influence may not be seen immediately, but ultimately it will create serious problems.

Second Peter 2:14 makes it clear that the apostates attend these church meetings for two reasons: first, to satisfy their own lusts; second, to capture converts for their cause.

They keep their eyes open, looking for "loose women" whom they can entice into sin. Paul warned about similar apostates who "creep into houses and lead captive silly women laden with sins, led away with divers lusts" (2 Tim. 3:6). More than one "minister" has used religion as a cloak to cover his own lusts. Some women, in particular, are vulnerable in "counseling sessions," and these men take advantage of them.

In one of the churches I pastored, I noticed that a young man in the choir was doing his utmost to appear a "spiritual giant" to the other choir members, especially the younger women. He prayed with fervency and often talked about his walk with the Lord. Some of the people were impressed by him, but I felt that something was wrong and that danger was in the air. Sure enough, he began to date one of the fine young ladies who happened to be a new believer. In spite of my warnings, she continued the friendship, which ended in her being seduced. I praise God that she was rescued and is now faithfully serving God, but she could have avoided that terrible experience.

The satisfying of their lusts is the false teachers' main ambition: they *cannot cease from sin*. The verb suggests "they are unable to stop." Why? Because they are in bondage (2 Peter 2:18-19). The apostates consider themselves to be "free," yet they are in the most terrible kind of slavery. Whatever they touch, they defile; whoever they enlist, they enslave.

"Beguiling unstable souls" presents the picture of a fisherman baiting a hook or a hunter baiting a trap. The same image is used in James 1:14 where James presents temptation as "the baiting of the trap." Satan knows that he could never trap us unless there is some fine bait to attract us in the first place. Satan promised Eve that she and Adam would become "like gods" if they ate of the forbidden

tree (Gen. 3:4-5), and they "took the bait" and were trapped.

What kind of "bait" do the apostates use to catch people? For one thing, they offer them "liberty" (2 Peter 2:19). This probably means a perversion of the grace of God, "turning the grace of our God into lasciviousness" (Jude 4). "Since you are saved by grace," they argued, "then you have the freedom to sin. The more you sin, the more of God's grace you will experience!" Paul answered their false arguments in Romans 6, a portion of Scripture that every believer ought to master.

Along with "freedom" they also bait the trap with "fulfillment." This is one of the "buzz words" of our generation, and it goes right along with "doing your own thing" and "having it your way." They say, "The Christian life that the church offers is old-fashioned and outdated. We have a new lifestyle that makes you feel fulfilled and helps you find your true self!" Alas, like the prodigal son, these unstable souls try to find themselves, but they end up *losing* themselves (Luke 15:11-24). In their search for fulfillment they become very self-centered and lose the opportunities for growth that come from serving others.

There can be no freedom or fulfillment apart from submission to Jesus Christ. "The purpose of life," said P.T. Forsyth, "is not to find your freedom, but to find your master." Just as a gifted musician finds freedom and fulfillment putting himself or herself under the discipline of a great artist, or an athlete under the discipline of a great coach, so the believer finds true freedom and fulfillment under the authority of Jesus Christ.

Who are the people who "take the bait" that the apostates put into their subtle traps? Peter called them "unstable souls." Stability is an important factor in a successful Christian life. Just as a child must learn to stand before he can walk or run, so the Christian must learn to "stand firm in the Lord." Paul and the other Apostles sought to establish their converts in the faith (Rom. 1:11; 16:25; 1 Thes. 3:2, 13). Peter was certain that his readers were "established in the present truth" (2 Peter 1:12), but he still warned them.

### Their Revolting (2 Peter 2:14b-16)

"They have abandoned the right road" is the way the Phillips translation expresses it. The apostates know the right road, the straight path that God has established, but they deliberately abandon God's way for their own. No wonder Peter called them "natural brute beasts" (2 Peter 2:12) and compared them to animals (2 Peter 2:22). "Be ye not as the horse, or as the mule!" warned the psalmist (Ps. 32:9). The horse likes to rush ahead and the mule likes to lag behind; both can get you off the right path. Believers are sheep, and sheep need to stay close to the shepherd or they will stray.

We have already learned one reason for the apostates' godless conduct: they want to satisfy the cravings of their flesh. But there is a second reason: they are covetous and want to exploit people for personal gain. Peter mentioned this in 2 Peter 2:3 and now develops the thought. Not only is the false teacher's outlook controlled by his passions (2 Peter 2:14a), but his heart is controlled by covetousness. He is in bondage to lust for pleasure and money!

In fact, he has perfected the skill of getting what he wants. "They are experts in greed" says the *New International Version*, and the Phillips translation is even more graphic: "Their technique of getting what they want is, through long practice, highly developed." They know exactly how to motivate people to give. While the true servant of God trusts the Father to meet his needs and seeks to help people grow through their giving, the apostate trusts his "fund-raising skills" and leaves people in worse shape than he found them. He knows how to exploit the unstable and the innocent.

There is certainly nothing wrong with a ministry sharing its opportunities and needs with its praying friends. My wife and I receive many publications and letters of this kind, and, quite frankly, some of them we throw away without reading. We have learned that these ministries cannot be trusted, that their dramatic appeals are not always based on fact, and that the funds donated are not always used as they should be. The other letters and publications we read carefully, pray about, discuss, and see if God would have us invest in their work. We know we cannot support every good work that God has raised up, so we try to exercise discernment, and invest in the ministries God has chosen for us.

As Peter wrote about the devious practices of these people, he could only exclaim, "Cursed children!" They were not the "blessed" children of God but the cursed children of the devil (John 8:44). They might succeed in building up their bank accounts, but in the end, at the throne of God, they would be declared bankrupt. "Depart from me, ye cursed, into everlasting fire, prepared for the devil and his angels" (Matt. 25:41). "For what is a man profited, if he shall gain the whole world, and lose his own soul?" (Matt. 16:26)

Covetousness is the insatiable desire for more—more money, more power, more prestige. The covetous heart is never satisfied. This explains why the love of money is a root of all kinds of evil (1 Tim. 6:10), for when a person craves more money, he will commit any sin to satisfy that craving. He has already broken the first two of the Ten Commandments, because money is already his god and idol. It is then a simple step to break the others—to steal, lie, commit adultery, take God's name in vain, and so on. No wonder Jesus warned, "Take heed and beware of covetousness" (Luke 12:15).

I have read that the people in North Africa have devised a clever way to catch monkeys. They make a hole in a gourd just large enough for the monkey's paw, then fill the gourd with nuts and tie it to a tree. At night, the monkey reaches into the gourd for the nuts, only to find he cannot pull his paw out of the gourd! Of course, he could let go of the nuts and escape quite easily—but he doesn't want to forfeit the nuts! He ends up being captured because of his covetousness. We might expect this kind of stupidity in a dumb animal, but certainly not in a person made in the image of God; yet it happens every day.

Peter knew his Old Testament Scriptures. He had already used Noah and Lot to illustrate his words, and in 2 Peter 2:15-16, he used the Prophet Balaam. The story of Balaam is found in Numbers 22–25; take time now to read it.

Balaam is a mysterious character, a Gentile prophet who tried to curse the Jews. Balak, the king of the Moabites, was afraid of Israel, so he turned to Balaam for help. Balaam knew it was wrong to cooperate with Balak, but his heart was covetous and he wanted the money and honor that Balak promised him. Balaam knew the truth of God and the will of God, yet he deliberately abandoned the right way and went astray. He is a perfect illustration of the apostates in their covetous practices.

From the outset, God told Balaam not to help Balak and, at first, Balaam obeyed and sent the messengers home. But when Balak sent more princes and promised more money and honor, Balaam decided to "pray about it again" and reconsider the matter. The second time, God tested Balaam and permitted him to go with the princes. This was not God's direct will; it was His permissive will, designed to see what the prophet would do.

Balaam jumped at the chance! But when he started to go astray, God rebuked the disobedient prophet through the mouth of his donkey. How remarkable that the animals obey God, even when their masters do not! (read Isa. 1:3) God permitted Balaam to set up his altars and offer his sacrifices, but God did not permit him to curse Israel. Instead, God turned Balaam's curse into a blessing (Deut. 23:4-5; Neh. 13:2).

Balaam was not able to curse Israel, but he was able to tell Balak how to defeat Israel. All the Moabites had to do was invite the Jews to be "friendly neighbors" and share in their feasts (Num. 25). Instead of maintaining its separated position, Israel compromised and joined the pagan orgies of the Moabites. God had to discipline the people and thousands of them died.

You can see in Balaam the two aspects of apostasy that Peter emphasized in this chapter: sensual lust and covetousness. He loved money and he led Israel into lustful sin. He was a man who could get messages from God, yet he led people away from God! When you read his oracles, you cannot help but be impressed with his eloquence; yet he deliberately disobeyed God! Balaam said, "I have sinned" (Num. 22:34), but his confession was not sincere. He even prayed, "Let me die the death of the righteous" (Num. 23:10), yet he did not want to live the life of the righteous.

Because Balaam counseled Balak to seduce Israel, God saw to it that Balaam was judged. He was slain by the sword when Israel defeated the Midianites (Num. 31:8). We wonder who received all the wealth that he had "earned" by his devious ways. Peter called his hire "the wages of unrighteousness." This phrase reminds us of another pretender, Judas, who received "the reward of iniquity" (Acts 1:18), and who also perished in shame.

We will have more to say about Balaam when we study Jude 11, but we must not ignore the main lesson: he was a rebel against the will of God. Like the false teachers that Peter described, Balaam knew the right way, but deliberately chose the wrong way because he wanted to make money. He kept "playing with the will of God" by trying to get "a different viewpoint" (Num. 22:41; 23:13, 27). He no doubt had a true gift from God because he

uttered some beautiful prophecies about Jesus Christ, but he prostituted that gift to base uses just to gain honor and wealth.

A bank officer approached a junior clerk and secretly asked, "If I gave you $50,000, would you help me alter the books?"

"Yes, I guess I would," the man replied.

"Would you do it for $100?"

"Of course not!" the man said. "What do you think I am, a common thief?"

"We've already determined that," said the officer. "Now we're talking about price."

The person who is covetous does have his price, and when it is met, he will do whatever is asked, even revolt against the will of God. Peter called this attitude *madness*. The word means "to be deranged, out of your mind." But Balaam thought he was doing the wise thing; after all, he was taking advantage of a situation that might never come along again. But any rebellion against God is madness and can only lead to tragedy. It was when the prodigal son "came to himself" that he realized how stupid he had been (Luke 15:17).

Peter has condemned three sins of the false teachers: their reviling, their reveling, and their revolting. All of these sins spring from pride and selfish desire. A true servant of God is humble and seeks to serve others (see the contrast in Phil. 2:20-21). The true servant of God does not think about praise or pay, because he serves God from a loving and obedient heart. He honors God and the authority that God has established in this world. In short, the true servant of God patterns himself after Jesus Christ.

In these last days there will be an abundance of false teachers pleading for support. They are gifted and experienced when it comes to deceiving people and getting their money. It is important that God's people be established in the truth, that they know how to detect when the Scriptures are being twisted and the people exploited. I thank God for agencies that help to expose "religious rackets," but there is still the need for spiritual discernment and a growing knowledge of the Word of God.

Not all of these "religious frauds" will be discovered and put out of business. But God will one day deal with all of them! Like animals, they will be "taken and destroyed" (2 Peter 2:12). They will receive "the reward of unrighteousness" (2 Peter 2:13) to compensate for the wages they have exploited from others. As "cursed children" (2 Peter 2:14) they will be banished from the presence of the Lord forever.

They are marked men and women; they will not escape.

# CHAPTER FIVE
# FALSE FREEDOM
*2 Peter 2:17-22*

It is a frightening fact that many people who are now zealous members of cults were at one time attending churches that at least professed to believe the Christian Gospel. They participated in the Communion service and saw the death of the Lord Jesus portrayed in the loaf and the cup. They even recited the Apostles' Creed and the Lord's Prayer. Yet today, these people will tell you that they "feel free" now that they have been "liberated" from the Christian faith.

At the same time, you will meet people who have rejected all religious faith and now profess to enjoy a new freedom. "I used to believe that stuff," they will boldly confess, "but I don't believe it anymore. I've got something better and I feel free for the first time in my life."

*Freedom* is a concept that is very important in today's world, yet not everybody really understands what the word means. In fact, everybody from the Communist to the "playboy" seems to have his own definition. Nobody is completely free in the sense of having the ability and the opportunity to do whatever he wants to do. For that matter, doing whatever you please is *not* freedom—it is the worst kind of bondage.

The apostates offer freedom to their converts, and this "bait" entices them to abandon the true faith and follow the false teachers. The teachers promise them liberty, but this promise is never fulfilled; the unstable converts only find themselves in terrible bondage. The freedom offered is a *false* freedom, and Peter gave three reasons that explain why it is false.

## It Is Based on False Promises
### (2 Peter 2:17-18)
Faith is only as good as the object. A pagan may have great faith in his idol, but the idol

can do nothing for him. I have a friend who put his faith in a certain investment scheme and lost almost everything. His faith was strong but the company was weak. When you put your faith in Jesus Christ, that faith will accomplish something, because God always keeps His promises. "There hath not failed one word of all His good promise" (1 Kings 8:56).

Peter uses three vivid illustrations to emphasize the emptiness of the apostates' promises.

*"Wells without water" (v. 17a).* The Greek word actually means "a flowing spring" rather than a tranquil well. It is the word our Lord used when He ministered to the Samaritan woman (John 4:14) and that John used in describing the satisfaction the saints will experience for all eternity (Rev. 7:17; 21:6). A spring without water is not a spring at all! A well is still called a well even if the water is gone, but a spring ceases to exist if the water is not flowing.

There is in mankind an inborn thirst for reality, for God. "Thou hast made us for Thyself," said Augustine, "and our hearts are restless until they rest in Thee." People attempt to satisfy this thirst in many ways, and they end up living on substitutes. Only Jesus Christ can give inner peace and satisfaction.

"Whosoever drinketh [present tense, "keeps on drinking"] of this water [in the well] shall thirst again," said Jesus, "but whosoever drinketh [takes one drink once and for all] of the water that I shall give him shall never thirst" (John 4:13-14). What a contrast! You may drink repeatedly at the broken cisterns of the world and never find satisfaction, but you may take one drink of the Living Water through faith in Jesus Christ, and you will be satisfied forever. The false teachers could not make this kind of an offer, because they had nothing to offer. They could promise, but they could not produce.

*"Clouds that are carried with a tempest" (v. 17b).* The picture is that of clouds of fog or mist being driven by a squall over a lake or sea. Clouds ought to announce the possibility of rain, but these clouds only announce that a windstorm is coming. Jude's description is, "Clouds they are without water, carried about of winds" (Jude 12). Again, there is noise, motion, and something to watch, but nothing profitable happens. The farmer sees the clouds and prays they will empty rain on his parched fields. The false

teachers have nothing to give; they are empty.

***"The mist of darkness" (v. 17c-18).***
The word translated "mist" means "blackness, gloom," so "the blackness of the darkness" would be an accurate translation (see 2 Peter 2:4). These apostates promise to lead people into the light, but they themselves end up in the darkest part of the darkness! (see Jude 6 and 13) The atmosphere of hell is not uniform: some places will be darker than others. How tragic that innocent people will be led astray by these apostates and possibly end up in hell with them.

Since these false teachers really have nothing to give, how are they able to attract followers? The reasons are found in 2 Peter 2:18.

First, the teachers are eloquent promoters of their doctrines. They know how to impress people with their vocabulary, "inflated words that say nothing" (literal translation). The average person does not know how to listen to and analyze the kind of propaganda that pours out of the mouths and printing presses of the apostates. Many people cannot tell the difference between a religious huckster and a sincere servant of Jesus Christ.

Do not be impressed with religious oratory. Apollos was a fervent and eloquent religious speaker, but he did not know the right message to preach (Acts 18:24-28). Paul was careful not to build his converts' faith on either his words or his wisdom (1 Cor. 2:1-5). Paul was a brilliant man, but his ministry was simple and practical. He preached to *express* and not to *impress*. He knew the difference between *communication* and *manipulation*.

The second reason the apostates are so successful is that they appeal to the base appetites of the old nature. This is part of their bait! (2 Peter 2:14) We must not think of "the lusts of the flesh" only in terms of sexual sins, for the flesh has other appetites. Read the list given in Galatians 5:19-21 and you will see the many different kinds of "bait" the apostates have available for baiting their traps.

For example, *pride* is one of the sins of the flesh, and apostate teachers like to appeal to the human ego. A true servant of God will lovingly tell people that they are lost sinners, under the wrath of a holy God, but the apostate minister will try to avoid "putting people on a guilt trip." He will tell his listeners how good they are, how much God loves them *and needs them* and how easy it is to get into the

family of God. In fact, he may tell them they are already in God's family and just need to start living like it! The apostate avoids talking about repentance, because egotistical men do not want to repent.

The third reason they are successful is that they appeal to immature people, people who have "very recently escaped" from their old ways. The apostate has no message for the down-and-out sinner, but he does have a message for the new believer.

A pastor friend of mine was assisting some missionaries in the Philippines by conducting open-air meetings near the university. Students who wanted to decide for Christ were asked to step into a building near the square, and there they were counseled and also given follow-up material to help them get started in their Christian life.

No sooner did a new convert walk out the door and past the crowd than a cultist would join him and start to introduce his own religion! All the apostates had to do was look for the people carrying follow-up material! This same procedure is often used in large evangelistic crusades: the false teachers are ready to pounce on new believers carrying decision packets.

This is why it is important that soul-winners, pastors, and other Christian workers ground new converts in the faith. Like newborn babies, new Christians need to be protected, fed, and established before they can be turned loose in this dangerous world. One reason Peter wrote this letter was to warn the church to care for the new Christians, because the false teachers were out to get them! We cannot blame new believers for being "unstable" (2 Peter 2:14) if we have not taught them how to stand.

The freedom the apostates offer is a false freedom because it is based on false promises. There is a second reason why it is false.

### It Is Offered by False Christians (2 Peter 2:19-20)
You cannot set someone free if you are in bondage yourself, and these false teachers were in bondage. Peter made it clear that these men had temporarily disentangled themselves from the pollutions of the world, but then they went right back into bondage again! They professed to be saved but had never really been redeemed (set free) at all!

The tenses of the verbs in 2 Peter 2:19 are present: "While they *promise* them [the new believers] liberty, they themselves [the apostates] *are* the servants of corruption" (italics mine). They claim to be the servants of God, but they are only the servants of sin. It is bad enough to be a slave, but when sin is your master, you are in the worst possible condition a person can experience.

As you review what Peter has written so far, you can see the kinds of sins that enslave the false teachers. For one thing, they were in bondage to money (2 Peter 2:3, 14). Their covetousness forced them to use every kind of deceptive technique to exploit innocent people. They were also in bondage to fleshly lust (2 Peter 2:10, 14). They had their eyes on weak women whom they could seduce. (In view of what Peter and Jude wrote about Sodom and Gomorrah, perhaps we should also include weak men and boys.)

They were also enslaved by pride (2 Peter 2:10-12). They thought nothing of speaking evil of those in places of authority, including the angels and God! They promoted themselves and derided everybody else. Sad to say, there are people who admire this kind of arrogance, who follow these proud men and support them.

It is interesting to compare the three men Peter named in this chapter—Noah, Lot, and Balaam. Noah kept himself completely separated from the apostasy of the world of his day. He boldly preached God's righteousness and was faithful in his walk and witness, even though no one but his family followed the Lord.

Lot knew the truth and kept himself pure, but he did not keep himself separated; he lost his family as a result. Lot hated the wickedness of Sodom, yet he lived in the midst of it and, by doing so, exposed his daughters and wife to godless influences.

Balaam not only followed the ways of sin, but he encouraged other people to sin! He told Balak how to seduce the nation Israel and his plan almost succeeded. Lot lost his family, but Balaam lost his life.

Beware of "the deceitfulness of sin" (Heb. 3:13). Sin always promises freedom but in the end brings bondage. It promises life but instead brings death. Sin has a way of gradually binding a person until there is no way of escape, apart from the gracious intervention of the Lord. Even the bondage that sin creates is deceitful, for the people who are bound actually think they are free! Too late they discover that they are prisoners of their own appetites and habits.

Jesus Christ came to bring freedom. In His first sermon in the synagogue at Nazareth, our Lord sounded forth the trumpet call of freedom and the advent of the "Year of Jubilee" (Luke 4:16ff). But Christ's *meaning* of freedom is different from the apostates' as is His method for accomplishing it.

In the Bible, freedom does not mean "doing your own thing" or "having it your way." That attitude is the very essence of sin. The freedom that Jesus Christ offers means *enjoying fulfillment in the will of God*. It means achieving your greatest potential to the glory of God. The Quaker leader Rufus Jones, paraphrasing Aristotle, said, "The true nature of a thing is the highest that it can become." Jesus Christ frees us to become our very best in this life, and then to be like Him in the next.

The apostates brought their followers into bondage by means of lies, but our Lord brings us into freedom by means of truth. "And ye shall know the truth, and the truth shall make you free" (John 8:32). He was speaking, of course, about the truth of the Word of God. "Sanctify them through Thy truth," He prayed; "Thy Word is truth" (John 17:17). Through the Word of God, we discover the truth about ourselves, our world, and our God. As we face this truth honestly, we experience the liberating power of the Spirit of God. We cease living in a world of fantasy and enter a world of reality, and through the power of God, we are able to fulfill His will, grow in grace, and "reign in life by one, Jesus Christ" (Rom. 5:17).

Those who live by God's truth enter into more and more freedom, but those who live by lies experience more and more bondage, until "the latter end is worse with them than the beginning" (2 Peter 2:20). This reminds us of our Lord's parable in Matthew 12:43-45, the truth of which parallels what Peter has written. *Temporary reformation without true repentance and rebirth only leads to greater sin and judgment.* Reformation cleans up the outside, but regeneration changes the inside.

Sinful tendencies do not disappear when a person reforms; they merely hibernate *and get stronger.* Holiness is not simply refusing to do evil things, for even unsaved people can practice self-control. True holiness is more than conquering temptation: it is conquering even *the desire* to disobey God. When my doctor told me to lose weight, he said, "I'll tell you how to do it: learn to hate the things that aren't good for you." His advice worked!

You can expect nothing but "false freedom" from false Christians who offer false promises. But there is a third reason why this freedom is false.

### It Involves a False Experience
### (2 Peter 2:21-22)

Peter called these apostates "natural brute beasts" (2 Peter 2:12), and then ended the warning by describing them as pigs and dogs! But he was not simply showing his personal disdain for them; rather, he was teaching a basic spiritual lesson.

It is very important that we understand that the pronoun *they* in this entire paragraph (2 Peter 2:17-22) refers to the false teachers and not to their converts. It is also important that we remember that these teachers are not truly born-again people. Jude described these same people in his letter and stated clearly that they were "sensual, having not the Spirit" (Jude 19). It is not *profession* of spirituality that marks a true believer but *possession* of the Spirit of God within (Rom. 8:9).

But these apostates did have a "religious experience"! And they would boldly claim that their experience brought them into fellowship with the Lord. They would be able to explain "the way of righteousness," and would use the Word of God to support their teachings. If they had not experienced some kind of "religious conversion," they would never have been able to get into the fellowship of the local assemblies.

But their experience, like their promises, was false.

Since Peter wrote both of his letters to the same group of believers we may assume that they had the doctrinal foundation presented so clearly in his first letter. Peter emphasized the new birth (1 Peter 1:3, 22-25). He reminded his readers that they were "partakers of the divine nature" (2 Peter 1:4). In his first letter, Peter described the believers as sheep (1 Peter 2:25; 5:1-4). Our Lord used this same image when He reinstated Peter into the apostleship after his denials (John 21:15-17).

There is no indication that the false teachers had ever experienced the new birth. They had *knowledge* of salvation and could use the language of the church, but they lacked that true saving experience with the Lord. At one time they had even received the Word of God (2 Peter 2:21), but then they turned away from it. *They never trusted Christ and became His sheep.*

Instead of being sheep, they were pigs and dogs—and keep in mind that the dogs in that day were not pampered pets! The Jews called the Gentiles "dogs" because a dog was nothing but a filthy scavenger who lived on garbage! It was hardly a title of respect and endearment!

These men could point to "an experience," but it was a *false* experience. Satan is the counterfeiter. We have already seen that Satan has a false gospel (Gal. 1:6-9), preached by false ministers (2 Cor. 11:13-15), producing false Christians (2 Cor. 11:26—"in perils among false brethren"). In His Parable of the Tares, our Lord taught that Satan plants his counterfeits ("the children of the wicked one") wherever God plants true believers (Matt. 13:24-30, 36-43).

What kind of "experience" did these false teachers have? To use Peter's vivid images, the pig was washed on the outside, but remained a pig; the dog was "cleaned up" on the inside, but remained a dog. The pig *looked* better and the dog *felt* better, but neither one had been changed. They each had the same old nature, not a new one.

This explains why both animals returned to the old life: it was part of their nature. A pig can stay clean only a short time and then must head for the nearest mudhole. We do not condemn a pig for acting like a pig because it has a pig's nature. If we saw *a sheep* heading for the mire, we would be concerned!

When I was a youngster, one of our neighbors owned a scrubby black mutt with the imaginative name of "Blackie." He had the habit of eating what dogs should not eat, and then regurgitating somewhere in the neighborhood, usually on our sidewalk. But that was not all. Blackie would then return to the scene of the crime and start all over again! Apparently dogs have been doing this for centuries, for Solomon mentioned it in Proverbs 26:11, the text that Peter quoted.

Certainly the dog feels better after emptying his stomach, *but it is still a dog.* "Having an experience" did not change his nature. Quite the contrary, it only gave further evidence of his "dog nature," because he came back and (just like a dog) lapped up his own vomit. It is a disgusting picture, but that is exactly the response Peter wanted to produce.

In my ministry, I have met people who have told me about their "spiritual experiences," but in their narratives I detected no evidence of a new nature. Like the sow, some of them were cleaned up on the outside. Like the dog, some of them were cleaned up temporarily on the inside and actually felt better. But in no case had they become "partakers of the divine nature" (2 Peter 1:4). They thought they were free from their problems and sins, when really they were still in bondage to an old sinful nature.

According to 2 Peter 2:20, these apostates "escaped the pollutions of the world." Pollution is defilement on the outside. But true believers have "escaped the corruption that is in the world through [because of] lust" (2 Peter 1:4). Corruption is much deeper than defilement on the outside: it is decay on the inside. True believers have received a new nature, a divine nature, and they have new and different appetites and desires. They have been transformed from pigs and dogs into sheep!

Imagine the disappointment of the person who thinks he has been delivered, only to discover that, in the end, he is in worse shape than when he started! The apostates promise freedom, but all they can give is bondage. True freedom must come from within; it has to do with the inner nature of the person. Because the true nature of a thing is the highest that it can become, a pig and dog can never rise higher than *Sus scrofa* and *Canis familiaris*.

I realize that there are some who believe that these apostate teachers were true believers who, in turning from the knowledge of Christ, forfeited their salvation. Even a casual reading of 2 Peter 2 and Jude would convince the impartial reader that these teachers never had a true experience of salvation through faith in Jesus Christ. Peter would never have compared them to swine and dogs had they once been members of the Lord's true flock, nor would he have called them "cursed children" (2 Peter 2:14). If they were true believers who had gone astray, it would have been Peter's responsibility to encourage his readers to rescue these backsliders (James 5:19-20), but Peter did not command them to do so. Instead, he condemned the apostates in some of the most forceful language found in the New Testament!

Now we better understand why this "freedom" offered by these teachers is a *false* freedom, a "freedom" that only leads to bondage. It is based on false promises, empty words that sound exciting but that have no divine authority behind them. It is offered by false Christians who were involved in a false experience. From start to finish, this "freedom" is the product of our adversary, the devil!

Now we can appreciate Peter's admonition in 2 Peter 1:10—"Wherefore the rather, brethren, give diligence to make your calling and election sure." In other words, "Has your spiritual experience been genuine?" It is a startling fact that there are many people in our churches who have never truly been born again, but who are convinced that they are saved and going to heaven! They have had "an experience," and perhaps look better (like the sow) and feel better (like the dog), but they have not been *made better* as "partakers of the divine nature."

Perhaps Peter recalled Judas, one of the Twelve, who was a tool of the devil and was never born again. Up to the very end, the other disciples did not know the truth about Judas and thought he was a spiritual man!

The apostates appear to have successful ministries, but in the end, they are bound to fail.

The important thing is that you and I have the assurance of a true experience with the Lord, and that we have nothing to do with these counterfeit ministries, no matter how popular they may be.

Christ is "the truth" (John 14:6) and following Him leads to freedom. The apostates are liars and following them leads to bondage. There can be no middle ground!

# CHAPTER SIX
# SCOFFING AT THE SCOFFERS
*2 Peter 3:1-10*

"Everybody is ignorant," said Will Rogers, "only on different subjects."

How true, and yet that is not the whole story because there is more than one kind of ignorance. Some people are ignorant because of lack of opportunity to learn, or perhaps lack of ability to learn; others are (to use Peter's phrase in 2 Peter 3:5) "willingly . . . ignorant." "Not ignorance, but ignorance of ignorance, is the death of knowledge," said a famous philosopher, and he is right.

Peter has dealt with the character and conduct of the apostates in 2 Peter 2, and now he deals with their false teaching. Peter affirmed the certainty of Christ's coming in glory (2 Peter 1:16ff), a truth that the apostates questioned and denied. In fact, they were scoffing at the very idea of the return of the Lord, the judgment of the world, and the establishment of a glorious kingdom.

How important it is for us as Christians to understand God's truth! Today we are surrounded by scoffers, people who refuse to take the Bible seriously when it speaks about Christ's return and the certainty of judgment. In this paragraph, Peter admonished his readers to understand three important facts about God and the promise of Christ's coming.

## God's Word Is True (2 Peter 3:1-4)

It is possible to have a pure and sincere mind and yet have a bad memory! Peter wrote this second letter primarily to awaken and arouse his readers (2 Peter 1:12-15). It is easy for Christians to "get accustomed to God's truth." Eutychus went to sleep listening to Paul preach! (Acts 20:7-10) Our Heavenly Father sacrificed so that we might have the truth of the Word and the freedom to practice it, but too often we take this for granted and become complacent. The church needs to be aroused regularly lest the enemy find us asleep and take advantage of our spiritual lethargy.

Because God's Word is true, we must pay attention to it and take its message seriously. New converts must be taught the Word and established in the doctrines of the faith, for new Christians are the apostate teacher's primary targets. But older Christians must also be reminded of the importance of Bible doctrine and, in particular, the doctrines that relate to the return of Christ. Prophetic teaching must not lull us to sleep. Rather, it must awaken us to live godly lives and to seek to win the lost (Rom. 13:11-14).

What the Bible teaches about the Day of the Lord was not invented by the Apostles. The prophets taught it and so did our Lord Jesus Christ (2 Peter 3:2). Peter emphasized the *unity* of the Word of God. When the scoffers denied "the power and coming" of Jesus Christ, they were denying the truth of the prophetic books, the teaching of our Lord in the Gospels, and the writing of the Apostles! Like our Lord's seamless garment, the Scriptures cannot be cut apart without ruining the whole.

As far back as the days of Enoch, God warned that judgment was coming (Jude 14-15). Many of the Hebrew prophets announced the Day of the Lord and warned that the world would be judged (Isa. 2:10-22; 13:6-16; Jer. 30:7; Dan. 12:1; Joel; Amos 5:18-20; Zeph.; Zech. 12:1–14:3). This period of judgment is also known as "the time of Jacob's trouble" (Jer. 30:7) and the Tribulation.

Our Lord taught about this day of judgment in His sermon on the Mount of Olives (Matt. 24–25). Paul discussed it in 1 Thessalonians 5 and 2 Thessalonians 1–2. The Apostle John described this terrible day in Revelation 6–19. It will be a time when God's wrath will be poured out on the nations, and when Satan will be free to give vent to his anger and malice. It will culminate with the return of Jesus Christ in glory and victory.

While I do not make it a test of fellowship or spirituality, I personally believe that the people of God will be taken to heaven *before* this "great and terrible day" dawns.

I think we should carefully distinguish the various "days" mentioned in the Bible. "The Day of the Lord" is that day of judgment that climaxes with the return of Christ to the earth. "The Day of God" (2 Peter 3:12) is the period when God's people enjoy the new heavens and the new earth, when all evil has been judged (1 Cor. 15:28). "The Day of Christ" relates to the coming of Christ for His church (1 Cor. 1:7-9; Phil. 1:10; 2:16).

Prophetic students seem to fall into three categories: those who believe the church will be raptured ("caught up together," 1 Thes. 4:13ff) *before* the Day of the Lord; those who see this event taking place *in the middle of* the Day of the Lord, so that the church experiences the first half of the Tribulation; and those who believe the church will be raptured when the Lord returns *at the Tribulation's close.* There are good and godly people in each group and our differences of interpretation must not create problems in fellowship or in sharing Christian love.

Not only does the Word of God predict the coming Day of the Lord, but it also predicts the appearance of the very scoffers who deny that Word! Their presence is proof that the Word they deny is the true Word of God! We should not be surprised at the presence of these apostate mockers (see Acts 20:28-31; 1 Tim. 4; 2 Tim. 3).

A scoffer is someone who treats lightly that which ought to be taken seriously. The people in Noah's day scoffed at the idea of a judgment, and the citizens of Sodom scoffed at the possibility of fire and brimstone destroying their sinful city. If you have tried at all to witness for Jesus Christ, you have no doubt met people who scoff at the idea of hell or a future day of judgment for this world.

Why do these apostates scoff? Because they want to continue living in their sins. Peter made it clear that false teachers cultivate "the lust of uncleanness" (2 Peter 2:10) and allure weak people by means of "the lusts of the flesh" (2 Peter 2:18). If your lifestyle contradicts the Word of God, you must either change your lifestyle or change the Word of God. The apostates choose the latter approach, so they scoff at the doctrines of judgment and the coming of the Lord.

What is their argument? The uniformity of the world. "Nothing cataclysmic has happened in the past," they argue, "so there is no reason to believe it will happen in the future." They take the "scientific approach" by examining evidence, applying reason, and drawing a conclusion. The fact that they *willfully ignore* a good deal of evidence does not seem to disturb them.

The scientific approach works admirably in matters that relate to the material universe, but you cannot take Bible prophecy into a laboratory and treat it as though it were another hypothesis. For that matter, the so-called "laws of science" are really only educated conclusions based on a limited number of experiments and tests. These laws are generalizations, always subject to change, because no scientist can perform an infinite number of experiments to prove his claim. Nor can he completely control all the factors involved in the experiments and in his own thinking.

The Word of God is still "a light that shineth in a dark [squalid] place" (2 Peter 1:19). We can trust it. No matter what the scoffers may claim, God's day of judgment will come on the world, and Jesus Christ shall return to establish His glorious kingdom.

### God's Work Is Consistent
### (2 Peter 3:5-7)

How did Peter refute the foolish argument of the apostate scoffers? "God does not interrupt the operation of His stable creation!" they argued. "The promise of Christ's coming is not true!" All Peter did was remind them of what God had done in the past and thus prove that His work is consistent throughout the ages. Peter simply presented evidence that the false teachers *deliberately* ignored. It is amazing how so-called "thinkers" (scientists, liberal theologians, philosophers) will be *selective* and deliberately refuse to consider certain data.

Peter cited two events in history to prove his point: the work of God at Creation (2 Peter 3:5), and the flood in Noah's day (2 Peter 3:6).

God created the heavens and the earth by His word. The phrase "and God said" occurs nine times in Genesis 1. "For He spake, and it was done; He commanded, and it stood fast" (Ps. 33:9). Not only was Creation *made* by the word of God, but it was *held together* by that same word. Kenneth Wuest translates 2 Peter 3:5 to bring out this subtle meaning: "For concerning this they willfully forget that heavens existed from ancient times, and land [standing] out of water, and by means of water cohering by the word of God."

Peter's argument is obvious: the same God who created the world by His word can also intervene in His world and do whatever He wishes to do! It is His word that made it and that holds it together, and His word is all-powerful.

The second event Peter cited was Noah's flood (2 Peter 3:6). He had already referred to the Flood as an illustration of divine judgment (2 Peter 2:5), so there was no need to go into detail. The Flood was a cataclysmic event; in fact, the Greek word translated "overflowed" gives us our English word *cataclysm*. The people living on earth had probably never seen a rainstorm or the fountains of the deep broken up, but these events happened just the same. Their "scientists" could have argued as the scoffers argued, "Everything goes on as it did from the beginning. Life is uniform so nothing unusual can happen." But it happened!

God has the power to "break in" at any time and accomplish His will. He can send rain from heaven or fire from heaven. "But our God is in the heavens: He hath done whatsoever He hath pleased" (Ps. 115:3).

Having established the fact that God has in the past "interrupted" the course of history, Peter was then ready for his application in 2 Peter 2:7. The same word that created and sustains the world is now holding it together, stored with fire, being preserved and reserved for that future day of judgment. God promised that there would be no more floods to destroy the world (Gen. 9:8-17). The next judgment will be a judgment of fire.

The phrase "stored with fire" used by Kenneth Wuest ("reserved unto fire," KJV) sounds very modern. Modern atomic science has revealed that the elements that make up the world are stored with power. There is enough atomic energy in a glass of water to run a huge ocean liner. Man has discovered this great power and, as a result, the world seems to teeter on the brink of atomic destruction. However, Peter seems to indicate that *man* will not destroy the world by his sinful abuse of atomic energy. It is *God* who will "push the button" at the right time and burn up the old creation and all the works of sinful man with it; then He will usher in the new heavens and earth and reign in glory.

Everything in God's original creation was good. It is man's sin that has turned a good creation into a *groaning* creation (Rom. 8:18-22). God could not permit sinful man to live in a perfect environment, so He had to curse the ground because of man (Gen. 3:14-19). Since that time, man has been busy polluting and destroying God's creation. For years, it appeared that this exploitation would not cause too much trouble, but now we are changing our minds. The balance of nature has been upset; valuable resources have been wasted; the supply of energy is running down; and civilization is facing a crisis. The prophets of doom today are not only preachers and evangelists, but also sociologists, ecologists, and atomic scientists.

Peter proved his point: God is able to intervene in the course of history. He did it in the past and He is able to do it again. The Day of the Lord that was promised by the prophets and Apostles, as well as by Jesus Christ, will come just as surely as the Flood came in Noah's day and the fire and brimstone came to destroy Sodom and Gomorrah.

But the scoffers had their argument ready: "Then why the delay?" The promise of Christ's coming and the judgment of the world has been around for centuries, and it is yet to be fulfilled. Has God changed His mind? The world today is certainly ripe for judgment! Thus, Peter's third fact.

**God's Will Is Merciful (2 Peter 3:8-10)**
Once again, Peter exposed the ignorance of the scoffers. Not only were they ignorant of

what God had done in the past (2 Peter 3:5), but they were also ignorant of what God was like. They were making God in their own image and ignoring the fact that God is eternal. This means that He has neither beginning nor ending. Man is immortal: he has a beginning but not an ending. He will live forever either in heaven or hell. But God is eternal, without beginning or ending, and He dwells in eternity. Eternity is not just "extended time." Rather, it is existence *above and apart from time.*

Peter was certainly referring to Psalm 90:4—"For a thousand years in Thy sight are but as yesterday when it is past, and as a watch in the night." Isaac Watts used Psalm 90 as the basis for the familiar hymn, "O God, Our Help in Ages Past."

A thousand ages, in Thy sight
Are like an evening gone;
Short as the watch that ends the night,
Before the rising sun.

Since a thousand years are as one day to the Lord, we cannot accuse Him of delayed fulfillment of His promises. In God's sight, the whole universe is only a few days old! He is not limited by time the way we are, nor does He measure it according to man's standards. When you study the works of God, especially in the Old Testament, you can see that He is never in a hurry, but He is never late.

He could have created the entire universe in an instant, yet He preferred to do it over a period of six days. He could have delivered Israel from Egypt in a moment, yet He preferred to invest eighty years in training Moses. For that matter, He could have sent the Saviour much sooner, but He waited until "the fullness of the time was come" (Gal. 4:4). While God works *in* time, He is not limited *by* time.

To God, a thousand years is as one day, and one day as a thousand years. God can accomplish in one day what it would take others a millennium to accomplish! He waits to work, but once He begins to work, He gets things done!

The scoffers did not understand God's eternality nor did they understand His mercy. Why was God delaying the return of Christ and the coming of the Day of the Lord? It was not because He was *unable* to act or *unwilling* to act. He was not tardy or off schedule! Nobody on earth has the right to decide when

God must act. God is sovereign in all things and does not need prodding or even counsel from sinful man (Rom. 11:33-36).

God delays the coming of Christ and the great day of fiery judgment because He is long-suffering and wants to give lost sinners the opportunity to be saved. "And account that the long-suffering of our Lord is salvation" (2 Peter 3:15).

God's "delay" is actually an indication that He has a plan for this world and that He is working His plan. There should be no question in anybody's mind whether God *wants* sinners to be saved. God "is not willing that any should perish" (2 Peter 3:9). First Timothy 2:4 affirms that God "will have all men to be saved, and to come unto the knowledge of the truth." These verses give both the negative and the positive, and together they assure us that God has no pleasure in the death of the wicked (Ezek. 18:23, 32; 33:11). He shows His mercy to all (Rom. 11:32) even though not all will be saved.

It is worth noting that God revealed this same long-suffering in the years before the Flood (1 Peter 3:20). He saw the violence and wickedness of man and could have judged the world immediately; yet He held back His wrath and, instead, sent Noah as a "preacher of righteousness." In the case of Sodom and Gomorrah, God patiently waited while Abraham interceded for the cities and He would have spared them had He found ten righteous people in Sodom.

If God is long-suffering toward lost sinners, why did Peter write, "The Lord . . . is long-suffering to us-ward"? Who is meant by "us-ward"? It would appear that God is long-suffering *to His own people!*

Perhaps Peter was using the word *us* in a general way, meaning "mankind." But it is more likely that he was referring to his readers as the elect of God (1 Peter 1:2; 2 Peter 1:10). God is long-suffering toward lost sinners because some of them *will* believe and become a part of God's elect people. We do not know who God's elect are among the unsaved people of the world, nor are we supposed to know. Our task is to make our *own* "calling and election sure" (2 Peter 1:10; cf. Luke 13:23-30). The fact that God has His elect people is an encouragement to us to share the Good News and seek to win others to Christ.

God was even long-suffering toward the scoffers of that day! They needed to repent and He was willing to save them. This is the only place where Peter used the word *repentance* in either of his letters, but that does not minimize its importance. To repent simply means "to change one's mind." It is not "regret," which usually means "being sorry I got caught." Nor is it "remorse," which is a hopeless attitude that can lead to despair.

Repentance is a change of mind that results in an action of the will. If the sinner honestly changes his mind about sin, he will turn from it. If he sincerely changes his mind about Jesus Christ, he will turn to Him, trust Him, and be saved. "Repentance toward God, and faith toward our Lord Jesus Christ" (Acts 20:21) is God's formula for salvation.

The word translated "come" at the end of 2 Peter 3:9 carries the meaning of "make room for." It is translated "contain" in John 2:6 and 21:25. The lost sinner needs to "make room" for repentance in his heart by putting away his pride and meekly receiving the Word of God. Repentance is a gift from God (Acts 11:18; 2 Tim. 2:25), but the unbeliever must make room for the gift.

As you review Peter's arguments, you can see that his evidence is irrefutable. He pointed out that the scoffers willfully rejected evidence in order that they might continue in their sins and scoffing. He proved from the Scriptures that God has intervened in past history, and that He has the power to do it today. He showed that the scoffers had a very low view of God's character because they thought He delayed in keeping His promises just as men do. Finally, he explained that God does not live in the realm of human time, and that His so-called "delay" only gives more opportunity for lost sinners to repent and be saved.

Having refuted their false claims, Peter then reaffirmed the certainty of the coming of the Day of the Lord. When will it come? Nobody knows when, because it will come to the world "as a thief in the night." Our Lord used this phrase (Matt. 24:43; Luke 12:39) and so did the Apostle Paul (1 Thes. 5:2ff). When the world is feeling secure, then God's judgment will fall. The thief does not warn his victims that he is coming! "For when they shall say, 'Peace and safety'; then sudden destruction cometh upon them, as travail upon a woman with child; and they shall not escape" (1 Thes. 5:3).

We do not know *when* it will happen, but we are told *what* will happen. Kenneth Wuest gives an accurate and graphic translation of these words: "In which the heavens with a rushing noise will be dissolved, and the elements being scorched will be dissolved, and the earth also and the works in it will be burned up" (2 Peter 3:10).

Many Bible students believe that Peter here described the action of atomic energy being released by God. The word translated *a great noise* in the *King James Version* means "with a hissing and a crackling sound." When the atomic bomb was tested in the Nevada desert, more than one reporter said that the explosion gave forth "a whirring sound," or a "crackling sound." The Greek word Peter used was commonly used by the people for the whirring of a bird's wings or the hissing of a snake.

The word *melt* in 2 Peter 3:10 means "to disintegrate, to be dissolved." It carries the idea of something being broken down into its basic elements, and that is what happens when atomic energy is released. "Heaven and earth shall pass away," said our Lord (Matt. 24:35), and it appears that this may happen by the release of the atomic power stored in the elements that make up the world. The heavens and earth are "stored with fire" (2 Peter 3:7, WUEST), and only God can release it.

For this reason, I do not personally believe that God will permit sinful men to engage in an earth-destroying atomic war. He will, I believe, overrule the ignorance and foolishness of men including well-meaning but unbelieving diplomats and politicians, so that He alone will have the privilege of "pushing the button" and dissolving the elements to make way for a new heaven and a new earth. Peter no doubt had in mind Old Testament passages such as Isaiah 13:10-11; 24:19; 34:4; and 64:1-4 when he wrote these words. The first passage is especially emphatic that *God* will bring judgment and not sinful man. "And I will punish the world for their evil, and the wicked for their iniquity," says the Lord. It does not sound as though He will give this task to some nervous military leader or some angry politician.

Of course, this great explosion and conflagration will not touch the "heaven of heavens" where God dwells. It will destroy the earth and the atmospheric heavens around it, the universe as we know it; this will make room for the new heavens and earth (2 Peter 3:13; Rev. 21:1ff).

Man's great works will also be burned up!

All of the things that man boasts about—his great cities, his great buildings, his inventions, his achievements—will be destroyed in a moment of time. When sinners stand before the throne of God, they will have nothing to point to as evidence of their greatness. It will all be gone.

This is certainly a solemn truth, and we dare not study it in cavalier fashion. In the remaining verses of this letter, Peter will apply this truth to our daily living. But it would be wise for us to pause now and consider: where will I be when God destroys the world? Is what I am living for only destined to go up in an atomic cloud, to vanish forever? Or am I doing the will of God so that my works will glorify Him forever?

Make your decision now—before it is too late.

# CHAPTER SEVEN
# BE DILIGENT!
## *2 Peter 3:11-18*

The purpose of prophetic truth is not speculation but motivation; thus Peter concluded his letter with the kind of practical admonitions that all of us must heed. It is unfortunate when people run from one prophetic conference to another, filling their notebooks, marking their Bibles, drawing their charts, and yet not living their lives to the glory of God. In fact, some of the saints battle each other more over prophetic interpretation than perhaps any other subject.

All true Christians believe that Jesus Christ is coming again. They may differ in their views of when certain promised events will occur, but they all agree that He is returning as He promised. Furthermore, all Christians agree that this faith in future glory ought to motivate the church. As one pastor said to me, "I have moved off the Planning Committee and joined the Welcoming Committee!" This does not mean that we should stop studying prophecy, or that every opposing viewpoint is correct, which is an impossibility. But it does mean that, whatever views we hold, they ought to make a difference in our lives.

"Be diligent!" is the admonition that best summarizes what Peter wrote in this closing paragraph. He used this word before in 2 Peter 1: "Giving all diligence, add to your faith" (2 Peter 1:5); "Give diligence to make your calling and election sure" (2 Peter 1:10); "Moreover I will endeavor [be diligent] that ye may be able" (2 Peter 1:15). If we are going to be successful Christians, we must learn to be diligent.

Peter gave three admonitions to encourage the readers in Christian diligence in the light of our Lord's return.

## Be Diligent to Live Godly Lives (2 Peter 3:11-14)

The key word in this paragraph is *look*. It means "to await eagerly, to be expectant." You find it in Luke 3:15 ("And as the people were in expectation") and Acts 3:5 ("expecting to receive something of them"). It describes an attitude of excitement and expectation as we wait for the Lord's return. Because we realize that the world and its works will be dissolved, and that even the very elements will be disintegrated, we fix our hope, not on anything in this world, but only on the Lord Jesus Christ.

Because we do not know the day or the hour of our Lord's return, we must constantly be ready. The believer who starts to neglect the "blessed hope" (Titus 2:13) will gradually develop a cold heart, a worldly attitude, and an unfaithful life (Luke 12:35-48). If he is not careful, he may even become like the scoffers and laugh at the promise of Christ's coming.

This expectant attitude ought to make a difference in our *personal conduct* (2 Peter 3:11). The word translated "manner" literally means "exotic, out of this world, foreign." Because we have "escaped the corruption that is in the world" (2 Peter 1:4), we must live differently from the people in the world. To them, we should behave like "foreigners." Why? Because this world is not our home! We are "strangers and pilgrims" (1 Peter 2:11) headed for a better world, the eternal city of God. Christians should be different, not odd. When you are different, you attract people; when you are odd, you repel them.

Our conduct should be characterized by holiness and godliness. "But as He which hath called you is holy, so be ye holy in all manner of conversation [behavior]; because it is written, 'Be ye holy; for I am holy' " (1 Peter 1:15-16). The word *holy* means "to separate, to cut off." Israel was a "holy nation" because God called the Jews out from among the Gentiles and kept them separated. Christians are called out from the godless world around them and are set apart for God alone.

The word *godliness* could be translated "piety." It is the same word we met in 2 Peter 1:6-7, "to worship well." It describes a person whose life is devoted to pleasing God. It is possible to be separated from sin positionally and yet not enjoy living for God personally. In the Greek world, the word translated *godliness* meant "respect and awe for the gods and the world they made." It is that attitude of reverence that says with John the Baptist, "He must increase, but I must decrease" (John 3:30).

Other New Testament writers also teach that an eager expectancy of the Lord's return ought to motivate us to live pure lives (see Rom. 13:11-14; 2 Cor. 5:1-11; Phil. 3:17-21; 1 Thes. 5:1-11; Titus 2:11-15; 1 John 2:28–3:3). However, it is not simply knowing the doctrine *in the mind* that motivates the life; it is having it *in the heart,* loving His appearing (2 Tim. 4:8).

Not only should this expectant attitude make a difference in our conduct, but it should also make a difference in our *witness*. The phrase *looking for and hasting unto* can be translated "looking for and hastening the coming of the Day of God." Peter affirms that it is possible for us to hasten the return of Jesus Christ.

The word translated "hasten unto" means "hasten" in the other five places where it is used in the New Testament. The shepherds "came with haste" (Luke 2:16). Jesus told Zaccheus to "make haste and come down" and "he made haste and came down" (Luke 19:5-6). Paul "hasted . . . to be at Jerusalem" (Acts 20:16); and the Lord told Paul to "make haste and get . . . out of Jerusalem" (Acts 22:18). To make this word a synonym for "eager anticipation" is to have Peter repeat himself in 2 Peter 2:12, for that is what the word *looking* means.

There are two extremes in ministry that we must avoid. One is the attitude that we are "locked into" God's sovereign plan in such a way that nothing we do will make any difference. The other extreme is to think that God cannot get anything done unless we do it! While God's sovereign decrees must never become an excuse for laziness, neither must our plans and activities try to take their place.

Perhaps two illustrations from Old Testament history will help us better understand the relationship between God's plans and man's service. God delivered Israel from Egypt and told the people He wanted to put them into their inheritance, the land of Canaan. But at Kadesh-Barnea all except Moses, Joshua, and Caleb rebelled against God and refused to enter the land (Num. 13–14). Did God force them to go in? No. Instead, He had them wander in the wilderness for the next forty years while the older generation died off. He adjusted His plan to their response.

When Jonah preached to the people of Nineveh, his message was clear: "Yet forty days, and Nineveh shall be overthrown!" (Jonah 3:4) It was God's plan to destroy the wicked city, but when the people repented, from the king on down, God adjusted His plan and spared the city. Neither God nor His basic principles changed, but His application of those principles changed. God responds when men repent.

How, then, can we as Christians hasten the coming of the Day of God? For one thing, we can pray as Jesus taught us, "Thy kingdom come" (Matt. 6:10). It would appear from Revelation 5:8 and 8:3-4 that the prayers of God's people are related in some way to the pouring out of God's wrath on the nations.

If God's work today is calling out a people for His name (Acts 15:14), then the sooner the church is completed, the sooner our Lord will return. There is a suggestion of this truth in Acts 3:19-21. While Matthew 24:14 relates primarily to the Tribulation, the principle is the same: man's ministry cooperates with God's program so that promised events can take place.

There are mysteries here that our minds cannot fully understand or explain, but the basic lesson is clear: the same God who ordains the end also ordains the means to the end, and we are a part of that means. Our task is not to speculate but to serve.

Finally, this expectant attitude will make a difference *when we meet Jesus Christ* (2 Peter 3:14). It will mean that He will greet us "in peace" and have no charges against us so that we are "ashamed before Him at His coming" (1 John 2:28). The Judgment Seat of Christ will be a serious event (2 Cor. 5:8-11) as we give an account of our service to Him (Rom. 14:10-13). It is better to meet Him "in peace" than for Him to fight against us with His Word! (Rev. 2:16)

If we are diligent to watch for His return, and to live holy and godly lives, then we will not be afraid or ashamed. We will meet Him "without spot and blameless." Jesus Christ is "a Lamb without blemish and without spot" (1 Peter 1:19), and we should be careful to follow His example. Peter had warned his readers against the defilement that the apostates bring: "Spots they are and blemishes" (2 Peter 2:13). The separated Christian will not permit himself to be "spotted and blemished" by the false teachers! He wants to meet his Lord wearing pure garments.

How do we maintain this eager expectancy that leads to holy living? By keeping "His promise" before our hearts (2 Peter 3:13). The promise of His coming is the light that shines in this dark world (2 Peter 1:19), and we must be sure that "the day star" is aglow in our hearts because we love His appearing.

## Be Diligent to Win the Lost (2 Peter 3:15-16)

Second Peter 3:15 ties in with verse 9, where Peter explained why the Lord had delayed fulfilling His promise. God had every reason long ago to judge the world and burn up its works, but in His mercy, He is long-suffering with us, "not willing that any should perish, but that all should come to repentance." This is the day of salvation, not the day of judgment.

Peter made reference to Paul's writings, because it is Paul, more than any other New Testament writer, who explained God's plan for mankind during this present age. Especially in Romans and Ephesians, Paul explained the relationship between Israel and the church. He pointed out that God used the nation Israel to prepare the way for the coming of the Saviour. But Israel rejected its King and asked to have Him crucified. Did this destroy God's plan? Of course not! Today, Israel is set aside nationally, but God is doing a wonderful new thing: He is saving Jews and Gentiles, and making them one in Christ in the church!

For centuries, if a Gentile wanted to be saved, he had to come by way of Israel. This same attitude persisted even in the early church (Acts 15). Paul made it clear that *both* Jews and Gentiles stand condemned before God and that both must be saved by faith in Jesus Christ. In Jesus Christ, saved Jews and Gentiles belong to the one body, the church. The church is a "mystery" that was hidden in God's counsels and later revealed through the

New Testament prophets and Apostles (see Eph. 3).

The Jewish nation was God's great testimony to Law, but the church is His witness for grace (see Eph. 1–2). Law prepared the way for grace, and grace enables us to fulfill the righteousness of the Law (Rom. 8:1-5). This does not mean that there was no grace under the Old Covenant, or that New Covenant believers are lawless! Anyone who was saved under the administration of Law was saved by grace, through faith, as Romans 4 and Hebrews 11 make clear.

Now, unlearned and unstable people have a difficult time understanding Paul's teachings. Even some learned and stable people who have spiritual discernment can find themselves floundering in great passages like Romans 9–11! Some Bible students, in their attempt to "harmonize" seeming contradictions (Law and grace, Israel and the church, faith and works) twist the Scriptures and try to make them teach what is really not there. The Greek word translated "wrest" means "to torture on the rack, to distort and pervert."

Even in Paul's day, there were those who twisted his words and tried to defend their ignorance. They accused Paul of teaching that, since we are saved by grace, it makes no difference how we live! It was "slanderously reported" that Paul taught, "Let us do evil that good may come" (Rom. 3:8; cf. Rom. 6:1ff). Others accused Paul of being against the Law because he taught the equality of Jews and Gentiles in the church (Gal. 3:28) and their liberty in Christ.

Most heresies are the perversion of some fundamental doctrine of the Bible. False teachers take verses out of context, twist the Scriptures, and manufacture doctrines that are contrary to the Word of God. Peter probably had the false teachers in mind, but the warning is good for all of us. We must accept the teaching of the Scriptures and not try to make them say what we want them to say.

Note that Peter classified Paul's letters as *Scripture,* that is, the inspired Word of God. Not only did the teaching of the Apostles agree with that of the prophets and our Lord (2 Peter 3:2), but the Apostles also agreed with each other. Some liberal scholars try to prove that the Apostles' doctrine was different from that of Jesus Christ, or that Peter and Paul were at variance with each other. The recipients of Peter's second letter had also read some of Paul's epistles, and Peter assured them that there was agreement.

What happens to people who blindly twist the Scriptures? They do it "unto their own destruction." Peter was not writing about Christians who have a difficult time interpreting the Word of God, because nobody understands *all* of the Bible perfectly. He was describing the false teachers who "tortured" the Word of God in order to prove their false doctrines. I once listened to a cultist "explain" why the group's leader was the "new Messiah" by manipulating the "weeks" in Daniel 9:23-27. He twisted the prophecy unmercifully!

The word *destruction* is repeated often in this letter (2 Peter 2:1-3; 3:7, 16). In the *King James Version,* it is translated "damnable," "pernicious," and "perdition," as well as "destruction." It means the rejection of eternal life, which results in eternal death.

Since this is the day of salvation, we must be diligent to do all we can to win the lost. We do not know how long the Lord will be "long-suffering" toward this evil world. We must not presume on His grace. We must understand what the Bible teaches about God's program for this present age, and we must be motivated by a love for the lost (2 Cor. 5:14) and a desire to be pleasing to Him when He returns.

The false teachers are multiplying and their pernicious doctrines are infecting the church. God needs separated men and women who will resist them, live godly lives, and bear witness of the saving grace of Jesus Christ. The time is short!

### Be Diligent to Grow Spiritually (2 Peter 3:17-18)

There are four "beloved" statements in 2 Peter 3 which summarize what Peter wanted to get across as he brought his second letter to a close.

> "Beloved . . . be mindful" (3:1-2).
> "Beloved, be not ignorant" (3:8).
> "Beloved . . . be diligent" (3:14).
> "Beloved . . . beware" (3:17).

The word translated "beware" means "be constantly guarding yourself." Peter's readers knew the truth, but he warned them that knowledge alone was not sufficient protection. They had to be on their guard; they had to be alert. It is easy for people who have a knowledge of the Bible to grow overconfident and to forget the warning, "Wherefore let him that thinketh he standeth take heed lest he fall" (1 Cor. 10:12).

What special danger did Peter see? That the true believers would be "led away together with the error of the wicked" (literal translation). He is warning us against breaking down the walls of separation that must stand between the true believers and the false teachers. There can be no communion between truth and error. The apostates "live in error" (2 Peter 2:18), while true believers live in the sphere of the truth (2 John 1-2).

The word *wicked* (2 Peter 3:17) means "the lawless." Peter's description of the apostates in 2 Peter 2 reveals how lawless they are. They even speak evil of the authorities that seek to enforce God's Law in this world! (2 Peter 2:10-11) They promise their converts freedom (2 Peter 2:19), but that freedom turns out to be lawlessness.

True Christians cannot fall from salvation and be lost, but they can fall from their own "steadfastness." What was this steadfastness? Being "established in the present truth" (2 Peter 1:12). The stability of the Christian comes from his faith in the Word of God, his knowledge of that Word, and his ability to use that Word in the practical decisions of life.

One of the great tragedies of evangelism is bringing "spiritual babies" into the world and then failing to feed them, nurture them, and help them develop. The apostates prey on young believers who have "very recently escaped" from the ways of error (2 Peter 2:18). New believers need to be taught the basic doctrines of the Word of God; otherwise, they will be in danger of being "led away with the error of the lawless."

How can we as believers maintain our steadfastness and avoid being among the "unstable souls" who are easily beguiled and led astray? By growing spiritually. "But be constantly growing" is the literal translation. We should not grow "in spurts," but in a constant experience of development.

We must grow "in grace." This has to do with Christian character traits, the very things Peter wrote about in 2 Peter 1:5-7, and that Paul wrote about in Galatians 5:22-23. We were saved by grace (Eph. 2:8-9), but grace does not end there! We must also be strengthened by grace (2 Tim. 2:1-4). God's grace can enable us to endure suffering (2 Cor. 12:7-10). His grace also helps us to give when giving is difficult (2 Cor. 8:1ff) and to sing when singing is difficult (Col. 3:16).

Our God is "the God of all grace" (1 Peter 5:10), who "giveth grace unto the humble" (James 4:6). As we study His Word, we learn about the various aspects of grace that are available to us as children of God. We are stewards of "the manifold grace of God" (1 Peter 4:10). There is grace for every situation and every challenge of life. "But by the grace of God I am what I am" wrote Paul (1 Cor. 15:10), and that should be our testimony as well.

Growing in grace often means experiencing trials and even suffering. We never really experience the grace of God until we are at the end of our own resources. The lessons learned in the "school of grace" are always costly lessons, but they are worth it. To grow in grace means to become more like the Lord Jesus Christ, from whom we receive all the grace that we need (John 1:16).

We must also grow in knowledge. How easy it is to grow in knowledge but not in grace! All of us know far more of the Bible than we really live. Knowledge without grace is a terrible weapon, and grace without knowledge can be very shallow. But when we combine grace and knowledge, we have a marvelous tool for building our lives and for building the church.

But note that we are challenged to grow, not just in knowledge of the Bible, as good as that is, but "in the knowledge of our Lord and Saviour Jesus Christ." It is one thing to "know the Bible," and quite another thing to know the Son of God, the central theme of the Bible. The better we know Christ through the Word, the more we grow in grace; the more we grow in grace, the better we understand the Word of God.

So, the separated Christian must constantly be *guarding* himself, lest he be led away into error; he also must be constantly *growing* in grace and knowledge. This requires diligence! It demands discipline and priorities. Nobody automatically drifts into spiritual growth and stability, but anybody can drift *out of* dedication and growth. "For this reason we must pay much closer attention to what we have heard, lest we drift away from it" (Heb. 2:1, NASB). Just as the boat needs the anchor, so the Christian needs the Word of God.

Physical growth and spiritual growth follow pretty much the same pattern. To begin with, we grow from the inside out. "As newborn babes" is the way Peter illustrated it (1 Peter 2:2). The child of God is born with everything he needs for growth and service (2 Peter 1:3). All he needs is the spiritual food and exercise that will enable him to develop. He needs to keep clean. We grow by nutrition, not by addition!

We grow best in a loving family, and this is where the local church comes in. A baby needs a family for protection, provision, and affection. Tests prove that babies who are raised alone, without special love, tend to develop physical and emotional problems very early. The church is God's "nursery" for the care and feeding of Christians, the God-ordained environment that encourages them to grow.

It is important that we grow in a balanced way. The human body grows in a balanced way with the various limbs working together; likewise the "spiritual man" must grow in a balanced way. We must grow in grace and knowledge (2 Peter 3:18), for example. We must keep a balance between worship and service, between faith and works. A balanced diet of the whole Word of God helps us to maintain a balanced life.

It is the Holy Spirit of God who empowers and enables us to keep things in balance. Before Peter was filled with the Spirit, he was repeatedly going to extremes. He would bear witness to Christ one minute and then try to argue with the Lord the next! (Matt. 16:13-23) He refused to allow Jesus to wash his feet, and then he wanted to be washed all over! (John 13:6-10) He promised to defend the Lord and even die with Him, yet he did not have the courage to *own* the Lord before a little servant girl! But when he was filled with the Spirit, Peter began to live a balanced life that avoided impulsive extremes.

What is the result of spiritual growth? Glory to God! "To Him be glory both now and forever." It glorifies Jesus Christ when we keep ourselves separated from sin and error. It glorifies Him when we grow in grace and knowledge, for then we become more like Him (Rom. 8:29). In his life and even in his death, Peter glorified God (John 21:18-19).

As you review this important epistle, you cannot help but be struck by the urgency of the message. The apostates are here! They are busy! They are seducing immature Christians! We must be guarding, growing, and glorifying the Lord, making the most of every opportunity to win the lost and strengthen the saved.

Be diligent! The ministry you save may be your own!

# 1 JOHN

## OUTLINE

**Key theme:** The tests of reality in the Christian life
**Key verse:** 1 John 5:13

I. **INTRODUCTION—1:1-4**

II. **THE TESTS OF TRUE FELLOW-SHIP: GOD IS LIGHT—1:5–2:29**
   A. Obedience—1:5–2:6
   ("saying" vs. "doing")
   B. Love—2:7-17
   C. Truth—2:18-29

III. **THE TESTS OF TRUE SONSHIP: GOD IS LOVE—chapters 3–5**
   A. Obedience—3
   B. Love—4
   C. Truth—5

## CONTENTS

# CHAPTER ONE
# IT'S REAL!
*1 John 1:1-4*

Once upon a time. . . ."
Remember how exciting those words used to be? They were the open door into an exciting world of make-believe, a dreamworld that helped you forget all the problems of childhood.

Then—*pow!* You turned a corner one day, and "Once upon a time" became kid stuff. You discovered that life is a battleground, not a playground, and fairy stories were no longer meaningful. You wanted something *real*.

The search for something real is not new. It has been going on since the beginning of history. Men have looked for reality and satisfaction in wealth, thrills, conquest, power, learning, and even in religion.

There is nothing really wrong with these experiences, except that *by themselves* they never really satisfy. *Wanting* something real and *finding* something real are two different things. Like a child eating cotton candy at the circus, many people who expect to bite into something real end up with a mouthful of nothing. They waste priceless years on empty substitutes for reality.

This is where the Apostle John's first epistle comes in. Written centuries ago, this letter deals with a theme that is forever up-to-date: *the life that is real.*

John had discovered that satisfying reality is not to be found in things or thrills, but in a Person—Jesus Christ, the Son of God. Without wasting any time, he tells us about this "living reality" in the first paragraph of his letter.

As you read 1 John 1:1-4, you learn three vital facts about the life that is real.

## This Life Is Revealed (1 John 1:1)
As you read John's letter, you will discover that he enjoys using certain words, and that the word "manifest" is one of them. "And the life was manifested" (1 John 1:2), he says. This life was not hidden so that we have to search for it and find it. No, it was *manifested*—revealed openly!

If you were God, how would *you* go about revealing yourself to men? How could you tell them about, and give them, the kind of life you wanted them to enjoy?

God has revealed Himself in creation (Rom. 1:20), but creation alone could never tell us the story of God's love. God has also revealed Himself much more fully in His Word, the Bible. But God's final and most complete revelation is in His Son, Jesus Christ. Jesus said, "He that hath seen Me hath seen the Father" (John 14:9).

Because Jesus is God's revelation of Himself, He has a very special name: "The Word of Life" (1 John 1:1).

This same title opens John's Gospel: "In the beginning was the Word, and the Word was with God, and the Word was God" (John 1:1).

Why does Jesus Christ have this name? Because Christ is to us what our words are to others. Our words reveal to others just what we think and how we feel. Christ reveals to us the mind and heart of God. He is the living means of communication between God and men. To know Jesus Christ is to know God!

John makes no mistake in his identification of Jesus Christ. Jesus is the Son of the Father—the Son of God (1 John 1:3). John warns us several times in his letter not to listen to the false teachers who tell lies about Jesus Christ. "Who is a liar but he that denieth that Jesus is the Christ?" (1 John 2:22) "Every spirit that confesseth that Jesus Christ is come in the flesh is of God; and every spirit that confesseth not that Jesus Christ is come in the flesh is not of God" (1 John 4:2-3). If a man is wrong about Jesus Christ, he is wrong about God, because Jesus Christ is the final and complete revelation of God to men.

For example, there are those who tell us that Jesus was a man but was not God. John has no place for such teachers! One of the last things he writes in this letter is, "We are in Him that is true, even in His Son Jesus Christ. This is *the true God,* and eternal life" (1 John 5:20).

False teaching is so serious a matter that John wrote about it in his second letter too, warning believers not to invite false teachers into their homes (2 John 9-10). And he makes it plain that to deny that Jesus is God is to follow the lies of Antichrist (1 John 2:22-23).

This leads to a basic Bible doctrine that has puzzled many people—the doctrine of the Trinity.

John mentions in his letter the Father, the Son, and the Holy Spirit. For example, he says, "By this know ye the Spirit of God: every spirit that confesseth that Jesus Christ is come in the flesh is of God" (1 John 4:2, sco). Here are references in one verse to God the Father, God the Son, and God the Holy Spirit. And in 1 John 4:13-15 is another statement that mentions the three Persons of the Trinity.

The word "Trinity" is a combination of *tri-,* meaning "three," and *unity,* meaning "one." A "trinity," then, is a three-in-one, or one-in-three. To be sure, the word "trinity" is not found in the Bible, but the truth is taught there (cf. also Matt. 28:19-20; John 14:16-17, 26; 2 Cor. 13:14; Eph. 4:4-6).

Christians do not believe that there are *three gods.* They believe that one God exists in three Persons—Father, Son, and Holy Spirit. Nor do Christians believe merely that one God reveals Himself in three different ways, much as one man may be a husband, a father, and a son. No, the Bible teaches that God is *one* but that He exists in *three* Persons.

One teacher of doctrine used to say, "Try to explain the Trinity and you *may* lose your mind. But try to explain it away and you *will* lose your soul!" And the Apostle John says, "Whoever denies the Son does not have the Father" (1 John 2:23, NASB). No Person of the Trinity is expendable!

As you read the Gospel records of the life of Jesus, you see the wonderful kind of life God wants us to enjoy. But it is not by *imitating* Jesus, our Example, that we may share in this life. No, there is a far better way.

### This Life Is Experienced (1 John 1:2)
Read the first four verses of John's letter again, and you will notice that the apostle had a *personal encounter with Jesus Christ.* His was no secondhand "religious experience" inherited from somebody else or discovered in a book! No, John knew Jesus Christ face-to-face. He and the other Apostles heard Jesus speak. They watched Him as He lived with them. In fact, they studied Him carefully, and even touched His body. They knew that Jesus was *real*—not a phantom, not a vision, but God in human corporeal form.

Some twentieth-century student may say: "Yes, and this means that John had an advantage. He lived when Jesus walked on earth. He knew Jesus personally. But I was born twenty centuries too late!"

But this is where our student is wrong! It was not the Apostles' *physical* nearness to Jesus Christ that made them what they were. It was their *spiritual* nearness. They had com-

mitted themselves to Him as their Saviour and their Lord. Jesus Christ was real and exciting to John and his colleagues because they had trusted Him. By trusting Christ, they had *experienced eternal life!*

Six times in this letter John uses the phrase "born of God." This was not an idea John had invented; he had heard Jesus use these words. "Except a man be born again," Jesus had said, "he cannot see the kingdom of God. . . . That which is born of the flesh is flesh; and that which is born of the Spirit is spirit. Marvel not that I said unto thee, 'Ye must be born again' " (John 3:3, 6-7). We can experience this "real life" only after we have believed the Gospel, put our trust in Christ, and been "born of God."

"Whosoever believeth that Jesus is the Christ is born of God" (1 John 5:1). Eternal life is not something we earn by good works or deserve because of good character. Eternal life, the life that is real, is a gift from God to those who trust His Son as their Saviour.

John wrote his Gospel to tell people how to receive this wonderful life (John 20:31). He wrote his first letter to tell people how to be sure they have really been born of God (1 John 5:9-13).

A college student returned to the campus after going home for a family funeral, and almost at once his grades began to go down. His counselor thought that the death of his grandmother had affected the boy, and that time would heal the wound, but the grades only became worse. Finally the boy confessed the real problem. While he was home, he happened to look into his grandmother's old Bible, and there he discovered in the family record that he was an adopted son.

"I don't know who I belong to," he told his counselor. "I don't know where I came from!"

The assurance that we are in God's family—that we have been "born of God"—is vitally important to all of us. Certain characteristics are true of all God's children. A person who is born of God lives a righteous life (1 John 2:29). A child of God does not *practice* sin (which is the meaning of the *King James* word "commit," 1 John 3:9). A believer will occasionally *commit* sin (cf. 1 John 1:8–2:2), but he will not make it a habit to sin.

God's children also love each other and their Heavenly Father (cf. 1 John 4:7; 5:1). They have no love for the world system around them (1 John 2:15-17), and because of this the world hates them (1 John 3:13). Instead of being overcome by the pressures of this world, and swept off balance, the children of God overcome the world (1 John 5:4). This is another mark of true children of God.

Why is it so important that we *know* that we have been born of God? John gives us the answer: if you are not a child of God, you a "child of wrath" (Eph. 2:1-3) and may become a "child of the devil" (1 John 3:10; and see Matt: 13:24-30, 36-43). A "child of the devil" is a counterfeit Christian who acts "saved" but has not been born again. Jesus called the Pharisees "children of the devil" (John 8:44) and they were very religious.

A counterfeit Christian—and they are common—is something like a counterfeit ten-dollar bill.

Suppose you have a counterfeit bill and actually think it is genuine. You use it to pay for a tank of gas. The gas station manager uses the bill to buy supplies. The supplier uses the bill to pay the grocer. The grocer bundles the bill up with forty-nine other ten-dollar bills and takes it to the bank. And the teller says, "I'm sorry, but *this* bill is a counterfeit."

That ten-dollar bill may have done a lot of good while it was in circulation, but when it arrived at the bank it was exposed for what it *really* was, and put out of circulation.

So with a counterfeit Christian. He may do many good things in this life, but when he faces the final judgment he will be rejected. "Many will say to Me in that day, 'Lord, Lord, have we not prophesied in Thy name? And in Thy name have cast out demons? And in Thy name done many wonderful works?' And then will I profess unto them, 'I never knew you; depart from Me, ye that work iniquity' " (Matt. 7:22-23, sco).

Each of us must ask himself honestly, "Am I a true child of God or am I a counterfeit Christian? Have I truly been born of God?"

If you have not experienced eternal life, this *real* life, you *can* experience it right now! Read 1 John 5:9-15 carefully. God has "gone on record" in His Word. He offers you the gift of eternal life. Believe His promise and ask Him for His gift. "For whosoever shall call upon the name of the Lord shall be saved" (Rom. 10:13).

We have discovered two important facts about "the life that is real": it is revealed in Jesus Christ and it is experienced when we put our trust in Him as our Saviour. But John does not stop here!

### This Life Is Shared (1 John 1:3-4)

"That which we have seen and heard declare we unto you" (1 John 1:3). And once *you* have experienced this exciting life that is real, *you* will want to share it with other people, just as John wanted to "declare" it to all his readers in the first century.

A pastor had a phone call from an angry woman. "I have received a piece of religious literature from your church," she shouted, "and I resent your using the mails to upset people!"

"What was so upsetting about a piece of mail from a church?" the pastor asked calmly.

"You have no right to try to change my religion!" the woman stormed. "You have your religion and I have mine, and I'm not trying to change yours!" (She really was, but the pastor didn't argue with her.)

"Changing your religion, or anybody else's religion, is not our purpose," the pastor explained. "But we have experienced a wonderful new life through faith in Christ, and we want to do all we can to share it with others."

Many people (including some Christians) have the idea that "witnessing" means wrangling over the differences in religious beliefs, or sitting down and comparing churches.

That isn't what John had in mind! He tells us that witnessing means sharing our spiritual experiences with others—both by the lives that we live and by the words that we speak.

John wrote this letter to share Christ with us. As you read it, you will discover that John had in mind *five* purposes for sharing.

*That we may have fellowship (v. 3).* This word *fellowship* is an important one in the vocabulary of a Christian. It simply means "to have in common." As sinners, men have nothing in common with the holy God. But God in His grace sent Christ to have something in common with men. Christ took on Himself a human body and became a man. Then He went to the cross and took on that body the sins of the world (1 Peter 2:24). Because He paid the price for our sins, the way is open for God to forgive us and take us into His family. When we trust Christ, we become "partakers of the divine nature" (2 Peter 1:4). The term translated "partakers" in Peter's epistle is from the same Greek root that is translated "fellowship" in 1 John 1:3.

What a thrilling miracle! Jesus Christ took on Himself the nature of man that by faith we may receive the very nature of God!

A famous British writer was leaving Liverpool by ship. He noticed that the other passengers were waving to friends on the dock. He rushed down to the dock and stopped a little boy. "Would you wave to me if I paid you?" he asked the lad, and of course the boy agreed. The writer rushed back on board and leaned over the rail, glad for someone to wave to. And sure enough, there was the boy waving back to him!

A foolish story? Perhaps—but it reminds us that *man hates loneliness.* All of us want to be wanted. The life that is *real* helps to solve the basic problem of loneliness, for Christians have genuine fellowship with God and with one another. Jesus promised, "Lo, I am with you always" (Matt. 28:20). In his letter, John explains the secret of fellowship with God and with other Christians. This is the first purpose John mentions for the writing of his letter—the sharing of his experience of eternal life.

***That we may have joy (v. 4).*** Fellowship is Christ's answer to the loneliness of life. Joy is His answer to the emptiness, the hollowness of life.

John, in his epistle, uses the word "joy" only once, but the idea of joy runs through the entire letter. Joy is not something that we manufacture for ourselves; joy is a wonderful by-product of our fellowship with God. David knew the joy which John mentions; he said, "In Thy presence is fullness of joy" (Ps. 16:11).

Basically, sin is the cause of the unhappiness that overwhelms our world today. Sin promises joy but it always produces sorrow. The pleasures of sin are temporary—they are only for a season (Heb. 11:25). God's pleasures last eternally—they are forevermore (Ps. 16:11).

The life that is real produces a joy that is real—not some limp substitute. Jesus said, the night before He was crucified, "Your joy no man taketh from you" (John 16:22). "These things have I spoken unto you, that My joy might remain in you, and that your joy might be full" (John 15:11).

Karl Marx wrote, "The first requisite for the people's happiness is the abolition of religion." But the Apostle John writes, in effect, "Faith in Jesus Christ gives you a joy that can never be duplicated by the world. I have experienced this joy myself, and I want to share it with you."

***That we may not sin (2:1).*** John faces the problem of sin squarely (cf. 1 John 3:4-9, for example) and announces the only answer to this enigma—the person and work of Jesus Christ. Christ not only died for us to carry the penalty of our sins, but rose from the dead in order to intercede for us at the throne of God: "If any man sin, we have an Advocate with the Father, Jesus Christ the righteous" (1 John 2:1).

Christ is our Representative. He defends us at the Father's throne. Satan may stand there as the accuser of the brethren (Zech. 3; Rev. 12:10), but Christ stands there as our Advocate—He pleads on our behalf! Continuing forgiveness, in response to His intercession, is God's answer to our sinfulness.

"I would like to become a Christian," an interested woman said to a visiting pastor, "but I'm afraid I can't hold out. I'm sure to sin again!"

Turning to 1 John 1, the pastor said, "No doubt you *will* sin again, because God says, 'If we say that we have no sin, we deceive ourselves, and the truth is not in us' (1 John 1:8). But if you *do* sin, God will forgive you if you will confess your sin to Him. But it isn't *necessary* for Christians to sin. As we walk in fellowship with God and in obedience to His Word, He gives us ability to resist and to have victory over temptation."

Then the pastor remembered that the woman had gone through surgery some months before.

"When you had your surgery," he asked, "was there a possibility of complications or problems afterward?"

"Oh, yes," she replied, "But whenever I had a problem, I went to see the doctor and he took care of it."

Then the truth hit her! "I see it!" she exclaimed. "Christ is always available to keep me out of sin or to forgive my sin!"

The life that is real is a life of *victory.* In this letter, John tells us how to draw on our divine resources to experience victory over temptation and sin.

***That we may not be deceived (2:26).*** As never before, Christians today need ability to distinguish between right and wrong, between truth and error. The notion is widespread in our generation that there are no "absolutes"—that *nothing* is *always* wrong and that *nothing* is *always* right. False doctrines, therefore, are more prevalent than at any time in history—and most men and women seem to be willing to accept almost any teaching except the truths of the Bible.

In John's epistles is a word that no other

New Testament writer uses—"antichrist" (1 John 2:18, 22; 4:3; 2 John 7). That prefix *anti-* has two meanings: "against" and "instead of." There are in this world teachers of lies who are opposed to Christ, and their method of "seducing" people is to use *lies.* They offer a substitute Christ, a substitute salvation, and a substitute Bible. They want to give you something *instead of* the real Word of God and real eternal life.

Christ is the Truth (John 14:6), but Satan is the liar (John 8:44). The devil leads people astray—not necessarily with gross sensual sins, but with half-truths and outright lies. He began his career by seducing man in the Garden of Eden. He asked Eve, "Yea, hath God said?" Even then, he did not appear to her in his true nature, but masqueraded as a beautiful creature (cf. 2 Cor. 11:13-15).

Satan today often spreads his lies even through religious groups! Not every man standing in a pulpit is preaching the truth of the Word of God. False preachers and false religious teachers have always been among the devil's favorite and most effective tools.

How can Christians today detect Satan's lies? How can they identify false teachers? How can they grow in their own knowledge of the truth so that they will not be victims of false doctrines?

John answers these questions. The life that is real is characterized by discernment.

The Holy Spirit, referred to by John as "the Anointing . . . ye have received of Him" (1 John 2:27), is Christ's answer to our need for discernment. The Spirit is our Teacher; it is He who enables us to detect truth and error and to remain ("abide") in Christ. He is our protection against ignorance, deception, and untruth.

The discernment of false doctrines and of false teachers will come to our attention again.

**That we may know we are saved (5:13).** We have already touched on this truth, but it is so important that it bears repeating. The life that is real is not built on the empty hopes—or wishes—based on human supposings. It is built on assurance. In fact, as you read John's letter you encounter the word *know* more than thirty times. No Christian, if he is asked whether or not he is going to heaven, needs to say "I *hope* so" or "I *think* so." He need have no doubt whatever.

The life that is real is such a free and exciting life because it is based on knowledge of solid *facts.* "You shall know the truth, and the truth shall make you free" (cf. John 8:32), promised Jesus. "We have not followed cunningly devised fables" (2 Peter 1:16), was the testimony of Jesus' disciples. These men, almost all of whom died for their faith, did not give their lives for a clever hoax of their own devising, as some critics of Christianity fatuously assert. They *knew* what they had seen!

Years ago a traveling entertainer billed himself as "The Human Fly." He would climb up the sides of buildings or monuments without the aid of ropes or the protection of nets. Usually the whole neighborhood would turn out to watch him.

During one performance, the Human Fly came to a point on the wall of the building and paused as though he didn't know what to do next. Then he reached with his right arm to take hold of a piece of mortar to lift himself higher. But instead of moving higher, he fell back with a scream and was killed on the pavement below.

When the police opened his right hand, it did not contain a piece of mortar. It contained a handful of dirty cobwebs! The Fly had tried to climb on cobwebs, and it just didn't work.

Jesus warned against such false assurance in the passage which we have already quoted. Many who profess to be Christians will be rejected in the day of God's judgment.

John is saying in his letter, "I want you to be *sure* that you *have* eternal life."

As you read this fascinating letter, you will discover that John frequently repeats himself. He weaves three themes in and out of these chapters: *obedience, love,* and *truth.* In 1 John 1 and 2, the apostle emphasizes *fellowship,* and he tells us that the conditions for fellowship are: obedience (1 John 1:5–2:6), love (1 John 2:7-17), and truth (1 John 2:18-29).

In the latter half of his letter, John deals primarily with *sonship*—our being "born of God." How can a person really know he is a child of God? Well, says John, sonship is revealed by obedience (1 John 3), love (1 John 4), and truth (1 John 5).

Obedience—love—truth. Why did John use these particular tests of fellowship and sonship? For a very practical reason.

When God made us, He made us in His own image (Gen. 1:26-27). This means that we have a personality patterned after God's. We have a *mind* to think with, a *heart* to feel with, and a *will* with which to make decisions. We sometimes refer to these aspects of our personality as *intellect, emotion,* and *will.*

The life that is real *must involve all the elements of the personality.*

Most people are dissatisfied today because their total personality has never been controlled by something real and meaningful. When a person is born of God through faith in Christ, God's Spirit comes into his life to live there forever. As he has fellowship with God in reading and studying the Bible and in prayer, the Holy Spirit is able to control his mind, heart, and will. And what happens then?

A Spirit-controlled *mind* knows and understands *truth.*

A Spirit-controlled *heart* feels *love.*

A Spirit-controlled *will* inclines us to *obedience.*

John wants to impress this fact on us, and that is why he uses a series of contrasts in his letter: truth vs. lies, love vs. hatred, and obedience vs. disobedience.

There is no middle ground in the life that is real. We must be on one side or on the other.

This, then, is the life that is real. It was revealed in Christ; it was experienced by those who trusted in Christ; and it can be shared today.

This life begins with *sonship* and continues in *fellowship.* First we are born of God; then we walk (live) with God.

This means that there are two kinds of people who cannot enter into the joy and victory about which we are thinking: those who have never been born of God and those who, though saved, are out of fellowship with God.

It would be a wise thing for us to take inventory spiritually (cf. 2 Cor. 13:5) and see whether or not we qualify to enjoy the spiritual experience with which John's letter deals.

We have already emphasized the importance of being born of God, but if you have any doubts or questions, a review of Fact 2 might be beneficial.

If a true believer is out of fellowship with God, it is usually for one of three reasons:

1. He has disobeyed God's will.
2. He is not getting along with fellow believers.
3. He believes a lie and therefore is living a lie.

Even a Christian can be mistaken in his understanding of truth. That's why John warns us, "Little children, let no man deceive you" (1 John 3:7).

These three reasons parallel John's three important themes: obedience, love, and truth. Once a believer discovers why he is out of fellowship with God, he should confess that sin (or those sins) to the Lord and claim His full forgiveness (1 John 1:9–2:2). A believer can never have joyful fellowship with the Lord if sin stands between them.

God's invitation to us today is, "Come and enjoy fellowship with Me and with each other! Come and share the life that is real!"

# CHAPTER TWO
# WALKING AND TALKING
*1 John 1:5–2:6*

Every form of life has its enemies. Insects have to watch out for hungry birds, and birds must keep an eye on hungry cats and dogs. Even human beings have to dodge automobiles and fight off germs.

The life that is real also has an enemy, and we read about it in this section. This enemy is *sin.* Nine times in these verses John mentions sin, so the subject is obviously not unimportant. John illustrates his theme by using the contrast between light and darkness: God is light; sin is darkness.

But there is another contrast here too—the contrast between *saying* and *doing.* Four times John writes, "If we say" or "He that saith" (1 John 1:6, 8, 10; 2:4). It is clear that our Christian life is to amount to more than mere "talk"; we must also "walk," or *live,* what we believe. If we are in fellowship with God (if we are "walking in the light"), our lives will back up what our lips are saying. But if we are living in sin ("walking in darkness"), then our lives will contradict what our lips are saying, making us hypocrites.

The New Testament calls the Christian life a "walk." This *walk* begins with a step of faith when we trust Christ as our Saviour. But salvation is not the end—it's only the beginning—of spiritual life. "Walking" involves progress, and Christians are supposed to advance in the spiritual life. Just as a child must learn to walk and must overcome many difficulties in doing so, a Christian must learn to "walk in the light." And the fundamental difficulty involved here is this matter of *sin*.

Of course, sin is not simply outward disobedience; sin is also inner rebellion or desire. For example, we are warned about the desires of the flesh and of the eyes and about the pride of life (1 John 2:16), all of which are sinful. Sin is also transgression of the Law (1 John 3:4), or literally, "lawlessness." Sin is refusal to submit to the Law of God. Lawlessness, or independence of the Law, is the very essence of sin. If a believer decides to live an independent life, how can he possibly walk in fellowship with God? "Can two walk together except they be agreed?" (Amos 3:3)

Neither in the Old Testament nor in the New does the Bible whitewash the sins of the saints. In escaping a famine, Abraham became weak in his faith and went down to Egypt and lied to Pharaoh (Gen. 12). Later, the patriarch tried to "help God" by marrying Hagar and begetting a son (Gen. 16). In both cases, God forgave Abraham his sin, but Abraham had to reap what he had sowed. God can and will cleanse the record, but He does not change the results. No one can unscramble an egg.

Peter denied the Lord three times and tried to kill a man in the Garden when Jesus was arrested. Satan is a liar and a murderer (John 8:44), and Peter was playing right into his hands! Christ forgave Peter (cf. John 21), of course, but what Peter had done hurt his testimony greatly and hindered the Lord's work.

The fact that Christians sin bothers some people—especially new Christians. They forget that their receiving the new nature does not eliminate the old nature they were born with. The old nature (which has its origin in our physical birth) fights against the new nature which we receive when we are born again (Gal. 5:16-26). No amount of self-discipline, no set of man-made rules and regulations, can control this old nature. Only the Holy Spirit of God can enable us to "put to death" the old nature (Rom. 8:12-13) and produce the Spirit's fruit (Gal. 5:22-23) in us through the new nature.

Sinning saints are not mentioned in the Bible to discourage us, but to warn us.

"Why do you keep preaching to us Christians about sin?" an angry church member said to her pastor. "After all, sin in the life of a Christian is different from sin in the life of an unsaved person!"

"Yes," replied the pastor, "it *is* different. It's *much worse!*"

All of us, therefore, must deal with our sins if we are to enjoy the life that is real. In this section, John explains three approaches to sin.

## We Can Try to Cover Our Sins (1 John 1:5-6, 8, 10; 2:4)

"God is light, and in Him is no darkness at all" (1 John 1:5). When we were saved, God called us out of darkness into His light (1 Peter 2:9). We are children of light (1 Thes. 5:5). Those who do wrong hate light (John 3:19-21). When light shines in on us, it reveals our true nature (Eph. 5:8-13).

Light produces life and growth and beauty, but sin is darkness; and darkness and light cannot exist in the same place. If we are walking in the light, the darkness has to go. If we are holding to sin, then the light goes. There is no middle ground, no vague "gray" area, where sin is concerned.

How do Christians try to cover up their sins? *By telling lies!* First, we tell lies to *others* (1 John 1:6). We want our Christian friends to think we are "spiritual," so we lie about our lives and try to make a favorable impression on them. We want them to think that we are walking in the light, though in reality we are walking in the darkness.

Once one begins to lie to others, he will sooner or later lie to *himself,* and our passage deals with this (1 John 1:8). The problem now is not deceiving others, but deceiving ourselves. It is possible for a believer to live in sin yet convince himself that everything is fine in his relationship to the Lord.

Perhaps the classic example of this is King David (2 Sam. 11–12). First David lusted after Bathsheba. Then he actually committed adultery. Instead of openly admitting what he had done, he tried to cover his sin. He tried to deceive Bathsheba's husband, made him drunk, and had him killed. He lied to himself and tried to carry on his royal duties in the usual way. When his court chaplain, the Prophet Nathan, confronted him with a similar hypothetical situation, David condemned the other man, though he felt no condemnation at all for himself. Once we begin to lie to others, it may not be long before we actually *believe* our lie.

But the spiritual decline becomes still worse: the next step is trying to lie *to God* (1 John 1:10). We have made ourselves liars; now we try to make God a liar! We contradict His Word, which says that *"all* have sinned," and we maintain that we are exceptions to the rule. We apply God's Word to others but not to ourselves. We sit through church services or Bible studies and are not touched by the Bible's teachings. Believers who have reached this low level are usually highly critical of other Christians, but they strongly resist applying the Word to their own lives.

The Holy Spirit's inspired picture of the human heart is devastating indeed! A believer lies about *his fellowship* (1 John 1:6); about *his nature*—"I could never do a thing like that!" (1 John 1:8) and about *his actions* (1 John 1:10).

Sin has a deadly way of spreading, doesn't it?

At this point we must discuss an extremely important factor in our experience of the life that is real. That factor is *honesty*. We must be honest with ourselves, honest with others, and honest with God. Our passage describes a believer who is living a dishonest life: he is a phony. He is playing a role and acting a part, but is not living a genuine life. He is insincere.

What losses does this kind of person experience?

For one thing, he loses *the Word*. He stops "doing the truth" (1 John 1:6); then the truth is no longer in him (1 John 1:8); and then he turns the truth into lies! (1 John 1:10) "Thy Word is truth" (John 17·17) said Jesus; but a person who lives a lie loses the Word. One of the first symptoms of walking in darkness is a loss of blessing from the Bible. You cannot read the Word profitably while you are walking in the dark.

But a dishonest person loses something else: he loses his fellowship with God and with God's people (1 John 1:6-7). As a result, prayer becomes an empty form to him. Worship is dull routine. He becomes critical of other Christians and starts staying away from church: "What communion hath light with darkness?" (2 Cor. 6:14)

A backslidden husband, for example, who is walking in spiritual darkness, out of fellowship with God, can never enjoy full fellowship with his Christian wife, who is walking in the light. In a superficial way, the couple can have companionship; but true spiritual fellowship is impossible. This inability to share spiritual experiences causes many personal problems in homes and between members of local churches.

A group of church members were discussing their new pastor.

"For some reason," said one man, "I really don't feel at ease with him. I believe he's a good man, all right—but something seems to stand between us."

Another member replied, "Yes, I think I know what you mean. I used to have that same problem with him, but now I don't have it anymore. The pastor and I have great fellowship."

"What did he do to make things better?"

"*He* didn't do anything," said the friend. "*I* did the changing."

"*You* did the changing?"

"Yes, I decided to be open and honest about things, the way our pastor is. You see, there isn't one stain of hypocrisy in his life, and there was so much pretending in *my* life that we just didn't make it together. He and I both knew I was a phony. Since I've started to live an honest Christian life, *everything* is better."

One problem with dishonesty is that just keeping a record of our lies and pretenses is a full-time job! Abraham Lincoln used to say that if a man is going to be a liar, he had better have a good memory! When a person uses up all his energy in *pretending*, he has nothing left for *living;* and life becomes shallow and tasteless. A person who pretends not only robs himself of reality, but he keeps himself from growing: his true self is smothered under the false self.

The third loss is really the result of the first two: the believer loses his character (1 John 2:4). The process starts out with his *telling* lies and it ends up with his *becoming a liar!* His insincerity, or lack of truthfulness, is at first a role that he plays. Then it is no longer a role—it has become the very essence of his life. His character has eroded. He is no longer a liar because he tells lies; he now tells lies because he is a confirmed liar.

Is it any wonder that God warns, "He that covereth his sins shall not prosper"? (Prov. 28:13) David tried to cover his sins and it cost him his health (Ps. 32:3-4), his joy (Ps. 51), his family, and almost his kingdom. If we want to enjoy the life that is real, we must *never* cover our sins.

What *should* we do?

## We Can Confess Our Sins (1 John 1:7, 9)

John gives two interesting titles to Jesus Christ: *Advocate* and *Propitiation* (1 John 2:1-2). It's important that we understand these two titles because they stand for two ministries that only the Lord Himself performs.

Let's begin with *Propitiation*. If you look this word up in the dictionary, you may get the wrong idea of its meaning. The dictionary tells us that "to propitiate" means "to appease someone who is angry." If you apply this to Christ, you get the horrible picture of an angry God, about to destroy the world, and a loving Saviour giving Himself to appease the irate God—and this is *not* the Bible picture of salvation! Certainly God is angry at sin; after all, He is infinitely holy. But the Bible reassures us that "God so *loved* [not *hated*] the world" (John 3:16, italics added).

No, the word "propitiation" does not mean the appeasing of an angry God. Rather, it means *the satisfying of God's holy law*. "God is light" (1 John 1:5) and, therefore, He cannot close His eyes to sin. But "God is love" (1 John 4:8) too and wants to save sinners.

How, then, can a holy God uphold His own justice and still forgive sinners? The answer is in the sacrifice of Christ. At the cross, God in His holiness judged sin. God in His love offers Jesus Christ to the world as Saviour. God was *just* in that He punished sin, but He is also *loving* in that He offers free forgiveness through what Jesus did at Calvary. (Read 1 John 4:10, and also give some thought to Rom. 3:23-26.)

Christ is the Sacrifice for the sins of the whole world, but He is Advocate only for believers. "We [Christians] have an Advocate with the Father." The word "advocate" used to be applied to lawyers. The word John uses is the very same word Jesus used when He was talking about the coming of the Holy Spirit (John 14:16, 26; 15:26). It means, literally, "one called alongside." When a man was summoned to court, he took an advocate (lawyer) with him to stand at his side and plead his case.

Jesus finished His work on earth (John 17:4)—the work of giving His life as a sacrifice for sin. Today He has an "unfinished work" in heaven. *He represents us before God's throne.* As our High Priest, He sympathizes with our weaknesses and temptations and gives us grace (Heb. 4:15-16; 7:23-28). As our Advocate, He helps us *when we sin.* When we confess our sins to God, because of Christ's advocacy God forgives us.

The Old Testament contains a beautiful picture of this. Joshua (Zech. 3:1-7) was the Jewish high priest after the Jews returned to their land following their Captivity in Babylon. (Don't confuse this Joshua with the Joshua who conquered the Promised Land.) The nation had sinned; to symbolize this, Joshua stood before God in filthy garments and Satan stood at Joshua's right hand to accuse him (cf. Rev. 12:10). God the Father was the Judge; Joshua, representing the people, was the accused; Satan was the prosecuting attorney. (The Bible calls him the accuser of the brethren.) It looked as if Satan had an open-and-shut case. But Joshua had an Advocate who stood at God's right hand, and this changed the situation. Christ gave Joshua a change of garments and silenced the accusations of Satan.

This is what is in view when Jesus Christ is called our "Advocate." He represents believers before God's throne, and the merits of His sacrifice make possible the forgiveness of the believer's sin. Because Christ *died* for His people, He satisfied the justice of God. ("The wages of sin is death.") Because He *lives* for us at God's right hand, He can apply His sacrifice to our needs day by day.

All He asks is that when we have failed we confess our sins.

What does it mean to "confess"? Well, to *confess* sins means much more than simply to "admit" them. The word *confess* actually means "to say the same thing [about]." To confess sin, then, means to say the same thing about it that God says about it.

A counselor was trying to help a man who had come forward during an evangelistic meeting. "I'm a Christian," the man said, "but there's sin in my life, and I need help." The counselor showed him 1 John 1:9 and suggested that the man confess his sins to God.

"O Father," the man began, "if we have done anything wrong—"

"Just a minute!" the counselor interrupted. "Don't drag *me* into your sin! My brother, it's not 'if' or 'we'—*you'd* better get down to business with God!"

The counselor was right.

Confession is not praying a lovely prayer, or making pious excuses, or trying to impress God and other Christians. True confession is naming sin—calling it by name what God calls it: envy, hatred, lust, deceit, or whatever it may be. Confession simply means being honest with ourselves and with God, and if others are involved, being honest with them too. It is more than *admitting* sin. It means *judging* sin and facing it squarely.

When we confess our sins, God promises to forgive us (1 John 1:9). But this promise is not a "magic rabbit's foot" that makes it easy for us to disobey God!

"I went out and sinned," a student told his campus chaplain, "because I knew I could come back and ask God to forgive me."

"On what basis can God forgive you?" the chaplain asked, pointing to 1 John 1:9.

"God is faithful and just," the boy replied.

"Those two words should have *kept you out of sin*," the chaplain said. "Do you know what it cost God to forgive your sins?"

The boy hung his head. "Jesus had to die for me."

Then the chaplain zeroed in. "That's right—forgiveness isn't some cheap sideshow trick God performs. God is faithful to His promise, and God is just, because Christ died for your sins and paid the penalty for you. Now, the next time you plan to sin, remember that you are going to sin against a faithful loving God!"

Of course, cleansing has two sides to it: the judicial and the personal. The blood of Jesus Christ, shed on the cross, delivers us from the guilt of sin and gives us right standing ("justification") before God. God is able to forgive because Jesus' death has satisfied His holy Law.

But God is also interested in cleansing a sinner inwardly. David prayed, "Create in me a clean heart, O God" (Ps. 51:10). When our confession is sincere, God does a cleansing work (1 John 1:9) in our hearts by His Spirit and through His Word (John 15:3).

The great mistake King David made was in trying to cover his sins instead of confessing them. For perhaps a whole year he lived in deceit and defeat. No wonder he wrote (Ps. 32:6) that a man should pray "in a time of finding out" (lit.).

When should we confess our sin? *Immediately when we discover it!* "He that covereth his sins shall not prosper; but whoso confesseth and forsaketh them shall have mercy" (Prov. 28:13). By walking in the light, we are able to see the "dirt" in our lives and deal with it immediately.

This leads to a third way to deal with sins.

## We Can Conquer Our Sins
## (1 John 2:1-3, 5-6)

John makes it clear that Christians do not *have* to sin. "I am writing these things unto you *that you may not sin*" (1 John 2:1, NASB).

The secret of victory over sin is found in the phrase "walk in the light" (1 John 1:7).

To walk in the light means to be open and honest, to be sincere. Paul prayed that his friends might "be sincere and without offense" (Phil. 1:10). The word *sincere* comes from two Latin words, *sine* and *cera*, which mean "without wax." It seems that in Roman days, some sculptors covered up their mistakes by filling the defects in their marble statues with wax, which was not readily visible—until the statue had been exposed to the hot sun awhile. But more dependable sculptors made certain that their customers knew that the statues they sold were *sine cera*—without wax.

It is unfortunate that churches and Bible classes have been invaded by insincere people, people whose lives cannot stand to be tested by God's light. "God is light," and when we walk in the light, there is nothing we can hide. It is refreshing to meet a Christian who is open and sincere and is not trying to masquerade!

To walk in the light means to be honest with God, with ourselves, and with others. It means that when the light reveals our sin to us, we immediately confess it to God and claim His forgiveness. And if our sin injures another person, we ask *his* forgiveness too.

But walking in the light means something else: it means obeying God's Word (1 John 2:3-4). "Thy Word is a lamp unto my feet and a light unto my path" (Ps. 119:105). To walk in the light means to spend time daily in God's Word, discovering His will; and then obeying what He has told us.

Obedience to God's Word is proof of our love for Him. There are three motives for obedience. We can obey because we *have to*, because we *need to*, or because we *want to*.

A slave obeys because he *has* to. If he doesn't obey he will be punished. An employee obeys because he *needs* to. He may not enjoy his work, but he *does* enjoy getting his paycheck! He needs to obey because he has a family to feed and clothe. But a Christian is to obey his Heavenly Father because he *wants* to—for the relationship between him and God is one of love. "If you love Me, keep My commandments" (John 14:15).

This is the way we learned obedience when we were children. First, we obeyed because we *had* to. If we didn't obey, we were spanked! But as we grew up, we discovered that obedience meant enjoyment and reward; so we started obeying because it met certain *needs* in our lives. And it was a mark of real maturity when we started obeying because of love.

"Baby Christians" must constantly be warned or rewarded. Mature Christians listen to God's Word and obey it simply because they love Him.

Walking in the light involves honesty, obedience, and love; it also involves following the example of Christ and walking as He walked (1 John 2:6). Of course, nobody ever *becomes* a Christian by following Christ's example; but *after* we come into God's family, we are to look to Jesus Christ as the one great Example of the kind of life we should live.

This means "abiding in Christ." Christ is not only the Propitiation (or sacrifice) for our sins (1 John 2:2) and the Advocate who represents us before God (1 John 2:1), but He is also the perfect Pattern (He is "Jesus Christ the righteous") for our daily life.

The key statement here is "as He is" (1 John 2:6). "Because *as He is,* so are we in this world" (1 John 4:17). We are to walk in the light "*as He is* in the light" (1 John 1:7). We are to purify ourselves "even *as He is* pure" (1 John 3:3). "He that doeth righteousness is righteous, even *as He is* righteous" (1 John 3:7). Walking in the light means living here on earth the way Jesus lived when He was here, and the way He is right now in heaven.

This has extremely practical applications in our daily lives. For example, what should a believer do when another believer sins against him? The answer is that believers should forgive one another "*even as* God for Christ's sake hath forgiven you" (Eph. 4:32; cf. Col. 3:13).

Walking in the light—following the example of Christ—will affect a home. Husbands are supposed to love their wives "even as Christ also loved the church" (Eph. 5:25). Husbands are supposed to care for their wives "even as the Lord" cares for the church (Eph. 5:29). And wives are to honor and obey their husbands (Eph. 5:22-24).

No matter what area of life it may be, our responsibility is to do what Jesus would do. "As He is, so are we in this world." We should "walk [live] even as He walked [lived]."

Jesus Himself taught His disciples what it means to abide in Him. He explains it in His illustration of the vine and its branches (John 15). Just as the branch gets its life by remaining in contact with the vine, so believers receive their strength by maintaining fellowship with Christ.

To abide in Christ means to depend completely on Him for all that we need in order to live for Him and serve Him. It is a living relationship. As He lives out His life through us, we are able to follow His example and walk as He walked. Paul expresses this experience perfectly: "Christ liveth in me" (Gal. 2:20).

This is a reference to the work of the Holy Spirit. Christ is our Advocate in heaven (1 John 2:1), to represent us before God when we sin. The Holy Spirit is God's Advocate for us here on earth. Christ is making intercession for us (Rom. 8:34), and the Holy Spirit is also making intercession for us (Rom. 8:26-27). We are part of a fantastic "heavenly party line": God the Son prays for us in heaven, and God the Spirit prays for us in our hearts. We have fellowship with the Father through the Son, and the Father has fellowship with us through the Spirit.

Christ lives out His life through us by the power of the Spirit, who lives within our bodies. It is not by means of *imitation* that we abide in Christ and walk as He walked. No, it is through *incarnation:* through His Spirit, "Christ liveth in me." To walk in the light is to walk in the Spirit and not fulfill the lusts of the flesh (cf. Gal. 5:16).

God has made provisions for us in these ways to conquer sin. We can never lose or change the sin nature that we were born with (1 John 1:8), but we need not obey its desires. As we walk in the light and see sin as it actually is, we will hate it and turn from it. And if we sin, we immediately confess it to God and claim His cleansing. By depending on the power of the indwelling Spirit, we abide in Christ and "walk as He walked."

But all this begins with openness and honesty before God and men. The minute we start to act a part, to pretend, to impress others, we step out of the light and into shadows. Sir Walter Scott puts it this way:

Oh, what a tangled web we weave
When first we practice to deceive!

The life that is real cannot be built on things that are deceptive. Before we can walk in the light, we must know ourselves, accept ourselves, and yield ourselves to God. It is foolish to try to deceive others because God already knows what we really are!

All this helps to explain why walking in the light makes life so much easier and happier. When you walk in the light, you live to please only one Person—God. This really simplifies things! Jesus said, "I do always those things that please *Him*" (John 8:29, italics added). We "ought to walk and to please God" (1 Thes. 4:1). If we live to please ourselves *and* God, we are trying to serve two masters, and this never works. If we live to please men, we will always be in trouble because no two men will agree and we will find ourselves caught in the middle. Walking in the light—living to please God—simplifies our goals, unifies our lives, and gives us a sense of peace and poise.

John makes it clear that the life that is real has no love for sin. Instead of trying to cover sin, a true believer confesses sin and tries to conquer it by walking in the light of God's Word. He is not content simply to know he is going to heaven. He wants to enjoy that heavenly life right here and now. "As He is, so are we in this world." He is careful to match his walk and his talk. He does not try to impress himself, God, or other Christians with a lot of "pious talk."

A congregation was singing, as a closing hymn, the familiar song, "For You I Am Praying." The speaker turned to a man on the platform and asked quietly, "For whom are *you* praying?"

The man was stunned. "Why, I guess I'm not praying for anybody. Why do you ask?"

"Well, I just heard you say, 'For you I am praying,' and I thought you meant it," the preacher replied.

"Oh, no," said the man. "I'm just singing."

Pious talk! A religion of words! To paraphrase James 1:22, "We should be doers of the Word as well as talkers of the Word." We must *walk* what we *talk*. It is not enough to know the language; we must also live the life. "If we say—" then we ought also *to do!*

# CHAPTER THREE
# SOMETHING OLD, SOMETHING NEW
## *1 John 2:7-11*

I just *love* that hat!"

"Man, I really *love* the old-fashioned kind of baked beans!"

"But, Mom, don't you realize that Tom and I *love* each other?"

Words, like coins, can be in circulation for such a long time that they start wearing out. Unfortunately, the word *love* (or, as it is now sometimes spelled, *luv)* is losing its value and is being used to cover a multitude of sins.

It is really difficult to understand how a man can use the same word to express his love for his wife as he uses to tell how he feels about baked beans! When words are used that carelessly they really mean little or nothing at all. Like the dollar, they have been devalued.

As John describes the life that is real, he uses three words repeatedly: *life, love,* and *light.* In fact, he devotes three sections of his letter to the subject of Christian love. He explains that *love, life,* and *light* belong together. Read these three sections (1 John 2:7-11; 3:10-24; 4:7-21) *without the intervening verses* and you will see that love, life, and light must not be separated.

In our present study (1 John 2:7-11), we learn how Christian love is affected by *light and darkness.* A Christian who is walking in the light (which simply means he is obeying God) is going to love his brother Christian.

In 1 John 3:10-24, we are told that Christian love is a matter of *life or death:* to live in hatred is to live in spiritual death. In 1 John 4:7-21 we see that Christian love is a matter of *truth or error* (cf. 1 John 4:6): because we *know* God's love toward us, we *show* God's love toward others.

In these three sections, then, we find three good reasons why Christians should love one another:

1. God has commanded us to love (1 John 2:7-11).

2. We have been born of God and God's love lives in us (1 John 3:10-24).

3. God first revealed His love to us (1 John 4:7-21). "We love . . . because He first loved us."

John not only *writes* about love but also *practices* it. One of his favorite names for his readers is "Beloved." He felt love for them. John is known as the "Apostle of Love" because in his Gospel and his epistles he gives such prominence to this subject. However, John was not *always* the "Apostle of Love." At one time Jesus gave John and his brother James, both of whom had hot tempers, the nickname "Boanerges" (Mark 3:17), which means "sons of thunder." On another occasion these two brothers wanted to call down fire from heaven to destroy a village (Luke 9:51-56).

Since the New Testament was written in Greek, the writers were often able to use more precise language. It is unfortunate that our English word *love* has so many shades of meaning (some of them contradictory). When we read in 1 John about "love," the Greek word used is *agape* (ah-GAH-pay), the word for God's love toward man, a Christian's love for other Christians, and God's love for His church (Eph. 5:22-33).

Another Greek word for love, *philia* (fee-LEE-ah), used elsewhere, carries the idea of "friendship love," which is not quite as profound or divine as *agape* love. (The Greek word for sensual love, *eros,* from which we get our word *erotic,* is not used at all in the New Testament.)

The amazing thing is that Christian love is both old and new (1 John 2:7-8). This seems to be a contradiction. Love itself, of course, is not new, nor is the commandment—that men love God and each other—a new thing. Jesus Himself combined two Old Testament commandments, Deuteronomy 6:5 and Leviticus 19:18, and said (Mark 12:28-34) that these two commandments summarize all the Law and the Prophets. Loving God and loving one's neighbor were old, familiar responsibilities before Jesus ever came to earth.

In what sense, then, *is* "love one another" a "new" (1 John 2:8) commandment? Again, a look at the Greek helps to answer the question.

The Greeks had two different words for "new"—one means "new in time," and the other means "new in quality." For example, you would use the first word to describe the latest car, a recent model. But if you purchased a car that was so revolutionary that it was *radically* different, you would use the second word—new in quality. (Our English words "recent" and "fresh" just about make this dis-

tinction: "recent" means new in time, "fresh" means new in character.)

The commandment to love one another is not new in time, but it is new in character. Because of Jesus Christ, the old commandment to "love one another" has taken on new meaning. We learn in these five brief verses (1 John 2:7-11) that the commandment is new in three important ways.

### It Is New in Emphasis (1 John 2:7)

In the previous paragraph (1 John 2:3-6), John has been talking about "the commandments" in general, but now he narrows his focus down to *one single commandment.* In the Old Testament, the command that God's people love one another was only one of *many,* but now this old commandment is lifted out and given a place of preeminence.

How is it possible for one commandment to stand head and shoulders above all the others? This is explained by the fact that love is the fulfillment of God's Law (Rom. 13:8-10).

Parents must care for their children according to law. Child neglect is a serious crime. But how many parents have a conversation like this when the alarm clock goes off in the morning?

*She:* "Honey, you'd better get up and go to work. We don't want to get arrested."

*He:* "Yeah, and you'd better get up and get breakfast for the kids, and get their clothes ready. The cops might show up and put us both in jail."

*She:* "You're right. Boy, it's a good thing they have a law, or we'd stay in bed all day!"

It's doubtful that the fear of the law is often the motive behind earning a living or caring for one's children. Parents fulfill their responsibilities (even if grudgingly on occasion) because they love each other and their children. To them, doing the right thing is not a matter of *law*—it's a matter of *love.*

The commandment "Love one another" is the fulfillment of God's Law in the same way. When you love people, you do not lie about them or steal from them. You have no desire to kill them. Love for God and love for others motivates a person to obey God's commandments *without even thinking about them!* When a person acts out of Christian love he obeys God and serves others—not because of fear, but because of his love.

This is why John says that "Love one another" is a new commandment—it is *new in emphasis.* It is not simply one of many commandments. No, it stands at the top of the list!

But it is new in emphasis in another way too. It stands at the very beginning of the Christian life. "The old commandment is the word which ye had from the beginning" (1 John 2:7). This phrase "from the beginning" is used in two different ways in John's letter, and it is important that you distinguish them. In 1 John 1:1, describing the eternality of Christ, we read that He existed "from the beginning." In John 1:1—a parallel verse—we read, "In the beginning was the Word."

But in 1 John 2:7, the subject is *the beginning of the Christian life*. The commandment to love one another is not an appendix to our Christian experience, as though God had an afterthought. No! It is in our hearts from the very beginning of our faith in Jesus Christ. If this were not so, John could not have written, "We know that we have passed out of death into life because we love the brethren" (1 John 3:14, NASB). And Jesus said, "By this all men will know that you are My disciples, if you have love for one another" (John 13:35, NASB).

By nature, an unsaved person may be selfish and even hateful. As much as we love a newborn baby, we must confess that the infant is self-centered and thinks the whole world revolves around his crib. The child is typical of an unsaved person. "We ourselves also were sometimes foolish, disobedient, deceived, serving divers lusts and pleasures, living in malice and envy, hateful and hating one another" (Titus 3:3). This unretouched photo of the unbeliever may not be beautiful, but it is certainly accurate! Some unregenerate persons do not display the traits here mentioned, but the works of the flesh (Gal. 5:19-21) are always potentially present in their dispositions.

When a sinner trusts Christ, he receives a new life and a new nature. The Holy Spirit of God comes to live in him and the love of God is "shed abroad in [his] heart" by the Spirit (Rom. 5:5). God does not have to give a new believer a long lecture about love! "For ye yourselves are taught of God [i.e., by the Holy Spirit within you] to love one another" (1 Thes. 4:9). A new believer discovers that he now hates what he used to love, and that he loves what he used to hate!

So the commandment to love one another is new in *emphasis:* it is one of the most important commandments Christ gave us (John 13:34). In fact, "love one another" is repeated at least a dozen times in the New Testament (John 13:34; 15:9, 12, 17; Rom. 13:8; 1 Thes. 4:9; 1 Peter 1:22; 1 John 3:11, 23; 4:7, 11-12; 2 John 5). And there are many other references to brotherly love.

It is important that we understand the meaning of Christian love. It is not a shallow sentimental emotion that Christians try to "work up" so they can get along with each other. It is a matter of the *will* rather than an *emotion*—an affection for and attraction to certain persons. It is a matter of determining—of making up your mind—that you will allow God's love to reach others through you, and then of acting toward them in loving ways. You are not to act "as if you loved them," but *because* you love them. This is not hypocrisy—it is obedience to God.

Perhaps the best explanation of Christian love is 1 Corinthians 13. You should read a modern translation of this chapter to get the full force of its message: the Christian life without love is NOTHING!

But the commandment "Love one another" is not only new in emphasis. It is new in another way.

### It Is New in Example (1 John 2:8)

"Love one another," John points out, was first true in Christ, and now it is true in the lives of those who are trusting Christ. Jesus Himself is the greatest Example of this commandment.

Later on we will think about that great statement, "God is love" (1 John 4:8), but it is anticipated here. When one looks at Jesus Christ, one sees love embodied and exemplified. In commanding us to love, Jesus does not ask us to do something that He has not already done Himself. The four Gospel records are the account of a life lived in the spirit of love—and that life was lived under conditions far from ideal. Jesus says to us, in effect, "I lived by this great commandment, and I can enable you to follow My example."

Jesus illustrated love by the very life that He lived. He *never* showed hatred or malice. His righteous soul hated all sin and disobedience, but He *never hated the people who committed such sins*. Even in His righteous announcements of judgment, there was always an undercurrent of love.

It is encouraging to think of Jesus' love for the twelve disciples. How they must have broken His heart again and again as they argued over who was the greatest, or tried to keep people from seeing their Master. Each of them was different from the others, and Christ's love was broad enough to include each one in a personal, understanding way. He was patient with Peter's impulsiveness, Thomas' unbelief, and even Judas' treachery. When Jesus commanded His disciples to love one another, He was only telling them to do as He had done.

Consider too our Lord's love for all kinds of people. The publicans and sinners were attracted (Luke 15:1) by His love, and even the lowest of the low could weep at His feet (Luke 7:36-39). Spiritually hungry rabbi Nicodemus could meet with Him privately at night (John 3:1-21), and 4,000 of the "common people" could listen to His teaching for three days (Mark 8:1-9) and then receive a miraculous meal from Him. He held babies in His arms. He spoke about children at play. He even comforted the women who wept as the soldiers led Him out to Calvary.

Perhaps the greatest thing about Jesus' love was the way it touched even the lives of His enemies. He looked with loving pity on the religious leaders who in their spiritual blindness accused Him of being in league with Satan (Matt. 12:24). When the mob came to arrest Him, He could have called on the armies of heaven for protection, but He yielded to His enemies. And then He died for them— for His enemies! "Greater love hath no man than this, that a man lay down his life for his *friends*" (John 15:13, italics added). But Jesus died not only for His friends, but also for *His foes!* And as they crucified Him, He prayed for them: "Father, forgive them, for they know not what they do."

In His life, in His teachings, and in His death, Jesus is the perfect Example of this new commandment, "Love one another." And this is what helps to make the commandment "new." In Christ we have a new illustration of the old truth that God is love and that the life of love is the life of joy and victory.

What is true in Christ ought to be true in each believer. "As He is, so are we in this world" (1 John 4:17). A believer should live a life of Christian love "because the darkness is passing away, and the true light is already shining" (1 John 2:8, NASB). This reminds us of the emphasis (1 John 1) on walking in the light. Two ways of life are contrasted: those who walk in the light practice love; those who walk in the darkness practice hatred. The Bible repeatedly emphasizes this truth.

"The darkness *is passing away,*" but the light does not yet shine fully all over the world, nor does it penetrate every area of even a believer's life.

When Christ was born, "the Dayspring from on high" visited the world (Luke 1:78). "Dayspring" means *sunrise.* The birth of Christ was the beginning of a new day for mankind! As He lived before men, taught them, and ministered to them, He spread the light of life and love. "The people who sat in darkness saw a great light; and to them which sat in the region and shadow of death light is sprung up" (Matt. 4:16).

But there is a conflict in this world between the forces of light and the forces of darkness. "And the light is shining in the darkness, and the darkness is not able to put it out" (John 1:5, lit.). Satan is the Prince of darkness, and he extends his evil kingdom by means of lies and hatred. Christ is the Sun of Righteousness (Mal. 4:2), and He extends His kingdom by means of truth and love.

The kingdoms of Christ and of Satan are in conflict today, but "the path of the just is as the shining light, that shineth more and more unto the perfect day" (Prov. 4:18). The darkness is passing away little by little, and the True Light is shining brighter and brighter in our hearts.

Jesus Christ is the standard of love for Christians. "A new commandment I give unto you, that ye love one another," He says; "as I have loved you, that ye also love one another" (John 13:34). And He repeats: "This is My commandment, that ye love one another, *as I have loved you*" (John 15:12, italics added). We are not to measure our Christian love against the love of some other Christian (and we usually pick somebody whose life is more of an excuse than an example!) but against the love of Jesus Christ our Lord. The old commandment becomes "new" to us as we see it fulfilled in Christ.

So the commandment, "Love one another," is new in emphasis and new in example. It is also new in a third way.

**It Is New in Experience (1 John 2:9-11)**
Our passage continues the illustration of light and darkness. If a Christian walks in the light and is in fellowship with God, he will also be in fellowship with others in God's family. *Love* and *light* go together, much as *hatred* and *darkness* go together.

It is easy to talk about Christian love, but

much more difficult to practice it. For one thing, such love is not mere talk (1 John 2:9). For a Christian to say (or sing!) that he loves the brethren, while he actually hates another believer, is for him to lie. In other words (and this is a sobering truth), *it is impossible to be in fellowship with the Father and out of fellowship with another Christian at the same time.*

This is one reason why God established the local church, the fellowship of believers. "You can't be a Christian alone"—a person cannot live a complete and developing Christian life unless he is in fellowship with God's people. The Christian life has two relationships: the vertical (Godward) and the horizontal (manward). And what God has joined together, man must not put asunder! And each of these two relationships is to be one of love, one for the other.

Jesus deals with this matter in the Sermon on the Mount (cf. Matt. 5:21-26). A gift on the altar was valueless as long as the worshiper had a dispute to settle with his brother. Note that Jesus does not say that the worshiper had something against his brother, but that the brother had something against the worshiper. But even when *we* have been offended, we should not wait for the one who has offended us to come to us; *we should go to him.* If we do not, Jesus warns us that we will end up in a prison of spiritual judgment where we will have to pay the last penny (Matt. 18:21-35). In other words, when we harbor an unforgiving, unloving spirit, we harm ourselves most.

The contrast between "saying" and "doing" is one we have met before (1 John 1:6, 8, 10; 2:4, 6). It is easy to practice a Christianity of "words"—singing the right songs, using the right vocabulary, praying the right prayers—and, through it all, deceiving ourselves into thinking we are spiritual. This mistake also ties into something Jesus taught in the Sermon on the Mount (Matt. 5:33-37). What we say should be the true expression of our character. We should not need extra words ("oaths") to fortify what we say. Our yes should mean yes and our no should mean no. So, if we *say* we are in the light, we will prove it by loving the brethren. Many Christians urgently need to be accepted, loved, and encouraged.

Contrary to popular opinion, Christian love is not "blind." When we practice true Christian love, we find life getting brighter and brighter. Hatred is what darkens life! When true Christian love flows out of our hearts, we will have greater understanding and perception in spiritual things. This is why Paul prays that our love may grow in knowledge and perception, "that ye may distinguish the things that differ" (cf. Phil. 1:9-10). A Christian who loves his brother is a Christian who sees more clearly.

No book in the Bible illustrates the blinding power of hatred like the Book of Esther. The events recorded there take place in Persia, where many of the Jews were living after the Captivity. Haman, one of the king's chief men, had a burning hatred for the Jews. The only way he could satisfy this hatred was to see the whole nation destroyed. He plunged ahead in an evil plot, completely blind to the fact that the Jews would win and that he himself would be destroyed.

Hatred is blinding people today too.

Christian love is not a shallow sentiment, a passing emotion that we perhaps experience in a church service. Christian love is a *practical* thing; it applies in the everyday affairs of life. Just consider the "one another" statements in the New Testament and you will see how practical it is to love one another. Here are just a few (there are over twenty such statements):

Wash one another's feet (John 13:14).

Prefer one another (Rom. 12:10).

Be of the same mind one to another (Rom. 12:16).

Do not judge one another (Rom. 14:13).

Receive one another (Rom. 15:7).

Admonish one another (Rom. 15:14).

Edify [build up] one another (1 Thes. 5:11).

Bear one another's burdens (Gal. 6:2).

Confess your faults to one another (James 5:16).

Use hospitality one to another (1 Peter 4:9).

In short, to love other Christians means to treat them the way *God* treats them—and the way God treats us. Christian love that does not show itself in action and in attitude (cf. 1 Cor. 13:4-7) is spurious.

What happens to a believer who does not love the brethren? We have already seen the first tragic result: he lives in the darkness, though he probably *thinks* he is living in the light (1 John 2:9). He *thinks* he sees, but he is actually blinded by the darkness of hatred. This is the kind of person who causes trouble in Christian groups. He thinks he is a "spiritual giant," with great understanding, when actually he is a babe with very little spiritual perception. He may read the Bible faithfully and pray fervently, but if he has hatred in his heart, he is living a lie.

The second tragic result is that such a believer becomes a cause of stumbling (cf. 1 John 2:10). It is bad enough when an unloving believer hurts himself (1 John 2:9); but when he starts to hurt *others* the situation is far more serious. It is *serious* to walk in the darkness. It is *dangerous* to walk in the darkness when stumbling blocks are in the way! An unloving brother stumbles himself, and in addition he causes others to stumble.

A man who was walking down a dark street one night saw a pinpoint of light coming toward him in a faltering way. He thought perhaps the person carrying the light was ill or drunk; but as he drew nearer he could see a man with a flashlight carrying *a white cane.*

"Why would a blind man be carrying a light?" the man wondered, and then he decided to ask.

The blind man smiled. "I carry my light, not so *I* can see, but so that *others* can see me. I cannot help being blind," he said, "but I can help being a stumbling block."

The best way to help other Christians not to stumble is to love them. Love makes us stepping-stones; hatred (or any of its "cousins," such as envy or malice) makes us stumbling blocks. It is important that Christians exercise love in a local church, or else there will always be problems and disunity. When we are falling over each other, instead of lifting each other higher, we will never become a truly happy spiritual family.

Apply this, for instance, to the delicate matter of "questionable things" (Rom. 14–15). Since believers come from different backgrounds, they do not always agree. In Paul's day, they differed on such matters as diets and holy days. One group said it was unspiritual to eat meat offered to idols. Another group wanted strict observance of the Sabbath. There were several facets to the problem, but basic to its solution was: "Love one another!" Paul puts it this way: "Let us not, therefore, judge one another anymore; but judge this, rather, that no man put a stumbling block or an occasion to fall in his brother's way. . . . But if thy brother be grieved with thy food, now walkest thou not in love" (Rom. 14:13, 15, sco).

A third tragic result of hatred is that it retards a believer's spiritual progress (1 John

2:11). A blind man—a person who is walking in darkness—can never find his way! The only atmosphere that is conducive to spiritual growth is the atmosphere of spiritual light—of love. Just as the fruits and flowers need sunshine, so God's people need love if they are going to grow.

The commandment, "Love one another," becomes new to us in our own day-by-day experience. It is not enough for us to recognize that it is new in emphasis and say, "Yes, love is important!" Nor is it enough for us to see God's love exemplified by Jesus Christ. We must know this love *in our own experience.* The old commandment, "Love one another," becomes a *new* commandment as we practice God's love in daily life.

Thus far, we have seen the *negative* side of 1 John 2:9-11; now let's look at the positive. If we practice Christian love, what will the wonderful results be?

First of all, we will be living in the light—living in fellowship with God and with our Christian brothers.

Second, we will not stumble or become stumbling blocks to others.

And, third, we will grow spiritually and will progress toward Christlikeness.

At this point, we should think about the contrast between the ugly "works of the flesh" (Gal. 5:19-21) and the beautiful fruit of the Spirit—"Love, joy, peace, patience, gentleness, goodness, faithfulness, meekness, and self-control" (Gal. 5:22-23).

When we are walking in the light, the "seed of the Word" (Luke 8:11) can take root and bear fruit. And the first cluster the Spirit produces is *love!*

But love does not live alone. Love produces *joy!* Hatred makes a man miserable, but love always brings him joy.

A Christian couple came to see a pastor because their marriage was beginning to fall apart. "We're both saved," the discouraged husband said, "but we just aren't happy together. There's no joy in our home." As the pastor talked with them and they considered together what the Bible has to say, one fact became clear: both the husband and wife were nursing grudges. Each recalled many annoying little things the other had done!

"If you two really loved each other," said the pastor, "you wouldn't file these hurts away in your hearts. Grudges fester in our hearts like infected sores, and poison the whole system."

Then he read, "[Love] thinketh no evil" (1 Cor. 13:5). He explained, "This means that love never keeps records of things others do that hurt us. When we truly love someone, our love covers their sins and helps to heal the wounds they cause." Then he read, "And above all things have fervent love among yourselves; for love shall cover the multitude of sins" (1 Peter 4:8, sco).

Before the couple left, the pastor counseled them: "Instead of keeping records of the things that hurt, start remembering the things that please. An unforgiving spirit always breeds poison, but a loving spirit that sees and remembers the best always produces health."

A Christian who walks in love is always experiencing some new joy because the "fruit of the Spirit" is love and joy. And when we blend "love" and "joy," we will have "peace"—and peace helps to produce "patience." In other words, walking in the light, walking in love, is the secret of Christian growth, which nearly always begins with love.

Now, all of us must admit that we cannot generate Christian love under our own power. By nature, we are selfish and hateful. It is only as God's Spirit floods our hearts with love that we, in turn, can love one another. "The love of God is shed abroad in our hearts by the Holy Ghost who is given unto us" (Rom. 5:5). The Spirit of God makes the commandment, "Love one another," into a new and exciting day-by-day experience. If we walk in the light, God's Spirit produces love. If we walk in darkness, our own selfish spirit produces hatred.

The Christian life—the life that is real—is a beautiful blending of "something old, something new." The Holy Spirit takes the "old things" and makes them "new things" in our experience. When you stop to think about it, the Holy Spirit never grows old! He is always young! And He is the only Person on earth *today* who was here centuries ago when Jesus lived, taught, died, and rose again. He is the only One who can take "old truth" and make it fresh and new in our daily experience at this present time.

There are other exciting truths in the rest of John's letter, but if we fail to obey in this matter of love, the rest of the letter may well be "darkness" to us. Perhaps the best thing we can do, right *now,* is to search our hearts to see if we hold anything against a brother, or if someone has anything against us. The life that is real is an honest life—and it is a life of

*doing,* not merely *saying.* It is a life of active love in Christ. This means forgiveness, kindness, long-suffering. But it also means joy and peace and victory.

The love life is the only life, because it is the life that is real!

# CHAPTER FOUR
# THE LOVE GOD HATES
## *1 John 2:12-17*

A group of first-graders had just completed a tour of a hospital, and the nurse who had directed them was asking for questions. Immediately a hand went up.

"How come the people who work here are always washing their hands?" a little fellow asked.

After the laughter had subsided, the nurse gave a wise answer:

"They are 'always washing their hands' for two reasons. First, they love health; and second, *they hate germs.*"

In more than one area of life, love and hate go hand in hand. A husband who loves his wife is certainly going to exercise a hatred for what would harm her. "Ye that love the Lord, hate evil" (Ps. 97:10). "Let love be without hypocrisy. Abhor what is evil; cleave to what is good" (Rom. 12:9, NASB).

John's epistle has reminded us to exercise love (1 John 2:7-11)—the right kind of love. Now it warns us that there is a *wrong* kind of love, a love that God hates. This is love for what the Bible calls "the world."

There are four reasons why Christians should not love "the world."

**Because of What the World Is**
The New Testament word *world* has at least three different meanings. It sometimes means the *physical* world, *the earth:* "God that made the world [our planet] and all things therein" (Acts 17:24). It also means the *human* world, *mankind:* "For God so loved the world" (John 3:16). Sometimes these two ideas appear together: "He [Jesus] was in the world, and the world [earth] was made by Him, and the world [mankind] knew Him not" (John 1:10).

But the warning, "Love not the world!" is not about the world of nature or the world of men. Christians ought to appreciate the beauty and usefulness of the earth God has made, since He "giveth us richly all things to enjoy" (1 Tim. 6:17). And they certainly ought to love people—not only their friends, but even their enemies.

This "world" named here as our enemy is an invisible spiritual system opposed to God and Christ.

We use the word *world* in the sense of *system* in our daily conversation. The TV announcer says, "We bring you the news from the world of sports." "The world of sports" is not a separate planet or continent. It is an organized system, made up of a set of ideas, people, activities, purposes, etc. And "the world of finance" and "the world of politics" are likewise systems of their own. Behind what we see, in sports or finance, is an invisible system that we cannot see; and it is the system that "keeps things going."

"The world," in the Bible, is Satan's system for opposing the work of Christ on earth. It is the very opposite of what is godly (1 John 2:16) and holy and spiritual. "We know that we are of God, and the whole world lies in the power of the evil one" (1 John 5:19, NASB). Jesus called Satan "the prince of this world" (John 12:31). The devil has an organization of evil spirits (Eph. 6:11-12) working with him and influencing the affairs of "this world."

Just as the Holy Spirit uses people to accomplish God's will on earth, so Satan uses people to fulfill his evil purposes. Unsaved people, whether they realize it or not, are energized by "the prince of the power of the air, the spirit that now worketh in the children of disobedience" (Eph. 2:1-2).

Unsaved people belong to "this world." Jesus calls them "the children of this world" (Luke 16:8). When Jesus was here on earth, the people of "this world" did not understand Him, nor do they now understand those of us who trust Him (1 John 3:1). A Christian is a member of the *human* world, and he lives in the *physical* world, but he does not belong to the *spiritual* world that is Satan's system for opposing God. "If ye were of the world [Satan's system], the world would love his own; but because ye are not of the world, but I have chosen you out of the world, therefore the world hateth you" (John 15:18).

"The world," then, is not a natural habitat for a believer. The believer's citizenship is in heaven (Phil. 3:20, NASB), and all his effective resources for living on earth come from his Father in heaven.

The believer is somewhat like a scuba diver. The water is not man's natural habitat, for he is not equipped for life in (or under) it. When a scuba diver goes under, he has to take special equipment with him so that he can breathe.

Were it not for the Holy Spirit's living within us, and the spiritual resources we have in prayer, Christian fellowship, and the Word, we could never "make it" here on earth. We complain about the pollution of earth's atmosphere—the atmosphere of "the world" is also so polluted spiritually that Christians cannot breathe normally!

But there is a second—and more serious—reason why Christians must not love the world.

## Because of What the World Does to Us (1 John 2:15-16)

"If any man love the world, the love of the Father is not in him" (1 John 2:15).

Worldliness is not so much a matter of *activity* as of *attitude*. It is possible for a Christian to stay away from questionable amusements and doubtful places and still love the world, for worldliness is a matter of the heart. To the extent that a Christian loves the world system and the things in it, he does *not* love the Father.

Worldliness not only affects your response to the love of God; it also affects your response *to the will of God*. "The world passeth away . . . but he that doeth the will of God abideth forever" (1 John 2:17).

Doing the will of God is a joy for those living in the love of God. "If ye love Me, keep My commandments." But when a believer loses his enjoyment of the Father's love, he finds it hard to obey the Father's will.

When you put these two factors together, you have a practical definition of worldliness: anything in a Christian's life that causes him to lose his enjoyment of the Father's love or his desire to do the Father's will is worldly and must be avoided. Responding to the Father's love (your personal devotional life), and doing the Father's will (your daily conduct)—these are two tests of worldliness.

Many things in this world are definitely wrong and God's Word identifies them as sins. It is wrong to steal and to lie (Eph. 4:25, 28). Sexual sins are wrong (Eph. 5:1-3). About these and many other actions, Christians can have little or no debate. But there are areas of Christian conduct that are not so clear and about which even the best Christians disagree. In such cases, each believer must apply the test to his own life and be scrupulously honest in his self-examination, remembering that even a *good* thing may rob a believer of his enjoyment of God's love and his desire to do God's will.

A senior student in a Christian college was known for his excellent grades and his effective Christian service. He was out preaching each weekend and God was using him to win the souls and challenge Christians.

Then something happened: his testimony was no longer effective, his grades began to drop, and even his personality seemed to change. The president called him in.

"There's been a change in your life and your work," the president said, "and I wish you'd tell me what's wrong."

The student was evasive for a time, but then he told the story. He was engaged to a lovely Christian girl and was planning to get married after graduation. He had been called to a fine church and was anxious to move his new bride into the parsonage and get started in the pastorate.

"I've been so excited about it that I've even come to the place where I don't want the Lord to come back!" he confessed. "And then the power dropped out of my life."

His plans—good and beautiful as they were—came between him and the Father. He lost his enjoyment of the Father's love. He was worldly!

John points out that the world system uses three devices to trap Christians: the lust (desire) of the flesh, the lust of the eyes, and the pride of life (1 John 2:16). These same devices trapped Eve back in the Garden: "And when the woman saw that the tree was good for food [*the lust of the flesh*], and that it was pleasant to the eyes [*the lust of the eyes*], and a tree to be desired to make one wise [*the pride of life*], she took of the fruit" (Gen. 3:6).

The lust of the flesh includes anything that appeals to man's fallen nature. "The flesh" does not mean "the body." Rather, it refers to the basic nature of unregenerate man that makes him blind to spiritual truth (1 Cor. 2:14). Flesh is the nature we receive in our physical birth; spirit is the nature we receive in the second birth (John 3:5-6). When we trust Christ, we become "partakers of the di-

vine nature" (2 Peter 1:4). A Christian has both the old nature (flesh) and the new nature (Spirit) in his life. And what a battle these two natures can wage! (Gal. 5:17-23)

God has given man certain desires, and these desires are good. Hunger, thirst, weariness, and sex are not at all evil in themselves. There is nothing wrong about eating, drinking, sleeping, or begetting children. But when the flesh nature controls them, they become sinful "lusts." Hunger is not evil, but gluttony is sinful. Thirst is not evil, but drunkenness is a sin. Sleep is a gift of God, but laziness is shameful. Sex is God's precious gift when used rightly; but when used wrongly, it becomes immorality.

Now you can see how the world operates. It appeals to the normal appetites and tempts us to satisfy them in forbidden ways. In today's world we are surrounded by all kinds of allurements that appeal to our lower nature—and "the flesh is weak" (Matt. 26:41). If a Christian yields to it, he will get involved in the "works of the flesh" (Gal. 5:19-21 gives us the ugly list).

It is important that a believer remember what God says about his old nature, the flesh. Everything God says about the flesh is *negative*. In the flesh there is *no good thing* (Rom. 7:18). The flesh profits *nothing* (John 6:63). A Christian is to put *no confidence* in the flesh (Phil. 3:3). He is to make *no provision* for the flesh (Rom. 13:14). A person who lives for the flesh is living a negative life.

The second device that the world uses to trap the Christian is called "the lust of the eyes." We sometimes forget that the eyes can have an appetite! (Have you ever said, "Feast your eyes on this"?)

The lust of the flesh appeals to the lower appetites of the old nature, tempting us to indulge them in sinful ways. The lust of the eyes, however, operates in a more refined way. In view here are pleasures that gratify the sight and the mind—sophisticated and intellectual pleasures. Back in the days of the Apostle John, the Greeks and Romans lived for entertainments and activities that excited the eyes. Times have not changed very much! In view of television, perhaps every Christian's prayer ought to be, "Turn away my eyes from looking at vanity" (Ps. 119:37, NASB).

Achan (Josh. 7), a soldier, brought defeat to Joshua's army because of the lust of his eyes. God had warned Israel not to take any spoils from the condemned city of Jericho, but Achan did not obey. He explained: "When I saw among the spoils a goodly Babylonish garment, and 200 shekels of silver, then I coveted them, and took them" (Josh. 7:21). The lust of the eyes led him into sin, and his sin led the army into defeat.

The eyes (like the other senses) are a gateway into the mind. The lust of the eyes, therefore, can include intellectual pursuits that are contrary to God's Word. There is pressure to make Christians *think* the way the world thinks. God warns us against "the counsel of the ungodly." This does not mean that Christians ignore education and secular learning; it *does* mean they are careful not to let intellectualism crowd God into the background.

The third device is the "boastful pride of life" (NASB). God's glory is rich and full; man's glory is vain and empty. In fact, the Greek word for "pride" was used to describe a braggart who was trying to impress people with his importance. People have always tried to outdo others in their spending and their getting. The boastful pride of life motivates much of what such people do.

Why is it that so many folks buy houses, cars, appliances, or wardrobes *that they really cannot afford?* Why do they succumb to the "travel now, pay later" advertising and get themselves into hopeless debt taking vacations far beyond their means? Largely because they want to impress other people—because of their "pride of life." They may want folks to notice how affluent or successful they are.

Most of us do not go that far, but it is amazing what stupid things people do just to make an impression. They even sacrifice honesty and integrity in return for notoriety and a feeling of importance.

Yes, the world appeals to a Christian through the lust of the flesh, the lust of the eyes, and the pride of life. And once the world takes over in one of these areas, a Christian will soon realize it. He will lose his enjoyment of the Father's love and his desire to do the Father's will. The Bible will become boring and prayer a difficult chore. Even Christian fellowship may seem empty and disappointing. It is not that there is something wrong with others, however—what's wrong is the Christian's worldly heart.

It is important to note that no Christian becomes worldly all of a sudden. Worldliness creeps up on a believer; it is a gradual process. First is the *friendship of the world* (James 4:4). By nature, the world and the Christian are enemies ("Marvel not, my brethren, if the world hate you," 1 John 3:13). A Christian who is a friend of the world is an enemy of God.

Next, the Christian becomes *"spotted by the world"* (James 1:27). The world leaves its dirty marks on one or two areas of his life. This means that gradually the believer accepts and adopts the ways of the world.

When this happens, the world ceases to hate the Christian and starts to love him! So John warns us, "Love not the world!"—but too often our friendship with the world leads to love. As a result, the believer becomes *conformed to the world* (Rom. 12:2) and you can hardly tell the two apart.

Among Christians, worldliness rears its ugly head in many subtle and unrecognized forms. Sometimes we tend to idolize great athletes, TV stars, or political leaders who profess to be Christians—as if these individuals were able to be of special help to Almighty God. Or we cater to wealthy and "influential" persons in our local church, as if God's work would fold up without their good will or financial backing. *Many* forms of worldliness do not involve reading the wrong books and indulging in "carnal" amusements.

Sad to say, being *conformed to* the world can lead a Christian into being *"condemned with* the world" (1 Cor. 11:32). If a believer confesses and judges this sin, God will forgive him; but if he does not confess, God must lovingly chasten him. When a Christian is "condemned with the world," he does not lose his sonship. Rather, he loses his testimony and his spiritual usefulness. And in extreme cases, Christians have even lost their lives! (read 1 Cor. 11:29-30)

The downward steps and their consequences are illustrated in the life of Lot (Gen. 13:5-13; 14:8-14; 19). First Lot looked toward Sodom. Then he pitched his tent toward Sodom in the well-watered plains of Jordan. Then he moved into Sodom. And when Sodom was captured by the enemy, Lot was captured too. He was a believer (2 Peter 2:6-8), but he had to suffer with the unbelieving sinners of that wicked city. And when God destroyed Sodom, everything Lot lived for went up in smoke! Lot was saved so as by fire and lost his eternal reward (1 Cor. 3:12-15).

No wonder John warns us not to love the world!

## Because of What a Christian Is
## (1 John 2:12-14)

This raises a practical and important question about the nature of a Christian and how he keeps from getting worldly.

The answer is found in the unusual form of address used in 1 John 2:12-14. Note the titles used as John addresses his Christian readers: "little children . . . fathers . . . young men . . . little children."

What is he referring to?

To begin with, "little children" (1 John 2:12) refers to *all believers*. Literally, this word means "born ones." *All* Christians have been born into God's family through faith in Jesus Christ, and their sins have been forgiven. The very fact that one is in God's family, sharing His nature, ought to discourage him from becoming friendly with the world. To be friendly with the world is treachery! "Friendship with the world is enmity with God . . . whosoever therefore will be [wants to be] a friend of the world is the enemy of God" (cf. James 4:4).

But something else is true: we begin as little children—born ones—*but we must not stay that way!* Only as a Christian grows spiritually does he overcome the world.

John mentions three kinds of Christians in a local church family: fathers, young men, and little children (1 John 2:12-14). The "fathers," of course, are mature believers who have an intimate personal knowledge of God. Because they know God, they know the dangers of the world. No Christian who has experienced the joys and wonders of fellowship with God, and of service for God, will want to live on the substitute pleasures this world offers.

The "young men" are the conquerors: they have overcome the wicked one, Satan, who is the prince of this world system. How did they overcome him? Through the Word of God! "I have written unto you, young men, because ye are strong, and the Word of God abideth in you" (1 John 2:14). The "young men," then, are not yet fully mature; but they are maturing, for they use the Word of God effectively. The Word is the only weapon that will defeat Satan (Eph. 6:17).

The "little children" addressed in 1 John 2:13 are not those addressed in 1 John 2:12; two different Greek words are used. The word in 1 John 2:13 carries the idea of "immature ones," or little children still under the authority of teachers and tutors. These are young Christians who have not yet grown up in Christ. Like physical children, these spiritu-

al children know their father, but they still have some growing to do.

Here, then, is the Christian family! All of them are "born ones," but some of them have grown out of infancy into spiritual manhood and adulthood. *It is the growing, maturing Christian to whom the world does not appeal.* He is too interested in loving his Father and in doing his Father's will. The attractions of the world have no allure for him. He realizes that the things of the world are only toys, and he can say with Paul, "When I became a man, I put away childish things" (1 Cor. 13:11).

A Christian stays away from the world because of what the world is (a satanic system that hates and opposes Christ), because of what the world does to us (attracts us to live on sinful substitutes), and because of what he (the Christian) is—a child of God.

## Because of Where the World Is Going
## (1 John 2:17)

"The world is passing away!" (cf. 1 John 2:17)

That statement would be challenged by many men today who are confident that the world—the system in which we live—is as permanent as anything can be. But the world is *not* permanent. The only sure thing about this world system is that it is not going to be here forever. One day the system will be gone, and the pleasant attractions within it will be gone: all are passing away. What is going to last?

*Only what is part of the will of God!*

Spiritual Christians keep themselves "loosely attached" to this world because they live for something far better. They are "strangers and pilgrims on the earth" (Heb. 11:13). "For here have we no continuing city, but we seek one to come" (Heb. 13:14). In Bible times, many believers lived in tents because God did not want them to settle down and feel at home in this world.

John is contrasting two ways of life: a life lived for eternity and a life lived for time. A worldly person lives for the pleasures of the flesh, but a dedicated Christian lives for the joys of the Spirit. A worldly believer lives for what he can see, the lust of the eyes; but a spiritual believer lives for the unseen realities of God (2 Cor. 4:8-18). A worldly minded person lives for the pride of life, the vainglory that appeals to men; but a Christian who does the will of God lives for God's approval. And he "abideth forever."

Every great nation in history has become

decadent and has finally been conquered by another nation. There is no reason why we should suppose that *our* nation will be an exception. Some nineteen world civilizations in the past have slipped into oblivion. There is no reason why we should think that our present civilization will endure forever. "Change and decay in all around I see," wrote Henry F. Lyte (1793–1847), and if our civilization is not eroded by change and decay it will certainly be swept away and replaced by a new order of things at the coming of Christ, which could happen at any time.

Slowly but inevitably, and perhaps sooner than even Christians think, the world is passing away; but the man who does God's will abides forever.

This does not mean that all God's servants will be remembered by future generations. Of the multitudes of famous men who have lived on earth, less than 2,000 have been remembered by any number of people for more than a century.

Nor does it mean that God's servants will live on in their writings or in the lives of those they influenced. Such "immortality" may be a fact, but it is equally true of unbelievers like Karl Marx, Voltaire, or Adolf Hitler.

No, we are told here (1 John 2:17) that Christians who dedicate themselves to doing God's will—to obeying God—"abide [remain] forever." Long after this world system, with its vaunted culture, its proud philosophies, its egocentric intellectualism, and its godless materialism, has been forgotten, and long after this planet has been replaced by the new heavens and the new earth, God's faithful servants will remain—sharing the glory of God for all eternity.

And this prospect is not limited to Moody, Spurgeon, Luther, or Wesley and their likes— it is open to each and every humble believer. If you are trusting Christ, it is for *you.*

This present world system is not a lasting one. "The fashion of this world passeth away" (1 Cor. 7:31). Everything around us is changing, but the things that are eternal never change. A Christian who loves the world will never have peace or security because he has linked his life with that which is in a state of flux. "He is no fool," wrote missionary martyr Jim Elliot, "who gives what he cannot keep to gain what he cannot lose."

The New Testament has quite a bit to say about "the will of God." One of the "fringe benefits" of salvation is the privilege of knowing God's will (Acts 22:14). In fact, God wants us to be "filled with the knowledge of His will" (Col. 1:9). The will of God is not something that we consult occasionally like an encyclopedia. It is something that completely controls our lives. The issue for a dedicated Christian is not simply, "Is it right or wrong?" or "Is it good or bad?" The key issue is, "Is *this* the will of God for me?"

God wants us to *understand* His will (Eph. 5:17), not just *know* what it is. "He made known His ways unto Moses, His acts unto the children of Israel" (Ps. 103:7). Israel knew *what* God was doing, but Moses knew *why* He was doing it! It is important that we understand God's will for our lives and see the purposes He is fulfilling.

After we know the will of God, we should *do it from the heart* (Eph. 6:6). It is not by talking about the Lord's will that we please Him, but by doing what He tells us (Matt. 7:21). And the more we obey God, the better able we are to "find and follow God's will" (Rom. 12:2, WMS). Discovering and doing God's will is something like learning to swim: you must get in the water before it becomes real to you. The more we obey God, the more proficient we become in knowing what He wants us to do.

God's goal for us is that we will "stand . . . complete in all the will of God" (Col. 4:12). This means to be *mature* in God's will.

A little child constantly asks his parents what is right and what is wrong and what they want him to do or not to do. But as he lives with his parents and experiences their training and discipline, he gradually discovers what their will for him is. In fact, a disciplined child can "read his father's mind" just by watching the parent's face and eyes! An immature Christian is always asking his friends what they think God's will is for him. A mature Christian stands complete in the will of God. He *knows* what the Lord wants him to do.

How does one discover the will of God? The process begins with *surrender:* "Present your bodies a living sacrifice . . . be not conformed to this world . . . that ye may prove [know by experience] what is that good, and acceptable, and perfect will of God" (Rom. 12:1-2). A Christian who loves the world will never know the will of God in this way. The Father shares His secrets with those who obey Him. "If any man is willing to do His will, he shall know of the doctrine" (John 7:17). And God's will is not a "spiritual cafeteria" where a Christian takes what he wants and rejects the rest! No, the will of God must be accepted in its entirety. This involves a personal surrender to God of one's entire life.

God reveals His will to us through His Word. "Thy Word is a lamp unto my feet, and a light unto my path" (Ps. 119:105). A worldly believer has no appetite for the Bible. When he reads it, he gets little or nothing from it. But a spiritual believer, who spends time daily reading the Bible and meditating on it, finds God's will there and applies it to his everyday life.

We may also learn God's will through circumstances. God moves in wonderful ways to open and close doors. We must test this kind of leading by the Word of God—and not test the Bible's clear teaching by circumstances!

Finally, God leads us into His will through prayer and the working of His Spirit in our hearts. As we pray about a decision, the Spirit speaks to us. An "inner voice" may agree with the leading of circumstances. We are never to follow this "inner voice" alone: we must always test it by the Bible, for it is possible for the flesh (or for Satan) to use circumstances—or "feelings"—to lead us completely astray.

To sum it up, a Christian is *in* the world physically (John 17:11), but he is not *of* the world spiritually (John 17:14). Christ has sent us *into* the world to bear witness of Him (John 17:18). Like a scuba diver, we must live in an alien element, and if we are not careful, the alien element will stifle us. A Christian cannot help being in the world, but when the world is in the Christian, trouble starts!

The world gets into a Christian through his heart: "Love not the world!" Anything that robs a Christian of his enjoyment of the Father's love, or of his desire to do the Father's will, is worldly and must be avoided. Every believer, on the basis of God's Word, must identify those things for himself.

A Christian must decide, "Will I live for the present only, or will I live for the will of God and abide forever?" Jesus illustrated this choice by telling about two men. One built on the sand and the other on the rock (Matt. 7:24-27). Paul referred to the same choice by describing two kinds of material for building: temporary and permanent (1 Cor. 3:11-15).

Love for the world is the love God hates. It is the love a Christian must shun at all costs!

# CHAPTER FIVE
# TRUTH OR CONSEQUENCES
## *1 John 2:18-29*

It makes no difference what you believe, just as long as you are sincere!"

That statement expresses the personal philosophy of many people today, but it is doubtful whether most of those who make it have really thought it through. Is "sincerity" the magic ingredient that makes something *true?* If so, then you ought to be able to apply it to any area of life, and not only to religion.

A nurse in a city hospital gives some medicine to a patient, and the patient becomes violently ill. The nurse is sincere but the medicine is wrong, and the patient almost dies.

A man hears noises in the house one night and decides a burglar is at work. He gets his gun and shoots the "burglar," who turns out to be his daughter! Unable to sleep, she has gotten up for a bite to eat. She ends up the victim of her father's "sincerity."

It takes more than "sincerity" to make something true. Faith in a lie will always cause serious consequences; faith in the truth is never misplaced. *It does make a difference what a man believes!* If a man wants to drive from Chicago to New York, no amount of sincerity will get him there if the highway is taking him to Los Angeles. A person who is *real* builds his life on truth, not superstition or lies. It is impossible to live a real life by believing lies.

God has warned the church family ("little children") about the conflict between light and darkness (1 John 1:1–2:6) and between love and hatred (1 John 2:7-17). Now He warns them about a third conflict: the conflict between truth and error. It is not enough for a believer to walk in the light and to walk in love; he must also walk in truth. The issue is truth—or consequences!

Before John explains the tragic consequences of turning from the truth, he emphasizes the seriousness of the matter. He does so by using two special terms: "the last time" and "antichrist." Both terms make it clear that Christians are living in an hour of crisis and must guard against the errors of the enemy.

"The last time" (or "the last hour") is a

term that reminds us that a new age has dawned on the world. "The darkness is past, and the true light now shineth" (1 John 2:8). Since the death and resurrection of Jesus Christ, God is doing a "new thing" in this world. All of Old Testament history prepared the way for the work of Christ on the cross. All history since that time is merely preparation for "the end," when Jesus will come and establish His kingdom. There is nothing more that God must do for the salvation of sinners.

You may ask, "But if it was 'the last hour' in John's day, why has Jesus not yet returned?"

This is an excellent question and Scripture gives us the answer. God is not limited by time the way His creatures are. God works *in* human time, but He is *above* time (cf. 2 Peter 3:8).

"The last hour" began back in John's day *and has been growing in intensity ever since.* There were ungodly false teachers in John's day, and during the intervening centuries they have increased both in number and in influence. "The last hour" or "the last times" are phrases that describe a *kind* of time, not a *duration* of time. "The latter times" are described in 1 Timothy 4. Paul, like John, observed characteristics of his time, and we see the same characteristics today in even greater intensity.

In other words, Christians have *always* been living in "the last time"—in crisis days. It is therefore important that you know what you believe and why you believe it.

The second term, "antichrist," is used in the Bible only by John (1 John 2:18, 22; 4:3; 2 John 7). It describes three things: 1. a *spirit* in the world that opposes or denies Christ; 2. the false teachers who embody this spirit; and, 3. a *person* who will head up the final world rebellion against Christ.

The "spirit of antichrist" (1 John 4:3) has been in the world since Satan declared war on God (cf. Gen. 3). The "spirit of antichrist" is behind every false doctrine and every "religious" substitute for the realities Christians have in Christ. That prefix *anti* actually has a dual meaning. It can mean, in the Greek, both "against" Christ and "instead of" Christ. Satan in his frenzy is *fighting* Christ and His eternal truth, and he is *substituting* his counterfeits for the realities found only in our Lord Jesus.

The "spirit of antichrist" is in the world today. It will eventually lead to the appearance of a "satanic superman" whom the Bible calls "Antichrist" (capital A). He is called (2 Thes.

2:1-12) "the man of sin" (or "lawlessness").

This passage explains that there are two forces at work in today's world: truth is working through the church by the Holy Spirit, and evil is working by the energy of Satan. The Holy Spirit in Christians, is holding back lawlessness; but when the church is removed at the Rapture (1 Thes. 4:13-18), Satan will be able to complete his temporary victory and take over the world. (John has more to say about this world ruler and his evil system in the Book of Rev., particularly 13:1-18; 16:13; and 19:20.)

Does it make any difference what you believe? It makes all the difference in the world! You are living in crisis days—in the last hour—and the spirit of antichrist is working in the world! It is vitally important that you know and believe the truth and be able to detect lies when they come your way.

John's epistle gives three outstanding marks of the false teacher who is controlled by the "spirit of antichrist."

## He Departs from the Fellowship (1 John 2:18-19)

"They went out from us, but they were not really of us; for if they had been of us, they would have remained with us" (1 John 2:19, NASB).

The word "us" refers, of course, to the fellowship of believers, the church. Not everyone who is part of an assembly of believers is necessarily a member of the family of God!

The New Testament presents the church in a twofold way: as one worldwide family, and as local units or assemblies of believers. There is a "universal" as well as "local" aspect of the church. The whole worldwide company of believers is compared with a *body* (1 Cor. 12) and with a *building* (Eph. 2:19-22). When a sinner trusts Christ as Saviour, he receives eternal life and immediately becomes a member of God's family and a part of Christ's spiritual body. He should then identify himself with a local group of Christians (a church) and start serving Christ (Acts 2:41-42). But the point here is that a person can belong to a local church and not be part of the true spiritual body of Christ.

One of the evidences of true Christian life is a desire to be with the people of God. "We know that we have passed from death unto life, because we love the brethren" (1 John 3:14). When people share the same divine nature (2 Peter 1:4) and are indwelt by the same Holy Spirit (Rom. 8:14-16), they want to enjoy fellowship and to share with one another. As we have seen, *fellowship* means "to have in common." When people have spiritual realities in common, they want to be together.

But the "counterfeit Christians" mentioned in 1 John 2 did not *remain* in the fellowship. They went out. This doesn't imply that "staying in the church" keeps a person saved; rather, it indicates that remaining in the fellowship is one evidence that a person is truly a Christian. In His Parable of the Sower (Matt. 13:1-9, 18-23), Jesus makes it clear that only those who produce fruit are truly born again. It is possible to be close to an experience of salvation, and even to have some characteristics that would pass for "Christian," and yet not be a child of God. The people in view in 1 John 2 left the fellowship because they did not possess the true life and the love of Christ was not in their hearts.

There are many unfortunate divisions among the people of God today, but all true Christians have things in common, regardless of church affiliation. They believe that the Bible is the Word of God and that Jesus is the Son of God. They confess that men are sinners and that the only way one can be saved is through faith in Christ. They believe that Christ died as man's substitute on the cross, and that He arose again from the dead. They believe that the Holy Spirit indwells true believers. Finally, they believe that one day in the future Jesus will come again. Christians may differ on other matters—church government, for example, or modes of baptism—but they agree on the basic doctrines of the faith.

If you will investigate the history of the false cults and antichristian religious systems in today's world, you will find that in most cases their founders started out *in a local church!* They were "with us" but not "of us," so they went out "from us" and started their own groups.

Any group, no matter how "religious," that for doctrinal reasons separates itself from a local church which holds to the Word of God, must immediately be suspect. Often these groups follow human leaders and the books men have written, rather than Jesus Christ and God's Word. The New Testament (e.g., 2 Tim. 3–4; 2 Peter 2) makes it clear that it is dangerous to depart from the fellowship.

## He Denies the Faith
## (1 John 2:20-25; 4:1-6)

The key question for a Christian is: Who is Jesus Christ? Is Christ merely "an Example," "a good Man," or "a wonderful Teacher"; or is He God come in the flesh?

John's readers knew the truth about Christ, or else they would not have been saved. "You all know the truth, because you have the Spirit of God, an unction, and the Spirit teaches you all things" (cf. 1 John 2:20, 27). "Now if any man have not the Spirit of Christ, he is none of His" (Rom. 8:9).

False Christians in John's day used two special words to describe their experience: "knowledge" and "unction." They claimed to have a special unction (anointing) from God which gave them a unique knowledge. They were "illuminated" and therefore living on a much higher level than anybody else. But John points out that *all* true Christians know God and have received the Spirit of God! And because they have believed the truth, they recognize a lie when they meet it.

The great assertion of the faith that sets a Christian apart from others is this: *Jesus Christ is God come in the flesh* (1 John 4:2).

Not all preachers and teachers who claim to be Christian are really Christian in their belief (1 John 4:1-6). If they confess that Jesus Christ is God come in the flesh, *then* they belong to the true faith. If they deny Christ, then they belong to Antichrist. They are *in* and *of* the world, and are not, like true believers, called *out of* the world. When they speak, the world (unsaved persons) hears them and believes them. But the unsaved world can never understand a true Christian. A Christian speaks under the direction of the Spirit of Truth; a false teacher speaks under the influence of the spirit of error—the spirit of antichrist.

To confess that "Jesus Christ is God come in the flesh" involves much more than simply to identify Christ. The demons did this (Mark 1:24) but it did not save them. True confession involves personal faith in Christ—in who He is and what He has done. A confession is not a mere intellectual "theological statement" that you recite; it is a personal witness from your heart of what Christ has done for you. If you have trusted Christ and have confessed your faith, you have eternal life (1 John 2:25). Those who cannot honestly make this confession do *not* have eternal life, which is an ultimately serious matter.

George Whitefield, the great British evangelist, was speaking to a man about his soul. He asked the man, "Sir, what do you believe?"

"I believe what my church believes," the man replied respectfully.

"And what does your church believe?"

"The same thing I believe."

"And what do *both* of you believe?" the preacher inquired again.

"We both believe the same thing!" was the only reply he could get.

A man is not saved by assenting to a church creed. He is saved by trusting Jesus Christ and bearing witness to his faith (Rom. 10:9-10).

False teachers will often say, "We worship the Father. We believe in God the Father, even though we disagree with you about Jesus Christ."

But to deny the Son means to deny the Father also. You cannot separate the Father and the Son, since both are one God. Jesus says, "I and My Father are One" (John 10:30). He also makes it clear that true believers honor *both* the Father and the Son: "That all men should honor the Son, even as they honor the Father. He that honoreth not the Son honoreth not the Father which hath sent Him" (John 5:23). If you say you "worship one God" but leave Jesus Christ out of your worship, you are not worshiping as a true Christian.

It is important that you stay with the truth of God's Word. The Word (or message) Christians have "heard from the beginning" is all you need to keep you true to the faith. The Christian life *continues* just as it *began:* through faith in the Bible's message. A religious leader who comes along with "something new," something that contradicts what Christians have "heard from the beginning," is not to be trusted. "Try the spirits, whether they are of God" (1 John 4:1). Let the Word abide in you (1 John 2:24), and abide in Christ (1 John 2:28); otherwise you will be led astray by the spirit of antichrist. No matter what false teachers may promise, you have the sure promise of eternal life (1 John 2:25). You need nothing more!

If false teachers were content to enjoy themselves in their own meetings, it would be bad enough; the tragedy is that they try earnestly to convert others to their antichristian doctrines. This is the third mark of a man who has turned away from God's truth.

## He Tries to Deceive the Faithful (1 John 2:26-29)

It is interesting to observe that antichristian groups rarely try to lead lost sinners to their false faith. Instead, they spend much of their time trying to convert professing Christians (and church members, at that) to their own doctrines. They are out to "seduce" the faithful.

The word "seduce" carries the idea of "being led astray." We have been warned that this would happen: "Now the Spirit speaketh expressly, that in the latter times some shall depart from the faith, giving heed to seducing spirits and teachings of demons" (cf. 1 Tim. 4:1).

Jesus calls Satan the "father of lies" (John 8:44), The devil's purpose is to lead Christians astray by teaching them false doctrines (2 Cor. 11:1-4, 13-15). We should not accept everything a person tells us simply because he claims to believe the Bible, for it is possible to "twist" the Bible to make it mean almost anything (2 Cor. 4:1-2).

Satan is not an originator; he is a counterfeiter. He imitates the work of God. For example, Satan has counterfeit "ministers" (2 Cor. 11:13-15) who preach a counterfeit gospel (Gal. 1:6-12) that produces counterfeit Christians (John 8:43-44) who depend on a counterfeit righteousness (Rom. 10:1-10). In the Parable of the Tares (Matt. 13:24-30, 36-43), Jesus and Satan are pictured as sowers. Jesus sows the true seed, the children of God; but Satan sows "the children of the wicked one." The two kinds of plants, while growing, look so much alike that the servants could not tell the difference until the fruit appeared! Satan's chief stratagem during this age is to plant the counterfeit wherever Christ plants the true. And it is important that you be able to detect the counterfeit and separate the teachings of Christ from the false teachings of antichrist.

How does a believer do this? By depending on the teaching of the Holy Spirit. Each believer has experienced the *anointing* (the *unction,* 1 John 2:20) of the Spirit, and it is the Spirit who teaches him truth (John 14:17; 15:26). False teachers are not led by the Spirit of Truth; they are led by the spirit of error (1 John 4:3, 6).

The word *anoint* reminds us of the Old Testament practice of pouring oil on the head of a person being set apart for special service. A priest was anointed (Ex. 28:41), and so was a king (1 Sam. 15:1) or a prophet (1 Kings 19:16). A New Testament Christian is anointed, not with literal oil, but by the Spirit of God—an anointing that sets him apart for his ministry as one of God's priests (1 Peter 2:5, 9). It is not necessary for you to pray for "an anointing of the Spirit"; if you are a Christian, you have already *received* this special anointing. This anointing "abides in us" and therefore does not need to be imparted to us.

We have seen that false teachers deny the Father and the Son; they also deny the Spirit. The Spirit is the Teacher God has given us (John 14:26), but these false Christians want to be teachers themselves and lead others astray. *They try to take the place of the Holy Spirit!*

We are warned against letting any *man* be our teacher, for God has given us the Spirit to teach us His truth. This does not deny the office of human teachers in the church (Eph. 4:11-12); but it means that under the guidance of the Spirit you must test the teaching of men as you search the Bible for yourself (cf. Acts 17:11).

A missionary to the American Indians was in Los Angeles with an Indian friend who was a new Christian. As they walked down the street, they passed a man on the corner who was preaching with a Bible in his hand. The missionary knew the man represented a cult, but the Indian saw only the Bible. He stopped to listen to the sermon.

"I hope my friend doesn't get confused," the missionary thought to himself, and he began to pray. In a few minutes the Indian turned away from the meeting and joined his missionary friend.

"What did you think of the preacher?" the missionary asked.

"All the time he was talking," exclaimed the Indian, "something in my heart kept saying, 'Liar! Liar!'"

That "something" in his heart was "Someone"—the Holy Spirit of God! The Spirit guides us into the truth and helps us to recognize error. This anointing of God is "no lie," because "the Spirit is truth" (1 John 5:6).

Why are some Christians led astray to believe false teachings? Because they are not *abiding* in the Spirit. The word "abide" occurs several times in this section of 1 John, and it would be helpful to review:

- False teachers do not abide ("continue") in the fellowship (1 John 2:19).
- The word (message) we have heard should abide in us (1 John 2:24).
- The anointing (the Holy Spirit) abides in us, and we should abide in the Spirit (1 John 2:27).
- As we abide in the Word and in the Spirit, we also abide in Christ (1 John 2:28).

We noticed this word *abide* earlier in John's letter too:

- If we say we abide in Christ, we should walk as He walked (1 John 2:6).
- If we love our brother, we abide in the light (1 John 2:10).
- If the Word abides in us, we will be spiritually strong (1 John 2:14).
- If we do the will of God, we shall abide forever (1 John 2:17).

"To abide" means *to remain in fellowship;* and "fellowship" is the key idea in the first two chapters of this epistle. From chapters 3 to 5, the emphasis is on *sonship,* or being "born of God."

It is possible to be a child in a family and yet be out of fellowship with one's father and with other members of the family. When our Heavenly Father discovers that we are out of fellowship with Him, He deals with us to bring us back into the place of abiding. This process is called "chastening"—child-training (Heb. 12:5-11).

A believer must allow the Spirit of God to teach him from the Bible. One of the major functions of a local church is the teaching of God's Word (2 Tim. 2:2; 4:1-5). The Spirit gives the gift of teaching to certain individuals in the fellowship (Rom. 12:6-7) and they teach others, but what they teach must be tested (1 John 4:1-3).

There is a difference between deliberate deception and spiritual ignorance. When Apollos preached in the synagogue at Ephesus, his message was correct as far as it went, but it was not complete. Priscilla and Aquila, two mature believers in the congregation, took him aside privately and instructed him in the full message of Christ (Acts 18:24-28). A Christian who spends time daily in the Bible and in prayer will walk in the Spirit and have the discernment he needs.

The Spirit teaches us "of *all things*" (1 John 2:27). False teachers have a way of "riding a hobby"—prophecy or sanctification or even diet—and neglecting the *whole* message of the Bible. Jesus implies that we are to live by *"every* word that proceedeth out of the mouth of God" (Matt. 4:4). Paul was careful to preach *"all* the counsel of God" (Acts 20:27).

"*All* Scripture is given by inspiration of God and is profitable" (2 Tim. 3:16).

If you ignore or neglect *any* part of the Bible, you invite trouble. You must read and study the *whole* Book, and be able to "rightly divide" it (2 Tim. 2:15); that is, you must "handle it accurately" (cf. NASB). You should discern in the Bible what God says to different people at different times; there are passages that apply specifically to the Jews, or to the Gentiles, or to the church (1 Cor. 10:32). You must be careful to distinguish between them. Though all of the Bible was written *for* you, not all of it was written *to* you. False teachers, however, pick (out of context) only what they want, and often apply to believers today passages that were given only for ancient Israel.

John's second epistle gives further warning about false teachers (2 John 7-11). A Christian who meddles with these deceivers is in danger of losing his full reward (2 John 8). You should not even say "good-bye" (which literally means "God be with you"). You are not to be rude or unkind, because that would not be Christian; but you are not to let them into your home to explain their views. Why? Because if you let them in, two consequences may follow: First, they will plant the seeds of false teaching in your mind, and Satan can water and nourish these seeds to produce bitter fruit. But even if this does not happen, by entertaining false teachers in your home you are giving them entrance into *other* homes! The deceiver will say to your neighbor down the street, "Mr. and Mrs. Smith let me into their home, and you know what good Christians *they* are!"

John has now concluded his message on fellowship and is about to begin his message on sonship. He has pointed out the contrasts between light and darkness (1 John 1:1–2:6), love and hatred (1 John 2:7-17), and truth and error (1 John 2:18-27). He has explained that a real Christian lives a life of *obedience* (walking in light, not darkness), *love,* and *truth.* It is impossible to live in fellowship with God if you are disobedient or hateful or untruthful. Any of these sins will lead you out of reality and into pretense. You will have an "artificial" life instead of an "authentic" life.

First John 2:28 and 29 are a "bridge" from the *fellowship* section into the *sonship* section ("born of God"); in these verses John uses three words that ought to encourage us to live in fellowship with the Father, the Son, and the Spirit.

● *Abide.* This is a word we have met twice before. You must recognize the importance of abiding in Christ. In fact, this has been the theme of the first two chapters of this epistle. You abide in Christ by believing the truth, obeying the truth, and loving other Christians—"the brethren." Obedience—love—truth. If you are a believer and find yourself out of fellowship with God, it is because you have disobeyed His Word, lacked love for a brother, or believed a lie. The solution is to confess your sin instantly and to claim God's forgiveness (1 John 1:9).

● *Appear.* This is the first mention in this epistle of the promised return of Christ. The Book of Revelation deals in detail with future events. The epistle (1 John 2:28–3:3; 4:17) merely mentions the return of Christ and a coming day of judgment.

Not all Bible students are agreed as to the details of future events, but evangelical Christians agree that Christ is returning for His church (1 Thes. 4:13-18). Though Christians will not then be judged for their sins, they will be judged on the basis of their faithfulness in serving Christ (1 Cor. 3:10-15). Those who have been faithful will receive rewards (1 Cor. 4:5); and those who have not been faithful will lose rewards. This event is called "the Judgment Seat of Christ" (Rom. 14:10; 2 Cor. 5:10); do not confuse it with the "Great White Throne Judgment" of unsaved people at the end of time (Rev. 20:11-15).

The fact that Jesus Christ may return at any moment ought to be an incentive for us to live in fellowship with Him and be obedient to His Word. For this reason, John uses a third word:

● *Ashamed.* Some Christians will be "ashamed before Him at His presence" (1 John 2:28). All believers are "accepted," but there is a difference between being "accepted" and being "acceptable." A disobedient child who goes out and gets dirty will be *accepted* when he comes home, but he will not be treated as though he were *acceptable.* "Therefore also we have as our ambition . . . to be pleasing to Him" (2 Cor. 5:9, NASB). A Christian who has not walked in fellowship with Christ in obedience, love, and truth will lose his rewards; and this will make him ashamed.

No matter in which direction a Christian looks, he finds reason to obey God. If he looks back, he sees Calvary, where Christ died for him. If he looks within, he sees the

Holy Spirit who lives within and teaches him the truth. If he looks around, he sees his Christian brethren whom he loves; he also sees a world lost in sin, desperately needing his godly witness. And if he looks ahead, he sees the return of Christ! "And every man that hath this hope in him purifieth himself, even as He is pure" (1 John 3:3). The return of Christ is a great inspiration for godly living.

John has written about light and darkness, love and hatred, and truth and error; and in 1 John 2:29 he sums up the whole matter of Christian living in one phrase—"doing righteousness."

The life that is *real* is a life of *doing*, not simply *talking* ("If we say," 1 John 1:8–2:9) or giving mental assent that a doctrine is correct. "Not every one that *saith* unto Me, 'Lord, Lord,' shall enter into the kingdom of heaven, but he that doeth the will of My Father which is in heaven" (Matt. 7:21, italics added). Christians do not simply *believe* the truth; they *do* it (1 John 1:6).

A person who *professes* to be a Christian, but who does not live in obedience, love, and truth, is either deceived or a deceiver. A child bears the nature of his father, and a person who has been "born of God" will reveal the characteristics of the Heavenly Father. "Therefore be imitators of God, as beloved children" (Eph. 5:1, NASB). "As obedient children, not fashioning yourselves according to the former lusts in your ignorance; but as He which hath called you is holy, so be ye holy" (1 Peter 1:14-15).

A Sunday School class seemed to be having constant problems. The pastor and the superintendent met with the teacher and officers, but made no apparent progress. Then, one Sunday morning, the teacher of the class came down the aisle during the closing hymn of the service. "I suppose she wants to dedicate her life to the Lord," the pastor thought.

"Pastor," she said, "I want to confess Christ as my Saviour. All these years I thought I was saved, but I wasn't. There was always something lacking in my life. The class problems were *my* problems, but now they've been solved. Now I *know* I'm saved."

"Test yourselves to see if you are in the faith; examine yourselves!" (2 Cor. 13:5, NASB) Does your life bear the marks of obedience, love, and truth? Is your Christian life something *real—genuine—authentic*? Or is it counterfeit?

It is a question of truth—or consequences!

And if you do not face the truth, you must pay the consequences!

# CHAPTER SIX
# THE PRETENDERS
*1 John 3:1-10*

The United States Treasury Department has a special group of men whose job it is to track down counterfeiters. Naturally, these men need to know a counterfeit bill when they see it.

How do they learn to identify fake bills?

Oddly enough, they are not trained by spending hours examining counterfeit money. Rather, they study *the real thing*. They become so familiar with authentic bills that they can spot a counterfeit by looking at it or, often, simply by feeling it.

This is the approach in 1 John 3, which warns us that in today's world there are counterfeit Christians—"children of the devil" (1 John 3:10). But instead of listing the evil characteristics of Satan's children, the Scripture gives us a clear description of God's children. The contrast between the two is obvious.

The key verse of this chapter is 1 John 3:10: a true child of God practices righteousness and loves other Christians despite differences. First John 3:1-10 deals with the first topic, and 1 John 3:11-24 takes up the second.

Practicing righteousness and loving the brethren, of course, are not new themes. These two important subjects are treated in the first two chapters of this epistle, but in 1 John 3 the approach is different. In the first two chapters the emphasis was on *fellowship:* a Christian who is in fellowship with God will practice righteousness and will love the brethren. But in 1 John 3–5, the emphasis is on *sonship:* because a Christian is "born of God," he will practice righteousness and will love the brethren.

"Born of God" is the idea that is basic to these chapters (cf. 1 John 2:29; 3:9; 4:7; 5:1, 4, 18).

When you read 1 John 3:1-10 in the *Authorized Version*, you may be startled by 1 John 3:6 and 9, which *seem* to contradict 1 John

1:8-9. The *Authorized* translation of the verbs here is not accurate. What the Greek text really says is: "No one who abides in Him *practices* sin; no one who *practices* sin has seen Him or knows Him" (1 John 3:6). "No one who is born of God *practices* sin . . . he cannot *practice* sin because he is born of God" (1 John 3:9). To "practice" sin is to sin consistently and as a way of life. It does not refer to committing an *occasional* sin. It is clear that no Christian is sinless (1 John 1:8-10), but God *expects* a true believer to sin less, not to sin *habitually*.

Every great personality mentioned in the Bible sinned at one time or another. Abraham lied about his wife (Gen. 12:10-20). Moses lost his temper and disobeyed God (Num. 20:7-13). Peter denied the Lord three times (Matt. 26:69-75). But sin was not the settled practice of these men. It was an *incident* in their lives, totally contrary to their normal habits. And when they sinned, they admitted it and asked God to forgive them.

An unsaved person (even if he professes to be a Christian but is a counterfeit) lives a life of *habitual sin.* Sin—especially the sin of unbelief—is the normal thing in his life (Eph. 2:1-3). He has no divine resources to draw on. His profession of faith, if any, is not real. This is the distinction in view in 1 John 3:1-10—a true believer does not live in habitual sin. He may *commit* sin—an occasional wrong act—but he will not *practice* sin—make a settled habit of it.

The difference is that a true Christian knows God. A counterfeit Christian may talk about God and get involved in "religious activities," but he does not really *know* God. The person who has been "born of God" through faith in Christ *knows* God the Father, God the Son, and God the Holy Spirit. And because he *knows* them, he lives a life of obedience: he does not practice sin.

John gives us three reasons for a holy life.

### God the Father Loves Us (1 John 3:1-3)

God's love for us is unique. First John 3:1 may be translated, "Behold, what peculiar, out-of-this-world kind of love the Father has bestowed on us." While we were *His enemies* God loved us and sent His Son to die for us!

The whole wonderful plan of salvation begins with the love of God.

Many translators add a phrase to 1 John 3:1: "That we should be called the sons of God, *and we are.*" "Sons of God" is not simply a high-sounding name that we bear; *it is a reality!* We *are* God's children! We do not expect the world to understand this thrilling relationship, because it does not even understand God. Only a person who knows God through Christ can fully appreciate what it means to be called a child of God.

First John 3:1 tells us *what we are* and 1 John 3:2 tells us *what we shall be.* The reference here, of course, is to the time of Christ's coming for His church. This was mentioned in 1 John 2:28 as an incentive for holy living, and now it is repeated.

God's love for us does not stop with the new birth. It continues throughout our lives and takes us right up to the return of Jesus Christ! When our Lord appears, all true believers will see Him and will become like Him (Phil. 3:20-21). This means, of course, that they will have new, glorified bodies, suited to heaven.

But the apostle does not stop here! He has told us what we *are* and what we *shall be.* Now, in 1 John 3:3, he tells us *what we should be.* In view of the return of Jesus Christ, we should keep our lives clean.

All this is to remind us of the Father's love. Because the Father loved us and sent His Son to die for us, we are children of God. Because God loves us, He wants us to live with Him one day. Salvation, from start to finish, is an expression of the love of God. We are saved by the *grace* of God (Eph. 2:8-9; Titus 2:11-15), but the provision for our salvation was originated in the love of God. And since we have experienced the love of the Father, we have no desire to live in sin.

An unbeliever who sins is a creature sinning against his Creator. A Christian who sins is a child sinning against his Father. The unbeliever sins against law; the believer sins against love.

This reminds us of the meaning of the phrase so often repeated in the Bible: "the fear of the Lord." This phrase does not suggest that God's children live in an atmosphere of terror, "for God hath not given us the spirit of fear" (2 Tim. 1:7). Rather, it indicates that God's children hold their Father in reverence and will not deliberately disobey Him or try His patience.

A group of teenagers were enjoying a party, and someone suggested that they go to a certain restaurant for a good time.

"I'd rather you took me home," Jan said to her date. "My parents don't approve of that place."

"Afraid your father will hurt you?" one of the girls asked sarcastically.

"No," Jan replied, "I'm not afraid my father will hurt me, but I am afraid I might hurt him."

She understood the principle that a true child of God, who has experienced the love of God, has no desire to sin against that love.

**God the Son Died for Us (1 John 3:4-8)**
John turns here from the *future* appearing of Jesus (1 John 3:2) to His *past* appearing (1 John 3:5, where the word "manifest," KJV, means "appear"). John gives two reasons why Jesus came and died: 1. to take away our sins (1 John 3:4-6), and 2. to destroy the works of the devil (1 John 3:7-8). For a child of God to sin indicates that he does not understand or appreciate what Jesus did for him on the cross.

***Christ appeared to take away our sins (vv. 4-6).*** There are several definitions of sin in the Bible: "Whatsoever is not of faith is sin" (Rom. 14:23). "The thought of foolishness is sin" (Prov. 24:9). "Therefore to him that knoweth to do good, and doeth it not, to him it is sin" (James 4:17). "All unrighteousness is sin" (1 John 5:17). But John's epistle defines sin as *lawlessness* (1 John 3:4). It views sin as *defilement* (1 John 1:9–2:2), but here it views it as *defiance*.

The emphasis here is not on *sins* (plural), but on *sin* (singular): "Whosoever *practices sin.*" Sins are the fruit, but *sin* is the root.

That God is love does not mean He has no rules and regulations for His family. "And hereby we do know that we know Him, if we keep His commandments" (1 John 2:3). "And whatsoever we ask, we receive of Him, because we keep His commandments, and do those things that are pleasing in His sight" (1 John 3:22). "By this we know that we love the children of God, when we love God and keep His commandments" (1 John 5:2).

God's children are not in bondage to the Old Testament Law, for Christ has set us free and has given us liberty (Gal. 5:1-6). But God's children are not to be lawless, either! They are "not without law to God, but under the law to Christ" (1 Cor. 9:21).

Sin is basically a matter of the will. For us to assert our will against God's will is rebellion, and rebellion is the root of sin. It is not simply that sin reveals itself in lawless behavior, but that the very *essence* of sin is lawlessness. No matter what his outward action may be, a sinner's inward attitude is one of rebellion.

Little Judy was riding in the car with her father. She decided to stand up in the front seat. Her father commanded her to sit down and put on the seat belt, but she declined. He told her a second time, and again she refused.

"If you don't sit down *immediately,* I'll pull over to the side of the road and spank you!" Dad finally said, and at this the little girl obeyed. But in a few minutes she said quietly, "Daddy, I'm still standing up inside."

Lawlessness! Rebellion! Even though there was constraint from the outside, there was still rebellion on the inside; and this attitude is the essence of sin.

But after a person has become a child of God, born again by faith in Jesus Christ, he cannot practice lawlessness! For one thing, Jesus Christ was without sin, and to abide in Him means to be identified with the One who is sinless. And even more than that, Jesus Christ died to *take away* our sins! If we know the person of Christ, and if we have shared in the blessing of His death, we cannot deliberately disobey God. The whole work of the Cross is denied when a professed Christian practices deliberate sin. This is one reason why Paul calls such people "enemies of the Cross of Christ" (Phil. 3:18-19).

"Whosoever abideth in Him does not practice sin" (1 John 3:6). "Abide" is one of John's favorite words. To *abide* in Christ means to be in fellowship with Him, to allow nothing to come between ourselves and Christ. *Sonship* (being born of God) brings about our *union* with Christ; but *fellowship* makes possible our *communion* with Christ. It is this communion (abiding) with Christ that keeps us from deliberately disobeying His Word.

A person who deliberately and habitually sins is proving that he does not know Christ and therefore cannot be abiding in Him.

There is more in the death of Christ on the cross than simply our salvation from judgment, as wonderful as that is. Through His death, Christ broke the power of the sin principle in our lives. The theme of Romans 6–8 is this identification with Christ in His death and resurrection. Christ not only died for me, but I died with Christ! Now I can yield myself to Him and sin will not have dominion over me.

***Christ appeared to destroy the works of the devil (vv. 7-8).*** The logic here is clear: if a man knows God, he will obey God; if he belongs to the devil, he will obey the devil.

John accepts the reality of a personal devil.

This enemy has many different names in Scripture: Satan (adversary, enemy), the devil (accuser), Abaddon or Apollyon (destroyer), the prince of this world, the dragon, etc. Whatever name you call him, keep in mind that his chief activity is to oppose Christ and God's people.

The contrast here is between Christ (who has no sin, 1 John 3:5) and the devil (who can do nothing but sin).

The origin of Satan is a mystery. Many scholars believe he was once one of the highest angels, placed by God over the earth and over the other angels, and that he sinned against God and was cast down (Isa. 14:9-17; Ezek. 28:12-14).

Satan is not eternal, as is God, for he is a created being. He was not *created* sinful. His present nature is a result of his past rebellion. Satan is not like God: he is not all-powerful, all-knowing, or everywhere present. However, he is assisted by an army of spirit creatures known as demons, who make it possible for him to work in many places at one time (Eph. 6:10-12).

Satan is a rebel, but Christ is the obedient Son of God. Christ was "obedient unto death, even the death of the cross" (Phil. 2:8). Christ is God but was willing to become a servant. Satan was a servant and wanted to become God. From the beginning of his career, Satan has been a sinner, and Christ came to destroy the works of the devil.

*Destroy* (1 John 3:8) does not mean "annihilate." Satan is certainly still at work today! *Destroy*, here, means "to render inoperative, to rob of power." Satan has not been annihilated, but his power has been reduced and his weapons have been impaired. He is still a mighty foe, but he is no match for the power of God.

Jesus compares this world to a palace that contains many valuable goods. A strong man is guarding this palace (Luke 11:14-23). Satan is the strong man, and his "goods" are lost men and women. The only way to release the "goods" is to bind the strong man, and that is just what Jesus did on the cross. Jesus, in coming to earth, invaded Satan's "palace." When He died, He broke Satan's power and captured his goods! Each time a lost sinner is won to Christ, more of Satan's "spoils" are taken from him.

For many months after the close of World War II, Japanese troops were discovered hidden in the caves and jungles of the Pacific islands. Some of these stragglers were living like frightened savages; they didn't know the war was over. Once they understood that it was no longer necessary for them to fight, they surrendered.

Christians may rest in the truth that Satan is a defeated enemy. He may still win a few battles here and there, *but he has already lost the war!* Sentence has been pronounced on him, but it will be awhile before the punishment is meted out. A person who knows Christ, and who has been delivered from the bondage of sin through Christ's death on the cross, has no desire to obey Satan and live like a rebel.

"Little children, let no man deceive you!" Counterfeit Christians were trying to convince true believers that a person could be "saved" and still practice sin. John does not deny that Christians sin, but he *does* deny that Christians can *live in sin*. A person who can *enjoy* deliberate sin and who does not feel convicted or experience God's chastening had better examine himself to see whether or not he is really born of God.

### God the Holy Spirit Lives in Us (1 John 3:9-10)

"Whosoever is born of God does not practice sin!"

Why? Because he has a new nature within him, and that new nature *cannot* sin. John calls this new nature God's "seed."

When a person receives Christ as his Saviour, tremendous spiritual changes take place in him. He is given a new standing before God, being accepted as righteous in God's sight. This new standing is called "justification." It never changes and is never lost.

The new Christian is also given a new position: he is set apart for God's own purposes to live for His glory. This new position is called "sanctification," and it has a way of changing from day to day. On some days we are much closer to Christ and obey Him much more readily.

But perhaps the most dramatic change in a new believer is what we call "regeneration." He is "born again" into the family of God. (*Re-* means "again," and *generation* means "birth.")

Justification means a new *standing* before God, sanctification means being *set apart* to God, and regeneration means a new *nature*— God's nature (cf. 2 Peter 1:4).

The only way to enter God's family is by trusting Christ and experiencing this new birth. "Whosoever believeth that Jesus is the Christ is born of God" (1 John 5:1).

Physical life produces only physical life; spiritual life produces spiritual life. "That which is born of the flesh is flesh; and that which is born of the Spirit is spirit" (John 3:6). Christians have been born again, "not of corruptible seed, but of incorruptible, by the Word of God, which liveth and abideth forever" (1 Peter 1:23). A Christian's "spiritual parents," so to speak, are the Word of God and the Spirit of God. The Spirit of God uses the Word of God to convict of sin and to reveal the Saviour.

We are saved by faith (Eph. 2:8-9), and "faith cometh by hearing, and hearing by the Word of God" (Rom. 10:17). In the miracle of the new birth, the Holy Spirit imparts new life—God's life—to a believing sinner, and as a result the individual is born into the family of God.

Just as physical children bear the nature of their parents, so God's spiritual children bear His nature. The divine "seed" is in them. A Christian has an old nature from his physical birth and a new nature from his spiritual birth. The New Testament contrasts these two natures and gives them various names:

| Old Nature | New Nature |
|---|---|
| "our old man" | "the new man" |
| (Rom. 6:6) | (Col. 3:10) |
| "the flesh" | "the Spirit" |
| (Gal. 5:24) | (Gal. 5:17) |
| "corruptible seed" | "God's seed" |
| (1 Peter 1:23) | (1 John 3:9) |

The old nature produces sin, but the new nature leads one into a holy life. A Christian's responsibility is to live according to his new nature, not the old nature.

One way to illustrate this is by contrasting the "outer man" with the "inner man" (2 Cor. 4:16). The physical man needs *food,* and so does the inner, or spiritual man. "Man shall not live by bread alone, but by every word that proceedeth out of the mouth of God" (Matt. 4:4). Unless a Christian spends time daily in meditating on the Word of God, his inner man will lack power.

A converted Indian explained, "I have two dogs living in me—a mean dog and a good dog. They are always fighting. The mean dog wants me to do bad things, and the good dog wants me to do good things. Do you want to know which dog wins? *The one I feed the most!*"

A Christian who feeds the new nature from the Word of God will have power to live a godly life. We are to "make not provision for the flesh, to fulfill the lusts thereof" (Rom. 13:14).

The physical man needs *cleansing,* and so does the inner man. We wash our hands and face frequently. A believer should look into the mirror of God's Word daily (James 1:22-25) and examine himself. He must confess his sins and claim God's forgiveness (1 John 1:9). Otherwise the inner man will become unclean and this uncleanness will breed infection and "spiritual sickness."

Unconfessed sin is the first step in what the Bible calls "backsliding"—gradually moving away from a close walk with Christ into a life filled with the alien world in which we live.

God's promise, "I will heal your backslidings" (Jer. 3:22), implies that backsliding resembles physical sickness. First is the secret invasion of the body by a disease germ. Then infection follows and there is a gradual decline: no pep, no appetite, no interest in normal activities. Then comes the collapse!

Spiritual decline works in a similar way. First sin invades us. Instead of fighting it, we yield to it (cf. James 1:14) and infection sets in. A gradual decline follows. We lose our appetite for spiritual things, we become listless and even irritable, and finally we collapse.

The only remedy is to confess and forsake our sin and turn to Christ for cleansing and healing.

The inner man not only needs food and cleansing, but he also needs *exercise.* "Exercise thyself . . . unto godliness" (1 Tim. 4:7). A person who eats but does not exercise will become overweight; a person who exercises without eating will kill himself. There must be proper balance.

"Spiritual exercise" for a believer, includes sharing Christ with others, doing good works in Christ's name, and helping to build up other believers. Each Christian has at least one spiritual gift which he is to use for the good of the church (1 Cor. 12:1-11). "As each one has received a special gift, employ it in serving one another, as good stewards of the manifold grace of God" (1 Peter 4:10, NASB).

Here is a vivid commentary on this whole process of temptation and sin:

"Let no one say when he is tempted, 'I am being tempted by God!' for God cannot be tempted by evil, and He Himself does not tempt anyone. But each one is tempted when he is carried away and enticed by his own lust. And when lust has conceived, it gives birth to sin; and when sin is accomplished, it brings forth death" (James 1:13-15, NASB).

Temptation appeals to our basic natural desires. There is nothing sinful about our desires, but temptation gives us an opportunity to satisfy these desires in an evil way. It is not sin to be hungry, but it is a sin to satisfy hunger out of the will of God. This was the first temptation Satan hurled at Jesus (Matt. 4:1-4).

The two terms, "carried away" and "enticed" (James 1:14), both relate to hunting or fishing: the putting of bait in a trap or on a hook. The animal (or fish) comes along and his natural desires attract him to the bait. But in taking the bait, he gets caught in the trap, or hooked. And the end is death.

Satan baits his traps with pleasures that appeal to the old nature, the flesh. But none of his bait appeals to the new divine nature within a Christian. If a believer yields to his old nature, he will hanker for the bait, take it, and sin. But if he follows the leanings of his new nature, he will refuse the bait and obey God. "This I say then, walk in the Spirit, and ye shall not fulfill the lust of the flesh" (Gal. 5:16).

Yielding to sin is the distinguishing mark of "the children of the devil" (1 John 3:10). They *profess,* or claim, one thing, but they *practice* another. Satan is a liar and the father of lies (John 8:44), and his children are like their father. "He that saith, 'I know [God],' and keepeth not His commandments, is a liar, and the truth is not in him" (1 John 2:4). The children of the devil try to deceive God's children into thinking that a person can be a Christian and still practice sin. "Little children, let no man deceive you; he that doeth righteousness is righteous, even as He [God] is righteous" (1 John 3:7).

False teachers in John's day taught that a Christian did not have to worry about sin because only the body sinned and what the body did in no way affected the spirit. Some of them went so far as to teach that sin is natural to the body, because the body is sinful.

The New Testament exposes the foolishness of such excuses for sin.

To begin with, "the old nature" is *not* the body. The body itself is neutral: it can be used either by the old sinful nature or by the new divine nature. "Therefore do not let sin reign in your mortal body, that you should obey its lusts, and do not go on presenting the members of your body to sin as instruments of unrighteousness; but present yourselves to God as those [who are] alive from the dead, and your members as instruments of righteousness to God" (Rom. 6:12-13, NASB).

How does a child of God go about overcoming the desires of the old nature? He must begin each day by yielding his body to God as a living sacrifice (Rom. 12:1). He must spend time reading and studying the Word of God, "feeding" his new nature. He must take time to pray, asking God to fill him with the Holy Spirit and give him power to serve Christ and glorify Him.

As he goes through the day, a believer must depend on the power of the Spirit in the inner man. When temptations come, he must immediately turn to Christ for victory.

The Word of God in his heart will help to keep him from sin if only he will turn to Christ. "Thy Word have I hid in mine heart, that I might not sin against Thee" (Ps. 119:11). If he *does* sin, he must instantly confess to God and claim forgiveness. But it is not *necessary* for him to sin. By yielding his body to the Holy Spirit within him, he will receive the power he needs to overcome the tempter.

A good practice is to claim God's promise: "No temptation has overtaken you but such as is common to man; and God is faithful, who will not allow you to be tempted beyond what you are able; but with the temptation will provide the way of escape also, that you may be able to endure it" (1 Cor. 10:13, NASB).

A Sunday School teacher was explaining the Christian's two natures—the old and the new—to a class of teenagers.

"Our old nature came from Adam," he explained, "and our new nature comes from Christ, who is called 'the Last Adam.' " He had the class read 1 Corinthians 15:45: "So also it is written, 'The first man, Adam, became a living soul.' The Last Adam became a life-giving spirit" (NASB).

"This means there are two 'Adams' living in me," said one of the teenagers.

"That's right," the teacher replied. "And what is the practical value of this truth?"

The class was silent for a moment, and then a student spoke up.

"This idea of the 'two Adams' really helps me in fighting temptation," he said. "When temptation comes knocking at my door, if I send the first Adam to answer, I'll sin. But if I send the Last Adam, I'll get victory."

A true believer does not practice sin; a counterfeit believer cannot help but practice sin, because he does not have God's new nature within him. The true believer also loves other Christians, which is discussed in detail in 1 John 3:11-24.

But these words were not written so that you and I might check on *other people*. They were inspired so that we may examine *ourselves*. Each of us must answer honestly before God:

1. Do I have the divine nature within me or am I merely *pretending* to be a Christian?

2. Do I cultivate this divine nature by daily Bible reading and prayer?

3. Has any unconfessed sin defiled my inner man? Am I willing to confess and forsake it?

4. Do I allow my old nature to control my thoughts and desires, or does the divine nature rule me?

5. When temptation comes, do I "play with it" or do I flee from it? Do I immediately yield to the divine nature within me?

The life that is real is honest with God about these vital issues.

# CHAPTER SEVEN
# LOVE OR DEATH
*1 John 3:11-24*

John's letter has been compared to a spiral staircase because he keeps returning to the same three topics: love, obedience, and truth. Though these themes recur, it is not true that they are merely repetitious. Each time we return to a topic, we look at it from a different point of view and are taken more deeply into it.

We have already learned about our love for other believers—"the brethren" (1 John 2:7-11)—but the emphasis in 1 John 2 was on *fellowship*. A believer who is "walking in the light" will evidence that fact by loving the brethren. In our present section, the emphasis is on his *relationship* with other believers.

Christians love one another because they have all been born of God, which makes them all brothers and sisters in Christ.

Obedience and love are both evidences of sonship and brotherhood. We have been reminded that a true child of God practices righteousness (1 John 3:1-10), and now we shall look into the matter of love for the brethren (1 John 3:11-24). This truth is first stated in the negative—"Whosoever doeth not righteousness is not of God, neither he that loveth not his brother" (1 John 3:10).

A striking difference should be noted between the earlier and the present treatment of love for the brethren. In the section on fellowship (1 John 2:7-11), we are told that loving the brethren is a matter of light and darkness. If we do not love one another, we cannot walk in the light, no matter how loud our profession. But in this section (1 John 3:11-24) on brotherhood, the epistle probes much deeper. We are told that loving the brethren is *a matter of life and death.* "He that loveth not his brother abideth in death" (1 John 3:14).

When it comes to this matter of love, there are four possible "levels of relationship," so to speak, on which a person may live: murder (1 John 3:11-12), hatred (1 John 3:13-15), indifference (1 John 3:16-17), and Christian compassion (1 John 3:18-24).

The first two are not Christian at all, the third is less than Christian, and only the last is compatible with true Christian love.

## Murder (1 John 3:11-12)
Murder, of course, is the lowest level on which one may live in relationship to someone else. It is the level on which Satan himself exists. The devil was a murderer from the beginning of his fallen career (John 8:44), but Christians have heard, from the beginning of their experience, that they are to "love one another." John emphasizes *origins:* "Go back to the beginning." If our spiritual experience originates with the Father, we *must* love one another. But if it originates with Satan, we will hate one another. "Let that therefore abide in you, which ye have heard from the beginning" (1 John 2:24).

Cain is an example of a life of hatred; we find the record in Genesis 4:1-16. It is important to note that Cain and Abel, being brothers, had the same parents, and they both brought sacrifices to God. Cain is not presented as an atheist; he is presented as a worshiper. And this is the point: children of the devil masquerade as true believers. They attend religious gatherings, as Cain did. They may even bring offerings. But these actions in themselves are not valid proof that a man is born of God. The real test is his love for the brethren—and here Cain failed.

Every man has a "spiritual lineage" as well as a physical, and Cain's "spiritual father" was the devil. This does not mean, of course, that Satan literally fathered Cain. It means, rather, that Cain's attitudes and actions originated with Satan. Cain was a murderer and a liar like Satan (John 8:44). He murdered his brother, and then he lied about it. "And the Lord said unto Cain, 'Where is Abel thy brother?' And he said, 'I know not'" (Gen. 4:9).

In contrast to this, God is love (1 John 4:8) and truth (John 14:6; 1 John 5:6); therefore, those who belong to God's family practice love and truth.

The difference between Cain's offering and Abel's offering was *faith* (Heb. 11:4), and faith is always based on the revelation God has given (Rom. 10:17). It seems clear that God must have given definite instructions concerning how He was to be worshiped. Cain rejected God's Word and decided to worship in his own way. This shows his relationship to Satan, for Satan is always interested in turning people away from the revealed will of God. The devil's "Yea, hath God said?" (Gen. 3:1) was the beginning of trouble for Cain's parents and for all mankind since.

We are not told by what outward sign the Lord accepted Abel's sacrifice and rejected Cain's. It may be that He sent fire from heaven to consume Abel's sacrifice of an animal and its blood. But we *are* told the results: Abel went away from the altar with God's witness of acceptance in his heart, but Cain went away angry and disappointed (Gen. 4:4-6). God warned Cain that sin was crouching at the door like a dangerous beast (Gen. 4:7) but promised that if Cain would obey God, he, like Abel, would enjoy peace.

Instead of heeding God's warning, Cain listened to Satan's voice and plotted to kill his brother. His envy had turned to anger and hatred. He knew that he was evil and that his brother was righteous. Rather than repent, as God commanded him to do, he decided to destroy his brother.

Centuries later, the Pharisees did the same thing to Jesus (Mark 15:9-10), and Jesus called them too children of the devil (John 8:44).

Cain's attitude represents the attitude of the present world system (1 John 3:13). The world hates Christ (John 15:18-25) for the same reason Cain hated Abel: Christ shows up the world's sin and reveals its true nature. When the world, like Cain, comes face-to-face with reality and truth, it can make only one of two decisions: repent and change, or destroy the one who is exposing it.

Satan is the "prince of this world" (John 14:30), and he controls it through murder and lies. How horrible to live on the same level as Satan!

A hunter took refuge in a cave during a rainstorm. After he had dried out a bit, he decided to investigate his temporary home and turned on his flashlight. Imagine his surprise when he discovered he was sharing the cave with an assortment of spiders, lizards, and snakes! His exit was a fast one.

If the unsaved world could only see, it would realize that it is living on the low level of murder and lies, surrounded by that old serpent Satan and all his demonic armies. Like Cain, the people of the world try to cover up their true nature with religious rites; but they lack faith in God's Word. People who continue to live on this level will eventually be cast into outer darkness with Satan to suffer apart from God forever.

### Hatred (1 John 3:13-15)

At this point, you are probably thinking, "But I have never murdered anyone!" And to this statement, God replies, "Yes, but remember that to a Christian hatred is the same as murder" (1 John 3:15; cf. Matt. 5:22). The only difference between Level 1 and Level 2 is the outward act of taking life. The inward intent is the same.

A visitor at the zoo was chatting with the keeper of the lion house.

"I have a cat at home," said the visitor, "and your lions act just like my cat. Look at them sleeping so peacefully! It seems a shame that you have to put those beautiful creatures behind bars."

"My friend," the keeper laughed, "these may *look* like your cat, but their disposition is radically different. There's murder in their hearts. You'd better be glad the bars are there."

The only reason some people have never actually murdered anyone is because of the "bars" that have been put up: the fear of arrest and shame, the penalties of the law, and the possibility of death. But we are going to be judged by "the law of liberty" (James 2:12). The question is not so much, "What did you do?" but "What did you *want* to do? What would you have done if you had been at liberty to do as you pleased?" This is why Jesus equates hatred with murder (Matt. 5:21-26) and lust with adultery (Matt. 5:27-30).

This does not mean, of course, that hatred in the heart does the same amount of damage, or involves the same degree of guilt, as actual murder. Your neighbor would rather you hate him than kill him! But in God's sight, hatred is the moral equivalent of murder, and if left unbridled it leads to murder. A Christian has passed from death to life (John 5:24), and the proof of this is that he loves the brethren. When he belonged to the world system, he hated God's people; but now that he belongs to God, he loves them.

These verses (1 John 3:14-15), like those that deal with habitual sin in a believer (1 John 1:5–2:6), concern a settled habit of life: a believer is *in the practice* of loving the brethren, even though on occasion he may be angry with a brother (Matt. 5:22-24). Occasional incidents of anger do not nullify the principle. If anything, they prove it true, because a believer out of fellowship with his fellow Christians is a miserable person! His feelings make clear to him that something is wrong.

Notice another fact: we are not told that murderers cannot be saved. The Apostle Paul himself took a hand in the stoning of Stephen (Acts 7:57-60) and admitted that his vote helped to put innocent people to death (Acts 26:9-11; 1 Tim. 1:12-15). But in His grace God saved Paul.

The issue here is not whether a murderer can become a Christian, but whether a man can *continue* being a murderer and still be a Christian. The answer is no. "And ye know that no murderer hath eternal life abiding in him" (1 John 3:15). The murderer did not once have eternal life and then lose it; he never had eternal life at all.

The fact that you have never actually murdered anyone should not make you proud or complacent. Have you ever harbored hatred in your heart?

Hatred does the hater far more damage than it does anyone else (Matt. 5:21-26). Jesus said that anger put a man in danger of facing the local court. Calling a brother an "empty-headed fool" put him in danger of the Sanhedrin, the highest Jewish council. But calling him a "cursed fool" put him in danger of eternal judgment in hell. Hatred that is not confessed and forsaken actually puts a man

into a spiritual and emotional prison! (Matt. 5:25)

The antidote for hatred is love. "Hateful and hating one another" is the normal experience of an unsaved person (Titus 3:3). But when a hateful heart opens to Jesus Christ, it becomes a loving heart. Then instead of wanting to "murder" others through hatred, one wants to love them and share with them the message of eternal life.

Evangelist John Wesley was stopped one night by a highwayman who robbed the Methodist leader of all his money. Wesley said to the man, "If the day should come that you desire to leave this evil way and live for God, remember that 'the blood of Jesus Christ cleanses from all sin.' "

Some years later, Wesley was stopped by a man after a church service. "Do you remember me?" the man asked. "I robbed you one night, and you told me that the blood of Jesus Christ cleanses from all sin. I have trusted Christ, and He has changed my life."

## Indifference (1 John 3:16-17)

But the test of Christian love is not simply failure to do *evil* to others. Love also involves doing them *good*. Christian love is both positive and negative. "Cease to do evil; learn to do well" (Isa. 1:16-17).

Cain is our example of false love; Christ is the example of true Christian love. Jesus gave His life for us that we may experience truth. Every Christian knows John 3:16, but how many of us pay much attention to 1 John 3:16? It is wonderful to experience the blessing of John 3:16; but it is even more wonderful to *share* that experience by obeying 1 John 3:16: Christ laid down life for us, and we ought to lay down our lives for the brethren.

Christian love involves sacrifice and service. Christ did not simply *talk* about His love; He died to prove it (Rom. 5:6-10). Jesus was not killed as a martyr; He willingly *laid down* His life (John 10:11-18; 15:13). "Self-preservation" is the first law of physical life, but "self-sacrifice" is the first law of spiritual life.

But God does not ask us to lay down our lives. He simply asks us to help a brother in need. John wisely turns from "the brethren" in 1 John 3:16 to the singular, "his brother," in 1 John 3:17.

It is easy for us to talk about "loving the brethren" and to neglect to help a single other believer. Christian love is personal and active. This is what Jesus had in mind in the Parable of the Good Samaritan (Luke 10:25-37). A lawyer wanted to talk about an abstract subject: "Who is my neighbor?" But Jesus focused attention on *one man in need,* and changed the question to, "To whom can I be a neighbor?"

Two friends were attending a conference on evangelism. During one of the sessions, Larry missed Pete. At luncheon, when he saw Pete, he said, "I missed you at the 10 o'clock session. It was really terrific! Where were you?"

"I was in the lobby talking to a bellhop about Christ. I led him to the Lord," said Pete.

There is nothing wrong with attending conferences, but it is easy to forget the individual and his needs while discussing generalities. The test of Christian love is not in loud professions about loving the whole church, but in quietly helping a brother who is in need. If we do not even help a brother, it is not likely we would "lay down our lives" for "the brethren."

A man does not have to murder in order to sin; hatred is murder in his heart. But a man need not even hate his brother to be guilty of sin. All he has to do is ignore him, or be indifferent toward his needs. A believer who has material goods and can relieve his brother's needs ought to do it. To "close the door of his heart" on his brother is a kind of murder!

If I am going to help my brother, I must meet three conditions. First, I must have the means necessary to meet his need. Second, I must know that the need exists. Third, I must be loving enough to want to share.

A believer who is too poor to help, or who is ignorant of his brother's need, is not condemned. But a believer who hardens his heart against his needy brother *is* condemned. One reason Christians should work is so that they may be able "to give to him that needeth" (Eph. 4:28).

In these days of multiplied social agencies, it is easy for Christians to forget their obligations. "So then, while we have opportunity, let us do good to all men, and especially to those who are of the household of the faith" (Gal. 6:10, NASB).

This "doing good" need not be in terms of money or material supplies. It may include personal service and the giving of oneself to others. There are many individuals in our churches who lack love and would welcome friendship.

A young mother admitted, in a testimony meeting, that she never seemed to find time for her own personal devotions. She had several little children to care for, and the hours melted away.

Imagine her surprise when two of the ladies from the church appeared at her front door.

"We've come to take over," they explained. "You go into the bedroom and get started on your devotions." After several days of this kind of help, the young mother was able to develop her devotional life so that the daily demands on her time no longer upset her.

If we want to experience and enjoy the love of God in our own hearts, we must love others, even to the point of sacrifice. Being indifferent to a brother's needs means robbing ourselves of what we need even more: the love of God in our hearts. It is a matter of love or death!

**Christian Love (1 John 3:18-24)**
True Christian love means loving in deed and in truth. The opposite of "in deed" is "in word," and the opposite of "in truth" is "in tongue." Here is an example of love "in word":

"If a brother or sister is without clothing and in need of daily food, and one of you says to them, 'Go in peace, be warmed and be filled'; and yet you do not give them what is necessary for their body, what use is that?" (James 2:15-16, NASB)

To love "in word" means simply to *talk* about a need, but to love "in deed" means to *do* something about meeting it. You may think, because you have discussed a need, or even prayed about it, that you have done your duty, but love involves more than words—it calls for sacrificial deeds.

To love "in tongue" is the opposite of to love "in truth." It means to love insincerely. To love "in truth" means to love a person genuinely, from the heart and not just from the tongue. People are attracted by genuine love, but repelled by the artificial variety. One reason why sinners were attracted to Jesus (Luke 15:1-2) was because they were sure He loved them sincerely.

"But does it not *cost* a great deal for the believer to exercise this kind of love?"

Yes, it does. It cost Jesus Christ His life. But the wonderful benefits that come to you as by-products of this love more than compensate for any sacrifice you make. To be sure, you do not love others because you want to get something in return, but the Bible principle, "Give and it shall be given unto you" (Luke 6:38), applies to love as well as to money.

John names three wonderful blessings that will come to a believer who practices Christian love.

**Assurance (vv. 19-20).** A believer's relationship with others affects His relationship with God. A man who is not right with his brother should go settle the matter before he offers his sacrifice on the altar (cf. Matt. 5:23-24). A Christian who practices love grows in his understanding of God's truth and enjoys a heart filled with confidence before God.

A "condemning heart" is one that robs a believer of peace. An "accusing conscience" is another way to describe it. Sometimes the heart accuses us wrongly, because it "is deceitful above all things, and desperately wicked; who can know it?" (Jer. 17:9) The answer to that question is, *"God* knows the heart!" More than one Christian has accused himself falsely, or been harder on himself than necessary; but God will never make such a mistake. A Christian who walks in love has a heart open to God ("God *is* love") and knows that God never judges wrongly.

John may have remembered two incidents from Jesus' life on earth that illustrate this important principle. When Jesus visited Bethany, He stayed at the home of Mary and Martha (Luke 10:38-42). Martha was busy preparing the meal, but Mary sat at His feet and listened to Him teach. Martha criticized both Mary and Jesus, but Jesus knew Mary's heart and defended her.

The Apostle Peter wept bitterly after he had denied his Lord, and no doubt he was filled with remorse and repentance for his sin. But Jesus knew that Peter had repented, and after His resurrection the Lord sent a special message (Mark 16:7) to Peter that must have assured the hot-headed fisherman that he was forgiven. Peter's heart may have condemned him, for he knew he had denied the Lord three times, but God was greater than his heart. Jesus, knowing all things, gave Peter just the assurance he needed.

Be careful lest the devil accuse you and rob you of your confidence (Rev. 12:10). Once you confess your sin and it is forgiven, you need not allow it to accuse you anymore. Peter was able to face the Jews and say, "But *ye* denied the Holy One and the Just!" (Acts 3:14) because his own sin of denying Christ had been taken care of and was forgiven and forgotten.

No Christian should treat sin lightly, but no Christian should be harder on himself than God is. There is a morbid kind of self-examination and self-condemnation that is not spiritual. If you are practicing genuine love for the brethren, your heart must be right before God, for the Holy Spirit would not "shed abroad" His love in you if there were habitual sin in your heart. When you grieve the Spirit, you "turn off" the supply of God's love (Eph. 4:30–5:2).

**Answered prayer (vv. 21-22).** Love for the brethren produces confidence toward God, and confidence toward God gives you boldness in asking for what you need. This does not mean that you *earn* answers to prayer by loving the brethren. Rather, it means that your love for the brethren proves that you are living in the will of God where God can answer your prayer. "And whatsoever we ask, we receive of Him, because we keep His commandments" (1 John 3:22). Love is the fulfilling of God's Law (Rom. 13:8-10); therefore, when you love the brethren, you are obeying His commandments and He is able to answer your requests.

A believer's relationship to the brethren cannot be divorced from his prayer life. If husbands and wives are not obeying God's Word, for example, their prayers will be hindered (1 Peter 3:7).

An evangelist had preached on the Christian home. After the meeting a father approached him.

"I've been praying for a wayward son for years," said the father, "and God has not answered my prayers."

The evangelist read Psalm 66:18—"If I regard iniquity in my heart, the Lord will not hear me."

"Be honest with yourself and the Lord," he said. "Is there anything between you and another Christian that needs to be settled?"

The father hesitated, then said, "Yes, I'm afraid there is. I've harbored resentment in my heart against another man in this church."

"Then go make it right," counseled the evangelist, and he prayed with the man. Before the campaign was over, the father saw his wayward son come back to the Lord.

These verses do not, of course, give us *all* the conditions for answered prayer, but they emphasize the importance of *obedience.* One great secret of answered prayer is obedience, and the secret of obedience is love. "If ye love Me, keep My commandments" (John 14:15).

"If ye abide in Me, and My words abide in you, ye shall ask what ye will, and it shall be done unto you. . . . If ye keep My commandments, ye shall abide in My love" (John 15:7, 10).

It is possible, of course, to keep God's commandments in a spirit of fear or servitude rather than in a spirit of love. This was the sin of the elder brother in the Parable of the Prodigal Son (Luke 15:24-32). A believer should keep His Father's commandments because this pleases Him. A Christian who lives to please God will discover that God finds ways to please His child. "Delight thyself also in the Lord, and He shall give thee the desires of thine heart" (Ps. 37:4). When our *delight* is in the love of God, our *desires* will be in the will of God.

**Abiding (vv. 23-24).** When a scribe asked Jesus to name the greatest commandment, He replied, "Thou shalt love the Lord thy God." Then He added a second commandment: "Thou shalt love thy neighbor as thyself" (Matt. 22:34-40). But God also gives us *one commandment* that takes in both God and man: "Believe in the name of His Son Jesus Christ, and love one another" (1 John 3:23, NASB). Faith toward God and love toward man sum up a Christian's obligations. Christianity is "faith which worketh by love" (Gal. 5:6).

Faith toward God and love toward men are two sides of the same coin. It is easy to emphasize faith—correct doctrine—and to neglect love. On the other hand, some say doctrine is not important and that love is our main responsibility. *Both doctrine and love are important.* When a person is justified by faith, he should know that the love of God is being shed abroad in his heart (Rom. 5:1-5).

"Abiding in Christ" is a key experience for a believer who wants to have confidence toward God and enjoy answers to prayer. Jesus, in His message to the disciples in the Upper Room (John 15:1-14) illustrated "abiding." He compared His followers to the branches of a vine. So long as the branch draws its strength from the vine, it produces fruit. But if it separates itself from the vine, it withers and dies.

Jesus was not talking about salvation; He was talking about fruit-bearing. The instant a sinner trusts Christ, he enters into *union* with Christ; but maintaining *communion* is a moment-by-moment responsibility. Abiding depends on our obeying His Word and keeping clean (John 15:3, 10).

As we have seen, when a believer walks in love, he finds it easy to obey God, and therefore he maintains a close communion with God. "If a man love Me, he will keep My words; and My Father will love him, and We will come unto him and make Our abode with him" (John 14:23).

The Holy Spirit is mentioned by name in 1 John for the first time in 3:24. John introduced us to the Holy One (1 John 2:20) with emphasis on the Spirit's anointing and teaching ministry. (This parallels John 14:26; 16:13-14.) But the Holy One is also the *abiding* Spirit (1 John 3:24; 4:13). When a believer obeys God and loves the brethren, the indwelling Holy Spirit gives him peace and confidence. The Holy Spirit abides with him forever (John 14:16), but when the Spirit is grieved, He withdraws His blessings.

The Holy Spirit is also the *attesting* Spirit (1 John 4:1-6), giving witness to those who are truly God's children. When a believer is abiding in Christ, the Spirit guides him and warns him of false spirits that would lead him astray.

He is also the *authenticating* Spirit (1 John 5:6-8), bearing witness to the person and work of Jesus Christ. This witness of the Spirit is mentioned in Romans 8:14-16.

Each member of the Triune Godhead is involved in the "love life" of a believer. God the Father commands us to love one another, God the Son gave His life on the cross, the supreme example of love. And God the Holy Spirit lives within us to provide the love we need (Rom. 5:5). To abide in love is to abide in God, and to abide in God is to abide in love. Christian love is not something we "work up" when we need it. Christian love is "shed abroad in our hearts by the Holy Spirit," and this is your constant experience as you abide in Christ.

There are four levels on which a person may live. He may choose the lowest level—Satan's level—and practice murder. Murderers "have their part in the lake which burneth with fire and brimstone, which is the second death" (Rev. 21:8).

Or, a person may choose the next level—hatred. But hatred, in God's sight, is the same as murder. A man who lives with hatred is slowly killing *himself*, not the other person! Psychiatrists warn that malice and hatred cause all kinds of physical and emotional problems. In fact, one specialist has entitled his book *Love or Perish!*

The third level—indifference—is far better

than the first two, because the first two are not Christian at all. A man who has constant hatred in his heart, or who habitually murders, proves he has never been born of God. But it is possible to be a Christian and be indifferent to the needs of others.

A man who murders belongs to *the devil,* like Cain. A man who hates belongs to *the world* (1 John 3:13), which is under Satan's control. But a Christian who is indifferent is living for *the flesh,* which serves Satan's purposes.

The only happy, holy way to live is on the highest level, the level of Christian love. This is the life of joy and liberty, the life of answered prayer. It assures you confidence and courage in spite of the difficulties of life.

Dr. Rene Spitz of New York made a study of children in foundling homes to determine what effect love and neglect had on them. The survey proved that children who were neglected and unloved were much slower in their development, and some of them even died. Even in a physical sense, love is the very atmosphere of life and growth.

It is even more so in the spiritual sense.

In fact, it is a matter of love or death!

# CHAPTER EIGHT
# GETTING TO THE BOTTOM OF LOVE
## 1 John 4:1-16

For the third time, we are considering the subject of love!

This does not mean John has run out of ideas and has to repeat himself. It means that the Holy Spirit, who inspired John, presents the subject once more, from a deeper point of view.

First, love for the brethren has been shown as proof of *fellowship with God* (1 John 2:7-11); then it has been presented as proof of *sonship* (1 John 3:10-14). In the earlier passage, love for the brethren is a matter of light or darkness; in the second it is a matter of life or death.

But in 1 John 4:7-16, we get down to the very foundation of the matter. Here we dis-

cover *why* love is such an important part of the life that is real. Love is a valid test of our fellowship and our sonship because "God is love." Love is part of the very being and nature of God. If we are united to God through faith in Christ, we share His nature. And since His nature is love, love is the test of the reality of our spiritual life.

A navigator depends on a compass to help him determine his course. But *why* a compass? Because it shows him his directions. And *why* does the compass point north? Because it is so constituted that it responds to the magnetic field that is part of the earth's makeup. The compass is responsive to the nature of the earth.

So with Christian love. The nature of God is love. And a person who knows God and has been born of God will respond to God's nature. As a compass naturally points north, a believer will naturally practice love because love is the nature of God. This love will not be a forced response; it will be a natural response. A believer's love for the brethren will be proof of his sonship and fellowship.

Three times, in this section, John encourages us to love one another (1 John 4:7, 11-12). He supports these admonitions by giving us three foundational facts about God.

## What God Is: "God Is Love"
### (1 John 4:7-8)

This is the third of three expressions in John's writings that help us understand the nature of God: "God is spirit" (John 4:24, NASB); "God is light" (1 John 1:5); and "God is love." None of these is a *complete* revelation of God, of course, and it is wrong to separate them.

*God is spirit* as to His essence; He is not flesh and blood. To be sure, Jesus Christ now has a glorified body in heaven, and one day we shall have bodies like His body. But being by nature spirit, God is not limited by time and space the way His creatures are.

*God is light.* This refers to His holy nature. In the Bible, light is a symbol of holiness and darkness is a symbol of sin (John 3:18-21; 1 John 1:5-10). God cannot sin because He is holy. Because we have been born into His family, we have received His holy nature (1 Peter 1:14-16; 2 Peter 1:4).

*God is love.* This does *not* mean that "love is God." And the fact that two people "love each other" does not mean that their love is necessarily holy. It has accurately been said that "love does not define God, but God defines love." God is love and God is light; therefore, His love is a *holy* love, and His holiness is expressed in love. All that God *does* expresses all that God *is*. Even His judgments are measured out in love and mercy (Lam. 3:22-23).

Much that is called "love" in modern society bears no resemblance or relationship to the holy, spiritual love of God. Yet we see banners saying "God is love!" displayed at many festivals, particularly where young people are "doing their own thing"—as if one could dignify immorality by calling it "love."

Christian love is a special kind of love. First John 4:10 may be translated: "In this way is seen the true love." There is a false love, and this kind of love God must reject. Love that is born out of the very essence of God *must* be spiritual and holy, because "God is spirit" and "God is light." This true love is "poured out within our hearts through the Holy Spirit who was given to us" (Rom. 5:5, NASB).

Love, therefore, is a valid test of true Christian faith. Since God is love, and we have claimed a personal relationship with God, we must of necessity reveal His love in how we live. A child of God has been "born of God," and therefore he shares God's divine nature. Since "God is love," Christians ought to love one another. The logic is unanswerable!

Not only have we been "born of God," but we also "know God." In the Bible, the word *know* has a much deeper meaning than simply intellectual acquaintance or understanding. For example, the verb *know* is used to describe the intimate union of husband and wife (Gen. 4:1). To know God means to be in a deep relationship to Him—to share His life and enjoy His love. This knowing is not simply a matter of understanding facts; it is a matter of perceiving truth (cf. 1 John 2:3-5).

We must understand "he that loveth not knoweth not God" (1 John 4:8) in this light. Certainly many unsaved people love their families and even sacrifice for them. And no doubt many of these same people have some kind of intellectual understanding of God. What, then, do they lack? They lack *a personal experience* of God. To paraphrase 1 John 4:8, "The person who does not have this divine kind of love has never entered into a personal, experiential knowledge of God. What he knows is in his head, but it has never gotten into his heart."

What *God* is determines what we ought to be. "As He is, so are we in this world" (1 John 4:17). The fact that Christians love one another is evidence of their fellowship with God and their sonship from God, and it is also evidence that they *know God*. Their experience with God is not simply a once-for-all crisis; it is a daily experience of getting to know Him better and better. True theology (the study of God) is not a dry, impractical course in doctrine—it is an exciting day-by-day experience that makes us Christlike!

A large quantity of radioactive material was stolen from a hospital. When the hospital administrator notified the police, he said: "Please warn the thief that he is carrying death with him, and that the radioactive material cannot be successfully hidden. As long as he has it in his possession, it is affecting him disastrously!"

A person who claims he knows God and is in union with Him must be personally affected by this relationship. A Christian ought to become what God is, and "God is love." To argue otherwise is to prove that one does not really know God!

## What God Did: "He Sent His Son" (1 John 4:9-11)

Because God is love, He must communicate—not only in words but in deeds. True love is never static or inactive. God reveals His love to mankind in many ways. He has geared all of creation to meeting men's needs. Until man's sin brought creation under bondage, man had on earth a perfect home in which to love and serve God.

God's love was revealed in the way He dealt with the nation of Israel. "The Lord did not set His love upon you, nor choose you, because ye were more in number than any people; for ye were the fewest of all people. But because the Lord loved you . . . hath the Lord brought you out with a mighty hand" (Deut. 7:7-8).

The greatest expression of God's love is in the death of His Son. "But God demonstrates His own love toward us, in that while we were yet sinners, Christ died for us" (Rom. 5:8, NASB).

The word *manifested* means "to come out in the open, to be made public." It is the opposite of "to hide, to make secret." Under the Old Covenant, God was hidden behind the shadows of ritual and ceremony (Heb. 10:1); but in Jesus Christ "the life was manifested" (1 John 1:2). "He that hath seen Me," said Jesus, "hath seen the Father" (John 14:9).

Why was Jesus Christ manifested? "And you know that He was manifested to take away our sins" (1 John 3:5). "For this purpose the Son of God was manifested, that He might destroy the works of the devil" (1 John 3:8). Where did Jesus take away our sins and destroy (render inoperative) the works of the devil? *At the cross!* God manifested His love at the cross when He gave His Son as a sacrifice there for our sins.

This is the only place in the epistle where Jesus is called God's only-begotten Son. The title is used in John's Gospel (John 1:14). It means "unique, the only one of its kind." The fact that God *sent* His Son into the world is one evidence of the deity of Jesus Christ. Babies are not *sent* into the world from some other place; they are *born* into the world. As the perfect Man, Jesus was born into the world, but as the eternal Son, He was sent into the world.

But the sending of Christ into the world, and His death on the cross, were not prompted by man's love for God. They were prompted by His love for man. The world's attitude toward God is anything but love!

Two purposes are given for Christ's death on the cross: that we might live through Him (1 John 4:9) and that He might be the propitiation for our sins (1 John 4:10). His death was not an accident; it was an appointment. He did not die as a weak martyr, but as a mighty conqueror.

Jesus Christ died that we might live "through Him" (1 John 4:9), "for Him" (2 Cor. 5:15), and "with Him" (1 Thes. 5:9-10). A sinner's desperate need is for *life,* because he is "dead in trespasses and sins" (Eph. 2:1). It is something of a paradox that Christ had to die so that we may live! We can never probe the mystery of His death, but this we know: He died for us (Gal. 2:20).

The death of Christ is described as a "propitiation." John has used this word before (1 John 2:2), so there is no need to study it in detail again. We should remember that propitiation does not mean that men must do something to appease God or to placate His anger. Propitiation is something God does to make it possible for men to be forgiven. "God is light," and therefore He must uphold His holy Law. "God is love," and therefore He wants to forgive and save sinners. How can God forgive sinners and still be consistent with His holy nature? The answer is the cross. There Jesus Christ bore the punishment for sin and met the just demands of the holy Law. But there, also, God reveals His love and makes it possible for men to be saved by faith.

It is important to note that the emphasis is on the *death* of Christ, not on His birth. The fact that Jesus was "made flesh" (John 1:14) is certainly an evidence of God's grace and love, but the fact that He was "made sin" (2 Cor. 5:21) is *underscored* for us. The example of Christ, the teachings of Christ, the whole earthly life of Christ, find their true meaning and fulfillment in the cross.

For the second time, believers are exhorted to "love one another" (1 John 4:11). This exhortation is a commandment to be obeyed (1 John 4:7), and its basis is the nature of God. "God is love; we know God; therefore, we should love one another." But the exhortation to love one another is presented as a privilege as well as a responsibility: "If God so loved us, we ought also to love one another" (1 John 4:11). We are not saved by *loving* Christ; we are saved by *believing on* Christ (John 3:16). But after we realize what He did for us on the cross, our normal response ought to be to love Him and to love one another.

It is important that Christians progress in their understanding of love. To love one another simply out of a sense of duty is good, but to love out of appreciation (rather than obligation) is even better.

This may be one reason why Jesus established the Lord's Supper, the Communion service. When we break the bread and share the cup, we remember His death. Few men, if any, want their deaths remembered! In fact, we remember *the life* of a loved one and try to forget the sadness of his death. Not so with Christ. He *commands* us to remember His death: "This do in remembrance of Me!"

We should remember our Lord's death in a spiritual way, not merely sentimentally. Someone has defined sentiment as "feeling without responsibility." It is easy to experience solemn emotions at a church service and yet go out to live the same defeated life. True spiritual experience involves the whole man. *The mind* must understand spiritual truth; *the heart* must love and appreciate it; and *the will* must *act on it.* The deeper we go into the meaning of the Cross, the greater will be our love for Christ and the greater our active concern for one another.

We have discovered what God is and what God has done; but a third foundation fact takes us even deeper into the meaning and implications of Christian love.

## What God Is Doing: "God Abides in Us" (1 John 4:12-16)

At this point it would be good for us to review what John has been saying about the basic truth that "God is love."

This truth is revealed to us in the Word, but it was also revealed on the cross, where Christ died for us. "God is love" is not simply a doctrine in the Bible; it is an eternal fact clearly demonstrated at Calvary. God has said something *to us,* and God has done something *for us.*

But all this is preparation for the third great fact: God does something *in us!* We are not merely students reading a book, or spectators watching a deeply moving event. We are *participants* in the great drama of God's love!

In order to save money, a college drama class purchased only a few scripts of a play and cut them up into the separate parts. The director gave each player his individual part in order and then started to rehearse the play. But nothing went right. After an hour of missed cues and mangled sequences, the cast gave up.

At that point, the director sat the actors all on the stage and said: "Look, I'm going to read the entire play to you, so don't any of you say a word." He read the entire script aloud, and when he was finished, one of the actors said:

"So that's what it was all about!"

And when they understood the entire story, they were able to fit their parts together and have a successful rehearsal.

When you read 1 John 4:12-16, you feel like saying, "So that's what it's all about!" Because here we discover what God had in mind when He devised His great plan of salvation.

To begin with, God's desire is to *live in us.* He is not satisfied simply to *tell* us that He loves us, or even *show* us that He loves us.

It is interesting to trace God's dwelling places as recorded in the Bible. In the beginning, God had fellowship with man in a personal, direct way (Gen. 3:8), but sin broke that fellowship. It was necessary for God to shed the blood of animals to cover the sins of Adam and Eve so that they might come back into His fellowship.

One of the key words in the Book of Genesis is *walked.* God walked with men, and men walked with God. Enoch (Gen. 5:22), Noah (Gen. 6:9), and Abraham walked with God

(Gen. 17:1; 24:40).

But by the time of the events recorded in Exodus, a change had taken place: God did not simply *walk* with men, He *lived,* or dwelt, with them. God's commandment to Israel was, "And let them make Me a sanctuary; that I may dwell among them" (Ex. 25:8). The first of those sanctuaries was the tabernacle. When Moses dedicated it, the glory of God came down and moved into the tent (Ex. 40:33-35).

God dwelt in the camp, but He did *not* dwell in the bodies of the individual Israelites.

Unfortunately, the nation sinned and God's glory departed (1 Sam. 4:21). But God used Samuel and David to restore the nation; and Solomon built God a magnificent temple. When the temple was dedicated, once again the glory of God came to dwell in the land (1 Kings 8:1-11).

But history repeated itself, and Israel disobeyed God and was taken into Captivity. The gorgeous temple was destroyed. One of the prophets of the Captivity, Ezekiel, saw the glory of God depart from it (Ezek. 8:4; 9:3; 10:4; 11:22-23).

Did the glory ever return? Yes—in the Person of God's Son, Jesus Christ! "And the Word became flesh, and tabernacled among us, and we beheld His glory" (John 1:14, lit.). The glory of God dwelt on earth in the body of Jesus Christ, for His body was the temple of God (John 2:18-22). But wicked men nailed His body to a cross. They crucified "the Lord of glory" (1 Cor. 2:8). All this was part of God's thrilling plan, and Christ arose from the dead, returned to heaven, and sent His Holy Spirit *to dwell in men.*

The glory of God now lives in the bodies of God's children. "Or do you not know that your body is a temple of the Holy Spirit who is in you, whom you have from God, and that you are not your own?" (6:19, NASB) The glory of God departed from the tabernacle and the temple when Israel disobeyed God, but Jesus has promised that the Spirit will abide in us *forever* (John 14:16).

With this background, we can better understand what 1 John 4:12-16 is saying to us. God is invisible (1 Tim. 1:17), and no man can see Him in His essence. Jesus is "the image of the invisible God" (Col. 1:15). By taking on Himself a human body, Jesus was able to reveal God to us. But Jesus is no longer here on earth. How, then, does God reveal Himself to the world?

He reveals Himself through the lives of His children. Men cannot see God, *but they can see us.* If we abide in Christ, we will love one another, and our love for one another will reveal God's love to a needy world. God's love will be experienced *in us* and then will be expressed *through us.*

That important little word *abide* (or *dwell,* KJV) is used six times in 1 John 4:12-16. It refers to our personal fellowship with Jesus Christ. To abide in Christ means to remain in spiritual oneness with Him, so that no sin comes between us. Because we are "born of God," we have *union* with Christ; but it is only as we trust Him and obey His commandments that we have *communion* with Him. Much as a faithful husband and wife "abide in love" though they may be separated by miles, so a believer abides in God's love. This abiding is made possible by the indwelling of the Holy Spirit (1 John 4:13).

Imagine the wonder and the privilege of having God abide in you! The Old Testament Israelite would look with wonder at the tabernacle or temple, because the presence of God was in that building. No man would dare to enter the holy of holies, where God was enthroned in glory! But *we* have God's Spirit *living in us!* We abide in this love, and we experience the abiding of God in us. "If a man love Me, he will keep My words; and My Father will love him, and We will come unto him, and make Our abode with him" (John 14:23).

God's love is *proclaimed* in the Word ("God is love") and *proved* at the cross. But here we have something deeper: God's love is *perfected* in the believer. Fantastic as it may seem, God's love is not made perfect in angels, but in sinners saved by His grace. We Christians are now the tabernacles and temples in which God dwells. He reveals His love through us.

Dr. G. Campbell Morgan, famous British preacher, had five sons, all of whom became ministers of the Gospel. One day a visitor in their home dared to ask a personal question: "Which of you six is the best preacher?"

Their united answer was, "Mother!"

Of course, Mrs. Campbell Morgan had never preached a formal sermon in a church; but her life was a constant sermon on the love of God. The life of a Christian who abides in God's love is a potent witness for God in the world. Men cannot see God, but they can see His love moving us to deeds of helpfulness and kindness.

Three different witnesses are suggested in these verses: 1. The witness *of* the believer that Jesus Christ is God's Son (1 John 4:15); 2. the witness *in* the believer by the Spirit (1 John 4:13); and 3. the witness *through* the believer that God is love and that He sent His Son to die for the world (1 John 4:14).

These witnesses cannot be separated. The world will not believe that God loves sinners until they see His love at work in His children's lives.

A Salvation Army worker found a derelict woman alone on the street and invited her to come into the chapel for help, but the woman refused to move. The worker assured her: "We love you and want to help you. God loves you. Jesus died for you." But the woman did not budge.

As if on divine impulse, the Army lassie leaned over and kissed the woman on the cheek, taking her into her arms. The woman began to sob, and like a child was led into the chapel, where she ultimately trusted Christ.

"You *told* me that God loved me," she said later, "but it wasn't till you *showed* me that God loved me that I wanted to be saved."

Jesus did not simply preach the love of God; He proved it by giving His life on the cross. He expects His followers to do likewise. If we abide in Christ, we will abide in His love. If we abide in His love, we must share this love with others. Whenever we share this love, it is proof in our own hearts that we are abiding in Christ. In other words, there is no separation between a Christian's inner life and his outer life.

Abiding in God's love produces two wonderful spiritual benefits in the life of a believer: 1. He grows in knowledge, and 2. He grows in faith (1 John 4:16). The more we love God, the more we understand the love of God. And the more we understand His love, the easier it is for us to trust Him. After all, when you know someone intimately and love him sincerely, you have no problem putting your confidence in him.

A man standing in the greeting card section of a store was having trouble picking out a card. The clerk asked if she could help, and he said:

"Well, it's our fortieth wedding anniversary, but I can't find a card that says what I want to say. You know, forty years ago it wouldn't have been any problem picking out a card, because back then I thought I knew what love was. But we love each other so much more today, I just can't find a card that says it!"

This is a growing Christian's experience with God. As he abides in Christ and spends time in fellowship with Him, he comes to love God more and more. He also grows in his love for other Christians, for the lost, and even for his enemies. As he shares the Father's love with others, he experiences more of the Father's love himself. He understands the Father's love better and better.

"God is love," then, is not simply a profound biblical statement. It is the basis for a believer's relationship with God and with his fellowman. Because God is love, *we* can love. His love is not past history; it is present reality. "Love one another" begins as *a commandment* (1 John 4:7), then it becomes *a privilege* (1 John 4:11). But it is more than a commandment or a privilege. It is also the thrilling *consequence* and evidence of our abiding in Christ (1 John 4:12). Loving one another is not something we simply *ought* to do; it is something we *want* to do.

Some practical applications grow out of this basic truth:

First, the better we know God's love, the easier it will be to live as a Christian. Bible knowledge alone does not take the place of personal experience of God's love. In fact, it can be a dangerous substitute if we are not careful.

Helen came home from a youth retreat greatly enthused over what she had learned. "We had some terrific sessions on how to have personal devotions," she told her sister Joyce. "I plan to have my devotions every single day."

A week later, while Joyce was running the vacuum cleaner, she heard Helen screaming, "Do you have to make all that noise? Don't you know I'm trying to have my devotions?" And the verbal explosion was followed by the slamming of a door.

Helen still had to learn that personal devotions are not an end in themselves. If they do not help us love God and love one another, they are accomplishing little. The Bible is a revelation of God's love; and the better we understand His love, the easier it should be for us to obey Him and love others.

A second consideration is that unless we *love* the lost, our verbal witness to them will be useless. The Gospel message is a message of love. This love was both declared and demonstrated by Jesus Christ. The only way we can effectively win others is to declare the Gospel and demonstrate it in how we live. Too much "witnessing" today is a mere mouthing of words. People need an expression of love.

One reason why God permits the world to hate Christians is so that Christians may return love for the world's hatred. "Blessed are you when men revile you, and persecute you, and say all kinds of evil against you falsely, on account of Me. . . . But I say to you, love your enemies, and pray for those who persecute you" (Matt. 5:11, 44, NASB).

"Pastor, the Bible tells us to love our neighbors, but I doubt that *anybody* could love *my* neighbors," Mrs. Barton said at the close of a Sunday School lesson. "I've tried to be nice to them, but it just doesn't work."

"Perhaps 'being nice to them' isn't the real answer," the pastor explained. "You know, it's possible to be nice to people with the wrong motive."

"You mean as though you're trying to buy them off?"

"Something like that. I think you and I had better pray that God will give you a true *spiritual* love for your neighbors. If you love them in a Christian way, you'll not be able to do them any damage," the pastor pointed out.

It took some weeks, but Mrs. Barton grew in her love for her neighbors; and she also found herself growing in her own spiritual life.

"My neighbors haven't changed a whole lot," she told the prayer group, "but *my* attitude toward them has really changed. I used to do things for them to try to win their approval. But now I do things for Jesus' sake, because He died for them—and it makes all the difference in the world!"

In this paragraph of his letter, John has taken us to the very foundation of Christian love. But he still has more to teach us. In the next section, he deals with our own personal love for God and how God perfects that love in us.

These two aspects of Christian love cannot be separated from one another: if we love God, we will love one another; and if we love one another, we will grow in our love for God.

And both statements are true because "God is love."

# CHAPTER NINE
# LOVE, HONOR,
# AND OBEY
*1 John 4:17–5:5*

The prospective bridegroom was extremely nervous as he and his fiancée were discussing their wedding plans with their pastor.

"I'd like to see a copy of the wedding vows," the young man said; and the pastor handed him the service. He read it carefully, handed it back, and said, "That won't do! There's nothing written in there about her obeying me!"

His fiancée smiled, took his hand, and said, "Honey, the word *obey* doesn't have to be written in a book. It's already written in love in my heart."

This is the truth in view in this portion of 1 John. Up to this point, the emphasis has been on Christians loving *one another;* but now we turn to a deeper—and more important—topic: a believer's love *for the Father.* We cannot love our neighbor or our brother unless we love our Heavenly Father. We must first love God with all our hearts; then we can love our neighbor as ourselves.

The key word in this section is *perfect.* God wants to perfect in us His love for us and our love for Him. The word *perfect* carries the idea of *maturity* and *completeness.* A believer is not only to grow in grace and knowledge (2 Peter 3:18), but he is also to grow in his love for the Father. He does this in response to the Father's love for him.

How much does God love us? Enough to send His Son to die for us (John 3:16). He loves His children in the same way as *He loves Christ* (John 17:23). And Jesus tells us that the Father wants the love with which He loved the Son to be in His children (John 17:26).

In other words, the Christian life is to be a daily experience of growing in the love of God. It involves a Christian's coming to know his Heavenly Father in a much deeper way as he grows in love.

It is easy to fragment the Christian life and become preoccupied with individual pieces instead of the total picture. One group may emphasize "holiness" and urge its members to get victory over sin. Another may stress witnessing, or "separation from the world." But each of these emphases is really a by-product of something else: a believer's growing love for the Father. Mature Christian love is the great universal need among God's people.

How can a believer know that his love for the Father is being perfected? This paragraph of 1 John suggests four evidences.

## Confidence (1 John 4:17-19)
Two brand-new words come into John's vocabulary here: *fear* and *torment.* And this is written to *believers!* Is it possible that Christians can actually live in fear and torment? Yes, unfortunately, many professed believers experience both fear and torment day after day. And the reason is that they are not growing in the love of God.

The word *boldness* can mean "confidence" or "freedom of speech." It does not mean brazenness or brashness. A believer who experiences perfecting love grows in his confidence toward God. He has a reverential fear of God, not a tormenting fear. He is a son who respects his Father, not a prisoner who cringes before a judge.

We have adopted the Greek word for *fear* into our English vocabulary: *phobia.* All sorts of phobias are listed in psychology books; for instance, *acrophobia*—"fear of heights," and *hydrophobia*—"fear of water." John is writing about *krisisphobia*—"fear of judgment." John has already mentioned this solemn truth in 1 John 2:28; and now he deals with it again.

If people are afraid, it is because of something in the past that haunts them, or something in the present that upsets them, or something in the future that they feel threatens them. Or it may be a combination of all three. A believer in Jesus Christ does not have to fear the past, present, or future, for he has experienced the love of God and this love is being perfected in him day by day.

"It is appointed unto men once to die, but after this the judgment" (Heb. 9:27). But a Christian does not fear future judgment, because Christ has suffered his judgment for him on the cross. "Truly, truly I say to you, he who hears My word, and believes Him who sent Me, has eternal life, and does not come into judgment, but has passed out of death into life" (John 5:24, NASB). "There is therefore now no condemnation for those who are in Christ Jesus" (Rom. 8:1, NASB). For a Christian, judgment is not future; *it is past.*

His sins have been judged already at the cross, and they will never be brought against him again.

The secret of our boldness is, "As He is, so are we in this world" (1 John 4:17). We know that "we shall be like Him" when He returns (1 John 3:1-2), but that statement refers primarily to the glorified bodies believers will receive (Phil. 3:20-21). *Positionally,* we are right now "as He is." We are so closely identified with Christ, as members of His body, that our position in this world is like His exalted position in heaven.

This means that the Father deals with us as He deals with His own beloved Son. How, then, can we ever be afraid?

We do not have to be afraid of *the future,* because our sins were judged in Christ when He died on the cross. The Father cannot judge our sins again without judging His Son, for "as He is, so are we in this world."

We do not have to be afraid of *the past,* because "He first loved us." From the very first, our relationship to God was one of love. It was not that we loved Him, but that He loved us (cf. 1 John 4:10). "For if, while we were enemies, we were reconciled to God through the death of His Son, much more, having been reconciled, we shall be saved by His life" (Rom. 5:10, NASB). If God loved us when we were outside the family, disobeying Him, how much more does He love us now that we are His children!

We do not need to fear *the present* because "perfect love casteth out fear" (1 John 4:18). As we grow in the love of God, we cease to be fearful of what He will do.

Of course there is a proper "fear of God," but it is not the kind of fear that produces torment. "For you have not received a spirit of slavery leading to fear again, but you have received a spirit of adoption as sons, by which we cry out, 'Abba! Father!' " (Rom. 8:15, NASB) "For God hath not given us a spirit of fear; but of power, and of love, and of a sound mind" (2 Tim. 1:7).

Fear is actually the beginning of torment. We torment ourselves as we contemplate what lies ahead. Many people suffer acutely when they contemplate a visit to the dentist. Think of how an unsaved person must suffer as he contemplates the day of judgment. But since a Christian has boldness in the day of judgment, he can have boldness as he faces life today, for there is no situation of life today that begins to compare with the terrible severity of the day of judgment.

God wants His children to live in an atmosphere of love and confidence, not fear and torment. We need not fear life or death, for we are being perfected in the love of God. "Who shall separate us from the love of Christ? Shall tribulation, or distress, or persecution, or famine, or nakedness, or peril, or sword? But in all these things we overwhelmingly conquer through Him who loved us. For I am convinced that neither death, nor life, nor angels, nor principalities, nor things present, nor things to come, nor powers, nor height, nor depth, nor any other created thing shall be able to separate us from the love of God, which is in Christ Jesus our Lord" (Rom. 8:35, 37-39, NASB).

Imagine! Nothing *in all creation*—present or future—can come between us and God's love!

The perfecting of God's love in our lives is usually a matter of several stages. When we were lost, we lived in fear and knew nothing of God's love. After we trusted Christ, we found a perplexing mixture of both fear and love in our hearts. But as we grew in fellowship with the Father, gradually the fear vanished and our hearts were controlled by His love alone. An immature Christian is tossed between fear and love; a mature Christian rests in God's love.

A growing confidence in the presence of God is one of the first evidences that our love for God is maturing. But confidence never stands alone; it always leads to other moral results.

### Honesty (1 John 4:20-21)

Here it is for the seventh time: "If a man say. . . !"

We have met this important phrase several times, and each time we knew what was coming: a warning against pretending.

Fear and pretense usually go together. In fact, they were born together when the first man and woman sinned. No sooner did Adam and Eve sense their guilt than they tried to hide from God and cover their nakedness. But neither their coverings nor their excuses could shelter them from God's all-seeing eye. Adam finally had to admit, "I heard Thy voice in the Garden, and I was afraid" (Gen. 3:10).

But when our hearts are confident toward God, there is no need for us to pretend, either to God or to other people. A Christian who lacks confidence with God will also lack confidence with God's people. Part of the torment that fear generates is the constant worry, "How much do others really know about me?" But when we have confidence with God, this fear is gone and we can face both God and men without worry.

"How many members do you have in your church?" a visitor asked the pastor.

"Somewhere near a thousand," the pastor replied.

"That certainly is a lot of people to try to please!" the visitor exclaimed.

"Let me assure you, my friend, that I have never tried to please all my members, or even some of them," the pastor said with a smile. "I aim to please *one* Person—the Lord Jesus Christ. If I am right with Him, then everything should be right between me and my people."

An immature Christian who is not growing in his love for God may think he has to impress others with his "spirituality." This mistake turns him into a liar! He is professing something that he is not really practicing; he is playing a role instead of living a life.

Perhaps the best example of this sin is seen in the experience of Ananias and Sapphira (Acts 5). They sold a piece of property and brought *part* of the money to the Lord, but they gave the impression that they were bringing *all* the money. The sin of this couple was not in taking money from God, for Peter made it clear that the disposal of the money was up to them (Acts 5:4). Their sin was hypocrisy. They were trying to make people think they were more generous and spiritual than they really were.

Pretending is one of the favorite activities of little children, but it is certainly not a mark of maturity in adults. Adults must *know* themselves and *be* themselves, fulfilling the purposes for which Christ saved them. Their lives must be marked by honesty.

Spiritual honesty brings peace and power to the person who practices it. He does not have to keep a record of the lies he has told, and he is not using his energy to cover up. Because he lives in open honesty with the Father, he can live in honesty with other people. Love and truth go together. Because he knows God loves him and accepts him (even with all his faults), he is not trying to impress others. He loves God, and therefore he loves his fellow Christians.

Jerry's grades were far below his usual performance and, on top of that, his health seemed to be failing. His new roommate was concerned about him and finally persuaded him to talk to the campus psychologist.

"I can't figure myself out," Jerry admitted. "Last year I was sailing through school, and this year it is like fighting a war."

"You're not having trouble with your new roommate, are you?" the counselor asked.

Jerry did not reply right away, and this gave the counselor a clue.

"Jerry, are you concentrating on living your life as a good student, or on trying to impress your new roommate with your abilities?"

"Yeah, I guess that's it," Jerry answered with a sigh of relief. "I've worn myself out acting and haven't had enough energy left for living."

Confidence toward God and honesty with others are two marks of maturity that are bound to show up when our love for God is being perfected.

## Joyful Obedience (1 John 5:1-3)

Not simply *obedience*—but *joyful* obedience! "His commandments are not burdensome" (1 John 5:3, NASB).

Everything in creation—except man—obeys the will of God. "Fire and hail, snow, and vapor, stormy wind fulfilling His Word" (Ps. 148:8). In the Book of Jonah, you see the winds and waves, and even the fish, obeying God's commands; but the prophet persisted in disobeying. Even a plant and a little worm did what God commanded. But the prophet stubbornly wanted his own way.

Disobedience to God's will is a tragedy—but so is reluctant, grudging obedience. God does not want us to disobey Him, but neither does He want us to obey out of fear or necessity. What Paul wrote about *giving* also applies to *living*: "not grudgingly or under compulsion, for God loves a cheerful giver" (2 Cor. 9:7, NASB).

What is the secret of *joyful* obedience? It is to recognize that obedience is a family matter. We are serving a loving Father and helping our brothers and sisters in Christ. We have been born of God, we love God, and we love God's children. And we demonstrate this love by keeping God's commandments.

A woman visited a newspaper editor's office, hoping to sell him some poems she had written.

"What are your poems about?" the editor asked.

"They're about love!" gushed the poetess.

The editor settled back in his chair and said,

"Well, read me a poem. The world could certainly use a lot more love!"

The poem she read was filled with *moons* and *Junes* and other sticky sentiments, and it was more than the editor could take.

"I'm sorry," he said, "but you just don't know what love is all about! It's not moonlight and roses. It's sitting up all night at a sickbed, or working extra hours so the kids can have new shoes. The world doesn't need your brand of poetical love. It needs some good old-fashioned *practical* love."

D.L. Moody often said, "Every Bible should be bound in shoe leather." We show our love to God, not by empty words but by willing works. We are not slaves obeying a master; we are children obeying a Father. And our sin is a family affair.

One of the tests of maturing love is our personal attitude toward the Bible, because in the Bible we find God's will for our lives revealed. An unsaved man considers the Bible an impossible book, mainly because he does not understand its spiritual message (1 Cor. 2:14). An immature Christian considers the demands of the Bible to be burdensome. He is somewhat like a little child who is learning to obey, and who asks, "*Why* do I have to do that?" or "Wouldn't it be better to do *this?*"

But a Christian who experiences God's perfecting love finds himself enjoying the Word of God and truly loving it. He does not read the Bible as a textbook, but as a love letter.

The longest chapter in the Bible is Psalm 119, and its theme is the Word of God. Every verse but two (Ps. 119:122, 132) mentions the Word of God in one form or another, as "law," "precepts," "commandments," etc. But the interesting thing is that the psalmist *loves* the Word of God and enjoys telling us about it! "O how love I Thy Law!" (Ps. 119:97) He rejoices in the Law (Ps. 119:14, 162) and delights in it (Ps. 119:16, 24). It is honey to his taste (Ps. 119:103). In fact, he turns God's Law into a song: "Thy statutes have been my songs in the house of my pilgrimage" (Ps. 119:54).

Imagine turning *statutes* into *songs*. Suppose the local symphony presented a concert of the traffic code set to music! Most of us do not consider laws a source of joyful song, but this is the way the psalmist looked at God's Law. Because he loved the Lord, he loved His Law. God's commandments were not grievous and burdensome to him. Just as a loving son or daughter happily obeys his father's command, so a Christian with perfecting love joyfully obeys God's command.

At this point, we can review and understand the practical meaning of "maturing love" in our daily lives. As our love for the Father matures, we have confidence and are no longer afraid of His will. We also are honest toward others and lose our fear of being rejected. And we have a new attitude toward the Word of God: it is the expression of God's love, and we enjoy obeying it. Confidence toward God, honesty toward others, and joyful obedience are the marks of perfecting love and the ingredients that make up a happy Christian life.

We can see too how sin ruins all this. When we disobey God we lose our confidence toward Him. If we do not immediately confess our sin and claim His forgiveness (1 John 1:9), we must start pretending in order to cover up. Disobedience leads to dishonesty, and both turn our hearts away from the Word of God. Instead of reading the Word with joy to discover the Father's will, we ignore the Word or perhaps read it in a routine way.

The burden of religion (man trying to please God in his own strength) is a grievous one (cf. Matt. 23:4); but the yoke that Christ puts on us is not burdensome at all (Matt. 11:28-30). Love lightens burdens. Jacob had to work for seven years to win the woman he loved, but the Bible tells us that "they seemed unto him a few days, for the love he had to her" (Gen. 29:20). Perfecting love produces joyful obedience.

### Victory (1 John 5:4-5)

The Greek goddess of victory was Nike, which also happens to be the name of a United States aerial missile. Both of them are named for the Greek word *nike* (NEE-kay) which simply means victory. But what does victory have to do with maturing love?

Christians live in a real world and are beset with formidable obstacles. It is not *easy* to obey God. It is much easier to drift with the world, disobey Him, and "do your own thing."

But the Christian is "born of God." This means he has the divine nature within him, and it is impossible for this divine nature to disobey God. "For whatever is born of God overcomes the world" (1 John 5:4, NASB). If the old nature is in control of us, we disobey God; but if the new nature is in control, we obey God. The world appeals to the old nature (1 John 2:15-17) and tries to make God's commandments seem burdensome.

Our *victory* is a result of *faith,* and we grow in faith as we grow in love. The more you love someone, the easier it is to trust him. The more our love for Christ is perfected, the more our faith in Christ is perfected too; because faith and love mature together.

The word *overcome* is a favorite with John; he uses it in 1 John 2:13-14 with reference to overcoming the devil. He uses it seven times in Revelation to describe believers and the blessings they receive (Rev. 2:7, 11, 17, 26; 3:5, 12, 21). He is not describing a special class of believers. Rather, he is using the word *overcomer* as a name for the true Christian. Because we have been born of God, we are overcomers.

We are told that a soldier in the army of Alexander the Great was not acting bravely in battle. When he should have been pressing ahead, he was lingering behind.

The great general approached him and asked, "What is your name, soldier?"

The man replied, "My name, sir, is Alexander."

The general looked him straight in the eye and said firmly: "Soldier, get in there and fight—or change your name!"

What is *our* name? "Children of God—the born-again ones of God." Alexander the Great wanted his name to be a symbol of courage; our name carries with it assurance of victory. To be born of God means to share God's victory.

This is a victory of faith, but faith in what? Faith in Jesus Christ, the Son of God! The person who overcomes the world is the one "who believes that Jesus is the Son of God" (1 John 5:5, NASB). It is not faith in ourselves, but faith in Christ, that gives us the victory. "In the world ye shall have tribulation, but be of good cheer; I have overcome the world" (John 16:33).

Identification with Christ in His victory reminds us of the several times we have read "as He is" in John's letter. "As He is, so are we in this world" (1 John 4:17). We should walk in the light "as He is in the light" (1 John 1:7). If we claim to abide in Him, then we should conduct ourselves as He conducted Himself (1 John 2:6). His children are to be, on earth, what He is in heaven. It is only necessary for us to claim this wonderful position *by faith*—and to *act* on it.

When Jesus Christ died, we died with Him. Paul said, "I have been crucified with Christ" (Gal. 2:20, NASB). When Christ was buried, we were buried with Him. And when He arose, we arose with Him. "Therefore we have been buried with Him through baptism into death, in order that as Christ was raised from the dead through the glory of the Father, so we too might walk in newness of life" (Rom. 6:4, NASB).

When Christ ascended to heaven, we ascended with Him and are now seated with Him in heavenly places (Eph. 2:6). And when Christ returns, we shall share His exaltation. "When Christ, who is our life, is revealed, then you also will be revealed with Him in glory" (Col. 3:4, NASB).

All these verses describe our spiritual position in Christ. When we claim this position by faith, we share His victory. When God raised Jesus from the dead, He "seated Him at His right hand in the heavenly places, far above all rule and authority and power and dominion, and every name that is named . . . and He put all things in subjection under His feet" (Eph. 1:20-22, NASB). This means that, positionally, each child of God is privileged to sit far above all his enemies!

Where a man sits determines how much authority he may exercise. The man who sits in the general manager's chair has a restricted sphere of authority; the man who sits in the vice president's chair exercises more control. But the man behind the desk marked *president* exercises the most authority. No matter where he may be in the factory or office, he is respected and obeyed because of where he sits. His power is determined by his position, not by his personal appearance or the way he feels.

So with a child of God: his authority is determined by his position in Christ. When he trusted Christ, he was identified with Him by the Holy Spirit and made a member of His body (1 Cor. 12:12-13). His old life has been buried and he has been raised to a new life of glory. In Christ, he is sitting on the very throne of the universe!

A Civil War veteran used to wander from place to place, begging a bed and bite to eat and always talking about his friend "Mr. Lincoln." Because of his injuries, he was unable to hold a steady job. But as long as he could keep going, he would chat about his beloved President.

"You say you knew Mr. Lincoln," a skeptical bystander retorted one day. "I'm not so sure you did. Prove it!"

The old man replied, "Why, sure, I can

prove it. In fact, I have a piece of paper here that Mr. Lincoln himself signed and gave to me."

From his old wallet, the man took out a much-folded piece of paper and showed it to the man.

"I'm not much for reading," he apologized, "but I know that's Mr. Lincoln's signature."

"Man, do you know what you have here?" one of the spectators asked. "You have a generous federal pension authorized by President Lincoln. You don't have to walk around like a poor beggar! Mr. Lincoln has made you rich!"

To paraphrase what John wrote: "You Christians do not have to walk around defeated, because Jesus Christ has made you victors! He has defeated every enemy and you share His victory. Now, *by faith*, claim His victory."

The key, of course, is *faith*, but this has always been God's key to victory. The great men and women named in Hebrews 11 all won their victories "by faith." They simply took God at His word and acted on it, and He honored their faith and gave them victory. Faith is not simply *saying* that what God says is true; true faith is *acting* on what God says because it is true. Someone has said that faith is not so much believing in spite of evidence, but obeying in spite of consequence.

Victorious faith is the result of maturing love. The better we come to know and love Jesus Christ, the easier it is to trust Him with the needs and battles of life. It is important that this maturing love become a regular and a practical thing in our daily lives.

How does a believer go about experiencing this kind of love and the blessings that flow from it?

To begin with, this kind of love must be cultivated. It is not the result of a hit-or-miss friendship! A previous study pointed out that a believer slips back into the world by stages:

1. Friendship with the world (James 4:4)
2. Spotted by the world (James 1:27)
3. Loving the world (1 John 2:15-17)
4. Conformed to the world (Rom. 12:2)

Our relationship to Jesus Christ, in a similar way, grows by stages.

**We must cultivate friendship with Christ.** Abraham was "the friend of God" (James 2:23) because he separated himself from the world and did what God told him. His life was not perfect, but when he sinned, he confessed and went right back to walking with God.

**This friendship will begin to influence our lives.** As we read the Word and pray, and as we fellowship with God's people, Christian graces will start to show up in us. Our thoughts will be cleaner, our conversation more meaningful, our desires more wholesome. But we will not be suddenly and totally changed; it will be a gradual process.

**Our friendship with Christ and our becoming like Him will lead to a deeper love for Christ.** On the human level, friendship *often* leads to love. On the divine level, friendship with Christ *ought* to lead to love. "We love Him because He first loved us" (1 John 4:19). The Word of God reveals His love to us, and the indwelling Spirit of God makes this love more and more real to us. Furthermore, this love is worked out in our lives in daily obedience. Christian love is not a passing emotion; it is a permanent devotion, a deep desire to please Christ and to do His will.

**The more we know Him the better we love Him, and the better we love Him the more we become like Him—"conformed to the image of His Son" (Rom. 8:29).** Of course we will not be completely conformed to Christ until we see Him (1 John 3:1-3); but we are to begin the process now.

What an exciting way to live! As God's love is perfected in us, we have confidence toward Him and do not live in fear. Because fear is cast out, we can be honest and open; there is no need to pretend. And because fear is gone, our obedience to His commands is born out of love, not terror. We discover that His commandments are not burdensome. Finally, living in this atmosphere of love, honesty, and joyful obedience, we are able to face the world with victorious faith and to overcome instead of *being* overcome.

The place to begin is not in some daring, dramatic experience. The place to begin is in the quiet, personal place of prayer. Peter wanted to give his life for Jesus, but when he was asked to pray, Peter went to sleep (Luke 22:31-33, 39-46). A believer who begins the day reading the Word, meditating on it, and worshiping Christ in prayer and praise will experience this perfecting love.

When it begins, he will know it—and others will know it. His life will be marked by confidence, honesty, joyful obedience, and victory.

# CHAPTER TEN
# WHAT DO YOU KNOW FOR SURE?
*1 John 5:6-21*

**N**othing is certain but death and taxes."

Benjamin Franklin wrote those words in 1789. Of course, a wise man like Franklin knew that many other things are also certain. The Christian also knows that there are many certainties. Of spiritual truth, Christians are not afraid to say, "We *know!*" In fact, the word *know* occurs thirty-nine times in John's brief letter, eight times in this closing chapter.

Man has a deep desire for certainty, and he will even dabble in the occult in his effort to find out something for sure. A businessman having dinner with his pastor said to him, "Do you see those offices across the street? In them sit some of the most influential business leaders in this town. Many of them used to come over here regularly to consult a fortune-teller. She isn't here anymore, but a few years ago you could count up the millions of dollars in this room as men waited to consult her."

The life that is real is built on the divine certainties that are found in Jesus Christ. The world may accuse the Christian of being proud and dogmatic, but this does not keep him from saying, "I know!" In these closing verses of John's letter we find five Christian certainties on which we can build our lives with confidence.

## Jesus Is God (1 John 5:6-10)

In 1 John 5:1-5, emphasis is placed on trusting Jesus Christ. A person who trusts Christ is born of God and is able to overcome the world. To believe that Jesus Christ is the Son of God is basic to Christian experience.

But *how* do we know that Jesus Christ is God? Some of His contemporaries called Him a liar and a deceiver (Matt. 27:63). Others have suggested He was a religious fanatic, a madman, or perhaps a Jewish patriot who was sincere but sadly mistaken. The people to whom John was writing were exposed to a popular false teaching that Jesus was merely a man on whom "the Christ" had come when Jesus was baptized. On the cross, "the Christ" left Jesus ("My God, My God, why hast Thou forsaken Me?") and so He died like any other human being.

John's epistle refutes this false teaching. It presents three infallible witnesses to prove that Jesus is God.

***First witness—the water.*** Jesus came "by water and blood." The water refers to His baptism in Jordan, when the Father spoke from heaven and said, "This is My beloved Son, in whom I am well pleased" (Matt. 3:13-17). At the same time the Spirit descended like a dove and rested on Him. This was the Father's attestation of His Son at the beginning of Jesus' ministry.

***Second witness—the blood.*** But the Father gave further witness as the time drew near for Jesus to die. He spoke audibly to Jesus from heaven, and said, "I have both glorified [My name], and will glorify it again" (John 12:28). Furthermore, the Father witnessed in miracle power when Jesus was on the cross: the supernatural darkness, the earthquake, and the rending of the temple veil (Matt. 27:45, 50-53). No wonder the centurion cried out, "Truly this was the Son of God!" (Matt. 27:54)

Jesus did not receive "the Christ" at His baptism and lose it at the cross. On both occasions, the Father witnessed to the deity of His Son.

***Third witness—the Spirit.*** The Spirit was given to bear witness to Christ (John 15:26; 16:14). We can trust the Spirit's witness because "the Spirit is truth." We were not present at the baptism of Christ or at His death, but the Holy Spirit was present. The Holy Spirit is the only Person active on earth today who was present when Christ was ministering here. The witness of the Father is past history, but the witness of the Spirit is present experience. The first is external, the second is internal—and both agree.

How does the Spirit witness within the heart of a believer? "For you have not received a spirit of slavery leading to fear again, but you have received a spirit of adoption as sons, by which we cry out, 'Abba! Father!' The Spirit Himself bears witness with our spirit that we are children of God" (Rom. 8:15-16, NASB). His witness is our inner confidence that we belong to Christ—not a confidence that we "work up" for ourselves, but a confidence that God gives us.

The Spirit also witnesses to us through the

Word. As we read God's Word, He speaks to us and teaches us. This is not true of an unsaved man (1 Cor. 2:14); it is true only of a believer.

A Christian feels "at home" with God's people because the Spirit dwells in him. This is another way the Spirit bears witness.

The Law required two or three witnesses for a matter to be settled (Deut. 19:15). The Father witnessed at the baptism and at the cross, and the Spirit witnesses today within the believer. The Spirit, the water, and the blood settle the matter: Jesus is God.

(Most scholars agree that 1 John 5:7 of the *Authorized Version* does not belong in the letter, but omitting it does not affect the teaching at all.)

We receive the witness of men, so why should we reject the witness of God?

People often say, "I wish I could have faith!" But everybody *lives* by faith! All day long, people trust one another. They trust the doctor and the pharmacist; they trust the cook in the restaurant; they even trust the fellow driving in the other lane on the highway. If we can trust men, why can we not trust God? And *not* to trust Him is to make Him a liar!

Jesus is God: this is the first Christian certainty, and it is foundational to everything else.

## Believers Have Eternal Life (1 John 5:11-13)

The key word in 1 John 5:6-10 is *witness,* sometimes translated "record" or "testifieth." God gave witness to His Son, but He has also given witness to His sons—to individual believers. We *know* that we have eternal life! Not only is there the witness of the Spirit within; but there is the witness of the Word of God. "These things have I written to you who believe in the name of the Son of God, in order that you may know that you have eternal life" (1 John 5:13, NASB).

Eternal life is a gift; it is not something that we earn (John 10:27-29; Eph. 2:8-9). But this gift is a Person—Jesus Christ. We receive eternal life not only *from* Christ, but *in* Christ. "He who has the Son has the life" (1 John 5:12, NASB). Not just "life" but "*the* life"—the life "which is life indeed" (1 Tim. 6:19, NASB).

This gift is received by faith. God has gone on record in His Word as offering eternal life to those who will believe on Jesus Christ. Millions of Christians have proved that God's record is true. Not to believe it is to make

God a liar. And if God is a liar, *nothing* is certain.

God wants His children to *know* that they belong to Him. John was inspired by the Spirit to write his Gospel to assure us that "Jesus is the Christ, the Son of God" (John 20:31). He wrote this epistle so that we may be sure that we are the children of God (1 John 5:13).

It would be helpful at this point to review the characteristics of God's children:

- "Everyone also who practices righteousness is born of Him" (1 John 2:29, NASB).
- "No one who is born of God practices sin" (1 John 3:9, NASB).
- "We know that we have passed out of death into life, because we love the brethren" (1 John 3:14, NASB).
- "Beloved, let us love one another, for love is from God; and everyone who loves is born of God and knows God" (1 John 4:7, NASB).
- "For whatsoever is born of God overcometh the world" (1 John 5:4).

If you bear these "birthmarks," you can say with confidence that you are a child of God.

When Sir James Simpson, the discoverer of chloroform, was on his deathbed, a friend asked him, "Sir, what are your speculations?"

Simpson replied: "Speculations! I have no speculations! 'For I know whom I have believed, and am persuaded that He is able to keep that which I have committed unto Him against that day.' "

## God Answers Prayer (1 John 5:14-15)

It is one thing to know that Jesus is God and that we are God's children; but what about the needs and problems of daily life? Jesus helped people when He was here on earth; does He still help them? Earthly fathers take care of their children; does the Heavenly Father respond when *His* children call on Him?

Christians have confidence in prayer, just as they have confidence as they await the judgment (1 John 2:28; 4:17). As we have seen, the word *confidence* means "freedom of speech." We can come to the Father freely and tell Him our needs.

Of course, there are conditions we must meet.

First, we must have a heart that does not condemn us (1 John 3:21-22). Unconfessed sin is a serious obstacle to answered prayer (Ps. 66:18). It is worth noting that differences between a Christian husband and his wife can hinder their prayers (1 Peter 3:1-7). If there is anything between us and any other Christian, we must settle it (Matt. 5:23-25). And unless a believer is abiding in Christ, in love and obedience, his prayers will not be answered (John 15:7).

Second, we must pray in God's will. "Thy will be done" (Matt. 6:10). "Prayer is a mighty instrument, not for getting man's will done in heaven, but for getting God's will done on earth," wrote Robert Law. George Mueller, who fed thousands of orphans with food provided in answer to prayer, said: "Prayer is not overcoming God's reluctance. It is laying hold of God's willingness."

There are times when we can only pray, "Not my will but Thine be done," because we simply do not know God's will in a matter. But most of the time we can determine God's will by reading the Word, listening to the Spirit (Rom. 8:26-27), and discerning the circumstances around us. Our very faith to ask God for something is often proof that He wants to give it (Heb. 11:1).

There are many promises in the Bible that we can claim in prayer God has promised to supply our needs (Phil. 4:19)—not our greeds! If we are obeying His will and really need something, He will supply it in His way and in His time.

"But if it is God's will for me to have a thing, then why should I pray about it?" Because prayer is the way God wants His children to *get* what they need. God not only ordains the end, but He also ordains the means to the end—prayer. And the more you think about it, the more wonderful this arrangement becomes. Prayer is really the thermometer of the spiritual life. God has ordained that I maintain a close walk with Him if I expect Him to meet my needs.

John does not write, "We *shall have* the requests," but, "We *know* that we have the requests" (cf. 1 John 5:15). The verb is present tense. We may not *see* the answer to a prayer immediately, but we have inner confidence that God has answered. This confidence, or faith, is "the evidence of things not seen" (Heb. 11:1). It is God witnessing to us that He has heard and answered.

What breathing is to a physical man, prayer is to a spiritual man. If we do not pray, we "faint" (Luke 18:1). Prayer is not only the utterance of the lips; it is also the desire of the heart. "Pray without ceasing" (1 Thes. 5:17) does not mean that a Christian is always saying an audible prayer. We are not heard for our much speaking (Matt. 6:7). No, "Pray without ceasing" suggests the attitude of the heart as well as the words of the lips. A Christian who has his heart fixed on Christ and is trying to glorify Him is praying constantly even when he is not conscious of it.

Charles Spurgeon, the famous preacher, was working hard on a message but was unable to complete it. It grew late and his wife said, "Why don't you go to bed. I'll wake you up early and you can finish your sermon in the morning."

Spurgeon dozed off and in his sleep began to preach the sermon that was giving him so much trouble! His wife wrote down what he said and the next morning gave her preacher-husband the notes.

"Why, that's exactly what I wanted to say!" exclaimed the surprised preacher. The message had been in his heart; it had simply needed expression. So with prayer: if we are abiding in Christ, the very desires of our heart are heard by God whether we voice them or not.

The pages of the Bible and the pages of history are filled with reports of answered prayer. Prayer is not spiritual self-hypnosis. Nor do we pray because it makes us feel better. We pray because God has commanded us to pray and because prayer is the God-appointed means for a believer to receive what God wants to give him. Prayer keeps a Christian in the will of God and living in the will of God keeps a Christian in the place of blessing and service. We are not beggars; we are children coming to a wealthy Father who loves to give His children what they need.

Though He was God in the flesh, Jesus depended on prayer. He lived on earth, as we must, in dependence on the Father. He arose early in the morning to pray (Mark 1:35), though He had been up late the night before healing the multitudes. He sometimes spent all night in prayer (Luke 6:12). In the Garden of Gethsemane, He prayed with "strong crying and tears" (Heb. 5:7). On the cross He prayed three times. If the sinless Son of God needed to pray, how much more do we?

The most important thing about prayer is the will of God. We must take time to ascertain what God's will is in a matter, especially searching in the Bible for promises or principles that apply to our situation. Once we know the will of God, we can pray with confidence and then wait for Him to reveal the answer.

## Christians Do Not Practice Sin
## (1 John 5:16-19)

"We know that no one who is born of God sins" (1 John 5:18, NASB). "No one who is born of God practices sin" (1 John 3:9, NASB). Occasional sins are not here in view, but habitual sins, the practice of sin. Because a believer has a new nature ("God's seed," 1 John 3:9), he has new desires and appetites and is not interested in sin.

A Christian faces three enemies, all of which want to lead him into sin: the world, the flesh, and the devil.

The world "lies in the power of the evil one" (1 John 5:19, NASB), Satan—the god of this age (2 Cor. 4:3-4, lit.) and the prince of this world (John 14:30). He is the spirit who works in the children of disobedience (Eph. 2:2).

*Satan* has many devices for leading a believer into sin. He tells lies, as he did to Eve (Gen. 3; 2 Cor. 11:1-3), and when men believe his lies they turn away from and disobey God's truth. Or, Satan may inflict physical suffering, as he did with Job and Paul (2 Cor. 12:7-9). In David's case, Satan used pride as his weapon and urged David to number the people and in this way defy God (1 Chron. 21). Satan is like a serpent who deceives (Rev. 12:9) and a lion who devours (1 Peter 5:8-9). He is a formidable enemy.

Then there is the problem of the *flesh*, the old nature with which we were born and which is still with us. True, we have a new nature (the divine seed, 1 John 3:9) within us, but we do not always *yield* to our new nature.

The *world* is our third enemy (1 John 2:15, 17). It is easy for us to yield to the desires of the flesh, the desires of the eyes, and the pride of life! The atmosphere around us makes it hard for us to keep our minds pure and our hearts true to God.

Then *how* does a believer keep from sinning?

First John 5:18 gives the answer: Jesus Christ keeps the believer so that the enemy cannot get his hands on him. "He [Christ] who was born of God keeps him [the believer] and the evil one does not touch him" (NASB). The *Authorized Version* here gives the impression that a believer keeps himself from sin, but this is not what the verse says. Of course, it is true that a Christian must keep himself in the love of God (Jude 21); but it is not true that a Christian must depend on himself to overcome Satan.

Peter's experience with Satan helps us to understand this truth.

"Simon, Simon," said Jesus, "behold, Satan has demanded permission to sift you like wheat; but I have prayed for you, that your faith may not fail; and you, when once you have turned again, strengthen your brothers" (Luke 22:31-32, NASB).

To begin with, Satan cannot touch any believer without God's permission. Satan wanted to sift *all* the disciples, and Jesus gave him permission. But Jesus prayed especially for Peter, and His prayer was answered. Peter's faith did not ultimately fail, even though his courage failed. Peter was restored and became a mighty and effective soul-winner.

Whenever Satan attacks us, we can be sure that God gave him permission. And if God gave him permission He will also give us power to overcome, because God will never permit us to be tested above our strength (1 Cor. 10:13).

One of the characteristics of "spiritual young men" is their ability to overcome the evil one (1 John 2:13-14). Their secret? "The word of God abides in you" (1 John 2:14, NASB). Part of the armor of God is the sword of the Spirit (Eph. 6:17), and this sword overcomes Satan.

When a believer sins, he can confess his sin and be forgiven (1 John 1:9). But a believer dare not play with sin, because sin is lawlessness (1 John 3:4, where "transgression of the Law" means "lawlessness"). A person who practices sin proves that he belongs to Satan (1 John 3:7-10). Furthermore, God warns that sin can lead to physical death!

"*All* unrighteousness is sin," but some sin is worse than other sin. *All* sin is hateful to God, and should be hateful to a believer; but some sin is punished with death. John tells us (1 John 5:16-17) about the case of a brother (a believer) whose life was taken because of sin.

The Bible mentions people who died because of their sin. Nadab and Abihu, the two sons of Aaron the priest, died because they deliberately disobeyed God (Lev. 10:1-7). Korah and his clan opposed God and died (Num. 16). Achan was stoned because he disobeyed Joshua's orders from God at Jericho (Josh. 6–7). A man named Uzzah touched the ark and God killed him (2 Sam. 6).

"But those are Old Testament examples!" someone may argue. "John is writing to New Testament believers who live under grace!"

To whom much is given, much shall be required. A believer today has a far greater responsibility to obey God than did the Old Testament saints. We have a complete Bible, we have the full revelation of God's grace, and we have the Holy Spirit living within us to help us obey God. But there are cases in the New Testament of believers who lost their lives because they disobeyed God.

Ananias and Sapphira lied to God about their offering, and they both died (Acts 5:1-11). Some believers at Corinth died because of the way they had acted at the Lord's Supper (1 Cor. 11:30). And 1 Corinthians 5:1-5 suggests that a certain offender would have died had he not repented and confessed his sin (2 Cor. 2:6-8).

If a believer does not judge, confess, and forsake sin, God must chasten him. This process is described in Hebrews 12:1-13, which suggests that a person who does *not* subject himself to the Father *will not live* (Heb. 12:9). In other words, first God "spanks" his rebellious children, and if they do not yield to His will, He may remove them from the world lest their disobedience lead others astray and bring further disgrace to His name.

"The sin unto death" is not some one *specific* sin. Rather, it is a *kind* of sin—it is the sort of sin that leads to death. With Nadab and Abihu, it was their presumption in taking the priest's office and entering the holy of holies. In the case of Achan it was covetousness. Ananias and Sapphira were guilty of hypocrisy and even of lying to the Holy Spirit.

If a Christian sees a brother committing sin, he should pray for him (1 John 5:16), asking that he confess his sin and return to fellowship with the Father. But if in his praying, he does not sense that he is asking in God's will (as instructed in 1 John 5:14-15), then he should not pray for the brother. "Therefore, pray not thou for this people, neither lift up cry nor prayer for them, neither make intercession to Me; for I will not hear thee" (Jer. 7:16).

James 5:14-20 somewhat parallels 1 John 5:16-17. James describes a believer who is sick, possibly because of his sin. He sends for the elders, who come to him and pray for him. The prayer of faith heals him and if he has sinned his sins are forgiven. "The prayer of faith" is prayer in the will of God, as described in 1 John 5:14-15. It is "praying in the Holy Spirit" (Jude 20).

Christians do not deliberately practice sin. They have the divine nature within; Jesus Christ guards them, and they do not want God's discipline.

## The Christian Life Is the Real Life (1 John 5:20-21)

Jesus Christ is the true God. We know Him who is true, and we are *in* Him who is true. We have "the real thing"!

"We know that our real life is in the true One, and in His Son, Jesus Christ. This is the real God and this is real, eternal life" (1 John 5:20, PH). *Reality* has been the theme throughout John's letter, and now we are reminded of it again.

John was probably writing to believers in the city of Ephesus, a city given over to the worship of idols. The temple of Diana, one of the wonders of the ancient world, was located in Ephesus, and the making and selling of idols was one of the chief occupations of the people there (Acts 19:21-41). Surrounded by idolatry, Christians there were under tremendous pressure to conform.

But "we know that there is no such thing as an idol in the world, and that there is no God but one" (1 Cor. 8:4, NASB). That is, "an idol has no real existence" (NASB, marg.). The tragedy of idolatry is that a dead image can do a worshiper no good because it is not genuine. Hebrew writers in the Old Testament called idols "nothings, vain things, vapors, emptiness." An idol is a lifeless, useless *substitute* for the real thing.

The Psalms contain caustic indictments of idolatry (Pss. 115:1-8; 135:15-18). To human vision, an idol looks real—eyes, ears, mouth, nose, hands, feet—but these are but useless imitations of the real thing. The eyes are blind, the ears are deaf, the mouth is silent, the hands and feet are paralyzed. But the real tragedy is that "those who make them will become like them; everyone who trusts in them" (Ps. 115:8, NASB). We become like the god we worship!

This is the secret of the life that is real. Because we have met the true God, through His Son Jesus Christ, we are in contact with reality. Our fellowship is with a God who is genuine. As we have seen, the word "real" means "the original as opposed to a copy" and "the authentic as opposed to an imitation." Jesus Christ is the true Light (John 1:9), and true Bread (John 6:32), and true Vine (John 15:1), and Truth itself (John 14:6). He is the Original; everything else is a copy. He is authentic; everything else is only an imitation.

Christians live in an atmosphere of reality. Most unsaved people live in an atmosphere of pretense and sham. Christians have been given spiritual discernment to know the true from the false, but the unsaved do not have this understanding. Christians do not simply choose between good and bad; they choose between true and false. An idol represents that which is false and empty; and a person who lives for idols will himself become false and empty.

Few people today bow to idols of wood and metal. Nevertheless, other idols capture their attention and affection. *Covetousness,* for example, is idolatry (Col. 3:5). A man may worship his bankbook or his stock portfolio just as fervently as a so-called heathen worships his ugly idol. "Thou shalt worship the Lord thy God, and Him only shalt thou serve" (Matt. 4:10). *The thing we serve is the thing we worship!* Whatever controls our lives and "calls the signals" is our god.

This explains why God warns us against the sin of idolatry. Not only is it a violation of His commandment (Ex. 20:1-6), but it is a subtle way for Satan to take control of us. When "things" take God's place in our lives, we are guilty of idolatry. This means we are living for the *un*real instead of for the *real.*

To a man of the world, the Christian life is unreal and the worldly life is real. This is because a man of the world lives by what he sees and feels (things) and not by what God says in His Word. An idol is a temporal *thing,* Jesus Christ is eternal God. "For the *things* which are seen are temporal, but the things which are *not seen* are eternal" (2 Cor. 4:18, NASB).

Like Moses, a Christian endures "as seeing Him who is invisible" (Heb. 11:27). Faith is "the evidence of things not seen" (Heb. 11:1). Noah had never seen a flood, yet by faith he "saw" it coming and did what God told him to do. Abraham "saw" a heavenly city and country by faith, and was willing to forsake his own earthly home to follow God. All of the great heroes of faith named in Hebrews 11 accomplished what they did because they "saw the invisible" by faith. In other words, they were in contact with reality.

The world boasts of its enlightenment, but a Christian walks in the *real* light, because God is light. The world talks about love, but it knows nothing of the *real* love which a Christian experiences because "God is love." The world displays its wisdom and learning, but a Christian lives in truth because "the Spirit is truth." God is light, love, and truth; and these together make a life that is *real.*

"But it makes no difference what a man believes so long as he is sincere!"

This popular excuse hardly needs refutation. Does it make any difference what the pharmacist believes, or the surgeon, or the chemist? It makes all the difference in the world!

> Shed a tear for Jimmy Brown;
> Poor Jimmy is no more.
> For what he thought was $H_2O$*
> Was $H_2SO_4$!†

A Christian has "turned to God from idols to serve the living and true God" (1 Thes. 1:9). Idols are dead, but Christ is the living God. Idols are false, but Christ is the true God. This is the secret of the life that is real!

So John's admonition, "Keep yourselves from idols," can be paraphrased, "Watch out for the imitation and the artificial and be real!"

---

\* Water
† Sulphuric acid

# 2 JOHN

## OUTLINE

**Key theme:** Loving and living the truth
**Key verse:** 2 John 4

I.  INTRODUCTION—verses 1-3

II. PRACTICING THE TRUTH—
    verses 4-6

III. PROTECTING THE TRUTH—
     verses 7-11

IV. CONCLUSION—verses 12-13

## CONTENTS

# CHAPTER ONE
# A FAITHFUL FAMILY
## 2 John

The apostate teachers not only invaded the churches, but they also tried to influence Christian homes. Titus faced this problem in Crete (Titus 1:10-11) and Timothy faced it in Ephesus (2 Tim. 3:6). As goes the home, so goes the church and the nation; thus the family is an important target in Satan's war against truth.

This brief letter was written to a godly mother and her children. Some Bible students have concluded that "the elect lady" refers to a local church and that "her children" are the believers fellowshipping in the church. "Thy elect sister" (2 John 13) would then refer to a sister church that was sending Christian greetings.

While it is true that John does address a group in this letter (note the plural in 2 John 6, 8, 10, 12), it is also true that he addresses an individual (2 John 1, 4-5, 13). Perhaps the solution is that a Christian assembly was meeting in this home, along with the family of the "elect lady," so that John had both the family and the congregation in mind (see Rom. 16:5; 1 Cor. 16:19; Col. 4:15; Phile. 2). He was concerned that this godly woman not permit anything false to come into her house (2 John 10) or into the assembly.

The dominant feelings in this little epistle are those of friendship and joy, even though these are mixed with concern and warning. If you and I are to keep our homes true to Christ, then we must have the same characteristics as this family to which John wrote.

**We Must Know the Truth (2 John 1-3)**
John used the word *truth* four times in this salutation, so it is an important word. Basically, it means "reality" as opposed to mere appearance, the *ultimate* that is the basis for all that we see around us. Jesus Christ is "the truth" (John 14:6) and God's Word is "truth" (John 17:17). God has revealed truth in the person of His Son and in the pages of His Word. He has given us "the Spirit of Truth" to teach us and to enable us to know truth (John 14:16-17; 16:13).

But the truth is not only an objective revelation from the Father, but also a subjective experience in our personal lives. We cannot only *know* the truth, but we can "love in the truth" and live "for the truth's sake." The truth "lives in us, and shall be with us forever." This means that "knowing the truth" is much more than giving assent to a body of doctrines, though that is important. It means that the believer's life is controlled by a love for the truth and a desire to magnify the truth.

John opened his letter on this note of "truth" because there were false teachers abroad who were spreading error. He called them deceivers and antichrists (2 John 7). John was not one to say that all religious teachings are true in one way or another, and that we should not be critical just as long as people are sincere. To John, there was a great difference, in fact, a deadly difference, between truth and error; and he would not tolerate error.

Since the truth will be with us forever, we certainly ought to get acquainted with it now and learn to love it. Of course, all truth centers in Jesus Christ, the eternal Son of God, with whom we shall live forever (John 14:1-6). It is wonderful to contemplate the fact that we shall spend eternity surrounded by truth, growing in our knowledge of truth, and serving the God of truth.

How did this elect lady and her children come to know the truth and become children of God? Through the grace and mercy of God (2 John 3). God is rich in mercy and grace (Eph. 2:4, 7), and He has channeled His mercy and grace to us in Jesus Christ. We are not saved by God's love, but by God's grace, which is "love that paid a price" (Eph. 2:8-9). God loves the whole world, yet the whole world is not saved. Only those who receive His abundant grace experience salvation from sin.

When you receive grace and mercy from God, you experience His peace. "Therefore, being justified [declared righteous] by faith, we have peace with God through our Lord Jesus Christ" (Rom. 5:1). God is not at war with lost sinners; it is sinners who are at war with God (Rom. 5:10; 8:7). God has been reconciled to sinners because of Christ's work on the cross. Now sinners must repent and be reconciled to God by faith in Jesus Christ (2 Cor. 5:14-21).

It is significant that at the very outset of his second letter John affirmed the deity of Jesus Christ. He did so by joining "the Lord Jesus Christ" with "God the Father." Suppose

2 John 3 read "from God the Father, and from the Prophet Amos." You would immediately respond, "Amos must not be joined with the Father's name in that fashion! It makes it appear that Amos is equal with God!"

But that is exactly why John joined the Father and the Son together: they are equally God! And then, to make certain that his readers did not miss the emphasis, John added "the Son of the Father." It is impossible to separate the two. If God is the Father, then He must have a Son; Jesus Christ is that Son. "Whosoever denieth the Son, the same hath not the Father" (1 John 2:23).

Many false teachers argue, "But Jesus is the 'son of God' in the same way all of us are God's sons, made in the image of God! When Jesus claimed to be God's Son, He was not really claiming to be God." But when Jesus said to the Jews, "I and My Father are One," they threatened to stone Him! Why? Because He had blasphemed! "Because that Thou, being a man, makest Thyself God" (John 10:30-33). They knew what He meant when He called Himself the "Son of God" and claimed equality with God.

The Christian faith stands or falls on the doctrine of the deity of Jesus Christ. If He is only man, then He cannot save us, no matter how gifted or unique He might be. If He is not God come in human flesh, then the Christian faith is lies—not truth—and John opened this letter with the wrong emphasis.

The great American statesman Daniel Webster was dining in Boston with a group of distinguished men, some of whom had Unitarian leanings. (The Unitarians deny the Trinity and the deity of both the Son and the Spirit.) When the subject of religion came up at the table, Webster boldly affirmed his belief in the deity of Jesus Christ and his confidence in His work of atonement.

"But Mr. Webster," said one man, "can you comprehend how Christ could be both God and man?"

"No, sir, I cannot comprehend it," Webster replied. "If I could comprehend Him, He would be no greater than myself. I feel that I need a superhuman Saviour!"

If our homes and churches are to be true to Christ and oppose the false teachers, we must know the truth. How do we learn the truth? By carefully studying God's Word and allowing the Spirit to teach us; by listening to others who are true to the faith; and then by practicing what we learn. We must not only *learn* the truth with our minds, but we must also *love* the truth in our hearts and *live* the truth by our wills. Our total persons must be yielded to the truth.

How important it is for parents to teach their children to love the truth! While we thank God for Sunday Schools and Christian day schools, in the final analysis, it is the home that must instill in children a love for truth and the knowledge of God's truth.

**We Must Walk in the Truth (2 John 4-6)**
To "walk in the truth" means to obey it, to permit it to control every area of our lives. This paragraph opens and closes with an emphasis on obedience, walking in the truth. It is much easier to study the truth, or even argue about the truth, than it is to practice it! In fact, sometimes zealous Christians disobey the truth in the very way they try to defend it.

When I was pastoring in Chicago, a strange young man often stood on the sidewalk in front of the church, passing out leaflets that denounced many evangelical leaders who were my friends. Of course, we could not stop him from distributing literature, so I instructed our people to take as many copies as he would give them and then destroy them!

One of our men decided to "shadow" the young man one evening, and he saw him walk to the nearby park, sit down under a tree, and light up a cigarette! Yet just a few minutes before, the young man had been shouting in front of the church, "I'm a fighting fundamentalist, and I'm not ashamed of it!" My guess is that most of the fundamentalists I know would have been ashamed of him. He thought he was promoting truth and opposing error, yet he was not walking in the truth himself. By his actions and belligerent attitude, he was denying the truth he sought to defend.

***The apostle's joy (v. 4a).*** John's joy was that the elect lady's children were walking in truth. John did not know all of them, however; the literal translation is "some of thy children." Somewhere in his travels, John had met some of her children and learned of their obedient walk with the Lord. "I have no greater joy than to hear that my children walk in truth" (3 John 4). We have no reason to believe that John was hinting that others of the children had gone astray after the false teachers. If by "children" John was including the members of the "house church," then it is possible that some of them had left the fellowship and joined with the deceivers.

It certainly brings great joy to the Father when He sees His children obeying His Word. I know personally what it means to the pastor when the church family is submissive to the Word and doing the will of God. Few things break the heart of a pastor like a disobedient and rebellious member who will not submit to the authority of God's Word.

When the great Baptist preacher Charles Spurgeon was a lad, he lived with his grandfather who pastored a church in Stambourne, England. A church member named Roads used to sit in the local pub and drink beer and smoke, and this practice grieved the pastor very much.

One day young Charles said to his grandfather, "I'll kill old Roads, that I will! I shall not do anything bad, but I'll kill him though, that I will!"

What did young Spurgeon do? He confronted Roads in the pub with these words: "What doest thou here, Elijah? Sitting with the ungodly, and you a member of a church and breaking your pastor's heart. I'm ashamed of you! I wouldn't break my pastor's heart, I'm sure!"

It was not long before Roads showed up at the pastor's home, confessing his sins and apologizing for his behavior. Young Spurgeon had "killed him" indeed!

**The apostle's argument (v. 4b).** He argued that God has commanded us to walk in truth and love. The word *commandment* is used five times in these few verses. God's commandments *focus* "the truth" on specific areas of life. "The truth" can be vague and general if we are not careful, but "the commandments" make that truth specific and binding.

Note that the commandments are given by "the Father." Each commandment is an expression of love and not simply law. The will of God is the revelation of God's heart (Ps. 33:11), not just His mind. Consequently, obedience to His Word should be a revelation of *our* love, not an expression of fear. "For this is the love of God, that we keep His commandments: and His commandments are not grievous" (1 John 5:3).

The false teachers try to make God's commandments appear harsh and difficult and then they offer their converts "true" freedom (2 Peter 2:19). But the greatest freedom is in obedience to God's perfect will. No believer who loves God would ever consider His commandments to be harsh and unbearable.

**The apostle's appeal (vv. 5-6).** John wanted the elect lady and her family to love one another and this appeal applies to us as well. "A new commandment I give unto you, 'That ye love one another' " (John 13:34). But John wrote that it was *not* a new commandment (see 1 John 2:7-11). Is this a contradiction?

The commandment "Love one another" is certainly not new in time, because even Old Testament Jews were instructed to love their neighbors (Lev. 19:18, 34) and the strangers within their gates (Deut. 10:19). But with the coming of God's Son to earth, this commandment is new in emphasis and in example. Jesus Christ gave new emphasis to brotherly love, and He exemplified it in His own life. It is also new in experience, for we have the Holy Spirit of God living within, enabling us to obey. "But the fruit of the Spirit is love" (Gal. 5:22; cf. Rom. 5:5).

Is it possible to *command* love? Yes, when you understand what Christian love really is. Many people have the mistaken idea that Christian love is a feeling, a special kind of "religious emotion" that makes us reach out and accept others. Certainly emotion is involved, but basically, Christian love is *an act of the will.* It simply means treating other people the same way God treats you! In fact, it is possible to love people that we really do not "like."

We may not be able to will our affections at all times, but we can will our attitudes and actions. When people are rude to us, we can be kind in return. When people persecute us, we can pray for them and, when the opportunity comes, do good to them. If we followed our feelings, we would probably retaliate! But if we ask the Spirit to control our wills, then we can act toward them as Jesus would have acted, in Christian love.

John went on to explain that love and obedience must go together (2 John 6). It is impossible to divorce our relationship with God from our relationship with people. If we say that we love God, but we hate our brother, then we can be sure that we do not really love God (1 John 4:20). If we obey God, then His love is perfected in us, and we have no problem loving our brother (1 John 2:3-5).

As you review this paragraph, you note three themes that blend: truth, love, and obedience. It is by believing the truth—in Christ and in the Word—that we are saved. The evidence of that salvation is love and obedience, but love and obedience are strengthened as we grow in our knowledge of truth. We speak the truth in love (Eph. 4:15) and we obey God's commandments because we love Him. Obedience enables us to learn more truth (John 7:17), and the more truth we learn, the more we love Jesus Christ who is truth!

Instead of living in a "vicious circle," we live in a "victorious circle" of love, truth, and obedience!

## We Must Abide in the Truth
## (2 John 7-11)

From encouraging truth, John turned to opposing error. He joined his voice with Peter's to warn that there are deceivers in the world. The word *deceiver* implies much more than teaching false doctrine. It also includes leading people into wrong living. John has already made it clear that *truth and life go together*. What we believe determines how we behave. Wrong doctrine and wrong living always go together.

Where did these false teachers come from originally? "For many deceivers have gone out into the world" (literal translation). They went out *from the church!* At one time, they professed to believe "the faith which was once delivered unto the saints" (Jude 3), but they turned from that faith and abandoned the truth and the church. "They went out from us, but they were not of us" (1 John 2:19). "Also of your own selves shall men arise, speaking perverse things, to draw away disciples after them" (Acts 20:30).

It takes constant spiritual vigilance to protect a family or a local church from the insidious attacks of false teachers. One very successful pastor told me, "If I took my eyes off this work for twenty-four hours and stopped praying, it would be invaded before we knew it." He was not emphasizing his own importance (though godly pastors are essential to spiritual churches) but the importance of diligence and vigilance.

Note that there are *many* deceivers! Why? Second Peter 2:2 gives the answer: "And many shall follow their pernicious ways." I think it was Mark Twain who said that a lie runs around the world while truth is putting on her shoes. Fallen human nature wants to believe lies and resist God's truth. We have already learned from 2 Peter 2 the devious methods the apostates use to seduce unwary and unstable people. No wonder they are successful!

These deceivers are also "antichrists" (see 1 John 2:18-29). The Greek prefix *anti* means both "instead of" and "against." These teachers are *against* Christ because they deny that He is indeed God come in the flesh (see 1 John 4:1-6). They not only deny the truth about Christ, but they give their converts a "substitute Christ" who is not the Christ of the Christian faith. The first question you want to ask any teacher, preacher, or author is, "What do you think about Christ? Is He God come in the flesh?" If he hesitates, or if he denies that Jesus is God come in the flesh, then you can be sure you have a false teacher.

I was preaching at Carrubers Close Mission in Edinburgh, Scotland, and before the meeting started, a young man came up to me. Without even introducing himself, he said, "Do you believe in the virgin birth of Jesus Christ?" I replied emphatically that I did, and that I preached that Jesus Christ was the Son of God come in the flesh. While I did not appreciate his arrogant manner, I did appreciate his concern that the man in the pulpit was "abiding in the truth."

To *abide in the truth* means to remain true to the basic doctrines of the Christian faith. The false teachers had departed from the truth and from the church fellowship and, therefore, they were dangerous. John pointed out three dangers the church and its members face because of deceivers in the world.

*The danger of going back (v. 8).* This is the danger of losing what has already been gained. *Look to yourselves* means "Beware! Take heed!" The false teachers offer something you do not have, when in reality they take away what you already have!

Satan is a thief and so are his helpers. John wanted his readers to receive "a full reward," which is his equivalent of 2 Peter 1:11, an abundant entrance into the eternal kingdom. What a tragedy it is when God's servants labor faithfully to build up a church, and then the work is destroyed by false teaching. No wonder Paul wrote to the Galatian assemblies, "I am afraid of [for] you, lest I have bestowed upon you labor in vain" (Gal. 4:11).

"Do not lose the things we accomplished" is the way Kenneth Wuest translates 2 John 8. Church members need to respect the work of faithful pastors and teachers and do everything to protect it and extend it. God's servants must one day give an account of their ministries, and they want to do it "with joy and not with grief" (Heb. 13:17). When the church goes backward, losing what it has gained, then it also will lose part of the reward at the Judgment Seat of Christ. It is essential that we hold fast to the truth of the Word of God!

**The danger of going ahead (v. 9).** The danger here is that of going beyond the limits of the Word of God and adding to it. The word translated "transgress" means "to run ahead too far, to pass beyond the assigned limits." It is false progress! The apostates like to make us believe that they are "progressive" while the church is "in a rut." They invite us to join them because they have something "new and exciting" to share. But their "progress" is such that they abandon the doctrine that Jesus Christ is the Son of God come in the flesh.

Fifty years ago, the American press was filled with news about "the fundamentalist-modernist controversy." Those who were true to the faith were opposing "modernism" in the mainline denominations and seeking to bring the schools and the leadership of these denominations back to historic Christianity. The "progressive" group called themselves "modernists," when actually there was nothing "modern" about their denials of Christian doctrine. These denials are as old as the church itself! One of their leaders, Dr. Harry Emerson Fosdick, said in one of his sermons, "Fundamentalism is still with us but mostly in the backwaters." If he were alive today, he would not make that statement; today the largest Sunday Schools, churches, seminaries, and missionary agencies are fundamental in doctrine.

If a person does not abide in the true doctrine, then he does not have either the Father or the Son. It is impossible to honor the Father and ignore the Son (or call Him a mere man) at the same time. "That all men should honor the Son, even as they honor the Father. He that honoreth not the Son honoreth not the Father which hath sent Him" (John 5:23). "Progressive theology" that denies Christ is not progressive at all; it is regressive—all the way back to Genesis 3:1, "Yea, hath God said?"

In giving this warning, however, John was not condemning "progress" as such. "The Lord has yet more light to shine forth from His Word." God gave us the Holy Spirit to teach us and to lead us into new understanding and application of the truth (John 16:12-16), and we must constantly grow (2 Peter 3:18).

But if our "learning" leads us away from the fundamental doctrines of the person and work of Jesus Christ, then we are on dangerous ground.

**The danger of going with (vv. 10-13).** John warned the family (and the church in their house) not to accept false teachers who visited them, wanting to fellowship with them or perhaps enjoy hospitality. Hospitality was a very important Christian ministry in that day, because there were very few inns where travelers could safely stay, especially Christians who wanted to keep away from the evil influences of the world. Christians were admonished to open their homes to visitors (Rom. 12:13; 1 Tim. 3:2; 5:3-10; Heb. 13:2; 1 Peter 4:8-10).

It was also true that traveling pastors and teachers needed homes to stay in (3 John 5-8). Believers who showed hospitality to these servants of God were "fellowhelpers to the truth," but believers who assisted false teachers were only sharing in their evil works. The doctrine of Jesus Christ is a test of truth, a basis for fellowship, and a bond for mutual cooperation.

Certainly this principle applies today. Often professed Christians come to our doors, wanting to play cassettes for us or offering us magazines or books. We must exercise discernment. If they do not agree with the true doctrine of Christ, not only must we not let them in, but we must not even say "goodbye," which means "God be with you."

Why was John so adamant about this? Because he did not want any of God's children to: (1) give a false teacher the impression that his heretical doctrine was acceptable; (2) become infected because of association and possible friendship; and (3) give the false teacher ammunition to use at the next place he stopped. If I entertain a cultist, for example, he will only say to the neighbors, "There's no reason why you shouldn't let me in. After all, Pastor Wiersbe let me in and we had a wonderful talk!" My disobedience could very well lead to somebody else's destruction.

Let me make it clear that John was not saying only born-again people should enter our houses! "Friendship evangelism" around the table is a wonderful way to win people to Christ. Christians need to be neighborly and hospitable. The apostle is admonishing us not to receive or encourage *false teachers who represent antichristian groups,* people who have left the church and are now trying to seduce others away from the truth. You can be sure that apostates use every opportunity they can to secure the endorsement of true Christians.

There is a tradition about the Apostle John that illustrates his position concerning false doctrine. When he was living in Ephesus, one day he went to the public baths, and there he saw Cerinthus, the leader of a heretical sect. John ran from the buildings lest they should fall down as a judgment from God! Cerinthus taught that Jesus was the natural son of Joseph and Mary, not God come in the flesh.

John's closing words (2 John 12-13) are almost identical to the farewell in 3 John, and they require no explanation. They do, however, express the importance of Christian fellowship and the joy that it should bring to our hearts (see 1 John 1:4). It is wonderful to receive letters, but even more wonderful to receive God's people into our homes and hearts.

This little epistle, written to a Christian mother and her family (and perhaps the church in their house), is a perfect gem of sacred correspondence. But we must not forget the major thrust of the letter: be alert! There are many deceivers in the world!

# 3 JOHN

## OUTLINE

**Key theme:** Having a good witness in the church
**Key verse:** 3 John 3

I.  GAIUS, A BELOVED BELIEVER—
    verses 1-8

II. DIOTREPHES, A PROUD
    BELIEVER—verses 9-10

III. DEMETRIUS, AN EXEMPLARY
     BELIEVER—verses 11-12

IV. CONCLUSION—verses 13-14

## CONTENTS

# CHAPTER ONE
# IT'S THE TRUTH
*3 John*

The battle for truth and against apostasy is fought not only in the home (2 John) but especially in the local church; and that is where 3 John comes in. This little letter (the shortest New Testament epistle in the original Greek) gives us a glimpse into an early assembly, its people, and its problems. As you read this brief letter, you find yourself saying, "Times have not changed very much!" We have similar people and problems today!

One of the key words in this letter is *witness* (3 John 3, "testified"; 3 John 6, 12, "report, bear record, record"). It means not only the words that we say but the lives that we live. Each Christian is a witness, either a good one or a bad one. We are either helping the truth (3 John 8) or hindering it.

This letter was addressed to Gaius, one of the leaders of the assembly. But John also discussed two other men in these verses— Diotrephes and Demetrius. Wherever there are people, there are problems—and the potential for *solving* problems. Each of us must honestly face the question, "Am I a part of the problem or a part of the answer?"

Consider the three men involved in this letter and note the kinds of Christians they were.

## Gaius the Encourager (3 John 1-8)

There is no question that the Apostle John dearly loved this man! He called him "the well beloved" in his greeting, and "beloved" in 3 John 5. It is unlikely that these were merely formal terms, like our "Dear Mr. Jones." (We may not even know Mr. Jones personally!) Third John 4 suggests that Gaius may have been one of John's converts, and, of course, those we lead to faith in Christ are especially precious to us. However, the beloved apostle looked on all the believers as his "little children" (1 John 2:1, 12, 18), so we must not press this too far.

If Gaius were a member of a church that I pastored, I would certainly have no trouble loving him! Consider the personal qualities of this excellent man.

*Spiritual health (v. 2).* John may be hinting here that his dear friend was not well and that John was praying for restored health: "I want you to be as healthy in body as you are in soul!" If this is the case, then it is evidence that it is possible to be spiritually healthy and physically sick. However, this kind of a greeting was very common in that day, so we must not build too much on it.

However, it is clear that Gaius was a man whose "spiritual health" was evident to all. "Though our outward man perish, yet the inward man is renewed day by day" (2 Cor. 4:16). Physical health is the result of nutrition, exercise, cleanliness, proper rest, and the disciplined order of a balanced life. Spiritual health is the result of similar factors. We must nourish ourselves with the Word, and then "work out" that nourishment in godly exercise (1 Tim. 4:6-7). We must keep ourselves clean (2 Cor. 7:1) and avoid the contamination and pollution that is in the world (2 Peter 1:4; James 1:27). While exercise and service are important, .it is also important that we rest in the Lord and gain new strength through fellowship with Him (Matt. 11:18-30). A balanced life is a healthy and happy life, a life that honors God.

*A good testimony (vv. 3-4).* Gaius was recognized as a man who obeyed the Word of God and "walked in truth" (see 2 John 4). Some of the brethren had made several visits to John, and they had joyfully reported that Gaius was a glowing example of what a Christian ought to be. In my own pastoral experience, I must confess that I have often been a bit "on edge" when people have said to me, "Is Mrs. _____ a member of your church?" Or, even worse, "I know one of your members quite well!" John never had to fear when Gaius' name came up!

What made Gaius such a good testimony? *God's truth.* The truth was "in him" and enabled him to walk in obedience to God's will. Gaius read the Word, meditated on it, delighted in it, and then practiced it in his daily life (see Ps. 1:1-3). What digestion is to the body, meditation is to the soul. It is not enough merely to *hear* the Word or *read* the Word. We must inwardly "digest it" and make it part of our inner persons (see 1 Thes. 2:13).

It is clear that Gaius' entire life was wrapped up in the truth. True living comes from the living truth. Jesus Christ, the truth (John 14:6), is revealed in the Word, which is God's truth (John 17:17). The Holy Spirit is also truth (1 John 5:6), and He teaches us the truth. The Spirit of God uses the Word of God to reveal the Son of God, and then to enable us to obey the will of God and "walk in truth."

**Practical ministry (vv. 5-8).** Gaius was also a fellowhelper to the truth (3 John 8). In practical ways, he assisted those who were ministering the Word. We have no indication that Gaius himself was a preacher or teacher, but he opened his heart and home to those who were.

We have learned from John's second letter the importance of Christian hospitality in that day. John warned "the elect lady" against entertaining false teachers (2 John 7-11), but in this letter he commended Gaius for showing hospitality to the true ministers of the Word. Gaius was an encouragement, not only to the brethren in general, but especially to "strangers" who came to fellowship with the church and to minister (see Heb. 13:2).

In this day of fear and violence, it is not easy to welcome strangers into our homes. Of course, in the early church, traveling ministers carried letters of recommendation from their own assemblies (Rom. 16:1); so it is important that we know something about the people we plan to entertain. However, it does take faith and love. As much as my wife and I enjoy sharing our home, we must confess that there have been times when bidding our guests good-bye brought a sense of happy relief! For the most part, however, our guests have truly been "angels unawares" whose presence was a blessing in our home.

Gaius not only opened his home, but he also opened his heart and his hand to give financial help to his guests. The phrase *bring forward on their journey* means "to assist on their journey." This could have included providing money and food as well as washing and mending clothing (see 1 Cor. 16:6; Titus 3:13). After all, our faith must be proved by our works (James 2:14-16), and our love must be expressed by deeds, not just words (1 John 3:16-18).

What is the motivation for this kind of practical ministry to the saints? First of all, *it honors God.* The phrase *after a godly sort* in 3 John 6 means "worthy of God, as befits God." We are never more "godlike" than when we are sacrificing to serve others. "That ye might walk worthy of the Lord unto all pleasing" (Col. 1:10). Since these itinerant ministers were representing the name of the Lord, any ministry to them was really a service to Jesus Christ (Matt. 10:40; 25:34-40).

A second motive is that the support of God's servants is *a witness to the lost* (3 John 7). Keep in mind that there were many wandering teachers in that day, sharing their ideas and begging for money. While the Lord Jesus taught definitely that God's servants deserve support (Luke 10:7), the standard in the New Testament is that this support comes from God's people. "Taking nothing of the Gentiles" means that these itinerant workers would not solicit help from the unsaved. Abraham had this same policy (Gen. 14:21-24), though he did not force his associates to adopt his policy. Many pastors make it clear, when the offering is being received, that they are not asking anything from the unbelievers in the congregation.

When God's people adequately support God's servants, it is a powerful testimony to the lost. But when ministers, churches, and other religious organizations go about *soliciting* from unsaved people and various businesses, it makes Christianity look cheap and commercial. This does not mean that God's servants should refuse a *voluntary* gift from an unconverted person, as long as the person understands that the gift will not purchase salvation. Even then, we must be very cautious. The king of Sodom's offer was voluntary, but Abraham rejected it! (Gen. 14:17-24)

The third motivation for serving is *obedience to God.* "We therefore ought to receive such" (3 John 8). This ministry of hospitality and support is not only an opportunity, but also an obligation. Galatians 6:6-10 makes it clear that those who receive *spiritual* blessings from the minister of the Word ought to share with him in *material* blessings; 1 Corinthians 9:7-11 further explains this principle. As a deacon expressed it to me in the first church I pastored, "You pay your board where you get your food!" It is unbiblical for church members to send their tithes and offerings all over the world and neglect to support the ministry of their own local church.

John gave a fourth motivation in 3 John 8: "That we might be fellowhelpers to the truth." Gaius not only received the truth and walked in the truth, but he was a "jointworker" who helped to further the truth. We do not know what his spiritual gifts were or how he served in the congregation, but we do know that Gaius helped extend and defend the truth by assisting those who taught and preached it.

In my itinerant ministry, I have stayed in many homes and been encouraged in my work. The host and hostess may not have been especially gifted people, but their ministry of gracious hospitality enabled me to exercise my gifts in the church. Whatever blessings came in the ministry will certainly be credited to their accounts! (Phil. 4:17)

It is one thing to fight apostasy and refuse to entertain false teachers, but quite another thing to open our homes (and wallets) to *promote the truth*. We need both the negative and the positive. We need more people like Gaius who are spiritually healthy, obedient to the Word, and sharing what they have for the furtherance of the truth. But, alas, not everybody is a Gaius! We turn now to an entirely different kind of Christian.

### Diotrephes the Dictator (3 John 9-10)
It seems like many churches have members who insist on "being boss" and having their own way. I must confess that sometimes it is the pastor who assumes dictatorial powers and forgets that the word *minister* means "a servant." But sometimes it is an officer, perhaps a longtime member of the church who thinks he or she has "seniority rights."

Our Lord's disciples often argued over which of them would be the greatest in the kingdom (Matt. 18:1ff). Jesus had to remind them that their model for ministry was not the Roman official who "lorded it over" people, but the Saviour Himself who came as a humble servant (Phil. 2:1ff). During my many years of ministry, I have seen the model for ministry change, and the church is suffering because of it. It appears that the "successful minister" today is more like a Madison Avenue tycoon than a submissive servant. In his hand he holds a wireless telephone, not a towel; in his heart is selfish ambition, not a love for lost souls and for God's sheep.

Diotrephes was motivated by pride. Instead of giving the preeminence to Jesus Christ (Col. 1:18), he claimed it for himself. He had the final say-so about everything in the church, and his decisions were determined by one thing: "What will this do for Diotrephes?" He was most unlike John the Baptist who said, "He [Jesus Christ] must increase, but I must decrease" (John 3:30). The Greek verb indicates that it was the *constant attitude* of Diotrephes to promote himself.

Whenever a church has a resident dictator in its membership there are bound to be problems, because people who are spiritually minded will not tolerate that kind of leadership.

The Holy Spirit is grieved when the members of the body are not permitted to exercise their gifts because one member must have his own way. At the Judgment Seat of Christ, we will discover how many hearts have been broken and churches destroyed because of the arrogant "ministries" of people like Diotrephes. Consider what this man was doing.

*He would not receive John (v. 9)*. It is incredible to think that a church leader (Diotrephes may have been an elder) would not have fellowship with one of our Lord's own apostles! How much Diotrephes could have learned from John! But Jesus Christ was not preeminent in his life, therefore Diotrephes could afford to treat the aged apostle this way.

Why did Diotrephes reject John? The obvious reason seems to be that John challenged the man's right to be dictator in the church. John was a threat to Diotrephes, because John had the authority of an apostle. John knew the truth about Diotrephes and was willing to make it known. Satan was at work in the church because Diotrephes was operating on the basis of pride and self-glorification, two of the devil's chief tools. If John appeared on the scene, Satan would be the loser.

*He lied about John (v. 10a)*. The phrase *prating against us with malicious words* means "bringing false and empty charges against us." What Diotrephes was saying about John was sheer nonsense, but there are people who love to hear such talk and who will believe it! Apparently, Diotrephes had made these accusations against John at one of the church meetings when John was not present to defend himself. But John warned that the day would soon come when he would settle accounts with Diotrephes the dictator.

Christians must be careful not to believe everything that they read or hear about God's servants, particularly those servants who have a wide ministry and are well known. I have quit reading certain publications because all they print are undocumented accusations about people whose ministries God is blessing in a singular way. I mentioned a certain publication to a friend of mine one day, and he said, "Yes, I know the editor quite well. He's like a blotter: he takes everything in *and gets it backward!*" We would all do well to filter these reports through Philippians 4:8.

*He rejected John's associates (v. 10b)*. Diotrephes would not even receive the other brethren because they were in fellowship with

John! It was "guilt by association." It is impossible to practice this kind of "separation" with any degree of consistency, because nobody can always know all that he needs to know about what his brother is doing! If I refuse to fellowship with you because you have fellowshipped with somebody I disapprove of, how do I know the extent of your fellowship? How can I keep track of what you have done? A person would need a computer and a full-time staff if he ever hoped to do a good job of keeping his associations pure!

Scripture makes it clear that we should have no fellowship with apostates (we studied this in 2 Peter), and that we must refrain from entangling alliances with unbelievers (2 Cor. 6:14ff). We must also avoid those whose doctrinal position is contrary to Scripture (Rom. 16:17-19). This does not mean that we cooperate only with those believers who interpret Scripture exactly as we do, because even good and godly people disagree on some matters such as church government or prophecy. All true Christians can agree on the fundamental doctrines of the faith and, in love, give latitude for disagreement on other matters.

However, to break personal fellowship with a brother because I disagree with his circle of friends is, to me, going beyond Scripture. Diotrephes rejected John, and then rejected the believers associated with John! But he went even further.

*He disciplined those who disagreed with him (v. 10c).* The church members who received John's associates were dismissed from the church! Again, it was guilt by association. Diotrephes had neither the authority nor the biblical basis for throwing these people out of the church, but he did it. Even "religious dictators" have to be careful lest the opposition become too strong!

The New Testament does teach church discipline, and these instructions ought to be obeyed. But church discipline is not a weapon for a dictator to use to protect himself. It is a tool for a congregation to use to promote purity and glorify God. It is not a pastor "throwing weight around," or a church board acting like a police court. It is the Lord exercising spiritual authority through a local church in order to rescue and restore an erring child of God.

Church "dictators" are dangerous people but, fortunately, they are easy to recognize. They like to talk about themselves and what they have "done for the Lord." They also have the habit of judging and condemning those who disagree with them. They are experts in putting labels on other Christians and classifying them into neat little categories of their own intention. They base their fellowship on personalities, not the doctrines that are fundamental to the faith. The tragedy is that these "dictators" actually believe that they are serving God and glorifying Jesus Christ.

It has been my experience that most of the distress and division in local churches, and between churches, has resulted from personalities more than anything else. If only we would return to the New Testament principle of making the person and work of Jesus Christ our test for fellowship, rather than associations and interpretations of nonessential doctrines. But people like Diotrephes will always have their enthusiastic followers because many sincere but immature and untaught believers prefer to follow such leaders.

## Demetrius the Exemplar (3 John 11-14)

According to the dictionary, an *exemplar* is "an ideal, a model, an example worthy to be imitated." Demetrius was that kind of a Christian. John warned his readers not to imitate Diotrephes. "If you want to imitate an example, then follow Demetrius!"

But is it right for us to imitate human leaders? Yes, if they in turn are imitating Jesus Christ. "Brethren, be followers together of me, and mark them which walk so as ye have us for an example" (Phil. 3:17). "Be ye followers of me, even as I also am of Christ" (1 Cor. 11:1). You and I cannot see God, but we can see God at work in the lives of His children. The godly life and dedicated service of another believer is always an encouragement and a stimulus to me. By our good example, we can "consider one another to provoke unto love and to good works" (Heb. 10:24).

Demetrius was a man worth imitating because he had a "good report" (witness) from the church fellowship. All the members knew him, loved him, and thanked God for his consistent life and ministry. While it is a dangerous thing when "all men shall speak well of you" (Luke 6:26), it is a wonderful thing when all the believers in a local church can agree to commend your life and testimony. If all men, saved and lost, good and evil, speak well of us, it may mean that we are compromising and masquerading.

But Demetrius not only had a good witness from the believers in the church, he also had a good witness from the Word (truth) itself.

Like Gaius, Demetrius walked in the truth and obeyed the Word of God. This does not mean that either of these men was perfect, but it does mean that they were consistent in their lives, seeking to honor the Lord.

Both the church and the Word bore witness to Demetrius' Christian life, and so did the Apostle John himself. (This meant that Demetrius would be in trouble with Diotrephes!) The beloved apostle knew firsthand that Demetrius was a man of God, and John was not ashamed to confess it.

John had warned that he was going to visit the church and confront Diotrephes (3 John 10), and no doubt both Gaius and Demetrius would stand with John in opposing the "dictator." They were the kind of men who would support the truth and submit themselves to authentic spiritual authority. Because they followed the truth, they could safely be imitated by other believers.

The conclusion of the letter (3 John 13-14) is similar to the conclusion of 2 John, and perhaps was a standard way to end letters in John's day. The apostle planned to visit the church "shortly" (soon), which certainly was a warning to Diotrephes and an encouragement to Gaius and Demetrius. The beloved John had "many things" to discuss with the assembly and its leaders, things he would rather deal with personally rather than by means of a letter.

"Peace be to thee" (3 John 14) must have been a benediction of real encouragement to Gaius! No doubt his own heart and mind were distressed because of the division in the church and the unspiritual way Diotrephes was abusing its members. George Morrison of Glasgow wrote, "Peace is the possession of adequate resources." The believer can enjoy the "peace of God" because he has adequate resources in Jesus Christ (Phil. 4:6-7, 13, 19).

John was careful to send greetings from the believers in the assembly with which he was associated at that time. "The friends send their greeting!" (NIV) What a blessing it is to have Christian friends! When Paul arrived near Rome, some of the brethren went to meet him, "whom when Paul saw, he thanked God and took courage" (Acts 28:15). Both Paul and John were not only soul winners, but also friend-makers. Diotrephes was so dictatorial that he had fewer and fewer friends, but John had more and more friends as he shared the love of Christ.

"Greet the friends by name" (NASB). The aged apostle did not want to write a long letter; besides, he was planning a visit. Paul sometimes ended his letters with a list of personal greetings (see Rom. 16), but John did not do this, at least in this letter. He wanted to have Gaius convey his greetings to his friends personally and individually, as though John were doing it himself. John was not concerned about a church only, but also the individuals within that church.

It is interesting to contrast these two little letters and to see the balance of truth that John presented. Second John was written to a godly woman about her family, while 3 John was written to a godly man about his church. John warned "the elect lady" about false teachers from the outside, but he warned Gaius about dictatorial leaders inside the fellowship. The false teachers in 2 John would appeal to *love* so that they might deny *truth*, while Diotrephes would appeal to *truth* as, in a most unloving way, he would attack the brethren.

How important it is to walk "in truth and love" (2 John 3) and hold the truth in love! (Eph. 4:15) To claim to love the truth and yet hate the brethren is to confess ignorance of what the Christian life is all about.

When God's people love Him, the truth, and one another, then the Spirit of God can work in that assembly to glorify Jesus Christ. But when any member of that assembly, including the pastor, becomes proud and tries to have "the preeminence," then the Spirit is grieved and He cannot bless. The church may *outwardly* appear successful, but inwardly it will lack the true unity of the Spirit that makes for a healthy fellowship.

What we need are more people like Gaius and Demetrius—and fewer like Diotrephes!

# JUDE

## OUTLINE

**Key theme:** Overcoming the apostates
**Key verses:** Jude 3-4

I. INTRODUCTION—verses 1-2

II. THE ALARM—verses 3-4

III. THE ARGUMENT—verses 5-16

IV. THE ADMONITION—verses 17-25

## CONTENTS

# CHAPTER ONE
# A CALL TO ARMS!
*Jude 1-7*

Since the author of this epistle was the brother of James, this would make him the half brother of our Lord Jesus Christ (see Mark 6:3). Our Lord's brothers in the flesh did not believe in Him while He was ministering (John 7:5). But after the Resurrection, James was converted (see 1 Cor. 15:7), and we have every reason to believe that Jude was also saved at that time. Acts 1:14 informs us that "His brethren" were part of the praying group that was awaiting the Holy Spirit; 1 Corinthians 9:5 states that "the brethren of the Lord" were known in the early church.

So much for the identification of the author. Why did Jude write this letter? To warn his readers that the apostates were already on the scene! Peter had prophesied that they would come (2 Peter 2:1-3; 3:3ff), and his prophecy had been fulfilled. Apparently Jude wrote to the same believers who had received Peter's letters, intending to stir them up and remind them to take Peter's warnings to heart. You will discover a number of parallels between Jude and 2 Peter as you study this fascinating but neglected letter.

He wrote to "exhort" them (Jude 3). In the Greek language, this word was used to describe a general giving orders to the army; hence the atmosphere of this letter is "military." Jude had started to write a quiet devotional letter about salvation, but the Spirit led him to put down his harp and sound the trumpet! The Epistle of Jude is a call to arms.

## The Army (Jude 1-2)
The Captain of the army is Jesus Christ, and the soldiers He commands are people who share a "common salvation" through faith in Him. Jude called them *saints* (Jude 3), which simply means "set-apart ones." He addressed them as *sanctified*, which, again, means "set apart." (Some manuscripts read "beloved in God the Father.") Perhaps there is an echo here of 1 Peter 1:2 where all three Persons of the Godhead are seen to be involved in our salvation.

Certainly salvation begins in the heart of God and not in the will of man (Rom. 9:16).

The mysteries of God's sovereign electing grace are beyond us in this life and will never be understood until we enter His glorious presence. For that reason, we are wise not to make them the basis for arguments and divisions. "The secret things belong unto the Lord our God" (Deut. 29:29).

Second Thessalonians 2:13-14 makes it clear that the same God who chose us also set us apart by the Spirit and then called us by the Gospel to trust in Jesus Christ. God's choosing and God's calling go together, for the God who ordains the end (our salvation) also ordains the *means to the end* (someone calling us to Christ). We did not understand how God's Spirit was working in our lives prior to our conversion, but He was working just the same to "set us apart" for Jesus Christ.

Not only are God's saints set apart, but they are also *preserved*. This means "carefully watched and guarded." The believer is secure in Jesus Christ. This same word is used in Jude 6 and 13 ("reserved") and also in Jude 21 ("keep yourselves"). God is preserving the fallen angels and the apostates for judgment, but He is preserving His own children for glory. Meanwhile, He is able to preserve us in our daily walk and keep us from stumbling.

Because they are set apart and preserved, God's soldiers are the recipients of God's choicest blessings: mercy, peace, and love. Like the Apostle Peter, Jude wanted these special blessings to be *multiplied* in their lives (1 Peter 1:2; 2 Peter 1:2). God in His mercy does not give us what we deserve. Instead, He gave our punishment to His own Son on the cross. "Surely He hath borne our griefs, and carried our sorrows. . . . But He was wounded for our transgressions, He was bruised for our iniquities" (Isa. 53:4-5).

Because of Christ's work on the cross, believers enjoy *peace*. The unsaved person is at war with God and cannot please Him (Rom. 8:7-8); but when he trusts the Saviour, the war ends and he receives God's peace (Rom. 5:1).

He also experiences God's *love* (Rom. 5:5). The Cross is God's demonstration of love (Rom. 5:8), but His love is not experienced within until His Spirit comes into the believing heart. As the believer grows in his spiritual life, he enters into a deeper relationship of love (John 14:21-24).

Certainly those who know Christ as their Saviour enjoy a unique position. They are called *by* God to be set apart *for* God that they might enjoy love *with* God. While their fellowship with the Father might change from day to day, their relationship as children cannot change. They are "preserved in Jesus Christ." Because Jude would write a great deal in this letter about sin and judgment, he was careful at the very outset to define the special place that believers have in the heart and plan of God. The apostates would sin, fall, and suffer condemnation; but the true believers would be kept safe in Jesus Christ for all eternity.

It bears repeating that an apostate is not a true believer who has abandoned his salvation. He is a person who has professed to accept the truth and trust the Saviour, and then turns from "the faith which was once delivered unto the saints" (Jude 3). Jude would not contradict what Peter wrote, and Peter made it clear that the apostates were not God's sheep, but were instead pigs and dogs (2 Peter 2:21-22). The sow had been cleaned on the outside, and the dog on the inside, but neither had been given that new nature which is characteristic of God's true children (2 Peter 1:3-4).

Here, then, we have the "spiritual army" that Jude was addressing. If you have trusted Jesus Christ, you are in this army. God is not looking for volunteers; He has already enlisted you! The question is not, "Shall I become a soldier?" Rather, it is, "Will I be a *loyal* soldier?"

Isaac Watts once preached a sermon on 1 Corinthians 16:13: "Watch ye, stand fast in the faith, quit you [act] like men, be strong." When he published the sermon, he added a poem to it; we sing it today as one of our spiritual songs.

Am I a soldier of the Cross,
A follower of the Lamb?
And shall I fear to own His cause,
Or blush to speak His name?

Must I be carried to the skies
On flowery beds of ease?
While others fought to win the prize
And sailed through bloody seas?

### The Enemy (Jude 3-4)

We have already noted that Jude set out to write an encouraging letter about "the common salvation." The name *Jude* (Judah) means "praise," and he was anxious to praise God and rejoice in the salvation God gives in Jesus Christ. But the Spirit of God changed his mind and led Jude to write about the battle against

the forces of evil in the world. Why? Because it was "needful" for the church.

I must confess that I sympathize with Jude. In my own ministry, I would much rather encourage the saints than declare war on the apostates. But when the enemy is in the field, the watchmen dare not go to sleep. The Christian life is a battleground, not a playground.

Jude wasted no time in identifying the enemy.

**They were ungodly (v. 4b).** This is one of Jude's favorite words. While these men *claimed* to belong to God, they were, in fact, ungodly in their thinking and their living. They might have "a form of godliness," but they lacked the *force* of godliness that lives in the true Christian (2 Tim. 3:5).

**They were deceitful (v. 4c).** They "crept in unawares." The Greek word means "to slip in secretly, to steal in undercover." Sometimes Satan's undercover agents are *"brought in* secretly" by those already on the inside (Gal. 2:4), but these men came in on their own. Peter warned that these men were coming (2 Peter 2:1) and now they had arrived on the scene.

How could false brethren get into true assemblies of the saints? *The soldiers had gone to sleep at the post!* The spiritual leaders in the churches had grown complacent and careless. This explains why Jude had to "blow the trumpet" to wake them up. Our Lord and His Apostles all warned that false teachers would arise, yet the churches did not heed the warnings. Sad to say, some churches are not heeding the warnings today.

**They were enemies of God's grace (v. 4d).** Why did they enter the churches? To attempt to change the doctrine and "turn the grace of our God into lasciviousness" (Jude 4). The word *lasciviousness* simply means "wantonness, absence of moral restraint, indecency." A person who is lascivious thinks *only* of satisfying his lusts, and whatever he touches is stained by his base appetites. Lasciviousness is one of the works of the flesh (Gal. 5:19) that proceeds from the evil heart of man (Mark 7:21-22).

Peter had already warned these people that the apostates would argue, "You have been saved by grace, so you are free to live as you please!" They promised the people freedom, but it was the kind of freedom that led to terrible bondage (2 Peter 2:13-14, 19). The readers both Peter and Jude addressed knew what Paul had written (2 Peter 3:15-16), so they should have been fortified with Romans 6 and 1 Corinthians 5–6.

The apostates, like the cultists today, use the Word of God to promote and defend their false doctrines. They seduce young, immature Christians who have not yet been grounded in the Scriptures. Every soldier of the Cross needs to go through "basic training" in a local church so that he knows how to use the weapons of spiritual warfare (2 Cor. 10:4-5).

**They denied God's truth (v. 4e).** "Even denying the Lord that bought them," Peter had warned (2 Peter 2:1). Jude was not writing about two different persons when he wrote "the only Lord God, and our Lord Jesus Christ" for the Greek construction demands that these two names refer to one Person. In other words, Jude was affirming strongly the deity of Jesus Christ. Jesus Christ is God!

But the apostates would deny this. They would agree that Jesus Christ was a good man and a great teacher, but not that He was eternal God come in human flesh. The first test of any religious teacher, as we have seen, is, "What do you think of Jesus Christ? Is He God come in the flesh?" Anyone who denies this cardinal doctrine is a false teacher *no matter how correct he may be in other matters*. If he denies the deity of Christ, something will always be missing in whatever he affirms.

**They were ordained to judgment (v. 4a).** Jude did not write that these men were ordained to become apostates, as though God were responsible for their sin. They became apostates because they willfully turned away from the truth. But God did ordain that such people would be judged and condemned. The Old Testament prophets denounced the false prophets of their day, and both Jesus Christ and His Apostles pronounced judgment on them.

Why should these men be judged by God? To begin with, they had denied His Son! That is reason enough for their condemnation! But they had also defiled God's people by teaching them that God's grace permitted them to practice sin. Furthermore, they derided the doctrine of Christ's coming (2 Peter 3). "Where is the promise of His coming?" They mocked the very promise of Christ's coming and the judgment He would bring against the ungodly.

Of course, they did all these things under the guise of religion, and this made their sin even greater. They deceived innocent people so that they might take their money and enjoy it in godless living. Jesus compared them to wolves in sheep's clothing (Matt. 7:15).

How, then, should the church respond to the presence of this insidious enemy? *By earnestly contending for the faith.*

"The faith" refers to that body of doctrine that was given by God through the Apostles to the church. The word *doctrine* is found at least sixteen times in the Pastoral Epistles alone. Paul admonished both Timothy and Titus to make sure the believers were being taught "sound doctrine," which means "healthy doctrine," doctrine that promotes the spiritual health of the local church. While individual teachers and preachers may disagree on the fine points of theology, there is a basic body of truth to which all true Christians are committed.

This body of truth was *delivered* (Jude 3) to the saints. The word means "to be entrusted with." The church collectively, and each Christian personally, has a stewardship to fulfill. "But as we were allowed of God to be put in trust with the Gospel, even so we speak" (1 Thes. 2:4). God committed the truth to Paul (1 Tim. 1:11), and he shared it with others, such as Timothy (1 Tim. 6:20). He exhorted Timothy to entrust the Word to other faithful men (2 Tim. 2:2). You and I would not have the Word today were it not for faithful believers down through the ages who guarded this precious deposit and invested it in others.

The church is always one generation short of extinction. If *our* generation fails to guard the truth and entrust it to our children, then that will be the end! When you think of the saints and martyrs who suffered and died so that we might have God's truth, it makes you want to take your place in God's army and be faithful unto death.

What does it mean to "contend for the faith"? The Greek word is an athletic term that gives us our English word *agonize*. It is the picture of a devoted athlete, competing in the Greek games and stretching his nerves and muscles to do his very best to win. You never fight the Lord's battles from a rocking chair or a soft bed! Both the soldier and the athlete must concentrate on doing their best and giving their all. There must also be teamwork, believers working together to attack and defeat the enemy.

Sometimes you hear well-meaning people say, "Well, it's fine to contend for the faith, but don't be so contentious!" While it is true that some of God's soldiers have been the cause of quarrels and divisions, it is also true that some of them have paid a great price to defend the faith. As Christian soldiers, we must not fight each other or go around looking for trouble. But when the banner of Christ is in danger of being taken by the enemy, we cannot sit idly by, nor can we ever hope to win the victory by wearing kid gloves.

Charles Spurgeon once said that "the new views are not the old truth in a better dress, but deadly errors with which we can have no fellowship." False doctrine is a deadly poison that must be identified, labeled, and avoided. Spurgeon also said, "I cannot endure false doctrine, however neatly it may be put before me. Would you have me eat poisoned meat because the dish is of the choicest ware?"

We must always speak the truth in love, and the weapons we use must be spiritual. At the same time, we must dare to take our stand for "the faith" even if our stand offends some and upsets others. We are not fighting personal enemies, but the enemies of the Lord. It is the honor and glory of Jesus Christ that is at stake. "Fight the good fight of faith" (1 Tim. 6:12).

## The Victory (Jude 5-7)

Like the Apostle Peter, Jude reached back into Old Testament history and gave three examples of God's victory over those who had resisted his authority and turned from the truth. Peter referred to the fallen angels, Noah, and Lot (2 Peter 2:4-9) and followed the historical order. He also emphasized God's deliverance of the righteous as well as His judgment of the ungodly. Jude, however, did not mention Noah and the Flood, but instead used the nation Israel as his example.

The point Jude was making is that *God judges apostates.* Therefore, the false teachers who had crept into the church would also one day be judged. Their seeming success would not last; God would have the last word.

*Israel (v. 5).* Both Paul (1 Cor. 10) and the author of Hebrews (Heb. 3–4) used the experiences of Israel to illustrate important spiritual truths. The nation was delivered from Egypt by the power of God and brought to the border of the Promised Land. But the people were afraid and did not have the faith to enter in and possess the land (see Num. 13–14). Moses, Joshua, and Caleb tried to encourage the people to obey God by faith, but the people refused. In fact, the leaders of the tribes

even wanted to organize and go back to Egypt, the place of bondage!

This was rebellion against the will and the Word of God, and God cannot tolerate rebellion. As a result, everybody in the camp twenty years and older was destined to die at some time in the next forty years. Their unbelief led to their extermination.

Keep in mind that Jude was using a historical event as an illustration, and we must not press every detail. The entire nation was delivered from Egypt, but that does not mean that each individual was personally saved through faith in the Lord. The main point of the account is that privileges bring responsibilities, and God cannot lightly pass over the sins of His people. If any of Jude's readers dared to follow the false teachers, they too would face the discipline of God. "Wherefore let him that thinketh he standeth take heed lest he fall" (1 Cor. 10:12).

*The fallen angels (v. 6).* We studied this illustration in 2 Peter 2:4, but Jude seems to add a new dimension to it by associating the fall of the angels with the destruction of Sodom and Gomorrah (Jude 7, "even as . . . in like manner"). Some Bible students believe that Jude was teaching not only a revolt of the angels against God, but also an invasion of earth by these fallen angels. They point to Genesis 6:1-4 and claim that "the sons of God" were fallen angels who assumed human bodies, cohabited with the daughters of men, and produced a race of giants on the earth. This was one reason that God sent the Flood.

As attractive and popular as this view is, I must confess that I have a difficult time accepting it. It is true that "the sons of God" is a title for angels (Job 1:6; 2:1; 38:7), but always for *unfallen* angels. Would the Holy Spirit, writing through Moses, call *rebellious* angels "the sons of God"? I doubt it.

My second problem is that angels are spirits and do not have bodies. In the Old Testament record, we do read of angels who *appeared* in human form, but this was not incarnation. How could a spirit being have a physical relationship with a woman, even if that being assumed a temporary body of some kind? Our Lord taught that the angels were sexless (Matt. 22:30).

Third, it appears that God sent the Flood because of what *man* did, not what angels did. "My Spirit shall not always strive with *man.* . . . And God saw that the wickedness of *man* was great in the earth. . . . And it repented [grieved] the Lord that He had made *man* on the earth" (Gen. 6:3, 5-6, italics mine). If this "fallen angel" view is correct, God should have repented that He created *the angels!*

Fourth, the phrases "even as" and "in like manner" in Genesis 6:7 need not be interpreted to say that the angels did what the Sodomites did, namely, "going after strange flesh." Notice the grammatical connections in the verse, and you will get the message: "Even as Sodom and Gomorrah . . . in like manner . . . are set forth for an example." The angels are an example of God's judgment and so are Sodom and Gomorrah.

I might add that Genesis 6:4 presents a strong argument *against* the view that fallen angels cohabited with women and produced a race of giants. "There were giants in the earth in those days; *and also after that*" (italics mine). This would mean that a *second* invasion of fallen angels had to take place! We have no record of this in Scripture.

Finally, both Peter and Jude state clearly that these rebellious angels are chained in darkness and reserved for judgment. They would have to have invaded the earth *prior* to being arrested and chained by God. We wonder why God would have permitted them to "run loose" long enough to get the women into sin and help to cause the great Flood. The whole explanation, though held by teachers whom I respect, to me seems a bit fantastic. The simplest explanation of Genesis 6 is that the godly line of Seth ("the sons of God") began to mingle with the ungodly line of Cain, and this broke down the walls of separation, resulting in compromise and eventually degrading sin. But regardless of which interpretation you accept, keep the main lesson in mind: the angels rebelled and were punished for their rebellion.

**Sodom and Gomorrah (v. 7).** Both Peter and Jude state that God made these cities an example to warn the ungodly that God does indeed judge sin (see 2 Peter 2:6). When you combine their descriptions, you discover that the citizens of Sodom and Gomorrah (and the other cities involved) were: ungodly, filthy, wicked, unlawful, unjust, and given over to fornication. They did not *occasionally* commit unnatural sexual sins; they indulged in them and gave themselves over to the pursuit of lust. The Greek verb is intensive: "to indulge in excessive immorality." This was their way of life—and death!

*Strange flesh* means "different flesh." The bent of their life was constantly downward, indulging in unnatural acts (see Rom. 1:24-27). Those who hold the "fallen angel" interpretation of Genesis 6 make the "strange flesh" refer to angels in human form; but when did the angels invade Sodom and Gomorrah? And, if fallen angels are meant, how can their sin and the sin of the Sodomites apply to us today, for we have no fallen angels to tempt or seduce us? Indeed, the men at Lot's door did want to engage in homosexual activity with his angelic guests, but the Sodomites did not know they were angels. Another possibility is that the Sodomites were guilty not only of unnatural sex with each other, but also with animals, which would be "strange flesh." Both homosexuality and beastiality are condemned by God (Lev. 18:22-25).

These cities were *set forth* by God as an example and warning to ungodly people today. The verb *set forth* means "to expose openly to public view." (Interestingly enough, the word was used to describe a corpse lying in state!) But the cities of the plain are not *today* in public view. It is generally agreed among archeologists that Sodom and Gomorrah are buried under the southern end of the Dead Sea. How, then, do they serve as an example? *In the pages of the Word of God.* No one can read Genesis 18–19 without clearly seeing God's hatred for sin and, at the same time, His patience and willingness to postpone judgment. This certainly ties in with Peter's explanation for God's seeming delay in fulfilling the promise of Christ's return (2 Peter 3:8ff).

The sin of Israel was rebellious unbelief (Heb. 3:12). The sin of the angels was rebellion against the throne of God. The sin of Sodom and Gomorrah was indulging in unnatural lust. Unbelief, rebellion against authority, and sensual indulgence were sins characteristic of the false teachers. The conclusion is obvious: the apostates will be judged. But, meanwhile, God's soldiers must stay on duty and see to it that these false teachers do not creep into the ranks and start to lead people astray. "Take heed unto thyself, and unto the doctrine" (1 Tim. 4:16).

What can we do practically to oppose the enemy and maintain the purity and unity of the church? For one thing, we must know the Word of God and have the courage to defend it. Every local church ought to be a Bible institute, and every Christian ought to be a Bible student. The pulpit needs to declare positive truth as well as denounce error.

Second, we must "watch and pray." The enemy is already here and we dare not go to sleep! Spiritual leaders in local congregations need to be alert as they interview candidates for baptism and church membership. Committees need to seek the mind of Christ as they appoint Sunday School teachers, youth sponsors, and other church leaders. Congregations must exercise discernment as they select officers.

Third, congregations and members must be careful where they send their money. "Should you help the wicked and love those who hate the Lord?" (see 2 Chron. 19:2)

Finally, we must have the courage to maintain a position of biblical separation from those who deny Christ and the fundamental doctrines of the Word (Rom. 16:17-20; 2 Tim. 2:15ff; 2 John 6-11). This does not mean that we separate from fellow believers over minor doctrinal differences, or that we practice "guilt by association." God's true army needs to stand together in the battle for truth.

Have you heeded the call to arms?

# CHAPTER TWO
# MEET THE
# APOSTATES!
*Jude 8-16*

Jude was not content simply to remind his readers to pay attention to what Peter had written. He wanted to add his own words of warning by describing what the false teachers were like and what they would do to the church. The Spirit of God led Jude to describe the characteristics of the apostates, reinforcing Peter's words and, at the same time, adding information. Jude 8-16 and 2 Peter 2 parallel and supplement each other.

But why this seemingly needless repetition? The Apostle Paul gave the answer: "To write the same things to you, to me indeed is not grievous, but for you it is safe" (Phil. 3:1). Parents repeat warnings and instructions to their children, and sometimes the children reply, "I know that! You've already told me a million times!" But wise parents know that some things *must* be said again and again for the safety and welfare of their children—whether the children want to hear them or not!

All that Jude wrote about the apostates in these verses may be summarized in three statements.

## They Reject Divine Authority
## (Jude 8-11)

All authority comes from the throne of God, whether it is authority in the home, the church, or the state. Those who exercise authority must first be *under* authority, accountable to God. But the false teachers reject divine authority and set themselves up as their own authority.

The *cause* of their rebellion is found in the word *dreamers* (Jude 8). These people live in a dreamworld of unreality and delusion. They believe Satan's lie, "Ye shall be as gods" (Gen. 3:5). Having turned away from God's truth, they feed their minds on false doctrine that inflates their egos and encourages their rebellion. Jude 10 informs us that the apostates are ignorant people who do not know what they are talking about! Jude echoed Peter's description of these men as "brute beasts" (2 Peter 2:12, 22). Animals live by natural instinct, and so do the apostates. When men rebel against God, they sink to the level of beasts.

The *course* of their rebellion was clearly described by Jude. As a result of their rebellion and pride, they "defile the flesh," living to satisfy their animal lusts. When a person despises God's authority, he feels free to disobey God's Laws and live as he pleases. What he forgets is that those laws have penalties attached to them so that he cannot disobey and escape the consequences.

They also use their tongues to express their rebellion against God. "With our tongue will we prevail; our lips are our own: who is lord over us?" (Ps. 12:4) The phrase *speak evil* in Jude 8 and 10 simply means "to blaspheme." Blasphemy involves much more than taking God's name in vain, though that is at the heart of it. A person blasphemes God when he takes His Word lightly and even jests about it, or when he deliberately defies God to judge him. "They set their mouth against the heavens, and their tongue walketh through the earth. And they say, 'How doth God know? and is there knowledge in the Most High?' " (Ps. 73:9, 11)

The *consequence* of their rebellion is seen in their own ruin: "they corrupt [destroy] themselves" (Jude 10). They defile themselves (Jude 8) and they destroy themselves, yet they have the idea they are promoting themselves! "Because sentence against an evil work is not executed speedily, therefore the heart of the sons of men is fully set in them to do evil" (Ecc. 8:11). The way of rebellion is but the way to ruin.

Arrogant speech is a dangerous thing, and so is despising the authority that God has established. Even the Archangel Michael (Dan. 10:13) did not dare to rebuke Satan, but respected the authority given to him by God. The name *Michael* means "Who is like God?" Ironically, Satan had said in his rebellion, "I will be like the Most High!" (Isa. 14:14) and his offer to men is, "Ye shall be as gods" (Gen. 3:5).

We have no information about the conflict between Satan and Michael over the body of Moses. When Moses died, the Lord buried him and no one knew where the sepulcher was located (Deut. 34:5-6). No doubt the Jewish people would have made a shrine out of the sepulcher and fallen into idolatry, so God kept the information to Himself. The text tells us that "not any man" knew the place, so perhaps Satan did know the place and tried to claim Moses' body for himself. Inasmuch as Satan does have a certain amount of authority in the realm of death he may have felt he had a right to interfere (Heb. 2:14-15).

The point is that Michael did not rebuke Satan, but left that to the Lord. It is a dangerous thing for God's people to confront Satan directly and to argue with him, because he is much stronger than we are. If an archangel is careful about the way he deals with the devil, how much more cautious ought we to be! While it is true that we share in the victory of Christ, it is also true that we must not be presumptuous. Satan is a dangerous enemy, and when we resist him, we must be sober and vigilant (1 Peter 5:8-9).

"The Lord rebuke thee!" has a parallel in Zechariah 3:1-5. The prophet had a vision of the high priest standing before God's throne in defiled garments, symbolizing the sinful condition of the nation Israel after the Babylonian Captivity. Satan had every right to accuse the people (see Rev. 12:9-11), except for one thing: they were the chosen ones of God, His covenant people, and He would not go back on His Word. God forgave His people, gave them clean garments, and warned them to walk in His ways. This is an Old Testament illustration of 1 John 1:5–2:2.

The *condemnation* of the false teachers is given in Jude 11: "Woe unto them!" Jude cited three examples from the Old Testament to illustrate the enormity of their sins, three men who rebelled against God's authority and who suffered for it.

Cain rebelled against God's way of salvation (Gen. 4; 1 John 3:11-12). By clothing Adam and Eve with the skins of slain animals (Gen. 3:21), God made it clear that the only way of forgiveness is through the shedding of blood. This is the way of faith, not the way of good works (Eph. 2:8-10). But Cain rejected this divinely authorized way and came to the altar with the fruits of his own labor. God rejected Cain's offering because God rejected Cain: his heart was not right before God. It was *by faith* that Abel's sacrifice was offered, and that was why God accepted it (Heb. 11:4).

The "way of Cain" is the way of religion without faith, righteousness based on character and good works. The "way of Cain" is the way of pride, a man establishing his own righteousness and rejecting the righteousness of God that comes through faith in Christ (Rom. 10:1-4; Phil. 3:3-12). Cain became a fugitive and tried to overcome his wretchedness by building a city and developing a civilization (Gen. 4:9ff). He ended up with everything a man could desire everything except God, that is.

We have already studied "the way of Balaam" (see 2 Peter 2:15-16). The "way of Balaam" is merchandising one's gifts and ministry just for the purpose of making money. It is using the spiritual to gain the material (see 1 Thes. 2:5-6; 1 Tim. 6:3-21). The false teachers were greedy for material gain and, like Balaam, would do anything for money. The "error of Balaam" is thinking that they can get away with this kind of rebellion. Balaam was a true prophet of God, but he prostituted his gifts and sought to destroy God's people. God turned Balaam's curses into blessings (Deut. 23:4-5).

While we are on the subject of Balaam, we might note the "doctrine of Balaam" (Rev. 2:14) which is, "You can violate your separated position and get away with it!" He told King Balak that the fastest way to destroy Israel would be to corrupt the nation by having the people defile themselves with the heathen nations around them. "You are God's chosen people," was the argument. "Certainly a little friendship with your neighbors will not hurt you!" It was "turning the grace of . . . God into lasciviousness" (Jude 4), and God judged both Israel and Balaam.

The story of Core (Korah) is found in Numbers 16, and it too centers on rebellion against authority. Korah and his followers resented the leadership of Moses and dared God to do anything about their rebellion. In speaking against ("gainsaying") Moses, they were speaking against the Lord who had given Moses his authority. This is a warning to us today, for it is so easy to speak against spiritual or governmental leaders in a careless way (see Titus 3:1-2). God judged Korah and his followers and established clearly the authority of His servant, Moses.

Cain rebelled against God's authority in *salvation,* for he refused to bring a blood sacrifice as God had commanded. Balaam rebelled against God's authority in *separation,* for he prostituted his gifts for money and led Israel to mix with the other nations. Korah rebelled against God's authority in *service,* denying that Moses was God's appointed servant and attempting to usurp his authority.

It is interesting to note the verbs that Jude used in this verse. The apostates "traveled on the road" of Cain, "gave themselves over to" the error of Balaam, and "perished" in the rebellion of Korah. The tragedy of rejecting authority!

## They Resort to Deliberate Hypocrisy (Jude 12-13, 16)

Jude 12 and 13 present six vivid pictures of the false teachers and help to explain why they are dangerous to the church.

***Filthy spots (v. 12a).*** Peter called them spots and blemishes (2 Peter 2:13). These men had invaded the "love feasts" in the local assemblies, but all they did was defile them. Instead of adding to the sanctity of the occasion, they detracted from it, like Judas at the last Passover that Jesus celebrated with His disciples. The tragedy is that the members of the assembly did not realize the true character of these men! They thought the men were spiritual!

The Greek word translated "spots" can also mean "hidden rocks." The mariner who is unaware of the hidden rocks can quickly wreck his ship. The pilot must always be alert, for waters that look calm and safe can contain treacherous reefs. Spiritual leaders must constantly be on guard.

***Selfish shepherds (v. 12b).*** The word translated "feeding" means "shepherding." Instead of shepherding the flock and caring for the needs of the people, these apostates only take care of themselves. Jude may have had in mind Isaiah 56:10-12 and Ezekiel 34, where the prophets condemned the political and spiritual leaders of the nation ("shepherds") for exploiting the people and caring only for themselves.

It is a serious thing to be a shepherd over God's flock. Our example must be Jesus Christ, the Good Shepherd who gave His life for the sheep. False shepherds *use* and *abuse* people in order to get what they want, and yet all the while, *the people love it!* Paul marveled at this when he wrote 2 Corinthians 11:20—"You don't mind, do you, if a man takes away your liberty, spends your money, takes advantage of you, puts on airs, or even smacks your face?" (PH)

These selfish shepherds do all of this "without fear." They are an arrogant lot! This is the difference between a true shepherd and a hireling: the true shepherd cares for the sheep, while the hireling cares only for himself. "Woe be to the shepherds of Israel that do feed themselves! Should not the shepherds feed the flocks?" (Ezek. 34:2) But these apostates *ought* to be afraid, for their judgment is coming.

***Empty clouds (v. 12c).*** Clouds that promise rain, but fail to produce, are a disappointment to the farmer whose crops desperately need water. The apostates look like men who can give spiritual help, and they boast of their abilities, but they are unable to produce. "Whoso boasteth himself of a false gift [a gift he does not give] is like clouds and wind without rain" (Prov. 25:14). They promise liberty, but they can only give bondage (2 Peter 2:19).

The Word of God is sometimes compared to the rain and the dew. "My doctrine shall drop as the rain, my speech shall distill as the dew" (Deut. 32:2). Isaiah 55:10 compares God's Word to the rain and snow from heaven that bring fruit on the earth. Like the clouds in the sky, the false teachers may be prominent and even attractive; but if they cannot bring rain, they are useless.

***Dead trees (v. 12d).*** The picture is that of an orchard in autumn, the time when the farmer expects fruit. But these trees are fruitless! "Ye shall know them by their fruits" (Matt. 7:16). Those who teach and preach the Word have the responsibility of feeding others, but the false teachers have nothing to give. Not only are they fruitless, but they are also rootless ("plucked up by the root"); this is why they are "twice dead." What a contrast to the godly man in Psalm 1:3!

One of the evidences of true salvation is producing spiritual fruit. The seed that fell on the hard soil, the shallow soil, and the crowd-cd soil did not produce fruit; but the seed that fell on the "good ground" did produce fruit (Matt. 13:1-9, 18-23). No matter how much of the Bible the false teachers may quote, the seed is not producing fruit in their own lives or through their ministries. Why? Because they have no spiritual roots. They lack spiritual life.

Fruit has in it the seed for more fruit (Gen. 1:11-12). One of the evidences that a ministry is truly of God is that the fruit multiplies. Manufactured "results" are sterile and dead, but true fruit continues to grow and reproduce itself in the lives of others.

**Raging waves (v. 13a).** I personally do not enjoy being *in* or *on* the ocean (I am not a good swimmer). However, I do enjoy sitting *by* the ocean and contemplating its grandeur and power. But I certainly would not want to be either in or on the ocean in a storm! There is great power in those waves, as many a mariner has discovered. But Jude compared the apostates to "raging waves of the sea" not because of their power, but because of their pride and arrogant speech. "Their mouth speaketh great swelling words" (Jude 16). Like the swelling of the sea, they make a lot of noise, *but what do they produce?* Have you ever walked along the beach the morning after a storm and seen the ugly refuse that has been deposited on the shore?

Jude may have had Isaiah 57:20 in mind: "But the wicked are like the troubled sea, when it cannot rest, whose waters cast up mire and dirt." All that the "great swelling words" of the apostates can produce is foam and flotsam! The true teachers of the Word bring up the treasures of the deep, but the false teachers produce only refuse. And what they boast about, they really ought to be ashamed of! (see Phil. 3:19)

**Wandering stars (v. 13b).** Jude was not referring to fixed stars, planets, or comets, because they have definite positions and orbits. He was referring to meteors, falling stars that suddenly appear and then vanish into the darkness, never to be seen again. Our Lord is compared to a star (Rev. 2:28; 22:16), and Christians are to shine as stars in this dark world (Phil. 2:15). Fixed stars can be depended on to guide the traveler through the darkness, but wandering stars can only lead him astray.

One of my hobbies is collecting books of sermons, not only by famous preachers, but also by obscure and forgotten men whose names once were famous. I have noticed that many a "pulpit beacon" has turned out to be a fallen star! It is disturbing to read histories and biographies and see how "the mighty have fallen." For the most part, those who have been true to the Word are ministering yet today as lights shining in the darkness, while the preachers of false doctrine have fallen into oblivion.

God has reserved chains of darkness for the rebellious angels (Jude 6), and He has reserved "the blackness of darkness forever" for apostate teachers. Beware of following a falling star! It will lead you into eternal blackness!

As you review these six pictures of the false teachers, you can easily see how dangerous they are and how important it is for the church to keep them out.

**Murmurers and complainers (v. 16).** Jude 16 completes the description and emphasizes even more why they are so dangerous: they are out to please themselves by taking advantage of others. This reminds us of Peter's statement (2 Peter 2:14), "A heart they have exercised with covetous practices" or, as Phillips translates it, "Their technique of getting what they want is, through long practice, highly developed." They give the impression that they are out to help you, but they are interested only in gratifying their own lusts.

What is their approach? For one thing, they murmur and complain and cause people to become dissatisfied with life. While each of us should do all we can, as God enables us, to improve our lot in life, at the same time we must be careful not to criticize God's providences or hinder His plans. The nation Israel was judged because of her complaining (1 Cor. 10:1-10), and Christians are commanded not to complain (Phil. 2:14-16). If a false teacher can make a person critical of his pastor or church, or dissatisfied with his situation, he then can lead him astray into false doctrine.

The false teachers also use "great swelling words" to impress ignorant people. Peter called their speeches "great swelling words of vanity" (2 Peter 2:18). They impress people with their vocabularies and oratory, but what they say is just so much "hot air." They also use flattery to manipulate their listeners. They "bow and scrape" and pay compliments to others, *if* it is to their advantage.

Knowing these things, we are amazed that anybody would listen to these apostates and follow them; but many people are doing it today! There is something in fallen human nature that loves a lie and is willing to follow it, no matter where it may lead. But the success of the apostates is only temporary, for their judgment is coming.

### They Receive Their Due Penalty (Jude 14-15)

All that we know about Enoch from Scripture is found in Genesis 5:18-24; Hebrews 11:5; and these two verses in Jude. He is called "the seventh from Adam" to identify him as the *godly* Enoch, since Cain had a son of the same name (Gen. 4:17). In a society that was rapidly being polluted and destroyed by sin, Enoch walked with God and kept his life clean. He also ministered as a prophet and announced the coming judgment.

Bible scholars tell us that this quotation is from an apocryphal book called *The Book of Enoch.* The fact that Jude quoted from this nonbiblical book does not mean the book is inspired and trustworthy, any more than Paul's quotations from the Greek poets put God's "seal of approval" on everything they wrote. The Spirit of God led Jude to use this quotation and make it a part of the inspired Scriptures.

When Enoch originally gave this message, it is possible that he was also referring to the coming judgment of the Flood. He certainly lived in an ungodly age, and it seemed that sinners were getting away with their evil deeds. But Enoch made it clear that judgment was coming and that the ungodly would get what was coming to them!

However, the final application of this prophecy is to the world in the end times, the very judgment that Peter wrote about in 2 Peter 3. The false teachers mocked this prophecy and argued that Jesus Christ would never come and God would never send judgment. But their very attitude was proof that the Word is true, for both our Lord and His Apostles, as well as the prophets, said that scoffers and mockers would appear in the last days (2 Peter 3:1-4). Enoch gave his prophecy thousands of years ago! See how patient God has been with those who have rebelled against Him!

What does Enoch's prophecy say about the coming judgment? It will be a *personal* judgment: God Himself will come to judge the world. He will not send a famine or a flood, nor will He assign the task to an angel. He Himself will come. This shows the seriousness of the event, and also its finality. "Behold, the Judge standeth before the door" (James 5:9).

Though it is a personal judgment, our Lord will not judge alone; the saints of God will be with Him. The word *saints* in Jude 14 means "holy ones" and can also refer to the angels (Deut. 33:2; Matt. 25:31). However, we know from Revelation 19:14; Colossians 3:4; and 1 Thessalonians 3:13 that the people of God will accompany the Lord when He returns to earth to defeat His enemies and establish His righteous kingdom (cf. 1 Cor. 6:2-3). Over the centuries, the people of God have suffered at the hands of the ungodly, but one day the tables will be turned.

It will be a *universal* judgment. He will execute judgment "upon all"—none will escape. Just as the Flood destroyed all who were outside the ark, and the fire and brimstone destroyed all in Sodom and Gomorrah except Lot and his wife and two daughters, so the last judgment will encompass all the ungodly. The word *ungodly* is used four times in this one verse! It will be "the day of judgment and perdition [ruin, destruction] of ungodly men" (2 Peter 3:7).

It will be a *just* judgment. God will convict ("convince") them of their sins, declare them guilty, pass sentence on them, and then execute the punishment. There will be a Judge, Jesus Christ (John 5:22), but no jury. There will be prosecution, but no defense; for every mouth will be stopped (Rom. 3:19). There will be a sentence, but no appeal, for there can be no higher court than God's final judgment. The entire procedure will be just, for the righteous Son of God will be in charge.

The Lord will have the record of their "ungodly deeds." He will also have a record of their motives and hidden desires as they committed these deeds and even these will be ungodly! He will recall the "hard speeches" (Jude 15) that they uttered against the Lord. The word *hard* carries the idea of "rough, harsh, stern, uncivil." After all, these people were "murmurers" and "complainers" (Jude 16) and spoke harsh things against God. They were not "afraid to speak evil of dignities" (2 Peter 2:10), but at the judgment their words will testify against them. They spoke "great swelling words" (2 Peter 2:18; Jude 16), but at the judgment their great words will bring great wrath.

There are times when God's children ask, "Lord, how long shall the wicked, how long shall the wicked triumph? How long shall they utter and speak hard things? and all the workers of iniquity boast themselves?" (Ps. 94:3-4) The answer is given in Psalm 50:3—"Our God shall come, and shall not keep silence: a fire shall devour before Him, and it shall be very tempestuous round about Him."

The words are familiar, but what James Russell Lowell wrote in "The Present Crisis" certainly applies today.

> Careless seems the great Avenger;
>    history's pages but record
> One death-grapple in the darkness
>    'twix old systems and the Word;
> Truth forever on the scaffold,
>    Wrong forever on the throne—
> Yet that scaffold sways the future,
>    and, behind the dim unknown,
> Standeth God within the shadow,
>    keeping watch above His own. . . .

"Nevertheless we, according to His promise, look for new heavens and a new earth, wherein dwelleth righteousness" (2 Peter 3:13).

"Even so, come, Lord Jesus!"

# CHAPTER THREE
# YOU DON'T HAVE TO STUMBLE
*Jude 17-25*

I read somewhere that the Great Wall of China was penetrated at least three times by the enemy, and each time the guards were bribed!

A strong defense depends on strong people, and this applies to spiritual battles as well as military contests. If the church is to oppose and defeat the false teachers, then all of us in the church must be strong and able to "stand against the wiles of the devil" (Eph. 6:11). There is always the danger of stumbling (Jude

24) and a stumble is the first step toward a fall.

In this closing paragraph, Jude addressed his beloved readers and gave them four instructions to follow if they would stand firm and resist the apostates.

## Remember God's Word (Jude 17-19)
From the very beginning, Satan has attacked the Word of God. "Yea, hath God said?" was his opening thrust when he led Eve into disobedience in the Garden (Gen. 3:1). Once we begin to question God's Word, we are vulnerable to Satan's other attacks, for only the truth of the Word can protect us from the lies of the devil. "To the Law and to the testimony: if they speak not according to this Word, it is because there is no light in them" (Isa. 8:20).

***Remember who gave the Word (v. 17).*** While our Lord had many disciples, He selected only a few to be *apostles*. The word means "one who is sent with a commission." In order to qualify, a believer had to be a witness of the resurrection of Christ (Acts 1:21-22; 1 Cor. 9:1). The Apostles lived with Christ during His ministry, learned from Him, and were sent by Him into all the world to carry the Good News of salvation.

Wherever there is the authentic, the counterfeit will appear; this happened in the early church. False apostles and teachers began to appear, and it was necessary to develop a system to protect the church against false prophecies and forged letters. Since Christ had committed "the faith" (Jude 3) to His Apostles, one of the main tests in the early church was, "Is this what the Apostles taught?" When the church assembled the New Testament books, it was required that each book be written either by an apostle or by someone closely associated with an apostle. Apostolic teaching was, and still is, the test of truth.

Jude mentioned the words that were "spoken" by the Apostles, because originally there were no New Testament epistles. Over the years, inspired letters were written by Paul, Peter, and John; we have these letters in our New Testament. We also have a record of some of their sermons in the Book of Acts. We no longer depend on tradition since we have the completed Scriptures, both the Old Testament and the New.

Whenever somebody offers you a "new revelation," test it by what the Apostles wrote and by what Jesus Christ taught. You will soon discover that the "revelation" is a lie.

**Remember what they said (v. 18).**
They prophesied that, in these last days,
mockers would come who would deny the
Word of God. Jude echoed what Peter had
written (2 Peter 3:3ff), but Paul and John also
warned their readers about the apostates
(1 Tim. 4; 2 Tim. 3; 1 John 2:18ff; 4:1-6).
When a warning is given so many times, it
behooves us to take it seriously!

The phrase "walking after their own lusts"
appears in 2 Peter 3:3 and Jude 16 and 18,
and it explains *why* the apostates deny God's
truth: they do not want God to tell them how
to live. They want to satisfy their own sinful
desires, and the Word of God condemns their
selfish way of life. When a person says, "I
have intellectual problems with the Bible," he
probably has *moral* problems because the
Bible contradicts what he is doing. The only
sure way to know the truth of the Bible is by
obeying it (John 7:17).

Before Satan can substitute his own lies, he
must get rid of the truth of God's Word. If he
cannot argue it away, he will laugh it away,
and he can usually find somebody to laugh
with him.

**Remember why they said it (v. 19).**
The false teachers want to divide the church
and lead people out of the true fellowship into
their false fellowship. "Also of your own
selves shall men arise, speaking perverse
things, to draw away disciples after them"
(Acts 20:30). Their appeal is usually, "We
have a deeper knowledge of the Word that
your church doesn't have! We have a better
understanding of prophecy, or of the Christian
life, than you do." They offer a "higher quality" religion than that of the Apostles.

Not only do false teachers divide the
church, but they also deceive the church, because they are "sensual, having not the
Spirit." The word *sensual* means the opposite
of "spiritual." This is the way Paul used it in
1 Corinthians 2:14-16, where it is translated
"natural." (The Greek word is *psukikos*, which
means "soulish.") Because the false teachers
do not have the Spirit of God, they must function on their natural "soul power" alone.

One of the tragedies in ministry today is
that some of God's people cannot discern between "soul ministry" and the true ministry of
the Spirit. There is so much "religious show-
manship" these days that the saints are confused and deceived. Just as there was "false
fire" in the tabernacle (Lev. 10), so there is

"false fire" today in the church; therefore we
must exercise careful discernment.

How can we discern between the "soulish"
and the "spiritual"? By using the Word of God
which is able to divide soul and spirit (Heb.
4:12); and by paying close attention to the
witness of the Spirit of God within (Rom.
8:16). A "soulish" ministry magnifies man, but
the Spirit glorifies Jesus Christ. When the
Spirit is ministering through the Word, there
is edification; but when the soul is merely
"manufacturing" a ministry, there is entertainment or, at best, only intellectual education. It
takes the Spirit of God to minister to our spirits and to make us more like Jesus Christ.

## Build Your Christian Life (Jude 20-21)

The Christian life must never stand still; if it
does, it will go backward. A house left to itself
falls apart. The apostates are in the business
of tearing down, but each Christian must be
involved in building up—first, his own spiritual
life and then his local assembly.

*The foundation* for our Christian life is our
"most holy faith" (Jude 20), which is the same
as "the faith which was once delivered unto
the saints" (Jude 3). There is a sense, of
course, in which our faith in Jesus Christ is the
basis for our growth, but even that faith depends on what God has revealed to us in His
Word. Subjective faith depends on objective
revelation of truth.

The Word of God is certainly central in spiritual growth. I have yet to meet a strong,
fruitful Christian who ignores his Bible. We
must daily spend devotional time in the Word,
seeking the mind of God. We must also study
the Word regularly, in a disciplined way, so
that we better understand what it teaches.
The gifted Chinese preacher, Watchman Nee,
used to read through the New Testament
once a month. This becomes apparent when
you read his books, for you are struck with his
wonderful insights into God's Word. The
members of the Chinese church used to have
a saying, "No Bible—no breakfast!" If we followed that motto in America, I wonder how
many Christians would go hungry.

*The power* for building the Christian life
comes from prayer: "praying in the Holy
Ghost" (Jude 20). The Word of God and
prayer go together in spiritual growth. If all
we do is read and study the Bible, we will
have a great deal of light, but not much power. However, if we concentrate on prayer and
ignore the Bible, we may be guilty of zeal

without knowledge. We read the Word to grow in faith (Rom. 10:17), then we use that faith to ask God for what we need and what His Word tells us we may have.

The Word of God and prayer certainly go together (Acts 6:4). Evangelist Billy Sunday used to give his converts three rules for success in the Christian life. Each day they were to read the Bible and let God talk to them. They were to pray; in other words, they were to talk to God. And they were to witness and talk to others about God. It would be difficult to improve on those rules.

What does it mean to "pray in the Holy Spirit"? (Note the contrast with Jude 19—"having not the Spirit.") It means to pray according to the leading of the Spirit. It has well been said, "Prayer is not getting man's will done in heaven—it is getting God's will done on earth." This agrees with 1 John 5:14-15.

As Christians, we may pray in solitude (Matt. 6:6), but we never pray *alone;* the Spirit of God joins with us as we pray (Rom. 8:26-28) because He knows the mind of God and can direct us. He can give us wisdom and knowledge from the Word (Eph. 1:15ff). He can also help us approach the Father through the access we have in Jesus Christ (Eph. 2:18). We worship God "in the Spirit" (Phil. 3:3), and the Spirit motivates us to pray, for He is "the Spirit of grace and of supplications" (Zech. 12:10). When the believer is yielded to the Spirit, then the Spirit will assist him in his prayer life, and God will answer prayer.

This "building process" in the Christian life involves the Word of God, the Spirit of God, and prayer. But these things, as precious as they are, can become somewhat routine; so Jude added another factor: *abiding in God's love* (Jude 21). He did not write, "Keep yourselves saved!" because he had already assured them that they were "preserved in Jesus Christ" (Jude 1). He wrote, "Keep yourselves in the love of God." Our Lord made a similar statement recounted in John 15:9—"Continue ye in My love."

To love God means much more than to enjoy a special kind of feeling. Of course, as we grow in grace, we do experience deeper fellowship with the Father (John 14:21-24), and we do have times when He seems very near. The Bible compares this to the love of a husband and wife (Eph. 5:22ff). Any happily married couple can tell you that love deepens over the years.

But it takes more than ecstatic feelings to make a successful marriage—or a successful Christian life! There must also be obedience and mutual concern. "But whoso keepeth His Word, in him verily is the love of God perfected" (1 John 2:5). "If ye keep My commandments, ye shall abide in My love" (John 15:10). We grow in our love for God as we listen to His Word, obey it, and delight in doing what pleases Him. That is how we keep ourselves in God's love.

God's love is a holy love; it is not shallow sentiment. "Ye that love the Lord, hate evil" (Ps. 97:10). To love God is to love what He loves and hate what He hates! We please Him by doing those things that He commands. It is the dedicated, separated Christian who enjoys the deepest fellowship with the Father in the family (2 Cor. 6:14-18).

We build our Christian life on the foundation of faith and through the motivation of love. But we also need hope: "looking for the mercy of our Lord Jesus Christ unto eternal life." The believer's eyes must be lifted heavenward. "Looking for that blessed hope, and the glorious appearing of the great God and our Saviour Jesus Christ" (Titus 2:13). "Looking for and hasting unto the coming of the day of God" (2 Peter 3:12).

The word translated "looking" (Jude 21) means "earnestly expecting." It describes an attitude of life that is motivated by the promise of our Lord's return. The apostates can only look for judgment, but God's people are looking for mercy. Not only is our salvation from sin the gift of God's mercy, but so also is the deliverance of His church from this evil world. In His mercy, He will come for us and take us to Himself.

We have already noted that looking for the coming of the Lord is a great encouragement to Christian living. It makes us want to keep pure (1 John 3:3) and to avoid the things of the flesh and the world (Phil. 3:17-21). Our hope in Christ is like an anchor (Heb. 6:19) that holds us in the storms of life, and like a helmet that protects us in the battles of life (1 Thes. 5:8).

The three "Christian graces" of faith, hope, and love enable us to grow in our spiritual walk. We are able to build on a solid foundation with materials that will not decay. Mere profession with the lips will not suffice. "Not everyone that saith unto Me, 'Lord, Lord,' shall enter into the kingdom of heaven; but he that doeth the will of My Father which is in heaven" (Matt. 7:21). The Parable of the Two

Builders (Matt. 7:24-27) makes it clear that to obey the will of God means to build on a foundation that cannot fail.

## Exercise Spiritual Discernment (Jude 22-23)

What should be the attitude of the growing Christian toward those who are being influenced by the apostates? Jude instructed his readers to exercise discernment and to act on the basis of that discernment. He described three different kinds of people who need spiritual help. The *New American Standard Bible* makes this clear:

> And have mercy on some, who are doubting; save others, snatching them out of the fire; and on some have mercy with fear, hating even the garment polluted by the flesh.

*The doubting (v. 22).* These are the people who are wavering. They are probably the "unstable souls" Peter wrote about (2 Peter 2:14). These people are converted, but they are not grounded in the faith. Our responsibility is to have mercy on them, or show compassion toward them, by seeking to lead them away from the influences of the apostates. This kind of ministry demands a great deal of love and patience, and we must keep in mind that immature believers are like little children who think they know right from wrong. If you say no to them, they will only rebel and become more stubborn!

One of the best ways to draw them away from the false teachers is to magnify all that they have in Christ and to share His love for them in practical ways. Make their salvation so wonderful and the Word so exciting that they will lose interest in the teachings of the apostates. It is not enough merely to refute the false doctrines. There must also be a warmth of love that assures the young believer, "We care for you."

It is an open secret that false teachers prey especially on disgruntled church members. (Note Jude 16—"murmurers" and "complainers.") It is important that the pastor and the people show special love and concern to new Christians and that they also minister to the mature members of the church, lest somebody stray because of neglect. Paul sent Timothy to the young believers in Thessalonica so that he might establish them in their faith (1 Thes. 2). Every young Christian needs a more mature believer to teach him how to stand and walk.

*The burning (v. 23a).* Apparently these are the people who have left the fellowship and are now a part of the apostate group. They need to be snatched out of the fire! The angels took Lot by the hand and pulled him out of Sodom (Gen. 19:16), and sometimes that must be done in order to rescue ignorant and unstable believers from the clutches of false teachers.

There is probably a reference here to Zechariah 3:2 and also Amos 4:11. In the Zechariah passage, the "brand" was the nation Israel brought back from the Babylonian Captivity and resettled in their land. God saw the people as a brand saved from the fire. In Amos 4, God was reproving the people for not heeding His warnings and judgments—poverty, poor crops, drought, pestilences, war, and even judgments like those that overthrew Sodom and Gomorrah. They were as a brand plucked out of the fire, yet they did not appreciate God's mercy.

*The dangerous (v. 23b).* The phrase *with fear* means "with caution." In trying to help those who have erred, we must be careful not to be trapped ourselves! Many a would-be rescuer has been drowned himself. When an unstable believer has been captured by false doctrine, we must be very careful as we try to help him, for Satan can use him to defile us. In trying to save him, we may be stained or burned ourselves!

The principle Jude was laying down was that stronger believers must never think they are beyond satanic influence. Even while serving the Lord and seeking to rescue one of His children, we can become defiled by those we want to help. The Old Testament Jews had to be very careful to avoid ceremonial defilement, and this included even their clothing (Lev. 13:47ff; 14:47; 15:17). If a "clean" person touched an "unclean" garment, then he was defiled.

We certainly must love God's people, but we must also hate sin. Wherever there is sin, Satan has a foothold and can go to work. Defilement spreads rapidly and secretly, and it must be dealt with drastically. If the Jewish priest thought that a garment was infected with leprosy, he had the garment burned.

Not every Christian is equipped to deal with false teachers or with those they have influenced and captured. It takes a good knowledge of the Word, a faithful walk with God, an understanding of Satan's devices, and certainly the fullness of the Spirit of God. It also demands spiritual discernment. It is much easier to instruct new Christians and keep them away from the false teachers than it is to snatch them out of the fire.

## Commit Yourself to Jesus Christ (Jude 24-25)

This well-known benediction contains a wealth of spiritual truth for the believer to receive. If we want to keep our feet on the ground spiritually, walk straight, and not stumble, then we must yield ourselves fully to the Saviour. He alone is able to guard us, but we must "keep ourselves in the love of God" (Jude 21). He is *able* if we are *willing!*

Jude was not writing about the possibility of the believer sinning and falling from God's family. We have noted before that he made it clear in Jude 1 that true believers are "preserved" and cannot be lost. He was writing about the believer's daily walk with the Lord and the danger of going astray and stumbling. If we do disobey God, we may confess our sins and receive His forgiveness (1 John 1:9). If we persist in disobedience, He will chasten us in love (Heb. 12:5-11). He will never permit one of His own to be lost.

The Father has covenanted with the Son that all of His people will one day *see* and *share* His glory (see John 17:22-24). Jesus Christ will have the special joy of presenting His bride, the church, before the Father's throne! It was the anticipation of this "joy" that helped Him endure the sufferings of the Cross (Heb. 12:2). The purpose of salvation is not simply to rescue sinners from hell, as wonderful as that is. The grand purpose is that God may be glorified for all eternity (Eph. 1:6, 12, 14).

Today, there are spots and blemishes in the church, but on that day God's people shall be blameless. Satan will find nothing to accuse. The bride will be arrayed in the righteousness of Christ to the glory of God.

Knowing this, the believer has a strong motive for living for Christ and obeying His Word. We want to bring joy to His heart today as we anticipate the joy He will have when He welcomes His bride to heaven! This is the significance of 1 John 3:3—"And every man that hath this hope in him purifieth himself, even as He is pure" (cf. Eph. 5:27; Phil. 2:15).

Jude 25 is the only place in this little letter where Jude called our Lord "Saviour." Peter used this title five times. But Jude *opened* his letter by reminding his readers of "the common salvation" (Jude 3) that they shared because of their faith in Jesus Christ. It is not enough to say that Jesus Christ is *"a savior,"* or *"the* Saviour"; we must say that He is *"our* Saviour—*my* Saviour."

He is not only our Saviour, but He is "the only wise God." He can give you the wisdom you need to live your life to the glory of God. The false teachers boasted of their special knowledge, but they lacked spiritual wisdom. God gives wisdom to those who ask Him (James 1:5), provided they are sincerely willing to obey Him. If Christians would seek the wisdom of God in the Word of God, they would not stumble into the traps of the false teachers, but would walk to please the Lord (Col. 1:9-10).

Why should we walk in obedience to God's will? So that Christ might receive the glory!

*Glory* is the sum total of all that God is and all that God does. Everything about Him is glorious! The glory of man fades as the mown grass, but the glory of God goes on eternally.

*Majesty* means "greatness, magnificence." Only God is great. When we praise God, we praise the most magnificent Person in the universe. He is not simply King; He is King of kings! He is not simply Lord; He is Lord of lords!

*Dominion* has to do with God's sovereignty and rule over all things. The Greek word means "strength, might," but it carries the idea of complete control over all things.

*Power* means "authority," which is the right to use power. All authority belongs to Jesus Christ (Matt. 28:18), including authority over the powers of darkness (Eph. 1:19-23). As we yield to Him, we share His authority and accomplish His will.

What a magnificent doxology this is! Knowing the purpose Jude had in mind when he wrote this letter, this doxology takes on even greater significance. Jude was reminding his readers of the greatness of Jesus Christ. If only they could catch that, they would never be led astray by false teachers. Like the young man who falls in love and marries, and is no longer interested in his old girlfriends, so the believer who keeps himself "in the love of God" (Jude 21), caught up in the glories of the Saviour, will never want to turn to Satan's substitutes.

You don't have to stumble.

If you will remember the Word, build your

# REVELATION

## OUTLINE

**Key theme:** Jesus Christ is Victor
**Key verses:** Revelation 1:19; 17:14

I. **THE THINGS WHICH THOU HAST SEEN—chapter 1**
John's vision of the exalted Christ

II. **THE THINGS WHICH ARE—chapters 2–3**
The messages to the seven churches

III. **THE THINGS WHICH SHALL BE HEREAFTER—chapters 4–22**
A. The throne in heaven—4–5
B. The Tribulation on earth—6–19
   1. The first half—6–9
   2. The middle—10–14
   3. The last half—15–19
C. The kingdom of Christ—20
D. The new heavens and earth—21–22

## CONTENTS

# CHAPTER ONE
# A VERY SPECIAL BOOK
*Revelation 1*

D on't ever prophesy," said American humorist Josh Billings, "for if you prophesy wrong, nobody will forget it; and if you prophesy right, nobody will remember it."

Over the centuries, prophecies have come and gone; yet the book that the Apostle John wrote near the close of the first century is with us still. I can recall reading it as a child and wondering what it was all about. Even today, with many years of concentrated study behind me, I am still fascinated by its message and mysteries.

In Revelation 1, John introduces his book and gives us the data essential for appreciating and understanding this prophecy.

## The Title (Rev. 1:1a)

The word translated "revelation" simply means "unveiling." It gives us our English word *apocalypse* which, unfortunately, is today a synonym for chaos and catastrophe. The verb simply means "to uncover, to reveal, to make manifest." In this book, the Holy Spirit pulls back the curtain and gives us the privilege of seeing the glorified Christ in heaven and the fulfillment of His sovereign purposes in the world.

In other words, Revelation is an *open* book in which God reveals His plans and purposes to His church. When Daniel finished writing his prophecy, he was instructed to "shut up the words, and seal the book" (Dan. 12:4); but John was given opposite instructions: "Seal not the sayings of the prophecy of this book" (Rev. 22:10). Why? Since Calvary, the Resurrection, and the coming of the Holy Spirit, God has ushered in the "last days" (Heb. 1:1-2) and is fulfilling His hidden purposes in this world. "The time is at hand" (Rev. 1:3; 22:10).

John's prophecy is primarily the revelation of Jesus Christ, not the revelation of future events. You must not divorce the Person from the prophecy, for without the Person there could be no fulfillment of the prophecy. "He is not incidental to its action," wrote Dr. Merrill Tenney. "He is its chief Subject." In Revelation 1–3, Christ is seen as the exalted Priest-King ministering to the churches. In Revelation 4–5, He is seen in heaven as the glorified Lamb of God, reigning on the throne. In Revelation 6–18, Christ is the Judge of all the earth; and in Revelation 19, He returns to earth as the conquering King of kings. The book closes with the heavenly Bridegroom ushering His bride, the church, into the glorious heavenly city.

Whatever you do as you study this book, get to know your Saviour better.

## The Author (Rev. 1:1b-2, 4, 9; 22:8)

The Holy Spirit used the Apostle John to give us three kinds of inspired literature: the Gospel of John, the three epistles, and the Book of Revelation. His purposes may be outlined as follows:

| Gospel of John | Epistles | Revelation |
|---|---|---|
| Believe, 20:31 | Be sure, 1 John 5:13 | Be ready, 22:20 |
| Life received | Life revealed | Life rewarded |
| Salvation | Sanctification | Sovereignty |
| The Prophet | The Priest | The King |

John wrote Revelation about A.D. 95, during the reign of the Roman emperor Titus Flavius Domitian. The emperor had demanded that he be worshiped as "Lord and God," and the refusal of the Christians to obey his edict led to severe persecution. Tradition says that it was Domitian who sent John to the Isle of Patmos, a Roman penal colony off the coast of Asia Minor. This being the location of John's exile, perhaps it is not surprising that the word *sea* is found twenty-six times in his book.

During Christ's earthly ministry, John and his brother James asked Jesus for special places of honor by His throne. The Lord told them that they would have to merit their thrones by sharing in His suffering. James was the first apostle martyred (Acts 12:1-2); John was the last of the Apostles to die, but he suffered on Patmos before his death (see Matt. 20:20-23).

How did the Lord convey the contents of this book to His servant? According to Revelation 1:1-2, the Father gave the revelation to the Son, and the Son shared it with the apostle, using "His angel" as intermediary. Sometimes Christ Himself conveyed information to John (Rev. 1:10ff); sometimes it was an elder (Rev. 7:13); and often it was an angel (Rev. 17:1; 19:9-10). Sometimes a "voice from heaven" told John what to say and do (Rev. 10:4). The book came from God to John, no matter what the various means of communication were; and it was all inspired by the Spirit.

The word *signified* (Rev. 1:1) is important; it means "to show by a sign." In Revelation, the noun is translated as *sign* (Rev. 15:1), *wonder* (Rev. 12:1, 3), and *miracle* (Rev. 19:20). This is the same word used in the Gospel of John for the miracles of Jesus Christ, for His miracles were events that carried a deeper spiritual message than simply the display of power. As you study Revelation, expect to encounter a great deal of symbolism, much of it related to the Old Testament.

Why did John use symbolism? For one thing, this kind of "spiritual code" is understood only by those who know Christ personally. If any Roman officers had tried to use Revelation as evidence against Christians, the book would have been a puzzle and an enigma to them. But an even greater reason is that symbolism is not weakened by time. John was able to draw on the great "images" in God's revelation and assemble them into an exciting drama that has encouraged persecuted and suffering saints for centuries. However, you must not conclude that John's use of symbolism indicates that the events described are not real. They are real!

There is a third reason why John used symbolism: symbols not only convey information, but also impart values and arouse emotions. John could have written, "A dictator will rule the world," but instead he described *a beast*. The symbol says much more than the mere title of "dictator." Instead of explaining a world system, John simply introduced "Babylon the Great" and contrasted the "harlot" with the "bride." The very name "Babylon" would convey deep spiritual truth to readers who knew the Old Testament.

In understanding John's symbolism, however, we must be careful not to allow our imaginations to run wild. Biblical symbols are consistent with the whole of biblical revelation. Some symbols are explained (Rev. 1:20; 4:5; 5:8); others are understood from Old Testament symbolism (Rev. 2:7, 17; 4:7); and some symbols are not explained at all (the "white stone" in Rev. 2:17). Nearly 300 references to the Old Testament are found in Revelation! This means that we must anchor our interpretations to what God has already revealed, lest we misinterpret this important prophetic book.

## The Readers (Rev. 1:3-4)

While the book was originally sent to seven actual local churches in Asia Minor, John makes it clear that *any* believer may read and profit from it (Rev. 1:3). In fact, God promised a special blessing to the one who would read the book and obey its message. (The verb *read* means "to read out loud." Revelation was first read aloud in local church meetings.) The Apostle Paul had sent letters to seven churches—Rome, Corinth, Galatia, Ephesus, Philippi, Colossae, and Thessalonica—and now John sent one book to seven different churches. Early in the book, he had a special message from Christ to each church.

John did not send this book of prophecy to the assemblies in order to satisfy their curiosity about the future. God's people were going through intense persecution and they needed encouragement. As they heard this book, its message would give them strength and hope. But even more, its message would help them examine their own lives (and each local assembly) to determine those areas needing correction. They were not only to *hear* the Word, but they were also to keep it—that is, guard it as a treasure and practice what it said. The blessing would come, not just by *hearing*, but even more so by *doing* (see James 1:22-25).

It is worth noting that there are seven "beatitudes" in Revelation: 1:3; 14:13; 16:15; 19:9; 20:6; 22:7, 14. The number seven is important in this book because it signifies fullness and completeness. In Revelation, God tells us how He is going to complete His great work and usher in His eternal kingdom. In Revelation, you will find seven seals (Rev. 5:1), seven trumpets (Rev. 8:6), seven vials (Rev. 16:1), seven stars (Rev. 1:16), and seven lampstands (Rev. 1:12, 20). Other "sevens" in this book will be discussed as we study.

The special messages to each of the seven churches are given in Revelation 2-3. Some students see in these seven churches a "panorama of church history," from apostolic times (Ephesus) to the apostate days of the twentieth century (Laodicea). While these churches may *illustrate* various stages in the history of the church, that was probably not the main reason why these particular assemblies were selected. Instead, these letters remind us that the exalted Head of the church knows what is going on in each assembly, and that our relationship to Him and His Word determines the life and ministry of the local body.

Keep in mind that the churches in Asia Minor were facing persecution and it was important that they be rightly related to the Lord and to each other. They are pictured as seven separate lampstands, each giving light in a dark world (Phil. 2:15; Matt. 5:14-16). The darker the day, the greater the light must shine; unfortunately situations existed in at least five of these assemblies that required correction if their lights were to shine brightly. As you read Revelation 2-3, note that the Lord always reminded them of who He is, and encouraged them to be "overcomers."

What's more, the promise of Jesus Christ's coming should be to all Christians at all times a motivation for obedience and consecration (Rev. 1:3, 7; 2:5, 25; 3:3, 11; 22:7, 12, 20; see also 1 John 1:1-33). No believer should study prophecy merely to satisfy his curiosity. When Daniel and John received God's revelations of the future, both fell down as dead men (Dan. 10:7-10; Rev. 1:17). They were overwhelmed! We need to approach this book as wonderers and worshipers, not as academic students.

### The Dedication (Rev. 1:4-6)

"If you don't stop writing books," a friend said to me, "you will run out of people to dedicate them to!" I appreciated the compliment, but I did not agree with the sentiment. John had no problem knowing to whom his book should be dedicated! But before he wrote the dedication, he reminded his readers that it was the Triune God who had saved them and would keep them as they faced the fiery trials of suffering.

God the Father is described as the Eternal One (see Rev. 1:8; 4:8). All history is part of His eternal plan, including the world's persecution of the church. Next, the Holy Spirit is seen in His fullness, for there are not seven spirits, but one. The reference here is probably to Isaiah 11:2.

Finally, Jesus Christ is seen in His threefold office as Prophet (faithful Witness), Priest (First-begotten from the dead), and King (Prince of the kings of the earth). *First-begotten* does not mean "the first one raised from the dead," but "the highest of those raised from the dead." *Firstborn* is a title of honor (see Rom. 8:29; Col. 1:15, 18).

But of the three Persons of the Trinity, it is to Jesus Christ alone that this book is dedicated. The reason? Because of what He has done for His people. To begin with, *He loves us* (present tense in most manuscripts). This parallels the emphasis in John's Gospel. He also *washed us from our sins,* or, as some texts read, *freed us* from our sins. This parallels the message of John's epistles (see 1 John 1:5ff). As a grand climax, Christ has *made us a kingdom of priests,* and this is the emphasis of Revelation. Today, Jesus Christ is a Priest-King like Melchizedek (Heb. 7), and we are seated with Him on His throne (Eph. 2:1-10).

In His love, God called Israel to be a kingdom of priests (Ex. 19:1-6), but the Jews failed God and their kingdom was taken from them (Matt. 21:43). Today, God's people (the church) are His kings and priests (1 Peter 2:1-10), exercising spiritual authority and serving God in this world.

### The Theme (Rev. 1:7-8)

The overriding theme of the Book of Revelation is the return of Jesus Christ to defeat all evil and to establish His reign. It is definitely a book of victory and His people are seen as "overcomers" (see Rev. 2:7, 11, 17, 26; 3:5, 12, 21; 11:7; 12:11; 15:2; 21:7). In his first epistle, John also called God's people "overcomers" (1 John 2:13-14; 4:4; 5:4-5). Through eyes of unbelief, Jesus Christ and His church are defeated in this world; but through eyes of faith, He and His people are the true victors. As Peter Marshall once said, "It is better to fail in a cause that will ultimately succeed than to succeed in a cause that will ultimately fail."

The statement in Revelation 1:7, "Behold, He cometh with clouds," describes our Lord's return *to the earth,* and is amplified in Revelation 19:11ff. This is not the same as His return *in the air* to catch away His people (1 Thes. 4:13-18; 1 Cor. 15:51ff). When He comes to catch away (rapture) His church, He will come "as a thief" (Rev. 3:3; 16:15) and only those who are born again will see Him (1 John 3:1-3). The event described in Revelation 1:7 will be witnessed by the whole world, and especially by a repentant nation of Israel (see Dan. 7:13; Zech. 12:10-12). It will be public, not secret (Matt. 24:30-31), and will climax the Tribulation period described in Revelation 6–19.

Godly Bible students have not always agreed as to the order of events leading up to the establishment of God's eternal kingdom (Rev. 21–22). I personally believe that the next event on God's calendar is the Rapture, when Christ shall return in the air and take His church to glory. Christ's promise to the church in Revelation 3:10-11 indicates that the church will not go through the Tribulation, and this is further supported by Paul in 1 Thessalonians 1:10; 5:9-10. It is significant to me that there is no mention of the word *church* between Revelation 3:22 and 22:16.

After the church is raptured, the events depicted in Revelation 6–19 will occur: the Tribulation, the rise of the "man of sin," the Great Tribulation (the wrath of God) and the destruction of man-made world government, and then Christ's return to the earth to set up His kingdom. Daniel indicates that this period of worldwide trouble will last seven years (Dan. 9:25-27). Throughout the Book of Revelation, you will find measurements of time that coincide with this seven-year time span (Rev. 11:2-3; 12:6, 14; 13:5).

The titles given to God in Revelation 1:8 make it clear that He is certainly able to work out His divine purposes in human history. *Alpha* and *Omega* are the first and last letters of the Greek alphabet; so, God is at the beginning of all things and also at their end. He is the eternal God (see Rev. 1:4), unlimited by time. He is also the Almighty, able to do anything. *Almighty* is a key name for God in Revelation (Rev. 1:8; 4:8; 11:17; 15:3; 16:7, 14; 19:6, 15; 21:22).

God the Father is called "Alpha and Omega" in Revelation 1:8 and 21:6; but the name also is applied to His Son (Rev. 1:11; 22:13). This is a strong argument for the deity of Christ. Likewise, the title "the first and the last" goes back to Isaiah (Isa. 41:4; 44:6; 48:12-13) and is another proof that Jesus is God.

### The Occasion (Rev. 1:9-18)

This book was born out of John's profound spiritual experience while exiled on Patmos.

*What John heard (vv. 9-11).* On the Lord's Day, John heard a trumpetlike voice behind him. It was Jesus Christ speaking! As far as we know, the apostle had not heard his Lord's voice since Christ had returned to heaven more than sixty years before. The Lord commissioned John to write this book and to send it to the seven churches He had selected. Later John would hear another trumpetlike voice, summoning him to heaven (Rev. 4:1). (Some students relate this to 1 Thes. 4:13-18 and see John's "rapture" as a picture of the rapture of the church.)

*What John saw (vv. 12-16).* He saw a vision of the glorified Christ. Revelation 1:20 makes clear that we must not interpret this vision literally, for it is made up of symbols. The seven lampstands represent the seven churches that would receive the book. Each local church is the bearer of God's light in this dark world. Compare this vision with Daniel's (Dan. 7:9-14).

Christ's garments are those of a Judge-King, One with honor and authority. The white hair symbolizes His eternality, "the Ancient of Days" (Dan. 7:9, 13, 22). His eyes see all (Rev. 19:12; Heb. 4:12), enabling Him to judge righteously. His feet of burning brass also suggest judgment, since the brazen altar was the place where the fire consumed the sin offering. The Lord had come to judge the churches, and He would also judge the evil world system.

The "sound of many waters" (Rev. 1:15) makes me think of Niagara Falls! Perhaps two ideas are suggested here: (1) Christ gathers together all the "streams of revelation" and is the Father's "last Word" to man (Heb. 1:1-3); (2) He speaks with power and authority and must be heard. The sword from His mouth certainly represents the living Word of God (Heb. 4:12; Eph. 6:17). He fights His enemies by using His Word (Rev. 2:16; 19:19-21).

Revelation 1:20 informs us that the seven stars in His hand represent the angels (*messengers,* see Luke 7:24 where the Greek word is so translated), or perhaps pastors, of the seven churches. God holds His servants and places them where He wants them to "shine" for Him. In Daniel 12:3, wise soul winners are compared to shining stars.

The Lord's shining countenance reminds us of His transfiguration (Matt. 17:2) and also the prophecy of Malachi 4:2 ("the Sun of righteousness [shall] arise"). The sun is a familiar image of God in the Old Testament (Ps. 84:11), reminding us not only of blessing, but of judgment. The sun can burn as well as bless!

This vision of Christ was totally different in appearance from the Saviour that John knew "in the flesh" when He was ministering on earth. He was not the "gentle Jewish carpenter" that sentimentalists like to sing about. He is the risen, glorified, exalted Son of God, the Priest-King who has the authority to judge all men, beginning with His own people (1 Peter 4:17).

*What John did (vv. 17-18).* He fell at the Lord's feet as though he were dead! And this is the apostle who leaned on Jesus' breast! (John 13:23) A vision of the exalted Christ can only produce awe and fear (Dan. 10:7-9). We need this attitude of respect today when so many believers speak and act with undue familiarity toward God. John's response illustrates what Paul wrote in 2 Corinthians 5:16: "Though we have known Christ after the flesh, yet now henceforth know we Him no more." John no longer "nestled" next to the Lord's heart, relating to Him as he had done before.

The Lord reassured John by touching him and speaking to him (note Dan. 8:18; 9:21; 10:10, 16, 18). "Fear not!" is a great encouragement for any child of God. We need not fear life, because He is "The Living One." We need not fear death, because He died and is alive, having conquered death. And we need not fear eternity because He holds the keys of hades (the world of the dead) and of death. The One with the keys is the One who has authority.

At the very beginning of this book, Jesus presented Himself to His people in majestic glory. What the church needs today is a new awareness of Christ and His glory. We need to see Him "high and lifted up" (Isa. 6:1). There is a dangerous absence of awe and worship in our assemblies today. We are boasting about standing on our own feet, instead of breaking and falling at His feet. For years, Evan Roberts prayed, "Bend me! Bend me!" and when God answered, the great Welsh Revival resulted.

## The Outline (Rev. 1:19)

To the best of my knowledge, the Book of Revelation is the only book in the Bible that contains an inspired outline of the contents. "The things which thou hast seen" refers to the vision in Revelation 1. "The things which are" refers to Revelation 2–3, the special messages to the seven churches. "The things which shall be hereafter" covers the events described in Revelation 4–22. What John heard in Revelation 4:1 substantiates this interpretation.

In review, we can summarize the basic characteristics of this remarkable book as follows:

*It is a Christ-centered book.* To be sure, *all* Scripture speaks of the Saviour; but the Book of Revelation especially magnifies the greatness and glory of Jesus Christ. The book is, after all, the revelation of Jesus Christ and not simply the revelation of future events.

*It is an "open" book.* John was told not to seal the book (Rev. 22:10) because God's people need the message it contains. Revelation *can* be understood, despite the fact that it contains mysteries that may never be comprehended until we meet at the throne of God. John sent the book to the seven churches of Asia Minor with the expectation that, when it was read aloud by the messengers, the listening saints would understand enough of its truths so as to be greatly encouraged in their own difficult situations.

*It is a book filled with symbols.* Biblical symbols are timeless in their message and limitless in their content. For instance, the symbol of "Babylon" originates in Genesis 10–11, and its meaning grows as you trace it through Scripture, climaxing with Revelation 17–18. The same is true of the symbols of "the Lamb" and "the bride." It is exciting to seek to penetrate deeper into the rich meanings that are conveyed by these symbols.

*It is a book of prophecy.* This is definitely stated in Revelation 1:3; 22:7, 10, 18-19; note also 10:11. The letters to the seven churches of Asia Minor dealt with immediate needs in those assemblies, needs that are still with us in churches today; but the rest of the book is devoted almost entirely to prophetic revelations. It was by seeing the victorious Christ presented that the persecuted Christians found encouragement for their difficult task of witnessing. When you have assurance for the future, you have stability in the present. John himself was suffering under the hand of Rome (Rev. 1:9), so the book was born out of affliction.

*It is a book with a blessing.* We have already noted the promise in Revelation 1:3, as well as the six other "beatitudes" scattered throughout the book. It is not enough simply to hear (or read) the book; we must respond to its message from the heart. We must take the message personally and say a believing "Amen!" to what it says. (Note the many "Amens" in the book: Rev. 1:6-7, 18; 3:14; 5:14; 7:12; 19:4; 22:20-21.)

*It is a relevant book.* What John wrote about would "shortly come to pass" (Rev. 1:1) because "the time is at hand" (Rev. 1:3). (Note also Rev. 22:7, 10, 12, 20.) The word *shortly* does not mean "soon" or "immediately," but "quickly, swiftly." God does not measure time as we do (2 Peter 3:1-10). No one knows when our Lord shall return; but when He begins to open the seals of the scroll (Rev. 6:1ff), events will occur with speed and without interruption.

*It is a majestic book.* Revelation is the book of "the throne," for the word *throne* is found forty-six times throughout. This book magnifies the sovereignty of God. Christ is presented in His glory and dominion!

*It is a universal book.* John saw nations and peoples (Rev. 10:11; 11:9; 17:15) as part of God's program. He also saw the throne room of heaven and heard voices from the ends of the universe!

*It is a climactic book.* Revelation is the climax of the Bible. All that began in Genesis will be completed and fulfilled in keeping with God's sovereign will. He is "Alpha and Omega, the beginning and the ending" (Rev. 1:8). What God starts, He finishes!

But before visiting the throne room of heaven, we must pause to listen to "the Man among the lampstands" as He reveals the personal needs in our churches and in our own hearts. "He that hath an ear, let him hear what the Spirit saith unto the churches!"

# CHAPTER TWO
# CHRIST AND THE
# CHURCHES, PART 1
*Revelation 2*

If you have ever moved to a new community and had to select a new church home, you know how difficult it is to examine and evaluate a church and its ministry. Imposing buildings may house dying or dead congregations, while modest structures might belong to virile assemblies on the march for the Lord. The church we think is "rich" may turn out to be poor in God's sight (Rev. 3:17), while the "poor" church is actually rich (Rev. 2:9).

Only the Head of the church, Jesus Christ, can accurately inspect each church and know its true condition, because He sees the internals, not only the externals (Rev. 2:23b). In these special messages to the seven churches in Asia Minor, the Lord gave each

assembly an "X ray" of its condition. But He intended for *all* the churches to read these messages and benefit from them. (Note the plural "churches" in Rev. 2:7, 11, 17, 29; 3:6, 13, 22.)

But the Lord was also speaking to *individuals,* and this is where you and I come in. "He that hath an ear, let him hear." Churches are made up of individuals, and it is individuals who determine the spiritual life of the assembly. So, while reading these messages, we must apply them personally as we examine our own hearts.

Finally, we must keep in mind that John was a pastor at heart, seeking to encourage these churches during a difficult time of persecution. Before Christ judges the world, He must judge His own people (Ezek. 9:6; 1 Peter 4:17). A purified church need never fear the attacks of Satan or men. "It is a very remarkable thing," wrote G. Campbell Morgan, "that the church of Christ persecuted has been the church of Christ pure. The church of Christ patronized has always been the church of Christ impure."

### Ephesus, the Careless Church
### (Rev. 2:1-7)
Each of the seven messages begins with a personal description or designation of Jesus Christ taken from the vision of Christ given in Revelation 1. (In the case of Ephesus, see Rev. 1:12, 16, 20.) The Ephesian assembly had enjoyed some "stellar" leadership—Paul, Timothy, and the Apostle John himself—but the Lord reminded them that *He* was in control of the ministry, placing the "stars" where He pleased. How easy it is for a church to become proud and forget that pastors and teachers are God's gifts (Eph. 4:11) who may be taken away at any time. Some churches need to be cautioned to worship the Lord and not their pastor!

*Approval (vv. 2-3, 6).* How gracious of the Lord to start with words of commendation! To begin with, this was a *serving* church, busy doing the works of the Lord. No doubt their weekly schedule was filled with activities. It was also a *sacrificing* church, for the word *labor* means "toil to the point of exhaustion." The Ephesian Christians paid a price to serve the Lord. They were a *steadfast* assembly, for the word *patience* carries the meaning of "endurance under trial." They kept going when the going was tough.

The Ephesian church was a *separated* people, for they carefully examined the visiting ministers (see 2 John 7-11) to see if they were genuine. Paul had warned the Ephesian elders that false teachers would come in from the outside and even arise from within the church (Acts 20:28-31), and John had instructed them to "try the spirits" (1 John 4:1-6). Indeed, Satan has his false ministers and the church must be constantly alert to detect them and reject them (2 Cor. 11:1-4, 12-15).

Ephesian Christians separated themselves not only from false doctrine but also from false deeds (Rev. 2:6). The word *Nicolaitan* means "to conquer the people." Some Bible students believe this was a sect who "lorded it over" the church and robbed the people of their liberty in Christ (see 3 John 9-11). They initiated what we know today as "clergy" and "laity," a false division that is taught nowhere in the New Testament. All God's people are "kings and priests" (1 Peter 2:9; Rev. 1:6) and have equal access to the Father through the blood of Christ (Heb. 10:19ff). We shall meet this dangerous sect again when we study the message to the church at Pergamos.

The believers at Ephesus were a *suffering* people who patiently bore their burdens and toiled without fainting. And they did all of this for His name's sake! No matter how you examine this congregation, you conclude that it is just about perfect. However, the One among the lampstands saw into their hearts, and He had a different diagnosis from ours.

***Accusation (v. 4).*** This busy, separated, sacrificing church really suffered from "heart trouble"—they had abandoned their first love! They displayed "works . . . labor . . . and patience" (Rev. 2:2), but these qualities were not motivated by a love for Christ. (Compare 1 Thes. 1:3—"work of faith, and labor of love, and patience of hope.") What we do for the Lord is important, *but so is why we do it!*

What is "first love"? It is the devotion to Christ that so often characterizes the new believer: fervent, personal, uninhibited, excited, and openly displayed. It is the "honeymoon love" of the husband and wife (Jer. 2:1-2). While it is true that mature married love deepens and grows richer, it is also true that it should never lose the excitement and wonder of those "honeymoon days." When a husband and wife begin to take each other for granted, and life becomes routine, then the marriage is in danger.

Just think of it: it is possible to serve, sacrifice, and suffer "for My name's sake" and yet not really love Jesus Christ! The Ephesian believers were so busy maintaining their separation that they were neglecting adoration. Labor is no substitute for love; neither is purity a substitute for passion. The church must have both if it is to please Him.

By reading Paul's epistle to the Ephesians, you discover at least twenty references to *love.* You also discover that Paul emphasized the believer's exalted position "in Christ . . . in the heavenly places." But the Ephesian church had fallen and was not living up to its heavenly position in Christ (Rev. 2:5). It is only as we love Christ fervently that we can serve Him faithfully. Our love for Him must be pure (Eph. 6:24).

***Admonition (vv. 5-7).*** "First love" can be restored if we follow the three instructions Christ gave. First, we must *remember* (literally "keep on remembering") what we have lost and cultivate a desire to regain that close communion once again. Then we must *repent*—change our minds—and confess our sins to the Lord (1 John 1:9). Third, we must *repeat the first works*, which suggests restoring the original fellowship that was broken by our sin and neglect. For the believer, this means prayer, Bible reading and meditation, obedient service, and worship.

In spite of the privileges it had enjoyed, the church of Ephesus was in danger of losing its light! The church that loses its love will soon lose its light, no matter how doctrinally sound it may be. "I will come" (Rev. 2:5) is not referring to the Lord's return, but to His coming judgment *then and there.* The glorious city of Ephesus is today but a heap of stones and no light is shining there.

Revelation 2:7 makes it clear that individual believers within the church may be true to the Lord, no matter what others may do. In these seven messages, the "overcomers" are not a "spiritual elite," but rather the true believers whose faith has given them victory (1 John 5:4-5). Sinful man was banned from the tree of life (Gen. 3:22-24), but in Christ we have eternal abundant life (John 3:16; 10:10). We enjoy this blessing now, and we shall enjoy it in greater measure in eternity (Rev. 22:1-5).

The church of Ephesus was the "careless church," made up of careless believers who neglected their love for Christ. Are we guilty of the same neglect?

## Smyrna, the Crowned Church
## (Rev. 2:8-11)

The name *Smyrna* means "bitter" and is related to the word *myrrh*. The city remains a functioning community today called Izmir. The assembly at Smyrna was persecuted for the faith, which explains why the Lord emphasized His death and resurrection as He opened His message. No matter what experiences God's people may have, their Lord identifies with them.

*Approval (v. 9).* The church at Smyrna was not having an easy time of it! The members were persecuted, probably because they refused to compromise and say, "Caesar is Lord." Smyrna was an important center of the Roman imperial cult, and anyone refusing to acknowledge Caesar as Lord would certainly be excluded from the guilds. This would mean unemployment and poverty. The word used here for *poverty* means "abject poverty, possessing absolutely nothing."

A large Jewish community also thrived in Smyrna. The Jews, of course, did not have to patronize the imperial cult since their religion was accepted by Rome; but they certainly would not cooperate with the Christian faith. So, from both Jews and Gentiles, the Christians in Smyrna received slander and suffering.

But they were rich! They lived for eternal values that would never change, riches that could never be taken away. "As poor, yet making many rich" (2 Cor. 6:10; 8:9). In fact, their suffering for Christ only increased their riches.

Our struggles are not with flesh and blood, but with the enemy, Satan, who uses people to accomplish his purposes. The Jewish synagogue was actually a synagogue of Satan. A true Jew is not one physically or racially, but spiritually (Rom. 2:17-29). Any religious group, Jewish or Gentile, that does not acknowledge Jesus Christ as God's Son is certainly acting contrary to God's will.

*Admonition (vv. 10-11).* No words of accusation are given to the congregation in Smyrna! They may not have enjoyed the approval of men, but they certainly received the praise of God. However, the Lord did give them solemn words of admonition as they faced increased suffering: "Don't be afraid!"

He assured them that He knew the devil's plans and was in complete control of the situation. Some of the believers would be imprisoned and tried as traitors to Rome. Yet their

tribulation would not be long; in the Bible, *ten days* signifies "a brief time" (Gen. 24:55; Acts 25:6). The important thing was *faithfulness,* standing true to Christ no matter what the government might threaten to do.

The "crown of life" is the winner's crown awarded at the annual athletic games. Smyrna was a key participant in the games, so this promise would be especially meaningful to believers living there. The Lord reinforced the promise given by James (James 1:12) and assured His people that there was nothing to fear. Because they had trusted Him, they were overcomers—victors in the race of faith (Heb. 12:1-3)—and, as overcomers, they had nothing to fear. Even if they were martyred, they would be ushered into glory, wearing crowns! They would never face the awful judgment of the second death, which is the lake of fire (Rev. 20:14; 21:8).

It costs to be a dedicated Christian, in some places more than others. As end-time pressures increase, persecution will also increase; and God's people need to be ready (1 Peter 4:12ff). The world may call us "poor Christians," but in God's sight we are rich!

## Pergamos, the Compromising Church
## (Rev. 2:12-17)

Called "the greatest city in Asia Minor," Pergamos had the first temple dedicated to Caesar and was a rabid promoter of the imperial cult. This is probably what is meant by "Satan's seat" in Revelation 2:13. The city also had a temple dedicated to Aesculapius, the god of healing, whose insignia was the entwined serpent on the staff. (This is still a medical symbol today.) Satan, of course, is likewise symbolized as the serpent (2 Cor. 11:3; Rev. 12:9; 20:2).

*Approval (v. 13).* Like their brothers and sisters in Smyrna, the believers in Pergamos had suffered persecution, and one of their men had died for the faith. In spite of intense suffering, this church had remained true to God. They refused to drop incense on the altar and say, "Caesar is Lord." The Lord's description of Himself ("He which hath the sharp sword," Rev. 2:12) would surely encourage the people, for the sword was also the symbol of the Roman proconsul. It was more important that the church fear Christ's sword than the Roman sword (Rev. 2:16).

*Accusation (vv. 14-15).* Despite their courageous stand against persecution, the believers in Pergamos were not faultless before the Lord. Satan had not been able to destroy them by coming as the roaring lion (1 Peter 5:8), but he was making inroads as the deceiving serpent. A group of compromising people had infiltrated the church fellowship, and Jesus Christ hated their doctrines and their practices.

These infiltrators are called "Nicolaitans," whom we met already at Ephesus (Rev. 2:6). The name means "to rule the people." What they taught is called "the doctrine of Balaam" (Rev. 2:14). The Hebrew name *Balaam* also means "lord of the people" and is probably synonymous with *Nicolaitans*. Sadly, this group of professed believers "lorded it over" the people and led them astray.

Understanding the story of Balaam helps us interpret this insidious group more accurately (see Num. 22–25). Balaam was a true prophet who prostituted his gifts in order to earn money from King Balak, who hired him to curse the people of Israel. God prevented Balaam from actually cursing the nation—in fact, God turned the curses into blessings!—but Balak still got his money's worth. How? By following Balaam's advice and making friends with Israel, and then inviting the Jews to worship and feast at the pagan altars. "If you can't beat 'em, join 'em!"

The Jewish men fell right into the trap and many of them became "good neighbors." They ate meat from idolatrous altars and committed fornication as part of heathen religious rites. Twenty-four thousand people died because of this disobedient act of compromise (Num. 25:1-9).

Why did this bit of ancient history apply to the believers at Pergamos? Because a group in that church said, "There is nothing wrong with being friendly to Rome. What harm is there in putting a pinch of incense on the altar and affirming your loyalty to Caesar?" Antipas refused to compromise and was martyred; but others took the "easy way" and cooperated with Rome.

It is unlikely that "things sacrificed to idols" is the same problem Paul dealt with in 1 Corinthians 8 and 10. The accusation here left no room for personal choice as did Paul. The Lord accused the Christians in Pergamos of sinning, of committing "spiritual fornication" by saying, "Caesar is Lord." Of course, this compromise made them welcome in the Roman guilds and protected them from Roman persecution, but it cost them their testimony and their crown.

Believers today also face the temptation to achieve personal advancement by ungodly compromise. The name *Pergamos* means "married," reminding us that each local church is "engaged to Christ" and must be kept pure (2 Cor. 11:1-4). We shall see later in Revelation that this present world system is pictured as a defiled harlot, while the church is presented as a pure bride. The congregation or the individual Christian that compromises with the world just to avoid suffering or achieve success is committing "spiritual adultery" and being unfaithful to the Lord.

*Admonition (vv. 16-17).* Antipas had felt the sword of Rome, but the church at Pergamos would feel the sword of Christ—the Word (Heb. 4:12)—if they did not repent. This is not a reference to our Lord's return but to a *present* judgment that comes to a church when it is disobedient to the Word of God. The Lord had presented Himself as "He which hath the sharp sword" (Rev. 2:12), so the church could not have been ignorant of its danger.

As with the previous churches, the closing appeal is to *the individual:* "*He* that hath an ear. . . . To *him* that overcometh" (Rev. 2:17, italics added). God fed the Israelites with manna during their wilderness travels, and a pot of the manna was placed in the ark of the covenant (Ex. 16:32-36; Heb. 9:4). Instead of eating "things sacrificed to idols" (Rev. 2:14), the believers in Pergamos needed to feast on God's holy food, the bread of life found in Jesus Christ through the Word (Matt. 4:4; John 6:32ff). The ark of the covenant was the throne of God (2 Sam. 6:2; Ps. 80:1; Isa. 37:16; all NASB), in contrast to Satan's throne which held authority in Pergamos (Rev. 2:13).

In those days, a white stone was put into a vessel by a judge to vote acquittal for a person on trial. It was also used like a "ticket" to gain admission to a feast. Both would certainly apply to the believer in a spiritual sense: he has been declared righteous through faith in Christ, and he feasts with Christ today (Rev. 3:20) and will feast with Him in glory (Rev. 19:6-9).

## Thyatira, the Corrupted Church (Rev. 2:18-29)

The longest message was sent to the church in the smallest city! Thyatira was a military town as well as a commercial center with many trade guilds. Wherever guilds were found, idolatry and immorality—the two great enemies of the early church—were almost always present too.

The city boasted a special temple to Apollo, the "sun god," which explains why the Lord introduced Himself as "the Son of God" (the only time in Revelation this title is used). John had to deliver a message of severe warning and judgment to this congregation, which explains the description of the Lord's eyes and feet.

**Approval (v. 19).** The believers in Thyatira were a busy lot! They were involved in sacrificial ministry for the sake of others. What's more, their works were increasing and characterized by faith, love, and patience; so the church was not guilty of mere "religious activity."

**Accusation (vv. 20-23).** Alas, the Lord found much to expose and condemn in the assembly at Thyatira. No amount of loving and sacrificial works can compensate for tolerance of evil. The church was permitting a false prophetess to influence the people and lead them into compromise. It is not likely that this woman was actually called "Jezebel," since such an infamous name would not be given to a child. The name is symbolic: Jezebel was the idolatrous queen who enticed Israel to add Baal worship to their religious ceremonies (see 1 Kings 16–19). The seductive teaching of Jezebel was similar to the "doctrine of Balaam" that the Lord condemned in the church of Pergamos (Rev. 2:14). She taught believers how to compromise with the Roman religion and the practices of the guilds, so that Christians would not lose their jobs or their lives.

It is interesting to contrast the churches at Ephesus and Thyatira. The Ephesian church was weakening in its love, yet faithful to judge false teachers; while the people in the assembly at Thyatira were growing in their love, but too tolerant of false doctrine. Both extremes must be avoided in the church. "Speaking the truth in love" is the biblical balance (Eph. 4:15). Unloving orthodoxy and loving compromise are both hateful to God.

Not only was the church at Thyatira tolerant of evil, but it was proud and unwilling to repent. The Lord gave the false prophetess time to repent, yet she refused. Now He was giving her followers opportunity to repent. His eyes of fire had searched out their thoughts and motives, and He would make no mistake.

In fact, the Lord threatened to use this assembly as a solemn example to "all the churches" not to tolerate evil. Jezebel and her children (followers) would be sentenced to tribulation and death! Idolatry and compromise are, in the Bible, pictured as fornication and unfaithfulness to the marriage vows (Jer. 3:6ff; Hosea 9:1ff). Jezebel's bed of sin would become a bed of sickness! To *kill with death* means "to kill with pestilence" (see NASB). God would judge the false prophetess and her followers once and for all.

**Admonition (vv. 24-29).** Not everyone in the assembly was unfaithful to the Lord, and He had a special word for them. They had separated themselves from the false doctrine and compromising practices of Jezebel and her followers, which Christ denounces as "the depths of Satan" (note the contrast in 1 Cor. 2:10). The Lord had no special demands to make; He simply wanted them to hold fast in their resistance to evil. "Till I come" refers to Christ's return for His people, at which time He will reward them for their faithfulness (see Rev. 3:3; 16:15; 22:7, 17, 20). This is the first mention in Revelation of the Lord's coming for the church, the event we commonly call the Rapture (see 1 Thes. 4:13-18). In contrast, the reference in Revelation 1:7 is to Christ's return to earth in judgment, to defeat His enemies and establish His kingdom (see Rev. 19:11ff).

The believers in Thyatira are promised authority over the nations, which probably refers to the fact that God's people will live and reign with Christ (see Rev. 20:4). When the Lord sets up His kingdom on earth, it will be a righteous kingdom with perfect justice. He will rule with a rod of iron (Ps. 2:8-9). Rebellious men will be like clay pots, easily broken to pieces!

Jesus Christ is "the Bright and Morning Star" (Rev. 22:16). The promise in Revelation 2:28 suggests that God's people shall be so closely identified with Christ that He will "belong" to them! But perhaps there is also an allusion here to Satan, who wanted the kingdom for himself and who offered the world's kingdoms to Christ if He would worship him but once (Matt. 4:8-11). In Isaiah 14:12, Satan is named *Lucifer,* which in Hebrew means "brightness, bright star." The compromising people in Thyatira were following "the depths of Satan," which would lead to darkness and death. God's overcomers, on the other hand, would share the Morning Star!

As you review these first four messages to the churches, you can see the dangers that still exist for the people of God. Like Ephesus, we can be zealous and orthodox, but at the same time lose our devotion to Christ. Or, like Thyatira, our love can be increasing yet lacking in the kind of discernment that is necessary to keep the church pure (see Phil. 1:9-11). Like Pergamos and Thyatira, we may be so tolerant of evil that we grieve the Lord and invite His judgment.

Would we have selected Smyrna as the most spiritual church of the four? Probably not, yet the Lord did! We need to remind ourselves not to judge God's people by wrong standards, because only the Lord can see the heart (see 1 Cor. 4:5).

God's exhortation to these churches (except Smyrna) is, "Repent! Change your minds!" It is not only lost sinners who need to repent, but also disobedient Christians. If we do not repent and deal with sin in our lives and in our assemblies, the Lord may judge us and remove our lampstand (Rev. 2:5). How tragic it is when a local church gradually abandons the faith and loses its witness for Christ!

"He that hath an ear, let him hear what the Spirit saith unto the churches!"

# CHAPTER THREE
# CHRIST AND THE
# CHURCHES, PART 2
*Revelation 3*

We are still listening to what the Holy Spirit has to say to the churches; for these messages from Christ belong to our day as well as to the first century. Churches are people, and human nature has not changed. So, as we continue our study, we must not look on these letters as ancient relics. On the contrary, they are mirrors in which we see ourselves!

**Sardis, the Feeble Church (Rev. 3:1-6)**
Ancient Sardis, the capital of Lydia, was a most important city. It lay about fifty miles east of Ephesus at the junction of five main roads; so it was a center for trade. It was also a military center, for it was located on an almost inaccessible plateau. The acropolis of

Sardis was about 1,500 feet above the main roads, and it formed an impregnable fortress. The main religion in the city was the worship of Artemis, one of the "nature cults" that built on the idea of death and rebirth.

Sardis was also known for its manufacture of woolen garments, a fact that has bearing on Christ's message to the church. Sad to say, the city at that time was but a shadow of its former splendor; and the church, unfortunately, had become like the city—it was alive in name only.

The message to Sardis is a warning to all "great churches" that are living on past glory. Dr. Vance Havner has frequently reminded us that spiritual ministries often go through four stages: a man, a movement, a machine, and then a monument. Sardis was at the "monument" stage, but there was still hope!

There was hope because Christ was the Head of the church and He was able to bring new life. He described Himself as the one possessing the seven Spirits and the seven stars. There is only one Holy Spirit (Eph. 4:4), but the number seven demonstrates fullness and completeness. The Holy Spirit gives life to the church, and life is exactly what the people at Sardis needed. The sevenfold Spirit of God is pictured as seven burning lamps (Rev. 4:5) and as seven all-seeing eyes (Rev. 5:6).

All of the church's man-made programs can never bring life, any more than a circus can resurrect a corpse. The church was born when the Spirit of God descended on the Day of Pentecost (Acts 2), and its life comes from the Spirit. When the Spirit is grieved, the church begins to lose life and power. When sin is confessed and church members get right with God and with each other, then the Spirit infuses new life—revival!

Christ also controls the seven stars, the messengers of the churches (Rev. 1:20), referring most likely to the pastors. Sometimes it is a pastor's fault that a church is dying, and the Lord of the church must remove the star and put another in his place.

There are no words of commendation to the believers at Sardis. Nor did the Lord point out any doctrinal problems that required correction. Neither is there any mention of opposition or persecution. The church would have been better off had there been some suffering, for it had grown comfortable and content and was living on its past reputation. There was reputation without reality, form without force. Like the city itself, the church at Sardis gloried in past splendor, but ignored present decay.

In fact, even what they did have was about to die! Why? Because the believers had gone to sleep. Twice in its long history, the citadel at Sardis had been captured, each time because sentries had failed to do their jobs faithfully. It is when the church's leaders and members get accustomed to their blessings and complacent about their ministry that the enemy finds his way in.

The impression is that the assembly in Sardis was not aggressive in its witness to the city. There was no persecution because there was no invasion of the enemy's territory. No friction usually means no motion! The unsaved in Sardis saw the church as a respectable group of people who were neither dangerous nor desirable. They were decent people with a dying witness and a decaying ministry.

Our Lord's counsel to the church began with, "Be watchful! Wake up!" (see Rom. 13:11ff) The "sentries" were asleep! The first step toward renewal in a dying church is honest awareness that something is wrong. When an organism is alive, there is growth, repair, reproduction, and power; if these elements are lacking in a church, then that church is either dying or already dead.

The Lord warned the Ephesian saints that He would come and remove their lampstand if they did not repent (Rev. 2:5). He warned the church at Pergamos that He would come and make war with the sword of the Spirit (Rev. 2:16). If the believers at Sardis did not follow His orders, He would come as a thief, when they least expected Him; and this would mean judgment.

However, a remnant of dedicated people often exists in even a dying church. The Christians at Sardis had life, even though it was feeble. They were working, even though their works were not all that they could have been. The Lord admonished them to strengthen what remained and not to give up because the church was weak. Where there is life, there is hope!

What was different about this dedicated remnant? They had not defiled their garments (Rev. 3:4). There is some evidence from antiquity that temple worshipers were not permitted to approach their gods and goddesses wearing dirty garments. The remnant in the church at Sardis had not compromised with the pagan society around them, nor had they

grown comfortable and complacent. It was this devoted spiritual remnant that held the future of the church's ministry.

"Wake up! Be watchful! Repent! Remember the Word you have received and obey it!" This is the formula for revival. It is good to guard our spiritual heritage, but we must not embalm it. It is not enough to be true to the faith and have a great history. That faith must produce life and works.

The promise in Revelation 3:5 ("clothed in white raiment") would have been especially meaningful to people who lived in a city where woolen garments were manufactured. And the statement about the names being blotted out would also be significant to people in the Roman Empire, where citizenship was vitally important (see Acts 22:24-30).

Is there a warning here that a true believer might lose his salvation? I don't think so. It would appear that God's "Book of Life" contains the names of all the living, the wicked as well as the righteous (Ps. 69:28). Revelation 13:8 and 17:8 suggest that the names of the saved are written in the book from the foundation of the world—that is, before they had done anything good or bad. By God's grace, they have been chosen in Christ before the beginning of time (Eph. 1:4; see also Matt. 25:34).

Jesus told His disciples to rejoice because their names were "written in heaven" (Luke 10:20). The Greek verb is in the perfect tense, which means it can be translated (as Kenneth Wuest does in his *Expanded Translation*), "your names have been written in heaven and are on permanent record up there." It is not likely that Jesus would contradict Himself in this important matter!

If the names of believers (the elect) are written from the foundation of the world, and if God knows all things, why would He enter the name of somebody who would one day fall and have to be removed from the book? We are enrolled in heaven because we have been born again (Heb. 12:23), and no matter how disobedient a child may be, he or she cannot be "unborn."

As unbelievers die, their names are removed from the book; thus, at the final judgment, the book contains only the names of believers (Rev. 20:12-15). It then becomes "the Lamb's Book of Life" (Rev. 21:27), because only those saved by the Lord Jesus Christ have their names in it. All the others have been blotted out, something God would never do for any true child of God (see Ex. 32:32; Rom. 9:3). It is a book of *life,* and lost sinners are *dead* (Eph. 2:1).

The warning here is that we not grow comfortable in our churches, lest we find ourselves slowly dying. The encouragement is that no church is beyond hope as long as there is a remnant in it, willing to strengthen the things that remain.

## Philadelphia, the Faithful Church (Rev. 3:7-13)

As most people know, *Philadelphia* means "love of the brethren." Certainly, brotherly love is an important mark of the Christian. We are "taught of God to love one another" (1 Thes. 4:9): by God the Father (1 John 4:19), God the Son (John 13:34), and God the Spirit (Rom. 5:5). But it is not enough to love God and our fellow believers; we must also love a lost world and seek to reach unbelievers with the Good News of the Cross. This church had a vision to reach a lost world, and God set before them an open door.

Philadelphia was situated in a strategic place on the main route of the Imperial Post from Rome to the East, and thus was called "the gateway to the East." It was also called "little Athens" because of the many temples in the city. The church was certainly located in a place of tremendous opportunity.

The only major problem with the location was that the area was prone to earthquakes. Philadelphia sat on a geological fault, and in 17 B.C. it was destroyed by a severe earthquake that also destroyed Sardis and ten other cities. Afterward, some of the citizens refused to move back into the city and remained in the surrounding countryside, which they called "the burnt land." There did not seem to be much security in the city of brotherly love!

Jesus Christ presented Himself to the church at Philadelphia as "He that is holy." This is tantamount to declaring that He is God, which, of course, He is. Jesus Christ is holy in His character, His words, His actions, and His purposes. As the Holy One, He is uniquely set apart from everything else, and nothing can be compared to Him.

But He is also the One who is true—that is, genuine. He is the original, not a copy; the authentic God and not a manufactured one. There were hundreds of false gods and goddesses in those days (1 Cor. 8:5-6), but only Jesus Christ could rightfully claim to be the true God.

It is worth noting that when the martyrs in heaven addressed the Lord, they called Him "holy and true" (Rev. 6:10). Their argument was that, because He was holy, He had to judge sin, and because He was true, He had to vindicate His people who had been wickedly slain.

Not only is He holy and true, but He has the authority to open and close doors. The background of this imagery is Isaiah 22:15-25. Assyria had invaded Judah (as Isaiah had warned), but the Jewish leaders were trusting Egypt, not God, to deliver the nation. One of the treacherous leaders was a man named Shebna who had used his office, not for the good of the people, but for his own private gain. God saw to it that Shebna was removed from office and that a faithful man, Eliakim, was put in his place and given the keys of authority. Eliakim was a picture of Jesus Christ, a dependable administrator of the affairs of God's people. Jesus Christ also has the keys of hades and of death (Rev. 1:18).

In the New Testament, an "open door" speaks of opportunity for ministry (Acts 14:27; 1 Cor. 16:9; 2 Cor. 2:12; Col. 4:3). Christ is the Lord of the harvest and the Head of the church, and it is He who determines where and when His people shall serve (see Acts 16:6-10). He gave the church at Philadelphia a great opportunity for ministry.

But could they take advantage of it? There were at least two obstacles to overcome, the first being their own lack of strength (Rev. 3:8). Apparently, this was not a large or a strong church; however, it was a faithful one. They were true to God's Word and unafraid to bear His name. Revelation 3:10 suggests that they had endured some special testing and had proved faithful.

It is not the size or strength of a church that determines its ministry, but faith in the call and command of the Lord. "God's commandments are God's enablements." If Jesus Christ gave them an open door, then He would see to it that they were able to walk through it! Martin Luther put it perfectly in his well-known hymn:

Did we in our own strength confide,
Our striving would be losing.
Were not the right Man on our side,
The Man of God's own choosing.

The second obstacle was the opposition of the Jews in the city (Rev. 3:9). This was really the opposition of Satan, for we do not battle against flesh and blood (Eph. 6:12). These people may have been Jews in the flesh, but they were not "true Israel" in the New Testament sense (Rom. 2:17-29). Jewish people certainly have a great heritage, but it is no guarantee of salvation (Matt. 3:7-12; John 8:33ff).

How were these Jews opposing the church at Philadelphia? For one thing, by excluding Jewish believers from the synagogue. Another weapon was probably false accusation, for this is the way the unbelieving Jews often attacked Paul. Satan is the accuser and he uses even religious people to assist him (Rev. 12:10). It is not easy to witness for Christ when the leading people in the community are spreading lies about you. The church at Smyrna faced the same kind of opposition (Rev. 2:9).

The believers in Philadelphia were in a similar situation to that of Paul when he wrote 1 Corinthians 16:9—there were both opportunities and obstacles! Unbelief sees the obstacles, but faith sees the opportunities! And since the Lord holds the keys, He is in control of the outcome! So what do we have to fear? Nobody can close the doors as long as He keeps them open. Fear, unbelief, and delay have caused the church to miss many God-given opportunities.

The Saviour gave three wonderful and encouraging promises to this church. First, He would take care of their enemies (Rev. 3:9). One day, these people would have to acknowledge that the Christians were right! (see Isa. 60:14; Phil. 2:10-11) If we take care of God's work, He will take care of our battles.

Second, He would keep them from Tribulation (Rev. 3:10). This is surely a reference to the time of Tribulation that John described in Revelation 6–19, "the time of Jacob's trouble." This is not speaking about some local trial, because it involves "them that dwell on the earth" (see Rev. 6:10; 8:13; 11:10; 12:12; 13:8, 12, 14; 14:6; 17:2, 8). The immediate reference would be to the official Roman persecutions that would come, but the ultimate reference is to the Tribulation that will encompass the earth before Jesus Christ returns to establish His kingdom. In many Bible scholars' understanding, Revelation 3:10 is a promise that the church will not go through the Tribulation, but will be taken to heaven before it begins (see 1 Thes. 4:13–5:11). The admonition, "Behold, I come quickly," would strengthen this view.

The third promise to the Philadelphians is that God would honor them (Rev. 3:12). The symbolism in this verse would be especially meaningful to people who lived in constant danger of earthquakes: the stability of the pillar, no need to go out or to flee, a heavenly city that nothing could destroy. Ancient cities often honored great leaders by erecting pillars with their names inscribed on them. God's pillars are not made of stone, because there is no temple in the heavenly city (Rev. 21:22). His pillars are faithful people who bear His name for His glory (Gal. 2:9).

In a very real sense, the church today is like the Philadelphian church, for God has set before us many open doors of opportunity. If He opens the doors, we must work; if He shuts the doors, we must wait. Above all, we must be faithful to Him and see the opportunities, not the obstacles. If we miss our opportunities, we lose our rewards (crowns), and this means being ashamed before Him when He comes (1 John 2:28).

## Laodicea, the Foolish Church (Rev. 3:14-22)

As with some of the previous churches, the Lord adapted His words to something significant about the city in which the assembly was located. In this case, Laodicea was known for its wealth and its manufacture of a special eye salve, as well as of a glossy black wool cloth. It also was located near Hieropolis, where there were famous hot springs, and Colossae, known for its pure, cold water.

The Lord presented Himself as "the Amen," which is an Old Testament title for God (see Isa. 65:16, where the word *truth* is the Hebrew word *amen*). He is the truth and speaks the truth, because He is "the faithful and true Witness" (Rev. 3:14). The Lord was about to tell this church the truth about its spiritual condition; unfortunately, they would not believe His diagnosis.

"Why is it that new Christians create problems in the church?" a young pastor once asked me.

"They don't create problems," I replied. "They *reveal* them. The problems have always been there, but we've gotten used to them. New Christians are like children in the home: they tell the truth about things!"

The Laodicean church was blind to its own needs and unwilling to face the truth. Yet honesty is the beginning of true blessing, as we admit what we are, confess our sins, and receive from God all that we need. If we want God's best for our lives and churches, we must be honest with God and let God be honest with us.

"The beginning of the creation of God" (Rev. 3:14) does not suggest that Jesus was created, and therefore not eternal God. The word translated *beginning* means "source, origin" (see John 1:3; Col. 1:15, 18).

The Lord demonstrated four areas of need in the church at Laodicea.

**They had lost their vigor (vv. 16-17).** In the Christian life, there are three "spiritual temperatures": a burning heart, on fire for God (Luke 24:32), a cold heart (Matt. 24:12), and a lukewarm heart (Rev. 3:16). The lukewarm Christian is comfortable, complacent, and does not realize his need. If he were cold, at least he would feel it! Both the cold water from Colossae and the hot water from Hieropolis would be lukewarm by the time it was piped to Laodicea.

As believers in Jesus Christ, we have every reason to be "fervent in spirit" (Rom. 12:11). Fervent prayer is also vital (Col. 4:12). It was as the Emmaus disciples listened to the Word that their hearts were warmed. No wonder Paul commanded that his letter to Colossae be sent to the Laodicean church! (Col. 4:16)

We enjoy a beverage that is either hot or cold, but one that is tepid is flat and stale. That's why the waitress keeps adding hot coffee or fresh iced tea to our cups and glasses. The second law of thermodynamics requires that a "closed system" eventually moderates so that no more energy is being produced. Unless something is added from the outside, the system decays and dies. Without added fuel, the hot water in the boiler becomes cool; without electricity, the refrigerant in the freezer becomes warm.

The church cannot be a "closed system." Jesus said, "Without Me ye can do nothing" (John 15:5). The Laodicean church was independent, self-satisfied, and secure. "We have need of nothing!" But all the while, their spiritual power had been decaying; their material wealth and glowing statistics were but shrouds hiding a rotting corpse. Their Lord was *outside the church,* trying to get in (Rev. 3:20).

**They had lost their values (vv. 17-18a).** The church at Smyrna thought itself poor, when it was really rich (Rev. 2:9); the Laodiceans boasted that they were rich, when in fact they were poor. Perhaps we have here a hint of why this church declined spiritually:

they had become proud of their ministry and had begun to measure things by human standards instead of by spiritual values. They were, in the eyes of the Lord, "wretched, and miserable, and poor."

Laodicea was a wealthy city and a banking center. Perhaps some of the spirit of the marketplace crept into the church so that their values became twisted. Why is it that so many church bulletins and letterheads show pictures of *buildings?* Are these the things that are most important to us? The board at the Laodicean church could proudly show you the latest annual report with its impressive statistics; yet Jesus said He was about to vomit them out of His mouth!

The solution? Pay the price to get true "gold tried in the fire." This suggests that the church needed some persecution; they were too comfortable (1 Peter 1:7). Nothing makes God's people examine their priorities faster than suffering!

**They had lost their vision (v. 18b).** The Laodiceans were "blind." They could not see reality. They were living in a fool's paradise, proud of a church that was about to be rejected. The Apostle Peter teaches that when a believer is not growing in the Lord, his spiritual vision is affected (2 Peter 1:5-9). "Diet" has bearing on the condition of one's eyes, in a spiritual sense as well as a physical one.

These people could not see themselves as they really were. Nor could they see their Lord as He stood outside the door of the church. Nor could they see the open doors of opportunity. They were so wrapped up in building their own kingdom that they had become lukewarm in their concern for a lost world.

The solution? Apply the heavenly eye salve! The city of Laodicea was noted for its eye salve, but the kind of medication the saints needed was not available in the apothecary shop. The eye is one of the body's most sensitive areas, and only the Great Physician can "operate" on it and make it what it ought to be. As He did with the man whose account is told in John 9, He might even irritate before He illuminates! But we must submit to His treatment and then maintain good spiritual "health habits" so that our vision grows keener.

**They had lost their vesture (vv. 17-22).** Like the emperor in Hans Christian Andersen's story, these Christians thought they were clothed in splendor when they were really naked! To be naked meant to be defeated and humiliated (2 Sam. 10:4; Isa. 20:1-4). The Laodiceans could go to the market and purchase fine woolen garments, but that would not meet their real need. They needed the white garments of God's righteousness and grace. According to Revelation 19:8, we should be clothed in "fine linen, clean and white," and this symbolizes "the righteous acts of the saints" (NASB). Salvation means that Christ's righteousness is *imputed* to us, put to our account; but sanctification means that His righteousness is *imparted* to us, made a part of our character and conduct.

There is no divine commendation given to this church. Of course, the Laodiceans were busy commending themselves! They thought they were glorifying God, when in reality they were disgracing His name just as though they had been walking around naked.

The Lord closed this letter with three special statements:

First, *an explanation:* "As many as I love, I rebuke and chasten" (Rev. 3:19a). He still loved these lukewarm saints, even though their love for Him had grown cold. He planned to chasten them as proof of His love (Prov. 3:11-12; Heb. 12:5-6). God permits churches to go through times of trial so that they might become what He wants them to become.

Second, *an exhortation:* "Be zealous therefore, and repent" (Rev. 3:19b). The church at Laodicea had to repent of their pride and humble themselves before the Lord. They had to "stir up that inner fire" (2 Tim. 1:6, PH) and cultivate a burning heart.

Finally, *an invitation* (Rev. 3:20-22). We often use these verses to lead lost people to Christ, but the basic application is to the believer. The Lord was outside the Laodicean church! He spoke to the individual—"if any man"—and not to the whole congregation. He appealed to a small remnant in Sardis (Rev. 3:4-5), and now He appeals to the individual. God can do great things in a church, even through one dedicated individual.

Christ was not impatient. "I have taken My stand" is the sense of the verb. He "knocks" through circumstances and He calls through His Word. For what is He appealing? Fellowship and communion, the people's desire to abide in Him. The Laodiceans were an independent church that had need of nothing, but they were not abiding in Christ and drawing their power from Him. They had a "successful

program" but it was not fruit that comes from abiding in Christ (John 15:1-8).

Note that when we invite Him in, the supper room becomes a throne room! It is through communion with Christ that we find victory and become overcomers indeed.

The letters to the seven churches are God's X rays, given to us so that we might examine our own lives and ministries. Judgment is going to come to this world, but it first begins at God's house (1 Peter 4:17). In these letters we find encouragement as well as rebuke.

May the Lord help us to hear what the Spirit is saying *today* to the church, and to the individuals in the churches!

# CHAPTER FOUR
# COME, LET US ADORE HIM!
*Revelation 4–5*

True spiritual worship is perhaps one of the greatest needs in our individual lives and in our churches. There is a constant emphasis today on witnessing for Christ and working for Christ, but not enough is said about worshiping Him. To *worship* means "to ascribe worth" (see Rev. 4:11; 5:12). It means to use all that we are and have to praise God for all that He is and does.

Heaven is a place of worship, and God's people shall worship Him throughout all eternity. Perhaps it would be good for us to get in practice now! A study of Revelation 4–5 will certainly help us better understand how to worship God and give Him the glory that He deserves.

If Revelation 1:19 is God's inspired outline of this book, then Revelation 4 ushers us into the third division: "the things which shall be hereafter." In fact, that is exactly what God said to John when He summoned him to heaven! It would appear that, in this experience, John illustrates what will happen to God's people when the Church Age has run its course: heaven will open; there will be a voice and the sound of a trumpet; and the saints will be caught up to heaven (1 Cor. 15:52; 1 Thes.

4:13-18). Then, God's judgment of the earth can begin.

But before God pours out His wrath, He gives us a glimpse into glory and permits us to hear the worshiping creatures in heaven as they praise God. Two aspects of their worship are presented for our instruction and imitation.

### They Worship the Creator (Rev. 4)

The key word in this chapter is *throne;* it is used fourteen times. In fact, this is a key word in the entire book, appearing forty-six times. No matter what may happen on earth, God is on His throne and is in complete control. Various teachers interpret Revelation in different ways, but all agree that John is emphasizing the glory and sovereignty of God. What an encouragement that would be to the suffering saints of John's day and of every age in history.

Using the throne as the focal point, we can easily understand the arrangement of this exciting chapter.

*On the throne—Almighty God (vv. 2-3a).* This is God the Father, since the Son approaches the throne in Revelation 5:6, and the Spirit is pictured before the throne in Revelation 4:5. There is no possible way for human words to describe what God is like in His essence. John can only use comparisons. Jasper is a clear gem (see Rev. 21:11) and the sardine is red. The Lord is robed in light, according to Psalm 104:2 and 1 Timothy 6:16. Both the jasper and the sardius (sardine) were found in the breastplate of the high priest (Ex. 28:17-21).

*Around the throne—a rainbow (v. 3b).* This rainbow was a complete circle, not merely an arc, for in heaven all things are completed. The rainbow reminds us of God's covenant with Noah (Gen. 9:11-17), symbolic of His promise that He would never again destroy the earth with a flood. God's covenant, as we shall see, was not only with Noah, but with all of His creation.

Judgment is about to fall, but the rainbow reminds us that God is merciful, even when He judges (Hab. 3:2). Usually, a rainbow appears *after* the storm; but here, we see it *before* the storm.

*Around the throne—elders and living creatures (vv. 3-4, 6-7).* The rainbow was around the throne vertically, while these heavenly beings were around the throne horizontally. They are, as it were, the king's court.

Who are these twenty-four elders seated on thrones? It is unlikely that they are angels, because angels are not numbered (Heb. 12:22), crowned, or enthroned. Besides, in Revelation 7:11, the elders are distinguished from the angels (see also Rev. 5:8-11). The crowns they wear are the "victor's crowns" (the Greek word *stephanos;* see Rev. 2:10); and we have no evidence that angels receive rewards.

These elders probably symbolize the people of God in heaven, enthroned and rewarded. There were twenty-four courses of priests in the Old Testament temple (1 Chron. 24:3-5, 18; see also Luke 1:5-9). God's people are "kings and priests" (Rev. 1:6), reigning and serving with Christ. Note especially their praise (Rev. 5:9-10). When Daniel (Dan. 7:9) saw the thrones set up (not "cast down" as in the *King James Version*), they were empty; but when John saw them, they had been filled. Since there were twelve tribes of Israel and twelve Apostles, perhaps the number twenty-four symbolizes the completion of God's people.

The white robes and palm branches speak of victory (see Rev. 7:9). These are the "overcomers" who have conquered because of their faith in Christ (1 John 5:4-5).

Also around the throne, John saw four "living creatures" ("beasts" in the *King James Version*) who were nearer to God than the angels and the elders. They resemble the cherubim that the Prophet Ezekiel saw (Ezek. 1:4-14; 10:20-22), but their praise (Rev. 4:8) reminds us of the seraphim of Isaiah 6. I believe that these special creatures symbolize God's creation and are related to God's covenant with Noah (Gen. 9:8-17). The faces of the living creatures parallel God's statement in Genesis 9:10—His covenant is with Noah (the face of the man), the fowl (the face of the eagle), the cattle (the face of the calf), and the beasts of the earth (the face of the lion).

These creatures signify the wisdom of God ("full of eyes") and proclaim the holiness of God. They are heavenly reminders that God has a covenant with His creation and that He rules His creation from His throne. The presence of the emerald rainbow further enhances this image, since the rainbow was given as the sign of the creation covenant. No matter what terrible judgments may fall on God's earth, He will be faithful to keep His Word. Men may curse Him during the judgments (Rev. 16:9,

11, 21), but nature will praise Him and magnify His holiness.

The cherubim described in Ezekiel 1 seem to have a part in the providential workings of God in the world, pictured by the "wheels within the wheels." God uses the forces of nature to accomplish His will (Ps. 148), and all nature praises and thanks Him.

Some students see in the four faces described (Rev. 4:7) an illustration of the fourfold picture of Christ given in the Gospel accounts. Matthew is the royal Gospel of the King, illustrated by the lion. Mark emphasizes the servant aspect of the Lord's ministry (the calf). Luke presents Christ as the compassionate Son of man. John magnifies the deity of Christ, the Son of God (the eagle).

Finally, the name used by these creatures, "Lord God Almighty," emphasizes the power of God. As mentioned in chapter 1, the name *Almighty* is used nine times in Revelation. The only other such usage in the New Testament is 2 Corinthians 6:18, but it is found at least thirty-one times in Job, a book that magnifies the power of God in nature.

**Out of the throne—storm signals (v. 5a).** "And from the throne proceed flashes of lightning and sounds and peals of thunder" (NASB). These are indications of a coming storm and reminders of God's awesome power (see Ex. 9:23, 28; 19:16). These "storm signals" will be repeated during the time of judgment, always proceeding from the throne and temple of God (Rev. 8:5; 11:19; 16:18). God has indeed prepared His throne for judgment (Ps. 9:7; note also 77:18).

Our world does not like to think of God as a God of judgment. They prefer to look at the rainbow around the throne and ignore the lightning and thunder out of the throne. He certainly is a God of grace, but His grace reigns *through righteousness* (Rom. 5:21). This was made clear at the cross where God manifested both His love for sinners and His wrath against sin.

**Before the throne—lamps and a sea (vv. 5b-6a).** The seven lamps connote completeness and symbolize the Holy Spirit of God (Rev. 1:4; note also Ezek. 1:13). John also seems to suggest in Revelation that the "heavenly sanctuary" follows the pattern of the earthly tabernacle and temple (see Heb. 9:23). The parallels are as follows:

| Earthly temple | Heavenly sanctuary |
| --- | --- |
| Holy of holies | The throne of God |
| Seven-branched candlestick | Seven lamps of fire before the throne |
| Bronze laver | Sea of glass |
| Cherubim over the mercy seat | Four living creatures around the throne |
| Priests | Elders (kings and priests) |
| Brazen altar | Altar (Rev. 6:9-11) |
| Incense altar | Incense altar (Rev. 8:3-5) |
| Ark of the covenant | Ark of the covenant (Rev. 11:19) |

There is no temple in heaven in a material sense. All of heaven is God's sanctuary for those who serve before His holy throne (Rev. 7:15). However, John indicates in Revelation 15:5-8 that there is a special "sanctuary" of God (note also Rev. 11:19). In the eternal state, there will be no temple (Rev. 21:22).

A pure crystal sea symbolizes God's holiness, and the mingled fire speaks of His holy judgment. The crystal "firmament" in Ezekiel's vision also comes to mind (Ezek. 1:22); it was the foundation for God's throne. We shall meet this "sea of glass" again in Revelation 15 where it is connected with Israel's victory over Egypt.

**Praise to the throne (vv. 9-11).** Whenever the living creatures glorified God, the elders would fall before the throne and praise Him. The Book of Revelation is filled with hymns of praise (Rev. 4:8, 11; 5:9-13; 7:12-17; 11:15-18; 12:10-12; 15:3-4; 16:5-7; 18:2-8; 19:2-6). The emphasis on praise is significant when you remember that John wrote this book to encourage people who were going through suffering and persecution!

The theme of this hymn is *God the Creator*, while in Revelation 5 the elders praise *God the Redeemer*. The praise in Revelation 4 is given to the Father on the throne, while in Revelation 5 it is directed to the Son (the Lamb) before the throne. The closing hymn (Rev. 5:13) is expressed to both, another proof of the deity of Jesus Christ.

If the twenty-four elders typify the people of God in heaven, then we must ask, "Why should God's people praise God the Creator?" If the heavens are declaring the glory of God, why shouldn't God's heavenly people join the chorus? Creation bears constant witness to the power, wisdom, and glory of God (Ps. 19). Acknowledging the Creator is the first step toward trusting the Redeemer (see Acts 14:8-18; 17:22-31). "All things were created by Him

[Christ] and for Him . . . and by Him all things consist [hold together]" (Col. 1:16-17).

But sinful man worships and serves the creature rather than the Creator, and this is idolatry (Rom. 1:25). Furthermore, sinful man has polluted and destroyed God's wonderful creation; and he is going to pay for it (see Rev. 11:18). Creation is for God's praise and pleasure, and man has no right to usurp that which rightfully belongs to God. Man plunged creation into sin, so that God's *good* creation (Gen. 1:31) is today a *groaning* creation (Rom. 8:22); but because of Christ's work on the cross, it will one day be delivered and become a *glorious* creation (Rev. 8:18-24).

It is unfortunate that the church today often neglects to worship the God of creation. The real answer to the ecological problem is not financial or legal, but spiritual. It is only when man acknowledges the Creator and begins to use creation to God's glory that the problems will be solved.

### They Worship the Redeemer (Rev. 5)

The focus of attention now shifts to a seven-sealed scroll in the hand of God. The scroll could not be read because it was rolled up and sealed (like a Roman will) with seven seals. John could see writing on both sides of the scroll, which meant that nothing more could be added. What was written was completed and final.

The scroll represents Christ's "title deed" to all that the Father promised Him because of His sacrifice on the cross. "Ask of Me, and I shall give Thee the heathen [nations] for Thine inheritance, and the uttermost parts of the earth for Thy possession" (Ps. 2:8). Jesus Christ is the "Heir of all things" (Heb. 1:2). He is our beloved "Kinsman-Redeemer" who was willing to give His life to set us free from bondage and to restore our lost inheritance (see Lev. 25:23-46; the Book of Ruth; Jer. 32:6-15).

As Christ removed the seals, various dramatic events took place. The seventh seal introduced the seven trumpet judgments (Rev. 8:1-2). Then, when the seventh trumpet had blown, the great day of God's wrath was announced, ushering in the "vial [bowl] judgments" that brought to a climax the wrath of God (Rev. 11:15ff; 15:1). It is possible that the trumpet judgments were written on one side of the scroll and the bowl judgments on the other.

A title deed or will can be opened only by the appointed heir, and this is Jesus Christ. No one in all the universe could be found worthy enough to break the seals. No wonder John wept, for he realized that God's glorious redemption plan for mankind could never be completed until the scroll was opened. The redeemer had to be near of kin, willing to redeem, and able to redeem. Jesus Christ meets all of the qualifications. He became flesh, so He is our Kinsman. He loves us and is willing to redeem; and He paid the price, so He is able to redeem.

Now we are able to enter into the worship experience described in the remainder of Revelation 5. And we'll discover four compelling reasons why we worship Jesus Christ.

***Because of who He is (vv. 5-7).*** Three unique titles are given to our Lord to describe who He is. First, He is *the Lion of the tribe of Judah.* The reference here is to Genesis 49:8-10, where Jacob prophetically gave the scepter to Judah and made it the tribe of the kings. (God never meant for Saul to establish a dynasty, because he came from the tribe of Benjamin. God *used him* to discipline Israel because the people asked for a king; then He *gave them* David from the tribe of Judah.)

The image of "the lion" speaks of dignity, sovereignty, courage, and victory. Jesus Christ is the only living Jew who can prove His kingship from the genealogical records. "Son of David" was a title often used when He was ministering on earth (see Matt. 1).

But He is also *the Root of David,* which means He brought David (and David's line) into existence. As far as His humanity is concerned, Jesus had His roots *in* David (Isa. 11:1, 10); but as far as His deity is concerned, Jesus is the Root *of* David. This speaks, of course, of our Lord's eternality; He is indeed the "Ancient of Days." How the Messiah could both be David's Lord and David's son was a problem Jesus presented to the Pharisees, and they could not (or would not) answer Him (Matt. 22:41-46).

When John turned to see, he saw not a lion but *a lamb!* Jesus Christ is called "the Lamb" at least twenty-eight times in the Book of Revelation (the Greek word used means "a little pet lamb") and the emphasis is not hard to miss. God's wrath is "the wrath of the Lamb" (Rev. 6:16). Cleansing is by "the blood of the Lamb" (Rev. 7:14). The church is "the bride of the Lamb" (Rev. 19:7; 21:9).

The theme of "the Lamb" is an important one throughout Scripture, for it presents the person and work of Jesus Christ, the Redeemer. The Old Testament question, "Where is the lamb?" (Gen. 22:7) was answered by John the Baptist who cried, "Behold the Lamb of God, which taketh away the sin of the world" (John 1:29). The choirs of heaven sing, "Worthy is the Lamb!" (Rev. 5:12)

The description of the Lamb (Rev. 5:6), if produced literally by an artist, would provide a grotesque picture; but when understood symbolically, conveys spiritual truth. Since seven is the number of perfection, we have here perfect power (seven horns), perfect wisdom (seven eyes), and perfect presence (seven Spirits in all the earth). The theologians would call these qualities omnipotence, omniscience, and omnipresence; and all three are attributes of God. The Lamb is God the Son, Christ Jesus!

We worship Jesus Christ because of who He is. But there is a second reason why we worship Him.

**Because of where He is (v. 6).** To begin with, Jesus is in heaven. He is not in the manger, in Jerusalem, on the cross, or in the tomb. He is ascended and exalted in heaven. What an encouragement this is to suffering Christians, to know that their Saviour has defeated every enemy and is now controlling events from glory! He too suffered, but God turned His suffering into glory.

But where is Christ in heaven? He is *in the midst.* The Lamb is the center of all that transpires in heaven. All creation centers in Him (the four living creatures), as do all of God's people (the elders). The angels around the throne encircle the Saviour and praise Him.

He is also *at the throne.* Some sentimental Christian poetry and hymnody dethrones our Saviour and emphasizes only His earthly life. These poems and songs glamorize "the gentle Carpenter" or "the humble Teacher," but they fail to exalt the risen Lord! We do not worship a Babe in a manger or a corpse on a cross. We worship the living, reigning Lamb of God who is in the midst of all in heaven.

**Because of what He does (vv. 8-10).** When the Lamb came and took the scroll (see Dan. 7:13-14), the weeping ended and the praising began. God's people and the representatives of God's creation joined their voices in a new song of praise. Note that praise *and prayer* were united, for incense is a picture of prayer rising to the throne of God (Ps. 141:2; Luke 1:10). We shall meet the "incense prayers" of the saints again (Rev. 6:9-11; 8:1-6).

What kind of song did they sing? To begin with, it was *a worship hymn,* for they said, "Thou art worthy!" To *worship* means "to ascribe worth," and Jesus alone is worthy. When I was in the pastorate, I tried to open each morning worship service with a hymn that lifted the congregation's minds and hearts upward to the Lord Jesus Christ. Too many contemporary songs are "I" centered rather than "Christ" centered. They so emphasize the believer's experience that they almost ignore the Lord's glory. Certainly there is a place for that kind of song, but nothing can compare with adoring Christ in spiritual worship.

But this song was also *a Gospel song!* "Thou wast slain, and hast redeemed us [some texts read *them*] by Thy blood." The word translated *slain* means "violently slain" (Rev. 5:6). Heaven sings about the Cross and the blood! I read about a denomination that revised its official hymnal and removed all songs about the blood of Christ. That hymnal could never be used in heaven, because there they glorify the Lamb slain for the sins of the world.

In Genesis 22, a ram was substituted for Isaac, a picture of Christ giving His life for *the individual* (see Gal. 2:20). At Passover, the lamb was slain for each *family* (Ex. 12:3). Isaiah states that Jesus died for *the nation of Israel* (Isa. 53:8; see also John 11:49-52). John affirms that the Lamb died for *the whole world!* (John 1:29) The more you meditate on the power and scope of Christ's work on the cross, the more humbled and worshipful you become.

This song was also *a missionary song.* Sinners were redeemed "out of every kindred, and tongue, and people, and nation" (Rev. 5:9). *Kindred* refers to a common ancestor and *tongue* to a common language. *People* means a common race, and *nation* a common rule or government. God loves a whole world (John 3:16) and His desire is that the message of redemption be taken to a whole world (Matt. 28:18-20).

Perhaps you heard about the Christian who was against foreign missions but somehow happened to attend a missionary rally. When they passed the offering plate, he told the usher, "I don't believe in missions!" "Then take something out," said the usher. "It's for the heathen."

This heavenly hymn was also *a devotional hymn,* for it announced our unique position in Christ as "a kingdom of priests." Like Melchizedek of old, believers are kings and priests (Gen. 14:17ff; Heb. 7; 1 Peter 2:5-10). The veil of the temple was torn when Jesus died, and the way is opened to God (Heb. 10:19-25). We "reign in life" as we yield to Christ and allow His Spirit to work in us (Rom. 5:17).

Finally, this song was *a prophetic hymn:* "We shall reign on the earth" (Rev. 5:10). When Jesus Christ returns to earth, He will establish His righteous kingdom for 1,000 years; and we shall reign with Him (Rev. 20:1-6). The prayers of the saints, "Thy kingdom come!" will then be fulfilled. Creation shall then be set free from bondage to sin (Isa. 11:1-10; Rom. 8:17-23), and Christ shall reign in justice and power.

What a marvelous hymn! How rich would be our worship if only we would blend all these truths in honoring Him!

**Because of what He has (vv. 11-14).** In this closing burst of praise, all the angels and every creature in the universe joined together to worship the Redeemer. What a cascade of harmony John heard! In this hymn, they stated those things that Jesus Christ deserved to receive because of His sacrificial death on the cross. When He was on earth, people did not ascribe these things to Him; for many of these things He deliberately laid aside in His humiliation.

He was born in weakness and He died in weakness; but He is the recipient of all power. He became the poorest of the poor (2 Cor. 8:9), and yet He owns all the riches of heaven and earth. Men laughed at Him and called Him a fool; yet He is the very wisdom of God (1 Cor. 1:24; Col. 2:3).

He shared in the sinless weaknesses of humanity as He hungered, thirsted, and became weary. Today in glory, He possesses all strength. On earth, He experienced humiliation and shame as sinners ridiculed and reviled Him. They laughed at His kingship and attired Him in a mock robe, crown, and scepter. But all of that is changed now! He has received all honor and glory!

And blessing! He became a curse for us on the cross (Gal. 3:13), so that we can never be under the curse of the broken Law. (Some translations read "praise" instead of "blessing," but the Greek word carries both meanings.) He is worthy of all praise!

The worship service climaxed with all of the universe praising the Lamb of God and the Father seated on the throne!

And there was even a loud "Amen!" from the four living creatures! In heaven, we are permitted to say "Amen!"

Keep in mind that all of this praise centered on the Lord Jesus Christ, the Redeemer. It is not Christ the Teacher, but Christ the Saviour, who is the theme of their worship. While an unconverted person could praise the Creator, he certainly could not sincerely praise the Redeemer.

All of heaven's praise came because the Lamb took the scroll from the Father's hand. God's great eternal plan would now be fulfilled and creation would be set free from the bondage of sin and death. One day the Lamb will break the seals and put in motion events that will eventually lead to His coming to earth and the establishment of His kingdom.

As you share in these heavenly worship services, do you find your own heart saying "Amen!" to what they have sung? You may believe in Christ as the Creator, but have you trusted Him as your Redeemer?

If not, will you do so right now?

"Behold, I stand at the door and knock: if any man hear My voice, and open the door, I will come in to him, and will sup with him, and he with Me" (Rev. 3:20).

# CHAPTER FIVE
# THE SEALS AND
# THE SEALED
*Revelation 6–7*

The worship described in Revelation 4–5 is preparation for the wrath described in Revelation 6–19. It seems strange to us that worship and judgment should go together, but this is because we do not fully understand either the holiness of God or the sinfulness of man. Nor do we grasp the total picture of what God wants to accomplish and how the forces of evil have opposed Him. God is long-suffering, but eventually He must judge sin and vindicate His servants.

According to Daniel 9:27, seven years are assigned to Israel in God's prophetic calendar, beginning with the signing of an agreement with the world dictator (the Antichrist), and ending with Christ's return to earth to judge evil and establish His kingdom. It is this period that is described in Revelation 6–19. By referring to John's outline (Rev. 1), you will see that his description is in three parts: the first three and a half years (Rev. 6–9), the events at the middle of the period (Rev. 10–14), and the last three and a half years (Rev. 15–19).

What is so significant about the middle of the Tribulation? That is when the Antichrist breaks his covenant with Israel and becomes their persecutor instead of their protector (Dan. 9:27).

As you study these fourteen action-filled chapters, keep in mind that John wrote to encourage God's people in every age of history. He was not only writing *prophecy* that would be fulfilled in the end times; but he was also writing great *theology* and dramatically revealing the character of God and the principles of His kingdom. These chapters describe the cosmic conflict between God and Satan, the New Jerusalem and Babylon; and no matter what "key" a student may use to unlock Revelation, he cannot help but see the exalted King of kings as He vindicates His people and gives victory to His overcomers.

Since the church never knows when Christ will return, each generation must live in expectancy of His coming. Therefore the Book of Revelation must be able to communicate truth to each generation, not just to the people who will be alive when these events occur. Verses like Revelation 13:9; 16:15; and 22:7, 18-20 all indicate the timelessness of John's message. This also explains why the apostle used so much symbolism, for symbols never lose their meaning. In every era of its history, the church has had to contend with Babylon (compare Rev. 18:4 with Jer. 50–51) and Antichrist (see 1 John 2:18ff). Revelation 6–19 is merely the climax of this conflict.

In Revelation 6–7, John characterized the opening days of the Tribulation as a time of retribution, response, and redemption.

## Retribution (Rev. 6:1-8)

In this section, John recorded the opening of the first four seals; and as each seal was opened, one of the four living creatures summoned a rider on a horse. ("Come and see" should read, "Come!") In other words, events take place on earth because of the sovereign direction of God in heaven.

The horse imagery is probably related to the vision described in Zechariah 1:7-17.

Horses represent God's activity on earth, the forces He uses to accomplish His divine purposes. The center of His program is Israel, particularly the city of Jerusalem. (Jerusalem is mentioned thirty-nine times in Zech.) God has a covenant purpose for Israel, and that purpose will be fulfilled just as He promised.

Now, let's try to identify these horses and their riders.

*Antichrist (vv. 1-2).* Daniel states that there is a "prince that shall come," who will make a covenant with Israel to protect her from her enemies (Dan. 9:26-27). In other words, the future world dictator begins his career as a peacemaker! He will go from victory to victory and finally control the whole world.

Some have suggested that the rider on the white horse is actually a symbol of the "conquering Christ" who today is defeating the forces of evil in the world. They point to Revelation 19:11 as proof, but the only similarity is the presence of a white horse. If this rider is indeed Jesus Christ, it seems strange that He should be named *at the end of the book* and not at the beginning!

We would expect the Antichrist to resemble *the* Christ, because Antichrist is Satan's great imitation! Even the Jews (who ought to know the Scriptures) will be deceived by him (John 5:43; 2 Thes. 2:1-12). This great deceiver will come as a peaceful leader, holding a bow but no arrows! (Our Lord's weapon is a sword; Rev. 19:15.) Antichrist will solve the world's problems and be received as the Great Liberator.

The word for *crown* in Revelation 6:2 is *stephanos,* which means "the victor's crown." The crown that Jesus Christ wears is *diadema,* "the kingly crown" (Rev. 19:12). Antichrist could never wear the diadem, because it belongs only to the Son of God.

Certainly, there is a sense in which Jesus Christ is conquering today, as He releases people from the bondage of sin and Satan (Acts 26:18; Col. 1:13). But this conquest began with His victory on the cross and certainly did not have to wait for the opening of a seal! We shall note later that the sequence of events in Revelation 6 closely parallels the sequence given by our Lord in His Olivet discourse; and the first item mentioned is the appearance of false Christs (Matt. 24:5).

*War (vv. 3-4).* Antichrist's conquest begins in peace, but soon he exchanges the empty bow for a sword. The color red is often associated with terror and death: the red dragon (Rev. 12:3), the red beast (Rev. 17:3). It is a picture of wanton bloodshed. War has been a part of man's experience since Cain killed Abel, so this image would speak to believers in every age, reminding them that God is ultimately in control, even though He is not responsible for the lawless deeds of men and nations.

**Famine (vv. 5-6).** The color black is often connected with famine (Jer. 14:1-2; Lam. 5:10). Famine and war go together. A shortage of food will always drive up prices and force the government to ration what is available. "To eat bread by weight" is a Jewish phrase indicating that food is scarce (Lev. 26:26). A penny (denarius) a day was a standard wage for laborers (Matt. 20:2) but, of course, it had much greater buying power than the common penny does today. A "measure" of wheat was about two pints, sufficient for the daily needs of one person. Ordinarily, a person could buy eight to twelve measures for a penny, and much more of barley, which was the cheaper grain.

However, during the Tribulation, a man will have to work all day just to secure food for himself! There will be nothing for his family! At the same time, the rich will be enjoying plenty of oil and wine. No wonder Antichrist will eventually be able to control the economy (Rev. 13:17) as he promises to feed the hungry masses.

**Death (vv. 7-8).** John saw two personages: Death riding a pale horse and hades (the realm of the dead) following him. Christ has the keys of death and hades (Rev. 1:18), and both will one day be cast into hell (Rev. 20:14). Death claims the body while hades claims the soul of the dead (Rev. 20:13). John saw these enemies going forth to claim their prey, armed with weapons of the sword, hunger, pestilence (death), and wild beasts. In ancient times, hunger, pestilence, and the ravages of beasts would be expected to accompany war (note also Jer. 15:2; 24:10; Ezek. 14:21).

Conquering tyrants who bring the world war, famine, and pestilence are certainly nothing new. Suffering people from the days of the Roman Empire to the most recent war can easily recognize anticipations of these four dreaded horsemen. This is why the Book of Revelation has been a source of encouragement to suffering believers throughout history. As they see the Lamb opening the seals,

they realize that God is in control and that His purposes will be accomplished.

**Response (Rev. 6:9-17)**
John recorded two responses to the opening of the seals, one in heaven and the other on earth.

**The martyrs (vv. 9-11).** When the Old Testament priest presented an animal sacrifice, the victim's blood was poured out at the base of the brazen altar (Lev. 4:7, 18, 25, 30). In Old Testament imagery, blood represents life (Lev. 17:11). So, here in Revelation, the souls of the martyrs "under the altar" indicates that their lives were given sacrificially to the glory of God. The Apostle Paul had the same idea in mind when he wrote Philippians 2:17 and 2 Timothy 4:6.

The Greek word *martus,* which gives us our English word *martyr,* simply means "a witness" (see Rev. 2:13; 17:6). These saints were slain by the enemy because of their witness to the truth of God and the message of Jesus Christ. The forces of Antichrist do not accept the truth, because Satan wants them to be deceived and accept his lies (see Rev. 19:20; 20:10; also 2 Thes. 2:9-12).

Since their murderers are still alive on earth, these martyrs are apparently from the early part of the Tribulation. But they represent *all* who have laid down their lives for Jesus Christ and the cause of God's truth, and they are an encouragement to all today who may be called to follow them. They assure us that the souls of the martyrs are in heaven, awaiting the resurrection (Rev. 20:4), and that they are at rest, robed in heavenly glory.

But is it "Christian" for these martyred saints to pray for vengeance on their murderers? After all, both Jesus and Stephen prayed that God would forgive those who killed them. I have no doubt that, when they were slain on earth, these martyrs also prayed for their slayers; and this is the right thing to do (Matt. 5:10-12, 43-48).

The great question, however, was not *whether* their enemies would be judged, but *when.* "How long, O Lord?" has been the cry of God's suffering people throughout the ages (see Pss. 74:9-10; 79:5; 94:3-4; also Hab. 1:2). The saints in heaven know that God will eventually judge sin and establish righteousness in the earth, but they do not know God's exact schedule. It is not personal revenge that they seek, but vindication of God's holiness and the establishment of God's justice. Every believer today who sincerely prays, "Thy kingdom come!" is echoing their petition.

God made clear to these martyrs that their sacrifice was an appointment, not an accident; and that others would join them. Even in the death of His people, God is in control (Ps. 116:15); so there is nothing to fear.

Many others would be slain for their faith before the Lord would return and establish His kingdom (see Rev. 11:7; 12:11; 14:13; and 20:4-5). Then as today, it appears that the enemy is winning; but God will have the last word. Even in our "enlightened" twentieth century, multiplied thousands of true believers have laid down their lives for Christ; certainly they will receive the crown of life (Rev. 2:10).

**The earth-dwellers (vv. 12-17).** The martyrs cried, "Avenge us!" but the unbelievers on earth will cry, "Hide us!" The opening of the sixth seal will produce worldwide convulsions and catastrophes, including the first of three great earthquakes (Rev. 6:12; 11:13; 16:18-19). All of nature will be affected: the sun, moon, and stars, as well as the heavens, the mountains, and the islands. Compare this scene with Joel 2:30-31 and 3:15 as well as with Isaiah 13:9-10 and 34:2-4.

Even though John wrote using symbolic language, these verses describe a scene that would frighten even the most courageous person. People will try to hide from the face of God and from the face of the Lamb! Imagine wanting to hide from *a lamb!* I once heard Dr. Vance Havner say that the day would come when the most expensive piece of real estate would be a hole in the ground, and he was right.

We will see more of "the wrath of God" as we progress through Revelation (Rev. 11:18; 14:10; 16:19; 19:15). We will also encounter the wrath of Satan (Rev. 12:17) and the wrath of the nations as they oppose God (Rev. 11:18). If men and women will not yield to the love of God, and be changed by the grace of God, then there is no way for them to escape the wrath of God.

Rank and wealth will not deliver anyone in that terrible day. John's list included kings, captains, and slaves, the rich and the poor. "Who shall be able to stand?"

The phrase "wrath of the Lamb" seems a paradox. "Wrath of the lion" would be more consistent. We are so accustomed to emphasizing the meekness and gentleness of Christ (Matt. 11:28-30) that we forget His holiness

and justice. The same Christ who welcomed the children also drove the merchants from the temple. God's wrath is not like a child's temper tantrum or punishment meted out by an impatient parent. God's wrath is the evidence of His holy love for all that is right and His holy hatred for all that is evil. Only a soft and sentimental person would want to worship a God who did not deal justly with evil in the world.

Furthermore, the people mentioned here are *impenitent.* They refuse to submit to God's will. They would rather hide from God in fear (remember Adam and Eve?) than run to Him in faith. They are proof that judgment *by itself* does not change the human heart. Not only will men seek to hide from God, but they will blaspheme Him as well! (Rev. 16:9, 11, 21)

But is there any hope for believers during this terrible time of judgment? And what about God's special people, the Jews, who made a covenant with the Antichrist? Certainly people will trust the Lord even after the church is taken to heaven, but how will they manage? We turn to Revelation 7 for some of the answers.

But before considering John's third theme in this section—redemption—we must note the parallels that exist between Christ's prophetic words recorded in Matthew 24 and what John wrote in Revelation 6. The following summary outline makes this clear.

| *Matthew 24* | *Revelation 6* |
|---|---|
| False Christs (vv. 4-5) | White horse rider (vv. 1-2) |
| Wars (v. 6) | Red horse—war (vv. 3-4) |
| Famines (v. 7a) | Black horse—famine (vv. 5-6) |
| Death (vv. 7b-8) | Pale horse—death (vv. 7-8) |
| Martyrs (v. 9) | Martyrs under the altar (vv. 9-11) |
| Worldwide chaos (vv. 10-13) | Worldwide chaos (vv. 12-17) |

Matthew 24:14 introduces the preaching of the Gospel of the kingdom throughout the whole world, and this may well be where Revelation 7 fits in. God may use the sealed 144,000 Jews to share His Word with the world, resulting in the salvation of multitudes.

## Redemption (Rev. 7:1-17)

It is important that we contrast the two groups of people described in this chapter.

| 7:1-8 | 7:9-17 |
|---|---|
| Jews | Gentiles from all nations |
| Numbered—144,000 | Not numbered, nor could be |
| Sealed on earth | Standing in heaven before God |

While we are not told explicitly in Scripture that the 144,000 Jews are God's special witnesses, and that the Gentile host is saved through their ministry, this appears to be a logical deduction; otherwise, why are they associated in this chapter? The parallel with Matthew 24:14 also indicates that the 144,000 will witness for the Lord during the Tribulation.

**The sealed Jews (vv. 1-8).** Angels are associated with the forces of nature: the wind (Rev. 7:1), fire (Rev. 14:18), and water (Rev. 16:5). Stopping the winds implies a "lull before the storm." God controls all of nature. During the day of His wrath, He will use the forces of nature to judge mankind. The phrase "four corners of the earth" is no more "unscientific" here than it is in Isaiah 11:12 or the daily newspaper.

In Scripture, a seal indicates ownership and protection. Today, God's people are sealed by the Holy Spirit (Eph. 1:13-14). This is God's guarantee that we are saved and safe, and that He will one day take us to heaven. The 144,000 Jews will receive the Father's name as their seal (Rev. 14:1), in contrast to the "mark of the beast" that Antichrist will give those who follow him (Rev. 13:17; 14:11; 16:2; 19:20).

This seal will protect these chosen Jews from the judgments that will "hurt the earth and the sea" (Rev. 7:2), and occur when the first four angels blow their trumpets (Rev. 8). The judgments are intensified when the horrible locusts are released from the pit (Rev. 9:1-4). Protected from these awesome judgments, the 144,000 will be able to do their work and glorify the Lord.

In every age, God has had His faithful remnant. Elijah thought he was alone, but God had 7,000 who were yet faithful to Him (1 Kings 19:18). The sealing described in Revelation 7 certainly has its background in Ezekiel 9:1-7, where the faithful were sealed before God's judgment fell. So, while these 144,000 Jews are an elect people in the last days with a special task from God, they also symbolize God's faithful elect in every age of history.

The number 144,000 is significant because it signifies perfection and completeness (144 = 12 x 12). Some see here the completeness of *all* God's people: the twelve tribes of Israel (Old Testament saints) and the twelve Apostles (New Testament saints). This may be a good *application* of this passage, but it is not the basic *interpretation;* for we are told that these 144,000 are all Jews, and even their tribes are named.

A man once told me he was one of the 144,000; so I asked him, "To which tribe do you belong, and can you prove it?" Of course, he could not prove it, no more than a Jew today can prove the tribe from which he or she descended. The genealogical records have all been destroyed. Even the fact that ten of the tribes were taken by the Assyrians and "lost" is no problem to God. He knows His people and their whereabouts (see Matt. 19:28; Acts 26:7; James 1:1).

This is not to say that our literal interpretation of this passage is not without problems. Why is Levi included when it had no inheritance with the other tribes? (Num. 18:20-24; Josh. 13:14) Why is Joseph named but not his son Ephraim, who is usually connected with his brother Manasseh? Finally, why is the tribe of Dan omitted here and yet included in Ezekiel's list for the apportionment of the land? (Ezek. 48:1) Many suggestions have been made, but we do not know the answers. Even if we interpreted this passage in a spiritual sense (i.e., Israel is the church), we would be no more certain. We must permit God to know "the secret things," and not allow our ignorance of them to hinder us from obeying what we *do* know (Deut. 29:29).

**The saved Gentiles (vv. 9-17).** You cannot read the Book of Revelation without developing a global outlook, for the emphasis is on what God does for people in the *whole* world. The Lamb died to redeem people "out of every kindred, and tongue, and people, and nation" (Rev. 5:9). The great multitudes pictured here came from "all nations, and kindreds, and people, and tongues" (Rev. 7:9). "Go ye into all the world, and preach the Gospel to every creature" was our Lord's mandate (Mark 16:15).

There is no doubt as to who this multitude

is, because one of the elders explained it to John (Rev. 7:14): they are Gentiles who have been saved through faith in Christ during the Tribulation. (We will meet this same group again in Rev. 14.) While today, in most parts of the world, it is relatively easy to confess Christ, this will not be the case during the Tribulation, at least during the last half of it. Then, unless persons wear the "mark of the beast," they will not be able to buy or sell; and this would leave them without even life's bare necessities. Revelation 7:16 indicates that they suffered hunger (see Rev. 13:17), thirst (see Rev. 16:4), and lack of shelter. (On the heat of the sun, see Rev. 16:8-9.)

The fact that they are *standing* before the throne and not seated around it indicates that these people are not identified with the twenty-four elders. In fact, John himself did not know who they were! If they had been Old Testament believers, or the church, John would have recognized them. That the elder had to tell John who they were suggests that they are a special people, which, indeed, they are.

Of course, in the heavenly city (Rev. 21–22), all distinctions will cease and we shall all simply be the people of God in glory. But while God is working out His program in human history, distinctions still exist between the Jews, the Gentiles, the church, and the Tribulation saints.

John gave a beautiful description of these people.

First, they were *accepted*, for they stood before God's throne and the Lamb. No doubt they had been rejected on earth for they stood for truth at a time when lies were popular and Satan was in charge. Their white robes and palms symbolize victory: they were true overcomers! The Jews used palm branches at their Feast of Tabernacles (Lev. 23:40-43), which was a special time of national rejoicing.

Then, they were *joyful*. They sang praises to the Father and to the Lamb; and their worship was joined by all those who surrounded the throne.

Third, they were *rewarded*. They had the privilege of being before God's throne and of serving Him. When God's people get to heaven, there will be work to do! We shall be able to serve Him perfectly! The Lamb will shepherd us and satisfy us with every good thing (see Isa. 49:10; Rev. 21:4).

The opening of the seventh seal will introduce the seven "trumpet judgments" (Rev.

8–11) and the wrath of God will increase both in intensity and scope. But before that occurs, we are assured that in His wrath, God will remember mercy (Hab. 3:2). Despite the wrath of God and the terror inspired by Satan and his helpers, multitudes will be saved through the blood of Jesus Christ. No matter what the age or dispensation, God's way of salvation has always been the same: faith in Jesus Christ, the Lamb of God.

Sad to say, however, multitudes during that time will also reject the Saviour and trust "the beast." But are there not people *today* who prefer Satan to Christ and this world to the world to come? They are just as condemned as the Tribulation sinners who receive the "mark of the beast."

If you have never trusted the Saviour, do so now.

If you have trusted Him, then share the Good News of salvation with others that they might be delivered from the wrath to come.

# CHAPTER SIX
# BLOW THE TRUMPETS!
*Revelation 8–9*

The seal judgments now over, the trumpet judgments are about to begin. These will be followed by the bowl (vial) judgments, culminating in the destruction of Babylon and Christ's return to earth. Note that from the seals to the trumpets to the bowls, the judgments increase in their intensity. Note also that the trumpet and the bowl judgments touch on the same areas, as the following summary illustrates:

| The Trumpets | The Judgment | The Bowls |
|---|---|---|
| 1. 8:1-7 | The earth | 16:1-2 |
| 2. 8:8-9 | The sea | 16:3 |
| 3. 8:10-11 | The rivers | 16:4-7 |
| 4. 8:12-13 | The heavens | 16:8-9 |
| 5. 9:1-2 | Mankind— torment | 16:10-11 |
| 6. 9:13-21 | An army | 16:12-16 |
| 7. 11:15-19 | Angry nations | 16:17-21 |

The trumpet judgments are released during the first half of the Tribulation, and the bowl judgments during the last half, which is also called "the wrath of God" (Rev. 14:10; 15:7). The trumpet judgments parallel the plagues that God sent on the land of Egypt. And why not? After all, the whole world will be saying, as did Pharaoh, "Who is the Lord that we should serve Him?"

The opening of the seventh seal, and the blowing of the first six trumpets, brought about three dramatic results.

### Preparation (Rev. 8:1-6)

This preparation involves two factors: silence (Rev. 8:1) and supplication (Rev. 8:2-6).

The hosts in heaven had just worshiped the Father and the Lamb with a tremendous volume of praise (Rev. 7:10-12). But when the Lamb opened the seventh seal, heaven was silent for about thirty minutes. John does not tell us what caused the silence, but several possibilities exist. The scroll had now been opened completely, and perhaps even turned over; and all of heaven could see God's glorious plan unfolding. Perhaps the heavenly hosts were simply awestruck at what they saw.

Certainly, this silence was "the lull before the storm," for God's intensified judgments were about to be hurled to the earth. "Hold thy peace at the presence of the Lord God: for the day of the Lord is at hand" (Zeph. 1:7; note also vv. 14-18, especially v. 16, "A day of the trumpet"). "Be silent, O all flesh, before the Lord: for He is raised up out of His holy habitation" (Zech. 2:13). "The Lord is in His holy temple: let all the earth keep silence before Him" (Hab. 2:20).

During this silence, the seven angels were given trumpets, significant to John, because he was a Jew and understood the place of trumpets in Israel's national life. According to Numbers 10, trumpets had three important uses: they called the people together (Num. 10:1-8); they announced war (Num. 10:9); and they announced special times (Num. 10:10). The trumpet sounded at Mount Sinai when the Law was given (Ex. 19:16-19), and trumpets were blown when the king was anointed and enthroned (1 Kings 1:34, 39). Of course, everyone familiar with the Old Testament would remember the trumpets at the conquest of Jericho (Josh. 6:13-16).

The voice of the Lord Jesus Christ sounded to John like a trumpet (Rev. 1:10). The voice of a trumpet summoned John to heaven (Rev. 4:1), and some relate this to the promise of the Rapture of the church given in 1 Thessalonians 4:13-18. Sounding seven trumpets certainly would announce a declaration of war, as well as the fact that God's anointed King was enthroned in glory and about to judge His enemies (Ps. 2:1-5). As trumpets declared defeat to Jericho, they will ultimately bring defeat to Babylon.

The awesome silence was followed by the actions of a special angel at the golden altar in heaven (see Rev. 9:13; 14:18; 16:7). In the tabernacle and temple, the golden altar stood before the veil and was used for burning incense (Ex. 30:1-10). This was the ministry Zacharias was performing when the angel told him that he and Elizabeth would have a son (Luke 1:5ff). Burning incense on this altar was a picture of prayer ascending to God (Ps. 141:2).

The "prayers of the saints" (Rev. 8:4) are not the prayers of a special group of people in heaven who have arrived at "sainthood." To begin with, *all* God's children are saints—set apart for God—through faith in Jesus Christ (2 Cor. 1:1; 9:1, 12; 13:13). And there is no definite teaching in the Scriptures that people in heaven pray for believers on earth, or that we can direct our prayers to God through them. We pray to the Father through the Son, for He alone is worthy (Rev. 5:3). For centuries, God's people have been praying, "Thy kingdom come, Thy will be done!" and now those prayers are about to be answered. Likewise, the Tribulation martyrs prayed for God to vindicate them (Rev. 6:9-11), a common plea of David in the Psalms (see Pss. 7; 26; 35; 52; 55; and 58 for example). These "imprecatory psalms" are not expressions of selfish personal vengeance, but rather cries for God to uphold His holy Law and vindicate His people.

On the great Day of Atonement, the high priest would put incense on the coals in the censer and, with the blood of the sacrifice, enter the holy of holies (Lev. 16:11-14). But in this scene, the angel put the incense on the altar (presented the prayers before God) and then *cast the coals* from the altar to the earth! The parallel in Ezekiel 10 indicates that this symbolized God's judgment; and the effects described in Revelation 8:5 substantiate this view. A storm is about to begin! (see Rev. 4:5; 11:19; 16:18)

Like it or not, the prayers of God's people

are involved in the judgments that He sends. The throne and the altar are related. The purpose of prayer, it has often been said, is not to get man's will done in heaven, but to get God's will done on earth—even if that will involves judgment. True prayer is serious business, so we had better not move the altar too far from the throne!

## Desolation (Rev. 8:7-13)

The first four trumpet judgments are "natural" in that they affect the land, the saltwater, the fresh water, and the heavenly bodies. The fifth and sixth judgments involve the release of demonic forces that first torment, and then kill. The last of the trumpet judgments (Rev. 11:15-19) creates a crisis among all the nations of the world.

**Desolation on earth (v. 7).** "Hail and fire mingled with blood" reminds us of the seventh plague that God sent against Egypt (Ex. 9:18-26). The Prophet Joel also promised "blood and fire" in the last days (Joel 2:30). Since this is a supernatural judgment, it is not necessary to try to explain how hail, fire, and blood become mingled. "Fire" could refer to the lightning of a severe electrical storm.

The target for this judgment is green vegetation, the trees and the grass, one third of which is burned up. One can well imagine how this would affect not only the balance of nature, but also the food supply. The Greek word for *trees* usually means "fruit trees"; and the destruction of pasture lands would devastate the meat and milk industries.

**Desolation in the seas (vv. 8-9).** Turning water into blood reminds us of the first Egyptian plague (Ex. 7:19-21). Note that John did not say that an actual burning mountain was cast out of heaven, but that the fiery object was like a great mountain. A triple judgment resulted: a third part of the saltwater turned to blood, a third part of the marine life died, and a third of the ships were destroyed. This will be an ecological and an economic disaster of unprecedented proportions.

Considering that the oceans occupy about three fourths of the earth's surface, you can imagine the extent of this judgment. The pollution of the water and the death of so many creatures would greatly affect the balance of life in the oceans, and this would undoubtedly lead to further insoluble problems. As of January 1, 1981 there were 24,867 ocean-going merchant ships registered. Imagine the shock waves that would hit the shipping industry if

8,289 valuable ships were suddenly destroyed! And what about their cargoes!

Some interpreters take "the sea" to mean the Mediterranean Sea. However, this would make a relatively small impact on the world, since the Mediterranean covers only 969,100 square miles and averages just 5,000 feet deep. It is likely that all the major bodies of saltwater are included in this judgment.

**Desolation in the fresh water (vv. 10-11).** God's wrath next reaches *inland* and touches the rivers and fountains of water (wells and sources of the rivers), making the fresh water taste bitter like wormwood. The National Geographic Society lists about 100 principal rivers in the world, ranging in length from the Amazon (4,000 miles long) to the Rio de la Plata (150 miles long). The U.S. Geological Survey reports thirty large rivers in the United States, beginning with the mighty Mississippi (3,710 miles long). One third of these rivers, and their sources, will become so bitterly polluted that drinking their water could produce death.

God has His stars numbered and named (Job 9:9-10). It is likely that this fallen star is molten and that, as it nears the earth, it begins to disintegrate and fall into the various bodies of water. If a star actually struck the earth, our globe would be destroyed; so this star must "come apart" as it enters the atmosphere. Of course, this event is a divinely controlled judgment; therefore, we must not try to limit it by the known laws of science.

The word translated "wormwood" gives us our English word *absinthe*, which is a popular liqueur in some countries of the world. The word means "undrinkable," and in the Old Testament was synonymous with sorrow and great calamity. Jeremiah, "the Weeping Prophet," often used it (Jer. 9:15; 23:15; Lam. 3:15, 19), and so did Amos (Amos 5:7, "those who turn justice into wormwood," NASB). Moses warned that idolatry would bring sorrow to Israel, like a root producing wormwood (Deut. 29:18). Solomon warned that immorality might seem pleasant, but in the end, it produces bitterness like wormwood (Prov. 5:4).

If the people who *drink from* these waters are in danger of dying, what must happen to the fish and other creatures that *live in* these waters? And what would happen to the vegetation near these rivers? If the ecologists are worried about the deadly consequences of water pollution today, what will they think when the third trumpet blows?

There is no direct parallel here to any of the plagues of Egypt. However, after the Exodus, Israel encountered bitter waters at Marah (which means "bitter") and Moses had to purify the water supply (Ex. 15:23-27). But no supernatural purification will be available during the Tribulation.

**Desolation in the heavens (vv. 12-13).** The judgments from the first three trumpets affected only a third part of the land and waters, but this fourth judgment affects the entire world. Why? Because it gets to the very source of the earth's life and energy, the sun. With one third less sunlight on the earth, there will be one third less energy available to support the life systems of man and nature.

This judgment parallels the ninth plague in Egypt (Ex. 10:21-23), which lasted three days. "The Day of the Lord is darkness, and not light" (Amos 5:18). Think of the vast changes in temperatures that will occur and how these will affect human health and food growth.

It is possible that this particular judgment is temporary, for the fourth bowl judgment will reverse it, and the sun's power will be intensified (Rev. 16:8-9). Then, at the close of the Tribulation, the sun and moon will be darkened again to announce the Saviour's return (Matt. 24:29-30; see also Luke 21:25-28).

"Blow ye the trumpet in Zion," said the Prophet Joel, "for the Day of the Lord cometh . . . a day of darkness and of gloominess" (Joel 2:1-2). Darkness, indeed! Not only will nature suffer loss, but human nature will take advantage of the long darkness and no doubt indulge in crime and wickedness. "Everyone that doeth evil hateth the light" (John 3:20).

At this point, a remarkable messenger will appear in the sky, proclaiming woe to the earth's inhabitants. Most manuscripts have "eagle" here instead of "angel," but either one would certainly get people's attention! Could this be the eaglelike living creature that John saw worshiping before the throne? (Rev. 4:7-8) Will God send it on this special mission? We cannot say for sure, but it is a possibility.

The three "woes" in Revelation 8:13 refer to the judgments yet to come when the remaining three angels blow their trumpets. It is as though the messenger cried, "If you think this has been terrible, just wait! The worst is yet to come!"

The phrase "inhabiters of the earth" (or "them that dwell on the earth") is found twelve times in Revelation (3:10; 6:10; 8:13; 11:10 [twice]; 12:12; 13:8, 12, 14; 14:6; 17:2, 8). It means much more than "people who live on the earth," for that is where *all* living people reside. Instead, it refers to a *kind* of people: those who live *for* the earth and the things *of* the earth. These are just the opposite of people who have their citizenship in heaven (Phil. 3:18-21). John described this worldly sort well in his first epistle (1 John 2:15-17), and later in this prophecy he again makes it clear that "earth-dwellers" are not born again (Rev. 13:8).

At the beginning of human history, heaven and earth were united because our first parents honored God and obeyed His will. Satan tempted them to focus on the earth; they disobeyed God; and ever since, a great gulf has been fixed between heaven and earth. This chasm was bridged when the Son of God came to earth and died for the sins of the world.

### Liberation (Rev. 9:1-21)

The late Dr. Wilbur M. Smith, who made the Book of Revelation his special study, once wrote: "It is probable that, apart from the exact identification of Babylon in Revelation 17 and 18, the meaning of the two judgments in this chapter represents the most difficult major problem in the Revelation" (*Wycliffe Bible Commentary*, p. 1509). Revelation 9 describes two frightening armies that are liberated at just the right time and permitted to judge mankind.

**The army from the pit (vv. 1-12).** The "bottomless pit" is literally "the pit of the abyss." Luke makes it clear that this "pit" is the abode of the demons (Luke 8:31), and John states that Satan will be temporarily "jailed" there during our Lord's reign on the earth (Rev. 20:1-3). The Antichrist (i.e., "the beast") will ascend out of this pit (Rev. 11:7; 17:8). It is not the lake of fire, for that is the final "prison" for Satan and all who follow him (Rev. 20:10), but part of that hidden underworld under the Lord's authority. Today, the fearsome army described here is already incarcerated, waiting for the hour of liberation.

This fallen star is a person, the king over the beings in the pit (Rev. 9:11). He does not have *complete* authority, for the key to the pit had to be given to him before he could loose his army. This "star" is probably Satan and the army, his demons (Eph. 6:10ff). One of the names for Satan is *Lucifer,* which means "brightness"; he also is compared to the "morning star" (Isa. 14:12-14). Jesus said to His disciples, "I beheld Satan as lightning fall from heaven" (Luke 10:18).

When the pit was opened, smoke emerged as though the door of a furnace had been loosened. Jesus compared hell to a furnace of fire (Matt. 13:42, 50), an image that ought to make people stop and think before they jest about it. The smoke polluted the air and darkened the sun, which had already been darkened when the fourth trumpet sounded.

But it is what came out of the smoke that truly terrorized mankind: an army of demons, compared to locusts. The eighth plague in Egypt was a devastating swarm of locusts (Ex. 10:1-20). People who have never encountered these insects have little idea of the damage they can do. When God wanted to judge His people, He would sometimes send locusts to devour the harvests (Deut. 28:38, 42; Joel 2).

These are not literal locusts, because locusts do not have scorpionlike stings in their tails. These creatures do not devour the green vegetation; in fact, they are prohibited from doing so. This demonic army is given the assignment of tormenting all who have not been protected by the seal of God. The 144,000 men from the tribes of Israel would therefore escape this painful judgment (Rev. 7:1-8). In fact, it is likely that all who have trusted the Lord will be sealed in some special way and protected from torment.

The normal lifespan of the locust is about five months (May to September), and this is the length of time that the judgment will last. These demons will sting people and thus create such pain that their victims will actually want to die, but death will flee from them (Jer. 8:3).

Reading the detailed description of these creatures, we realize that John is not writing about ordinary locusts. Yet, despite its obvious symbolism, it aptly portrays a powerful enemy armed for battle. With bodies like horses but faces like men, the demons' heads are crowned and covered with long hair. They have teeth like those of lions, and their skin is like a coat of mail. When they fly, the noise is like an army of chariots rushing by. It is unnecessary to try to "spiritualize" these symbols, or to interpret them in light of modern means of warfare. John is heaping image upon image to force us to feel the horror of this judgment.

Real locusts do not have a king (Prov. 30:27), but this army follows the rule of Satan, the angel of the bottomless pit. His name is "Destroyer." "The thief [Satan] cometh not, but for to steal, and to kill, and to destroy" (John 10:10). Real locusts are pervasive destroyers, but this army only tortures those who do not belong to the Lord.

As God's people, we can be thankful that Jesus Christ holds the keys of hell and death (Rev. 1:18) and exercises divine authority even over Satan. God has His timetable for all these events, and nothing will happen too soon or too late (2 Thes. 2:6; note also Rev. 9:15).

***The army from the east (vv. 13-21).*** It was at the golden altar of incense that the angel offered the prayers of the saints (Rev. 8:3-5); now from this same altar a voice speaks, commanding that four angels be loosed. These angels are apparently wicked, because no holy angel would be bound. Each angel is in charge of part of the vast army that follows them at their liberation, an army of 200 million beings! The army is released at a precise time, for a special purpose: to kill (not just torment) a third of the world's population. Since a fourth of mankind has already been killed (Rev. 6:8), this means that *half of the world's population will be dead* by the time the sixth trumpet judgment is completed.

Are we to identify this as a literal army of men, moving in conquest across the globe? Probably not. For one thing, the emphasis in this paragraph is not on the riders, but on the horses. The description cannot fit war-horses as we know them or, for that matter, modern warfare equipment, such as tanks. To assert that this is a literal army, and to point to some nation (such as China) that claims to have 200 million soldiers, is to miss the message John is seeking to convey.

The deadly power of these horses is in their mouths and tails, not in their legs. Fire, smoke, and brimstone issue from their mouths, and their tails are like biting serpents. They can attack men from the front as well as from the rear.

I take it that this is another demonic army, headed by four fallen angels; and that all of them are today bound by the Lord, unable to act until God gives them permission. Why they are bound at the Euphrates River is not explained, though that area is the cradle of civilization (Gen. 2:14), not to mention one of the boundaries for Israel (Gen. 15:18).

One would think that the combination of five months of torment and then death (from fire, smoke, and brimstone) would bring men and women to their knees in repentance; but such is not the case. These judgments are not remedial but retributive: God is upholding His holy Law and vindicating His suffering people (see Rev. 6:9-11). Even a casual reading of Revelation 9:20-21 reveals the awful wickedness of mankind, even in the midst of God's judgments. The most frightening thing about Revelation 9 is not the judgments that God sends but the sins that men persist in committing *even while God is judging them.*

Consider the sins that men and women will be committing:

*Demon worship,* which goes hand-in-hand with *idolatry* (see 1 Cor. 10:19-21), will be the leading sin. Satan will be at work (always under the permissive will of God), and Satan has always wanted to be worshiped (Isa. 14:12-15; Matt. 4:8-10). A great deal of "religion" will be practiced at this time, but it will be false religion. People will worship the works of their own hands, which could well include the buildings they construct, the machines they make, and the cities they build, as well as their idols.

Here are dead sinners worshiping dead gods! (see Ps. 115) Their gods will not be able to protect or deliver them, yet these people will continue to reject the true God and worship Satan and idols!

*Murder* and *theft* will also be rife in those days. So will various kinds of *sexual immorality.* The word translated "sorcery" is the Greek word *pharmakia,* which means "the use of drugs." Drugs are often used in pagan religious rites and demon worship. As we see the expansion of today's "drug culture," we have no problem envisioning a whole society given over to these demonic practices.

Mankind will be breaking the first two Mosaic commandments by making and worshiping idols. In their murders, they will violate the sixth commandment, and in their thefts, the eighth. By their fornication, they will break the seventh commandment. It will be an age of lawlessness with "every man doing that which is right in his own eyes" (see Jud. 21:25).

But God is working out His plan; and neither the sins of mankind nor the schemes of Satan will hinder Him from accomplishing His will.

We have come now to the midpoint of the Tribulation (Rev. 10–14), a time during which some important events must take place. Thus far, we have covered about three-and-a-half years of this seven-year period (Dan. 9:27). During this time, Antichrist began his career as a peacemaker and a special friend to Israel; but now, his true character will be revealed. He will become a peace-breaker and a persecutor of the people of God.

Things will not look bright for God's people during this middle stage of the prophetic journey, but they will still be overcomers through the power of the King of kings and Lord of lords!

# CHAPTER SEVEN
# A TIME FOR TESTIMONY
*Revelation 10–11*

Revelation 10–14 describes the events that will occur at the middle of the seven-year Tribulation. This explains John's repeated mention of the three-and-a-half-year time segment in one form or another (Rev. 11:2-3; 12:6, 14; 13:5). At the beginning of this period, the Antichrist began to make his conquest by promising to protect the Jews and assist in their rebuilding of the temple in Jerusalem. But after three-and-a-half-years, he will break his agreement, invade the temple, and begin to persecute the Jewish people.

However depressing the events of this middle segment of the Tribulation may be, God is not without His witness to the world. In Revelation 10–11 are three important testimonies: from a mighty angel (Rev. 10:1-11), from the two special witnesses (Rev. 11:1-14), and from the elders in heaven (Rev. 11:15-19).

## The Testimony of the Mighty Angel (Rev. 10:1-11)

More than sixty references to angels are made in Revelation. They are God's army sent to accomplish His purposes on earth. Believers today seldom think about these servants (Heb. 1:14), but one day in heaven we shall learn about all they did for us here.

***The description of the angel (vv. 1-4).***
This angel amazes us, for he has some of the
characteristics that belong especially to the
Lord Jesus Christ. John had seen and heard a
"strong angel" (Rev. 5:2), and the same
Greek word is here translated "mighty." All
angels excel in strength (Ps. 103:20), but apparently some have greater power and authority than others.

We first saw the rainbow around the throne
of God (Rev. 4:3); now it sits like a crown on
the head of this messenger. The rainbow was
God's sign to mankind that He would never
again destroy the world with a flood. Even in
wrath, God remembers His mercy (Hab. 3:2).
Whoever this angel is, he has the authority of
God's throne given to him.

God is often identified with clouds. God led
Israel by a glorious cloud (Ex. 16:10), and
dark clouds covered Sinai when the Law was
given (Ex. 19:9). When God appeared to Moses, it was in a cloud of glory (Ex. 24:15ff;
34:5). "[He] maketh the clouds His chariot"
(Ps. 104:3). A cloud received Jesus when He
ascended to heaven (Acts 1:9); and, when He
returns, it will be with clouds (Rev. 1:7).

The fact that the angel's face is "as the sun"
corresponds to the description of Jesus Christ
in Revelation 1:16; his feet correspond to the
Lord's description in Revelation 1:15. His
voice like a lion suggests Revelation 5:5. This
being could well be our Lord Jesus Christ,
appearing to John as a kingly angel. Jesus often appeared in the Old Testament as "the
Angel of the Lord" (Ex. 3:2; Jud. 2:4; 6:11-
12, 21-22; 2 Sam. 24:16). This was a temporary manifestation for a special purpose, not a
permanent incarnation.

Two other characteristics would suggest
identifying the angel as Jesus Christ: the book
in his hand and the awesome posture that he
assumed. The little book contains the rest of
the prophetic message that John will deliver.
Since our Lord was the only One worthy to
take the scroll and break the seals (Rev.
5:5ff), it might well be concluded that He is
the only One worthy to give His servant the
rest of the message.

The angel's posture is that of a conqueror
taking possession of his territory. He is claiming the whole world (see Josh. 1:1-3). Of
course, only the victorious Saviour could make
such a claim. The Antichrist will soon complete his conquest and force the whole world
to submit to his control. But before that happens, the Saviour will claim the world for Him-

self, the inheritance that His Father promised
Him (Ps. 2:6-9). Satan roars like a lion to
frighten his prey (1 Peter 5:8), but the Lion of
Judah roars to announce victory (see Ps. 95:3-
5; Isa. 40:12-17).

We are not told why John was forbidden to
write what the seven thunders uttered, the
only "sealed" thing in an otherwise "unsealed"
book (see Dan. 12:9; Rev. 22:10). God's
voice is often compared to thunder (Ps. 29;
Job 26:14; 37:5; John 12:28-29). It is useless
for us to speculate when God chooses to veil
His truth (Deut. 29:29).

***The declaration of the angel (vv. 5-
11).*** This declaration fills us with awe, not
only because of what the angel declares, but
also because of the way he declares it. It is a
solemn scene, with his hand lifted to heaven
as though he were under oath.

But if this angel is our Lord Jesus Christ,
why would He take an oath? In order to affirm
the solemnity and certainty of the words spoken. God put Himself "under oath" when He
made His covenant with Abraham (Heb. 6:13-
20) and when He declared His Son to be High
Priest (Heb. 7:20-22). He also took an oath
when He promised David that the Christ
would come from his family (Acts 2:29-30).

The emphasis in Revelation 10:6 is on God
the Creator. Various judgments have already
been felt by the heavens, the earth, and the
sea; and more judgments are to come. The
word that is translated "time" actually means
"delay." God has been delaying His judgments
so that lost sinners will have time to repent
(2 Peter 3:1-9); now, however, He will accelerate His judgments and accomplish His purposes.

Recall that the martyred saints in heaven
were concerned about God's seeming delay in
avenging their deaths (Rev. 6:10-11). "How
long, O Lord, how long?" has been the cry of
God's suffering people from age to age. God's
seeming delay in fulfilling His promises has
given the scoffers opportunity to deny God's
Word and question His sincerity (see 2 Peter
3). God's Word is true and His timing, perfect. This means comfort to saints—but judgment to sinners.

In the Bible, a *mystery* is a "sacred secret,"
a truth hidden to those outside but revealed
to God's people by His Word (Matt. 13:10-
12). The "mystery of God" has to do with the
age-old problem of evil in the world. Why is
there both moral and natural evil in the world?
Why doesn't God do something about it? Of

course, the Christian knows that God did "do something about it" at Calvary when Jesus Christ was made sin and experienced divine wrath for a sinful world. We also know that God is permitting evil to increase until the world is ripe for judgment (2 Thes. 2:7ff; Rev. 14:14-20). Since God has already paid the price for sin, He is free to delay His judgment, and He cannot be accused of injustice or unconcern.

The signal for this mystery's completion is the sounding of the seventh trumpet (Rev. 11:14-19). The last half of the Tribulation begins when the angels start to pour out the bowls, in which "is filled up [completed] the wrath of God" (Rev. 15:1).

*The directions* that the angel gave to John (Rev. 10:8-11) should remind us of our responsibility to assimilate the Word of God and make it a part of the inner man. It was not enough for John to see the book or even know its contents and purpose. He had to *receive* it into his inner being.

God's Word is compared to food: bread (Matt. 4:4), milk (1 Peter 2:2), meat (1 Cor. 3:1-2), and honey (Ps. 119:103). The Prophets Jeremiah (Jer. 15:16) and Ezekiel (Ezek. 2:9–3:4) knew what it was to "eat" the Word before they could share it with others. The Word must always "become flesh" (John 1:14) before it can be given to those who need it. Woe unto that preacher or teacher who merely echoes God's Word and does not incarnate it, making it a living part of his very being.

God will not thrust His Word into our mouths and force us to receive it. He hands it to us and we must take it. Nor can He change the effects the Word will have in our lives: there will be both sorrow and joy, bitterness and sweetness. God's Word contains sweet promises and assurances, but it also contains bitter warnings and prophecies of judgment. The Christian bears witness of both life and death (2 Cor. 2:14-17). The faithful minister will declare all of God's counsel (Acts 20:27). He will not dilute the message of God simply to please his listeners (2 Tim. 4:1-5).

The angel commissioned John to prophesy *again;* his work was not yet completed. He must declare God's prophetic truth concerning (not "before") many peoples, and nations, and tongues, and kings (Rev. 5:9). The word *nations* usually refers to the Gentile nations. John will have much to say about the nations of the world as he presents the rest of this prophecy.

## The Testimony of the Two Witnesses (Rev. 11:1-14)

*The ministry of the witnesses (vv. 1-6).* The place is Jerusalem and the time is the first half of the Tribulation. Israel is worshiping again at its restored temple, built under the protection of the Antichrist, whose true character has not yet been revealed. To spiritualize Revelation 11:1-2 and make the temple refer to the church creates a number of serious problems. For one thing, how could John measure an invisible body of people, even if the church were still on earth? If the temple is the church, then who are the worshipers and what is the altar? And since the church unites Jews and Gentiles in one body (Eph. 2:11ff), why are the Gentiles segregated in this temple? It seems wisest to interpret this temple as an actual building in the holy city of Jerusalem (Neh. 11:1, 18; Dan. 9:24).

John's measurement of the temple is a symbolic action. To measure something means to claim it for yourself. When we sold our house in Chicago, the new owners brought in an architect to measure various areas and recommend possible changes. Had the architect shown up previous to the buyers' commitment, we would have thrown him out. The Lord was saying through John, "I own this city and this temple, and I claim both for Myself!" The Old Testament background is found in Ezekiel 40–41 and Zechariah 2:1-3.

What John did was especially significant because the Gentiles had taken over Jerusalem. Antichrist had broken his agreement with Israel (Dan. 9:27) and now he was about to use the temple for his own diabolical purposes (2 Thes. 2:3-4). All of this will be elaborated in Revelation 13. "Jerusalem shall be trodden down of the Gentiles," said Jesus, "until the times of the Gentiles be fulfilled" (Luke 21:24). The "times of the Gentiles" began in 606 B.C. when Babylon began to devastate Judah and Jerusalem, and it will continue until Jesus Christ returns to deliver the Holy City and redeem Israel (Zech. 14).

Note that the two witnesses minister during the *first* half of the Tribulation (Rev. 11:3; 1,260 days). Jerusalem is then overrun by the Gentiles for forty-two months, the *last* half of the Tribulation.

Their witness is related to Israel and the temple. How tragic that the power of God and the Word of God will be *outside* the temple and not within as in former ages. Like the temple that Jesus left, this new house will be desolate (see Matt. 23:38). These two men are specifically called prophets (Rev. 11:3, 6), and I take this to mean prophetic ministry in the Old Testament sense, calling the nations to repent and return to the true God of Israel.

Not only do these witnesses declare God's words, but they also do God's works and perform miracles of judgment, reminding us of both Moses and Elijah (Ex. 7:14-18; 1 Kings 17:1ff; 2 Kings 1:1-12). Some students cite Malachi 4:5-6 as evidence that one of the witnesses may be Elijah, but Jesus applied that prophecy to John the Baptist (Matt. 17:10-13). John the Baptist, however, denied that he was Elijah returned to earth (John 1:21, 25; see also Luke 1:16-17). This confusion may be explained in part by realizing that throughout Israel's history, God sent special messengers—"Elijahs"—to call His people to repentance; so in this sense, Malachi's prophecy will be fulfilled by the witnesses.

Instead of relating the ministry of the witnesses to Moses and Elijah, the angel who spoke to John connected their ministry with Zerubbabel and Joshua the high priest (Zech. 4). These two men helped to reestablish Israel in Palestine and to rebuild the temple. It was a discouraging task, and the Gentiles made it even more difficult; but God provided the special power they needed to get the work done. This truth is an encouragement to God's servants in all ages, for the work of the Lord is never easy.

**The martyrdom of the witnesses (vv. 7-10).** This comes only when they have finished their testimony. God's obedient servants are immortal until their work is done. "The beast" (Antichrist) is now in power and wants to take over the temple; but he cannot succeed until the two witnesses are out of the way. God will permit him to slay them, for no one will be able to make war against "the beast" and win (Rev. 13:4).

The witnesses will not even be permitted decent burial (see Ps. 79:1-3). But even this indecency will be used by God to bear witness to mankind. No doubt the TV cameras in Jerusalem will transmit the scene to people around the world, and the news analysts will discuss its significance. The earth-dwellers will rejoice at their enemies' removal and will celebrate a "satanic Christmas" by sending gifts to one another. It thus would appear that the power of the two witnesses will not be limited to Jerusalem, but that they will be able to cause things to happen in other parts of the world.

These two prophets will definitely have a relationship with Israel; and the world, for the most part, has not approved of the nation Israel. In the middle of the Tribulation, "the beast" will turn against Israel and begin to persecute the Jews. The two witnesses will not be around to protect the nation and a frightening anti-Semitic movement will ensue.

Jerusalem is called a "great city" (Rev. 11:8); and from a human viewpoint, this is a true statement. But God looks at men and nations from a *spiritual* viewpoint. To Him, Jerusalem will be considered as polluted and worldly as Sodom and as rebellious and proud as Egypt.

**The resurrection of the witnesses (vv. 11-14).** Miraculously, the two witnesses are not only raised from the dead, but caught up into heaven! God rescues them from their enemies and gives a solemn witness to the watching world. The world's great joy suddenly becomes great fear. (Note the word *great* in Rev. 11, repeated eight times.)

Are we to interpret the three-and-a-half days literally? Or does the phrase simply mean "after a short time"? It seems too specific to mean that. Does it symbolize a longer period, say three-and-a-half years? It is not likely that two dead bodies would be kept lying in a city street for more than three years. Perhaps this is a picture of a rapture of all the saints in the midst of the Tribulation, and the three-and-a-half years covers the first half of the period. If so, then what is symbolized by the *death* of the two witnesses? This interpretation solves one problem only to create another.

These days appear to be literal days, just as the forty-two months in Revelation 11:2 are literal months. The Bible does not explain why this length of time was chosen and it is useless for us to speculate.

Our Lord's *friends* watched Him ascend to heaven (Acts 1:9-12), but the witnesses' *enemies* will see them resurrected and will be shaken with fear. Their fear will increase when a great earthquake occurs, killing 7,000 men and destroying a tenth part of Jerusalem. A great earthquake occurred when the sixth seal was opened (Rev. 6:12), and there will be a greater one when the seventh vial is poured out (Rev. 16:18-20).

## The Testimony of the Elders (Rev. 11:15-19)

We have been waiting since Revelation 8:13 for this third "woe" to arrive and now it is here. When the seventh angel blew the trumpet, three dramatic events occurred.

*An announcement of victory (v. 15).* These "great voices" were probably the choirs of heaven. The great announcement is that the kingdom (John uses the singular because "the beast" now has the world under his control) of this world belongs to Jesus Christ. Of course, Christ does not *claim* His royal rights until He returns; but the victory has already been won. Satan offered Him the world's kingdoms, but He refused the offer (Matt. 4:8-9). Instead, He died on the cross, arose, and returned victoriously to heaven; and there the Father gave Him His inheritance (Ps. 2:4-9).

However, we must not incorrectly assume that our Lord is not reigning *today*, because He is. According to Hebrews 7:1-2, Jesus Christ is "King of righteousness" and "King of peace." He is enthroned with the Father (Rev. 3:21), and He will reign until He defeats all His foes (1 Cor. 15:25). Today, He rules over a spiritual kingdom; but in that future day, He will reign over the nations of the world and rule with a rod of iron.

No matter how difficult the circumstances might be, or how defeated God's people may think they are, Jesus Christ is still King of kings and Lord of lords, and He is in control. One day, we shall triumph!

*An acclamation of praise (vv. 16-18).* The elders left their own thrones and prostrated themselves in worship before God's throne. They gave thanks for three special blessings: that Christ reigns supremely (Rev. 11:17), that He judges righteously (Rev. 11:18), and that He rewards graciously (Rev. 11:18).

In Revelation 4:10-11, the elders praised the Creator; and in Revelation 5:9-14, they worshiped the Redeemer. Here the emphasis is on the Conqueror and the King. Keep in mind that in John's day the church on earth looked as though it were defeated, for Rome was the conqueror and king. John was reminding the saints that *they* were "a kingdom of priests" reigning with the Saviour (Rev. 1:5-6). It may seem at times that the throne of heaven is empty, but it is not. Jesus Christ has both power and authority—in fact, *all* authority (Matt. 28:18, where the word *power* means "authority"). "Thou . . . hast begun to reign" is a good translation.

Christ not only reigns supremely, but He judges righteously (Rev. 11:18). The Lamb is

also the Lion! In Revelation 11:18, we have a "table of contents" for the remainder of the Book of Revelation. These events did not take place the instant the angel blew his trumpet; he simply signaled the beginning of the process, and now these events would take place as planned.

"The nations were angry." What do the nations have to be angry about? Certainly the Lord has been good and gracious to them. He has provided their needs (Acts 14:15-17; 17:24-31), assigned their territories, and graciously postponed His judgment to give men opportunity to be saved. Even more, He sent His Son to be the Saviour of the world. Today, God offers forgiveness to the nations! What more could He do for them?

Then, why are the nations angry? *Because they want to have their own way.* "Why do the heathen [the nations] rage, and the people imagine a vain thing? The kings of the earth set themselves, and the rulers take counsel together, against the Lord, and against His anointed [Christ], saying, 'Let us break Their bands asunder, and cast away Their cords from us' " (Ps. 2:1-3). They want to worship and serve the creature instead of the Creator (Rom. 1:25). Like adolescent children, the nations want to cast off all restraint; *and God will permit them to do so.* The result will be another "Babylon" (Rev. 17–18), man's last attempt to build his Utopia, a "heaven on earth."

Note the change in attitude shown by the nations of the world. In Revelation 11:2, the nations ruthlessly take over Jerusalem. In Revelation 11:9, they rejoice at the death of the two witnesses. But now they are angry; their arrogance and joy did not last very long. This belligerent attitude finally will cause the nations to unite to fight God at the great battle of Armageddon.

"And Thy wrath is come." The word translated "angry" in Revelation 11:18 is the verb form of the word translated "wrath." But man's wrath can never equal the wrath of the Lamb (Rev. 6:16-17). Even Satan's wrath, as cruel as it is, is no match for God's wrath (Rev. 12:17). There was intense suffering in the first half of the Tribulation, but only the last half will reveal the wrath of God (Rev. 11:18; 14:10; 16:19; 19:15). There are two Greek words for anger: *thumos*, which means "rage, passionate anger," and *orgē*, used here, which means "indignation, a settled attitude of wrath." God's anger is not an outburst of temper; it is holy indignation against sin. Both of these Greek words are used in Revelation to describe God's anger: *orgē* is used only four times; *thumos*, seven (Rev. 14:10, 19; 15:1, 7; 16:1, 19; 19:15). God's anger is not dispassionate, for He hates sin and loves righteousness and justice; but neither is it temperamental and unpredictable.

"And the time of the dead, that they should be judged" takes us to the very end of God's prophetic program. In one sense, every day is a "day of the Lord" because God is always judging righteously. God is long-suffering toward lost sinners and often postpones judgment, but there will be a final judgment of sinners and none will escape. This judgment is described in Revelation 20:11-15.

There will also be a judgment of God's children, known as "the Judgment Seat of Christ" (Rom. 14:10-13; 1 Cor. 3:9-15; 2 Cor. 5:9-11). God will reward His faithful servants (Matt. 25:21) and the sufferings they experienced on earth will be forgotten in the glory of His presence. Though God's children will not be judged for their sins (that judgment took place on the cross), they will be judged for their works and rewarded generously by the Master.

The Judgment Seat of Christ will take place in heaven after Christ has called His people home. When He returns to earth to establish His kingdom, the saints will be ready to reign with Him, with every blemish of the church removed (Eph. 5:25-27; Rev. 19:7-8). Today, we groan as we serve God, because we know only too well our handicaps and blemishes; but one day, we shall serve Him *perfectly!*

"Them that destroy the earth" refers to the rebellious earth-dwellers who will not submit to God. How ironic that these people live for the earth and its pleasures, yet at the same time are *destroying* the very earth that they worship! When man forgets that God is the Creator and he is the creature, he begins to exploit his God-given resources, and this brings destruction. Man is a steward of creation, not the owner.

As mentioned before, Revelation 11:18 is a summary statement of events yet to come. It is heaven's song of praise for the Lord's faithfulness to accomplish His purposes in the world. Again, it appears strange to us that heavenly beings can sing about judgment. Perhaps if we had more of the throne's perspective, we would be able to join their praises.

*An assurance of God's faithfulness (v. 19).* This chapter opened with a temple on earth, but now we see the temple in heaven. The focus of attention is on the ark of God, the symbol of God's presence with His people.

In the Old Testament tabernacle and temple, the ark stood behind the veil, in the holy of holies. God's glory rested on the ark, and God's Law was within the ark, beautifully illustrating that the two must never be separated. He is the holy God and must deal righteously with sin. But He is also the faithful God who keeps His promises to His people. It was the ark of God that led Israel through the Jordan and into their inheritance (Josh. 3:11-17). This vision of the ark would greatly encourage God's suffering people to whom John sent this book. "God will fulfill His promises!" John was saying to them. "He will reveal His glory! Trust Him!"

Once again, John saw and heard the portents of a storm (see Rev. 4:5; 8:5). Greater judgment is about to fall on the rebellious people of earth! But God's people need not fear the storms for He is in control. The ark reminds them of His presence and the faithfulness of His promises. And on that ark was the mercy seat on which the blood was sprinkled each Day of Atonement (Lev. 16:15-17). Even in wrath, God remembers His mercy (Hab. 3:2).

The stage is now set for the dramatic appearance of "the beast," Satan's masterpiece, the false Christ who will control the world.

# CHAPTER EIGHT
# THE TERRIBLE TRIO
## *Revelation 12–13*

Revelation 12–13 introduces us to the three key characters in the drama of the last half of the Tribulation: Satan the dragon, the false Christ, and the false prophet. These three are, in a sense, an evil trinity, opposing the true God and His people on earth. While these events will be of special significance to God's people at that time, the message of these two chapters can encourage suffering saints during any age.

Satan is the great enemy of the church, and he fights against God and His people by accusing the saints in heaven and attacking them on earth. However, Christ has overcome the old serpent, and He gives victory to His people.

The adversary always works through human means, in this case, "the beast" (false Christ or Antichrist) and the false prophet. Satan is an imitator, a counterfeiter; and he seeks to control men by means of deception. "The beast" is the future world dictator who promises to solve the pressing problems of the nations; the false prophet is his "propaganda minister." For a time, it appears that the satanic trio is succeeding; but then their world empire begins to collapse, the nations assemble for one final battle, Jesus Christ appears, and the battle is over.

Has this not been the pattern for the church's conflict with evil over the centuries? Whether the ruler has been a Caesar, a Hitler, a Stalin, or an agnostic humanist, Satan has energized and motivated him. The ruler has promised the people all that they want and need, only to lead them into slavery. He has usually had an associate to promote his program to the people and to entice them, if not force them, to obey. Often their submission amounted almost to worship.

God has permitted His people to suffer under the despotism of these rulers, but He has also enabled His people to experience great victories, even in martyrdom. They have been true overcomers! Then He has brought deliverance, only to have the cycle repeat itself, with each succeeding dictatorship worse than the previous one. The climax will come with the appearance of the Antichrist in his time (2 Thes. 2).

**The Dragon (Rev. 12)**

John's vision opens with *two wonders in heaven* (Rev. 12:1-6). The first is a woman giving birth to a son. Since this child is identified as Jesus Christ (compare Rev. 12:5 with Rev. 19:15 and Ps. 2:9), this symbolic woman can be none other than the nation Israel. It was through Israel that Jesus Christ came into the world (Rom. 1:3; 9:4-5). By further comparing the description in Revelation 12:1 with Genesis 37:9-10, the identification seems certain.

In the Old Testament, Israel is often compared to a woman, and even a woman in travail (Isa. 54:5; 66:7; Jer. 3:6-10; Micah 4:10; 5:2-3). The apostate world system is compared to a harlot (Rev. 17:1ff), and the church to a pure bride (Rev. 19:7ff).

The son is born and is then caught up to the throne of God (Rev. 12:5). We have symbolized here the birth of Christ and His victorious ascension, but nothing is said about either His life or His death. The colon in the middle of the verse represents thirty-three years of history!

The woman with child is the first wonder; the great red dragon is the second. Revelation 12:9 makes it clear that this is Satan. The color red is associated with death (Rev. 6:4) and Satan is a murderer (John 8:44). The heads, horns, and crowns will appear again in Revelation 13:1 and 17:3. The heads represent mountains (Rev. 17:9), and the horns represent kings (Rev. 17:12). We shall study the meaning of these symbols in more detail later.

The dragon was cast out of heaven (Rev. 12:9), and he took with him a third of the angels (Rev. 12:7, 9). They are spoken of as "stars" in Revelation 12:4 (see also Dan. 8:10). This is evidently a reference to the fall of Satan (Isa. 14:12-15), when he and his hosts revolted against God. However, the casting out described in Revelation 12:7-10 is yet future.

Just as soon as the child was born, Satan tried to destroy Him. This conflict between Satan and "the woman" began soon after man fell (Gen. 3:15). Throughout Old Testament history, Satan tried to prevent the birth of the Redeemer. There was always a "dragon" standing by, waiting to destroy Israel or the ancestors of the Messiah. Pharaoh is called a "dragon" (Ezek. 29:3), and so is Nebuchadnezzar (Jer. 51:34). At one critical point, the royal line was limited to one little boy (2 Kings 11:1-3). When Jesus Christ was born, Satan used King Herod to try to destroy Him (Matt. 2). Satan thought that he had succeeded when he used Judas to betray the Lord and hand Him over to be crucified. But the Cross was actually Satan's defeat! "And they overcame him [Satan] by the blood of the Lamb" (Rev. 12:11).

Even today Satan has access to heaven, where he accuses God's people; but he cannot dethrone the exalted Saviour. His strategy is to persecute God's people and devour them if possible (1 Peter 5:8). He has a special hatred for the Jewish people and has been the power behind anti-Semitism from the days of Pharaoh and Haman (see the Book of Esther) to

Hitler and Stalin. Finally, in the middle of the Tribulation, there will come a wave of anti-Semitism such as the world has never seen (Rev. 12:6). But God will protect His people during those three-and-a-half years (1,260 days; see Rev. 11:2; 13:5).

Apart from the 144,000 (who are sealed and protected), a believing remnant of Jews will survive this very troublesome time. We are not told where God will protect them or who it is that will care for them. Matthew 24:15-21 will take on special meaning for those believing Jews who live in the end days. Note especially the parenthesis in Revelation 12:15.

You and I are involved in a similar conflict today (see Eph. 6:10ff). Satan is out to destroy the church, and our victory can come only through Jesus Christ.

The next scene in this cosmic drama is *a war in heaven* (Rev. 12:7-12). Scripture makes it clear that Satan has access to heaven even today (Job 1-2). Once he was the highest of God's angels, but he rebelled against God and was cast down (Isa. 14:12-15). Interestingly, as God's church faithfully serves Christ and wins the lost, Satan is also cast down and defeated (Luke 10:1-2, 17-20; Matt. 16:18; note also 12:29).

Of course, when Jesus Christ died on the cross, it meant Satan's ultimate defeat (John 12:31-33). Satan will one day be cast out of heaven (Rev. 12:7-10), and then finally cast into hell (Rev. 20:10).

What is this celestial conflict all about? The fact that Michael led God's angels to victory is significant, because Michael is identified with the nation Israel (Dan. 10:10-21; 12:1; note also Jude 9). The name *Michael* means "who is like God?" and this certainly parallels Satan's egocentric attack on Jehovah—"I will be like the Most High" (Isa. 14:14). Apparently, the devil's hatred of Israel will spur him to make one final assault against the throne of God, but he will be defeated by Michael and a heavenly host.

But perhaps there is another factor involved in this war. After the church is taken to heaven, believers will stand before the Judgment Seat of Christ and have their works examined. On the basis of this judgment, rewards will be given (Rom. 14:10-12; 1 Cor. 3:10-15; 2 Cor. 5:10-11). It seems likely that Satan will be present at this event and will accuse the saints, pointing out all the "spots and wrinkles" in the church (Eph. 5:24-27).

The name *devil* means "accuser," and *Satan* means "adversary." Satan stands at the throne of God and fights the saints by accusing them (see Job 1-2; Zech. 3). But Jesus Christ, the "heavenly Advocate" (1 John 2:1-2), represents the church before God's holy throne. Because Jesus Christ died for us, we can overcome Satan's accusations "by the blood of the Lamb." Our salvation is secure, not because of our own works, but because of His finished work at Calvary.

How furious Satan will be when the church comes forth in glory "without spot or wrinkle, or any such thing." When the accuser sees that his tactics have failed, he will become angry and threaten the very peace of heaven.

How does this future war apply to the church today? The same serpent who accuses the saints in heaven also deceives the nations on earth (Rev. 12:9); and one of his strategies is to lie about the church. He deceives the nations into thinking that the people of God are dangerous, deluded, even destructive. It is through Satan's deception that the leaders of the nations band together against Christ and His people (Ps. 2; Acts 4:23-30). God's people *in every age* must expect the world's opposition, but the church can always defeat the enemy by being faithful to Jesus Christ.

Christ's shed blood gives us our perfect standing before God (1 John 1:5–2:2). But our witness to God's Word and our willingness to lay down our lives for Christ defeats Satan as well. Satan is not equal to God; he is not omnipotent, omnipresent, or omniscient. His power is limited and his tactics must fail when God's people trust the power of the blood and of the Word. Nothing Satan does can rob us of "salvation, and strength, and the kingdom of our God, and the power of His Christ" (Rev. 12:10), if we are yielded to Him. God's great purposes will be fulfilled!

Believers in any age or situation can rejoice in this victory, no matter how difficult their experiences may be. Our warfare is not against flesh and blood, but against the spiritual forces of the wicked one; and these have been defeated by our Saviour (Eph. 6:10ff; note also Eph. 1:15-23).

Heaven will rejoice when Satan is cast out, but the earth-dwellers will not; for the last half of the Tribulation will mean intense suffering for the world. The "woe" in Revelation 12:12 reminds us of the "three woes" referred to in Revelation 8:13. The first "woe" is described in Revelation 9:1-12, and the second in Revelation 9:13-21. The third "woe" is referred to in Revelation 11:14ff, but this passage only summarizes the events that will climax God's plan for the earth. It may be that part of this third "woe" is casting out Satan and permitting his terrible wrath on earth.

This, then, is the third scene in the drama: *Satan's wrath on earth* (Rev. 12:13-16). Knowing that his time is short, and having no more access to heaven, the adversary must vent all of his anger earthward. He begins with Israel (the woman), and creates a wave of anti-Semitism. Satan has always hated the Jews because they are God's chosen people and the vehicle through which salvation came into the world. Satan would like to destroy the nation, particularly as the time draws near for the Messiah to return to earth to establish the promised kingdom. A Jewish remnant must be ready to receive Him and form the nucleus for the kingdom (Zech. 12:9–14:21; Rev. 1:7).

God will prepare a special place where the Jewish remnant will be protected and cared for. It is interesting that the remnant's escape from Satan is described in terms of a flying eagle, for this is a repeated image in the Old Testament with reference to Israel. God delivered Israel from Egypt "on eagles' wings" (Ex. 19:4), and cared for the people in the wilderness as an eagle would her young (Deut. 32:11-12). Their return from Babylonian Captivity was like "mounting up with wings as eagles" (Isa. 40:31).

Note that the remnant will be sheltered for the last half of the Tribulation. We do not know where this sheltered place will be, nor do we need to know. But the lesson for all of us is clear: God cares for those whom He wants to use to accomplish His purposes on earth. True, some people will give their lives (Rev. 12:11), but others will be spared (see Acts 12 for an example of this principle).

The phrase "water as a flood" is not explained, but there is a parallel in Psalm 124. (Also note the phrase "escaped as a bird" in verse 7 of this same Psalm.) This "flood" is probably an outpouring of hatred and anti-Semitic propaganda. Or it may symbolize armies that invade Israel and seek to defeat the remnant. If that is the meaning, then the earth opening up could well be an earthquake that God sends to destroy the invaders. When Satan discovers that the people he seeks to kill are protected, then he turns on those who were not carried to the hidden place of safety. He will declare war, and God will permit him

to have victory for a time (Rev. 13:7); but ultimately, the old serpent will be defeated.

**The Beast from the Sea (Rev. 13:1-10)**
Some texts read, "And he [Satan] stood upon the sand of the sea." The sea symbolizes the Gentile nations (Rev. 17:15). From one of them, Satan will bring forth his "Super Leader," the man we call "Antichrist." Up to this point, Antichrist has headed a ten-nation European league; but now he is about to embark on a new career as Satan's world dictator.

You will remember that Antichrist began his career as a peacemaker (Rev. 6:2) and even "settled" the Arab-Israeli problem by making a covenant with the Jews to protect them for seven years (Dan. 9:27). This protection would permit the nation to rebuild the temple and reinstitute religious rituals (Dan. 9:27; Rev. 11:1). But in the middle of the seven-year period (the time we are studying now in Rev. 10–14) he will break that covenant, stop the ceremonies, and set up himself as god in the temple (Dan. 9:27; 2 Thes. 2:1-12).

The symbolic description of "the beast" enables us to learn something about his origin and character. God does not see him as a man, made in the divine image, but as a wild animal, under the control of Satan. He is a man (Rev. 13:18); but he is energized from hell, for he comes out of the pit (Rev. 11:7; 17:8). Just as Jesus Christ is God in the flesh, so "the beast" will be Satan in a human body (see John 13:2, 27).

The seven heads represent seven mountains (Rev. 17:9); and since Rome was built on seven hills, this must be a veiled reference to that powerful city (see Rev. 17:18). It would be a most meaningful allusion in John's day!

The ten horns represent ten kingdoms (Dan. 7:24; Rev. 17:12). It appears that "the beast" will head a "United States of Europe," a revived Roman Empire, before taking over as world dictator. All nations will no doubt admire and thank him for the "peace" he has achieved, little realizing the sorrow and destruction he will bring to the world.

The three animals named in Revelation 13:2 remind us of the four beasts Daniel saw in his dream (Dan. 7): a lion (Babylon), a bear (Media-Persia), a leopard (Greece), and a "terrible beast" (the Antichrist). John saw these animals, or kingdoms, in reverse order since he was looking *back*, while Daniel was looking *ahead*. The final world empire will be rooted in all the previous empires and unite in one their evil and power. Added to the ferocity of these beasts will be Satan's own power, throne, and authority!

Once Satan presents his great "masterpiece," the counterfeit Christ, to the world, what will happen next?

First, there will be *wonder* (Rev. 13:3). Certainly a terrified world will wonder at Antichrist's power and his sudden rise to international fame and authority. But mankind will also wonder at the healing of his "wound." What is this "wound"? John does not explain it, but perhaps what he later wrote (Rev. 17:9-13) can help interpret the symbolism. This "wound" must be important, because John mentioned it three times (Rev. 13:3, 12, 14), including the fact that it was sword-inflicted.

The seven heads represent seven mountains, but also seven kings or kingdoms (Rev. 17:10). Antichrist or "the beast" is one of these seven kings (Rev. 17:11), but he is also the eighth. Apparently, he reigns twice; but how can this be? The suggestion has been made that "the beast" will be a European leader who will form a ten-nation federation (Rev. 17:12), but be slain in the process. Revelation 11:7 and 17:8 state that "the beast" will ascend out of the abyss. Is it possible that Satan will (with God's permission) resurrect a man from the dead? If Satan has power to give life to a dead idol (Rev. 13:15), could he not also give life to a dead body?

If "the beast" ruled as one of the seven kings, was slain, and then raised up again, he could rule as the eighth king. If, on the other hand, the image is seen representing *kingdoms* rather than individuals, we would have the reemergence of a "dead kingdom" on the world scene. However, it would be difficult to understand how a kingdom could be slain by a sword. It is best, I think, to apply this prophecy to individual persons.

Not only will there be wonder, but there will also be *worship* (Rev. 13:4). Worship is the one thing Satan has always wanted (Matt. 4:8-10), and he will receive it through "the beast." The second "beast," described in the last half of this chapter, will organize and promote the worship of Antichrist, making it the official religion of the world!

There will also be *words* (Rev. 13:5-6). Almost all dictators have risen to power by controlling people with their words. Some of us can recall when Adolf Hitler was rising to power, and know now how he mesmerized huge crowds with his speeches. Satan will make "the beast" a great orator, whose addresses will blaspheme God, His name, His tabernacle (heaven), and the saints in heaven. Since Satan will have recently been cast out of heaven, this blasphemy is to be expected.

Satan can do nothing without God's permission (see Job 1-2; Luke 22:31-32), so "the beast's" authority is *delegated*, not inherent. It will last for three-and-a-half years, the last half of the Tribulation.

In his night vision, Daniel saw "the beast" as the fourth and final empire (Dan. 7:19-28). There, as in John's vision, is the same image of the ten horns with the added revelation that "the beast" must defeat three of the kings to gain control. Daniel also heard "the beast's" blasphemous words (Dan. 7:25).

Finally, there will be *war* (Rev. 13:7-10). God will permit Antichrist to war against His people ("wear out the saints," Dan. 7:25) and even to defeat some of them. John prophesied that some of the saints will be captured and some will be martyred. But because of their faith, they will have patience, or endurance (see Heb. 6:12; Rev. 1:9), and will not deny the Lord in spite of persecution and death.

The world's population will be divided: those who are saved, with their names in God's book, will not submit to "the beast"; those who are lost—the earth-dwellers—will worship "the beast" and do his bidding. Note that Revelation 13:9 applies this truth to "any man," no matter in which age he may live. Certainly in John's day, this was meaningful; for every Roman citizen had to acknowledge, "Caesar is Lord." Likewise in every age of the church, true believers have had to take their stand for Christ, come what may.

Keep in mind that "the beast" is a counterfeit Christ. The world would not receive Christ, but it will receive Antichrist (John 5:43). The world would not believe the truth, but they will believe the lie (2 Thes. 2:8-12). Jesus spoke (and still speaks) gracious words of salvation, and men turn a deaf ear; but they will listen to the blasphemous words of "the beast." The world will not worship *the* Christ, but they will bow down to Antichrist.

In Revelation 17, we will learn that "the beast" rises to power by means of "the harlot," a symbol of the apostate world church. This is not any one denomination or faith, but a world religious system that has rejected God's Son and God's truth. However, when "the beast" rises to universal power, he will no longer need "the harlot" and shall subsequently destroy her and establish his own satanic religion.

## The Beast from the Earth
## (Rev. 13:11-18)

In Revelation 16:13; 19:20; and 20:10, the beast from the earth is called "the false prophet." The dragon or Satan is the counterfeit Father ("I will be like the Most High"), "the beast" is the counterfeit Christ, and the false prophet is the counterfeit Holy Spirit. This completes the satanic trinity.

One of the ministries of the Holy Spirit is to glorify Christ and lead people to trust and worship Him (John 16:7-15). The false prophet will point to Antichrist and his image and compel people to worship Satan through "the beast."

The image of the horns (Rev. 13:11) suggests that the false prophet has authority, but the absence of a crown indicates that his authority is not political. Our Lord warned that there would be false prophets (Matt. 24:11, 24), and this one will be the greatest. He will have the "character" of a lamb but the voice of the dragon. What a deceiver he will be—and all the world will listen to him!

When our Lord ministered on earth, Jewish leaders often asked Him to perform some sign to prove that He was indeed their Messiah; and Jesus refused. But the false prophet will perform deceptive signs that will lead the world into devil-worship (see 2 Thes. 2:9). His greatest sign will be "the abomination of desolation" mentioned by Daniel (Dan. 9:27; 11:36), Jesus (Matt. 24:15), and Paul (2 Thes. 2:4).

What is "the abomination of desolation"? It is the image of "the beast," set up in the temple in Jerusalem. An idol is bad enough; but setting it up in the temple is the height of all blasphemy. Since Satan could not command worship in heaven, he will go to the next best place—the Jewish temple in the Holy City (see Dan. 8:9-14).

The false prophet, energized by Satan, will perform his "lying wonders" and even duplicate some of the signs performed by the two witnesses (Rev. 13:13; see also 11:5). Up to this time, the two witnesses have been ministering at the temple in Jerusalem, but "the beast" will slay them and take over the temple. When God raises the two witnesses from the dead and takes them to heaven, the false prophet will answer that challenge by giving life to the image of "the beast." Not only will the image move, but it will speak!

Not content to control people through religious deceit, the false prophet will institute strong economic measures as well. Everybody (except believers; Rev. 20:4) will receive a special mark in order to buy or sell; but the only way to get that mark is to submit to "the beast" and worship him. Surely this is a strong allusion to the Caesar worship in the Roman Empire, but this same policy has been used by political leaders throughout history.

This special mark is the name or number of "the beast"—the mystical 666. In the ancient world, the letters of the alphabet were used for numbers, both in Greek and Hebrew; and Bible students have been attempting for years to unravel the mystery of this name and number. If you work at it hard enough, almost *any* name will fit!

Since man was created on the sixth day, six is the number of man. Creation was made for man and likewise has the number six stamped on it: twenty-four hours to a day (4 x 6), twelve months to a year (2 x 6). Seven is the number of perfection and fullness, but six is the "human number," just short of perfection.

Despite all man's imaginative calculations, we must confess that no one knows the meaning of this number and name. No doubt believers on earth at that time will understand it clearly. The "satanic trinity" cannot claim the number seven; it must settle for 666.

This much is sure: in recent years, we have seen a worldwide increase in the use of numbers for identification. In the United States, a person's Social Security number is indispensable. In fact, numbers are more important to computers than names! Perhaps this is an advance warning of what will happen on earth when "the beast" is in control.

We have reached the middle of the Tribulation in our study, but we are not yet ready for the return of the Lord. Before John revealed how the great drama will climax, he paused to overview great events to come; and that will be our next topic.

An antichristian system pervades our world, and true believers must not be a part of it (1 John 2:15-17). We must shun false worship (1 Cor. 10:14-22), that we may be found faithful to the Lord in these last days! (2 Tim. 3)

# CHAPTER NINE
# VOICES OF VICTORY
*Revelation 14–16*

One of the themes that links Revelation 14–16 together is expressed by the word *voice*, which is used eleven times. In the events recorded, God speaks to His people or to the lost world, or His creatures speak out in praise of the Lord or in warning to the world. As the world moves into the last half of the Tribulation, heaven is not silent.

## The Voice of the 144,000 (Rev. 14:1-5)
This special group of Jewish men was sealed by God before the seventh seal was opened (Rev. 7), and now they are seen on Mount Zion with the Lord Jesus Christ. Contrast this picture to the one described in Revelation 13: the followers of "the beast" whose mark is on their foreheads (Rev. 13:16). God always has His faithful people, no matter how wicked the world may become.

The 144,000 are *standing* with Christ on Mount Zion, but which Mount Zion: the heavenly one (Heb. 12:22-24) or the earthly one? I personally believe that this is the heavenly Mount Zion, and that the scene anticipates Christ's coronation and the establishment of His kingdom when He returns to earth (Zech. 14:4ff). Christ today is enthroned in the heavenly Zion (Ps. 2:6), and we are enthroned with Him (Eph. 2:6). The scene in Revelation 14 is the assurance to God's people that He cares for His own and finally will take them to glory.

Not only are the 144,000 standing, but they are also *singing* (Rev. 14:2-3). Because of the special experiences they had during the Tribulation, they have a new song to sing that others cannot share (see Pss. 33:3; 40:3; 96:1; 98:1; 144:9; 149:1). They are accompanied by heavenly harps and other heavenly voices. It is encouraging to know that one day our sorrows will be transformed into songs!

John also pointed out their *separation* (Rev. 14:4-5). The 144,000 did not belong *to* the earth because they had been redeemed *out of* the earth. They were not earth-dwellers, but citizens of heaven. Believers today do not belong to this very special group but, like them, we have been redeemed and are not part of

this world system (see John 17:14-19; Phil. 3:17-21).

The phrase "defiled with women" does not imply that sex within marriage is evil, because it is not (Heb. 13:4). It merely indicates that these 144,000 Jewish men were unmarried. In the Bible, fornication and adultery are pictures of idolatry (Ex. 34:15; James 4:4). While most of the world bowed down to the image of "the beast," the 144,000 were faithful to the true God. While others lied to get what they needed, the 144,000 were without guile and blemish.

The term *firstfruits* means "the very finest." But it also carries the idea of an expected harvest. On the Feast of Firstfruits, the priest waved the sheaf before the Lord as a sign that the entire harvest belonged to Him (Lev. 23:9-14). The 144,000 may be the firstfruits of the harvest yet to come; they may be the nucleus of the coming kingdom. However, it would seem difficult for a *heavenly* company such as this to establish an earthly kingdom.

## The Voices of the Angels (Rev. 14:6-20)
At least six different angels are involved in this scene, each with a particular message to proclaim.

*"Judgment is come!" (vv. 6-7)* During the present age, the angels are not privileged to preach the Gospel. That responsibility has been given to God's people. While the nations will fear "the beast" and give honor to him, this heavenly messenger will summon them to fear and honor God alone. It is a reminder that God is the Creator and He alone deserves worship. This is not the Gospel message as we know it (1 Cor. 15:1-4); rather, it is a return to the message of Romans 1:18ff, what theologians call "natural theology."

All creation bears witness to God's existence as well as to His power and wisdom. Nonetheless, "the beast" will convince men that he is in charge of the world, and that their destinies are in his hands. The message of the angel calls men back to basics: God is Creator—worship and serve Him. The fear of the Lord, not the fear of "the beast," is the source of wisdom (Prov. 9:10).

*"Babylon is fallen!" (v. 8)* This proclamation anticipates the events of Revelation 18 (see also Rev. 16:18-19). We will consider it in detail then. "Babylon" is God's name for the world system of "the beast," the entire economic and political organization by which he rules. "The harlot" (Rev. 17) is the religious

system that "the beast" uses to help build his organization. When Antichrist establishes his own religion (Rev. 13:11-15), he will destroy the "harlot"; but it is God who will destroy Babylon.

**"Escape God's wrath!" (vv. 9-13)** The third message is directed especially to those who are deciding about following "the beast." It is a warning that "the easy way" is really the hard way, that to "go along with the world" means to go away from God. The Greek text reads, "If any man continues to worship the beast," suggesting that there is still opportunity for repentance and salvation.

"Drinking the cup" is sometimes used as an image of judgment (Jer. 25:15ff; 51:7ff; note also Rev. 14:8). God's final judgments on mankind will be "vials of wrath" poured out from heaven (Rev. 16). God will not mix mercy with this judgment (Ps. 75:8; Hab. 3:2), but will pour out His undiluted indignation on a rebellious world.

Images like "fire and brimstone" (Rev. 14:10) and "smoke" (Rev. 14:11) upset some people. They ask, "How can a God of love actually permit His creatures to suffer eternal torment?" But we must keep in mind that God's love is a *holy* love, not one based on sentimentality, and therefore He *must* justly deal with sin. We may not like the word *torment*, but it is here just the same (Rev. 14:10; see also 9:5; 11:10; 20:10).

We must also keep in mind that God has repeatedly warned sinners and given them opportunity to repent. The first angel in this series invited sinners to turn to God, and the second one warned that the whole "Babylonian" system would be destroyed. If people persist in their sins even after God sends judgments and warnings, then they have only themselves to blame.

John intended for his readers to see the contrast between Revelation 14:11 and 13: no rest for the wicked, but eternal rest for the saints (see 2 Thes. 1:3-12). Better to reign with Christ forever than with Antichrist for a few short years! Better to endure persecution patiently now than to escape it and suffer throughout eternity!

**"The harvest is ripe!" (vv. 14-20)** The Person pictured here on the white cloud is undoubtedly our Lord Jesus Christ (see Dan. 7:13-14; Rev. 1:13). We have had the image of the cup, and now we have the image of the harvest, both of the grain (Rev. 14:14-16) and of the grape (Rev. 14:17-20). Again, this an-

ticipates the final judgment of the world.

While winning lost souls to Christ is sometimes pictured as a harvest (John 4:34-38), this image is also used of God's judgment (Matt. 13:24-30, 36-43; Luke 3:8-17). God permits the seeds of iniquity to grow until they are ripe, and then He judges (Gen. 15:16).

The grape harvest is often a picture of judgment (see Joel 3:13ff, which anticipates the Day of the Lord). In actuality, Scripture portrays three different "vines." Israel was God's vine, planted in the land to bear fruit for God's glory; but the nation failed God and had to be cut down (Ps. 80:8-16; Isa. 5:1-7; see also Matt. 21:33-46). Today, Christ is the Vine and believers are branches in Him (John 15). But the world system is also a vine, "the vine of the earth" in contrast to Christ, the heavenly Vine; and it is ripening for judgment. The wicked system—Babylon—that intoxicates people and controls them, will one day be cut down and destroyed in "the winepress of the wrath of God."

Some see in this image an anticipation of the "battle of Armageddon," when the armies of the world will gather against Jerusalem (Zech. 14:1-4; Rev. 16:16). Certainly, John is using hyperbole when he describes a river of blood four feet deep and 200 miles long (see also Isa. 63:1-6). Today, God is speaking to the world in grace, and men will not listen. One day hence, He must speak in wrath. The bitter cup will be drunk, the harvest of sin reaped, and the vine of the earth cut down and cast into the winepress.

**The Voice of the Victors (Rev. 15:1-4)**
At this point, John saw the seven angels holding the seven vials of God's wrath, poised for action. The wicked world is about to "drink of the wine of the wrath of God" (Rev. 14:10); but before the angels pour out their judgments, there is an "interlude" of blessing. Before sending the "third woe" (Rev. 11:14), God once again reassures His faithful people.

John saw the believers from the Tribulation who had overcome "the beast" and his system. These are the people who "loved not their lives unto the death" (Rev. 12:11). Since they did not cooperate with the satanic system and receive the mark of "the beast," they were unable to buy or sell (Rev. 13:17). They were totally dependent on the Lord for their daily bread. Some of them were put into prison and some were slain (Rev. 13:10); but all of them practiced faith and patience.

This entire scene is reminiscent of Israel following the Exodus. The nation had been delivered from Egypt by the blood of the lamb, and the Egyptian army had been destroyed at the Red Sea. In thankfulness to God, the Israelites stood by the sea and sang "the song of Moses."

The Tribulation saints whom John saw and heard were standing by the "sea of glass" in heaven (Rev. 4:6), just as the Israelites stood by the Red Sea. They were singing "the song of Moses" and also "the song of the Lamb." "The song of Moses" is recorded in Exodus 15, and its refrain is: "The Lord is my strength and song, and He is become my salvation" (Ex. 15:2). The 144,000 sang a song that nobody else could sing; but this is a song *all* saints can sing.

When Israel returned from Babylonian Captivity and reestablished their government and restored temple worship, they used this same refrain at the dedication services (Ps. 118; see especially v. 14).

In the future, when God shall call His people back to their land, Isaiah prophesied that they will sing this song again (Isa. 11:15–12:6). "The song of Moses" is indeed an important song in the hymnal of the Jewish nation.

This scene would give great assurance and endurance to suffering saints in any age of the church. It is possible to be victorious over the world system! One does not have to yield to the "mark of the beast." Through the blood of the Lamb, we have deliverance. Our Lord's work on the cross is a "spiritual exodus" accomplished by His blood. (Note Luke 9:31, where the word "decease" is *exodus* in the Greek.)

In their song, the Tribulation saints praise God's works as well as His ways. The earth-dwellers certainly would not praise God for His works, and they would never understand His ways. God's works are great and marvelous, and His ways are just and true. There is no complaint here about the way God permitted these people to suffer! It would save us a great deal of sorrow if we would acknowledge God's sovereignty in this same way today! "The Lord is righteous in all His ways, and holy in all His works" (Ps. 145:17).

The phrase "king of saints" can also be read "king of ages." God is the eternal King, but He is also in charge of history. Nothing happens by accident. The singers seek to glorify God and honor Him, the very praise the first

angel proclaimed in Revelation 14:7. Antecedents of this song may be found in Psalms 86:9; 90:1-2; 92:5; 98:2; 111:9; and 145:17.

Revelation 15:4 is another anticipation of the kingdom, foretelling the time when all nations shall worship the Lamb and obey Him. This verse also announces that God's judgments are about to be manifested.

## The Voice of Fulfillment (Rev. 15:5–16:21)

The "great voice" out of the temple commands the seven angels to pour out the contents of their vials (Rev. 16:1), after which he announces "It is done!" (Rev. 16:17) The "mystery of God" is finished! (Rev. 10:7) The martyrs in glory had asked, "How long?" (Rev. 6:9-11) and now their cry would be answered.

The seven angels emerge from the heavenly temple (see Rev. 11:19), because their work is holy as are the judgments they bring. The angels' clothing reminds us of the priestly garments, for their service is a divine ministry. When the Old Testament tabernacle and temple were dedicated, these earthly buildings were filled with God's glory (Ex. 40:34-35; 2 Chron. 7:1-4); but now the *heavenly* temple is filled with smoke (see Isa. 6:4; Ezek. 10:4). This smoke likewise is evidence of God's glory and power.

Each of the angels has a specific "target" for the contents of his vial. The earth-dwellers have already suffered from the seal and trumpet judgments, but this final series of judgments will climax God's plan, leading to Babylon's fall and Jesus Christ's return to earth.

*Grievous sores (v. 2).* This vial judgment reminds us of the sixth plague in Egypt (Ex. 9:8-12; note also Deut. 28:27, 35). Only those who have submitted to "the beast" and who have rejected the warning of the first angel will experience this judgment (Rev. 14:6-7).

Revelation 16:10-11 suggests that these sores do not disappear; for by the time of the fifth vial, people are still in pain from the first judgment. Yet their pain will not cause them to repent (see Rev. 9:20-21). William R. Newell used to say, "If men are not won by grace, they will never be won."

It is an awesome thought to consider almost the entire population of the world suffering from a painful malady that nothing can cure. Constant pain affects a person's disposition so that he finds it difficult to get along with other people. Human relations during that period will certainly be at their worst.

**Waters turned to blood (vv. 3-6).** The second and third vials parallel the first plague in Egypt (Ex. 7:14-25). The second vial will center on the sea, and the third will turn the inland waters (rivers and fountains) into blood. When the second trumpet judgment occurred, a third part of the sea became blood; but with this judgment, the entire system of seas and oceans will be polluted. The third trumpet made a third part of the inland waters bitter as wormwood; but the third vial will turn all of those bitter waters into blood.

Heaven gives justification for this terrible judgment: the earth-dwellers have shed the blood of God's people, so it is only right that they should drink blood. In God's government, the punishment fits the crime. Pharaoh tried to drown the Jewish boy babies, but it was his own army that eventually drowned in the Red Sea. Haman planned to hang Mordecai on the gallows and to exterminate the Jews; but he himself was hanged on the gallows, and his family was exterminated (Es. 7:10; 9:10). King Saul refused to obey God and slay the Amalekites, so he was slain by an Amalekite (2 Sam. 1:1-16).

**Great heat from the sun (vv. 8-9).** All earthly life depends on the light of the sun. In previous judgments, a part of the sun had been dimmed (Rev. 8:12), but now the heat of the sun is increased. Anyone who has been on the desert knows how merciless the sun's heat can be. Remembering too that the water system is now useless, you can imagine how people will suffer from thirst. Alas, even this judgment will not bring men to their knees! (see Mal. 4:1)

**Darkness (vv. 10-11).** This is not worldwide darkness; only "the beast," his throne, and his kingdom are affected. This reminds us of the fifth trumpet (Rev. 9:2) and the ninth plague (Ex. 10:21-23). Where is the throne of "the beast"? His image is in the temple in Jerusalem, so that may be the center of his operation. Or perhaps he is ruling from Rome, in cooperation with the apostate church headquartered there.

When God sent the ninth plague to Egypt, the entire land was dark, except for Goshen where the Israelites lived. The judgment of the fifth vial is just the opposite: there is light for the world, but darkness reigns at the headquarters of "the beast"! Certainly this will be a great blow to his "image" throughout the earth.

**The Euphrates dried up (vv. 12-16).** This famous river was mentioned earlier in Revelation, when the sixth trumpet sounded (Rev. 9:13ff) and the angels were loosed who were bound therein. At that time, an army of demonic horsemen was also released. Now, an army from the nations of the world gathers for the great battle at Armageddon. The drying up of the river will make it possible for the army of the "kings of the East" to come to Palestine and invade the Holy Land.

We often speak of "the battle of Armageddon," but nowhere does the Bible use that phrase. On September 2, 1945, when General Douglas MacArthur supervised signing the peace treaty with Japan, he said: "We have had our last chance. If we will not devise something greater and more equitable [than war], Armageddon will be at our door."

The name *Armageddon* comes from two Hebrew words, *har Megiddo,* the hill of Megiddo. The word *Megiddo* means "place of troops" or "place of slaughter." It is also called the Plain of Esdraelon and the Valley of Jezreel. The area is about fourteen miles wide and twenty miles long, and forms what Napoleon called "the most natural battlefield of the whole earth." Standing on Mount Carmel and overlooking that great plain, you can well understand why it would be used for gathering the armies of the nations.

It was on this plain that Barak defeated the armies of Canaan (Jud. 5:19). Gideon met the Midianites there (Jud. 7) and it was there that King Saul lost his life (1 Sam. 31). Titus and the Roman army used this natural corridor, as did the Crusaders in the Middle Ages. British General Allenby used it when he defeated the Turkish armies in 1917.

From a human viewpoint, it appears that the armies of the nations are gathering on their own; but John makes it clear that the military movement is according to God's plan. The satanic trinity, through demonic powers, will influence the nations and cause the rulers to assemble their armies. They will even work miracles that will impress the rulers and cause them to cooperate. But all this will merely fulfill the will of God and accomplish His purposes (see Rev. 17:17). The Gentile nations will look on Armageddon as a battle, but to God, it will be only a "supper" for the fowls of the air (Rev. 19:17-21).

Zechariah 12 and 14 describe this event from Israel's point of view. Since "the beast" has set up his image in the temple at Jerusalem, and since many of the Jews will not bow down to him, it is natural that the Holy City should be the object of attack. However, not only the Jews are involved; for God has a purpose for the Gentile nations as well. Joel 3:9-21 parallels the Zechariah references, and Joel 3:19 makes clear that God will punish the Gentiles for the way they have treated the Jews (see also Isa. 24; Zeph. 3:8ff).

The outcome of the "battle" is recorded in Revelation 19: the Lord returns and defeats His enemies. Obviously, the assembling and marching armies create no problem for Almighty God. When the nations rage and defy Him, "He that sitteth in the heavens shall laugh: the Lord shall have them in derision. Then shall He speak unto them in His wrath, and vex them in His sore displeasure" (Ps. 2:4-5).

*"It is done!" (vv. 17-21)* The devil is "the prince of the power of the air," so perhaps this seventh vial has a special effect on his dominion (Eph. 2:2). But the immediate result is a devastating earthquake that affects the cities of the nations. Satan's entire system is now about to be judged by God: his religious system (the harlot, Rev. 17), his political and economic system (Babylon, Rev. 18), and his military system (the armies, Rev. 19).

The "great city" (Rev. 16:19) is probably Jerusalem (see Rev. 11:8). The Prophet Zechariah prophesied an earthquake that would change the topography of Jerusalem (Zech. 14:4). But the key idea here is that Babylon would fall (see Jer. 50–51). "The beast's" great economic system, which subjugated the people of the world, would be completely destroyed by God.

Added to the earthquake will be a hailstorm with hailstones of tremendous weight. (A talent of silver weighs about 125 pounds!) This judgment is reminiscent of the seventh plague in Egypt (Ex. 9:22-26). Just as Pharaoh and the Egyptian leaders did not repent, so the earth-dwellers will not repent; in fact, they will blaspheme God! No wonder the hail comes, for blasphemers are supposed to be stoned to death (Lev. 24:16).

Reviewing these three chapters, we see the encouragement they give to suffering Christians. The sealed 144,000 will arrive on Mount Zion and praise God (Rev. 14:1-5). The martyrs will also be in glory, praising God (Rev. 15:1-4). John's message is clear: it is possible to be victorious over "the beast" and be an overcomer!

Movements of armies, confederations of nations, and worldwide opposition to God cannot hinder the Lord from fulfilling His Word and achieving His purposes. Men think they are free to do as they please, but in reality, they are accomplishing the plans and purposes of God!

Every generation of Christians has been able to identify with the events in Revelation 14–16. There has always been a "beast" to oppress God's people and a false prophet to try to lead them astray. We have always been on the verge of an "Armageddon" as the nations wage war.

But in the last days, these events will accelerate and the Bible's prophecies will be ultimately fulfilled. I believe the church will not be on the scene at that time, but both Jewish and Gentile believers will be living who will have to endure Antichrist's rule.

The admonition in Revelation 16:15 applies to us all: "Behold, I [Jesus] come as a thief. Blessed is he that watcheth, and keepeth his garments, lest he walk naked, and they see his shame." Jesus Christ may return at any time, and it behooves us to keep our lives clean, to watch, and to be faithful.

# CHAPTER TEN
# DESOLATION AND DESTRUCTION!
## *Revelation 17–18*

Beginning in Revelation 17, John describes the Lamb's step-by-step victory over "the beast" and his kingdom. In Revelation 17, the religious system is judged; in Revelation 18, the political and economic system fall victim. Finally, the Lord Himself returns to earth; judges Satan, "the beast," and the false prophet (Rev. 19:19-20); and then establishes His kingdom.

One reason John used symbolism was so that his message would encourage believers in any period of church history. The true church is a pure virgin (Rev. 19:7-8; see also 2 Cor. 11:2), but the false religious system is a "harlot" who has abandoned the truth and prostituted herself for personal gain. In every age, there has been a "harlot" who has persecuted God's people; and this will culminate in the last days in a worldwide apostate religious system.

Likewise, every age has featured a "Babylon," a political and economic system that has sought to control people's minds and destinies. Just as the contrast to the "harlot" is the pure bride, so the contrast to "Babylon" is the City of God, the New Jerusalem, the eternal home prepared for the Lamb's wife (Rev. 21:9ff). Each generation of believers must keep itself pure from the pollution of both the "harlot" and "Babylon."

In these two chapters, John prophesies two divine judgments.

**The Desolation of the Harlot (Rev. 17)**
The scene begins with *an invitation* (Rev. 17:1-2). One of the angels asks John to come and see what God will do with "the beast's" worldwide religious system. Four times in this chapter, the woman is called a "harlot" (Rev. 17:1, 5, 15-16); and her sin is called "fornication" (Rev. 17:2, 4). Her evil influence has extended to the whole world, reaching even into high places ("the kings of the earth").

Following the invitation, John was carried away "in the Spirit" into the wilderness. There he saw "the harlot" and wrote down *the description* of what he saw (Rev. 17:3-6). Genesis 2 speaks of a pure bride in a lovely Garden; but by the Bible's end, civilization has degenerated to an impure harlot in a wilderness! That is what sin does to the world.

The description is very full. The woman is dressed in expensive garments, decorated with gold and precious stones. She is holding a golden cup in her hand and is drunk with the blood of the saints. On her forehead (see Rev. 13:16; 14:1) she wears a special name.

Her posture is important. She is seated upon "many waters" (Rev. 17:1), and upon a scarlet beast with seven heads and ten horns. No wonder John was "greatly astonished" (NIV) when he beheld the woman and "the beast."

But what did it all mean? Thankfully, the angel gave John (and all believers) *the explanation* of these symbols (Rev. 17:7-18).

Let's begin with *the woman*. Revelation 17:18 makes clear that she is identified with a city that existed in John's day ("reigns" is present tense). This city is prosperous and powerful, but also idolatrous ("blasphemy") and dangerous. For one thing, it pollutes the

nations with its filth and abomination (pictured by the golden wine cup); for another, it persecutes those who belong to the Lord (Rev. 17:6). Power, wealth, pollution, persecution: these words summarize the "great harlot's" involvement on a worldwide scale.

The woman's name also involves "mystery" (Rev. 17:5). In the New Testament, a "mystery" is a hidden truth that only the spiritually initiated can understand. To grasp one of God's mysteries requires spiritual intelligence and discernment. In this case, the mystery has to do with Babylon.

The city of Babylon was founded by Nimrod (Gen. 10:8-11). The name *Bab-el* means "the gate of God." Ironically, the famous tower of Babel (Gen. 11:1-9) was an idolatrous attempt by man to defy God. When the Lord sent judgment on the builders by making mankind's one language into many, the word *bab-el* came to mean "confusion." Later in history, Babylon became a great empire before finally falling to Media-Persia. But from the beginning of Nimrod's city in Genesis 10, an insidious anti-God "Babylonian influence" has been felt throughout history.

The woman is "the great harlot," but she is also "the mother of harlots." The Babylonian system has, in one way or another, given birth to all false religions. She has also seduced men into opposing God and persecuting His servants.

The seven mountains (Rev. 17:9) probably symbolize the city of Rome, built on seven hills. Certainly in John's day, the Roman Empire was living in luxury, spreading false religion, polluting the nations with its idolatry and sin, and persecuting the church.

John's readers would not be surprised when he used an evil harlot to symbolize a wicked city or political system. God even called Jerusalem a harlot (Isa. 1:21). Isaiah said that Tyre was a harlot (Isa. 23:16-17), and Nahum used this same designation for Nineveh (Nahum 3:4). (Read Jer. 50–51 for further historical parallels to John's prophetic message.)

As noted earlier, scarlet is the color of Satan (Rev. 12:3) and of sin (Isa. 1:18). Scarlet was a popular color in Rome, and both scarlet and purple were associated with rank and riches.

But the woman must not be separated from "the beast" that carries her. "The beast" has seven heads and ten horns. The seven heads symbolize seven mountains (Rev. 17:9) and also seven kings or kingdoms (Rev. 17:10), in keeping with Old Testament imagery (Ps. 30:7; Dan. 2:35). I have already suggested that the seven mountains can be interpreted geographically as the seven hills of Rome, but they may also be interpreted historically as seven kingdoms.

According to Revelation 17:10, five of these kings (or kingdoms) had passed off the scene, one was present in John's day, and one was yet to come. If so, then the five *past* kingdoms would be Egypt, Assyria, Babylon, Persia, and Greece. The *present* kingdom would be Rome, and the *future* kingdom would be that of "the beast." In order to understand Revelation 17:10-11, we must consider Revelation 17:12.

"The beast" not only has seven heads, but also ten horns, which represent ten kings. But these are very special kings: they enable "the beast" to rise to power and are even willing to yield their authority to him. Recall that at the opening of the first seal (Rev. 6:1-2), Antichrist began his "peaceful" conquest of the nations. He organized a "United States of Europe," brought peace to the Middle East, and appeared to be the great leader the troubled world was seeking.

But in the midst of the seven-year period, this ruler broke his covenant with Israel (Dan. 9:27) and began to persecute the people of God as well as the nation Israel. Energized by Satan and assisted by the false prophet, "the beast" became the world's dictator and its god. In this way, "the beast" was both "one of the seven [kings, kingdoms]" but also "the eighth." His kingdom was nothing but a revival of the Roman Empire ("one of the seven"), but it was a new kingdom ("the eighth").

But how does all this relate to Babylon? The "Babylonian system" of false religion has been a part of history since Nimrod founded his empire. Scholars have discovered it is amazingly like the true Christian faith! Alas, it is Satan's counterfeit of God's truth. Babylonians practiced the worship of mother and child, and even believed in the death and resurrection of the son.

Readers in John's day would identify "the harlot" with the Roman Empire. Readers in the Middle Ages might identify it as the Roman ecclesiastical system. Today, some believers see "the harlot" and the Babylonian system in an apostate "world church" that minimizes doctrinal truth, rejects the authority of the Word, and tries to unite professed believers on some other basis than faith in Jesus Christ.

However, in the days when John's prophecy will be fulfilled, an amazing thing will happen: "the harlot" will be made desolate by the very system that carried her! It is important to note that *"the beast" carries "the harlot."* Satan (and Antichrist) will use the apostate religious system to accomplish his own ends (i.e., attain world power); but then he will do away with "the harlot" and establish his own religious system. And all of this will be the fulfillment of God's Word (Rev. 17:17).

Since "the beast" sets up his image in the temple about the middle of the Tribulation, we can assume that "the harlot" and "the beast" work together during those first three-and-a-half years. This is corroborated by the fact that the ten kings assist him in desolating "the harlot" (Rev. 17:16). These are the same ten kings associated with "the beast" when he sets up the "United States of Europe" during the first half of the Tribulation.

Throughout history, political systems have "used" religious bodies to further their political causes. At the same time, church history reveals that religious groups have used politics to achieve their purposes. The marriage of church and state is not a happy one, and has often spawned children that have created serious problems. When dictators are friendly with religion, it is usually a sign that they want to make use of religion's influence and then destroy it. The church of Jesus Christ has been most influential in the world when it has maintained a separated position.

Compare the description of "the harlot's" desolation with that of the death of Jezebel (2 Kings 9:30-37).

Finally, note that those who trust the Lord are not influenced by "the harlot" or defeated by the kings (Rev. 17:14). Once again, John points out that the true believers are the "overcomers."

Satan's counterfeit religion is subtle, requiring spiritual discernment to recognize. It was Paul's great concern that the local churches he founded not be seduced away from their sincere devotion to Christ (2 Cor. 11:1-4). In every age, there is the tremendous pressure to conform to "popular religion" and to abandon the fundamentals of the faith. In these last days, we all need to heed the admonitions in 1 Timothy 4 and 2 Timothy 3 and remain true to our Lord.

## The Destruction of Babylon (Rev. 18)

Babylon was not only an ancient city and a powerful empire, but also the symbol of mankind's rebellion against God. In Revelation 18, Babylon represents the world system of "the beast," particularly in its economic and political aspects. At the same time, John calls Babylon a "city" at least eight times (Rev. 14:8; 17:18; 18:10, 16, 18-21). Old Testament prophecy seems to make clear that the city itself will not be rebuilt (Isa. 13:19-22; Jer. 51:24-26, 61-64). Some equate Babylon with Rome, particularly since "the harlot" and "the beast" cooperate during the first half of the Tribulation. Perhaps Peter was using *Babylon* as a "code name" for Rome when he wrote his first letter (1 Peter 5:13). Certainly, John's readers would think of the Roman Empire as they read these words about Babylon.

John heard four voices give four important announcements.

**The voice of condemnation (vv. 1-3).** This announcement was anticipated in Revelation 14:8 (some commentators would also include Rev. 16:19, but I have interpreted the "great city" in that context as Jerusalem). There is a definite reference here to Jeremiah 51–52, where the prophet saw the fall of historical Babylon. But here John saw the destruction of spiritual Babylon, the world system organized by "the beast." It was no ordinary angel that made this announcement, for he had great power and a glory that radiated throughout the whole earth. Despite Satan's devices and the opposition of evil men, "the earth shall be filled with the knowledge of the glory of the Lord" (Hab. 2:14).

The phrase "is fallen, is fallen" not only adds dramatic effect to the announcement, but suggests a dual judgment: ecclesiastical Babylon, "the harlot," in Revelation 17, and political Babylon here in Revelation 18. This thought is amplified in Revelation 18:6 when God announces that Babylon will receive "double" for her many sins.

The church, the bride of the Lamb, is the habitation of God (Eph. 2:22); Babylon, on the other hand, is the habitation of Satan (Rev. 18:2). This parallels the judgment on ancient Babylon (Isa. 13:21ff; Jer. 51:37ff). Furthermore, John called the city "a cage of every unclean and hateful bird" (Rev. 18:2). In Christ's Parable of the Sower, He also used the birds as a picture of Satan (Matt. 13:31-32).

This judgment has come because the Baby-lonian "system" has polluted the whole world. As in the judgment of "the harlot," the sin is that of "fornication" or idolatry. The system intoxicated the people of the world with all the riches and pleasures it had to offer. It catered to those who were "lovers of pleasures more than lovers of God" (2 Tim. 3:4).

Christians in every age have had to heed the warning of 1 John 2:15-17. How easy it is to become fascinated by the things the world has to offer. Like a person taking a sip of wine, we can soon find ourselves drinking deeply and then wanting more. The world system that opposes Christ has always been with us, and we must beware of its subtle influence.

The world system satisfies the desires of the earth-dwellers who follow "the beast" and reject the Lamb. But worldly things never permanently satisfy or last. The love of pleasures and possessions is but an insidious form of idolatry, demonic in its origin and destructive in its outcome.

**The voice of separation (vv. 4-8).** This admonition parallels Jeremiah 50:8 and 51:6, 45. In all ages, God's true people have had to separate themselves from that which is worldly and anti-God. When God called Abraham, He ordered him to get out of his country (Gen. 12:1). God separated the Jewish nation from Egypt and warned the Israelites not to go back. The church today is commanded to separate itself from that which is ungodly (Rom. 16:17-18; 2 Cor. 6:14–7:1).

John offered two reasons for God's people separating themselves from the diabolical system. The first is that they might avoid pollution, becoming "partakers of her sins" (Rev. 18:4). "Neither be partaker of other men's sins" (1 Tim. 5:22). The word means "joint fellowship or partnership." There is a *good* partnership in the Lord (Phil. 4:14), but there is also an evil partnership that we must avoid (Eph. 5:11). True unity of the Spirit exists among believers, but we must not compromise by joining forces with that which is opposed to Christ.

The second reason is that God's people might be spared the terrible plagues He will send on Babylon. God had patiently endured the growing sins of the evil system, but now the time had come for His wrath to be poured out. He would treat Babylon just as she treated His people.

What specific sins would God judge? We have already noted Babylon's evil influence on the nations of the world, seducing them with *idolatry*. Another sin that will be judged is *pride:* "She hath glorified herself!" (Rev. 18:7) She saw herself as a queen who could never be dethroned, and this false confidence and pride could never be accepted by the Lord (see Isa. 47 for the parallel, especially vv. 7-9).

A third sin is Babylon's *worship of pleasures and luxury*. To "live deliciously" (Rev. 18:7) is to live proudly in luxury while others go without. It means to make possessions and pleasures the most important things in life, and to ignore the needs of others. John summarized this attitude as "the lust of the flesh, and the lust of the eyes, and the pride of life" (1 John 2:16).

God's people must not delay in separating themselves from this evil system, because God's judgment will come suddenly and Babylon will be destroyed in a single day. Sometimes God's judgments work silently "as a moth" (Hosea 5:12), but at other times they are "as a lion" (Hosea 5:14) and spring suddenly, and there is no escape. In one day, the entire economic empire will collapse! But those who have their citizenship in heaven will rejoice at the judgment of God.

**The voice of lamentation (vv. 9-19).** This long paragraph describes the mourning of the merchants as they see Babylon go up in smoke and all their wealth destroyed. The image here is that of a prosperous ancient city that is visited by many ships. The wealth of the city provides for many nations and employs many people. It is worth noting that not only do the merchants lament the fall of Babylon (Rev. 18:11), but also the kings of the earth (Rev. 18:9). Business and government are so intertwined that what affects one affects the other.

Certainly, the city of Rome was the center for world trade and government in John's day, and it was known for its extravagance and luxury. Politically and economically, the people in the Empire were dependent on Rome. Today, with the complex connections that exist between governments and businesses, and with the interrelated computer systems, it would not take long for "Babylon" to collapse and the world's economic system to be destroyed.

The word translated "wail" (Rev. 18:9) means "a loud lamentation" as opposed to silent weeping. In fact, the same word is translated "weep" in Revelation 18:11. Note that the merchants are not feeling sorry for the city, but for themselves: they have lost valuable customers! God had brought an end to their life of luxury and wealth. Even their employees weep (Rev. 18:17-18).

John gave an inventory of some of the commodities that brought wealth to these kings, merchants, and shipmasters. Gold, silver, and precious stones led the list. Then he described costly garments (see also Rev. 18:16) and items made of different materials. "Thyine wood" (Rev. 18:12) was valued highly by the Romans who used it for decorative cabinets and other luxury furnishings.

Imported spices were greatly sought in that day, both for foods and for personal use as perfumes. The city of Rome had to depend on imported foods, just as many nations do today. In fact, our great cities would starve were it not for trucks and trains that daily bring in fresh produce and meats.

Last on the list, and most disturbing, is "slaves and the souls of men" (Rev. 18:13). It has been estimated that one third of Rome's population was enslaved; and it was not unusual for 10,000 human beings to be auctioned off *in one day* in the great slave markets of the Empire. There were probably over 60 million slaves throughout the Empire, people who were treated like pieces of furniture, bought and sold, used and abused.

Is John suggesting that there will, in the end times, be a return to slavery? Perhaps not in the ancient sense, but certainly we can see an increasing loss of freedom in our world today. Persons are "bought and sold" (and even traded!) by athletic teams; and our great corporations more and more seek to control the lives of their officers and workers. As people become more enslaved to luxury, with more bills to pay, they find themselves unable to break loose from the "system."

It would take little imagination to conceive of a universal enslavement under the rule of "the beast." We have already seen that he required his mark on everyone who would buy or sell (Rev. 13:16-17), and he also demanded that all people worship his image. He will promise "freedom," but put men and women in bondage (2 Peter 2:19). He will take advantage of the people's appetites (Rev. 18:14) and use their appetites to enslave them.

John may also have had in mind Ezekiel 27, the lament over the fall of Tyre. As you read that chapter, you will find a number of parallels.

***The voice of celebration (vv. 20-24).***
In contrast to the lament of the kings and merchants is the rejoicing of heaven's inhabitants that Babylon has fallen. How important it is that God's people look at events from God's point of view. In fact, we are commanded to rejoice at the overthrow of Babylon, because in this judgment God will vindicate His servants who were martyred (see Rev. 6:9-11).

Note the repeated refrain, "No more!" Jeremiah used a similar approach when he warned Judah of the nation's coming judgment at the hands of the Babylonians (Jer. 25:8-10). Now that same judgment comes to Babylon herself! This description of Babylon's losses indicates to us that both the luxuries *and* the necessities will be removed. Both music and manufacturing, work and weddings, will come to a violent end.

Revelation 18:24 should be compared with Revelation 17:6 and Matthew 23:35. Satan has used religion and business to persecute and slay the people of God. During the first half of the Tribulation, as "the beast" rises to power, ecclesiastical and political-economic Babylon will work together in opposing the Lord and His people. It will seem that God does not care; but at the right time, the Lord will vindicate His people and destroy both "the harlot" and the great city. God is patient with His enemies; but when He does begin to work, He acts suddenly and thoroughly.

We must not think that this voice of celebration calls us to be glad because sinners are judged. The fact of divine judgment ought always to break our hearts, knowing that lost sinners are condemned to eternal punishment. The joy in this section centers on God's righteous judgment, the fact that justice has been done. It is easy for comfortable Bible students to discuss these things in their homes. If you and I were with John on Patmos, or with the suffering saints to whom he wrote, we might have a different perspective. We must never cultivate personal revenge (Rom. 12:17-21), but we must rejoice at the righteous judgments of God.

At this point in our study, the political and economic system of "the beast" has at last been destroyed. All that remains is for Jesus Christ to come from heaven and personally meet and defeat "the beast" and his armies. This He will do, and then establish His righteous kingdom on earth.

But the important question is: "Are we citizens of 'Babylon' or citizens of heaven?"

Can you rejoice because your name is written in heaven? If not, then the time has come for you to trust Jesus Christ and "get out of Babylon" and into the family of God.

# CHAPTER ELEVEN
# THE KING AND
# HIS KINGDOM
*Revelation 19–20*

How will it all end?" has been mankind's major question for centuries. Historians have studied the past, hoping to find a clue to understanding the future. Philosophers have tried to penetrate the meaning of things, but they have yet to find the key. No wonder perplexed people have turned in desperation to astrology and spiritism!

The prophetic Word of God shines like a "light . . . in a dark place" (2 Peter 1:19), and on that we can depend. Here in Revelation 19–20, John has recorded five key events that will take place before God "wraps up" human history and ushers in His new heavens and earth.

## Heaven Will Rejoice (Rev. 19:1-10)
When Babylon fell on the earth, the command was given in heaven, "Rejoice over her!" (Rev. 18:20) and what we read in this section is heaven's response to that command. The word *alleluia* is the Greek form of the Hebrew word *hallelujah,* which means "praise the Lord." This is heaven's "Hallelujah Chorus" and it will be sung for three reasons.

***God has judged His enemies (vv. 1-4).***
Since the "great whore [harlot]" of Revelation 17 was destroyed by "the beast" and his fellow rulers (Rev. 17:16) in the middle of the Tribulation, the "great whore" referred to here must be Babylon the Great. Comparing Revelation 17:2 with 18:3 and 9, the connection is obvious. Both the apostate religious system and the satanic economic-political system led the world astray and polluted mankind. Both were guilty of persecuting God's people and martyring many of them.

The song emphasizes God's attributes,

which is the proper way to honor Him. We do not rejoice at the sinfulness of Babylon, or even the greatness of Babylon's fall. We rejoice that God is "true and righteous" (Rev. 15:3; 16:7; 17:6) and that He is glorified by His holy judgments. As we discovered in Revelation 8:1-6, God's throne and altar are related to His judgments. Revelation 19:3 should be compared with Revelation 14:10-11, and Revelation 19:4 with Revelation 5:6-10.

*God is reigning (vv. 5-6).* The literal translation is, "The Lord God omnipotent has begun to reign." This does not suggest that heaven's throne has been empty or inactive, because that is not the case. The Book of Revelation is the "book of the throne," and the omnipotent God has indeed been accomplishing His purposes on earth. This burst of praise is an echo of Psalm 97:1—"The Lord reigneth; let the earth rejoice!"

God has been reigning on the throne of heaven, but He is now about to conquer the thrones of earth as well as the kingdom of Satan and "the beast." In His sovereignty, He has permitted evil men and evil angels to do their worst; but now the time has come for God's will to be done on earth as it is in heaven. Domitian was emperor of Rome when John was on Patmos, and one of his assumed titles was "Lord and God." How significant it must have been, then, to John's readers that he used the word *alleluia* four times in the first six verses of this chapter—truly, only Jehovah is worthy of worship and praise.

*The bride is ready (vv. 7-10).* The bride, of course, is the church (2 Cor. 11:2; Eph. 5:22-33); and Jesus Christ, the Lamb, is the Bridegroom (John 3:29). At a wedding, it is customary to focus attention on the bride; but in this case, it is the *Bridegroom* who receives the honor! "Let us be glad and rejoice, and give honor to Him."

"What did the bride wear?" is the usual question asked after a wedding. The Lamb's bride is dressed "in the righteous acts of the saints" (literal translation). When the bride arrived in heaven at the Judgment Seat of Christ, she was not at all beautiful (in fact, she was covered with spots, wrinkles, and blemishes according to Paul in Eph. 5:27); but now she is radiant in her glory. She has "made herself ready" for the public ceremony.

Jewish weddings in that day were quite unlike weddings in the Western world. First, there was an engagement, usually made by the parents when the prospective bride and groom were quite young. This engagement was binding and could be broken only by a form of divorce. Any unfaithfulness during the engagement was considered adultery.

When the public ceremony was to be enacted, the groom would go to the bride's house and claim her for himself. He would take her to his home for the wedding supper, and all the guests would join the happy couple. This feast could last as long as a week.

Today, the church is "engaged" to Jesus Christ; and we love Him even though we have not seen Him (1 Peter 1:8). One day, He will return and take His bride to heaven (John 14:1-6; 1 Thes. 4:13-18). At the Judgment Seat of Christ, her works will be judged and all her spots and blemishes removed. This being completed, the church will be ready to return to earth with her Bridegroom at the close of the Tribulation to reign with Him in glory (see Luke 13:29; Matt. 8:11). Some students believe that the entire Kingdom Age will be the "marriage supper."

Revelation 19:9 contains the fourth of the seven "beatitudes" found in the book (see Rev 1:3). Certainly the bride is not invited to her own wedding! This invitation goes out to the guests, believers from the Old Testament era and the Tribulation. During the eternal state, no distinctions will be made among the people of God; but in the Kingdom Age, differences will still exist as the church reigns with Christ and as Israel enjoys the promised messianic blessings.

John was so overwhelmed by all of this that he fell down to worship the angel who was guiding him, an act that he later repeats! (Rev. 22:8-9) Of course, worshiping angels is wrong (Col. 2:18) and John knew this. We must take into account the tremendous emotional content of John's experience. Like John himself, this angel was only a servant of God (Heb. 1:14); and we do not worship servants (see Acts 10:25-26).

### Christ Will Return (Rev. 19:11–20:3)

First, John described the Conqueror (Rev. 19:11-16) and then His conquests (Rev. 19:17–20:3). The rider on the white horse (Rev. 6:2) is the false Christ, but this Rider is the true Christ. He is not coming *in the air* to take His people home (1 Thes. 4:13-18), but *to the earth* with His people, to conquer His enemies and establish His kingdom.

Note the emphasis on Jesus' names (Rev. 19:11-13, 16). He is "Faithful and True" (see

Rev. 3:14), in contrast to "the beast" who was unfaithful (he broke the covenant with Israel) and false (he ruled by means of deception and idolatry). Suffering saints need to be reminded that God is faithful and will not desert them, because His promises are true.

Perhaps the "secret name" (see Rev. 19:12) is the same as the "new name" (Rev. 3:12). Not knowing what this name is, we cannot comment on it; but it is exciting to know that, even in heaven, we shall learn new things about our Lord Jesus!

"The Word of God" is one of the familiar names of our Lord in Scripture (John 1:1-14). Just as we reveal our minds and hearts to others by our words, so the Father reveals Himself to us through His Son, the incarnate Word (Rev. 14:7-11). A word is made up of letters, and Jesus Christ is "Alpha and Omega" (Rev. 21:6; 22:13). He is the "divine alphabet" of God's revelation to us.

The Word of God is "living and powerful" (Heb. 4:12); what's more, it fulfills His purposes on earth (Rev. 17:17; note also Rev. 6:11; 10:7; 15:1). Jehovah Himself says, "I am watching to see that My Word is fulfilled" (Jer. 1:12, NIV). Just as the Word was the Father's Agent in Creation (John 1:1-3), so the Word is His Agent for judgment and consummation.

Christ's most important name is "King of kings, and Lord of lords" (Rev. 19:16). This is His victorious name (Rev. 17:14), and it brings to mind references such as Daniel 2:47 and Deuteronomy 10:17. Paul used this same title for our Lord Jesus Christ in 1 Timothy 6:15. The title speaks of Christ's sovereignty, for all kings and lords must submit to Him. No matter who was on the throne of the Roman Empire, Jesus Christ was his King and Lord!

The greatness of Christ is seen not only in His names, but also in John's description of the conquering King (Rev. 19:12-16). The eyes "as a flame of fire" symbolize His searching judgment that sees all (Rev. 1:14). The many crowns (diadems) indicate His magnificent rule and sovereignty. The vesture dipped in blood speaks of judgment and probably relates to Isaiah 63:1-6 and Revelation 14:20, the conquest of His enemies. It is not our Lord's blood that marks His vesture, but that of His foes.

The sharp sword is a symbol of God's Word (Rev. 19:21; see also Eph. 6:17; Heb. 4:12; Rev. 1:16). This is in keeping with the fact that Christ will consume the enemy "with the spirit of His mouth" (2 Thes. 2:8; note also

Isa. 11:4). We have met with the "rod of iron" before (Rev. 2:27; 12:5), a symbol of His justice as He rules over the earth. The image of the winepress must be associated with the judgment at Armageddon (Rev. 14:14-20; see also Isa. 63:1-6).

Jesus is not alone in His conquest, for the armies of heaven ride with Him. Who are they? Certainly the angels are a part of this army (Matt. 25:31; 2 Thes. 1:7); but so are the saints (1 Thes. 3:13; 2 Thes. 1:10). Jude describes the same scene (Jude 14-15). The word *saints* means "holy ones" and could refer to believers or angels.

It will be unnecessary for the army to fight, for Christ Himself will defeat the enemy through three great victories.

**He will defeat the armies of the kings of the earth (vv. 17-19, 21).** These warriors have assembled to fight "against the Lord and against His anointed" (Ps. 2:1-3), but their weapons prove futile. The battle turns out to be a slaughter—a "supper" for the scavenger birds! The first half of Revelation 19 describes the marriage supper of the Lamb; the last half describes the "supper of the great God" (see Matt. 24:28; Luke 17:37).

The word *flesh* occurs six times in this paragraph. While John's immediate reference is to the human body, eaten by the vultures, there is certainly a deeper meaning here: man fails because he is flesh and relies on flesh. The Bible has nothing good to say about fallen human nature. Recall the Lord's words before the Flood: "My spirit shall not always strive with man, for that he also is flesh" (Gen. 6:3). (See also John 3:6; 6:63; Rom. 7:18; Phil. 3:3.) "All flesh is as grass" (1 Peter 1:24) and must be judged.

This is the account of the well-known "battle of Armageddon," which was anticipated earlier (Rev. 14:14-20; 16:13-16). All that our Lord has to do is speak the Word, and "the sword of His mouth" will devour His enemies.

**He will defeat "the beast" and false prophet (v. 20).** Since Satan's "henchmen" are the leaders of the revolt, it is only right that they be captured and confined. They are cast into the lake of fire (see Rev. 20:10, 14-15), the final and permanent place of punishment for all who refuse to submit to Jesus Christ. "The beast" and false prophet are the first persons to be cast into hell. Satan will follow 1,000 years later (Rev. 20:10), to be joined by those whose names are not recorded in the Book of Life (Rev. 20:15).

Today, when an unbeliever dies, his spirit goes to a place called *hades,* which means "the unseen world"—that is, the realm of the dead. When believers die, they go immediately into the presence of the Lord (2 Cor. 5:6-8; Phil. 1:19-23). Hades will one day be emptied of its dead (Rev. 20:13), who will then be cast into hell to join Satan, the beast, and the false prophet.

***Satan will be defeated (vv. 1-3).*** The "bottomless pit" spoken of in Revelation 20:1 is not the same as hell; it is the "abyss" that we have met before in our studies (Rev. 9:1-2, 11; 11:7; 17:8). Satan is not cast into hell immediately, because God still has one more task for him to perform. Rather, Satan is confined in the bottomless pit for 1,000 years. First, Satan was cast out of *heaven* (Rev. 12:9), and now he is cast out of *earth!*

Some Bible students feel that the "chaining" of Satan took place when Jesus died on the cross and arose from the dead to ascend to heaven. While it is true that Jesus won His decisive victory over Satan at the cross, the sentence against the devil has not yet been effected. He is a defeated foe, but he is still free to attack God's people and oppose God's work (1 Peter 5:8). I think it was Dr. James M. Gray who suggested that, if Satan is bound today, it must be with a terribly long chain! Paul was sure that Satan was loose (Eph. 6:10ff), and John agreed with him (Rev. 2:13; 3:9).

Having taken care of His enemies, the Lord is now free to establish His righteous kingdom on the earth.

## Saints Will Reign (Rev. 20:4-6)

The phrase "thousand years" occurs six times in Revelation 20:1-7. This period in history is known as "the Millennium," from two Latin words, *mille* ("thousand") and *annum* ("year")—the 1,000-year kingdom of Christ on earth. At last, Christ and His church will reign over the nations of the earth, and Israel will enjoy the blessings promised by the prophets (see Isa. 2:1-5; 4:1-6; 11:1-9; 12:1-6; 30:18-26; 35:1-10).

Is this a literal kingdom on earth, or should these verses be "spiritualized" and applied to the church today? Some interpreters say that the term "a thousand years" is simply a number meaning "ultimate perfection" (10 x 10 x 10 = 1,000). They assert that it is a symbol of Christ's victory and the church's wonderful

blessings now that Satan has been defeated and bound. This view is known as *amillennialism,* which means "no millennium"—that is, no literal kingdom.

The problem with this view is that it does not explain why John introduced the period with a resurrection of the dead. He was certainly not writing about a "spiritual" resurrection, because he even told how these people died! And in Revelation 20:5, John wrote of another literal resurrection. If we are now in the 1,000-year kingdom of victory, when did this resurrection take place? It seems reasonable to assume that John wrote about a literal physical resurrection of the dead, and a literal kingdom on earth.

What is the purpose of the millennial kingdom? For one thing, it will be the fulfillment of God's promises to Israel *and to Christ* (Ps. 2; Luke 1:30-33). Our Lord reaffirmed them to His own Apostles (Luke 22:29-30). This kingdom will be a worldwide display of Christ's glory, when all nature will be set free from the bondage of sin (Rom. 8:19-22). It will be the answer to the prayers of the saints, "Thy kingdom come!" It will also be God's final demonstration of the sinfulness of sin and the wickedness of the human heart apart from God's grace, but more on this later.

The Tribulation martyrs will be raised from the dead and given glorious thrones and rewards. The church will share in this reign, as symbolized by the twenty-four elders (Rev. 5:10; see also 2:26-28; 3:12, 21; 1 Thes. 4:13-18; 2 Tim. 2:12). Some Bible students believe that the Old Testament saints will also be a part of this "first resurrection" (Dan. 12:1-4).

The phrase "general resurrection" is not found in the Bible. On the contrary, the Bible teaches *two* resurrections: the first is of the saved and leads to blessing; the second is of all the lost and leads to judgment (note especially John 5:28-29; Dan. 12:2). These two resurrections will be separated by 1,000 years.

Revelation 20:6 describes the special blessings of those who share in the first resurrection. They did not *earn* these blessings; they are part of the believer's inheritance in Jesus Christ. This is the sixth of the seven "beatitudes" in Revelation; the final one is in Revelation 22:7. These resurrected believers will share Christ's glorious life, reigning as kings and priests with Him, and never experience the "second death," the lake of fire (hell, Rev. 20:14).

During the Millennium, the inhabitants of the earth will include not only glorified saints, but also citizens of the nations who bow in submission to Jesus Christ (see Matt. 25:31-40; also 8:11). Because of the earth's perfect conditions, people will live long lives (Isa. 65:17-25, especially v. 20). They will marry and have children who will outwardly conform to our Lord's righteous rule. But not all of them will be truly born again as the Millennium progresses; and this explains why Satan will be able to gather a great army of rebels at the close of the Kingdom Age (Rev. 20:8).

For many centuries, man has dreamed of a "golden age," a "utopia" in which the human race will be free from war, sickness, and even death. Men have tried to achieve this goal on their own and have failed. It is only when Jesus Christ reigns on David's throne that the kingdom will come and the earth be delivered from the oppression of Satan and sin.

### Satan Will Revolt (Rev. 20:7-10)

At the close of the Millennium, Satan will be released from the pit and permitted to lead one last revolt against the Lord. Why? As final proof that the heart of man is desperately wicked and can be changed only by God's grace. Imagine the tragedy of this revolt: people who have been living in a perfect environment, under the perfect government of God's Son, will finally admit the truth and rebel against the King! Their obedience will be seen as mere *feigned* submission, and not true faith in Christ at all.

The naming of "Gog and Magog" (Rev. 20:8) does not equate this battle with the one described in Ezekiel 38–39; for that army invades from the north, while this one comes from the four corners of the earth. These two events are related, however, inasmuch as in both battles, Israel is the focal point. In this case, Jerusalem will be the target ("beloved city," Pss. 78:68; 87:2). God will deal with this revolt very quickly and efficiently, and Satan will be cast into hell. Note that "the beast" and false prophet will still be suffering in the lake of fire after 1,000 years! (see Matt. 25:41)

In one sense, the millennial kingdom will "sum up" all that God has said about the heart of man during the various periods of history. It will be a reign of law, and yet law will not change man's sinful heart. Man will still revolt against God. The Millennium will be a period of peace and perfect environment, a time when disobedience will be judged swiftly and with justice; and yet in the end the subjects of the King will follow Satan and rebel against the Lord. A perfect environment cannot produce a perfect heart.

God is now about to "wrap up" human history. One great event remains.

### Sinners Are Recompensed (Rev. 20:11-15)

There shall be a second resurrection, and the unsaved will be raised and will stand before God's judgment. Do not confuse this judgment at the White Throne with the Judgment Seat of Christ, where believers will have their works judged and rewarded. At this judgment, there will be only unbelievers; and there will be no rewards. John described here an awesome scene. Heaven and earth will flee away and no place will be left for sinners to hide! All must face the Judge!

The Judge is Jesus Christ, for the Father has committed all judgment to Him (Matt. 19:28; John 5:22-30; Acts 17:31). These lost sinners rejected Christ in life; now they must be judged by Him and face eternal death.

From where do these "dead" come? Death will give up the bodies, and hades (the realm of the spirits of the dead) will give up the spirits. There will even be a resurrection of bodies from the sea. No sinner will escape.

Jesus Christ will judge these unsaved people on the basis of what is written "in the books." What books? For one thing, God's Word will be there. "The Word that I have spoken, the same shall judge him in the last day" (John 12:48). Every sinner will be held accountable for the truth he or she has heard in this life.

There will also be a book containing the works of the sinners being judged, though this does not suggest that a person can do good works sufficient to enter heaven (Eph. 2:8-9; Titus 3:5). Why, then, will Jesus Christ consider the works, good and bad, of the people before the White Throne? To determine the degree of punishment they will endure in hell. All of these people will be cast into hell. Their personal rejection of Jesus Christ has already determined their destiny. But Jesus Christ is a righteous Judge, and He will assign each sinner the place that he deserves.

There are degrees of punishment in hell (Matt. 11:20-24). Each lost sinner will receive just what is due him, and none will be able to argue with the Lord or question His decision.

God knows what sinners are doing, and His books will reveal the truth.

"The Book of Life" will be there, containing the names of God's redeemed people (Phil. 4:3; Rev. 21:27; note also 13:8; 17:8). No unsaved person will have his or her name in the Lamb's Book of Life; only true believers are recorded there (Luke 10:20).

When the judgment is finished, all of the lost will be cast into hell, the lake of fire, the second death. Many people reject the biblical doctrine of hell as being "unchristian," and yet Jesus clearly taught its reality (Matt. 18:8; 23:15, 33; 25:46; Mark 9:46). A sentimental kind of humanistic religion will not face the reality of judgment, but teaches a God who loves everyone into heaven and sends no one to hell.

Hell is a witness to the righteous character of God. He must judge sin. Hell is also a witness to man's responsibility, the fact that he is not a robot or a helpless victim, but a creature able to make choices. God does not "send people to hell"; they send themselves by rejecting the Saviour (Matt. 25:41; John 3:16-21). Hell is also a witness to the awfulness of sin. If we once saw sin as God sees it, we would understand why a place such as hell exists.

In light of Calvary, no lost sinner can condemn God for casting him into hell. God has provided a way of escape, patiently waiting for sinners to repent. He will not lower His standards or alter His requirements. He has ordained that faith in His Son is the only way of salvation.

The White Throne Judgment will be nothing like our modern court cases. At the White Throne, there will be a Judge but no jury, a prosecution but no defense, a sentence but no appeal. No one will be able to defend himself or accuse God of unrighteousness. What an awesome scene it will be!

Before God can usher in His new heavens and earth, He must finally deal with sin; and this He will do at the Great White Throne.

You can escape this terrible judgment by trusting Jesus Christ as your personal Saviour. By so doing, you never will be a part of the second resurrection or experience the terrors of the second death, the lake of fire.

"He that heareth My Word," said Jesus, "and believeth on Him that sent Me, hath everlasting life, and shall not come into condemnation [judgment], but is passed from death unto life" (John 5:24).

Have you trusted Him and passed from death unto life?

# CHAPTER TWELVE
# ALL THINGS NEW!
*Revelation 21–22*

Human history begins in a Garden and ends in a City that is like a garden paradise. In the Apostle John's day, Rome was the admired city; yet God compared it to a harlot. "That which is highly esteemed among men is abomination in the sight of God" (Luke 16:15). The eternal city of God is compared to a beautiful bride (Rev. 21:9), because it is the eternal home for God's beloved people.

God's statements recorded in Revelation 21:5-6 aptly summarize these final two chapters: "Behold, I make all things new. . . . It is done!" What began in Genesis is brought to completion in Revelation, as the following summary shows:

| *Genesis* | *Revelation* |
|---|---|
| Heavens and earth created, 1:1 | New heavens and earth, 21:1 |
| Sun created, 1:16 | No need of the sun, 21:23 |
| The night established, 1:5 | No night there, 22:5 |
| The seas created, 1:10 | No more seas, 21:1 |
| The curse announced, 3:14-17 | No more curse, 22:3 |
| Death enters history, 3:19 | No more death, 21:4 |
| Man driven from the tree, 3:24 | Man restored to paradise, 22:14 |
| Sorrow and pain begin, 3:17 | No more tears or pain, 21:4 |

**The Citizens of the City (Rev. 21:1-8)**
John gives us a threefold description of the citizens of the city.

***They are God's people (vv. 1-5).*** The first heaven and earth were prepared for the first man and woman and their descendants. God had readied everything for them when He placed them in the Garden. Unfortunately, our first parents sinned, ushering death and decay into God's beautiful world. Creation is in bondage and travail (Rom. 8:18-23), and even the heavens "are not clean in His sight" (Job 15:15).

God has promised His people a new heaven and earth (Isa. 65:17; 66:22). The old creation must make way for the new creation if God is to be glorified. Jesus called this event "the regeneration" of the earth (Matt. 19:28), and Peter explained it as a cleansing and renewing by fire (2 Peter 3:10-13). Bible students are not agreed as to whether the old elements will be renewed or whether the old will be destroyed and a whole new creation ushered in. The fact that the Greek word translated *new* means "new in character" (Rev. 21:1, 5) may lend credence to the former explanation.

"No more sea" does not mean "no more water." It simply indicates that the new earth will have a different arrangement as far as water is concerned. Three fourths of our globe consists of water, but this won't be the case in the eternal state. In John's day, the sea meant danger, storms, and separation (John himself was on an island at the time!); so perhaps John was giving us more than a geography lesson.

Even despite Scripture's description, it is difficult to imagine what the eternal city will be like. John characterizes it as a *holy* city (see Rev. 21:27), a *prepared* city (see John 14:1-6), and a *beautiful* city, as beautiful as a bride on her wedding day. He amplifies these characteristics in Revelation 21–22.

But the most important thing about the city is that God dwells there with His people. The Bible gives an interesting record of the dwelling places of God. First, God walked with man in the Garden of Eden. Then He dwelt with Israel in the tabernacle and later the temple. When Israel sinned, God had to depart from those dwellings. Later, Jesus Christ came to earth and "tabernacled" among us (John 1:14). Today, God does not live in man-made temples (Acts 7:48-50), but in the bodies of His people (1 Cor. 6:19-20) and in the church (Eph. 2:21-22).

In both the tabernacle and the temple, the veil stood between men and God. That veil was torn in two when Jesus died, thus opening a "new and living way" for God's people (Heb. 10:19ff). Even though God dwells in believers today by His Spirit, we still have not begun to understand God or fellowship with Him as we would like; but one day, we shall dwell in God's presence and enjoy Him forever.

The eternal city is so wonderful that the best way John found to describe it was by contrast—"no more." The believers who first read this inspired book must have rejoiced to know that, in heaven, there would be no more pain, tears, sorrow, or death; for many of their number had been tortured and slain. In every age, the hope of heaven has encouraged God's people in times of suffering.

*The citizens of heaven are a satisfied people (v. 6).* People who live in modern cities do not think much about water, but this was a major concern in John's day. No doubt John himself, working in the Roman mines, had known the meaning of thirst. Tortured saints throughout the ages would certainly identify with this wonderful promise from the Lord. Free and abundant living water for all!

*These heavenly citizens are an overcoming people (vv. 7-8).* "He that overcometh" is a key phrase in this book (Rev. 2:7, 11, 17, 26; 3:5, 12, 21; note also 12:11). As John pointed out in his first epistle, all true believers are overcomers (1 John 5:4-5), so this promise is not just for the "spiritually elite." Because we are the children of God, we shall inherit all things.

After the great Chicago fire of 1871, evangelist Dwight L. Moody went back to survey the ruins of his house. A friend came by and said to Moody, "I hear you lost everything."

"Well," said Moody, "you understood wrong. I have a good deal more left than I lost."

"What do you mean?" the inquisitive friend asked. "I didn't know you were that rich."

Moody then opened his Bible and read to him Revelation 21:7—"He that overcometh shall inherit all things, and I will be his God."

In contrast to the overcomers, Revelation 21:8 describes the people who *were overcome* by sin and would not trust the Lord. What is their destiny? The lake of fire! The world considers Christians as "losers," but it is the unbelievers who are the losers!

The fearful are the cowardly, the people who did not have the courage to stand up for Christ (see Matt. 10:32-33). The word *abominable* means "polluted," and refers to those who indulged in sin and were thus polluted in mind, spirit, and body (2 Cor. 7:1). The other characteristics mentioned in Revelation 21:8 need no special explanation, except to note that all of them would be true of "the beast's" followers (note Rev. 17:4, 6; 18:3, 9; 19:2).

## The Character of the City
### (Rev. 21:9–22:5)

The eternal city is not only the home of the bride; it *is* the bride! A city is not buildings; it is people. The city John saw was holy and heavenly; in fact, it descended to earth from heaven, where it was prepared. John's description staggers the imagination, even accepting the fact that a great deal of symbolism is involved. Heaven is a real place of glory and beauty, the perfect home for the Lamb's bride.

We have already noted that "the glory of God" has appeared in different places throughout history. God's glory dwelt in the tabernacle and then in the temple. Today, His glory dwells in believers and in His church. For all eternity, the glory of God will be seen in His holy city. It is the only light the city will need.

The city's description follows the pattern of cities with which John's readers were familiar: foundations, walls, and gates. The foundations speak of *permanence,* in contrast to the tents in which "pilgrims and strangers" lived (Heb. 11:8-10). The walls and gates speak of *protection.* God's people will never have to fear any enemies. Angels at the gates will act as sentries!

In this city, saints of the Old Covenant and the New Covenant will be united. The twelve gates are identified with the twelve tribes of Israel, and the twelve foundations with the 12 Apostles (see Eph. 2:20). Including the tribe of Levi, there were actually thirteen tribes; and, including Paul, there were thirteen Apostles. When John listed the tribes in Revelation 7, both Dan and Ephraim were omitted, perhaps indicating that we should not press these matters too literally. John is simply assuring us that all of God's believing people will be included in the city (Heb. 11:39-40).

John had measured the earthly Jerusalem (Rev. 11), but now he is invited to measure the heavenly city. *Foursquare* means "equal on all sides," so the city might be a cube or a pyramid. More importantly, the fact that it is equal on all sides indicates the perfection of God's eternal city: nothing is out of order or balance.

The measurements are staggering! If we take a cubit as eighteen inches, then the city walls are 216 feet high! If a furlong is taken as 600 feet (measures differed in ancient days), the city would be about 1,500 miles square! There will be plenty of room for everyone!

The city's construction cannot but fascinate us. The walls are jasper, which is a clear crystal; but the city itself will be made of pure gold, as clear as crystal. The light of God's glory will shine throughout the city, resembling a huge holy of holies.

Building foundations are usually underground, but these foundations will not only be visible but beautifully garnished with precious stones. Each separate foundation will have its own jewel, and the blending of the colors will be magnificent as God's light shines through.

No one can be dogmatic about the colors of these gems, and it really does not matter. Jasper, as we have seen, is a clear crystal. Sapphire is a blue stone, and chalcedony is probably greenish-blue. The emerald, of course, is green; and the sardonyx is like our onyx, a white stone streaked with brown, though some scholars describe it as red and white.

Sardius is a red stone (sometimes described as "blood red"), and chrysolite a yellow quartz like our modern topaz. Beryl is green and topaz a yellow-green. We are not sure about the chrysoprasus; some think it is a golden-tinted stone, others, an apple-green color. The jacinth is probably blue, though some claim it was yellow; and the amethyst is a rich purple, or blue-red.

Our God is a God of beauty, and He will lavish His beauty on the city He is preparing for His people. Perhaps Peter had the holy city in mind when he wrote about the "manifold grace of God" (1 Peter 4:10), for the word translated "manifold" means "many colored, variegated."

In ancient times, the pearl was considered a "royal gem," produced by a mollusk covering an irritating grain of sand within its shell. But the pearl gates of the heavenly city will never be closed (Rev. 21:25) because there will be no danger of anything entering that would disturb or defile her citizens.

John noted that some items were missing from the city, but their absence only magnified its glory. There will be no temple, since the entire city will be indwelt by God's presence. Indeed, "secular" and "sacred" will be indistinguishable in heaven. The sun and moon will be absent since the Lord is the light of the city, and there will never be any night (see Isa. 60:19).

The mention of nations in Revelation 21:24 and 26 suggests that there will be *peoples* (plural) on the new earth. Since in the eternal state there will be only glorified beings, we must not think that the earth will be populated with various nations such as exist today. Instead, these verses reflect the ancient practice of kings and nations bringing their wealth and glory to the city of the greatest king. In the heavenly city, everyone will honor the "King of kings" (see Pss. 68:29; 72:10-11; Isa. 60).

In Revelation 22:1-5, we move inside the city to discover that it is like a beautiful garden, reminiscent of the Garden of Eden. There were four rivers in Eden (Gen. 2:10-14), but there is only one river in the heavenly city. Ezekiel saw a purifying river flowing from the temple, certainly a millennial scene (Ezek. 47); but this river will flow directly from God's throne, the very source of all purity. Man was prohibited from eating of the tree of the knowledge of good and evil, and prevented from eating of the tree of life (Gen. 2:15-17; 3:22-24). But in the eternal home, man will have access to the tree of life. The river and the tree symbolize abundant life in the glorious city.

"No more curse" takes us back to Genesis 3:14-19 where the curse began. Interestingly, even the Old Testament closes with the statement, "Lest I come and smite the earth with a curse" (Mal. 4:6). But the New Testament announces, "And there shall be no more curse!" Satan will be consigned to hell; all of creation will be made new; and the curse of sin will be gone forever.

What will we do in heaven for all eternity? Certainly, we shall praise the Lord, but we shall also serve Him. "His servants shall serve Him" (Rev. 22:3) is a great encouragement to us, for in heaven our service will be perfect. As we seek to serve the Lord here on earth, we are constantly handicapped by sin and weakness; but all hindrances will be gone when we get to glory. Perfect service in a perfect environment!

What will this service be? We are not told, nor do we need to know now. It is sufficient that we know what God wants us to do *today*. Our faithfulness in life prepares us for higher service in heaven. In fact, some students think that we shall have access to the vast universe and perhaps be sent on special missions to other places. But it is useless to speculate, because God has not seen fit to fill in the details.

Not only shall we be servants in heaven, but we shall also be kings. We shall reign forever and ever! This speaks of sharing Christ's authority in glory. As believers, we are seated with Christ in the heavenlies today (Eph. 2:1-10); but in the eternal state, we shall reign as kings over the new heavens and earth. What an honor! What grace!

Certainly, many interesting questions could be asked about our future abode in heaven, but most must go unanswered until we reach our glorious home. In fact, John closed his book by reminding us that we have responsibilities today *because* we are going to heaven.

## The Challenge of the City (Rev. 22:6-21)

Heaven is more than a destination; it is a motivation. Knowing that we shall dwell in the heavenly city ought to make a difference in our lives here and now. The vision of the heavenly city motivated the patriarchs as they walked with God and served Him (Heb. 11:10, 13-16). Knowing that He was returning to the Father in heaven also encouraged Jesus Christ as He faced the cross (Heb. 12:2). The assurance of heaven must not lull us into complacency or carelessness, but spur us to fulfill our spiritual duties.

*We must keep God's Word (vv. 6-11, 18-19).* Because what John wrote is the Word of God, his words are faithful and true (see Rev. 19:11). The same God who spoke through the prophets also spoke through the Apostle John. As the "capstone" of God's revelation, John's book cannot be divorced from the rest of the Bible. If we deny that John wrote the truth, then we must also deny the prophets.

What does it mean to "keep the sayings of the prophecy of this book"? (Rev. 22:7) Basically, it means to guard, to watch over, to preserve intact. We must not add to the Word of God or take anything from it (see Deut. 4:2; Prov. 30:5-6). And this responsibility is especially great in light of Christ's return. The word *shortly* in Revelation 22:6 means "quickly come to pass." The church has expected Christ to return since the days of the Apostles, and He has not yet come; but when John's prophecies begin to be fulfilled, they will happen very quickly. There will be no delay.

The warnings in Revelation 22:18-19 do not suggest that people who tamper with the Bible will be brought back to earth to suffer the Tribulation's plagues, or that they will lose their salvation. Nobody fully understands the Bible or can explain everything in it; and those of us who teach the Word sometimes have to change our interpretations as we grow in knowledge. God sees the heart, and He can separate ignorance from impudence and immaturity from rebellion.

It was customary in ancient days for writers to put this kind of warning at the close of their books, because the people who copied them for public distribution might be tempted to tamper with the material. However, John's warning was not addressed to a writer, but to the hearer, the believer in the congregation where this book was read aloud. By analogy, however, it would apply to anyone reading and studying the book today. We may not be able to explain the penalties given, but we do know this: it is a dangerous thing to tamper with the Word of God. The one who guards the Word and obeys it will be blessed; the one who alters it will be disciplined in some way.

For a second time, John was overwhelmed by what he saw and heard; and he fell down to worship the angel who was speaking to him (see Rev. 19:10). The angel gave John three words of counsel: do not worship angels; worship God; and do not seal up the Revelation. The Prophet Daniel was commanded to seal his book (Dan. 12:4), because the time was not yet ready. John's book was an "apocalypse," an unveiling (Rev. 1:1); and, therefore, it must not be sealed.

Once again, the Holy Spirit is reminding us of the living unity of God's Word. We have seen in our study how John, led by the Spirit, reached back into the Old Testament and used many of the images found there, including Daniel's prophecy. Scripture is its own best interpreter.

Does Revelation 22:11 suggest that God does not want men to repent and change their ways? No, because that would be contrary to the message of Revelation and of the Gospel itself. The angel's words must be understood in light of the repeated statement, "Behold, I come quickly" (Rev. 22:7, 12), as well as his statement, "For the time is at hand" (Rev. 22:10). Jesus Christ's coming will occur so quickly that men will not have time to change their characters.

Revelation 22:11, therefore, is a solemn warning that decision determines character, and character determines destiny. Suffering believers might ask, "Is it worth it to live a godly life?" John's reply is, "Yes! Jesus is returning, and He will reward you!" Next comes John's second admonition.

*We have the responsibility of serving the Lord (vv. 12-14).* "My reward is with Me" implies that God is mindful of our sufferings and our service, and nothing will ever be done in vain if it is done for Him. At the Judgment Seat of Christ, believers will be judged according to their works; and rewards will be given to those who have been faithful.

Throughout church history, there have been those who have (to use Dwight L. Moody's words) become "so heavenly minded that they were no earthly good." They quit their jobs, sold their property, and sat and waited for Jesus to return. All of them have been embarrassed, of course, because it is unbiblical to set dates for His coming. It is also unbiblical to become careless and lazy just because we believe Jesus is coming soon. Paul faced this problem with some of the believers in Thessalonica (2 Thes. 3).

No wonder John added, "Blessed are they that do His commandments" (Rev. 22:14). If we really believe that Jesus is coming soon, we will watch and be faithful (Luke 12:35ff).

Revelation 22:13 is a great encouragement to anyone who seeks to serve the Lord. Whatever God starts, He will finish; for He is the Alpha and Omega, the beginning and the ending, the first and the last (see Phil. 1:6; 2:12-13).

*We must keep our lives clean (vv. 15-16).* The contrast here is between those who do God's commandments and enter the city, and those who reject His Word and are excluded from the city (see Rev. 21:8, 27). It is not likely that those who "do His commandments" are a special or an elite group of saints. The phrase is similar to "them that overcome" and characterizes all the people of God. Obedience to God's Word is a mark of true salvation.

Our Lord's titles in Revelation 22:16 are most interesting. The "root" is buried in the ground where no one can see it, but the "star" is in the heavens where everyone can see it. In "the Root and Offspring of David" we have Jesus' Jewish, national name, but in "the Bright and Morning Star" we have His universal name. One speaks of humility, the other of majesty and glory.

As "the Root . . . of David," Jesus Christ brought David into existence. As "the Offspring of David," Jesus came into this world, born a Jew from David's line. Both the deity and the humanity of Jesus are evident here. For a parallel, see Matthew 22:41-46.

The "morning star" announces dawn's soon arrival. Jesus Christ will come for His church as "the Morning Star." But when He returns to judge, it will be as "the Sun of righteousness" in burning fury (Mal. 4:1-3). Because God's people look for their Lord's return, they keep their lives clean and dedicated to Him (1 John 2:28–3:3).

*We must keep expecting Jesus Christ to return (vv. 17, 20-21).* Three times in this closing chapter John wrote, "I [Christ] come quickly" (Rev. 22:7, 12, 20). But He has "delayed" His return for nearly 2,000 years! Yes, He has; and Peter tells us why: God wants to give this sinful world opportunity to repent and be saved (2 Peter 3:1ff). In the meantime, the Spirit of God, through the church (the bride), calls for Jesus to come; for the bride wants to meet her Bridegroom and enter into her home. "Even so, come, Lord Jesus" (Rev. 22:20).

But believers ought also to invite lost sinners to trust Christ and drink the water of life. Indeed, when the church lives in expectancy of Christ's return, such an attitude provokes ministry and evangelism as well as purity of heart. We want to tell others of the grace of God. A true understanding of Bible prophecy should both motivate us to obey God's Word and to share God's invitation with a lost world.

If our study of Revelation has been truly led by the Spirit, then we will join John in the Bible's last prayer:

"Even so, come, Lord Jesus!"

Are you ready?